AUTOCOURSE™

THE WORLD'S LEADING GRAND PRIX ANNUAL

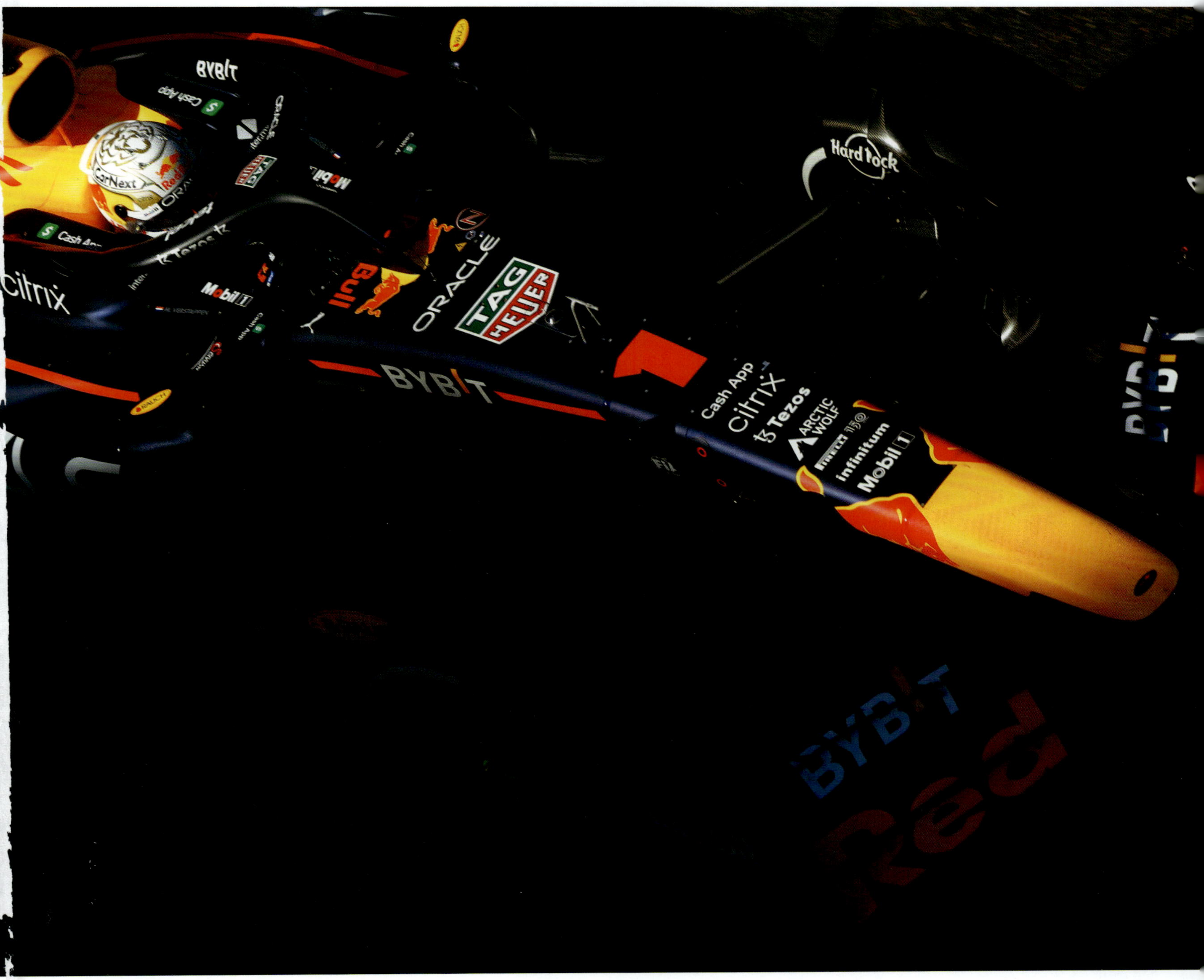

icon
PUBLISHING LIMITED

ROLEX

CONTENTS

AUTOCOURSE 2022–2023
is published by:
Icon Publishing Limited
4 Suffolk Villas
Suffolk Road
Cheltenham
Gloucestershire
GL50 2AX
United Kingdom

Tel: +44 (0)1242 245329

Email: info@autocourse.com
Website: www.autocourse.com

Printed in the United Kingdom by
Gomer Press Ltd
Llandysul Enterprise Park
Llandysul, Ceredigion, SA44 4JL
Tel: 01559 362371
email: sales@gomer.co.uk

ISBN: 978-1910584-50-7

DISTRIBUTORS
Gardners Books
1 Whittle Drive, Eastbourne
East Sussex BN23 6QH
Tel: +44 (0)1323 521555
email: sales@gardners.com

Chaters Wholesale Ltd
25/26 Murrell Green Business Park
Hook, Hampshire RG27 9GR
Tel: +44 (0)1256 765443
Fax: +44 (0)1256 769900
email: books@chaters.co.uk

NORTH AMERICA
National Book Network
NBN
4501 Forbes Boulevard
Suite 200
Lanham, MD 20706
Tel: (301) 459-3366
Fax: (301) 429-5746

AUTOCOURSE™
www.autocourse.com

publisher
STEVE SMALL
steve.small@iconpublishinglimited.com

commercial director
BRYN WILLIAMS
bryn.williams@iconpublishinglimited.com

editor
TONY DODGINS

grand prix correspondents
TONY DODGINS
MAURICE HAMILTON

f1 technical editor
MARK HUGHES

text editor
IAN PENBERTHY

results and statistics
DAVID HAYHOE

lap chart compiler
PETER McLAREN

f1 car and circuit illustrations
ADRIAN DEAN
f1artwork@blueyonder.co.uk

Acknowledgements

France: ACO; Fédération Française du Sport Automobile; FIA (Mohammed Ben Sulayem, Tom Wood, Roman De Lauw); **Germany:** Formula 3 Vereinigung; Mercedes-Benz (Toto Wolff, James Allison, Mike Elliott, James Vowles, Bradley Lord, Richard Wilson, Rosa Herrero Venegas, Charlotte Davies). **Great Britain:** Formula One Group (Stefano Domenicali, Ross Brawn, Liam Parker); Maurice Hamilton, Mark Hughes; McLaren (Zak Brown, James Key, Andreas Seidl, Andrea Stella, Sophie Ogg, Harry Bull, Charlie Russell, Sophie Almeida); Red Bull Racing (Christian Horner, Helmut Marko, Pierre Wache, Paul Monaghan, Paul Smith, Gemma Lusty); Alpine F1 (Laurent Rossi, Otmar Szafnauer, Pat Fry, Matt Harman, Alan Permane, James Lloyd); Aston Martin (Mike Crack, Andrew Green, Tom McCullough, Andy Stevenson, Matt Bishop, Will Hings, Eve Merrell, Britta Roeske); Williams F1 (Jost Capito, Dave Robson, Rebecca Banks); **Italy:** Commissione Sportiva Automobilistica Italiana; Scuderia Ferrari (Mattia Binotto, Laurent Mekies, Silvia Hoffer, Roberta Colleluori, Mia Djacic); AlphaTauri Honda (Franz Tost, Jody Egginton, Jonathan Eddolls, Fabiana Valenti, Carolyn Paterson); Pirelli (Mario Isola, Matteo Bonciani, Anthony Peacock). **Switzerland:** Alfa Romeo ORLEN (Frédéric Vasseur, Jan Monchaux, Will Ponissi). **USA:** Haas (Guenther Steiner, Simone Resta, Stuart Morrison); IndyCar Series; Indianapolis Motor Speedway.

Photographs published in AUTOCOURSE 2022–2023 have been contributed by:

Alfa Romeo ORLEN; Alpine F1 Team; Aston Martin Cognizant Aramco F1 Team; Haas F1 Team; Mercedes-AMG Petronas F1 Team; McLaren F1 Team; Red Bull Content Pool/Getty Images; Scuderia Ferrari; Williams Racing; Pirelli; DTM; F2 Media; Japanese Super Formula; British GP3; Japanese Regional F3; Australian F3; Formula E/LAT; WEC; BTCC/Jacob Ebrey; WTCR/ETCR; Audi Communications Motorsport; BMW Motorsport; LAT Images; Motorsport Images; IndyCar/Penske Entertainment Corp.; Grand Prix Photo/Peter Nygaard; Lukas Gorys; Motor Sport; Peter J. Fox; Atsuo Sakurai; Bryn Williams; XPB Images.

Dust jacket: 2022 FIA World Drivers' Champion Max Verstappen.
Photo: Bryn Williams

Title page: The number '1' on the Red Bull of Max Verstappen, who powered his way to a record-breaking 15 wins during the 2022 season.
Photo: Red Bull Content Pool/Getty Images

STILL LEADING THE FIELD

www.autocourse.com

1
Red Bull
RACING

Photo: Red Bull Content Pool/Getty Images

FOREWORD by MAX VERSTAPPEN

THIS year has been incredible, and as a team we've enjoyed some really special moments as we secured the Drivers' and Constructors' Championships. I'd like to thank the whole team for providing such an incredible car. To win 15 races personally and 17 as a team is just unbelievable. I'm grateful to everyone for the hard work optimising the car each weekend.

It should not be underestimated how tough it is to fight to the wire one season and then to take in a different set of regulations, yet still turn up for the following year with a car capable of giving our team the most competitive season in its history!

We consistently pushed the boundaries, and even in the difficult moments at the beginning of the season, everyone stayed calm and we kept working in the same direction – and that's why we are champions.

I'm confident we can keep this going. I really believe in Red Bull Racing, and our ability to fight for even more wins and championships together in the coming years.

It's also important for everyone to spend some time away from racing, with family and friends, to recharge our batteries and come back to try to do it all again next year in what will be the longest season in F1 history.

Finally, it was incredibly tough to lose our founder and key member of our team, Dietrich Mateschitz. Dietrich believed in me from such a young age and gave incredible opportunities to so many young drivers, and sportsmen and women. For that, I will always be thankful.

EDITOR'S INTRODUCTION

SHUFFLING THE PACK

Above: After Miami, America can't get enough of Formula 1. The record crowd at the United States Grand Prix in Austin paves the way for another extravaganza planned at Las Vegas in 2023.
Photo: Red Bull Content Pool/Getty Images

Top right: Wielders of power. F1's Stefano Domenicali and the FIA's Mohammed Ben Sulayem.
Photo: XPB Images

Above right: In torrential conditions, Pierre Gasly could have had a close call in Japan.

Right: Father-and-son racers. Proud father Jos Verstappen with two-time world champion son Max.
Photos: Red Bull Content Pool/Getty Images

TAKE a look back at relatively recent F1 history, and during the last 20-odd years, there have been three lengthy periods of domination by three different entities: Ferrari, 2000–04 inclusive; Red Bull, 2010–13; and a record-breaking eight-year Mercedes spell from 2014 through 2021.

Ferrari's was brought to an end by a combination of Renault and Fernando Alonso, a tyre regulation change, and the loss of its senior management – Ross Brawn and Jean Todt – and its outstanding driver, Michael Schumacher.

Red Bull's domination was ended by a change of regulations and the ushering in of F1's new hybrid power unit era, with Mercedes having stolen a decisive early march.

Max Verstappen had overcome Mercedes to win his first world title in controversial circumstances at Abu Dhabi in 2021, but in the constructors' championship, the team was still on top. But there was every chance that swingeing chassis alterations, with a return to ground-effect aerodynamics for the first time in 40 years might upset that, and so it proved. Once again, a major rule change shuffled the pack.

Ultimately, Red Bull did a tremendous job of transitioning late on to its new 2022 car after the demands of the '21 season, yet served up the most dominant year of its 18-year history. Sadly, team founder Dietrich Mateschitz (see page 50) passed away just a couple of weeks after Verstappen had sealed his second successive title in Japan.

Suzuka was a bit of a shambles for very different reasons, one important, one less so. In the aftermath of the 2021 Abu Dhabi controversy, where Lewis Hamilton and Mercedes had felt robbed, with some justification, the governing FIA dispensed with the services of Michael Masi as race director, instead rotating former DTM race director Niels Wittich and Portuguese former WEC race director Eduardo Freitas in the role.

Freitas was in charge in Japan, where, in conditions mirroring those of 2014 – when Jules Bianchi had been fatally injured when he struck a recovery vehicle out on the circuit – another course vehicle was despatched to recover Carlos Sainz's Ferrari. Pierre Gasly had been in the pits at the time of its deployment, something that was overlooked by race control, and was apoplectic when, running hard on full wets to catch the pack behind a safety car, he encountered the recovery vehicle in the gloom. Most drivers shared Gasly's dismay, none more so than Charles Leclerc, who had been mentored by Bianchi.

It was a sad and poignant moment when Bianchi's father took to social media with the message, "No respect for the life of the driver, no respect for Jules' memory."

The other issue at Suzuka was the points distribution for shortened races, which had been amended after the Spa '21 debacle, when half-points had been awarded for a race that never actually got under way, other than for three exploratory laps behind the safety car.

Everyone – drivers, teams, broadcasters, media – believed that a 28-lap Japanese GP was between 50 and 75 per cent of the scheduled 53 laps when it timed out, and therefore the new points allocation pertinent to that (see page 28) meant that the victorious Verstappen had fallen one point

short of his second title. But the bit in the rules about it only applying to races that had been red-flagged and could not be restarted had been left in place erroneously. The FIA went by the book – how could it do otherwise after the fallout from Abu Dhabi in 2021? – awarded full points, and Max was champion.

One of new FIA president Mohammed Ben Sulayem's election manifesto pledges had been greater transparency. We certainly got that, with a prompt and full investigation into Suzuka under FIA deputy president for sport Robin Reid. As a result, measures were put in place to better track the positions of all cars on-circuit and moves to tidy up the rulebook were confirmed. Freitas, meanwhile, was sidelined, with Wittich taking over full charge of F1 race direction thereafter.

That apart, there were a few gripes about track limits and the consistency of penalty applications, but nothing of the scale of Abu Dhabi '21 to be concerned with.

Commercially, F1 went from strength to strength. Miami played host to its first grand prix and was a success, even if fake marinas didn't quite do it for you! How much is attributable to the 'Netflix effect' and *Drive to Survive* is difficult to ascertain, but races were practically sold out across the board.

With Las Vegas part of a 24-race schedule in 2023, the calendar has grown by 50 per cent from the relatively recent past, when 16-race seasons were typical. China has bitten the dust once again for 2023, due to Covid restrictions. Whether or not it is replaced, the New Year will offer a record number of races. The sport is in rude health.

Above: IndyCar provided some thrilling racing in a season when Will Power and Josef Newgarden disputed the championship. The Penske pair leads the field at Iowa.
Photo: IndyCar/Penske Entertainment Corp.

Top right: Stoffel Vandoorne might have scored only a single victory at Monaco, but his consistency took him to the FormulaE title.
Photo: FormulaE

Above right: Toyota triumphed again at Le Mans. The drivers of the victorious No.8 car, Sébastien Buemi, Brendon Hartley and Ryu Hirakawa, celebrate their success.
Photo: WEC

Right: There was controversy in the final WTCC season of its current guise. Mikel Azcona and Hyundai took the honours after the Lynk & Co team had withdrawn mid-season.
Photo: WTCC

In Sportscars, Toyota took its Hypercar to a fifth consecutive World Endurance Championship and Le Mans 24 Hours win, with the No.8 Toyota Gazoo Racing entry, shared by Kiwi Brendon Hartley, Ryu Hirakawa and Sébastien Buemi, taking the spoils. The champions won the six-round series by seeing off the Alpine challenge of André Negrão, Mathieu Vaxivière and Nicolas Lapierre, who took wins at Sebring and Monza.

Brazilian Felipe Drugovich was a comfortable winner of the FIA Formula 2 championship. Driving for MP Motorsport, the 22-year-old took the title by 101 points, winning feature races in Jeddah, Barcelona, Monaco and Zandvoort. He was rewarded with a reserve-driver role at Aston Martin.

Runner-up Théo Pourchaire, Alfa Romeo's reserve, won feature races in Bahrain, Imola and Budapest, while third-placed driver Liam Lawson won sprint races in Jeddah, Paul Ricard, Spa and Abu Dhabi.

In fourth place, American Logan Sargeant won the Silverstone feature and secured enough F1 superlicence points to claim a seat alongside Alex Albon at Williams in 2023.

Frenchman Victor Martins claimed the FIA F3 crown, with feature-race victories in Bahrain and Spain. It was a close-fought season with Barbadian Zane Maloney, who won at Zandvoort, and Briton Oliver Bearman, who claimed the Spa sprint race.

The ABB FIA Formula E series, now in its eighth season, fell to Mercedes driver Stoffel Vandoorne. The Belgian took a lone win in Monaco, but his consistency won out against Kiwi Jaguar Racing driver Mitch Evans, who recorded a Rome double and a win in South Korea. Swiss Edoardo Mortara claimed third in the series.

In the World Touring Car Cup, which was in its fifth and final season under the current format, Spanish Hyundai driver Mikel Azcona triumphed, ahead of Argentine Nestor Girolami with his Honda Civic, and the Audi of Frenchman Nathanaël Berthon. Going forward, a new touring car World Tour series is planned.

In the USA, Will Power won his second IndyCar title with Team Penske, beating team-mate Josef Newgarden to the crown after a Monterrey finale where five drivers were in contention. Scott Dixon finished third in the series with Chip Ganassi, while 2021 champion Alex Palou won at Laguna Seca on the way to fifth overall. He also impressed McLaren with his handling of its MCL36 in the first free practice session for the US GP in Austin, earning himself an F1 third driver role with the team in non-clashing weekends in 2023.

The 106th running of the Indy 500 resulted in a win for former F1 driver Marcus Ericsson, with Chip Ganassi, after team-mate Scott Dixon started from his fifth 500 pole.

In the 51st season of the NASCAR Cup, Joey Logano took the title, ahead of Ross Chastain, Christopher Bell and regular season champion Chase Elliott. Some 19 different race winners throughout the year equalled a modern-era record set in 2001.

Tony Dodgins
December, 2022

Simon Arron

Photo: Courtesy of Motor Sport

IT is with great regret and sadness that I have to record the sudden passing of good friend, colleague, ex-AUTOCOURSE editor and all-round good guy, Simon Arron, at 61.

It actually feels wrong to use the word 'sadness' in the same sentence as Simon. He was the most upbeat, positive person you could ever come across, with an unquenchable love and enthusiasm for every single form of motor racing. He would think nothing of stepping off a 12-hour post-Brazilian GP flight from São Paulo to London – in the cheap seats – and climbing straight into his car to go and meet a mate testing a Ford Anglia classic saloon at Oulton Park.

Over 20-odd years of oft-tiring worldwide travel, deadline pressures, funny moments, poignant moments, room sharing and mickey-taking, there was truthfully never a wrong or angry word. Only a month before the awful news, he emailed me to ask what I thought of IBM Thinkpads. He'd just bought 15,000 motor racing negatives – many obscure, no doubt – and needed to archive them.

We're all privileged to work in a fabulous sport, but it won't be quite the same without him. To his son Tom, daughter Lucy, family and many, many friends, AUTOCOURSE and I extend our most sincere condolences.

Tezos
Red Bull
ORACLE
BYBIT

FIA F1 WORLD CHAMPIONSHIP 2022

TOP TEN DRIVERS

THE EDITOR'S CHOICE

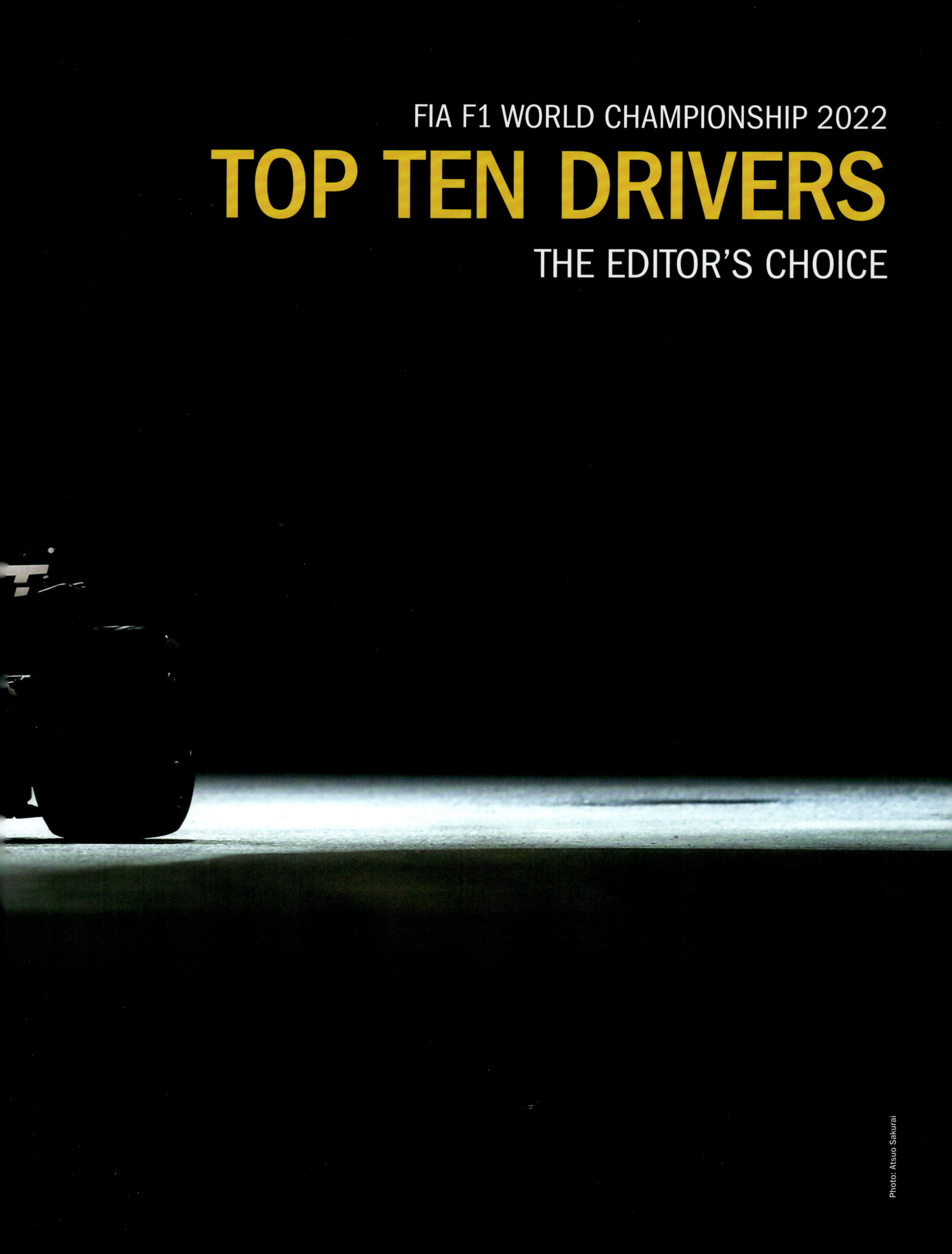

Photo: Atsuo Sakurai

Photo: Red Bull Content Pool/Getty Images

MAX VERSTAPPEN

1

SO conclusively did Max Verstappen dominate the 2022 season that there can be no other choice as No.1.

At the beginning, when reliability bugs plagued Red Bull, and he retired in Bahrain and Australia, it looked as though Max had a fight on his hands with Charles Leclerc and Ferrari. But he parlayed a tricky start into a record 15 wins in a single season.

Post-Melbourne, round three of 22, he was almost admitting defeat, already 46 points behind Leclerc at a point where it seemed that he could only take eight points per race, at best, out of that deficit. But the season turned, and quicker than anyone could have anticipated.

Imola was key. After Leclerc was quickest in wet qualifying, Max passed him assertively and won the season's first sprint race, putting him on the drier pole side for the main race. From there, he won comfortably as Leclerc spun down to sixth in pursuit of second. It was the first win of a hat trick, followed by victories in Miami and Barcelona.

As the pendulum swung, it seemed as though Verstappen could win from anywhere on the grid – tenth in Hungary and even 14th at Spa. Both were sublime performances. Okay, the Red Bull was undeniably the class of the field in Belgium, but even so, Max was on an entirely different level to team-mate Pérez.

At Suzuka, he was on a different level to everyone, a 27s victory in a 28-lap race ridiculously good. That clinched him a second title.

Verstappen and Leclerc had karting 'history', but the racing between them was notably clean and respectful. Max seemingly cut Charles more slack than he ever allowed Lewis Hamilton, a point reinforced in Brazil. The refusal to switch positions with Pérez at Interlagos was not his finest hour, the only real blot on the season. The team was not blameless, but even if he had his reasons for not obliging Sergio, it was perhaps surprising that he didn't embrace the bigger picture.

CHARLES LECLERC

2

LECLERC is world champion material. Initially, it looked as though 2022 would be the year. Probably the quickest single-lap driver in F1, when he converted Bahrain and Australian poles into race victories, and finished second to Verstappen in Saudi Arabia, opening a 46-point advantage over the Dutchman, few would have bet against him.

But part of the reason for his stunning one-lap qualifying speed, the Ferrari's ability to bring its tyres in quickly, worked against him on Sunday afternoon. Especially after the Spa technical directive, which resulted in Ferrari running the car higher, with less tyre-protecting downforce. Whereas Red Bull took a step forward in the race, Ferrari went backwards with higher tyre degradation. And while Red Bull was spot on operationally, the same could not be said of Maranello.

The year degenerated quickly: an engine failure while leading comfortably at Barcelona; his Monaco pole negated by a lack of strategic sharpness on the Ferrari pit wall; Azerbaijan another retirement after his sixth pole in eight races (he took nine over the season); engine frailty in Canada limiting him to fifth on a day when team-mate Sainz had pushed Verstappen. Then frustration at not being prioritised at Silverstone and ending up on the wrong tyre. Angry didn't make a start on it. I mean, who passes Hamilton around the outside of Copse on old tyres...

There was only one more win, a fine race in Austria where he had to pass Verstappen on-track three times. By that point, Max had turned that large deficit into a 38-point championship lead, and it was crucial that Leclerc kept the momentum going in France. Instead, under pit-stop pressure from Max, he crashed out of the lead. After spinning down to sixth in Imola, it was Leclerc's second driving error as Verstappen went on a five-race win streak.

But if – and it's a big if – Ferrari gets the job done, Leclerc will deliver. Make no mistake.

Photo: Scuderia Ferrari

Photo: McLaren F1 Team

LANDO NORRIS

3

IT was a close call as to whether Norris deserved to be second in the rankings, so consistently good was his level in 2022.

Outside the 'Big Three' teams, Lando was 'best of the rest' by a country mile, helped by Fernando Alonso's myriad reliability issues at Alpine. The lowest points-scorer from the top six was Lewis Hamilton, on 240; Norris, seventh, finished on 122, with Alpine's Esteban Ocon and Alonso on 92 and 81 respectively.

Whenever conditions or circuit layout put more emphasis on the driver in the overall car/driver performance equation, Norris stood out. In a chaotic qualifying session at Imola, which was red-flagged five times, only Verstappen and Leclerc were quicker. In wet conditions at Silverstone, he lined up sixth; in the one-hit Brazilian session, he was fourth and at Monaco, fifth.

A podium at Imola was the race highlight, but fourth place in Singapore was fabulous, too. Marina Bay is the toughest physical challenge of the season anyway, without a driver having to alter his line at Turn Six to avoid exceeding the FIA's aerodynamic oscillation metric! The last place in the world he would want bad porpoising... A VSC stop helped, but to finish fourth, not far behind old team-mate Sainz's Ferrari, mentally spent through intense concentration, was outstanding.

The McLaren MCL36 was not an easy chassis – entry instability and mid-corner understeer – but Norris adapted while Daniel Ricciardo was lost. The 20–2 qualifying superiority in his favour was the biggest across the grid, and the average 0.326s between them was exceeded only by Bottas's margin over rookie Zhou and Albon's over Latifi. Effectively, it ended Daniel's F1 career.

It's time that Lando was competing for race wins and championships. His speed and talent look absolutely top drawer, and it will be a big ask for Oscar Piastri to sit alongside him, irrespective of the young Aussie's own potential. Simulators are sophisticated these days, but there's still no substitute for real on-track mileage. A fascinating partnership.

LEWIS HAMILTON

4

AFTER enjoying the best/equal-best car for the previous eight seasons, Hamilton was presented with a Mercedes W13 that was not on the same level as the Red Bull or Ferrari, and, in George Russell, his quickest team-mate since Fernando Alonso.

Early season, F1's new ground-effect regulations resulted in bouncing or 'porpoising' dominating the paddock lexicon, and the Mercedes was most seriously affected. If any justification is needed for putting Hamilton ahead of Russell in an end-of-season analysis, with fewer points, no poles and fewer front-row starts, it goes back to the early-season experimentation that his experience and working relationships with the technical team, dictated he conduct. As far as Azerbaijan, Russell was more impressive and 5–3 ahead in the qualifying head-to-head.

But as the team began to get a handle on the car and development brought it closer to the ultimate pace, so Lewis became stronger. It might not have been his greatest year: he went out in Q1 at Jeddah in a car he labelled "undrivable", but that goes back to the previous point; he was out on the opening lap at Spa, at fault for a contact with Alonso; and Singapore was messy and uncharacteristic. On other occasions, however, Russell beat him through advantages such as fortuitous safety car timing.

By season's end, Hamilton led in Austin and, with bolder team strategy, could have won in Mexico City. He'd turned around the qualifying head-to-head and followed his team-mate over the line in Brazil for Mercedes' only win of the year.

It might all have added up to just the third time in 16 years that Hamilton had been out-pointed by a team-mate over a full season (Jenson Button and Nico Rosberg achieved it), but, as he said, it was for fourth and fifth. If it had been about first and second, that's different. His work ethic and motivational presence are still mighty and, who knows, Mercedes could be shooting for the titles again in 2023.

Photo: XPB Images

Photo: Mercedes-AMG Petronas F1 Team

GEORGE RUSSELL

5

IT was Russell's misfortune that, after three years at the back with Williams, his move to eight-time consecutive constructors' champions, Mercedes, coincided with significant rule changes and a fall-off in level from the three-pointed star.

'Mr Saturday's' qualifying performances at Williams had led many to believe that he might even have had Lewis Hamilton's number for single-lap pace. He didn't quite, but it was mighty close. By season's end, he was 13–9 down over the year, by an average of just 0.02s – the closest team-mate differential across the grid.

Aboard a difficult car, he finished the first nine races in the top five, with podiums in Melbourne, Barcelona and Baku. He wasn't remotely fazed by having a seven-time champion on the other side of the garage. Rather, he relished the opportunity to prove his credentials as a top-liner.

Why does a man with more points, and his team's lone race win and pole position under his belt, not outrank his team-mate? You could actually build a case for any driver ranked second through sixth to occupy the P2 slot behind Verstappen.

In George's case, there was a mid-season drop-off just after the summer break. Starting at the Belgian GP, he qualified eighth, sixth, sixth, eleventh and eighth at five successive races, behind Hamilton every time. In addition to his retirement on the opening lap at Silverstone, there was a first-lap collision with pole-man Sainz in Austin. Hamilton led that race and was the stronger Mercedes driver in Mexico, too, despite George outqualifying him.

But by any measure, it was a massively impressive first year at Mercedes. The Budapest pole was the most unexpected of the year, save Kevin Magnussen's in Brazil, and Russell's Interlagos win was simply fabulous. A restart with a dozen laps remaining and Lewis Hamilton right behind trying to keep his win-every-season record alive, and potentially with DRS? You'd have bet on Lewis. But George was cucumber cool. A champion in the making.

FERNANDO ALONSO

6

YOU wouldn't think that Fernando Alonso had made his F1 debut almost 22 years ago, at the Australian GP in 2001.

The season-closing Abu Dhabi GP was his 355th F1 start, with only five other drivers qualifying for F1's '300 Club' – Kimi Räikkönen, 349; Rubens Barrichello, 325; Lewis Hamilton, 310; and Michael Schumacher and Jenson Button, 306 each.

It remains true that no driver has managed to win a GP after passing the 300 mark. Hamilton must be favourite to do that, but Alonso, in the right car, would be more than capable of it, too. But perhaps the 41-year-old's shelf life was all part of the thinking when Alpine baulked at offering the multi-year contract extension that he had sought. Aston Martin quickly swooped.

There wasn't much between Alonso and team-mate Esteban Ocon for one-lap speed, Fernando 12–10 up with less than a tenth between them for average qualifying pace over the year. But over a race distance, he was as feisty and relentless as ever. His fifth place at Silverstone ranks as possibly the best of many excellent performances in 2022, a result he matched at Spa and Brazil, more of which anon. He was sixth in France and the Netherlands, and seventh in Monaco, Azerbaijan, Canada, Japan and USA.

Alonso's Achilles heel was Alpine unreliability, which led to retirements in Saudi Arabia, Imola, Monza, Singapore, Mexico and Abu Dhabi. Without that, undoubtedly he would have been battling Lando Norris for 'best of the rest' honours in the championship, behind drivers from 'The Big Three' teams.

"Last year, I wasn't 100 per cent happy with how it went, but this year, I was much happier with the car and with my performance. You need a few races or even a whole season to feel 100 per cent again," he admitted.

There were some spiky on-track moments with Ocon, none more so that in Brazil, where they took each other out of contention in the sprint. Given their mutual combative spirit, it was inevitable. Make no mistake, Alonso still has it.

Photo: Alpine F1 Team

CARLOS SAINZ

7

THE highlight of Sainz's year was pole position and a first grand prix win in his 150th start at the British Grand Prix at Silverstone.

The Ferrari F1-75 was quickest of all at the start of the season, Charles Leclerc winning two of the first three races. Initially, however, Carlos found it snappy and tricky, his confidence taking an early-season battering. He was second to Leclerc in the Bahrain season-opener, and then a podium finisher behind Verstappen and his team-mate in Saudi. But then came a spin in Australia and a retirement after a collision at Imola.

While Leclerc is acknowledged as one of the outright quickest over a single lap, Sainz did a fine job to qualify an average of just a tenth behind him in their first season together. That margin was more like a quarter of a second over the first third of 2022, but his adaptability and work ethic brought it back to 2021 levels over the latter part of the year.

As Carlos himself said, "It was a bit of a nightmare with the early-season retirements. I was slow when the car was fast, and by the end of the year, I was fast, but, relatively, we were not as fast as before, so nothing was quite right."

Austin was his season in microcosm. So often within a few hundredths of Verstappen and Leclerc, he finally claimed a second pole in Texas, but was taken out by Russell at the first corner…

Early season, Leclerc established himself as very much 'The Man' at Ferrari, and once he was in that position, it was difficult for Carlos to fight back. He tried hard, at times the calmest head in the place and a guiding light when there was strategy doubt on the pit wall.

He finished the season fifth in the championship, and it will be interesting to see what he can achieve in 2023 if he makes a better start. That's always key at Ferrari. In Leclerc, though, he faces a formidable foe.

SERGIO PÉREZ

8

EDDIE IRVINE once described being Michael Schumacher's team-mate as akin to being hit around the head with a cricket bat every couple of weeks. It's an invidious position to be on the opposite side of the garage to a true elite performer, which Verstappen is undeniably.

At the start of 2022, Pérez made quite a good fist of it. We'd become used to average team-mate qualifying deficits to Verstappen being in the order of 0.4–0.5s, but Checo qualified 0.24s adrift in Bahrain, took an almost unbelievable pole in Jeddah, then lined up just 0.09s adrift in Melbourne and within 0.04s in Miami. Some even talked of him challenging for the title.

But there were reasons. Red Bull's late transition on to its '22 car, after its to-the-wire 2021 season, meant that initially RB18 was a bit flabby, some 20kg over an already increased weight limit. It was lazier and understeered, the exact opposite to how Verstappen likes a car. It wasn't so much Sergio making a step as Max being reduced to the lowest common denominator.

As the season progressed, that changed. The car wasn't being deliberately developed in Max's direction rather than Sergio's, it was rather the natural result of weight saving and balance change effectively amounting to the same thing.

Pérez has always been great on street circuits, where precision, consistency and economy of effort, rather than outright flamboyance, can reap reward. His Monaco win was a career highlight, but evidently it upset his team-mate, who believed that Checo's Q3 spin at Portiers, after a first run that was 0.04s quicker than his own, was no accident. Pérez went on to win the race, with Verstappen third. At that stage, some seven races in, the Mexican was still within 15 points of the championship lead.

After Verstappen's Singapore weekend went pear-shaped, Pérez took the best win of his career under intense pressure from Leclerc. But two wins versus 15 tells the story. And the end-of-season spat, Monaco payback, was a shame.

Photo: Red Bull Content Pool/Getty Images

Photo: XPB Images

ESTEBAN OCON

9

EVER since they were thrown together as Alpine team-mates, it had been nip and tuck for one-lap pace between Esteban Ocon and Fernando Alonso. There had been an average of just 0.07s between them in Fernando's favour in 2021, and in 2022, Alonso shaded their qualifying battles 12–10 by an average of just 0.09s. Only the 0.02s margin separating Hamilton and Russell was tighter.

It meant that often they found themselves disputing the same pieces of tarmac early in races. And occasionally it wasn't pretty! Esteban is not slow, but Alonso's relentless race pace is even quicker, only sometimes the other Alpine was not easy to negotiate.

Ocon is a tough – sometimes more than tough – racer, as Sergio Pérez could attest after their two seasons together at Racing Point in 2017 and '18. Remember Spa, Baku and Singapore?

Then, as now, Otmar Szafnauer was the long-suffering referee! Among the 'highlights' of the season were Saudi, where Ocon's defence against Alonso could have been described as marginal, and Hungary, where his opening-lap defence moved Alonso to claim, "Never in my life have I seen defence like Esteban's today. Never!"

Then came Brazil, when, while embroiled in a tight constructors' battle with McLaren, they took chunks out of each other in the sprint race, and started the main event 17th and 18th! Big boss Laurent Rossi was apoplectic.

Ocon is feisty and uncompromising, and he won't be bowed – a bit like his nemesis. There were some fine results in 2022: sixth in Saudi and Canada, fifth in Austria, and the highlight, a brilliant fourth at Suzuka defending from Hamilton.

The Frenchman always professed the utmost respect for Alonso, even if things had become a bit lukewarm by the end of their two years together. It just makes you wonder how it might be when Pierre Gasly, a man with whom Esteban has a bit of history, arrives… Ready, Otmar?

VALTTERI BOTTAS

10

DECIDING on the final spot in the 2022 Top Ten was a tough call. Both Pierre Gasly and Alex Albon had decent claims. At Williams, Albon's 0.6s average qualifying gap to team-mate Nicholas Latifi was the biggest differential across the entire grid, and even more impressive than the 0.42s average by which 'Mr Saturday', George Russell, had bested the Canadian in 2021.

Ultimately, though, the first half of Valtteri Bottas's season just shades it. Far from being disillusioned by losing his Mercedes seat to Russell, Bottas hit the ground running with Alfa Romeo and took full advantage of the only car to be on the weight limit at the start of the season.

He scored points in seven of the first nine races: Bahrain, Australia, Imola, Miami, Spain, Monaco and Canada. He qualified as high as fifth in Miami, and might even have beaten the Mercs but for a spin.

A fifth place at Imola proved more crucial than anyone could have anticipated. When Alfa found itself out-developed comprehensively – I suppose you can't get any lighter when you've started on the weight limit! – the second half of its season went backwards at about the same rate as Aston Martin advanced. They ended the year tied on 55 points after Abu Dhabi. Alfa took an estimated extra $10m, thanks to Bottas's Imola result bettering the sixth places achieved by Sebastian Vettel in Azerbaijan and Suzuka, and by Lance Stroll in Singapore.

The average qualifying margin of 0.4s that the experienced Bottas had over Zhou Guanyu was the second biggest differential across the grid, which was to be expected in the Chinese driver's rookie F1 season. But the fact that Zhou actually managed to outqualify Valtteri eight times over the season reflects very well on his level and ability to quickly take on board the lessons and complications of F1, despite a very nasty accident at Silverstone. He deserves his second year at Alfa.

Photo: Alfa Romeo ORLEN

A NEW WORLD ORDER

A combined study between F1 and the FIA gave rise to new technical and financial regulations designed to improve the quality of racing and level the F1 playing field over time. The pecking order was likely to change, and did. TONY DODGINS reviews the 2022 season...

Above: The sparks flew between Red Bull and Ferrari in the opening races of the season.
Photo: Atsuo Sakurai

Right: Adrian Newey's mastery of the black art of aerodynamics was put to good use on the RB18.
Photo: Red Bull Content Pool/Getty Images

Far right: Ferrari racing director Laurent Mekies and his team were up for the challenge.
Photo: Scuderia Ferrari

AFTER eight years of record-breaking domination by Mercedes, dating back to the start of F1's hybrid era in 2014, it is not disrespecting the three-pointed star's stunning achievements to say that a press of the 'reset' button was anticipated with relish. Red Bull's Max Verstappen might have clinched the 2021 drivers' title in that controversial Abu Dhabi finale, but Mercedes had ended the season with the quickest car once again.

The 2022 regulations, heralding a return to ground-effect aerodynamics, was probably the biggest rule change to hit the sport for 40 years, since the switch *away* from ground effect for 1983! The question was whether the Mercedes juggernaut could navigate such new territory. Or, as is so often the case with such a conceptual change, would there be a new world order?

Pre-season testing at Sakhir in Bahrain and then the opening races pointed firmly to the latter. It was a resurgent Ferrari team and Charles Leclerc who won in Bahrain and Australia, and finished runner-up to Verstappen at Jeddah in between. Meanwhile, Mercedes could not qualify higher than fifth.

In terms of 'the show', the greatest relief and probably biggest surprise was the closeness of the competition. Historically, whenever there is such a fundamental change, someone gets it very right and dominates, while the rest take time to copy and catch up. But despite clearly differing approaches in the key downforce-producing sidepod area of the cars, there was little to choose between the Ferrari and the Red Bull, while Mercedes was a good seven-tenths away in qualifying trim.

Leclerc's Ferrari took pole for the Bahrain opener with 1m 30.558s, Verstappen's Red Bull alongside him on 1m 30.681s, and Carlos Sainz just 0.006s adrift in the second Ferrari. Lewis Hamilton's 1m 31.238s showed that Mercedes had work to do, the team badly affected by the paddock's new buzzwords – 'porpoising' and 'bouncing'.

Winston Churchill once told Parliament that those who fail to learn from history are condemned to repeat it. When Colin Chapman's Lotus team dominated in 1978 with its Lotus 79 ground-effect car, the innovative designer pursued the belief that 'more is better'. He went in search of maximum downforce with his extreme Lotus 80. Initially, he wanted downforce-creating venturis under the nose as well as the main sidepods, which, on the Type 80, extended beyond even the rear wheels, all sealed by full-length skirts.

The skirt area around the rear wheels proved an insurmountable problem, and the front venturis were abandoned in favour of small wings front and rear. Chapman's original thinking had been that if he could produce so much downforce from the venturis, why did he need wings at all? Indeed, the car did produce lots of downforce, but it wasn't consistent. Lotus knew it had a problem when, testing at Silverstone, Mario Andretti reported that he could see daylight under the front wheels while flat-out on the straight!

The 80 was bouncing all over the place, and it was Mario who coined the term 'porpoising'.

The condition is caused by aero-elasticity, as Peter Wright, conductor of much of the pioneering work behind the Lotus ground-effect cars, described it. The Lotus 80, he explained, was so sensitive that above a certain critical speed, it became aerodynamically unstable in pitch.

The 2022 cars were always likely to be prone to it, too, with much more downforce generated by the underbodies and running so close to the track surface. If the air separates sufficiently, the aero stalls and the ride height rises, until the airflow reattaches and the ride height drops again. The process repeats, hence the porpoising.

You could perhaps accuse the Mercedes W13 of being a modern-day Lotus 80. The team had taken an adventurous approach to the letter of the regulations (*see* Team Review, page 68) and, with its 'zero' pods, had gone down a path not trodden by anyone else. Like Chapman, they were hamstrung by aero inconsistency and the mechanical limitations of suspension. They improved to the point where George Russell and Hamilton could finish 1-2 at Interlagos, but were realistic enough to admit that Brazil was probably the season's only weekend when Red Bull had underperformed seriously.

When the return to ground effects was announced, you couldn't help but think that it was right up Red Bull chief technical officer (CTO) Adrian Newey's street. In his exclusive interview with AUTOCOURSE (*see* page 42), team principal Christian Horner explained that Adrian "just missed" ground effects the first time around. Well, yes, but…

Newey specifically undertook a course in Aeronautics and Astronautics at Southampton University because he could see the way the wind was blowing, excuse the pun, and wanted to design race-cars rather than to work in the motor industry, in which case he'd have opted for mechanical engineering.

He chose Southampton because he knew that the Brabham and March F1 teams used its wind tunnel and hoped that it would add some credibility to future job applications! And his final year project, which helped him to a first-class honours degree, was 'Ground effect aerodynamics as applied to a sports car'.

Realising that the super-stiff and hence uncomfortable suspension needed to cope with the downforce was impractical for a sports car, Newey had proposed a variable-geometry spring system linked to the car's speed, or what would later become known as active suspension, now banned in F1 of course.

Forty years on, while 60-odd-year-old mere mortals having some sort of life crisis might buy themselves a Mk1 Escort Twincam or a Ducati 900SS, how satisfying must the career symmetry be for Newey to be given the time and budget to finally indulge himself in a lifetime's ambition, Red Bull's RB17 hypercar (*see* page 42), splitting his time with F1?

Even though F1 teams are now 800-strong rather than 30-strong as they would have been 40 years ago, with modern simulation tools to boot, having Newey as CTO amid such a swingeing change can only have been a huge benefit. It's perhaps no surprise that his main input to the 2022 car was the suspension – key to achieving consistent downforce.

Red Bull was on top of porpoising from the start, and given the myriad wind tunnels and simulation tools available today, it was perhaps surprising that others were not. Ferrari team principal Mattia Binotto, who ultimately would end the year falling on his sword, explained: "Such behaviour is normal with this type of car. And it cannot be simulated in the wind tunnel because it occurs at 250–270km/h, and the regulations limit wind-tunnel speed to 180km/h."

Red Bull's early-season failings – if, indeed, circumstances that gave them 'only' the equal-fastest car can be couched in such terms – were down to reliability problems and additional weight, both caused by the rapid transition on to the '22 car after a '21 season that had gone right down to the wire as far as 12th December. It all added up to a slightly lazy RB18 without the kind of sharp front end preferred by Verstappen.

It was an opening for Ferrari, which had turned heads at Red Bull with its quick and consistent pre-season testing performances. And initially the Scuderia made the most of it. Leclerc was the qualifying king of 2022, with nine pole positions and the quickest average qualifying time over the year. Quite often, his pole time would come on a second Q3 run when he would throw caution to the wind, flirting with the walls and barriers, the Ferrari alive and a joy to behold.

But he converted front-row starts into wins on only three occasions. After those two victories in the first three rounds at Sakhir and Melbourne, the only other win came mid-season in Austria.

But that's far from the full story. While Leclerc was not blameless himself, turning a potential second into sixth at Imola when he lost the Ferrari at Variante Alta chasing Pérez, he could quite easily have won another seven consecutive

Above: Both Charles Leclerc and Carlos Sainz felt that they were championship contenders after the Ferrari's show of pace in the Middle East.
Photo: Scuderia Ferrari

Above right: One step forward and one step back for Mercedes, but Lewis Hamilton never gave up. A Barcelona first-lap collision with Kevin Magnussen left him in last place, but he brought the car home fifth.
Photo: Mercedes-AMG Petronas F1 Team

Right: By the time of the French Grand Prix in July, Max Verstappen had won his seventh race of the season, and the writing was on the wall for the opposition.
Photo: Atsuo Sakurai

races, four of which fell to arch rival Verstappen, between round six in Spain and round 12 in France.

In Barcelona, he led comfortably from pole before the engine failed. At Monaco, Ferrari managed to lose the race on strategy, despite locking out the front row. That takes some doing at Monte Carlo, even if variable conditions throw in a curveball!

"Box now, for hards," Leclerc was told over the radio in the Principality. Then, too late, just as he arrived in the pit lane: "Stay out, stay out, stay out!"

"Why? What?" was the irate response, followed – after trailing home fourth in a race he should have won – by a calm, more resigned, "I have no words… no words. The season is long, but we cannot do that."

In Azerbaijan, another pole, another retirement. Canada: a replacement engine, grid drop and fifth place in a race when team-mate Carlos Sainz had pushed Verstappen all the way to the flag.

Then Silverstone, where Ferrari chose not to move Sainz out of the way to prioritise the quicker Leclerc, resulting in him ending up on the wrong tyres, condemned to finish fourth in a race he'd had the pace to win. That put him on a collision course with Binotto. He was so annoyed that he managed to overtake Lewis Hamilton around the outside of Copse on old tyres! Probably not recommended for anyone targeting old age, but ballsy in the extreme and phenomenal to witness.

"The amount of race time we have lost during this race… Oh, my God!" lamented the frustrated Monégasque on the slow-down lap.

Austria he did win, after passing Verstappen three times, reversing the Saturday sprint result and, rarely, having the more benign tyre usage. Then came France, where undercut pressure from Verstappen forced a costly error from Leclerc himself, who spun away the lead on his own at Turn 11.

"Nooooooooooooo!" he screamed from the cockpit. For one so level headed and grounded out of the cockpit, it was a quite shocking example of his competitive instincts and emotions laid bare. One race after half-distance, it was all but over, Verstappen 63 points clear in the championship at that point.

Max was sublime all season, though. When he won his first championship, he had said that anything afterwards was a bonus. Since he is so naturally quick and innately competitive, you wrote that off as PR-speak, but actually he did seem more relaxed in 2022. He was never exactly a bundle of nerves to start with, but who knew what had gone on in the head when faced with the pressure cooker of Abu Dhabi '21?

Some of the early-season racing with Leclerc was tremendous, both of them fully committed, but respectful and affording each other racing room. They'd had their karting spats in the past, but in Jeddah, it was great to see Leclerc acknowledge his rival's driving with "that was good," despite having to settle for second. Whether it would have remained the same between them if Ferrari had continued as it had started and the fight had gone to the wire is a different matter, but it did seem as though Verstappen was prepared to cut Leclerc more slack than ever he had done Hamilton. Putting that observation to father Jos in Abu Dhabi, just a week after the latest Lewis/Max contact at Interlagos, brought a wry smile. "I think it might be the other way around," Verstappen Sr said.

While Ferrari was left to contemplate potential winning streaks for Leclerc that didn't happen, Red Bull could savour those that did for Verstappen. Between Miami in early May and Canada in mid-June, he took victories in four out of five races, and from France at the end of June until Mexico in October, he won eight out of nine. That meant a new record 15 wins in a single season, beating the 13 of Michael Schumacher at Ferrari in 2004, and Sebastian Vettel, with Red Bull again, in 2013. Schumacher's 13 from 18

represented a 72.2 per cent strike rate, while Max's 15 from 22 worked out at 68.2 per cent, so there's still something for him to aim for!

It was 'Mercedes-plus' dominance from Red Bull, giving the team its first constructors' championship since 2013 and, with 17 wins (Sergio Pérez having claimed Monaco and Singapore), the most successful season in its history.

Early-season, as drivers felt the physical effects of the porpoising aboard stiffly-suspended cars, the need to address it mid-season became a political hot potato. The teams not so badly affected by it resisted, claiming that it was motivated by those teams unable to run their cars low enough to maximise ground effect.

After round four at Imola, George Russell, in his debut season with Mercedes and one of those suffering most, said, "The bouncing really takes your breath away. It's the most extreme I've ever felt it. I really hope we find a solution because it's not sustainable for the drivers. This is the first weekend I've truly been struggling with my back and almost like, chest pains, from the severity of the bouncing."

There were those who pooh-poohed the safety element, pointing out that it was the only justifiable means of initiating what would effectively become an in-season rule change (read 'interpretation') not otherwise agreed upon by sufficient teams.

Post-Azerbaijan, Hamilton was suffering badly with back pain from severe porpoising down Baku's long main straight and struggled to get out of the car, claiming that there was no way that he could have done so in an emergency within the FIA's required time frame.

"I was actually biting down on my teeth," he said. "I can't express the pain you experience, particularly on the straight, and I was just praying for the race to end."

Some might have been inclined to nominate the seven-time champion for an Oscar, but they wouldn't have been in the cockpit! For those of a certain age, however, it brought

Above: With the opposition on the ropes, they were well and truly floored in Spa, where Red Bull's Max Verstappen and Sergio Pérez delivered a dominant 1-2 finish.

Top right: Pérez produced the lap of his career to claim pole position in Saudi Arabia.
Photos: Red Bull Content Pool/Getty Images

Above right: After the early flyaway races, normality returned to the paddock, and the wearing of masks was no longer obligatory.
Photo: XPB Images

Right: Due to the weather, the race in Suzuka was a shambles; the points awarded after the truncated race even more so.
Photo: Pirelli

to mind just how much drivers had hated the super-stiff ground-effect cars of the early eighties. Forty years ago, Keke Rosberg, no shrinking violet, had spoken of the potential long-term impact on the spine and how it had almost been necessary to have a chiropractor permanently on hand.

There were two ways of looking at the moves to have bouncing regulated. One was that it was politically motivated in the hope that any Technical Directive (TD) might rob the quick teams of some downforce. On the other hand, it was entirely feasible that fitting cars with sensors to measure vertical oscillations that could not exceed a certain metric would be even tougher for teams, such as Mercedes, that were already struggling with it most.

Health-and-safety considerations have moved on in 40 years, and once the FIA had acknowledged the issue and sought medical opinion, it was duty bound to do something. Hence, much anticipation surrounded the implementation of TD39, issued mid-June, but with implementation delayed from that month's French GP until Spa after the summer break. It addressed both oscillations, and the mountings of the underbody plank and skid plates, amid suspicions that some rule interpretations had facilitated 'cushioning' of the underbody plank around the stall point of the venturi tunnels, effectively allowing a car to be run lower without illegally wearing the plank.

The great irony? At Spa, Red Bull and Verstappen produced their most dominant performance of the year so far, the TD having zero effect on the team's performance. Or, if anything, cementing its superiority, as Ferrari seemed to have taken a hit, qualifying more than six-tenths from Verstappen. Having already won from tenth on the grid at Hungaroring, Max started 14th in Belgium after sundry engine and gearbox penalties had been applied, and was in the lead after a dozen laps, beating team mate Pérez by 17s! Okay, the Red Bull was in its absolute element around Spa, but Verstappen himself was on an entirely different level.

We saw it again at Suzuka, where he won a delayed 28-lap race by 27s. That clinched a second successive title, even though that took a while to be fully understood…

There was confusion over points allocation when not only race broadcasters, but the entire paddock got it wrong. For the first time in F1 history, drivers were awarded full points for a race that had not completed 75 per cent distance.

It's perfectly true that the wording of the rule in question was not new and said, "If a race is suspended *and cannot be resumed*… half-points will be awarded if the leader has completed more than two laps, but less than 75 per cent of the original race distance, and full points will be awarded if the leader has completed 75 per cent or more of the original race distance."

The important bit is "cannot be resumed". The Japanese GP was resumed, so none of it applies.

You can argue that it's all perfectly clear, nobody read the rulebook properly and the FIA got it completely right. In fact, after the aggravation following Abu Dhabi the previous year, it was imperative that they did everything by the book.

But there are a couple of supplementaries. First, after the Spa debacle in 2021, where half-points were awarded after three laps behind a safety car with no actual racing, a new regulation was introduced in 2022 that was intended to prevent a repeat and to award points commensurate with race distance completed.

A more complex rule said that for any points to be allocated, a minimum of two laps had to be completed by the leader without safety car or VSC intervention. If at least two laps, but less than 25 per cent of the scheduled distance had been completed, points would be 6-4-3-2-1 to the first five finishers. If between 25 and 50 per cent was completed,

the points allocation would change to 13-10-8-6-5-4-3-2-1 for the first nine. If at least 50 per cent of the distance, but less than 75 per cent, it became 19-14-12-9-8-6-5-3-2-1 to the top ten, with anything over 75 per cent of the distance bringing full points.

The intent made sense, but only if the "cannot be resumed" part of the regulation had been removed, which it hadn't been. Otherwise, taking things to extremes, in a Suzuka situation, where the rain delay had lasted long enough that only three laps had been possible before the race timed out, full points would still have been awarded. Clearly not the intention and a total nonsense. The rule is to be tidied up going forward.

Pérez fought a battle with Leclerc for distant runner-up spot in the championship as Red Bull pursued its first ever drivers' championship 1-2. In Jeddah, he became the first Mexican to start a GP from pole, even though it had taken him 217 qualifying attempts to do it. It was a stunning lap. "I can do 1,000 laps and not beat that!" he beamed.

Just as impressive was the way he led the opening 14 laps, unflustered and in control, before the racing gods let him down with a safety car just after he'd made his pit stop. That relegated him to an eventual fourth as Verstappen and Leclerc fought out the win again.

Much of Max and Charles's enjoyment of their lead scrap was rooted in the raceability of cars that could follow more closely, as intended.

"It looks like the new rules are working," Leclerc said. And for that, Ross Brawn's Motorsport team at F1, in association with the FIA, deserved a pat on the back. Formula 1 has always been about the bottom line, dollars, but hard cash had finally been invested in improving the spectacle, from those with the brains and tools to make a difference. Improve the product, and even more people will watch it.

While previous cars had lost around 35 per cent of their total downforce when running three car lengths (around 20m) behind a rival, with that loss increasing to 47 per cent

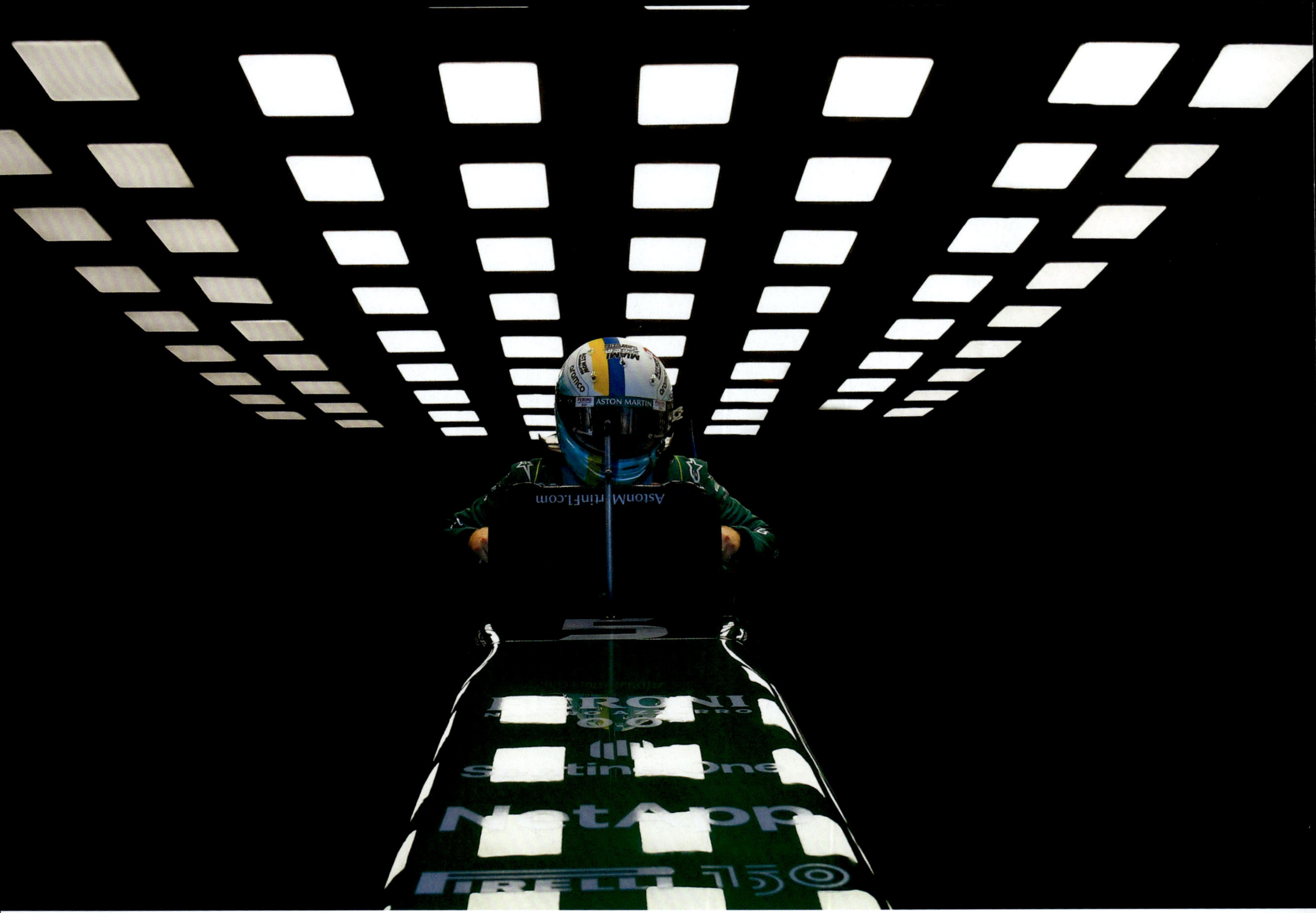

Above: Set the controls for the heart of the sun. Sebastian Vettel looks as though he is about to go into orbit in his Aston Martin.
Photo: Peter Nygaard/GP Photo

Above right: The season produced some major crashes, but none more dramatic than the accident that befell Zhou Guanyu. Without doubt, the Halo proved a life-saver.
Photo: Autocourse

Right: Lewis Hamilton didn't get much opportunity to fight with Max Verstappen over the same bits of tarmac, but when he did, in Brazil, the old rivals made contact again…
Photo: Peter Nygaard/GP Photo

if the gap came down to a single car length, the respective targets under the new regulations were 4 per cent and 18 per cent. Suddenly, you had racing. With a few caveats, as Verstappen explained.

"The cars are better to follow," he explained, "but it just depends on the tyres. The hard tyre was capable of following closer, but the other compounds – and this depends on the track – just fall apart. As soon as you follow for a few laps, they just open up.

"It's probably the tyres, but also the weight of the car [almost 800kg without fuel] pushes you over the tyre edge. It's something we need to look at for the future. We've improved the following and the racing, but if the tyres don't let you, for whatever reason, that's a bit of a shame."

Pérez made amends for Saudi by taking his first win of the year in Monaco. When Ferrari, which had locked out the front row, messed up its race strategy, his third place on the grid, ahead of Verstappen, was the foundation of his victory. He'd achieved it via a spin on his final Q3 run, which had blocked the track and prevented Verstappen, who was quicker behind, from completing his lap…

Shades of Schumacher at Rascasse in 2006? A closer look at Sergio's steering and throttle inputs made it highly questionable whether the spin had been an accident. From that point on, although we didn't know it at the time, any help for Checo from Max… well, Red Bull could whistle for it.

When Verstappen hit trouble in Singapore qualifying, Pérez picked up the baton and won his second race of the year – perhaps his career-best drive – under the heaviest pressure from Leclerc. It took him to within a point of the Monégasque in the championship. And when, in Japan, Leclerc outbraked himself at the chicane on the final lap and earned a 5s penalty, handing second place to Pérez, the Mexican was ahead. Post-USA, at home in Mexico, could he expect any help from Verstappen, with the latter's championship in the bag? Behind closed doors, apparently, Max had told them to forget it, but the situation never arose because, at a race that Mercedes might have won with bolder strategy, Hamilton put himself between Verstappen and Pérez on the road.

But in Brazil, we found out in no uncertain terms. At the final sprint qualifying event of the year, Verstappen had a weaker Saturday than anticipated, then a clash with Hamilton early in the main race, leading to another recovery drive. Red Bull had not envisaged being in sixth and seventh places in the final laps at Interlagos…

Pérez was asked not to resist Verstappen as he came through, allowing the Dutchman to close down Alonso's fifth-placed Alpine. His understanding was that if Max failed to pass Alonso, he would return the position on the last lap. But he didn't, despite being told to do so.

"What happened, Max?" asked race engineer Gianpiero Lambiase.

On the surface, the refusal to let Pérez repass looked petty and graceless after Checo's efforts to hold back Hamilton at Abu Dhabi in 2021, particularly. But now came the evidence of prior discussion.

"I told you already last time, you guys, don't ask that again to me. Okay?" Verstappen radioed. "Are we clear about that? I gave my reason and I stand by it."

Max had kind of thrown Red Bull under the bus, just weeks after it had been centre stage over a cost-cap breach (*see* page 38). The world would want to know Max's reason, it would come out and then Red Bull could face a 'crashgate' enquiry over Monaco. Verstappen and team principal Christian Horner were still trending on Twitter 12 hours later…

"Just when you think you're cruising nicely to the end of the year," Horner grimaced wryly in a reflective moment a few days later, after all hell had broken loose internally. The FIA said that it was quite happy to investigate Monaco if anyone so wished, but, six months down the road and with nothing at stake, nobody did. As McLaren's Zak Brown said, "That train has long since left the station."

The Leclerc/Pérez battle for second place went down

BYBIT
PETRONAS

kimoa
Castrol EDGE
citi
Private Bank
MAPFRE
RCi
BANK AND SERVICES
PIRELLI

VELAS

AMG
PETRONAS
TeamViewer

to the last lap of the last race in Abu Dhabi, with Leclerc winning out. The only problem was that it had been the other Red Bull driver whom Charles had been battling with back in March.

Amid widespread speculation about sacking, Mattia Binotto received the dreaded Ferrari chairman's vote of confidence, so it was no surprise when, post-season in late November, the news came of his departure at the end of the year.

"I am leaving a company that I love, which I have been part of for 28 years, with the serenity that comes from the conviction that I have made every effort to achieve the objectives set," said Binotto in a statement. "I think it's the right time to take this step as hard as this decision has been for me."

As F1 chief and former Ferrari team principal Stefano Domenicali said, speaking from experience, finishing second is never good enough at Maranello. Ferrari has not had a drivers' champion since Kimi Räikkönen in 2007 and, although most prolific in terms of constructors' championship successes, with 16, it has not triumphed in the teams' competition since 2008.

In its recent history, 53-year-old Binotto, having headed the engine and technical departments during his long career, had been involved with championship challenges in 2017/18 and, early-season at any rate, in 2022. In the absence of an obvious team principal to replace Maurizio Arrivabene, almost reluctantly, he had assumed a dual technical/leadership role in January 2019. He is very different from a Christian Horner or Toto Wolff.

Having put a square peg in a round hole, Ferrari couldn't reverse the process and put Binotto back into a square one. As a result, it might have taken a Kalashnikov to its own foot and given itself two significant holes to fill, rather than one. Binotto's forced departure could be manna for an organisation like Audi, preparing its 2026 F1 entry...

Elsewhere, one of the stories of the year was George Russell's fabulous first season with Mercedes, where he proved himself all but Lewis Hamilton's equal, claiming the team's lone victory in Brazil and taking its only pole position in Budapest. But after three seasons at the back with Williams, it was his misfortune to join Mercedes just as it lost its competitive edge.

"We lost months of development to the porpoising issues," Toto Wolff admitted. "There was effectively a six-month delay putting performance on the car, so, for us, it was like starting a 100m sprint 10m behind everyone."

With noises coming out of Brackley that the team has identified and corrected its issues with the '22 car, many are predicting a full championship challenge again in 2023, but Wolff cautioned, "You can't be sure at all, but we'll do all in our power to be in that position."

Hamilton lost none of his competitive spirit, despite such a character-building year. "He's been really good," Wolff confirmed. "He held us up when the energy levels got a little bit down in the briefing room. He and George developed the car well and, okay, if he finished the season behind in the championship when it's fourth and fifth, I don't think that means a lot. If it's about first, that's different."

There can be little doubt that the Mercedes driver line-up is the strongest on the grid, and if the team does step up over the winter, that is one intra-team battle that promises to be mouth watering.

Russell's performance level, and that of Lando Norris at McLaren, where effectively he might have ended the F1 career of eight-time race winner Daniel Ricciardo, led one commentator to suggest that Hamilton, Russell and Norris are the strongest combination of British talent to be on the grid at the same time, better even than Clark, Surtees and Stewart from the sixties. High praise indeed, but it's certainly a discussion worth having.

Then there was Fernando Alonso. At 41, 20-plus years into an F1 career, how does he sustain such competitive intensity? Okay, he was nip and tuck with Alpine team-mate Esteban Ocon for single-lap pace, but his race performances were as relentless as ever and still absolutely top drawer. Talk to many a retired driver, and they will admit that, with age, the absolute hair's-breadth judgement can fall away a fraction. Gaps that a driver might think are there, perhaps might not be. Alonso's rear-ending incidents with Stroll in Austin and Ocon in Brazil might raise a question, but that's probably nonsense. Alpine's loss is Aston Martin's gain.

Formula 1 is in a good place. And, over time, as the effects of the budget cap and reduced aero development time for the front-running teams take full effect, it promises to be even better. As Wolff said, "I don't think anyone will run away with eight championships in a row ever again, and that is how the regulations have been framed." You can't put that all down to the efforts of one man, but Ross Brawn should certainly enjoy a fulfilled retirement.

Above: Fernando Alonso brought much to Alpine in his two-year stint, but now he takes his massive experience to Aston Martin.
Photo: Alpine F1 Team

Left: Lewis Hamilton congratulates team-mate George Russell on his win in Brazil.
Photo: Mercedes-AMG Petronas F1 Team

Far left: Loyal company man Mattia Binotto resigned, or did Ferrari chairman John Elkann wield the axe?
Photo: Scuderia Ferrari

Right: Going fishing? Ross Brawn decided to call it a day from the rigours of Formula 1.
Photo: XPB Images

MARRIAGE OF CONVENIENCE

It was very much a time of change as new FIA president Mohammed Ben Sulayem began his first term as successor to Jean Todt. Both on and off track, there was more than enough to occupy the sport's movers and shakers, as DIETER RENCKEN explains...

Above: Stefano Domenicali and Mohammed Ben Sulayem are both locked into a partnership.

Right: Formula 1 returned to Australia in 2022. Domenicali takes a track walk with F1's Jonathan Nicholas and Roberto Dalla.

Photos: XPB Images

IF the 2021 season had been about Covid, and the appointment as Formula 1 CEO and president of former Ferrari team principal Stefano Domenicali by F1 commercial rights holder Liberty Media, 2022 was about F1's 'new era' regulations, the arrival of Mohammed Ben Sulayem and budget caps.

The election of the 61-year-old Emirati as FIA president marked a first for a non-European, and to claim that the 14-time Middle East Rally champion and WRC competitor instituted change would be akin to suggesting that Max Verstappen is merely speedy. To MBS, as he is known, the health of the FIA (and its 300-odd clubs) is paramount, and his administration's decisions flow from this premise.

Thus, when, in June, Formula 1 proposed a doubling of sprint races to six, Domenicali assumed it to be *fait accompli* – as matters usually had been under Jean Todt, who had stepped down on 15th December, 2021, after reaching both the Federation's age and office limits. Instead, Ben Sulayem placed the matter on hold until the governing body had analysed the impact on race officials – effectively FIA proxies.

Indeed, that MBS puts the clubs first was underscored by a refusal to sanction a 2023 F1 calendar asterisk-pocked by provisional dates: "Our clubs and fans deserve certainty," he insisted, and thus approved the final calendar in mid-September – in stark contrast to previous seasons when differing draft schedules containing 'Subject to promoter agreement' or similar clauses had been released on a serial basis by F1.

Todt had represented the last thread of continuity harking back 25 years to the rule of Bernie Ecclestone and Max Mosley – long-standing friends who had cut the original FIA/F1 commercial rights agreement in 1998, arguably weighted in favour of the former. When Mosley retired from the FIA presidency in 2009 and made way for Todt – who had been Ferrari team boss and thus was *au fait* with the deal – Ecclestone continued to head F1.

Liberty acquired the rights in 2017 and took F1 public, forcing Ecclestone aside. Todt mentored Liberty's (primarily US) executives in F1's ways, building solid rapport. Then Domenicali, who had reported to Todt at Ferrari and served on FIA commissions, came in and further bonds were in place. Todt departed, to be succeeded by a Middle East rally champion who had had few dealings with F1.

To Liberty (and most fans), F1 is what it's all about, whereas for Ben Sulayem and his cabinet – deputy president for sport Robert Reid was 2001 world champion rally co-driver – F1 is but a chapter in a portfolio that encompasses myriad on- and off-track series, karting, mobility and political lobbying on behalf of global motoring communities. F1 is the portfolio's primary chapter, but a chapter it is, nonetheless.

Thus, shocks within the corridors of F1's swanky St James's Market offices were felt all the way to the Place de la Concorde in Paris and led to a rapid recalibration of the relationship between 'landlord' and 'tenant' – the FIA owns F1, and Liberty holds a 113-year 'lease' on its commercial rights, with 88 years remaining. Indeed, some suggest that the relationship is at its lowest ebb, that a break-away series is planned.

Such rumours, though, overlook a crucial aspect: as a stock-market-listed entity, Liberty desperately needs the global recognition facilitated by the FIA, which is prohibited by EU decree from commercialising its championships – hence the various CRH agreements for its respective categories. The fact is that the FIA and F1 need each other to survive and are currently establishing new boundaries after 25-odd years of utter cosiness.

Understandably, both sides play down any rifts. In September, Domenicali said, "The new president took office in January, he is building his team. We talk to each other almost every day, the relationship must continue to be [strong] while respecting each other's responsibilities. The important thing is to stay united and have a common vision of F1."

For his part, as his first year in office came to a close, MBS told AUTOCOURSE in Abu Dhabi, "I'll tell you about my relationship with [F1]. First of all, I speak to Stefano at least every two days; if I don't, he calls [me]. This is the way even before any meeting or before any decisions; it's a marriage, and this marriage is going to last and strongly.

"I listen to [Domenicali], he listens to me. We both know this marriage has to be sustainable and go further, and honestly, it's going from strength to strength."

Regardless of any ups and downs – which, according to sources on both sides, are regular – the duo was aligned on the tricky question of Russia. No sooner had initial shots been targeted at Ukraine than a joint statement spelled the end of the Sochi race, adding that Russian drivers would be required to sign FIA peace commitments.

If MBS thought the FIA presidency was an easy trip to Paris, he was in for a rude awakening. Not only was the election tightly fought against Todt loyalists, but his administration inherited the mess that was Abu Dhabi, 2021, plus teething issues associated with F1's 'new era' and its budget cap, the latter introduced in 2021 with a reporting deadline of end-March 2022.

All three factors returned to bite the FIA, but, by then, Todt was long gone. These were not the only unwelcome legacies, however: after 100 days in office, the FIA Senate issued a 'progress report' claiming that the organisation faced a budgetary shortfall of $25m, and that various previous regime soft-core projects – such as low-cost moped helmets and myriad road-safety initiatives – were to be scrapped.

Crucially, buried in the document was an item the Senate could not scrap: looming litigation in Waco, Texas, over the rights to the halo, the safety device mandated for single-seater categories. Allegedly developed in-house, it transpired that halo had been patented by a Norwegian, who was seeking royalties. When these were denied, he went legal, claiming hundreds of millions. Eventually, MBS's team settled for an estimated $3.5m.

One of Ben Sulayem's first tasks after taking office was to visit F1 team bosses individually, with *that* Abu Dhabi finale topping agendas. Clearly, the trickiest to appease was Toto Wolff, boss of the aggrieved Mercedes outfit. He and Lewis Hamilton had refused to attend the FIA Gala celebrations held on the eve of the elections and were seeking coherent answers if not full-bodied revenge.

Hamilton went into ultra-low-profile mode, refusing even to respond to Ben Sulayem's texts. Then, shortly before testing began, he announced, "I've been gone; now I'm back!" It was a dramatic act from a driver not short of theatrics and clearly calculated to keep 'AD2021' front and centre to ensure folk continued the debate about his title loss to Verstappen.

What transpired behind closed doors in Brackley during MBS's meeting with Wolff will never be public. It is likely, though, that a deal was struck for Shaila-Ann Rao – Mercedes F1's legal counsel before switching to the role of Wolff special adviser – to rejoin the FIA, initially as F1 adviser to Ben Sulayem before being appointed interim secretary-general for sport as replacement for Peter Bayer.

Bayer, who oversaw the investigation into AD2021, also led the 2026 F1 power unit project. According to sources, it was slow progress on the latter, rather than the contentious Abu Dhabi report, that led to his hasty departure after seemingly losing the confidence of MBS. The FIA gave little away, however.

"The FIA warmly thanks him for the achievements he has contributed to the development of motorsport over the past five years," it said in a brief statement. "In particular, he supervised, with the entire sporting division, the building of the single-seater pyramid from karting to F1, the creation of the new World Rally Raid Championship, as well as improving safety and sustainability in all disciplines."

By then, the FIA had parted ways with Michael Masi, the F1 race director who, in 2019, had replaced the late lamented Charlie Whiting. Masi's creative interpretation of the safety car regulations had resulted in the Abu Dhabi debacle. Still, MBS refused to blame the Australian publicly, saying only that he had committed a human error. In his place came two rotating race directors.

"Our race structure was wrong organisationally," explained MBS. "Although we brought in two new race directors [DTM's Niels Wittich and WEC's Eduardo Freitas], I wouldn't say we have got it all right yet. We needed to clean the stables.

"It's not like going to a supermarket and ordering more stewards. You need firm and fair people, tolerant people. I am thinking of, for example, bringing in rally co-drivers, who have plenty of the multi-tasking skills that are required, and training them up."

By September, his former co-driver, Ronan Morgan, was leading a race-director seminar in Monza. But, to be fair, the Irishman is a seasoned F1 clerk of course.

Wittich, though, drew much paddock mirth by insisting that the letter of the FIA's International Sporting Code, which demands that drivers don (only) fireproof underwear beneath race suits and don't wear jewellery while in the car, be respected.

Hamilton refused to remove his (embedded) studs, so it became a show of strength: race director versus race driver. The latter backed down, then obtained medical advice that fixed nose studs are healthier than regular removal. It was a fight that the FIA never was going to win convincingly, so one wonders why Wittich bothered.

Rao had been FIA legal director before moving to Mercedes, but her return in an F1 oversight role understandably perturbed team principals, including Ferrari's Mattia Binotto, who said, "It's a concern, but it's only a concern. It's down to the FIA to ensure there will be no conflicts of interest, to behave properly, and it's down to the president to ensure it. I've got the trust they will do it."

Wolff saw matters differently: "The FIA is changing its structure and organisation, and the president has to make his decisions, and we certainly shouldn't interfere in any of the decisions."

A month later, a highly contentious Technical Directive, which effectively amended regulations on ride height, was introduced during the Canadian Grand Prix. The consensus was that it favoured Mercedes, who had suffered more than most from the dreaded 'porpoising' – the car bouncing that accompanied the switch to ground-effect aerodynamics.

This phenomenon had a humorous side effect. Both the FIA and F1 were keen to take credit for the success of the 'new era' regulations – largely proposed by F1, but framed by the FIA – until the P-word was mentioned, when eyes glazed over and teams were blamed for not identifying the issue during simulations. For the record, overtaking increased by over 30 per cent year on year, and racing was closer across the season.

Through it all, Domenicali worked immensely hard on F1's commercial packages, signing agreements for 24 grands prix in 2023. The word is that China's inclusion in the face of continuing Covid restrictions is a contractual tactic. He renewed TV deals, including Sky's mega package. He also worked on persuading former employer VW (after Ferrari, he had joined Lamborghini, from whence he had been recruited) to enter as a power-unit supplier (if no more), preferably with two brands.

Indeed, the Italian was all but invisible to the media until the Belgian GP, where inexplicably he stated, "I don't see a girl in F1 in the next five years unless something like a meteorite hits earth." Shortly thereafter, W Series withdrew from two North American F1 support races it planned to stage, citing transatlantic travel costs. A month later, F1 announced an in-house women's feeder series. Confusing…

The good news at Spa-Francorchamps, though, was two-fold: Audi confirmed an entry, initially as 2026 PU supplier, while F1 announced a reprieve for this most scenic of circuits after talks for a race at Kyalami had collapsed. A week later, however, Porsche announced that its much-mooted partnership with Red Bull was over, but that it was seeking an alternative. At the time of writing, the 2026 PU entry deadline had come and gone. Twice.

However, the year's bombshell scandal was but a fortnight away. As F1 decamped in Singapore, rumours broke that two teams had been found in breach of 2021's $145m budget cap, with Rao said to have been in the thick of things. So convoluted (and complex) is this saga that it is analysed separately (see page 38).

Then F1 travelled to Suzuka, Japan, where the sport collectively proved that it had learned little from previous incidents. Max Verstappen scored a second title, but only after much toing and froing about truncated races, while Pierre Gasly – who had been mentored by Jules Bianchi, who had succumbed to injuries suffered when he hit a recovery vehicle at Suzuka in teeming rain in 2014 – could easily have collided with a tractor…

To the FIA's credit, Reid took charge immediately, demanding an investigation. The net effect was that Freitas was relieved of rotational race-director duties and a detailed report released to the media within two weeks. Ben Sulayem had promised transparency in his election manifesto, and now F1 got it. If the collective intakes of breath as the report landed were any guide, F1 was not ready for such brutal honesty.

As AUTOCOURSE closed for press, news filtered through that Rao was leaving the FIA. In the minds of (too) many in the paddock, it is none too soon, for hers had been an uneasy relationship with F1's key players. Now, MBS faces the task of slotting yet another senior head into this crucial role, one that administers the present while preparing for motor sport's future. F1's 2026 'newer era' is three years hence, as are FIA elections…

The news encapsulated F1, 2022: Mercurial highs dragged down by avoidable lows as sporting, technical and financial issues collided under a new FIA administration that skirted around crucial issues as it established a (still uneasy) working 'marriage' with its commercial partner. Yet, MBS deserves top marks for putting heart and soul into this, at times, thankless task, even if some of his attempts have proved misguided.

That Mohammed Ben Sulayem takes the FIA presidency extremely seriously is evident from his sacrifices since acceding to global motoring's top job: "I am a motor sport person, and of course mobility is equally important for me," he told AUTOCOURSE. "I have no other job, I have no XYZ. I left our [UAE] Federation, I left the [UAE] Olympic Committee. I have only the FIA. My passion is here, my heart is here."

Above: Mohammed Ben Sulayem. The face of fierce determination.
Photo: XPB Images

Left: A symbolic announcement at Spa that Audi would be entering F1 in 2026.
Photo: Audi Communications Motorsport

Mohammed Ben Sulayem

Education
Bachelor's Degree in Business, American University in Washington, DC, USA, and Ulster University (UK).

Sporting career
Fourteen-time FIA Middle East Rally champion; won 61 international events as driver (1983–2002).

Hobbies, interests and charities
Patron of a wide range of charities and ambassador for road safety in the UAE; supporter of motor sport officials' and young drivers' education, training and research to promote motor sport safety; supporter of classic vehicle movements and automotive heritage.

FIA history
Vice president for sport and member of the World Motor Sport Council (2008–2013, re-elected 2017); founding member and chairman of FIA Region I; vice president for Automobile Mobility and Tourism (2013–2017); member of Innovation Fund Steering Committee.

Motor sport's next big thing?
"Sustainability – that's our biggest challenge. I believe we can do it if we do it right, are part of the solution and export the knowledge. There are so many good things in the FIA that we haven't been exporting."

STRETCHING THE CAP

The newly introduced F1 cost cap is a fundamental part of levelling the F1 playing field, as well as making the sport sustainable in the long term. There were always likely to be bumps in the road for such a complex undertaking, and so it proved. DIETER RENCKEN examines the timeline of events...

Above: Max Verstappen takes to the track in his Red Bull. Despite persistent rumours, his 2021 title would not be taken away from him.
Photo: Red Bull Content Pool/Getty Images

Top right: Lewis Hamilton voiced his concerns about leniency when it came to overspending by rival teams.
Photo: Mercedes-AMG Petronas F1 Team

Above right: Aston Martin's Mike Krack preferred to keep his counsel.
Photo: Aston Martin Aramco Cognizant F1 Team

Right: Austin, Texas. During a testy press conference, McLaren's Zak Brown has his say while Jost Capito of Williams and Red Bull's Christian Horner await their turn to speak.
Photo: Red Bull Content Pool/Getty Images

Monday 6th June, Paris
The FIA announces that it has entered into an Accepted Breach Agreement (ABA) with Williams, after the team committed a procedural (ie. timing or reporting) breach of the 2021 Financial Regulations, which imposed a cap of $145m (excluding accommodation, marketing, hospitality, travel costs and top three executive salaries). The reporting deadline is 31st March for the previous year.

No details of the breach are released, save that the team is fined $25,000 and ordered to pay costs of the process.

Friday 30th September, Singapore
16:00: Rumours emerge that two teams, including a top-three team, have committed transgressions of the 2021 Financial Regulations.

Mercedes and Ferrari hit out at the alleged transgressors, creating suspicions that Red Bull and one unnamed (later mooted to be Aston Martin) are the teams involved. Outlandish overspends of up to $10m are claimed by some Italian and German media outlets.
18:00: Both Red Bull and Aston Martin deny culpability, claiming to have filed support documentation well under the cap, but offer no further comment. They demand an investigation into the source of the leaks.

Saturday 1st October, Singapore
The governing body slams "unwarranted speculation" and denies that its personnel leaked the information. It promises to publish its budget-cap findings that week. Subsequently, these are delayed.

Monday, 10th October, Paris
The FIA confirms that Red Bull overspent by an unspecified amount, albeit under five per cent – a so-called minor breach – and committed paperwork irregularities, while Aston Martin is found to be in procedural breach.

The governing body undertakes to reveal details after consultative processes with the respective teams. These will begin before the United States Grand Prix (20–23rd October), then continue as required.

Red Bull team boss Christian Horner again demands an enquiry into the Singapore leaks, with suspicion falling on the FIA's (interim) secretary for sport, Shaila-Ann Rao, formerly Mercedes F1 legal counsel and special adviser, and said still to have an open door to the team. The FIA denies the allegations.

Monday 17th October, Woking
McLaren CEO Zak Brown addresses a letter to the FIA, in which he accuses teams who overspent of "cheating". In the letter – seen by AUTOCOURSE – he writes, "One team was guilty of a minor overspend breach plus a procedural breach, and two further teams were also in procedural breach. The overspend breach, and possibly the procedural breaches, constitute cheating by offering significant advantages across the technical, sporting and financial regulations."

Significantly, the letter is copied to the six teams who received clearance certificates, but not to Red Bull Racing, Aston Martin or Williams.

Thursday 20th October, Austin
14:00: Seven-time world champion Lewis Hamilton – who had narrowly lost the 2021 championship to Max Verstappen and previously had suggested that a $1m overspend could make 0.30s lap-time difference to car performance – wades into the controversy during the FIA's driver press conference.

"I think the sport needs to do something about this," he says. "Otherwise, if they're relaxed with these rules, then all the teams will just go over. Spending millions more and then only having a slap on the wrist is obviously not going to be great for the sport. F1 might as well not have a cost cap [in that case]."

16:00: Upon arrival in Austin for the USGP, Red Bull declines to comment, save for protesting its innocence and stressing that its original submissions were approximately $4m under the cap. It emerges that overspends on staff catering, failure to claim engineering rebates correctly, incorrect allocations of severance pay and sick leave combined to push the team $5.8m over the cap, resulting in a swing of $1.8m.

Aston Martin refuses to comment, save for an admission by team principal Mike Krack that, "We are in discussion with the FIA. I think it will be something we try to conclude in the next days. We had some discussions over the weekend as well with them and I'm quite confident we'll get it solved."

Saturday 22nd October, Austin

10:00: Horner, Brown and Williams team boss Jost Capito attend the FIA's Saturday press conference. Capito says that his team's breach arose due to a supplier not filing paperwork prior to 31st March, 2022.

Horner reveals that Red Bull's submissions ran to 75,000 individual line items, all of which needed to be checked internally and by the FIA's head of cost cap administration, Frederico Lodi, and his team.

He hits back at Brown, saying of his letter, "For a fellow competitor to be accusing you of cheating, to accuse you of fraudulent activity is shocking. It's absolutely shocking that without the facts, without any knowledge of the details, it can make that kind of accusation. We've been on trial because of public accusations since Singapore.

"Numbers have been put out in the media that are miles out of reality, and the damage that does to the brand, to our partners, to our drivers, to our workforce... In an age where mental health is prevalent, we're seeing significant issues within our workforce."

Below right: Lance Stroll in action for Aston Martin. His team was found guilty of breaching the cost cap, along with Red Bull and Williams
Photo: Aston Martin Aramco Cognizant F1 Team

Below: Red Bull called a press conference in Mexico, where Christian Horner expressed dissatisfaction with the penalty his team had been given.
Photo: Red Bull Content Pool/Getty Images

Brown defends the letter, saying, "If a team spends more than the cap, they're going to get an advantage. The cap is a rule, no different than technical rules in the sport. We're not taking a view whether they did or didn't.

"My letter was: if someone has [overspent], then here are the things that we think should be addressed. No different than if a ride height is incorrect, or a flexi wing, or whatever the case may be."

However, the trio agrees that the 5 per cent window for minor overspend breaches – which trigger ABAs to save teams from appearing before the Cost Cap Adjudication Committee, effectively the High Court for financial matters – is too high, given that minor breaches could run up to $7.25m within a $145m cap.

12:00: Talks between the FIA and Red Bull are scheduled for noon, with shuttling of key personnel between Red Bull's hospitality and the FIA's offices. Meetings are held between senior FIA officials, including president Mohammed Ben Sulayem, Lodi and Rao, and Red Bull senior management.

The presence of technical chief Adrian Newey at these meetings suggests sporting or technical penalties in addition to a fine.

14:00: It emerges that Red Bull co-founder Dietrich Mateschitz, not seen in public for a year, has succumbed to a long illness at his home in Austria. Talks are postponed out of respect for the man who was arguably this century's biggest motor sport benefactor being not only a double F1 team owner and Austria's grand prix promoter, but also sponsor of numerous teams competing in international two- and four-wheel series.

Tuesday 25th October
Talks resume via teleconferencing – Red Bull executives are congregated in Cancun, Austria and Milton Keynes; Aston Martin's are in Silverstone and Mexico City, while FIA officials are spread across Paris, Mexico and Geneva.

Sources advise AUTOCOURSE that both teams are prepared to enter into ABAs with the governing body. Talk is of a heavy fine for Aston Martin, with Red Bull probably facing heavier fines and aerodynamic restrictions.

Wednesday 26th October
ABAs and applicable sanctions are formally agreed, but need to be ratified by FIA president Ben Sulayem with support from the FIA WMSC. Mateschitz's passing complicates Red Bull's reporting structures, but a deal is done; Aston Martin chairman and CEO Martin Whitmarsh also accepts the breach and sanction.

Thursday 27th October
Red Bull calls a press conference for 11am Mexican time on Friday, after the FIA grants permission to use the room usually reserved for official gatherings.

Friday 28th October
09:00: The FIA releases details of Red Bull's breach, finding that the team overspent in four main areas amounting to a total of $5.8m, which, after the $4m under-submission, created an overspend as follows:

BUDGET CAP: THE OPINION

FORMULA 1 director of motor sports Ross Brawn, one of the cost cap's architects, gave his verdict:

"I think that the budget cap is a great success, thanks to the fact that it's regulated within the FIA's system. We made an attempt at it 10–15 years ago, but that was an agreement between teams, which is very difficult to make stick. We've seen with the issues we had this year with Red Bull and Aston Martin [that] if it wasn't for the regulatory process, we would have struggled.

"The hiccups we've had were predictable, but they're not severe. The teams now know where the limit is, they know the consequences of breaching the budget cap, both in terms of penalties and adverse publicity. Nobody wants to be seen to be breaching the cap in future, so it's a huge success."

• Internal costs incorrectly booked for severance payments and sick leave.
• Overspend on catering costs, which should have been split into F1 departments and other.
• Incorrect allocation of development and excess parts.
• Tax rebates for research and development also outside the cap if correctly accounted for.
• Clerical errors pertaining to charges booked to Red Bull Powertrains (which is outside the cap).

However, the FIA found that certain errors had been incurred due to differing interpretations of the regulations. Crucially, it found that the team "had not acted in bad faith or in a dishonest or fraudulent manner, nor wilfully concealed information from the Cost Cap Administration or gained or sought to gain any advantage from inaccurate exclusions or adjustments of certain costs."

After adjustments for interpretations, Red Bull incurred an overspend of $400,000, or 0.37 per cent of the cap. However, the team is fined $7m and has its aerodynamic testing allowance reduced by 10 per cent for a period of 12 months, effective immediately. The team is also ordered to pay the assessed costs of the ABA process.

10:00: Details of Aston Martin's breach are released. Despite finding that the team underspent (by $2m), it is found in procedural breach due to understatements for research and development tax credits (as per Red Bull).

As with Red Bull, the FIA also found no evidence that the team had "acted in bad faith or in a dishonest or a fraudulent manner, nor had it wilfully concealed information from the Cost Cap Administration or gained or sought to gain any advantage from inaccurate exclusions or adjustments of certain costs."

The team is fined $450,000 plus the costs of the ABA process.

11:00: Red Bull calls a media conference, during which Horner clarifies Red Bull's position and explains the background to the breach. He calls the penalties "draconian" and claims that aerodynamic restrictions could amount to a loss of half a second in lap time. He says that Red Bull accepts the sanctions albeit not as an admission of guilt – but due to interpretative differences within immature regulations.

Horner also reveals that on Japanese GP Sunday (9th October), immediately after Max Verstappen had clinched his second title, he received a call from Rao advising him of the breach. She is said to have congratulated him on the team's success, then suggested, "Do not celebrate too hard, as you were found in breach…"

He continued, "Had we dragged it through the administration process, then gone to appeal, that could have taken months. Beyond that, the International Court of Appeal. We could have been looking at a 12-month period to have this situation closed.

"With the amount of speculation, commenting and sniping that has been going on in the paddock, we felt that it was in everybody's interests – our's, the FIA's, Formula 1's – to close the book. We close the book here, today. We accept the penalties begrudgingly, but we accept them."

Note: As per FIA convention, all values expressed in US$.

FAITH IN THE FUTURE

In a watershed year for Red Bull Racing, team founder Dietrich Mateschitz died, the team claimed its first constructors' championship since 2013 and an impressive new in-house Powertrains facility was established at its Milton Keynes base. Team Principal Christian Horner sat down to discuss it all with TONY DODGINS...

Above: Christian Horner – constantly looking forward and determined to achieve more success.

Top right: Christian Horner and Adrian Newey discuss the design ace's limited-run RB17 hypercar at it's June launch.

Above centre right: Max Verstappen saw off Charles Leclerc's challenge in Jeddah to kickstart his season.

Above right: Chief engineer Paul Monaghan *(left)* and technical director Pierre Waché, just some of the formidable Red Bull talent.

Right: The end of a long season approaches for Verstappen's crew. They played a vital role in his record run of 15 race wins.

Photos: Red Bull Racing/Getty Images

WHEN Red Bull Racing suffered three retirements in the first three races of 2022, two for Max Verstappen and one for Sergio Pérez, and faced a resurgent Ferrari, it was impossible to envisage that the Milton Keynes-based team would convert that into the most dominant season in its illustrious history. Come Abu Dhabi in November, it had won no fewer than 17 of the season's 22 races, and the RB18 became the most successful car ever under the stewardship of technical chief Adrian Newey.

"I think the year is right up there with our very best," said Horner. "The 2021 season was an epic, and it took so much energy. It was like a heavyweight bout from start to finish. I think we finished on the 14th December, just in time for me to get Covid over Christmas!

"Then it was straight into January, a new year with the biggest F1 regulation changes in 40 years. Because of the '21 fight, we were the last team to transition on to the '22 car and felt we were going to be a bit on the back foot. We accepted that based on what we'd managed to do in '21.

"But, at the second Bahrain test, when we bolted on the first update, suddenly we thought, hang on, we're 20kg overweight, but the times still look pretty good!

"It was an incredible effort by the team over that winter to produce such a competitive car, albeit a bit on the chubby side. Twenty kilos is actually a massive amount [translating to around 0.6s per lap]."

Reliability in Formula 1 is now so strong, and Red Bull among the very sharpest operationally, that those early-race fuel-system issues were quite shocking. They were down to simple things such as a lack of rig testing amid the rush.

"Bahrain was a brilliant race between Max and Charles Leclerc. We could see that Ferrari had their car together in winter testing. They did loads of miles, were quick, it looked right, and we thought, Christ, those guys have got it together! We knew they'd started hugely earlier than us. They'd written off '21 to concentrate on '22, so we were really encouraged, even though we left Bahrain with zero points. It was just great to be on the pace. We should at least have finished second, and potentially third as well.

"Our strike back came at round two in Saudi, where Checo put in the lap of his career for pole. Max, again, had a massive race with Charles and managed to get the job done. Suddenly, our campaign was under way. We had a tough ride in Australia with Max, but thereafter, winning both the sprint race and main GP at Imola to beat Ferrari at home was crucial. If Ferrari had beaten us there, they would have started to find their confidence, and then everything starts to grow. But we were able to keep them under pressure, and then the mistakes started coming."

With no disrespect to Pérez, his pole at Saudi was one of the year's biggest surprises. One of the abiding memories of

2021 was Verstappen's speed and commitment at the same Jeddah circuit, which even had Fernando Alonso's eyes out on stalks as he watched a replay. In 2022, it was almost as though Max and Checo had swapped cars!

Show Pérez some walls – be it in Jeddah, Monaco, Baku or Singapore – and he's dynamite. Quick and precise. Early-season, he was unexpectedly nip and tuck with Verstappen for one-lap pace, too. Initially, Max did not get on too well with the RB18. That was rooted in its flabbiness. It was ponderous, without the sharp, strong front-end turn-in that he so relishes and can cope with.

"The car was very benign," Horner said. "I think Alex Albon had done a brilliant job in the simulator, working with the engineers through '21, and had probably developed a car that he would have driven very well. But it was a little too neutral for Max. The one thing that he hates is understeer. It just makes the car more predictable, and that suited Checo at that stage of the year. It was only as we started to get weight out of the car, and the balance started to shift, that we started to get more front end, which was definitely a quicker race-car. Max was then able to really exploit it to the max, you might say."

Eventually, the chassis came within 4kg of the minimum weight limit before some of the old bits went back on to get through the year, and it ended up back at around 12kg over the limit, a slightly worrying admission for the team's rivals.

The overarching feature of the early season and the return to ground-effect aerodynamics, not seen for nigh on 40 years, was the bouncing, or 'porpoising', phenomenon that afflicted teams to varying degrees – Mercedes very badly, but Red Bull barely at all. Some pointed to Adrian Newey being the only man in the paddock with experience of the effect from the first time around, back in the late seventies and early eighties, but Horner put the record straight.

"I think Adrian just missed it first time around. He came in at the end of skirts, so we didn't even have his knowledge to really draw upon. It's 100 per cent true that we were less badly affected, but I think we just got on top of it quicker. We understood the issues and addressed them very quickly. That was just the technical team doing a great job of understanding what was going on."

Newey's achievements are legendary and rightly applauded, but Horner was keen to recognise some of the unsung heroes within his organisation. Red Bull's head of aerodynamics is Italian Enrico Balbo, who spent seven years at Williams and was the designer of the double-diffuser concept on that team's 2009 car, also run by Toyota and Brawn, allowing the latter to dominate the year and win the championship. From there, he became an aerodynamics group leader at Mercedes for four years, before joining Red Bull in 2017.

"He's a fantastically talented engineer who stepped up when Dan Fallows joined Aston Martin," Horner explained. "He was the natural successor, and it was the right time for him to make that step. That technical group, with Pierre Waché [technical director since 2018], Enrico, Craig Skinner [chief designer] and Ben Waterhouse [head of performance engineering] is super-strong, highly integrated and by far, I think, our strongest ever technical group.

"Then you have Adrian. He was there to give guidance and for the big decisions on things like wheelbase and suspension, and as a great sounding board to bounce ideas off. But, obviously, he's been splitting his time between RB17 and F1. So, it was a big step up for the guys with RB18, and it enabled Adrian to drift in and out."

RB17, for those unaware, is Newey's ambitious 2020 lock-down hypercar project. With the F1 rule change delayed a year until 2022, and the 2020 car carried over into '21 due to Covid, the RB16 became the RB16B, and the RB17 designation was given to Newey's car. It will be built with ground-effect technology as a track car, non-road-legal. A blisteringly fast two-seater designed and built without compromise, it will feature an 1100bhp twin-turbo V8 and

Above: Dozens of cameras capture the moment as Sergio Pérez jumps from his Red Bull, having just won the Singapore Grand Prix.

Right: Yas Marina. More than 120 men and women (yes, we counted 'em) contributed to the team's outstanding year.

Photos: Red Bull Racing/Getty Images

come with a £5m-plus price tag! A production run of 50 is scheduled for 2025.

When Leclerc won two of the first three races and Verstappen had those retirements, Max was despondent about his championship chances, given that Ferrari was consistently quick. However, a combination of shortcomings – reliability, strategy and driver mistakes – at Maranello turned the tables quicker than he could ever have believed. Four wins in five races between Imola and Azerbaijan turned the season on its head.

"He's just been outstanding all year," Horner acknowledged. "Winning that championship in '21 took the pressure off his shoulders, and he just made another step. Every big pressure point he stepped up: the early racing with Charles in Bahrain and Saudi, the racing they had in Miami – the pressure there was massive. Then coming back to win after an off in Barcelona. In Azerbaijan, he was untouchable. He had an incredible season and just got stronger and stronger as the year went on.

"Sergio, too, has had a great year. The races he won in Monaco and Singapore, the five 1-2 finishes he's had, that pole in Saudi – tremendous. At Singapore in particular, he did an unbelievable job."

It would not be F1 without a couple of bumps in the road along the way. Horner was forced to marshal a bit of internal strife that erupted at the penultimate round in Brazil, where Verstappen refused to cede to Pérez to assist his bid to claim second in the championship (covered elsewhere), simultaneously implicating his team-mate in some Monaco hanky-panky.

"Yeah, just when you think you're cruising along nicely to the end of the year…" Christian said with a wry smile. "Look, Max's season has been on another planet this year, so we're not going to let the events of a couple of laps in Brazil dictate the year for us." The first ever Red Bull drivers' championship 1-2 fell at the final couple of hurdles, and that must have been a regret, however much it is sugar-coated.

But at Red Bull in '2022, it was as busy off-track as it was on. Team founder Dietrich Mateschitz was ill, and the news of his death, at 78, came on the Saturday of the Austin GP weekend in October, just as Red Bull was embroiled in controversy over breaking F1's inaugural cost cap in 2021 (covered elsewhere). Talk of a potential future link-up with Porsche was much discussed, even presented as a done deal in some quarters, as, back at base, the team was in the process of building and staffing its new Powertrains division, which will provide engines for F1's new 2026 engine regulations.

The decision to pursue the massive undertaking will make Red Bull the only F1 team with a chassis and engine division on-site, although Mercedes F1 has Brixworth and Brackley separated by just a few miles. It dates back to Honda's decision to withdraw from F1 during the Covid period.

"Basically, we had a simple choice: do we do it or do we go back to being a customer?" Horner explained. "And we're not a very good customer! We're very demanding. Mercedes wouldn't supply, Renault didn't want to supply, and Ferrari were the only ones that would potentially have us. Either we took control of our destiny or it was time to stop, basically. That's the crossroads we were at, and stopping wasn't an option.

"It was and is a massive task, but Dietrich's commitment

was absolute. Applying the same spirit that we have done with the chassis, just the encouragement he gave us, right up to the last budget that he signed off in September, which sets the team up for the next ten years, was tremendous. In terms of the facilities, the infrastructure we have, wind tunnels that will be coming on-site."

Initially, Horner said, it was Mateschitz himself who had driven the Porsche talks.

"I think he was nervous that potentially we wouldn't have the skillset to be able to race against a Mercedes or a Ferrari. There was discussion back in January of this year and then more over a period of time. But the more we looked at it, the more it became apparent that, actually, we've got what it needs. There wasn't anything on the technical side that Porsche was bringing that we didn't feel we had access to. Indeed, we were a long way ahead of where they were. So, in the end, the discussions just came to a natural conclusion to remain independent."

In the wake of Mateschitz's death, his heir, 30-year-old son Mark, has a net worth put at $16bn by Bloomberg, with operations now to be run by a three-man structure, including CEO for corporate projects and investments Oliver Mintzlaff, a 47-year-old German. An ex-elite runner, he was board chairman and MD of Bundesliga team RB Leipzig. At a time of change, it is easy to understand why perhaps the team's key figures were wary of any joint partnership with Porsche. Although Mercedes has been a key investor in F1 and a stable influence for the past 25-plus years, as well as a works outfit for the past 12, F1 history is littered with manufacturers who come and go to suit their own agendas. Not to mention partnerships that simply didn't work, such as that between Williams and BMW in the early noughties.

"There were discussions about a 50/50 partnership, and that was always going to be more complicated," Horner admitted. "And with Dietrich not around, it was the right decision for us to remain independent. Porsche is a wonderful company, incredibly capable, but it wasn't the right fit or structure for us to embark on a partnership."

Having taken that decision, what's the status of Red Bull Powertrains today?

"We're over 300 people now. We've recruited aggressively and wisely, and have some phenomenal talent in the group. We've got people from the electrical side of Honda because we inherited all their English staff. We've also recruited aggressively from our neighbours, people already in the sport. We've created a factory in 55 weeks, fully equipped with seven dynos, and had a prototype V6 running within a year. They are making big strides, but we're on a hugely steep curve and working against a tight timescale – 2026 might seem some way away, but it's tomorrow."

When Mateschitz tasked Horner with looking after his ambitious F1 entry at the back end of 2004, Christian had entered the paddock at 31, F1's youngest team principal. Having secured the services of Newey, where Jaguar had famously failed – although it was close! – the team and Sebastian Vettel won four successive world championships between 2010 and 2013. The birth of the hybrid era in 2014 and Mercedes superiority served up a seven-year period of domination before the unforgettable 2021 season, when Verstappen gave Milton Keynes its first championship title in eight years. In 2022, they took the constructors' championship as well, the one that pays the money.

In 2023, Horner will doff his own personal cap and raise his bat as he reaches the big 5-0. With his team back on top, might it be time to pursue fresh ambitions, perhaps within the sport's administration itself, especially with Ross Brawn stepping back?

"I'm a racer and have always enjoyed that side," he said. "The next challenge for me is obviously Powertrains. The scale of the task shouldn't be underestimated, and it takes some balls to take on Ferrari and Mercedes as a subsidiary of a fizzy drinks manufacturer!

"We have to be competitive. We don't have a choice. There's a lot going on. It's an exciting time for Formula 1. The sport's never been more popular, the commercial opportunities are huge. We've got 42 partners involved with the team now, we're producing track cars, Adrian's dream car, the RB17 – a full Red Bull car with a Red Bull engine – we're involved with an America's Cup project, doing all kinds of big stuff. It's a very exciting time for the business. I'm still enjoying the competition too much at the moment."

FEET ON THE GROUND

After 15 full seasons and 299 GP starts, Sebastian Vettel called time on his F1 career. JOE SAWARD profiles a man who thinks it is time to move on to pastures new...

Above: The 'wildman' look. Sebastian Vettel, 2022 vintage.
Photo: Aston Martin Aramco Cognizant F1 Team

Top right: A sensational first win in the Toro Rosso at Monza, 2008.
Photo: XPB Images

Above right: When we were young. The fresh-faced trio of Lewis Hamilton, Seb and Fernando Alonso after qualifying at Yas Marina, 2010.

Right: Heading to victory, leading team-mate Mark Webber in the 2010 Malaysian Grand Prix.
Photos: Red Bull Racing/Getty Images

SEBASTIAN VETTEL struggled to describe what he feels about retiring after spending 15 years as a grand prix driver. It would be better to ask him later, he says, once the process is complete. He has always been someone who has tried very hard to put his feelings into words. He was never the petulant "No comment" type, even when things were going badly. He was always funny and smart, but picking a high or low point of his career was too much of a challenge.

"I think I've been lucky that there's been so many moments to choose from," he admitted. "It's impossible to remember everything after so many years. I guess the firsts, in a way, always stand out. But I think every time had its highlights. I also enjoyed the last two years, even though from a sporting point of view, maybe they weren't really a highlight. There was nothing to celebrate, but I think I learned a lot. I progressed and I grew, and had a good time with Aston Martin."

Vettel had a similar problem when asked to put his career into perspective, to rank himself among the greats. He is one of the few of the modern generation who are interested by the history of the sport, but he is not comfortable trying to put himself into historical perspective.

"It is like if someone takes a picture of you and publishes it," he explained. "Do you like the picture if you do not choose it? I feel a little embarrassed to do that."

It was no surprise that he is a little self-conscious. How can one judge oneself? How can one put oneself into a historical perspective, without risking being seen as arrogant at best, delusional at worst. Better to say nothing and let others decide. Seb has always had his feet on the ground, more than many of his rivals. He has often made the point that he comes from an "ordinary family", and this mattered.

His father, Norbert, was a carpenter, but they always loved to go racing together. Seb was always a perfectionist.

"Even outside the race-car, I constantly find myself wanting everything to be perfect," he admitted. "Things always have to be completely accurate. I can't stand a picture hanging crookedly on the wall. It bothers me, distracts me and has to be corrected."

Vettel has always seemed to be a man with solid values, although occasional petulant moments means that one needs to remember that he has been in the F1 spotlight since he was only 19 years old, when he became the youngest man ever to take part in a grand prix weekend.

Nine seconds into his F1 career, he was fined $1,000 for speeding in the pit lane. Clearly he was impatient...

At the same time, he appreciated that he was lucky. His father had raced karts and taken part in hillclimbs, and when Seb was only three, Norbert bought him a small kart, which he would drive around the garden. He could not compete until he was seven, but quickly he began winning races and was carried through the junior formulas by support from Red Bull. He did a solid job, and by 2006 had been named BMW Sauber's third driver. The following year, Robert Kubica had his major accident in Canada, and the team turned to Vettel for the US Grand Prix at Indianapolis. He became the

youngest driver ever to score a point in F1, in his debut race. It was a great start.

A few weeks later, Red Bull ran out of patience with Scott Speed, and Vettel was called in to race for Scuderia Toro Rosso from Hungary onwards. Up against Tonio Liuzzi, he made little impact early on, but in Japan, he found himself running third behind the safety car. It was an opportunity, but disaster struck. He ran into the back of Red Bull Racing's Mark Webber and punted the Australian out of the race. Keen to make amends, he finished fourth in China a week later, his one-stop strategy working out better than Liuzzi's two-stopper after the weather conditions changed. It was the team's best performance of the year – and that's what goes into the history books.

There is no law against good fortune. His next team-mate was the highly-rated, four-time Champ Car champion Sébastian Bourdais, but the Frenchman crumbled quickly. Vettel scored a few points mid-season, but then at Monza, the cards all fell in his favour. The Toro Rosso was quick on the straights, and he did a perfect job in qualifying in damp conditions, taking pole position. Then he ran away with the race as his rivals tripped over one another. Everyone loves an underdog, and it was an amazing and emotional victory for the small Italian team.

Seb was 21 years and 74 days old, almost a year younger than Fernando Alonso had been when he won his first F1 victory. After that, he was quickly promoted to Red Bull Racing. He made some mistakes, but soon started winning, helped by the fact that team-mate Mark Webber was suffering from the after-effects of a cycling accident. Seb quickly became a popular figure, thanks to his love of British humour, his ability as a driver and his cheerful character. There were times when his rivalry with Webber boiled over, when he was given new parts and Webber was not, but generally he emerged as being the more successful driver. He lost his cool from time to time, but he was as he was.

"I am not very patient," he admitted, "but generally I have my feelings quite under control. I am naturally happy. I am not angry. I enjoy what I am doing. I love Formula 1, but there are some things that make me angry – if things do not go according to my wishes or plans."

He had settled in Switzerland, in an old mill house, off the beaten track, not far from the German border in Konstanz, and only 200 miles by road from his hometown. It was close

Above: Singapore, 2019. Vettel's 53rd grand prix win would be his last.
Photo: XPB Images

Top right: Contrasting emotions. Joy for Seb and his father, Norbert, as they celebrate his win in the 2011 Monaco Grand Prix…
Photo: Red Bull Racing/Getty Images

Above right: …And anger in Montreal. Seb storms from the stewards' room after being penalised for a manoeuvre by Lewis Hamilton, which cost him the victory. Mattia Binotto tries to assuage the livid Ferrari driver.
Photo: XPB Images

Right: Seb bids an emotional farewell at Yas Marina.
Photos: Aston Martin Aramco Cognizant F1 Team

enough to the airport in Zurich to take the sting out of the international flying one must do in modern Formula 1. When he was not racing, he would shut the door on the world outside and live a quiet life. Talking about his private life was always off-limits. His wife, Hanna, who was with him before he became famous, has remained a constant presence. They have two daughters, born in 2014 and 2015, and a son born in 2019. The names of his two daughters came out by accident, when a conversation he was having was overheard, but the name of his son is still not known publicly. He does not want his children to be in the public eye.

He was not on social media until the last few months of his F1 career, when he accepted that if he is to have any relevance in the world after he leaves the sport, he must at least engage with the world.

"I don't consider myself to be famous," he explained. "Politicians are famous. Presidents, Kings, Queens – they are famous. I think that with the way I grew up and the way I live. There are some advantages with being famous, but on the other hand, the private life is the most important thing. It is not always easy."

But Vettel never let fame get to him. He took Formula 1 in his stride.

"One thing that I have learned in F1 is that nothing is fixed," he explained. "You never know what happens. Some things change so quickly, it is impossible to predict. So many things happen. It is difficult to know what is true and what is not true. Even though it is all based on contracts, nothing is fixed."

He has accumulated a considerable fortune over time, but it has made no difference.

"When I grew up, I was always told that as long as you have something to eat, you are healthy and you have a roof over your head, then it is fine," he explained. "There are some things that you can fulfil with money, but at the end of the day, these are not the things that make you happy. It is the small things that make life good. I am sure that you can ask most of the drivers about the things they remember, and it will not be when they got a large cheque and went to the bank, but it would be things like standing on the podium at Monza, seeing the joy in the team and the faces. Those things stay with you forever and they make you happy. You are not there thinking, 'Oh yeah, I have finished first, I will get a big bonus' when you cross the line…"

As a grand prix driver, you have money, but there is always pressure from the teams to be what they want you to be.

"I am who I am," Vettel says. "If people like it, that is fine. If other people don't like it, then there is nothing that I can do about it. You cannot keep everyone happy."

He admits that he was not always perfect, particularly in 2017 in Baku, where he wrongly accused Lewis Hamilton of a giving him a brake test under the safety car, lost his temper, drove his Ferrari alongside Hamilton's Mercedes and deliberately banged wheels.

"I'm actually quite sorry," he says now. "Baku wasn't a great moment, because what I did wasn't right. So I want that moment to… not happen, if you see what I mean."

There was another petulant moment, in Canada in 2019, when it was ruled that he had earned a punishment for blocking Hamilton after making a mistake and running off the track. When they got to *parc fermé*, he swapped the P1 and P2 signs to indicate his discontent. At 31, he could still have moments when emotions got the better of him.

But in the end, F1 careers often come down to numbers. Vettel's are impressive: 122 podiums, 53 victories, plus dozens of pole positions and fastest laps. He won four back-to-back titles with Red Bull between 2010 and 2013. He left at the end of 2014, when it became clear that with the

new engine regulations, the team could not offer him world championship success. Ferrari was interested and seemed a better choice. But after five years, during which he won 14 victories, he had failed to win another title. The mighty Mercedes team was unbeatable.

"I had a fantastic time at Ferrari," Seb said. "I was close to the world title twice, but we failed. There are reasons why we didn't, win but I'm calm about it. I spent a lot of time at Ferrari, and I have a lot of respect for the team and for everyone there."

But in 2020, it became clear that it was time to change. He was happy to receive an offer from Aston Martin.

"Obviously, 2020 wasn't a good year for me," he admitted. "It was the first time when I was really at the point of, you know: Do I have a drive? Do I want to drive? Should I stop? I felt like I wanted to drive, and I was very grateful for the opportunity. Hopes were high, because the team was performing so well in 2020. The target was to keep doing that, but it worked out differently.

"But I think those years have been very important for me: one for the driving, but also, maybe to have the room and the possibility to grow even more off-track."

He decided to use the platform that F1 had provided to speak out for causes he believed in. He stood alongside Lewis Hamilton on a number of issues, notably inequality, racism, freedom of sexual expression and the need to preserve the planet. His whole image changed, with a new scruffier look, no longer the clean-cut youngster of his earlier days. With his long shaggy hair and headband, he looked more 1970s than 2020s, but that was all part of the freedom he felt to express his views.

"My passion comes with certain aspects of F1 that I've learned to dislike," he said. "They might be solved in the future, but the will to apply that change has to grow much, much stronger, and has to be leading to action today. I've asked myself in recent years how I can deal with the fact that I fly to Japan, Brazil or Abu Dhabi and consume resources. But I couldn't change that as a Formula 1 driver. I'm increasingly caught in a dichotomy between what my views and values are, and what I'm doing. It doesn't fit together. In retrospect, it bothers me that I didn't realise until so late that I could use my voice to draw attention to issues. Talk is not enough and we cannot afford to wait. There is no alternative. We live in very decisive times, and how we all shape the next years will determine our lives."

Vettel admits that retiring was a difficult decision.

"I have spent a lot of time thinking about it," he said. "I want to take some more time to reflect on what I will focus on next; it's very clear to me that, being a father, I want to spend more time with my family, but it is a bundle of motives. As far as my children are concerned, I've been living in a conflict for years. They are a priority to me, but on the other hand, I'm very consistent in my sport, and it's become more difficult every year to do right by them – not just because there are more and more races per season.

"I quite look forward to the idea of doing nothing, at first, and then see what it does to me," he said. "I mean, there are lots of other things in my head as well. Other interests and ideas outside racing. But I've done this for so long and it's central to my life. So, it will be difficult to say that I'm not going to miss it. I love racing. There's been many moments this year where I loved what I was doing so much. But I think I see it as a challenge. I see it as an opportunity to learn a lot about myself, and to put myself in exactly that position that I haven't been in before and I'm not comfortable with. I think I look forward to not having the calendar and then obviously at some point, I need to find a lot of things that will keep me busy because I'm a busy, busy bee, busy mind.

"In general, we have to pursue our ambition because of our talents. And from that point of view, I am satisfied because I made my dreams come true. We drivers love to race, we want to take on a challenge. I would even have paid to be able to do what I have done..."

THE GIVER OF WINGS

More than once, leading lights of the F1 paddock have been a little sniffy about a 'fizzy drinks company' trying to win grands prix. They underestimated the vision and commitment of one of the sport's greatest benefactors, Dietrich Mateschitz, who passed away just days after his company had taken its sixth F1 drivers' championship in 12 years. MAURICE HAMILTON outlines his amazing story...

Above: Aerobatics at the Abu Dhabi round of the Red Bull Air Race World Championship in the United Arab Emirates in 2019.

Top right: The Red Bull Racing facility at Milton Keynes.

Photos: Red Bull Content Pool

Above right: Man with a vision. Dietrich Mateschitz at the Monaco Grand Prix in 2005, when his F1 plans were just beginning to take shape.

Photo: Autocourse Archive

Right: Danke Didi. Members of the Red Bull team, in the pit lane at Austin, Texas, lead the applause in honour of the team's late founder.

Photo: Red Bull Content Pool

FOR a markedly quiet man, Dietrich Mateschitz's influence within motor sport was, if not loud, then abundantly clear. As benefactors and financial allies go, the Austrian's impact on global competition was colossal. His energy drinks company changed the dynamic for high-risk sports, from skydivers and base-jumpers to a world-beating team in Formula 1.

Red Bull Racing has been, at one and the same time, the spectacular symbol of Mateschitz's patronage and the tip of a fiscal sporting iceberg. You could say that the cool, hidden image associated with the latter suited him just as well as the dynamic high-speed symbolism that proved so attractive to consumers of his product. A billion cans of Red Bull are sold each year, contributing to a personal wealth of several billion. A reasonable return, you could say, for a $500,000 investment made 40 years before.

After studying business and economics at Vienna University, Mateschitz set off on his travels, not only to see the world as the salesman for a cosmetics company, but also to keep an astute eye out for business opportunities. It was while in Hong Kong in 1982 that he came across Krating Daeng, a local drink that helped provide energy and, as he discovered, cope with jet lag. Krating Daeng, which translated into 'Red Water Buffalo', was made by two brothers from the Yoovidhya family. Mateschitz formed a partnership with Chaleo Yoovidhya, which allowed Dietrich to run the business from Austria and adapt the recipe of guarana, taurine, caffeine, sucrose and ginseng by adding carbonated water to suit the European palate.

Being a marketing man at heart, and having Jochen Rindt, Austria's first world champion, as a role model, Mateschitz was quick to appreciate the benefits that would come from associating an energy drink with motor sport. After all, the purpose of Red Bull (as the new product would be known) was to charge adrenaline in the same way that an F1 car on full noise could instantly quicken the pulse.

"I would say it's a pretty prefect fit between them," Mateschitz told Anthony Rowlinson, former editor of *F1 Racing*, during a rare interview in 2006. "Motorsport generally fits with what we're trying to do with Red Bull, which is why you see us in NASCAR, MotoGP, WRC and many other branches of motor sport. But F1 is the pinnacle of that. Right from the start, we could see that F1 was a good marketing platform, one of the very best in fact."

That feeling wasn't always reciprocated within the sometimes self-important F1 paddock. Mateschitz had made the logical first step by supporting Gerhard Berger, the astute fellow Austrian being alert to his benefactor's enthusiasm and his company's potential, particularly when Red Bull quickly embraced markets in Hungary and Slovenia. Karl Wendlinger was next to benefit from Mateschitz's espousal of home drivers, a move that brought Dietrich into contact with Sauber and led to the appearance of Red Bull Team Sauber Petronas on the F1 entry list in 1995.

That relationship soured in 2001, however, when Peter Sauber chose Kimi Räikkönen at the expense of Mateschitz's preference for Enrique Bernoldi and the Brazilian's link with the untapped South American market. Red Bull moved on to support Bernoldi at Arrows, an association that led to Mateschitz giving serious thought to rescuing the beleaguered

British team and renaming it Red Bull Team USA (with obvious positive implications for reaching another major part of the American market). That fell foul of complications created by the necessary clearing of Arrows' debts to banks and suppliers. (It was also rumoured that a British High Court judge found it difficult to accept that an unknown fizzy drinks company 'from abroad' could have $30m to throw at a failed motor racing team).

Obstacles continued to appear along other potential paths to team ownership, in one case, despite the best efforts of a man highly qualified to offer a sound opinion. Niki Lauda had been appointed by the Ford Motor Company in 2001 to help turn around the dithering progress of Jaguar Racing, a resuscitation process that had been necessary almost since the F1 team's birth, following the purchase of Stewart Grand Prix by Ford at the end of 1999. Lauda was obviously aware of Mateschitz, a fellow Austrian clearly going places in the focused and successful manner embraced by Lauda.

"I knew that budget was always a problem at Jaguar," said Lauda. "At one stage, I went to Richard Parry-Jones [a vice-president within the Ford Motor Company] and I said I had this guy, Mateschitz, who wants to go into the American market. I said Mr Mateschitz owns Red Bull and he would be interested in sponsoring the team, maybe investing in half of it. Richard agreed to see him. Mateschitz flew to England and we showed Parry-Jones the proposal. Richard said he would have to think about it. Then he called me and said Ford could never accept having a drink like Red Bull on the car. These people would rather close down the team than have an energy drink on their car. Completely stupid!"

In November, 2004, Ford decided to end its involvement with Jaguar Racing and save an estimated $50 million per annum. Within days, the team was sold to Red Bull. The following year, Mateschitz also bought Minardi and renamed the small Italian team Toro Rosso (later to become AlphaTauri in deference to a fashion brand).

"We knew that F1 had the best image," said Mateschitz. "Whatever sort of analysis we did – qualitative, quantitative, any type – whenever we assessed it, we could see what it might be able to offer."

Although Mateschitz had saved more than 1,000 jobs within the motor sport industry, his obvious business

Above: This massive charging-bull sculpture has become the symbol of the Red Bull Ring.

Top right: Wings for Life CEO Anita Gerhardter at the organisation's World Run press conference in Salzburg, January, 2022.

Top far right: The Red Bull Ring has been transformed into a five-star facility.

Above right: The superbly restored Douglas DC-6B, flagship of the Flying Bulls fleet, on one of its traditional race-day flypasts.

Above far right: Red Bull supports a bewildering variety of sporting endeavours. Here, Alberto Ginés López performs during the Red Bull Dual Ascent of the dam face in Verzasca, Switzerland, October, 2022.

Right: Dietrich Mateschitz has left a huge legacy in the sporting world.
Photos: Red Bull Content Pool

priorities led to cynical observations that Red Bull Racing and Toro Rosso would be no more than marketing exercises far removed from the ambition of any serious racing team. Mateschitz was ahead of that game, too, particularly when he showed an acute understanding of the importance of delegating by making Dr Helmut Marko his personal representative in Red Bull's motor sport division. Employing an old friend and ex-F1 driver was one thing, quite another later to appoint ex-F2 racer Christian Horner to run the team and then bring on board Adrian Newey with his championship design credentials. It took a couple of years for Red Bull Racing to begin edging towards front-line competitiveness. Then came four world titles on the trot with Sebastian Vettel between 2010 and 2013.

In tandem with this, the establishment of a young driver scheme (ruled with an iron rod by Marko) brought Red Bull sponsorship to the junior ranks and provided a feeder of potential talent for the F1 teams. A casebook study would be written around the remarkable progress of Max Verstappen, bypassing F2, taken under the Toro Rosso wing in 2014, promoted to the senior team, winning first time out for Red Bull in Spain, 2016, and clinching his second world championship ten days before Mateschitz passed away on 22nd October, 2022, at the age of 78. Despite such a heartfelt loss, it was clear that the Mateschitz legacy would remain evident on several fronts.

He had introduced the slogan 'Red Bull Gives You Wings'. Apart from an obvious connation with the drink's enhancing qualities for late-night revellers, the catchphrase had a more serious intent. In 2004, Mateschitz had formed an alliance with Heinz Kinigadner, an Austrian Motocross world champion whose brother and son had been paralysed in separate accidents. By forming 'Wings for Life', Kinigadner and Mateschitz were determined to make the non-profit organisation accelerate much-needed research into the seemingly impossible repair of spinal-cord injuries. Kinigadner was grateful, not just for the support, but also for Mateschitz's determination that Wings for Life should remain cost-free and the investment continuous.

"When he came out with his Red Bull product, Dietrich helped me doing some events in South America, and we became good friends before real sponsorship," Kinigadner told Tom Tremayne in an interview in 2014. "He likes motorcycles. When KTM in 1989 was in bankruptcy, he was preparing himself to buy it. This was his dream. With Mateschitz, we have a guy who is really doing a lot. He's so clever and focused to make Wings for Life independently living. He says, 'It makes no sense that each year I'm giving 20 million dollars to you and, next year, when I'm not there anymore, the next guy says, "Okay, we stop."' Thanks to Dietrich, this will not stop." That pragmatic observation is now being seamlessly fulfilled.

Mateschitz's motives went beyond altruism. He used his accumulating wealth to build Hangar-7, a museum at Salzburg airport dedicated to his passion for classic aircraft and helicopters. Not for Mateschitz a converted maintenance building with aircraft hanging from the ceiling. Hangar-7 was a complex engineering project using 1,754 panes of glass, some curved and all different sizes, to combine technology, art and entertainment under a stunning overarching structure representing a completely different vision in every respect.

Not all the exhibits are static. A beautifully restored Douglas DC-6B, flagship of the Flying Bulls fleet, has been used to overfly the grid at the start of the Austrian Grand Prix and serve as a reminder that the former Österreichring (later, A1-Ring) had been saved and modernised by Mateschitz to rightly justify a change to the 'Red Bull Ring' title.

The massive bull on a hilltop within the stunning environs not only readily identifies ownership, but also is perfectly in tune with Mateschitz's wish to bring a smile. That much is also evident within the F1 paddock's multi-layer Energy Station, with its high standard of catering. Almost as an

aside in this bewildering catalogue of personal investment, Mateschitz established the Red Bull Media House, basically his own media empire, which spawned Servus TV, Red Bull TV, magazines, books and Red Bull Records.

All this was driven by the need to keep the vision of the simple, but effective Red Bull can to the forefront. Where Red Bull Racing was concerned, that meant winning. Mateschitz's reluctance to create a high personal profile in the paddock might have placed the onus on the team to do the talking for him, but he understood exactly what was needed to make Red Bull Racing's conversation worth listening to.

"We invested in Red Bull Racing's wind tunnel to make it state of the art," Mateschitz told Anthony Rowlinson in 2006. "We invested in the facilities. We have almost doubled the number of employees and we have gone out to get the best of what is available, whether that is Adrian Newey to design the car, or Renault and Ferrari engines to power it. [And, more recently, the massive commitment to Red Bull Powertrains]. Everybody realises that is more than just marketing to do this.

"We have to win," he continued. "At the very least, we have to compete at the front. When you are an energy drink, and it's an energy drink that gives you wings, you have to be competing with the winners. Actually, you maybe don't have to win as long as you lose in the right way. There are some losers who are the race heroes, and it's an essential part of sport to lose as well as win. But if we lose for too long, then people will ask questions. They will be shouting from the back of the grandstand, 'Get us another energy drink!' Our expectations are extremely high."

Those expectations were met once more in 2021 and 2022. The fickle and cyclical nature of this sport means that there will be another dip in years to come. But the boss's legacy will remain unimpeachable. For someone with a light personal touch, 'Didi' Mateschitz has left a massive footprint.

APPRECIATIONS 2022

By MAURICE HAMILTON

1958 Belgian Grand Prix, Spa-Francorchamps.

1959 French Grand Prix, Reims.

TONY BROOKS

TONY BROOKS, who died on 3rd May, 2022, at the age of 90, was the last of the motor racing greats of the 1950s. The Englishman might have been one of the less well known, but his natural modesty and charm could not hide the fact that three of his six grand prix wins had been at Spa-Francorchamps, the Nürburgring Nordschleife and Monza – very different, but nonetheless tough and demanding racetracks. Brooks did not set out to be a racing driver. He had been studying dentistry and racing for fun in his spare time, but such had been his obvious latent talent that he was invited to race sports cars for Aston Martin and subsequently Connaught's Formula 1 car at Syracuse on 23rd October, 1955. When he beat the works Maseratis on that day in Sicily, to score the first victory for a British car in a grand prix (albeit non-championship) since 1924, the relatively inexperienced Brooks made an impact that was significant enough to attract an offer from BRM for 1956. The only moment of note typifying a disappointing season was a huge accident at Silverstone – from which he was lucky to escape serious injury – during his single grand prix outing for the British team.

A switch to Vanwall for 1957 was more rewarding. He finished second at Monaco a few weeks before he was scheduled to drive for Aston Martin in the Le Mans 24 Hours. At 2.30am, Brooks took over a DBR1, which he knew had become stuck in fourth gear, thinking that he could sort the problem while on the move. However, an attempt to free the transmission resulted in him running wide, overturning and being trapped beneath a car brim-full of fuel. He was only freed when the following car inadvertently knocked the Aston to one side. A deep-seated religious belief heightened his appreciation of the sanctity of life and led to a determination never again to race a car he knew to be mechanically compromised. Shortly after, while continuing to recover from his injuries, he took part in the British Grand Prix at Aintree and was happy to hand over his car when the Vanwall driven by Stirling Moss ran into trouble. Moss and Brooks would rightly share the credit for giving a British car its first win in a world championship grand prix. Vanwall went on to even greater things in 1958, when Brooks took the three aforementioned memorable victories and finished third in the championship, each drive being a consummate display of the precise, graceful and unflurried style that had become his hallmark.

A move to Ferrari for 1959 led to Brooks being in the running for the championship at the final race in Sebring, Florida. However, his personal criterion of caution prompted him to have his Dino 246 checked following a bump from behind at the start. He rejoined to finish third in a race that he had needed to win to become champion. His final two seasons in F1 were spent with the British Racing Partnership and BRM, before he decided to concentrate on a burgeoning garage business and spend more time with his family.

MAURO FORGHIERI

MAURO FORGHIERI, who died, aged 87, on 2nd November, 2022, was the technical powerhouse behind Ferrari's success across 20 years, starting in the mid-1960s. A bespectacled genius, Forghieri's work was not only responsible for four drivers' and seven constructors' titles, but also notable for the fact that the Italian was unique in creating every aspect of the car – from chassis to engine, transmission and gearbox.

Forghieri, a former student at Bologna University, found himself suddenly elevated to technical chief, at the age of 27, after a mass walk-out by Ferrari's engineering team. Two years later, John Surtees won the 1964 world title at the wheel of the Ferrari 158, powered by a 1.5-litre V8. It took time for Ferrari to get to grips with the 3-litre formula in 1966, partly because of a poor budget and Ferrari's insistence on competing in F2, sports cars, hill climbs and CanAm, alongside F1.

Fiat ownership in 1969 changed the financial dynamic and led to Forghieri producing the outstanding flat-12, which, coupled with a clever transverse gearbox, would power Niki Lauda to world titles and a run of constructors' championships in the mid-1970s. Jody Scheckter also used a flat-12 to win the championship in 1979. Forghieri managed to maintain a tricky, but productive working relationship with the boss, largely because the irascible Enzo Ferrari knew the worth of his talented engineer. Ferrari's failing health and the increase of political intrigue led to Forghieri's resignation in 1986.

He created a Lamborghini V12 for Larrousse-Lola in F1 and took on work through his respected consultancy. His name, however, will long be remembered for classic racing cars, not just in F1, but also in sports cars, the Ferrari 330P4 being one particularly graceful epitaph for a colourful character with outstanding engineering intellect.

1948
1948
Weltmeisterschaftslauf
1958
AvD

VIC ELFORD

DURING an extraordinary season in 1968, VIC ELFORD demonstrated a combination of speed and versatility that will never be equalled. In January, as reigning European Rally Champion, he won the Monte Carlo Rally in a Porsche 911T. A week later, he shared the winning long-tail Porsche 907 in the Daytona 24 Hours – on a track he had never seen before and in a car he knew little about.

In July, the Englishman finished fourth on his F1 debut at the wheel of a Cooper-BRM in the wet French Grand Prix, on the road circuit at Rouen. The Cooper team had seen better days, and Elford persevered to finish fifth in Canada – significantly, on the challenging Ste Jovite track – and score points twice in 1969 during four outings with the Antique Automobiles-entered McLaren M7B.

Although he never won Le Mans outright, Elford is best remembered for victories at just about every classic sports car venue of the day. Of those, his win in the 1968 Targa Florio was outstanding. Sharing a Porsche 907 with Umberto Maglioli, he set about recouping time lost due to a puncture. Relying on his memory (through rally driver experience) of the 45 miles of Sicilian roads, he pulverised the lap record and the 18-minute loss to score one of the event's greatest victories. One of the few fans among Porsche drivers of the 917, he led development of the legendary machine and frequently established lap records, often on his way to victory in championship sports car races.

Having shown his exceptional versatility by racing for, among others, Alfa Romeo, Ferrari, Chaparral, Shadow and Chevrolet, Elford retired from driving in 1972, becoming manager of the ATS F1 team for a short period in 1977 before moving to Florida. He died, aged 86, on 13th March, 2022.

PATRICK TAMBAY

PATRICK TAMBAY might have won just two of the 114 grands prix entered by the Frenchman during nine seasons, but he will be fondly remembered for the emotional significance attached to both victories.

Tambay's racing career got off to a flying start when victory in the Pilote Elf competition guaranteed a drive in Formule Renault. Although he didn't win the championship in either 1972 or 1973, he was propelled straight into F2, where he enjoyed modest success.

A sideways step in 1977 brought the CanAm title and paved the way for F1, first with Theodore and then a frustrating two seasons with the struggling McLaren team. In 1981, he returned to Theodore and had eight unproductive races with Ligier. Not for the first time, Tambay appeared to have been relegated to the sidelines. But when his friend, Gilles Villeneuve, was killed during qualifying for the 1982 Belgian Grand Prix, he received the call from Ferrari.

Patrick scored his first F1 podium two races later at Brands Hatch and stood on the top step during a highly charged weekend at Hockenheim. Didier Pironi, Ferrari's apparent champion elect, had suffered terrible injuries during practice, but Tambay's victory raised the morale of the shattered team and helped secure not only the constructors' title, but also his place for 1983.

At the end of the fourth round at Imola, Tambay was in tears as he took Ferrari No.27 (the number forever associated with Villeneuve) across the line to score a poignant win 12 months on from the French-Canadian's fraught and final appearance in front of the *tifosi*. Although in the reckoning for the championship early in the season, Tambay suffered a string of retirements that defeated the promise of three pole positions. He finished fourth in the table – which would be as good as it would get.

Having been dropped by Ferrari, two deeply disappointing years with recalcitrant and unreliable Renaults were summed up by 11th in both the 1984 and 1985 championships before Renault withdrew. His final year in F1 would be even worse as the new Beatrice Haas team failed to deliver, Tambay scoring points just once. Racing for the Silk Cut Jaguar team in 1989 brought some good placings with Jan Lammers, before he moved briefly into PR and a more rewarding role as a TV commentator.

After struggling with ill health for many years, Patrick Tambay died, aged 73, on 4th December, 2022.

BRUCE JOHNSTONE

WHEN motor racing in South Africa received a long-awaited boost with the staging of two international events in 1960, BRUCE JOHNSTONE made his name in the second, the Cape GP at Killarney. At the wheel of a Cooper-Alfa Romeo, previously raced with success by another local driver, the 23-year-old from Durban finished fourth on the same lap as the winning works F2 Porsche of Stirling Moss. Runner-up in the 1961 South African Championship, Johnstone was invited to drive for the Yeoman Credit team in the Springbok Series. He crashed his Cooper-Climax during the 1961 Natal GP and didn't get to race in the South African GP after going off during practice.

A busy season in Europe in 1962 (including a class win in the Nürburgring 1,000km) led to the promise of drives with BRM, for whom he had been testing. He finished fourth in the Oulton Park Gold Cup, but was hugely disappointed when given a semi-works BRM, which blew up during the Natal GP. It was no better in his home GP, which he finished six laps behind.

Despite sharing David Piper's winning Ferrari 250 GTO in the Rand Nine Hours at Kyalami, Johnstone had become disillusioned by the BRM experience and quit racing. He passed away on 3rd March, 2022, aged 85.

DANNY ONGAIS

DANNY ONGAIS, who died on 26th March, 2022, aged 79, made his name initially as a drag racer, and later in USAC and IMSA. Compared to his often spectacular success in the United States, his brief forays into F1 were disappointing. Born in Honolulu, Ongais was noted for a dramatic driving style, which he brought to F1 in late 1977 when Interscope Racing entered the Hawaiian for the two North American GPs in a Penske-Cosworth PC4. He crashed out in the wet after moving up to seventh place at Watkins Glen, but brought the year-old car home seventh, two laps behind, at Mosport.

He came to an arrangement with Morris Nunn to drive the Englishman's Ensign-Cosworth in the opening two races of the 1978 season, but retired in both Argentina and Brazil when the under-funded car suffered mechanical trouble.

Interscope obtained a Shadow-Cosworth DN9 for the United States GP (West), but Ongais failed to qualify on the streets of Long Beach. It was a similar story later in the year when the American team travelled to Zandvoort for the Dutch GP.

All of this was in sharp contrast to his burgeoning career in USAC, and a disappointment for European race fans, who would be mesmerised by his dramatic efforts when IndyCar made a rare visit to the tight club circuit at Brands Hatch in the same year. *(Also see an appreciation by Gordon Kirby on page 394).*

KUNIMITSU TAKAHASHI

THE motorsport career of KUNIMITSU TAKAHASHI, who passed away on 16th March, 2022, at the age of 82, was as long as it was diverse.

Aged just 21, he became the first Japanese rider to win a world championship grand prix on a 250cc Honda. That victory, at Hockenheim in 1961, was followed by three more (on 125cc bikes), but his career was interrupted in 1962 by a serious accident during the Isle of Man TT. Racing Datsuns brought a switch to four wheels, followed by wins in the Japanese championship for sports cars in 1966 and 1971.

Takahashi became a stalwart of the country's premier single-seater series (Formula 2000), finishing second in the 1977 championship. His one and only F1 appearance was at Fuji in the same year, when he qualified 22nd for the Japanese Grand Prix and finished ninth, two laps behind, in a well-used Tyrrell-Cosworth 007 entered by a local team. After racing F2 in Japan for the Kojima team, he won the Japanese sports car championship on four occasions in the 1980s (including 1987 with Kenneth Acheson in a Nova-run Porsche 962C) as well as taking a class win at Le Mans in 1995 with a Honda NSX.

After competing regularly in the local F3000 series, Takahashi formed his own GT team and raced a Honda NSX GT2 before finally retiring from competition in 2000.

REINE WISELL

RACING in the shadow of fellow Swede Ronnie Peterson had a significant effect on the career of REINE WISELL. Having competed successfully in touring cars and F3, he moved beyond Scandinavia, winning 11 races in F3 in 1968. He frequently went head-to-head with Peterson the following year, their epic battle in the Monaco F3 race summing up the pecking order when Peterson won and became the first to reach F1. Wisell switched to sports cars and did enough in Sid Taylor's F5000 McLaren to warrant a drive with Lotus, as the team hastily regrouped following the death of Jochen Rindt at Monza in 1970 and the subsequent departure of John Miles. He joined an elite club when he finished on the podium on his F1 debut at Watkins Glen, the USGP having been won by Emerson Fittipaldi in the other Lotus 72. That was enough to earn a full-time seat with Lotus, and he had a busy 1971 with a full programme of F2 (including a fine win at Pau), but little of note in terms of F1 results. Wisell became a member of an over-ambitious BRM team that was spread too thinly, a return to Lotus for the final two races of 1972 doing little to resurrect a F1 career that was losing momentum. Three subsequent appearances in a variety of March F1 cars, in 1973 and 1974, were complemented by various sports car and F2 drives before Wisell returned to touring cars, followed by historic racing. He died at the age of 80 on 20th March, 2022.

TEAM-BY-TEAM

FORMULA 1 REVIEW

Team Reviews: MARK HUGHES

Car Illustrations: ADRIAN DEAN

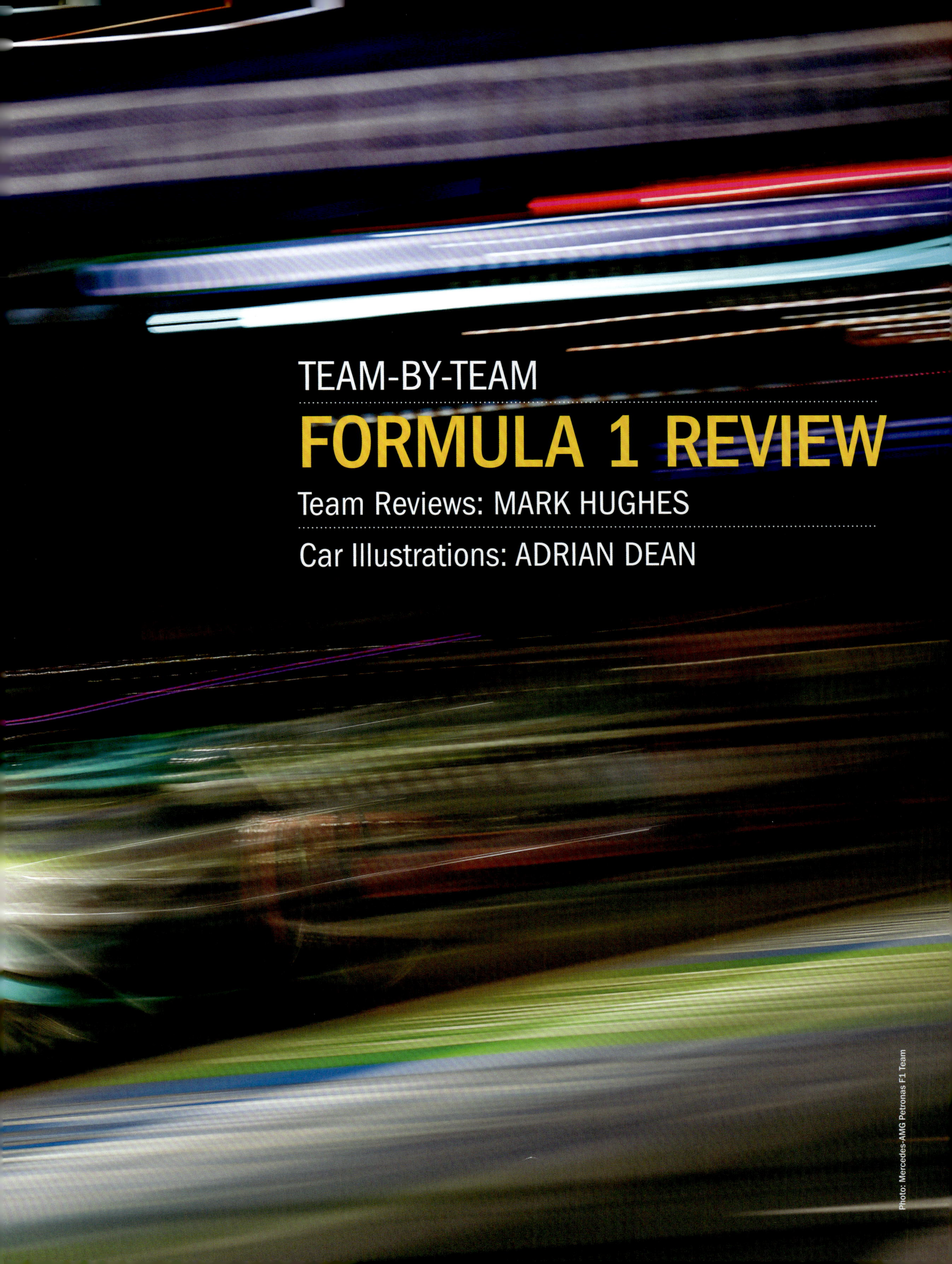

Photo: Mercedes-AMG Petronas F1 Team

ORACLE RED BULL RACING

33

MAX VERSTAPPEN

11

SERGIO PÉREZ

As well as taking Max Verstappen to a world title and a record number of grand prix victories in a season, Red Bull won the constructors' championship for the first time in nine years. It was a resounding performance, directly comparable to its V8-era glory days.

Although it failed to win only five of the season's 22 races (with Verstappen on 15 victories, Sergio Pérez on two), it was only in the second half of the season that the victories came by sheer overwhelming performance superiority. For much of the first half, they were the product of Ferrari's reliability problems and strategy errors, which Red Bull and Verstappen punished without mercy.

This stunning season was delivered courtesy of the Honda-powered RB18. Originally, the Japanese engine manufacturer had been set to leave F1 officially in 2022, although still preparing and supplying the RA621 power unit, which had first raced in 2021. There was a shift in policy on that, and the Honda insignia had reappeared on the engine cover in the latter part of the season. For two reasons, it was especially fitting that Verstappen sealed his second world title at Suzuka: first, because it is Honda's own circuit, and secondly because it was the last race that the ailing owner of the team, Dietrich Mateschitz, watched before his passing.

The all-new aerodynamic regulations offered an opportunity to steal a march on the competition, and with Adrian Newey as a key member of the technical team, it's perhaps not so surprising that it did so. But head of aero Enrico Balbo (who, once upon a time, had designed the double diffuser of the 2009 Williams) should be given full credit, together with technical director Pierre Waché, chief engineering officer Rob Marshall, chief designer Craig Skinner, head of performance engineering Ben Waterhouse and chief engineer (car) Paul Monaghan.

"I'm lucky enough to have a really good group of people at Milton Keynes," said Newey, "and it's a very good team. All F1 teams are big engineering teams, but in terms of the involvement in meetings, I put my tuppence-worth in, but it's the guys who bat those ideas around, and maybe come up with a list and go away and do the work. Specifically, on this car, I did the front and rear suspension, and a few other bits and pieces."

The very start of Newey's F1 career had coincided with the end of F1's last ground-effect era. So he was mindful of some of the potential hazards. Whether that was the reason the RB18 did not suffer from the porpoising that so troubled most of the others is impossible to know. But the whole concept of the car was based around a floor that was intended to provide good downforce over a wide range of operating conditions, rather than maximum peak downforce.

"If you have an aero map which, as you get closer to the ground, generates more downforce, eventually the flow structure breaks down and loses downforce. Then it's going to porpoise," explained Newey. "With these regs, you could see that was a possibility, but

RED BULL RACING RB18

TITLE PARTNERS	Red Bull • Oracle **PRINCIPAL TEAM PARTNER** ByBit
TEAM PARTNERS	TAG Heuer • Puma • Rauch • Tezos • BMC • Cash App • Claro • Hard Rock International • Pirelli • Walmart • América Móvil Interprotección • Poly • Therabody • Ocean Bottle • Pokerstars • Armor All • Gold Standard • AlphaTauri • Inter.mx
TECHNICAL PARTNERS	Honda • Mobil 1 • Esso • Citrix • Siemens • Hewlett Packard Enterprise • Arctic Wolf • AT&T • DMG Mori • Hexagon • Ansys • PWR OZ • Sabelt
POWER UNIT	**Type:** Red Bull RBPTH001 1.6-litre turbo **No. of cylinders (vee angle):** V6 (90°) **No. of valves:** 24 **Max rpm (ICE):** 15,000 **Power output:** 900+bhp **Electronics:** MESL standard electronic control unit/Honda Racing Development **Fuel:** Esso Synergy **Oil:** Mobil 1
TRANSMISSION	Longitudinally-mounted eight-speed gearbox, hydraulic power-shift and clutch operation
CHASSIS	**Monocoque:** Carbon-fibre composite with engine as fully stressed member **Front suspension:** Aluminium uprights, carbon-fibre double wishbones with pull-rod-actuated torsion springs, dampers and anti-roll bar **Rear suspension:** Aluminium uprights, carbon-fibre double wishbones with push-rod-actuated torsion springs, dampers and anti-roll bar **Wheels:** OZ Racing, 18in diameter **Tyres:** Pirelli P Zero **Brakes:** Brembo Calipers, pads and discs
DIMENSIONS	Not disclosed **Formula weight:** 798kg, including driver and camera

MAX VERSTAPPEN

CHRISTIAN HORNER

Photos: Red Bull Content Pool/Getty Images

ORACLE RED BULL RACING: PERSONNEL

Chairman: Dietrich Mateschitz

Team Principal & CEO: Christian Horner OBE

Red Bull Motorsport Consultant: Helmut Marko

Chief Technical Officer: Adrian Newey OBE

Technical Director: Pierre Waché

Chief Engineering Officer: Rob Marshall

Chief Designer: Craig Skinner

Chief Engineer, Car Engineering: Paul Monaghan

Sporting Director: Jonathan Wheatley

Head of Aerodynamics: Enrico Balbo

Head of Performance Engineering: Ben Waterhouse

Principal Strategy Engineer: Hannah Schmitz

Head of Driver Academy: Guillaume Roquelin

Race Engineer *(Verstappen)***:** Gianpiero Lambiase

Race Engineer *(Perez)***:** Hugh Bird

Chief Mechanic: Phil Turner

No.1 Mechanic *(Verstappen)***:** Chris Gent

No.1 Mechanic *(Perez)***:** Adam Chamberlain

Chief Marketing Officer: Oliver Hughes

Brand Director: Kelly Brittain

Commercial Director: Nick Stocker

Head of Strategic Partnerships: Zoe Chilton

Head of Red Bull Relations: Paul Hendrix

Head of Communications: Paul Smith

Above: Street-race ace. Sergio Pérez won under mixed weather conditions at Monaco.

Top right: Principal strategy enginner Hannah Schmitz is credited with playing an important part in Red Bull's flexible race tactics.

Above centre right: Sporting director Jonathan Wheatley and chief engineer Paul Monaghan have been integral to the team's success over many years.

Above right: Chief engineering officer Rob Marshall.

Right: Max Verstappen lofts the winner's trophy at Imola, just one of a record-breaking 15 race wins taken by the Dutchman through the season.

Far right: Race engineer Hugh Bird gives Sergio Pérez the lowdown.

Photos: Red Bull Content Pool/Getty Images

whether they would and how you model that was the difficulty."

The underfloor was shaped very differently to that of any other car, and the rear suspension system was given the travel and layout to facilitate a fantastic ride quality that was a crucial part in maintaining consistent downforce without triggering the bouncing seen elsewhere. In that sense, the RB18 seemed a better integrated concept than any other.

A high nose (the regulations stipulate that the distance between the nose tip and the ground should be between 125 and 250mm) was incorporated to maximise airflow to the inlets of the underfloor venturis, but the further above the ground, the less effective the wing itself tends to be, so there is always a trade-off to be made there. There are also dimensional requirements that stipulate the range of the front axle position relative to the nose tip, so there were variations between cars in the distance between the axle line and the venturi inlets. It is notable that the fastest three cars of the season had the axle mounted well forward.

The airflow around this entire area is considered by aerodynamicists as a three-dimensional challenge, and this was very much part of what drove the choice of pull-rod operation for the front suspension, after years of push-rod. Similarly, at the rear, the traditional pull-rod arrangement was replaced by push-rod in reaction to the different aerodynamic priorities the new regulations created.

Sidepods, which swept gracefully downwards with a significant undercut at the front, housed smaller radiators than on the Ferrari, as the radiator area was supplemented by further cooling around the centreline of the car, beneath the engine cover. The car tended to run a smaller rear wing than its competition for any given circuit, though it was being fed from below by very aggressively-profiled lower beam wing elements.

In its initial form, the RB18 was not quite as quick over a qualifying lap as the higher-downforce Ferrari, but its straight-line performance was better. The car that began the season in Bahrain was as much as 20kg over the minimum weight (costing around 0.6s per lap) and the front didn't have the grip sought by Verstappen, perhaps through a combination of wing height choice and how the excess weight in the car was distributed, though chief engineer Paul Monaghan cautioned against attributing too much to that: "By regulation, the front-to-rear weight distribution can only be varied by 1 per cent. A few kilos off here or there isn't even going to shift it the full 1 per cent. Incrementally, it shifted rearwards a bit as we developed the car. But they're very sensitive these cars, and the decimal places will have a small effect on the balance, but it wasn't our sole tool for dealing with the front end. We found various ways of addressing it."

Underfloor designs are the most closely-guarded secrets of this generation of car, as the floor is by far the dominant mechanism of performance. But inevitably they are photographed, either when being moved between truck and garage or when a car is craned off the track after an accident. The tunnels of the RB18's floor appeared to be higher-roofed (and more arched) than others, and the central keel separating left- and right-hand tunnels was not uniformily teardrop-shaped, as on other cars. The sides of the three inlet vanes to the tunnels were variable in their geometry and occasionally reshaped between races, together with the various flicks and vortex generators of the external edges of the floor. A higher tunnel, in theory, would not accelerate the air as strongly towards the venturi throats, but would be much more tolerant of changes in ride height and airflow speed without stalling. The shaping of the floor's central keel would appear to maintain a more consistent tunnel volume along its varying height, and the profiling of the inlet vanes is used to accurately condition the airflow to the various parts of the tunnel.

Probably as a result of such careful profiling and a deep understanding of how the various flows of the floor interract with each other, the RB18 seemed able to retain a greater proprtion of its downforce at low speed, when the ride height naturally increases. Its peak high-speed downforce (when the rear ride height is at its lowest) appeared from GPS to be less than that of Ferrari at most tracks, but the payback was the low-speed performance, great straight-line speed and relative immunity from porpoising. The rear suspension, though by definition of the regulations much stiffer than in previous years, was probably soft relative to the others – and with enough travel to allow for a big variation in ride height at low speed and high, without inducing the vertical bouncing seen elsewhere.

"Clearly, you run these cars much lower at the rear," said Monaghan. "So if we've reduced the hub travel at the back, we must have changed the stiffness for a given load. The aerodynamics of the car are very different through the ride height range. Being a ground-effect car, by definition there's an interest in running it low. If you want to run the car lower, we've had to change the stiffness of the car. So the suspension still plays a massive part, but is operated very differently to that of 2021 and before. The way you go about the discipline of supporting the car, and doing your heave and roll rates, and the ratio between front and rear, is driven by the differences in the aero of the car."

The outermost of the tunnel inlet vanes actually direct airflow out of the side of the car, giving a small wing effect on that part of the bodywork and helping to acclerate the airflow down the sides. Only the inboard vanes direct flow to the tunnels. Varying the arrangement of those vanes allowed the team to vary the proportion of the total airflow going through the tunnels and thus the aero distribution between front and rear axles. So when weight came off the front of the car, so the aero distribution was matched to the new weight distribution. The most significant change came with the new floor introduced at the French Grand Prix in July. By that time, a lot of weight had been saved and hence the rearrangement of the vane geometry to make the accompanying aero balance shift.

That initial 20kg weight penalty was reduced to as little as 4kg in the early part of the season's second half, but further aero performance devlopments resulted in it creeping back up to 12kg by the end of the season. By that time, however, the car, the team and its lead driver had rewritten the record books.

16

CHARLES LECLERC

55

CARLOS SAINZ

SCUDERIA FERRARI

FERRARI produced a super-fast car in the F1-75, quick enough to set a glittering sequence of pole positions. But its performance dominance in the first half-season was not fully maintained into the latter half, and not converted into as many victories as should have been the case – for a variety of reasons.

In the first ten races, Charles Leclerc had the performance to win at least seven of them on his own terms, but he won only three. Two of those were in the opening trio of races. Likely victories in Spain and Baku were lost to power-unit failures. Potential Leclerc victories in Monaco and Silverstone were lost to poor strategic decisions on the pit wall (though in the latter case, team-mate Carlos Sainz at least was the beneficiary, rather than Red Bull, as was the case in Monaco). Without the PU and strategy problems, in the sequence between Spain and Austria, Leclerc might reasonably have won five consecutive races. Which would have formed a great platform for a title challenge, even against the ever improving performance of Red Bull, which unquestionably was a faster car in the season's second half.

The Ferrari was highly original in both its aerodynamic response to the new regulations and its new power unit. The most visually distinctive feature was the deep channel on the upper surface of the sidepods, creating a low-pressure area that hurried the airflow towards the rear wing. Those sidepods had a very bluff frontal shape, without the traditional undercuts, the idea being to maximise the air out-wash around them, to give the floor a cleaner flow. It was extremely effective, GPS traces showing that it carried a significant downforce advantage over the competition for much of the season. Opting for the wide, out-washing sidepods meant that there was no necessity to have any supplementary radiator surface area higher up around the centreline, as on many others, allowing a lower centre of gravity. The suspension remained push-rod front/pull-rod rear, and at the front, it was virtually indistinguishable from that of the previous couple of years.

The new 066/7 power unit was almost completely new, retaining only the ERS system and battery introduced late in the 2021 season. With concept by Wolf Zimmermann and development undertaken by a PU team headed by Enrico Gualtieri, it was highly innovative. Partly in response to the requirement of 10 per cent biofuel, it featured a relatively small turbo and long inlet tracts, with the aim of more than recovering the low-speed power delivery lost to the new fuel. Indeed, its low-speed acceleration was terrific – better than any of the other three rival PUs – even though it tended to use up its battery deployment a little earlier at the end of the straights than the Honda. Although the turbo was new, it retained the traditional combined turbine/compressor layout (making it the only one of the four PUs not with a split turbo).

There were seven poles from the first ten races,

FERRARI F1-75

PREMIUM PARTNERS	Shell • Santander • Velas • Snapdragon
TEAM PARTNERS	Ray Ban • AWS • Richard Mille • Ceva Logistics • Mission Winnow • Bitdefender • Etrella Galicia • HCL Software • Palantir
TECHNICAL PARTNERS	OMR • Mahle • Pirelli • SKF • NGK Spark Plug • Brembo • Riedel • Garrett Motion • Öhlins Racing • Sabelt
OFFICIAL PARTNERS	Puma • Radiobook • Vistajet • Armani • Riva • Frecciarossa • Manpower Group • Technogym • Iveco • Bell Helmets
POWER UNIT	**Type:** Ferrari 066/7 1.6-litre turbo hybrid **No. of cylinders (vee angle):** V6 (90°) **Bore and stroke:** 80 x 53mm **No. of valves:** 24 **Max rpm:** 15,000 **MGU-K rpm:** 50,000 **MGU-H rpm:** 125,000
TRANSMISSION	Ferrari eight-speed plus reverse longitudinal gearbox, sequential semi-automatic, hydraulically-controlled rear differential
CHASSIS	**Monocoque:** Carbon-fibre and honeycomb composite construction with Halo cockpit protection **Front suspension:** Push-rod-actuated inboard springs **Rear suspension:** Pull-rod-actuated inboard springs **Wheels:** OZ Racing, 18in diameter **Tyres:** Pirelli P Zero **Brake system:** Ventilated carbon discs, rear brake-by-wire
DIMENSIONS	Not disclosed **Formula weight:** 798kg, including driver and camera

CHARLES LECLERC

MATTIA BINOTTO

Photos: Scuderia Ferrari

SCUDERIA FERRARI: PERSONNEL

Chairman: John Elkann

Chief Executive Officer: Benedetto Vigna

Team Principal: Mattia Binotto

Racing Director: Laurent Mekies

External Relations: Gino Rosato

Head of Power Unit Area: Enrico Gualtieri

Head of Chassis Area: Enrico Cardile

Head of Supply Chain & Manufacturing: Enrico Racca

Head of Strategy & Sporting: Iñaki Rueda

Head of PU Operations & Electronics: Luigi Fraboni

Head of Track Engineering: Matteo Togninalli

Key Relations Executive Manager: Jonathan Giacobazzi

Race Operations Manager: Claudio Albertini

Race Engineer *(Leclerc)*: Xavier Marcos Padros

Performance Engineer *(Leclerc)*: Bryan Bozzi

Race Engineer *(Sainz)*: Riccardo Adami

Performance Engineer *(Sainz)*: Steven Petrik

Chief Mechanic: Fabio Bellosi

No.1 Mechanic *(Leclerc)*: Alessandro Fusaro

No.1 Mechanic *(Sainz)*: Andrea Di Musciano

Head of Communications: Silvia Frangipane Hoffer

Above: The Ferrari in its 75th-anniversary livery, as it appeared in Monza.
Illustration: Adrian Dean

Top: Carlos Sainz was top dog at the British Grand Prix.

Top right: Charles Leclerc holds aloft the winner's trophy at Red Bull Ring.

Above right: A magical moment for Sainz as he takes his first GP win.

Right: The season began with much promise for Ferrari, as Leclerc won the opener in Bahrain.

Far right: Second place in the drivers' and constructors' championships was progress for the Ferrari squad, pictured at the Abu Dhabi finale. It was not enough to save team principal Mattia Binotto.
Photos: Scuderia Ferrari

but it was at the 12th round in France that both Ferrari and Red Bull made significant upgrades to their floors. Ferrari's form tailed off a little from this point and led the team to question whether its new floor was under-performing. So for the next few races, it was tested back to back in the practices with the original floor – and found to be performing pretty much as in simulation. The problem was more to do with how much Red Bull had improved. That Paul Ricard floor featured a higher inlet on the inboard side with a separate step-down to the outboard inlet. It was designed to feed a greater proportion of the airflow through the underfloor tunnels.

In general, the car ran with more wing than the Red Bull with each car at their respective optimum. In Montreal, the team introduced a more efficient rear wing, which surrendered some raw downforce for a greater gain in straight-line speed, to give a better trade-off relative to its main rival. But the very low downforce demands of Spa and Monza later in the year revealed that when the wing level was trimmed to the minimum, the car lost way too much downforce to remain competitive with the Red Bull.

The tailing off of the car's raw competitiveness coincided not only with the continued highly-productive development of the Red Bull, but also the imposition of the FIA technical directive concerning bouncing. An imposed limit on vertical loads and a more specific regulation about how the plank had to be mounted to the floor seemed to impact upon the Ferrari more than other cars.

The Technical Directive (039) was introduced for Spa. One race before that, in Hungary, Ferrari had struggled with tyre degradation, which was an issue that continued for much of the remainder of the season. Even leading from pole at Monza, with Verstappen starting a penalised seventh, the Ferrari's front left tyre degradation left Leclerc defenceless against the advancing Red Bull. The same trait was even evident in the rain of Suzuka, where initially Leclerc was able to match Verstappen's pace – but only for four laps, after which the front intermediates surrendered.

A tweaked version of the Ricard floor was introduced at Suzuka, optimised around the generally greater rear ride height that car was obliged to carry after TD039 was imposed.

The power-unit failures of the early season were linked to the MGU-H system, and team boss Mattia Binotto admitted at the time that the technical solution to the weakness was not a short-term one. This had been corrected by the latter half of the season. Carlos Sainz's fiery exit from the Austrian Grand Prix was unconnected to this, however. The problem was traced to a catastrophic turbo failure in the circuit's high altitude. This had implications for the much higher altitude of Mexico City later in the season, when the turbos were turned down significantly to prevent a repeat.

In the thinner air of higher altitudes, the higher shaft speeds needed to meet the usual boost levels were a potential problem for the Ferrari. The smaller turbo can struggle to meet the boost targets set by the mapping when the resistance at the output end of the compressor is greater than the turbine can overcome, in which case the airflow reverses until conditions stabilise and the compressor is able to work once more. This is known as turbo surge, and the oscillations it creates can place unbearable extra stresses on the moving parts. Using the MGU-H to limit the turbo's speed resulted in the Ferraris being well down on power and finishing a distant fifth and sixth, far behind Red Bull and Mercedes.

By that time, aero development had been switched off, as the team sought to stay within the cost-cap limits. This was a contributory factor to the improving Mercedes generally assuming the status of second-fastest car in the last few races.

There were many upsides to Ferrari's 2022 season – not least that it had delivered a big competitive leap over the previous two years, with a highly original, technically creative design. But the unavoidable conclusion is that it could have been so much more.

44

LEWIS HAMILTON

63

GEORGE RUSSELL

Photos: Mercedes-AMG Petronas F1 Team

MERCEDES-AMG PETRONAS F1 TEAM

MERCEDES fell to earth dramatically in 2022. The run of eight consecutive world constructors' championships was brought to an end by a dominant Red Bull. For much of the season, the Mercedes W13 wasn't even the second-fastest car, as Red Bull and Ferrari vied for the status of being fastest. It was only in the penultimate race, in Brazil, that the car even claimed a win.

It had looked so exciting for the team in pre-season simulation, with a unique aero concept promising enormous downforce and a likely big advantage over the competition. That remained forever a dream, hidden within simulation tools that did not adequately predict the real-world porpoising hazards of such big ground-effect downforce. Furthermore, because the car had been designed around this idealised aero, it had built-in limitations, which extended beyond simply the failure to match the simulated downforce.

The 'zero sidepods' concept, which had made these misleading promises, was facilitated by a unique reading of the dimensional regulations around the front of the sidepods and cockpit.

An unusual tall, narrow radiator inlet allowed the regulation upper impact structure to be exposed to the air and sheathed in a contoured cover (on to which the mirrors were mounted), which directed airflow from above down to the outer floor area, helping to accelerate the crucial flow at that point.

This contoured 'sis' (side impact system) bar is allowed by regulation to extend as far outwards as the bodywork directly beneath it. The triangular section of the bodywork forming the front of the W13 sidepods – in contrast to the conventional undercut in this area – meant that the bottom was far wider than on conventional cars. Consequently, the bar could extend correspondingly further outwards and thus be more powerful in down-washing the airflow to the exposed lower floor edges.

Together with the packaging of the radiators, this allowed Mercedes to ditch the conventional downward ramp of sidepod bodywork, which in a conventional sidepod is used to accelerate the air to the gap between the rear wheel and the top of the diffuser. Instead, the reduction of bodywork area aft of the radiator inlet left an enormously wide channel of exposed floor for the airflow to feed to that space between the wheel and diffuser.

It was an ingenious interpretation, and the front triangular-section sidepod, which almost dissolved into nothing behind, gave it the dramatic look of a radar-evading stealth fighter jet.

It didn't perform like one, however, not initially at any rate.

When the car was tested for the first time on-track, its porpoising was extreme. As the downforce pulled the rear close to the ground, the ground effect of the tunnels was enhanced, pulling it yet further down until eventually the flow was too restrict-

MERCEDES-AMG F1 W13

TITLE PARTNER	Petronas **PRINCIPAL PARTNER** INEOS
TEAM PARTNERS	UBS • Team Viewer • CrowdStrike • Akkodis • Hewlett Packard Enterprise • IWC Schaffhausen • The Ritz-Carlton • Einhell • AMD Monster Energy • Pure Storage • Tommy Hilfiger • Tibco • Fastly • Crestron
TEAM SUPPLIERS	Puma • Police • OZ Racing • Endless • Axalta • Belstaff • Eight Sleep • Pirelli
POWER UNIT	**Type:** Mercedes-AMG F1 M13 E Performance **No. of cylinders (vee angle):** V6 (90°) **No. of valves:** 24 **Max rpm (ICE):** 15,000 **Electronics:** FIA standard ECU and FIA homologated electronic & electrical system **Instrumentation:** McLaren Electronic Systems (MES) **Fuel:** Petronas Primax **Lubricants and fluids:** Petronas Tutela
TRANSMISSION	**Gearbox:** Eight forward gears plus one reverse, carbon-fibre main case, sequential, semi-automatic, hydraulic activation **Clutch:** Carbon plate
CHASSIS	**Monocoque:** Moulded carbon-fibre and honeycomb composite structure **Front suspension:** Carbon-fibre wishbone and push-rod-actuated torsion springs and rockers **Rear suspension:** Carbon-fibre wishbone and pull-rod-actuated inboard springs and rockers **Brake system:** Carbone Industrie carbon/carbon discs and pads, Brembo calipers, rear brake-by-wire **Steering:** Power-assisted rack-and-pinion **Wheels:** BBS forged magnesium, 18in diameter **Tyres:** Pirelli P Zero
DIMENSIONS	**Length:** Over 5000mm **Width:** 2000mm **Height:** 970mm **Formula weight:** 798kg, including driver and camera

LEWIS HAMILTON

TOTO WOLFF

Photos: Mercedes-AMG Petronas F1 Team

MERCEDES-AMG PETRONAS F1 TEAM: PERSONNEL

Team Principal & CEO: Toto Wolff

Chief Technical Officer: James Allison

Managing Director, High Performance Powertrains: Hywel Thomas

Technical Director: Mike Elliott

Chief Operating Officer: Rob Thomas

Performance Director: Loic Serra

Chief Designer: John Owen

Sporting Director: Ron Meadows

Aerodynamics Director: Jarrod Murphy

Motorsport Strategy Director: James Vowles

Trackside Engineering Director: Andrew Shovlin

Race Engineer ***(Hamilton)*****:** Peter Bonnington

Performance Engineer ***(Hamilton)*****:** Marcus Dudley

Race Engineer ***(Russell)*****:** Riccardo Musconi

Performance Engineer ***(Russell)*****:** Hugues Bretonnier

Chief Mechanic: Matt Deane

Chief Engineer Trackside: Simon Cole

Strategic Communications Director: Bradley Lord

ed and it stalled, increasing the ride height and allowing it to unstall, at which point, the process would begin all over again. This was a generic problem faced by all the teams, but on the W13, it was exacerbated by the sheer area of exposed floor at the rear, without any bodywork above, effectively making it a cantilever.

But this was just the beginning of the problem, for the stiffness of the chassis and suspension brought the whole structure into conflict with the phasing of the porpoising (which is an aerodynamic trait), initiating bouncing (which is a mechanical trait).

Technical director Mike Elliott explained the fundamental conflict of forces involved: "There are two issues. The aerodynamic issue is there's effectively a phasing between the aerodynamic force and the motion of the car. And the phasing between the two means that you get an energy input. So once you hit a bump and you initiate an oscillation, the aerodynamics are such that they add energy to the oscillation, rather than damp it. With the previous generations of cars, the aerodynamics would have damped the oscillation, but this year's cars don't.

"So even when you've cured the aerodynamic input, the fact that you've got a net less damping means that you struggle to run the cars as stiffly as you'd want to do to run them close to the ground. And so you end up with a level of bounce, and it just comes from the road input. These cars are fundamentally very stiff; you want to run them as low as you can, and that's the compromise you're making between the aerodynamics and the ride of the car."

Or as Lewis Hamilton put it, "The stiffness of the car is to the point where the suspension is pretty useless and stiffer than the tyres. The tyres are then squashing and bouncing, so we're bouncing on the tyres as well."

Even running the suspension that stiff still wasn't stiff enough for the aero. In turn, this was a function of the restriction of the rear suspension travel, which had been defined by the pick-up points designed into the car in the expectation of a smooth aerodynamic performance, with no account having been taken of the porpoising and bouncing problem that emerged. Thus a suspension inappropriate to the car's aero traits was baked into it.

As was a floor that only added to the problem, as Elliott admitted: "To try and make a stiff floor is more challenging, the more overhang you've got. And when floor stiffness was a significant effect on bouncing, then that had a consequence."

Relative to most of the rest of the field, it produced good downforce, so it was still comfortably the third-fastest car. But its deficit to Red Bull and Ferrari over the season averaged around 0.7s. It tended to be more competitive on race-days than in qualifying, largely on account of how effectively it controlled front tyre temperatures. A highly sophisticated arrangement of ducting within the outer carbon-fibre 'cake tins' was probably responsible for this.

Initially, to keep the car from reaching the porpoising threshold, it had to be run higher than it had been designed to do (but still not high enough to banish the bouncing), losing it the sort of downforce that would have been needed to compete at the front. Floor updates for Barcelona (and a new front wing introduced in Miami) were key to obtaining a much better handle on the bouncing, and on race pace, it was genuinely competitive with Ferrari. But that was a false dawn, as chief of trackside engineering Andrew Shovlin explained: "Those changes and a better understanding enabled us to run the car where it was designed to run. But then, when we had the clarity which that brought, we realised we were working much better on high-downforce tracks than low. We weren't able to fix that."

That was a function of the drag levels induced by the car. Keeping the floor away from porpoising territory meant running bigger wings to compensate. The W13 simply could not be run practically with as big a proportion of its total downforce derived from the underbody as Red Bull or, initially, Ferrari. It was notable that when Ferrari's way of cushioning the plank-to-floor mounting was outlawed by TD039 (from Spa onwards), its performance became quite similar to that of Mercedes.

Further updates of the floor appeared at Silverstone and Paul Ricard in July, but probably the biggest breakthrough occurred with the Austin upgrade, comprising a new floor and front wing, together with a significant weight loss and a reliability upgrade to the power unit, with a strengthened crankshaft. These, along with continued excellent race-day tyre usage (which often brought a handicap in qualifying), suddenly made the car a contender. Hamilton led for a time in Austin, while George Russell vied for pole in Mexico before going on to lead a team 1-2 in Brazil.

No one was kidding themselves, though. That victory came on a weekend when Red Bull had been struggling, and a week later, in the season finale at Abu Dhabi, Mercedes was again trailing by 0.7s, around a track that punished high drag and at which, in the high-speed sweeps, the roll was enough to make the floor edges trigger the dreaded porpoising.

Elliott: "The longer-term issues that we baked into the car, there were opportunities to see those in hindsight. I think a number of us would look back and go, 'I wish we'd spotted that.' But I think, inevitably, these things never come down to one thing. It's normally a consequence of a few things that go together. In order to have spotted the original problem, you'd have to learn about some of the other things that came later, if that makes sense. So, in hindsight, yes, it could have been fixed; in practicality, it would have been very tough."

Above: The car's systems are checked on the grid in Baku.

Left: A momentous day for George Russell in Brazil.

Far left: The unique concept of the W13 is well illustrated by this overhead shot from Abu Dhabi.

Right: A season without a win was unthinkable for Lewis, who seemed to handle it with good grace.

Below: Pit-stop action in Austin.

Photos: Mercedes-AMG Petronas F1 Team

ALPINE F1 TEAM

14

FERNANDO ALONSO

31

ESTEBAN OCON

Photos: Alpine F1 Team

ALPINE moved ahead of McLaren in the late-season races for fourth in the constructors' championship, but it was harder than it should have been, given the consistency of raw performances of their respective cars.

The Alpine A522 was a step-change improvement on the team's efforts of the previous few years, and represented the fruits of the technical team at Enstone really beginning to gel and the efforts at Viry in creating the new split-turbo power unit, which was a significant improvement. A few reliability glitches (and probably some overperformances from Lando Norris in qualifying at McLaren) made things tougher than they might have been.

The response of the technical team, guided by chief technical officer Pat Fry and technical director Matt Harmon, to the new regulations was a car based on two fundamentals of wide bodywork and a stiff floor. This turned out to be the foundation of the car's very consistent performance from track to track, and its relative immunity to the porpoising and bouncing encountered elsewhere.

Fry explained what had led them down that path: "We were very nervous of the flow structures under the car and how they were blowing up in CFD, and we were quite worried about the stability of these structures. It wasn't that we were super-clever and thought about porpoising – we didn't. Where we ended up, with the wide bodywork and stiff floor, was purely to stiffen the car's structure because that improves the stability of the flow, which is what we were worried about under these regulations. If the floor moves, you can have real problems. So it meant we went in with a car that we knew was going to be overweight, but was worth that effort to make it stable so that we could know that the car on the track was what we had in the tunnel. I think that was a good thing, and you can see that we didn't need to change our ride height to alleviate any problems. We pretty much ran with what we started with."

Thus it was somewhat galling when the porpoising problem through the field led to the FIA allowing extra floor stays on the eve of the season. "Yes, I'm still annoyed that they allowed the extra fixings," said Fry. "That was a change of rules. The others who didn't have wide bodywork and stiff floor could have thrown kilos at their cars or raised their ride heights and fixed the problem. It was kind of a let-off for a lot of teams, and we could probably have had a better season if they had to lift their cars another 10mm or so. It was all within the realms of they could have fixed it – but the FIA chose not to."

Although the bodywork was wide, the actual skeleton of the car was super-slim, which had been very much a design aim from the beginning, at both Viry and Enstone.

Photo: Bryn Williams

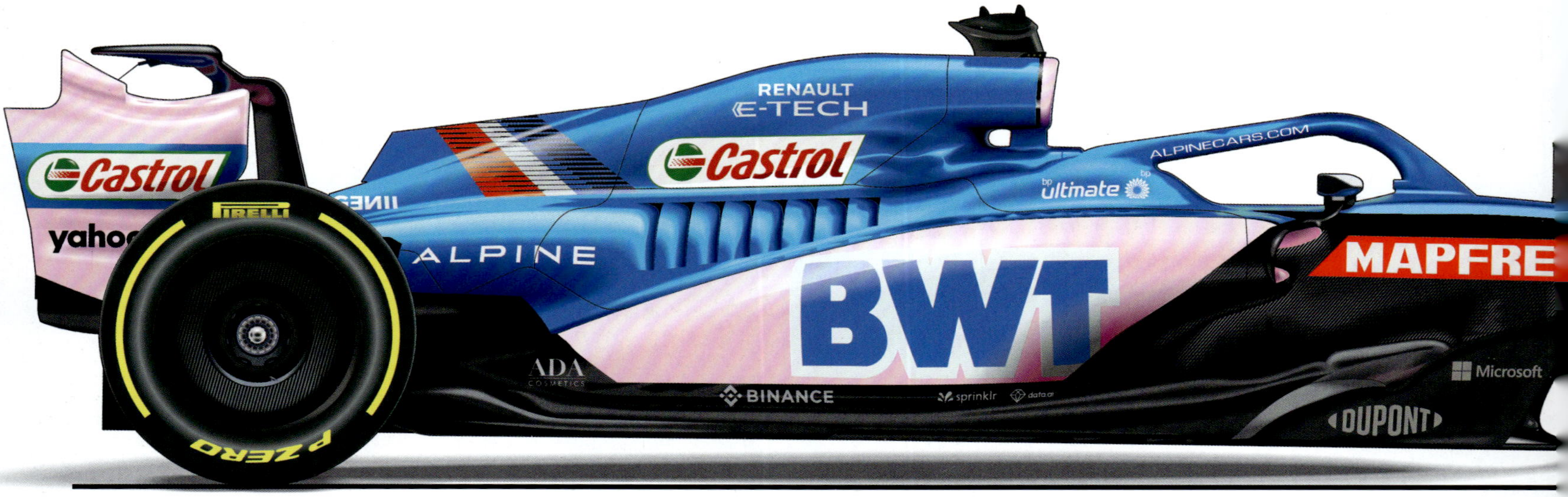

ALPINE A522

TITLE PARTNER	BWT **PREMIUM PARTNERS** Castrol • BP Ultimate • Mobilize Financial Services • MAPFRE • Renault E-Tech
OFFICIAL PARTNERS	Microsoft • Mandiant • Binanace • Dupont • Plug • Delphi Technologies • Plug Power . Data.ai • Bell & Ross • Kappa Sprinklr Boeing • Genii Business Exchange
TECHNICAL PARTNERS	Eurodatacar • PerkinElmer • Shamir • Siemens • 3d Systems • Alpinestars • Boeing • Elysium • GF Machining Solutions • Yahoo
OFFICIAL SUPPLIERS	Alpinestars • Alpine Eyewear • Elysium • GCaps • Hexis • KX • K.Way • Linde • Matrix Volume Graphics • Pirelli • Roland Trak Racer • Volume Graphics
POWER UNIT	**Type:** Renault E-Tech RE22 Hybrid **No. of cylinders (vee angle):** V6 (90°) **No. of valves:** 24 **Max rpm (ICE):** 15,000 **Electronics:** MES-Microsoft standard electronic control unit **Fuel:** BP **Oil:** Castrol
TRANSMISSION	**Gearbox:** Eight-speed semi-automatic with reverse gear and quick-shift system **Clutch:** AP Racing
CHASSIS	**Monocoque:** Moulded carbon-fibre and aluminium honeycomb composite **Front suspension:** Upper and lower carbon-fibre wishbones, push-rod-actuated torsion-bar springs, dampers and anti-roll bar **Rear suspension:** Upper and lower carbon-fibre wishbones, pull-rod actuated torsion-bar springs and transverse-mounted damper units inside gearbox casing, aluminium uprights **Wheels:** OZ magnesium, 18in dia. **Tyres:** Pirelli P Zero **Brakes:** Brembo calipers, carbon discs and pads **Master cylinders:** AP Racing
DIMENSIONS	**Length:** 5620mm **Width:** 2000mm **Front track:** 2000mm **Rear track:** 2000mm **Height:** 1100mm
	Formula weight: 798kg, including driver and camera

FERNANDO ALONSO

OTMAR SZAFNAUER

Photo: XPB Images

ALPINE F1 TEAM: PERSONNEL

CEO Alpine: Laurent Rossi

Team Principal: Otmar Szafnauer

Director of Racing Expansion Projects: Davide Brivio

Chief Technical Officer: Pat Fry

Technical Director: Matthew Harmon

Engine Technical Director: Bruno Famin

Sporting Director: Alan Permane

Chief Engineer: Simon Virrill

Head of Aerodynamics: Dirk de Beer

Chief Mechanic: Rob Cherry

Head of Performance Systems: Pierre Genon

Chief Race Engineer: Ciaron Pilbeam

Race Engineer (*Alonso*)**:** Karel Loos

Race Engineer (*Ocon*)**:** Josh Peckett

Head of Race Strategy: Matthieu Dubois

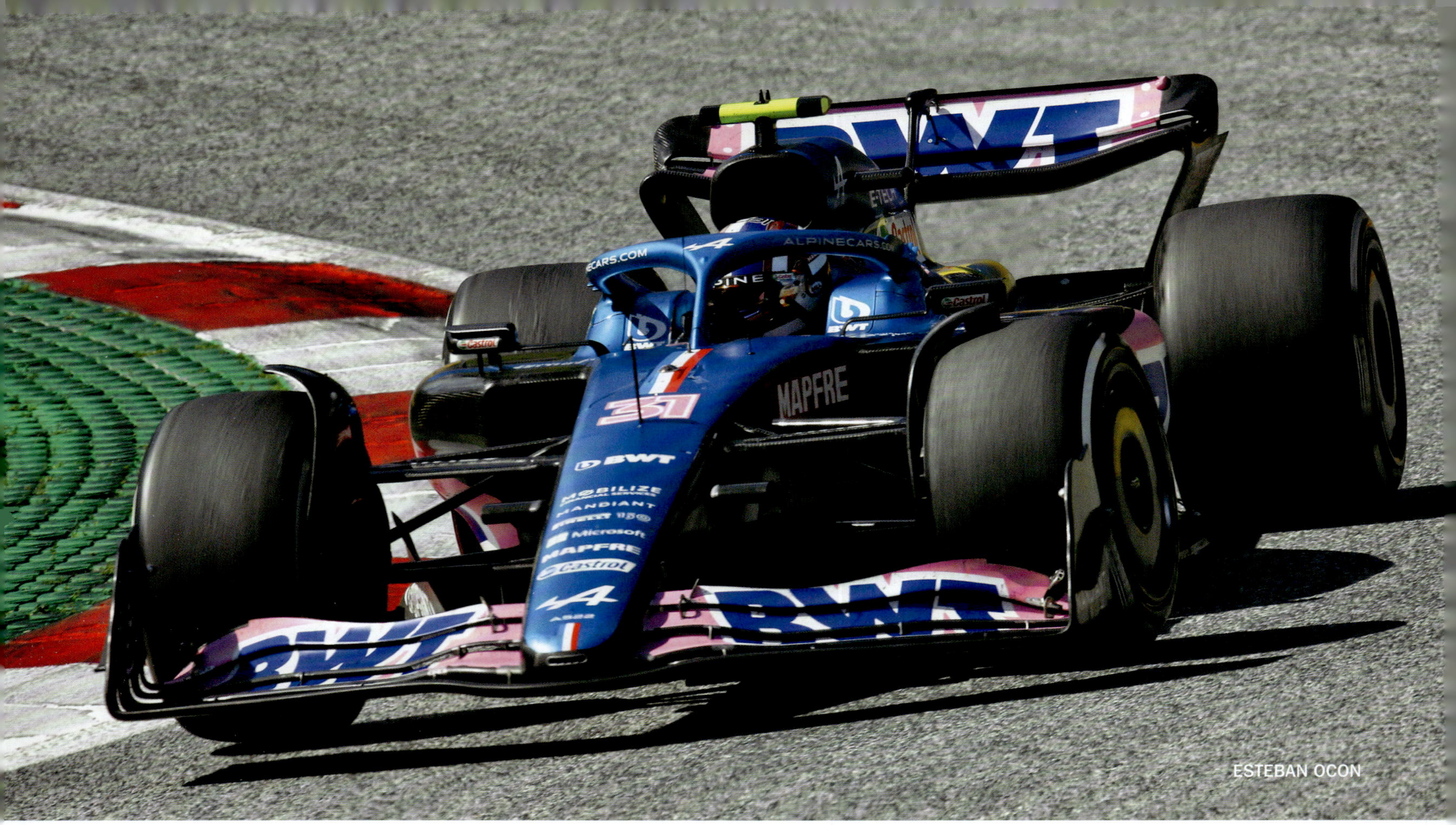

Above: The BWT-liveried car that ran in the opening two races of the year.
Illustration: Adrian Dean

Right: Ocon and Alonso enjoyed a feisty duel in Saudi Arabia, setting the tone for the season.
Photo: XPB Images

Top right: The experienced Fernando Alonso's departure from the team will be keenly felt.
Photo: Alpine F1 Team

Far right: The Alpine team celebrates after taking fourth place in the constructors' championship ahead of McLaren.
Photo: XPB Images

LAURENT ROSSI

PAT FRY

MATTHEW HARMON

Bruno Famin is in charge of the project at Viry and spoke of the new split-turbo power unit, which brought not only a significant power increase, but also other benefits: "It's a better packaging mainly. That's about the type of choice we made together with Enstone, but it's not the only one.

"It's one of the examples of improving packaging of the car to have a better aero, to have a lower centre of gravity and to have, at the end, a better car – because the Alpine car will make the result and score points.

"It's not only power which has improved, but also chassis integration to enable the aerodynamicists and the chassis guys to make a better car, because our goal is to do the best car, not only the best engine.

"We made some choices on the PU to have the best car, maybe we could have done a better figure on the dyno with a slower car at the end. The A522 has been designed on the engine to get the best compromise to have the best car. We will keep working in that way."

"That's helped give us that very strong backbone," said Harmon, "which has maximised the real estate available for our aerodynamicists to work with."

It's a theme that Fry expanded upon: "When you lay the car out, and you don't actually know what your aero routes are going to be, you have to try to get it so that the only things in the radiator ducts are the radiators and nothing else. So all the boxes and stuff you have there are all inside the car, all on the centreline. It means when you come to upgrade something, if you want to undercut the floor or whatever, in the past, that would have meant cutting through all your box mountings, and it's huge job. So we could keep our options open. If you look at the gap between the radiators and how we've increased the bodywork since the start, and there's a 50mm gap there. Look at the other cars, it's exactly the same, particularly the Red Bull. You have to freeze certain things, but then you end up growing the car. Particularly by the side of the radiators. That gave us a lot of freedom. It's just floor and body panels, makes it nice and easy."

The car received regular updates, notably to its sidepods and floor. The car was deliberately engineered to allow modular additions, particularly around the floor, so as to have a cost-efficient development in the era of the cost cap.

A water-pump failure took Fernando Alonso out of the points in Jeddah, and a hydraulics failure in Q3 caused him to crash just as he was about to complete a lap that would have put him third on the grid. He lost good race positions to further cooling-system failures at Monza, Singapore and Mexico. The qualifying highlight was the Spaniard's second-fastest time in the wet of Montreal, but he was unable to capitalise fully on that because of an air leak in the hydraulics. It was such niggling problems that made sealing fourth in the constructors' championship more difficult than it might have been.

By late season, the Enstone wind tunnel was working full-time on the 2023 car, but there was still useful development going on to the A522, as Harmon explained at Zandvoort: "We've tried to target technologies more towards simulation tools, making sure we are understanding what we're putting on the car and not scatter-gunning it. We're very careful about what we choose, and our correlation is excellent at the moment. It has meant we can develop the car without necessarily needing to use the tunnel."

A new floor brought a very significant step at Suzuka, where the cars qualified fifth and seventh, with a handy 0.3s margin over McLaren, and where Esteban Ocon raced to a strong fourth place. Fifth and eighth in Brazil, where McLaren non-scored, effectively sealed the place with one round remaining.

Alpine is in an interesting situation at the moment, with a head count perhaps better suited to the cost cap than the top three teams, giving it more scope for in-season development. From that perspective, it seems doubly unfortunate that it has lost the services of double world champion Alonso, who, of course, joins Aston Martin for 2023.

3

DANIEL RICCIARDO

4

LANDO NORRIS

Photos: McLaren F1 Team

McLAREN F1 TEAM

McLAREN actually had a stronger year than the tricky MCL36A had promised. Certainly, a disastrous start to the season with a brake overheating issue, which curtailed any useful testing at Bahrain prior to the opening race there, suggested trouble ahead. What with that and the car's drivers both complaining of its difficult balance, it was quite remarkable that the team was fighting Alpine for fourth in the constructors' championship until late in the season. There would be no repeat of the victory and pole of 2021, however, the nearest being Lando Norris's third place in the semi-wet of Imola early in the year. And it's probably fair to say that his sometimes brilliant qualifying performances flattered the car just as much as Alpine's iffy reliability.

Created in Toyota's Cologne wind tunnel while the team's own more modern facility was still being constructed, the car had a different set of aero-related quirks to its predecessor, but they were perhaps even more debilitating, especially for Daniel Ricciardo, who just could not gel with the car and left at the end of the season, a year short of his contract time.

The car appeared conventional enough, with a teardrop-shaped upper body in plan view, not much undercut to the sidepods, but an extensively profiled coke-bottle section at the back. Mercedes continued to supply the power unit, but the team made its own gearbox casing. There was a change in the suspension layout both front and rear.

Like Red Bull, McLaren chose to go from push-rod front/pull-rod rear suspension actuation to the opposite. Technical director James Key didn't see that as an important factor in the car's performance, but explained the thinking behind it: "There are now so few devices at the front to help condition flow to the all-important big inlet to the floor. The front wing is very regulated, so we haven't seen much front wing development compared to previous years, and that's just because you're very constrained there. So all you have left is the front suspension. We did a fair bit of thinking what would be right for our car, and for aero reasons, we went pull-rod. There are pros and cons aerodynamically. There are definitely mechanical downsides, and we worked hard at eradicating those until it wasn't a talking point and hopefully gave us a bit of aero improvement at the front.

"Then the reverse at the rear. Mechanically, the push-rod is definitely nicer, tends to be a more direct and stiffer installation, and we knew the cars would inevitably be lower and stiffer than last year, and actually one of the reasons the rear pull-rod became fashionable from 2009 was because the lower area of the brake ducts tended to be quite heavily developed, and you didn't want a push-rod to interfere. All of that disappeared when the brake duct became a standard component with no development scope. We looked at both – they were running in parallel right to the end – but decided on push-rod for that and various packaging reasons; it was better for the gearbox we had, etc."

McLAREN MCL36A

FORMULA 1 PARTNERS	OKX • BAT • Dell Technologies • Darktrace • Goldman Sachs • Arrow • Tezos • Google • Cisco/Webex • Unilever • Splunk Jack Daniel's • Stanley, Black & Decker • alteryx • cadence • Smartsheet • DataRobot • Gopuff • Coca Cola • FXPro • Richard Mille Hilton • Entain • CNBC • Gulf • Medallia • VMware • Castore • Easypost • Immersive Labs • Klipsch • K-Swiss • Heineken • TUMI Deloitte • Sikkens (AzkoNobel) • Mind • Sparco • Logitech • SunGod • FAI Aviation Group • Ashurst • Pirelli • Stratasys • Kaust Techno Gym • Hookit • Buzz • Volvo Trucks • Enkei • New Era • Ultimotive Group • L'Amy Luxe
POWER UNIT	**Type:** Mercedes-AMG M13 E Performance **No. of cylinders (vee angle):** V6 (90°) **No. of valves:** 24 **Max rpm (ICE):** 15,000 **Electronics:** McLaren Applied, including chassis control, power unit control, data acquisition, sensors, data analysis and telemetry **Fuel:** Gulf E10 **Lubricants:** Gulf
TRANSMISSION	**Gearbox:** Eight forward speeds and one reverse, seamless-shift, carbon-composite casing **Clutch:** Carbon multi-plate
CHASSIS	**Monocoque:** Carbon-fibre composite, incorporating driver controls and fuel cell **Front suspension:** Carbon-fibre wishbone and pull-rod suspension elements operating inboard torsion-bar and damper system **Rear suspension:** Carbon-fibre wishbone and push-rod suspension elements operating inboard torsion-bar and damper system **Wheels:** BBS, 18in diameter **Tyres:** Pirelli P Zero **Brakes:** AP Racing calipers and master cylinders, carbon discs and pads, AP Racing brake-by-wire rear control system **Steering:** Power-assisted rack-and-pinion **Instruments:** McLaren Applied dashboard
DIMENSIONS	Not disclosed **Formula weight:** 798kg, including driver and camera

LANDO NORRIS

ZAK BROWN

Photos: McLaren F1 Team

McLAREN F1 TEAM: PERSONNEL

Chief Executive Officer: Zak Brown

Team Principal: Andreas Seidl

Chief People Officer: Daniel Gallo

Chief Communications Officer: Steve Atkins

Chief Financial Officer: Laura Bowden

Executive Director, Technical: James Key

Executive Director, Racing: Andrea Stella

Executive Director, Operations: Piers Thynne

Executive Director, Brand & Marketing: Louise McEwen

Executive Director, Partnerships & Accelerator: Matt Dennington

Executive Director, Business Development: Nick Martin

Director, Race Engineering: Hiroshi Imai

Director, Car Operations & Engineering: Charlie Hooper

Director, F1 Communications: Sophie Ogg

Race Engineer *(Ricciardo)***:** Tom Stallard

Race Engineer *(Norris)***:** Will Joseph

Above: Team principal Andreas Seidl brought a welcome breath of sanity to the turmoil that often surrounds F1.

Above right: Executive Director, Racing Andrea Stella was a steady hand in a team that was still emerging from its lean years.

Right: James Key was given the unenviable task of producing a car to match the likes of the 'Big Three'.

Far right: Daniel Ricciardo generally put a smiley face on a year for frowns.

Photos: McLaren F1 Team

Above: Andretti Autosport's star driver, Colton Herta, took a test for McLaren in Portimão. Subsequently, he signed a long-term deal to stay in the USA with his current team.

Right: Pato O'Ward was another IndyCar star hopeful of breaking into F1 via Zak Brown's multiple McLaren racing teams. The Mexican hotshot tested at the Red Bull Ring.

Left: The real deal? Oscar Piastri was the chosen one. Having spurned Alpine '*bleu*' in favour of 'papaya' orange, the much sought-after youngster heads for his F1 debut in 2023.

Far right: Cause for celebration? The team's best placing of the year was Lando's podium at Imola.

Photos: McLaren F1 Team

Testing at Barcelona went smoothly enough, and the car was notably untroubled by the porpoising seen on others, but Norris was somewhat sanguine about that, observing that perhaps it didn't have as much downforce as some of those that were troubled by porpoising, notably Mercedes and Ferrari. But it was at the following Bahrain test where the team suddenly came face to face with a crisis, as the car could not run without the front brake temperatures getting wildly out of control.

"Fundamentally, it was a bit of an ambitious design, with not quite enough cross-sectional area in the exit ducts for very energised, high-temperature air to always guarantee it was going to pass through," explained Key. "Even though we went through the standard process of proving the cooling would be okay, even dyno running, what we concluded was a) the brake energies were higher than predicted, and b) we were right on the edge, but didn't know it – and that's where we really made the mistake. We'd seen them running slightly high in Barcelona, but just reasoned that away. It was a failure on our part, a failure of process. At a certain air temperature, in certain circuit conditions with a certain exit configuration, we discovered you could choke the whole system. That's why it was okay at Barcelona, then we get to Bahrain, and, 'Gee, what's gone wrong?'"

New ducts fashioned in metal, rather than carbon fibre, were readied in time for the race one week later. "The teamwork and effort that went into recovering and giving us a car we could race in Bahrain was impressive," said Key. "Brake ducts are nightmare parts, so coming up with a way of solving the problem, designing it full scale, making it and getting it to the track all in five days was an extraordinary team effort. But it worked, lasted the race and stayed on the car all the way through to Imola."

It was only with that problem out of the way that energy could be devoted to understanding the car's somewhat inconsistent handling traits between corner entry and apex. Entry instability combined with mid-corner understeer was the worst of both worlds. Key acknowledged that there were questions surrounding the car's genesis. "The problems were in different windows compared to '21," he said. "Some of those comments sound a bit familiar from '21, but for different reasons. It's made us step back and think, 'Are we missing something here? We're waiting for this new wind tunnel to come along and we know we're going to learn a huge amount from that with all the new technology. So is there something we're not understanding with this one?' Having said that, there are certain developments which give you more downforce, but make the situation worse and other developments which reduce the downforce but make the balance situation better. There's a conflict from entry to apex, and I think various teams are at various stages with that. Some others have got the best of both worlds – the downforce and the characteristics. Others have got better characteristics, but a bit lower downforce. Some of that is the immaturity of this generation of cars; there's still more to come. There are probably mechanical aspects as well."

Somehow, Norris found a way to drive around the peculiar traits, and by Australia, for round three, he was able to finish fifth, 'best of the rest' behind the big three teams. One race later at Imola, probably aided by the wet conditions prevailing throughout the weekend, he was a terrific third. More usually, he'd be found in the lower reaches of the top ten, with Ricciardo as much as half a minute behind. The car was relatively quick around the slow turns of Monaco and Hungary, relatively slow around the more aerodynamically demanding Barcelona and Paul Ricard. Its aero efficiency didn't seem to be as good as Alpine's, and it wasn't great under braking because of that rear instability. Yet Norris was the leading finisher after the top three teams on six occasions, with Ricciardo achieving the feat with a strategy-aided seventh place in Mexico.

Bodywork developments came thick and fast, typically around the floor area, and while downforce was gradually improved, the basic traits of the car remained. It was notably good at switching on its front tyres in the early part of the season, which sometimes helped flatter its qualifying performance, but usually there would be a penalty to be paid in the race with degradation. This was another area of development. "It's really complicated with the corners of the car now," said Key. "You've got a prescribed rim geometry, and you can have the [carbon-fibre shroud within the sealing disc] on or off. If you've got it on, you have this enclosed area of hot air, so any unsealing of that makes it much cooler, but you take an aero hit, and it's that sort of domain where you're asking, 'Can we cool the rims better without just relying on the very basic on or off?' Mercedes has been really good with this; they can take the high-speed corners really aggressively and still hang on to everything with the tyre temps. They are one end of the scale. We've crept up to about the middle of that scale, I'd say. Our performance at Monza, where we had some new developments, gave us the closest qually to race performance we've had. It's not all about the tyres, but a fair chunk of it is."

The new McLaren wind tunnel doesn't come on line until the middle of 2023, so the new season's car will have been created in the Toyota tunnel again. The team must hope that having an understanding of the quirks of the 2022 car will have given it a better starting point.

24

ZHOU GUANYU

77

VALTTERI BOTTAS

ALFA ROMEO RACING ORLEN

THE Alfa Romeo-badged Sauber team had a promising, but frustrating season. It produced a car, the C42, that at its best was capable of running ahead of Alpine and McLaren as 'best of the rest' behind the big three. But too often, that potential wasn't converted into points because of either reliability or operational issues. It steadily lost competitiveness through the season as others developed more, but enjoyed a late-season resurgence through some delayed aero upgrades.

Jan Monchaux oversaw the creation of the car as technical director, and right from the conception stage, he understood how, under the regulations, the car's weight would be a battleground almost as significant as the usual one of aerodynamics. Consequently, the C42 was the only car that began the season on the minimum weight limit, despite the bigger wheels, tyres and brakes, and the requirement for a much stiffer floor to withstand the ground-effect loads it induced.

"There's no magic recipe for the weight," he said. "From the very first moment you start drafting how to focus on the weight, the discipline, especially for the mechanical designers to try even in the early stages before concepts are fully mature to make the effort on the weight. Depending what you see, either put more resources or consider different avenues, even if it wasn't an obvious direction otherwise. Just relentlessly chasing every gram."

Part of that concept was keeping the car's wheelbase to the absolute minimum, so that physically there was less car! The regulations stipulate a wheelbase of between 3460 and 3600mm. Almost every other car was at the maximum, but the Alfa was just over 3500mm. It was further helped by the fact that the new Ferrari power unit produced a weight saving compared to other PUs. This was mated to a gearbox with Ferrari internals, but Alfa's own casing, giving it the freedom to define its own rear suspension pick-up points – which was essential, as it had chosen a rear push-rod system in contrast to Ferrari's pull-rod. The fuel tank was also Alfa's own, specially tailored to the car's shorter wheelbase.

The cooling system, however, was pure Ferrari, with all the radiator area mounted down low in the sidepods and no higher supplementary coolers within the engine cover, as on other cars. As with Ferrari, this defined the sidepods as bluff and outwash-generating. In plan view, it had a distinct teardrop shape (like the Ferrari and the Ferrari-powered Haas), but because of the shorter wheelbase, that teardrop had a fatter head to accommodate all the components.

The front wing was very distinctive, with the outboard elements reducing in area quite dramatically to aid outwash around the front tyre. On the inboard side, between the nose and the flap adjusters, the flaps were very heavily cambered. Those of the mid-section were somewhere in between. Matching these

ALFA ROMEO C42

TITLE SPONSORS	Alfa Romeo • ORLEN
OFFICIAL PARTNERS	Accelleron • Acer • Adler Pelzer Group • AMX • aximtrade • Camozzi • Cielo • Ciesse Piumini • Code Zero • Curam Domi Delsey • DRF Bets • Edelweiss • Everdome • Floki • Georg Fischer • Globeair • Hyland • Jig Space • Lemo • Marelli mindmaze • Mitsubishi Electric • Modere • Path • Pirelli • Puma • Rebellion • Sabelt • Sauber Technologies • Save the Children • Seagate • SenseTime • Singha • Socios • Vauld • Walter Meier • Web Eyewear • WhistlePig • ZCG
TEAM SUPPLIERS	Additive Industries • Assos • Brütsch-Rüegger • Ferrari Trento • Floyd • Iveco • Protech Monte-Carlo • Riedel • Salt • Virtek
POWER UNIT	**Type:** Ferrari Hybrid 1.6-litre turbo **No. of cylinders** (vee angle): V6 (90°) **No. of valves:** 24 **Max rpm:** 15,000
TRANSMISSION	Alfa Romeo F1 Team ORLEN carbon-fibre maincase with Ferrari cassette containing eight forward speeds and one reverse **Clutch:** Carbon composite
CHASSIS	Carbon-fibre monocoque **Front suspension:** Carbon-fibre double wishbone, push-rod-actuated inboard torsion springs, rockers and damper units **Rear suspension:** Carbon-fibre double wishbone, push-rod-actuated inboard torsion springs, rockers and damper units **Dampers:** Öhlins **Wheels:** BBS, 18in diameter **Tyres:** Pirelli P Zero **Brake system:** Brembo brake calipers, carbon discs and pads, rear brake by wire **Steering:** Power-assisted rack-and-pinion **Instruments:** Alfa Romeo F1 Team ORLEN
DIMENSIONS	**Length:** 5500mm **Width:** 2000mm **Height:** 970mm **Formula weight:** 798kg, including driver and camera

VALTTERI BOTTAS

FRÉDÉRIC VASSEUR

ALFA ROMEO RACING ORLEN: PERSONNEL

Team Principal & CEO: Frédéric Vasseur

Operations Director: Axel Kruse

Technical Director: Jan Monchaux

Head of Aerodynamics: Alessandro Cinelli

Chief Designer: Eric Gandelin

Sporting Manager: Beat Zehnder

Senior Strategy Engineer: Ruth Buscombe

Head of Track Engineering: Xevi Pujolar

Race Engineer *(Bottas)*: Alex Chan

Race Engineer *(Zhou)*: Jörn Becker

Chief Mechanic: Reto Camenzind

Senior Communications Manager: Will Ponissi

BEAT ZEHNDER

Photos: Alfa Romeo Racing ORLEN

three distinct phases, the lower edge of the wing was contoured, varying its clearance from the ground. The closer to the ground, the harder the underside of the wing element is worked, and in this way there was a compensating effect for the variation in flap area over the wing's span. Front suspension remained push-rod.

Early testing of the car at Fiorano and Barcelona revealed a serious porpoising problem. This was partly a function of the focus on weight saving, as the car's relatively light floor was flexing excessively. "We had a kangaroo car during shakedown in Fiorano," said Monchaux. "We were struggling in testing with it at Barcelona, damaged the floor, even the chassis. It took us until the end of that test to sort it out. Initially, the solution was to run the car higher. Then we used the stiffeners on the floor. But we realised the floor was too light and was vibrating too much or deflecting. So we had to try to stay away from the [ride height] zone where it starts and becomes exponentially bad."

Most other teams were going through a similar process, so it didn't have too much effect competitively, and the newly-recruited Valtteri Bottas qualified a good sixth (splitting the two cars from his former team, Mercedes) and finished strongly in sixth, pushing Magnussen's Haas hard for fifth after falling a long way back at the start with a clutch problem. This would become something of a recurring theme and was never fully resolved. "It's mainly driven by the driver, and our drivers struggled a bit with the hardware we are supplied by our PU supplier," said Monchaux. "The start and lap-one performance we are not happy with and are working on hard for next year. It's a very expensive problem in such a tight midfield, losing hard-won grid places."

During this early part of the season, when the car's weight advantage over the competition was at its greatest, it was at its most competitive. Bottas qualified and raced the C42 to unofficial 'best of the rest' status at both Miami and Barcelona. In addition to his super-strong performance in the wet of Imola, it made for a sequence of fifth, seventh and sixth places, which helped put the team in a strong fifth place in the constructors' championship after the first seven races.

Points became rather harder to come by in subsequent races, with PU problems and strategy errors combining with other midfield teams making bigger development strides.

Speed of production was revealed as a bottleneck in developing the car. Parts were being developed in the wind tunnel, but couldn't be manufactured quickly. "We are trying to catch up," said Monchaux, "but we are production-limited. We are only 400 people, not 7–800, so it takes longer."

A new front wing showed great promise in the tunnel shortly after the summer break, but wasn't actually introduced until the Japanese Grand Prix in October. It had been conceived to improve the flow to the underfloor, the main flaps being slimmed down while the flap adjusters were moved further inboard to ensure that the span of flap that was adjusted increased, with the narrower elements still allowing a better through-flow to the tunnel inlets of the floor.

It produced an immediate upturn in the Alfa's performance, and Bottas qualified a strong sixth in Mexico after languishing in the Q2 part of the grid for several races. Points there and in Brazil a week later confirmed the underlying quality of the car apparent at the start of the season. With the team's future purchase by Audi, a lot of investment is looming.

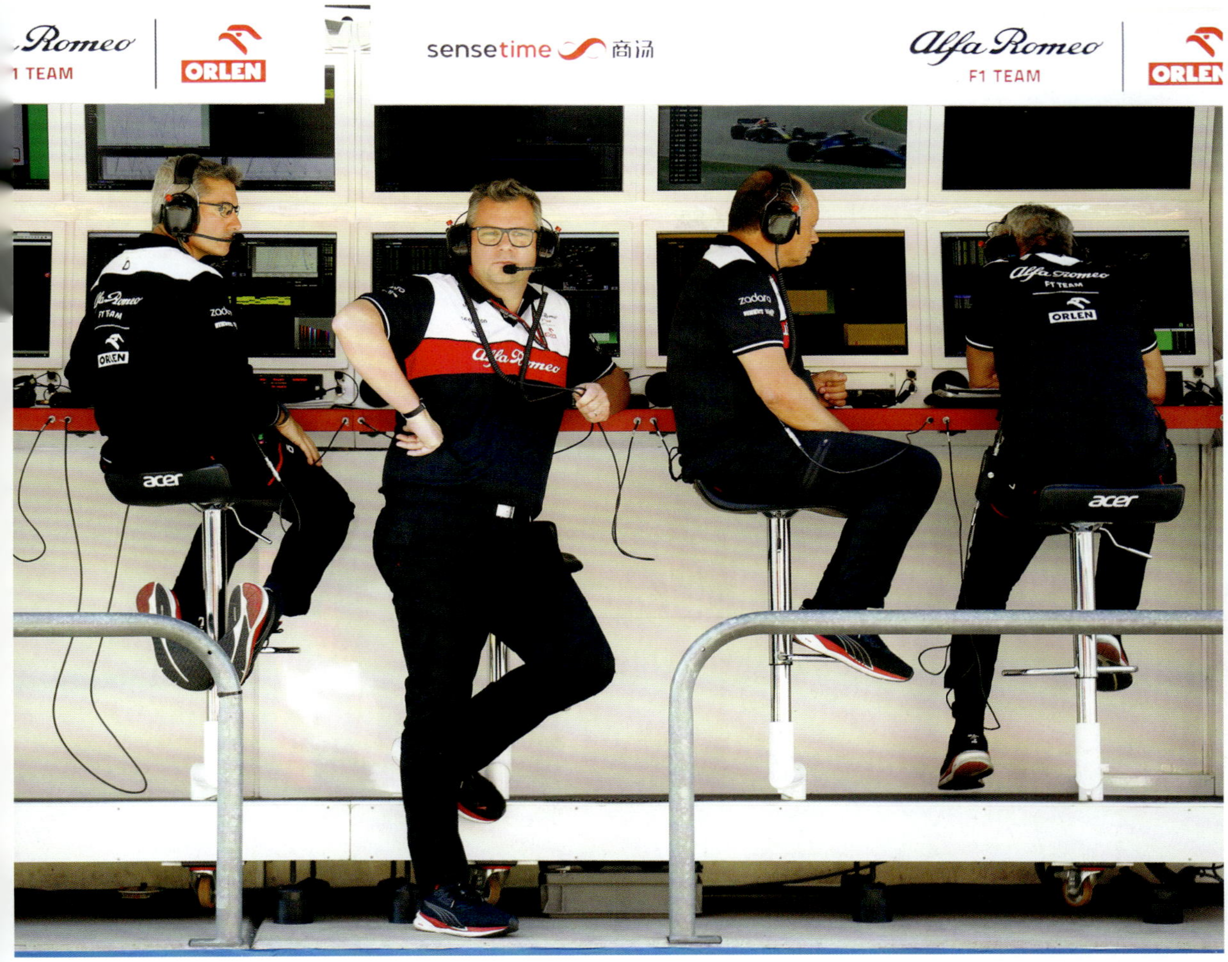

Left: Technical director Jan Monchaux on the pit wall.

Far left: Zhou Guanyu locks a wheel in the race in Saudi Arabia.

Below far left, from left: Senior strategy engineer Ruth Buscombe on the grid; Xevi Pujolar was head of track engineering; Alex Chan was race engineer for Valtteri Bottas.

Below: Once again, Robert Kubica acted as the team's third driver.

Bottom: Alfa Romeo clinched sixth place over Aston Martin in the constructors' battle.

Photos: Alfa Romeo Racing ORLEN

5

SEBASTIAN VETTEL

18

LANCE STROLL

27

NICO HÜLKENBERG

ASTON MARTIN COGNIZANT F1 TEAM

THE second season of Aston Martin branding for the Silverstone-based team did not go well, its response to the new aero regulations, in the shape of the AMR22, proving ill-conceived, so much so that an extensively redesigned version of the car was readied for Spain in May. Although better than the original, it was far too new, putting the team effectively half a season or more behind the others. A series of lower top-ten points scores was salvaged by Sebastian Vettel and Lance Stroll, but the car averaged almost 2s off the ultimate qualifying pace, with both cars going out in the Q1 part of qualifying on eight occasions.

"We went down the wrong path with the initial concept," admitted technical director Andy Green. "Our tools definitely misled us, and we did well to recover and change direction. But it was very late. And when you're in a cost cap, you can't just keep developing. You have a couple of shots at it and then that's it, and that's where we got to."

The original car was based on the concept of running the rear bodywork super-low, in theory to maximise the ground effect of the floor's big venturi tunnels. It was a very distinctive-looking machine, with wide upper body and extensive cooling slats for high-mounted, heavily inclined radiators to allow for a heavily undercut lower bodywork. That required the Mercedes power unit to be sited quite far back within the wheelbase. As usual, Mercedes supplied not only the power unit, but also the gear-

ASTON MARTIN AMR22

TITLE PARTNER	Cognizant
STRATEGIC PARTNER	Aramco
GLOBAL PARTNERS	Peroni • crypto.com • JCB • SentinelOne • Juniper • NetApp • Epos • Girard Perregaux • Socios.com • Pirelli • Bombardier • TikTok
OFFICAL SUPPLIERS	Oakley • Ogio • Hackett • IFS • Altair • ebb3 • Pelmark • Voip unlimited • Alpinestars • Schuberth
POWER UNIT	**Type:** Mercedes-AMG F1 M13 EQ Power+ **No. of cylinders (vee angle):** V6 (90°) **No. of valves:** 24 **Max rpm (ICE):** 15,000 **Electronics:** FIA standard ECU and FIA homologated electronics & electrical system **Fuel:** E10
TRANSMISSION	**Gearbox:** Mercedes-AMG F1 eight-speed, semi-automatic, seamless-shift **Clutch:** AP Racing
CHASSIS	**Monocoque:** Carbon-fibre composite with Zylon anti-intrusion panels **Front Suspension:** Carbon-fibre wishbone and push-rod suspension elements operating inboard torsion-bar and damper system **Rear suspension:** Carbon-fibre wishbone and pull-rod suspension elements operating inboard torsion-bar and damper system **Wheels:** BBS alloy, 18in diameter **Tyres:** Pirelli P Zero **Brake system:** Brembo calipers, carbon discs and pads, brake-by-wire system
DIMENSIONS	**Length:** 5600mm **Width:** 2000mm **Wheelbase** 3600mm **Formula weight:** 798kg, including driver and camera

SEBASTIAN VETTEL

MIKE KRACK

Photos: Aston Martin Cognizant F1 Team

ASTON MARTIN COGNIZANT F1 TEAM: PERSONNEL

Chairman: Lawrence Stroll

Group CEO: Martin Whitmarsh

Team Principal: Mike Krack

Chief Technical Officer: Andrew Green

Technical Director: Dan Fallows

Deputy Technical Director: Eric Blandin

Sporting Director: Andy Stevenson

Performance Director: Tom McCullough

Engineering Director: Luca Furbatto

Chief Designers: Akio Haga/Ian Hall

Head of Aerodynamic Development: Ian Greig

Head of Trackside Performance: Bradley Joyce

Chief Operations Officer: Bob Halliwell

Head of Build and Car Assembly: Mark Gray

Head of Race Strategy: Bernadette Collins

Race Engineer *(Vettel/Hülkenberg)***:** Chris Cronin

Race Engineer *(Stroll)***:** Ben Michell

Chief Mechanic: Curtis Stones

No.1 Mechanic *(Vettel/Hülkenberg)***:** Michael Brown

No.1 Mechanic *(Stroll)***:** Scott Taggart

Managing Director, Commercial: Jefferson Slack

Chief Communications Officer: Matt Bishop

Head of Media & Communications: Will Hings

Senior Partner Media Officer: Steve Cooper

Media & Communications Officer: Eve Merrell

LANCE STROLL

box and rear suspension. The high siting of the radiators meant that the lower bodywork could be profiled to maximise the pressure differential between the upper and lower surfaces, and thus the downforce created. That was the theory, at least.

A preliminary test at Silverstone revealed the reality of severe aerodynamic porpoising. Almost from that moment, several weeks before the season even began, it became clear that the car was fundamentally flawed and a redesign was hurriedly initiated for later in the season. But the team would be obliged to do the opening five races with the original car.

"Our tools had led us down the garden path in telling us there were no issues with running the car down low in ground effect," said Green. "It wasn't showing any instabilities down there. And the reality was very, very different… It was just so fundamental in the design of the car that there was no option but just to have another stab at it. And at that time, we didn't know a lot more than we did at the beginning of the season. All we knew at the time was we've gone in the wrong direction. We didn't really have a good understanding of what the right direction was, on what a good car should really look like."

The positioning of the radiators and the higher centre of gravity they conferred only intensified the bouncing problem on the suspension and tyres, something the Mercedes rear suspension did not have the travel to accommodate. "There was nothing inherently wrong with the suspension," Green pointed out. "The main issue was the car couldn't run in the [ride-height] region that it was supposed to run in. The issue with the suspension was more like it didn't have enough room to get us out of that problem. So the problem was self-induced; the suspension just didn't have the freedom to get us out of the problem. We had to design our way out of it aerodynamically.

"With the original car, we were locked in. We couldn't run it high enough to get us out of that porpoising range. So, unfortunately, we had to run the car stiff as well, which doesn't help with the bouncing. We'd really forced ourselves into a corner."

Such was the tightness of the midfield group behind the top three or four teams that even with a car as flawed as the Aston, the nuances of tyre preparation could occasionally alleviate its fundamental lack of pace, and in Miami, Vettel even managed to put it into the lower reaches of Q3. But no one was kidding themselves that there was any potential in the original car. The rejigged machine (still called AMR22), which appeared at the Spanish Grand Prix, featured an all-new bodywork that closely resembled the Red Bull. Gone was the wide upper body, and in its place was a more conventional heavily ramped sidepod.

This had involved a resiting of the whole cooling package and was a very extensive re-engineering job, not simply a new set of body panels. Although the bodywork was very close to that of the pace-setting Red Bull, the original monocoque shape meant that there were still fundamental aerodynamic limitations. It would also take the team some time to completely understand the behaviour of the updated car. In Monaco and Baku, it was able to make the lower part of the Q3 grid, but in the next three races – Canada, Britain and Austria – neither car was able to breach the Q1 hurdle.

"The car introduced in Spain was incredibly underdeveloped, by definition," said Green. "I wouldn't have even classified it as a launch-spec car; it was lower than that. Had we started from a clean sheet, it would have ended up with a completely different chassis shape. A lot of the chassis ended up restricting what we now believe we need to do. And a lot of it is just time, time understanding the problem, time developing around the problem, and understanding what's good and what's bad."

There was enough budget for one further – more minor – upgrade, in time for the British Grand Prix in July. It concerned detailing around the floor edges and rear brake ducts, but did not have a transformative effect on the car's competitiveness.

In Hungary, the team introduced an all-new rear wing with a highly original interpretation of the regulations, which had sought to eliminate endplates and their disruptive wake. Without breaking the wording of the regs, Aston had effectively reintroduced endplates by way of rolling the surfaces at the outer edges of the wing into a tight area to form an endplate (which increases downforce by limiting the spillage off the side of the wing). The regulations prohibit vertical straight lines in this part of the wing and define the minimum curvature required. This gave the barrier effect of an endplate without contravening the curvature requirements. The car did show some very good performance in low-speed corners with this wing.

It was developed with the full knowledge of the FIA, which accepted that it met the letter of the regs, despite subverting their intent, and the feature is set to be banned for 2023. "We were just trying to exploit

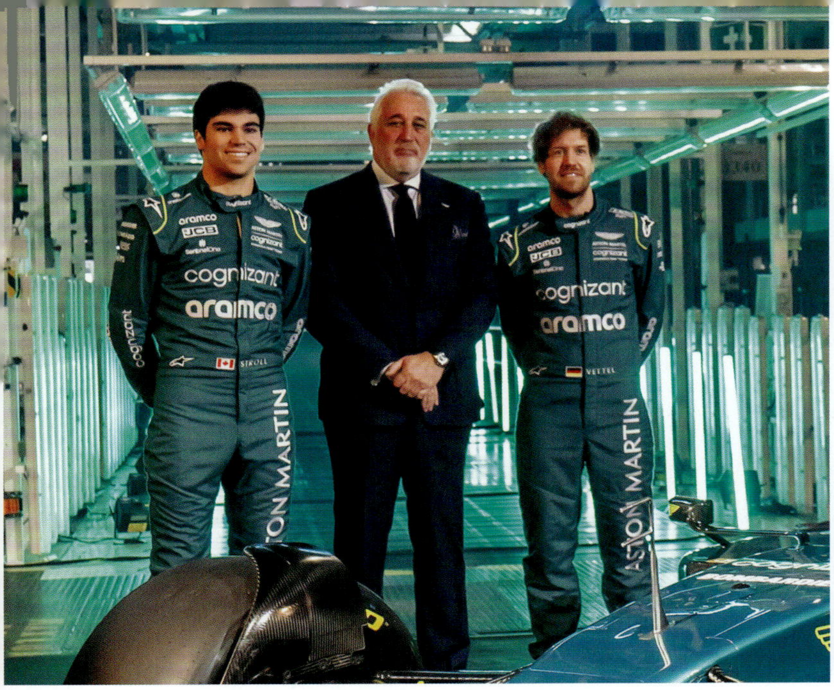

the regulations free of prejudice," said Green. "When you're given FOM's generic model of a car signalling, 'This is what your car's going to look like with these regulations', it's very difficult to forget that. They are trying to force you into a certain design, so it's really difficult to read the regulations and come up with a solution that's different. But you can do it, you have to just wipe your mind clean of the knowledge of the FOM solution. That's what we came up with. We went through the process with the FIA over many months to make sure that we were interpreting it right, and they, reluctantly I should say, agreed that we had interpreted it as written, and they wouldn't prevent us from running it. It was a good little mini morale boost for the team, to show the rest of them that we do come up with our own ideas, we do have a clever bunch of people working here."

Hopefully for the team, that will carry forward into 2023 and combine with a better understanding of the nuances of these aero regulations, helped by the recruitment of Dan Fallows from Red Bull and Eric Blandin from Mercedes to add strength to the aero department. "This season has given us a really good foundation for '23," said Green of the harsh lessons that had been learned.

"I think we're a lot more stable now than we were when we were designing the '22 car," he continued. "In terms of facilities and recruitment, we've done all the growing we need to do now, we've been stable now for quite a while, and it takes time to gel, and that's the process we've been going through over the last six to twelve months. It's a really exciting time for the team, I believe."

Above: Nico Hülkenberg stood in for Vettel in Bahrain and Saudi Arabia, after the team's lead driver contracted Covid.

Above left: Plenty to ponder for Lance Stroll and his engineers.

Top left: Chairman Lawrence Stroll poses with his drivers at the launch of the AMR22.

Top right: The long serving Tom McCullough occupied the role of performance director.

Top centre: F2 champion Felipe Drugovich was appointed the third driver for the team in 2023.

Left: Vettel ensconsed in his cockpit and ready for action.

Photos: Aston Martin Cognizant F1 Team

20

KEVIN MAGNUSSEN

47

MICK SCHUMACHER

HAAS F1 TEAM

EIGHTH in the constructors' championship undersells the strength of the Haas competitive comeback after two seasons of treading water. Although it was a relatively infrequent scorer (seven points scores) and averaged around 0.7s adrift of the Alpine/McLaren level of qualifying, at its best, it was quick enough to be 'best of the rest' behind the big three, as was the case in the opening round in Bahrain. The team's season was also given an edge of glory with a great opportunistic grab of pole position by Kevin Magnussen in Brazil.

Haas retained its unique structure, a car being created from a base within the Ferrari factory, using the Ferrari wind tunnel, with several of the technical team on secondment from there. Among them was technical chief Simone Resta. The VF-22 was the first car created by the new group, which had been brought together in 2021.

It was similar in concept to the Ferrari, which was not surprising given that it shared the layout-defining components – power unit, gearbox, cooling system, and front and rear suspension. Its overall form, with teardrop-shaped sidepods in plan view and bluff outwash-prioritising forward surfaces, was much the same, but without the sophistication of Ferrari's deep channels.

The VF-22 shared with the top three cars a generous gap between front axle and sidepods, and there was a general feeling that this would become a trend confirmed with the 2023 generation of cars, as it offers better opportunities for controlling the wake from the front wheels to better feed the venturi tunnel inlets. It went well on aerodynamically demanding tracks, notably Barcelona (where Magnussen spoilt his chances of good points with a first-lap collision with Lewis Hamilton).

It was a relatively vice-free car, without the narrow set-up limitations of the McLaren or AlphaTauri, and with a bigger team might well have been able to show more consistently well than it did. Budget considerations meant that it received very little development, with just a single update package coming at the Hungarian Grand Prix just before the summer shutdown. For the same reasons, there was not much opportunity to shed the excess weight that the bigger teams were able to do. The quality of the car tended to shine through the financial circumstances of the team in randomly timed favourable moments.

The car had much the same traits as the Ferrari in terms of its balance, strong low-speed acceleration and an ability to switch on the front tyres relatively quickly. Like the Ferrari, it was also afflicted by early-season porpoising, though it needed to be run higher than the red car to keep it away from that threshold, losing it more downforce.

"At the beginning, that was a mess," admitted Resta. "In testing at Barcelona, we were damaging

HAAS VF-22

PARTNERS	Haas Automation Inc. • MoneyGram • 1 & 1 • Haas Tooling.com • Alpinestars • Cyrus • Hantec Markets • Home Deluxe • Lunar • Ionos Maui Jim • Pirelli • Schuberth • Taittinger Champagne • OAKBERRY • Transfer Mate • Tricorp workwear • Under Armour
POWER UNIT	**Type:** Ferrari 066/7 Hybrid 1.6-litre turbo **No. of cylinders (vee angle):** V6 (90°) **No. of valves:** 24 **Max rpm (ICE):** 15,000 **Electronics:** FIA standard ECU and FIA homologated electronics & electrical system **Fuel & lubricants:** Shell
TRANSMISSION	Ferrari servo-controlled hydraulic limited-slip differential, semi-automatic sequential and electronically-controlled gearbox, quick-shift (eight gears plus reverse) **Clutch:** AP Racing
CHASSIS	**Monocoque:** Carbon-fibre and honeycomb composite structure **Front suspension:** Double wishbones, push-rod-actuated torsion-bar springs, anti-roll bar **Rear suspension:** Double wishbones, pull-rod actuated torsion-bar springs, anti-roll bar **Dampers:** ZF Sachs/Öhlins **Steering:** Ferrari **Wheels:** BBS, 18in diameter **Tyres:** Pirelli P Zero **Brake system:** Six-piston calipers, carbon discs and pads **Cockpit instrumentation:** Ferrari **Fuel cell:** ATL
DIMENSIONS	**Length:** Not disclosed **Height:** Not disclosed **Width:** 2000mm **Wheelbase:** Not disclosed
	Formula weight: 798g, including driver and camera

KEVIN MAGNUSSEN

GUENTHER STEINER

Photos: Haas F1 Team

HAAS F1 TEAM: PERSONNEL

Founder & Chairman: Gene Haas

Chief Operating Officer: Joe Custer

Team Principal: Guenther Steiner

Technical Director: Simone Resta

Chief Designer: Andrea De Zordo

Team Manager: Peter Crolla

F1 Race Programme Manager: Nick Burns

Head of Aerodynamics: Arron Melvin

Performance Engineer *(Schumacher)***:** Ronan O'Hare

Performance Engineer *(Magnussen)***:** Trevor Green-Smith

Director of Engineering: Ayao Komatsu

Race Engineer *(Schumacher)***:** Gary Gannon

Race Engineer *(Magnussen)***:** Mark Slade

Chief Mechanic: Matt Scott

Race Mechanic *(Schumacher)***:** Toby Brown

Race Mechanic *(Magnussen)***:** Elliot Parkes

Head of Communications: Stuart Morrison

20
KEVIN MAGNUSSEN
47
20
Magnussen
P5
47
Schumacher
P11

Left: Gary Gannon acted as Mick Schumacher's race engineer.

Far left: With Magnussen fifth and Schumacher 11th, the team celebrates its brilliant start to the season in Bahrain.

Below centre: Popular reserve driver Pietro Fittipaldi gave his all for the team, although he would be overlooked for a full-time drive in 2023.

Below left: Ayao Komatsu continued in his role as director of engineering.

Bottom far left: Work progresses in a calm and orderly fashion on Schumacher's car in the Haas garage.

Below: Ferrari ties brought in Antonio Giovinazzi for a couple of outings in free practice.

Photos: Haas F1 Team

Bottom: Mick Schumacher's performances improved as the season progressed, but eventually the German youngster was dropped in favour of the hugely experienced Nico Hülkenberg, who was seen as a safer pair of hands.

Photo: Bryn Williams

the floor and even the bodywork with the bouncing. The thing that was really crucial was the support that the FIA has given, allowing the teams to introduce some stiffening stays on the rear that were very, very helpful in the way that they were considered, approved and implemented very early."

The problem was sorted sufficiently quickly that Haas qualified seventh and finished fifth, representing 'best of the rest' and emphasising that the car was very sound in its underlying qualities while others in the midfield were dealing with varying degrees of imbalance. That advantage steadily disappeared as others developed while Haas did not.

"There's been cars developing a lot in the season," acknowledged Resta. "It is obvious to see that Aston Martin has had quite a significant recovery, for example. We started decently well with the car... Being a younger and smaller team, clearly we have much more limited resources about how we can push things, optimisation, etc. We were paying the price for that also with the weight."

There was another possibly quite significant budget-related restriction, as Resta explained: "If you start counting the number of rear wings that some people out there have introduced this year, you can understand how much people decided to invest on race-specific items, like, for example, two, three, five or even more level of rear wings. And other people like ourselves, we really haven't introduced anything. So we decided to try to focus our attention on to the most common downforce levels on all tracks, and we pay the price in the tracks where you start to drop downforce. Not too much in tracks like Baku, Belgium, Canada, but elsewhere quite a lot."

The Hungary upgrade comprised an all-new floor better resolved in its performance at various ride heights. The floor's tunnel inlet fences were realigned for the new underfloor geometry, as was the leading edge of the floor to better feed those tunnel inlets. There was a new engine cover with more of a ducktail profile in plan view and a smoother transition to the coke-bottle section of the rear lower bodywork. This required a change in the arrangement of the cooling louvres on the top surfaces of the sidepods, and new shrouds were designed for the rear suspension legs to align them with the airflow around the new bodywork and floor. The rear brake ducts were new and were said to provide not only more downforce at that point, but also better airflow to the rear lower beam wing.

Even discounting the peculiar circumstances of Magnussen's pole in Brazil, the car was slightly more competitive after the upgrade than it had averaged before. The single big upgrade had effectively clawed back what had been lost to the steady developments seen elsewhere. This had cost competitiveness in the intervening races, but that's what the team could afford, given its unique structure and limited size.

10

PIERRE GASLY

22

角田裕毅

YUKI TSUNODA

SCUDERIA ALPHATAURI

THE all-new regulations perhaps represented an even bigger challenge to AlphaTauri than to the larger teams, as all cumulative development, the sort of things that the team had been so good at, was wiped clean. Amid this clean-sheet restart, the team was operating from Red Bull's 60 per cent model scale wind tunnel for the first time, after many years in its own 50 per cent tunnel. So there was a lot for the little team to be putting its arms around, and it did not enjoy as competitive a season as in the previous few years. It was ninth in the constructors' championship, trailed by only Williams, though it was actually more competitive than a couple of teams ahead of it in that table in terms of its qualifying performance.

Technical director Jody Egginton oversaw the creation of the Honda-powered AT03 model, taking the then-new 2022 Red Bull rear end, which meant a switch to push-rod actuation for the rear suspension. But at the front of the car, the team created its own, rather than taking the Red Bull pull-rod. So the AT03 was one of only two cars on the grid with push-rod actuation for both front and rear. There was probably less to that than meets the eye, and it was driven as much by cost factors as for any significant difference in performance. In the cost-cap regulations, proprietary parts have an assigned value, which, in some cases, might be higher than the cost of a team producing its own. Such was the case here, and at the time it was obliged to make the choice, because of the lead times involved, AlphaTauri's aero numbers were suggesting that remaining with push-rod at the front would be slightly more favourable.

Aerodynamically, the car was quite conventional, using a centreline cooling package within the engine cover to supplement the sidepod radiators to minimise sidepod frontal area – and also to make for more flexibility in bodywork development as the team headed into unknown territory with the new regulations. Space freed up from the sidepod internals was potential aero-development space.

That said, the dominant development component by far – for all teams – was the floor. Under these regulations, maximising the load from the ground-effect floor, without tripping over into the instability of porpoising, was the main preoccupation. This was almost a whole new science for the team, at a time when it was working in a different tunnel. The biggest issue in developing the car turned out to be a conflict between maintaining consistent balance through corners while continuing to put more aero load on it. Frequently, the drivers complained of entry understeer, but mid-corner instability. Circuits with long corners did not show the car at its best, and it was at its most competitive at Baku and Monaco. In Azerbaijan, Pierre Gasly qualified sixth and finished fifth, having kept Lewis Hamilton's Mercedes behind for a time. This was an untypically strong performance,

Photos: Red Bull Content Pool/Getty Images

ALPHATAURI AT03

PARTNERS AlphaTauri • Honda • Fantom • DAZN • Rapid API • Buzz • Epicor • Randstad Italia • ICM.com • Ziba Foods • Pirelli • Ravenol • Riedel Siemens • GMG

SUPPLIERS Pirelli • Randstad • Riedel • RDS • Siemens • Epicor

POWER UNIT **Type:** Red Bull RBPTH001 **No. of cylinders (vee angle):** V6 (90°) **No. of valves:** 24 **Max rpm (ICE):** 15,000
Electronics: MESL standard electronic control unit **Fuel:** E10

TRANSMISSION Red Bull eight-speed gearbox, carbon-composite main case, longitudinally mounted with hydraulic power-shift
Clutch: Carbon multi-plate

CHASSIS **Monocoque:** Carbon composite
Front suspension: Carbon-composite wishbones and uprights, push-rod-actuated inboard torsion bars and dampers
Rear suspension: Carbon-composite wishbones, push-rod-actuated inboard torsion bars and dampers
Steering: Power-assisted rack-and-pinion **Wheels:** 18in diameter **Tyres:** Pirelli P Zero **Brakes:** Brembo calipers, carbon discs and pads
Fuel system: Scuderia Toro Rosso/Red Bull Technology

DIMENSIONS Not disclosed **Formula weight:** 798kg, including driver and camera

YUKI TSUNODA

FRANZ TOST

SCUDERIA ALPHATAURI: PERSONNEL

Team Owner: Dietrich Mateschitz

Team Principal: Franz Tost

Technical Director: Jody Egginton

Head of Sporting Direction: Marco Perrone

Head of Vehicle Performance: Guillaume Dezoteux

Chief Race Engineer: Jonathan Eddolls

Logistics Manager: Michela Fabbri

Race Engineer *(Gasly)***:** Pierre Hamelin

Race Engineer *(Tsunoda)***:** Mattia Spini

Chief Mechanic: Domiziano Facchinetti

Head of Quality and Reliability: Philip Mitchell

Director of Partnerships & Business Development: Fabian Wrabetz

Head of Communications: Fabiana Valenti

Press Officer: Carolyn Paterson

Digital Manager: Diego Mandolfo

though – and occasional lower top-ten points were the norm.

The newness of both regulations and the aero department's working environment meant that there was a lot of adapting to do, and the team could not maintain its previous efficiencies in verifying new components in the tunnel and producing them quickly. Updates tended to come in round-up packages of changes, rather than the previous incremental system. That gave less time for the fine-tuning the car really needed to combine any increases in load with the through-corner balance the drivers were seeking. Such is the overwhelming aerodynamic power of the floor that small changes have a big effect. Thus the previous incremental approach to changes would have been preferable, but couldn't be achieved.

"Priority number one was floor development," stressed Egginton. "That's the battleground. So any changes we did with front wing, etc were just trying to tune around that, seeking to improve response, particularly low-speed yaw." That was the main limitation defining the AT03's balance problem. With a better initial response, it could have been better balanced through the corner.

The biggest of the upgrade packages came ahead of the French Grand Prix. It featured a heavily revised engine cover/coke-bottle section with a taller, wider shoulder. The surface behind that area remained unchanged, creating a gulley in the bodywork that was used to better link the flow around the front tyres with that being fed to the rear of the car. The diffuser was modified, including the removal of the previous cutout, which was no longer needed because of the improved flow from the front of the car. The floor edges and fences were also changed as part of the rechannelled underfloor flow.

But even that didn't have a noticeable effect on the car's competitiveness, and in general, it was less competitive in the season's first half than the second, as the aero riddle was never properly solved. Egginton was determined to get the team back on its former trajectory for 2023.

"It's not easy moving wind tunnels," he said. "We didn't have to make that decision, but we did and it was the right thing to do, and in year two, the expectation is that we get back to business and operating the way we showed in 2020 and '21. We've just got to do it, and we've got most of the tools. We're a little bit smaller team, we have to work a little bit harder and a little bit more efficiently. But what we might lose in firepower, I like to think we can recover with quick reactions and tenacity. That's the goal."

Left: Illuminated by torchlight, local hero Yuki Tsunoda was the centre of attention in Suzuka.

Far left: Poetry in motion. An Alpha-Tauri pit stop for Gasly at Zandvoort.

Below centre left: Liam Lawson had a couple of Friday runs for the team.

Below left: After excellent service to AlphaTauri, Gasly netted himself a dream move to Alpine for 2023.

Bottom far left: Technical director Jody Egginton.

Below: Gasly's AT03 sparking at speed in qualifying at Silverstone.

Bottom: Tsunoda had a roller coaster of a season and faces the challenge of Nyck de Vries for 2023.

Photos: Scuderia AlphaTauri/Getty Images

23

ALEX ALBON

Photos: Williams Racing

NYCK DE VRIES

45

6

NICHOLAS LATIFI

WILLIAMS RACING

DESPITE the clean-sheet opportunity of the new aero regulations, Williams was not notably more competitive than it had been in 2021, generally the slowest car on the grid and qualifying an average of 2.2s off the ultimate pace. One car – invariably that of Alex Albon – graduated from Q1 in half of the races, with Q3 reached twice. Lower-end points were scored on five occasions, but not enough to keep the team from being last in the constructors' championship.

In its original form, the FW44 was highly distinctive, with 'size zero' sidepods not dissimilar to those used on the Mercedes W13, with no undercut, but a fairly extreme ramp downwards. This was packaged around a cooling system with radiators around the centreline that were mounted quite high in the car and that supplemented the traditional ones, pushed towards the front of the sidepods.

The Mercedes power unit drove through the Mercedes gearbox, a first for Williams, which, traditionally, had always built its own gearbox. The rear suspension (conventional pull-rod) remained Williams' own, together with the push-rod front.

Head of Vehicle Dynamics Dave Robson explained the reasoning behind taking the Mercedes gearbox: "It allowed us to have designers look at other things. It's a cost, though, and it's not cheap. That's an ongoing trade. It influenced what we did in those opening tests because you have a whole new piece of kit to understand. Mercedes GP supplied people to operate it from

Photo: Bryn Williams

WILLIAMS FW44

PARTNERS Sofina • Lavazza • Acronis • Dorilton Ventures • Bang &Olufsen • Virtua • Versa Integrity • Honibe • Financial Times • Broadcom/Symantec Bremont • Thales • U-Earth • Pirelli • Umbro • ZIESS • PPG • OMP Racing • KX Systems • Dtex • B&R Industrial Automation • Crew Clothing MEI Rigging and Crating • Life Fitness • Nexa3D • Spinal Injuries Association

POWER UNIT **Type:** Mercedes-AMG F1 M13 EQ Power **No. of cylinders (vee angle):** V6 (90°) **No. of valves:** 24 **Max rpm (ICE):** 15,000
Fuel injection: High-pressure direct injection (max 500 bar, one injector/cylinder) **Max fuel flow rate:** 100kg/hr (above 10,500rpm)
Pressure charging: Single-stage compressor and exhaust turbine on common shaft **Exhaust turbine max rpm:** 125,000
Electronics: FIA standard SECU control unit **ERS:** Mercedes AMG HPP

TRANSMISSION Mercedes-AMG F1: eight-speed forward, one reverse unit with carbon-fibre maincase, sequential, semi-automatic, hydraulic activation gear selection

CHASSIS **Monocoque:** Moulded carbon-fibre and honeycomb composite structure surpassing FIA impact and strength requirements
Front suspension: Double wishbone, push-rod-actuated springs and anti-roll bar **Rear suspension:** pull-rod-actuated springs and anti-roll bar
Wheels: F1 Standard Supply Component **Tyres:** Pirelli P Zero **Brakes:** Brembo six-piston front and rear calipers, carbon discs and pads
Steering: Williams power-assisted rack-and-pinion **Fuel system:** Kevlar-reinforced rubber bladder

DIMENSIONS **Length:** Not disclosed **Width:** 2000mm **Height:** 970mm **Wheelbase:** Not disclosed **Formula weight:** 798kg, including driver and camera

ALEX ALBON

Photo: Williams Racing

JOST CAPITO

WILLIAMS RACING: PERSONNEL

Co-founders: Sir Frank Williams & Sir Patrick Head

Williams Board: Matthew Savage, Darren Fultz, James Matthews

Chief Executive Officer & Team Principal: Jost Capito

Sporting Director: Sven Smeets

General Counsel: Mark Biddle

Chief Finance Officer: Steve Cripps

Chief Marketing Director: Claudia Schwarz

Commercial Director: James Bower

HR Director: Nicola Salter

Technical Director: François-Xavier Demaison

Design Director: Dave Worner

Head of Vehicle Performance: Dave Robson

Aerodynamics Director: David Wheater

Head of Engineering Co-ordination: George Henson

Chief Race Engineer: Paul Williams

Head of Strategy: Richard Lockwood

Performance Engineers: Andrew Vizard/George Britton

Operations Director: James Colgate

Senior Race Engineer ***(Albon)*****:** James Urwin

Senior Race Engineer ***(Latifi)*****:** Gaeten Jago

Team Manager: Dave Redding

Race Team Co-ordinator: Bryan Hart

Head of Communications: Rebecca Banks

Above: The team convenes for the traditional end-of-season photograph at Yas Marina.

Top right: Logan Sargeant will be in Williams F1 overalls in 2023, having successfully gained his superlicence.

Above right: The role of head of performance was in the experienced hands of Dave Robson.

Top far right: Nicholas Latifi enjoyed two seasons with the team, but for 2023, he must look for opportunities outside F1.

Above far right: Nyck de Vries was a late substitute for the indisposed Alex Albon and grabbed an F1 lifeline with his drive to ninth.

Right: So much to learn. The hi-tech steering wheel of the Williams reflects the technical nature of the modern F1 car.

Photos: Williams Racing

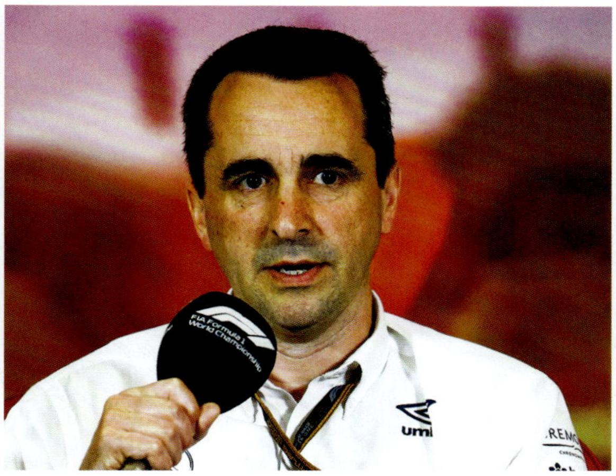

a reliability point of view. You get some settings, and it's our job to work out how to use them. The impact on tyres of shifting settings can be significant, for example, so there was quite a lot to catch up on.

"The rear suspension, because it's fixed to a Mercedes gearbox, meant there were restrictions on the loads we can put in it, and some of the inboard pick-up points are defined. So we didn't have full freedom to do what we wanted. But I don't think it's been a big limitation. Next year, it will look a bit different, but not much."

Like many teams, Williams discovered the reality of ground-effect porpoising at the first winter test, around Barcelona. "Seeing it the first time, it looks dreadful, but the drivers weren't really finding it disturbing," Robson continued. "But you are hitting the ground quite hard, so there's reliability problems, and in that test, we wore the plank quite heavily at the rear. So we couldn't have raced like that. There was a bit of a redesign of the plank and where you put the skid material before we arrived in Bahrain, so if we had that problem again, we could at least finish the race legally. By Bahrain, there wasn't any porpoising, but it has come and gone at different circuits. It does harm performance under braking, and a few occasions prior to the metric [FIA technical directive, introduced at Spa], we could porpoise enough to wear the plank. But since the metric's been introduced, we've not troubled it."

Testing and the early races revealed a downforce shortfall and difficult corner balance, with contrasting traits between turn-in and mid-corner (a common theme among the 2022 crop of cars behind the top three). In reaction to this, the team began pressing ahead early on a heavily-revised car, with much more conventional (Red Bull-like) sidepods. and this was introduced at Silverstone.

"Having seen what others had done, and with a better understanding of how that whole rear corner area – with the winglet on the brake duct, the floor and air being fed to it – worked as a system, we could see there was opportunity to do something better," said Robson. "Not just short term, but something with more potential going forwards.

"That inspired the wind-tunnel work, which got us to the Silverstone upgrade. We'd have liked to have pushed them further, but with cost-cap restrictions, we opted not to change the radiators, which are the same as the launch car. We'd have liked to have changed those and the shape of the sidepod a bit more, but that would have been quite expensive. What we got was better than the launch car in terms of feeding that corner, but also something we can work on and build on for next year when we have a bit more freedom to push a bit harder.

"The winglet cluster at the rear corner changed as part of that update and has changed again since. There are lots of different ways to make that work. That winglet cluster sits and works with the suspension links as well, so there's always scope to crank it up harder."

Albon reported that although there was definitely more downforce, the car was even more demanding to drive in terms of the balance changes, something that Nicholas Latifi really struggled with. Nonetheless, the updated car was undoubtedly quicker than the original, to the tune of over 0.5s when measured by the deficit to pole in dry qualifying sessions.

"Yes, the extra downforce did wind up the sensitivities a bit," said Robson. "In a way that the wind tunnel said it would, so it wasn't a big surprise. Typically, you'll always have to trade those two. The sensitivity can be a problem. At tracks where the wind is calm, we do tend to do quite a lot better. Even at tracks where certain corners are sheltered, our relative performance is better. It's there on all cars, but, yes, it's something we probably haven't got optimised."

The downforce shortfall, even to the cars around it on the grid, was usually apparent. At high-downforce-demanding tracks, the car was at its least competitive; habitually, it was the fastest through the speed traps, unencumbered by the extra drag that extra downforce brings. According to the team's hierarchy of tracks on how the car should perform, Monza was firmly at the top, so it was particularly galling for Albon when he had to stand down for the Italian Grand Prix because of a bout of appendicitis. That was the background to the great stand-in job made by Nyck de Vries who, on his debut, took the car through to Q2 and finished ninth in the race. It was back to reality, however, at the downforce-demanding Singapore three weeks later, where the two FW44s populated the back of the grid. Earlier, Albon had succeeded in getting the car through to Q3 at Spa, a feat also achieved by Latifi in the wet of Silverstone.

This is a team still transitioning under the third year of new owners. A lot of changes are being made to the facilities in Grove, which will determine its future trajectory.

"It's a huge project, which is starting to make a difference," said Robson. "A lot of the upgrading going on there hasn't yet made its way to the car. The tunnel is in a good state; it's had some upgrades and is pretty close to state of the art. With the cost cap in terms of head count, it depends how much we want to outsource or manufacture – invest in people or other things. In terms of total resource, we're heading in the right direction, and we are fighting against teams who've spent a lot in the last decade, so they will still have a lasting, albeit decaying, advantage."

CHASSIS LOGBOOK 2022

COMPILED BY DAVID HAYHOE

RED BULL RB18

ROUND 1 BAHRAIN GP

	MERCEDES	
44	Lewis Hamilton	F1 W13/03
63	George Russell	F1 W13/02
	RED BULL	
1	Max Verstappen	RB18/03
11	Sergio Pérez	RB18/01
	FERRARI	
16	Charles Leclerc	F1-75/
55	Carlos Sainz	F1-75/
	McLAREN-MERCEDES	
3	Daniel Ricciardo	MCL36/
4	Lando Norris	MCL36/
	ALPINE-RENAULT	
14	Fernando Alonso	A522/02
31	Esteban Ocon	A522/01
	ALPHATAURI-RED BULL	
10	Pierre Gasly	AT03/03
22	Yuki Tsunoda	AT03/02
	ASTON MARTIN-MERCEDES	
18	Lance Stroll	AMR22/01
27	Nico Hülkenberg	AMR22/02
	WILLIAMS-MERCEDES	
6	Nicholas Latifi	FW44/03
23	Alexander Albon	FW44/02
	ALFA ROMEO-FERRARI	
24	Zhou Guanyu	C42/02
77	Valtteri Bottas	C42/01
	HAAS-FERRARI	
20	Kevin Magnussen	VF-22/01
47	Mick Schumacher	VF-22/02

ROUND 2 SAUDI ARABIAN GP

	MERCEDES	
44	Lewis Hamilton	F1 W13/03
63	George Russell	F1 W13/02
	RED BULL	
1	Max Verstappen	RB18/03
11	Sergio Pérez	RB18/01
	FERRARI	
16	Charles Leclerc	F1-75/
55	Carlos Sainz	F1-75/
	McLAREN-MERCEDES	
3	Daniel Ricciardo	MCL36/
4	Lando Norris	MCL36/
	ALPINE-RENAULT	
14	Fernando Alonso	A522/02
31	Esteban Ocon	A522/01
	ALPHATAURI-RED BULL	
10	Pierre Gasly	AT03/01
22	Yuki Tsunoda	AT03/02
	ASTON MARTIN-MERCEDES	
18	Lance Stroll	AMR22/01
27	Nico Hülkenberg	AMR22/02
	WILLIAMS-MERCEDES	
6	Nicholas Latifi	FW44/03
23	Alexander Albon	FW44/02
	ALFA ROMEO-FERRARI	
24	Zhou Guanyu	C42/02
77	Valtteri Bottas	C42/01
	HAAS-FERRARI	
20	Kevin Magnussen	VF-22/01
47	Mick Schumacher	VF-22/02

ROUND 3 AUSTRALIAN GP

	MERCEDES	
44	Lewis Hamilton	F1 W13/03
63	George Russell	F1 W13/02
	RED BULL	
1	Max Verstappen	RB18/03
11	Sergio Pérez	RB18/01
	FERRARI	
16	Charles Leclerc	F1-75/
55	Carlos Sainz	F1-75/
	McLAREN-MERCEDES	
3	Daniel Ricciardo	MCL36/
4	Lando Norris	MCL36/
	ALPINE-RENAULT	
14	Fernando Alonso	A522/02
31	Esteban Ocon	A522/01
	ALPHATAURI-RED BULL	
10	Pierre Gasly	AT03/01
22	Yuki Tsunoda	AT03/02
	ASTON MARTIN-MERCEDES	
5	Sebastian Vettel	AMR22/02
18	Lance Stroll	AMR22/01
	WILLIAMS-MERCEDES	
6	Nicholas Latifi	FW44/03
23	Alexander Albon	FW44/02
	ALFA ROMEO-FERRARI	
24	Zhou Guanyu	C42/02
77	Valtteri Bottas	C42/01
	HAAS-FERRARI	
20	Kevin Magnussen	VF-22/01
47	Mick Schumacher	VF-22/03

ROUND 4 EMILIA ROMAGNA GP

	MERCEDES	
44	Lewis Hamilton	F1 W13/03
63	George Russell	F1 W13/01
	RED BULL	
1	Max Verstappen	RB18/04
11	Sergio Pérez	RB18/03
	FERRARI	
16	Charles Leclerc	F1-75/
55	Carlos Sainz	F1-75/
	McLAREN-MERCEDES	
3	Daniel Ricciardo	MCL36/
4	Lando Norris	MCL36/
	ALPINE-RENAULT	
14	Fernando Alonso	A522/02
31	Esteban Ocon	A522/01
	ALPHATAURI-RED BULL	
10	Pierre Gasly	AT03/04
22	Yuki Tsunoda	AT03/02
	ASTON MARTIN-MERCEDES	
5	Sebastian Vettel	AMR22/02
18	Lance Stroll	AMR22/01
	WILLIAMS-MERCEDES	
6	Nicholas Latifi	FW44/03
23	Alexander Albon	FW44/02
	ALFA ROMEO-FERRARI	
24	Zhou Guanyu	C42/02
77	Valtteri Bottas	C42/03 (01-Fri P1)
	HAAS-FERRARI	
20	Kevin Magnussen	VF-22/01
47	Mick Schumacher	VF-22/03

ROUND 5 MIAMI GP

	MERCEDES	
44	Lewis Hamilton	F1 W13/03
63	George Russell	F1 W13/02
	RED BULL	
1	Max Verstappen	RB18/04
11	Sergio Pérez	RB18/03
	FERRARI	
16	Charles Leclerc	F1-75/
55	Carlos Sainz	F1-75/
	McLAREN-MERCEDES	
3	Daniel Ricciardo	MCL36/
4	Lando Norris	MCL36/
	ALPINE-RENAULT	
14	Fernando Alonso	A522/02
31	Esteban Ocon	A522/01
	ALPHATAURI-RED BULL	
10	Pierre Gasly	AT03/04
22	Yuki Tsunoda	AT03/02
	ASTON MARTIN-MERCEDES	
5	Sebastian Vettel	AMR22/03
18	Lance Stroll	AMR22/01
	WILLIAMS-MERCEDES	
6	Nicholas Latifi	FW44/03
23	Alexander Albon	FW44/04
	ALFA ROMEO-FERRARI	
24	Zhou Guanyu	C42/02
77	Valtteri Bottas	C42/01
	HAAS-FERRARI	
20	Kevin Magnussen	VF-22/01
47	Mick Schumacher	VF-22/02

ROUND 6 SPANISH GP

	MERCEDES	
44	Lewis Hamilton	F1 W13/03
63	George Russell	F1 W13/02
	RED BULL	
1	Max Verstappen	RB18/04
11	Sergio Pérez	RB18/01
36	Jüri Vips	RB18/01 (Fri P1)
	FERRARI	
16	Charles Leclerc	F1-75/
55	Carlos Sainz	F1-75/
	McLAREN-MERCEDES	
3	Daniel Ricciardo	MCL36/
4	Lando Norris	MCL36/
	ALPINE-RENAULT	
14	Fernando Alonso	A522/02
31	Esteban Ocon	A522/03
	ALPHATAURI-RED BULL	
10	Pierre Gasly	AT03/04
22	Yuki Tsunoda	AT03/02
	ASTON MARTIN-MERCEDES	
5	Sebastian Vettel	AMR22/01
18	Lance Stroll	AMR22/02
	WILLIAMS-MERCEDES	
6	Nicholas Latifi	FW44/03
23	Alexander Albon	FW44/04
45	Nyck de Vries	FW44/04 (Fri P1)
	ALFA ROMEO-FERRARI	
24	Zhou Guanyu	C42/04
88	Robert Kubica	C42/04 (Fri P1)
77	Valtteri Bottas	C42/03
	HAAS-FERRARI	
20	Kevin Magnussen	VF-22/03
47	Mick Schumacher	VF-22/02

ROUND 7 MONACO GP

	MERCEDES	
44	Lewis Hamilton	F1 W13/01
63	George Russell	F1 W13/02
	RED BULL	
1	Max Verstappen	RB18/04
11	Sergio Pérez	RB18/01
	FERRARI	
16	Charles Leclerc	F1-75/
55	Carlos Sainz	F1-75/
	McLAREN-MERCEDES	
3	Daniel Ricciardo	MCL36/
4	Lando Norris	MCL36/
	ALPINE-RENAULT	
14	Fernando Alonso	A522/02
31	Esteban Ocon	A522/03
	ALPHATAURI-RED BULL	
10	Pierre Gasly	AT03/04
22	Yuki Tsunoda	AT03/02
	ASTON MARTIN-MERCEDES	
5	Sebastian Vettel	AMR22/01
18	Lance Stroll	AMR22/02
	WILLIAMS-MERCEDES	
6	Nicholas Latifi	FW44/03
23	Alexander Albon	FW44/02
	ALFA ROMEO-FERRARI	
24	Zhou Guanyu	C42/04
77	Valtteri Bottas	C42/03
	HAAS-FERRARI	
20	Kevin Magnussen	VF-22/03
47	Mick Schumacher	VF-22/02

ROUND 8 AZERBAIJAN GP

	MERCEDES	
44	Lewis Hamilton	F1 W13/01
63	George Russell	F1 W13/02
	RED BULL	
1	Max Verstappen	RB18/04
11	Sergio Pérez	RB18/03
	FERRARI	
16	Charles Leclerc	F1-75/
55	Carlos Sainz	F1-75/
	McLAREN-MERCEDES	
3	Daniel Ricciardo	MCL36/
4	Lando Norris	MCL36/
	ALPINE-RENAULT	
14	Fernando Alonso	A522/02
31	Esteban Ocon	A522/03
	ALPHATAURI-RED BULL	
10	Pierre Gasly	AT03/04
22	Yuki Tsunoda	AT03/02
	ASTON MARTIN-MERCEDES	
5	Sebastian Vettel	AMR22/01
18	Lance Stroll	AMR22/02
	WILLIAMS-MERCEDES	
6	Nicholas Latifi	FW44/03
23	Alexander Albon	FW44/04
	ALFA ROMEO-FERRARI	
24	Zhou Guanyu	C42/04
77	Valtteri Bottas	C42/03
	HAAS-FERRARI	
20	Kevin Magnussen	VF-22/03
47	Mick Schumacher	VF-22/01

Red Bull Content Pool/Getty Images

FERRARI F1-75

Scuderia Ferrari

MERCEDES-AMG F1 W13 - LAUNCH CAR

MERCEDES-AMG F1 W13

Mercedes-AMG Petronas F1 Team

ROUND 9 CANADIAN GP

	MERCEDES	
44	Lewis Hamilton	F1 W13/01
63	George Russell	F1 W13/02
	RED BULL	
1	Max Verstappen	RB18/04
11	Sergio Pérez	RB18/03
	FERRARI	
16	Charles Leclerc	F1-75/
55	Carlos Sainz	F1-75/
	McLAREN-MERCEDES	
3	Daniel Ricciardo	MCL36/
4	Lando Norris	MCL36/
	ALPINE-RENAULT	
14	Fernando Alonso	A522/02
31	Esteban Ocon	A522/03
	ALPHATAURI-RED BULL	
10	Pierre Gasly	AT03/04
22	Yuki Tsunoda	AT03/02
	ASTON MARTIN-MERCEDES	
5	Sebastian Vettel	AMR22/01
18	Lance Stroll	AMR22/02
	WILLIAMS-MERCEDES	
6	Nicholas Latifi	FW44/03
23	Alexander Albon	FW44/04
	ALFA ROMEO-FERRARI	
24	Zhou Guanyu	C42/04
77	Valtteri Bottas	C42/01
	HAAS-FERRARI	
20	Kevin Magnussen	VF-22/03
47	Mick Schumacher	VF-22/01

ROUND 10 BRITISH GP

	MERCEDES	
44	Lewis Hamilton	F1 W13/03
63	George Russell	F1 W13/02
	RED BULL	
1	Max Verstappen	RB18/03
11	Sergio Pérez	RB18/01
	FERRARI	
16	Charles Leclerc	F1-75/
55	Carlos Sainz	F1-75/
	McLAREN-MERCEDES	
3	Daniel Ricciardo	MCL36/
4	Lando Norris	MCL36/
	ALPINE-RENAULT	
14	Fernando Alonso	A522/02
31	Esteban Ocon	A522/03
	ALPHATAURI-RED BULL	
10	Pierre Gasly	AT03/04
22	Yuki Tsunoda	AT03/03
	ASTON MARTIN-MERCEDES	
5	Sebastian Vettel	AMR22/04
18	Lance Stroll	AMR22/02
	WILLIAMS-MERCEDES	
6	Nicholas Latifi	FW44/02
23	Alexander Albon	FW44/04
	ALFA ROMEO-FERRARI	
24	Zhou Guanyu	C42/04
77	Valtteri Bottas	C42/01
	HAAS-FERRARI	
20	Kevin Magnussen	VF-22/03
47	Mick Schumacher	VF-22/01

ROUND 11 AUSTRIAN GP

	MERCEDES	
44	Lewis Hamilton	F1 W13/01
63	George Russell	F1 W13/02
	RED BULL	
1	Max Verstappen	RB18/03
11	Sergio Pérez	RB18/01
	FERRARI	
16	Charles Leclerc	F1-75/
55	Carlos Sainz	F1-75/
	McLAREN-MERCEDES	
3	Daniel Ricciardo	MCL36/
4	Lando Norris	MCL36/
	ALPINE-RENAULT	
14	Fernando Alonso	A522/02
31	Esteban Ocon	A522/03
	ALPHATAURI-RED BULL	
10	Pierre Gasly	AT03/01
22	Yuki Tsunoda	AT03/03
	ASTON MARTIN-MERCEDES	
5	Sebastian Vettel	AMR22/04
18	Lance Stroll	AMR22/02
	WILLIAMS-MERCEDES	
6	Nicholas Latifi	FW44/02
23	Alexander Albon	FW44/04
	ALFA ROMEO-FERRARI	
24	Zhou Guanyu	C42/03
77	Valtteri Bottas	C42/01
	HAAS-FERRARI	
20	Kevin Magnussen	VF-22/03
47	Mick Schumacher	VF-22/01

ROUND 12 FRENCH GP

	MERCEDES	
44	Lewis Hamilton	F1 W13/03
19	Nyck de Vries	F1 W13/03 (Fri P1)
63	George Russell	F1 W13/02
	RED BULL	
1	Max Verstappen	RB18/04
11	Sergio Pérez	RB18/03
	FERRARI	
16	Charles Leclerc	F1-75/
55	Carlos Sainz	F1-75/
	McLAREN-MERCEDES	
3	Daniel Ricciardo	MCL36/
4	Lando Norris	MCL36/
	ALPINE-RENAULT	
14	Fernando Alonso	A522/02
31	Esteban Ocon	A522/03
	ALPHATAURI-RED BULL	
10	Pierre Gasly	AT03/01
22	Yuki Tsunoda	AT03/03
	ASTON MARTIN-MERCEDES	
5	Sebastian Vettel	AMR22/04
18	Lance Stroll	AMR22/02
	WILLIAMS-MERCEDES	
6	Nicholas Latifi	FW44/02
23	Alexander Albon	FW44/04
	ALFA ROMEO-FERRARI	
24	Zhou Guanyu	C42/02
77	Valtteri Bottas	C42/01
88	Robert Kubica	C42/01 (Fri P1)
	HAAS-FERRARI	
20	Kevin Magnussen	VF-22/03
47	Mick Schumacher	VF-22/02

HAAS VF-22 - LAUNCH CAR

ROUND 13 HUNGARIAN GP

	MERCEDES	
44	Lewis Hamilton	F1 W13/03
63	George Russell	F1 W13/02
	RED BULL	
1	Max Verstappen	RB18/04
11	Sergio Pérez	RB18/03
	FERRARI	
16	Charles Leclerc	F1-75/
55	Carlos Sainz	F1-75/
	McLAREN-MERCEDES	
3	Daniel Ricciardo	MCL36/
4	Lando Norris	MCL36/
	ALPINE-RENAULT	
14	Fernando Alonso	A522/02
31	Esteban Ocon	A522/03
	ALPHATAURI-RED BULL	
10	Pierre Gasly	AT03/01
22	Yuki Tsunoda	AT03/03
	ASTON MARTIN-MERCEDES	
5	Sebastian Vettel	AMR22/04
18	Lance Stroll	AMR22/02
	WILLIAMS-MERCEDES	
6	Nicholas Latifi	FW44/02
23	Alexander Albon	FW44/04
	ALFA ROMEO-FERRARI	
24	Zhou Guanyu	C42/02
77	Valtteri Bottas	C42/01
88	Robert Kubica	C42/01 (Fri P1)
	HAAS-FERRARI	
20	Kevin Magnussen	VF-22/03
47	Mick Schumacher	VF-22/0

ALPHATAURI AT03

ALPINE A522

BWT LIVERY - LAUNCH CAR

McLAREN MCL36

McLaren F1 Team

ROUND 14 BELGIAN GP

	MERCEDES	
44	Lewis Hamilton	F1 W13/03
63	George Russell	F1 W13/02
	RED BULL	
1	Max Verstappen	RB18/04
11	Sergio Pérez	RB18/01
	FERRARI	
16	Charles Leclerc	F1-75/
55	Carlos Sainz	F1-75/
	McLAREN-MERCEDES	
3	Daniel Ricciardo	MCL36/
4	Lando Norris	MCL36/
	ALPINE-RENAULT	
14	Fernando Alonso	A522/02
31	Esteban Ocon	A522/03
	ALPHATAURI-RED BULL	
10	Pierre Gasly	AT03/04
40	Liam Lawson	AT03/04 (Fri P1)
22	Yuki Tsunoda	AT03/03
	ASTON MARTIN-MERCEDES	
5	Sebastian Vettel	AMR22/04
18	Lance Stroll	AMR22/02
	WILLIAMS-MERCEDES	
6	Nicholas Latifi	FW44/02
23	Alexander Albon	FW44/04
	ALFA ROMEO-FERRARI	
24	Zhou Guanyu	C42/03
77	Valtteri Bottas	C42/01
	HAAS-FERRARI	
20	Kevin Magnussen	VF-22/03
47	Mick Schumacher	VF-22/0

ROUND 15 DUTCH GP

	MERCEDES	
44	Lewis Hamilton	F1 W13/03
63	George Russell	F1 W13/02
	RED BULL	
1	Max Verstappen	RB18/04
11	Sergio Pérez	RB18/01
	FERRARI	
16	Charles Leclerc	F1-75/
55	Carlos Sainz	F1-75/
	McLAREN-MERCEDES	
3	Daniel Ricciardo	MCL36/
4	Lando Norris	MCL36/
	ALPINE-RENAULT	
14	Fernando Alonso	A522/02
31	Esteban Ocon	A522/03
	ALPHATAURI-RED BULL	
10	Pierre Gasly	AT03/04
22	Yuki Tsunoda	AT03/03
	ASTON MARTIN-MERCEDES	
5	Sebastian Vettel	AMR22/04
18	Lance Stroll	AMR22/02
	WILLIAMS-MERCEDES	
6	Nicholas Latifi	FW44/02
23	Alexander Albon	FW44/04
	ALFA ROMEO-FERRARI	
24	Zhou Guanyu	C42/03
77	Valtteri Bottas	C42/01
	HAAS-FERRARI	
20	Kevin Magnussen	VF-22/03
47	Mick Schumacher	VF-22/02

ROUND 16 ITALIAN GP

	MERCEDES	
44	Lewis Hamilton	F1 W13/03
63	George Russell	F1 W13/02
	RED BULL	
1	Max Verstappen	RB18/04
11	Sergio Pérez	RB18/01
	FERRARI	
16	Charles Leclerc	F1-75/
55	Carlos Sainz	F1-75/
	McLAREN-MERCEDES	
3	Daniel Ricciardo	MCL36/
4	Lando Norris	MCL36/
	ALPINE-RENAULT	
14	Fernando Alonso	A522/02
31	Esteban Ocon	A522/03
	ALPHATAURI-RED BULL	
10	Pierre Gasly	AT03/04
22	Yuki Tsunoda	AT03/03
	ASTON MARTIN-MERCEDES	
5	Sebastian Vettel	AMR22/04
34	Nyck de Vries	AMR22/04 (Fri P1)
18	Lance Stroll	AMR22/02
	WILLIAMS-MERCEDES	
6	Nicholas Latifi	FW44/02
23	Alexander Albon	FW44/04 (Fri)
45	Nyck de Vries	FW44/04 (Sat-Sun)
	ALFA ROMEO-FERRARI	
24	Zhou Guanyu	C42/03
77	Valtteri Bottas	C42/01
	HAAS-FERRARI	
20	Kevin Magnussen	VF-22/03
47	Mick Schumacher	VF-22/02
99	Antonio Giovinazzi	VF-22/02 (Fri P1)

ROUND 17 SINGAPORE GP

	MERCEDES	
44	Lewis Hamilton	F1 W13/03
63	George Russell	F1 W13/02
	RED BULL	
1	Max Verstappen	RB18/04
11	Sergio Pérez	RB18/03
	FERRARI	
16	Charles Leclerc	F1-75/
55	Carlos Sainz	F1-75/
	McLAREN-MERCEDES	
3	Daniel Ricciardo	MCL36/
4	Lando Norris	MCL36/
	ALPINE-RENAULT	
14	Fernando Alonso	A522/02
31	Esteban Ocon	A522/03
	ALPHATAURI-RED BULL	
10	Pierre Gasly	AT03/04
22	Yuki Tsunoda	AT03/03
	ASTON MARTIN-MERCEDES	
5	Sebastian Vettel	AMR22/04
18	Lance Stroll	AMR22/05
	WILLIAMS-MERCEDES	
6	Nicholas Latifi	FW44/02
23	Alexander Albon	FW44/04
	ALFA ROMEO-FERRARI	
24	Zhou Guanyu	C42/03
77	Valtteri Bottas	C42/01
	HAAS-FERRARI	
20	Kevin Magnussen	VF-22/03
47	Mick Schumacher	VF-22/02

Alfa Romeo ORLEN

Williams Racing

WILLIAMS FW44

ROUND 18 JAPANESE GP

	MERCEDES	
44	Lewis Hamilton	F1 W13/03
63	George Russell	F1 W13/02
	RED BULL	
1	Max Verstappen	RB18/04
11	Sergio Pérez	RB18/03
	FERRARI	
16	Charles Leclerc	F1-75/
55	Carlos Sainz	F1-75/
	McLAREN-MERCEDES	
3	Daniel Ricciardo	MCL36/
4	Lando Norris	MCL36/
	ALPINE-RENAULT	
14	Fernando Alonso	A522/02
31	Esteban Ocon	A522/03
	ALPHATAURI-RED BULL	
10	Pierre Gasly	AT03/04
22	Yuki Tsunoda	AT03/03
	ASTON MARTIN-MERCEDES	
5	Sebastian Vettel	AMR22/04
18	Lance Stroll	AMR22/05
	WILLIAMS-MERCEDES	
6	Nicholas Latifi	FW44/02
23	Alexander Albon	FW44/04
	ALFA ROMEO-FERRARI	
24	Zhou Guanyu	C42/03
77	Valtteri Bottas	C42/01
	HAAS-FERRARI	
20	Kevin Magnussen	VF-22/03
47	Mick Schumacher	VF-22/01 (02-Fri)

ALFA ROMEO C42

ROUND 19 UNITED STATES GP

	MERCEDES	
44	Lewis Hamilton	F1 W13/03
63	George Russell	F1 W13/02
	RED BULL	
1	Max Verstappen	RB18/04
11	Sergio Pérez	RB18/01
	FERRARI	
16	Charles Leclerc	F1-75/
39	Robert Shwartzman	F1-75/ (Fri P1)
55	Carlos Sainz	F1-75/
	McLAREN-MERCEDES	
3	Daniel Ricciardo	MCL36/
28	Alex Palou	MCL36/ (Fri P1)
4	Lando Norris	MCL36/
	ALPINE-RENAULT	
14	Fernando Alonso	A522/02
31	Esteban Ocon	A522/03
	ALPHATAURI-RED BULL	
10	Pierre Gasly	AT03/01
22	Yuki Tsunoda	AT03/03
	ASTON MARTIN-MERCEDES	
5	Sebastian Vettel	AMR22/04
18	Lance Stroll	AMR22/05
	WILLIAMS-MERCEDES	
6	Nicholas Latifi	FW44/02
45	Logan Sargeant	FW44/02 (Fri P1)
23	Alexander Albon	FW44/04
	ALFA ROMEO-FERRARI	
24	Zhou Guanyu	C42/03
77	Valtteri Bottas	C42/04
98	Théo Pourchaire	C42/04 (Fri P1)
	HAAS-FERRARI	
20	Kevin Magnussen	VF-22/03
99	Antonio Giovinazzi	VF-22/03 (Fri P1)
47	Mick Schumacher	VF-22/01

ROUND 20 MEXICO CITY GP

	MERCEDES	
44	Lewis Hamilton	F1 W13/03
63	George Russell	F1 W13/02
19	Nyck de Vries	F1 W13/02 (Fri P1)
	RED BULL	
1	Max Verstappen	RB18/04
11	Sergio Pérez	RB18/01
	FERRARI	
16	Charles Leclerc	F1-75/
55	Carlos Sainz	F1-75/
	McLAREN-MERCEDES	
3	Daniel Ricciardo	MCL36/
4	Lando Norris	MCL36/
	ALPINE-RENAULT	
14	Fernando Alonso	A522/02
31	Esteban Ocon	A522/03
82	Jack Doohan	A522/03 (Fri P1)
	ALPHATAURI-RED BULL	
10	Pierre Gasly	AT03/01
22	Yuki Tsunoda	AT03/03
40	Liam Lawson	AT03/03 (Fri P1)
	ASTON MARTIN-MERCEDES	
5	Sebastian Vettel	AMR22/04
18	Lance Stroll	AMR22/05
	WILLIAMS-MERCEDES	
6	Nicholas Latifi	FW44/02
23	Alexander Albon	FW44/04
45	Logan Sargeant	FW44/04 (Fri P1)
	ALFA ROMEO-FERRARI	
24	Zhou Guanyu	C42/03
77	Valtteri Bottas	C42/01
	HAAS-FERRARI	
20	Kevin Magnussen	VF-22/03
51	Pietro Fittipaldi	VF-22/03 (Fri P1)
47	Mick Schumacher	VF-22/01

ROUND 21 SÃO PAULO GP

	MERCEDES	
44	Lewis Hamilton	F1 W13/03
63	George Russell	F1 W13/02
	RED BULL	
1	Max Verstappen	RB18/04
11	Sergio Pérez	RB18/01
	FERRARI	
16	Charles Leclerc	F1-75/
55	Carlos Sainz	F1-75/
	McLAREN-MERCEDES	
3	Daniel Ricciardo	MCL36/
4	Lando Norris	MCL36/
	ALPINE-RENAULT	
14	Fernando Alonso	A522/02
31	Esteban Ocon	A522/03
	ALPHATAURI-RED BULL	
10	Pierre Gasly	AT03/01
22	Yuki Tsunoda	AT03/03
	ASTON MARTIN-MERCEDES	
5	Sebastian Vettel	AMR22/04
18	Lance Stroll	AMR22/05
	WILLIAMS-MERCEDES	
6	Nicholas Latifi	FW44/02
23	Alexander Albon	FW44/04
45	Logan Sargeant	FW44/04 (Sat P2)
	ALFA ROMEO-FERRARI	
24	Zhou Guanyu	C42/03
77	Valtteri Bottas	C42/04
	HAAS-FERRARI	
20	Kevin Magnussen	VF-22/03
47	Mick Schumacher	VF-22/02

ROUND 22 ABU DHABI GP

	MERCEDES	
44	Lewis Hamilton	F1 W13/03
63	George Russell	F1 W13/02
	RED BULL	
1	Max Verstappen	RB18/04
36	Liam Lawson	RB18/04 (Fri P1)
11	Sergio Pérez	RB18/01
	FERRARI	
16	Charles Leclerc	F1-75/
55	Carlos Sainz	F1-75/
39	Robert Shwartzman	F1-75/ (Fri P1)
	McLAREN-MERCEDES	
3	Daniel Ricciardo	MCL36/
4	Lando Norris	MCL36/
28	Patricio O'Ward	MCL36/ (Fri P1)
	ALPINE-RENAULT	
14	Fernando Alonso	A522/02
82	Jack Doohan	A522/02 (Fri P1)
31	Esteban Ocon	A522/03
	ALPHATAURI-RED BULL	
10	Pierre Gasly	AT03/01
22	Yuki Tsunoda	AT03/03
	ASTON MARTIN-MERCEDES	
5	Sebastian Vettel	AMR22/04
18	Lance Stroll	AMR22/05
34	Felipe Drugovich	AMR22/05 (Fri P1)
	WILLIAMS-MERCEDES	
6	Nicholas Latifi	FW44/02
45	Logan Sargeant	FW44/02 (Fri P1)
23	Alexander Albon	FW44/04
	ALFA ROMEO-FERRARI	
24	Zhou Guanyu	C42/03
88	Robert Kubica	C42/03 (Fri P1)
77	Valtteri Bottas	C42/04
	HAAS-FERRARI	
20	Kevin Magnussen	VF-22/03
47	Mick Schumacher	VF-22/02
51	Pietro Fittipaldi	VF-22/02 (Fri P1)

Atsuo Sakurai

ASTON MARTIN AMR22 - LAUNCH CAR

Aston Martin Aramco Cognizant F1 Team

FIA FORMULA 1 WORLD CHAMPIONSHIP

GRANDS PRIX 2022

BY TONY DODGINS and MAURICE HAMILTON

FIA FORMULA 1 WORLD CHAMPIONSHIP · ROUND 1

BAHRAIN GRAND PRIX

SAKHIR CIRCUIT

Charles Leclerc crosses the line to take victory in the opening race of the season.
Photo: Atsuo Sakurai

SAKHIR QUALIFYING

RED BULL team principal Christian Horner called the new 2022 F1 ground-effect regulations the biggest chassis change in 40 years. The biggest, therefore, since ground effect had been banned in 1983.

As such, the level of excitement and anticipation was off the charts. Unless you happen to be a blinkered fan of a driver blessed by a superior car, any prolonged period of single-team domination can be a turn-off. The great thing about 2021 had been two evenly matched teams and drivers. Would the new era redefine the pecking order?

Apparently, yes, although it would take time for teams to get a handle on their new cars. In-season development would be even more important in 2022.

Pre-season testing in Barcelona and Bahrain had pointed to Red Bull and Ferrari stealing an early march, with the order somewhat fluid behind. Opening-round qualifying, as ever, was the first glimpse of cars in comparable specs.

Defending champion Max Verstappen appeared to be a likely pole-winner. Red Bull had put its definitive aero package on its new car on the last day of the final Bahrain test, and the RB18 had moved the goalposts. But Ferrari was close, after test days that Charles Leclerc and Carlos Sainz agreed had been unbelievably smooth running. But, nobody knew definite fuel loads.

When the chips were down, it was the Monégasque who repeated his 2019 Sakhir pole position, heading Verstappen by 0.13s.

"I was pretty sure that Red Bull would be quicker than us in qualifying," Leclerc admitted, "so that was a good surprise. Until my last Q3 run, I wasn't happy with my driving. I knew the lap was in there somewhere, but I just hadn't put it together. These cars feel completely different: I've tried many different styles and still needed to find the perfect one."

It was an interesting point. More stringent crash test requirements, and the change to 18-inch wheels and tyres had bloated cars to almost 800kg, which is more like sports car weight. Consider that a Niki Lauda championship-winning Ferrari 312T from the mid-seventies, complete with flat-12 engine, weighed just 575kg.

"Race tyre degradation, with fuel weight on top, will be important," Leclerc added.

That was a point of view shared by the new world champion: "Here in Bahrain, you really need to make sure that the car is working in the race. My qualifying was a bit hit and miss: Q2 [which Max topped] felt good, but in Q3, it was tough to get a balance. But I think we've got a good race car."

Sainz was happy with third place, just 0.007s behind Verstappen. Scratching for most of the weekend, sometimes as much as seven-tenths adrift of Leclerc, he was happy to be close when it mattered, reflecting the average margin between the Ferrari pairing in 2021.

Also the norm, Sergio Pérez was around four-tenths shy of Verstappen, which was good enough for the second row and 0.31s ahead of Lewis Hamilton.

Enter the 2022 buzzword: 'porpoising'. It is a phenomenon that was prevalent during the previous ground-effect era, and there aren't too many technical brains in the paddock with experience dating back that far, notwithstanding Red Bull's Adrian Newey, which might or might not have been significant.

Basically, when the underfloor is responsible for a much higher percentage of the downforce, porpoising, or bouncing, arises when airflow separation occurs as a car approaches maximum speed and load. If the separation is sufficient, downforce reduces, the ride height rises and then, when the airflow re-attaches, the ride height reduces until separation occurs again and the process repeats itself. It rocks back and forth, like a porpoise dipping in and out of the sea.

The term was coined by Mario Andretti back in 1979 when he tested Colin Chapman's extreme Lotus 80 ground-effect car, which the design ace and Lotus founder could not persuade to work. But why was it still a factor 40-odd years later, given the sophistication of today's wind tunnels and simulation tools?

The answer was simple, as Ferrari's team principal Mattia Binotto explained: "Such behaviour is normal with this type of car. It cannot be simulated in the wind tunnel because it occurs at 250–270km/h, and the regulations limit wind tunnel speed to 180km/h."

It affected everyone to a greater or lesser degree. Red Bull seemed to suffer least, Ferrari a little more, and Mercedes significantly. But, as Binotto added, he didn't expect it to be an issue four or five races in.

Lewis Hamilton, fifth, and seven-tenths off the pace, fervently hoped so.

"I'm not going to say I'm relieved," he said, "because the guys ahead of us are in another league, but I'm really happy considering where we've been in testing." Realistically, Toto Wolff figured that the Mercs were missing around half a second, not the seven-tenths suggested by the time sheet.

For George Russell, though, it was more like 1.7s after a disastrous Q3. He was sixth in Q2, just a couple of tenths behind his team-mate, having been quicker in every practice session. But, in Q3, almost a full second slower, he dropped to ninth.

"We have to take the blame," Wolff explained. "We told him to push on the out-lap and he lost the tyre." To such an extent, Russell said, that he had no grip by Turn 11 on his preparation lap.

If, the previous autumn, you had told Valtteri Bottas, sixth, that he would split the Mercs on the grid on his Alfa Romeo debut, he would have laughed, but that was the situation.

And, ditto, seventh-placed Kevin Magnussen, who just ten days earlier had been on a beach in Miami with his mates when he got the call from Guenther Steiner to resume his Haas career in place of Nikita Mazepin, following Russia's invasion of Ukraine. The Netflix portrayal of 'K-Mag' shattering Guenther's glass paddock door in a fit of pique obviously had not precluded career advancement!

"It's crazy. I'm super-happy," the Dane beamed. "It's been a massive roller coaster. I was really surprised by the call from Guenther. I feel so unbelievably happy to be in F1 with a good car. I had an issue in Q2 with the hydraulics and thought I couldn't get out for Q3, so seventh is fantastic! My neck has been giving up, but that will improve quickly. The car wasn't bad on a long run either, but my concern is reliability."

Fernando Alonso put his Alpine eighth on the grid, 0.02s quicker than Russell, with AlphaTauri's Pierre Gasly completing the top ten.

Esteban Ocon missed out on Q3 by 0.07s, a couple of tenths clear of Mick Schumacher, for whom Magnussen was going to be a decent yardstick.

If James Allison had some head scratching to do at Mercedes, so did McLaren technical chief James Key, the new MCL36 lacking grip and qualifying 13th with Lando Norris, while Daniel Ricciardo, who had missed the final Bahrain test with Covid, was only 18th.

Zhou Guanyu, the first ever Chinese driver in F1, did a respectable job to make Q2 on his debut with the second Alfa, albeit eight-tenths behind team leader Bottas.

Williams had work to do. New signing Alexander Albon was a creditable 14th, while Nicholas Latifi propped up the grid.

It was not a dream start to 2022 for Aston Martin either, with Sebastian Vettel forced to miss the season-opener due to Covid. Once again, super-sub Nico Hülkenberg stepped up. It was to his great credit that despite not having raced anything for 18 months, 'The Hulk' went a quarter of a second quicker than the boss's boy, Nico and Lance Stroll lining up 17th and 19th.

Above: The Ferraris of Charles Leclerc and Carlos Sainz show their pace under the Bahrain floodlights.
Photo: Scuderia Ferrari

Left: Lewis Hamilton's Mercedes suffered from extreme porpoising during practice and qualifying.
Photo: Mercedes-AMG Petronas F1 Team

Far left: The ever dependable Nico Hülkenberg was pressed into action following Vettel's indisposition.
Photo: Peter Nygaard

Below far left: Kevin Magnussen was delighted to be a member of the Formula 1 circus once again.
Photo: Haas F1 Team

Above: Max Verstappen dives to the inside of Carlos Sainz in their battle for second place.
Photo: Atsuo Sakurai

Top right: Points on his debut for Zhou Guanyu, the first Chinese driver to start a grand prix.
Photo: Pirelli

Above right: Sixth place marked a satisfactory debut for Valtteri Bottas in the Alfa Romeo team.
Photo: Alfa Romeo ORLEN

Right: Alpine and Fernando Alonso had plenty to work on to climb out of the tightly-contested midfield.
Photo: Atsuo Sakurai

REVISED tyre rules for 2022 meant that drivers were no longer obliged to start the race on the tyre they had used to record their fastest lap in Q2. Instead, tyre choice was free for all, not just those who had qualified outside the top ten. Under the new initiative, everyone except the two McLarens (on mediums) lined up on Pirelli's soft-compound rubber (the C1/C2/C3 from the hardest end of the range were the offerings at Sakhir). Pole-man Charles Leclerc, alone among the top four, opted for new softs.

When the starting lights went out on F1's new dawn, Leclerc made no mistake and immediately eased the Ferrari over to the right on the run down to Turn One to cover off the inside from Max Verstappen's Red Bull.

Carlos Sainz had a brief look at the outside of Verstappen in Turn One, but thought better of it, while Lewis Hamilton got the jump on Sergio Pérez, who had to lift briefly out of T2/3, leaving himself vulnerable to Kevin Magnussen's Haas, the Dane further demoting the Mexican. George Russell was immediately up a couple of places to seventh, followed by Pierre Gasly's AlphaTauri, and the Alpines of Fernando Alonso and Esteban Ocon. Alex Albon had the first Williams in 11th place, ahead of Yuki Tsunoda and Mick Schumacher's Haas, which lost a couple of places after being clipped into a quick spin by Ocon's Alpine, an incident that the stewards adjudged needed no further investigation.

The big opening-lap loser was Valtteri Bottas who, down eight places from his excellent sixth on the grid, suffered again from an Alfa testing bugbear, a vibrating/slipping clutch.

"There's unfortunately no quick fix," he explained. "We are trying to look into it because in 50 per cent of our starts, it happens. But avoiding it, in terms of holding the revs, where you drop the clutch, the driver inputs, trying to be as consistent as possible, is not easy."

It wasn't a good opening lap for McLaren either, Lando Norris down four places to 17th, while Daniel Ricciardo was dead last.

Pérez made some early progress when a lap-three lock-up from Magnussen in Turn One gave Sergio a run into Turn Four. When the Dane had to cover the inside, his exit was compromised and the Red Bull knifed ahead on the run down the hill. A couple of laps later, the Haas locked up into T1 once again, allowing Russell to demote him further.

Also new for 2022 were bigger 18-inch wheels and lower-profile Pirelli rubber, and it was only a few laps into the race that Red Bull was on the phone to Verstappen, telling him to lift-and-coast to keep his brake temperatures in check.

Ten laps into the 57, Leclerc was circulating comfortably out of DRS range of the second-placed Red Bull, his lead almost 3s, with Sainz a further 3.5s adrift in the second Ferrari. Carlos had a similar margin in hand over Pérez, who had managed to demote Hamilton into Turn Four with the aid of DRS to run fourth. Russell was sixth, 4.5s clear of Magnussen, who had Gasly's AlphaTauri just 1.5s behind. The Alpines of Ocon and Alonso completed the top ten, Esteban ahead as Fernando complained about his tyres from early on.

After just 12 laps, Hamilton was into the pits for a set of hard-compound Pirellis, which some had speculated might not be used at all. The Mercedes was a bit squirrelly until Lewis got them up to temperature. Alonso, too, pitted for new boots.

The first move at the front came three laps later when Verstappen peeled into the pit lane for a set of soft-compound Pirellis. Sainz, Magussen, Bottas and Ocon among the top ten followed him in on the same lap. Having started on used softs, Verstappen accelerated back into the fray on a shiny set of new ones.

Ferrari responded with the race leader a lap later, with Red Bull also pitting Pérez from his fourth place. When Leclerc rejoined, he had Verstappen right with him through Turns 1/2/3, the Red Bull's tyres fully up to temperature. Charles did a good job of defending Turn Four, but Verstappen stayed with him for the rest of the lap and, with DRS, got down the inside of the leading Ferrari into Turn One.

With the second DRS detection point immediately after Turn One, however, Leclerc was able to get a better exit from T3 and repay the compliment just in time to cut back across the Red Bull's bows and claim the line through T4.

The same thing occurred on the very next lap, Leclerc jinking right this time and going inside Verstappen into T4. Undeterred, Max tried again on the following lap, so late on the brakes into T1 that he locked up the right front as he went by, and Leclerc was back ahead before T2. This was great stuff. Undoubtedly the Sakhir layout helps, with action between T1 and T4 hardly a new phenomenon, but at least the frequency was an early pointer to the 2022 regs having the desired effect of spicing up the racing.

Verstappen's lock-up meant that when approaching the final corner on to the main straight for the 20th time, he was 1.2s behind the Ferrari, did not get the added 12mph advantage of DRS and was no longer able to trouble Lerclerc. They were now very much in their own race, Sainz some 8.2s behind the Red Bull.

An early indication of just how high the degradation was (Daniel Ricciardo had abandoned his starting set of mediums after 17 laps, although the team made Lando Norris do 24 on his) came when Sainz radioed in on lap 24 and suggested to Ferrari that they ought to start thinking about three stops.

A few laps later, as the race reached half-distance, Verstappen told Red Bull, "The tyres are almost dead again." Given the caning he'd given them in his attempts to demote Leclerc, however, it wasn't entirely surprising!

Hamilton, meanwhile, had just made his second stop, jettisoning a set of used hards for medium-compound Pirellis, engineer Pete Bonnington telling him, "Lewis, important that we don't push this tyre too hard on the out-lap," which, with half the race remaining, did seem a little optimistic if they were thinking about making it through to the flag.

At this point, the bottom six comprised Lance Stroll's Aston Martin, the Alex Albon/Nicholas Latifi Williams, and the McLarens of Ricciardo and Norris, sandwiching Nico Hülkenberg with the second Aston – all of them powered by Mercedes engines.

That might just have been a coincidence and a reflection of a disappointing start to the season for McLaren, Williams and Aston, but Mercedes engine chief Hywel Thomas had already admitted that the change from 5.75 per cent bio component in the fuel to 10 per cent ethanol had been the biggest regulation challenge on the engine side since 2014.

"Some areas of performance we're really happy with, and other areas less happy," he admitted.

Above: Charles Leclerc and Carlos Sainz gave Ferrari a 1-2 finish, bringing an end to the team's 45-race winless streak.
Photo: Scuderia Ferrari

Top right: Max Verstappen walks away from his Red Bull after retiring just four laps from the end.

Above right: Sergio Pérez stands by his stricken Red Bull, which ran out of fuel just one lap from the finish.
Photos: XPB Images

Centre right: George Russell's fourth place brought a healthy haul of championship points to his team.
Photo: Mercedes-AMG Petronas F1 Team

Centre far right: A dogged performance by Lewis Hamilton salvaged an unexpected podium for Mercedes.
Photo: Pirelli

Right: Thrown back into the F1 fray at short notice, Kevin Magnussen enjoyed a cut-and-thrust battle with Hamilton before taking an excellent fifth place.
Photo: Haas F1 Team

At the front, while Verstappen had fitted another set of softs when he made his first stop, team-mate Pérez had gone on to the medium tyre and was running competitively. Max dictated the second stops, too, when he pitted on lap 30 after 16 laps on his new softs and changed them for a set of the yellow-walled tyres.

"Box, box," was the instruction to Leclerc in response. He was neatly in and out for his own set of mediums after a fine 2.5s stop by the Ferrari crew.

This time, he rejoined with a little more in hand. Verstappen, who obviously had been told not to push the rubber too hard on his out-lap, was tantalisingly close, but not close enough to demote the Ferrari this time, and unimpressed.

"Okay, this is two times I've been told not to push on the out-lap when I could easily have been in front! I'm never ever doing it again," he radioed in.

In the third-place battle, both Sainz and Pérez were in two laps later, lap 33, and, as with their respective team leaders, the Ferrari stop was around half a second quicker. Carlos had a new set of mediums bolted on, Sergio a used set of softs, and they rejoined in the same order.

It looked as though Ferrari had its respective battles under control, but after another ten laps, Red Bull pitted both Verstappen and Pérez for sets of used softs. That took any immediate pressure away from Leclerc and Sainz, but heaped it on should there be a late-race safety car!

Would Ferrari respond? Yes. Sainz was called in first, just 11 laps into his third (medium) stint, swapping them for a set of used softs. Hamilton, too, made a third stop for a final stint on used softs.

It was as though they'd had a crystal ball, because, just as Verstappen radioed in complaining about heavy steering, Gasly's AlphaTauri expired in flames out of Turn Three with 11 laps to go. What initially was a virtual safety car soon became a full safety car, and Leclerc pitted, maintaining his lead.

Thus at the end of a fascinating opening encounter, we were presented with a seven-lap shootout. The order as the safety car period came to an end was Leclerc, Verstappen, Sainz, Pérez, Hamilton, Russell, Magnussen, Bottas, Ocon, Schumacher, Tsunoda, Alonso, Zhou, Stroll, Albon, Ricciardo, Norris and Latifi.

Verstappen's attempt to crowd Leclerc's restart by drawing almost alongside into the last corner actually worked against him, as Charles bolted and Max's compromised exit left him vulnerable to Sainz.

"Hey, what's going on with the battery?" asked Verstappen.

"Battery's fine," responded engineer 'GP' Lambiase.

"No it's not!" replied a rattled Verstappen.

With three to go, Sainz pulled out with DRS on the run from T10 to T11 and made it a Ferrari 1-2.

"We can see the issue Max, and it's not battery related," Lambiase told Verstappen.

"What do you want me to do?" asked the world champion.

"There's not a lot we can do," came the response. Suddenly, the No.1 Red Bull was crawling, passed by all and sundry; Verstappen was left to trickle into the pits to retire.

On the penultimate lap, it was team-mate Pérez's turn to report bad news: "I'm losing power."

"Two laps to go, get your elbows out," instructed race engineer Hugh Bird.

Heartbreakingly for Pérez, though, out of Turn One for the last time, the engine stopped, which pitched him into a spin. It would be a double DNF for Red Bull. Subsequent investigation revealed that although there was fuel in both RB18s, the last of it wasn't being picked up.

The resurgent Ferrari team was ecstatic about starting the year with a 1-2, Leclerc claiming a third win to add to his back-to-back victories at Spa and Monza in 2019. Ferrari's 45-race winless streak, the second longest in its history, had come to an end.

Had you offered Hamilton the damage limitation of a 183rd podium before the race, he'd have snapped your arm off. Team-mate Russell's fourth place made it a decent haul of points for the eight-time constructors' champions, even if the ultimate pace had been missing.

There was a real feel-good factor surrounding fifth and sixth places for Magnussen and Bottas, ahead of Ocon's Alpine and Yuki Tsunoda's sole surviving AlphaTauri. Alonso and debutant Zhou completed the points scorers, while Mick Schumacher only just missed out on claiming a first F1 championship point.

Tony Dodgins

VIEWPOINT
DÉJÀ VU DISCOMFORT

THERE'S nothing like a major change of regulations to shake things up. Even a minor revision (compared to 2022) can do the job, as Brawn's double diffuser proved in 2009. Having got the rough end of that particular stick, Lewis Hamilton at least was accustomed to the effect of the new season's sudden performance deficit for the reigning constructors' champions.

There were quite a few uncomfortable parallels here. In 2008, Hamilton and McLaren had been involved in that incredible last-lap grab of the championship at the final race in Brazil. Fast forward to 2021, and he had been in a similar scenario with Mercedes in Abu Dhabi, only this time, bad luck, misfortune, highly questionable official decision making – call it what you will – had given him an understanding of how poor Felipe Massa and Ferrari must have felt at Interlagos 13 years before.

Hamilton had won five grands prix in 2008. In 2009, it had taken ten races before he had stood on the podium – albeit on the top step in Hungary. This had been the start of a sluggish recovery from having the slowest car in the field – three seconds off the pace during pre-season testing – to one that was barely half-decent as a dire lack of downforce was gradually overcome. Hamilton had finished fifth in the 2009 championship; the winner, Jenson Button, had scored almost twice as many points.

The revival in 2022 would be even more difficult thanks to 'porpoising' (which kicked in at 250km/h and beyond) being impossible to replicate in a wind tunnel with a regulatory 180km/h limit. Added to which, the restriction on testing meant that four Friday practice sessions would be needed to accumulate the same feedback as a single day of testing.

Hamilton and George Russell were literally in for a rough ride thanks to a fundamental error in Mercedes' interpretation of the new rules. Unlike in 2009, the pessimistic view at this stage was that Mercedes would be lucky to see the top of a podium at any point, never mind ten races into the season.

Maurice Hamilton

1

FORMULA 1 GULF AIR BAHRAIN GRAND PRIX 2022

ROLEX

Official Timepiece

SAKHIR 18–20 MARCH

RACE DISTANCE: 57 laps, 191.530 miles/308.238km

RACE WEATHER: Dry/dark (track 26–29°C, air 22–24°C)

BAHRAIN INTERNATIONAL CIRCUIT, SAKHIR

Circuit: 3.363 miles/5.412km, 57 laps

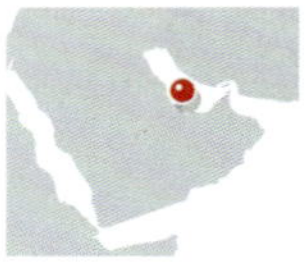

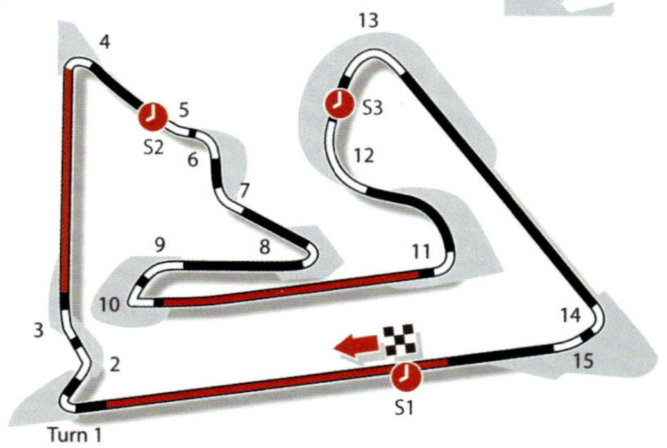

RACE – OFFICIAL CLASSIFICATION

Pos.	Driver	Nat.	No.	Entrant	Car/Engine	Laps	Time/Retirement	Speed (mph/km/h)	Gap to winner	Fastest race lap	
1	**Charles Leclerc**	MC	16	Scuderia Ferrari	Ferrari F1-75-066/7 V6	57	1h 37m 33.584s	117.792/189.568		1m 34.570s	51
2	**Carlos Sainz**	E	55	Scuderia Ferrari	Ferrari F1-75-066/7 V6	57	1h 37m 39.182s	117.680/189.387	5.598s	1m 35.740s	52
3	**Lewis Hamilton**	GB	44	Mercedes-AMG Petronas F1 Team	Mercedes-AMG F1 W13-M13 E Perf. V6	57	1h 37m 43.259s	117.598/189.255	9.675s	1m 36.228s	53
4	**George Russell**	GB	63	Mercedes-AMG Petronas F1 Team	Mercedes-AMG F1 W13-M13 E Perf. V6	57	1h 37m 44.795s	117.567/189.206	11.211s	1m 36.302s	56
5	**Kevin Magnussen**	DK	20	Haas F1 Team	Haas VF-22-Ferrari 066/7 V6	57	1h 37m 48.338s	117.496/189.092	14.754s	1m 36.623s	53
6	**Valtteri Bottas**	FIN	77	Alfa Romeo F1 Team ORLEN	Alfa Romeo C42-Ferrari 066/7 V6	57	1h 37m 49.703s	117.469/189.048	16.119s	1m 36.599s	53
7	**Esteban Ocon**	F	31	BWT Alpine F1 Team	Alpine A522-Renault E-Tech RE22 V6	57	1h 37m 53.007s *	117.402/188.941	19.423s	1m 37.110s	53
8	**Yuki Tsunoda**	J	22	Scuderia AlphaTauri	AlphaTauri AT03-RBPTH001 V6	57	1h 37m 53.970s	117.383/188.910	20.386s	1m 37.104s	53
9	**Fernando Alonso**	E	14	BWT Alpine F1 Team	Alpine A522-Renault E-Tech RE22 V6	57	1h 37m 55.974s	117.343/188.846	22.390s	1m 36.733s	44
10	**Zhou Guanyu**	CHN	24	Alfa Romeo F1 Team ORLEN	Alfa Romeo C42-Ferrari 066/7 V6	57	1h 37m 56.648s	117.330/188.824	23.064s	1m 36.685s	39
11	Mick Schumacher	D	47	Haas F1 Team	Haas VF-22-Ferrari 066/7 V6	57	1h 38m 06.158s	117.140/188.519	32.574s	1m 36.956s	37
12	Lance Stroll	CDN	18	Aston Martin Aramco Cognizant F1 Team	Aston Martin AMR22-Mercedes F1 M13 E Perf. V6	57	1h 38m 19.457s	116.876/188.094	45.873s	1m 37.146s	49
13	Alexander Albon	T	23	Williams Racing	Williams FW44-Mercedes F1 M13 E Perf. V6	57	1h 38m 27.516s	116.717/187.838	53.932s	1m 37.355s	50
14	Daniel Ricciardo	AUS	3	McLaren F1 Team	McLaren MCL36-Mercedes F1 M13 E Perf. V6	57	1h 38m 28.559s	116.696/187.804	54.975s	1m 37.261s	50
15	Lando Norris	GB	4	McLaren F1 Team	McLaren MCL36-Mercedes F1 M13 E Perf. V6	57	1h 38m 29.919s	116.669/187.761	56.335s	1m 36.988s	51
16	Nicholas Latifi	CDN	6	Williams Racing	Williams FW44-Mercedes F1 M13 E Perf. V6	57	1h 38m 35.379s	116.562/187.588	1m 01.795s	1m 38.251s	51
17	Nico Hülkenberg	D	27	Aston Martin Aramco Cognizant F1 Team	Aston Martin AMR22-Mercedes F1 M13 E Perf. V6	57	1h 38m 37.413s	116.521/187.523	1m 03.829s	1m 38.201s	49
18	Sergio Pérez	MEX	11	Oracle Red Bull Racing	Red Bull RB18-RBPTH001 V6	56	*fuel system*		1 lap	1m 36.089s	52
19	Max Verstappen	NL	1	Oracle Red Bull Racing	Red Bull RB18-RBPTH001 V6	54	*fuel system*		3 laps	1m 35.440s	51
	Pierre Gasly	F	10	Scuderia AlphaTauri	AlphaTauri AT03-RBPTH001 V6	44	*power unit*			1m 37.324s	34

* Ocon: 5s time penalty for causing a collision with Schumacher (served at pit stop).

DHL Fastest race lap (scores 1 point): Charles Leclerc on lap 51, 1m 34.570s, 128.014mph/206.018km/h.

Lap record: Michael Schumacher (Ferrari F2004 V10), 1m 30.252s, 134.263mph/216.074km/h (2004, 3.366-mile/5.417km circuit).

Lap record (current configuration): Pedro de la Rosa (McLaren MP4-20-Mercedes V10), 1m 31.447s, 132.386mph/213.054km/h (2005).

19 · STROLL · Aston Martin

17 · HÜLKENBERG · Aston Martin

15 · ZHOU · Alfa Romeo

13 · NORRIS · McLaren

11 · OCON · Alpine

20 · LATIFI · Williams

18 · RICCIARDO · McLaren

16 · TSUNODA · AlphaTauri

14 · ALBON · Williams

12 · SCHUMACHER · Haas

Grid order	1	2	3	4	5	6	7	8	9	10	11	12	13	14	15	16	17	18	19	20	21	22	23	24
16 LECLERC	16	16	16	16	16	16	16	16	16	16	16	16	16	16	16	16	16	16	16	16	16	16	16	16
1 VERSTAPPEN	1	1	1	1	1	1	1	1	1	1	1	1	1	1	11	1	1	1	1	1	1	1	1	1
55 SAINZ	55	55	55	55	55	55	55	55	55	55	55	55	55	11	63	55	55	55	55	55	55	55	55	55
11 PÉREZ	44	44	44	44	44	44	44	44	44	11	11	11	11	55	1	11	11	11	11	11	11	11	11	11
44 HAMILTON	20	20	11	11	11	11	11	11	11	44	44	63	63	63	55	44	44	44	44	44	44	44	44	44
77 BOTTAS	11	11	20	20	63	63	63	63	63	63	63	20	20	20	44	63	63	63	63	63	63	63	63	63
20 MAGNUSSEN	63	63	63	63	20	20	20	20	20	20	20	10	10	10	22	20	20	20	20	20	20	20	20	20
14 ALONSO	10	10	10	10	10	10	10	10	10	10	10	31	31	31	24	10	10	10	10	10	10	10	10	10
63 RUSSELL	14	14	14	14	14	14	14	31	31	31	31	22	22	22	20	14	14	14	14	14	14	14	14	14
10 GASLY	31	31	31	31	31	31	31	14	14	14	22	77	77	44	18	18	18	31	31	31	31	31	31	31
31 OCON	23	23	23	23	22	22	22	22	22	22	14	24	44	77	14	31	31	22	22	22	22	22	22	22
47 SCHUMACHER	22	22	22	22	23	23	23	77	77	77	77	44	24	24	10	27	22	18	77	77	77	77	77	77
4 NORRIS	47	47	47	47	47	77	77	23	23	24	24	23	18	18	27	4	77	77	24	24	24	24	24	24
23 ALBON	77	77	77	77	77	47	24	24	24	23	23	18	23	14	4	22	4	4	47	47	47	47	47	47
24 ZHOU	27	27	27	27	24	24	47	47	47	18	18	27	27	27	3	3	27	24	4	4	4	23	23	23
22 TSUNODA	4	18	18	24	27	27	27	27	18	47	47	4	4	4	31	77	24	47	23	23	23	4	4	18
27 HÜLKENBERG	18	4	24	18	18	18	18	18	27	27	27	47	14	3	77	47	47	27	27	6	18	18	18	4
3 RICCIARDO	6	24	4	4	4	4	4	4	4	4	4	3	3	6	47	24	3	23	6	18	6	6	6	6
18 STROLL	24	6	6	6	6	3	6	6	6	6	6	6	6	47	23	23	23	6	18	3	3	3	3	3
6 LATIFI	3	3	3	3	3	6	3	3	3	3	3	14	47	23	6	6	6	3	3	27	27	27	27	27

Grid order	25	26	27	28	29	30	31	32	33	34	35	36	37	38	39	40	41	42	43	44	45	46	47
16 LECLERC	16	16	16	16	16	16	16	55	55	16	16	16	16	16	16	16	16	16	16	16	16	16	16
1 VERSTAPPEN	1	1	1	1	1	1	55	11	11	1	1	1	1	1	1	1	1	1	1	55	1	1	1
55 SAINZ	55	55	55	55	55	55	11	16	16	55	55	55	55	55	55	55	55	55	55	1	55	55	55
11 PÉREZ	11	11	11	11	11	11	1	1	1	11	11	11	11	11	11	11	11	11	11	44	11	11	11
44 HAMILTON	44	44	44	63	63	63	63	63	63	44	44	44	44	44	44	44	44	44	44	11	63	44	44
77 BOTTAS	63	63	63	20	20	20	20	20	44	20	63	63	63	63	63	63	63	63	63	63	44	63	63
20 MAGNUSSEN	20	20	20	10	10	10	44	44	20	63	77	77	20	20	20	20	20	20	20	20	20	20	20
14 ALONSO	10	10	10	44	44	44	10	10	77	77	24	24	10	10	10	10	10	10	10	10	77	77	77
63 RUSSELL	31	31	31	31	31	31	77	77	24	24	10	20	24	31	31	31	31	31	31	77	24	31	31
10 GASLY	14	22	22	22	77	77	24	24	10	10	20	10	14	14	14	22	22	22	22	22	31	47	47
31 OCON	22	77	77	77	22	24	14	14	14	14	14	14	31	22	22	14	14	77	77	24	47	22	22
47 SCHUMACHER	77	24	24	24	24	14	47	31	31	31	31	31	22	77	77	77	77	14	24	31	22	14	14
4 NORRIS	24	47	47	47	47	47	31	47	22	22	22	22	77	24	24	24	24	24	47	47	14	24	24
23 ALBON	47	14	14	14	14	22	22	22	47	47	47	18	18	18	47	47	47	47	14	14	18	23	18
24 ZHOU	23	23	18	18	18	18	18	18	18	18	18	47	47	47	4	4	18	18	18	18	23	18	23
22 TSUNODA	18	18	23	23	23	23	23	23	23	23	23	4	4	4	18	18	4	23	23	23	4	3	3
27 HÜLKENBERG	6	6	6	3	3	3	3	3	3	4	4	27	27	23	23	23	23	3	3	3	6	4	4
3 RICCIARDO	3	3	3	6	6	6	6	27	27	27	27	23	23	3	3	3	3	6	4	4	3	6	6
18 STROLL	27	27	27	27	27	27	27	4	4	3	3	3	3	6	6	6	6	4	6	6	27	27	27
6 LATIFI	4	4	4	4	4	4	4	6	6	6	6	6	6	27	27	27	27	27	27	27			
																						SC	SC

TIME SHEETS

PRACTICE 1 (FRIDAY)

Weather: Dry/sunny

Temperatures: track 32-36°C, air 19-20°C

Pos.	Driver	Laps	Time
1	Pierre Gasly	23	1m 34.193s
2	Charles Leclerc	22	1m 34.557s
3	Carlos Sainz	23	1m 34.611s
4	George Russell	23	1m 34.629s
5	Max Verstappen	22	1m 34.742s
6	Lance Stroll	22	1m 34.814s
7	Lewis Hamilton	17	1m 34.943s
8	Fernando Alonso	14	1m 35.000s
9	Yuki Tsunoda	20	1m 35.028s
10	Sergio Pérez	23	1m 35.050s
11	Zhou Guanyu	20	1m 35.053s
12	Esteban Ocon	15	1m 35.151s
13	Nicholas Latifi	15	1m 35.644s
14	Nico Hülkenberg	23	1m 35.815s
15	Alexander Albon	17	1m 35.923s
16	Lando Norris	22	1m 36.304s
17	Daniel Ricciardo	20	1m 36.402s
18	Mick Schumacher	23	1m 36.536s
19	Kevin Magnussen	21	1m 36.804s
20	Valtteri Bottas	2	no time

PRACTICE 2 (FRIDAY)

Weather: Dry/dark

Temperatures: track 22-24°C, air 17-18°C

Pos.	Driver	Laps	Time
1	Max Verstappen	20	1m 31.936s
2	Charles Leclerc	20	1m 32.023s
3	Carlos Sainz	22	1m 32.520s
4	George Russell	25	1m 32.529s
5	Fernando Alonso	24	1m 32.877s
6	Valtteri Bottas	30	1m 32.951s
7	Sergio Pérez	20	1m 32.958s
8	Mick Schumacher	24	1m 33.085s
9	Lewis Hamilton	23	1m 33.144s
10	Kevin Magnussen	23	1m 33.183s
11	Lando Norris	27	1m 33.280s
12	Esteban Ocon	25	1m 33.360s
13	Pierre Gasly	24	1m 33.621s
14	Yuki Tsunoda	26	1m 33.789s
15	Zhou Guanyu	27	1m 33.953s
16	Lance Stroll	25	1m 33.958s
17	Nico Hülkenberg	28	1m 34.061s
18	Daniel Ricciardo	12	1m 34.166s
19	Nicholas Latifi	28	1m 34.486s
20	Alexander Albon	22	1m 34.735s

PRACTICE 3 (SATURDAY)

Weather: Dry/sunny

Temperatures: track 34-38°C, air 22°C

Pos.	Driver	Laps	Time
1	Max Verstappen	15	1m 32.544s
2	Charles Leclerc	16	1m 32.640s
3	Sergio Pérez	20	1m 32.791s
4	George Russell	19	1m 32.935s
5	Carlos Sainz	20	1m 33.053s
6	Lewis Hamilton	15	1m 33.121s
7	Kevin Magnussen	15	1m 33.437s
8	Valtteri Bottas	21	1m 33.733s
9	Zhou Guanyu	18	1m 33.880s
10	Lance Stroll	14	1m 33.920s
11	Lando Norris	18	1m 33.955s
12	Nico Hülkenberg	18	1m 33.971s
13	Pierre Gasly	18	1m 34.176s
14	Mick Schumacher	17	1m 34.295s
15	Daniel Ricciardo	20	1m 34.378s
16	Fernando Alonso	15	1m 34.628s
17	Alexander Albon	15	1m 34.868s
18	Esteban Ocon	16	1m 34.957s
19	Nicholas Latifi	14	1m 35.667s
-	Yuki Tsunoda	-	-

QUALIFYING (SATURDAY)

Weather: Dry/dark Temperatures: track 24-26°C, air 19°C

Pos.	Driver	First	Second	Third	Qualifying Tyre
1	Charles Leclerc	1m 31.471s	1m 30.932s	1m 30.558s	Soft (n)
2	Max Verstappen	1m 31.785s	1m 30.757s	1m 30.681s	Soft (n)
3	Carlos Sainz	1m 31.567s	1m 30.787s	1m 30.687s	Soft (n)
4	Sergio Pérez	1m 32.311s	1m 31.008s	1m 30.921s	Soft (n)
5	Lewis Hamilton	1m 32.285s	1m 31.048s	1m 31.238s	Soft (n)
6	Valtteri Bottas	1m 31.919s	1m 31.717s	1m 31.560s	Soft (n)
7	Kevin Magnussen	1m 31.955s	1m 31.461s	1m 31.808s	Soft (n)
8	Fernando Alonso	1m 32.346s	1m 31.621s	1m 32.195s	Soft (n)
9	George Russell	1m 32.269s	1m 31.252s	1m 32.216s	Soft (n)
10	Pierre Gasly	1m 32.096s	1m 31.635s	1m 32.338s	Soft (n)
11	Esteban Ocon	1m 32.041s	1m 31.782s		
12	Mick Schumacher	1m 32.380s	1m 31.998s		
13	Lando Norris	1m 32.239s	1m 32.008s		
14	Alexander Albon	1m 32.726s	1m 32.664s		
15	Zhou Guanyu	1m 32.493s	1m 33.543s		
16	Yuki Tsunoda	1m 32.750s			
17	Nico Hülkenberg	1m 32.777s			
18	Daniel Ricciardo	1m 32.945s			
19	Lance Stroll	1m 33.032s			
20	Nicholas Latifi	1m 33.634s			

QUALIFYING: head to head

Hamilton	1	0	Russell
Verstappen	1	0	Pérez
Ricciardo	0	1	Norris
Leclerc	1	0	Sainz
Gasly	1	0	Tsunoda
Hülkenberg	1	0	Stroll
Alonso	1	0	Ocon
Bottas	1	0	Zhou
Albon	1	0	Latifi
Magnussen	1	0	Schumacher

Pirelli

FOR THE RECORD

1st GRAND PRIX & 1st POINT: Zhou Guanyu , (the first Chinese driver to start an F1 GP).

10th POLE POSITION: Charles Leclerc

250th WORLD CHAMPIONSHIP GP START: Mercedes

30th FRONT ROW: Max Verstappen

Alfa Romeo ORLEN

DID YOU KNOW?

Verstappen was the first driver to use No.1 on his car since Vettel in 2014.

Red Bull were only using one digit for their drivers' car numbers (1 and 11). Previous occasions were at Red Bull, 2016–18 (3 and 33) and McLaren at the 2017 Monaco GP (2 and 22).

POINTS

DRIVERS

1	Charles Leclerc	26
2	Carlos Sainz	18
3	Lewis Hamilton	15
4	George Russell	12
5	Kevin Magnussen	10
6	Valtteri Bottas	8
7	Esteban Ocon	6
8	Yuki Tsunoda	4
9	Fernando Alonso	2
10	Zhou Guanyu	1

CONSTRUCTORS

1	Ferrari	44
2	Mercedes	27
3	Haas	10
4	Alfa Romeo	9
5	Alpine	8
6	AlphaTauri	4

9 · RUSSELL · Mercedes

7 · MAGNUSSEN · Haas

5 · HAMILTON · Mercedes

3 · SAINZ · Ferrari

1 · LECLERC · Ferrari

10 · GASLY · AlphaTauri

8 · ALONSO · Alpine

6 · BOTTAS · Alfa Romeo

4 · PÉREZ · Red Bull

2 · VERSTAPPEN · Red Bull

48	49	50	51	52	53	54	55	56	57	
16	16	16	16	16	16	16	16	16	16	1
1	1	1	1	1	1	55	55	55	55	2
55	55	55	55	55	55	11	11	11	44	3
11	11	11	11	11	11	44	44	44	63	4
44	44	44	44	44	44	63	63	63	20	5
63	63	63	63	63	63	20	20	20	77	6
20	20	20	20	20	20	77	77	77	31	7
77	77	77	77	77	77	31	31	31	22	8
31	31	31	31	31	31	22	22	22	14	9
47	47	47	22	22	22	14	14	14	24	10
22	22	22	14	14	14	24	24	24	47	
14	14	14	47	24	24	47	47	47	18	
24	24	24	24	47	47	1	18	18	23	
18	18	18	18	18	18	18	23	23	3	
23	23	23	23	23	23	23	3	3	4	
3	3	3	3	3	3	3	4	4	6	
4	4	4	4	4	4	4	6	6	27	
6	6	6	6	6	6	6	27	27		
27	27	27	27	27	27	27				
SC	SC	SC								

33 = Pit stop *27 = One lap or more behind*

SC Safety car deployed on laps shown

RACE TYRE STRATEGIES

PIRELLI

	Driver	Race Stint 1	Race Stint 2	Race Stint 3	Race Stint 4
1	Leclerc	Soft (n): 1-15	Soft (u): 16-31	Medium (n): 32-46	Soft (u): 47-57
2	Sainz	Soft (u): 1-14	Soft (n): 15-33	Medium (n): 34-44	Soft (u): 45-57
3	Hamilton	Soft (u): 1-11	Hard (u): 12-27	Medium (n): 28-45	Soft (u): 46-57
4	Russell	Soft (u): 1-15	Hard (u): 16-33	Medium (n): 34-45	Soft (u): 46-57
5	Magnussen	Soft (n): 1-14	Soft (u): 15-34	Medium (n): 35-46	Soft (u): 47-57
6	Bottas	Soft (u): 1-14	Medium (n): 15-36	Medium (n): 37-45	Soft (u): 46-57
7	Ocon	Soft (n): 1-14	Medium (n): 15-30	Hard (n): 31-43	Soft (u): 44-57
8	Tsunoda	Soft (u): 1-15	Medium (n): 16-29	Soft (n): 30-44	Soft (u): 45-57
9	Alonso	Soft (u): 1-14	Medium (n): 15-25	Hard (n): 26-42	Soft (n): 43-57
10	Zhou	Soft (u): 1-15	Medium (n): 16-37	Medium (n): 38-45	Soft (u): 46-57
11	Schumacher	Soft (n): 1-12	Medium (n): 13-35	Soft (u): 36-57	
12	Stroll	Soft (n): 1-18	Soft (n): 19-38	Medium (n): 39-45	Soft (n): 46-57
13	Albon	Soft (n): 1-19	Medium (n): 20-35	Medium (u): 36-46	Soft (u): 47-57
14	Ricciardo	Medium (n): 1-17	Soft (n): 18-33	Hard (n): 34-44	Soft (n): 45-57
15	Norris	Medium (n): 1-24	Hard (n): 25-41	Soft (n): 42-45	Soft (n): 46-57
16	Latifi	Soft (n): 1-14	Soft (n): 15-32	Medium (n): 33-45	Soft (n): 46-57
17	Hülkenberg	Soft (n): 1-19	Soft (n): 20-37	Medium (n): 38-44	Soft (n): 45-57
18	Pérez	Soft (u): 1-15	Medium (n): 16-33	Soft (u): 34-43	Soft (u): 44-56 (dnf)
19	Verstappen	Soft (u): 1-14	Soft (n): 15-30	Medium (n): 31-43	Soft (u): 44-54 (dnf)
	Gasly	**Soft (u): 1-14**	Medium (n): 15-32	Hard (n): 33-44 **(dnf)**	

The tyre regulations stipulate that at least two of three dry tyre specifications must be used during a dry race.

Selected compounds for Sakhir: Red = Soft (C3); Yellow = Medium (C2); White = Hard (C1). (n) new (u) used

Scuderia Ferrari

Insets: From the Paddock Club to photographers at sunset and glistening trophies, colour abounds.
Photos: XPB Images

Main photo: A flurry of tyre smoke as the late-braking Max Verstappen takes the lead from Charles Leclerc.
Photo: Red Bull Content Pool/Getty Images

FIA FORMULA 1 WORLD CHAMPIONSHIP · ROUND 2

SAUDI ARABIAN GRAND PRIX

JEDDAH CIRCUIT

AT Jeddah Corniche three short months previously, the racing world, Fernando Alonso in particular, had marvelled at Max Verstappen's speed and commitment over nine-tenths of a very special qualifying lap before he clouted the wall at the final corner.

That final turn had been widened by a metre-and-a-half, and the walls moved back in the high-speed sweepers at a track that combines blind corners and a 157mph average speed. The intention had been to improve sightlines, but nobody thought it made much difference. Ultimately, it was still a big-balls lap that demanded total commitment. Thus when Sergio Pérez managed to wrest his first F1 pole from Charles Leclerc, he was absolutely thrilled. "I can do 1,000 laps and not beat that!" he beamed.

His team principal was delighted, too. "To put in that lap, at a track that's so fast and dangerous, was phenomenal," Christian Horner enthused. "This car seems more suited to Checo's style, not quite so quirky as last year's. But to deliver that, at this circuit, will do his confidence a lot of good."

Leclerc had failed in his quest for a second successive 2022 pole by just 0.02s, but, being the sportsman he is, he was highly appreciative of Pérez's efforts: "That was a good lap from Sergio. My first Q3 lap felt good and I was happy with it, so just went for it on the second lap and more or less put everything together. I don't think I left anything behind."

Team-mate Carlos Sainz, having topped Q1 and Q2, was a couple of tenths adrift in the final analysis, but six-hundredths clear of Verstappen's Red Bull.

"Used softs were actually giving me a better feeling," Sainz said. "I had a new set for the last Q3 run and I just didn't seem to have any rear grip."

Given that Ferrari's F1-75 was showing early indications of being a championship challenger, Maranello's intra-team competition was displaying additional spice.

Verstappen was a nailed-on pole favourite, so fourth place, behind both Ferraris and his team-mate, was unexpected. "After Q1 and Q2, it looked okay, and with the ambient going down, you should improve, but I didn't find as much as I thought. I did something different with the tyre warm-up in Q3, and it didn't work," he explained.

Alpine was in good shape in Saudi, with Esteban Ocon – so close to a podium three months earlier – a fine fifth on the grid, with Fernando Alonso seventh, just 0.08s slower. They were the only team other than Ferrari and Red Bull to have two cars in Q3. Ocon survived a big snap-oversteer moment in the middle of Turns 9–10, which could have ended in the kind of accident that befell poor Mick Schumacher.

The Haas driver, pushing hard to match new team-mate Kevin Magnussen, red-flagged Q2 after a big impact that totally destroyed the Haas. After checks at the circuit's medical facility and a nearby hospital, Mick was deemed okay, but he would take no further part in the weekend.

"Hard-core bouncing?" the Mercedes pit wall crew asked George Russell early in Friday's first free practice session.

"Yes," was the one-word response.

Mercedes was experiencing the same tricky situation that had afflicted the team in pre-season testing and the Bahrain season-opener, and Russell did a very solid job to split the Alpines and qualify sixth.

"As a team, not a good day for us," he grimaced. "We just don't have a handle on the car and we're fighting a very small set-up window. We managed to get inside it, but Lewis didn't."

That was something of an understatement. Hamilton's predicament was so bad that when Lance Stroll found a few hundredths at the end of Q1, it was sufficient to bounce out the seven-time champion!

In trying to solve the porpoising conundrum, Hamilton had gone a bit more extreme on set-up and found himself lacking any rear grip at a track with close walls that demanded full commitment. If the car doesn't stick, a driver can't give that commitment, and Lewis's plight was that simple.

Valtteri Bottas continued Alfa Romeo's impressive start to the new season with eighth place, just 0.08s shy of the man who had taken his place at Mercedes.

An impressive reflection of F1's current strength in depth was the presence of seven different makes of car in the top ten Saudi qualifiers, right after such swingeing regulation changes. As well as the Red Bull, Ferrari and Alpine pairs, there was Mercedes, Alfa, AlphaTauri (for whom Pierre Gasly had qualified ninth) and Haas, with Kevin Magnussen completing the top ten.

After his 11th-hour return to the US team, the Dane was honest enough to admit that, actually, he thought he had a potential top-six car. "I think I was half a second behind the car because my neck was giving out, but that will improve soon," he explained.

McLaren made a more optimistic showing than in Bahrain, with Lando Norris and Daniel Ricciardo qualifying 11th and 12th, until the Aussie was demoted three grid slots for impeding Lance Stroll. Zhou Guanyu lined up 13th with the second Alfa, ahead of the non-starting Schumacher and Stroll's Aston Martin. Sebastian Vettel missed his second successive race due to Covid, with Nico Hülkenberg substituting again.

'The Hulk' joined Hamilton, Williams drivers Alexander Albon and Nicholas Latifi, and AlphaTauri's Yuki Tsunoda (whose car ground to an early halt with a hydraulic issue) as Q1 eliminees.

Left: A brilliant lap brought a first pole position for Sergio Pérez.
Photo: Red Bull Content Pool/Getty Images

Top left: The sportsmanlike Charles Leclerc had no answer to the Mexican's speed in qualifying.
Photo: Scuderia Ferrari

Below left: Toto Wolff and Mercedes found themselves trapped in a vicious set-up circle.
Photo: Mercedes-AMG Petronas F1 Team

Far left: The high-speed track was challenging, with concrete walls waiting for the tiniest of errors.
Aston Martin Aramco Cognizant F1 Team

Below: Techpro barriers on specific corners brought some level of protection for the likes of Carlos Sainz.
Photo: Scuderia Ferrari

Above: Starting from pole position, Sergio Pérez led the race's early stages before losing out after pitting before a safety car was deployed. The Mexican trailed Verstappen and the two Ferraris to finish fourth.
Photo: Red Bull Content Pool/Getty Images

Right: In deference to title sponsor BWT, Alpine ran both of their cars in the all-pink livery for the second of two races.
Photo: Alpine F1 Team

RACE-DAY in Jeddah, on 27th March, was 11 years to the day since Sergio Pérez had made his GP debut for Sauber in the Australian GP, becoming the first Mexican in F1 since Héctor Rebaque in the 1981 Caesar's Palace GP.

Since then, Pérez had made 215 starts – and taken part in 217 qualifying sessions – before finally becoming the first Mexican driver to take an F1 pole position. It was only the second time that he had managed to outqualify Max Verstappen, but when the lights went out, he looked as though he'd been doing it every week, promptly moving across to cover off Charles Leclerc's Ferrari on the short 230m run down to Jeddah's Turn One.

Behind, Verstappen managed to outfumble Carlos Sainz, while Esteban Ocon kept hold of his fifth starting slot, ahead of George Russell and Fernando Alonso. Valtteri Bottas was next with the first Alfa Romeo, but team-mate Zhou Guanyu dropped to the back when he mistakenly hit the anti-stall button, negating all the good work he had done in narrowly missing out on Q3. Kevin Magnussen ran ninth after bravely pulling off an outside pass of Pierre Gasly's AlphaTauri.

On lap four, with DRS now in play, Russell managed to put the first Mercedes into fifth, ahead of Ocon, with team-mate Lewis Hamilton still languishing down in 14th after his problematic qualifying hour.

A spiky little tussle was developing between the Alpines, with Ocon rather rudely moving left a tad late as Alonso tried to demote him across the start/finish line on the fifth lap. The Spaniard got it done next time around, then ran Esteban wide on exit as payback. Ocon was not done, though, and ran too deep into T1 on the following lap trying to retake the place. He did so, but, having run off the track, was obliged to hand it back, with Bottas now becoming interested as well!

At the front, Pérez was doing a fine job, opening a 2s advantage over Leclerc's Ferrari. With the whole field having started on the medium-compound Pirellis, save for the McLaren pair (on hards), it looked as though Ferrari was going to launch an undercut attempt when they radioed a message to Leclerc: "Box to overtake."

The Ferrari pit crew emerged, as did Red Bull's, but they had been sold a dummy, as Charles carried on while Sergio appeared in the pit lane. The likelihood was that Leclerc had been instructed to do the opposite of Pérez, so carried on when the Red Bull pitted to cover him. The Mexican rejoined just behind Russell's Mercedes. It was at this point that the racing gods dealt him a cruel blow.

Nicholas Latifi, who had found the Williams a handful in qualifying and crashed, had brought out a yellow in sector three when he lost it again. That soon became a virtual, then a full safety car while the Canadian's car was retrieved, giving all those behind Pérez a cheap stop.

Leclerc *et al* dived in next time around, Charles becoming the new race leader as the field duly lined up behind the safety car. It was a close call between Sainz, coming out of the pits after his stop, and Pérez, coming through the Turn One complex. The Spaniard was soon on the radio, complaining that he'd reached the safety car line first and therefore should be third, Pérez having caused him to lift as he chopped across the Red Bull's bows. It looked a fairly open-and-shut case, but Race Control, rather unfathomably, did not address it until after the restart.

The order behind Bernd Maylander's safety car was

Leclerc, Verstappen, Pérez, Sainz, Russell, Magnussen, Hamilton, Alonso, Hülkenberg, Bottas, Ocon, Ricciardo, Norris, Gasly, Zhou, Stroll and Albon.

As the safety car lights went off and it prepared to pull in, Verstappen began jinking around for the second successive race, at times almost alongside Leclerc's Ferrari. A regulation clarification would soon put a stop to that in future. The idea, presumably, was to crowd Leclerc and prevent him from using the full width of the track in the hope of slowing his exit on to the main straight, facilitating a tow. Charles coped with it, though, bolted decisively, went left, then right to break the tow and managed to maintain his lead into Turn One.

Behind, the frustrated Pérez, informed by his team that Sainz had beaten him to the safety car line when emerging from the pits, pulled over and let the Ferrari into third place. In their wake behind Russell, Hamilton was trying to get the second Mercedes up into sixth, ahead of Magnussen's Haas, but the Dane was boxing clever. Approaching the final corner, he lifted off to make sure that the Mercedes was ahead crossing the DRS detection line and then passed it again on the front straight.

Next time around, half-distance in the 50-lap race, Hamilton ensured it did not happen again, got the benefit of DRS this time and outbraked the Haas into Turn One.

With 14 laps remaining, Alonso's feisty drive came to a premature end when he suddenly felt a loss of power accompanied by a 'cool the car' message on the steering wheel. He was left with no option but to trundle slowly around to the pits, not something particularly comfortable amid the fast sweeps and blind corners at Jeddah Corniche.

Almost simultaneously, Daniel Ricciardo's McLaren began crawling slowly as well, finally coming to a halt with no drive just before the pit-lane entry. Bottas was into the pit lane to retire as well, his engine temperatures having climbed alarmingly.

"A bit frustrating because we were looking good for P6 at least," said the Finn, who had been re-energised by his start to the season at Alfa Romeo.

With a yellow in sector three, Haas called in Magnussen to jettison his hard tyres and bolt on a set of mediums, which appeared to be a good call when Race Control closed the pit lane shortly afterwards and the race went to a VSC, the Dane getting a cheap stop.

Hamilton, meanwhile, radioed in, "The car is slowing," and was told to "Box, box," but just too late, and he was forced to drive past the now closed pit-lane entry. Seemingly okay again, however, he would have to wait until the race went green once more to make his tyre stop from sixth.

When racing was resumed, there were nine laps remaining. Leclerc led by just over a second from Verstappen. Sainz, in the second Ferrari, was 8.5s behind the lead Red Bull with 2.5s in hand over Pérez in the second. Russell, 'best of the rest' in the non-Ferrari/Red Bull race, was a further 12s in arrears. Ocon's Alpine ran sixth, ahead of Norris's McLaren and Gasly's AlphaTauri. Hamilton pitted out behind a gaggle comprising Stroll, Albon and Magnussen, now in 12th place.

On lap 42 of the 50, suddenly Verstappen was all over Leclerc, the Red Bull seemingly possessing more grip. The Monégasque had been quicker through the first sector of the lap all race, but the straight-line speed advantage of the Red Bull was giving it the edge in sectors two and three. Sure enough, Verstappen had sufficient speed with DRS to take the race lead around the outside of the Ferrari on the run down to the final corner, before flicking back across to protect the inside.

But Leclerc, now with DRS, countered down the main straight and, despite running a little deep into Turn One, managed to retake the lead.

Next time around, it was a similar scenario, except that this time neither man wanted to lead across the DRS detection line into the final corner, both locking up in their endeavours not to do so. Verstappen won out, but had locked up more heavily. Leclerc, meanwhile, got off the brakes, maximised his line through the last corner and got a sufficiently better exit to be able to protect himself down into Turn One.

"He crossed the line again!" Verstappen snitched on the radio to draw the stewards' attention to Leclerc crossing the pit-lane entry line – illegal unless a driver is pitting – to reduce the length of the main straight as much as possible.

Despite Leclerc's best efforts, when Verstappen hung back into the final turn and picked up the DRS this time, he was able to drive by the Ferrari on the main straight at the

Right: Third-placed Carlos Sainz surveys the rear of Verstappen's race-winning Red Bull.
Photo: Peter Nygaard/GP Photo

Below: George Russell hustled his Mercedes to fifth.
Photo: Mercedes-AMG Petronas F1 Team

Bottom right: Not for the first time in the Middle East, Nicholas Latifi's accident changed the complexion of the race.
Photo: XPB Images

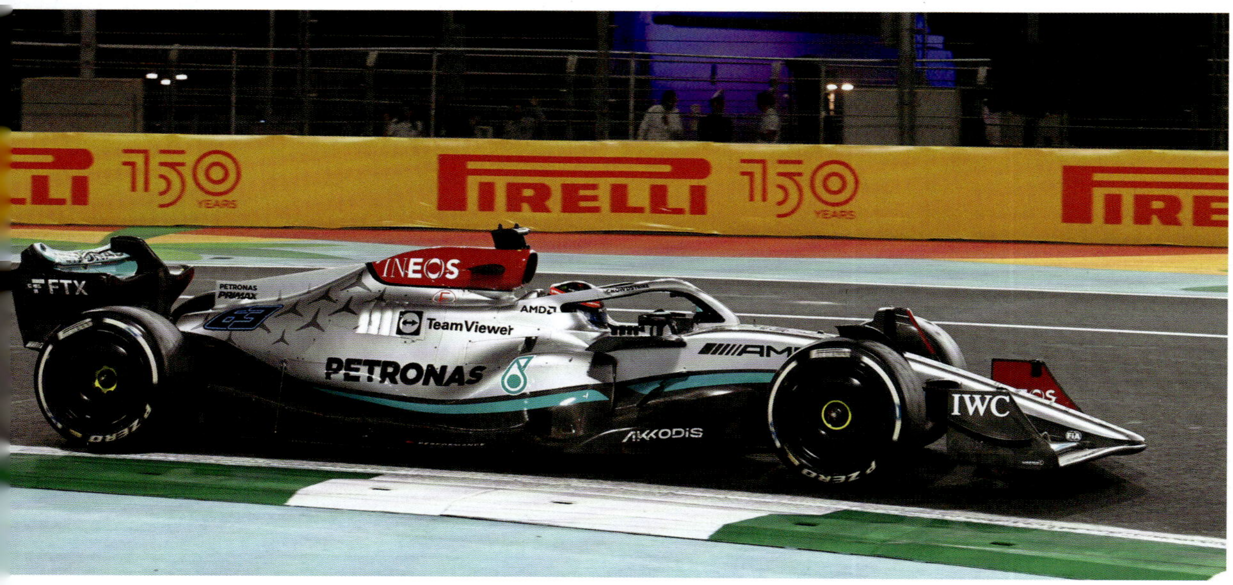

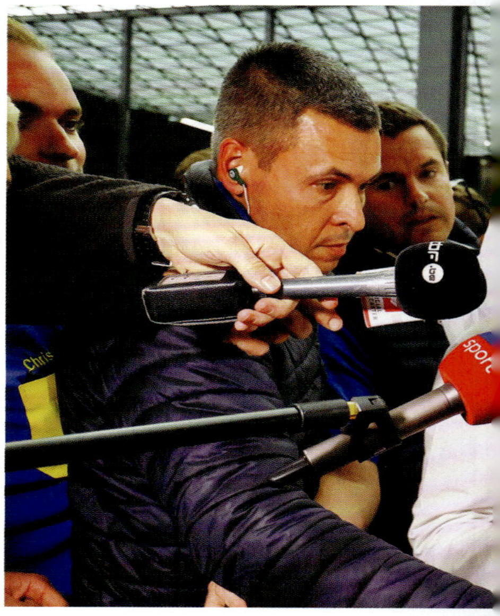

start of lap 46. Leclerc did his level best to stay with him and come back on the next lap, but the Red Bull's straight-line speed advantage proved decisive. Verstappen, giving it everything in an attempt to ensure that the Ferrari could not strike back, claimed the race's fastest lap in the process.

As they started the penultimate lap, a yellow flag in sector one, just where Leclerc would have attempted to repass, was a lucky break for Verstappen. It had been caused by contact between Lance Stroll and Alexander Albon when the Anglo-Thai had tried to go inside the Canadian, but run into the Aston Martin.

"The idiot just dive-bombed me," an unimpressed Stroll reported over the radio.

Starting the very last lap, Verstappen sounded rattled as Leclerc got close in sector one, where the yellow was. "How did he get so close?" Verstappen shouted. "That's so unfair!"

But the only realistic overtaking spot was on the run down to the final corner, with DRS. The Red Bull had enough straight-line speed to make it unfeasible for Leclerc to launch a bid down the inside, and it was a relieved Verstappen who booted the Red Bull out of the last turn and took the chequered flag. He was a couple of car lengths clear of the Ferrari, which reclaimed the additional point for fastest lap.

Around 10s in arrears, Sainz made it a Ferrari 1-3, ahead of the luckless Pérez. Some 22s behind him, Russell was rewarded with ten points for a fine drive to fifth. A similar distance behind the first Mercedes, Ocon, who had been cruelly robbed of a podium over the line by Bottas first time up in Jeddah, hung on this time to take his Alpine across the line just in front of Norris's McLaren. Gasly pipped Magnussen to eighth, with Hamilton tenth. It had been a long afternoon for a single point for the seven-time champion.

After the double DNF in the season-opener, the Red Bull pit wall crew was delighted. "What a great race!" beamed Christian Horner. "Thankfully, we just had enough to bring it home. Max drove a very patient race, looked after the tyres and then, after that last safety car, really went for it. But it was such bad luck for Checo. He'd done all the hard work at the beginning of the race, and then to have the safety car come out at the wrong time… you can't do anything about that. He'd driven brilliantly all weekend."

The winner had enjoyed himself, too – eventually. "It was a tricky one," Verstappen explained. "On the mediums, I didn't have enough front grip. I was understeering quite a bit and they opened up really quickly, so that was all about managing and not a lot of fun. Checo got unlucky with the safety car, but as soon as we put the hard tyre on, I had a much better feeling and could finally push a bit.

"Ferrari were extremely quick in the high-speed because of their wing level. With a VSC, you never quite know who is going to come off best with tyres cooling down, but it seemed like I had good pace afterwards. Charles played it smart, but I eventually passed him, and then it felt like four qualifying laps because he was constantly in my DRS trying to get back at me. We managed to stay on top, but it's super-close between the two of us. The battles have been really hard, but cool. We have a lot of respect for each other."

That was evident and good to see. What was also clear was that the 2022 regulations appeared to be working as intended and had spiced up the racing.

Tony Dodgins

Left: The drivers convened to discuss track safety issues.
Photo: Lukas Gorys

Below left: Mohammed Ben Sulayem and Stefano Domenicali meet the press to allay fears over the safety of F1 participants.
Photo: XPB Images

Below: Flames billow into the sky after a missile attack during practice for the 2022 Saudi Arabian Grand Prix at the Jeddah Corniche Circuit.
Photo: GP Photo/Peter Nygaard

VIEWPOINT
CASH AND CRASHES

THE discomfort many felt when Formula 1 attracted bad press by visiting Saudi Arabia was not helped – admittedly in a minor way compared to accusations of 'sports washing' – by pictures of substantial changes to the landscape at Spa-Francorchamps.

It was not so much that the classic track in Belgium would be celebrating its 97th birthday in 2022 and, therefore, was due for a facelift, but more the need to eliminate the hazard created by ever increasing speed over the blind brow at Eau Rouge. If that was rightly considered dangerous, then what about the track at Jeddah?

The reasons for major pieces of scene shifting at Spa were ridiculed in Jeddah by F1 being happy to send drivers into very fast, unsighted curves more numerous and hazardous than Eau Rouge. Moving the walls back a few centimetres in a couple of places at Jeddah was purely cosmetic. It led to easy editorial narrative suggesting that generous Saudi fees filling F1's Covid-depleted coffers had the side effect of making Liberty Media go blind in one eye.

The question of being in Jeddah at all took an even more serious turn on Friday, when a column of black smoke announced an attack on an oil refinery owned by Aramco, coincidentally a global partner in F1 and sponsor of the Aston Martin team. It gave ironic meaning to the 'No War' messages being carried on drivers' crash helmets following Russia's invasion of Ukraine. This was closer to home in every sense.

A lengthy drivers' meeting failed to reach a unanimous conclusion. It was only after considerable persuasion by team bosses and Liberty Media, backed by security assurances from the local authorities, that the drivers were persuaded to stay.

Mick Schumacher probably wished he'd gone home early when a small misjudgement while trying to get into Q3 for the first time led to a massive accident as his Haas destroyed itself against the ever present concrete. Yet another pause for thought, seemingly lost in the powerful backwash of a $55 million annual payout.

Maurice Hamilton

2

Official Timepiece

FORMULA 1 STC SAUDI ARABIAN GRAND PRIX 2022

JEDDAH 25–27 MARCH

RACE DISTANCE: 50 laps, 191.662 miles/308.450km

RACE WEATHER: Dry/dark (track 27–29°C, air 25°C)

JEDDAH CORNICHE CIRCUIT

Circuit: 3.836 miles/6.174km, 50 laps

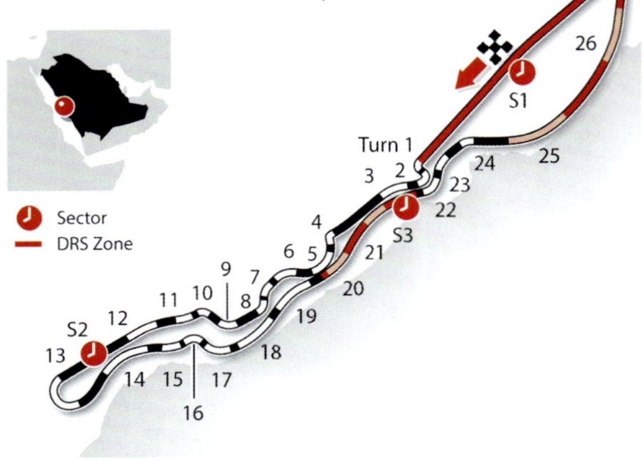

RACE – OFFICIAL CLASSIFICATION

Pos.	Driver	Nat.	No.	Entrant	Car/Engine	Laps	Time/Retirement	Speed (mph/km/h)	Gap to winner	Fastest race lap
1	**Max Verstappen**	NL	1	Oracle Red Bull Racing	Red Bull RB18-RBPTH001 V6	50	1h 24m 19.293s	136.379/219.481		1m 31.772s 50
2	**Charles Leclerc**	MC	16	Scuderia Ferrari	Ferrari F1-75-066/7 V6	50	1h 24m 19.842s	136.364/219.457	0.549s	1m 31.634s 48
3	**Carlos Sainz**	E	55	Scuderia Ferrari	Ferrari F1-75-066/7 V6	50	1h 24m 27.390s	136.161/219.130	8.097s	1m 31.905s 48
4	**Sergio Pérez**	MEX	11	Oracle Red Bull Racing	Red Bull RB18-RBPTH001 V6	50	1h 24m 30.093s	136.088/219.013	10.800s	1m 32.042s 46
5	**George Russell**	GB	63	Mercedes-AMG Petronas F1 Team	Mercedes-AMG F1 W13-M13 E Perf. V6	50	1h 24m 52.025s	135.502/218.070	32.732s	1m 32.821s 43
6	**Esteban Ocon**	F	31	BWT Alpine F1 Team	Alpine A522-Renault E-Tech RE22 V6	50	1h 25m 15.310s	134.885/217.077	56.017s	1m 33.103s 46
7	**Lando Norris**	GB	4	McLaren F1 Team	McLaren MCL36-Mercedes F1 M13 E Perf. V6	50	1h 25m 15.417s	134.883/217.073	56.124s	1m 32.753s 46
8	**Pierre Gasly**	F	10	Scuderia AlphaTauri	AlphaTauri AT03-RBPTH001 V6	50	1h 25m 22.239s	134.703/216.784	1m 02.946s	1m 33.468s 42
9	**Kevin Magnussen**	DK	20	Haas F1 Team	Haas VF-22-Ferrari 066/7 V6	50	1h 25m 23.601s	134.667/216.726	1m 04.308s	1m 32.779s 48
10	**Lewis Hamilton**	GB	44	Mercedes-AMG Petronas F1 Team	Mercedes-AMG F1 W13-M13 E Perf. V6	50	1h 25m 33.241s	134.414/216.319	1m 13.948s	1m 32.997s 47
11	Zhou Guanyu	CHN	24	Alfa Romeo F1 Team ORLEN	Alfa Romeo C42-Ferrari 066/7 V6	50	1h 25m 41.508s*	134.198/215.971	1m 22.215s	1m 33.924s 45
12	Nico Hülkenberg	D	27	Aston Martin Aramco Cognizant F1 Team	Aston Martin AMR22-Mercedes F1 M13 E Perf. V6	50	1h 25m 51.035s	133.950/215.572	1m 31.742s	1m 33.651s 47
13	Lance Stroll	CDN	18	Aston Martin Aramco Cognizant F1 Team	Aston Martin AMR22-Mercedes F1 M13 E Perf. V6	49			1 lap	1m 34.446s 46
14	Alexander Albon	T	23	Williams Racing	Williams FW44-Mercedes F1 M13 E Perf. V6	47	*accident*		3 laps	1m 34.368s 46
	Valtteri Bottas	FIN	77	Alfa Romeo F1 Team ORLEN	Alfa Romeo C42-Ferrari 066/7 V6	36	*overheating*			1m 33.979s 31
	Fernando Alonso	E	14	BWT Alpine F1 Team	Alpine A522-Renault E-Tech RE22 V6	35	*mechanical*			1m 33.831s 33
	Daniel Ricciardo	AUS	3	McLaren F1 Team	McLaren MCL36-Mercedes F1 M13 E Perf. V6	35	*mechanical*			1m 34.487s 34
	Nicholas Latifi	CDN	6	Williams Racing	Williams FW44-Mercedes F1 M13 E Perf. V6	14	*accident*			1m 37.530s 9
NS	Yuki Tsunoda	J	22	Scuderia AlphaTauri	AlphaTauri AT03-RBPTH001 V6		*transmission before the parade lap*			
NS	Mick Schumacher	D	47	Haas F1 Team	Haas VF-22-Ferrari 066/7 V6		*car damaged in qualifying*			

* Zhou: 5s time penalty for leaving the track and gaining an advantage; drive-through penalty for failing to serve earlier penalty during pit stop.

DHL Fastest race lap (scores 1 point): Charles Leclerc on lap 48, 1m 31.634s, 150.717mph/242.556km/h.

Lap record: Lewis Hamilton (Mercedes F1 W12 V6), 1m 30.734s, 152.212mph/244.962km/h (2021).

18 · LATIFI · Williams

16 · ALBON · Williams

14 · RICCIARDO · McLaren
3-place grid penalty for impeding Ocon in qualifying

12 · ZHOU · Alfa Romeo

19 · TSUNODA · AlphaTauri

17 · HÜLKENBERG · Aston Martin

15 · HAMILTON · Mercedes

13 · STROLL · Aston Martin

11 · NORRIS · McLaren

Grid order	1	2	3	4	5	6	7	8	9	10	11	12	13	14	15	16	17	18	19	20	21	22	23	24	25	26	27	28	29	30	31	32	33	34	35	36	37	38
11 PÉREZ	11	11	11	11	11	11	11	11	11	11	11	11	11	11	16	16	16	16	16	16	16	16	16	16	16	16	16	16	16	16	16	16	16	16	16	16	16	16
16 LECLERC	16	16	16	16	16	16	16	16	16	16	16	16	16	16	11	1	1	1	1	1	1	1	1	1	1	1	1	1	1	1	1	1	1	1	1	1	1	1
55 SAINZ	1	1	1	1	1	1	1	1	1	1	1	1	1	1	1	55	11	11	11	11	55	55	55	55	55	55	55	55	55	55	55	55	55	55	55	55	55	55
1 VERSTAPPEN	55	55	55	55	55	55	55	55	55	55	55	55	55	55	55	11	55	55	55	55	11	11	11	11	11	11	11	11	11	11	11	11	11	11	11	11	11	11
31 OCON	31	31	63	63	63	63	63	63	63	63	63	63	63	63	63	63	63	63	63	63	63	63	63	63	63	63	63	63	63	63	63	63	63	63	63	63	63	63
63 RUSSELL	63	63	31	31	31	31	14	14	14	14	14	14	14	14	14	14	20	20	20	20	20	20	44	20	44	44	44	44	44	44	44	44	44	44	44	44	44	44
14 ALONSO	14	14	14	14	14	14	31	31	31	31	31	31	31	77	77	77	44	44	44	44	44	44	20	44	20	20	20	20	20	20	20	20	20	20	14	20	20	31
77 BOTTAS	77	77	77	77	77	77	77	77	77	77	77	77	77	31	31	20	14	14	14	14	14	14	14	14	14	14	14	14	14	14	14	14	14	14	20	31	31	4
10 GASLY	20	20	20	20	20	20	20	20	20	20	20	20	20	20	20	31	27	27	27	27	27	27	27	77	77	77	77	77	77	77	77	77	77	77	31	4	4	10
20 MAGNUSSEN	10	4	4	10	10	10	10	10	10	10	10	10	10	44	44	44	77	77	77	77	77	77	77	27	31	31	31	31	31	31	31	31	31	31	77	10	10	18
4 NORRIS	4	10	10	4	4	4	4	4	4	4	44	44	44	10	10	4	31	31	31	31	31	31	31	31	3	3	3	3	3	3	3	3	3	3	3	27	18	23
24 ZHOU	18	18	18	18	18	18	18	18	44	44	4	4	4	4	4	24	3	3	3	3	3	3	3	3	27	27	27	4	4	4	4	4	4	4	4	18	23	20
18 STROLL	3	3	3	3	3	3	3	44	18	18	24	24	24	24	24	27	4	4	4	4	4	4	4	4	4	4	4	27	10	10	10	10	10	10	10	23	27	24
3 RICCIARDO	44	44	44	44	44	44	44	24	24	24	18	27	27	27	27	3	10	10	10	10	10	10	10	10	10	10	10	10	27	27	27	27	27	27	27	24	24	27
44 HAMILTON	23	23	23	23	24	24	24	3	27	27	27	18	18	6	3	10	24	24	24	24	24	24	24	24	24	24	18	18	18	18	18	18	18	18	18	77		
23 ALBON	27	27	24	24	23	23	27	27	23	23	23	23	6	3	18	18	18	18	18	18	18	18	18	18	18	18	24	23	23	23	23	23	23	23	23			
27 HÜLKENBERG	6	24	27	27	27	27	23	23	6	6	6	6	23	18	23	23	23	23	23	23	23	23	23	23	23	23	23	24	24	24	24	24	24	24	24			
6 LATIFI	24	6	6	6	6	6	6	6	3	3	3	3	3	23																								
22 TSUNODA																																						
																VSC	SC	SC	SC	SC																		VSC

VSC Virtual safety car deployed on laps shown

SC Safety car deployed on laps shown

11 = Pit stop *18 = One lap or more behind*

TIME SHEETS

PRACTICE 1 (FRIDAY)

Weather: Dry/sunny

Temperatures: track 27-29°C, air 22-23°C

Pos.	Driver	Laps	Time
1	Charles Leclerc	17	1m 30.772s
2	Max Verstappen	24	1m 30.888s
3	Valtteri Bottas	22	1m 31.084s
4	Carlos Sainz	14	1m 31.139s
5	Pierre Gasly	28	1m 31.317s
6	Yuki Tsunoda	26	1m 31.505s
7	Sergio Pérez	25	1m 31.563s
8	Esteban Ocon	26	1m 32.026s
9	Lewis Hamilton	20	1m 32.364s
10	Fernando Alonso	23	1m 32.821s
11	Daniel Ricciardo	24	1m 32.506s
12	Lance Stroll	23	1m 32.582s
13	Lando Norris	24	1m 32.594s
14	Zhou Guanyu	26	1m 32.608s
15	George Russell	19	1m 32.839s
16	Nico Hülkenberg	23	1m 33.034s
17	Alexander Albon	25	1m 33.087s
18	Nicholas Latifi	26	1m 33.529s
19	Mick Schumacher	22	1m 34.429s
20	Kevin Magnussen	2	no time

PRACTICE 2 (FRIDAY)

Weather: Dry/dark

Temperatures: track 26-29°C, air 22-23°C

Pos.	Driver	Laps	Time
1	Charles Leclerc	15	1m 30.074s
2	Max Verstappen	23	1m 30.214s
3	Carlos Sainz	12	1m 30.320s
4	Sergio Pérez	24	1m 30.360s
5	Lewis Hamilton	24	1m 30.513s
6	George Russell	29	1m 30.664s
7	Lando Norris	26	1m 30.735s
8	Esteban Ocon	26	1m 30.760s
9	Valtteri Bottas	14	1m 30.832s
10	Yuki Tsunoda	26	1m 30.886s
11	Fernando Alonso	27	1m 30.944s
12	Pierre Gasly	29	1m 30.963s
13	Mick Schumacher	27	1m 31.169s
14	Lance Stroll	28	1m 31.372s
15	Daniel Ricciardo	23	1m 31.527s
16	Nico Hülkenberg	30	1m 31.615s
17	Zhou Guanyu	27	1m 31.615s
18	Nicholas Latifi	26	1m 31.814s
19	Alexander Albon	29	1m 31.866s
20	Kevin Magnussen	13	1m 32.344s

PRACTICE 3 (SATURDAY)

Weather: Dry/sunny

Temperatures: track 28-30°C, air 24°C

Pos.	Driver	Laps	Time
1	Charles Leclerc	23	1m 29.735s
2	Max Verstappen	12	1m 29.768s
3	Sergio Pérez	16	1m 29.833s
4	Carlos Sainz	22	1m 30.009s
5	Valtteri Bottas	22	1m 30.030s
6	Esteban Ocon	16	1m 30.139s
7	Pierre Gasly	11	1m 30.148s
8	Kevin Magnussen	18	1m 30.262s
9	Fernando Alonso	17	1m 30.296s
10	Yuki Tsunoda	19	1m 30.415s
11	Lewis Hamilton	17	1m 30.707s
12	Mick Schumacher	17	1m 30.765s
13	Zhou Guanyu	20	1m 30.946s
14	George Russell	15	1m 30.983s
15	Lance Stroll	18	1m 31.067s
16	Daniel Ricciardo	16	1m 31.186s
17	Alexander Albon	26	1m 31.374s
18	Nico Hülkenberg	18	1m 31.424s
19	Lando Norris	17	1m 31.529s
20	Nicholas Latifi	13	1m 31.992s

QUALIFYING (SATURDAY)

Weather: Dry/dark Temperatures: track 24-29°C, air 23-24°C

Pos.	Driver	First	Second	Third	Qualifying Tyre
1	Sergio Pérez	1m 29.705s	1m 28.924s	1m 28.200s	Soft (n)
2	Charles Leclerc	1m 29.039s	1m 28.780s	1m 28.225s	Soft (n)
3	Carlos Sainz	1m 28.855s	1m 28.686s	1m 28.402s	Soft (u)
4	Max Verstappen	1m 28.928s	1m 28.945s	1m 28.461s	Soft (n)
5	Esteban Ocon	1m 30.093s	1m 29.584s	1m 29.068s	Soft (u)
6	George Russell	1m 29.680s	1m 29.618s	1m 29.104s	Soft (n)
7	Fernando Alonso	1m 29.978s	1m 29.295s	1m 29.147s	Soft (n)
8	Valtteri Bottas	1m 29.683s	1m 29.404s	1m 29.183s	Soft (n)
9	Pierre Gasly	1m 29.891s	1m 29.418s	1m 29.254s	Soft (u)
10	Kevin Magnussen	1m 29.831s	1m 29.546s	1m 29.588s	Soft (u)
11	Lando Norris	1m 29.957s	1m 29.651s		
12	Daniel Ricciardo	1m 30.009s	1m 29.773s		
13	Zhou Guanyu	1m 29.978s	1m 29.819s		
14	Mick Schumacher	1m 30.167s	1m 29.920s		
15	Lance Stroll	1m 30.256s	1m 31.009s		
16	Lewis Hamilton	1m 30.343s			
17	Alexander Albon	1m 30.492s			
18	Nico Hülkenberg	1m 30.543s			
19	Nicholas Latifi	1m 31.817s			
20	Yuki Tsunoda	no time			

QUALIFYING: head to head

Hamilton	1	1	Russell
Verstappen	1	1	Pérez
Ricciardo	0	2	Norris
Leclerc	2	0	Sainz
Gasly	2	0	Tsunoda
Hülkenberg	1	1	Stroll
Alonso	1	1	Ocon
Bottas	2	0	Zhou
Albon	2	0	Latifi
Magnussen	2	0	Schumacher

FOR THE RECORD

1st POLE POSITION: Sergio Pérez

Red Bull Content Pool/Getty Images

POINTS

DRIVERS

1	Charles Leclerc	45
2	Carlos Sainz	33
3	Max Verstappen	25
4	George Russell	22
5	Lewis Hamilton	16
6	Esteban Ocon	14
7	Sergio Pérez	12
8	Kevin Magnussen	12
9	Valtteri Bottas	8
10	Lando Norris	6
11	Yuki Tsunoda	4
12	Pierre Gasly	4
13	Fernando Alonso	2
14	Zhou Guanyu	1

CONSTRUCTORS

1	Ferrari	78
2	Mercedes	38
3	Red Bull	37
4	Alpine	16
5	Haas	12
6	Alfa Romeo	9
7	AlphaTauri	8
8	McLaren	6

10 · MAGNUSSEN · Haas

8 · BOTTAS · Alfa Romeo

6 · RUSSELL · Mercedes

4 · VERSTAPPEN · Red Bull

2 · LECLERC · Ferrari

9 · GASLY · AlphaTauri

7 · ALONSO · Alpine

5 · OCON · Alpine

3 · SAINZ · Ferrari

1 · PÉREZ · Red Bull

39	40	41	42	43	44	45	46	47	48	49	50	•
16	16	16	1	16	16	16	1	1	1	1	1	1
1	1	1	16	1	1	1	16	16	16	16	16	2
55	55	55	55	55	55	55	55	55	55	55	55	3
11	11	11	11	11	11	11	11	11	11	11	11	4
63	63	63	63	63	63	63	63	63	63	63	63	5
44	44	31	31	31	31	31	31	31	4	4	31	6
31	31	4	4	4	4	4	4	4	31	31	4	7
4	4	10	10	10	10	10	10	10	10	10	10	8
10	10	18	18	20	20	20	20	20	20	20	20	9
18	18	20	20	18	18	44	44	44	44	44	44	10
23	23	23	23	44	44	18	18	18	24	24	24	
20	20	44	44	23	23	23	23	23	27	27	27	
24	24	24	24	24	24	24	24	24	*18*	*18*		
27	27	27	27	27	27	27	27	27				
VSC	VSC											

RACE TYRE STRATEGIES

PIRELLI

	Driver	Race Stint 1	Race Stint 2	Race Stint 3
1	Verstappen	Medium (n): 1-16	Hard (n): 17-50	
2	Leclerc	Medium (n): 1-16	Hard (n): 17-50	
3	Sainz	Medium (n): 1-16	Hard (n): 17-50	
4	Pérez	Medium (n): 1-15	Hard (n): 16-50	
5	Russell	Medium (n): 1-16	Hard (n): 17-50	
6	Ocon	Medium (n): 1-16	Hard (n): 17-50	
7	Norris	Medium (n): 1-16	Hard (n): 17-50	
8	Gasly	Medium (n): 1-15	Hard (n): 16-50	
9	Magnussen	Hard (u): 1-37	Medium (u): 38-50	
10	Hamilton	Hard (u): 1-40	Medium (u): 41-50	
11	Zhou	Medium (n): 1-16	Hard (n): 17-50	
12	Hülkenberg	Hard (u): 1-37	Medium (u): 38-50	
13	Stroll	Medium (n): 1-13	Hard (n): 14-49	
14	Albon	Medium (n): 1-13	Hard (n): 14-47 (dnf)	
	Bottas	Medium (n): 1-16	Hard (n): 17-35	Medium (n): 36 **(dnf)**
	Alonso	Medium (n): 1-16	Hard (n): 17-35 **(dnf)**	
	Ricciardo	Medium (n): 1-8	Hard (n): 9-35 **(dnf)**	
	Latifi	Medium (n): 1-8	Hard (n) 10-14 **(dnf)**	
ns	Tsunoda			
ns	Schumacher			

The tyre regulations stipulate that at least two of three dry tyre specifications must be used during a dry race. Selected compounds for Jeddah: Red = Soft (C4); Yellow = Medium (C3); White = Hard (C2). (n) new (u) used

Mercedes-AMG Petronas F1 Team

FIA FORMULA 1 WORLD CHAMPIONSHIP · ROUND 3

AUSTRALIAN GRAND PRIX

MELBOURNE CIRCUIT

POWERED BY
HYBRID
SINCE 2014
The world's most efficient engine
aramco
aramco
aramco
aramco
NEVER DRINK

MELBOURNE QUALIFYING

ALBERT PARK had undergone the biggest changes since it had appeared on the F1 calendar in 1996, replacing Adelaide. The idea had been to increase the chances of overtaking at a circuit that had gained a reputation for being challenging for drivers, but on which actual racing was more than difficult.

The track had been resurfaced for the first time, Turns 1, 2, 6 and 11 had been widened and reprofiled, while the old chicane was gone, making a longer flat-out run from T6 all the way down to a new-look T9/10. The initial plan had been for a record four DRS zones, but one before the new section was removed after the opening day's practice when some drivers had reported instability there, not aided by porpoising.

The good news for Aston Martin was that Sebastian Vettel was fit again, after missing the season's first two races with Covid. But there was plenty of bad news, too... Both Vettel and Lance Stroll crashed in Saturday practice, giving the Aston crew a scramble to get the cars out for qualifying. Stroll's car was ready first, but no sooner had he left the garage than he had a misunderstanding with fellow Canadian Nicholas Latifi.

The latter, on a prep lap, let the Aston through, then realised that Stroll, too, was going slowly, just as Zhou Guanyu arrived on the scene. The Williams driver was attempting to repass the Aston on the inside just as Stroll got a warning about the Alfa and, without checking his mirrors, jinked right and straight into Latifi, who suffered his second heavy impact of the weekend. Meanwhile, in the Aston pit, they surveyed the garage monitors with disbelief. But not for long. The resultant red flag gave them some extra time to get Vettel out, but practically his first flying lap of the weekend was insufficient for him to get out of Q1. So both Astons and both Williams bit the Q1 dust, along with Kevin Magnussen. Haas, after such a great start to the season, was struggling to generate tyre temperature in Melbourne.

The AlphaTauris of Pierre Gasly and Yuki Tsunoda were eliminated in Q2, the Frenchman missing out on the top-ten shootout to countryman Esteban Ocon by less than a tenth. Out, too, went Valtteri Bottas (ending an amazing 103-race streak of Q3 appearances), Zhou and Mick Schumacher with the second Haas.

Max Verstappen's Red Bull topped Q1, while Sergio Pérez's RB18 headed Q2, with Charles Leclerc's Ferrari third in both sessions. But the championship leader emerged as the man to beat in Q3 and claimed his 11th F1 pole, in the process becoming the first man other than Lewis Hamilton to take an Australian pole in the hybrid era.

"The car feels really good," he said, "because Melbourne is a track at which I've always struggled. I had a messy FP3 session, but finally managed to put everything together. But the Red Bull race pace looked good on the high-fuel runs, so let's see."

Team-mate Carlos Sainz couldn't buy any luck. On his first Q3 run, he was nip and tuck with Leclerc's provisional pole pace before a red flag caused by Fernando Alonso, who had suffered a hydraulics issue. The Alpine's steering was heavy and the gears refused to shift, running the Spaniard wide and off at Turn 11 after he had just set the fastest sector-two time.

Alonso, who had been bang on the pace since first thing Friday, was deeply frustrated: "I was having my best weekend in years and had saved two sets of tyres for Q3. I'm not sure we could have fought for pole, but for sure the top three."

The incident tripped up fellow countryman Sainz at a time when the intra-team battle at Ferrari was at an important stage. After being forced to back off due to the yellows, he had his second Q3 run scuppered when a steering-wheel electronics issue caused a delay in firing up the car. By the time Carlos left the pits, there was not enough time for a proper tyre preparation lap and, struggling for grip, he could do no better than ninth. The frustration was palpable. "We shouldn't really be having trouble starting," he lamented.

That left the way clear for Verstappen to follow up his Saudi win by putting his Red Bull on the front row, just 0.09s clear of team-mate Pérez. A final-sector lock-up cost him three-tenths, however, without which he'd have been in the pole fight.

"Not good," Verstappen admitted. "I didn't really feel confident in the car. So far, it's been a bit of a struggle. I don't feel able to push to the limit. I've had a bit of understeer, and the weekend has felt a little all over the place."

Given McLaren's start to the season, fourth on the grid was a great outcome for Lando Norris. The team seemed to be on top of the brake issues that had troubled them and were vindicated in their hopes that Melbourne would be better suited to the car. Home hero Daniel Ricciardo qualified seventh, three slots and 0.33s behind Norris. "I'm generally satisfied with a first Q3 of the year," he said, "but on the last run, I went around 1s slower with a new set of tyres, and I'm not sure why."

Mercedes would have taken a third-row lockout if they'd been offered it before Melbourne kicked off. Hamilton outqualified Russell by a tenth to claim fifth, with George one of those who would have preferred the fourth DRS zone to remain. "The DRS open through 8/9 actually reduced the porpoising on our car and made it feel safer," he explained.

Eighth, between Ricciardo and Sainz, was Ocon, just 0.03s slower than the Australian as Alpine appeared to be in really good shape. Alonso's hydraulic problem had prevented him from setting a Q3 time, which meant tenth place on race-day as Ferrari, Red Bull, McLaren, Mercedes and Alpine each put both cars through to the final stage of qualifying.

Left: After missing the opening two races, Sebastian Vettel was back in action for Aston Martin.
Photo: Aston Martin Aramco Cognizant F1 Team

Centre left: Alpine reserve driver, and 2021 Formula 2 champion, Oscar Piastri relaxes on home soil ahead of a mid-season, off-track saga.
Photo: Alpine F1 Team

Below centre left: Mattia Binotto had the satisfaction of watching Charles Leclerc's strong start to the season.
Photo: Scuderia Ferrari

Far left: After the opening two night races, the sun shone down on the Melbourne pit lane.
Photo: Atsuo Sakurai

Below: Leclerc scorches to pole position in his Ferrari.
Photo: Scuderia Ferrari

Opening spread: A bird's eye view of the final preparations for the cars on the starting grid.
Photo: Red Bull Content Pool/Getty Images

Above: Carlos Sainz is plagued by electronics issues as Yuki Tsunoda and Zhou Guanyu take advantage.
Photo: XPB Images

Top right: A warm welcome home for Daniel Ricciardo, who qualified his McLaren in the top ten and finished sixth, just behind team-mate Norris.
Photo: McLaren F1 Team

Above right: A hydraulics issue in qualifying left Fernando Alonso deeply frustrated and compromised on race-day.
Photo: Alpine F1 Team

Right: Lance Stroll drew the displeasure of the stewards with his moves on Valtteri Bottas, the Canadian gaining penalty points on his licence.
Photo: Alfa Romeo ORLEN

Below right: An inspired drive by Alex Albon, who ran on hard tyres for 57 of the 58 laps to take a point for Williams, putting them on the 2022 constructors' board.
Photo: XPB Images

THERE was pressure of differing sorts on the two Ferrari drivers as they sat eyeing the starting lights in Melbourne. For Charles Leclerc, it was about re-establishing his superiority after Max Verstappen's win in Jeddah. For Carlos Sainz, it was about recovering from the frustration of qualifying, after the steering-wheel electronics issue had turned a potential pole position into a slot on the fifth row.

Both Sainz and Alonso were well out of starting position, so while the top eight all started on the medium-compound Pirelli, both Spaniards went for the alternative strategy and took the hard compound. They were matched by the Aston Martins of Sebastian Vettel and Lance Stroll, Kevin Magnussen's Haas and Alexander Albon's Williams.

The decision meant a tricky opening lap, as the hard did not generate temperature as quickly, especially on the Ferrari. Sainz soon came under pressure, dropping from ninth to 14th. He was not helped by more electronic issues, which had demanded a change of steering wheel (see Viewpoint).

Meanwhile, Leclerc had managed to convert his pole position and completed the first lap 0.6s ahead of Verstappen. Sergio Pérez had actually got a better start than Max, but, finding himself close to his team-mate's rear wing on the run to Turn One, had been forced to lift, allowing a fast-starting Lewis Hamilton to snaffle third place.

George Russell was also well away and managed to jump old mate Lando Norris into Turn One. Then came Daniel Ricciardo, Esteban Ocon, Pierre Gasly, Fernando Alonso, Yuki Tsunoda, Valtteri Bottas, Mick Schumacher, Sainz, Zhou Guanyu, Magnussen, Vettel, Nicholas Latifi, Stroll and Albon.

Sainz, in a hurry to make up lost time, ran around the outside of Schumacher approaching the tricky new T9/10 section. However, with his tyres not yet properly in and a dusty surface off-line, he ran off across the grass, spun across the road and ended up beached in the gravel, facing from whence he had come – race over.

After an initial VSC came a full safety car, with Stroll taking the opportunity to duck into the pits and swap his starting hard-compound Pirellis for mediums. Meanwhile, Verstappen was reminded of the new rule for following a car in front – The Verstappen Rule? He could position himself to the side of Leclerc, but could put no part of his car in front of the Ferrari's rear wing.

We were under way again on lap seven, Leclerc's Ferrari making a quick sideways twitch as he booted it out of the penultimate corner, but not enough to allow Verstappen a superior enough exit from the final turn to enable an overtake attempt into T1.

Once DRS was re-enabled, Hamilton quickly came under pressure from Pérez, the Red Bull seizing third place with a comfortable move down the inside of Turn Three. The Mexican was already 4s behind his team-mate as Leclerc and Verstappen appeared to be fighting an individual battle once more.

Meanwhile, Vettel, with precious little meaningful running across the entire weekend, lost time going wide through the Turn 11 gravel. "Sorry for that," he radioed. "So difficult to judge the car under braking." After such a tricky weekend for the team, they had all been called together on race morning so that Vettel and Stroll could thank them for their efforts after giving them so much damage to contend with!

A dozen laps into the race, Leclerc had managed to put 3.5s between himself and Verstappen, who was telling the Red Bull pit-wall crew, "My left front is completely grained." That was somewhat contrary to expectations that the Red Bull was likely to be easier on its stressed left front tyre than the Ferrari. Pitting was not yet an option, however, because Max did not have a window to Alonso's hard-tyred, longer-running Alpine.

Hamilton had dropped a couple of seconds behind Pérez and had team-mate Russell within DRS range, with the Norris/Ricciardo McLarens right in touch. Ocon was just 1.5s adrift with the first of the Alpines, while Gasly's AlphaTauri was a similar distance behind and under pressure from Alonso. Further back, Bottas was pressuring Tsunoda's AlphaTauri, successfully demoting it a couple of laps later.

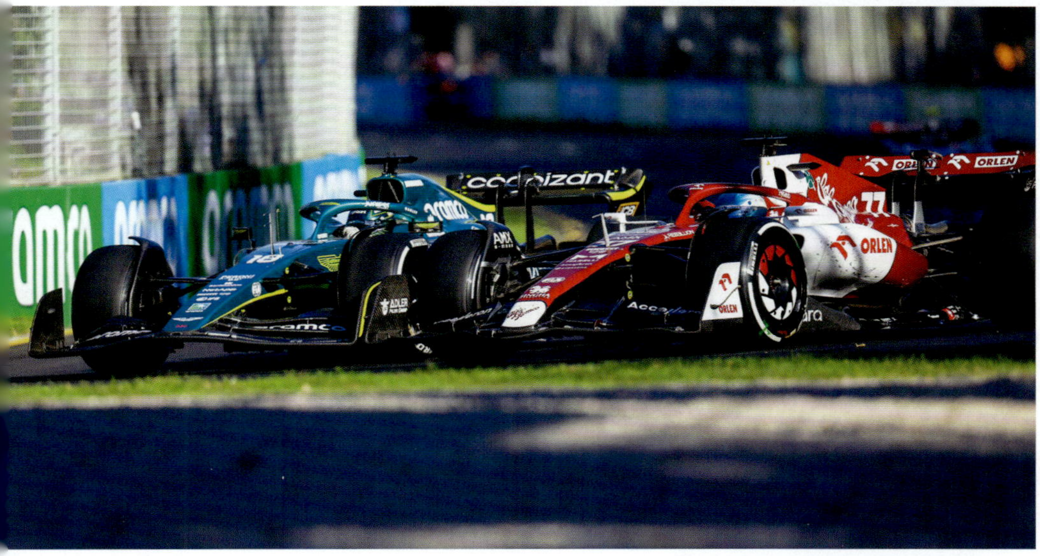

Magnussen soon began leaning on Tsunoda, too, almost running into the back of the Japanese driver on the high-speed run to T9/10 on lap 17. Like Sainz, he was forced to head for the grass, but managed to keep the car pointing in the right direction. "Sorry, my bad…" he radioed in.

At just over one-third-distance, lap 19 of the 58, with Leclerc enjoying a sizeable gap in the lead, Red Bull pitted Verstappen, who rejoined just in front of a battling Gasly and Alonso. The twice world champion grabbed the opportunity to go down the Frenchman's inside into Turn Three to take eighth, just behind Verstappen, with whom it had been a close call.

By lap 20, Pérez, some 17s behind Leclerc's race-leading Ferrari, was struggling with his left front Pirelli, just as his team-mate had, to the extent that he had fallen back into Hamilton's clutches. Meanwhile, the McLarens had dropped 4s behind the Mercs after shadowing them so closely, Norris and Ricciardo running in tandem.

"Lando will pit this lap," Ricciardo was informed on lap 21. "Verstappen is 4.5s behind on new tyres, and so we want maximum pace as soon as Lando is out of your way."

Pérez was in for his tyre stop, too, to protect against any undercut threat by Mercedes or McLaren. Meanwhile, Leclerc continued to circulate serenely at the front, with a 27.5s margin over Verstappen. With a stop time of around 20s, Ferrari could afford to run him a couple of laps further, but needed to be aware that the reshod Red Bull had just set the race's fastest lap.

Crowd favourite Ricciardo was in on lap 22, from fourth place. After making the fastest stops in the first two races, his McLaren crew was on top form again with another 2.4s pit stop. Daniel pitted out still behind his team-mate, and just ahead of Albon and Stroll. They were almost three abreast on the run down to Turn Three, with Albon losing out to Stroll for 11th as he was forced wide. Vettel, in the second Aston Martin, was taking a look at the Williams, too.

Leclerc was in next time around, the Ferrari crew turning around the race leader in a drama-free 2.7s. Mercedes stopped Hamilton on the next lap, and he pitted out just ahead of Pérez's Red Bull. However, with tyre warm-up taking time on the hards, he was passed by the Mexican around the outside on the run to T9/10.

Hamilton had a go back as soon as his rubber was up to temperature, but was thwarted by the second safety car of the afternoon. Unbelievably, in more drama for Aston Martin, Vettel had suffered an embarrassing shunt when he lost the car on the kerb exiting Turn Four. Unexpected, from a four-time world champion in his 280th race…

That all worked perfectly for Russell, who was able to make his tyre stop and lose only 12s instead of 19s, leapfrogging him ahead of Hamilton. As the field jinked around behind the safety car, Schumacher had the narrowest of escapes after nearly ramming Tsunoda. "Holy cow, that was close," Mick acknowledged. It had been.

The interruption wiped out Leclerc's 6s advantage over Verstappen at the front of the field. And with Max now off a medium tyre that had been fragile on the Red Bull, it was time to see whether the performance dynamic changed on the harder compound.

Leclerc didn't get the best of restarts, suffering understeer in the final turn and having to lift. Verstappen drew alongside down the straight and looked at the outside into Turn One. Charles, though, braked deep enough into the corner to repel him.

Russell was third and had to defend against a feisty Alonso as he brought his new tyres in. The timing of the safety car, while great for the Mercedes driver, was not kind to the Spaniard who, having started on the hard Pirelli, was too far out (31 laps) from the chequered flag to be able take advantage of a cheap stop for mediums. Three slots further back, Magnussen was in the same boat.

It didn't take long for Leclerc to establish that he was just as comfortable on the hard tyre as on the medium, quickly

Above: Reliability reaped rewards for Mercedes, with George Russell claiming third place ahead of team-mate Lewis Hamilton.
Photo: Mercedes-AMG Petronas F1 Team

Top right: On top of the world, down under for Charles Leclerc.

Above right: A first-lap retirement ended a weekend to forget for Ferrari's Carlos Sainz.

Right: It was joy for the Ferrari crew as they celebrated a second win in just three races.
Photos: Scuderia Ferrari

putting a couple of seconds between himself and Verstappen as the race reached half-distance.

Now Pérez was putting Alonso under pressure in an effort to reclaim fourth place and got down the inside of the Alpine into Turn Three with relative ease. Hamilton was next to have Fernando in his sights, getting a move done down the inside into Turn One to claim fifth.

With 20 laps to go, Pérez had hunted down Russell in his quest to put the second Red Bull back into a podium position. Mercedes was quickly on the radio: "George, important: management is more important than position. If you're hurting the tyres to keep Pérez behind, you can let him by."

"Not what I want to hear!" Russell responded. Whatever, there was precious little he could do when Pérez came around his outside on the way into Turn 11.

It was now that Verstappen received a message from Gianpiero Lambiase that he didn't want to hear: "Okay, Max, stop the car." Able to smell burning fluid, he pulled off on the exit of Turn Two, prompting another VSC period as he registered his second DNF in the season's first three races. Post-race analysis discovered a fuel leak – a separate issue from the one that had caused his retirement in Bahrain.

With ten laps remaining, Leclerc had a comfortable 14s lead over Pérez's Red Bull and was in a class of his own. Some 6s behind, Sergio, Russell and Hamilton were running together, with a 15s gap to the two McLarens behind. Albon's Williams, still on its starting hards, was seventh with a pit stop to make, closely followed by Ocon's Alpine. After an 8s gap came a four-car train comprising Stroll, Gasly, Bottas and, at the back of it following his stop for softs, Alonso.

After receiving a three-place grid penalty for his part in the qualifying collision with Latifi, Stroll had now attracted a 5s penalty and a point on his licence for making two moves on the main straight while defending from Bottas. Lance claimed that he had been merely trying to break the tow and not turning into Valtteri, but that's not the way the stewards saw it. It would prove expensive, dropping him to 12th in a final kick in the teeth for Aston Martin.

With four laps remaining and approaching a batch of backmarkers, a confident Leclerc asked, "Can we go for fastest lap now before I reach the traffic?"

"No. Negative," replied the Ferrari pit-wall crew. "We have the fastest lap and we don't think anyone can beat it."

"Okay, but... Okay," said Leclerc, who was not convinced that his extra point was safe.

Hamilton, who positively hates to finish a race behind a team-mate, was also not so happy on the radio: "You guys put me in a really difficult position." Perhaps following an instruction to stay behind Russell?

It was probably a transmission for the benefit of the listening public, but it did seem a little unfair. It was not as though Mercedes had instructed Vettel to crash and hand Russell a cheap stop. In what had been its best showing of the season so far, the three-pointed star would have a driver on the podium for the second time in 2022, but this time, it would be George.

Leclerc ignored team instructions and set a new quickest time on the very last lap, and it was fortunate that he did, given that Alonso had beaten his previous time after a late stop to swap his starting hards for softs. The Ferrari took the flag 20.5s in front of Pérez, with Russell 5s behind the Red Bull. Hamilton was 2.5s behind his team-mate, and comfortably clear of the Norris and Ricciardo McLarens. Ocon finished seventh for Alpine, ahead of Bottas's Alfa Romeo and Gasly's AlphaTauri. And after a brilliant 57-lap stint on hards, and a last-lap stop for softs, Albon's fine drive was rewarded with the final point.

Leclerc's consummate victory gave him a 34-point lead in the championship after just three races – over a most unlikely second-place man, George Russell!

Tony Dodgins

VIEWPOINT
CHARLES VICTORIOUS; TORMENT FOR CARLOS

YOU had to feel for Carlos Sainz. Going into qualifying, he had genuine hopes of claiming his first pole position. And yet 24 hours later, he would have been forgiven for thinking that his 2022 championship was as good as over. Ferrari team-mate Charles Leclerc was on his way to opening a 34-point series lead, and Sainz had ended a points-scoring streak lasting 17 races.

Apart from the impetuous error that had put him in the gravel, none of this was the Spaniard's fault. In fact, the sequence of disasters had been triggered by his hero and fellow countryman crashing early in Q3 just as he was about to complete a provisional pole lap, which he was forced to back out of because of the red flag to deal with Fernando Alonso's damaged Alpine.

Problems in firing up the Ferrari for the restart meant that there was no time for Sainz to complete the two laps required to bring his soft tyres into their operating window. The inevitable penalty of cold rubber resulted in P9 instead of what should have been P2 – at the very least.

Any thoughts of making up lost ground were scuppered when a problem with his steering wheel required a swap less than a minute before the formation lap. Sainz found the positioning of some switches unfamiliar, resulting in anti-stall kicking in and 14th place at the end of the first lap. Leclerc was already 9.3 seconds down the road in the leading sister car.

Sainz had been one of only six drivers to choose the hard tyre, but a combination of frustration and over-enthusiasm to get going led to a spin into retirement. The only good thing to say was that he hadn't collected anyone else and was left to suffer in his misery on the far side of the circuit.

Looking at the bigger picture, it probably crossed Sainz's mind – however briefly – that this combination of events during a 24-hour period might have consigned him to a support role for the rest of the season.

Maurice Hamilton

3

FORMULA 1 HEINEKEN AUSTRALIAN GRAND PRIX 2022

ROLEX

Official Timepiece

MELBOURNE 8–10 APRIL

RACE DISTANCE: 58 laps, 190.217 miles/306.124km

RACE WEATHER: Dry/sunny (track 33–39°C, air 26–28° C)

ALBERT PARK GRAND PRIX CIRCUIT, MELBOURNE

Circuit: 3.280 miles/5.278km
58 laps

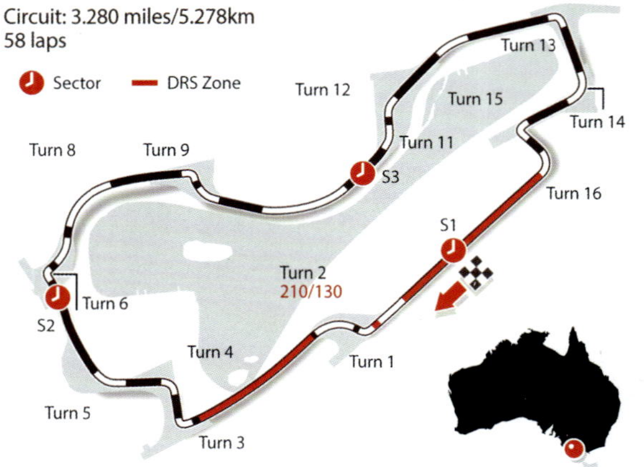

RACE – OFFICIAL CLASSIFICATION

Pos.	Driver	Nat.	No.	Entrant	Car/Engine	Laps	Time/Retirement	Speed (mph/km/h)	Gap to winner	Fastest race lap	
1	**Charles Leclerc**	MC	16	Scuderia Ferrari	Ferrari F1-75-066/7 V6	58	1h 27m 46.548s	130.024/209.254		1m 20.260s	58
2	**Sergio Pérez**	MEX	11	Oracle Red Bull Racing	Red Bull RB18-RBPTH001 V6	58	1h 28m 07.072s	129.519/208.441	20.524s	1m 21.094s	58
3	**George Russell**	GB	63	Mercedes-AMG Petronas F1 Team	Mercedes-AMG F1 W13-M13 E Perf. V6	58	1h 28m 12.141s	129.396/208.242	25.593s	1m 21.495s	53
4	**Lewis Hamilton**	GB	44	Mercedes-AMG Petronas F1 Team	Mercedes-AMG F1 W13-M13 E Perf. V6	58	1h 28m 15.091s	129.324/208.126	28.543s	1m 21.886s	51
5	**Lando Norris**	GB	4	McLaren F1 Team	McLaren MCL36-Mercedes F1 M13 E Perf. V6	58	1h 28m 39.851s	128.721/207.157	53.303s	1m 22.848s	55
6	**Daniel Ricciardo**	AUS	3	McLaren F1 Team	McLaren MCL36-Mercedes F1 M13 E Perf. V6	58	1h 28m 40.285s	128.711/207.140	53.737s	1m 22.451s	54
7	**Esteban Ocon**	F	31	BWT Alpine F1 Team	Alpine A522-Renault E-Tech RE22 V6	58	1h 28m 48.231s	128.519/206.831	1m 01.683s	1m 22.469s	58
8	**Valtteri Bottas**	FIN	77	Alfa Romeo F1 Team ORLEN	Alfa Romeo C42-Ferrari 066/7 V6	58	1h 28m 54.987s	128.356/206.569	1m 08.439s	1m 21.651s	54
9	**Pierre Gasly**	F	10	Scuderia AlphaTauri	AlphaTauri AT03-RBPTH001 V6	58	1h 29m 02.769s	128.169/206.268	1m 16.221s	1m 22.731s	52
10	**Alexander Albon**	T	23	Williams Racing	Williams FW44-Mercedes F1 M13 E Perf. V6	58	1h 29m 05.930s	128.093/206.146	1m 19.382s	1m 22.589s	54
11	Zhou Guanyu	CHN	24	Alfa Romeo F1 Team ORLEN	Alfa Romeo C42-Ferrari 066/7 V6	58	1h 29m 08.243s	128.038/206.057	1m 21.695s	1m 22.541s	55
12	Lance Stroll	CDN	18	Aston Martin Aramco Cognizant F1 Team	Aston Martin AMR22-Mercedes F1 M13 E Perf. V6	58	1h 29m 15.146s *	127.873/205.792	1m 28.598s	1m 23.592s	48
13	Mick Schumacher	D	47	Haas F1 Team	Haas VF-22-Ferrari 066/7 V6	57			1 lap	1m 23.006s	55
14	Kevin Magnussen	DK	20	Haas F1 Team	Haas VF-22-Ferrari 066/7 V6	57			1 lap	1m 23.071s	44
15	Yuki Tsunoda	J	22	Scuderia AlphaTauri	AlphaTauri AT03-RBPTH001 V6	57			1 lap	1m 23.342s	56
16	Nicholas Latifi	CDN	6	Williams Racing	Williams FW44-Mercedes F1 M13 E Perf. V6	57			1 lap	1m 23.882s	49
17	Fernando Alonso	E	14	BWT Alpine F1 Team	Alpine A522-Renault E-Tech RE22 V6	57			1 lap	1m 20.846s	57
	Max Verstappen	NL	1	Oracle Red Bull Racing	Red Bull RB18-RBPTH001 V6	38	*fuel system*			1m 21.677s	37
	Sebastian Vettel	D	5	Aston Martin Aramco Cognizant F1 Team	Aston Martin AMR22-Mercedes F1 M13 E Perf. V6	22	*accident*			1m 25.189s	17
	Carlos Sainz	E	55	Scuderia Ferrari	Ferrari F1-75-066/7 V6	1	*accident*			no time	

* Stroll: 5s time penalty for making more than one change of direction to defend a position.

DHL Fastest race lap (scores 1 point): Charles Leclerc on lap 59, 1m 20.260s, 147.104mph/236.740km/h (new record).

Lap record: Michael Schumacher (Ferrari F2004 V10), 1m 24.125s, 141.010mph/226.933km/h (2004, 3.295-mile/5.303km circuit).

19 · STROLL · Aston Martin
3-place grid penalty for causing a collision with Latifi in qualifying

17 · VETTEL · Aston Martin

15 · SCHUMACHER · Haas

13 · TSUNODA · AlphaTauri

11 · GASLY · AlphaTauri

ALBON · Williams
3-place grid penalty for causing a collision with Stroll in the Saudi GP. Disqualified from qualifying for not being able to provide a 1-litre fuel sample

18 · LATIFI · Williams

16 · MAGNUSSEN · Haas

14 · ZHOU · Alfa Romeo

12 · BOTTAS · Alfa Romeo

Grid order	1	2	3	4	5	6	7	8	9	10	11	12	13	14	15	16	17	18	19	20	21	22	23
16 LECLERC	16	16	16	16	16	16	16	16	16	16	16	16	16	16	16	16	16	16	16	16	16	16	16
1 VERSTAPPEN	1	1	1	1	1	1	1	1	1	1	1	1	1	1	1	1	1	11	11	44	44	63	1
11 PÉREZ	44	44	44	44	44	44	44	44	44	11	11	11	11	11	11	11	11	44	44	63	63	1	63
4 NORRIS	11	11	11	11	11	11	11	11	11	44	44	44	44	44	44	44	44	63	63	3	1	44	14
44 HAMILTON	63	63	63	63	63	63	63	63	63	63	63	63	63	63	63	63	63	4	4	1	14	14	11
63 RUSSELL	4	4	4	4	4	4	4	4	4	4	4	4	4	4	4	4	4	3	3	11	77	11	44
3 RICCIARDO	3	3	3	3	3	3	3	3	3	3	3	3	3	3	3	3	3	1	1	14	11	20	20
31 OCON	31	31	31	31	31	31	31	31	31	31	31	31	31	31	31	31	10	10	14	10	20	4	4
55 SAINZ	10	10	10	10	10	10	10	10	10	10	10	10	10	10	10	10	14	14	10	77	3	3	3
14 ALONSO	14	14	14	14	14	14	14	14	14	14	14	14	14	14	14	14	77	77	77	4	4	18	23
10 GASLY	22	22	22	22	22	22	22	22	22	22	22	22	22	22	22	77	22	24	20	20	23	23	31
77 BOTTAS	77	77	77	77	77	77	77	77	77	77	77	77	77	77	77	22	24	20	24	24	18	5	18
22 TSUNODA	47	47	47	47	47	47	47	47	47	47	47	20	20	20	20	24	20	23	23	23	5	31	77
24 ZHOU	55	24	24	24	24	24	24	24	24	24	20	24	24	24	24	20	23	18	18	18	31	77	10
47 SCHUMACHER	24	20	20	20	20	20	20	20	20	20	24	47	47	23	23	23	18	5	5	5	10	10	22
20 MAGNUSSEN	20	5	5	5	5	5	5	5	5	6	6	6	23	18	18	18	5	31	31	31	24	22	47
5 VETTEL	5	6	6	6	6	6	6	6	6	23	23	23	18	5	5	5	31	22	22	22	22	47	24
6 LATIFI	6	18	23	23	23	23	23	23	23	18	18	18	5	47	47	47	47	47	47	47	47	24	6
18 STROLL	18	23	18	18	18	18	18	18	18	5	5	5	6	6	6	6	6	6	6	6	6	6	
23 ALBON	23																						
			SC	SC	SC	SC																	SC

Grid order	24	25	26	27	28	29	30	31	32	33	34	35	36	37	38	39	40	41	42	43	44	45	46
16 LECLERC	16	16	16	16	16	16	16	16	16	16	16	16	16	16	16	16	16	16	16	16	16	16	16
1 VERSTAPPEN	1	1	1	1	1	1	1	1	1	1	1	1	1	1	1	11	11	11	11	11	11	11	11
11 PÉREZ	63	63	63	63	63	63	63	63	63	63	63	63	11	11	11	63	63	63	63	63	63	63	63
4 NORRIS	14	14	14	14	14	14	11	11	11	11	11	11	63	63	63	44	44	44	44	44	44	44	44
44 HAMILTON	11	11	11	11	11	11	14	44	44	44	44	44	44	44	44	4	4	4	4	4	4	4	4
63 RUSSELL	44	44	44	44	44	44	44	14	14	14	14	14	14	14	14	3	3	3	3	3	3	3	3
3 RICCIARDO	20	20	20	20	20	20	20	20	20	20	4	4	4	4	4	23	23	23	23	23	23	23	23
31 OCON	4	4	4	4	4	4	4	4	4	4	20	3	3	3	3	31	31	31	31	31	31	31	31
55 SAINZ	3	3	3	3	3	3	3	3	3	3	3	20	20	20	20	77	18	18	18	18	18	18	18
14 ALONSO	23	23	23	23	23	23	23	23	23	23	23	23	23	23	23	18	10	10	10	10	10	10	10
10 GASLY	31	31	31	31	31	31	31	31	31	31	31	31	31	31	31	10	77	77	77	77	77	77	77
77 BOTTAS	77	77	77	77	18	18	18	18	18	18	18	18	18	18	18	14	47	47	47	47	47	14	14
22 TSUNODA	18	18	18	18	77	77	77	77	77	77	77	77	77	77	77	47	14	14	14	14	14	47	47
24 ZHOU	10	10	10	10	10	10	10	10	10	10	10	10	10	10	10	24	24	24	24	24	24	24	24
47 SCHUMACHER	22	22	22	22	22	22	22	47	47	47	47	47	47	47	47	22	22	22	22	22	22	20	20
20 MAGNUSSEN	47	47	47	47	47	47	47	22	22	22	24	24	24	24	24	20	6	6	20	20	20	22	22
5 VETTEL	24	24	24	24	24	24	24	24	24	24	22	22	22	22	22	6	20	20	6	6	6	6	6
6 LATIFI	6	6	6	6	6	6	6	6	6	6	6	6	6	6	6								
18 STROLL																							
23 ALBON																							
	SC	SC	SC													VSC	VSC						

TIME SHEETS

PRACTICE 1 (FRIDAY)

Weather: Dry/sunny

Temperatures: track 36–39°C, air 21–22°C

Pos.	Driver	Laps	Time
1	Carlos Sainz	24	1m 19.806s
2	Charles Leclerc	21	1m 20.377s
3	Sergio Pérez	20	1m 20.399s
4	Max Verstappen	22	1m 20.626s
5	Lando Norris	22	1m 20.878s
6	Esteban Ocon	27	1m 21.004s
7	Lewis Hamilton	26	1m 21.027s
8	Daniel Ricciardo	23	1m 21.155s
9	Fernando Alonso	21	1m 21.229s
10	Valtteri Bottas	23	1m 21.247s
11	Yuki Tsunoda	26	1m 21.289s
12	George Russell	26	1m 21.457s
13	Sebastian Vettel	18	1m 21.661s
14	Pierre Gasly	26	1m 21.701s
15	Zhou Guanyu	21	1m 21.821s
16	Lance Stroll	24	1m 21.869s
17	Alexander Albon	25	1m 22.754s
18	Kevin Magnussen	18	1m 23.186s
19	Nicholas Latifi	25	1m 23.924s
20	Mick Schumacher	15	1m 24.349s

PRACTICE 2 (FRIDAY)

Weather: Dry/sunny

Temperatures: track 26–29°C, air 22–23°C

Pos.	Driver	Laps	Time
1	Charles Leclerc	27	1m 18.978s
2	Max Verstappen	22	1m 19.223s
3	Carlos Sainz	27	1m 19.376s
4	Fernando Alonso	22	1m 19.537s
5	Sergio Pérez	20	1m 19.658s
6	Esteban Ocon	25	1m 19.842s
7	Valtteri Bottas	25	1m 20.055s
8	Lando Norris	24	1m 20.100s
9	Pierre Gasly	27	1m 20.142s
10	Daniel Ricciardo	24	1m 20.203s
11	George Russell	25	1m 20.212s
12	Yuki Tsunoda	30	1m 20.424s
13	Lewis Hamilton	23	1m 20.521s
14	Lance Stroll	28	1m 20.611s
15	Zhou Guanyu	23	1m 21.063s
16	Kevin Magnussen	23	1m 21.191s
17	Alexander Albon	28	1m 21.912s
18	Mick Schumacher	22	1m 21.974s
19	Nicholas Latifi	24	1m 22.307s
-	Sebastian Vettel	-	-

PRACTICE 3 (SATURDAY)

Weather: Dry/overcast

Temperatures: track 31–32°C, air 24°C

Pos.	Driver	Laps	Time
1	Lando Norris	12	1m 19.117s
2	Charles Leclerc	15	1m 19.249s
3	Sergio Pérez	17	1m 19.265s
4	Fernando Alonso	15	1m 19.275s
5	Carlos Sainz	17	1m 19.419s
6	Daniel Ricciardo	14	1m 19.693s
7	Max Verstappen	16	1m 19.809s
8	Lewis Hamilton	13	1m 19.896s
9	Valtteri Bottas	17	1m 20.008s
10	Yuki Tsunoda	12	1m 20.071s
11	George Russell	16	1m 20.096s
12	Pierre Gasly	14	1m 20.133s
13	Esteban Ocon	14	1m 20.205s
14	Mick Schumacher	17	1m 20.692s
15	Zhou Guanyu	16	1m 20.836s
16	Alexander Albon	16	1m 20.958s
17	Kevin Magnussen	14	1m 21.025s
18	Nicholas Latifi	14	1m 21.050s
19	Lance Stroll	11	1m 21.636s
20	Sebastian Vettel	5	no time

QUALIFYING (SATURDAY)

Weather: Dry/partly cloudy Temperatures: track 26–31°C, air 22–24°C

Pos.	Driver	First	Second	Third	Qualifying Tyre
1	Charles Leclerc	1m 18.881s	1m 18.606s	1m 17.868s	Soft (n)
2	Max Verstappen	1m 18.580s	1m 18.611s	1m 18.154s	Soft (n)
3	Sergio Pérez	1m 18.834s	1m 18.340s	1m 18.240s	Soft (n)
4	Lando Norris	1m 19.280s	1m 19.066s	1m 18.703s	Soft (n)
5	Lewis Hamilton	1m 19.401s	1m 19.106s	1m 18.825s	Soft (n)
6	George Russell	1m 19.405s	1m 19.076s	1m 18.933s	Soft (n)
7	Daniel Ricciardo	1m 19.665s	1m 19.130s	1m 19.032s	Soft (u)
8	Esteban Ocon	1m 19.605s	1m 19.136s	1m 19.061s	Soft (n)
9	Carlos Sainz	1m 18.983s	1m 18.469s	1m 19.408s	Soft (n)
10	Fernando Alonso	1m 19.192s	1m 18.815s	no time	
11	Pierre Gasly	1m 19.580s	1m 19.226s		
12	Valtteri Bottas	1m 19.251s	1m 19.410s		
13	Yuki Tsunoda	1m 19.742s	1m 19.424s		
14	Zhou Guanyu	1m 19.910s	1m 20.155s		
15	Mick Schumacher	1m 20.104s	1m 20.465s		
16	Alexander Albon	1m 20.135s			
17	Kevin Magnussen	1m 20.254s			
18	Sebastian Vettel	1m 21.149s			
19	Nicholas Latifi	1m 21.372s			
20	Lance Stroll	no time			

QUALIFYING: head to head

Hamilton	2	1	Russell
Verstappen	2	1	Pérez
Ricciardo	0	3	Norris
Leclerc	3	0	Sainz
Gasly	3	0	Tsunoda
Hülkenberg	1	1	Stroll
Vettel	1	0	Stroll
Alonso	1	2	Ocon
Bottas	3	0	Zhou
Albon	3	0	Latifi
Magnussen	2	1	Schumacher

Alpine F1 Team

FOR THE RECORD

1st GP LEADING EVERY LAP: Charles Leclerc

25th GRAND PRIX: Melbourne

Aston Martin Aramco Cognizant F1 Team

POINTS

DRIVERS

1	Charles Leclerc	71
2	George Russell	37
3	Carlos Sainz	33
4	Sergio Pérez	30
5	Lewis Hamilton	28
6	Max Verstappen	25
7	Esteban Ocon	20
8	Lando Norris	16
9	Kevin Magnussen	12
10	Valtteri Bottas	12
11	Daniel Ricciardo	8
12	Pierre Gasly	6
13	Yuki Tsunoda	4
14	Fernando Alonso	2
15	Zhou Guanyu	1
16	Alexander Albon	1

CONSTRUCTORS

1	Ferrari	104
2	Mercedes	65
3	Red Bull	55
4	McLaren	24
5	Alpine	22
6	Alfa Romeo	13
7	Haas	12
8	AlphaTauri	10
9	Williams	1

9 · SAINZ · Ferrari   7 · RICCIARDO · McLaren   5 · HAMILTON · Mercedes   3 · PÉREZ · Red Bull   1 · LECLERC · Ferrari

10 · ALONSO · Alpine   8 · OCON · Alpine   6 · RUSSELL · Mercedes   4 · NORRIS · McLaren   2 · VERSTAPPEN · Red Bull

47	48	49	50	51	52	53	54	55	56	57	58	
16	16	16	16	16	16	16	16	16	16	16	16	1
11	11	11	11	11	11	11	11	11	11	11	11	2
63	63	63	63	63	63	63	63	63	63	63	63	3
44	44	44	44	44	44	44	44	44	44	44	44	4
4	4	4	4	4	4	4	4	4	4	4	4	5
3	3	3	3	3	3	3	3	3	3	3	3	6
23	23	23	23	23	23	23	23	23	23	31	31	7
31	31	31	31	31	31	31	31	31	31	77	77	8
18	18	18	10	10	10	77	77	77	77	23	10	9
10	10	10	18	77	77	10	10	10	10	10	23	10
77	77	77	77	18	18	18	18	18	24	24	24	
14	14	14	14	14	24	24	24	24	18	18	18	
47	47	47	24	24	20	20	20	20	47	47		
24	24	24	20	20	14	47	47	47	20	20		
20	20	20	47	47	47	22	22	22	22	22		
22	22	22	22	22	22	6	6	6	6	6		
6	6	6	6	6	6	14	14	14	14	14		

18 = Pit stop   *6 = One lap or more behind*

SC Safety car deployed on laps shown

VSC Virtual safety car deployed on laps shown

RACE TYRE STRATEGIES

PIRELLI

	Driver	Race Stint 1	Race Stint 2	Race Stint 3	Race Stint 4
1	Leclerc	Medium (n): 1–22	Hard (n): 23–58		
2	Pérez	Medium (n): 1–20	Hard (n): 21–58		
3	Russell	Medium (n): 1–23	Hard (n): 24–58		
4	Hamilton	Medium (n): 1–22	Hard (n): 23–58		
5	Norris	Medium (n): 1–20	Hard (n): 21–58		
6	Ricciardo	Medium (n): 1–21	Hard (n): 22–58		
7	Ocon	Medium (n): 1–17	Hard (n): 18–58		
8	Bottas	Medium (n): 1–22	Hard (n): 23–58		
9	Gasly	Medium (n): 1–21	Hard (n): 22–58		
10	Albon	Hard (n): 1–57	Soft (n): 58		
11	Zhou	Medium (n): 1–21	Hard (n): 22–58		
12	Stroll	Medium (n): 1–2	Medium (u): 3	Hard (u): 4–23	Hard (u): 24–58
13	Schumacher	Medium (u): 1–14	Hard (n): 15–57		
14	Magnussen	Hard (n): 1–39	Medium (u): 40–57		
15	Tsunoda	Medium (n): 1–18	Hard (n): 19–57		
16	Latifi	Medium (n): 1–13	Medium (u): 14–23	Hard (n): 24–57	
17	Alonso	Hard (n): 1–39	Medium (n): 40–53	Medium (n): 54–57	
	Verstappen	Medium (n): 1–18	Hard (n): 19–38 (dnf)		
	Vettel	Hard (u): 1–22 (dnf)			
	Sainz	Medium (u): 1 (dnf)			

The tyre regulations stipulate that at least two of three dry tyre specifications must be used during a dry race. Selected compounds for Melbourne: Red = Soft (C5); Yellow = Medium (C3); White = Hard (C2). (n) new (u) used

McLaren F1 Team

FIA FORMULA 1 WORLD CHAMPIONSHIP · ROUND 4

EMILIA ROMAGNA GRAND PRIX

IMOLA CIRCUIT

Advantage Max. Verstappen's sprint-race victory put him on the grippier side of the track for the start of the grand prix proper.
Photo: Atsuo Sakurai

IMOLA QUALIFYING/SPRINT QUALIFYING

A GRAND PRIX at Imola, just down the road from Maranello, with Ferrari's Charles Leclerc leading the world championship and having won two of the first three races. Enough to put the fervent *tifosi* into the highest of spirits. They were dampened slightly by a soggy opening practice session on a dank, misty Friday morning, but a couple of espressos and Ferraris dominant in the wet were more than enough to shore things up.

The Emilia Romagna GP featured the first 2022 sprint qualifying format, with a couple of tweaks. There was still a one-hour Friday qualifying session to determine the grid for a 100km Saturday sprint 'race', the result of which would set the grid for Sunday's main event.

The FIA had planned to double the number of sprint events from three to six in 2022, but the teams knocked that back on the grounds of unwanted additional expense amid a budget cap. And the consensus was that whoever was quickest in regular qualifying on Friday should be credited with pole position, not the winner of the Saturday sprint if they turned out to be different. But only as far as the record books were concerned. Sunday's grid positions would still be determined exclusively by Saturday's sprint. Confused? You should be...

The other change was the scoring system. Instead of just 3-2-1 championship points on offer for the first three sprint finishers, the first eight finishers would now be rewarded 8-7-6-5-4-3-2-1.

When qualifying began on Friday afternoon, the rain had gone, but the track was still damp and there was a mix of Q1 tyre choice between Pirelli's intermediate treaded rubber and soft-compound slicks. It was not long before a red flag interrupted proceedings, with Alex Albon suffering overheating Williams brakes, an affliction that had hit team-mate Nicholas Latifi in pre-season testing in Bahrain. A fire, followed by a small explosion, damaged the upright and rear suspension, scattering debris. Albon would start at the back for the second consecutive 'race'.

The two Mercedes had struggled to generate tyre temperature in the wet conditions of practice and, with the ambient at just 12 degrees, suffered the same problem in qualifying, to the extent that George Russell and Lewis Hamilton only just scraped out of Q2, 12th and 15th respectively, with Yuki Tsunoda's AlphaTauri failing to bump Hamilton by just 0.004s! AlphaTauri team-mate Pierre Gasly was another Q1 eliminee, along with Latifi, the hobbled Albon and Esteban Ocon, who had suffered a gearbox problem.

In Q2, it was Max Verstappen who set the initial pace a couple of tenths clear of Carlos Sainz. But the Spaniard, who had just signed a Ferrari contract extension to the end of 2024, continued his troubled start to the season when he lost the Ferrari at the second Rivazza and ended his session in the wall, bringing out a second red flag. While the Ferrari was being recovered, the rain came down once again, and there would be no further improvements, as both Mercedes drivers, Mick Schumacher, Zhou Guanyu and Lance Stroll bit the dust.

Thus for the first time since the Japanese GP of 2012, Q3 took place without any Mercedes representation. On a drying track, the intermediate was the tyre of choice, but Kevin Magnussen's Haas was caught out at Acque Minerale and brought out the third red flag of the session, although the Dane managed to extricate himself from the gravel and continue.

The fourth red, equalling the record number in Hungary, 2016 and Baku, 2021, was caused by Valtteri Bottas with just three minutes of the session remaining, as Verstappen topped the times from Leclerc. The new record fifth came when Lando Norris lost his McLaren at Acque Minerali in the final minute of the session. He wasn't too disheartened, as it confirmed P3 on the grid for the McLaren.

The final interruption confirmed a first pole of the season for Verstappen, ahead of Leclerc, Norris, an excellent fourth from Magnussen, then Fernando Alonso's Alpine, Daniel Ricciardo in the second McLaren, Sergio

Above: Max Verstappen drives around Charles Leclerc to take control of the sprint race on the penultimate lap.
Photo: Red Bull Content Pool/Getty Images

Left: On the soft-compound Pirellis, Leclerc gets the drop on Verstappen on the opening lap.
Photo: Lukas Gorys

Right: Carlos Sainz takes flight at the chicane in his Ferrari.
Photo: Atsuo Sakurai

Below: Sergio Pérez made up ground from his lowly starting position to take the third-place sprint gong.
Photo: Red Bull Content Pool/Getty Images

Pérez's Red Bull, Bottas's Alfa Romeo, Sebastian Vettel's Aston Martin, and Sainz.

The Haas drivers and Nicholas Latifi apart, the soft-compound Pirelli was the choice for the sprint, and it was Leclerc who delighted the crowd by beating Verstappen off the line to lead the 21-lapper.

Zhou Guanyu prompted an opening-lap safety car when he lost his Alfa Romeo after contact with Pierre Gasly's AlphaTauri, and we were racing again on lap five, the laps behind the safety car easing fears that the softs might go away before the end. A man on the move was Pérez. After taking advantage of some argy-bargy between Ricciardo and Alonso at the Tamburello chicane on the opening lap, he was quickly past Magnussen and up into fourth place.

Sainz, after his qualifying incident, was also making progress with the second Ferrari, up to seventh by lap nine. That became fifth when he displaced Magnussen and Ricciardo, and set his sights on his old mate Norris's McLaren, which he demoted with two to go.

With five laps remaining, Verstappen started to apply pressure to Leclerc's leading Ferrari, getting within DRS range for the first time. The Red Bull was slightly quicker through the opening two sectors of the lap, but Leclerc's traction out of the second Rivazza and good use of battery deployment kept him ahead until Verstappen gave it his all as they began the penultimate lap, silencing the home crowd with a good move around the outside into the Tamburello chicane to claim the eight points.

Pérez, after a very strong run, was actually catching the championship pace-setters en route to third, ahead of Sainz – another good recovery – the McLarens of Norris and Ricciardo, Bottas's Alfa Romeo and Magnussen, for whom the choice of the medium Pirelli did not really work, although it allowed the Dane to claim the final point. Alonso and Mick Schumacher just missed out, while Mercedes had to be content with 11th place for Russell and 14th for Hamilton.

Above: With Max Verstappen away in the lead, Sergio Pérez, Lando Norris and Charles Leclerc dispute second place, while behind, mayhem is about to be caused by the spinning Ferrari of Carlos Sainz.
Photo: XPB Images

Top right: Yuki Tsunoda enjoyed a strong race for AlphaTauri, finishing seventh.
Photo: Red Bull Content Pool/Getty Images

Above right: Valtteri Bottas overcame his collision with Sainz in the first-lap mêlée to take an unexpected fifth.
Photo: Alfa Romeo ORLEN

Above far right: Lando Norris had the satisfaction of an unexpected first podium of the season for McLaren.
Photo: Pirelli

Right: Norris's crew applaud him as he crosses the line to take a splendid third place.
Photo: XPB Images

AS the grid assembled for the main event at Imola, the track was damp and the entire field was on Pirelli's intermediate tyre. Red flares signalled the all-consuming passion for Ferrari, and all eyes were on the front row to see if Charles Leclerc could repeat his feat from the sprint race and beat pole-man Max Verstappen's Red Bull into the Tamburello chicane.

This time, though, Leclerc did not get the same grip and traction on the wet asphalt that he'd enjoyed in the dry, his last-lap sprint-race demotion proving costly. Rather than challenging the lead Red Bull, he was demoted by the second RB18 as Sergio Pérez barged past, and then by Lando Norris's McLaren, which came down the Ferrari's inside after a brilliant getaway.

Further back, there was more drama for Carlos Sainz as the Spaniard's left rear wheel was clipped by Daniel Ricciardo's right front as they piled into the chicane, the Ferrari heading backwards into the gravel to the dismay of the home fans. Ricciardo managed to extricate himself and keep going.

As everyone behind took evasive action, George Russell made up no fewer than five places to put the first Mercedes into the top six from 11th on the grid! The Aston Martins benefited, too, both up four places.

With Sainz beached and out of his second successive race early on, the safety car was deployed, with the order behind it: Verstappen, Pérez, Norris, Leclerc, Kevin Magnussen, Russell, Valtteri Bottas, Fernando Alonso, Sebastian Vettel, Yuki Tsunoda, Lance Stroll, Lewis Hamilton, Esteban Ocon, Pierre Gasly, Alex Albon, Nicholas Latifi, Mick Schumacher, Zhou Guanyu and Ricciardo.

With the race under way again on lap five of the 61, Vettel nipped by Alonso to go eighth, the Alpine soon afflicted by a missing section of its right sidepod, which had parted company with the car after opening-lap contact with an out-of-shape Mick Schumacher. The two-time champion dropped down the order and ultimately into retirement.

There was a huge roar from the *tifosi* as Leclerc got a run on Norris on lap eight, demoting the McLaren into the Tamburello chicane. By this stage, Charles was some 6s behind Verstappen's fleeing Red Bull.

With a dozen laps down, Verstappen led team-mate Pérez by 5s, with Leclerc 2.5s behind the second Red Bull. Norris's McLaren had dropped 6s to the Ferrari, and Magnussen's fifth-place Haas was under severe pressure from Russell's Mercedes. George got a move done around the outside of the Dane into the Tamburello chicane, but ran wide on exit, allowing Bottas to close in on the pair. Russell went by again into the Variante Alta chicane, now renamed Curva Gresini in honour of Italian motorcycle rider/team manager Fausto Gresini, who had succumbed to Covid-19 in 2021, aged 60. A lap later, Bottas also demoted Magnussen with a committed, brave move around the outside on the approach to the first Rivazza.

By lap 18, a drier line was emerging, and both Vettel and Ricciardo made early stops for medium-compound dry tyres. Red Bull soon made the call with Pérez, who had Leclerc breathing down his neck. Rather than follow Sergio in, Charles stayed out. The pit lane became super-busy as half the field piled in, poor Bottas losing the benefit of his Rivazza heroics after a problem with the right front gun cost him 8s. Hamilton also lost out with a tardy 5s stop and was jumped by Ocon for 11th.

On lap 20, both race leader Verstappen and Leclerc pitted. The Red Bull stop was 1.4s better than Ferrari's, which was crucial. The Ferrari rejoined just ahead of Pérez on the track and went through the Tamburello chicane narrowly in front, but not by a sufficient margin to prevent Pérez from retaking second into the Villeneuve chicane as Leclerc's tyres went through the warm-up phase.

On lap 29, Pérez had a moment at Variante Alta, running across the chicane, which allowed Leclerc right on to his rear wing. But, despite the Ferrari coming out of the second Rivazza very close and picking up DRS, the Red Bull's straight-line speed was strong enough to repel any attack into Tamburello.

Further down, Yuki Tsunoda was going well in AlphaTauri's home race, moving up into eighth, ahead of Magnussen's Haas with 15 laps remaining, then beginning to chase Vettel's Aston.

On lap 50, Ferrari rolled the dice and brought in Leclerc for

ORLEN

splunk>
ACCELERATING
TRANSFORMATION
sparco

ROLEX
ROLEX

Above: With the track now dry, the Red Bull crew executes another perfect tyre change as Verstappen takes on soft Pirellis at his final stop.
Photo: Red Bull Content Pool/Getty Images

Above right: Leclerc rues the costly error that left him to scramble home in sixth place.
Photo: Scuderia Ferrari

Right: Delighted Verstappen and Pérez celebrate their 1-2 finish.
Photo: Red Bull Content Pool/Getty Images

a set of soft-compound tyres, losing track position to Norris's McLaren in the process. Red Bull responded with Pérez on the next lap and had the Mexican rolling again in just 2.2s, good enough to pit out ahead of the flying Leclerc, who had just blown by Norris. Playing it safe in case of a late-race safety car, Red Bull also pitted Verstappen next time around for a set of softs.

"I think we should have gone for mediums," Leclerc told the Ferrari pit-wall crew, despite setting a new race fastest lap as he attempted to close down Pérez with 11 laps to go. But, trying to stay within DRS range as they closed in to lap Mick Schumacher, Leclerc took way too much kerb into Variante Alta and spun backwards into the tyres, to the dismay of the flag-waving Ferrari fans.

He extricated himself and managed to continue, but damage to the front wing endplate gave him major understeer and a car that was reluctant to turn left. With hindsight, he might have been better staying out, but the Ferrari headed for the pits once more, for a new nose, which dropped him to ninth.

Tsonoda, meanwhile, had caught Vettel and promptly moved up into seventh.

Leclerc was now into damage limitation, trying to salvage whatever he could from a disastrous afternoon. He repassed Magnussen with eight to go and set his sights on Vettel.

Verstappen was more comfortable than he could ever have hoped, almost 14s clear of his team-mate, with Norris now up into a podium position for McLaren. Some 6.5s down, Russell was unable to close down the McLaren and, hampered by understeer as a result of not getting a front wing adjustment at his stop, had his hands full defending against Bottas's Alfa.

With three laps remaining, Leclerc had caught Vettel and taken seventh from the Alfa. Next on his radar was Tsunoda's AlphaTauri, which he managed to relieve of sixth place on the last lap.

But a comfortable Red Bull 1-2 on Ferrari's home turf at Imola, after such a dominant performance in Australia, was not what the prancing horse had been hoping for. Leclerc had had decent pace, but it was Verstappen who claimed the additional point for fastest lap. Losing the lead of the sprint race had been costly for Leclerc, as had his mistake behind Pérez.

A podium from Norris, meanwhile, was a great fillip for McLaren after such a tough start to the season. "It's a bit unbelievable when you consider where we were in Bahrain," he said. "Personally, I honestly didn't think I'd be on the podium all year – that's how bad it was! But to be standing up there in just the fourth race of the season is quite remarkable, how much we've been able to turn it around and make some good improvements." Italy was proving to be a happy hunting ground for Lando after his third place

in the corresponding race a year earlier, followed by second at Monza.

Russell, meanwhile, did a fine job to fend off the luckless Bottas for fourth, ahead of the chastened Leclerc, Tsunoda, Vettel, Magnussen and, making it two Astons in the top ten as the team scored its first points of the year, Stroll.

"That was a very lovely Sunday!" Verstappen radioed in as he contemplated a much more palatable 27-point championship deficit to Leclerc after claiming every point on offer at Imola.

In the constructors' championship, Ferrari still led, but it's margin of superiority over Red Bull was down to just 11 points. Leclerc was not slow to beat himself up: "I believe that the spin shouldn't have happened today," he grimaced. "P3 was the best I could do, we didn't have the pace to do much more, and I was too greedy and paid the price for it. I lost seven potential points compared with the third place I was in before. It's a shame because it's seven points that are valuable at the end of the championship for sure, and it shouldn't happen again."

Red Bull's reliability problems at two of the first three races had gifted Leclerc and Ferrari a great start to the campaign, and they didn't want to hand any of it back. Heading to Barcelona, they were hoping it was a blip and not the start of a significant shift in momentum.

Tony Dodgins

VIEWPOINT
A SMALL, BUT EXPENSIVE MISTAKE

WITH Ferrari leading both championships and having dominated the previous race, it was a return to the good old days for the *tifosi*. And here they were at Imola, 50 miles from Maranello. Talk about an excuse for a party.

In 2021, you might have suggested that Charles Leclerc's tendency to make small mistakes at vital moments would go against him when the pressure was on. But that seemed to be a thing of the past, judging by the way he had calmly embraced the competitiveness of the 2022 Ferrari.

With Red Bull closing the performance gap to almost nothing, pole for Imola's first 2022 sprint race was decided by a small error as Leclerc locked up at Acque Minerale. That didn't seem to matter when he took the lead and pulled away – perhaps too enthusiastically as his right front opened up and allowed Max Verstappen to take the lead on the last lap.

What should have been a minor setback became a major one when, as the race report explains, there was a good side of the grid and a bad one. Leclerc was on the latter. The knock-on effect was third behind the fast-starting Red Bulls. With Charles unable to find a way past Sergio Pérez, Ferrari rolled the dice in the closing stages and brought him in for fresh rubber, Pérez following suit.

Urged on by the sea of red at every corner, Leclerc pushed hard and, in his enthusiasm, took too much kerb at Curva Gresini (formerly Variante Alta) and sent the F1-75 into a spin that ended against the barrier.

Whether or not he should have stopped for a new nose is irrelevant in terms of the mental kicking he was giving himself as he climbed back to score six points. It could have been zero points, but that was no consolation. The crestfallen Monégasque was his usual honest self when analysing the massive disappointment all round, only too aware that, when up against Verstappen, a few more mistakes like that would cost him the championship.

Maurice Hamilton

4

FORMULA 1 ROLEX GRAN PREMIO DEL MADE IN ITALY E DELL'EMILIA ROMAGNA 2022

IMOLA 22–24 APRIL

RACE DISTANCE: 63 laps, 192.034 miles/309.049km

RACE WEATHER: Wet-dry, overcast (track 15–18°C, air 12–14°C)

AUTODROMO ENZO E DINO FERRARI, IMOLA

Circuit: 3.050 miles/4.909km, 63 laps

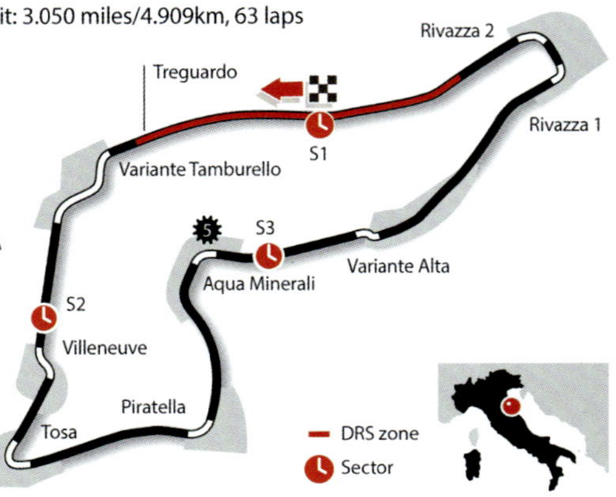

Rolex

Official Timepiece

RACE – OFFICIAL CLASSIFICATION

Pos.	Driver	Nat.	No.	Entrant	Car/Engine	Laps	Time/Retirement	Speed (mph/km/h)	Gap to winner	Fastest race lap	
1	**Max Verstappen**	NL	1	Oracle Red Bull Racing	Red Bull RB18-RBPTH001 V6	63	1h 32m 07.986s	125.058/201.262		1m 18.446s	55
2	**Sergio Pérez**	MEX	11	Oracle Red Bull Racing	Red Bull RB18-RBPTH001 V6	63	1h 32m 24.513s	124.686/200.662	16.527s	1m 18.949s	52
3	**Lando Norris**	GB	4	McLaren F1 Team	McLaren MCL36-Mercedes F1 M13 E Perf. V6	63	1h 32m 42.820s	124.275/200.002	34.834s	1m 20.903s	61
4	**George Russell**	GB	63	Mercedes-AMG Petronas F1 Team	Mercedes-AMG F1 W13-M13 E Perf. V6	63	1h 32m 50.492s	124.104/199.726	42.506s	1m 20.962s	57
5	**Valtteri Bottas**	FIN	77	Alfa Romeo F1 Team ORLEN	Alfa Romeo C42-Ferrari 066/7 V6	63	1h 32m 51.167s	124.089/199.702	43.181s	1m 20.758s	43
6	**Charles Leclerc**	MC	16	Scuderia Ferrari	Ferrari F1-75-066/7 V6	63	1h 33m 04.058s	123.803/199.241	56.072s	1m 18.574s	63
7	**Yuki Tsunoda**	J	22	Scuderia AlphaTauri	AlphaTauri AT03-RBPTH001 V6	63	1h 33m 09.096s	123.691/199.061	1m 01.110s	1m 20.544s	61
8	**Sebastian Vettel**	D	5	Aston Martin Aramco Cognizant F1 Team	Aston Martin AMR22-Mercedes F1 M13 E Perf. V6	63	1h 33m 18.878s	123.475/198.714	1m 10.892s	1m 21.211s	47
9	**Kevin Magnussen**	DK	20	Haas F1 Team	Haas VF-22-Ferrari 066/7 V6	63	1h 33m 23.246s	123.379/198.559	1m 15.260s	1m 21.238s	61
10	**Lance Stroll**	CDN	18	Aston Martin Aramco Cognizant F1 Team	Aston Martin AMR22-Mercedes F1 M13 E Perf. V6	62			1 lap	1m 21.750s	46
11	Alexander Albon	T	23	Williams Racing	Williams FW44-Mercedes F1 M13 E Perf. V6	62			1 lap	1m 21.757s	61
12	Pierre Gasly	F	10	Scuderia AlphaTauri	AlphaTauri AT03-RBPTH001 V6	62			1 lap	1m 21.713s	34
13	Lewis Hamilton	GB	44	Mercedes-AMG Petronas F1 Team	Mercedes-AMG F1 W13-M13 E Perf. V6	62			1 lap	1m 21.419s	50
14	Esteban Ocon	F	31	BWT Alpine F1 Team	Alpine A522-Renault E-Tech RE22 V6	62	*		1 lap	1m 21.887s	37
15	Zhou Guanyu	CHN	24	Alfa Romeo F1 Team ORLEN	Alfa Romeo C42-Ferrari 066/7 V6	62			1 lap	1m 21.286s	61
16	Nicholas Latifi	CDN	6	Williams Racing	Williams FW44-Mercedes F1 M13 E Perf. V6	62			1 lap	1m 21.338s	62
17	Mick Schumacher	D	47	Haas F1 Team	Haas VF-22-Ferrari 066/7 V6	62			1 lap	1m 18.999s	55
18	Daniel Ricciardo	AUS	3	McLaren F1 Team	McLaren MCL36-Mercedes F1 M13 E Perf. V6	62			1 lap	1m 21.577s	61
	Fernando Alonso	E	14	BWT Alpine F1 Team	Alpine A522-Renault E-Tech RE22 V6	6	*accident/floor and sidepod*			1m 39.685s	5
	Carlos Sainz	E	55	Scuderia Ferrari	Ferrari F1-75-066/7 V6	0	*accident*			no time	

* Ocon: 5s time penalty for unsafe release from a pit stop (originally finished 11th).

DHL Fastest race lap (scores 1 point): Max Verstappen on lap 55, 1m 18.446s, 139.983mph/225.281km/h.

Lap record: Lewis Hamilton (Mercedes F1 W11 V6), 1m 15.484s, 145.476mph/234.121km/h (2020).

19 · LATIFI · Williams

17 · GASLY · AlphaTauri

15 · STROLL · Aston Martin

13 · VETTEL · Aston Martin

11 · RUSSELL · Mercedes

20 · ZHOU · Alfa Romeo
Car modified in *parc fermé*; required to start from the pit lane

18 · ALBON · Williams

16 · OCON · Alpine

14 · HAMILTON · Mercedes

12 · TSUNODA · AlphaTauri

Grid order		1	2	3	4	5	6	7	8	9	10	11	12	13	14	15	16	17	18	19	20	21	22	23	24	25	26	27	28	29	30	31	32	33	34	35	36	37	38	39	40	41	42	43	44	45	46	47	48	49	50	51
1	VERSTAPPEN	1	1	1	1	1	1	1	1	1	1	1	1	1	1	1	1	1	1	1	1	1	1	1	1	1	1	1	1	1	1	1	1	1	1	1	1	1	1	1	1	1	1	1	1	1	1	1	1	1	1	1
16	LECLERC	11	11	11	11	11	11	11	11	11	11	11	11	11	11	11	11	11	16	16	11	11	11	11	11	11	11	11	11	11	11	11	11	11	11	11	11	11	11	11	11	11	11	11	11	11	11	11	11	11	11	11
11	PÉREZ	4	4	4	4	4	4	4	16	16	16	16	16	16	16	16	16	16	11	4	16	16	16	16	16	16	16	16	16	16	16	16	16	16	16	16	16	16	16	16	16	16	16	16	16	16	16	16	16	16	4	16
55	SAINZ	16	16	16	16	16	16	16	4	4	4	4	4	4	4	4	4	4	4	11	4	4	4	4	4	4	4	4	4	4	4	4	4	4	4	4	4	4	4	4	4	4	4	4	4	4	4	4	4	4	16	4
4	NORRIS	20	20	20	20	20	20	20	20	20	20	20	63	63	63	63	63	63	63	63	63	63	63	63	63	63	63	63	63	63	63	63	63	63	63	63	63	63	63	63	63	63	63	63	63	63	63	63	63	63	63	63
3	RICCIARDO	63	63	63	63	63	63	63	63	63	63	63	20	77	77	77	77	77	77	77	77	77	77	77	77	77	77	77	77	77	77	77	77	77	77	77	77	77	77	77	77	77	77	77	77	77	77	77	77	77	77	77
77	BOTTAS	77	77	77	77	77	77	77	77	77	77	77	77	20	20	20	20	20	20	5	5	5	5	5	5	5	5	5	5	5	5	5	5	5	5	5	5	5	5	5	5	5	5	5	5	5	5	5	5	5	5	5
20	MAGNUSSEN	14	14	14	14	5	5	5	5	5	5	5	5	5	5	5	5	22	22	20	20	20	20	20	20	20	20	20	20	20	20	20	20	20	20	20	20	20	20	20	20	20	20	20	20	20	20	22	22	22	22	22
14	ALONSO	5	5	5	5	22	22	22	22	22	22	22	22	22	22	22	22	5	18	22	22	22	22	22	22	22	22	22	22	22	22	22	22	22	22	22	22	22	22	22	22	22	22	22	22	22	22	20	20	20	20	20
47	SCHUMACHER	22	22	22	22	18	18	18	18	18	18	18	18	18	18	18	18	18	44	18	18	18	18	18	18	18	18	18	18	18	18	18	18	18	18	18	18	18	18	18	18	18	18	18	18	18	18	18	18	18	18	18
63	RUSSELL	18	18	18	18	14	44	44	44	44	44	44	44	44	44	44	44	44	31	31	31	31	31	31	31	31	31	31	31	31	31	31	31	31	31	31	31	31	31	31	31	31	31	31	31	31	31	31	31	31	31	31
22	TSUNODA	44	44	44	44	44	31	31	31	31	31	31	31	31	31	31	31	31	6	10	23	23	23	23	23	23	23	23	23	23	23	23	23	23	23	23	23	23	23	23	23	23	23	23	23	23	23	23	23	23	23	23
5	VETTEL	31	31	31	31	31	10	10	10	10	10	10	10	10	10	10	10	10	24	23	10	10	10	10	10	10	10	10	10	10	10	10	10	10	10	10	10	10	10	10	10	10	10	10	10	10	10	10	10	10	10	10
44	HAMILTON	10	10	10	10	10	23	23	23	23	23	23	23	23	23	23	23	6	47	44	44	44	44	44	44	44	44	44	44	44	44	44	44	44	44	44	44	44	44	44	44	44	44	44	44	44	44	44	44	44	44	44
18	STROLL	23	23	23	23	23	6	6	6	6	6	6	6	6	6	6	6	24	5	3	3	3	3	3	3	3	3	3	3	3	3	6	6	6	6	6	6	6	6	6	24	24	24	24	24	24	24	24	24	24	24	24
31	OCON	6	6	6	6	6	47	47	47	47	47	47	47	47	24	24	24	47	10	6	6	6	6	6	6	6	6	6	6	6	6	24	24	24	24	24	24	24	24	24	6	6	6	6	6	6	6	6	6	6	6	6
10	GASLY	47	47	47	47	47	24	24	24	24	24	24	24	24	47	47	47	23	23	47	47	47	47	47	24	24	24	24	24	24	47	47	47	47	47	47	47	47	47	47	47	47	47	47	47	47	47	47	47	47	47	47
23	ALBON	24	24	24	24	24	3	3	3	3	3	3	3	3	3	3	3	3	3	24	24	24	24	24	47	47	47	47	47	47	47	3	3	3	3	3	3	3	3	3	3	3	3	3	3	3	3	3	3	3	3	3
6	LATIFI	3	3	3	3	3	14																																													
24	ZHOU																																																			
		SC	SC	SC	SC																																															

TIME SHEETS

PRACTICE 1 (FRIDAY)

Weather: Wet/overcast

Temperatures: track 14–15°C, air 11–12°C

Pos.	Driver	Laps	Time
1	Charles Leclerc	24	1m 29.402s
2	Carlos Sainz	25	1m 30.279s
3	Max Verstappen	21	1m 30.867s
4	Kevin Magnussen	23	1m 32.439s
5	Mick Schumacher	23	1m 32.988s
6	Sergio Pérez	17	1m 33.012s
7	Fernando Alonso	13	1m 33.160s
8	Sebastian Vettel	22	1m 33.365s
9	Yuki Tsunoda	18	1m 33.611s
10	George Russell	21	1m 34.262s
11	Valtteri Bottas	19	1m 34.615s
12	Pierre Gasly	19	1m 35.104s
13	Esteban Ocon	14	1m 35.420s
14	Lando Norris	12	1m 35.502s
15	Daniel Ricciardo	15	1m 35.625s
16	Lance Stroll	23	1m 36.033s
17	Alexander Albon	17	1m 36.461s
18	Lewis Hamilton	17	1m 36.464s
19	Zhou Guanyu	22	1m 37.450s
20	Nicholas Latifi	15	1m 39.698s

PRACTICE 2 (SATURDAY)

Weather: Dry/sunny

Temperatures: track 30–31° C, air 19–20°C

Pos.	Driver	Laps	Time
1	George Russell	32	1m 19.457s
2	Sergio Pérez	33	1m 19.538s
3	Charles Leclerc	35	1m 19.740s
4	Lewis Hamilton	34	1m 19.992s
5	Fernando Alonso	29	1m 20.174s
6	Carlos Sainz	31	1m 20.258s
7	Max Verstappen	36	1m 20.371s
8	Yuki Tsunoda	35	1m 20.381s
9	Pierre Gasly	37	1m 20.439s
10	Zhou Guanyu	32	1m 20.498s
11	Alexander Albon	34	1m 20.591s
12	Kevin Magnussen	30	1m 20.740s
13	Mick Schumacher	29	1m 20.977s
14	Lance Stroll	38	1m 21.149s
15	Sebastian Vettel	38	1m 21.155s
16	Esteban Ocon	30	1m 21.179s
17	Nicholas Latifi	31	1m 21.263s
18	Lando Norris	6	1m 23.821s
-	Valtteri Bottas	-	-
-	Daniel Ricciardo	-	-

QUALIFYING (FRIDAY)

Weather: Dry-wet/mostly overcast Temperatures: track 13–15°C, air 12–13°C

Pos.	Driver	First	Second	Third	Qualifying Tyre
1	Max Verstappen	1m 19.295s	1m 18.793s	1m 27.999s	Intermediate (n)
2	Charles Leclerc	1m 18.796s	1m 19.584s	1m 28.778s	Intermediate (n)
3	Lando Norris	1m 20.168s	1m 19.294s	1m 29.131s	Intermediate (u)
4	Kevin Magnussen	1m 20.147s	1m 19.902s	1m 29.164s	Intermediate (n)
5	Fernando Alonso	1m 20.198s	1m 19.595s	1m 29.202s	Intermediate (n)
6	Daniel Ricciardo	1m 19.980s	1m 20.031s	1m 29.742s	Intermediate (n)
7	Sergio Pérez	1m 19.773s	1m 19.296s	1m 29.808s	Intermediate (n)
8	Valtteri Bottas	1m 20.419s	1m 20.192s	1m 30.439s	Intermediate (u)
9	Sebastian Vettel	1m 20.364s	1m 19.957s	1m 31.062s	Intermediate (n)
10	Carlos Sainz	1m 19.305s	1m 18.990s	no time	
11	George Russell	1m 20.383s	1m 20.757s		
12	Mick Schumacher	1m 20.422s	1m 20.916s		
13	Lewis Hamilton	1m 20.470s	1m 21.138s		
14	Zhou Guanyu	1m 19.730s	1m 21.434s		
15	Lance Stroll	1m 20.342s	1m 28.119s		
16	Yuki Tsunoda	1m 20.474s			
17	Pierre Gasly	1m 20.732s			
18	Nicholas Latifi	1m 21.971s			
19	Esteban Ocon	1m 22.338s			
20	Alexander Albon	no time			

POINTS

DRIVERS

1	Charles Leclerc	86
2	Max Verstappen	59
3	Sergio Pérez	54
4	George Russell	49
5	Carlos Sainz	38
6	Lando Norris	35
7	Lewis Hamilton	28
8	Valtteri Bottas	24
9	Esteban Ocon	20
10	Kevin Magnussen	15
11	Daniel Ricciardo	11
12	Yuki Tsunoda	10
13	Pierre Gasly	6
14	Sebastian Vettel	4
15	Fernando Alonso	2
16	Zhou Guanyu	1
17	Alexander Albon	1
18	Lance Stroll	1

For the Sprint, additional points are allocated to the top eight drivers for both championships, with the winner earning eight points. P2 through to P8 earn seven, six, five, four, three, two and one point respectively.

CONSTRUCTORS

1	Ferrari	124
2	Red Bull	113
3	Mercedes	77
4	McLaren	46
5	Alfa Romeo	25
6	Alpine	22
7	AlphaTauri	16
8	Haas	15
9	Aston Martin	5
10	Williams	1

QUALIFYING: head to head

Hamilton	2	2	Russell
Verstappen	3	1	Pérez
Ricciardo	0	4	Norris
Leclerc	4	0	Sainz
Gasly	3	1	Tsunoda
Hülkenberg	1	1	Stroll
Vettel	2	0	Stroll
Alonso	2	2	Ocon
Bottas	4	0	Zhou
Albon	3	1	Latifi
Magnussen	3	1	Schumacher

SPRINT QUALIFYING (SATURDAY)

RACE DISTANCE: 21 laps, 63.921miles/102.871km RACE WEATHER: Dry/overcast (track 27–28°C, air 20–21°C)

Pos.	Driver	Tyre	Laps	Time/Retirement	Speed (mph/km/h)	Gap to leader	Fastest race lap	
1	**Max Verstappen**		21	30m 39.567s	125.092/201.316		1m 19.154s	14
2	**Charles Leclerc**		21	30m 42.542s	124.890/200.991	2.975s	1m 19.044s	11
3	**Sergio Pérez**		21	30m 44.288s	124.772/200.801	4.721s	1m 19.012s	14
4	**Carlos Sainz**		21	30m 57.145s	123.908/199.411	17.578s	1m 19.251s	14
5	**Lando Norris**		21	31m 04.128s	123.444/198.664	24.561s	1m 20.030s	9
6	**Daniel Ricciardo**		21	31m 07.307s	123.234/198.326	27.740s	1m 20.328s	12
7	**Valtteri Bottas**		21	31m 07.700s	123.208/198.284	28.133s	1m 20.219s	9
8	**Kevin Magnussen**		21	31m 10.279s	123.038/198.010	30.712s	1m 20.557s	6
9	Fernando Alonso		21	31m 11.845s	122.935/197.845	32.278s	1m 20.639s	10
10	Mick Schumacher		21	31m 13.340s	122.837/197.687	33.773s	1m 20.567s	15
11	George Russell		21	31m 15.851s	122.672/197.422	36.284s	1m 20.756s	19
12	Yuki Tsunoda		21	31m 17.865s	122.541/197.210	38.298s	1m 20.909s	20
13	Sebastian Vettel		21	31m 19.744s	122.418/197.013	40.177s	1m 21.044s	8
14	Lewis Hamilton		21	31m 21.026s	122.335/196.879	41.459s	1m 20.663s	9
15	Lance Stroll		21	31m 22.477s	122.240/196.727	42.910s	1m 20.948s	14
16	Esteban Ocon		21	31m 23.084s	122.201/196.664	43.517s	1m 20.995s	14
17	Pierre Gasly		21	31m 23.361s	122.183/196.635	43.794s	1m 20.599s	18
18	Alexander Albon		21	31m 28.438s	121.855/196.106	48.871s	1m 21.020s	14
19	Nicholas Latifi		21	31m 31.584s	121.652/195.780	52.017s	1m 21.437s	16
	Zhou Guanyu		0	accident			no time	

Fastest race lap: Sergio Pérez on lap 14, 1m 19.012s, 138.980mph/223.667km/h.

9 · ALONSO · Alpine

7 · BOTTAS · Alfa Romeo

5 · NORRIS · McLaren

3 · PÉREZ · Red Bull

1 · VERSTAPPEN · Red Bull

10 · SCHUMACHER · Haas

8 · MAGNUSSEN · Haas

6 · RICCIARDO · McLaren

4 · SAINZ · Ferrari

2 · LECLERC · Ferrari

52	53	54	55	56	57	58	59	60	61	62	63	·
1	1	1	1	1	1	1	1	1	1	1	1	1
11	11	11	11	11	11	11	11	11	11	11	11	2
16	4	4	4	4	4	4	4	4	4	4	4	3
4	63	63	63	63	63	63	63	63	63	63	63	4
63	16	77	77	77	77	77	77	77	77	77	77	5
77	77	22	22	22	22	22	22	22	22	16	16	6
5	5	5	5	5	5	5	16	16	16	22	22	7
22	22	20	20	16	16	16	5	5	5	5	5	8
20	20	16	16	20	20	20	20	20	20	20	20	9
18	18	18	18	18	18	18	18	18	18	18		10
31	31	31	31	31	31	31	31	31	31	31		
23	23	23	23	23	23	23	23	23	23	23		
10	10	10	10	10	10	10	10	10	10	10		
44	44	44	44	44	44	44	44	44	44	44		
24	24	24	24	24	24	24	24	24	24	24		
6	6	6	6	6	6	6	6	6	6	6		
47	3	3	47	47	47	47	47	47	47	47		
3	47	47	3	3	3	3	3	3	3	3		

31 = Pit stop *20 = One lap or more behind*

SC Safety car deployed on laps shown

RACE TYRE STRATEGIES

PIRELLI

	Driver	Race Stint 1	Race Stint 2	Race Stint 3	Race Stint 4
1	Verstappen	Intermediate (n): 1-19	Medium (n): 20-51	Soft (n): 52-63	
2	Pérez	Intermediate (n): 1-18	Medium (n): 19-50	Soft (n): 51-63	
3	Norris	Intermediate (n): 1-19	Medium (n): 20-63		
4	Russell	Intermediate (n): 1-18	Medium (n): 19-63		
5	Bottas	Intermediate (n): 1-18	Medium (n): 19-63		
6	Leclerc	Intermediate (n): 1-19	Medium (n): 20-49	Soft (n): 50-53	Soft (u): 54-63
7	Tsunoda	Intermediate (n): 1-18	Medium (n): 19-63		
8	Vettel	Intermediate (n): 1-17	Medium (u): 18-63		
9	Magnussen	Intermediate (n): 1-18	Medium (u): 19-63		
10	Stroll	Intermediate (n): 1-18	Medium (u): 19-62		
11	Albon	Intermediate (n): 1-17	Medium (n): 18-62		
12	Gasly	Intermediate (n): 1-17	Medium (n): 18-62		
13	Hamilton	Intermediate (u): 1-18	Medium (n): 19-62		
14	Ocon	Intermediate (n): 1-18	Medium (n): 19-62		
15	Zhou	Intermediate (n): 1-18	Medium (n): 19-62		
16	Latifi	Intermediate (n): 1-18	Medium (n): 19-62		
17	Schumacher	Intermediate (n): 1-18	Medium (n): 19-52	Soft (n): 53-62	
18	Ricciardo	Intermediate (n): 1-2	Intermediate (u): 3-16	Medium (u): 17-30	Hard (n) 31-62
	Alonso	Intermediate (n): 1-6 (dnf)			
	Sainz	Intermediate (n): 0 (dnf)			

The tyre regulations stipulate that at least two of three dry tyre specifications must be used during a dry race. Selected compounds for Imola: Red = Soft (C4); Yellow = Medium (C3); White = Hard (C2). (n) new (u) used

Scuderia Ferrari

FIA FORMULA 1 WORLD CHAMPIONSHIP · ROUND 5

MIAMI GRAND PRIX

MIAMI CIRCUIT

Main photo: The moment of truth as Max Verstappen's Red Bull passes Charles Leclerc's Ferrari to take the lead only nine laps into the race.

Inset, right: Max reflects on a job well done.

Inset, far right: The podium was on a grand scale, dwarfing the drivers and dignitaries somewhat.

Photos: Red Bull Content Pool/Getty Images

FORMULA 1
CRYPTO.COM
MIAMI GRAND PRIX
crypto.com
FERRARI
aramco
FIA Formula 1 World Championship
crypto.com
MSC

MIAMI QUALIFYING

AND so, from one of the more traditional tracks, Imola, to one of Liberty Media's new 'signature' venues – Miami. With Las Vegas confirmed for November, 2023, grand prix racing was finally gaining a proper foothold in the USA. The 2022 season was the first since 1984 to feature two US races.

Around 15 miles north of downtown Miami, the new International Autodrome features a 3.36-mile, 19-turn layout around the Hard Rock Stadium, home of the Miami Dolphins football team.

The first phenomenon the drivers experienced was a serious lack of grip off the racing line as the track rubbered in, which was not unusual at a new street track. That and the close proximity of walls added up to considerable jeopardy. Carlos Sainz was the first to fall foul of it when he lost the rear end of his Ferrari out of Turn 13 after 20 minutes of FP2 on Friday afternoon.

Despite the relatively low-speed second-gear corner, Sainz went into a concrete wall rather than a Tecpro barrier, and was left with a headache and a sore, knotted neck for the rest of the weekend, as well as another dent to his confidence. Esteban Ocon was a victim of the same turn in FP3, the Frenchman suffering a 51g impact in an accident that cracked his Alpine chassis and ruled him out of qualifying. He expressed similar sentiments to Sainz: "We said in the drivers' briefing that it should be Tecpro there, but it wasn't listened to, which is unacceptable."

The Frenchman's misfortune meant that only an additional four drivers were eliminated in Q1. After looking impressive up to that point for Williams, it was perhaps a surprise that Alex Albon was one of them, the Anglo Thai left frustrated by a poor tyre preparation lap. Zhou Guanyu also had bad luck with traffic and suffered the same fate, joined on the sidelines by Kevin Magnussen – out in Q1 for the second time in three races – and Nicholas Latifi.

Sainz was not the only front-runner to suffer limited running on the opening day at a new track. Max Verstappen encountered a hydraulic issue in the opening practice session on Friday morning and brushed the wall as the steering tightened up. The rear brakes also caught fire, and Red Bull made a precautionary gearbox change, meaning that the frustrated Dutchman was only able to run a handful of quick laps and was playing catch-up going into qualifying.

The standout performance on Friday was none other than George Russell topping FP2 for Mercedes! Had the world champions solved their porpoising issues and joined the battle up front? Apparently not. Russell did not know why he was quick and, on Saturday, after a few overnight changes, found the Merc an entirely different proposition. To the extent that he was eliminated in Q2, only 12th fastest.

You could sense the annoyance. "Sorry guys," he said, after a big snap of oversteer on a bump in T6 ruined his best lap. "I just didn't have the same confidence in the car today." Educated guesswork was that in trying to run the car lower, the team had overdone things.

The midfield was super-tight as ever. Fernando Alonso's Alpine missed out on Q3 by just 0.032s, Russell by 0.045s, and Sebastian Vettel's Aston Martin by 0.086s as the frustrated four-time champion made a hash of the tight T14/15 chicane. Both Ferraris, Red Bulls and AlphaTauris made the cut, along with Valtteri Bottas's Alfa Romeo, Lewis Hamilton's Mercedes, Lando Norris's McLaren and Lance Stroll's Aston.

Despite his problematic opening day, it seemed that Verstappen was doing just fine, the first to break 1m 29s as he took provisional pole with his first Q3 run, eight-hundredths clear of Charles Leclerc's Ferrari, with Sainz third and Sergio Pérez half a second adrift with the second Red Bull.

When it mattered, though, Leclerc hit back, overcoming time lost in catching the Ferrari after a snap in Turn Four that resulted in his team-mate being almost a quarter of a second faster in the lap's opening sector. Sainz, though, had been slower than Leclerc all weekend out of T13, scene of his Friday shunt, and through the tight final sector. Great commitment and accuracy through the second and third sectors were enough to give Charles his third pole in five races as Ferrari took its first front-row lockout since Mexico, 2019.

"The lap wasn't great, but it was enough, so I can't complain," smiled Leclerc, who no doubt was happy to see his team-mate join him on the front row to potentially give him a race-day buffer to championship rival Verstappen.

The Dutchman's attempt to hang on to pole was scuppered when he became a bit too greedy in Turn Six and the car stepped out on him, ruining the lap. Again, though, the Red Bulls seemed to have a significant straight-line speed advantage, and the long straight between Turns 16 and 17 looked like affording plenty of opportunity to pass.

If Verstappen hadn't been able to improve on his final run, team-mate Pérez had, putting the second RB18 fourth, just five-hundredths behind the world champion.

Bottas continued his fine form, achieving a season-best fifth for Alfa, also the team's best qualifying performance since 2019, 0.15s ahead of Hamilton's Mercedes, no doubt providing Valtteri with great satisfaction.

After a below-par Imola, Gasly qualified the first AlphaTauri seventh, 0.06s clear of Norris's McLaren. In deference to the location, Lando was sporting a one-off helmet paint scheme in the design of a basketball.

Yuki Tsunoda, ninth, was a top-ten qualifier for the first time in 2022, a quarter of a second behind team-mate Pierre Gasly, with Stroll completing the top ten.

Above: With downtown Miami in the distance, the new F1 track was laid out around the Miami Dolphins football stadium.
Photo: Red Bull Content Pool/Getty Images

Top left: Miami mover and shaker David Beckham with Ferrari chairman John Elkann.
Photo: Scuderia Ferrari

Above far left: Sales pitch. Yachts were marooned on a sea of plastic.
Photo: Alfa Romeo ORLEN

Left: FIA president Mohammed Ben Sulayem chats with Michael Andretti on the grid.
Photo: Lukas Gorys

Centre left: Azure blue was the colour.
Photo: Alfa Romeo ORLEN

Centre far left: Jackie Stewart and Emerson Fittipaldi, legendary drivers from a bygone age, were still enjoying the modern-day glamour of F1.

Bottom far left: The Williams sisters, Venus and Serena, were among a multitude of personalities to take to the grid before the start.
Photos: XPB Images

Left: The 3.36-mile, 19-turn layout around the Hard Rock Stadium was a stern test for the drivers.
Photo: Pirelli

Above: Pole-sitter Charles Leclerc takes the lead from the start, while Max Verstappen's Red Bull pinches second place from the Ferrari of Carlos Sainz.
Photo: Pirelli

Top right: The walls were unforgiving, leaving Verstappen very little margin for error.
Photo: Atsuo Sakurai

Above right: Alex Albon brought some cheer to Williams by taking tenth and the final point on offer.
Photo: Pirelli

Right: Valtteri Bottas ran as high as fifth for much of the race, before a late error dropped him to seventh, behind Mercedes pair George Russell and Lewis Hamilton.
Photo: XPB Images

WITH the inaugural Miami GP the hottest ticket in town, predictably, the grid was awash with 'celebrities' – although identifying them was not the work of a moment for those not familiar with US pop culture. Two rather more fundamental things were missing, in the shape of the Aston Martins of tenth-placed Lance Stroll and his 13th-placed, four-time world champion team-mate, Sebastian Vettel. The team had made an error with the freezing of its fuel and, to avoid taking a penalty, had no option but to make pit-lane starts with both cars. Frustrating after Aston's best combined qualifying performance of the season.

As the lights went out, Charles Leclerc aced his start and converted his pole position, but team-mate Carlos Sainz was slower than Max Verstappen off the grid. Fully committed, Verstappen went around the outside of the Ferrari at the right-hand Turn One to pinch an important second place. Arguably, Sainz could have used his elbows a bit more, but given his recent incident count and Verstappen's uncompromising approach, it was perhaps no surprise that he gave ground. Without the hoped-for buffer, Ferrari was faced with the question of whether Leclerc would fall prey to the Red Bull's superior straight-line speed once more. Even without any DRS assistance, which would not come into play until the third lap, the RB18 was 5–6mph quicker on the straight than the Ferrari.

Valtteri Bottas ran fifth, while Lewis Hamilton, with a brief right-front lock-up and a tap from Fernando Alonso, lost a couple of places to the fast-starting Pierre Gasly and the Spaniard, the latter up four places. Lando Norris's McLaren was ninth, from Yuki Tsunoda's AlphaTauri, Daniel Ricciardo's McLaren, Haas twins Mick Schumacher and Kevin Magnussen, then Zhou Guanyu, George Russell (down three slots on the hard-compound Pirelli), Williams pair Alex Albon and Nicholas Latifi, Esteban Ocon's Alpine and the pit-lane-starting Astons of Stroll and Vettel.

In terms of tyre strategy, the first 14 had all chosen the medium compound, with Russell joined on the longer-running harder tyre by Ocon, Latifi and the two Aston Martin drivers.

The first indication that DRS-assisted overtaking would not prove too problematic came when Hamilton relieved Alonso of seventh place with relative ease between Turns 11 and 12 on the third lap.

Up front, Leclerc opened a small margin early on, but it soon became apparent that Verstappen could go with him. The pair had a 4s margin over Sainz by the eighth lap, when Verstappen, within DRS range, had his first serious look at the leading Ferrari on the long straight from T16 to T17. That wasn't quite on and he dropped back into line, following Leclerc closely through Turns 18 and 19 before using the main straight DRS zone to comfortably go inside the Ferrari into Turn One.

Leclerc was able to stay with the Red Bull, but despite the Ferrari having DRS this time on the long back straight and the shorter main one, it was insufficient to overcome the Red Bull's inherent pace advantage.

As the medium-tyre opening stint wore on, it was evident that the Ferraris were taking more out of the rubber than the Red Bulls. On lap 13, Leclerc ran very deep into T17 and dropped to 2.5s behind Verstappen, while Pérez closed to within a second-and-a-half of third-placed Sainz.

"The tyres feel okay," Verstappen told Red Bull 15 laps in.

"Yep," replied engineer Gianpiero Lambiase. "You've done an excellent job on the front right."

Meanwhile, Ferrari told Leclerc, "We are planning to go to Plan D for delta, and the hard is as expected." Which, presumably, given the lap times of those who'd started on it, meant not as quick.

As Verstappen set fastest lap of the race, Leclerc was able to match it, despite his earlier lock-up, so Ferrari had not shot its bolt.

Meanwhile, further back, Bottas was still running an

excellent fifth, a couple of seconds clear of Hamilton, while Alonso was into the pits on lap 16 to try to undercut Gasly's seventh-placed AlphaTauri. But that plan went awry when a problem with the right rear wheel left a frustrated Fernando stationary for 5.7s. He pitted out just ahead of a hard-tyred gaggle comprising Stroll, Latifi and Vettel. The former champion pulled off a fine move around the outside of the Canadian at Turn 11, giving him the inside line for T12. It was tight, but fair, and all over 15th place. The glory days might have gone, but Vettel was still enjoying his racing!

At one-third-distance, 19 laps into the race's 57, McLaren brought in seventh-placed Norris from 11s behind Hamilton's Mercedes, to swap his starting set of medium Pirellis for a set of hards. Again, it wasn't the smoothest of stops, and Lando dropped places to Vettel and Magnussen as he brought his new rubber up to temperature.

Pérez, meanwhile, had dropped to 5s behind Sainz's third-placed Ferrari and was on the radio to Red Bull complaining about a loss of power.

"Yes, we're looking into it," was the response from race engineer Hugh Bird.

"What's going on?" Pérez wanted to know.

"It's looking good. Power unit's all looking good."

"I'm losing power, man! How can you say it's good?"

"You've lost the tow. You've dropped back and lost the tow," explained Bird.

"Man, I'm losing power," Sergio insisted. "I'm losing three seconds per straight." There was now a 7.5s gap to Sainz, and Bottas was just a similar distance behind the second Red Bull.

Hamilton brought his Mercedes in for hards on lap 23 and was on his way after a typically efficient 2.7s stop by the Mercedes team. It dropped him behind team-mate Russell who, of course, had started on the hard tyre.

By lap 24, Leclerc had fallen almost 5s behind Verstappen and appeared to be in tyre trouble. "This car is so difficult to drive," he informed the Ferrari pit-wall crew, despite having just recorded the fastest lap of the race. He was in for the hard-compound Pirelli next time around, the Ferrari stationary for 3.2s.

Red Bull responded by bringing in Verstappen next lap. Despite having an extra set of new mediums compared to Ferrari, which Christian Horner thought might prove important if degradation drove the race towards a two-stopper, they also fitted the hard-compound tyre to cover Leclerc, with a 2.4s stop.

After a couple of laps leading, Sainz pitted on lap 28, with Pérez following the second Ferrari in at the same time. The Spaniard's stop occupied 5.4s due to a sticking front right wheel, while the Mexican was on his way again in just 3.1s. Pérez's power-loss issues had been resolved, but a sensor problem was costing him around 25bhp, which meant that Ferrari's pit-stop problem had not lost them a position.

With 20 laps remaining, Verstappen reclaimed the race's fastest lap and led Leclerc by 7.5s. Sainz was a further 15s in arrears, with Pérez some 6.5s adrift of the second Red Bull, but with a 12s cushion to Russell's Mercedes, which still had a stop to make. Bottas, his stop done, was 2s behind the man who had replaced him at Mercedes, with Hamilton a similar distance adrift of the Alfa. Ocon, Gasly and Alonso completed the top ten.

The next bit of action involved Fernando when the Alpine driver had a look at the inside of Gasly into Turn One and made contact with the AlphaTauri's right rear as the Frenchman closed the door. Alonso stole the place as Gasly sorted himself out and Stroll demoted him further.

A couple of laps later, with 16 to go, the struggling Gasly ran deep into Turn Eight and, as he came off the marbles and regained the track, made contact with Norris, sending him spinning wildly out of the race as the McLaren lost its punctured right rear tyre, spreading debris down the track.

"I'm out boys, sorry about that, I don't know what happened," Norris informed his team.

Left: Pirelli provided NFL helmets for the drivers to wear on the podium.
Photo: Pirelli

Below: Ferrari's Carlos Sainz managed to keep the Red Bull of Sergio Pérez at bay in their battle for third.
Photo: Scuderia Ferrari

Right: The track layout was imaginative given the tight confines within which it was built.
Photo: Alfa Romeo ORLEN

Below right: Despite the high ticket prices, a massive crowd flocked to the circuit for Miami's inaugural F1 race.
Photo: Lukas Gorys

An initial VSC and then a full safety car was a good break for Russell, allowing him a cheap stop. Red Bull elected to bring in Pérez and bolt on a fresh set of mediums.

This was going to be interesting. At the lap-46 restart, the first three – Verstappen, Leclerc and Sainz – were all on used hard-compound Pirellis, but fourth-placed Pérez had fresh mediums, Bottas and Hamilton were on hards, Russell had his mediums, Alonso and the Schumacher/Magnussen Haas cars were on hards, with Ocon's Alpine behind on fresh softs.

Pérez, with better tyre warm-up, was all over Sainz, but he went defensive and managed to hold off the Red Bull into Turn One. Their respective team-mates were at it as well. While Leclerc might have had no answer to Verstappen on the medium compound, he was relatively stronger on the harder tyre and, with quicker warm-up on the Ferrari, hassled Max hard as he attempted to stay within range for the reintroduction of DRS after two laps. Verstappen, though, had things under control. Just.

With seven laps to go, Bottas was kicking himself. After a fine performance all weekend, he ran too deep on the brakes at the end of the back straight, allowing both Mercedes past. At the same time, Russell also attacked Hamilton on his better rubber, getting by on the inside of T12 after his team-mate had run him wide at the previous corner.

Pérez now tried down the inside of Sainz into Turn One, made it by, but outbraked himself and was repassed on the way out.

Further back, the fatherly relationship that had developed between Schumacher and Vettel, who had been helped by Michael Schumacher when he had arrived on the F1 scene, was tested when Mick launched an optimistic bid down the inside of Turn One. When Vettel turned in, his right rear wheel was hit firmly by the Haas's left front, spinning the Aston Martin across the kerb and out of the race.

"What gap was that?" radioed a frustrated Vettel.

"I mean, that was clearly my corner," Mick told the Haas pit-wall crew, with absolutely no conviction whatsoever.

Thus, after starting third on the grid, Verstappen won his second successive race to reduce Leclerc's world championship lead to 19 points and bring Red Bull to within six points of Ferrari at the top of the constructors' championship table. Ferrari had to be content with second and third places, with Pérez a close fourth as 2022's 'big two' dominated once again.

The quirks of strategy and safety car timing meant that for the fourth race in succession, Russell was able to get the better of Hamilton on race-day, with Bottas left to rue a mistake that robbed him of the satisfaction of beating both silver cars. Ocon benefited likewise and brought his Alpine home eighth, an outcome he would happily have signed for on Saturday when his shunt in FP3 had resulted in him missing qualifying and starting at the back. Alonso made it a double helping of points for the Enstone team, with another fine performance from Albon giving Williams the final point.

After one of the most hyped races in living memory, it was time to contemplate the upcoming familiarity of Barcelona, so often a decent barometer of car performance across the season. But as we'd seen so far, it looked as though there was the proverbial fag paper's width between Verstappen and Leclerc, Red Bull and Ferrari, with the former's better straight-line speed decisive this time.

Tony Dodgins

VIEWPOINT
MARMITE OR MAGIC?

IT was the Marmite Grand Prix: you were either satisfied by the way the weekend had played out, or it left a disagreeable taste. Miami established a new commercial model in race promotion with unprecedented levels of VIP hospitality. If success was measured by the bottom line, then a sell-out crowd appeared to tick that box, even though the vast total outlay did not leave much fat on the fiscal bone. But the overarching question remained: did F1 really need this?

Liberty Media had made no secret of wishing to bring F1 to an American audience that went beyond the many dedicated race fans. The inevitable choice was a street race or, as with the Miami International Autodrome (MIA), the closest equivalent.

Given the basic material available – a multi-purpose stadium and surrounding car parks – the organisers created an imaginative layout that managed to incorporate two high-speed straights and fast, tricky curves. The tight, off-camber turns beneath the turnpike flyover might have irritated many drivers, but it kept them busy and induced the mistakes intended by the track's designers.

Judging by the state of the first three finishers, they knew they had been tested physically, even if the actual racing element was only saved by the late safety car. But that was nothing new. There had been better F1 races before this. And much worse. The problem was that some of the criticism was self-inflicted.

By hyping the Miami Grand Prix to an unprecedented level (it was described by one gushing TV presenter as the most anticipated race in living memory), the continuing close contest between Red Bull and Ferrari was bound to fall short in the minds of the same naive punters Liberty Media was trying to attract.

The scene on the starting grid summed it up. This was either the most impressive collection of A-listers, proving F1 to be the hottest ticket in town, or it was a mishmash of so-called celebrities who brought nothing to what, after all, was a round of a prestigious sporting world championship.

Maurice Hamilton

5

FORMULA 1 CRYPTO.COM MIAMI GRAND PRIX 2022

MIAMI 6–8 MAY

RACE DISTANCE: 57 laps, 191.683 miles/308.326km

RACE WEATHER: Dry/sunny-overcast (track 38–48°C, air

MIAMI INTERNATIONAL AUTODROME, FLORIDA

Circuit: 3.363 miles/5.412km, 57 laps

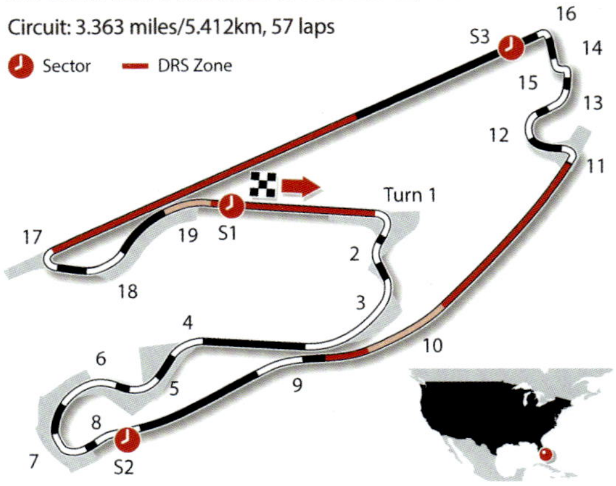

RACE – OFFICIAL CLASSIFICATION

Pos.	Driver	Nat.	No.	Entrant	Car/Engine	Laps	Time/Retirement	Speed (mph/km/h)	Gap to winner	Fastest race lap	
1	**Max Verstappen**	NL	1	Oracle Red Bull Racing	Red Bull RB18-RBPTH001 V6	57	1h 34m 24.258s	121.764/195.960		1m 31.361s	54
2	**Charles Leclerc**	MC	16	Scuderia Ferrari	Ferrari F1-75-066/7 V6	57	1h 34m 28.044s	121.683/195.830	3.786s	1m 31.488s	53
3	**Carlos Sainz**	E	55	Scuderia Ferrari	Ferrari F1-75-066/7 V6	57	1h 34m 32.487s	121.587/195.676	8.229s	1m 31.790s	56
4	**Sergio Pérez**	MEX	11	Oracle Red Bull Racing	Red Bull RB18-RBPTH001 V6	57	1h 34m 34.896s	121.536/195.593	10.638s	1m 31.819s	54
5	**George Russell**	GB	63	Mercedes-AMG Petronas F1 Team	Mercedes-AMG F1 W13-M13 E Perf. V6	57	1h 34m 42.840s	121.366/195.320	18.582s	1m 32.195s	56
6	**Lewis Hamilton**	GB	44	Mercedes-AMG Petronas F1 Team	Mercedes-AMG F1 W13-M13 E Perf. V6	57	1h 34m 45.626s	121.307/195.224	21.368s	1m 32.941s	55
7	**Valtteri Bottas**	FIN	77	Alfa Romeo F1 Team ORLEN	Alfa Romeo C42-Ferrari 066/7 V6	57	1h 34m 49.331s	121.228/195.097	25.073s	1m 33.184s	56
8	**Esteban Ocon**	F	31	BWT Alpine F1 Team	Alpine A522-Renault E-Tech RE22 V6	57	1h 34m 52.644s	121.157/194.983	28.386s	1m 33.163s	56
9	**Alexander Albon**	T	23	Williams Racing	Williams FW44-Mercedes F1 M13 E Perf. V6	57	1h 34m 56.623s	121.072/194.847	32.365s	1m 33.447s	57
10	**Lance Stroll**	CDN	18	Aston Martin Aramco Cognizant F1 Team	Aston Martin AMR22-Mercedes F1 M13 E Perf. V6	57	1h 35m 01.284s	120.974/194.688	37.026s	1m 33.312s	52
11	Fernando Alonso	E	14	BWT Alpine F1 Team	Alpine A522-Renault E-Tech RE22 V6	57	1h 35m 01.386s *	120.971/194.684	37.128s	1m 33.331s	53
12	Yuki Tsunoda	J	22	Scuderia AlphaTauri	AlphaTauri AT03-RBPTH001 V6	57	1h 35m 04.404s	120.907/194.581	40.146s	1m 33.035s	55
13	Daniel Ricciardo	AUS	3	McLaren F1 Team	McLaren MCL36-Mercedes F1 M13 E Perf. V6	57	1h 35m 05.160s *	120.891/194.556	40.902s	1m 33.265s	56
14	Nicholas Latifi	CDN	6	Williams Racing	Williams FW44-Mercedes F1 M13 E Perf. V6	57	1h 35m 14.194s	120.700/194.248	49.936s	1m 34.169s	53
15	Mick Schumacher	D	47	Haas F1 Team	Haas VF-22-Ferrari 066/7 V6	57	1h 35m 37.563s	120.209/193.457	1m 13.305s	1m 32.528s	57
16	Kevin Magnussen	DK	20	Haas F1 Team	Haas VF-22-Ferrari 066/7 V6	56	*accident damage* *		1 lap	1m 33.511s	52
17	Sebastian Vettel	D	5	Aston Martin Aramco Cognizant F1 Team	Aston Martin AMR22-Mercedes F1 M13 E Perf. V6	54	*accident damage*		3 laps	1m 33.479s	50
	Pierre Gasly	F	10	Scuderia AlphaTauri	AlphaTauri AT03-RBPTH001 V6	45	*accident damage*			1m 34.487s	38
	Lando Norris	GB	4	McLaren F1 Team	McLaren MCL36-Mercedes F1 M13 E Perf. V6	39	*accident*			1m 33.411s	37
	Zhou Guanyu	CHN	24	Alfa Romeo F1 Team ORLEN	Alfa Romeo C42-Ferrari 066/7 V6	6	*water pump*			1m 35.731s	4

* Alonso: 5s time penalty for causing a collision with Gasly; 5s time penalty for leaving the track and gaining an advantage (originally finished 8th).

* Magnussen: 5s time penalty for causing a collision with Stroll. * Ricciardo: 5s time penalty for leaving the track and gaining an advantage (originally finished 11th).

DHL Fastest race lap (scores 1 point): Max Verstappen on lap 54, 1m 31.361s, 132.511mph/213.255km/h.

Lap record: No previous race.

19 · LATIFI · Williams

17 · ZHOU · Alfa Romeo

15 · SCHUMACHER · Haas

13 · VETTEL · Aston Martin
Started from the pit lane

11 · ALONSO · Alpine

20 · OCON · Alpine

18 · ALBON · Williams

16 · MAGNUSSEN · Haas

14 · RICCIARDO · McLaren

12 · RUSSELL · Mercedes

Grid order	1	2	3	4	5	6	7	8	9	10	11	12	13	14	15	16	17	18	19	20	21	22	23
16 LECLERC	16	16	16	16	16	16	16	16	1	1	1	1	1	1	1	1	1	1	1	1	1	1	1
55 SAINZ	1	1	1	1	1	1	1	1	16	16	16	16	16	16	16	16	16	16	16	16	16	16	16
1 VERSTAPPEN	55	55	55	55	55	55	55	55	55	55	55	55	55	55	55	55	55	55	55	55	55	55	55
11 PÉREZ	11	11	11	11	11	11	11	11	11	11	11	11	11	11	11	11	11	11	11	11	11	11	11
77 BOTTAS	77	77	77	77	77	77	77	77	77	77	77	77	77	77	77	77	77	77	77	77	77	77	77
44 HAMILTON	10	10	10	10	10	44	44	44	44	44	44	44	44	44	44	44	44	44	44	44	44	44	63
10 GASLY	14	14	44	44	44	10	10	10	10	10	10	10	10	10	10	10	4	63	63	63	63	63	44
4 NORRIS	44	44	14	14	14	14	14	14	14	14	14	14	14	14	4	4	63	4	3	3	3	3	3
22 TSUNODA	4	4	4	4	4	4	4	4	4	4	4	4	4	4	14	63	3	3	31	31	31	31	31
18 STROLL	22	22	22	22	22	47	47	47	47	47	20	47	47	63	63	3	31	31	10	10	10	10	10
14 ALONSO	3	47	47	47	47	20	20	20	20	20	47	3	63	3	3	31	10	10	14	14	14	14	14
63 RUSSELL	47	3	20	20	20	22	22	22	22	3	3	63	3	47	23	23	14	14	18	18	18	18	18
5 VETTEL	20	20	3	3	3	3	3	3	3	22	63	20	23	23	31	14	18	18	5	5	5	5	5
3 RICCIARDO	24	24	24	24	24	63	23	63	63	63	23	23	31	31	18	18	5	5	20	20	20	20	20
47 SCHUMACHER	63	63	63	63	63	23	63	23	23	23	31	31	6	6	6	5	20	20	47	47	47	47	47
20 MAGNUSSEN	23	23	23	23	23	31	31	31	31	31	22	6	18	18	5	20	47	47	4	4	4	4	4
24 ZHOU	6	31	31	31	31	6	6	6	6	6	6	18	5	5	20	6	6	6	6	23	23	23	23
23 ALBON	31	6	6	6	6	18	18	18	18	18	18	5	20	20	47	47	22	22	23	6	6	6	6
6 LATIFI	18	18	18	18	18	5	5	5	5	5	5	22	22	22	22	22	23	23	22	22	22	22	22
31 OCON	5	5	5	5	5	24																	

Grid order	24	25	26	27	28	29	30	31	32	33	34	35	36	37	38	39	40	41	42	43	44	45	46
16 LECLERC	1	1	1	55	1	1	1	1	1	1	1	1	1	1	1	1	1	1	1	1	1	1	1
55 SAINZ	55	55	55	1	16	16	16	16	16	16	16	16	16	16	16	16	16	16	16	16	16	16	16
1 VERSTAPPEN	16	11	11	16	55	55	55	55	55	55	55	55	55	55	55	55	55	55	55	55	55	55	55
11 PÉREZ	11	16	16	11	11	11	11	11	11	11	11	11	11	11	11	11	11	11	11	11	11	11	11
77 BOTTAS	77	77	77	63	63	63	63	63	63	63	63	63	63	63	63	63	77	77	77	77	77	77	77
44 HAMILTON	63	63	63	77	77	77	77	77	77	77	77	77	77	77	77	77	44	44	44	44	44	44	44
10 GASLY	44	44	44	44	44	44	44	44	44	44	44	44	44	44	44	44	63	63	63	63	63	63	63
4 NORRIS	3	3	3	3	3	3	31	31	31	31	31	31	31	31	31	31	31	31	14	14	14	14	14
22 TSUNODA	31	31	31	31	31	31	10	10	10	10	10	10	10	10	10	14	14	14	47	47	47	47	47
18 STROLL	10	10	10	10	10	10	3	14	14	14	14	14	14	14	14	18	47	47	31	31	31	31	31
14 ALONSO	14	14	14	14	14	14	14	18	18	18	18	18	18	18	18	10	18	20	20	23	23	23	23
63 RUSSELL	18	18	18	18	18	18	18	20	20	20	47	47	47	47	47	47	20	23	23	18	18	18	18
5 VETTEL	5	5	5	20	20	20	5	47	47	47	20	20	20	20	20	20	5	18	18	20	20	20	20
3 RICCIARDO	20	20	20	5	5	5	20	5	5	5	5	4	4	4	4	4	23	5	5	5	5	5	5
47 SCHUMACHER	47	47	47	47	47	47	47	4	4	4	4	5	5	5	5	5	10	3	3	3	3	3	3
20 MAGNUSSEN	4	4	4	4	4	4	4	23	23	23	23	23	23	23	23	23	3	*10*	*10*	*10*	10	6	6
24 ZHOU	23	23	23	23	23	23	23	3	3	3	3	3	3	3	3	3	*22*	*22*	*6*	*6*	6	22	22
23 ALBON	22	22	22	22	22	22	22	22	22	22	22	22	22	22	*22*	*22*	6	6	*22*	*22*	22	10	
6 LATIFI	6	6	6	6	6	6	6	6	6	6	6	*6*	*6*	*6*	*6*	*6*							
31 OCON																							
																		VSC	SC	SC	SC	SC	SC

TIME SHEETS

PRACTICE 1 (FRIDAY)

Weather: Dry/sunny

Temperatures: track 38-44°C, air 22-23°C

Pos.	Driver	Laps	Time
1	Charles Leclerc	26	1m 31.098s
2	George Russell	23	1m 31.169s
3	Max Verstappen	14	1m 31.277s
4	Sergio Pérez	22	1m 31.301s
5	Pierre Gasly	27	1m 31.498s
6	Carlos Sainz	25	1m 31.528s
7	Alexander Albon	20	1m 31.854s
8	Lewis Hamilton	23	1m 31.956s
9	Kevin Magnussen	20	1m 32.559s
10	Daniel Ricciardo	21	1m 32.592s
11	Lando Norris	26	1m 32.615s
12	Fernando Alonso	31	1m 32.884s
13	Zhou Guanyu	23	1m 33.020s
14	Sebastian Vettel	24	1m 33.024s
15	Esteban Ocon	27	1m 33.417s
16	Lance Stroll	23	1m 33.576s
17	Valtteri Bottas	13	1m 33.773s
18	Yuki Tsunoda	27	1m 34.043s
19	Mick Schumacher	20	1m 34.945s
20	Nicholas Latifi	27	1m 35.637s

PRACTICE 2 (FRIDAY)

Weather: Dry/sunny

Temperatures:: track 44-54°C, air 33-34°C

Pos.	Driver	Laps	Time
1	George Russell	18	1m 29.938s
2	Charles Leclerc	21	1m 30.044s
3	Sergio Pérez	19	1m 30.150s
4	Lewis Hamilton	18	1m 30.179s
5	Fernando Alonso	20	1m 30.372s
6	Lando Norris	20	1m 30.535s
7	Pierre Gasly	20	1m 30.547s
8	Zhou Guanyu	24	1m 30.860s
9	Esteban Ocon	20	1m 30.861s
10	Kevin Magnussen	19	1m 30.921s
11	Carlos Sainz	9	1m 30.964s
12	Daniel Ricciardo	23	1m 31.208s
13	Yuki Tsunoda	23	1m 31.260s
14	Sebastian Vettel	23	1m 31.393s
15	Mick Schumacher	21	1m 31.587s
16	Lance Stroll	23	1m 31.631s
17	Alexander Albon	21	1m 31.710s
18	Nicholas Latifi	14	1m 32.913s
19	Max Verstappen	1	no time
-	Valtteri Bottas	-	-

PRACTICE 3 (SATURDAY)

Weather: Dry/partly cloudy

Temperatures: track 48-49°C, air 33°C

Pos.	Driver	Laps	Time
1	Sergio Pérez	21	1m 30.304s
2	Charles Leclerc	23	1m 30.498s
3	Max Verstappen	20	1m 30.649s
4	Fernando Alonso	18	1m 31.036s
5	Sebastian Vettel	24	1m 31.049s
6	Mick Schumacher	19	1m 31.050s
7	Carlos Sainz	24	1m 31.172s
8	Kevin Magnussen	20	1m 31.227s
9	Alexander Albon	14	1m 31.501s
10	Lando Norris	18	1m 31.594s
11	Yuki Tsunoda	24	1m 31.659s
12	Lance Stroll	22	1m 31.665s
13	Daniel Ricciardo	19	1m 31.728s
14	Valtteri Bottas	26	1m 31.885s
15	Lewis Hamilton	20	1m 31.890s
16	Pierre Gasly	18	1m 31.901s
17	George Russell	19	1m 31.924s
18	Zhou Guanyu	16	1m 32.051s
19	Nicholas Latifi	16	1m 32.376s
20	Esteban Ocon	3	-

QUALIFYING (SATURDAY)

Weather: Dry/sunny Temperatures: track 49-53°C, air 33-34°C

Pos.	Driver	First	Second	Third	Qualifying Tyre
1	Charles Leclerc	1m 29.474s	1m 29.130s	1m 28.796s	Soft (n)
2	Carlos Sainz	1m 30.079s	1m 29.729s	1m 28.986s	Soft (n)
3	Max Verstappen	1m 29.836s	1m 29.202s	1m 28.991s	Soft (n)
4	Sergio Pérez	1m 30.055s	1m 29.673s	1m 29.036s	Soft (n)
5	Valtteri Bottas	1m 30.845s	1m 29.751s	1m 29.475s	Soft (n)
6	Lewis Hamilton	1m 30.388s	1m 29.797s	1m 29.625s	Soft (n)
7	Pierre Gasly	1m 30.779s	1m 30.128s	1m 29.690s	Soft (n)
8	Lando Norris	1m 30.761s	1m 29.634s	1m 29.750s	Soft (n)
9	Yuki Tsunoda	1m 30.485s	1m 30.031s	1m 29.932s	Soft (n)
10	Lance Stroll	1m 30.441s	1m 29.996s	1m 30.676s	Soft (n)
11	Fernando Alonso	1m 30.407s	1m 30.160s		
12	George Russell	1m 30.490s	1m 30.173s		
13	Sebastian Vettel	1m 30.677s	1m 30.214s		
14	Daniel Ricciardo	1m 30.583s	1m 30.310s		
15	Mick Schumacher	1m 30.645s	1m 30.423s		
16	Kevin Magnussen	1m 30.975s			
17	Guanyu Zhou	1m 31.020s			
18	Alexander Albon	1m 31.266s			
19	Nicholas Latifi	1m 31.325s			
20	Esteban Ocon	no time			

QUALIFYING: head to head

Hamilton	3	2	Russell
Verstappen	4	1	Pérez
Ricciardo	0	5	Norris
Leclerc	5	0	Sainz
Gasly	4	1	Tsunoda
Hülkenberg	1	1	Stroll
Vettel	2	1	Stroll
Alonso	3	2	Ocon
Bottas	5	0	Zhou
Albon	4	1	Latifi
Magnussen	3	2	Schumacher

Alpine F1 Team

DID YOU KNOW?

The United States extended its record of most circuits hosting world championship races to 11.

Scuderia Ferrari

POINTS

DRIVERS

1	Charles Leclerc	104
2	Max Verstappen	85
3	Sergio Pérez	66
4	George Russell	59
5	Carlos Sainz	53
6	Lewis Hamilton	36
7	Lando Norris	35
8	Valtteri Bottas	30
9	Esteban Ocon	24
10	Kevin Magnussen	15
11	Daniel Ricciardo	11
12	Yuki Tsunoda	10
13	Pierre Gasly	6
14	Sebastian Vettel	4
15	Alexander Albon	3
16	Fernando Alonso	2
17	Lance Stroll	2
18	Zhou Guanyu	1

CONSTRUCTORS

1	Ferrari	157
2	Red Bull	151
3	Mercedes	95
4	McLaren	46
5	Alfa Romeo	31
6	Alpine	26
7	AlphaTauri	16
8	Haas	15
9	Aston Martin	6
10	Williams	3

9 · TSUNODA · AlphaTauri

7 · GASLY · AlphaTauri

5 · BOTTAS · Alfa Romeo

3 · VERSTAPPEN · Red Bull

1 · LECLERC · Ferrari

10 · STROLL · Aston Martin
Started from the pit lane

8 · NORRIS · McLaren

6 · HAMILTON · Mercedes

4 · PÉREZ · Red Bull

2 · SAINZ · Ferrari

47	48	49	50	51	52	53	54	55	56	57	·
1	1	1	1	1	1	1	1	1	1	1	1
16	16	16	16	16	16	16	16	16	16	16	2
55	55	55	55	55	55	55	55	55	55	55	3
11	11	11	11	11	11	11	11	11	11	11	4
77	77	44	63	63	63	63	63	63	63	63	5
44	44	63	44	44	44	44	44	44	44	44	6
63	63	77	77	77	77	77	77	77	77	77	7
14	14	14	14	14	14	14	14	14	14	14	8
47	47	47	47	47	47	5	31	31	31	31	9
31	31	31	31	31	31	47	23	23	23	23	10
23	23	5	5	5	5	31	20	20	3	3	
5	5	23	23	23	23	23	18	18	18	18	
3	3	3	3	3	3	3	3	3	20	22	
20	20	18	20	20	20	20	22	22	22	6	
18	18	20	18	18	18	18	6	6	6	47	
6	6	22	22	22	22	22	47	47	47		
22	22	6	6	6	6	6	5				

24 = Pit stop *6 = One lap or more behind*

SC Safety car deployed on laps shown

VSC Virtual safety car deployed on laps shown

RACE TYRE STRATEGIES

PIRELLI

	Driver	Race Stint 1	Race Stint 2	Race Stint 3
1	Verstappen	Medium (n): 1-26	Hard (n): 27-57	
2	Leclerc	Medium (n): 1-24	Hard (n): 25-57	
3	Sainz	Medium (n): 1-27	Hard (n): 28-57	
4	Pérez	Medium (n): 1-27	Hard (n): 28-41	Medium (n): 42-57
5	Russell	Hard (n): 1-40	Medium (n): 41-57	
6	Hamilton	Medium (n): 1-22	Hard (n): 23-57	
7	Bottas	Medium (n): 1-26	Hard (n): 27-57	
8	Ocon	Hard (n): 1-41	Soft (n): 42-57	
9	Alonso	Medium (n): 1-15	Hard (n): 16-57	
10	Albon	Medium (n): 1-16	Hard (n): 17-57	
11	Ricciardo	Medium (n): 1-30	Hard (n): 31-41	Soft (n): 42-57
12	Stroll	Hard (u): 1-40	Medium (u): 41-57	
13	Tsunoda	Medium (n): 1-11	Hard (n): 12-41	Soft (u): 42-57
14	Latifi	Hard (n): 1-34	Medium (n): 35-57	
15	Schumacher	Medium (n): 1-14	Hard (n): 15-54	Medium (n): 55-57
16	Magnussen	Medium (n): 1-12	Hard (n): 13-42	Medium (n): 43-56 (dnf)
17	Vettel	Hard (n): 1-41	Medium (u): 42-54 (dnf)	
	Gasly	Medium (n): 1-18	Hard (n): 19-39	Soft (u): 40-45 **(dnf)**
	Norris	Medium (n): 1-18	Hard (n): 19-39 (dnf)	
	Zhou	Medium (n): 1-6 (dnf)		

The tyre regulations stipulate that at least two of three dry tyre specifications must be used during a dry race. Selected compounds for Miami: Red = Soft (C4); Yellow = Medium (C3); White = Hard (C2). (n) new (u) used

Alpine F1 Team

Red Bull Content Pool/Getty Images

FIA FORMULA 1 WORLD CHAMPIONSHIP · ROUND 6

SPANISH GRAND PRIX

BARCELONA-CATALUNYA CIRCUIT

Inset: Victory for Max Verstappen took him to the top of the drivers' championship standings for the first time in 2022.

Main photo: With Ferrari in trouble, the Red Bulls ran riot in Catalunya.
Photos: Red Bull Content Pool/Getty Images

CATALUNYA QUALIFYING

AFTER the ballyhoo of Miami, it was back to more familiar territory, the Circuit de Catalunya in Barcelona. There were car upgrades galore, with every team save Haas running modified cars.

The most controversial was the heavily revised Aston Martin, which bore a striking similarity to Red Bull's RB18. That was not entirely surprising, given that Red Bull's former head of aerodynamics, Dan Fallows, had joined Aston in April as technical director.

"Imitation is the biggest form of flattery," said Red Bull team principal Christian Horner. "It's no coincidence that a few individuals have transferred from Red Bull to Aston Martin over the winter and the early part of the season. It was brought to our attention by the FIA early on in the week when they said, 'We have a car that looks remarkably like yours. Can we have a list of your leavers to see where they went?' That immediately raises alarm bells.

"We see all along the paddock personnel moving from team to team after gardening leave. What they take in their head is fair game, but what isn't fair, and what we wouldn't accept, is if there has been any transfer of IP. We won't disclose where we are with certain personnel, but a breach of IP is a criminal offence. We invest millions and millions into it."

Helmut Marko added, "It's not just Dan Fallows, there is evidence that data has been downloaded. Copying is not prohibited, but is it possible to do such a detailed copy of our car with no documentation?"

Aston Martin, meanwhile, claimed that it had prepared two designs over the winter, which the FIA had investigated and been satisfied that the work had been done at Aston's Silverstone base.

However, the new car did not run like a Red Bull on track, Sebastian Vettel and Lance Stroll being 16th and 18th as they joined Williams men Alex Albon and Nicholas Latifi as F1 eliminees along with, sadly, home hero Fernando Alonso. The Alpine had hit traffic on its second Q1 run during a hugely competitive session when just over half a second had covered seventh-placed Valtteri Bottas through to 15th-placed Esteban Ocon.

"You must be kidding!" Vettel replied when informed by the Aston Martin pit-wall crew that he would take no further part in qualifying.

"We didn't manage the session too well internally," explained Alonso for his part. "I started the run just behind Lando [Norris] and thought I had just a couple of seconds' margin, but in fact I had more like 20s and could have created a bit more of a gap. Unfortunate and a high price to pay, because when you start at the back in Barcelona, everything becomes a lot more difficult."

He was not wrong: track position is king at the circuit, where 28 of the previous 31 winners had come from the front row. Lewis Hamilton's record was pretty astounding, never having lost a race in Barcelona since his 2016 coming-together with Mercedes team-mate Nico Rosberg. And in the Merc camp, there was optimism that its upgrade, allied to the fast, flowing track layout, would boost competitiveness.

As ever, when the track temperature approaches 50 degrees at Circuit de Catalunya, striking the right balance between attacking in sector one and having enough tyre left for sector three was key to a quick lap.

The Q2 battle was tight. With Max Verstappen topping the times, the two Red Bulls went through, as did the two Ferraris, the two Mercedes, and Bottas's Alfa Romeo, leaving a four-way fight for three Q3 slots between the two Haas cars and the two McLarens. With Kevin Magnussen quick enough for fifth, it looked as though Mick Schumacher had missed out on his first Q3 appearance when Norris's second flying lap put him eighth. But that lasted as long as it took the stewards to delete the McLaren's final effort for exceeding track limits at Turn 12.

When it turned serious, Mercedes faced an uphill struggle to maintain a Barcelona record, the team chasing its tenth successive pole and Hamilton a tenth consecutive front-row start. Lewis's Friday optimism, however, did not extend as far as challenging right at the very front. Carlos Sainz set the initial Q3 pace, with championship leader Charles Leclerc losing the Ferrari's rear in sector three and spinning on his first run. Then Verstappen moved the goalposts with a lap that was three-tenths quicker than Sainz's, suggesting that he was on course to take pole.

But that was counting without Leclerc. Second time up, his lap was totally committed, despite not having a banker lap on the board. While Sainz stopped the clock in 1m 19.166s, just behind Verstappen's 1m 19.073s, Leclerc, after a mighty second sector, was the only man to dip well into the 1m 18s with a 1m 18.750s, claiming Ferrari's first Spanish GP pole since 2008.

"The car felt great," Leclerc said, "and hopefully we can get on top of the tyre management in the race."

Ultimately, Verstappen was unable to wrest back pole, complaining of a lack of power – actually a failure of his DRS to open – on his final run.

A fabulous fourth was George Russell's Mercedes, albeit 0.64s shy of Leclerc's pole time. But beating Hamilton around Barcelona in every qualifying session certainly caught the attention.

Sergio Pérez split the two Mercs with the second Red Bull, while Bottas lapped his Alfa just 0.09s slower than Hamilton to take seventh on the grid. Kevin Magnussen was a similar distance behind with the first Haas, as Ricciardo and Schumacher completed the top ten.

It looked like Leclerc vs Verstappen at the front once more, but Mercedes was closer. "We've made a solid step, but let's keep expectations at a reasonable level," said Toto Wolff. "Lewis says it finally drives like an F1 car and, being positive, we normally have a better race than qualifying car, so let's see."

Right: Charles Leclerc celebrates his pole position, which made him the pre-race favourite.
Photo: Atsuo Sakurai

Below: Aston Martin's Andrew Green fields questions from the press about the upgrades on his team's car.
Photo: Lukas Gorys

Below centre: The revised Aston Martin's sidepods closely followed the Red Bull's.
Photo: Aston Martin Aramco Cognizant F1 Team

Bottom: Mick Schumacher, like all of the drivers, had to combat the sizzling temperatures.
Photo: Haas F1 Team

Left: Mercedes-backed Nyck de Vries was given practice time with Williams and ran quicker than team-mate Nicholas Latifi.
Photo: Williams Racing

Centre left: Centre of attention. Lewis Hamilton and George Russell make their way to their garage for practice.
Photo: Atsuo Sakurai

Below left: Estonian Formula 2 challenger Juri Vips was given his first taste of F1 action with Red Bull.
Photo: Red Bull Content Pool/Getty Images

Above: Following his spin and first pit stop, Max Verstappen hunts down George Russell to retake the lead.
Photo: Pirelli

Top right: Race leader Charles Leclerc pits his Ferrari on lap 21, only to suffer engine failure six laps later.

Top far right: Mattia Binotto consoles his crestfallen driver.
Photos: Scuderia Ferrari

Above right: Lewis Hamilton is congratulated on his great drive to fifth following his first-lap collision with Kevin Magnussen.

Above far right: Hamilton's car is checked for damage.
Photos: Mercedes-AMG Petronas F1 Team

Centre right: Pierre Gasly's AlphaTauri tips the Aston Martin of Lance Stroll into a spin, earning the Frenchman a five-second penalty.
Photo: Red Bull Content Pool/Getty Images

Right: Sergio Pérez would briefly lead the race on two occasions before deferring to Verstappen.
Photo: Bryn Williams

IN the past, Barcelona had served up many an insomniac's cure, since it is a track where following closely and overtaking are particularly difficult. Thus there was interest in whether the 2022 regulations would offer much in the way of salvation.

From pole position, though, Charles Leclerc was determined not to have anyone to follow and made a strong start, immediately chopping across to the right to control the inside line at Turn One. The Ferrari was soon a length clear of Max Verstappen's Red Bull, allowing Leclerc to move back across and take the racing line through Turn One, ahead of the Red Bull, a fast-starting George Russell, Sergio Pérez and Lewis Hamilton who, despite starting on the harder medium-compound Pirellis, got down the inside of a slow-starting Carlos Sainz in Turn Three, forcing the Ferrari to go all the way around the outside before slamming back across to claim the line into Turn Four.

Kevin Magnussen sought to take advantage of the slightly compromised Hamilton by going around the outside of Turn Four, but they made contact and the Haas ended up in the gravel. Hamilton suffered a punctured left front in the incident, and both faced a long, slow tour back to the pits. Lewis also had a lengthy 10s stop as the crew checked for damage and fitted a new set of soft tyres.

Leclerc led across the line on the opening lap, from Verstappen, then Russell, Pérez, Sainz, Mick Schumacher (sixth place the highest he'd ever run in F1), Valtteri Bottas, Daniel Ricciardo, Esteban Ocon, Lando Norris, Yuki Tsunoda, Pierre Gasly, Sebastian Vettel, Lance Stroll, Fernando Alonso, Alex Albon, Zhou Guanyou, Nicholas Latifi and, some 53s behind the leader, Hamilton.

The seven-time champion did not sound too enamoured at the prospect of a long crawl back through the field when he told the Mercedes pit, "I would save this engine, guys, if I was you. I'm sorry."

Race engineer Peter Bonnington replied, "Lewis, we still think we can achieve points here today: P8, maybe better."

It might have been Fernando Alonso's home GP and he might have been in a lowly 14th place, but he is a racer and he gave his home fans something to cheer when he dummied Sebastian Vettel around the outside down the main straight with DRS, before diving back inside the Aston into Turn One at the start of lap eight. The margin was narrow…

But, just as there were wild cheers for that, there were groans when Carlos Sainz ploughed through the Turn Four gravel, his sixth place becoming 11th between the AlphaTauris of Tsunoda and Gasly. It was a strange incident, with Sainz all on his own, neither attacking nor defending, a strong crosswind the most credible explanation.

With ten laps down, Leclerc was 2s clear of Verstappen, the Red Bull safely out of DRS range, with Russell 7.5s behind the leading Ferrari. Mercedes had hoped that the W13's race pace would be stronger than in qualifying, but it didn't look that way for George, who was under heavy pressure from Pérez. Bottas was another 8s adrift, some 3s ahead of Ocon's Alpine. There was a similar gap to Mick Schumacher, who had the Ricciardo/Norris McLarens dogging his wheel tracks.

Bizarrely, second-place man Verstappen then suffered an almost carbon copy of Sainz's incident at Turn Four, the Red Bull off into the gravel and losing enough time that he rejoined in fourth place, just behind the Russell/Pérez battle. Engineer 'GP' Lambiase was soon on the radio with the explanation: "That was a large gust on entry to Turn Four there, Max."

Lando Norris's track-limits violation in qualifying meant that he was outqualified by McLaren team-mate Daniel Ricciardo for just the second time in 2022, but despite feeling unwell, he overtook the Australian, who soon lost another place to Yuki Tsunoda.

With Leclerc's Ferrari almost 10s clear up front, Pérez allowed Verstappen back past him to have a go at Russell, who was on the radio to the team asking, "Why have I got 'cool the car' warnings? I've got no one in front of me."

"The alarms are real," the team responded.

Behind him, though, Verstappen had problems of his own.

"Max, the DRS flap did not open last time. Keep trying," Lambiase told his frustrated driver.

Both the Mercedes and the Red Bull pitted 13 laps into the 66 for Pirelli mediums. As Verstappen tried to line up the Mercedes down the main straight, the DRS opened for the shortest instant and then closed again as Max continued to have problems with its activation, much to his frustration. Even with the DRS in full operation, he did not find it easy to oust Russell, who resolutely defended the inside at Turn One for lap after lap.

With a handy lead, Leclerc was under no kind of undercut threat and did not stop until lap 22, one-third-distance, for a set of mediums. He rejoined comfortably in front of Russell and Verstappen as the Dutchman received some more advice from the pit wall: "Max, try pressing the DRS after your kerbing." Down the main straight on lap 24, it was working perfectly as he finally got down the inside of Russell's Mercedes into Turn One. Russell, though, was robust and fought back on the inside of T3, running the Red Bull wide on exit.

Suddenly, on lap 27, there was a despairing cry from Leclerc – "No, No, no, no! What happened?" – as the leading Ferrari lost power and was called into the pits, its race run. It was a crushing blow for the Monégasque as the Russell/Verstappen fight immediately became about the lead.

On lap 29, Red Bull called in Verstappen for a second stop after just 16 laps on his mediums, bolting on a set of soft-compound Pirellis in an attempt to undercut Russell. But 37 laps remaining suggested that he would be in for a third time.

Two laps later, Pérez had caught Russell and swooped around the outside to take the lead into Turn One. Zhou Guanyou, meanwhile, posted a retirement – further evidence of some fragility in the Ferrari power unit division.

Verstappen, on his fresh softs, was now on a charge, relieving Bottas of third place with a rarely seen move around the outside of Turn 12! There was definitely something to be said for these new regulations.

Above: Russell gamely tries to keep Verstappen's Red Bull at bay.
Photo: Mercedes-AMG Petronas F1 Team

Top right: Fernando Alonso struggled for pace all weekend, but managed to put his Alpine in the points, albeit a lap down.
Photo: XPB Images

Above right: Alpine team-mate Esteban Ocon fared better on his lonely run to seventh.
Photo: Bryn Wiliams

Right: Russell maintained his run of points-scoring finishes with a well-earned podium for Mercedes.
Photo: Pirelli

"Our strategy here is to have the tyre advantage we need in that final stint, Max," Lambiase told Verstappen as he closed in on his team-mate.

Pérez made his second stop after 38 laps, putting Verstappen into the lead, with a 17s margin, but with an additional stop to make. Russell ran 4s behind the second Red Bull, with Bottas a further 10s in arrears, and Sainz closing in after his second stop. Hamilton, from the very back, remember, had now made an additional stop for mediums, having run the softs when he'd made his unscheduled opening-lap pit visit. His pace was impressive and he was just 10s behind the Ferrari.

As the race reached two-thirds-distance, lap 44, Red Bull called in Verstappen for his third and final stop, the world champion resuming on mediums, behind team-mate Pérez, but ahead of Russell's third-placed Mercedes.

Four laps later, as Verstappen closed the gap to almost within DRS range, Red Bull was soon on the radio to Pérez. "You're on a different strategy to Max," they told him. "If he's quicker, let him through."

"That's very unfair, but okay," Pérez replied. And maybe he had a point. Verstappen had been off the road earlier, and now they were on the same medium-compound tyres, Sergio's being six laps older, but both clearly able to run to the flag without problem. Pérez did as he was bid, throttling back between T3 and T4 to allow Verstappen back in front on lap 49.

A couple of laps later, Lewis Hamilton exceeded the expectations of his team and put his Mercedes into the top six as he went by Esteban Ocon's Alpine on the front straight. He was on another set of softs after a third pit stop.

Russell also made a third stop (a strategy followed by more than half the field), rejoining just 5s behind Valtteri Bottas's now third-placed Alfa. Russell made short work of the man whose seat he had taken, down the inside into T1 as Bottas momentarily locked his right front.

With the first three positions seemingly secure, interest turned to the battle for fourth as the medium-tyred, two-stopping Bottas was closed down by the three-stopping Sainz and Hamilton, both on softs, with eight laps remaining. The difference in grip meant that Valtteri was pretty much a sitting duck, Carlos going by into Turn One, and Lewis comfortably around the outside of T3.

Hamilton now took a fancy to Sainz's fourth place and swooped around the outside of the Ferrari into Turn One with six to go. The fact that he had been 53s adrift when he rejoined after his first-lap mishap, and was now just 40s behind Verstappen's Red Bull, showed just how strong a pace he had been able to run all afternoon. Okay, so after Leclerc's demise, there was no great pressure on the Red Bulls, but it was promising nonetheless. A good job Mercedes hadn't retired the car!

The drama wasn't quite over for Lewis, though, as he started to receive warnings of cooling issues and a DNF risk, the team telling him to lift and coast as often as possible, and even to give the place back to Sainz if need be. Which is precisely what happened down the main straight heading on to the penultimate lap, to the delight of the home fans.

At the scene of his Red Bull debut and first F1 victory six years earlier, Verstappen calmly closed out the second Red Bull 1-2 in three races with a 13s margin over team-mate Sergio Pérez. Russell joined them in celebration with his second F1 podium, just over half a minute behind the race winner.

Sainz finished his home race in fourth place, ahead of Hamilton, whose race pace had shown that, while hopes that Mercedes could join the lead battle were optimistic, Lewis himself was as relentless as ever.

Behind the big three, Bottas took 'best of the rest' honours for Alfa Romeo, albeit a minute down, with Ocon 15s further behind with the first Alpine, which got to the line just 8s adrift, despite feeling unwell. Alonso and Tsunoda completed the points-scorers.

Leclerc's engine failure was a crushing blow for the young Monégasque, whose impressive early-season championship lead had been wiped out: he was left contemplating a six-point deficit. One small saving grace was an interval of just five days before the cars were on track again at his home race in Monte Carlo.

Tony Dodgins

VIEWPOINT
A FALSE DAWN FOR MERCEDES?

A PODIUM for George Russell; a powerful comeback by Lewis Hamilton; second and third fastest race laps for the Mercedes pair. 'Silver Arrows Comeback' headlines were as inevitable as they were welcome after the Mercedes W13 had literally been bounced all over the place during the previous five races. Would this dramatic recovery continue? Despite Toto Wolff's bold assurance that his team would be fighting for the championship, cautious voices inside and outside Mercedes AMG Petronas F1 hinted that Barcelona might have flattered slightly to deceive.

The flow and comparative smoothness of Circuit de Barcelona-Catalunya had always suited Mercedes, and 2022 was no different, helped on this occasion by the raft of developments that made the W13 a very different car to the one that had struggled so visibly during the pre-season test on the same circuit. Most noticeable to the naked eye was a reduction in porpoising, so much so that, for the first time in 2022, the drivers and engineers had a car that responded to set-up changes in the way they had come to expect in seasons past.

Hamilton's hopes of making the most of it were scuppered straight away, however, by contact with Kevin Magnusson, and a puncture that necessitated a pit stop and the massive loss of 45 seconds. Fortunately, the aero had not been damaged, allowing Hamilton to haul himself back into contention after rejoining at the rear of the field.

Up front, Russell was being mighty in his clean defence of a podium position from heavy attacks at various stages by both Red Bulls. He might have been helped by Verstappen's intermittent trouble with his DRS, but the Englishman had his own problems with an overheating power unit. The same applied to Hamilton as he became embroiled in traffic, both drivers coping with alarm signals constantly flashing on their readouts, and employing 'lift-and-coast' when they could.

The 25 points for Mercedes might have been twice as many as Ferrari's total, and the performance deficit might have been slashed. But the fact remained that the former champions were still half a second off the pace.

Maurice Hamilton

6

FORMULA 1 PIRELLI GRAN PREMIO DE ESPAÑA 2022

CIRCUIT DE BARCELONA-CATALUNYA

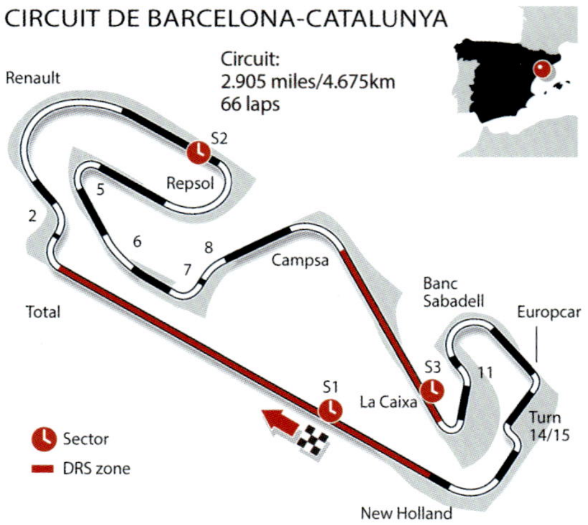

BARCELONA 20–22 MAY

RACE DISTANCE: 66 laps, 190.646 miles/308.424km

RACE WEATHER: Dry/sunny (track 47–49°C, air 36–37°C)

RACE – OFFICIAL CLASSIFICATION

Pos.	Driver	Nat.	No.	Entrant	Car/Engine	Laps	Time/Retirement	Speed (mph/km/h)	Gap to winner	Fastest race lap
1	**Max Verstappen**	**NL**	**1**	**Oracle Red Bull Racing**	Red Bull RB18-RBPTH001 V6	66	1h 37m 20.475s	118.128/190.108		1m 25.456s 46
2	**Sergio Pérez**	**MEX**	**11**	**Oracle Red Bull Racing**	Red Bull RB18-RBPTH001 V6	66	1h 37m 33.547s	117.864/189.684	13.072s	1m 24.108s 55
3	**George Russell**	**GB**	**63**	**Mercedes-AMG Petronas F1 Team**	Mercedes-AMG F1 W13-M13 E Perf. V6	66	1h 37m 53.402s	117.466/189.043	32.927s	1m 24.636s 53
4	**Carlos Sainz**	**E**	**55**	**Scuderia Ferrari**	Ferrari F1-75-066/7 V6	66	1h 38m 05.683s	117.220/188.648	45.208s	1m 25.985s 49
5	**Lewis Hamilton**	**GB**	**44**	**Mercedes-AMG Petronas F1 Team**	Mercedes-AMG F1 W13-M13 E Perf. V6	66	1h 38m 15.009s	117.035/188.350	54.534s	1m 24.253s 51
6	**Valtteri Bottas**	**FIN**	**77**	**Alfa Romeo F1 Team ORLEN**	Alfa Romeo C42-Ferrari 066/7 V6	66	1h 38m 20.451s	116.927/188.176	59.976s	1m 26.395s 36
7	**Esteban Ocon**	**F**	**31**	**BWT Alpine F1 Team**	Alpine A522-Renault E-Tech RE22 V6	66	1h 38m 35.872s	116.623/187.686	1m 15.397s	1m 25.935s 54
8	**Lando Norris**	**GB**	**4**	**McLaren F1 Team**	McLaren MCL36-Mercedes F1 M13 E Perf. V6	66	1h 38m 43.710s	116.468/187.437	1m 23.235s	1m 25.619s 53
9	**Fernando Alonso**	**E**	**14**	**BWT Alpine F1 Team**	Alpine A522-Renault E-Tech RE22 V6	65			1 lap	1m 26.599s 56
10	**Yuki Tsunoda**	**J**	**22**	**Scuderia AlphaTauri**	AlphaTauri AT03-RBPTH001 V6	65			1 lap	1m 26.828s 59
11	Sebastian Vettel	D	5	Aston Martin Aramco Cognizant F1 Team	Aston Martin AMR22-Mercedes F1 M13 E Perf. V6	65			1 lap	1m 27.629s 59
12	Daniel Ricciardo	AUS	3	McLaren F1 Team	McLaren MCL36-Mercedes F1 M13 E Perf. V6	65			1 lap	1m 27.285s 54
13	Pierre Gasly	F	10	Scuderia AlphaTauri	AlphaTauri AT03-RBPTH001 V6	65	*		1 lap	1m 26.987s 51
14	Mick Schumacher	D	47	Haas F1 Team	Haas VF-22-Ferrari 066/7 V6	65			1 lap	1m 27.447s 32
15	Lance Stroll	CDN	18	Aston Martin Aramco Cognizant F1 Team	Aston Martin AMR22-Mercedes F1 M13 E Perf. V6	65			1 lap	1m 26.876s 54
16	Nicholas Latifi	CDN	6	Williams Racing	Williams FW44-Mercedes F1 M13 E Perf. V6	64			2 laps	1m 27.246s 52
17	Kevin Magnussen	DK	20	Haas F1 Team	Haas VF-22-Ferrari 066/7 V6	64			2 laps	1m 27.537s 3
18	Alexander Albon	T	23	Williams Racing	Williams FW44-Mercedes F1 M13 E Perf. V6	64	*		2 laps	1m 28.281s 56
	Zhou Guanyu	CHN	24	Alfa Romeo F1 Team ORLEN	Alfa Romeo C42-Ferrari 066/7 V6	28	*power unit*			1m 28.415s 12
	Charles Leclerc	MC	16	Scuderia Ferrari	Ferrari F1-75-066/7 V6	27	*power unit*			1m 27.030s 25

* Albon: 5s time penalty for leaving the track without a justifiable reason multiple times. * Gasly: 5s time penalty for causing a collision with Stroll (served at pit stop).

DHL Fastest race lap (scores 1 point): Sergio Pérez on lap 55, 1m 24.108s, 124.336mph/200.099km/h.

Lap record: Giancarlo Fisichella (Renault R25 V10), 1m 15.641s, 136.835mph/220.213km/h (2005, 2.875-mile/4.627km circuit).

Lap record (current configuration): Max Verstappen (Red Bull RB16B-Honda V6), 1m 18.149s, 133.817mph/215.357km/h (2021).

19 · LATIFI · Williams

17 · STROLL · Aston Martin

15 · ZHOU · Alfa Romeo

13 · TSUNODA · AlphaTauri

11 · NORRIS · McLaren

20 · ALONSO · Alpine
Used additional power unit elements; required to start from the back of the grid

18 · ALBON · Williams

16 · VETTEL · Aston Martin

14 · GASLY · AlphaTauri

12 · OCON · Alpine

	Grid order	1	2	3	4	5	6	7	8	9	10	11	12	13	14	15	16	17	18	19	20	21	22	23	24	25	26
16	LECLERC	16	16	16	16	16	16	16	16	16	16	16	16	16	16	16	16	16	16	16	16	16	16	16	16	16	16
1	VERSTAPPEN	1	1	1	1	1	1	1	1	63	63	63	63	11	11	11	11	11	63	63	63	63	63	63	63	63	63
55	SAINZ	63	63	63	63	63	63	63	63	11	11	1	1	63	77	63	63	63	1	1	1	1	1	1	1	1	1
63	RUSSELL	11	11	11	11	11	11	11	11	1	1	11	11	1	63	1	1	1	11	11	11	11	11	11	11	11	11
11	PÉREZ	55	55	55	55	55	55	77	77	77	77	77	77	77	1	77	77	77	77	77	77	77	77	77	77	77	77
44	HAMILTON	47	47	47	77	77	77	31	31	31	31	31	31	31	5	5	5	31	31	31	31	31	31	31	55	55	55
77	BOTTAS	77	77	77	47	47	31	47	47	47	4	4	4	5	31	31	31	5	55	55	55	55	55	55	31	31	31
20	MAGNUSSEN	3	3	3	3	31	47	3	3	4	47	47	47	18	55	55	55	55	5	5	5	4	4	4	4	4	4
3	RICCIARDO	31	31	31	31	3	3	4	4	3	3	22	5	4	18	4	4	4	4	4	4	22	22	22	22	22	22
47	SCHUMACHER	4	4	4	4	4	4	22	22	22	22	3	18	55	4	22	22	22	22	22	22	5	14	14	14	14	14
4	NORRIS	22	22	22	22	22	22	55	55	55	55	5	55	14	22	14	14	14	14	14	14	14	47	47	47	47	47
31	OCON	10	10	10	10	10	10	10	10	14	5	18	6	22	14	3	3	3	3	47	47	47	3	3	3	3	3
22	TSUNODA	5	5	5	5	5	5	14	14	10	14	6	14	3	3	47	47	47	47	3	3	3	24	24	24	24	24
10	GASLY	18	18	18	18	14	14	5	5	5	10	23	22	47	47	10	10	10	10	10	10	10	10	10	10	10	10
24	ZHOU	14	14	14	14	18	24	24	24	24	18	55	3	10	10	24	24	24	24	24	24	24	18	18	18	18	18
5	VETTEL	23	23	24	24	24	18	18	18	18	24	14	10	24	24	44	44	44	44	44	44	44	44	5	5	5	5
18	STROLL	24	24	23	23	23	23	23	23	23	23	10	24	44	44	23	18	18	18	18	18	18	5	6	6	44	44
23	ALBON	6	6	6	6	6	6	6	6	6	6	24	44	23	23	18	23	23	23	23	23	6	6	23	44	6	6
6	LATIFI	44	44	44	44	44	44	44	44	44	44	44	23	6	6	6	6	6	6	6	6	23	23	44	23	23	20
14	ALONSO	20	20	20	20	20	20	20	20	20	20	20	20	20	20	20	20	20	20	20	20	20	20	20	20	20	23

	Grid order	27	28	29	30	31	32	33	34	35	36	37	38	39	40	41	42	43	44	45	46	47	48	49	50	51	52
16	LECLERC	63	63	63	63	11	11	11	11	11	11	11	1	1	1	1	1	1	1	11	11	11	11	1	1	1	1
1	VERSTAPPEN	1	11	11	11	63	63	63	63	63	1	1	11	11	11	11	11	11	11	1	1	1	1	11	11	11	11
55	SAINZ	11	1	77	77	1	1	1	1	1	63	63	63	63	63	63	63	63	63	63	63	63	63	63	63	63	77
63	RUSSELL	16	77	1	1	77	77	77	77	77	77	77	77	77	77	77	77	77	77	77	77	77	77	77	77	77	63
11	PÉREZ	77	55	55	55	55	31	31	31	55	55	55	55	55	55	55	55	55	55	55	44	44	44	55	55	55	55
44	HAMILTON	55	31	31	31	31	4	4	55	31	44	44	44	44	44	44	44	44	44	44	31	55	55	31	31	44	44
77	BOTTAS	31	4	4	4	4	55	55	44	44	31	31	31	31	31	31	31	31	31	31	55	31	31	44	44	31	31
20	MAGNUSSEN	4	22	22	22	22	22	44	5	5	5	5	5	4	4	4	4	4	4	4	4	4	4	4	4	4	14
3	RICCIARDO	22	14	14	14	14	44	5	4	4	4	4	4	5	5	5	14	14	14	14	14	14	14	14	14	14	22
47	SCHUMACHER	14	47	47	3	44	5	22	14	14	14	14	14	14	14	14	22	22	22	22	22	22	22	22	22	22	4
4	NORRIS	47	3	3	47	3	14	14	22	22	22	22	22	22	22	22	5	47	47	47	47	47	47	47	47	47	47
31	OCON	3	10	5	44	5	47	47	47	47	47	47	47	47	47	47	47	3	3	3	3	3	5	5	5	5	5
22	TSUNODA	24	5	44	5	47	3	3	3	3	3	3	3	3	3	3	3	10	10	5	5	5	3	3	3	3	3
10	GASLY	10	44	10	10	10	10	10	10	10	10	10	10	10	10	10	10	5	5	10	10	10	10	10	10	10	10
24	ZHOU	5	24	18	18	18	18	18	18	18	18	18	18	18	18	18	18	18	18	18	18	6	6	6	6	18	18
5	VETTEL	44	20	6	6	6	6	6	6	6	6	6	6	6	6	6	6	6	6	6	6	20	20	20	20	20	20
18	STROLL	18	18	20	23	23	23	23	23	23	23	23	23	23	20	20	20	20	20	20	20	18	18	18	18	6	6
23	ALBON	20	6	23	20	20	20	20	20	20	20	20	20	20	23	23	23	23	23	23	23	23	23	23	23	23	23
6	LATIFI	6	23																								
14	ALONSO	23																									

TIME SHEETS

PRACTICE 1 (FRIDAY)

Weather: Dry/sunny

Temperatures: track 45-47° C, air 29-30° C

Pos.	Driver	Laps	Time
1	Charles Leclerc	27	1m 19.828s
2	Carlos Sainz	27	1m 19.907s
3	Max Verstappen	28	1m 20.164s
4	George Russell	28	1m 20.590s
5	Fernando Alonso	24	1m 20.768s
6	Lewis Hamilton	27	1m 20.811s
7	Lando Norris	24	1m 21.279s
8	Pierre Gasly	23	1m 21.422s
9	Daniel Ricciardo	23	1m 21.737s
10	Yuki Tsunoda	28	1m 21.814s
11	Esteban Ocon	26	1m 21.891s
12	Lance Stroll	23	1m 21.920s
13	Robert Kubica	20	1m 21.975s
14	Kevin Magnussen	16	1m 22.089s
15	Mick Schumacher	21	1m 22.146s
16	Sebastian Vettel	20	1m 22.164s
17	Valtteri Bottas	25	1m 22.614s
18	Nyck de Vries	28	1m 22.920s
19	Nicholas Latifi	27	1m 23.011s
20	Jüri Vips	23	1m 24.138s

PRACTICE 2 (FRIDAY)

Weather: Dry/sunny

Temperatures: track 42-45°C, air 30-31°C

Pos.	Driver	Laps	Time
1	Charles Leclerc	29	1m 19.670s
2	George Russell	27	1m 19.787s
3	Lewis Hamilton	26	1m 19.874s
4	Carlos Sainz	31	1m 19.990s
5	Max Verstappen	27	1m 20.006s
6	Fernando Alonso	26	1m 20.203s
7	Sergio Pérez	30	1m 20.632s
8	Sebastian Vettel	31	1m 20.703s
9	Esteban Ocon	27	1m 20.745s
10	Mick Schumacher	25	1m 20.757s
11	Pierre Gasly	28	1m 20.917s
12	Kevin Magnussen	24	1m 21.013s
13	Lance Stroll	32	1m 21.249s
14	Yuki Tsunoda	29	1m 21.285s
15	Daniel Ricciardo	22	1m 21.385s
16	Valtteri Bottas	3	1m 21.828s
17	Zhou Guanyu	30	1m 21.866s
18	Alexander Albon	31	1m 22.319s
19	Nicholas Latifi	25	1m 23.197s
20	Lando Norris	6	1m 23.388s

PRACTICE 3 (SATURDAY)

Weather: Dry/sunny

Temperatures: track 43-46°C, air 31-32°C

Pos.	Driver	Laps	Time
1	Charles Leclerc	23	1m 19.772s
2	Max Verstappen	12	1m 19.844s
3	George Russell	16	1m 19.920s
4	Lewis Hamilton	18	1m 20.002s
5	Carlos Sainz	23	1m 20.129s
6	Sergio Pérez	19	1m 20.260s
7	Lando Norris	18	1m 20.403s
8	Kevin Magnussen	21	1m 20.646s
9	Valtteri Bottas	24	1m 20.781s
10	Esteban Ocon	18	1m 20.882s
11	Daniel Ricciardo	17	1m 20.910s
12	Sebastian Vettel	24	1m 20.944s
13	Fernando Alonso	17	1m 20.981s
14	Zhou Guanyu	19	1m 21.201s
15	Yuki Tsunoda	22	1m 21.449s
16	Lance Stroll	23	1m 21.520s
17	Alexander Albon	18	1m 21.572s
18	Nicholas Latifi	18	1m 22.419s
19	Mick Schumacher	4	1m 25.467s
20	Pierre Gasly	1	no time

Alfa Romeo Racing ORLEN

QUALIFYING (SATURDAY)

Weather: Dry/sunny Temperatures: track 46-47°C, air 34-35°C

Pos.	Driver	First	Second	Third	Qualifying Tyre
1	Charles Leclerc	1m 19.861s	1m 19.969s	1m 18.750s	Soft (n)
2	Max Verstappen	1m 20.091s	1m 19.219s	1m 19.073s	Soft (n)
3	Carlos Sainz	1m 19.892s	1m 19.453s	1m 19.166s	Soft (n)
4	George Russell	1m 20.218s	1m 19.470s	1m 19.393s	Soft (n)
5	Sergio Pérez	1m 20.447s	1m 19.830s	1m 19.420s	Soft (n)
6	Lewis Hamilton	1m 20.252s	1m 19.794s	1m 19.512s	Soft (n)
7	Valtteri Bottas	1m 20.355s	1m 20.053s	1m 19.608s	Soft (n)
8	Kevin Magnussen	1m 20.227s	1m 19.810s	1m 19.682s	Soft (n)
9	Daniel Ricciardo	1m 20.549s	1m 20.287s	1m 20.297s	Soft (n)
10	Mick Schumacher	1m 20.683s	1m 20.436s	1m 20.368s	Soft (n)
11	Lando Norris	1m 20.838s	1m 20.471s		
12	Esteban Ocon	1m 20.880s	1m 20.638s		
13	Yuki Tsunoda	1m 20.707s	1m 20.639s		
14	Pierre Gasly	1m 20.719s	1m 20.861s		
15	Zhou Guanyu	1m 20.476s	1m 21.094s		
16	Sebastian Vettel	1m 20.954s			
17	Fernando Alonso	1m 21.043s			
18	Lance Stroll	1m 21.418s			
19	Alexander Albon	1m 21.645s			
20	Nicholas Latifi	1m 21.915s			

QUALIFYING: head to head

Hamilton	3	3	Russell
Verstappen	5	1	Pérez
Ricciardo	1	5	Norris
Leclerc	6	0	Sainz
Gasly	4	2	Tsunoda
Hülkenberg	1	1	Stroll
Vettel	3	1	Stroll
Alonso	3	3	Ocon
Bottas	6	0	Zhou
Albon	5	1	Latifi
Magnussen	4	2	Schumacher

Aston Martin Aramco Cognizant F1 Team

POINTS

DRIVERS

1	Max Verstappen	110
2	Charles Leclerc	104
3	Sergio Pérez	85
4	George Russell	74
5	Carlos Sainz	65
6	Lewis Hamilton	46
7	Lando Norris	39
8	Valtteri Bottas	38
9	Esteban Ocon	30
10	Kevin Magnussen	15
11	Daniel Ricciardo	11
12	Yuki Tsunoda	11
13	Pierre Gasly	6
14	Sebastian Vettel	4
15	Fernando Alonso	4
16	Alexander Albon	3
17	Lance Stroll	2
18	Zhou Guanyu	1

CONSTRUCTORS

1	Red Bull	195
2	Ferrari	169
3	Mercedes	120
4	McLaren	50
5	Alfa Romeo	39
6	Alpine	34
7	AlphaTauri	17
8	Haas	15
9	Aston Martin	6
10	Williams	3

9 · RICCIARDO · McLaren

7 · BOTTAS · Alfa Romeo

5 · PÉREZ · Red Bull

3 · SAINZ · Ferrari

1 · LECLERC · Ferrari

10 · SCHUMACHER · Haas

8 · MAGNUSSEN · Haas

6 · HAMILTON · Mercedes

4 · RUSSELL · Mercedes

2 · VERSTAPPEN · Red Bull

53	54	55	56	57	58	59	60	61	62	63	64	65	66	
1	1	1	1	1	1	1	1	1	1	1	1	1	1	1
11	11	11	11	11	11	11	11	11	11	11	11	11	11	2
63	63	63	63	63	63	63	63	63	63	63	63	63	63	3
77	77	77	77	77	55	55	44	44	44	44	44	55	55	4
55	55	55	55	55	44	44	55	55	55	55	55	44	44	5
44	44	44	44	44	77	77	77	77	77	77	77	77	77	6
14	31	31	31	31	31	31	31	31	31	31	31	31	31	7
31	4	4	4	4	4	4	4	4	4	4	4	4	4	8
4	47	14	14	14	14	14	14	14	14	14	14	14		9
47	14	47	22	22	22	22	22	22	22	22	22	22		10
22	22	22	47	47	47	5	5	5	5	5	5	5		
5	5	5	5	5	5	47	47	47	47	47	3	3		
3	3	3	3	3	3	3	3	3	3	3	47	10		
10	10	10	10	10	10	10	10	10	10	10	10	47		
18	18	18	18	18	18	18	18	18	18	18	18	18		
20	20	20	20	20	20	20	20	20	6	6	6			
6	6	6	6	6	6	6	6	6	20	20	20			
23	23	23	23	23	23	23	23	23	23	23	23			

44 = Pit stop *6 = One lap or more behind*

RACE TYRE STRATEGIES

PIRELLI

	Driver	Race Stint 1	Race Stint 2	Race Stint 3	Race Stint 4	Race Stint 5
1	Verstappen	Soft (u): 1-13	Medium (n): 14-28	Soft (u): 29-44	Medium (n): 45-66	
2	Pérez	Soft (u): 1-17	Medium (n): 18-37	Medium (n): 38-53	Soft (u): 54-66	
3	Russell	Soft (u): 1-13	Medium (n): 14-36	Medium (n): 37-51	Soft (u): 52-66	
4	Sainz	Soft (u): 1-10	Medium (n): 11-31	Medium (n): 32-45	Soft (u): 46-66	
5	Hamilton	Medium (n): 1	Soft (u): 2-22	Medium (n): 23-48	Soft (u): 49-66	
6	Bottas	Soft (u): 1-14	Medium (n): 15-34	Medium (n): 35-66		
7	Ocon	Soft (n): 1-13	Medium (n): 14-35	Soft (u): 36-52	Soft (u): 53-66	
8	Norris	Soft (n): 1-12	Medium (n): 13-33	Soft (u): 34-51	Soft (u): 52-66	
9	Alonso	Soft (u): 1-10	Medium (n): 11-31	Soft (u): 32-53	Soft (u): 54-65	
10	Tsunoda	Soft (n): 1-11	Medium (n): 12-32	Soft (n): 33-52	Soft (u): 53-65	
11	Vettel	Soft (u): 1-21	Soft (u): 22-42	Medium (n): 43-65		
12	Ricciardo	Soft (u): 1-11	Soft (u): 12-31	Medium (n): 32-48	Soft (u): 49-65	
13	Gasly	Soft (n): 1-10	Medium (n): 11-29	Soft (u): 30-46	Soft (u): 47-65	
14	Schumacher	Soft (u): 1-12	Soft (u): 13-30	Medium (n): 31-65		
15	Stroll	Soft (u): 1-12	Soft (u): 13-27	Medium (u): 28-46	Soft (u): 47-65	
16	Latifi	Soft (n): 1-12	Medium (n): 13-26	Soft (n): 27-50	Soft (u): 51-64	
17	Magnussen	Soft (u): 1	Medium (n): 2-29	Hard (n): 30-64		
18	Albon	Soft (n): 1-11	Medium (n): 12-25	Soft (n): 26-45	Medium (n): 46-54	Soft (u): 55-64
	Zhou	Soft (n): 1-10	Medium (n): 11-28 (dnf)			
	Leclerc	Soft (u): 1-21	Medium (n): 22-27 (dnf)			

The tyre regulations stipulate that at least two of three dry tyre specifications must be used during a dry race.

Selected compounds for Barcelona: Red = Soft (C3); Yellow = Medium (C2); White = Hard (C1). (n) new (u) used

FIA FORMULA 1 WORLD CHAMPIONSHIP · ROUND 7

MONACO GRAND PRIX

MONTE CARLO CIRCUIT

TIP TOP
24H/24H
FIRE

MONTE CARLO QUALIFYING

AS Formula 1 arrived in the Principality, the unthinkable was being discussed: an F1 calendar without the Monaco GP. Automobile Club de Monaco president Michel Boeri was busy pouring cold water on suggestions that the race was in serious jeopardy because the club did not want to pay a hosting fee in line with other venues, plus hand over signage rights and give up host broadcasting to F1. But the powers that be were insistent: things would have to change.

For their part, the drivers were contending that the circuit itself actually had a different feel in 2022, a symptom of the grounding and porpoising that had resulted from F1's new regulations. The challenge, though, was the same as ever: how to extract the absolute maximum from what had become a heavier and more unwieldy package without clouting the barriers that punish any mistake so heavily.

There was incident from first to last. Yuki Tsunoda brought out the red flag in Q1 when he clipped the barrier into the harbour-front chicane, just enough to puncture the left front and send him crawling back to the pits.

The Q1 eliminees were the two Williams drivers, Alexander Albon and Nicholas Latifi, Aston Martin's Lance Stroll and, unsurprisingly perhaps, Alfa Romeo's Monaco virgin, Zhou Guanyu. Much more of a surprise was Pierre Gasly, who had been P5 in FP3 on Saturday morning and full of confidence.

"I'm just so disappointed," he grimaced. "We decided to do just two laps in Q1 when the others did three or four. When I did my lap, I was P4/5, but the track rubbers in and then we had the red flag [ironically, for his team-mate]. We left too late for the last run: Yuki crossed the line with 1s on the clock, and I missed it by 2s. We are making too many mistakes these last few race weekends. Here, it's cost us big time. We deserved way more."

It can't have helped Gasly's mood when his team-mate just missed out on the top-ten shootout as the fastest of those to go out in Q2, joined by Valtteri Bottas, Haas pair Kevin Magnussen and Mick Schumacher, and Daniel Ricciardo, the 2018 Monaco winner still struggling at McLaren relative to team-mate Lando Norris.

And so, to the most important Q3 session of the year. As Maurice Hamilton points out in *Viewpoint*, Charles Leclerc's fortunes in Monte Carlo are certainly no match for his pace. In 2021, he had suffered the crushing disappointment of taking pole and then being unable to capitalise on it when Ferrari gambled on sending him out without a gearbox change after an off in the final sector.

In 2022, however, with a Ferrari that was even better suited to the downforce and traction needs of the narrow streets, there was no denying Leclerc. He set a hugely impressive lap on his first Q3 run, and this time it would be others who brought the session to a premature end, ensuring that his 1m 11.376s lap would be more than enough.

Sergio Pérez, another who always had shown well in Monaco, had topped the times on the opening day and actually shown his world champion team-mate the way for much of the weekend. After the first Q3 run, he was third quickest, a quarter of a second from Leclerc, but just 0.03s down on Carlos Sainz in the second Ferrari and four-hundredths quicker than Verstappen.

But then it all went wrong. On his final run, he lost the rear end as he turned into Portiers and pirouetted backwards into the barrier. Just behind him on the road was Sainz, who tried to take evasive action, but spun in sympathy. The result was a roadblock and a session-ending red flag with just 30s left on the clock. The Ferraris would start from the front row, with the two Red Bulls on row two, Sergio ahead of Max for the second time in 2022.

Best of the rest, within half a second of Leclerc's pole, was a fine effort by Norris, who took the honour of quickest Brit, a quarter of a second faster than George Russell's Mercedes. The W13 was a bit of a handful around the Principality, and for Russell to go almost half a second quicker than Lewis Hamilton around Monaco was a performance that should not be underestimated.

Likewise, Fernando Alonso, who was seventh quickest for Alpine, 0.14s adrift of Russell, but he ended his session in the tyres at Mirabeau as he attempted to improve. "The brakes were still a bit too cold in the first sector," he explained.

Between the two Alpine drivers, seventh and tenth, were two men with 11 world championships between them – Hamilton and Sebastian Vettel, who did a fine job to put the first Aston Martin ninth on the grid. Esteban Ocon, though, was frustrated.

"There was definitely a lot more potential," he said. "I didn't get my final lap in because of the red flag, and it was shaping up to be a good one. From where we came from on Friday, when the car was moving around all over the place and we were lacking confidence in it, we did a really good job. I think P7 was possible, which Fernando proved, so yes, a bit of frustration..."

After his blow-up while leading in Spain, Leclerc was hopeful that he could crack his Monaco jinx and hit straight back in the championship fight, but a look at the weather forecast revealed that Sunday might not be so straightforward. He would get to see the lights this time after his second successive Monte Carlo pole, but there could be challenges ahead, both in the cockpit and on the pit wall...

Above: Crunch! Daniel Ricciardo makes a mess of his McLaren in Friday's second free practice.
Photo: Lukas Gorys

Above left: Millimetres to spare for Alex Albon in his Williams.
Photo: Peter Nygaard/Grand Prix Photo

Top: Charles Leclerc acknowledges the crowd after taking pole position for Ferrari.
Photo: Scuderia Ferrari

Top left: Qualifying was brought to a halt after Sergio Pérez hit the barriers and blocked the track.
Photo: XPB Images

Left: Not seen on TV. Massive building works on reclaimed land were skilfully edited out of the broadcasts.

Above far left: Nicholas Latifi and Pierre Gasly search for space in their battle to escape Q1.
Photos: Red Bull Content Pool/Getty Images

Opening spread: With the race restarted, Pérez, on medium Pirellis, assumed control.
Photo: XPB Images

Above: The race finally got under way behind the safety car, with everyone on full wets.
Photo: Pirelli

Top right: Fernando Alonso hustles his Alpine up towards Casino Square.
Photo: Alpine F1 Team

Above right: Mick Schumacher brought proceedings to a halt by splitting his Haas in two.
Photo: Haas F1 Team

Right: Sebastian Vettel took home the final point for tenth place.
Photo: Aston Martin Aramco Cognizant F1 Team

THE times, it seemed, were a changing. As well as the rumours concerning Monaco's future – it has been something of an anachronism for as long as 50 years – there had already been a first, which had eliminated the 'free' Friday. Instead, the event was hosted over three consecutive days, in keeping with everywhere else, rather than having the first practice day on Thursday.

Then, as race start time approached, there was another first, with a delay of nine minutes so that the teams could prepare for heavy rain that radar had identified approaching the circuit. There were tyre trolleys everywhere as they switched the cars to intermediates. After a further short delay, it was announced that two formation laps would be run behind the safety car, which demands that everyone must be on extreme wets. Cue more grid chaos.

It was all a bit bizarre, given that the circuit was barely wet and only light drizzle was falling.

"What are we waiting for, complete dry?" Max Verstappen asked on the radio as he sat on the grid. He wasn't the only one who was a little perplexed.

A message came through from race control to the effect that they had been monitoring a severe downpour that was approaching rapidly. Since it was due to arrive during the starting procedure, the safety car start and its associated procedures had been implemented for safety reasons, considering that there had been no previous wet running during the weekend.

The downpour duly arrived and the red flag appeared, the cars returning to the pit lane. Eventually, the message came through that the race would resume behind the safety car, some 65 minutes after the scheduled start. Some opined that the 'health and safety' attitude had been a bit overdone. Weren't these men supposed to be the greatest drivers in the world, on a relatively low-speed circuit? It transpired, however, that there was also a problem with the starting gantry's electronics, understandable perhaps given the Hollywood-style downpour, and a rolling start was probably the safest option in more ways than one.

It was not long before there was clear demonstration of just how tricky F1 cars are on cold tyres and brakes. Behind Bernd Maylander's safety car, Nicholas Latifi went into the barrier at Loews (now Fairmont) hairpin – "The car just wouldn't turn!" – and Lance Stroll clipped the barrier on the outside into Massenet, puncturing his right rear and sending him to the pits. Double Canada high and dry. On second thoughts, make that wet…

With the race distance reduced to 77 laps and the safety car in, we were under way at last. Pierre Gasly immediately did something about his unrepresentative qualifying slot by rolling the dice and making an early stop for a switch to intermediate Pirellis.

After a few hairy moments, Gasly's AlphaTauri became the quickest car by lap seven, which was the cue for Yuki Tsunoda and Sebastian Vettel to pit for inters, too.

"How are conditions, Max?" Red Bull race engineer Gianpiero 'GP' Lambiase asked Verstappen.

"Drying, but still a bit tricky on these tyres," was the reply.

With ten laps down, Charles Leclerc led team-mate Carlos Sainz by 3.8s, with Sergio Pérez just 1.2s behind the second Ferrari and Verstappen adopting a watching brief a similar distance further back. Lando Norris was running 6.6s behind the Red Bull for McLaren, with George Russell reporting that he thought he was quicker. An attempt to get by, however, resulted in a straight-on moment at the chicane. Fernando Alonso's Alpine was a further 4s back, with a similar gap behind him to Lewis Hamilton. Esteban Ocon had dropped 10s to the seven-time champion, and Valtteri Bottas's Alfa completed the top ten an additional 3s in arrears. Gasly, on his intermediates, meanwhile, was 14th. Vettel, Mick Schumacher, Tsunoda, Stroll and Latifi had all copied his move on to the intermediates.

With a dry line emerging and the leaders now actively looking for damp patches to keep the full wets alive, the thinking was to extend as far as making a switch straight to slicks feasible. By lap 13, Leclerc had his lead out to 5s over team-mate Sainz.

With 14 laps on the board, Pérez was on the radio to Red Bull: "It's definitely inters now." Proving his point, Gasly got better traction on his inters than Daniel Ricciardo's McLaren on its wets between Tabac and the entry to the Swimming Pool complex, to move up to 12th. A lap later, however, Sainz was on the radio to Ferrari with a different message: "We are going to go straight to dries."

Hamilton's Mercedes had pitted on lap 15, and he had

opted for a set of the intermediate tyres. Clearly, opinion was divided.

After 16 laps, out went the message to Pérez: "Box, box." In he came, and the Red Bull crew turned him around in just 2.3s, sending him back out on the inters. Importantly, he rejoined just ahead of Russell's Mercedes.

It was not long before Pérez was turning the timing screens purple, but, crucially, Ferrari did not respond for two laps. When Leclerc pitted for intermediates, he rejoined third, behind his team-mate, who had yet to pit, and Pérez. Further back, Hamilton was flying until he became stuck behind the wet-shod Esteban Ocon, suffering some front wing damage as he tried to force his way through.

Ferrari left Sainz out until lap 21, when they had no choice but to go straight on to slicks if they were to have a chance of resisting the flying Pérez. They also made the decision to stop Leclerc again after just three laps on his intermediates, stacking him behind Carlos, although there did appear to be confusion, as they told him late to stay out when he was already in the pit lane.

"What happened?" yelled a furious Leclerc, who had done everything right, but now was behind his team-mate. Worse than that, Red Bull pitted Pérez again after six laps on inters, bringing in Verstappen on the same lap. Max had stopped for inters on the same lap as Charles, but had run an extra lap on them before having hard-compound slicks fitted. As they all got back up to speed on slicks, there had been a complete reshuffle at the front: Pérez led fractionally from Sainz, with a 5s gap to Verstappen, who had emerged from the pits just in front of Leclerc, who was fit to be tied.

Sainz, right in Pérez's wheel tracks, gunned it out of the Antony Hoghes corner and, jinking this way and that, survived a big tank-slapper on the front straight before tucking in behind the Red Bull again at Ste Devote.

VIEWPOINT
A VICTIM OF CIRCUMSTANCE

MONACO, a race Charles Leclerc loves, had not been paying him in kind. He knows the place like the back of his hand – as you would when arguably the world's most famous grand prix track is in your front yard. Time and again, the Monégasque had been in impressive command, only to be knocked back by circumstances that were often beyond his control.

On his first time out in F2 in 2017, the chance of a brilliant victory had been scuppered by a safety car and, eventually, a suspension problem. The subsequent sprint race brought more suspension trouble, this time after a clash of wheels.

The step up to F1 with Alfa Romeo the following year had been a learning process that appeared to be paying off until a solid 12th place at Monaco was wiped out against the back of a Toro Rosso, thanks to brake failure on the Alfa. The pressure associated with the move to Ferrari for 2019 began to tell when he locked up and damaged his tyres early in qualifying. Believing that Leclerc had done enough to make Q2, Ferrari kept him in the pits, only to watch their man's time slide into the drop zone. The race was not much better, thanks to damage inflicted by a collision.

With Monaco absent from the Covid-affected 2020 calendar, Leclerc was raring to go in 2021. Fastest time in Q3 was followed by an off that brought qualifying to an end – and also his hopes for the race. Internal damage became evident while on his way to the grid, the much prized pole position having to remain unoccupied. Surely his luck had to come good in 2022?

Despite the mixed conditions, Leclerc appeared to have everything under control until Ferrari miscued on pit-stop strategy, his disappointment being made worse by the way the cards fell in relation to his team-mate's track position. At least he hadn't far to go when it came to closing his front door on a race that seems destined to cause frustration at every turn.

Maurice Hamilton

It was a bad afternoon for Haas. With Kevin Magnussen already out of the race after 19 laps due to a power unit issue, team-mate Schumacher dropped it exiting the Swimming Pool complex. "I'm okay," he told the team, "I just don't understand it." The car was in two parts, the gearbox capsule, rear wing and rear wheels completely separate from the monocoque after what had looked like a relatively innocuous impact with the Tecpro barrier.

There was an inevitable red flag while the debris was cleared and the barrier repaired, everyone lining up in the pit lane and fitting new tyres after 30 laps of the scheduled 77. It would be another restart, again behind the safety car.

"No more rain expected until the end of the race," Leclerc's race engineer told him. "Everyone expected to go to the end."

"Perfect," replied the fourth-placed pole-man with a heavy dose of sarcasm.

The order was now Pérez, Sainz, Verstappen, Leclerc, Russell, Norris, Alonso, Hamilton, Ocon, Bottas, Vettel, Gasly, Ricciardo, Stroll, Tsunoda, Zhou, Latifi and Albon.

There was some divergence on tyre strategy among the top ten: both Red Bull drivers were on mediums, as were Russell, Alonso, Hamilton and Ocon, while both Ferrari drivers, Norris and Bottas had opted for hards. This being Monaco, though, it probably wasn't going to make a lot of difference. Chances are a driver could run on the rims themselves and still not be overtaken!

After two laps heading the field, Bernd Maylander pulled off to leave Pérez leading the Monaco GP, the Mexican surviving a quick lock-up into Mirabeau. The three-hour race maximum was clearly going to come into play on this day, Red Bull telling its drivers on lap 35 that instead of the scheduled 77, they anticipated another 29 laps.

In an incident that now seemed to have happened in a different age, Ocon was informed that he had been awarded a 5s penalty for turning in on Lewis Hamilton at Ste Devote. Ultimately, it would drop him out of the top ten. Meanwhile, Zhou Guanyu pulled off a tremendous save after losing the rear end of his Alfa Romeo while trying to get down the inside of Tsunoda for 16th into the chicane.

As the laps ticked down, it was the expected stalemate at the front, although Sainz was making Pérez work for it, and you could have thrown the proverbial blanket over the first four. With five laps to go, Russell had managed to keep his Mercedes within 8s of the leading quartet and was comfortably clear of Norris.

The Red Bull computers had been spot on, the clock running out on lap 63, with one further lap required for Pérez to win his third grand prix, surpassing Pedro Rodriguez's two to make him the winningest Mexican in F1 history.

"Yes, great job guys!" he radioed in appreciation.

A couple of seconds back, behind Sainz and Verstappen, Leclerc, fourth, was in a much different frame of mind.

"No words. No words. Oi, oi, oi," he said quietly.

"The season is long," Mattia Binotto replied.

"But we cannot do that," Leclerc pointed out. The seven-point loss at Imola had been down to him; the 13-point loss here was down to the pit-wall crew.

"As a driver, you dream of winning here," beamed a delighted Pérez, who had taken his 19th F1 podium. "After your home race, this is the most special weekend to win. With the rain, it was tough not to make a mistake, and keeping Carlos behind was not easy."

Russell maintained his record of top-five finishes just ahead of a closing Norris, with Alonso, seventh, backing off to protect his mediums, safe in the knowledge that Hamilton couldn't pass. Bottas and Vettel completed the scorers.

Verstappen now had a nine-point lead at the top of the championship table, with Pérez only six points adrift of Leclerc. Red Bull led Ferrari by 36 in the constructors' chase.

Attention now turned to a very different type of street track – Baku – where Pérez had always excelled. Could he make it two Azerbaijans in succession as well as two races in a row?

Tony Dodgins

Above: Charles Leclerc was in command from the start – until Ferrari's pit-stop strategy consigned him to fourth place and no hope of victory.
Photo: Pirelli

Left: A dream come true for Sergio Pérez as the Mexican joins the elite list of drivers to have won the Monaco Grand Prix.
Photo: Red Bull Content Pool/Getty Images

7

FORMULA 1 GRAND PRIX DE MONACO 2022

ROLEX

Official Timepiece

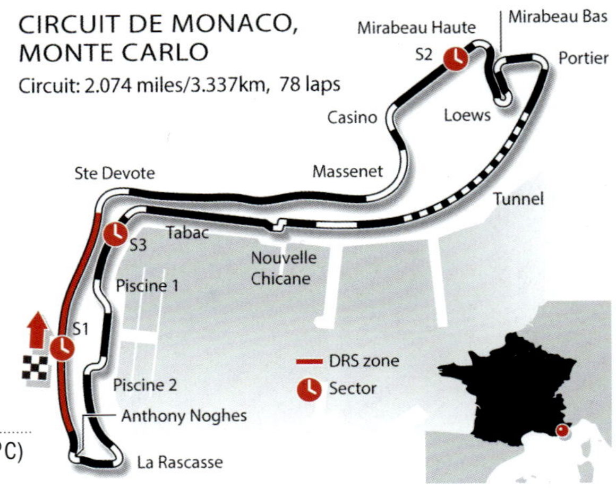

MONTE CARLO 27–29 MAY

RACE DISTANCE: 64 laps, 132.705 miles/213.568km

RACE WEATHER: Wet track-drying/cloudy (track 26–32°C, air 20–23°C)

RACE – OFFICIAL CLASSIFICATION

Pos.	Driver	Nat.	No.	Entrant	Car/Engine	Laps	Time/Retirement	Speed (mph/km/h)	Gap to winner	Fastest race lap	
1	**Sergio Pérez**	MEX	11	Oracle Red Bull Racing	Red Bull RB18-RBPTH001 V6	64	1h 56m 30.265s	68.343/109.987		1m 16.028s	46
2	**Carlos Sainz**	E	55	Scuderia Ferrari	Ferrari F1-75-066/7 V6	64	1h 56m 31.419s	68.332/109.969	1.154s	1m 16.421s	47
3	**Max Verstappen**	NL	1	Oracle Red Bull Racing	Red Bull RB18-RBPTH001 V6	64	1h 56m 31.756s	68.328/109.964	1.491s	1m 16.052s	47
4	**Charles Leclerc**	MC	16	Scuderia Ferrari	Ferrari F1-75-066/7 V6	64	1h 56m 33.187s	68.314/109.941	2.922s	1m 16.249s	46
5	**George Russell**	GB	63	Mercedes-AMG Petronas F1 Team	Mercedes-AMG F1 W13-M13 E Perf. V6	64	1h 56m 42.233s	68.226/109.799	11.968s	1m 16.830s	42
6	**Lando Norris**	GB	4	McLaren F1 Team	McLaren MCL36-Mercedes F1 M13 E Perf. V6	64	1h 56m 42.496s	68.223/109.795	12.231s	1m 14.693s	55
7	**Fernando Alonso**	E	14	BWT Alpine F1 Team	Alpine A522-Renault E-Tech RE22 V6	64	1h 57m 16.623s	67.893/109.263	46.358s	1m 15.882s	50
8	**Lewis Hamilton**	GB	44	Mercedes-AMG Petronas F1 Team	Mercedes-AMG F1 W13-M13 E Perf. V6	64	1h 57m 20.653s	67.854/109.200	50.388s	1m 17.203s	51
9	**Valtteri Bottas**	FIN	77	Alfa Romeo F1 Team ORLEN	Alfa Romeo C42-Ferrari 066/7 V6	64	1h 57m 22.790s	67.833/109.167	52.525s	1m 17.600s	57
10	**Sebastian Vettel**	D	5	Aston Martin Aramco Cognizant F1 Team	Aston Martin AMR22-Mercedes F1 M13 E Perf. V6	64	1h 57m 23.801s	67.823/109.151	53.536s	1m 17.558s	54
11	Pierre Gasly	F	10	Scuderia AlphaTauri	AlphaTauri AT03-RBPTH001 V6	64	1h 57m 24.554s	67.816/109.140	54.289s	1m 17.344s	61
12	Esteban Ocon	F	31	BWT Alpine F1 Team	Alpine A522-Renault E-Tech RE22 V6	64	1h 57m 25.909s *	67.803/109.119	55.644s	1m 17.571s	50
13	Daniel Ricciardo	AUS	3	McLaren F1 Team	McLaren MCL36-Mercedes F1 M13 E Perf. V6	64	1h 57m 27.900s	67.784/109.088	57.635s	1m 17.532s	59
14	Lance Stroll	CDN	18	Aston Martin Aramco Cognizant F1 Team	Aston Martin AMR22-Mercedes F1 M13 E Perf. V6	64	1h 57m 31.067s	67.754/109.039	1m 00.802s	1m 17.672s	56
15	Nicholas Latifi	CDN	6	Williams Racing	Williams FW44-Mercedes F1 M13 E Perf. V6	63			1 lap	1m 18.579s	43
16	Zhou Guanyu	CHN	24	Alfa Romeo F1 Team ORLEN	Alfa Romeo C42-Ferrari 066/7 V6	63			1 lap	1m 18.200s	52
17	Yuki Tsunoda	J	22	Scuderia AlphaTauri	AlphaTauri AT03-RBPTH001 V6	63			1 lap	1m 15.334s	61
	Alexander Albon	T	23	Williams Racing	Williams FW44-Mercedes F1 M13 E Perf. V6	48	*handling* *			1m 18.023s	40
	Mick Schumacher	D	47	Haas F1 Team	Haas VF-22-Ferrari 066/7 V6	24	*accident*			1m 24.778s	24
	Kevin Magnussen	DK	20	Haas F1 Team	Haas VF-22-Ferrari 066/7 V6	19	*power unit*			1m 33.754s	18

Initially the race was abandoned after the formation lap, due to very wet conditions, and restarted with a rolling start for 77 laps, 65 minutes later. It was red-flagged on lap 30, following Schumacher's accident and resumed after about 20 minutes with a rolling start. The race ended at 64 laps on reaching the two-hour limit.

* Albon: 5s time penalty for leaving the track and gaining an advantage. * Ocon: 5s time penalty for causing a collision with Hamilton (originally finished 9th).

DHL Fastest race lap (scores 1 point): Lando Norris on lap 55, 1m 14.693s, 99.938mph/160.834km/h.

Lap record: Lewis Hamilton (Mercedes F1 W12 V6), 1m 12.909s, 102.383mph/164.769km (2021).

20 · ZHOU · Alfa Romeo

18 · STROLL · Aston Martin

16 · ALBON · Williams

14 · RICCIARDO · McLaren

12 · BOTTAS · Alfa Romeo

19 · LATIFI · Williams

17 · GASLY · AlphaTauri

15 · SCHUMACHER · Haas

13 · MAGNUSSEN · Haas

11 · TSUNODA · AlphaTauri

	Grid order	1	2	3	4	5	6	7	8	9	10	11	12	13	14	15	16	17	18	19	20	21	22	23	24	25	26
16	LECLERC	16	16	16	16	16	16	16	16	16	16	16	16	16	16	16	16	16	55	55	55	11	11	11	11	11	11
55	SAINZ	55	55	55	55	55	55	55	55	55	55	55	55	55	55	55	55	55	11	11	11	1	55	55	55	55	55
11	PÉREZ	11	11	11	11	11	11	11	11	11	11	11	11	11	11	11	1	1	16	16	16	55	1	1	1	1	1
1	VERSTAPPEN	1	1	1	1	1	1	1	1	1	1	1	1	1	1	1	4	11	1	1	1	16	16	16	16	16	16
4	NORRIS	4	4	4	4	4	4	4	4	4	4	4	4	4	4	4	11	63	63	63	63	4	4	63	63	63	63
63	RUSSELL	63	63	63	63	63	63	63	63	63	63	63	63	63	63	63	63	14	14	14	14	63	63	4	4	4	4
14	ALONSO	14	14	14	14	14	14	14	14	14	14	14	14	14	14	14	14	4	4	4	4	14	14	14	14	14	14
44	HAMILTON	44	44	44	44	44	44	44	44	44	44	44	44	44	44	31	31	31	31	31	31	44	44	44	44	44	44
5	VETTEL	5	5	5	5	5	31	31	31	31	31	31	31	31	31	44	44	44	44	44	44	31	5	31	31	31	31
31	OCON	31	31	31	31	31	77	77	77	77	77	77	77	77	77	77	77	77	77	77	10	10	31	18	77	77	77
22	TSUNODA	22	22	22	22	22	20	20	20	20	20	20	20	20	20	20	20	20	20	10	5	5	18	77	5	5	5
77	BOTTAS	77	77	77	77	77	3	3	3	3	3	3	3	10	10	10	10	10	10	20	18	18	77	5	10	10	10
20	MAGNUSSEN	20	20	20	20	20	23	23	23	23	23	24	10	3	3	3	3	3	3	5	77	77	10	10	3	3	3
3	RICCIARDO	3	3	3	3	3	24	24	24	24	24	10	24	24	24	24	24	5	5	18	22	3	3	3	18	18	18
47	SCHUMACHER	47	47	47	23	23	10	10	10	10	10	5	5	5	5	5	5	24	24	22	3	22	22	22	22	22	22
23	ALBON	23	23	23	24	24	5	5	5	5	5	23	23	23	23	23	23	23	22	3	24	23	24	24	24	24	24
10	GASLY	10	24	24	47	10	22	47	47	47	47	47	47	47	47	47	47	22	18	24	23	24	47	47	47	6	6
18	STROLL	24	10	10	10	47	47	22	22	22	22	22	22	22	22	22	22	18	6	23	47	47	6	6	6	23	23
6	LATIFI	18	18	18	18	18	18	18	18	18	18	18	18	18	18	18	18	6	23	6	6	6	23	23	23		
24	ZHOU	6	6	6	6	6	6	6	6	6	6	6	6	6	6	6	6	47	47	47							
		SC	SC																								

	Grid order	27	28	29	30	31	32	33	34	35	36	37	38	39	40	41	42	43	44	45	46	47	48	49	50	51	52	53
16	LECLERC	11	11	11	11	11	11	11	11	11	11	11	11	11	11	11	11	11	11	11	11	11	11	11	11	11	11	11
55	SAINZ	55	55	55	55	55	55	55	55	55	55	55	55	55	55	55	55	55	55	55	55	55	55	55	55	55	55	55
11	PÉREZ	1	1	1	1	1	1	1	1	1	1	1	1	1	1	1	1	1	1	1	1	1	1	1	1	1	1	1
1	VERSTAPPEN	16	16	16	16	16	16	16	16	16	16	16	16	16	16	16	16	16	16	16	16	16	16	16	16	16	16	16
4	NORRIS	63	63	63	63	63	63	63	63	63	63	63	63	63	63	63	63	63	63	63	63	63	63	63	63	63	63	63
63	RUSSELL	4	4	4	4	4	4	4	4	4	4	4	4	4	4	4	4	4	4	4	4	4	4	4	4	4	4	4
14	ALONSO	14	14	14	14	14	14	14	14	14	14	14	14	14	14	14	14	14	14	14	14	14	14	14	14	14	14	14
44	HAMILTON	44	44	44	44	44	44	44	44	44	44	44	44	44	44	44	44	44	44	44	44	44	44	44	44	44	44	44
5	VETTEL	31	31	31	31	31	31	31	31	31	31	31	31	31	31	31	31	31	31	31	31	31	31	31	31	31	31	31
31	OCON	77	77	77	77	77	77	77	77	77	77	77	77	77	77	77	77	77	77	77	77	77	77	77	77	77	77	77
22	TSUNODA	5	5	5	5	5	5	5	5	5	5	5	5	5	5	5	5	5	5	5	5	5	5	5	5	5	5	5
77	BOTTAS	10	10	10	10	10	10	10	10	10	10	10	10	10	10	10	10	10	10	10	10	10	10	10	10	10	10	10
20	MAGNUSSEN	3	3	3	3	3	3	3	3	3	3	3	3	3	3	3	3	3	3	3	3	3	3	3	3	3	3	3
3	RICCIARDO	18	18	18	18	18	18	18	18	18	18	18	18	18	18	18	18	18	18	18	18	18	18	18	18	18	18	18
47	SCHUMACHER	22	22	22	22	22	22	22	22	22	22	22	22	22	22	22	22	22	22	22	22	22	22	22	22	22	22	22
23	ALBON	24	24	24	24	24	24	24	24	24	24	24	24	24	24	24	24	24	24	24	24	24	24	6	6	6	6	6
10	GASLY	6	6	6	6	6	6	6	6	6	6	6	6	6	6	6	6	6	6	6	6	6	6	24	24	24	24	24
18	STROLL	23	23	23	23	23	23	23	23	23	23	23	23	23	23	23	23	23	23	23	23	23	23					
6	LATIFI																											
24	ZHOU																											
		SC	SC	SC	SC	SC	SC																					

SC Safety car deployed on laps shown

TIME SHEETS

PRACTICE 1 (FRIDAY)

Weather: Dry/sunny

Temperatures: track 52–55°C, air 31–33°C

Pos.	Driver	Laps	Time
1	Charles Leclerc	29	1m 14.531s
2	Sergio Pérez	30	1m 14.570s
3	Carlos Sainz	28	1m 14.601s
4	Max Verstappen	26	1m 14.712s
5	Lando Norris	31	1m 15.056s
6	Pierre Gasly	33	1m 15.083s
7	Daniel Ricciardo	33	1m 15.157s
8	George Russell	34	1m 15.211s
9	Sebastian Vettel	33	1m 15.387s
10	Lewis Hamilton	29	1m 15.499s
11	Yuki Tsunoda	36	1m 15.536s
12	Lance Stroll	26	1m 15.539s
13	Fernando Alonso	28	1m 15.749s
14	Kevin Magnussen	30	1m 15.806s
15	Alexander Albon	39	1m 16.110s
16	Esteban Ocon	24	1m 16.315s
17	Zhou Guanyu	27	1m 16.417s
18	Nicholas Latifi	30	1m 17.714s
19	Mick Schumacher	12	1m 18.636s
20	Valtteri Bottas	2	no time

PRACTICE 2 (FRIDAY)

Weather: Dry/sunny

Temperatures: track 46–52°C, air 30–33°C

Pos.	Driver	Laps	Time
1	Charles Leclerc	30	1m 12.656s
2	Carlos Sainz	32	1m 12.700s
3	Sergio Pérez	31	1m 13.035s
4	Max Verstappen	33	1m 13.103s
5	Lando Norris	24	1m 13.294s
6	George Russell	31	1m 13.406s
7	Pierre Gasly	32	1m 13.636s
8	Fernando Alonso	31	1m 13.912s
9	Sebastian Vettel	32	1m 14.059s
10	Yuki Tsunoda	27	1m 14.134s
11	Kevin Magnussen	32	1m 14.239s
12	Lewis Hamilton	29	1m 14.267s
13	Valtteri Bottas	28	1m 14.468s
14	Alexander Albon	33	1m 14.486s
15	Zhou Guanyu	23	1m 14.525s
16	Lance Stroll	29	1m 14.623s
17	Mick Schumacher	33	1m 14.894s
18	Esteban Ocon	34	1m 15.216s
19	Nicholas Latifi	33	1m 16.276s
20	Daniel Ricciardo	2	no time

PRACTICE 3 (SATURDAY)

Weather: Dry/sunny

Temperatures: track 51–53°C, air 27°C

Pos.	Driver	Laps	Time
1	Sergio Pérez	27	1m 12.476s
2	Charles Leclerc	29	1m 12.517s
3	Carlos Sainz	28	1m 12.846s
4	Max Verstappen	29	1m 12.881s
5	Pierre Gasly	22	1m 13.210s
6	Lando Norris	19	1m 13.226s
7	Lewis Hamilton	26	1m 13.375s
8	Kevin Magnussen	24	1m 13.436s
9	George Russell	26	1m 13.476s
10	Fernando Alonso	23	1m 13.585s
11	Yuki Tsunoda	25	1m 13.645s
12	Mick Schumacher	26	1m 13.827s
13	Sebastian Vettel	28	1m 13.838s
14	Valtteri Bottas	25	1m 13.849s
15	Alexander Albon	22	1m 13.882s
16	Daniel Ricciardo	29	1m 14.104s
17	Esteban Ocon	22	1m 14.260s
18	Lance Stroll	20	1m 14.639s
19	Zhou Guanyu	25	1m 14.861s
20	Nicholas Latifi	26	1m 14.910s

QUALIFYING (SATURDAY)

Weather: Dry/mostly sunny Temperatures: track 44–51°C, air 26–29°C

Pos.	Driver	First	Second	Third	Qualifying Tyre
1	Charles Leclerc	1m 12.569s	1m 11.864s	1m 11.376s	Soft (n)
2	Carlos Sainz	1m 12.616s	1m 12.074s	1m 11.601s	Soft (n)
3	Sergio Pérez	1m 13.004s	1m 11.954s	1m 11.629s	Soft (n)
4	Max Verstappen	1m 12.993s	1m 12.117s	1m 11.666s	Soft (n)
5	Lando Norris	1m 12.927s	1m 12.266s	1m 11.849s	Soft (n)
6	George Russell	1m 12.787s	1m 12.617s	1m 12.112s	Soft (n)
7	Fernando Alonso	1m 13.394s	1m 12.688s	1m 12.247s	Soft (n)
8	Lewis Hamilton	1m 13.444s	1m 12.595s	1m 12.560s	Soft (u)
9	Sebastian Vettel	1m 13.313s	1m 12.613s	1m 12.732s	Soft (n)
10	Esteban Ocon	1m 12.848s	1m 12.528s	1m 13.047s	Soft (u)
11	Yuki Tsunoda	1m 13.110s	1m 12.797s		
12	Valtteri Bottas	1m 13.541s	1m 12.909s		
13	Kevin Magnussen	1m 13.069s	1m 12.921s		
14	Daniel Ricciardo	1m 13.338s	1m 12.964s		
15	Mick Schumacher	1m 13.469s	1m 13.081s		
16	Alexander Albon	1m 13.611s			
17	Pierre Gasly	1m 13.660s			
18	Lance Stroll	1m 13.678s			
19	Nicholas Latifi	1m 14.403s			
20	Zhou Guanyu	1m 15.606s			

QUALIFYING: head to head

Hamilton	3	4	Russell
Verstappen	5	2	Pérez
Ricciardo	1	6	Norris
Leclerc	7	0	Sainz
Gasly	4	3	Tsunoda
Hülkenberg	1	1	Stroll
Vettel	4	1	Stroll
Alonso	4	3	Ocon
Bottas	7	0	Zhou
Albon	6	1	Latifi
Magnussen	5	2	Schumacher

McLaren F1 Team

FOR THE RECORD

1,000th POINT: **Sergio Pérez**

80th WIN: **Red Bull**

10th PODIUM: **Carlos Sainz**

DID YOU KNOW?

With the first four being separated by less than 3 seconds, this race produced the 7th-closest top four of all time; the closest since Abu Dhabi, 2016; the 8th shortest-distance race in the World Championship.

POINTS

DRIVERS

1	Max Verstappen	125
2	Charles Leclerc	116
3	Sergio Pérez	110
4	George Russell	84
5	Carlos Sainz	83
6	Lewis Hamilton	50
7	Lando Norris	48
8	Valtteri Bottas	40
9	Esteban Ocon	30
10	Kevin Magnussen	15
11	Daniel Ricciardo	11
12	Yuki Tsunoda	11
13	Fernando Alonso	10
14	Pierre Gasly	6
15	Sebastian Vettel	5
16	Alexander Albon	3
17	Lance Stroll	2
18	Zhou Guanyu	1

CONSTRUCTORS

1	Red Bull	235
2	Ferrari	199
3	Mercedes	134
4	McLaren	59
5	Alfa Romeo	41
6	Alpine	40
7	AlphaTauri	17
8	Haas	15
9	Aston Martin	7
10	Williams	3

10 · OCON · Alpine

8 · HAMILTON · Mercedes

6 · RUSSELL · Mercedes

4 · VERSTAPPEN · Red Bull

2 · SAINZ · Ferrari

9 · VETTEL · Aston Martin

7 · ALONSO · Alpine

5 · NORRIS · McLaren

3 · PÉREZ · Red Bull

1 · LECLERC · Ferrari

54	55	56	57	58	59	60	61	62	63	64	
11	11	11	11	11	11	11	11	11	11	11	1
55	55	55	55	55	55	55	55	55	55	55	2
1	1	1	1	1	1	1	1	1	1	1	3
16	16	16	16	16	16	16	16	16	16	16	4
63	63	63	63	63	63	63	63	63	63	63	5
4	4	4	4	4	4	4	4	4	4	4	6
14	14	14	14	14	14	14	14	14	14	14	7
44	44	44	44	44	44	44	44	44	44	44	8
31	31	31	31	31	31	31	31	31	31	31	9
77	77	77	77	77	77	77	77	77	77	77	10
5	5	5	5	5	5	5	5	5	5	5	
10	10	10	10	10	10	10	10	10	10	10	
3	3	3	3	3	3	3	3	3	3	3	
18	18	18	18	18	18	18	18	18	18	18	
22	22	6	6	6	6	6	6	6	6		
6	6	24	24	24	24	24	24	24	24		
24	24	22	22	22	22	22	22	22	22		

20 = Pit stop *3 = One lap or more behind*

Race red-flagged

RACE TYRE STRATEGIES

	Driver	Race Stint 1	Race Stint 2	Race Stint 3	Race Stint 4	Race Stint 5
1	Pérez	Wet (n): 1–16	Intermediate (n): 17–22	Hard (n) 23–30	Medium (n): 31–64	
2	Sainz	Wet (n): 1–21	Hard (n) 22–64			
3	Verstappen	Wet (n): 1–18	Intermediate (n): 19–22	Hard (n) 23–30	Medium (n): 31–64	
4	Leclerc	Wet (n): 1–18	Intermediate (n): 19–21	Hard (n) 22–64		
5	Russell	Wet (n): 1–21	Hard (n): 22–30	Medium (n) 31–64		
6	Norris	Wet (n): 1–17	Intermediate (n): 18–22	Hard (n): 23–51	Medium (n): 52–64	
7	Alonso	Wet (n): 1–21	Hard (n): 22–30	Medium (n) 31–64		
8	Hamilton	Wet (n): 1–15	Intermediate (n): 16–22	Hard (n) 23–30	Medium (n): 31–64	
9	Bottas	Wet (n): 1–20	Hard (n): 21–64			
10	Vettel	Wet (n): 1–6	Intermediate (n): 7–23	Hard (u): 24–64		
11	Gasly	Wet (n): 1–2	Intermediate (n): 3–22	Hard (n): 23–64		
12	Ocon	Wet (n): 1–21	Hard (n): 22–30	Medium (n): 31–64		
13	Ricciardo	Wet (n): 1–19	Hard (n): 20–64			
14	Stroll	Wet (n): 1	Wet (u): 2	Intermediate (n): 3–24	Hard (u): 25–64	
15	Latifi	Wet (n): 1	Wet (u): 2	Intermediate (n): 3–19	Hard (n): 20–29	Medium (n): 30–63
16	Zhou	Wet (n): 1–19	Hard (n): 20–29	Medium (n): 30–63		
17	Tsunoda	Wet (n): 1–6	Intermediate (n): 7–21	Hard (n) 22–29	Medium (n): 30–56	Soft (n) 57–63
	Albon	Wet (n): 1–18	Hard (n): 19–22	Medium (n): 23–48 (dnf)		
	Schumacher	Wet (n): 1–4	Intermediate (n): 5–17	Hard (n) 18–24 (dnf)		
	Magnussen	Wet (n): 1–19 (dnf)				

The tyre regulations stipulate that at least two of three dry tyre specifications must be used during a dry race.

Selected compounds for Monaco: Red = Soft (C5); Yellow = Medium (C4); White = Hard (C3). (n) new (u) used

PIRELLI

FIA FORMULA 1 WORLD CHAMPIONSHIP · ROUND 8

AZERBAIJAN GRAND PRIX

BAKU CITY CIRCUIT

Max Verstappen eases his Red Bull past team-mate Sergio Pérez.
Photo: Red Bull Content Pool/Getty Images

BAKU QUALIFYING

BAKU, with its tight confines and long, long front straight, almost guarantees incident. Drivers need downforce for the parts of the circuit where the corners are tight and the barriers close, but as slippery and raceable a car as possible with strong straight-line speed for that straight. The temptation is to run less wing than ideal.

Lance Stroll had claimed a memorable podium with Williams at Baku in 2017, and it's a circuit he likes, but this time the Canadian provided all the Q1 drama. He went straight on at Turn Seven, flat-spotting his left front, then did it properly and clouted the barriers at Turn Two, bringing out a red flag with two minutes and thirty seconds on the clock. That prompted a mad scramble by everyone to make their second runs. Joining Stroll's Aston Martin as Q1 casualties were the two Haas cars of Kevin Magnussen and Mick Schumacher, and the two Williams of Alexander Albon and Nicholas Latifi.

After Sebastian Vettel's fabulous second place in 2021, Aston Martin's best result, he was on form again, despite a trip down the Turn 15 escape road. "Check the brakes, the pedal feels a bit long," he told the team by way of explanation. Lando Norris also overdid it and had to bail out at T15, but he survived after a quick spin-turn. While Vettel got it right on his next run and went through to Q3, Norris had to be content with P11, missing out on the top-ten shootout by just 0.03s.

Team-mate Daniel Ricciardo joined him on the sidelines, 12th, ahead of Esteban Ocon's Alpine, and the two Alfa Romeos of Zhou Guanyu and Valtteri Bottas.

When it turned serious in Q3, the smart money was on Charles Leclerc becoming the first 'multi-pole' winner at Baku, but it was Ferrari team-mate Carlos Sainz who was on provisional pole after the first runs, five-hundredths quicker than the Monégasque. On his final run, however, Leclerc produced one of those sensational laps that leaves rivals with distant looks and puzzled demeanours. His time was 0.455s quicker than Sainz, who thought he'd done a decent lap. Pole was in the bag. "Let's go, come on!" shouted the pumped-up Leclerc.

"It didn't feel like I left much on the table," Charles said, the Ferrari quickest in sectors one and two. "Turn Two was where I was losing all the time, and on my final lap, I just released the brakes and prayed that it was okay. It was a pretty close one there! Then the last corner was a bit trickier, but that was wind related. Overall, really happy with the lap."

The opening couple of race laps would be important for Leclerc if he was going to protect his position against Red Bull's superior straight-line speed before DRS became operational. Thus it was important for Red Bull to stop Ferrari from locking out the front row with such a relatively short run to Turn One. When the chips were down, both RB18s got between Leclerc and Sainz.

Sergio Pérez was actually the quicker, outqualifying Max Verstappen for the second time in 2022 at a circuit where he had won the previous year, slightly fortuitously after Lewis Hamilton's 'brake magic' *faux pas* at the restart following Verstappen's tyre blow-out. There is no denying that Checo is excellent around Baku, and he was driving with total confidence off the back of his Monaco win, just millimetres from the wall out of Turn 16. His lap was 0.28s behind Leclerc, but six-hundredths quicker than his team-mate.

"When you get to Q3 run one here, that's when you go balls out," Sergio explained, "and it was a little bit too much. I hit the wall a couple of times. Luckily, we managed to survive, which is the key really here. But it wasn't an ideal qualifying because at the end, we had a problem with the engine and couldn't turn it on. I was basically on my own, and a slipstream is very powerful around here. Who knows if it would have been enough for pole, because Charles had a very good lap."

Verstappen thought there had been more to come, too: "The start of the lap was good, but then it went away from me a little bit – tiny mistakes. In general, I was just struggling a bit to find front-to-rear balance over one lap. Not what I wanted, but as a team, being second and third, we still have a good opportunity for tomorrow."

There was a chasm between the two pace-setting cars of 2022 and the rest, topped by George Russell's Mercedes. He produced another great effort, despite being fully nine-tenths down on the second Ferrari, which was good enough to beat his seven-time world champion team-mate by a couple of tenths as the Mercs were split by Pierre Gasly's AlphaTauri.

The Faenza team was in decent shape around Baku, as Yuki Tsunoda claimed eighth place on the grid, his best qualifying performance of the season, one slot better than Miami.

Vettel was just four-hundredths down in ninth, providing the Aston Martin team with some cheer after Stroll's exit from Q1. The top ten was completed by Fernando Alonso's Alpine, the Spaniard having hustled the blue car through the twisty bits and taken full advantage of its strong speed on the straight.

Pierre Gasly took fifth for AlphaTauri.
Photo: Red Bull Content Pool/Getty Images

Left: Leclerc was on pole for Ferrari, but retired from the race with an engine failure.
Photo: Scuderia Ferrari

Below: Once again, George Russell took third place for Mercedes following the Ferrari retirements.
Photo: Mercedes-AMG Petronas F1 Team

Above: Charles Leclerc locks his Ferrari's left front wheel, allowing Sergio Pérez to take the lead in his Red Bull.
Photo: Red Bull Racing/Getty Images

Above right: Toto Wolff watched his Mercedes continue to struggle for race-winning pace.

Right: Lewis Hamilton leads Esteban Ocon's Alpine as he climbs through the field to an eventual fourth place.
Photos: Mercedes-AMG Petronas F1 Team

WITH Charles Leclerc on pole for the sixth time in eight 2022 races and a lover of street circuits, the question was whether Red Bull would challenge him for race pace. And, particularly, whether Sergio Pérez, Baku winner in 2021 and always strong in Azerbaijan, could follow up on his Monte Carlo victory and put himself squarely in the championship fight.

As the starting lights blinked out, both front-row men made a strong getaway. It was Pérez, however, who barged down the inside into Turn One and took the lead as Leclerc momentarily locked his left front and was forced to go defensive against Max Verstappen, in the second Red Bull, on the run to Turn Two.

With the DRS effect very strong at Baku, Pérez immediately got his head down and was already 1.3s clear of Leclerc as the field crossed the line at the end of the opening lap. Verstappen was next, from Carlos Sainz, George Russell, Pierre Gasly, Lewis Hamilton, Sebastian Vettel, Yuki Tsunoda, Fernando Alonso, Lando Norris, Daniel Ricciardo, Esteban Ocon, Zhou Guanyu, Valtteri Bottas, Alex Albon, Lance Stroll, Kevin Magnussen, Nicholas Latifi and Mick Schumacher. It was pretty much grid order, save for Vettel sneaking his Aston Martin ahead of Tsunoda's AlphaTauri.

Tyre-wise, the entire field had elected to start on the medium-compound Pirelli save for some of those outside the top ten, with Ricciardo, Ocon, Bottas, Stroll and Schumacher anticipating longer opening stints by starting on the hards.

All was orderly and well mannered, with Leclerc unable to do anything about Pérez, given the Red Bull's superior straight-line speed, but at least able to use the Ferrari's downforce and strong traction to get himself out of Turn 16 with a big enough margin that he was not vulnerable to the world champion down that long front straight.

The first incident of note involved Sainz in the second Ferrari, who ground to a halt in the escape road at Turn Four on lap nine. "Brake-by-wire failure," he told Ferrari on the radio. "Something failed..." It had sounded a lot more mechanical and clunky than that, though, and after Leclerc's engine failure in Barcelona, was further evidence that Ferrari had issues with its power unit.

The result was a virtual safety car ten laps into the race's 51, with Leclerc straight into the pit lane for a set of hard-compound Pirellis that would have to go 41 laps if the Ferrari was to get through on a one-stopper. It wasn't the quickest of pit stops, though, the Ferrari stationary for 5.4s after a problem releasing the front jack. Russell, Gasly, Hamilton, Vettel and Tsunoda all followed suit. With Hamilton stacked behind Russell, Vettel was able to relegate the second Mercedes.

"Did he have a free stop?" Verstappen enquired of arch-rival Leclerc?

"Most of the field hasn't pitted, but, yes, he has had a free stop. He's in P3," race engineer Gianpiero 'GP' Lambiase told him.

"How many laps are left?"

"Forty-two, including this one."

Vettel, meanwhile, was looking racy, closing in on Ocon's Alpine. Unable to quite get a move done into Turn One, he flew by in the second DRS zone between T2 and T3, but outbraked himself and took to the escape road. By the time he'd neatly executed a spin turn, the Aston had been relegated by Tsunoda's AlphaTauri.

At the front, by lap 14, Verstappen had closed in on team-mate Pérez and duly eased comfortably by on the inside of Turn One at the start of the following lap. No doubt, Red Bull was more than aware of 2018, when Verstappen had taken out Ricciardo as they battled, and had issued a 'no fighting' edict.

Meanwhile, Leclerc was about 10s down on the Red Bull pair after his stop, but was lapping quicker on his new rubber.

Two laps later, Red Bull brought in Pérez, the Mexican being given a somewhat tardy 5.7s stop to go on to the hard

Pirellis, getting out only just ahead of Russell's Mercedes.

After a number of laps stuck behind Esteban Ocon's rocket-in-a-straight-line Alpine, Hamilton finally made it by down the inside into T3 to put himself ninth, now some 13s behind his fourth-placed team-mate.

Behind Russell, Alonso in the other Alpine had also proven something of a roadblock to the McLarens of Norris and Ricciardo, which had Gasly with them, but the trio was freed when Fernando came in for his tyre stop.

Ricciardo was told on the radio, "Alonso pitted into traffic. Lando's trying to overcut him and we'd like you to sit behind Lando to give him that opportunity."

"If I sit behind any longer, I'm going to get eaten up by Gasly," Daniel responded.

"Copy."

With 19 laps on the board, Red Bull brought in Verstappen, handing the race lead to Leclerc for the first time. Being able to see what Max could do on hard tyres that were ten laps fresher than the Ferrari's was an interesting prospect. At least it would have been. No sooner had the Red Bull rejoined than Leclerc's Ferrari expired in plumes of smoke on the main straight, for the second time in three races, completing a disastrous day for Maranello. The championship chase was suddenly taking on a much different complexion from that at the start of the year.

Back to the McLarens, and when Norris pitted out of the way, Ricciardo, as he predicted, did get eaten up by Gasly, the Frenchman putting the AlphaTauri into what was now fourth place, given the demise of Leclerc.

Team-mate Tsunoda, 8.5s further back, was also on the move, passing Ocon's Alpine down the inside of Turn Three to claim seventh, just 5s behind Hamilton after 23 laps.

Then, a message from Alfa Romeo to Zhou Guanyou: "Joe, I'm afraid we have a technical issue, we have to box."

"Are you kidding me? Again?" With team-mate Valtteri Bottas already on his third power unit, it was yet more concern for the Ferrari engine department... It was more than a shame for Zhou, too, the Chinese driver doing a solid job in 12th place when he was passed the bad news.

As the race reached half-distance, Verstappen had a 7s advantage over team-mate Pérez; Russell's Mercedes was a comfortable third, 12s in arrears; then came Gasly, with a 3.5s margin over Ricciardo, yet to stop on his hard-compound starting tyres and soon to be passed by Hamilton. Tsunoda, Vettel, Ocon and the flying Alonso, who recorded 347km/h through the speed trap, completed the top ten.

Next up, a crawling Haas and an urgent call from the pit wall: "Okay, Kevin, stop the car. Stop the car."

Above: Sebastian Vettel had his best race of the season so far, taking sixth for Aston Martin.
Photo: Aston Martin Aramco Cognizant F1 Team

Top right: Alfa Romeo ran in an Italian-themed tri-colour livery for the race in Baku.
Photo: Alfa Romeo ORLEN

Above right: To preserve their points-paying positions, McLaren asked Lando Norris to surrender his eighth place to team-mate Daniel Ricciardo.
Photo: McLaren F1 Team

Right: The Red Bull team celebrates its crushing 1-2 finish.
Photo: Red Bull Content Pool/Getty Images

"Engine," said Magnussen. Even more food for thought for Maranello as Magnussen pulled off at Turn 15, prompting a second VSC period.

Red Bull took the opportunity to pit both cars; Russell and Hamilton followed them in, while Gasly stayed out. It worked well for Ricciardo, who jettisoned his starting set of hards for new mediums. Hamilton, on his fresh tyres, made short work of regaining fifth from Tsunoda and, lapping a second a lap faster, set off after Gasly's fourth-placed AlphaTauri. In fact, Yuki was struggling with a broken rear wing, only half of the main plane reacting to DRS, which, potentially, would have produced high-speed instability. Into the pits he came for fresh tyres and a 20s stop as the mechanics went to work with the gaffer tape!

"What is this?" enquired a rattled Tsunoda.

"It's for reliability," he was told. "From now on, no DRS." FIA technical chief Jo Bauer was on his way for a look, just as Tsunoda accelerated back into the fray!

With seven laps to go, Hamilton had caught Gasly and relieved the Frenchman of fourth place with the aid of DRS down the inside into Turn Three. Some 7s behind the AlphaTauri, Vettel was enjoying Aston Martin's best display thus far in the season and had a comfortable 6s cushion over Alonso's Alpine. Closing on Fernando on softer rubber was Ricciardo, with team-mate Norris, on his relatively fresh hard-compound Pirellis, just 2.7s further back and closing.

"Okay, Lando, here's the situation," Norris was told. "If you can close up on Daniel, and if Daniel can't close up on Alonso, we will let you through, but if we can't overtake Alonso, we will relinquish the position towards the end of the race. Happy?"

"Yeah, happy, but tell him to push more now," he replied.

Then, a lap or so later: "Alonso has said that is all the pace he has, and Daniel is trying his best."

"Yes, okay, I'm maximum pace, mate."

It had all been relatively simple for Verstappen, whose margin to Pérez was now out to almost 20s. On the penultimate lap, however, he came on the radio to tell the team, "Under braking at Turn Five, I felt something fall between my feet, a tiny piece. Can you check everything is normal?"

"Okay, copy that, Max."

At McLaren, meanwhile, it seemed that the excitement was over. "We think Alonso is too fast; we're going to hold position," Norris was told.

"Why hold position?" Lando asked.

"We held position in stint one [when Norris was ahead], and we're returning the favour."

"Yeah, but that was for strategy, this is for a finishing position," Norris calmly pointed out. McLaren wanted its double-points finish without undue drama at a track where they'd predicted they might struggle.

Despite the foreign object between his feet, Verstappen was still intent on pinching fastest lap from his team-mate. He didn't quite manage it: Pérez's mark was 1m 46.046s; Verstappen's penultimate lap was 1m 46.050. Close...

The world champion's 66th podium made him Red Bull's most successful driver in terms of that metric. "Was that a good race, or was that a good race? You tell me!" Verstappen enthused on his slow-down lap.

"Very mature drive today, Max," Christian Horner confirmed. "Great pace when you needed it. Well done. Brilliant result." For the team, it was indeed a brilliant result – maximum points on a day when the Ferrari challenge had imploded. For Verstappen, it was some kind of redemption after his tyre explosion within sight of victory 12 months earlier.

"We were maybe a tiny bit lucky with Charles's retirement," Verstappen admitted, "but nevertheless, our car was really quick today, and I think I could have closed that gap anyway."

The ever consistent Russell continued the impressive start to his Mercedes career by claiming a third podium of the season, maintaining his record of finishing in the top five at every race so far. His team-mate, Hamilton, crossed the line 25s down in fourth place, some 6s clear of Gasly's AlphaTauri.

Not quite reaching the heights of the previous year, Vettel was an excellent sixth for Aston, with Alonso, Ricciardo, Norris and Ocon completing the points-scorers.

Ferrari's dire day meant that Verstappen now enjoyed a 21-point championship lead from team-mate Pérez, with Leclerc 34 points in arrears. In the constructors' championship, Red Bull's advantage over Ferrari was out to 80 points. Canada was just seven days hence.

Tony Dodgins

VIEWPOINT
TYRE WHISPERER GONE QUIET

WITH Sergio Pérez out front, the race had seemed to be his for the taking, given Checo's reputation for taking care of his tyres. As it turned out, tyre degradation would be his downfall – and he wasn't sure why that should be.

Pérez had arrived in Baku buoyed by the victory at Monaco and happy that he was more at one with the 2022 Red Bull than the previous year's RB16B, from which only Verstappen had been able to extract the maximum. When Pérez took the lead from Charles Leclerc at the start and pulled away, he looked all set for two wins on the trot. Then events seemed to conspire against him, starting on lap nine.

The VSC prompted by Sainz's hobbled Ferrari came just as Pérez passed the pit entrance and denied the Mexican a cheap stop. When racing resumed, he discovered that his previous pace had gone. Had he pushed too hard on heavy fuel? Had something happened to the compound on his mediums during the slow laps? He didn't think so. Given his reputation for nursing rubber, conjuring points out of nowhere with Force India/Racing Point, you had to believe him.

As Verstappen closed in and passed with ease, a pit stop meant second place for Pérez (helped by Ferrari's day going up in smoke with Leclerc's failure). Hesitant – and at times confusing – radio communications between Sergio and his engineer not only added to the mystery, but also triggered the inevitable conspiracy theories. Here was Verstappen resuming command on a day when Red Bull management might have come under pressure with another maximum haul (plus fastest lap) for Pérez, whose struggle, coincidentally, was not helped by a stuck front jack at the first stop and a faulty wheel gun at the second.

That was pure bad luck, of course. The tyre problem, less so. It seemed that the 'Tyre Whisperer' had lost his voice just when he could have been shouting about Verstappen's lead being slashed to a mere seven points.

Maurice Hamilton

8

FORMULA 1 AZERBAIJAN GRAND PRIX 2022

ROLEX

Official Timepiece

BAKU CITY CIRCUIT

Circuit: 3.730 miles/6.003km , 51 laps

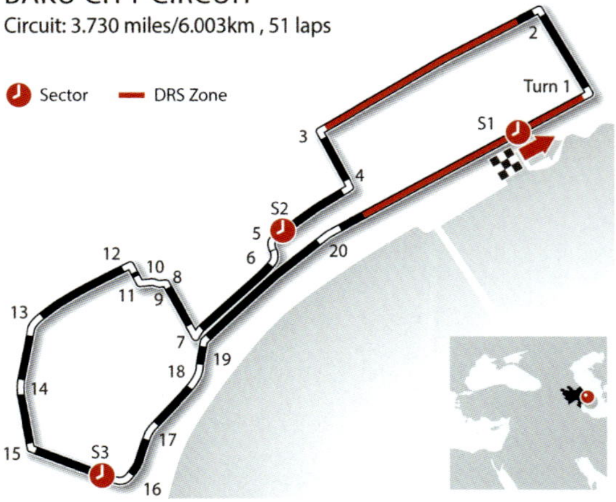

BAKU 10–12 JUNE

RACE DISTANCE: 51 laps, 190.170 miles/306.049km

RACE WEATHER: Dry/sunny (track 48–54°C, air 27–30°C)

RACE – OFFICIAL CLASSIFICATION

Pos.	Driver	Nat.	No.	Entrant	Car/Engine	Laps	Time/Retirement	Speed (mph/km/h)	Gap to winner	Fastest race lap
1	**Max Verstappen**	NL	1	Oracle Red Bull Racing	Red Bull RB18-RBPTH001 V6	51	1h 34m 05.941s	121.257/195.144		1m 46.050s 50
2	**Sergio Pérez**	MEX	11	Oracle Red Bull Racing	Red Bull RB18-RBPTH001 V6	51	1h 34m 26.764s	120.811/194.427	20.823s	1m 46.046s 36
3	**George Russell**	GB	63	Mercedes-AMG Petronas F1 Team	Mercedes-AMG F1 W13-M13 E Perf. V6	51	1h 34m 51.936s	120.277/193.567	45.995s	1m 47.177s 42
4	**Lewis Hamilton**	GB	44	Mercedes-AMG Petronas F1 Team	Mercedes-AMG F1 W13-M13 E Perf. V6	51	1h 35m 17.620s	119.737/192.698	1m 11.679s	1m 47.044s 39
5	**Pierre Gasly**	F	10	Scuderia AlphaTauri	AlphaTauri AT03-RBPTH001 V6	51	1h 35m 23.240s	119.620/192.509	1m 17.299s	1m 48.519s 39
6	**Sebastian Vettel**	D	5	Aston Martin Aramco Cognizant F1 Team	Aston Martin AMR22-Mercedes F1 M13 E Perf. V6	51	1h 35m 30.040s	119.477/192.280	1m 24.099s	1m 48.206s 41
7	**Fernando Alonso**	E	14	BWT Alpine F1 Team	Alpine A522-Renault E-Tech RE22 V6	51	1h 35m 34.537s	119.383/192.129	1m 28.596s	1m 47.989s 49
8	**Daniel Ricciardo**	AUS	3	McLaren F1 Team	McLaren MCL36-Mercedes F1 M13 E Perf. V6	51	1h 35m 38.148s	119.309/192.009	1m 32.207s	1m 48.276s 44
9	**Lando Norris**	GB	4	McLaren F1 Team	McLaren MCL36-Mercedes F1 M13 E Perf. V6	51	1h 35m 38.497s	119.301/191.997	1m 32.556s	1m 47.997s 37
10	**Esteban Ocon**	F	31	BWT Alpine F1 Team	Alpine A522-Renault E-Tech RE22 V6	51	1h 35m 54.125s	118.977/191.475	1m 48.184s	1m 48.297s 36
11	Valtteri Bottas	FIN	77	Alfa Romeo F1 Team ORLEN	Alfa Romeo C42-Ferrari 066/7 V6	50			1 lap	1m 48.179s 42
12	Alexander Albon	T	23	Williams Racing	Williams FW44-Mercedes F1 M13 E Perf. V6	50			1 lap	1m 47.966s 48
13	Yuki Tsunoda	J	22	Scuderia AlphaTauri	AlphaTauri AT03-RBPTH001 V6	50			1 lap	1m 47.523s 42
14	Mick Schumacher	D	47	Haas F1 Team	Haas VF-22-Ferrari 066/7 V6	50			1 lap	1m 48.410s 40
15	Nicholas Latifi	CDN	6	Williams Racing	Williams FW44-Mercedes F1 M13 E Perf. V6	50	*		1 lap	1m 49.583s 37
16	Lance Stroll	CDN	18	Aston Martin Aramco Cognizant F1 Team	Aston Martin AMR22-Mercedes F1 M13 E Perf. V6	46	*vibration*		5 laps	1m 48.038s 38
	Kevin Magnussen	DK	20	Haas F1 Team	Haas VF-22-Ferrari 066/7 V6	31	*power unit*			1m 48.789s 12
	Zhou Guanyu	CHN	24	Alfa Romeo F1 Team ORLEN	Alfa Romeo C42-Ferrari 066/7 V6	23	*hydraulics*			1m 48.723s 12
	Charles Leclerc	MC	16	Scuderia Ferrari	Ferrari F1-75-066/7 V6	21	*power unit*			1m 47.531s 13
	Carlos Sainz	E	55	Scuderia Ferrari	Ferrari F1-75-066/7 V6	8	*hydraulics*			1m 48.978s 3

* Latifi: 10s stop/go penalty for personnel touching the car after the 15s warning during the starting procedure; 5s time penalty for ignoring blue flags.

DHL Fastest race lap (scores 1 point): Sergio Pérez on lap 36, 1m 46.046s, 126.627mph/203.787km/h.

Lap record: Charles Leclerc (Ferrari SF90 V6), 1m 43.009s, 130.361mph/209.795km/h (2019).

20 · SCHUMACHER · Haas

18 · LATIFI · Williams

16 · MAGNUSSEN · Haas

14 · ZHOU · Alfa Romeo

12 · RICCIARDO · McLaren

19 · STROLL · Aston Martin

17 · ALBON · Williams

15 · BOTTAS · Alfa Romeo

13 · OCON · Alpine

11 · NORRIS · McLaren

Grid order	1	2	3	4	5	6	7	8	9	10	11	12	13	14	15	16	17	18	19	20
16 LECLERC	11	11	11	11	11	11	11	11	11	11	11	11	11	11	1	1	1	1	16	1
11 PÉREZ	16	16	16	16	16	16	16	16	1	1	1	1	1	1	11	11	16	16	1	11
1 VERSTAPPEN	1	1	1	1	1	1	1	1	16	16	16	16	16	16	16	16	11	11	11	63
55 SAINZ	55	55	55	55	55	55	55	55	63	63	63	63	63	63	63	63	63	63	63	3
63 RUSSELL	63	63	63	63	63	63	63	63	10	14	14	14	14	14	14	14	14	4	4	10
10 GASLY	10	10	10	10	10	10	10	10	44	4	4	4	4	4	4	4	4	3	3	16
44 HAMILTON	44	44	44	44	44	44	44	44	5	3	3	3	3	3	3	3	3	10	10	44
22 TSUNODA	5	5	5	5	5	5	5	5	22	10	10	10	10	10	10	10	10	14	44	4
5 VETTEL	22	22	22	22	22	22	22	22	14	31	31	31	31	31	31	31	31	44	31	31
14 ALONSO	14	14	14	14	14	14	14	14	4	5	5	5	44	44	44	44	44	31	22	22
4 NORRIS	4	4	4	4	4	4	4	4	3	44	44	44	22	22	22	22	22	22	5	5
3 RICCIARDO	3	3	3	3	3	3	3	3	31	22	22	22	5	5	5	5	5	5	24	24
31 OCON	31	31	31	31	31	31	31	31	24	77	77	77	77	77	24	24	24	24	20	20
24 ZHOU	24	24	24	24	24	24	24	24	20	18	18	18	24	24	77	77	20	20	77	14
77 BOTTAS	23	23	23	23	23	20	20	20	77	24	24	24	18	18	20	20	77	77	14	77
20 MAGNUSSEN	77	77	20	20	20	23	23	23	23	20	20	20	20	20	18	18	18	18	18	18
23 ALBON	18	20	77	77	77	77	77	77	18	23	23	23	23	23	23	23	23	23	23	23
6 LATIFI	20	18	18	18	18	18	18	18	47	47	47	47	47	47	47	47	47	47	47	47
18 STROLL	6	6	47	47	47	47	47	47	6	6	6	6	6	6	6	6	6	6	6	6
47 SCHUMACHER	47	47	6	6	6	6	6	6												
									VSC	VSC										

Grid order	21	22	23	24	25	26	27	28	29	30	31	32	33	34	35	36	37	38	39	40	41
16 LECLERC	1	1	1	1	1	1	1	1	1	1	1	1	1	1	1	1	1	1	1	1	1
11 PÉREZ	11	11	11	11	11	11	11	11	11	11	11	11	11	11	11	11	11	11	11	11	11
1 VERSTAPPEN	63	63	63	63	63	63	63	63	63	63	63	63	63	63	63	63	63	63	63	63	63
55 SAINZ	10	10	10	10	10	10	10	10	10	10	10	10	10	10	10	10	10	10	10	10	10
63 RUSSELL	3	3	3	3	3	44	44	44	44	44	44	44	44	22	22	44	44	44	44	44	44
10 GASLY	44	44	44	44	44	3	3	3	3	3	3	3	22	44	44	22	22	5	5	5	5
44 HAMILTON	31	22	22	22	22	22	22	22	22	22	22	22	3	5	5	5	5	22	14	14	14
22 TSUNODA	22	31	31	31	5	5	5	5	5	5	5	5	5	14	14	14	14	14	3	3	3
5 VETTEL	5	5	5	5	31	31	14	14	14	14	14	14	14	3	3	3	3	3	4	4	4
14 ALONSO	24	24	20	20	20	14	31	31	31	31	31	31	31	4	4	4	4	4	31	31	31
4 NORRIS	20	20	14	14	14	20	20	20	20	20	20	4	4	31	31	31	31	31	77	77	77
3 RICCIARDO	14	14	77	77	77	77	77	77	77	77	4	77	77	77	77	77	77	77	23	23	23
31 OCON	77	77	18	18	18	18	18	4	4	4	77	23	23	23	23	23	23	23	22	22	22
24 ZHOU	18	18	23	23	23	23	4	18	18	18	23	18	18	18	18	18	18	18	18	18	18
77 BOTTAS	23	23	4	4	4	4	23	23	23	23	18	47	47	47	47	47	47	47	47	47	47
20 MAGNUSSEN	4	4	24	47	47	47	47	47	47	47	47	6	6	6	6	6	6	6	6	6	6
23 ALBON	16	47	47	6	6	6	6	6	6	6	6										
6 LATIFI	47	6	6																		
18 STROLL	6																				
47 SCHUMACHER																					
													VSC	VSC	VSC						

TIME SHEETS

PRACTICE 1 (FRIDAY)

Weather: Dry/sunny/windy

Temperatures: track 44-47°C, air 25-28°C

Pos.	Driver	Laps	Time
1	Sergio Pérez	21	1m 45.476s
2	Charles Leclerc	21	1m 45.603s
3	Max Verstappen	25	1m 45.810s
4	Carlos Sainz	22	1m 46.012s
5	Fernando Alonso	22	1m 46.571s
6	Lewis Hamilton	21	1m 46.667s
7	Yuki Tsunoda	25	1m 46.696s
8	George Russell	24	1m 46.705s
9	Pierre Gasly	25	1m 46.830s
10	Esteban Ocon	21	1m 46.917s
11	Lando Norris	19	1m 47.691s
12	Lance Stroll	24	1m 47.847s
13	Kevin Magnussen	24	1m 47.946s
14	Sebastian Vettel	22	1m 47.970s
15	Valtteri Bottas	22	1m 48.078s
16	Zhou Guanyu	24	1m 48.222s
17	Alexander Albon	22	1m 48.419s
18	Daniel Ricciardo	22	1m 48.810s
19	Nicholas Latifi	7	1m 50.921s
20	Mick Schumacher	3	1m 58.332s

PRACTICE 2 (FRIDAY)

Weather: Dry/sunny

Temperatures: track 33-37°C, air 23-26°C

Pos.	Driver	Laps	Time
1	Charles Leclerc	24	1m 43.224s
2	Sergio Pérez	22	1m 43.472s
3	Max Verstappen	18	1m 43.580s
4	Fernando Alonso	22	1m 44.142s
5	Carlos Sainz	25	1m 44.274s
6	Pierre Gasly	26	1m 44.315s
7	George Russell	26	1m 44.548s
8	Yuki Tsunoda	24	1m 44.567s
9	Esteban Ocon	24	1m 44.609s
10	Lando Norris	23	1m 44.771s
11	Sebastian Vettel	27	1m 44.781s
12	Lewis Hamilton	25	1m 44.874s
13	Lance Stroll	26	1m 44.874s
14	Daniel Ricciardo	25	1m 45.059s
15	Valtteri Bottas	25	1m 45.115s
16	Zhou Guanyu	24	1m 45.264s
17	Kevin Magnussen	26	1m 45.588s
18	Alexander Albon	13	1m 46.397s
19	Mick Schumacher	21	1m 46.425s
20	Nicholas Latifi	26	1m 47.218s

PRACTICE 3 (SATURDAY)

Weather: Dry/sunny

Temperatures: track 50-53°C, air 27-30°C

Pos.	Driver	Laps	Time
1	Sergio Pérez	18	1m 43.170s
2	Charles Leclerc	19	1m 43.240s
3	Max Verstappen	14	1m 43.449s
4	Carlos Sainz	19	1m 43.596s
5	Lando Norris	13	1m 44.418s
6	Daniel Ricciardo	19	1m 44.476s
7	Pierre Gasly	21	1m 44.491s
8	George Russell	17	1m 44.573s
9	Esteban Ocon	15	1m 44.685s
10	Sebastian Vettel	18	1m 44.689s
11	Fernando Alonso	14	1m 44.842s
12	Lewis Hamilton	19	1m 44.845s
13	Lance Stroll	17	1m 44.879s
14	Zhou Guanyu	18	1m 44.913s
15	Kevin Magnussen	17	1m 44.919s
16	Yuki Tsunoda	20	1m 44.964s
17	Alexander Albon	17	1m 45.479s
18	Mick Schumacher	19	1m 45.532s
19	Valtteri Bottas	17	1m 45.574s
20	Nicholas Latifi	17	1m 46.070s

QUALIFYING (SATURDAY)

Weather: Dry/sunny Temperatures: track 36-40°C, air 25-28°C

Pos.	Driver	First	Second	Third	Qualifying Tyre
1	Charles Leclerc	1m 42.865s	1m 42.046s	1m 41.359s	Soft (n)
2	Sergio Pérez	1m 42.733s	1m 41.955s	1m 41.641s	Soft (n)
3	Max Verstappen	1m 42.722s	1m 42.227s	1m 41.706s	Soft (n)
4	Carlos Sainz	1m 42.957s	1m 42.088s	1m 41.814s	Soft (n)
5	George Russell	1m 43.754s	1m 43.281s	1m 42.712s	Soft (n)
6	Pierre Gasly	1m 43.268s	1m 43.129s	1m 42.845s	Soft (u)
7	Lewis Hamilton	1m 43.939s	1m 43.182s	1m 42.924s	Soft (n)
8	Yuki Tsunoda	1m 43.595s	1m 43.376s	1m 43.056s	Soft (n)
9	Sebastian Vettel	1m 43.279s	1m 43.268s	1m 43.091s	Soft (n)
10	Fernando Alonso	1m 44.083s	1m 43.360s	1m 43.173s	Soft (n)
11	Lando Norris	1m 44.237s	1m 43.398s		
12	Daniel Ricciardo	1m 44.437s	1m 43.574s		
13	Esteban Ocon	1m 43.903s	1m 43.585s		
14	Zhou Guanyu	1m 43.777s	1m 43.790s		
15	Valtteri Bottas	1m 44.478s	1m 44.444s		
16	Kevin Magnussen	1m 44.643s			
17	Alexander Albon	1m 44.719s			
18	Nicholas Latifi	1m 45.367s			
19	Lance Stroll	1m 45.371s			
20	Mick Schumacher	1m 45.775s			

QUALIFYING: head to head

Hamilton	3	5	Russell
Verstappen	5	3	Pérez
Ricciardo	1	7	Norris
Leclerc	8	0	Sainz
Gasly	5	3	Tsunoda
Hülkenberg	1	1	Stroll
Vettel	5	1	Stroll
Alonso	5	3	Ocon
Bottas	7	1	Zhou
Albon	7	1	Latifi
Magnussen	6	2	Schumacher

Alfa Romeo ORLEN

FOR THE RECORD

25th WIN: Max Verstappen

20th PODIUM: Sergio Pérez

80th FASTEST LAP: Red Bull

20th 1-2 FINISH: Red Bull

DID YOU KNOW?

This was the first time since 2002 (Montoya) that a driver had four consecutive poles without converting any to a win.

POINTS

DRIVERS

1	Max Verstappen	150
2	Sergio Pérez	129
3	Charles Leclerc	116
4	George Russell	99
5	Carlos Sainz	83
6	Lewis Hamilton	62
7	Lando Norris	50
8	Valtteri Bottas	40
9	Esteban Ocon	31
10	Pierre Gasly	16
11	Fernando Alonso	16
12	Kevin Magnussen	15
13	Daniel Ricciardo	15
14	Sebastian Vettel	13
15	Yuki Tsunoda	11
16	Alexander Albon	3
17	Lance Stroll	2
18	Zhou Guanyu	1

CONSTRUCTORS

1	Red Bull	279
2	Ferrari	199
3	Mercedes	161
4	McLaren	65
5	Alpine	47
6	Alfa Romeo	41
7	AlphaTauri	27
8	Haas	15
9	Aston Martin	15
10	Williams	3

10 · ALONSO · Alpine 8 · TSUNODA · AlphaTauri 6 · GASLY · AlphaTauri 4 · SAINZ · Ferrari 2 · PÉREZ · Red Bull

9 · VETTEL · Aston Martin 7 · HAMILTON · Mercedes 5 · RUSSELL · Mercedes 3 · VERSTAPPEN · Red Bull 1 · LECLERC · Ferrari

42	43	44	45	46	47	48	49	50	51	
1	1	1	1	1	1	1	1	1	1	1
11	11	11	11	11	11	11	11	11	11	2
63	63	63	63	63	63	63	63	63	63	3
10	10	44	44	44	44	44	44	44	44	4
44	44	10	10	10	10	10	10	10	10	5
5	5	5	5	5	5	5	5	5	5	6
14	14	14	14	14	14	14	14	14	14	7
3	3	3	3	3	3	3	3	3	3	8
4	4	4	4	4	4	4	4	4	4	9
31	31	31	31	31	31	31	31	31	31	10
77	77	77	77	77	*77*	*77*	*77*	*77*		
23	23	23	23	*23*	*23*	*23*	*23*	*23*		
22	*22*	*22*	*22*	*22*	*22*	*22*	*22*	*22*		
18	*18*	*18*	*18*	*47*	*47*	*47*	*47*	*47*		
47	*47*	*47*	*47*	*18*	*6*	*6*	*6*	*6*		
6	*6*	*6*	*6*	*6*						

16 = Pit stop *6 = One lap or more behind*

VSC Safety car deployed on laps shown

RACE TYRE STRATEGIES

PIRELLI

	Driver	Race Stint 1	Race Stint 2	Race Stint 3
1	Verstappen	Medium (n): 1-18	Hard (n): 19-33	Hard (n): 34-51
2	Pérez	Medium (n): 1-16	Hard (n): 17-33	Hard (n): 34-51
3	Russell	Medium (n): 1-9	Hard (n): 10-33	Hard (u): 34-51
4	Hamilton	Medium (n): 1-9	Hard (n): 10-33	Hard (u): 34-51
5	Gasly	Medium (n): 1-9	Hard (u): 10-51	
6	Vettel	Medium (u): 1-9	Hard (u): 10-51	
7	Alonso	Medium (n): 1-18	Hard (n): 19-51	
8	Ricciardo	Hard (n): 1-33	Medium (n): 34-51	
9	Norris	Medium (n): 1-20	Hard (n): 21-51	
10	Ocon	Hard (n): 1-33	Medium (n): 34-51	
11	Bottas	Hard (n): 1-33	Medium (n): 34-50	
12	Albon	Medium (n): 1-9	Hard (n): 10-29	Hard (n): 30-50
13	Tsunoda	Medium (n): 1-9	Hard (u): 10-38	Soft (u): 39-50
14	Schumacher	Hard (n): 1-9	Medium (u): 10-23	Hard (u): 24-50
15	Latifi	Medium (n): 1-17	Hard (n): 18-50	
16	Stroll	Hard (u): 1-30	Medium (u): 31-46 (dnf)	
	Magnusssen	Medium (u): 1-9	Hard (n): 10-31 (dnf)	
	Zhou	Medium (n): 1-9	Hard (n): 10-23 (dnf)	
	Leclerc	Medium (n): 1-9	Hard (n): 10-21 (dnf)	
	Sainz	Medium (n): 1-8 (dnf)		

The tyre regulations stipulate that at least two of three dry tyre specifications must be used during a dry race. Selected compounds for Baku: Red = Soft (C5); Yellow = Medium (C4); White = Hard (C3). (n) new (u) used

Photo: Mercedes AMG Petronas F1 Team

FIA FORMULA 1 WORLD CHAMPIONSHIP · ROUND 9

CANADIAN GRAND PRIX

MONTREAL CIRCUIT

aws
aws

MONTREAL QUALIFYING

THE knock-on effect of Charles Leclerc's second power unit failure in three races, while leading in Azerbaijan, was a fourth internal-combustion engine and a back-of-the-grid start in Canada. Yuki Tsunoda was in the same boat with his Honda-powered AlphaTauri.

With Montreal cold and wet on Saturday morning in the third session of free practice, full wets were the order of the day until conditions improved slightly, allowing Fernando Alonso to top the session on intermediate Pirellis. He was just five-hundredths quicker than Pierre Gasly's AlphaTauri and Sebastian Vettel's Aston Martin. An unlikely top three.

Not surprisingly, Gasly and Vettel were dismayed when, in the slightly wetter conditions of Q1, they found themselves among the eliminees, along with both home drivers, Lance Stroll and Nicholas Latifi, and Tsunoda, who would start from the back anyway with his fresh engine.

"That can't be!" Vettel responded when told that he hadn't made the Q2 cut. "I mean, it was just so different to this morning. I had no grip. It felt like the rear left was broken. Ah, man..."

Gasly's frustration was plain to see as well, the Frenchman unable to generate enough brake temperature: "After we boxed to change tyres, the front left brake just completely switched off. I'm really frustrated because we could have really done something today."

Full wets had been needed in Q1, but with the rain easing, drivers were opting for intermediates for the second session. It was still treacherously slippery in places, however. Alexander Albon skated off at Turn Five, and although the Williams was not badly damaged, he discovered that he couldn't engage reverse.

Then, Sergio Pérez couldn't get his Red Bull turned in and slid straight on at Turn Five, bringing out the red flag. The Mexican would start the race from a highly disappointing 13th. Albon, Valtteri Bottas, Lando Norris and Leclerc also fell at the second hurdle. The last had not bothered to record a time, knowing that he would start from the back with his fresh engine.

"Something's not right with the PU, like it's misfiring a bit," Norris had told McLaren.

"Yes, we can see it," the team responded. "Sorry Lando, but you have to box."

Thus Daniel Ricciardo would be the only team representative to progress to Q3.

The final session was one of those where intermediates appear to be the sensible choice, but with the track becoming quicker and a dry line emerging, it is tantalisingly close to slicks.

George Russell thought so, rolled the dice and paid the price. The wettest part of the circuit was T1/2, and Russell figured that if he could negotiate that, then a decent lap would be possible. With nothing to lose, he figured it might even give him pole. Unfortunately, Turn Two was just too wet, and the car swapped ends on him, ending up backed into the tyre wall. George's session was over.

It was a shame because he had been looking very impressive, six-tenths clear of team-mate Lewis Hamilton in both Q1 and Q2. Around Montreal of all places, a track Hamilton loves and on which he is always competitive.

Max Verstappen, always tremendous on a wet track, left his most impressive effort to the end of the session when the track was at its best, stopping the clock in 1m 21.299s. He was in a class of his own, with his nearest challenger 0.65s away.

"That's pole position, Max," 'GP' Lambiase told him.

"Not bad, then," said Verstappen, "but it was a tricky session."

"Yeah, I won't say masterclass, but you were on top of that all session. Nice job."

The nearest to him was none other than Fernando Alonso, who put the Alpine on the front row just a month before his 41st birthday. Had he been expecting that?

"I don't really know," he said. "We were P1 in FP3, so it seemed that we were okay in wet conditions, but it wasn't really wet. In Q3, it was nearly dry at the end, so, in a way, I was thinking, 'Why could it not be a little bit wetter and rain a little bit now.' But at the end, we were also okay in the semi-dry conditions. The car was fast yesterday in the dry, fast for long-run pace as well, and fast in the wet, so it's been a very competitive weekend."

A tenth-and-a-half down and heading the second row was Carlos Sainz. He appeared to be on course for the front row, but a mistake out of the Turn 13 final chicane lost the Ferrari time and meant that he qualified behind his childhood idol.

The rest were a long way off, headed by Lewis Hamilton on 1m 22.891s in fourth place. It was a strong effort, if not perhaps by the seven-time champion's regular Montreal standards.

Just seven-hundredths behind the Mercedes was Kevin Magnussen's Haas. When team-mate Mick Schumacher joined him on the second row, it added up to the best combined Haas qualifying performance since the German GP of 2018.

Esteban Ocon couldn't match the heroics of his team-mate, but ensured that both Alpines were in the top seven, just 0.03s quicker than the first run of the chastened Russell, who nonetheless was positive and convinced that his attempt on slicks had been worthwhile. "We're not here to finish fourth," he asserted.

Daniel Ricciardo would start ninth for McLaren, a couple of tenths behind Russell and a similar amount clear of Zhou Guanyu, who outqualified Bottas for the second successive race in the Alfa Romeo.

Above: Mick Schumacher took sixth place on the grid for Haas, alongside team-mate Kevin Magnussen.
Photo: Haas F1 Team

Above left: Fernando Alonso uses all his skills and experience to put his Alpine on the front row.
Photo: Alpine F1 Team

Left: George Russell's gamble on fitting slick tyres for Q3 failed to pay off.
Photo: Lukas Gorys

Below left: Claiming a place in Q3, Zhou Guanyu heads down the pit lane with inters on his Alfa.
Photo: Alfa Romeo ORLEN

Opening spread: Red Bull's Max Verstappen just had the measure of Ferrari's Carlos Sainz, giving him a strong lead in the championship.
Photo: Red Bull Content Pool/Getty Images

Above: After the rain in qualifying, race-day was blessed with sunny skies. Sebastian Vettel leads Pierre Gasly, Lance Stroll, Charles Leclerc, Nicholas Latifi and Yuki Tsunoda on the opening lap.
Photo: Aston Martin Aramco Cognizant F1 Team

Above right: Tsunoda hops from his AlphaTauri to trigger a late-race intervention by the safety car.
Photo: XPB Images

Above far right: Home-crowd favourite Stroll throws team caps to the crowd.
Photo: Aston Martin Aramco Cognizant F1 Team

Right: Best of the rest. More valuable points for Esteban Ocon, who took sixth for Alpine.
Photo: Alpine F1 Team

MUCH of the pre-race chat had been about whether Fernando Alonso, with nothing to lose, could lead a grand prix as a 40-year-old by arrowing his Alpine past Max Verstappen at the first corner of the Canadian GP.

The answer was that he couldn't. It's a relatively short run to Montreal's Turn One, and with pole on the inside, once Verstappen had made a decent getaway, there was no pressure and the Red Bull was securely in front as the field charged into the tight turn. It was Alonso who had to watch his mirrors to repel the advances of Carlos Sainz's Ferrari.

There was action behind as Lewis Hamilton locked up from fourth and Kevin Magnussen took a look around the outside of the Mercedes on the way out of T2 on the run into T3. Hamilton leaned on the Haas, giving Magnussen only just enough room. Kevin fought it a bit too far and, as he tucked in behind the seven-time champion, there was contact between the Haas's right front wing endplate and the left rear wheel of the Mercedes.

The Dane would need to stop for a new front wing. Falling to the back of the field after such a strong qualifying session was a bitter pill for team principal Guenther Steiner to swallow. While it was a huge positive that the rejuvenated team was racing Mercedes, another contact with Hamilton after an optimistic outside move, following the one in Barcelona, might have had them quietly requesting that K-Mag temper his approach slightly.

Behind this tussle, Mick Schumacher, in the second Haas, dropped a place to Esteban Ocon, who managed to get around his outside and across into T3 in exactly the manner that Magnussen had been trying with Hamilton.

Behind Verstappen, Sainz soon won the battle of the Spaniards to put his Ferrari into second and ensure that Max was not going to have things all his own way. And, after his optimistic qualifying punt on slick tyres, George Russell was busy fighting his way back through the field from eighth on the grid, soon passing Schumacher and Ocon to run fifth after Magnussen's demise, just 3s behind his team-mate.

After Sergio Pérez's disappointing qualifying, things went from bad to worse for the Mexican. "I've lost the engine," he told the Red Bull pit just nine laps into the race, prompting a virtual safety car while his car was removed. With the top ten having started on the medium-compound Pirellis, Verstappen took the opportunity to dive in for a set of hards, with Hamilton following suit. The rest, however, figured that it was a little too early for a one-stopper and stayed out.

Hamilton and Verstappen soon proved that new hards could cope with the still relatively new mediums, Lewis getting a better exit from T13 and powering past Ocon back into fifth place at the start of lap 13.

At the front, we now had a Spanish 1-2, with Sainz leading Alonso by almost 5s. It was short-lived, however, as Verstappen comfortably passed Alonso and set off after Sainz, retaking the lead when Carlos made his own stop for hards after 20 laps.

Which is when the afternoon turned completely sour for the Haas team, Schumacher grinding to a halt with some nasty mechanical noises emanating from the power unit. Cue immediate requirement of the radio 'bleep' machine from the cockpit as seventh place and hopes of Mick's first F1 points evaporated.

"Sorry man, you were on it," race engineer Gary Gannon told Schumacher appreciatively.

When Sainz rejoined, he did so behind Alonso and very close to Hamilton's already hard-compound-shod Mercedes.

Importantly, though, the Ferrari brought its rubber up to temperature without ceding a place to Lewis. Both soon went by Alonso, who extended his medium-tyred opening stint as far as lap 28.

Some 42 laps into the race's 70, Verstappen stopped again for his second set of hard-compound Pirellis, but pitted out just fractionally behind Hamilton as they accelerated down to Turn Three. Lewis gave the Red Bull a squeeze and led through the chicane.

"Why didn't you make sure I was in front?" radioed an angry Verstappen.

"Didn't have the pace," replied engineer 'GP' Lambiase matter-of-factly.

But Verstappen needn't have worried. Down the straight into Turn 13, the Red Bull comfortably went by again, and Hamilton immediately carried on into the pit lane to take his own second set of hards.

What of Charles Leclerc? He had been making steady progress from the back of the grid with his fresh engine, starting on the hard tyre, but as they degraded, he found some of the quicker midfield cars harder to deal with. He made his lone tyre stop for mediums after 41 laps and now was lapping much quicker, passing Yuki Tsunoda's AlphaTauri and Daniel Ricciardo's McLaren to move up into the top ten.

At the end of lap 47, with 23 to go, Sainz, who had stopped just the once of course, had an 8.7s lead over Verstappen, who was on fresher tyres and closing the gap, but not at the rate that might have been expected.

The race's complexion changed on lap 49, however, when Tsunoda accelerated out of the pit lane on cold tyres and went straight into the tyre barrier at T1/2. The yellow flags soon became a full safety car. As a result, Sainz lost his advantage and had to pit, losing track position to Verstappen, who had stopped six laps earlier. But it was a good break for others yet to make their second stops or, as in the case of hard-tyred starters like Bottas and Stroll, yet to make their first. Ocon, Alonso and Zhou Guanyu also benefited.

It was actually the first piece of good fortune Alonso had had all race. When the first VSC occurred, he was on the start/finish straight and couldn't take advantage of it, and he was actually in the pit lane when it ended. Then, from around lap 20, he encountered an issue with the car's battery deployment and reckoned that he was losing the best part of a second.

"At that point, we forgot about the podium and just did the best we could," Fernando explained. "I was able to defend while I was in a DRS train, but I was in trouble if I wasn't."

The final 15 laps looked like being tasty, with the whole

Above: Valtteri Bottas and team-mate Zhou Guanyu brought some cheer to Alfa Romeo with seventh and eighth places respectively.
Photo: Alfa Romeo ORLEN

Top right: Lewis Hamilton was back on the podium for the first occasion since Bahrain.

Above right: After his great qualifying effort, Kevin Magnussen's first-lap collision with Hamilton caused front wing damage to his Haas.
Photos: XPB Images

Right: Fernando Alonso was a front-row starter for the first time in nearly a decade!
Photo: Alpine F1 Team

field bunched behind the safety car in the order Verstappen, Sainz, Hamilton, Russell, Ocon, Alonso, Leclerc, Bottas, Vettel, Zhou, Ricciardo, Magnussen, Stroll, Gasly, Albon, Norris and Latifi.

Norris was having a highly frustrating afternoon in a McLaren that lacked straight-line speed, having been sentenced to 14th on the grid after his power unit issue in qualifying. He had lost further time being stacked in the pits and with a 5s pit-lane speeding penalty.

"We got had over a few times with the safety cars and, basically, nothing went our way at all. We shouldn't have been racing with some of the cars we were, but there was nothing I could do," explained the dejected Lando as a three-race points-scoring sequence came to an end.

At the front, Sainz was pushing Verstappen hard, chasing his first GP win, and with the benefit of DRS, which, of course, the Red Bull didn't have.

"I expected to have a bit more pace," Verstappen admitted, "but we seemed to lack a little bit compared to Carlos. It was a bit more difficult than I expected. But we did our strategy, and I think for us it was the right one.

"After that second stop, I had the fresher tyres, I was closing in on Carlos, but I wasn't sure if I actually would fully close the gap before the end. But then the safety car came out. I wasn't very happy with that because I knew that he'd have fresh tyres behind me. And already with a little bit more pace compared to me, so it was difficult to defend. The last 15 or 16 laps we were flat out, pushing to the limit. I knew I couldn't make a mistake and it was good racing. It's always more enjoyable to be able to be really pushing instead of just saving your tyres." Amen to that.

"It was a tough, intense battle with Max," Sainz agreed. "I knew I had a bit of a pace delta on him for the whole race, and I was on five- or six-lap-fresher tyres at the end, but I think to overtake around here, you need to have more than those two- or three-tenths, you know. I gave it all. I was risking everything over the kerbs, close to the wall and having a few moments out there in the dirty air. I got close a couple of times, but not enough to really throw a move down the inside anywhere. But I can tell you, I was pushing!"

There were a few raised eyebrows when Ferrari bolted on a second set of hards at Sainz's second stop. Had they not discussed mediums or even softs?

"I was just thinking about it," Sainz admitted with a smile in the post-race press conference. "The safety car stayed out a bit longer than maybe I or the team thought. By the time it was green flag, there were only 16 laps left, which was the right number of laps to maybe try and put on a soft, and try to overtake Max on the warm-up phase of the hard.

"It's easy to say that now! But at the time, with still 20-something laps to go, the hard was definitely the fastest option to the flag, especially knowing that it was a bit of a fresher tyre compared to Max. It's a shame. I felt like, also, without the safety car, as Max said, he wouldn't have caught me easy. I think it would have been a good battle at the end. I was ready to hang it out there until the chequered flag. I was in a good place, still doing 1m 17.3s, and I think we could have made it to a flag."

All ifs and buts. The reality was a sixth win in nine 2022 races for Verstappen and a 47-point championship advantage over Red Bull team-mate Pérez. Sainz had to be satisfied with his fifth F1 career second place, while Hamilton was back on the podium for the first time since the Bahrain season-opener.

Russell made it two Mercedes in the first four, while Leclerc had to be content with fifth place from the back. Given how close his team-mate was, it was yet another race where it seemed that Charles could have won, all things being equal. The Alpines of Ocon and Alonso took the flag sixth and seventh, after a race that had promised so much more for the front-row starter. The Alfas of Bottas and Zhou finished eighth and ninth, while Stroll kept Canadian honour alive by claiming the final point for Aston Martin.

Tony Dodgins

VIEWPOINT
YOU CAN'T BEAT EXPERIENCE

FERNANDO ALONSO'S race might have been compromised by a number of issues on Sunday, but that did not prevent the oldest man in the field from being the talk of the paddock on Saturday. The Spaniard's Alpine had felt good from the start of practice (third in FP1, fifth in FP2, quickest in FP3). Then tricky conditions during qualifying played into his hands on a track he knew very well.

Given F1's three-year absence from Circuit Gilles Villeneuve, Alonso had the benefit of experience over some of his younger rivals when it came to using skill and confidence to run close to the wall. He was a joy to watch as he chucked the blue car around the slippery track and claimed a place on the front row. At the post-qualifying press conference, he was asked to do more talking than the other two drivers (Verstappen and Sainz) put together.

"Yeah," grinned Fernando, "the car was good straight away. We didn't make huge set-up changes. So that was a help to build up confidence. It's also a circuit [where] you need some rhythm. You use a lot of kerb here and it's quite bumpy. There are a few things that are here for many, many years. I've been racing here 16 or 17 years. Experience is a help; it's never a downside."

Alonso used that knowledge to avoid making optimistic forecasts about taking on Ferrari and Red Bull. "Fifth would be like a win for us," he said. The faint hope of at least leading into the first corner was denied by Verstappen making a clean start. It was downhill from there on for Alonso, not helped by narrowly missing the pit lane when the VSC was deployed for a second time, and struggling from around one-third-distance when an engine air leak robbed the Renault of straight-line speed and sent temperatures skyward.

Fernando eventually finished ninth; not where he wanted to be. But a couple of psychological as well as championship points had been made.

Maurice Hamilton

9

FORMULA 1 AWS GRAND PRIX DU CANADA 2022

ROLEX Official Timepiece

MONTRÉAL 17–19 JUNE

RACE DISTANCE: 70 laps, 189.686 miles/305.270km

RACE WEATHER: Dry/sunny (track 41°C, air 20–22°C)

CIRCUIT GILLES VILLENEUVE, MONTRÉAL

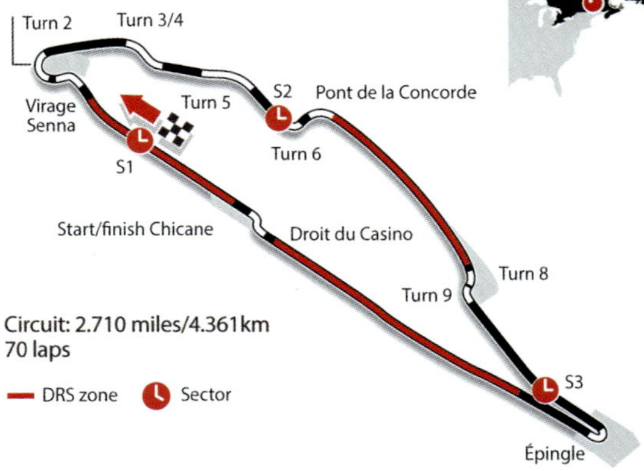

Circuit: 2.710 miles/4.361km
70 laps

RACE – OFFICIAL CLASSIFICATION

Pos.	Driver	Nat.	No.	Entrant	Car/Engine	Laps	Time/Retirement	Speed (mph/km/h)	Gap to winner	Fastest race lap	
1	**Max Verstappen**	NL	1	Oracle Red Bull Racing	Red Bull RB18-RBPTH001 V6	70	1h 36m 21.757s	118.107/190.075		1m 15.839s	64
2	**Carlos Sainz**	E	55	Scuderia Ferrari	Ferrari F1-75-066/7 V6	70	1h 36m 22.750s	118.087/190.043	0.993s	1m 15.749s	63
3	**Lewis Hamilton**	GB	44	Mercedes-AMG Petronas F1 Team	Mercedes-AMG F1 W13-M13 E Perf. V6	70	1h 36m 28.763s	117.964/189.845	7.006s	1m 16.167s	69
4	**George Russell**	GB	63	Mercedes-AMG Petronas F1 Team	Mercedes-AMG F1 W13-M13 E Perf. V6	70	1h 36m 34.070s	117.856/189.671	12.313s	1m 16.418s	63
5	**Charles Leclerc**	MC	16	Scuderia Ferrari	Ferrari F1-75-066/7 V6	70	1h 36m 36.925s	117.798/189.578	15.168s	1m 15.901s	62
6	**Esteban Ocon**	F	31	BWT Alpine F1 Team	Alpine A522-Renault E-Tech RE22 V6	70	1h 36m 45.647s	117.621/189.293	23.890s	1m 17.110s	62
7	**Valtteri Bottas**	FIN	77	Alfa Romeo F1 Team ORLEN	Alfa Romeo C42-Ferrari 066/7 V6	70	1h 36m 47.004s	117.594/189.249	25.247s	1m 16.927s	60
8	**Zhou Guanyu**	CHN	24	Alfa Romeo F1 Team ORLEN	Alfa Romeo C42-Ferrari 066/7 V6	70	1h 36m 48.709s	117.559/189.193	26.952s	1m 16.578s	63
9	**Fernando Alonso**	E	14	BWT Alpine F1 Team	Alpine A522-Renault E-Tech RE22 V6	70	1h 36m 51.702s *	117.499/189.096	29.945s	1m 17.010s	64
10	**Lance Stroll**	CDN	18	Aston Martin Aramco Cognizant F1 Team	Aston Martin AMR22-Mercedes F1 M13 E Perf. V6	70	1h 36m 59.979s	117.332/188.827	38.222s	1m 17.421s	64
11	Daniel Ricciardo	AUS	3	McLaren F1 Team	McLaren MCL36-Mercedes F1 M13 E Perf. V6	70	1h 37m 04.804s	117.235/188.671	43.047s	1m 17.932s	59
12	Sebastian Vettel	D	5	Aston Martin Aramco Cognizant F1 Team	Aston Martin AMR22-Mercedes F1 M13 E Perf. V6	70	1h 37m 06.002s	117.210/188.632	44.245s	1m 17.956s	63
13	Alexander Albon	T	23	Williams Racing	Williams FW44-Mercedes F1 M13 E Perf. V6	70	1h 37m 06.650s	117.197/188.611	44.893s	1m 17.951s	59
14	Pierre Gasly	F	10	Scuderia AlphaTauri	AlphaTauri AT03-RBPTH001 V6	70	1h 37m 06.940s	117.191/188.601	45.183s	1m 17.810s	60
15	Lando Norris	GB	4	McLaren F1 Team	McLaren MCL36-Mercedes F1 M13 E Perf. V6	70	1h 37m 13.902s *	117.051/188.376	52.145s	1m 17.495s	63
16	Nicholas Latifi	CDN	6	Williams Racing	Williams FW44-Mercedes F1 M13 E Perf. V6	70	1h 37m 21.735s	116.895/188.124	59.978s	1m 18.540s	61
17	Kevin Magnussen	DK	20	Haas F1 Team	Haas VF-22-Ferrari 066/7 V6	70	1h 37m 29.937s	116.731/187.860	1m 08.180s	1m 18.046s	11
	Yuki Tsunoda	J	22	Scuderia AlphaTauri	AlphaTauri AT03-RBPTH001 V6	47	*accident*			1m 18.309s	15
	Mick Schumacher	D	47	Haas F1 Team	Haas VF-22-Ferrari 066/7 V6	18	*hydraulics*			1m 18.967s	13
	Sergio Pérez	MEX	11	Oracle Red Bull Racing	Red Bull RB18-RBPTH001 V6	7	*hydraulics*			1m 18.844s	7

* Alonso: 5s time penalty for making more than one change of direction to defend a position (originally finished 7th). * Norris: 5s time penalty for pit lane speeding

DHL Fastest race lap (scores 1 point): Carlos Sainz on lap 63, 1m 15.749s, 128.784mph/207.258km/h.

Lap record: Valtteri Bottas (Mercedes F1 W10 V6), 1m 13.078s, 133.491mph/214.833km/h (2019).

19 · LECLERC · Ferrari
Used additional power unit elements; required to start from the back of the grid

17 · STROLL · Aston Martin

15 · GASLY · AlphaTauri

13 · PÉREZ · Red Bull

11 · BOTTAS · Alfa Romeo

20 · TSUNODA · AlphaTauri
Used additional power unit elements; required to start from the back of the grid

18 · LATIFI · Williams

16 · VETTEL · Aston Martin

14 · NORRIS · McLaren

12 · ALBON · Williams

Grid order	1	2	3	4	5	6	7	8	9	10	11	12	13	14	15	16	17	18	19	20	21	22	23	24	25	26	27	28	29	30	31	32	33	34	35	36	37	38	39	40	41	42	43	44	45	46	47	48	49	50	51	52	53	54
1 VERSTAPPEN	1	1	1	1	1	1	1	1	55	55	55	55	55	55	55	55	55	55	55	1	1	1	1	1	1	1	1	1	1	1	1	1	1	1	1	1	1	1	1	1	1	1	55	55	55	55	55	55	1	1	1	1	1	1
14 ALONSO	14	14	55	55	55	55	55	55	14	14	14	14	14	14	1	1	1	1	1	14	14	55	55	55	55	55	55	55	55	55	55	55	55	55	55	55	55	55	55	55	55	55	1	1	1	1	1	1	55	55	55	55	55	55
55 SAINZ	55	55	14	14	14	14	14	14	1	1	1	1	1	1	14	14	14	14	14	55	55	14	44	44	44	44	44	44	44	44	44	44	44	44	44	44	44	44	44	44	44	44	44	63	44	44	44	44	44	44	44	44	44	44
44 HAMILTON	44	44	44	44	44	44	44	44	63	63	63	63	63	63	63	63	63	63	44	44	44	44	14	14	14	14	14	63	63	63	63	63	63	63	63	63	63	63	63	63	63	63	63	44	63	63	63	63	63	63	63	63	63	63
20 MAGNUSSEN	20	20	20	20	63	63	63	63	31	31	31	44	44	44	44	44	44	44	63	63	63	63	63	63	63	63	63	31	31	31	31	31	31	31	31	31	31	31	31	31	31	31	31	31	31	31	31	31	31	31	31	31	31	31
47 SCHUMACHER	31	31	63	63	20	20	31	31	44	44	44	31	31	31	31	31	31	31	77	31	31	31	31	31	31	31	31	14	16	16	16	16	16	16	16	16	16	16	16	16	14	14	14	14	14	14	14	14	14	14	14	14	14	14
31 OCON	63	63	31	31	31	31	47	47	47	47	47	47	47	47	47	47	47	47	31	77	16	16	16	16	16	16	16	16	14	14	14	14	14	14	14	14	14	14	14	14	77	77	77	77	77	77	77	77	16	16	16	16	16	16
63 RUSSELL	47	47	47	47	47	47	24	24	24	24	24	24	24	24	24	24	24	24	16	16	77	77	77	77	77	77	77	77	77	77	77	77	77	77	77	77	77	77	77	77	18	18	18	18	18	18	16	16	77	77	77	77	77	77
3 RICCIARDO	3	3	3	24	24	24	3	3	3	3	3	3	3	3	3	3	3	3	18	18	18	18	18	18	18	18	18	18	18	18	18	18	18	18	18	18	18	18	18	18	16	24	24	24	24	24	24	24	5	5	5	5	5	5
24 ZHOU	24	24	24	3	3	3	11	23	23	23	23	23	23	23	23	23	77	77	24	24	24	24	24	24	24	24	24	24	24	24	24	24	24	24	24	24	24	24	24	24	24	22	22	16	16	16	3	3	24	24	24	24	24	24
77 BOTTAS	11	11	11	11	11	11	23	77	77	77	77	77	77	77	77	77	16	16	22	22	22	22	22	22	22	22	22	22	22	22	22	22	22	22	22	22	22	22	22	22	22	3	16	22	22	3	5	5	3	3	3	3	3	3
23 ALBON	23	23	23	23	23	23	77	4	4	4	4	4	16	16	16	16	23	4	3	3	3	3	3	3	3	3	3	3	3	3	3	3	3	3	3	3	3	3	3	3	3	16	3	3	3	22	20	20	20	20	20	20	20	20
11 PÉREZ	77	77	77	77	77	77	4	16	16	16	16	16	4	4	4	4	4	18	10	10	10	10	10	10	10	10	10	10	10	5	5	5	5	5	5	5	5	5	5	5	5	5	5	5	5	5	18	18	18	18	18	18	18	18
4 NORRIS	4	4	4	4	4	4	16	18	18	18	18	18	18	18	18	18	18	22	5	5	5	5	5	5	5	5	5	5	5	10	10	10	10	10	10	20	20	20	20	20	20	20	20	20	20	20	23	10	10	10	10	10	10	10
10 GASLY	5	5	5	5	16	16	18	22	22	22	22	22	22	22	22	22	22	5	20	20	20	20	20	20	20	20	20	20	20	20	20	20	20	20	20	23	23	23	23	23	23	23	23	23	23	23	22	23	23	23	23	23	23	23
5 VETTEL	18	18	16	16	18	18	22	6	5	5	5	5	5	5	5	5	5	10	23	23	23	23	23	23	23	23	23	23	23	23	23	23	23	23	23	4	4	4	4	4	4	10	10	10	10	10	10	4	4	4	4	4	4	4
18 STROLL	10	16	18	18	22	22	6	5	10	10	10	10	10	10	10	10	10	23	6	6	4	4	4	4	4	4	4	4	4	4	4	4	4	4	4	10	10	10	10	10	10	4	4	4	4	4	4	6	6	6	6	6	6	6
6 LATIFI	16	10	10	10	6	6	5	10	6	6	6	6	6	6	20	20	20	20	4	4	6	6	6	6	6	6	6	6	6	6	6	6	6	6	6	6	6	6	6	6	6	6	6	6	6	6	6							
16 LECLERC	22	22	22	22	5	5	10	20	20	20	20	20	20	20	6	6	6	6																																				
22 TSUNODA	6	6	6	6	10	10	20																																															
									VSC	VSC										VSC	VSC																												SC	SC	SC	SC	SC	SC

TIME SHEETS

PRACTICE 1 (FRIDAY)

Weather: Dry/sunny

Temperatures: track 41°C, air 25-26°C

Pos.	Driver	Laps	Time
1	Max Verstappen	27	1m 15.158s
2	Carlos Sainz	34	1m 15.404s
3	Fernando Alonso	31	1m 15.531s
4	Sergio Pérez	32	1m 15.619s
5	Charles Leclerc	30	1m 15.666s
6	George Russell	29	1m 15.822s
7	Lance Stroll	32	1m 15.877s
8	Lewis Hamilton	27	1m 15.877s
9	Sebastian Vettel	33	1m 16.041s
10	Daniel Ricciardo	29	1m 16.083s
11	Pierre Gasly	29	1m 16.165s
12	Lando Norris	17	1m 16.211s
13	Alexander Albon	29	1m 16.308s
14	Yuki Tsunoda	33	1m 16.322s
15	Esteban Ocon	26	1m 16.421s
16	Valtteri Bottas	27	1m 16.426s
17	Zhou Guanyu	30	1m 17.152s
18	Mick Schumacher	25	1m 17.223s
19	Nicholas Latifi	33	1m 17.241s
20	Kevin Magnussen	31	1m 17.555s

PRACTICE 2 (FRIDAY)

Weather: Dry/sunny

Temperatures: track 35-41°C, air 25-26°C

Pos.	Driver	Laps	Time
1	Max Verstappen	33	1m 14.127s
2	Charles Leclerc	32	1m 14.208s
3	Carlos Sainz	32	1m 14.352s
4	Sebastian Vettel	35	1m 14.442s
5	Fernando Alonso	24	1m 14.543s
6	Pierre Gasly	34	1m 14.879s
7	George Russell	31	1m 14.971s
8	Lando Norris	30	1m 14.987s
9	Daniel Ricciardo	31	1m 15.033s
10	Esteban Ocon	32	1m 15.119s
11	Sergio Pérez	29	1m 15.167s
12	Lance Stroll	34	1m 15.396s
13	Lewis Hamilton	25	1m 15.421s
14	Kevin Magnussen	34	1m 15.499s
15	Mick Schumacher	35	1m 15.516s
16	Zhou Guanyu	31	1m 15.526s
17	Yuki Tsunoda	37	1m 15.567s
18	Alexander Albon	30	1m 16.171s
19	Nicholas Latifi	27	1m 16.509s
20	Valtteri Bottas	3	no time

PRACTICE 3 (SATURDAY)

Weather: Wet/overcast

Temperatures: track 16°C, air 11°C

Pos.	Driver	Laps	Time
1	Fernando Alonso	15	1m 33.836s
2	Pierre Gasly	18	1m 33.889s
3	Sebastian Vettel	18	1m 33.891s
4	Esteban Ocon	16	1m 34.003s
5	Daniel Ricciardo	14	1m 34.110s
6	Lando Norris	13	1m 34.248s
7	George Russell	11	1m 34.259s
8	Sergio Pérez	10	1m 34.498s
9	Max Verstappen	10	1m 34.616s
10	Carlos Sainz	18	1m 34.778s
11	Valtteri Bottas	15	1m 35.016s
12	Zhou Guanyu	15	1m 35.213s
13	Lance Stroll	23	1m 35.531s
14	Kevin Magnussen	17	1m 35.643s
15	Lewis Hamilton	12	1m 35.692s
16	Alexander Albon	17	1m 35.761s
17	Yuki Tsunoda	27	1m 36.261s
18	Mick Schumacher	18	1m 37.388s
19	Nicholas Latifi	11	1m 38.394s
20	Charles Leclerc	5	no time

QUALIFYING (SATURDAY)

Weather: Rain, wet track drying/cloudy Temperatures: track 17°C, air 12°C

Pos.	Driver	First	Second	Third	Qualifying Tyre
1	Max Verstappen	1m 32.219s	1m 23.746s	1m 21.199s	Inter (n)
2	Fernando Alonso	1m 32.277s	1m 24.848s	1m 21.944s	Inter (n)
3	Carlos Sainz	1m 32.781s	1m 25.197s	1m 22.096s	Inter (n)
4	Lewis Hamilton	1m 33.841s	1m 25.543s	1m 22.891s	Inter (n)
5	Kevin Magnussen	1m 32.957s	1m 26.254s	1m 22.960s	Inter (n)
6	Mick Schumacher	1m 33.707s	1m 25.684s	1m 23.356s	Inter (n)
7	Esteban Ocon	1m 33.012s	1m 26.135s	1m 23.529s	Inter (n)
8	George Russell	1m 33.160s	1m 24.950s	1m 23.557s	Inter (n)
9	Daniel Ricciardo	1m 33.636s	1m 26.375s	1m 23.749s	Inter (n)
10	Zhou Guanyu	1m 33.692s	1m 26.116s	1m 24.030s	Inter (n)
11	Valtteri Bottas	1m 33.689s	1m 26.788s		
12	Alexander Albon	1m 34.047s	1m 26.858s		
13	Sergio Pérez	1m 33.929s	1m 33.127s		
14	Lando Norris	1m 34.066s	no time		
15	Charles Leclerc	1m 33.008s	no time		
16	Pierre Gasly	1m 34.492s			
17	Sebastian Vettel	1m 34.512s			
18	Lance Stroll	1m 35.532s			
19	Nicholas Latifi	1m 35.660s			
20	Yuki Tsunoda	1m 36.575s			

QUALIFYING: head to head

Hamilton	4	5	Russell
Verstappen	6	3	Pérez
Ricciardo	2	7	Norris
Leclerc	8	1	Sainz
Gasly	6	3	Tsunoda
Hülkenberg	1	1	Stroll
Vettel	6	1	Stroll
Alonso	6	3	Ocon
Bottas	7	2	Zhou
Albon	8	1	Latifi
Magnussen	7	2	Schumacher

Scuderia AlphaTauri/Getty Images

FOR THE RECORD

1st FRONT ROW: Alpine

150th GRAND PRIX START: Max Verstappen

DID YOU KNOW?

Alonso's interval between front rows of 9 years and 332 days beat Mario Andretti's record by over 2 years.

This was the first time that two Spaniards had lined up in the top three of a starting grid.

POINTS

DRIVERS

1	Max Verstappen	175
2	Sergio Pérez	129
3	Charles Leclerc	126
4	George Russell	111
5	Carlos Sainz	102
6	Lewis Hamilton	77
7	Lando Norris	50
8	Valtteri Bottas	46
9	Esteban Ocon	39
10	Fernando Alonso	18
11	Pierre Gasly	16
12	Kevin Magnussen	15
13	Daniel Ricciardo	15
14	Sebastian Vettel	13
15	Yuki Tsunoda	11
16	Zhou Guanyu	5
17	Alexander Albon	3
18	Lance Stroll	3

CONSTRUCTORS

1	Red Bull	304
2	Ferrari	228
3	Mercedes	188
4	McLaren	65
5	Alpine	57
6	Alfa Romeo	51
7	AlphaTauri	27
8	Aston Martin	16
9	Haas	15
10	Williams	3

9 · RICCIARDO · McLaren 7 · OCON · Alpine 5 · MAGNUSSEN · Haas 3 · SAINZ · Ferrari 1 · VERSTAPPEN · Red Bull

10 · ZHOU · Alfa Romeo 8 · RUSSELL · Mercedes 6 · SCHUMACHER · Haas 4 · HAMILTON · Mercedes 2 · ALONSO · Alpine

55	56	57	58	59	60	61	62	63	64	65	66	67	68	69	70	
1	1	1	1	1	1	1	1	1	1	1	1	1	1	1	1	1
55	55	55	55	55	55	55	55	55	55	55	55	55	55	55	55	2
44	44	44	44	44	44	44	44	44	44	44	44	44	44	44	44	3
63	63	63	63	63	63	63	63	63	63	63	63	63	63	63	63	4
31	31	31	31	31	16	16	16	16	16	16	16	16	16	16	16	5
14	14	14	16	16	31	31	31	31	31	31	31	31	31	31	31	6
16	16	16	14	14	14	14	14	14	14	14	14	14	14	14	14	7
77	77	77	77	77	77	77	77	77	77	77	77	77	77	77	77	8
5	5	24	24	24	24	24	24	24	24	24	24	24	24	24	24	9
24	24	3	3	3	3	3	3	18	18	18	18	18	18	18	18	10
3	3	5	5	5	18	18	18	3	3	3	3	3	3	3	3	
20	20	18	18	18	5	5	5	5	5	5	5	5	5	5	5	
18	18	23	23	23	23	23	23	23	23	23	23	23	23	23	23	
10	10	20	10	10	10	10	10	10	10	10	10	10	10	10	10	
23	23	10	4	4	4	4	4	4	4	4	4	4	4	4	4	
4	4	4	20	6	6	6	6	6	6	6	6	6	6	6	6	
6	6	6	6	20	20	20	20	20	20	20	20	20	20	20	20	

44 = Pit stop *6 = One lap or more behind*

VSC Virtual safety car deployed on laps

SC Safety car deployed on laps shown

RACE TYRE STRATEGIES

PIRELLI

	Driver	Race Stint 1	Race Stint 2	Race Stint 3
1	Verstappen	Medium (n): 1-9	Hard (n): 10-43	Hard (n): 44-70
2	Sainz	Medium (n): 1-20	Hard (n): 21-49	Hard (n): 50-70
3	Hamilton	Medium (n): 1-9	Hard (n): 10-44	Hard (n): 45-70
4	Russell	Medium (n): 1-19	Hard (n): 20-45	Hard (n): 46-70
5	Leclerc	Hard (n): 1-41	Medium (n): 42-70	
6	Ocon	Medium (n): 1-19	Hard (n): 20-49	Medium (n): 50-70
7	Alonso	Medium (n): 1-28	Hard (n): 29-49	Medium (n): 50-70
8	Bottas	Hard (n): 1-49	Medium (n): 50-70	
9	Zhou	Medium (n): 1-19	Hard (n): 20-49	Hard (n): 50-70
10	Stroll	Hard (n): 1-47	Medium (u): 48-70	
11	Ricciardo	Medium (n): 1-19	Hard (n): 20-49	Hard (n): 50-70
12	Vettel	Medium (u): 1-5	Hard (u): 6-19	Hard (u): 20-70
13	Albon	Medium (n): 1-18	Hard (n): 19-48	Hard (n): 49-70
14	Gasly	Medium (n): 1-5	Hard (n): 6-36	Hard (n): 37-70
15	Norris	Hard (n): 1-19	Hard (n): 20-42	Medium (n): 43-70
16	Latifi	Medium (n): 1-9	Hard (n): 10-37	Hard (n): 38-70
17	Magnusssen	Medium (n): 1-7	Hard (n): 8-70	
	Tsunoda	Medium (n): 1-9	Hard (n): 10-47 (dnf)	
	Schumacher	Medium (n): 1-18 (dnf)		
	Pérez	Hard (n): 1-7 (dnf)		

The tyre regulations stipulate that at least two of three dry tyre specifications must be used during a dry race. Selected compounds for Montreal: Red = Soft (C5); Yellow = Medium (C4); White = Hard (C3). (n) new (u) used

Aston Martin Cognizant F1 Team

PIRELLI

FIA FORMULA 1 WORLD CHAMPIONSHIP · ROUND 10

BRITISH GRAND PRIX

SILVERSTONE CIRCUIT

SILVERSTONE QUALIFYING

FOLLOWING on from Montreal, Silverstone served up another wet qualifying session, with Pirelli's green-walled intermediate tyre used by everyone throughout. For the second successive race, both Aston Martins struggled for grip and bit the dust in Q1, Sebastian Vettel not quite getting across the line in time to try one last lap to escape the bottom five.

"You got the flag, and ... we're out," Vettel was told.

"Not again, not again..." came the disbelieving, dejected response.

Joining the Astons in the elimination zone were the Haas cars of Kevin Magnussen and Mick Schumacher – in direct contrast to their great performances in Canada – and Alex Albon's Williams. But not, this time, Nicholas Latifi, who made it into Q2 and was destined to go even further.

Albon was very unhappy with his P16. "Why are we doing cool-down laps?" he wanted to know. "I really don't understand. I have no grip!"

With weather radar suggesting that heavier rain was on the way for Q2, there was real urgency to put an early time on the board. Latifi was one of those who did, and it secured his passage into the heady heights of Q3!

One of those who almost didn't was Carlos Sainz, who didn't figure in the top ten as the heavier rain came. Happily for the Spaniard, though, he took the Ferrari across the line to go P4 – just in time. The five Q2 casualties were the AlphaTauris of Pierre Gasly and Yuki Tsunoda, Valtteri Bottas's Alfa Romeo, Daniel Ricciardo's McLaren and Esteban Ocon's Alpine.

For the final session, it was the opposite way around, with rain consistent early on, but easing a little later so that the grid-defining laps came at the very end.

Max Verstappen, that wet-weather expert, indulged in a quick 360-degree spin out of Stowe, but controlled it superbly and carried on as though nothing had happened. With a couple of minutes to go, Sainz's Ferrari was on pole position, until Charles Leclerc moved the goalposts by beating his time by almost nine-tenths. Then, Verstappen shaved another quarter-second off that.

On their final attempts, Leclerc spun, the subsequent yellow flag tripping up Verstappen. That left the way clear for Sainz. Could he deliver? The answer was yes. He took his first F1 pole position at the 150th attempt, beating Verstappen's time by 0.072s.

"That's P1, baby," Riccardo Adami told him over the radio.

"Ha! I didn't expect that one," Sainz responded candidly. "I felt terrible out there. How did I do P1?"

"You kept it together," Adami said.

Sainz elaborated: "It wasn't easy out there – very, very tricky conditions. Especially in Q3, when I found it particularly tough to put the lap together. There was a lot of standing water on the racing line and it was difficult to get the tyres up to temperature.

"There wasn't a single lap where the track conditions were the same as the previous one. Every lap was a bit of a new adventure. I particularly struggled with the rears, just getting the traction. But towards the end, they started to switch on, and I managed to put in a couple of laps that were decent, but it was a big challenge."

Verstappen was fairly sure that the yellow for Leclerc's spin in the middle sector had cost him pole, but he was confident enough in the Red Bull's balance and feel. "Sunday is when I like to go racing," he smiled, full of confidence.

And so, it seemed, was Leclerc: "Unfortunately, I did the mistake on that last Q3 lap. I knew I had to put the lap together, and I just didn't do a good enough job. There was quite a lot of standing water and I lost it there. Apart from that, the car was competitive in those conditions, which is important to see because, the last few years, it hasn't been easy for us. It's good to see that we found a bit of a consistency in rainy conditions. And in the dry this morning, the car was good, so I'm looking forward to the race."

As the top three did their post-session interviews, there was considerable booing for Verstappen, the home fans obviously not having forgiven him for Abu Dhabi in 2021. The British crowd, appreciative in the past, much more Lords or Wimbledon than the Den at Millwall, seemed to be gravitating increasingly towards a football mentality.

Behind the top three, Sergio Pérez made it an all-Ferrari/Red Bull first couple of rows, despite the variable conditions, and fifth was the best that home hero Lewis Hamilton could do. Such was his British GP record, that nobody was ruling him out.

Lando Norris was in much better shape than in Montreal and qualified his McLaren in the top six, albeit 1.1s shy of the ultimate pace, with Fernando Alonso just three-hundredths behind for Alpine, narrowly pipping George Russell in his first British GP as a Mercedes driver.

"I definitely underperformed compared to where the car should have been," Russell admitted. "I made a mistake at T3 and lost three- or fourth-tenths at the start of the lap, which wasn't ideal. I should have been P4 or P5."

Zhou Guanyu turned in another fine performance to outqualify Alfa Romeo team-mate Bottas for the third successive race. And a spin into the gravel in Q3 could not dampen Nicholas Latifi's delight at making it all the way through to the shootout with his older-specification Williams.

FOR the second successive British GP, we had opening-lap drama. It was relatively straightforward among the first couple of rows, with Max Verstappen's Red Bull beating pole-man Carlos Sainz's Ferrari into Turn One. Lewis Hamilton managed to jump Charles Leclerc for third, but all hell broke loose mid-pack.

Pierre Gasly got a strong start in his AlphaTauri, and attempted to go between Zhou Guanyu's Alfa Romeo to the left and George Russell's Mercedes on the right. As Russell moved left, the gap Gasly was aiming for disappeared and they made contact, sending Russell into Zhou. The front left/right rear wheel contact flipped the Alfa.

Zhou came down hard upside down, the impact breaking the Alfa's roll hoop as it skated at high speed along the track, then through the gravel trap before rolling over the tyre barrier and coming to rest wedged between the barrier and the chain-link fence protecting the spectator area. A very nasty shunt indeed.

Out came the red flag before the race was even 25s old. Further back, Sebastian Vettel's Aston Martin had rear-ended Alex Albon amid the confusion, sending the Williams into the pit wall.

"I don't know how I survived, but looking at the replay, I saw that the halo saved me," Zhou said later. "Once I stopped, I didn't know where I was because I was upside down, and the next thing I felt was something leaking. I wasn't sure if it was from my body or from the car, so I just tried to switch the engine off. I knew that if a fire started, it would be difficult to get out."

So prompt had been the deployment of the red flag that the whole field had not tripped the first timing sensors, so the restart would take place from the original grid positions, meaning that the good work done by both Verstappen and Hamilton had been for nothing.

As the lights blinked out for the second time, Verstappen again tried to steal the inside line into Turn One, but this time Sainz swooped right, put the squeeze on the Red Bull and just managed to fend off Max.

Pérez was feisty, too, and Leclerc, who'd made a better start this time, had contact with the Mexican before having a look around the outside of Verstappen at Brooklands, where he had the door firmly slammed in his face. Pérez had a damaged front wing and was forced to pit for a replacement after five laps. Leclerc suffered slight right front wing endplate damage, costing him around five points of downforce, but was okay to continue.

Lando Norris had also made a great start, side by side with Hamilton around Brooklands and getting a good exit on to the straight that enabled him to snatch fifth place into Copse. Breathless stuff!

Sainz, Verstappen and Leclerc started to break away at the front, and Hamilton finally got a retaliatory move done on Norris down the inside into Brooklands on lap six, taking what was now fourth place, given Pérez's unscheduled stop.

The race order was Sainz, Verstappen, Leclerc, Hamilton, Norris, Fernando Alonso, Gasly, Yuki Tsunoda, Esteban Ocon, Nicholas Latifi, Valtteri Bottas, Daniel Ricciardo, Sebastian Vettel, Kevin Magnussen, Mick Schumacher and Stroll. Russell had been unable to take the restart, and joined Zhou and Albon as first-start casualties, bringing to an end his impressive run of consistent points-scoring from the start of the season.

The lead changed on lap ten, when Sainz's Ferrari ran wide in the Maggots/Becketts/Chapel sequence and Verstappen

Above: Just Stop Oil protestors were swiftly removed from the track.

Top left: Carlos Sainz overcame the difficult conditions to claim pole.
Photos: Bryn Williams

Top: A horrifying scenario is about to unfold as the Alfa Romeo of Zhou Guanyu barrel rolls in the pack.

Above left: The Alfa turns upside down as Albon's damaged Williams and Russell's Mercedes become *hors de combat.*

Centre left: Zhou's car heads across the run-off towards the barriers.
Photos: Lukas Gorys

Left: George Russell rushes to help, with Zhou in the Alfa trapped between the catch fencing and the tyre wall.
Photo: Mercedes-AMG Petronas F1 Team

Opening spread: A sweet moment at last for Carlos Sainz celebrating his maiden GP win in his 150th start.
Photo: Scuderia Ferrari

Above: The race was restarted after a delay of almost an hour. Sainz is already in control, ahead of Red Bull pair Verstappen and Pérez.
Photo: Bryn Williams

Top right: Celebrities were much in evidence. Aston Martin welcomed Keanu Reeves to its garage.
Photo: Aston Martin Aramco Cognizant F1 Team

Above right: Meanwhile, Dutch international Nathan Aké and Virgil van Djik were VIP guests of Red Bull.
Photo: Red Bull Content Pool/Getty Images

Right: In your face. Fernando Alonso's Alpine throws up gravel ahead of Lando Norris's pursuing McLaren.
Photo: Bryn Williams

needed no second invitation to go by as they shot out on to Hangar Straight.

The Red Bull's lead was short-lived, however, as Max slowed on Hangar Straight just a couple of laps later, allowing Sainz to retake the lead.

"I ran over a piece of carbon," Verstappen radioed in. "Keep checking the car. The tyres are not lovely. I think I've got a puncture." As he peeled off into the pits, the Ferraris were running 1-2.

The Red Bull didn't have a puncture, however, and the team sent Verstappen back into the fray on fresh mediums. A couple of laps later, engineer Lambiase told him, "Okay, Max, can confirm it's bodywork damage. Loss of rear [downforce]. It's not critical, so you're able to continue, but you will have a performance loss."

It was considerable, sentencing Verstappen to an afternoon of scrapping in the midfield that eventually yielded seventh place and just six points.

Silverstone's high-speed nature and relatively smooth surface suited the Mercedes well, and Hamilton, amazingly, started to make inroads into the Ferrari advantage. That was all it took for Leclerc, who had caught Sainz and evidently was quicker, to start asking his team to swap them, which also would have the effect of giving Leclerc priority at the first pit stop.

But there was no such instruction from the Ferrari pit-wall crew – evidence that, unlike previous policy, where the No.1 was prioritised at all times (think Austria, 2002 or Hockenheim, 2010), as yet there was no favouring of Leclerc. The pole-man would be allowed to try to claim his first GP win.

With the top ten all having started on the medium-compound Pirelli, Ferrari pitted Sainz some 20 laps into the race's 52 for a set of the hard-compound boots. Leclerc was brought in five laps later, emerging still just behind his Spanish team-mate. That put Hamilton into the lead and yet to make his stop. He still had good pace on his starting mediums, and Mercedes were aiming for as big a tyre offset as possible.

Leclerc was starting to fret once more, having been instructed to look after his tyres while still stuck behind Sainz, his lap time only a tenth quicker then Hamilton, despite his fresher rubber. Lewis had a 19s lead over the Spaniard, not far off the required pit-stop window.

Again, Leclerc got on the blower to ask Ferrari to swap them around. He was told that first the team would give Sainz a lap speed delta to drive to. It was 1m 32.2s.

Still, Leclerc was not pacified. "What do I need to do?" he asked calmly. "I'm fucking up my race. We are losing time to Hamilton. A 1:32.2 is not enough, in my opinion."

"Copy that," replied race engineer Xavier Marcos Padros.

Sainz asked for one more lap to hit the delta before the team swapped the cars, and his request was granted.

"It's not good enough," his race engineer, Riccardo Adami, told him a lap later. "We are swapping the cars."

"Copy," replied Sainz, and he let Leclerc by into Brooklands on lap 31. At that point, it seemed that his hope of a debut F1 win was history.

Hamilton finally made his tyre stop on lap 33, with just 19 laps to go and rejoined a couple of seconds behind Sainz on his fresher tyres. This was going to be interesting...

With 39 laps on the board and 13 to go, it appeared that Leclerc had everything under control, now 4.6s clear of his team-mate, who had Hamilton's Mercedes almost within DRS range. Then there was a 23.5s margin to Pérez, who'd run strongly after the early-race stop for a new wing; and a 14s gap to Norris's McLaren, running just 1.5s clear of another strong showing by Alonso's Alpine.

But it was Esteban Ocon's sister car that was about to throw in a curve ball and upset Leclerc's afternoon.

"I have a problem, guys," the Frenchman radioed. "I can't exit the corner." The Alpine ground to a halt out of Woodcote on to the front straight, coming to a stop beside the old pit wall. Cue a full safety car.

What to do? Ferrari had a conundrum. If they pitted Leclerc and Sainz, presumably for softs, given that there were only 13 laps remaining, then Hamilton would surely stay out, claiming track position and the lead. He had gone on to fresh hard-compound Pirellis just six laps previously. Ferrari had precious little soft-tyre data to go on from Friday, when there hadn't been as much gain as expected from them. And this was Hamilton and Silverstone, remember. Would they be able to get by? Maranello took the decision to split the call, leaving Leclerc out in the lead and pitting Sainz. Hamilton followed Carlos in, as did the remainder of the top ten.

It was another four laps before the safety car pulled in and we had green-flag conditions for a ten-lap sprint to the chequered flag. Realising that it would take Leclerc longer to generate tyre temperature on his hard tyres, Ferrari asked him to fall back the maximum ten car lengths from his team-mate to give Leclerc some breathing space.

"But, guys, I'm under pressure from Hamilton," Carlos responded. "Please don't ask these things. Please, please. Stop inventing, stop inventing. Trust me, there's more to lose like that."

"Copy that."

"Guys, I'm going to be much quicker than Charles at the restart."

Leclerc knew that, too, and wanted some estimation from the pits as to how long the soft would be the quicker tyre.

"We think it will be faster for two laps and then it will degrade more," he was told.

"It's going to be hard," Leclerc said as the field was released again. Immediately, he came under pressure from his team-mate, who got a better exit out on to the Wellington Straight and was ahead into Brooklands.

Behind, Pérez was all over Hamilton, whose Mercedes was taking longer with tyre warm-up, the Red Bull seizing third place into Brooklands as Alonso's Alpine also closed in.

Above: With Verstappen hobbled by bodywork damage, Sergio Pérez stepped up to the plate to take second place for Red Bull.
Photo: Atsuo Sakurai

Top right: Leclerc congratulates teammate Sainz on his first grand prix win.
Photo: XPB Images

Above right: That was fun. Sebastian Vettel and Mick Schumacher enjoyed their battle for eighth, which went the way of the Haas driver.
Photo: Aston Martin Aramco Cognizant F1 Team

Right: Lewis Hamilton and Leclerc put on a spectacular show of racecraft in front of an enthralled crowd.
Photo: Atsuo Sakurai

A couple of laps later, with DRS enabled, Pérez had hunted down Leclerc. Ferrari's estimation that the soft would only be quicker for a couple of laps was wide of the mark. As they went into Stowe, Pérez went for the inside. Leclerc gave him just enough room and stayed with the Red Bull as they swept through side by side, the Ferrari having the inside line for Vale. But Pérez kept his boot in around the outside, forcing the Ferrari wide on exit.

Hamilton, right behind, could see what was happening, went through on the proper racing line, got on the gas sooner and blasted the Merc past both of them on the inside on exit.

His moment of glory was short-lived, however. Pérez came back at him down the inside of Turn Three, compromising his exit, and Leclerc ran the Ferrari around his outside as they went out on to the Wellington Straight. This was fantastic.

Sainz was now in control, almost 4s clear of Pérez with four laps separating him from his first grand prix victory. Behind, things were becoming feisty between Leclerc and Hamilton for the final podium place.

After the first start, Leclerc had been asked for any observations and had told the team, "Exit of Turn Three: I was side by side with Hamilton, and Lewis just did as if I wasn't there, so I hope they are looking into that."

Now, on lap 46, nigh on a couple of hours later, as Hamilton tried to go around the Ferrari exiting Woodcote, it was his turn to receive a curt chop. It forced him out of the throttle momentarily and left him briefly vulnerable to Alonso.

Two laps later, they were still battling. Leclerc went deep into Brooklands to prevent Hamilton from going around his outside, whereupon Lewis switched back inside and passed the Ferrari around the outside of Luffield. Leclerc wasn't finished, however. It might have been frustration at the day in general, who knows, but he pulled off one of those moves that had you blinking in disbelief at what you had just witnessed (*see* Viewpoint). On 23-lap-old hard tyres, he passed Hamilton, on softs that had done just four racing laps, around the outside of Copse, at 180mph plus. Not just anyone. Lewis Hamilton!

It was reminiscent of Mark Webber passing Alonso at Spa's Eau Rouge, despite knowing that, due to DRS, it was probably all in vain. Just pure bloody-minded racer instinct. Because, just a few hundred yards further on, he was a sitting duck to a Mercedes with DRS, Hamilton completing the move comfortably before Stowe to secure his third 2022 podium and his second in succession. He also managed to snatch an extra point on the last lap by going three-tenths faster than Sainz's soft-compound fastest lap.

"He can have that," laughed delighted first-time GP winner Sainz. "We did it! Great job, guys."

Sentiments that were not quite mirrored in the cockpit of the other Ferrari, although nobody, not even the classy Leclerc, whose spell of dire luck continued, begrudged Carlos his moment.

"The amount of time we lost in this race," Charles radioed in, "is ... oh my God. The only good thing about today is that Carlos won. But, guys, frickin' 'ell. Anyway, enjoy the victory." This last bit was genuine, not sarcastic.

That said it all about a day when ruthless old Ferrari would have capitalised on misfortune striking its main opposition. That was the storyline. That, and some of the best, uncompromising, skilful racing witnessed for many a moon.

Tony Dodgins

VIEWPOINT
STUNNING LECLERC

MAGNIFICENT racing at Silverstone – and it's wheel to wheel!" Alex Jacques was describing the action thus far in the British Grand Prix as he shared the Channel 4 commentary box with David Coulthard and Mark Webber. This was on lap 43. If they thought that was good, their collective minds were about to be blown as Charles Leclerc lined up Lewis Hamilton and prepared to take a run around the outside of the Mercedes through the blind right-hander at Copse. At 180mph plus.

"That's committed!" enthused Jacques while urgently crouching forward, stabbing his finger at the screen. Coulthard and Webber reeled back in their seats, as if in anticipation of an enormous accident as the Ferrari reached the turn-in point – and kept coming, left wheels kicking up dust at the edge of the track as Hamilton also refused to back off.

"No way! No way has Charles Leclerc done that!" roared Jacques as he summed up the incredulity of the watching world. "Whao!" yelled Coulthard. Webber was momentarily speechless. "That is absolutely incredible stuff!" continued Jacques. "Unbelievable move," said Webber finally, his quieter tone reflecting that disbelief as the Ferrari emerged ahead of the Mercedes and the pair charged towards the Maggots-Becketts complex.

Leclerc was running Pirelli hards; Hamilton was on much newer softs, a detail that increased the gob-smacking element of a move that immediately entered the annals of 'F1's Greatest Moments'. It ranked alongside Mika Häkkinen's refusal to be intimidated by Michael Schumacher at 200mph into Les Combes at Spa in 2000; was on a par with Nigel Mansell swooping around the outside of Gerhard Berger at Peraltada during the 1990 Mexican GP; and matched Webber sitting it out with Fernando Alonso as they swooped downhill into Eau Rouge in 2011.

Leclerc's bold commitment and confidence brought the same sense of thrill generated in similar golden moments by the likes of Ayrton Senna, Gilles Villeneuve and Jochen Rindt. Magnificent indeed. At such times, however, mere words are barely enough to describe extrovert brilliance that has been a privilege to behold.

Maurice Hamilton

10

ROLEX

Official Timepiece

FORMULA 1 LENOVO BRITISH GRAND PRIX 2022

SILVERSTONE 1–3 JULY

RACE DISTANCE: 52 laps, 190.263 miles/306.198km

RACE WEATHER: Dry/overcast (track 28–36°C, air 18–22°C)

SILVERSTONE CIRCUIT

Circuit: 5.891km/3.660 miles, 52 laps

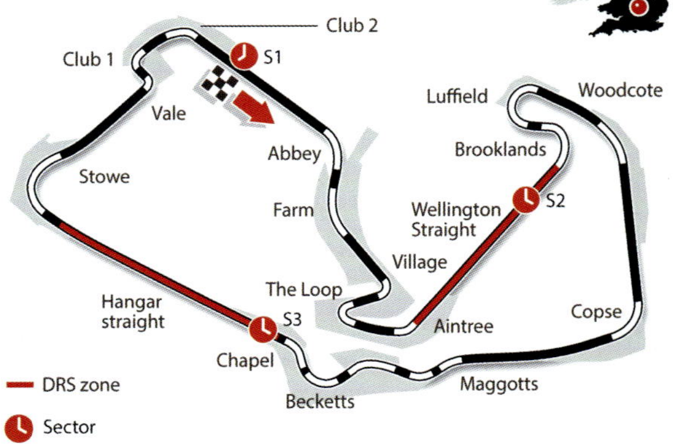

RACE – OFFICIAL CLASSIFICATION

Pos.	Driver	Nat.	No.	Entrant	Car/Engine	Laps	Time/Retirement	Speed (mph/km/h)	Gap to winner	Fastest race lap
1	**Carlos Sainz**	E	55	Scuderia Ferrari	Ferrari F1-75-066/7 V6	52	2h 17m 50.311s	82.819/133.285		1m 30.813s 44
2	**Sergio Pérez**	MEX	11	Oracle Red Bull Racing	Red Bull RB18-RBPTH001 V6	52	2h 17m 54.090s	82.782/133.224	3.779s	1m 30.937s 47
3	**Lewis Hamilton**	GB	44	Mercedes-AMG Petronas F1 Team	Mercedes-AMG F1 W13-M13 E Perf. V6	52	2h 17m 56.536s	82.757/133.185	6.225s	1m 30.510s 52
4	**Charles Leclerc**	MC	16	Scuderia Ferrari	Ferrari F1-75-066/7 V6	52	2h 17m 58.857s	82.734/133.147	8.546s	1m 31.282s 52
5	**Fernando Alonso**	E	14	BWT Alpine F1 Team	Alpine A522-Renault E-Tech RE22 V6	52	2h 17m 59.882s	82.724/133.131	9.571s	1m 31.609s 47
6	**Lando Norris**	GB	4	McLaren F1 Team	McLaren MCL36-Mercedes F1 M13 E Perf. V6	52	2h 18m 02.254s	82.700/133.093	11.943s	1m 31.645s 47
7	**Max Verstappen**	NL	1	Oracle Red Bull Racing	Red Bull RB18-RBPTH001 V6	52	2h 18m 09.088s	82.632/132.983	18.777s	1m 32.354s 45
8	**Mick Schumacher**	D	47	Haas F1 Team	Haas VF-22-Ferrari 066/7 V6	52	2h 18m 09.306s	82.630/132.980	18.995s	1m 32.109s 48
9	**Sebastian Vettel**	D	5	Aston Martin Aramco Cognizant F1 Team	Aston Martin AMR22-Mercedes F1 M13 E Perf. V6	52	2h 18m 12.666s	82.596/132.926	22.355s	1m 32.471s 52
10	**Kevin Magnussen**	DK	20	Haas F1 Team	Haas VF-22-Ferrari 066/7 V6	52	2h 18m 14.901s	82.574/132.890	24.590s	1m 32.661s 52
11	Lance Stroll	CDN	18	Aston Martin Aramco Cognizant F1 Team	Aston Martin AMR22-Mercedes F1 M13 E Perf. V6	52	2h 18m 16.458s	82.558/132.865	26.147s	1m 32.379s 52
12	Nicholas Latifi	CDN	6	Williams Racing	Williams FW44-Mercedes F1 M13 E Perf. V6	52	2h 18m 22.822s	82.495/132.763	32.511s	1m 33.286s 48
13	Daniel Ricciardo	AUS	3	McLaren F1 Team	McLaren MCL36-Mercedes F1 M13 E Perf. V6	52	2h 18m 23.128s	82.492/132.758	32.817s	1m 32.644s 34
14	Yuki Tsunoda	J	22	Scuderia AlphaTauri	AlphaTauri AT03-RBPTH001 V6	52	2h 18m 31.221s *	82.412/132.629	40.910s	1m 33.832s 51
	Esteban Ocon	F	31	BWT Alpine F1 Team	Alpine A522-Renault E-Tech RE22 V6	37	*fuel pump*			1m 33.537s 37
	Pierre Gasly	F	10	Scuderia AlphaTauri	AlphaTauri AT03-RBPTH001 V6	26	*accident/rear wing*			1m 34.614s 18
	Valtteri Bottas	FIN	77	Alfa Romeo F1 Team ORLEN	Alfa Romeo C42-Ferrari 066/7 V6	20	*gearbox*			1m 35.103s 19
	George Russell	GB	63	Mercedes-AMG Petronas F1 Team	Mercedes-AMG F1 W13-M13 E Perf. V6	0	*accident*			no time
	Guanyu Zhou	CHN	24	Alfa Romeo F1 Team ORLEN	Alfa Romeo C42-Ferrari 066/7 V6	0	*accident*			no time
	Alexander Albon	T	23	Williams Racing	Williams FW44-Mercedes F1 M13 E Perf. V6	0	*accident*			no time

The race was red-flagged following the first-lap multi-car collision at Turn 1, which resulted in Zhou overturning and flying over the tyre wall. After almost an hour, the race resumed from a standing start for the remaining laps.

* Tsunoda: 5s time penalty for causing a collision with Gasly (served at pit stop).

DHL Fastest race lap (scores 1 point): Lewis Hamilton on lap 52, 1m 30.510s, 145.595mph/234.312km/h.

Lap record: Max Verstappen (Red Bull RB16-Honda V6), 1m 27.097s, 151.300mph/243.494km/h (2020).

19 · SCHUMACHER · Haas

17 · MAGNUSSEN · Haas

15 · OCON · Alpine

13 · TSUNODA · AlphaTauri

11 · GASLY · AlphaTauri

20 · STROLL · Aston Martin

18 · VETTEL · Aston Martin

16 · ALBON · Williams

14 · RICCIARDO · McLaren

12 · BOTTAS · Alfa Romeo

Grid order	1	2	3	4	5	6	7	8	9	10	11	12	13	14	15	16	17	18	19	20	21	22	23	24	25	26	27	28	29	30	31	32	33	34	35	36	37	38	39	40	41
55 SAINZ	1	55	55	55	55	55	55	55	55	1	1	1	55	55	55	55	55	55	55	55	16	16	16	16	16	44	44	44	44	44	44	44	44	16	16	16	16	16	55	16	16
1 VERSTAPPEN	55	1	1	1	1	1	1	1	1	55	55	55	16	16	16	16	16	16	16	16	44	44	44	44	44	55	55	55	55	55	16	16	16	55	55	55	55	55	16	55	55
16 LECLERC	44	16	16	16	16	16	16	16	16	16	16	16	44	44	44	44	44	44	44	44	55	55	55	55	55	16	16	16	16	16	55	55	55	44	44	44	44	44	44	44	44
11 PÉREZ	16	11	11	11	11	44	44	44	44	44	44	44	4	4	4	4	4	4	4	4	4	4	4	4	4	4	4	4	4	4	4	4	4	4	11	11	11	11	11	11	11
44 HAMILTON	14	44	4	4	4	4	4	4	4	4	4	4	14	14	14	14	14	14	14	14	14	14	14	14	14	14	14	14	14	14	14	14	14	11	4	4	4	4	14	4	14
4 NORRIS	11	4	44	44	44	14	14	14	14	14	14	14	1	1	1	1	1	1	1	1	1	1	1	11	11	11	11	11	11	11	11	11	11	14	14	14	14	14	4	14	4
14 ALONSO	4	14	10	10	14	10	10	10	10	10	31	31	31	31	31	31	31	31	31	31	31	31	11	5	5	5	5	5	5	5	5	5	5	5	5	5	5	5	5	5	5
63 RUSSELL	6	6	14	14	10	22	22	22	22	22	6	6	6	6	6	6	6	6	6	11	11	11	5	1	1	1	1	1	1	1	1	1	1	1	1	31	31	1	1	20	20
24 ZHOU	77	10	22	22	22	31	31	31	31	31	77	77	77	77	77	77	77	77	77	3	20	20	6	6	6	6	6	6	31	31	31	31	31	31	31	1	1	47	47	18	1
6 LATIFI	3	77	6	31	31	6	6	6	6	6	3	3	3	3	3	3	3	3	47	20	5	5	31	31	31	31	31	31	6	6	6	47	47	47	47	47	47	20	20	1	47
10 GASLY	10	22	31	6	6	77	77	77	77	77	20	20	20	20	47	47	47	47	3	77	6	6	47	47	47	47	47	47	47	47	47	6	20	20	20	20	20	6	6	47	6
77 BOTTAS	20	3	3	77	77	5	3	3	3	3	47	47	47	47	20	20	20	11	11	5	47	47	20	20	20	20	20	20	20	20	20	20	6	6	6	6	6	18	18	6	18
22 TSUNODA	5	31	77	3	3	3	20	20	20	20	10	10	10	10	10	10	11	20	20	6	3	3	3	3	3	3	3	3	3	3	3	3	18	18	18	18	18	3	3	3	3
3 RICCIARDO	18	20	5	5	5	20	47	47	47	47	18	18	18	18	18	11	22	22	5	47	10	10	10	10	10	10	18	18	18	18	18	18	3	3	3	3	3	22	22	22	22
31 OCON	47	5	20	20	20	47	18	18	18	18	22	22	11	11	11	22	5	5	10	10	18	18	18	18	18	18	22	22	22	22	22	22	22	22	22	22	22				
23 ALBON	22	47	18	47	47	18	11	11	11	11	11	11	22	22	22	5	10	10	18	18	22	22	22	22	22	22															
20 MAGNUSSEN	31	18	47	18	18	11	5	5	5	5	5	5	5	5	5	18	18	18	22	22																					
5 VETTEL																																									
47 SCHUMACHER																																									
18 STROLL																																									
	SC	SC	SC																																				SC	SC	SC

TIME SHEETS

PRACTICE 1 (FRIDAY)

Weather: Wet/overcast

Temperatures: track 21–29°C, air 16–18°C

Pos.	Driver	Laps	Time
1	Valtteri Bottas	9	1m 42.249s
2	Lewis Hamilton	10	1m 42.781s
3	Carlos Sainz	8	1m 42.967s
4	Charles Leclerc	7	1m 43.801s
5	Mick Schumacher	3	1m 43.895s
6	Zhou Guanyu	4	1m 46.171s
7	Kevin Magnussen	3	1m 48.161s
8	Lance Stroll	5	1m 51.243s
9	Yuki Tsunoda	5	1m 51.373s
10	Sebastian Vettel	5	1m 59.168s
11	George Russell	2	no time
12	Sergio Pérez	3	no time
13	Esteban Ocon	2	no time
14	Fernando Alonso	1	no time
15	Alexander Albon	1	no time
16	Daniel Ricciardo	4	no time
17	Pierre Gasly	3	no time
18	Lando Norris	4	no time
19	Nicholas Latifi	1	no time
20	Max Verstappen	3	no time

PRACTICE 2 (FRIDAY)

Weather: Dry/overcast

Temperatures: track 26–31°C, air 18–21°C

Pos.	Driver	Laps	Time
1	Carlos Sainz	28	1m 28.942s
2	Lewis Hamilton	21	1m 29.105s
3	Lando Norris	29	1m 29.118s
4	Max Verstappen	18	1m 29.149s
5	Charles Leclerc	25	1m 29.404s
6	Fernando Alonso	19	1m 29.695s
7	Sergio Pérez	17	1m 29.753s
8	George Russell	29	1m 29.799s
9	Daniel Ricciardo	26	1m 29.902s
10	Lance Stroll	17	1m 29.942s
11	Valtteri Bottas	29	1m 30.000s
12	Sebastian Vettel	20	1m 30.057s
13	Esteban Ocon	12	1m 30.238s
14	Alexander Albon	14	1m 30.263s
15	Zhou Guanyu	27	1m 30.271s
16	Yuki Tsunoda	29	1m 30.338s
17	Kevin Magnussen	27	1m 30.480s
18	Pierre Gasly	28	1m 30.510s
19	Mick Schumacher	29	1m 30.609s
20	Nicholas Latifi	27	1m 31.326s

PRACTICE 3 (SATURDAY)

Weather: Dry/overcast

Temperatures: track 22–27°C, air 17–19°C

Pos.	Driver	Laps	Time
1	Max Verstappen	18	1m 27.901s
2	Sergio Pérez	21	1m 28.311s
3	Charles Leclerc	21	1m 28.348s
4	George Russell	21	1m 28.426s
5	Lewis Hamilton	24	1m 28.488s
6	Carlos Sainz	21	1m 28.689s
7	Lando Norris	20	1m 29.102s
8	Valtteri Bottas	20	1m 29.185s
9	Mick Schumacher	21	1m 29.510s
10	Fernando Alonso	20	1m 29.520s
11	Esteban Ocon	24	1m 29.552s
12	Sebastian Vettel	25	1m 29.593s
13	Zhou Guanyu	17	1m 29.752s
14	Alexander Albon	22	1m 29.780s
15	Pierre Gasly	23	1m 29.885s
16	Lance Stroll	26	1m 29.892s
17	Yuki Tsunoda	22	1m 30.039s
18	Daniel Ricciardo	21	1m 30.293s
19	Nicholas Latifi	16	1m 30.489s
20	Kevin Magnussen	19	1m 30.523s

QUALIFYING (SATURDAY)

Weather: Rain/overcast Temperatures: track 18–20°C, air 14–16°C

Pos.	Driver	First	Second	Third	Qualifying Tyre
1	Carlos Sainz	1m 40.190s	1m 41.602s	1m 40.983s	Inter (n)
2	Max Verstappen	1m 39.129s	1m 40.655s	1m 41.055s	Inter (n)
3	Charles Leclerc	1m 39.846s	1m 41.247s	1m 41.298s	Inter (n)
4	Sergio Pérez	1m 40.521s	1m 42.513s	1m 41.616s	Inter (n)
5	Lewis Hamilton	1m 40.428s	1m 41.062s	1m 41.995s	Inter (n)
6	Lando Norris	1m 41.515s	1m 41.821s	1m 42.084s	Inter (n)
7	Fernando Alonso	1m 41.598s	1m 42.209s	1m 42.116s	Inter (n)
8	George Russell	1m 40.028s	1m 41.725s	1m 42.161s	Inter (n)
9	Zhou Guanyu	1m 40.791s	1m 42.640s	1m 42.719s	Inter (n)
10	Nicholas Latifi	1m 41.998s	1m 43.273s	2m 03.095s	Inter (n)
11	Pierre Gasly	1m 41.680s	1m 43.702s		
12	Valtteri Bottas	1m 41.396s	1m 44.232s		
13	Yuki Tsunoda	1m 41.893s	1m 44.311s		
14	Daniel Ricciardo	1m 41.933s	1m 44.355s		
15	Esteban Ocon	1m 41.730s	1m 45.190s		
16	Alexander Albon	1m 42.078s			
17	Kevin Magnussen	1m 42.159s			
18	Sebastian Vettel	1m 42.666s			
19	Mick Schumacher	1m 42.708s			
20	Lance Stroll	1m 43.430s			

QUALIFYING: head to head

Hamilton	5	5	Russell
Verstappen	7	3	Pérez
Ricciardo	2	8	Norris
Leclerc	8	2	Sainz
Gasly	7	3	Tsunoda
Hülkenberg	1	1	Stroll
Vettel	7	1	Stroll
Alonso	7	3	Ocon
Bottas	7	3	Zhou
Albon	8	2	Latifi
Magnussen	8	2	Schumacher

Scuderia Ferrari

FOR THE RECORD

1st POLE POSITION & WIN: Carlos Sainz

1st POINTS: Mick Schumacher

150th GRAND PRIX START: Carlos Sainz

60th FASTEST LAP: Lewis Hamilton

2,000th POINT: Fernando Alonso

600th RACE WITH A PODIUM: Ferrari engine

POINTS

DRIVERS

1	Max Verstappen	181
2	Sergio Pérez	147
3	Charles Leclerc	138
4	Carlos Sainz	127
5	George Russell	111
6	Lewis Hamilton	93
7	Lando Norris	58
8	Valtteri Bottas	46
9	Esteban Ocon	39
10	Fernando Alonso	28
11	Pierre Gasly	16
12	Kevin Magnussen	16
13	Sebastian Vettel	15
14	Daniel Ricciardo	15
15	Yuki Tsunoda	11
16	Zhou Guanyu	5
17	Mick Schumacher	4
18	Alexander Albon	3
19	Lance Stroll	3

CONSTRUCTORS

1	Red Bull	328
2	Ferrari	265
3	Mercedes	204
4	McLaren	73
5	Alpine	67
6	Alfa Romeo	51
7	AlphaTauri	27
8	Haas	20
9	Aston Martin	18
10	Williams	3

9 · ZHOU · Alfa Romeo

7 · ALONSO · Alpine

5 · HAMILTON · Mercedes

3 · LECLERC · Ferrari

1 · SAINZ · Ferrari

10 · LATIFI · Williams

8 · RUSSELL · Mercedes

6 · NORRIS · McLaren

4 · PÉREZ · Red Bull

2 · VERSTAPPEN · Red Bull

42	43	44	45	46	47	48	49	50	51	52	
16	55	55	55	55	55	55	55	55	55	55	1
55	16	16	44	11	11	11	11	11	11	11	2
44	11	11	11	16	16	44	44	44	44	44	3
11	44	44	16	44	44	16	16	16	16	16	4
14	14	14	14	14	14	14	14	14	14	14	5
4	4	4	4	4	4	4	4	4	4	4	6
5	5	1	1	1	1	1	1	1	1	1	7
20	1	5	47	47	47	47	47	47	47	47	8
1	47	47	5	5	5	5	5	5	5	5	9
47	20	20	20	20	20	20	20	20	20	20	10
6	6	6	6	6	6	6	18	18	18	18	
18	18	18	18	18	18	18	6	6	6	6	
3	3	3	3	3	3	3	3	3	3	3	
22	22	22	22	22	22	22	22	22	22	22	

11 = Pit stop *22 = One lap or more behind*

SC Safety car deployed on laps shown

Race red-flagged on lap 1

SC

RACE TYRE STRATEGIES

PIRELLI

	Driver	Race Stint 1	Race Stint 2	Race Stint 3	Race Stint 4	Race Stint 5
1	Sainz	Medium (n): 1	Medium (n): 2-20	Hard (n): 21-39	Soft (n): 40-52	
2	Pérez	Medium (n): 1	Medium (n): 2-5	Medium (u): 6-39	Soft (n): 40-52	
3	Hamilton	Medium (n): 1	Medium (n): 2-33	Hard (n): 34-39	Soft (n): 40-52	
4	Leclerc	Medium (n): 1	Medium (n): 2-25	Hard (n): 26-52		
5	Alonso	Medium (n): 1	Medium (n): 2-33	Hard (n): 34-39	Soft (n): 40-52	
6	Norris	Medium (n): 1-34	Hard (n): 35-40	Soft (n): 41-52		
7	Verstappen	Soft (n): 1	Medium (n): 2-12	Medium (n): 13-23	Hard (n): 24-39	Soft (n): 40-52
8	Schumacher	Hard (u): 1	Medium (n): 2-19	Hard (n): 20-39	Soft (n): 40-52	
9	Vettel	Soft (n): 1	Soft (n): 2-6	Medium (u): 7-39	Medium (u): 40-52	
10	Magnusssen	Soft (n): 1	Medium (u): 2-22	Medium (n): 23-52		
11	Stroll	Soft (u): 1	Medium (u): 2-15	Hard (n): 16-40	Medium (u): 41-52	
12	Latifi	Soft (n): 1	Soft (n): 2-19	Medium (n): 20-39	Soft (u): 40-52	
13	Ricciardo	Medium (n): 1-20	Hard (n): 21-32	Soft (n): 33-38	Soft (n): 39-52	
14	Tsunoda	Medium (n): 1	Soft (n): 2-18	Hard (u): 19-38	Soft (n): 39-52	
	Ocon	Medium (n): 1	Soft (n): 2-22	Hard (n): 23-37 (dnf)		
	Gasly	Medium (n): 1	Soft (n): 2-16	Hard (u): 17-26 (dnf)		
	Bottas	Medium (n): 1	Medium (n): 2-20 (dnf)			
	Russell	Hard (n): 0 (dnf)				
	Zhou	Medium (n): 0 (dnf)				
	Albon	Hard (n): 0 (dnf)				

The tyre regulations stipulate that at least two of three dry tyre specifications must be used during a dry race.
Selected compounds for Silverstone: Red = Soft (C3); Yellow = Medium (C2); White = Hard (C1). (n) new (u) used

FIA FORMULA 1 WORLD CHAMPIONSHIP - ROUND 11

AUSTRIAN GRAND PRIX

RED BULL RING

Snapdragon
Snapdragon
Ray-Ban
Ray-Ban
VELAS
16
aws
Palantir
MAHLE
Santander
#WeRaceAsOne

SPIELBERG QUALIFYING/SPRINT QUALIFYING

THE Red Bull Ring played host to F1's second Saturday sprint race of 2022 after a qualifying session with its fair share of drama. For the third successive GP weekend, Aston Martin lost both cars in Q1. Sebastian Vettel finished up bottom of the pile after losing his last lap for exceeding track limits at Turn One, a recurring theme throughout the weekend when, in the main race alone, there would be 43 track-limits transgressions as drivers crossed white lines defining them, mostly at the lap-ending Turns Nine and Ten.

Joining Vettel as Q1 casualties were team-mate Lance Stroll, Nicholas Latifi, Zhou Guanyu and Daniel Ricciardo.

Another driver to fall foul of track limits in qualifying was Sergio Pérez, the Mexican having his best Q2 lap deleted, but not before he'd competed in and finished fourth in Q3! The stewards' decision to wipe out his Q2 best, and hence his Q3 times, too, meant that Pérez would start Saturday's Sprint 13th.

Had Pérez's time been deleted at the end of Q2, Pierre Gasly would have gone through to the top-ten shootout for AlphaTauri, but instead the Frenchman joined Alex Albon, Valtteri Bottas, Yuki Tsunoda and Lando Norris as Q2 eliminees.

The Q3 session began with the very unfamiliar sight of Lewis Hamilton losing control of his Mercedes and putting it into the tyre barrier at Turn Seven before he had a representative lap time on the board. He had lost the rear as he turned in and had no chance to catch it. "Sorry to damage the car, guys," he radioed in, sounding a little chastened.

He wasn't the only one who found the W13 to be a handful. George Russell, who nevertheless would end up fourth on the grid, spun backwards into the tyres out of the final corner, Turn Ten, on his second run, bringing out the red flag.

It was a close-run thing between Red Bull and Ferrari for pole. It looked as though Charles Leclerc would continue his strong qualifying form when he took provisional pole with a lap in 1m 05.013s, team-mate Carlos Sainz running him very close on 1m 05.066s as Ferrari made its bid to lock out the front row.

But that was counting without Max Verstappen, who snatched his third 2022 pole with a lap in 1m 04.984s. Behind fourth-placed Russell, Esteban Ocon put the first Alpine fifth in an incredibly tight mid-grid, ahead of the Haas pair, Kevin Magnussen and Mick Schumacher, whose level was back to Montreal standards rather than the disappointment of Silverstone.

Fernando Alonso was less than a tenth behind the second Haas as he took eighth for Alpine, with Hamilton and Gasly – promoted when Pérez was penalised – completing the top ten.

Just as the sprint race formation lap was about to start, we were treated to the bizarre sight of Alonso's car up on a jack, tyre blankets still fitted. There had been a problem firing up the engine, and the Spaniard would take no further part.

"It's frustrating," he shrugged. "This year, I feel probably at my highest level, driving-wise, thanks to the experience as well." But once again, he'd suffered misfortune.

As the Alpine was pushed away and the formation lap took place, it was Zhou Guanyu's turn to suffer a power unit issue, the Alfa being left stranded off the back as the grid formed up. The start was aborted and the sprint reduced by a lap to 23. Zhou, meanwhile, managed to get the car fired up, but now would start from the pit lane rather than his 18th grid slot, recovering to 16th before the end, a good effort in his first start since the frightening accident at Silverstone just six days previously.

When finally we got under way, Verstappen moved right from his outside-line pole, crowding Leclerc's Ferrari as the latter tried to get down the inside into T1. Sainz took advantage of their tussle by running around the outside of his team-mate, got a decent exit and slipstreamed Verstappen's leading Red Bull into Turn Three. Going around the outside was a big ask, and as Verstappen ran the Ferrari out wide, Leclerc cut back inside Sainz and kept his car there on the downhill run into Turn Four, retaking second on the brakes.

Behind, on the uphill run to Turn One, Gasly moved left from the right-hand side of the grid, but clipped Hamilton's right front wheel, the AlphaTauri spinning into the run-off area. Lewis would soon work his way back, passing Albon for tenth and ultimately claiming the final point for eighth.

At the front, Verstappen seemed to have things under control en route to his second 2022 Sprint win, but Leclerc didn't go away, despite also having to focus on a tussle with his own team-mate.

"The difference was just the first few laps when the Ferraris were fighting a little bit, so I had a bit of a gap," Max explained, "but after that, I think we were quite similar in pace. So I do expect tomorrow that it's going to be a very interesting battle again."

Leclerc was never quite able to get into DRS range and finished 1.6s down, with his team-mate a further 4s back.

"I had a good start, then a couple of good fights," Sainz explained. "First with Max into Turn Three, then Charles into T3 again a bit later, which was good. It was good racing, like it should be, but then I probably overheated the tyres a bit running behind Charles and had to back off to recover them."

Leclerc, meanwhile, agreed with Verstappen: "I think it was pretty close between the three of us for pace. I was probably the one managing the most at the beginning and the one maybe pushing the most at the end. I just tried something different. But it didn't work out. But tomorrow, it will be an exciting race." He seemed quietly confident that Ferrari would have the measure of Red Bull.

Around 8s behind the second Ferrari, Russell finished fourth in the first Mercedes, with the other points going to Pérez – a good recovery drive from 13th on the grid – Ocon, Magnussen and Hamilton, after his opening-lap brush with Gasly.

Left: Nicholas Latifi prepares for action.
Photo: Williams Racing

Top centre left: Pierre Gasly's AlphaTauri goes temporarily airborne at the start of the sprint race.
Photo: Lukas Gorys

Below centre left: After qualifying only ninth, Lewis Hamilton discusses his prospects for the sprint.
Photo: Mercedes-AMG Petronas F1 Team

Far left: Max Verstappen leads Sainz, Leclerc, Russell, Ocon, and Haas pair Magnussen and Schumacher.
Photo: Red Bull Content Pool/Getty Images

Below: Verstappen waves to the crowd after taking pole position.
Photo: Lukas Gorys

Opening spread: Despite pressure from Verstappen, Leclerc overcame technical issues with his Ferrari to score a third win of the season.
Photo: Pirelli

Above: Abandon ship! Carlos Sainz makes a swift exit from his burning Ferrari as a marshal attempts to bring the rolling car to a halt.
Photo: XPB Images

Right: Haas enjoyed a rewarding weekend in Styria, with Schumacher taking a career-best sixth place and team-mate Magnussen ninth.
Photo: Haas F1 Team

A VICTIM of Ferrari power unit reliability issues, Valtteri Bottas started the Austrian GP from the pit lane with a fresh engine, Alfa Romeo also having changed the rear wing. Fernando Alonso, meanwhile, was right at the back with a fresh Renault power unit after failing to start Saturday's Sprint race.

For the fifth time in the season, the front-row starters anxiously watching the lights were Max Verstappen and Charles Leclerc. Verstappen made a perfect start in the Red Bull, immediately moving right to cover Leclerc, with plenty of time to get back across on to the ideal line for the right-handed Turn One. Behind, Carlos Sainz and George Russell went into the first turn side by side, the Ferrari running wide on exit and regaining the track behind the Mercedes. But with superior grunt, Sainz was back inside the Mercedes by Turn Three, with Sergio Pérez's Red Bull having a look at the outside of Russell.

This continued all the way down to Turn Four, where the Mercedes made contact with the Red Bull and Pérez was tipped into a spin through the gravel. Arguably, it was a racing incident (*see* Viewpoint) – Russell certainly thought so, but he would be penalised five seconds.

"There was nothing I could do, he just turned into me," Russell radioed in.

Across the line, they streamed in the order Verstappen, Leclerc, Sainz, Russell, Esteban Ocon, Kevin Magnussen, Lewis Hamilton, Mick Schumacher, Daniel Ricciardo, Lando Norris, Lance Stroll, Pierre Gasly, Alex Albon, Zhou Guanyu, Yuki Tsunoda, Nicholas Latifi, Sebastian Vettel (reporting damage), Alonso, Bottas and, some 17s adrift, Pérez. The second Red Bull was soon in the pits, with a sizeable hole in the right-hand side pod, also switching to a set of hard tyres, the medium having been the starting tyre of choice among the front-runners.

Turn back the clock a year and no one could have countenanced Schumacher's Haas taking Hamilton's Mercedes for seventh position, but that was precisely the situation that unfolded on lap seven as Lewis got a bit twitchy out of Turn Three. "Their straight-line speed is crazy," Hamilton told the Mercedes pit.

Leclerc had been spot on with his prediction that tyre degradation would be key to the race, the cooler race-day conditions seemingly suiting Ferrari better. He was now hassling Verstappen, who had started to struggle a little with an understeering front end on his starting mediums. Ten laps into the 71, Leclerc went down the inside at Turn Three, but Verstappen fended him off.

"I can't hold this long," Verstappen warned his team.

"Understood, Max," replied race engineer GP Lambiase. Sainz, in the second Ferrari, was still well in touch, just 1.8s behind his team-mate.

Russell stopped on lap 11 to serve his 5s penalty, switch to hard tyres and take on a new front wing.

A lap later, Leclerc got a better exit from Turn Three than the leading Red Bull, ducked into Verstappen's slipstream and pulled off a late, brave move down the inside of Turn Four to take the lead.

Once the Ferrari was through, Verstappen headed straight for an early first pit stop, just 13 laps in, going on to the hard-compound Pirellis and rejoining eighth, a couple of seconds behind Lando Norris's McLaren.

The Ferraris were now 1-2, with Leclerc 2.5s ahead of Sainz and Ocon running a strong third for Alpine, 12.5s back. A couple of seconds behind the blue car, Magnussen was

a fine fourth for Haas, with team-mate Schumacher and Hamilton in line astern behind, then a 2s gap to Norris.

Proving that his tricky start to 2022 had done nothing to dampen his enthusiasm for racing, Hamilton, after a better exit from T6, pulled off a rarely seen move down the inside of Turn Seven to split the Haas pair.

With track limits an issue all weekend, Sainz had already received two warnings for exceeding them in his bid to stay with his team-mate. A third transgression would mean a black-and-white warning flag, and a further breach, a 5s penalty, which would hit Vettel, Gasly, Norris and Zhou before the end of the afternoon.

Magnussen proved relatively easy prey for Hamilton, the Dane running in clean air without the benefit of any DRS assistance, which Hamilton used to snatch fourth place down into Turn Four. Kevin then headed for the pits for tyres, with Norris having already done so in a bid to undercut the Haas. He got back out just ahead of the McLaren, while Schumacher had to wait another lap to pit, rejoining behind both McLarens, with Ricciardo having already made an early lap-12 stop.

By now, Verstappen had caught Hamilton and, after Lewis had defended for a few corners, went comfortably by with DRS into T4, while Schumacher immediately went back past Ricciardo on his fresh hards.

Ocon's lap-16 stop to switch from mediums to hards brought him out behind a couple of hard-tyred starters – Tsunoda's AlphaTauri and Zhou's Alfa Romeo – and just ahead of Alonso's sister Alpine, also on hards. The Spaniard was not scheduled to stop until lap 27, as he was doing all he could from his starting position of 19th.

On lap 23, Verstappen received a message from the Red Bull pit-wall crew: "Leclerc's last lap a 1:10.8, the same for Sainz. Looks like they're going on a one-stop, so we'll be pushing all the way to the end of the race here, Max." However, it wouldn't quite turn out like that.

The margin between the lead Ferrari and Verstappen was a tad over 17s at this point, meaning that the Red Bull was still on schedule to retake the lead when the red cars pitted.

There was a frantic midfield tussle going on. Ocon headed it on his fresh mediums, from Tsunoda and Zhou, on their starting hards, whom the Frenchman had just repassed. Then came Alonso on his starting hards and soon to pit, from Magnussen, Norris and Mick Schumacher, then Ricciardo a couple of seconds back, all on relatively fresh new hards.

When Alonso had to lift out of the throttle behind Zhou in Turn Ten, Magnussen got a run on the Alpine and down its inside into Turn One.

On lap 26, Pérez trailed into the pits to retire his Red Bull, too much damage having been done during his opening-lap skirmish with Russell to make it worth carrying on.

Not far behind him into the pit lane came race leader Charles Leclerc, who was on his way again in 2.6s, 6s behind Verstappen, but with a 13-lap tyre offset.

Then Ferrari brought in Sainz, sending him back into the fray after an accomplished 2.3s stop, just behind Hamilton's Mercedes, which would soon be pitting after a 28-lap opening stint on the medium tyre. It wasn't an ideal stop for the seven-time champion, however, a sticky right front wheel keeping him stationary for 4s and putting him back out behind, rather than in front of, Ocon. It was no problem, though, as his 12-lap tyre offset ensured he was comfortably back past with DRS into Turn Three.

Schumacher, meanwhile, repassed Norris into Turn Three, having been undercut. It looked like a straightforward move, but Norris had a few words to say over the radio. "I had to take avoiding action," he claimed. "He completely squeezed me under braking. He can't move under braking." Undeterred and displaying a strong turn of pace, Mick was soon past his team-mate as well, to go sixth.

Leclerc had now set the race's fastest lap and, by lap 32, he was right back on Verstappen's tail, the Ferrari comfortably retaking the race lead down the inside into Turn Three with no resistance.

Behind, there was a nice little cameo between F1's most experienced man and one of the least, Yuki Tsunoda. When the young Japanese driver edged the Alpine towards the grass on the run down to Turn Four, Alonso kept his foot in and had time to wave a warning finger at Tsunoda as he went by.

Above: Esteban Ocon scored valuable points for Alpine with his fifth place, putting them level with McLaren in their constructors' battle.
Photo: Alpine F1 Team

Top right: The victorious Charles Leclerc is mobbed by his Ferrari crew.
Photo: Scuderia Ferrari

Above right: Second best. The Orange Army streams away, after their man, for once, failed to take the race win.
Photo: Atsuo Sakurai

Right: George Russell closes in on the Red Bull of Sergio Pérez to renew hostilities begun at Paul Ricard.
Photo: XPB Images

Verstappen made his second stop on lap 37, another set of hard-compound rubber going on to the Red Bull.

Further back, Vettel found himself in the gravel for the second time during the weekend after he attempted to go around the outside of Pierre Gasly's AlphaTauri at Turn Four, only to be ushered wide.

"He has to give up the corner, I had the nose ahead," Vettel protested over the radio.

As at the first round of stops, Leclerc's second pit visit, on lap 49, gave him a handy tyre offset compared to Verstappen. Ferrari had also opted for the hard compound, Charles rejoining 3.6s behind the leading Red Bull. Sainz stopped a lap later and went back out still third, now just over 5s behind his team-mate.

It's a tricky task to pass Max Verstappen once in a race, but now Leclerc was faced with doing it for the third time. He shaped up to go around the outside of the Red Bull approaching Turn Three, and as Verstappen forced him wide, he flicked back to the inside and calmly accelerated past on exit with the aid of really strong traction. Drama-free, Ferrari No.16 led once again.

By lap 57, with 14 to go, Sainz also had Verstappen in his sights as Ferrari chased a 1-2. He tucked into the slipstream to launch a move into Turn Four, but at that moment his power unit expired in a cloud of smoke.

"No, no, engine, engine! No, no, no, no, no, no, no, no, no, no!" made clear exactly what Sainz thought about it as he pulled off in the Turn Four escape road, the Ferrari engine cover well ablaze. He climbed smartly out and sat dejectedly on the ground.

During the resulting VSC period, Leclerc pitted for a set of mediums, the time loss amounting to around just 10s, with Verstappen following him in, both choosing to put themselves in a stronger position in case a full safety car followed. The order was now Leclerc, Verstappen, Hamilton, Ocon, Russell, Schumacher, Magnussen, Norris, Alonso, Ricciardo, Albon, Bottas, Gasly, Stroll, Zhou, Tsunoda and Vettel.

As the VSC period ended, with ten laps to go, there was more anxiety for Ferrari. "The throttle pedal feels a bit strange," reported the race leader.

With five to go, Leclerc led Verstappen by 3.5s. They were in a race of their own, as Hamilton's Mercedes lagged half a minute behind in the final podium position.

"I cannot imagine what is happening with the pedal," Leclerc radioed, a bit more tension in his voice. "It's a mess."

"Sometimes, it is not coming back to zero per cent," the pit-wall crew told him.

Would there be a sting in the tail? Verstappen now had the gap down to less than 3s as he reclaimed the race's fastest lap.

"The downshifts are refused," Leclerc radioed suddenly. "Turn Three is so difficult."

"It's because of the throttle pedal," the team responded, the loud pedal remaining at 20–30 per cent every time Leclerc lifted off.

This time, though, it all held together for the Monégasque, who, for the first time, won a GP without having started it from pole. Behind, Hamilton, some 18s adrift, took a third consecutive podium. Russell was back to scoring points, in fourth place, after his Silverstone DNF, comfortably 8s clear of Ocon's Alpine, which had a delighted Schumacher – scoring for the second successive race – a similar distance behind. Norris's 5s track-limits penalty had cost him sixth place, but he beat Magnussen over the line by 3.5s, with Ricciardo and Alonso claiming the final points. Bottas just missed out after a strong drive following his pit-lane start.

"Yes, yes!" shouted Leclerc after taking the chequered just 1.5s to the good. "Oh, my God! I was really scared, really scared." As no doubt, had been Ferrari's Mattia Binotto over those final few laps. It was a fourth win of the year for Ferrari, but also a fourth mechanical breakage, with penalties no doubt looming. Food for thought as Leclerc now trailed Verstappen by 38 points in the championship.

Tony Dodgins

VIEWPOINT
OVER-REGULATING THE LIFE OUT OF RACING

THE stewards caused a familiar debate about inconsistency when they found George Russell to be the guilty party in an incident with Sergio Pérez at Turn Four. The official bulletin said that Russell had been "wholly at fault" because Pérez had been "at least fully alongside at the entry of the turn and all the way through the manoeuvre, including at the apex of the corner and left sufficient room for car 63 [Russell]."

According to that metric, Russell agreed that he had been at fault. But as the Mercedes driver pointed out, "The dynamic of every single incident is different. The fact was Checo was on my outside, and I needed to leave him space, but if he puts me in a position when I'm already at the limit of my car, and somebody turns in who has more grip, there's nowhere I can go. From the second I braked, I was on the limit of my car and there's nothing more I can do. Checo was in the clean air; I had Carlos [Sainz], [ahead] on the inside, defending. He's [Pérez] got a lot of experience; he knows how this goes."

The inference was that Pérez understood exactly how to compromise Russell in terms of the rules as he placed the Red Bull alongside and then marginally ahead. The Mexican would also have known that Russell, seeing this coming, would have been the last of the late brakers and heading for understeer city. Pérez did leave Russell room. But had it been enough under the circumstances? Would the Red Bull have made it around the corner without the contact? Probably. But we'll never know for sure.

Whatever happened to a driver's intuition in circumstances such as these? If he puts himself on the outside, there's always a chance that there could be contact. It should be his call, not a decision made by stewards impelled by the rule book rather than the unique circumstances created by two racers going at each other and knowing exactly how it might end up.

Maurice Hamilton

11

FORMULA 1 ROLEX GROSSER PREIS VON ÖSTERREICH 2022

ROLEX

Official Timepiece

SPIELBERG 8–10 JULY

RACE DISTANCE: 71 laps, 190.420 miles/306.452km

RACE WEATHER: Dry/cloudy (track 30–32°C, air 20–21°C)

RED BULL RING, SPIELBERG

Circuit: 2.683 miles/4.318km

71 laps

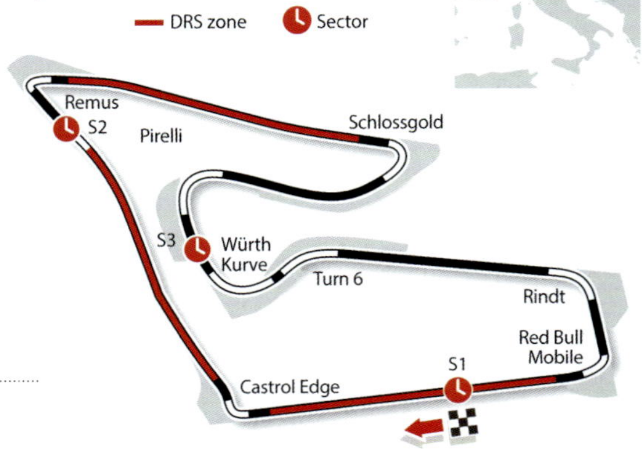

RACE – OFFICIAL CLASSIFICATION

Pos.	Driver	Nat.	No.	Entrant	Car/Engine	Laps	Time/Retirement	Speed (mph/km/h)	Gap to winner	Fastest race lap	
1	**Charles Leclerc**	MC	16	Scuderia Ferrari	Ferrari F1-75-066/7 V6	71	1h 24m 24.312s	135.361/217.843		1m 07.583s	62
2	**Max Verstappen**	NL	1	Oracle Red Bull Racing	Red Bull RB18-RBPTH001 V6	71	1h 24m 25.844s	135.320/217.777	1.532s	1m 07.275s	62
3	**Lewis Hamilton**	GB	44	Mercedes-AMG Petronas F1 Team	Mercedes-AMG F1 W13-M13 E Perf. V6	71	1h 25m 05.529s	134.268/216.084	41.217s	1m 09.000s	63
4	**George Russell**	GB	63	Mercedes-AMG Petronas F1 Team	Mercedes-AMG F1 W13-M13 E Perf. V6	71	1h 25m 23.284s *	133.803/215.335	58.972s	1m 09.075s	61
5	**Esteban Ocon**	F	31	BWT Alpine F1 Team	Alpine A522-Renault E-Tech RE22 V6	71	1h 25m 32.748s	133.556/214.938	1m 08.436s	1m 09.559s	62
6	**Mick Schumacher**	D	47	Haas F1 Team	Haas VF-22-Ferrari 066/7 V6	70			1 lap	1m 09.625s	50
7	**Lando Norris**	GB	4	McLaren F1 Team	McLaren MCL36-Mercedes F1 M13 E Perf. V6	70	*		1 lap	1m 09.304s	62
8	**Kevin Magnussen**	DK	20	Haas F1 Team	Haas VF-22-Ferrari 066/7 V6	70			1 lap	1m 09.938s	61
9	**Daniel Ricciardo**	AUS	3	McLaren F1 Team	McLaren MCL36-Mercedes F1 M13 E Perf. V6	70			1 lap	1m 09.924s	61
10	**Fernando Alonso**	E	14	BWT Alpine F1 Team	Alpine A522-Renault E-Tech RE22 V6	70			1 lap	1m 08.558s	62
11	Valtteri Bottas	FIN	77	Alfa Romeo F1 Team ORLEN	Alfa Romeo C42-Ferrari 066/7 V6	70			1 lap	1m 09.266s	61
12	Alexander Albon	T	23	Williams Racing	Williams FW44-Mercedes F1 M13 E Perf. V6	70			1 lap	1m 09.669s	60
13	Lance Stroll	CDN	18	Aston Martin Aramco Cognizant F1 Team	Aston Martin AMR22-Mercedes F1 M13 E Perf. V6	70			1 lap	1m 10.048s	64
14	Guanyu Zhou	CHN	24	Alfa Romeo F1 Team ORLEN	Alfa Romeo C42-Ferrari 066/7 V6	70	*		1 lap	1m 09.380s	50
15	Pierre Gasly	F	10	Scuderia AlphaTauri	AlphaTauri AT03-RBPTH001 V6	70	*		1 lap	1m 10.104s	61
16	Yuki Tsunoda	J	22	Scuderia AlphaTauri	AlphaTauri AT03-RBPTH001 V6	70			1 lap	1m 10.023s	62
17	Sebastian Vettel	D	5	Aston Martin Aramco Cognizant F1 Team	Aston Martin AMR22-Mercedes F1 M13 E Perf. V6	70	*		1 lap	1m 10.001s	62
	Carlos Sainz	E	55	Scuderia Ferrari	Ferrari F1-75-066/7 V6	56	*engine/fire*			1m 08.649s	55
	Nicholas Latifi	CDN	6	Williams Racing	Williams FW44-Mercedes F1 M13 E Perf. V6	48	*floor*			1m 10.890s	14
	Sergio Pérez	MEX	11	Oracle Red Bull Racing	Red Bull RB18-RBPTH001 V6	24	*accident damage*			1m 11.843s	5

* Gasly: 5s time penalty for leaving the track without a justifiable reason multiple times (served at pit stop); 5s time penalty for causing a collision with Vettel.

* Norris & Zhou: 5s time penalty for leaving the track without a justifiable reason multiple times (served at pit stop). * Russell: 5s time penalty for causing a collision with Pérez (served at pit stop).

* Vettel: 5s time penalty for leaving the track without a justifiable reason multiple times (originally finished 16th).

DHL Fastest race lap (scores 1 point): Max Verstappen on lap 62, 1m 07.275s, 143.576mph/231.063km/h.

Lap record record (current configuration): Carlos Sainz (McLaren MCL35-Renault V6), 1m 05.619s, 147.200mph/236.894km/h (2020).

19 · ALONSO · Alpine
Used additional power unit elements; required to start from the back of the grid

17 · LATIFI · Williams

15 · ALBON · Williams

13 · ZHOU · Alfa Romeo

11 · RICCIARDO · McLaren

20 · BOTTAS · Alfa Romeo
Car modified in *parc fermé*; required to start from the pit lane; used additional power unit elements

18 · VETTEL · Aston Martin

16 · TSUNODA · AlphaTauri

14 · GASLY · AlphaTauri

12 · STROLL · Aston Martin

Grid order	1	2	3	4	5	6	7	8	9	10	11	12	13	14	15	16	17	18	19	20	21	22	23	24	25	26	27
1 VERSTAPPEN	1	1	1	1	1	1	1	1	1	1	1	16	16	16	16	16	16	16	16	16	16	16	16	16	16	16	55
16 LECLERC	16	16	16	16	16	16	16	16	16	16	16	1	55	55	55	55	55	55	55	55	55	55	55	55	55	55	1
55 SAINZ	55	55	55	55	55	55	55	55	55	55	55	55	1	31	31	44	44	1	1	1	1	1	1	1	1	1	16
63 RUSSELL	63	63	63	63	63	63	63	63	63	63	31	31	31	20	44	1	1	44	44	44	44	44	44	44	44	44	44
11 PÉREZ	31	31	31	31	31	31	31	31	31	31	20	20	20	44	47	31	18	18	18	18	18	18	18	18	18	18	18
31 OCON	20	20	20	20	20	20	20	20	20	20	47	47	47	47	1	47	22	22	22	22	22	22	31	31	31	31	31
20 MAGNUSSEN	44	44	44	47	47	47	47	47	47	47	44	44	44	1	20	18	24	24	24	24	24	31	22	22	22	20	20
44 HAMILTON	47	47	47	44	44	44	44	44	44	44	63	4	4	4	18	22	14	14	14	14	31	24	24	20	20	4	47
47 SCHUMACHER	3	3	3	3	4	4	4	4	4	4	4	18	18	18	22	24	5	5	5	31	14	14	14	4	4	47	4
4 NORRIS	4	4	4	4	3	3	3	3	3	3	3	3	22	22	24	14	31	31	31	20	20	20	20	14	47	14	3
3 RICCIARDO	18	18	18	18	18	18	18	18	18	18	18	22	24	24	14	5	20	20	20	4	4	4	4	47	14	3	63
18 STROLL	10	10	10	10	10	10	10	10	10	10	10	10	14	14	5	20	4	4	4	47	47	47	47	3	3	63	14
24 ZHOU	23	23	23	23	23	23	23	23	23	23	22	24	5	5	4	4	3	3	47	5	3	3	3	63	63	22	23
10 GASLY	24	22	22	22	22	22	22	22	22	22	23	14	3	3	3	3	47	47	3	3	23	23	23	23	23	23	10
23 ALBON	22	24	24	24	24	24	24	24	24	24	24	5	23	23	23	23	23	23	23	23	63	63	63	24	10	10	77
22 TSUNODA	6	6	6	6	6	6	6	6	6	6	6	6	77	77	10	10	10	10	10	10	10	10	10	10	77	77	6
6 LATIFI	5	14	14	14	14	14	14	14	14	14	14	23	10	10	77	77	63	63	63	63	77	77	77	77	6	6	5
5 VETTEL	14	5	5	5	5	5	5	5	5	5	5	77	6	6	63	63	77	77	77	77	6	6	6	6	5	5	22
14 ALONSO	77	77	77	77	77	77	77	77	77	77	77	63	63	63	6	6	6	6	6	6	5	5	5	5	24	24	24
77 BOTTAS	11	11	11	11	11	11	11	11	11	11	11	11	11	11	11	11	11	11	11	11	11	11	11	11			

Grid order	28	29	30	31	32	33	34	35	36	37	38	39	40	41	42	43	44	45	46	47	48	49	50	51	52	53	54	55
1 VERSTAPPEN	1	1	1	1	1	16	16	16	16	16	16	16	16	16	16	16	16	16	16	16	16	16	55	1	1	16	16	16
16 LECLERC	16	16	16	16	16	1	1	1	55	55	55	55	55	55	55	55	55	55	55	55	55	55	1	16	16	1	1	1
55 SAINZ	55	55	55	55	55	55	55	55	1	1	1	1	1	1	1	1	1	1	1	1	1	1	16	55	55	55	55	55
63 RUSSELL	44	31	44	44	44	44	44	44	44	44	44	44	44	44	44	44	44	44	44	44	44	44	44	44	44	44	44	44
11 PÉREZ	18	44	31	31	31	31	31	31	31	31	31	31	31	31	31	31	31	14	14	14	14	14	14	14	31	31	31	31
31 OCON	31	20	20	20	47	47	47	47	47	47	47	47	47	47	47	47	3	31	31	31	31	31	31	31	14	14	63	63
20 MAGNUSSEN	20	18	47	47	20	20	20	20	20	20	20	20	20	4	4	4	14	63	63	63	63	63	63	63	63	63	14	14
44 HAMILTON	47	47	4	4	4	4	4	4	4	4	4	4	4	20	3	3	63	18	18	47	47	47	47	47	47	47	47	47
47 SCHUMACHER	4	4	63	63	63	63	63	63	63	63	63	63	63	3	14	14	18	47	47	20	20	20	20	20	20	20	20	20
4 NORRIS	3	63	3	3	3	3	3	3	3	3	3	3	3	23	18	18	47	20	20	18	4	4	4	4	4	4	4	4
3 RICCIARDO	63	3	23	23	23	23	23	23	23	23	23	23	23	14	63	63	20	24	4	4	3	3	3	3	3	3	3	3
18 STROLL	23	23	10	10	10	10	10	10	10	10	10	10	14	18	24	24	24	22	24	3	18	23	23	23	23	23	23	23
24 ZHOU	10	10	77	77	77	77	77	77	77	5	5	18	18	24	20	20	22	4	3	23	23	77	77	77	77	77	77	77
10 GASLY	77	77	5	5	5	5	5	5	5	77	77	14	10	63	22	22	4	3	23	77	77	10	10	10	10	10	10	10
23 ALBON	6	5	18	18	18	18	18	18	18	18	18	77	24	22	5	5	23	23	22	10	10	18	18	18	18	18	18	18
22 TSUNODA	5	6	6	6	22	14	14	14	14	14	14	24	22	5	23	23	77	77	77	22	22	22	22	22	22	22	24	24
6 LATIFI	22	22	22	22	14	22	22	22	22	24	24	22	5	77	77	77	5	10	10	5	5	5	24	24	24	24	22	22
5 VETTEL	14	14	14	14	24	24	24	24	24	22	22	5	77	10	10	10	10	5	5	24	24	24	5	5	5	5	5	5
14 ALONSO	24	24	24	24	6	6	6	6	6	6	6	6	6	6	6	6	6	6	6	6	6							
77 BOTTAS																												

23 = Pit stop 6 = *One lap or more behind*

TIME SHEETS

PRACTICE 1 (FRIDAY)

Weather: Dry/sunny

Temperatures: track 38–42°C, air 22–25°C

Pos.	Driver	Laps	Time
1	Max Verstappen	34	1m 06.302s
2	Charles Leclerc	32	1m 06.557s
3	George Russell	32	1m 06.702s
4	Sergio Pérez	27	1m 06.839s
5	Lewis Hamilton	31	1m 06.909s
6	Kevin Magnussen	32	1m 06.965s
7	Carlos Sainz	29	1m 07.039s
8	Fernando Alonso	32	1m 07.100s
9	Mick Schumacher	32	1m 07.246s
10	Yuki Tsunoda	33	1m 07.296s
11	Lance Stroll	26	1m 07.431s
12	Esteban Ocon	27	1m 07.462s
13	Sebastian Vettel	29	1m 07.476s
14	Valtteri Bottas	27	1m 07.522s
15	Alexander Albon	32	1m 07.582s
16	Pierre Gasly	33	1m 07.592s
17	Daniel Ricciardo	25	1m 07.743s
18	Guanyu Zhou	28	1m 07.889s
19	Nicholas Latifi	28	1m 08.149s
20	Lando Norris	14	1m 09.915s

PRACTICE 2 (SATURDAY)

Weather: Dry/cloudy

Temperatures: track 31–39°C, air 21–23°C

Pos.	Driver	Laps	Time
1	Carlos Sainz	40	1m 08.610s
2	Charles Leclerc	43	1m 08.660s
3	Max Verstappen	32	1m 08.778s
4	Fernando Alonso	21	1m 08.832s
5	Esteban Ocon	24	1m 08.848s
6	Sergio Pérez	36	1m 09.179s
7	George Russell	33	1m 09.240s
8	Valtteri Bottas	26	1m 09.251s
9	Lewis Hamilton	14	1m 09.350s
10	Lando Norris	38	1m 09.519s
11	Lance Stroll	43	1m 09.525s
12	Pierre Gasly	37	1m 09.579s
13	Sebastian Vettel	44	1m 09.602s
14	Guanyu Zhou	36	1m 09.665s
15	Mick Schumacher	32	1m 09.700s
16	Alexander Albon	34	1m 09.740s
17	Daniel Ricciardo	34	1m 09.852s
18	Kevin Magnussen	34	1m 09.960s
19	Yuki Tsunoda	39	1m 10.005s
20	Nicholas Latifi	36	1m 10.261s

QUALIFYING (FRIDAY)

Weather: Dry/sunny Temperatures: track 30–36°C, air 23–25°C

Pos.	Driver	First	Second	Third	Qualifying Tyre
1	Max Verstappen	1m 05.852s	1m 05.374s	1m 04.984s	Soft (n)
2	Charles Leclerc	1m 05.419s	1m 05.287s	1m 05.013s	Soft (u)
3	Carlos Sainz	1m 05.660s	1m 05.576s	1m 05.066s	Soft (u)
4	George Russell	1m 06.235s	1m 05.697s	1m 05.431s	Soft (n)
5	Esteban Ocon	1m 06.468s	1m 05.993s	1m 05.726s	Soft (u)
6	Kevin Magnussen	1m 06.366s	1m 05.894s	1m 05.879s	Soft (u)
7	Mick Schumacher	1m 06.405s	1m 06.151s	1m 06.011s	Soft (u)
8	Fernando Alonso	1m 06.016s	1m 06.082s	1m 06.103s	Soft (n)
9	Lewis Hamilton	1m 06.079s	1m 05.475s	1m 13.151s	Soft (n)
10	Pierre Gasly	1m 06.589s	1m 06.160s		
11	Alexander Albon	1m 06.516s	1m 06.230s		
12	Valtteri Bottas	1m 06.442s	1m 06.319s		
13	Sergio Pérez *	1m 06.143s	1m 06.458s	no time	Soft (n)
14	Yuki Tsunoda	1m 06.463s	1m 06.851s		
15	Lando Norris	1m 06.330s	1m 25.847s		
16	Daniel Ricciardo	1m 06.613s			
17	Lance Stroll	1m 06.847s			
18	Guanyu Zhou	1m 06.901s			
19	Nicholas Latifi	1m 07.003s			
20	Sebastian Vettel	1m 07.083s			

* Pérez: fastest Q2 times (the best, 1m 05.805s) and all Q3 times (the best, 1m 05.404s) were deleted for leaving the track without a justifiable reason in Q2.

POINTS

DRIVERS

1	Max Verstappen	208
2	Charles Leclerc	170
3	Sergio Pérez	151
4	Carlos Sainz	133
5	George Russell	128
6	Lewis Hamilton	109
7	Lando Norris	64
8	Esteban Ocon	52
9	Valtteri Bottas	46
10	Fernando Alonso	29
11	Kevin Magnussen	22
12	Daniel Ricciardo	17
13	Pierre Gasly	16
14	Sebastian Vettel	15
15	Mick Schumacher	12
16	Yuki Tsunoda	11
17	Guanyu Zhou	5
18	Alexander Albon	3
19	Lance Stroll	3

For the Sprint, additional points are allocated to the top eight drivers for both championships, with the winner earning eight points, and P2 through to p8 earning seven, six, five, four, three, two and one point respectively.

CONSTRUCTORS

1	Red Bull	359
2	Ferrari	303
3	Mercedes	237
4	McLaren	81
5	Alpine	81
6	Alfa Romeo	51
7	Haas	34
8	AlphaTauri	27
9	Aston Martin	18
10	Williams	3

QUALIFYING: head to head

Hamilton	5	6	Russell
Verstappen	8	3	Pérez
Ricciardo	2	9	Norris
Leclerc	9	2	Sainz
Gasly	8	3	Tsunoda
Hülkenberg	1	1	Stroll
Vettel	7	2	Stroll
Alonso	8	3	Ocon
Bottas	8	3	Zhou
Albon	9	2	Latifi
Magnussen	9	2	Schumacher

SPRINT QUALIFYING (SATURDAY)

RACE DISTANCE: 23 laps, 61.632 miles/99.188km RACE WEATHER: Dry/cloudy (track 33–37°C, air 25–26°C)

Pos.	Driver	Tyre	Laps	Time/Retirement	Speed (mph/km/h)	Gap to leader	Fastest race lap
1	**Max Verstappen**		23	26m 30.059s	139.540/224.568		1m 08.455s 5
2	**Charles Leclerc**		23	26m 31.734s	139.393/224.331	1.675s	1m 08.321s 4
3	**Carlos Sainz**		23	26m 35.703s	139.046/223.773	5.644s	1m 08.409s 4
4	**George Russell**		23	26m 43.488s	138.371/222.687	13.429s	1m 08.979s 4
5	**Sergio Pérez**		23	26m 48.361s	137.952/222.012	18.302s	1m 09.137s 14
6	**Esteban Ocon**		23	27m 01.091s	136.869/220.269	31.032s	1m 09.384s 4
7	**Kevin Magnussen**		23	27m 04.598s	136.573/219.793	34.539s	1m 09.232s 4
8	**Lewis Hamilton**		23	27m 05.506s	136.497/219.671	35.447s	1m 09.516s 7
9	Mick Schumacher		23	27m 07.222s	136.353/219.439	37.163s	1m 09.457s 4
10	Valtteri Bottas		23	27m 07.616s	136.320/219.386	37.557s	1m 09.674s 4
11	Lando Norris		23	27m 08.639s	136.234/219.248	38.580s	1m 09.909s 8
12	Daniel Ricciardo		23	27m 09.797s	136.137/219.092	39.738s	1m 09.996s 8
13	Lance Stroll		23	27m 18.300s	135.431/217.955	48.241s	1m 10.295s 4
14	Guanyu Zhou		23	27m 20.812s *	135.224/217.622	50.753s	1m 10.165s 11
15	Pierre Gasly		23	27m 22.184s	135.111/217.440	52.125s	1m 10.409s 4
16	Alexander Albon		23	27m 22.471s *	135.087/217.402	52.412s	1m 10.367s 5
17	Yuki Tsunoda		23	27m 24.615s	134.911/217.118	54.556s	1m 10.267s 4
18	Nicholas Latifi		23	27m 38.753s	133.761/215.268	1m 08.694s	1m 10.284s 4
19	Sebastian Vettel		21			2 laps	1m 10.317s 4
NS	Fernando Alonso			electrics			

The race was scheduled for 24 laps, but due to Zhou having an engine failure, the start was aborted and another formation lap was required.

* Albon: 5s time penalty for forcing Norris off the track (originally finished 13th). * Zhou: Started from the pit lane.

Fastest race lap: Charles Leclerc on lap 4, 1m 08.321s, 141.378mph/227.525km/h.

9 · SCHUMACHER · Haas

7 · MAGNUSSEN · Haas

5 · PÉREZ · Red Bull

3 · SAINZ · Ferrari

1 · VERSTAPPEN · Red Bull

10 · NORRIS · McLaren

8 · HAMILTON · Mercedes

6 · OCON · Alpine

4 · RUSSELL · Mercedes

2 · LECLERC · Ferrari

56	57	58	59	60	61	62	63	64	65	66	67	68	69	70	71	·
16	16	16	16	16	16	16	16	16	16	16	16	16	16	16	16	1
1	1	1	1	1	1	1	1	1	1	1	1	1	1	1	1	2
55	44	44	44	44	44	44	44	44	44	44	44	44	44	44	44	3
44	31	31	31	31	63	63	63	63	63	63	63	63	63	63	63	4
31	63	63	63	63	31	31	31	31	31	31	31	31	31	31	31	5
63	14	47	47	47	47	47	47	47	47	47	47	47	47	47		6
14	47	20	20	20	20	4	4	4	4	4	4	4	4	4		7
47	20	4	4	4	4	20	20	20	20	20	20	20	20	20		8
20	4	3	3	3	3	3	3	3	3	3	3	3	3	3		9
4	3	14	23	23	23	23	23	77	77	77	77	77	77	14		10
3	23	23	77	77	77	77	77	23	23	23	14	14	14	77		
23	77	77	10	10	10	14	14	14	14	14	23	23	23	23		
77	10	10	18	18	14	10	10	18	18	18	18	18	18	18		
10	18	18	14	14	18	18	18	10	10	10	24	24	24	24		
18	24	24	24	24	24	24	24	24	24	24	10	10	10	10		
24	22	22	22	22	22	22	22	22	22	22	5	5	5	5		
22	5	5	5	5	5	5	5	5	5	5	22	22	22	22		
5																

VSC Safety car deployed on laps shown

		VSC	VSC													

RACE TYRE STRATEGIES

PIRELLI

	Driver	Race Stint 1	Race Stint 2	Race Stint 3	Race Stint 4
1	Leclerc	Medium (n): 1-26	Hard (n): 27-49	Hard (n): 50-58	Medium (n): 59-71
2	Verstappen	Medium (n): 1-13	Hard (n): 14-36	Hard (n): 37-58	Medium (n): 59-71
3	Hamilton	Medium (n): 1-28	Hard (n): 29-51	Medium (n): 52-71	
4	Russell	Medium (u): 1-11	Hard (n): 12-40	Hard (u): 41-71	
5	Ocon	Medium (n): 1-16	Hard (n): 17-44	Hard (u): 45-71	
6	Schumacher	Medium (n): 1-16	Hard (n): 17-43	Hard (n): 44-70	
7	Norris	Medium (n): 1-14	Hard (n): 15-43	Hard (n): 44-70	
8	Magnussen	Medium (u): 1-15	Hard (n): 16-41	Hard (n): 42-70	
9	Ricciardo	Medium (u): 1-12	Hard (n): 13-44	Hard (n): 45-70	
10	Alonso	Hard (n): 1-27	Hard (n): 28-57	Hard (n): 58	Medium (n): 59-70
11	Bottas	Medium (n): 1-6	Hard (n): 7-39	Hard (n): 40-70	
12	Albon	Medium (n): 1-11	Hard (n): 12-41	Hard (n): 42-70	
13	Stroll	Medium (u): 1-29	Hard (u): 30-48	Medium (u): 49-70	
14	Zhou	Hard (n): 1-24	Hard (n): 25-46	Medium (n): 47-70	
15	Gasly	Medium (n): 1-12	Hard (n): 13-40	Hard (n): 41-70	
16	Tsunoda	Hard (n): 1-26	Medium (n): 27-46	Hard (n): 47-70	
17	Vettel	Hard (u): 1-20	Medium (u): 21-44	Medium (n): 45-70	
	Sainz	Medium (n): 1-27	Hard (n): 28-50	Hard (n): 51-56 (dnf)	
	Latifi	Medium (n): 1-12	Hard (n): 13-35	Hard (n): 36-48 (dnf)	
	Pérez	Medium (n): 1	Hard (n): 2-24 (dnf)		

The tyre regulations stipulate that at least two of three dry tyre specifications must be used during a dry race.

Selected compounds for Spielberg: Red = Soft (C5); Yellow = Medium (C4); White = Hard (C3). (n) new (u) used

pionship
DHL
MSC CRUISES
MYLAPS
MSC CRUISES
DHL
DHL
14
Hard Rock
citrix
Tezos
ARCTIC WOLF
Infinitum
Mobil 1

FIA FORMULA 1 WORLD CHAMPIONSHIP · ROUND 12

FRENCH GRAND PRIX

CIRCUIT PAUL RICARD

LE CASTELLET QUALIFYING

HAVING stopped the rot with a fine win in Austria, Charles Leclerc arrived at Paul Ricard hoping that he could continue the momentum and reduce his championship deficit to Max Verstappen. His Monaco home is just a couple of hours down the road and, to all intents and purposes, this was a home race, since he had done much of his junior karting at Brignoles, just 30 miles away.

He had some help, too. Carlos Sainz's spectacular engine failure at Red Bull Ring meant that he would start from the back in France with a new power unit and therefore was free to offer Leclerc a helpful tow down the Mistral Straight and through Signes into Le Beausset in qualifying. That was reckoned to be worth at least a couple of tenths.

Sainz did the job perfectly, and the result was a seventh 2022 pole for Leclerc, the 16th of his F1 career. He stopped the clock in 1m 30.872s, with Max Verstappen fully 0.3s away. And this after the Dutchman had finished Saturday morning's third free practice session three-and-a-half tenths in front of the Ferraris...

"I'm very happy," Leclerc said. "Overall, the weekend has been quite difficult. I struggled to find the right balance, the right driving style, and also it's very, very warm. So, whenever you get a small snap, the rest of the lap is compromised. It was very tricky, but I was really happy with my last lap. And, obviously, the help from Carlos was great teamwork.

"But, the Red Bull guys were very quick in the race simulations. We've worked a little bit on the car for the race, so hopefully it will go better for us tomorrow. Tyre management will be a big thing. We were good in Austria, but we struggled a bit more yesterday. I think we've made a significant step up in performance since then, so hopefully we can show that in the race."

Verstappen didn't believe that Leclerc's tow explained the whole margin between them. "My final run in Q3 was not a clean lap," he admitted. "Just by being on the limit, I had a couple of moments, which cost me lap time. We have to figure out why they happened and how to make the car more predictable, let's put it like that. Getting the tyres in the right window in the heat is tough, and it was a bit of a struggle to get the right balance, but we still have two cars in the top three."

Red Bull team-mate Sergio Pérez would start in the top three for the fifth time in 2022, but he also admitted to struggling with the car's balance throughout the weekend. Across the grid, though, the Red Bull men were far from alone.

Once again, Mercedes was almost a full second off the ultimate pace, but Lewis Hamilton made the best of what he had to put the first Silver Arrow on the second row, some 0.36s quicker than George Russell, who lined up sixth.

Into the gap between them went Lando Norris after a fine lap in the McLaren, team-mate Daniel Ricciardo having missed the top-ten shootout by just 0.08s. For qualifying pace at least, Norris had half a second in hand over Alpine, for whom Fernando Alonso qualified seventh.

Eighth was a fine effort from Yuki Tsunoda in the AlphaTauri, as team-mate Pierre Gasly had to contemplate a 16th-place start at his home race. "I don't fully understand," the Frenchman grimaced. "Yesterday, we were comfortably top ten, but this morning the car felt completely different, and I don't know why."

For Sainz, ninth with more engine penalties to come was something of a bitter pill to swallow after a Q2-topping time that indicated he would have been squarely in the pole fight, while Kevin Magnussen turned in a strong performance to start tenth for Haas. There were conflicting fortunes for Guenther Steiner's men, though. Team-mate Mick Schumacher had also looked good, but, along with Ricciardo, had a Q1 time deleted for exceeding track limits at Turn Three. In Mick's case, it was enough to eliminate him and spell 19th on the grid.

In the second Alpine, Esteban Ocon would line up 12th for his home GP, ahead of Valtteri Bottas's Alfa Romeo, the Aston Martin of Sebastian Vettel and Alex Albon in the Williams, the last having done a strong job to haul the car into Q2 once more.

The devastated Gasly apart, Lance Stroll, Zhou Guanyu, the aforementioned Schumacher and Nicholas Latifi also went out in Q1. The heat and the nature of the track meant that keeping the soft-compound rubber alive for the whole lap was a challenge throughout qualifying, so looking after the medium and hard compounds would be key to the race. Putting even greater emphasis on that was a pit-lane extension that took the average stop loss up to around 28s, which tipped the strategic balance even more in favour of the one-stopper.

FOR the sixth time in 2022, Charles Leclerc and Max Verstappen shared the front row as 30-degree ambient and 50-degree track temperatures greeted the drivers for a race that many felt would be all about tyres. The entire field had opted for the medium-compound Pirelli as the starting tyre, with the exception of Pierre Gasly, Valtteri Bottas and Carlos Sainz – starting from the back with engine penalties – who went for the white-walled hard. Degradation on the soft-compound tyre was reckoned to be too severe to make it compatible with the desired single-stop strategy.

Leclerc converted his pole and got the Ferrari into Turn One with its nose in front, Verstappen having to fend off the attentions of Lewis Hamilton, who, at Paul Ricard, became the sixth man to reach 300 GP starts (joining Kimi Räikkönen, Fernando Alonso, Rubens Barrichello, Jenson Button and Michael Schumacher). No driver had yet won a race after passing that milestone, however, so that was another record that Lewis was looking to claim!

Sergio Pérez tucked into fourth with the second Red Bull, ahead of a pro-active Fernando Alonso (who would pass Räikkönen's record number of laps raced in a GP career during the course of the race), up two places from his seventh grid slot with the Alpine. George Russell ran sixth, ahead of Lando Norris, Daniel Ricciardo, Yuki Tsunoda, Esteban Ocon, Sebastian Vettel, Lance Stroll, Alex Albon, Mick Schumacher, Gasly, Kevin Magnussen, Bottas, Sainz, Nicholas Latifi and Zhou Guanyu.

Into the chicane for the first time, Ocon took a bit too much inside kerb and made contact with Tsunoda's sidepod, spinning the AlphaTauri down to the back, the home driver awarded a 5s time penalty.

Magnussen was one of the most impressive early movers, up seven places from his penalised, back-of-the-grid starting slot to 13th, after just two laps! Stroll was on the move, too, up five places. Going in the opposite direction was Bottas, down six places in the Alfa.

With five laps completed, the championship protagonists had dropped Hamilton's Mercedes by 4s as Verstappen hovered around DRS distance of the leading Ferrari without quite being able to launch an attack. Pérez was keeping Hamilton honest and had Russell's Mercedes 2s adrift, George demoting Alonso's Alpine.

Helping to maintain the status quo at the front was Leclerc's speed through Turns Six/Seven, while Verstappen's Red Bull was quicker down the ensuing straights. When Leclerc missed the apex into the chicane on lap six and ran a tad wide, however, Verstappen got a good run through Signes and forced the Monégasque to defend the inside into Le Beausset.

Magnussen, running hard from the off, was into the pits to get rid of his starting mediums after just nine laps, while Sainz, from the back, was making impressive progress, up to 12th just ten laps into the 53-lap race.

"The pace is good, you're doing a good job," the Ferrari pit-wall crew told him.

"It doesn't feel that way," he replied.

A couple of laps later, Ferrari was on the phone to Leclerc, too: "We are thinking Plan B? Let me know your opinion."

"Yeah, copy that," Charles responded calmly. On lap 15, he was evidently pushing, opening his margin over Verstappen to almost 2s as blistering became evident on the inside shoulder of his right-front Pirelli.

Red Bull pulled the trigger first, stopping Verstappen after 16 laps, the Dutchman on his way again in just 2.4s. He

Above: Charles Leclerc holds the lead from Max Verstappen and Lewis Hamilton as the field blasts away.
Photo: Peter Nygaard/GP Photo

Top left: Nyck de Vries was given a run in Hamilton's Mercedes for Friday's FP1.
Photo: XPB Images

Above left: Meanwhile, Lewis takes a watching brief.
Photo: Mercedes-AMG Petronas F1 Team

Left: Thumbs up from pole-sitter Leclerc, who wore a special Jules Bianchi tribute helmet.
Photo: Scuderia Ferrari

Opening spread: Verstappen emerged victorious in the scorching heat of Le Castellet.
Photo: Red Bull Content Pool/Getty Images

ORACLE
10

ESSO

rejoined seventh, just behind Norris's McLaren.

Leclerc, meanwhile, was told by Ferrari, "Hard tyres are two-tenths slower than expected, still suffering from overheating." He did not come in immediately.

At Red Bull, 'GP' Lambiase told Verstappen, "You do need to push now, he [Leclerc] is not in." The gap between the Ferrari and the Red Bull was 27.1s, and the pit-stop loss time 27–28s. It was going to be tight…

But, next moment, on lap 18, the French crowd, and the many Leclerc and Ferrari fans within it, could not quite believe it when the circuit monitors showed Charles embedded in the tyre barrier at Turn 11. Out came the safety car, and the field prepared to take advantage of a cheap first pit stop. More bad news for Ferrari amid the scramble was a slow stop followed by an unsafe release of Sainz into the path of Albon's Williams.

When an anguished Leclerc shouted that he couldn't get off throttle, some wondered about a repeat of the problem that had given him such a nail-biting conclusion in Austria a fortnight earlier, but actually he was referring to an inability to select reverse and back the Ferrari out of the tyres.

"He's alright?" Verstappen enquired of Leclerc.

"Yes, I'm told he's okay, Max. Thanks for asking," Lambiase informed the world champion. Meanwhile, a forlorn Leclerc was on his way back to the pits on the back of a scooter, a drastic blow dealt to his championship aspirations.

With the field bunched anew, the order behind the safety car was Verstappen, Hamilton, Pérez, Russell, Alonso, Norris, Ricciardo, Sainz, Ocon, Stroll, Albon, Gasly, Vettel, Bottas, Latifi, Zhou, Magnussen and Schumacher. The first seven were now on the hard tyre, presumably to the end, while Sainz was on fresh mediums, but with a potential penalty hanging over him. Gasly, running 12th, was the only other driver on mediums.

Verstappen judged the lap-21 restart well and fended off any chance of a challenge from Hamilton, while Sainz got down the inside of Ricciardo into Turn One and then wasted little time in dispatching Norris in the second McLaren at the chicane to move into the top six. Next on his radar was compatriot Alonso, the Alpine unable to resist as Sainz arrowed the Ferrari down its inside at the chicane next time around, just as race control confirmed a 5s time penalty for the pit-lane indiscretion.

Further back, Schumacher came off worst when he tried to go around the outside of Zhou at the chicane, the Alfa's left front clipping the Haas's right rear and tipping it into a spin, for which the Chinese driver also attracted a 5s penalty.

Russell provided sterner opposition to Sainz, but ultimately the Spaniard utilised a better exit from Turn Eight to dive around the outside of the Mercedes at Signes to go fifth.

By lap 35, with 18 to go, Ocon had caught Ricciardo's McLaren as the two teams continued their close tussle for fourth in the constructors' championship.

Sainz was now with third-placed Pérez, but was unable to go by as the Ferrari's mediums started to degrade. "We cannot pass," he told the Maranello pit-wall crew.

"Okay, copy. Plan D confirmed," they replied.

"Do we know if those ahead are stopping?" Carlos wanted to know.

"I think they stay out to the end," was Riccardo Adami's response.

"Then let's stop," Sainz suggested.

"Stay out, stay out."

Above: Fernando Alonso briefly holds off the attentions of George Russell in the race's early stages.
Photo: XPB Images

Top: Hamilton held the lead after Leclerc's retirement, but was soon overhauled by Verstappen.
Photo: Mercedes-AMG Petronas F1 Team

Above left: Verstappen blasts his Red Bull down one of the circuit's long straights.
Photo: Red Bull Content Pool/Getty Images

Left: Sergio Pérez and Russell made contact in their battle over the final podium place.
Photo: XPB Images

Above: With Ferrari failing to deliver, Russell and Hamilton's podium placings ensured a healthy haul of constructor points for Mercedes.
Photo: Mercedes-AMG Petronas F1 Team

Top right: After starting from the back of the grid, Carlos Sainz had to settle for fifth place after an unsafe release from a pit stop earned him a five-second penalty.
Photo: Scuderia Ferrari

Above right: Daniel Ricciardo broke into the points for McLaren with a ninth-place finish.
Photo: McLaren F1 Team

Right: A crestfallen Charles Leclerc is comforted by team principal Mattia Binotto, after crashing out of the race when leading.
Photo: Scuderia Ferrari

Sainz launched renewed attempts to pass the Red Bull and, despite spirited defence from the Mexican, got the Ferrari around the outside of Turn 14 to snatch the place – brave stuff!

At that point, Ferrari instructed him, "Box, box."

"Not now, not now!" Sainz responded.

Russell sensed an opportunity to demote Pérez further and, late on the brakes, had a go down the inside of the Red Bull into the chicane. He overdid it slightly and made contact with the Red Bull's left sidepod, forcing the Mexican to take to the escape road. Sergio returned to the track well ahead and then, after consulting his lap delta, fell back to his rightful spot.

"He just turned into me," Russell radioed in, which did seem to be somewhat at odds with the situation.

"Ah, man, he just drove into me," was Pérez's take.

With ten to go, Sainz did indeed pit again, and by the time he had served his penalty and was on his way again, a podium position had become ninth. The Ferrari strategy came under the microscope once again, but there was solid logic behind it.

The team had thought that Sainz's mediums would degrade over the rest of the race, to the extent that he would not have been able to achieve a 5s margin – the extent of his penalty – over Russell/Pérez and would be destined to be classified fifth. By pitting for a second set of mediums, he would recover to fifth anyway and would likely claim an extra point for fastest lap, which is exactly how it played out.

With six laps remaining, Ocon gave the home crowd something to cheer when he pulled off a fine outside pass of Ricciardo's McLaren at Signes to take eighth.

Verstappen now had a comfortable 10s margin over Hamilton, who was confronted with a non-working drinks bottle in 35-degree ambient. Pérez and Russell were another 7s in arrears; Alonso's Alpine was a fine fifth, 22s back, but being caught by the recovering Sainz and about to be swallowed up as Carlos used his superior grip to great effect to also go around the outside of Signes.

With Russell repeatedly thwarted by Pérez for the final podium position, a VSC period intervened with three laps to go, with Zhou's stricken Alfa trackside. Russell knew he might have an opportunity when it disappeared, and so it was. After dropping back, he got the delta just right when the race came under green once again and arrowed past the Red Bull up into third. For the first time in 2022, we would have two Mercedes drivers on the podium.

Pérez was not impressed, "I don't know what was going on with the VSC," he explained. "It said it was ending at the exit of Turn Eight, and then it was at Turn 15, so there was something going on there, and I got caught out by it."

Behind fifth-placed Sainz, Alpine made handy gains to go ahead of McLaren for fourth in the constructors' championship, the quartet crossing the line in the order Alonso, Norris, Ocon, Ricciardo. Behind them, Stroll took the final point for Aston, only just having held off a few determined last-lap bids to take it away from him by team-mate Vettel.

As Verstappen contemplated a Jackie Stewart-equalling 27th GP win, he could enjoy a 63-point championship advantage over Leclerc after 12 of the season's 22 races. In the constructors', Red Bull now had an 82-point margin over Ferrari.

"The car was quick today," Verstappen said, "and it would have been interesting to see how it would have played out with Charles. It was very hot and the tyres overheated if you followed closely, so I had to back out early on and wait for later in the race. It would have been close."

Leclerc was brutally honest: "I think I'm performing at the highest level in my career, but if I keep making those mistakes, then it's pointless – I'm losing too many points. Seven it was in Imola, and 25 here because, honestly, we were probably the strongest car on track today. So, if we lose the championship by 32 points at the end of the season, I will know where they are coming from, and it's unacceptable. I need to get on top of those things."

Tony Dodgins

VIEWPOINT
FRENCH FOLLIES

CHARLES LECLERC might be Monégasque, but Paul Ricard represented a home grand prix of sorts. In which case, old hands from the heyday of the Ligier and Renault teams could have told him how a race in the heat of Le Castellet can cause havoc with what, at first sight, might appear to be a likely victory for a French team or driver.

In 1980, the two home teams held four of the first six places on the grid, Alan Jones and Williams starting from fourth and seemingly set to play a bit part. Both Renaults were in trouble from an early stage, but Jacques Laffite had everything in hand as he led the first half of the race. When the Ligier's front tyres began to lose grip, Jones was poised to delight Frank Williams by slicing into the lead and defeating the home favourites at a time when bad feeling was rife between the British teams and the French governing body.

There was no such political backdrop in 2022, but there was a similarity: despite Leclerc and Ferrari having marginally the fastest car, they combined to hand a clear victory to Max Verstappen and Red Bull when the British-based team did not expect such a generous gift.

In truth, the overall picture amounted to more than 25 points. The result of Leclerc's misjudgement as he strayed on to the dust could be added to the error at Imola. Throw in the mechanical failures in Spain and Azerbaijan, plus the team's tactical clumsiness in Monaco and Britain, and the total giveaway was edging towards 100 points.

No rival could afford to be so generous to Red Bull, a team that was ticking every box in terms of strategy and set-up. The RB18 might not have been the quickest car – we're talking fractions of a second that nevertheless add up over the course of a hot afternoon high above the Mediterranean – but the package was being maximised while Ferrari and Leclerc appeared to be doing the reverse.

(Purely as a matter of interest, Jones went on to win the 1980 championship, Williams scoring twice as many points as Ligier.)

Maurice Hamilton

12

FORMULA 1 LENOVO GRAND PRIX DE FRANCE 2022

LE CASTELLET 22-24 JULY

ROLEX

Official Timepiece

RACE DISTANCE: 53 laps, 192.432 miles/309.690km

RACE WEATHER: Dry/sunny (track 53-57°C, air 31-35°C)

CIRCUIT PAUL RICARD, LE CASTELLET

Circuit: 3.630 miles/5.842km, 53 laps

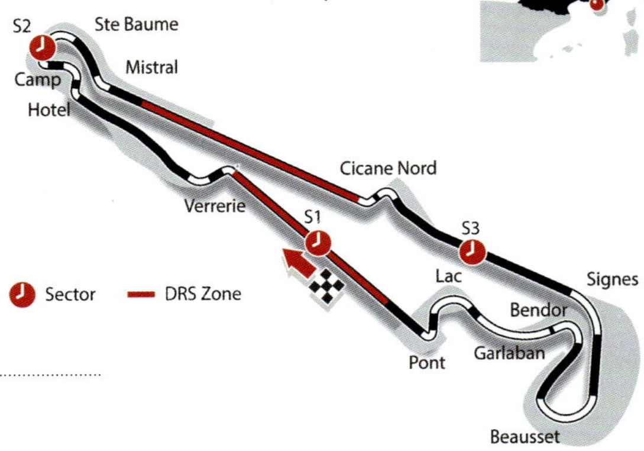

RACE – OFFICIAL CLASSIFICATION

Pos.	Driver	Nat.	No.	Entrant	Car/Engine	Laps	Time/Retirement	Speed (mph/km/h)	Gap to winner	Fastest race lap	
1	**Max Verstappen**	NL	1	Oracle Red Bull Racing	Red Bull RB18-RBPTH001 V6	53	1h 30m 02.112s	128.238/206.379		1m 37.491s	30
2	**Lewis Hamilton**	GB	44	Mercedes-AMG Petronas F1 Team	Mercedes-AMG F1 W13-M13 E Perf. V6	53	1h 30m 12.699s	127.987/205.975	10.587s	1m 37.668s	30
3	**George Russell**	GB	63	Mercedes-AMG Petronas F1 Team	Mercedes-AMG F1 W13-M13 E Perf. V6	53	1h 30m 18.607s	127.848/205.751	16.495s	1m 37.548s	51
4	**Sergio Pérez**	MEX	11	Oracle Red Bull Racing	Red Bull RB18-RBPTH001 V6	53	1h 30m 19.422s	127.828/205.720	17.310s	1m 37.780s	45
5	**Carlos Sainz**	E	55	Scuderia Ferrari	Ferrari F1-75-066/7 V6	53	1h 30m 30.984s *	127.556/205.282	28.872s	1m 35.781s	51
6	**Fernando Alonso**	E	14	BWT Alpine F1 Team	Alpine A522-Renault E-Tech RE22 V6	53	1h 30m 44.991s	127.228/204.754	42.879s	1m 38.160s	53
7	**Lando Norris**	GB	4	McLaren F1 Team	McLaren MCL36-Mercedes F1 M13 E Perf. V6	53	1h 30m 54.138s	127.014/204.410	52.026s	1m 39.037s	43
8	**Esteban Ocon**	F	31	BWT Alpine F1 Team	Alpine A522-Renault E-Tech RE22 V6	53	1h 30m 59.071s *	126.900/204.225	56.959s	1m 38.684s	53
9	**Daniel Ricciardo**	AUS	3	McLaren F1 Team	McLaren MCL36-Mercedes F1 M13 E Perf. V6	53	1h 31m 02.484s	126.821/204.098	1m 00.372s	1m 39.133s	27
10	**Lance Stroll**	CDN	18	Aston Martin Aramco Cognizant F1 Team	Aston Martin AMR22-Mercedes F1 M13 E Perf. V6	53	1h 31m 04.661s	126.770/204.017	1m 02.549s	1m 39.185s	52
11	Sebastian Vettel	D	5	Aston Martin Aramco Cognizant F1 Team	Aston Martin AMR22-Mercedes F1 M13 E Perf. V6	53	1h 31m 06.606s	126.725/203.944	1m 04.494s	1m 39.044s	43
12	Pierre Gasly	F	10	Scuderia AlphaTauri	AlphaTauri AT03-RBPTH001 V6	53	1h 31m 07.560s	126.703/203.908	1m 05.448s	1m 38.786s	53
13	Alexander Albon	T	23	Williams Racing	Williams FW44-Mercedes F1 M13 E Perf. V6	53	1h 31m 10.677s	126.630/203.792	1m 08.565s	1m 39.199s	53
14	Valtteri Bottas	FIN	77	Alfa Romeo F1 Team ORLEN	Alfa Romeo C42-Ferrari 066/7 V6	53	1h 31m 18.778s	126.443/203.491	1m 16.666s	1m 37.963s	52
15	Mick Schumacher	D	47	Haas F1 Team	Haas VF-22-Ferrari 066/7 V6	53	1h 31m 22.506s	126.357/203.352	1m 20.394s	1m 39.068s	48
16	Zhou Guanyu	CHN	24	Alfa Romeo F1 Team ORLEN	Alfa Romeo C42-Ferrari 066/7 V6	47	*power unit* *		6 laps	1m 39.368s	25
	Nicholas Latifi	CDN	6	Williams Racing	Williams FW44-Mercedes F1 M13 E Perf. V6	40	*accident damage*			1m 39.650s	40
	Kevin Magnussen	DK	20	Haas F1 Team	Haas VF-22-Ferrari 066/7 V6	37	*accident damage*			1m 39.265s	11
	Charles Leclerc	MC	16	Scuderia Ferrari	Ferrari F1-75-066/7 V6	17	*accident*			1m 38.088s	4
	Yuki Tsunoda	J	22	Scuderia AlphaTauri	AlphaTauri AT03-RBPTH001 V6	17	*accident damage*			1m 40.216s	4

* Ocon: 5s time penalty for causing a collision with Tsunoda (served at pit stop). * Sainz: 5s time penalty for unsafe release from a pit stop (served at pit stop).

* Zhou: 5s time penalty for causing a collision with Schumacher.

DHL Fastest race lap (scores 1 point): Carlos Sainz on lap 51, 1m 35.781s, 136.438mph/219.575km/h.

Lap record: Sebastian Vettel (Ferrari SF90 V6), 1m 32.740s, 140.912mph/226.775km/h (2019).

19 · SAINZ · Ferrari
Used additional power unit elements; required to start from the back of the grid

17 · SCHUMACHER · Haas

15 · STROLL · Aston Martin

13 · ALBON · Williams

11 · BOTTAS · Alfa Romeo

20 · MAGNUSSEN · Haas
Used additional power unit elements; required to start from the back of the grid·

18 · LATIFI · Williams

16 ·ZHOU · Alfa Romeo

14 · GASLY · AlphaTauri

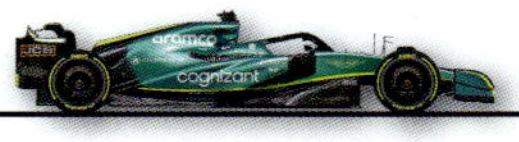

12 · VETTEL · Aston Martin

	Grid order	1	2	3	4	5	6	7	8	9	10	11	12	13	14	15	16	17	18	19	20	21	22	23	24	25	26	27	28	29	30	31	32	33	34	35	36	37	38	39	40	41	42
16	LECLERC	16	16	16	16	16	16	16	16	16	16	16	16	16	16	16	16	16	44	1	1	1	1	1	1	1	1	1	1	1	1	1	1	1	1	1	1	1	1	1	1	1	1
1	VERSTAPPEN	1	1	1	1	1	1	1	1	1	1	1	1	1	1	1	44	44	1	44	44	44	44	44	44	44	44	44	44	44	44	44	44	44	44	44	44	44	44	44	44	44	44
11	PEREZ	44	44	44	44	44	44	44	44	44	44	44	44	44	44	44	11	11	11	11	11	11	11	11	11	11	11	11	11	11	11	11	11	11	11	11	11	11	11	11	11	55	11
44	HAMILTON	11	11	11	11	11	11	11	11	11	11	11	11	11	11	11	63	63	63	63	63	63	63	63	63	63	63	63	63	63	55	55	55	55	55	55	55	55	55	55	55	11	63
4	NORRIS	14	14	63	63	63	63	63	63	63	63	63	63	63	63	63	1	14	14	14	14	14	55	55	55	55	55	55	55	55	63	63	63	63	63	63	63	63	63	63	63	63	14
63	RUSSELL	63	63	14	14	14	14	14	14	14	14	14	14	14	14	14	14	1	5	4	4	55	14	14	14	14	14	14	14	14	14	14	14	14	14	14	14	14	14	14	14	14	4
14	ALONSO	4	4	4	4	4	4	4	4	4	4	4	4	4	4	4	4	4	4	3	3	4	4	4	4	4	4	4	4	4	4	4	4	4	4	4	4	4	4	4	4	4	55
22	TSUNODA	3	3	3	3	3	3	31	31	31	31	31	31	31	31	31	31	31	6	55	55	3	3	3	3	3	3	3	3	3	3	3	3	3	3	3	3	3	3	3	3	3	3
3	RICCIARDO	31	31	31	31	31	31	3	3	3	3	3	3	3	3	3	3	55	3	31	31	31	31	31	31	31	31	31	31	31	31	31	31	31	31	31	31	31	31	31	31	31	31
31	OCON	18	18	18	18	18	18	18	18	18	18	18	18	55	55	55	55	3	55	18	18	18	18	18	18	18	18	18	18	18	18	18	18	18	18	18	18	18	18	18	18	18	18
77	BOTTAS	5	5	5	5	5	5	5	5	5	5	5	55	18	18	18	18	18	31	23	23	23	23	23	23	23	23	23	23	23	23	23	23	23	23	23	23	23	23	5	5	5	5
5	VETTEL	23	20	20	20	20	20	20	55	55	55	55	5	5	5	5	5	5	18	5	10	10	10	10	10	10	10	10	5	5	5	5	5	5	5	5	5	5	5	23	23	23	23
23	ALBON	20	23	23	23	55	55	55	23	23	23	23	23	23	23	23	23	23	23	10	5	5	5	5	5	5	5	5	77	77	77	77	77	77	77	77	10	10	10	10	10	10	10
10	GASLY	47	47	47	55	23	23	23	47	10	10	10	10	10	10	10	10	10	10	6	77	77	77	77	77	77	77	77	20	20	20	20	20	20	20	20	20	20	47	47	47	47	47
18	STROLL	10	10	55	47	47	47	47	10	77	77	77	77	77	6	6	6	6	77	77	6	6	6	20	20	20	20	20	10	10	10	10	10	10	10	10	6	6	77	77	77	77	77
24	ZHOU	77	55	10	10	10	10	10	77	6	6	6	6	6	77	77	77	77	24	24	24	24	20	6	6	6	6	6	6	6	6	6	6	6	6	6	47	47	6	*6*	*6*	*24*	*24*
47	SCHUMACHER	6	77	77	77	77	77	77	6	22	22	20	20	20	20	20	20	20	20	20	20	20	47	47	47	47	47	47	47	47	47	47	47	47	47	47	77	77	*24*	*24*	*24*		
6	LATIFI	55	6	6	6	6	6	6	24	47	20	47	47	47	47	47	47	47	47	47	47	47	24	24	24	24	24	24	24	24	24	24	24	24	24	24	24	*24*					
55	SAINZ	24	24	24	24	24	24	24	22	20	47	22	24	24	24	24	24	24																									
20	MAGNUSSEN	22	22	22	22	22	22	22	20	24	24	24	22	22	22	22	22	22																									
																			SC	SC	SC																						

TIME SHEETS

PRACTICE 1 (FRIDAY)

Weather: Dry/sunny

Temperatures: track 54-55°C, air 31-33°C

Pos.	Driver	Laps	Time
1	Charles Leclerc	23	1m 33.930s
2	Max Verstappen	19	1m 34.021s
3	Carlos Sainz	21	1m 34.268s
4	George Russell	25	1m 34.881s
5	Pierre Gasly	21	1m 34.979s
6	Sergio Pérez	21	1m 35.174s
7	Lando Norris	21	1m 35.232s
8	Alexander Albon	24	1m 35.414s
9	Nyck de Vries	23	1m 35.426s
10	Daniel Ricciardo	21	1m 35.660s
11	Zhou Guanyu	21	1m 35.676s
12	Lance Stroll	19	1m 35.810s
13	Esteban Ocon	21	1m 35.828s
14	Sebastian Vettel	24	1m 35.851s
15	Fernando Alonso	22	1m 35.875s
16	Mick Schumacher	19	1m 36.022s
17	Kevin Magnussen	22	1m 36.104s
18	Yuki Tsunoda	26	1m 36.127s
19	Robert Kubica	19	1m 36.332s
20	Nicholas Latifi	23	1m 37.043s

PRACTICE 2 (SATURDAY)

Weather: Dry/sunny

Temperatures: track 48-53°C, air 32-34°C

Pos.	Driver	Laps	Time
1	Carlos Sainz	22	1m 32.527s
2	Charles Leclerc	22	1m 32.628s
3	Max Verstappen	17	1m 33.077s
4	George Russell	20	1m 33.291s
5	Lewis Hamilton	23	1m 33.517s
6	Lando Norris	21	1m 33.607s
7	Pierre Gasly	24	1m 33.906s
8	Kevin Magnussen	24	1m 33.928s
9	Daniel Ricciardo	23	1m 33.984s
10	Sergio Pérez	16	1m 34.060s
11	Fernando Alonso	24	1m 34.259s
12	Valtteri Bottas	27	1m 34.264s
13	Sebastian Vettel	27	1m 34.420s
14	Yuki Tsunoda	24	1m 34.540s
15	Lance Stroll	26	1m 34.595s
16	Alexander Albon	23	1m 34.653s
17	Zhou Guanyu	26	1m 34.654s
18	Esteban Ocon	26	1m 34.660s
19	Mick Schumacher	22	1m 35.195s
20	Nicholas Latifi	27	1m 35.412s

PRACTICE 3 (SATURDAY)

Weather: Dry/sunny

Temperatures: track 48-52°C, air 31-34°C

Pos.	Driver	Laps	Time
1	Max Verstappen	23	1m 32.272s
2	Carlos Sainz	14	1m 32.626s
3	Charles Leclerc	20	1m 32.909s
4	Lewis Hamilton	22	1m 33.255s
5	Sergio Pérez	25	1m 33.293s
6	George Russell	18	1m 33.376s
7	Fernando Alonso	18	1m 33.505s
8	Alexander Albon	19	1m 33.558s
9	Lando Norris	16	1m 33.669s
10	Yuki Tsunoda	19	1m 33.751s
11	Daniel Ricciardo	17	1m 33.788s
12	Nicholas Latifi	16	1m 33.841s
13	Pierre Gasly	18	1m 33.869s
14	Valtteri Bottas	20	1m 33.872s
15	Zhou Guanyu	19	1m 33.911s
16	Kevin Magnussen	23	1m 34.031s
17	Esteban Ocon	18	1m 34.122s
18	Lance Stroll	20	1m 34.177s
19	Mick Schumacher	12	1m 34.222s
20	Sebastian Vettel	11	1m 34.536s

QUALIFYING (SATURDAY))

Weather: Dry/sunny Temperatures: track 50-55° C, air 31-33° C

Pos.	Driver	First	Second	Third	Qualifying Tyre
1	Charles Leclerc	1m 31.727s	1m 31.216s	1m 30.872s	Soft (n)
2	Max Verstappen	1m 31.891s	1m 31.990s	1m 31.176s	Soft (n)
3	Sergio Pérez	1m 32.354s	1m 32.120s	1m 31.335s	Soft (n)
4	Lewis Hamilton	1m 33.041s	1m 32.274s	1m 31.765s	Soft (n)
5	Lando Norris	1m 32.672s	1m 32.777s	1m 32.032s	Soft (n)
6	George Russell	1m 33.109s	1m 32.633s	1m 32.131s	Soft (n)
7	Fernando Alonso	1m 32.819s	1m 32.631s	1m 32.552s	Soft (n)
8	Yuki Tsunoda	1m 33.394s	1m 32.836s	1m 32.780	Soft (n)
9	Carlos Sainz	1m 32.297s	1m 31.081s	no time	
10	Kevin Magnussen	1m 32.756s	1m 32.649s	no time	
11	Daniel Ricciardo	1m 33.404s	1m 32.922s		
12	Esteban Ocon	1m 33.346s	1m 33.048s		
13	Valtteri Bottas	1m 33.034s	1m 33.052s		
14	Sebastian Vettel	1m 33.285s	1m 33.276s		
15	Alexander Albon	1m 33.423s	1m 33.307s		
16	Pierre Gasly	1m 33.439s			
17	Lance Stroll	1m 33.439s			
18	Zhou Guanyu	1m 33.674s			
19	Mick Schumacher	1m 33.701s			
20	Nicholas Latifi	1m 33.794s			

QUALIFYING: head to head

Hamilton	6	6	Russell
Verstappen	9	3	Pérez
Ricciardo	2	10	Norris
Leclerc	10	2	Sainz
Gasly	8	4	Tsunoda
Hülkenberg	1	1	Stroll
Vettel	8	2	Stroll
Alonso	9	3	Ocon
Bottas	9	3	Zhou
Albon	10	2	Latifi
Magnussen	10	2	Schumacher

Alfa Romeo/ORLEN

FOR THE RECORD

300th GRAND PRIX START: Lewis Hamilton (the sixth driver in F1 history to achieve this)

20th FRONT ROW: Charles Leclerc

6,000th POINT: Red Bull

1,500th LAP LED: Max Verstappen

DID YOU KNOW?

This was the 100th anniversary of Aston Martin making its GP racing debut at the 1922 French GP with the TT1

POINTS

DRIVERS

1	Max Verstappen	233
2	Charles Leclerc	170
3	Sergio Pérez	163
4	Carlos Sainz	144
5	George Russell	143
6	Lewis Hamilton	127
7	Lando Norris	70
8	Esteban Ocon	56
9	Valtteri Bottas	46
10	Fernando Alonso	37
11	Kevin Magnussen	22
12	Daniel Ricciardo	19
13	Pierre Gasly	16
14	Sebastian Vettel	15
15	Mick Schumacher	12
16	Yuki Tsunoda	11
17	Zhou Guanyu	5
18	Lance Stroll	4
19	Alexander Albon	3

CONSTRUCTORS

1	Red Bull	396
2	Ferrari	314
3	Mercedes	270
4	Alpine	93
5	McLaren	89
6	Alfa Romeo	51
7	Haas	34
8	AlphaTauri	27
9	Aston Martin	19
10	Williams	3

9 · RICCIARDO · McLaren

7 · ALONSO · Alpine

5 · NORRIS · McLaren

3 · PÉREZ · Red Bull

1 · LECLERC · Ferrari

10 · OCON · Alpine

8 · TSUNODA · AlphaTauri

6 · RUSSELL · Mercedes

4 · HAMILTON · Mercedes

2 · VERSTAPPEN · Red Bull

43	44	45	46	47	48	49	50	51	52	53	-
1	1	1	1	1	1	1	1	1	1	1	1
44	44	44	44	44	44	44	44	44	44	44	2
11	11	11	11	11	11	11	63	63	63	63	3
63	63	63	63	63	63	63	11	11	11	11	4
14	14	14	14	55	55	55	55	55	55	55	5
4	4	55	55	14	14	14	14	14	14	14	6
3	55	4	4	4	4	4	4	4	4	4	7
55	3	31	31	31	31	31	31	31	31	31	8
31	31	3	3	3	3	3	3	3	3	3	9
18	18	18	18	18	18	18	18	18	18	18	10
5	5	5	5	5	5	5	5	5	5	5	
23	23	23	23	10	10	10	10	10	10	10	
10	10	10	10	23	23	23	23	23	23	23	
47	47	47	47	47	47	47	47	47	77	77	
77	77	77	77	77	77	77	77	77	47	47	
24	*24*	*24*	*24*	*24*							

20 = Pit stop *24 = One lap or more behind*

SC Safety car deployed on laps shown

VSC Virtual safety car deployed on laps shown

VSC

RACE TYRE STRATEGIES

PIRELLI

	Driver	Race Stint 1	Race Stint 2	Race Stint 3
1	Verstappen	Medium (n): 1-16	Hard (n): 17-53	
2	Hamilton	Medium (n): 1-18	Hard (n): 19-53	
3	Russell	Medium (n): 1-18	Hard (u): 19-53	
4	Pérez	Medium (n): 1-18	Hard (n): 19-53	
5	Sainz	Hard (n): 1-18	Medium (n): 19-42	Medium (n): 43-53
6	Alonso	Medium (n): 1-18	Hard (n): 19-53	
7	Norris	Medium (n): 1-18	Hard (n): 19-53	
8	Ocon	Medium (n): 1-18	Hard (n): 19-53	
9	Ricciardo	Medium (n): 1-18	Hard (n): 19-53	
10	Stroll	Medium (u): 1-18	Hard (n): 19-53	
11	Vettel	Medium (u): 1-19	Hard (u): 20-53	
12	Gasly	Hard (n): 1-18	Medium (n): 19-53	
13	Albon	Medium (n): 1-18	Hard (n): 19-53	
14	Bottas	Hard (n): 1-18	Hard (n): 19-36	Medium (n): 37-53
15	Schumacher	Medium (n): 1-9	Hard (n): 10-18	Hard (n): 19-53
16	Zhou	Medium (n): 1-9	Hard (n): 10-22	Hard (n): 23-47 (dnf)
	Latifi	Medium (n): 1-19	Hard (n): 20-38	Medium (n): 39-40 (dnf)
	Magnussen	Medium (n): 1-8	Hard (n): 9-18	Hard (n): 19-37 (dnf)
	Leclerc	Medium (n): 1-17 (dnf)		
	Tsunoda	Medium (n): 1-11	Hard (n): 12-17 (dnf)	

The tyre regulations stipulate that at least two of three dry tyre specifications must be used during a dry race. Selected compounds for Le Castellet: Red = Soft (C4); Yellow = Medium (C3); White = Hard (C2). (n) new (u) used

Mercedes AMG Petronas F1 Team

FIA FORMULA 1 WORLD CHAMPIONSHIP · ROUND 13

HUNGARIAN GRAND PRIX

HUNGARORING CIRCUIT

Red Bull's perfect strategy and lightning-quick pit stops ensured that Max Verstappen could grab his chance of outright victory.
Photo: Red Bull Content Pool/Getty Images

HUNGARORING QUALIFYING

BUDAPEST gave us the most inexplicable grid of the season so far. Although Lewis Hamilton loves Hungaroring, and could boast eight poles and eight victories there, nobody at Mercedes was very optimistic. Although the circuit has a flow to it, there's a lot of slower-speed stuff with traction at a premium. A Silverstone or Barcelona it isn't, and there are also bumps at Turn Four and Turn 11. In short, it appeared to be Ferrari territory.

That's how it looked on Friday, when the ambient was 35 degrees and the track temperature approaching 55. At the head of the pack, it was Charles Leclerc on a 1m 18.3s from Lando Norris, who had delivered what McLaren admitted was a Friday lap with the engine turned up. Carlos Sainz was a hundredth slower in the second Ferrari, and the Mercs were eighth (George Russell) and 11th (Hamilton), the best part of a second away.

The weather forecast for Saturday was very different, though, with qualifying expected to be held in the rain. But as things turned out, only FP3 was affected, and by the time the 4pm qualifying hour ticked around, the track was dry and 'green.'

The first sign of an anomaly came when Mercedes topped Q1, with Hamilton managing 1m 18.374s, and Russell, 1m 18.407s. Sainz was four-hundredths away in the Ferrari, with Max Verstappen's Red Bull a further 0.07s down. Falling at the first hurdle were the two AlphaTauris, the two Williams and Sebastian Vettel's Aston Martin.

The Q2 session looked more representative, as Verstappen improved to 1m 17.7s and topped the times, six-hundredths quicker than Leclerc's Ferrari. Fernando Alonso, quick in the Alpine all weekend, was an excellent third, four-hundredths ahead of compatriot Sainz. But Hamilton was fifth, within three-tenths of the ultimate pace. An unanticipated casualty was Sergio Pérez, who had not been happy with his Red Bull's balance at any point in the weekend. His first run was erroneously deleted for track limits before being reinstated, but he lost time behind Kevin Magnussen on his second and would start 11th. Also taking no further part were Zhou Guanyu, Magnussen, Lance Stroll, who nevertheless had made it out of Q1 for the first time in eight races, and Mick Schumacher.

When it mattered in Q3, it looked as though it was all back to the original script. Ferrari found some additional pace, and it was Carlos Sainz who looked like claiming his second F1 pole with 1m 17.421s. This time, Leclerc had no answer, some 0.14s slower.

"It wasn't a good day for me," Leclerc admitted, after getting a bit crossed up out of Turn One. "I was struggling massively to get the tyres into the single-lap window in Q3. The track changed a bit, the sun came out, the car felt pretty inconsistent and the tyres weren't in the right window. The pace is there, we just need to understand the tyres and come back in the race."

With Pérez already out, there was more Red Bull drama for Verstappen. Having locked up on his first run, his second was scuppered by an MGU-K issue, which prompted more than one expletive. The world champion would start tenth, just one place ahead of his team-mate at a circuit reputed to be the most difficult for overtaking, after Monaco.

So, a gilt-edged opportunity for Ferrari, then? But hold on. When Russell steamed through Turn One, his Mercedes dash told him that he was 0.15s up on his previous best. By the time he was through Turn Two, that delta was up to 0.3s. 'Mr Saturday' had driven some pretty spectacular qualifying laps in his relatively short F1 career, in 2021 at Spa in particular. But this one, he felt, was even better, amazingly giving him his first ever F1 pole with 1m 17.377s! Cue disbelieving faces on the Ferrari pit wall.

"I can't quite believe it myself," Russell admitted. "We probably had the toughest Friday of the season: here until 11pm, scratching our heads and with morale pretty low. To get the pole just 24 hours later is just such a feeling! It's pretty huge for the team.

"Today, we got the car perfectly in the window. And the lap here feels very special because there is such a rhythm and flow to it, and when you get it completely hooked up, it's a fantastic feeling. No matter how many qualifying sessions I do, I don't think I'll ever have one that comes close to the feelings I had in Spa, and here. And this one is probably the best."

What of his team-mate? Hamilton could have been right in the mix, too, but had a DRS issue and aborted his second run. He would line up only seventh, three-quarters of a second behind Russell."

Although quick to congratulate Russell, Sainz's face betrayed his disappointment at not claiming a second F1 pole just three races after his first. "I thought I had things more or less under control, but my Q3 runs were nothing special. We were struggling a bit to get the tyres up to temperature over one lap, so I'm a bit disappointed," he admitted.

Fourth place on the grid was the reward for a great lap by Lando Norris in the first McLaren, more than six-tenths quicker than under-fire team-mate Daniel Ricciardo, who would start ninth.

It was a close scrap between the Alpine twins, with a 1m 18.018s lap from Esteban Ocon and 1m 18.078s from Fernando Alonso as *'les bleues'* continued their battle with McLaren over fourth place in the constructors' championship. Little did we know that in just a couple of days' time would come confirmation of Alonso's shock move to Aston Martin for 2023 after Vettel called time on his ultra-successful career (see Viewpoint).

Just a hundredth of a second behind Hamilton, there was a happy return to the top ten qualifiers for Valtteri Bottas in the Alfa Romeo, some six races after he had last achieved the feat.

AS race start time approached, there was a 40 per cent chance of rain over the following couple of hours, but it was just light spots as George Russell watched the lights intently from his first F1 pole. His reaction time was good and he steamed down to Turn One in front. Carlos Sainz had a look around the outside, but Russell covered him.

Tyre choice and strategy were interesting. Mercedes, concerned about opening-lap tyre warm-up, had sent Russell to the grid on used soft-compound Pirellis, while both Ferraris would start on new mediums. Fourth-placed Lando Norris had also gone for used softs, while both Alpines and Lewis Hamilton had opted for new mediums, as had Valtteri Bottas. Daniel Ricciardo, like his team-mate, was on used softs, as was Max Verstappen, starting tenth after his qualifying fiasco.

After just a lap, we had a VSC while debris from a damaged front wing on Alex Albon's Williams was removed, following contact with Sebastian Vettel. The first four across the line at the end of the opening lap were in grid order – Russell, Sainz, Charles Leclerc and Norris. Hamilton had jumped the Esteban Ocon/Fernando Alonso Alpines, which had rather tripped themselves up.

"Never in my life have I seen defence like Esteban," Alonso claimed, obviously unimpressed.

Verstappen was already up two places to eighth, as was team-mate Sergio Pérez behind him, with Kevin Magnussen tenth. Then came Ricciardo, Mick Schumacher, Bottas (down five places), Lance Stroll, Albon, Yuki Tsunoda, Zhou Guanyu, Vettel, Nicholas Latifi and Pierre Gasly, who had started from the back with a fresh Honda power unit.

Russell, on the softer tyres, was able to keep the Ferraris in check early on, while Verstappen moved up to seventh when he demoted Alonso's Alpine. Out of Turn Three, Fernando got a bit squirrely, and as he regained the track, he found the Red Bull already there and lifted, discretion being the better part of valour.

Vertappen's progress continued on lap seven, when he demoted Ocon's Alpine down the inside of Turn One and set off after Hamilton. Pérez, meanwhile, bravely drove around the outside of Alonso in Turn Two to move up into eighth.

After ten laps, Russell was still hanging on in front, with Sainz's Ferrari 2.3s back and Leclerc just 1.3s further in arrears. Norris was running 4s behind the second Ferrari, leading a three-car train that also included Hamilton and Verstappen, with Pérez some 2.5s behind his team leader.

Starting lap 12, Hamilton got a move done on Norris down the inside of Turn One to take fourth, Lando losing another slot as Verstappen followed his 2021 foe through on the run into Turn Two. Next lap, Norris lost another position as Pérez displaced him at Turn One once again.

McLaren was not in a race with Red Bull, however. More important was their constructors' fight with Alpine, and on that score, they were doing okay. Norris was 4s clear of Ocon, who had team-mate Alonso just 1.5s behind, then Ricciardo in the second McLaren 4s further back – so good symmetry there.

With 16 of the 71 laps completed, Ferrari instructed Sainz

Above: Carlos Sainz attempts to wrest the lead from George Russell at the first turn.
Photo: Lukas Gorys

Top left: Mike Krack and Tom McCullough discuss their options.
Photo: Aston Martin Aramco Cognizant F1 Team

Top centre: I can't quite believe it! Russell after taking his first pole.
Photo: XPB Images

Top: McLaren's Andreas Seidl keeps an eye on the weather.
Photo: McLaren F1 Team

Centre left: Williams' Nicholas Latifi topped the rain-lashed FP3 times.
Photo: Williams Racing

Left: A face like thunder. Sainz ponders losing pole position to Russell.
Photo: Peter Nygaard/GP Photo

Above: Having started on soft Pirellis from tenth on the grid, Red Bull's Max Verstappen soon carved his way through the field.
Photo: Red Bull Content Pool/Getty Images

Top right: A resigned look from a Ferrari crew member sums up Maranello's disappointing day.
Photo: Scuderia Ferrari

Top far right: Once again, Adrian Newey and the Red Bull team had all the answers on race-day.
Photo: Red Bull Content Pool/Getty Images

Above right: Sebastian Vettel snatched tenth place, and the final championship point, from team-mate Lance Stroll.
Photo: Aston Martin Aramco Cognizant F1 Team

Right: Good strategy and a controlled drive by Lewis Hamilton were rewarded with a very competitive second place for Mercedes.
Photo: Mercedes-AMG Petronas F1 Team

to "box". It proved to be a dummy call, however, with Russell heading to the pit lane, presumably to cover him, while Carlos stayed out!

Russell had a set of mediums bolted on and rejoined fifth, just managing to hold off Alonso's Alpine. Sainz was in next lap, a 3.7s stop not helping his cause, and putting him out still behind Russell and the yet-to-stop Ocon. He'd also gone on to a second set of mediums, which meant that Ferrari would be stopping again.

Less-than-perfect stops for both Russell and Sainz might have given an overcut opportunity – tough to achieve in Hungary – to Leclerc, who stayed circulating five laps longer than Russell.

Pérez pitted to jettison his used softs 18 laps into the race and, like Verstappen, took on mediums. Hamilton was in a lap later, Mercedes fitting another set of mediums, which told you that another stop was planned for Lewis, too.

Leclerc was finally called in on lap 21, and when Ferrari also fitted a second set of mediums, it confirmed that he was on a two-stopper as well. He had actually done enough to overcut his team-mate and emerge just 1.8s behind Russell's leading Mercedes.

When Ocon pitted, he came back out just as team-mate Alonso and Daniel Ricciardo were bearing down upon him. Both Alpines had been fitted with Pirelli's hard compound at their stops, with the obvious intention of running to the end, so this was important between them for track position.

When Alonso attempted to go around the outside of Turn Two, Ocon, still getting his tyres up to temperature, ran him wide, and a grateful Ricciardo slipped down the inside of both on exit. If Alonso had been unimpressed with Esteban's start, no doubt he was positively seething by now!

By one-third-distance, Leclerc, on tyres five laps fresher than Russell's, had closed down the leader and was looking to go by. George was not about to let go without a fight, though, and defended manfully for three or four laps, protecting the inside at Turn One and then driving Leclerc wide as the Ferrari looked at the outside of Turn Two.

With Sainz just 2.3s seconds behind and Verstappen closing in, and now just a similar distance behind the second Ferrari, Leclerc didn't want to waste any more time. Starting on lap 31, he came from quite a long way back with DRS, dummied inside into Turn One and then swept around the outside, giving Russell a quick chop to get his nose in front.

After a 22-lap stint on his mediums, Verstappen was called in again after 38 laps to go on to another set. He was on his way again in a rapid 2.4s, pitting out sixth, behind Hamilton and team-mate Pérez. The undercut looked set to leapfrog Verstappen ahead of Sainz and possibly Russell.

Mercedes responded by bringing in Russell, while Ferrari did the same with leader Leclerc, leaving Sainz out in the knowledge that they had probably already lost the Spaniard's position to Red Bull. But whereas Verstappen had been given mediums, having started on the softs, Leclerc had to take on something other than the yellow-walled tyre. With just over 30 laps remaining, Ferrari opted for hards rather than softs. Russell, having started on the soft, also went the medium-compound route.

Pérez, with a stop yet to make, was briefly ahead of Verstappen, but was moved smartly out of the way as the world champion started to close down the Ferrari on his quicker tyres. Given that the Alpines had struggled since going on to the hard tyre, Ferrari's decision seemed questionable, with even a conversion to a three-stopper and two sets of softs possibly the better option, or running Leclerc longer, then putting him on softs. With hindsight, easy to say perhaps.

It took Verstappen no time at all to displace the Ferrari into Turn One.

"The tyres are ****" Leclerc told the Ferrari pit-wall crew.

It wasn't quite over yet, though. Verstappen locked up and suffered a quick spin into the penultimate corner, letting Leclerc back in front. By the time he regained the track, he was just ahead of team-mate Pérez, while Russell was bearing down on them on the main straight. The Mercedes

CEVA

aramco
aramco
aramco
aramco
cognizant
cognizant

PETRONAS
PETRONAS
Syntium
PETRONAS
Syntium
INEOS

Above: Russell enjoyed a good mid-race tussle with Leclerc before the Ferrari challenge faded.
Photo: Mercedes-AMG Petronas F1 Team

Top right: All seemed sweetness and light between Alpine's Otmar Szafnauer and Fernando Alonso at the driver's 41st birthday celebrations.
Photo: Alpine F1 Team

Above right: A cheery Vettel announced his plans for retirement from Formula 1 at the end of the year, setting off a chain reaction in the driver market for 2023.
Photo: Aston Martin Aramco Cognizant F1 Team

Right: The victorious Verstappen jumps into the welcoming embrace of Red Bull's Helmut Marko and Christian Horner.
Photo: Red Bull Content Pool/Getty Images

demoted Pérez, but couldn't quite get Verstappen on lap 42.

The Dutchman was right back with Leclerc for third by lap 45. Ferrari's hope was that the latter's hards were properly in by now and, with Verstappen's mediums a few laps older, that passing might be a difficult proposition. It wasn't, though, Max going by out of Turn One as Charles struggled for traction.

Lewis Hamilton briefly led the Hungarian GP for three laps when Sainz made his second stop for used softs, no doubt a strategy Leclerc wished Ferrari had adopted for him, especially in view of a four-lap-longer starting stint. Not to mention the poor pace Alpine had shown since bolting on the hard tyre...

When Hamilton pitted on lap 51 and rejoined on softs, Verstappen was leading by 5.5s from Leclerc, who had his hands full with Russell. He managed to fend him off for a few laps before the Mercedes took second place around the outside into Turn One, whereupon Ferrari pitted Leclerc for a third time. They swapped the hard tyres for a set of used softs, but cost their driver 20s in the process. That would translate into a very disappointing sixth place.

With eight to go, Hamilton was with Sainz's third-placed Ferrari, blasting by on the main straight. Now he was only 1.4s behind team-mate Russell. After just a couple of laps, Lewis used the superior grip of his softs to switch back inside at Turn One, floored the throttle and accelerated past the pole-man into second place. Verstappen's Red Bull, on its harder medium-compound tyres, was 10s up the road, which looked like a bridge too far.

And so it proved, but not before a sprinkling of rain threatened to spice up the final lap. Verstappen tip-toed around it, being cautious with his throttle application, and took the chequer just under 8s ahead of a fine drive from Hamilton, who had also netted an additional point for fastest lap on his soft tyres.

Russell made it two Mercedes drivers on the podium, with Sainz fourth, a second clear of Pérez, the frustrated Leclerc and then a distant Norris. Next came the two Alpines, which had fallen away on the hard tyre, as had Ricciardo (all the way to 15th). Vettel scored the final point for Aston Martin right on Ocon's tail.

Post-race, Verstappen revealed how, once more, Red Bull's fleetness of foot had been important, given the lack of performance of the hard-compound rubber. Out of position, tenth on the grid, he had actually been planning to start on it and run a long opening stint.

"But then, when I went to the grid on the soft tyres, I was already struggling for grip," Max explained, "so I was like, 'No way we're going to start on the hards.' It's also credit to the team because we'd planned the strategy around them and then we switched to a soft. I had a lot of confidence in them just changing it around. I'm very happy that we did because the hard tyre was really, really tough. You could see that with Charles sliding around so much. After we made up our minds with the soft, the hard was never a consideration."

Hamilton was delighted with his best result of the season: "I was definitely struggling at the beginning and wasn't sure whether I'd be able to catch the guys up. But, bit by bit, I got more comfortable with the balance. And, really unlucky for George today. The other guys still have a bit of an edge, but we're clearly closing the gap. This is just an amazing way to go into the break with this performance."

And, after the summer break, at Spa, would the FIA's new porpoising rule amendments bring the multiple constructors' champions closer still? Interesting times.

Tony Dodgins

VIEWPOINT
SILLY SEASON GETS SERIOUS

ON the Thursday before the Hungarian Grand Prix, Sebastian Vettel revealed that he would be retiring at the end of the season. In many ways, this was no surprise. Seb had turned 35 a few weeks before, and the future was hardly bright for the four-time world champion, particularly with Aston Martin languishing near the bottom of the championship table, ninth. Making this decision just after the halfway point in the season would allow plenty of time for Aston to sort a replacement. They would do it faster than anyone imagined!

Early on the Monday following Hungary, it was announced that Fernando Alonso would swap teams for the seventh time. This was a surprise on many counts, not least to Alpine, who had departed for the summer break believing that Alonso had agreed terms and would be extending his contract to the end of 2023.

Apart from bringing an abrupt end to the Silly Season preoccupation with trying to guess the name of Vettel's replacement – Nico Hülkenberg and Nyck de Vries were mentioned – Alonso's announcement had torpedoed Alpine's plans. And it was about to get worse for the Anglo/French alliance.

The only good thing associated with Alonso's decision to leave was the solving of the 'What do we do with Oscar?' problem as Alpine sought to find a drive for Piastri, their F2 championship-winning reserve driver. The way was now clear for the Australian to join Esteban Ocon, who was staying on board for a fourth season. Alpine duly gathered themselves in the wake of the Alonso bombshell and confirmed Ocon/Piastri for 2023.

But not so fast! Piastri wasted no time in saying on social media that he had no contract with Alpine for 2023 and would be off someplace else. At least guessing his likely destination briefly gave Silly Season devotees some excitement, until it emerged that Daniel Ricciardo would not stay at McLaren in 2023, and that Piastri was likely to land there. It looked like being a busy summer break for the lawyers and the Contract Recognition Board...

Maurice Hamilton

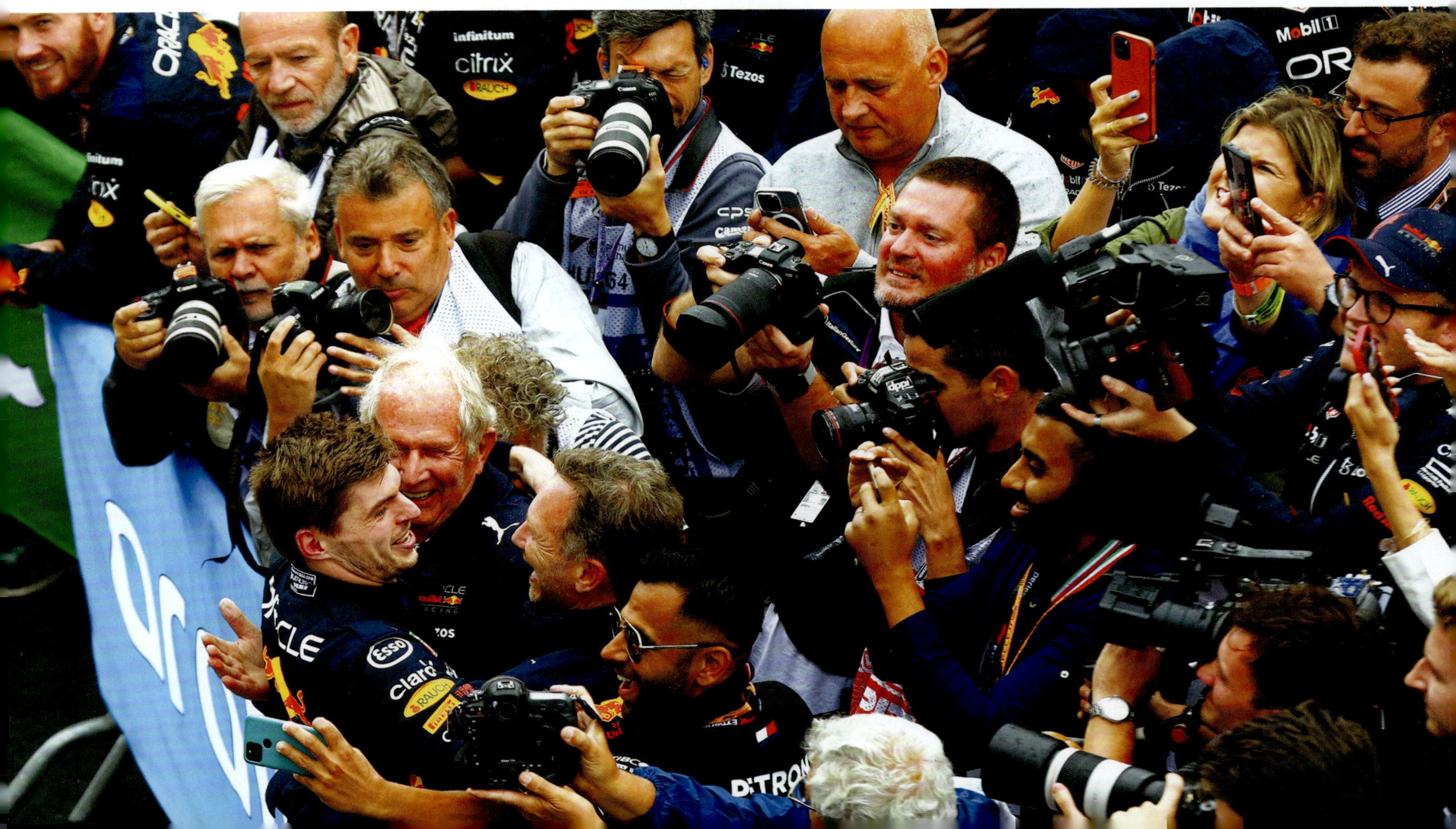

13

FORMULA 1 ARAMCO MAGYAR NAGYDÍJ 2022

ROLEX

Official Timepiece

HUNGARORING, MOGYORÓD, BUDAPEST
Circuit: 2.722 miles/4.381km, 70 laps

BUDAPEST 29-31 JULY

RACE DISTANCE: 70 laps, 190.531 miles/306.630km

RACE WEATHER: Dry/cloudy (track 24-29°C, air 19-21°C)

RACE – OFFICIAL CLASSIFICATION

Pos.	Driver	Nat.	No.	Entrant	Car/Engine	Laps	Time/Retirement	Speed (mph/km/h)	Gap to winner	Fastest race lap	
1	**Max Verstappen**	NL	1	Oracle Red Bull Racing	Red Bull RB18-RBPTH001 V6	70	1h 39m 35.912s	114.779/184.719		1m 22.126s	45
2	**Lewis Hamilton**	GB	44	Mercedes-AMG Petronas F1 Team	Mercedes-AMG F1 W13-M13 E Perf. V6	70	1h 39m 43.746s	114.629/184.477	7.834s	1m 21.386s	57
3	**George Russell**	GB	63	Mercedes-AMG Petronas F1 Team	Mercedes-AMG F1 W13-M13 E Perf. V6	70	1h 39m 48.249s	114.543/184.339	12.337s	1m 22.766s	57
4	**Carlos Sainz**	E	55	Scuderia Ferrari	Ferrari F1-75-066/7 V6	70	1h 39m 50.491s	114.500/184.270	14.579s	1m 22.000s	51
5	**Sergio Pérez**	MEX	11	Oracle Red Bull Racing	Red Bull RB18-RBPTH001 V6	70	1h 39m 51.600s	114.478/184.235	15.688s	1m 21.940s	44
6	**Charles Leclerc**	MC	16	Scuderia Ferrari	Ferrari F1-75-066/7 V6	70	1h 39m 51.959s	114.471/184.224	16.047s	1m 21.622s	57
7	**Lando Norris**	GB	4	McLaren F1 Team	McLaren MCL36-Mercedes F1 M13 E Perf. V6	70	1h 40m 54.212s	113.308/182.352	1m 18.300s	1m 23.043s	47
8	**Fernando Alonso**	E	14	BWT Alpine F1 Team	Alpine A522-Renault E-Tech RE22 V6	69			1 lap	1m 23.979s	47
9	**Esteban Ocon**	F	31	BWT Alpine F1 Team	Alpine A522-Renault E-Tech RE22 V6	69			1 lap	1m 24.149s	60
10	**Sebastian Vettel**	D	5	Aston Martin Aramco Cognizant F1 Team	Aston Martin AMR22-Mercedes F1 M13 E Perf. V6	69			1 lap	1m 22.824s	51
11	Lance Stroll	CDN	18	Aston Martin Aramco Cognizant F1 Team	Aston Martin AMR22-Mercedes F1 M13 E Perf. V6	69			1 lap	1m 22.437s	51
12	Pierre Gasly	F	10	Scuderia AlphaTauri	AlphaTauri AT03-RBPTH001 V6	69			1 lap	1m 23.199s	58
13	Zhou Guanyu	CHN	24	Alfa Romeo F1 Team ORLEN	Alfa Romeo C42-Ferrari 066/7 V6	69			1 lap	1m 22.029s	58
14	Mick Schumacher	D	47	Haas F1 Team	Haas VF-22-Ferrari 066/7 V6	69			1 lap	1m 23.151s	50
15	Daniel Ricciardo	AUS	3	McLaren F1 Team	McLaren MCL36-Mercedes F1 M13 E Perf. V6	69	*		1 lap	1m 23.654s	63
16	Kevin Magnussen	DK	20	Haas F1 Team	Haas VF-22-Ferrari 066/7 V6	69			1 lap	1m 23.511s	37
17	Alexander Albon	T	23	Williams Racing	Williams FW44-Mercedes F1 M13 E Perf. V6	69			1 lap	1m 23.047s	43
18	Nicholas Latifi	CDN	6	Williams Racing	Williams FW44-Mercedes F1 M13 E Perf. V6	69			1 lap	1m 22.478s	60
19	Yuki Tsunoda	J	22	Scuderia AlphaTauri	AlphaTauri AT03-RBPTH001 V6	68			2 laps	1m 23.538s	58
20	Valtteri Bottas	FIN	77	Alfa Romeo F1 Team ORLEN	Alfa Romeo C42-Ferrari 066/7 V6	65	*power unit*		5 laps		

* Ricciardo: 5s time penalty for causing a collision with Stroll (originally finished 13th).

DHL Fastest race lap (scores 1 point): Lewis Hamilton on lap 57, 1m 21.386s, 120.414mph/193.787km/h.

Lap record: Lewis Hamilton (Mercedes F1 W11 V6), 1m 16.627s, 127.892mph/205.823km/h (2020).

19 · LATIFI · Williams

17 · ALBON · Williams

15 · SCHUMACHER · Haas

13 · MAGNUSSEN · Haas

11 · PÉREZ · Red Bull

20 · GASLY · AlphaTauri
Car modified in parc fermé; required to start from the pit lane; additional power unit elements used

18 · VETTEL · Aston Martin

16 · TSUNODA · AlphaTauri

14 · STROLL · Aston Martin

12 · ZHOU · Alfa Romeo

Grid order		1	2	3	4	5	6	7	8	9	10	11	12	13	14	15	16	17	18	19	20	21	22	23	24	25	26	27
63	RUSSELL	63	63	63	63	63	63	63	63	63	63	63	63	63	63	63	55	16	16	16	16	16	63	63	63	63	63	63
55	SAINZ	55	55	55	55	55	55	55	55	55	55	55	55	55	55	55	16	55	44	44	63	63	16	16	16	16	16	16
16	LECLERC	16	16	16	16	16	16	16	16	16	16	16	16	16	16	16	63	44	11	63	55	55	55	55	55	55	55	55
4	NORRIS	4	4	4	4	4	4	4	4	4	4	4	44	44	44	44	44	11	63	55	31	1	1	1	1	1	1	1
31	OCON	44	44	44	44	44	44	44	44	44	44	44	1	1	1	1	1	31	31	31	1	31	31	44	44	44	44	44
14	ALONSO	31	31	31	31	31	31	1	1	1	1	1	4	11	11	11	11	63	55	14	14	14	44	31	11	11	11	11
44	HAMILTON	14	14	14	14	1	1	31	31	11	11	11	11	4	31	31	31	14	14	1	44	44	11	11	4	4	4	4
77	BOTTAS	1	1	1	1	14	14	11	11	31	31	31	31	31	14	14	14	1	1	47	47	11	4	4	77	77	24	3
3	RICCIARDO	11	11	11	11	11	11	14	14	14	14	14	14	14	4	47	47	47	47	77	11	4	77	77	24	24	77	24
1	VERSTAPPEN	20	20	20	20	20	3	3	3	3	3	3	3	3	3	77	77	77	77	11	77	77	24	24	3	3	3	31
11	PEREZ	3	3	3	3	3	47	47	47	47	47	47	47	47	47	3	24	24	24	24	4	24	14	14	31	31	31	18
24	ZHOU	47	23	47	47	47	20	77	77	77	77	77	77	77	77	24	4	4	4	4	24	47	3	3	14	14	14	14
20	MAGNUSSEN	77	47	77	77	77	77	18	18	18	18	18	18	18	5	5	10	6	6	3	3	3	18	18	18	18	18	5
18	STROLL	18	77	18	18	18	18	22	22	22	5	5	5	5	24	10	6	3	3	18	18	18	5	5	5	5	5	10
47	SCHUMACHER	23	18	22	22	22	22	5	5	5	22	22	22	24	18	6	23	23	18	5	5	5	47	22	22	22	10	77
22	TSUNODA	22	22	5	5	5	5	24	24	24	24	24	24	10	10	4	3	18	23	23	23	22	22	47	10	10	22	22
23	ALBON	24	24	24	24	24	24	6	6	10	10	10	10	22	6	23	18	5	5	22	22	10	10	10	47	47	47	47
5	VETTEL	5	5	6	6	6	6	10	10	6	6	6	6	6	23	18	5	22	22	20	10	23	20	20	20	20	20	20
6	LATIFI	6	6	10	10	10	10	23	23	23	23	23	23	23	20	22	22	20	20	10	20	20	6	6	6	6	6	6
10	GASLY	10	10	23	23	23	23	20	20	20	20	20	20	20	22	20	20	10	10	6	6	6	23	23	23	23	23	23
			VSC	VSC																								

Grid order		28	29	30	31	32	33	34	35	36	37	38	39	40	41	42	43	44	45	46	47	48	49	50	51	52	53	54
63	RUSSELL	63	63	63	16	16	16	16	16	16	16	16	16	55	55	55	55	55	55	55	44	44	44	44	1	1	1	1
55	SAINZ	16	16	16	63	63	63	63	63	63	63	63	55	44	44	44	44	44	44	44	55	1	1	1	44	16	16	63
16	LECLERC	55	55	55	55	55	55	55	55	55	55	55	63	16	16	16	16	16	1	1	1	16	16	16	16	63	63	55
4	NORRIS	1	1	1	1	1	1	1	1	1	1	1	44	1	1	1	1	1	16	16	16	63	63	63	63	55	55	16
31	OCON	44	44	44	44	44	44	44	44	44	44	44	11	11	11	63	63	63	63	63	63	55	55	55	55	44	44	44
14	ALONSO	11	11	11	11	11	11	11	11	11	11	11	1	63	63	11	11	11	11	11	11	11	11	11	11	11	11	11
44	HAMILTON	4	4	4	4	4	4	4	4	4	4	4	4	4	4	4	3	3	3	4	4	4	4	4	4	4	4	4
77	BOTTAS	3	3	3	3	3	3	3	3	3	3	3	3	3	3	3	18	18	18	3	14	14	14	14	14	14	14	14
3	RICCIARDO	31	18	18	18	18	18	18	18	18	18	18	18	18	18	18	4	4	4	18	31	31	31	31	31	31	31	31
1	VERSTAPPEN	18	31	31	31	31	31	31	31	31	31	5	5	5	5	5	5	5	5	14	77	77	77	77	77	77	77	77
11	PEREZ	14	14	14	5	5	5	5	5	5	5	31	31	31	14	14	14	14	14	31	3	3	18	18	18	18	18	18
24	ZHOU	5	5	5	14	14	14	14	14	14	14	14	14	14	31	31	31	31	31	5	24	18	3	3	5	5	5	5
20	MAGNUSSEN	10	10	10	10	10	10	10	10	10	10	10	10	10	10	10	10	10	10	77	18	24	5	5	3	3	3	3
18	STROLL	77	77	77	77	77	77	77	77	77	77	77	77	77	77	77	77	77	77	10	5	5	24	24	10	10	10	10
47	SCHUMACHER	22	22	22	22	22	47	47	47	47	47	24	24	24	24	24	24	24	24	24	10	10	10	10	24	47	47	47
22	TSUNODA	47	47	47	47	47	24	24	24	24	24	47	47	47	47	47	47	47	47	47	47	47	47	47	47	20	20	20
23	ALBON	24	24	24	24	24	22	6	6	6	6	6	6	23	20	20	20	20	20	20	20	20	20	20	20	6	6	6
5	VETTEL	6	6	6	6	6	6	20	20	23	23	23	23	20	6	6	6	6	6	6	6	6	6	6	6	23	23	23
6	LATIFI	20	20	20	20	20	20	23	23	20	20	20	20	6	22	22	22	22	23	23	23	23	23	23	23	24	24	24
10	GASLY	23	23	23	23	23	23	22	22	22	22	22	22	22	23	23	23	23	22	22	22	22	22	22	22	22	22	22

VSC Virtual safety car deployed on laps shown

TIME SHEETS

PRACTICE 1 (FRIDAY)

Weather: Dry/sunny

Temperatures: track 46-55°C, air 34-37°C

Pos.	Driver	Laps	Time
1	Carlos Sainz	26	1m 18.750s
2	Max Verstappen	24	1m 18.880s
3	Charles Leclerc	26	1m 19.039s
4	Lando Norris	21	1m 19.299s
5	George Russell	28	1m 19.606s
6	Sergio Pérez	24	1m 19.622s
7	Lewis Hamilton	25	1m 19.710s
8	Daniel Ricciardo	28	1m 19.841s
9	Esteban Ocon	30	1m 20.348s
10	Fernando Alonso	27	1m 20.377s
11	Sebastian Vettel	26	1m 20.383s
12	Lance Stroll	25	1m 20.414s
13	Pierre Gasly	28	1m 20.456s
14	Yuki Tsunoda	27	1m 20.695s
15	Zhou Guanyu	23	1m 20.810s
16	Alexander Albon	28	1m 20.834s
17	Kevin Magnussen	24	1m 20.921s
18	Mick Schumacher	25	1m 21.027s
19	Robert Kubica	20	1m 21.179s
20	Nicholas Latifi	27	1m 21.413s

PRACTICE 2 (FRIDAY)

Weather: Dry/sunny

Temperatures: track 45-50°C, air 35-37°C

Pos.	Driver	Laps	Time
1	Charles Leclerc	27	1m 18.445s
2	Lando Norris	29	1m 18.662s
3	Carlos Sainz	29	1m 18.676s
4	Max Verstappen	26	1m 18.728s
5	Daniel Ricciardo	27	1m 18.872s
6	Fernando Alonso	30	1m 19.049s
7	Sebastian Vettel	31	1m 19.253s
8	George Russell	28	1m 19.355s
9	Sergio Pérez	28	1m 19.397s
10	Valtteri Bottas	30	1m 19.411s
11	Lewis Hamilton	23	1m 19.547s
12	Zhou Guanyu	26	1m 19.605s
13	Esteban Ocon	27	1m 19.614s
14	Lance Stroll	30	1m 19.702s
15	Pierre Gasly	28	1m 19.730s
16	Kevin Magnussen	29	1m 19.818s
17	Mick Schumacher	28	1m 19.985s
18	Nicholas Latifi	30	1m 20.488s
19	Yuki Tsunoda	31	1m 20.521s
20	Alexander Albon	20	1m 20.615s

PRACTICE 3 (SATURDAY)

Weather: Wet/overcast

Temperatures: track 23-31°C, air 20-22°C

Pos.	Driver	Laps	Time
1	Nicholas Latifi	17	1m 41.480s
2	Mick Schumacher	14	1m 42.141s
3	Alexander Albon	19	1m 42.381s
4	Max Verstappen	10	1m 43.205s
5	George Russell	13	1m 43.434s
6	Fernando Alonso	16	1m 43.570s
7	Carlos Sainz	15	1m 43.589s
8	Lando Norris	13	1m 43.743s
9	Sebastian Vettel	14	1m 44.178s
10	Kevin Magnussen	20	1m 44.655s
11	Lewis Hamilton	11	1m 44.832s
12	Mick Schumacher	18	1m 45.156s
13	Esteban Ocon	17	1m 45.570s
14	Daniel Ricciardo	11	1m 45.624s
15	Lance Stroll	17	1m 45.638s
16	Zhou Guanyu	17	1m 45.691s
17	Yuki Tsunoda	17	1m 45.850s
18	Valtteri Bottas	20	1m 45.930s
19	Pierre Gasly	18	1m 46.091s
20	Sergio Pérez	11	1m 48.240s

QUALIFYING (SATURDAY))

Weather: Dry/cloudy Temperatures: track 30-33°C, air 21-25°C

Pos.	Driver	First	Second	Third	Qualifying Tyre
1	George Russell	1m 18.407s	1m 18.154s	1m 17.377s	Soft (n)
2	Carlos Sainz	1m 18.434s	1m 17.946s	1m 17.421s	Soft (n)
3	Charles Leclerc	1m 18.806s	1m 17.768s	1m 17.567s	Soft (n)
4	Lando Norris	1m 18.653s	1m 18.121s	1m 17.769s	Soft (n)
5	Esteban Ocon	1m 18.866s	1m 18.216s	1m 18.018s	Soft (n)
6	Fernando Alonso	1m 18.716s	1m 17.904s	1m 18.078s	Soft (n)
7	Lewis Hamilton	1m 18.374s	1m 18.035s	1m 18.142s	Soft (n)
8	Valtteri Bottas	1m 18.935s	1m 18.445s	1m 18.157s	Soft (n)
9	Daniel Ricciardo	1m 18.775s	1m 18.198s	1m 18.379s	Soft (n)
10	Max Verstappen	1m 18.509s	1m 17.703s	1m 18.823s	Soft (n)
11	Sergio Pérez	1m 19.118s	1m 18.516s		
12	Zhou Guanyu	1m 18.973s	1m 18.573s		
13	Kevin Magnussen	1m 18.993s	1m 18.825s		
14	Lance Stroll	1m 19.205s	1m 19.137s		
15	Mick Schumacher	1m 19.164s	1m 19.202s		
16	Yuki Tsunoda	1m 19.240s			
17	Alexander Albon	1m 19.256s			
18	Sebastian Vettel	1m 19.273s			
19	Pierre Gasly	1m 19.527s			
20	Nicholas Latifi	1m 19.570s			

QUALIFYING: head to head

Hamilton	6	7	Russell
Verstappen	10	3	Pérez
Ricciardo	2	11	Norris
Leclerc	10	3	Sainz
Gasly	8	5	Tsunoda
Hülkenberg	1	1	Stroll
Vettel	8	3	Stroll
Alonso	9	4	Ocon
Bottas	10	3	Zhou
Albon	11	2	Latifi
Magnussen	11	2	Schumacher

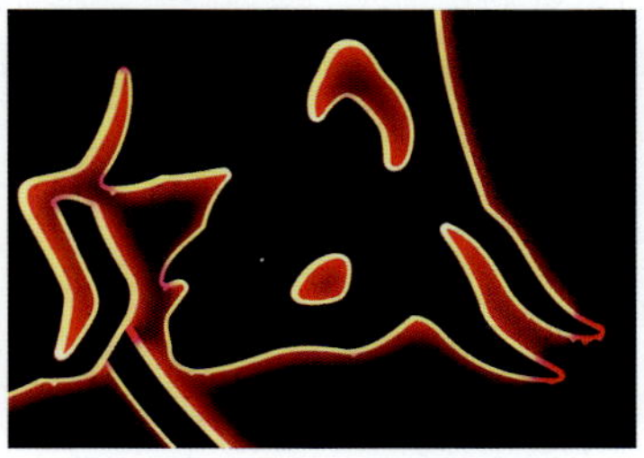

Red Bull Content Pool/Getty Images

FOR THE RECORD

1st POLE POSITION: George Russell

70th PODIUM: Max Verstappen

1,500th LAP LED: Max Verstappen

DID YOU KNOW?

Red Bull have previously only won one race from as low as 10th on the grid – Daniel Ricciardo at the 2017 Azerbaijan GP.

POINTS

DRIVERS

1	Max Verstappen	258
2	Charles Leclerc	178
3	Sergio Pérez	173
4	George Russell	158
5	Carlos Sainz	156
6	Lewis Hamilton	146
7	Lando Norris	76
8	Esteban Ocon	58
9	Valtteri Bottas	46
10	Fernando Alonso	41
11	Kevin Magnussen	22
12	Daniel Ricciardo	19
13	Pierre Gasly	16
14	Sebastian Vettel	16
15	Mick Schumacher	12
16	Yuki Tsunoda	11
17	Zhou Guanyu	5
18	Lance Stroll	4
19	Alexander Albon	3

CONSTRUCTORS

1	Red Bull	431
2	Ferrari	334
3	Mercedes	304
4	Alpine	99
5	McLaren	95
6	Alfa Romeo	51
7	Haas	34
8	AlphaTauri	27
9	Aston Martin	20
10	Williams	3

9 · RICCIARDO · McLaren

7 · HAMILTON · Mercedes

5 · OCON · Alpine

3 · LECLERC · Ferrari

1 · RUSSELL · Mercedes

10 · VERSTAPPEN · Red Bull

8 · BOTTAS · Alfa Romeo

6 · ALONSO · Alpine

4 · NORRIS · McLaren

2 · SAINZ · Ferrari

55	56	57	58	59	60	61	62	63	64	65	66	67	68	69	70	
1	1	1	1	1	1	1	1	1	1	1	1	1	1	1	1	1
63	63	63	63	63	63	63	63	63	63	44	44	44	44	44	44	2
55	55	55	55	55	55	55	55	44	44	63	63	63	63	63	63	3
44	44	44	44	44	44	44	44	55	55	55	55	55	55	55	55	4
11	11	11	11	11	11	11	11	11	11	11	11	11	11	11	11	5
16	16	16	16	16	16	16	16	16	16	16	16	16	16	16	16	6
4	4	4	4	4	4	4	4	4	4	4	4	4	4	4	4	7
14	14	14	14	14	14	14	14	14	14	14	14	14	14	14		8
31	31	31	31	31	31	31	31	31	31	31	31	31	31	31		9
77	77	77	77	77	77	77	18	18	18	5	5	5	5	5		10
18	18	18	18	18	18	18	5	5	5	18	18	18	18	18		
5	5	5	5	5	5	5	77	77	77	77	10	10	10	10		
10	10	10	10	10	10	10	10	10	10	10	3	3	3	3		
3	3	3	3	3	3	3	3	3	3	3	47	47	47	24		
47	47	47	47	47	47	47	47	47	47	47	24	24	24	47		
20	20	20	20	20	20	20	24	24	24	24	20	20	23	20		
6	23	23	24	24	24	24	20	20	20	20	23	23	20	23		
23	24	24	23	23	23	23	23	23	23	23	6	6	6	6		
24	6	6	6	6	6	6	6	6	6	6	22	22	22			
22	22	22	22	22	22	22	22	22	22	22						

23 = Pit stop *22 = One lap or more behind*

VSC VSC

RACE TYRE STRATEGIES

	Driver	Race Stint 1	Race Stint 2	Race Stint 3	Race Stint 4
1	Verstappen	Soft (u): 1-16	Medium (n): 17-38	Medium (n): 39-70	
2	Hamilton	Medium (n): 1-19	Medium (n): 20-51	Soft (u): 52-70	
3	Russell	Soft (u): 1-16	Medium (n): 17-39	Medium (n): 40-70	
4	Sainz	Medium (n): 1-17	Medium (n): 18-47	Soft (u): 48-70	
5	Pérez	Soft (n): 1-18	Medium (n): 19-42	Medium (n): 43-70	
6	Leclerc	Medium (n): 1-21	Medium (n): 22-39	Hard (n): 40-54	Soft (u): 55-70
7	Norris	Soft (n): 1-14	Medium (n): 15-42	Hard (n): 43-70	
8	Alonso	Medium (n): 1-21	Hard (n): 22-69		
9	Ocon	Medium (n): 1-23	Hard (n): 24-69		
10	Vettel	Soft (n): 1-15	Medium (u): 16-46	Medium (n): 47-69	
11	Stroll	Soft (n): 1-14	Medium (u): 15-46	Soft (u): 47-69	
12	Gasly	Soft (n): 1-16	Medium (n): 17-46	Soft (u): 47-69	
13	Zhou	Medium (n): 1-27	Hard (n): 28-51	Soft (u): 52-69	
14	Schumacher	Medium (n): 1-21	Hard (n): 22-41	Medium (n): 42-69	
15	Ricciardo	Soft (u): 1-15	Medium (n): 16-46	Hard (n): 47-69	
16	Magnussen	Medium (n): 1-6	Hard (n): 7-35	Medium (n): 36-67	Soft (n): 68-69
17	Albon	Soft (n): 1-2	Medium (n): 3-21	Medium (n): 22-40	Soft (n): 41-69
18	Latifi	Medium (n): 1-18	Medium (n): 19-39	Soft (n): 40-56	Soft (n): 57-69
19	Tsunoda	Soft (n): 1-13	Medium (n): 14-33	Soft (n): 34-51	Soft (u): 52-68
20	Bottas	Medium (n): 1-26	Hard (n): 27-65 (dnf)		

The tyre regulations stipulate that at least two of three dry tyre specifications must be used during a dry race. Selected compounds for Hungaroring : Red = Soft (C4); Yellow = Medium (C3); White = Hard (C2). (n) new (u) used

Alpine F1 Team

Williams Racing

ORACLE

FIA FORMULA 1 WORLD CHAMPIONSHIP · ROUND 14

BELGIAN GRAND PRIX

SPA-FRANCORCHAMPS CIRCUIT

SPA-FRANCORCHAMPS QUALIFYING

As the paddock reconvened in Belgium after F1's summer break, there was plenty going on. Fernando Alonso had surprised Alpine by jumping into Sebastian Vettel's vacant seat at Aston Martin for 2023. The catalyst for the move, apparently, was Alpine's reluctance to offer the Spaniard a new two-year deal rather than a single-year contract. This was based on his 41 years, but the way Fernando was driving, it seemed a bit short-sighted.

Alpine had then issued a statement confirming Oscar Piastri alongside Esteban Ocon, but without any input from Piastri, who was not slow to announce on social media that he had signed a contract elsewhere! This turned out to be with McLaren, and F1's Contract Recognition Board (CRB) subsequently ruled that the McLaren contract was the only valid one applicable to the promising young Australian.

Daniel Ricciardo, meanwhile, confirmed that he and McLaren were parting company after two disappointing seasons. "We put in a lot of effort trying to understand, but too many weekends were a bit of a struggle," he admitted. "It's not the nicest feeling, but I can hold my head high as far as trying to make it work goes. The team made the decision. It's tough, but I have some good memories – Monza and that first win for the team since 2012, I won't forget. I still love the sport. I haven't lost confidence in myself, and if it's the right opportunity, F1 is where I want to be. It's the only racing I'm interested in and where I see myself."

With the 2026 engine regulations now firmed up, the big news was Audi's confirmation that it would be entering F1 as an engine supplier that same year, a tie-up with the Hinwil-based Sauber team widely anticipated.

On track, there was plenty of interest, too. Revisions to the Spa circuit included a gravel trap at La Source, a slight reprofiling and ironing out of the bump at the bottom of the compression at Eau Rouge, gravel at Turn Nine and a big gravel trap, rather than tarmac run-off, at the fast, left-handed Pouhon. Also, an impressive new grandstand at Eau Rouge.

Much interest surrounded the FIA's new porpoising/ride-height 'safety' controls, which came into effect for the first time at Spa, postponed from Paul Ricard. The rumour was that some teams were allowing the underbody plank to move within the floor to facilitate lower ride heights. The new rules meant that six contact points would be subject to measurement, rather than just one, with conjecture that the pecking order might well change. But, as Friday practice showed, that turned out to be wishful thinking...

Amid a raft of power unit changes, Max Verstappen had his fourth internal-combustion engine, turbocharger, MGU-H and MGU-K of the season fitted for FP1, against the permitted three; Lando Norris took his third energy store and control electronics against a maximum of two; and Esteban Ocon had a batch of new components, each carrying a ten-place grid drop. All would start from the back.

Charles Leclerc also had several new engine components and would be faced with a drive through the field on Sunday. There were penalties, too, for Ferrari engine users Valtteri Bottas and Mick Schumacher.

Through it all, the overarching feature was the dominance of Verstappen's Red Bull. So much for the technical directive. At the end of qualifying, the world champion had gone around in 1m 43.665s. His nearest rival, Carlos Sainz, had stopped the clock in 1m 44.297s, with Sergio Pérez 0.17s behind with the second RB18.

Leclerc, knowing he had penalties and concentrating more on a race set-up, was fourth quickest, a tenth behind the Mexican. Then there was a half-second gap to the two Alpines, Ocon quicker than team-mate Alonso this time.

What of the Mercs and the team's optimism that the TD might put them back somewhere near the ball park? Well, the best that Lewis Hamilton could manage was a lap 1.84s adrift of the pace-setting Red Bull. Okay, Spa is a long lap, but... And George Russell was a quarter of a second behind Hamilton.

Alex Albon was only six-hundredths adrift of his old mate, doing a fine job for Williams, his best qualifying performance of the season, while Norris completed the top ten with the first McLaren.

The chastened Ricciardo was quickest of those who didn't make the top-ten shootout, some 0.05s quicker than Pierre Gasly, who would start his 100th GP in the first AlphaTauri. Zhou Guanyu was 13th, but would drop five places with a gearbox penalty, promoting Lance Stroll, who would end up ninth on the grid.

Out in Q1 went Sebastian Vettel (by just 0.002s), Nicholas Latifi, Kevin Magussen – the trio would end up starting tenth, 11th and 12th! – Yuki Tsunoda (who would start from the pit lane after work was performed under *parc fermé* conditions) and Bottas (who broke a 148-race run of always making it out of the first session of qualifying).

"It looks like we're going to see two races," enthused Christian Horner, referencing the fact that both Verstappen and Leclerc would start at or near the back. "It's going to be fascinating. Checo won't be taking any penalties, we assume that Sainz and the Mercs won't be, so we should be seeing those four guys at the front, and the other two coming through the pack and seeing how far they can get."

Given the devastating pace advantage shown by Verstappen, he was conceivably still in with a realistic shot at victory, even from the back... It looked as though the super-efficient Red Bull was made for Spa. And everyone except Verstappen and Norris at McLaren, the Ferraris included, was struggling to put their tyres in the correct temperature window. Advantage, Red Bull...

SUCH are the anomalies of modern-day F1 engine/gearbox grid penalties that at Spa, not one driver would start the race from the position in which he had qualified! The question was: could any of those at the front make a sufficiently decisive break before Max Verstappen arrived? The world champion would start 14th, with Charles Leclerc's Ferrari one place behind him.

As far as tyre choice was concerned, Ferrari's Charles Leclerc and Carlos Sainz, Verstappen and Valtteri Bottas had opted for the soft-compound Pirelli, with the rest of the field on the medium, apart from Yuki Tsunoda, who ran the hard.

When the lights changed, Sainz made no mistake, and the Ferrari completed the short run to the La Source hairpin with its nose in front. Sergio Pérez, despite angling the Red Bull to the right off grid slot two, could not manage to cover off a fine start from Fernando Alonso's Alpine. Not only the Spaniard, but also the two Mercedes drivers, Lewis Hamilton and George Russell, had demoted the Mexican by the time everyone was on the throttle for the plunge down the hill towards Eau Rouge.

Down the Kemmel Straight and into the Les Combes chicane, Hamilton tried to go around the outside of Alonso in what seemed like an optimistic move and, sure enough, contact was made. Fernando lost places to Pérez and Russell as he sorted himself out, while Hamilton, with significant damage to the underbody, dropped to the tail of the field and was out of the race.

"What an idiot!" Alonso radioed. "Closing the door from the outside. I mean, we had a mega-start, but this guy only knows how to drive and start in first!" Which did seem a tad harsh an assessment of the seven-time world champion.

Behind, there were lurid moments as cars avoided each other, with Lance Stroll on the grass, ushered there by team-mate Vettel, and Verstappen and Leclerc taking advantage of the confusion to make up ground from the back and complete the opening lap in eighth and tenth places respectively. The order across the line was Sainz, Pérez, Russell, Alonso, Sebastian Vettel (from tenth!), Daniel Ricciardo, Alex Albon, Verstappen, Stroll, Leclerc, Kevin Magnussen, Nicholas Latifi, Esteban Ocon, Bottas, Lando Norris, Zhou Guanyu, Mick Schumacher, then Tsunoda and Gasly, the latter hampered by an electrical issue.

Battling for 12th place with Ocon on the second lap, Latifi ran wide out of the Les Combes chicane, lost the rear end of the Williams on the kerb, spun back across the track and tagged the innocent Bottas. The Alfa Romeo ended up beached in the gravel and out of the race – not such a fine way to celebrate his 33rd birthday.

With the Alfa stranded and Hamilton's Mercedes at the side of the circuit further around the lap at Blanchimont, we had a full safety car.

Typical 2022 misfortune continued for Leclerc when, behind the safety car, he told the Ferrari pit-wall crew that he had some smoke from the front right. Believe it or not, he had collected a visor tear-off from great rival Verstappen and had to pit to have it removed, also taking on a set of new medium-compound Pirellis.

The pack closing up was great news for Verstappen. When the race resumed on lap five, he wasted no time in getting down the inside of Ricciardo's McLaren into the Bus Stop chicane to take sixth. Next time around, he repeated the same move to relieve Vettel's Aston Martin of fifth. And all this before DRS had even been re-enabled.

When it was, Verstappen drove past Alonso's Alpine on the Kemmel Straight as if it wasn't there and set his sights on Russell's third-placed Mercedes. George was unable to offer any meaningful resistance either, so, by lap eight, Verstappen was already up into the podium positions and just 4.1s off the race lead.

A couple of laps later, the world champion was on the

Above: Sainz takes control at the start, while Pérez is engulfed by Alonso and Russell to his right, and Hamilton to his left.
Photo: Atsuo Sakurai

Left: Liam Lawson prepares for his Friday first-practice duties for AlphaTauri.

Below left: Sergio Pérez inherited a front-row grid slot after team-mate Max Verstappen elected to take grid penalties.
Photos: Red Bull Content Pool/Getty Images

Opening spread: A study in speed. Verstappen and Red Bull were in a league of their own at Spa.
Photo: Atsuo Sakurai

Above: With a spanking-new grandstand, the reconfigured Eau Rouge was resplendent in the sunshine at Spa-Francorchamps.
Photo: Red Bull Content Pool/Getty Images

Right: Lewis Hamilton's race was over on the opening lap, after his Mercedes was in contact with Fernando Alonso's Alpine.
Photo: Mercedes-AMG Petronas F1 Team

tail of team-mate Pérez, who had Sainz's leading Ferrari just over a second further up the road. It did not take long before Max was on the radio: "We're losing a silly amount of time now..." The message was clear: "Get him out of my way."

At that same point, just 12 laps into the race's 44, Sainz made a much earlier pit stop than anticipated on his medium-compound Pirellis, having reported much higher degradation than expected. Of course, with Verstappen arriving from P14 so soon, an early stop also helped Ferrari protect what looked like a tenuous race lead. When Verstappen walked past Pérez on the Kemmel Straight to claim that lead, it had taken him just a dozen laps to hit the front.

Sainz was not helped by pitting back out just behind Ricciardo's fifth-placed McLaren. He remained bottled up behind the Australian for half a lap before forcing his way through down the inside into Pouhon of all places. Then Vettel's Aston Martin was dispatched down the inside into the Bus Stop chicane.

Russell made his first stop on lap 14, but despite Verstappen being on the soft red-walled Pirelli, there was no sign of Red Bull responding to Sainz's stop. Seemingly, they had sufficient pace to do whatever they pleased.

"Let's try to extend a little bit," Verstappen radioed.

"Understood, Max, keep it there," responded race engineer Lambiase.

When Red Bull did stop a car, it was team-mate Pérez, in response to Russell and Leclerc, whose early unscheduled stop under the safety car now had the Ferrari in fourth place. Sergio came back out comfortably clear of the Mercedes, but just in front of the Ferrari. Leclerc made a bid to go around the outside of the Red Bull into the Les Combes chicane, but was somewhat rudely rebuffed by Pérez.

Not for nothing is Pérez sometimes known as the Mexican Minister of Defence!

Verstappen made his pit stop on lap 16, jettisoning his starting softs in favour of a set of mediums, and was back on his way in 2.8s. He was almost 5s behind Sainz, who once again led for Ferrari, and 1s clear of his earlier-stopping team-mate. But, proving that Maranello was suffering much more than expected with thermal degradation on the yellow-walled tyre, Russell, who was not enjoying any sort of straight-line speed from his Mercedes, was still comfortably able to take fourth from Leclerc's Ferrari at the end of the Kemmel Straight on lap 16.

With speed from an entirely different stratosphere, Verstappen took just two laps to wipe out Sainz's 5s advantage and reclaim the lead down the Kemmel Straight on lap 18, to the delight of the travelling orange army.

Further back, Albon was continuing his fine weekend's work for Williams in eighth place, but he lost it to Ocon's Alpine with a lap-20 lock-up into La Source. It was credit to Albon's pace and the slipperiness of the Williams around Spa that Ferrari did not want Leclerc to fall behind it at his second stop, and was asking Charles how much further he could push his set of mediums to create a pit window, as well as keeping him informed of the Anglo-Thai's lap times – not the expected scenario if you wound back a few races. It was worth remembering that the Williams had set the fastest sector-one time during qualifying!

Just before half-distance, Pérez made it a Red Bull 1-2 when he eased past Sainz's Ferrari with the help of DRS. It was becoming something of a demonstration from Christian Horner's men.

On lap 26, however, after just a 14-lap stint, Ferrari

brought in Sainz for a second stop, sending him back out on the hard-compound Pirellis, while Leclerc stopped just afterwards, rejoining on another set of mediums, some 3s clear of an Albon/Ricciardo/Stroll/Norris/Zhou train. Alonso pitted, too, his Alpine being fitted with hards. He came out behind the train, but, on his fresh rubber, went through it like a hot knife through butter.

Pérez was in from his second place on lap 28, Red Bull also giving him hard-compound tyres, a slick 2.4s stop getting him back out ahead of Sainz.

Russell's Mercedes made its second stop on lap 30, and race leader Verstappen was in a lap later for a slick 2.3s stop to go on to his final set of medium-compound Pirellis.

With ten laps remaining, there was a tasty battle going on for seventh place. Into La Source, Gasly and Vettel were side by side, the Aston nipping the AlphaTauri tight on the inside, before Vettel opened his line and switched back inside on exit. The compromised speed of both, however, allowed Ocon to take full advantage through Eau Rouge and blast past down the Kemmel Straight to take the position, now some 9s behind team-mate Alonso. Vettel, without DRS, was also repassed by Gasly, but got him back down the inside into Rivage. Great stuff.

As the laps ticked by, Verstappen, imperious, was in a race of his own, 15s clear of team-mate Pérez, who also had a comfortable 10s margin over Sainz. Russell, though, was closing in on the Ferrari. Leclerc, once again struggling on the medium, had dropped fully 20s behind the hard-compound-shod Mercedes.

On the penultimate lap, Ferrari pulled in Leclerc for a set of soft-compound tyres to go for fastest lap, leaving themselves open to a bit more strategy ridicule as the Monégasque ceded his fifth place to Alonso's Alpine in the process. Charles pitted out just in front of Fernando, but could do little to stop the Alpine from towing past on the Kemmel Straight. With his new boots, he was always likely to go by again on the final lap, but a last-lap pass of Alonso is never a given.

Leclerc did retake the place without any drama on the last lap, but, guess what, he would be classified sixth after attracting a 5s time penalty for speeding in the pit lane! And, tellingly, despite his softs, he could not beat Verstappen's medium-compound fastest lap set with 12 laps of fuel on board! That was a reflection of just how superior Red Bull had been and just how much of a struggle Ferrari had endured in Belgium. Further evidence was Sainz claiming the final podium position, just 2s clear of Russell's Mercedes, which had qualified 2s from the ultimate pace.

"I don't think it was anything to do with the technical directive," Ferrari team principal Mattia Binotto said. "We simply didn't get the set-up right here and suffered much higher degradation on the medium tyre than expected, with both cars."

Just half a second behind Leclerc when the 5s penalty was applied, Ocon finished seventh for Alpine, ahead of Vettel and Gasly, with the final point deservingly going to Albon.

Thus Verstappen joined Jim Clark and Michael Schumacher as the only men to win at Spa from outside the top ten.

"The car was super-competitive from the get go," he acknowledged. "I knew we could have a really good result today. Winning from P14, even with that car, is always a bit difficult because you don't know how much you are going to lose on lap one or what's going to happen. Luckily, I stayed out of trouble while there was a lot of stuff going on. I just tried to avoid everything, and once it calmed down with the safety car, I was just overtaking cars every lap. Once I got to P3, I knew I had a good chance of winning the race."

Reflecting on it, team principal Christian Horner said, "I think it's one of our biggest ever team performances. I didn't expect Max to get to the front so quickly. It was one of those weekends where we were just right in the window with our car. The technical directive had no impact on the way we operate it. Max was exemplary, and it's right up there with the very best that we achieved in 2010."

In fact, it was the lowest position from which Red Bull had won a race. The team was now 1-2 in the drivers' championship – Verstappen enjoying a 93-point advantage, with Pérez five points ahead of Leclerc – and a huge 118 points clear of Ferrari in the constructors' championship. And next up was Max's home race at Zandvoort...

Tony Dodgins

PIRELLI
P ZERO
100
150

Above: George Russell salvaged fourth for Mercedes.
Photo: Mercedes-AMG Petronas F1 Team

Left: Birthday boy Bottas was out after just one lap, having been tagged by Latifi's Williams.
Photo: Alfa Romeo ORLEN

Far left: A fine drive by Alex Albon put his Williams into the points, ahead of Norris, Stroll and Ricciardo.
Photo: Williams Racing

Below left: Gasly, Vettel and Ocon run three abreast down the Kemmel Straight.
Photo: Pirelli

Below: A reflective Verstappen ponders his crushing victory at the post-race press conference.
Photo: Red Bull Content Pool/Getty Images

VIEWPOINT
GENIUS AT WORK

MAX VERSTAPPEN'S post-race interview said everything the opposition didn't need to hear and see. The Dutchman had about him a confidence that came not from his ninth win and an increasingly comfortable lead of the championship, but from the knowledge that his Red Bull felt superb, and he had the ability and racecraft to go with it.

He might have dragged his heels a little when leaving home in the knowledge that a grid penalty was in store once he reached Belgium, but all of that was forgotten from the moment he took to the track for the first time on Friday morning. His car seemed as though on rails, and there can be no better feeling for a driver when he knows there are 4.4 miles of Spa-Francorchamps on which to exploit it. The Red Bull might have been edgy, but the RB18 was exactly as Verstappen liked it. The timing screen provided proof during Q3, with a lap that was 0.65s clear of the field and almost casual in its execution. Nonetheless, a penalised 14th grid slot would surely shrink the comfort zone on Sunday.

Not a bit of it. Verstappen's poise and self-assurance was such that he knew the seventh-row start would not be a problem. You could see it on the first lap. Normally, the hectic opening minutes provide an opportunity for a driver out of position to make up a couple of places in a single lap. Later, Verstappen would talk about biding his time, letting others have their tyre-rubbing moments while he waited for opportunities that would surely come. This Verstappen was as different as it was possible to be from the fiery teenager who had provoked Kimi Räikkönen's ire while defending at Spa in 2016.

By lap 18, car No.1 was leading the race and pulling away with ease. He would beat his team-mate by 17.8 seconds. Fastest lap was almost a formality in what amounted to a demonstration of why Verstappen deserved to be declared the best driver of 2022.

Maurice Hamilton

14

FORMULA 1 ROLEX BELGIAN GRAND PRIX 2022

Official Timepiece

SPA-FRANCORCHAMPS 26-28 AUGUST

RACE DISTANCE: 44 laps, 191.415 miles/308.052km

RACE WEATHER: Dry/sunny (track 33-38°C, air 24-28°C)

CIRCUIT DE SPA-FRANCORCHAMPS

Circuit: 4.352 miles/7.004km

44 laps

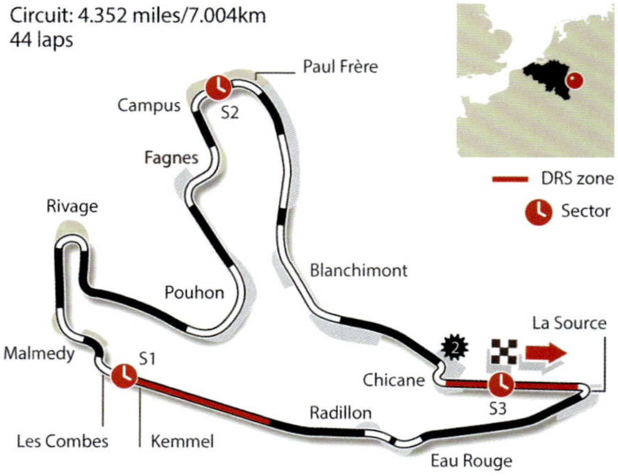

RACE – OFFICIAL CLASSIFICATION

Pos.	Driver	Nat.	No.	Entrant	Car/Engine	Laps	Time/Retirement	Speed (mph/km/h)	Gap to winner	Fastest race lap	
1	**Max Verstappen**	NL	1	Oracle Red Bull Racing	Red Bull RB18-RBPTH001 V6	44	1h 25m 52.894s	133.729/215.216		1m 49.354s	32
2	**Sergio Pérez**	MEX	11	Oracle Red Bull Racing	Red Bull RB18-RBPTH001 V6	44	1h 26m 10.735s	133.267/214.473	17.841s	1m 50.764s	29
3	**Carlos Sainz**	E	55	Scuderia Ferrari	Ferrari F1-75-066/7 V6	44	1h 26m 19.780s	133.035/214.099	26.886s	1m 51.977s	32
4	**George Russell**	GB	63	Mercedes-AMG Petronas F1 Team	Mercedes-AMG F1 W13-M13 E Perf. V6	44	1h 26m 22.034s	132.977/214.006	29.140s	1m 50.793s	31
5	**Fernando Alonso**	E	14	BWT Alpine F1 Team	Alpine A522-Renault E-Tech RE22 V6	44	1h 27m 06.150s	131.854/212.199	1m 13.256s	1m 52.868s	35
6	**Charles Leclerc**	MC	16	Scuderia Ferrari	Ferrari F1-75-066/7 V6	44	1h 27m 07.830s *	131.812/212.131	1m 14.936s	1m 49.984s	44
7	**Esteban Ocon**	F	31	BWT Alpine F1 Team	Alpine A522-Renault E-Tech RE22 V6	44	1h 27m 08.534s	131.794/212.102	1m 15.640s	1m 51.717s	36
8	**Sebastian Vettel**	D	5	Aston Martin Aramco Cognizant F1 Team	Aston Martin AMR22-Mercedes F1 M13 E Perf. V6	44	1h 27m 11.001s	131.732/212.002	1m 18.107s	1m 52.515s	40
9	**Pierre Gasly**	F	10	Scuderia AlphaTauri	AlphaTauri AT03-RBPTH001 V6	44	1h 27m 25.075s	131.379/211.434	1m 32.181s	1m 53.002s	24
10	**Alexander Albon**	T	23	Williams Racing	Williams FW44-Mercedes F1 M13 E Perf. V6	44	1h 27m 34.794s	131.135/211.042	1m 41.900s	1m 53.055s	28
11	Lance Stroll	CDN	18	Aston Martin Aramco Cognizant F1 Team	Aston Martin AMR22-Mercedes F1 M13 E Perf. V6	44	1h 27m 35.972s	131.106/210.995	1m 43.078s	1m 52.880s	29
12	Lando Norris	GB	4	McLaren F1 Team	McLaren MCL36-Mercedes F1 M13 E Perf. V6	44	1h 27m 37.633s	131.065/210.928	1m 44.739s	1m 51.678s	31
13	Yuki Tsunoda	J	22	Scuderia AlphaTauri	AlphaTauri AT03-RBPTH001 V6	44	1h 27m 38.111s	131.053/210.909	1m 45.217s	1m 52.436s	32
14	Zhou Guanyu	CHN	24	Alfa Romeo F1 Team ORLEN	Alfa Romeo C42-Ferrari 066/7 V6	44	1h 27m 39.146s	131.027/210.868	1m 46.252s	1m 52.317s	30
15	Daniel Ricciardo	AUS	3	McLaren F1 Team	McLaren MCL36-Mercedes F1 M13 E Perf. V6	44	1h 27m 40.057s	131.004/210.831	1m 47.163s	1m 53.080s	34
16	Kevin Magnussen	DK	20	Haas F1 Team	Haas VF-22-Ferrari 066/7 V6	43			1 lap	1m 53.332s	29
17	Mick Schumacher	D	47	Haas F1 Team	Haas VF-22-Ferrari 066/7 V6	43			1 lap	1m 52.646s	35
18	Nicholas Latifi	CDN	6	Williams Racing	Williams FW44-Mercedes F1 M13 E Perf. V6	43			1 lap	1m 52.256s	38
	Valtteri Bottas	FIN	77	Alfa Romeo F1 Team ORLEN	Alfa Romeo C42-Ferrari 066/7 V6	1	*accident*			no time	
	Lewis Hamilton	GB	44	Mercedes-AMG Petronas F1 Team	Mercedes-AMG F1 W13-M13 E Perf. V6	0	*accident damage*			no time	

* Leclerc: 5s time penalty for pit lane speeding (originally finished 5th).

DHL Fastest race lap (scores 1 point): Max Verstappen on lap 32, 1m 49.354s, 143.273mph/230.575km/h.

Lap record: Kimi Räikkönen (McLaren MP4-19B-Mercedes V8), 1m 45.108s, 148.465mph/238.931km/h (2004, 4.335-mile/6.976km circuit)

Lap record (current configuration): Valtteri Bottas (Mercedes F1 W09 V6), 1m 46.286s, 147.409mph/237.231km/h (2018)

19 · SCHUMACHER · Haas
Used additional power unit elements; required to start from the back of the grid; used additional restricted-number components; 10-place grid penalty

17 · NORRIS · McLaren
Used additional power unit elements; required to start from the back of the grid

15 · LECLERC · Ferrari
Used additional power unit elements; required to start from the back of the grid; used additional restricted-number components; 10-place grid penalty

13 · BOTTAS · Alfa Romeo
Used additional power unit elements and restricted-number component; 20-place grid penalty

11 · LATIFI · Williams

20 · TSUNODA · AlphaTauri
Car modified in parc fermé and additional power unit elements used; required to start from the pit lane

18 · ZHOU · Alfa Romeo
Used additional power unit elements; required to start from the back of the grid; used additional restricted-number components; 10-place grid penalty

16 · OCON · Alpine
Used additional power unit elements; required to start from the back of the grid

14 · VERSTAPPEN · Red Bull
Used additional power unit elements; required to start from the back of the grid; used additional restricted-number component; 5-place grid penalty

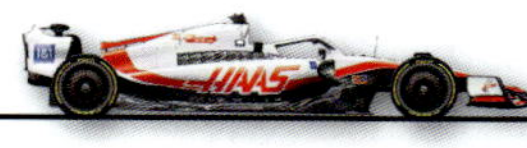

12 · MAGNUSSEN · Haas

Grid order	1	2	3	4	5	6	7	8	9	10	11	12	13	14	15	16	17	18	19	20	21	22	23	24	25	26	27	28	29	30	31	32	33	34	35
55 SAINZ	55	55	55	55	55	55	55	55	55	55	11	1	1	1	1	55	55	1	1	1	1	1	1	1	1	1	1	1	1	1	1	1	1	1	1
11 PEREZ	11	11	11	11	11	11	11	11	11	11	1	11	11	11	55	1	1	55	55	55	11	11	11	11	11	11	11	63	11	11	11	11	11	11	11
14 ALONSO	63	63	63	63	63	63	63	1	1	1	55	63	63	55	11	11	11	11	11	11	55	55	55	55	63	63	63	11	63	55	55	55	55	55	55
44 HAMILTON	14	14	14	14	14	14	1	63	63	63	63	5	55	5	16	63	63	63	63	63	63	63	63	63	55	55	55	55	55	63	63	63	63	63	63
63 RUSSELL	5	5	5	5	5	1	14	14	14	14	5	55	5	16	63	16	16	16	16	16	16	16	16	16	16	5	5	5	5	5	16	16	16	16	16
23 ALBON	3	3	3	3	1	5	5	5	5	5	14	18	18	63	18	14	14	14	14	14	14	14	14	14	5	31	31	31	16	16	5	5	5	14	14
3 RICCIARDO	23	23	23	23	3	23	23	23	23	3	3	16	16	18	22	22	22	5	5	5	5	5	5	5	31	16	16	16	31	31	31	31	14	10	31
10 GASLY	1	1	1	1	23	3	3	3	3	18	18	3	24	22	14	23	5	23	23	31	31	31	31	31	14	3	3	3	14	14	14	14	10	5	5
18 STROLL	18	16	18	18	18	18	18	18	18	31	31	4	22	14	23	5	23	31	31	23	23	23	23	23	23	4	4	14	3	3	3	10	31	31	10
5 VETTEL	16	18	20	20	20	20	31	31	31	4	4	31	14	24	5	31	31	22	3	3	3	3	3	3	3	24	14	4	22	10	10	3	23	23	23
6 LATIFI	20	20	31	31	31	31	20	20	4	23	16	24	4	6	31	3	3	3	10	10	18	18	18	18	18	23	24	22	10	22	23	23	18	18	18
20 MAGNUSSEN	6	31	16	4	4	4	4	4	20	16	24	22	6	23	3	10	10	10	18	18	10	4	4	4	4	14	22	10	4	23	18	18	4	4	4
77 BOTTAS	31	4	4	24	24	24	24	24	16	20	22	14	47	3	10	4	4	18	4	4	4	24	24	24	24	18	10	24	23	18	4	4	24	24	24
1 VERSTAPPEN	77	24	24	47	22	22	22	16	24	24	6	6	23	31	6	18	18	4	24	24	24	10	20	20	20	22	20	23	18	24	24	24	22	22	22
16 LECLERC	4	47	47	22	10	10	10	22	22	22	47	47	3	10	4	24	24	24	20	20	20	20	22	22	22	20	47	47	47	4	22	22	3	3	3
31 OCON	24	22	22	10	47	16	16	10	10	6	20	23	31	47	20	20	20	20	47	22	22	22	47	10	10	10	23	18	24	47	20	20	20	20	20
4 NORRIS	47	10	10	16	16	6	6	6	6	47	23	10	10	4	24	47	47	47	22	47	47	47	10	47	47	47	18	6	6	6	6	6	6	47	47
24 ZHOU	22	6	6	6	6	47	47	47	47	10	10	20	20	20	47	6	6	6	6	6	6	6	6	6	6	6	6	20	20	20	47	47	47	6	6
47 SCHUMACHER	10																																		
22 TSUNODA																																			

SC Safety car deployed on laps shown

SC · SC SC

TIME SHEETS

PRACTICE 1 (FRIDAY)

Weather: Dry-wet/cloudy

Temperatures: track 22-24°C, air 18-19°C

Pos.	Driver	Laps	Time
1	Carlos Sainz	16	1m 46.538s
2	Charles Leclerc	16	1m 46.607s
3	Max Verstappen	10	1m 46.755s
4	George Russell	13	1m 47.396s
5	Lance Stroll	13	1m 47.437s
6	Alexander Albon	15	1m 47.835s
7	Daniel Ricciardo	14	1m 48.081s
8	Yuki Tsunoda	16	1m 48.310s
9	Lewis Hamilton	10	1m 48.420s
10	Sergio Pérez	13	1m 48.474s
11	Nicholas Latifi	13	1m 48.485s
12	Zhou Guanyu	15	1m 48.672s
13	Lando Norris	15	1m 49.470s
14	Fernando Alonso	17	1m 49.664s
15	Sebastian Vettel	12	1m 49.813s
16	Esteban Ocon	5	1m 50.315s
17	Kevin Magnussen	9	1m 50.982s
18	Mick Schumacher	15	1m 51.259s
19	Liam Lawson	14	1m 52.065s
20	Valtteri Bottas	2	no time

PRACTICE 2 (FRIDAY)

Weather: Dry-wet/cloudy

Temperatures: track 21-23°C, air 18-20°C

Pos.	Driver	Laps	Time
1	Max Verstappen	20	1m 45.507s
2	Charles Leclerc	21	1m 46.369s
3	Lando Norris	17	1m 46.589s
4	Lance Stroll	16	1m 46.635s
5	Carlos Sainz	20	1m 46.649s
6	Lewis Hamilton	18	1m 46.893s
7	Fernando Alonso	19	1m 46.975s
8	George Russell	22	1m 47.042s
9	Daniel Ricciardo	18	1m 47.255s
10	Sergio Pérez	15	1m 47.346s
11	Alexander Albon	15	1m 47.520s
12	Zhou Guanyu	21	1m 47.617s
13	Yuki Tsunoda	16	1m 47.658s
14	Pierre Gasly	19	1m 47.782s
15	Sebastian Vettel	19	1m 47.867s
16	Esteban Ocon	21	1m 47.944s
17	Kevin Magnussen	19	1m 48.208s
18	Valtteri Bottas	21	1m 48.419s
19	Nicholas Latifi	14	1m 48.612s
20	Mick Schumacher	23	1m 49.941s

PRACTICE 3 (SATURDAY)

Weather: Dry/cloudy

Temperatures: track 20-22°C, air 15-18°C

Pos.	Driver	Laps	Time
1	Sergio Pérez	19	1m 45.047s
2	Max Verstappen	19	1m 45.184s
3	Carlos Sainz	13	1m 45.824s
4	Lando Norris	20	1m 45.965s
5	Fernando Alonso	16	1m 46.061s
6	George Russell	19	1m 46.071s
7	Charles Leclerc	12	1m 46.120s
8	Sebastian Vettel	18	1m 46.166s
9	Esteban Ocon	24	1m 46.601s
10	Pierre Gasly	19	1m 46.604s
11	Daniel Ricciardo	18	1m 46.646s
12	Lewis Hamilton	20	1m 46.769s
13	Nicholas Latifi	20	1m 46.811s
14	Alexander Albon	20	1m 46.836s
15	Valtteri Bottas	20	1m 46.881s
16	Lance Stroll	16	1m 46.975s
17	Kevin Magnussen	14	1m 46.982s
18	Yuki Tsunoda	23	1m 47.035s
19	Zhou Guanyu	20	1m 47.089s
20	Mick Schumacher	6	1m 52.494s

QUALIFYING (SATURDAY))

Weather: Dry/cloudy Temperatures: track 21-22°C, air 16-18°C

Pos.	Driver	First	Second	Third	Qualifying Tyre
1	Max Verstappen	1m 44.581s	1m 44.723s	1m 43.665s	Soft (n)
2	Carlos Sainz	1m 45.050s	1m 45.418s	1m 44.297s	Soft (n)
3	Sergio Pérez	1m 45.377s	1m 44.794s	1m 44.462s	Soft (n)
4	Charles Leclerc	1m 45.572s	1m 44.551s	1m 44.553s	Soft (n)
5	Esteban Ocon	1m 46.039s	1m 45.475s	1m 45.180s	Soft (n)
6	Fernando Alonso	1m 46.075s	1m 45.552s	1m 45.368s	Soft (n)
7	Lewis Hamilton	1m 45.736s	1m 45.420s	1m 45.503s	Soft (n)
8	George Russell	1m 45.650s	1m 45.461s	1m 45.776s	Soft (n)
9	Alexander Albon	1m 45.672s	1m 45.675s	1m 45.837s	Soft (n)
10	Lando Norris	1m 45.745s	1m 45.603s	1m 46.178s	Soft (u)
11	Daniel Ricciardo	1m 46.212s	1m 45.767s		
12	Pierre Gasly	1m 46.183s	1m 45.827s		
13	Zhou Guanyu	1m 46.178s	1m 46.085s		
14	Lance Stroll	1m 46.256s	1m 46.611s		
15	Mick Schumacher	1m 46.342s	1m 47.718s		
16	Sebastian Vettel	1m 46.344s			
17	Nicholas Latifi	1m 46.401s			
18	Kevin Magnussen	1m 46.557s			
19	Yuki Tsunoda	1m 46.692s			
20	Valtteri Bottas	1m 47.866s			

QUALIFYING: head to head

Hamilton	7	7	Russell
Verstappen	11	3	Pérez
Ricciardo	2	12	Norris
Leclerc	10	4	Sainz
Gasly	9	5	Tsunoda
Hülkenberg	1	1	Stroll
Vettel	8	4	Stroll
Alonso	9	5	Ocon
Bottas	10	4	Zhou
Albon	12	2	Latifi
Magnussen	11	3	Schumacher

Red Bull Content Pool/Getty Images

FOR THE RECORD

100th GRAND PRIX START: Pierre Gasly

20th FASTEST LAP: Max Verstappen

150th FRONT ROW POSITION: Red Bull

DID YOU KNOW?

This was Verstappen's second consecutive win from 10th or lower on the grid. The only other driver to have done so is Bruce McLaren at the 1959 United States GP and the following race, Argentina 1960. Apart from Max, John Watson is the only driver to have done so twice in a season.

POINTS

DRIVERS

1	Max Verstappen	284
2	Sergio Pérez	191
3	Charles Leclerc	186
4	Carlos Sainz	171
5	George Russell	170
6	Lewis Hamilton	146
7	Lando Norris	76
8	Esteban Ocon	64
9	Fernando Alonso	51
10	Valtteri Bottas	46
11	Kevin Magnussen	22
12	Sebastian Vettel	20
13	Daniel Ricciardo	19
14	Pierre Gasly	18
15	Mick Schumacher	12
16	Yuki Tsunoda	11
17	Zhou Guanyu	5
18	Alexander Albon	4
19	Lance Stroll	4

CONSTRUCTORS

1	Red Bull	475
2	Ferrari	357
3	Mercedes	316
4	Alpine	115
5	McLaren	95
6	Alfa Romeo	51
7	Haas	34
8	AlphaTauri	29
9	Aston Martin	24
10	Williams	4

9 · STROLL · Aston Martin

7 · RICCIARDO · McLaren

5 · RUSSELL · Mercedes

3 · ALONSO · Alpine

1 · SAINZ · Ferrari

10 · VETTEL · Aston Martin

8 · GASLY · AlphaTauri
Started from the pit lane

6 · ALBON · Williams

4 · HAMILTON · Mercedes

2 · PÉREZ · Red Bull

36	37	38	39	40	41	42	43	44	
1	1	1	1	1	1	1	1	1	1
11	11	11	11	11	11	11	11	11	2
55	55	55	55	55	55	55	55	55	3
63	63	63	63	63	63	63	63	63	4
16	16	16	16	16	16	16	14	16	5
14	14	14	14	14	14	14	16	14	6
31	31	31	31	31	31	31	31	31	7
5	5	5	5	5	5	5	5	5	8
10	10	10	10	10	10	10	10	10	9
23	23	23	23	23	23	23	23	23	10
18	18	18	18	18	18	18	18	18	
4	4	4	4	4	4	4	4	4	
24	24	24	24	24	22	24	24	22	
22	22	22	22	22	24	22	22	24	
3	3	3	3	3	3	3	3	3	
20	20	20	20	20	20	20	*20*		
47	47	47	47	47	47	*47*	*47*		
6	*6*	*6*	*6*	*6*	*6*	*6*	*6*		

16 = Pit stop *6 = One lap or more behind*

RACE TYRE STRATEGIES

PIRELLI

	Driver	Race Stint 1	Race Stint 2	Race Stint 3	Race Stint 4
1	Verstappen	Soft (n): 1-15	Medium (n): 16-30	Medium (n): 31-44	
2	Pérez	Medium (n): 1-14	Medium (n): 15-27	Hard (n): 28-44	
3	Sainz	Soft (u): 1-11	Medium (n): 12-25	Hard (n): 26-44	
4	Russell	Medium (n): 1-13	Medium (n): 14-29	Hard (n): 30-44	
5	Alonso	Medium (n): 1-11	Medium (n): 12-25	Hard (n): 26-44	
6	Leclerc	Soft (n): 1-3	Medium (n): 4-25	Medium (n): 26-42	Soft (u): 43-44
7	Ocon	Medium (n): 1-12	Hard (n): 13-32	Medium (n): 33-44	
8	Vettel	Medium (u): 1-14	Hard (u): 15-33	Medium (u): 34-44	
9	Gasly	Medium (n): 1-10	Hard (n): 11-22	Medium (n): 23-44	
10	Albon	Medium (n): 1-10	Hard (n): 11-26	Medium (n): 27-44	
11	Stroll	Medium (u): 1-15	Medium (u): 16-26	Hard (u): 27-44	
12	Norris	Medium (n): 1-13	Hard (n): 14-29	Medium (n): 30-44	
13	Tsunoda	Hard (n): 1-18	Medium (n): 19-30	Medium (n): 31-44	
14	Zhou	Medium (n): 1-14	Medium (n): 15-28	Soft (u): 29-44	
15	Ricciardo	Medium (n): 1-12	Hard (n): 13-32	Medium (n): 33-44	
16	Magnussen	Medium (n): 1-11	Hard (n): 12-27	Medium (n): 28-43	
17	Schumacher	Medium (n): 1-14	Hard (n): 15-30	Medium (n): 31-43	
18	Latifi	Medium (n): 1-3	Medium (n): 4-15	Hard (n): 16-34	Soft (n): 35-43
	Bottas	Soft (n): 1 (dnf)			
	Hamilton	Medium (n): 0 (dnf)			

The tyre regulations stipulate that at least two of three dry tyre specifications must be used during a dry race. Selected compounds for Spa: Red = Soft (C4); Yellow = Medium (C3); White = Hard (C2). (n) new (u) used

Mercedes AMG Petronas F1 Team

FIA FORMULA 1 WORLD CHAMPIONSHIP · ROUND 15

DUTCH GRAND PRIX

ZANDVOORT CIRCUIT

Tezos
Red Bull
ORACLE

ZANDVOORT QUALIFYING

THERE was never any doubt about Zandvoort being a sell-out, but Max Verstappen's performance at Spa meant that you could not move amid the sea of orange at the Dutch seaside resort, his home race of course. But things did not get off to the best of starts for the Dutchman, his Red Bull stranded out on the track with a gearbox issue after just ten minutes of the opening practice session on Friday. When he did get in some running, he was not entirely happy with the Red Bull's balance and finished the opening day down in eighth place. That was not in the script…

After its struggles in Belgium, Ferrari was offering more of a challenge around the tight, twisty track, which is universally popular with the drivers. After the first Q3 runs, Verstappen had a challenge on his hands if he was going to deliver the home supporters the pole position they craved. Charles Leclerc, already with seven 2022 pole positions to his name, had found more performance after understeer-afflicted Q1/Q2 runs. The Ferrari broke the timing beam in 1m 10.456s to go five-hundredths quicker than Verstappen on the first Q3 runs and silence the partying Dutch fans.

On his second run, Leclerc went quicker still, 1m 10.363s, but lost time with a bit of a twitch in Turn Ten, and it was Max who managed to put the Red Bull on pole by the skin of his teeth – 1m 10.343s! – to roars and cheers from the fans.

"It was really fine margins," he admitted, "and also the last run was a bit compromised on the out-lap because of getting one extra car in front of me and having to slow down a bit too much in the first sector. So, when I started my lap, I felt like the tyres were not really switched on. I managed to recover a bit in sector two, and that was just enough for pole. At Spa, we were dominant, but you can clearly see that on the higher-downforce tracks we struggle a little bit more to extract the best from the car. But it's still a quick car." Something of an understatement…

Leclerc was disappointed, but clearly not distraught: "In Turn Ten, I made a small mistake. It's tricky when there's a tailwind there, but to be honest, looking at the small gap to Max, I didn't expect that coming into Q3 after the Q1/Q2 runs we had, which were much trickier. But by the end of Q3, the car felt quite good. I haven't been completely at ease with the balance for a few races on qualifying runs."

Carlos Sainz was third quickest and, like his team-mate, was surprised by the level of extra grip Ferrari had managed to discover in Q3. He qualified just 0.07s behind Leclerc.

After its disappointment at Spa, Mercedes appeared to be a much bigger threat in The Netherlands, Sainz going as far as to say that he expected the silver cars to be at least as quick as the Ferraris in the race. Lewis Hamilton qualified just three-tenths from the ultimate pace, the team's best qualifying effort of the season, notwithstanding George Russell's somewhat bizarre and inexplicable pole position at a cold Budapest.

This time, though, George was fully half a second adrift of Lewis as Sergio Pérez split the Mercs with the second Red Bull. The Mexican, more than seven-tenths from his team-mate, knew that he could have performed better, overdoing it on his last run and spinning at the final corner.

Lando Norris took the honours as 'best of the rest' for McLaren, while Mick Schumacher, starting to come under a bit of pressure for his continued tenure of a Haas in 2023, achieved a timely third top-ten qualifying slot of the year.

Yuki Tsunoda also produced a solid qualifying effort to put the first AlphaTauri ninth on the grid, separated from team-mate Pierre Gasly's 11th place by Lance Stroll, who made it through to Q3 for just the second time in the season, showing a decent turn of pace for Aston Martin.

The slippery Alpines were not as strong a factor on a downforce track, qualifying 12th and 13th, Esteban Ocon a hundredth quicker than Fernando Alonso as he outqualified the two-time world champion for the third race in succession.

Zhou Guanyu furthered his case for a second season with Alfa Romeo by outqualifying Valtteri Bottas for the fifth time, the pair split by another fine effort from Alex Albon in hauling his Williams into Q2.

Daniel Ricciardo, meanwhile, plumbed new depths when he could manage no more than 17th, only one slot better off than in McLaren's worst showing at its problematic Melbourne season-opener.

"Someone kicked up dirt and a dust cloud ahead of me at the penultimate corner," Ricciardo explained. "I was hoping it wouldn't affect the grip, but it did, ultimately costing me about three-tenths, which was the difference between going out and going through to Q2. Not great at a track where overtaking is so difficult."

Joining him as Q1 eliminees were Kevin Magnussen, Sebastian Vettel and Nicholas Latifi. For Vettel, with team-mate Stroll showing strongly, it was particularly disappointing. His final run was an improvement and looking good enough to progress, but in the final sector, at the penultimate corner, the four-time champion ran wide and ended the session in the gravel trap.

The stage was set for another Verstappen versus Ferrari battle, although nobody was betting strongly on anything other than a second successive home win for the people's champion.

Right: Max Verstappen leads the two Ferraris of Leclerc and Sainz through the sweeping Zandvoort turns on the opening lap.
Photo: XPB Images

Below: Antonio Giovinazzi was on hand as Ferrari's reserve driver, but did not see any action.
Photo: Scuderia Ferrari

Bottom: The partisan fans turned the stands red, white and blue with flags supplied by the race organisers.
Photo: Red Bull Content Pool/Getty Images

Opening spread: Verstappen took his tenth win of the season, ahead of George Russell's Mercedes.
Photo: GP Photo/Peter Nygaard

AS the grid formed up for round 15 of the championship – record attendance 305,000 over the weekend – pole-man and home hero Max Verstappen had opted for the soft-compound Pirelli tyre, in keeping with both Ferraris (using scrubbed ones), while fourth-placed Lewis Hamilton was on the medium. A one-stop race was thought to be possible, but the soft tyres pointed towards a two-stop for the first three. Other medium runners down the grid were Lando Norris and George Russell, fifth and sixth, Mick Schumacher (tenth), Kevin Magnussen (15th) and Alex Albon (17th).

Verstappen got the power down well and immediately swooped right to take the inside line for Tarzan, with Charles Leclerc, Hamilton and Carlos Sainz in grid order behind. Hamilton had a brief look at the inside of Sainz into Turn One, making light contact with the Ferrari sidepod, but both emerged unscathed. Sergio Pérez ran fifth, Norris was up a place ahead of Russell, and then came a fast-starting Lance Stroll, Esteban Ocon (up three places), Schumacher, Yuki Tsunoda, Pierre Gasly, Fernando Alonso, Zhou Guanyu, Magnussen, Albon, Daniel Ricciardo, Sebastian Vettel, Valtteri Bottas and Nicholas Latifi.

Magnussen, up three places on the opening lap, ran wide in Turn Two the second time around, skating through the gravel and hitting the tyre barrier. He was able to continue, but dropped to the back.

Up front, the status quo remained for the first five laps, Leclerc staying just outside DRS range of the leading Red Bull, while Sainz had dropped 2.5s behind his team-mate and was under pressure from Hamilton, who appeared more comfortable on the medium tyre.

With overtaking not the work of a moment around Zandvoort, the drivers had figured that the qualifying hour was up there with Monaco and Budapest in terms of importance. On lap ten, though, Alonso got a move done on Tsunoda to take the AlphaTauri's 11th place.

Hamilton thought that he was quicker than Sainz's Ferrari, but there was precious little he could do about making progress until Carlos pitted to get rid of his starting softs after 15 laps, with Pérez's Red Bull following him in. It was a disastrous stop for Sainz. The left rear would not engage, and Pérez actually ran over a discarded Ferrari wheel gun as he jumped Carlos and accelerated back into the race.

"Oh my God," was Sainz's take on the situation.

Above: Verstappen is already breaking away as the field negotiates the banked Hugenholtz hairpin.
Photo: Alfa Romeo ORLEN

Right: Unsafe release for Carlos Sainz as he exits his pit box in front of Fernando Alonso's Alpine.
Photo: XPB Images

Team-mate Leclerc was on the radio a couple of laps later to report that his tyres were not great. Ferrari pitted him, and this time the stop was much better: he was on his way with a new set of medium-compound Pirellis after being stationary for just 2.5s.

At quarter-distance, Verstappen led Hamilton's Mercedes by 11.6s, with Russell 3s behind his team-mate. Then Red Bull responded to Leclerc by pitting the race leader, who rejoined still 2.5s clear of the Ferrari. Alpine, meanwhile, had pitted Alonso after 12 laps on his starting softs, the Spaniard now recording competitive laps on the hard-compound Pirelli.

At one-third-distance, 24 of the 72 laps completed, the two Mercedes were still happily circulating at the front of the field, Hamilton 2.6s clear of Russell, and it began to look like Mercedes was thinking about a single-stop race.

Red Bull, no doubt with the same idea, gave Verstappen the instruction to move up on to the tail of Russell. His second-placed Mercedes had now dropped a further second to Hamilton, and you wondered whether Mercedes was about to play strategy games.

Ferrari had also come to the conclusion that Mercedes could be trying a one-stop race, warning Leclerc after 26 laps. The Mercedes problem, though, was that Hamilton only had a 17s margin to Pérez's fifth-placed Red Bull, with a pit stop occupying around 20 seconds.

Russell, meanwhile, received a radio message from race engineer Riccardo Musconi: "This is looking good – Lewis, 1m 16.7s, Verstappen [on his new boots], 1m 16.0s." In other words, the Mercedes pace was good enough on used mediums to facilitate a one-stopper on to the hards and a shot at victory.

To Russell, though, it appeared as though the Red Bull was going quicker than that, Verstappen driving straight past him on the main straight as soon as he reached DRS range on lap 28. As he did so, Max claimed the race's fastest lap with a 1m 15.725s.

The Mercedes crew was out in the pit lane on the next lap, Hamilton indeed taking the durable hard-compound Pirelli for a likely one-stopper. He was on his way again after a 2.6s stop. A couple of laps later, Russell also came in for a set of the hard tyres.

As the race approached half-distance, Verstappen had a handy 8.3s lead over Leclerc's Ferrari, with Pérez a similar distance behind the Monégasque. Hamilton, though, had

closed to within just over 1s of Pérez and was in Verstappen's pit window. This was starting to look like it could be far from straightforward for the crowd favourite.

As he got DRS for the first time, Hamilton shaped up to go around Pérez's outside into Tarzan, but, after a quick lock-up, Sergio defended manfully and gave the Mercedes a healthy chop on exit. Meanwhile, fastest race lap from Russell on his new hards once again pointed to Mercedes being a serious threat. Hamilton, realising this, was much closer out of the final corner next time around and swooped past the outside of Pérez to take third place on lap 37. Just then, Vettel rather unhelpfully emerged from the pits in front of them. Pérez thought about a look down the inside of the banked Turn Three until Hamilton swiftly covered that off.

The time behind Pérez had cost Hamilton around 3s, and it was now nip and tuck as to whether Verstappen could get in and out a second time and still maintain his lead. But still he stayed out.

By lap 39, Russell had also caught Pérez, whose mediums were now 25 laps old, and pulled off a carbon copy of Hamilton's pass into Tarzan. The Mercs clearly had the beating of Pérez, but what about Verstappen?

Hamilton had now taken the race's fastest lap, with 1m 15.116s, and had closed to within 18.7s of the race leader, so Verstappen would lose the lead if he pitted.

Next time around, and 'GP' Lambiase was on the radio to Verstappen, asking for his thoughts on tyre compounds.

"This tyre doesn't really feel spectacular," the world champion said of his existing set of mediums.

"Understood," replied Lambiase.

Just a week after Mercedes boss Toto Wolff had described Spa qualifying as the worst in his ten years with the team, here were his cars pushing for a win! Most thought Russell had been optimistic when, post-qualifying, he had claimed that Mercedes might be able to clear Pérez and the two Ferraris in the race, but he had been spot on.

There was a Red Bull into the pits on lap 41 of the 72, but it was Pérez, the Mexican taking on a set of hards and rejoining seventh, behind Norris's McLaren.

On lap 44, Tsunoda pulled off the track, shouting on the radio, "Tyres not fitted!"

The yellow flag in sector one was not what Mercedes wanted to see. If it was upgraded to a VSC or even a full safety car, Verstappen would get a cheap second stop. The conspiracy theorists were quick to point out that AlphaTauri, of course, is the Red Bull junior team...

What had happened was that Tsunoda, after leaving the pits following a tyre stop, had been convinced that there was an issue and stopped the car near a gap in the barrier at the exit of Turn Three.

But the team's data indicated that all wheels were attached, and Tsunoda was instructed to return to the pits. Already preparing to get out, he'd loosened his belts, but he drove back to the AlphaTauri pit, where the belts were done up again and a set of soft tyres fitted before he was sent on his way.

Meanwhile, on lap 46, Leclerc, who had Hamilton within a couple of seconds of him, had stopped for a new set of hard-compound tyres.

The Tsunoda drama was not over, however. On rejoining, he thought that there was still an issue – it was attributed to a broken differential – and this time he stopped a little further around the lap. Later, he was reprimanded for driving without his belts done up. The immediate effect, though, was a VSC, which reduced the pit-stop loss time to around 12s, just when Hamilton was 13.7s behind leader Verstappen.

In came the Dutchman for a set of hards, Hamilton following him in for mediums. "That VSC has stuffed us," was Lewis's rather pointed message on the radio. There was no doubt that under normal circumstances, Verstappen would have pitted out behind him and potentially would have had to pass both Mercs on the track.

It looked as though Red Bull had been going for as big a

Above: The late-race safety car, caused by the removal of Valtteri Bottas's Alfa, left leader Hamilton out on medium Pirellis. The freshly-shod trio of Verstappen, Russell and Leclerc, on softs, prepare to pounce.
Photo: Atsuo Sakurai

Top right: Confusion abounds as Yuki Tsunoda pits and waits for his safety belts to be done up.
Photo: Red Bull Content Pool/Getty Images

Above right: On rejoining, Tsunoda, convinced that there was still an issue (it was attributed to a broken differential), stopped a little further around the lap, triggering a virtual safety car.
Photo: XPB Images

Right: A fourth win in a row for Max. The Dutchman was now more than 100 points clear of Leclerc in the drivers' championship.
Photo: Red Bull Content Pool/Getty Images

tyre offset as possible with Verstappen, and later Christian Horner claimed that the timing of the VSC had not been ideal for them either.

"It could not have come at a worse time, actually," he said, "because it forced Max on to the hard-compound tyre instead of extending his stint, rejoining on softs and passing the Mercs on track."

With 20 laps to go, Verstappen led Hamilton by 12.8s, with Russell just 2.3s behind Lewis. Leclerc's Ferrari was 8.8s in arrears, with a 5s margin in hand over Pérez; Ocon's Alpine was running sixth, 18s adrift and 3s clear of Sainz. Fourth to eighth places were all on the hard-compound Pirelli. Just 1.5s behind, both Norris and Alonso were on softs, with the hard-tyred Stroll completing the top ten.

The race was about to take another twist as Bottas's Alfa ground to a halt on the inside of the track, just before Turn One. On lap 56, with 16 to go, we had a full safety car. "I lost the engine," Valtteri reported.

"Box, box," was the immediate instruction to race leader Verstappen, Red Bull readying a set of used softs for him. While he was in, Hamilton did not pit and moved into the lead of the race. Then Russell reached the safety car line just before the rejoining Verstappen, so the Mercs were running 1-2. Leclerc and Pérez also pitted, for used softs and new mediums respectively.

As the safety car passed through the pit lane, Russell stopped for softs, as did Sainz, the Ferrari being released right into the path of Alonso's Alpine.

Circulating behind the safety car, on 12-lap-old mediums, Hamilton came to the realisation, "It's going to be hard to keep that car [Verstappen] behind me now, guys."

"Yes, copy Lewis," responded Pete Bonnington, "but let's give it everything." The only other driver still on mediums was fifth-placed Pérez.

Hamilton judged his restart well, but had the engine in the wrong mode, and Verstappen was instantaneously alongside down the main straight and ahead by the time they reached Turn One. A bit further back, Russell had his hands full with Leclerc's Ferrari, but hung on.

"That was the biggest **** up," a disgruntled Hamilton said over the radio. But there was worse to come as Russell closed in and went to his team-mate's right down the main straight on the next lap. Just as he did so, Lewis briefly moved that way, too, and contact was averted by a narrow margin. Russell had to lift briefly, but still managed to snatch second place down the inside into Turn One.

"I can't believe you guys ****** me. I can't tell you how ****** I am," Hamilton radioed. His next problem was Leclerc, the Ferrari further demoting the Mercedes on lap 66 to claim the final podium position.

The next soft-tyred car was Sainz, some 3.5s behind with two laps to go, but with a 5s penalty for that unsafe release. With the field bunched up, that was going to cost him, as Pérez, Alonso, Norris, Ocon and Stroll were running in line astern behind.

The home crowd cared little about that, however, as to a man and woman, they stood, cheering wildly as Max Verstappen took the 30th win of his F1 career and his tenth of 2022. Russell claimed his best result of the season, and Leclerc, somewhat unbelievably, was on the podium for just the second time in ten races.

The disappointed Hamilton had to be content with fourth, ahead of Pérez, Alonso, Norris, the penalised Sainz, Ocon and Stroll.

With Monza, the final leg of an F1 triple-header, just seven days away, could anyone stop Verstappen from making it five in a row?

Tony Dodgins

VIEWPOINT
ALPHATHEORY

AS the race strategies played out, a cracking finish beckoned. With Max Verstappen preparing to surrender his lead and make a late stop for softs, he would have to chase down and overtake the Mercedes of George Russell and Lewis Hamilton. All of this in front of a sell-out, passionate crowd expecting – demanding – one answer to that scenario. It was distinctly possible. But not inevitable. Then, on lap 44, Yuki Tsunoda changed everything.

The AlphaTauri driver had been struggling with what he thought was a loose wheel following a pit stop. A return to the pits to have his belts tightened (after stopping out on the circuit in the belief that his race was run) confirmed all four wheels to be secure. But he got no further than halfway around the next lap before pulling over once more. The triggering of a VSC afforded Verstappen a cheap pit stop and allowed him to remain in the lead. Game over.

It didn't take long for social media to begin spewing conspiracy theories, linking AlphaTauri with Red Bull and claiming that Tsunoda's parking had been a tactical ploy by the junior team at the behest of the mother ship. That claim didn't bear scrutiny on several counts.

On-board footage from Tsunoda's car clearly showed him struggling with handling problems created by a faulty diff, graunching noises providing the audio evidence. If this had been deliberately manufactured by the AlphaTauri engineers, it was an impressive trick.

This sequence of events might have made Verstappen's win easier, but given his comfortable lead in the championship, there was no need for desperate measures to secure maximum points. Red Bull and associates were not about to risk censure – and possible exclusion – for collusion. This was not some drama cooked up for Netflix, even though the continuing controversy over the nonsense in Abu Dhabi the previous December might have led some casual observers to believe that was actually the case. You reap what you sow.

Maurice Hamilton

15

FORMULA 1 HEINEKEN DUTCH GRAND PRIX 2022

ZANDVOORT 2-4 SEPTEMBER

RACE DISTANCE: 72 laps, 190.504 miles/306.587km

RACE WEATHER: Dry/overcast 33-34°C, air 23-25°C)

Official Timepiece

CIRCUIT ZANDVOORT

Circuit: 2.646 miles/4.259km, 72 laps

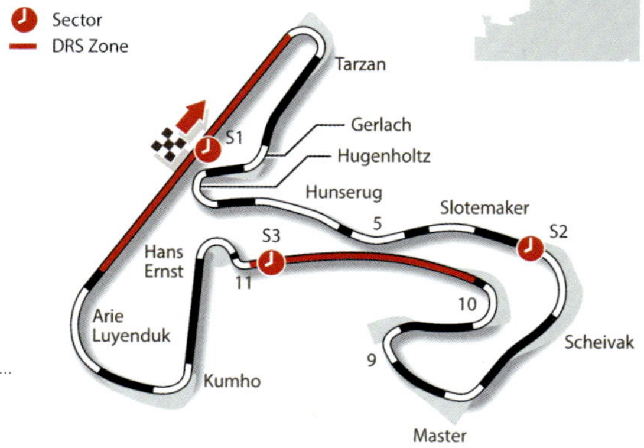

RACE – OFFICIAL CLASSIFICATION

Pos.	Driver	Nat.	No.	Entrant	Car/Engine	Laps	Time/Retirement	Speed (mph/km/h)	Gap to winner	Fastest race lap	
1	**Max Verstappen**	NL	1	Oracle Red Bull Racing	Red Bull RB18-RBPTH001 V6	72	1h 36m 42.773s	118.187/190.204		1m 13.652s	62
2	**George Russell**	GB	63	Mercedes-AMG Petronas F1 Team	Mercedes-AMG F1 W13-M13 E Perf. V6	72	1h 36m 46.844s	118.105/190.071	4.071s	1m 13.671s	72
3	**Charles Leclerc**	MC	16	Scuderia Ferrari	Ferrari F1-75-066/7 V6	72	1h 36m 53.702s	117.965/189.846	10.929s	1m 14.413s	62
4	**Lewis Hamilton**	GB	44	Mercedes-AMG Petronas F1 Team	Mercedes-AMG F1 W13-M13 E Perf. V6	72	1h 36m 55.789s	117.923/189.778	13.016s	1m 13.854s	54
5	**Sergio Pérez**	MEX	11	Oracle Red Bull Racing	Red Bull RB18-RBPTH001 V6	72	1h 37m 00.941s	117.818/189.610	18.168s	1m 14.404s	63
6	**Fernando Alonso**	E	14	BWT Alpine F1 Team	Alpine A522-Renault E-Tech RE22 V6	72	1h 37m 01.527s	117.806/189.591	18.754s	1m 14.144s	51
7	**Lando Norris**	GB	4	McLaren F1 Team	McLaren MCL36-Mercedes F1 M13 E Perf. V6	72	1h 37m 02.079s	117.795/189.573	19.306s	1m 14.706s	63
8	**Carlos Sainz**	E	55	Scuderia Ferrari	Ferrari F1-75-066/7 V6	72	1h 37m 03.689s *	117.763/189.521	20.916s	1m 14.643s	63
9	**Esteban Ocon**	F	31	BWT Alpine F1 Team	Alpine A522-Renault E-Tech RE22 V6	72	1h 37m 03.890s	117.759/189.514	21.117s	1m 15.084s	64
10	**Lance Stroll**	CDN	18	Aston Martin Aramco Cognizant F1 Team	Aston Martin AMR22-Mercedes F1 M13 E Perf. V6	72	1h 37m 05.232s	117.732/189.471	22.459s	1m 15.043s	65
11	Pierre Gasly	F	10	Scuderia AlphaTauri	AlphaTauri AT03-RBPTH001 V6	72	1h 37m 09.782s	117.640/189.323	27.009s	1m 15.165s	65
12	Alexander Albon	T	23	Williams Racing	Williams FW44-Mercedes F1 M13 E Perf. V6	72	1h 37m 13.163s	117.572/189.213	30.390s	1m 15.534s	65
13	Mick Schumacher	D	47	Haas F1 Team	Haas VF-22-Ferrari 066/7 V6	72	1h 37m 15.768s	117.519/189.129	32.995s	1m 15.233s	51
14	Sebastian Vettel	D	5	Aston Martin Aramco Cognizant F1 Team	Aston Martin AMR22-Mercedes F1 M13 E Perf. V6	72	1h 37m 18.780s *	117.458/189.031	36.007s	1m 14.862s	50
15	Kevin Magnussen	DK	20	Haas F1 Team	Haas VF-22-Ferrari 066/7 V6	72	1h 37m 19.642s	117.441/189.003	36.869s	1m 15.369s	53
16	Zhou Guanyu	CHN	24	Alfa Romeo F1 Team ORLEN	Alfa Romeo C42-Ferrari 066/7 V6	72	1h 37m 20.093s *	117.432/188.988	37.320s	1m 15.940s	63
17	Daniel Ricciardo	AUS	3	McLaren F1 Team	McLaren MCL36-Mercedes F1 M13 E Perf. V6	72	1h 37m 20.537s	117.423/188.974	37.764s	1m 15.577s	52
18	Nicholas Latifi	CDN	6	Williams Racing	Williams FW44-Mercedes F1 M13 E Perf. V6	71			1 lap	1m 16.066s	62
	Valtteri Bottas	FIN	77	Alfa Romeo F1 Team ORLEN	Alfa Romeo C42-Ferrari 066/7 V6	53	*fuel system*			1m 16.844s	51
	Yuki Tsunoda	J	22	Scuderia AlphaTauri	AlphaTauri AT03-RBPTH001 V6	43	*differential*			1m 17.138s	16

* Sainz: 5s time penalty for unsafe release from a pit stop (originally finished 5th). * Vettel: 5s time penalty for ignoring blue flags (originally finished 13th).

* Zhou: 5s time penalty for pit lane speeding (served at pit stop).

DHL Fastest race lap (scores 1 point): Max Verstappen on lap 62, 1m 13.652s, 129.353mph/208.173km/h.

Lap record: Lewis Hamilton (Mercedes F1 W12 V6), 1m 11.097s, 134.002mph/215.654km/h (2021).

19 · VETTEL · Aston Martin

17 · RICCIARDO · McLaren

15 · ALBON · Williams

13 · ALONSO · Alpine

11 · GASLY · AlphaTauri

20 · LATIFI · Williams

18 · MAGNUSSEN · Haas

16 · BOTTAS · Alfa Romeo

14 · ZHOU · Alfa Romeo

12 · OCON · Alpine

Grid order	1	2	3	4	5	6	7	8	9	10	11	12	13	14	15	16	17	18	19	20	21	22	23	24	25	26	27	28
1 VERSTAPPEN	1	1	1	1	1	1	1	1	1	1	1	1	1	1	1	1	1	1	44	44	44	44	44	44	44	44	44	44
16 LECLERC	16	16	16	16	16	16	16	16	16	16	16	16	16	16	16	16	16	44	63	63	63	63	63	63	63	63	63	1
55 SAINZ	55	55	55	55	55	55	55	55	55	55	55	55	55	44	44	44	44	63	1	1	1	1	1	1	1	1	1	63
44 HAMILTON	44	44	44	44	44	44	44	44	44	44	44	44	44	55	63	63	63	16	16	16	16	16	16	16	16	16	16	16
11 PEREZ	11	11	11	11	11	11	11	11	11	11	11	11	11	63	4	4	4	11	11	11	11	11	11	11	11	11	11	11
63 RUSSELL	4	4	4	63	63	63	63	63	63	63	63	63	63	11	18	18	31	31	23	55	55	55	55	55	55	55	55	55
4 NORRIS	63	63	63	4	4	4	4	4	4	4	4	4	4	4	31	31	11	23	55	23	4	4	4	4	4	4	4	4
47 SCHUMACHER	18	18	18	18	18	18	18	18	18	18	18	18	18	18	11	11	23	55	4	4	18	18	18	18	18	18	18	18
22 TSUNODA	31	31	31	31	31	31	31	31	31	31	31	31	31	31	23	23	55	4	18	18	23	14	14	14	14	14	14	14
18 STROLL	47	47	47	47	47	47	47	47	47	47	47	47	47	23	77	55	18	18	14	14	14	31	31	31	31	31	31	31
10 GASLY	22	22	22	22	22	22	22	22	22	22	22	22	22	77	55	77	14	14	31	31	31	22	22	22	22	22	22	22
31 OCON	10	10	10	10	10	10	10	10	10	14	14	14	23	20	14	14	22	22	22	22	22	10	10	10	10	10	10	10
14 ALONSO	14	14	14	14	14	14	14	14	14	10	24	23	77	14	22	22	10	10	10	10	10	24	24	24	24	24	24	24
24 ZHOU	24	24	24	24	24	24	24	24	24	24	23	77	20	22	10	10	24	24	24	24	24	47	47	47	47	47	47	47
23 ALBON	20	23	23	23	23	23	23	23	23	23	77	24	6	10	24	24	47	47	47	47	47	77	77	77	77	77	77	77
77 BOTTAS	23	3	3	3	3	3	3	3	3	3	10	20	14	24	47	47	5	5	77	77	77	23	23	23	23	23	23	23
3 RICCIARDO	3	5	5	5	5	5	5	5	77	77	3	6	10	5	5	5	77	77	5	5	5	5	5	5	5	5	5	5
20 MAGNUSSEN	5	77	77	77	77	77	77	77	5	6	20	10	24	47	3	3	3	3	3	3	3	3	3	3	3	3	20	20
5 VETTEL	77	6	6	6	6	6	6	6	6	20	6	5	5	3	20	20	20	20	20	20	20	20	20	20	20	20	3	3
6 LATIFI	6	20	20	20	20	20	20	20	20	5	5	3	3	6	6	6	6	6	6	6	6	6	6	6	6	6	6	6

Grid order	29	30	31	32	33	34	35	36	37	38	39	40	41	42	43	44	45	46	47	48	49	50	51	52	53	54	55
1 VERSTAPPEN	1	1	1	1	1	1	1	1	1	1	1	1	1	1	1	1	1	1	1	1	1	1	1	1	1	1	1
16 LECLERC	44	63	63	16	16	16	16	16	16	16	16	16	16	16	16	16	44	44	44	44	44	44	44	44	44	44	44
55 SAINZ	63	16	16	11	11	11	11	11	44	44	44	44	44	44	44	44	16	63	63	63	63	63	63	63	63	63	63
44 HAMILTON	16	11	11	44	44	44	44	44	11	11	63	63	63	63	63	63	63	16	16	16	16	16	16	16	16	16	16
11 PEREZ	11	44	44	63	63	63	63	63	63	63	11	11	55	55	55	11	11	11	11	11	11	11	11	11	11	11	11
63 RUSSELL	55	55	55	55	55	55	55	55	55	55	55	55	4	4	4	4	4	4	4	31	31	31	31	31	31	31	55
4 NORRIS	4	4	4	4	4	4	4	4	4	4	4	4	11	11	11	14	14	14	14	55	55	55	55	55	55	55	31
47 SCHUMACHER	18	18	18	18	18	18	18	18	18	14	14	14	14	14	14	31	31	31	31	4	4	4	4	4	4	4	4
22 TSUNODA	14	14	14	14	14	14	14	14	14	18	31	31	31	31	31	55	55	55	55	14	14	14	14	14	14	14	14
18 STROLL	31	31	31	31	31	31	31	31	31	31	22	22	22	18	18	18	18	18	18	18	18	18	18	18	18	18	18
10 GASLY	22	22	22	22	22	22	22	22	22	22	18	18	18	22	10	10	10	10	10	10	10	10	10	10	10	10	10
31 OCON	10	10	10	24	24	24	24	24	24	23	23	23	23	23	23	23	23	23	23	23	23	23	23	23	23	23	23
14 ALONSO	24	24	24	10	77	23	23	23	23	10	10	10	10	10	77	77	77	77	77	77	77	77	77	77	77	24	24
24 ZHOU	47	47	47	47	23	77	5	10	10	77	77	77	77	77	24	24	24	24	24	24	24	24	24	24	24	47	47
23 ALBON	77	77	77	77	47	5	10	77	77	24	24	24	24	24	5	5	5	5	5	5	47	47	47	47	47	5	5
77 BOTTAS	23	23	23	23	5	20	77	5	5	5	5	5	5	5	47	47	47	47	47	47	5	5	5	5	5	20	20
3 RICCIARDO	5	5	5	5	20	10	3	3	3	3	3	47	47	47	20	20	20	20	20	20	20	20	20	20	20	3	3
20 MAGNUSSEN	20	20	20	20	10	3	47	47	47	47	47	3	20	20	3	3	3	3	3	3	3	3	3	3	3	6	6
5 VETTEL	3	3	3	3	3	47	20	20	20	20	20	20	3	3	6	6	6	6	6	6	6	6	6	6	6		
6 LATIFI	6	6	6	6	6	6	6	6	6	6	6	6	6	6	22												

VSC Safety car deployed on laps shown

VSC VSC VSC

TIME SHEETS

PRACTICE 1 (FRIDAY)

Weather: Dry/sunny
Temperatures: track 30-36°C, air 23-25°C

Pos.	Driver	Laps	Time
1	George Russell	29	1m 12.455s
2	Lewis Hamilton	28	1m 12.695s
3	Carlos Sainz	30	1m 12.845s
4	Lando Norris	32	1m 12.929s
5	Daniel Ricciardo	31	1m 13.077s
6	Charles Leclerc	30	1m 13.127s
7	Sergio Pérez	30	1m 13.416s
8	Fernando Alonso	31	1m 13.633s
9	Esteban Ocon	33	1m 13.963s
10	Alexander Albon	29	1m 14.063s
11	Mick Schumacher	29	1m 14.163s
12	Lance Stroll	30	1m 14.257s
13	Kevin Magnussen	31	1m 14.405s
14	Pierre Gasly	28	1m 14.474s
15	Sebastian Vettel	28	1m 14.500s
16	Zhou Guanyu	18	1m 14.534s
17	Yuki Tsunoda	31	1m 14.630s
18	Valtteri Bottas	22	1m 14.695s
19	Max Verstappen	7	1m 14.714s
20	Nicholas Latifi	33	1m 15.122s

PRACTICE 2 (FRIDAY)

Weather: Dry/sunny
Temperatures: track 35-36°C, air 26-27°C

Pos.	Driver	Laps	Time
1	Charles Leclerc	27	1m 12.345s
2	Carlos Sainz	30	1m 12.349s
3	Lewis Hamilton	21	1m 12.417s
4	Lando Norris	24	1m 12.448s
5	George Russell	27	1m 12.655s
6	Lance Stroll	28	1m 12.746s
7	Fernando Alonso	25	1m 12.848s
8	Max Verstappen	22	1m 13.042s
9	Esteban Ocon	27	1m 13.305s
10	Daniel Ricciardo	10	1m 13.362s
11	Yuki Tsunoda	19	1m 13.419s
12	Sergio Pérez	23	1m 13.493s
13	Mick Schumacher	27	1m 13.604s
14	Sebastian Vettel	27	1m 13.611s
15	Zhou Guanyu	25	1m 13.624s
16	Pierre Gasly	16	1m 13.666s
17	Alexander Albon	26	1m 13.837s
18	Valtteri Bottas	27	1m 14.167s
19	Kevin Magnussen	25	1m 14.282s
20	Nicholas Latifi	24	1m 14.797s

PRACTICE 3 (SATURDAY)

Weather: Dry/sunny
Temperatures: track 33-37°C, air 24-27°C

Pos.	Driver	Laps	Time
1	Charles Leclerc	20	1m 11.632s
2	George Russell	24	1m 11.698s
3	Max Verstappen	22	1m 11.793s
4	Carlos Sainz	17	1m 11.971s
5	Lewis Hamilton	25	1m 12.156s
6	Sergio Pérez	29	1m 12.176s
7	Fernando Alonso	16	1m 12.327s
8	Sebastian Vettel	25	1m 12.491s
9	Mick Schumacher	15	1m 12.558s
10	Lando Norris	18	1m 12.591s
11	Kevin Magnussen	15	1m 12.606s
12	Lance Stroll	18	1m 12.773s
13	Alexander Albon	18	1m 12.775s
14	Esteban Ocon	20	1m 13.003s
15	Pierre Gasly	23	1m 13.046s
16	Yuki Tsunoda	22	1m 13.256s
17	Daniel Ricciardo	20	1m 13.299s
18	Valtteri Bottas	15	1m 13.359s
19	Zhou Guanyu	14	1m 13.421s
20	Nicholas Latifi	22	1m 13.625s

QUALIFYING (SATURDAY))

Weather: Dry/sunny Temperatures: track 40-41°C, air 29-30°C

Pos.	Driver	First	Second	Third	Qualifying Tyre
1	Max Verstappen	1m 11.317s	1m 10.927s	1m 10.342s	Soft (n)
2	Charles Leclerc	1m 11.443s	1m 10.988s	1m 10.363s	Soft (n)
3	Carlos Sainz	1m 11.767s	1m 10.814s	1m 10.434s	Soft (n)
4	Lewis Hamilton	1m 11.331s	1m 11.075s	1m 10.648s	Soft (n)
5	Sergio Pérez	1m 11.641s	1m 11.314s	1m 11.077s	Soft (u)
6	George Russell	1m 11.561s	1m 10.824s	1m 11.147s	Soft (u)
7	Lando Norris	1m 11.556s	1m 11.116s	1m 11.174s	Soft (n)
8	Mick Schumacher	1m 11.741s	1m 11.420s	1m 11.442s	Soft (n)
9	Yuki Tsunoda	1m 11.427s	1m 11.428s	1m 12.556s	Soft (u)
10	Lance Stroll	1m 11.568s	1m 11.416s	no time	
11	Pierre Gasly	1m 11.705s	1m 11.512s		
12	Esteban Ocon	1m 11.748s	1m 11.605s		
13	Fernando Alonso	1m 11.667s	1m 11.613s		
14	Zhou Guanyu	1m 11.826s	1m 11.704s		
15	Alexander Albon	1m 11.695s	1m 11.802s		
16	Valtteri Bottas	1m 11.961s			
17	Daniel Ricciardo	1m 12.081s			
18	Kevin Magnussen	1m 12.319s			
19	Sebastian Vettel	1m 12.391s			
20	Nicholas Latifi	1m 13.353s			

QUALIFYING: head to head

Hamilton	8	7	Russell
Verstappen	12	3	Pérez
Ricciardo	2	13	Norris
Leclerc	11	4	Sainz
Gasly	9	6	Tsunoda
Hülkenberg	1	1	Stroll
Vettel	8	5	Stroll
Alonso	9	6	Ocon
Bottas	10	5	Zhou
Albon	13	2	Latifi
Magnussen	11	4	Schumacher

Alfa Romeo ORLEN

FOR THE RECORD

30th WIN: Max Verstappen
5,000th LAP LED: Red Bull
600th RACE WITH A PODIUM: Ferrari
100th WIN: Honda engine (including Red Bull)

DID YOU KNOW?

Max Verstappen becomes the 16th driver to achieve four consecutive grand prix wins in the championship.

POINTS

DRIVERS

1	Max Verstappen	310
2	Charles Leclerc	201
3	Sergio Pérez	201
4	George Russell	188
5	Carlos Sainz	175
6	Lewis Hamilton	158
7	Lando Norris	82
8	Esteban Ocon	66
9	Fernando Alonso	59
10	Valtteri Bottas	46
11	Kevin Magnussen	22
12	Sebastian Vettel	20
13	Daniel Ricciardo	19
14	Pierre Gasly	18
15	Mick Schumacher	12
16	Yuki Tsunoda	11
17	Zhou Guanyu	5
18	Lance Stroll	5
19	Alexander Albon	4

CONSTRUCTORS

1	Red Bull	511
2	Ferrari	376
3	Mercedes	346
4	Alpine	125
5	McLaren	101
6	Alfa Romeo	51
7	Haas	34
8	AlphaTauri	29
9	Aston Martin	25
10	Williams	4

9 · TSUNODA · AlphaTauri

7 · NORRIS · McLaren

5 · PÉREZ · Red Bull

3 · SAINZ · Ferrari

1 · VERSTAPPEN · Red Bull

10 · STROLL · Aston Martin

8 · SCHUMACHER · Haas

6 · RUSSELL · Mercedes

4 · HAMILTON · Mercedes

2 · LECLERC · Ferrari

56	57	58	59	60	61	62	63	64	65	66	67	68	69	70	71	72	
1	44	44	44	44	1	1	1	1	1	1	1	1	1	1	1	1	1
44	63	1	1	1	44	44	44	63	63	63	63	63	63	63	63	63	2
63	1	63	63	63	63	63	63	44	44	16	16	16	16	16	16	16	3
16	16	16	16	16	16	16	16	16	16	44	44	44	44	44	44	44	4
11	11	11	11	11	55	55	55	55	55	55	55	55	55	55	55	55	5
55	55	55	55	55	11	11	11	11	11	11	11	11	11	11	11	11	6
4	4	14	14	14	14	14	14	14	14	14	14	14	14	14	14	14	7
14	14	4	4	4	4	4	4	4	4	4	4	4	4	4	4	4	8
31	31	31	31	31	31	31	31	31	31	31	31	31	31	31	31	31	9
18	18	18	18	18	18	18	18	18	18	18	18	18	18	18	18	18	10
10	10	10	10	10	10	10	10	10	10	10	10	10	10	10	10	10	
23	23	23	23	23	23	23	23	23	23	23	23	23	23	23	23	23	
47	47	47	47	47	47	47	47	47	47	47	47	47	47	5	5	5	
5	5	5	5	5	5	5	5	5	5	5	5	5	5	47	47	47	
20	20	20	20	20	20	20	20	20	20	20	20	20	20	20	20	20	
24	24	24	24	24	24	24	24	24	24	24	24	24	24	24	24	24	
3	3	3	3	3	3	3	3	3	3	3	3	3	3	3	3	3	
6	6	6	6	6	6	6	6	6	6	6	6	6	6	6	6		

5 = Pit stop   *6 = One lap or more behind*

SC Safety car deployed on laps shown

SC SC SC SC SC

RACE TYRE STRATEGIES

	Driver	Race Stint 1	Race Stint 2	Race Stint 3	Race Stint 4	Race Stint 5
1	Verstappen	Soft (n): 1-18	Medium (n): 19-48	Hard (n): 49-56	Soft (u): 57-72	
2	Russell	Medium (n): 1-31	Hard (n): 32-48	Medium (n): 49-57	Soft (u): 58-72	
3	Leclerc	Soft (u): 1-17	Medium (n): 18-45	Hard (n): 46-56	Soft (u): 57-72	
4	Hamilton	Medium (n): 1-29	Hard (n): 30-48	Medium (n): 49-57		
5	Pérez	Soft (u): 1-14	Medium (n): 15-40	Hard (n): 41-56	Medium (n): 57-72	
6	Alonso	Soft (n): 1-12	Hard (n): 13-47	Soft (n): 48-72		
7	Norris	Soft (n): 1-17	Hard (n): 18-47	Soft (u): 48-57	Soft (u): 58-72	
8	Sainz	Soft (u): 1-14	Medium (n): 15-43	Hard (n): 44-57	Soft (u): 58-72	
9	Ocon	Soft (n): 1-18	Hard (n): 19-56	Soft (u): 57-72		
10	Stroll	Soft (n): 1-16	Medium (u): 17-38	Hard (u): 39-56	Soft (u): 57-72	
11	Gasly	Soft (u): 1-11	Medium (u): 12-32	Hard (u): 33-56	Soft (n): 57-72	
12	Albon	Medium (n): 1-21	Medium (n): 22-42	Hard (n): 43-55	Soft (n): 56-72	
13	Schumacher	Medium (n): 1-13	Medium (n): 14-33	Hard (n): 34-47	Soft (u): 48-72	
14	Vettel	Soft (n): 1-9	Medium (u): 10-35	Hard (u): 36-48	Soft (n): 49-72	
15	Magnussen	Medium (n): 1-14	Medium (n): 15-34	Hard (n): 35-47	Soft (u): 48-72	
16	Zhou	Soft (n): 1-12	Soft (u): 13-37	Medium (n): 38-55	Soft (u): 56-72	
17	Ricciardo	Soft (n): 1-11	Medium (n): 12-27	Hard (n): 28-47	Soft (n): 48-55	Soft (n): 56-72
18	Latifi	Soft (n): 1-13	Medium (n): 14-26	Hard (n): 27-54	Soft (n): 55-71	
	Bottas	Soft (n): 1-16	Soft (n): 17-34	Medium (n): 35-53 (dnf)		
	Tsunoda	Soft (u): 1-13	Medium (u): 14-42	Hard (n): 43 (dnf)		

The tyre regulations stipulate that at least two of three dry tyre specifications must be used during a dry race.
Selected compounds for Zandvoort: Red = Soft (C3); Yellow = Medium (C2); White = Hard (C1). (n) new (u) used

FIA FORMULA 1 WORLD CHAMPIONSHIP · ROUND 16

ITALIAN GRAND PRIX

MONZA CIRCUIT

ROLEX
ROLEX
PIRELLI
PIRELLI
PIRELLI
PIRELLI
ALPHATAURI
VELAS

MONZA QUALIFYING

WITH the following two races on the F1 calendar to be run at Singapore and Suzuka, neither of which easily facilitates overtaking, there was a predictable plethora of engine/grid penalties in Italy.

Monza was celebrating its 100th anniversary, and Ferrari its 75th year as an independent manufacturer since its 125S first rolled off the production line in 1947. Fittingly, Charles Leclerc delighted the *tifosi* with pole position. He would end up being the only man on the grid to start where he had qualified!

"I think it was in 2014 when I first came here, for my first year in single-seaters," Leclerc recalled before the weekend got under way. "I've got a very bad memory, so this might be wrong, but I think it was my first victory in single-seaters, so I always liked Monza."

In fact, he was right. He had scored a Monza double en route to runner-up spot in that year's Formule Renault 2.0 Alps championship. The driver who had beaten him to the title was a certain Nyck de Vries (with George Russell fourth in the series, both driving for Korainen).

It was de Vries who also starred in Monza qualifying. After driving Sebastian Vettel's Aston Martin in FP1 on Friday morning, the former F2/Formula E champion and Mercedes reserve was having a coffee in F1's Paddock Club on Saturday morning when he was told he was wanted by Williams, to substitute for Alexander Albon, who had appendicitis.

Monza, with its low-downforce set-up, is always a challenge when it comes to late braking for the chicanes as downforce bleeds off. And that's for drivers who are in the groove and fully *au fait* with their chassis. It was a good thing that de Vries had been out in the Aston, but still he did an exceptional job to jump into a different car, have just FP3 for familiarisation and then put it into Q2 while regular driver Nicholas Latifi was eliminated in Q1. When penalties were applied to no fewer than nine drivers, de Vries would start eighth, and he was daring to entertain thoughts of points on his F1 debut as he pushed his claim for a permanent seat on the 2023 grid.

It appeared as though the pole fight would be between the two Ferraris and Max Verstappen, with Sergio Pérez a little way off, and that's how it transpired. Leclerc almost lost it through the Ascari chicane on his first Q3 run, but he put together a superb second attempt, super-quick through the second Lesmo, to stop the clock in 1m 20.161s.

The best that Verstappen could manage was a 1m 20.306s, which was enough to pip Carlos Sainz by just over a tenth. "We chose to go for a bit more downforce," Max explained, "and over one lap, it was maybe not the best. But for tomorrow, it can be quite strong. I think it will be an interesting battle." The Red Bull long-run pace on Friday afternoon had been superior to Ferrari's, but Red Bull had chosen to take a fifth engine, and the world champion would start seventh. Having recently won from tenth and 14th, that did not seem an insurmountable task...

For Carlos Sainz, however, it was a different matter. A fifth ICE, sundry other powertrain components and a gearbox penalty put the second Ferrari right at the back of the grid. While it enlivens races to have quick men coming through the field, with thousands and thousands of passionate fans thronging through the gates, it wasn't exactly ideal for one of the two cars they'd come to see to face the risk of being taken out of contention.

"I'm not going to lie," Sainz said. "It hurts to be starting at the back, especially with how competitive the car is and how good I'm feeling. I wish I was at the front with Charles, trying for a 1-2 for the *tifosi*."

You had to wonder if a much better solution would be to subtract constructors' championship points for additional components. The driver, after all, had not transgressed, so why should he have been penalised? The argument against this, apparently, is that a team with a significant points advantage would simply keep taking new components.

Pérez was fourth quickest with the second Red Bull, but had a ten-place drop for a fourth ICE.

Lewis Hamilton's Mercedes was 1.3s shy of the Ferrari pole-position pace as the seven-time champion pipped team-mate George Russell by a couple of hundredths after the latter had been quicker throughout the practices. Just four-hundredths further adrift was Lando Norris with the first McLaren, team-mate and 2021 winner Daniel Riccardo next up, but still 0.34s adrift, the typical margin between the pair throughout the year.

Fernando Alonso had looked strong all weekend, but admitted that his Q3 was "not well executed" after finishing tenth in the classification, having abandoned both Q3 runs. By the time the penalties had been applied, though, he would start sixth!

It was some considerable time before anyone fully understood what Sunday's grid would look like. Once the penalties had been applied, Leclerc shared the front row with Russell, and the two McLarens were on row two. Pierre Gasly's AlphaTauri and Alonso were on row three, ahead of Verstappen and de Vries. Zhou Guanyu and Nicholas Latifi lined up on row five, ahead of the Aston Martins of Sebastian Vettel and Lance Stroll.

The penalised Pérez would start 13th, ahead of Esteban Ocon's Alpine (five-place penalty for a fifth ICE), Valtteri Bottas's Alfa Romeo (15-place penalty for a sixth ICE

THE *tifosi* thronged to the Temple of Speed in their thousands, in the hope that Charles Leclerc could repeat his heroics of 2019 and give Ferrari its 20th Monza win. Charles had elected to start the 53-lap race on the soft-compound Pirelli tyres, in keeping with fellow front-row starter George Russell, Max Verstappen, Nyck de Vries and Esteban Ocon; the rest were on the yellow-walled medium tyre.

With a 450m dash down to the braking zone for the tight first chicane, Leclerc made a sufficiently strong getaway to flick right across the front of Russell's Mercedes and cover off the inside. Russell had a look at the outside, but was forced over the Turn Two kerb as Leclerc took his line, George keeping his boot in and emerging still second. There were huge cheers from the home faithful as their beloved Ferrari led the field through Curva Grande.

Behind, Daniel Ricciardo had made another strong getaway at the scene of his McLaren career highlight a year earlier, and was chased by Pierre Gasly (another Monza winner, of course), Verstappen, Lando Norris (who had gone into anti-stall off the line), then Fernando Alonso, de Vries, Zhou Guanyu, Sebastian Vettel, Lance Stroll, Kevin Magnussen, Ocon, Nicholas Latifi, Sergio Pérez, Carlos Sainz, Mick Schumacher, Yuki Tsunoda, Lewis Hamilton and Valtteri Bottas.

Verstappen did not even have to await the third-lap activation of DRS to utilise the Red Bull's superior straight-line speed to demote Gasly and Ricciardo, and move up into third, his five-place engine penalty appearing to be a small impediment. Further back, Sainz managed to barge by Pérez's Red Bull.

With Monza 'skinny wings', the effectiveness of DRS is much reduced, with an estimated gain of only around 5mph on the main straight, but by the end of the fourth lap, Verstappen was close enough through Parabolica to close down Russell's Mercedes and go inside into the first chicane to annexe second. Leclerc's leading Ferrari was only 2s up the road.

The *tifosi*, meanwhile, were appreciative of Sainz's progress as he came through the field, up into the top ten after relegating the Aston Martins of Vettel and Stroll.

Pérez was a very early stopper, into the pits after just seven laps with the second Red Bull. He'd flat-spotted his starting mediums in a late-braking contest with Sainz on the opening lap and was suffering serious vibrations. As he accelerated back into the race, smoke billowed from the right front wheel, some debris having lodged in his brake duct. It soon caught fire, the Mexican relying on the high-speed Monza lap to generate some airflow to put it out!

By lap ten, we had an all-Spanish battle for seventh place as Sainz closed in on Alonso, who was amid a DRS train also comprising Gasly and Norris, with the impressive de Vries and Zhou right behind. There was little that Fernando could do to resist, and a lap later, the same applied to Sainz's old McLaren team-mate, Norris, as Carlos arrowed down the inside into the first chicane to put the second Ferrari into the top six. Gasly's AlphaTauri succumbed next time around.

There followed a somewhat cryptic message to Leclerc from Ferrari: "If Verstappen goes to Plan C, we would like to go to Plan B. Are you happy with that?"

"Yes, happy," confirmed Leclerc.

The Scuderia had taken its fair share of strategy criticism throughout 2022, and here, again, was the suggestion that the pit-wall crew lacked confidence. Mattia Binotto countered that, however, claiming that they were well on top of their plan, but that driver input was valuable, too, which was fair enough.

On lap 12, suddenly a yellow flag appeared in sector two as Vettel ground to a halt. It quickly became a VSC so that the Aston could be recovered just after the second Lesmo.

"What do you think about boxing for Plan A?" Ferrari asked Leclerc.

Above: Charles Leclerc shuts the door on George Russell as the front-row pair attack the first chicane.
Photo: Peter Nygaard/GP Photo

Top left: Touching the badge. Dressed in unfamiliar yellow for the Ferrari anniversary celebrations, Leclerc took pole for Ferrari.
Photo: Scuderia Ferrari

Above left: A big day for Nyck de Vries, about to make his first grand-prix start.
Photo: Williams Racing

Centre left: The Monza track was celebrating its 100th anniversary.
Photo: Alfa Romeo ORLEN

Left: Piero Lardi Ferrari, the only living son of Enzo, was in attendance for the occasion.
Photo: Scuderia Ferrari

Opening spread: Anticlimax. The safety car leads the field across the line to conclude proceedings.
Photo: Pirelli

ORACLE
ESSO
citrix

PIRELLI

"Yeah, it will be tight, but probably the best solution," Leclerc agreed as the Ferrari came into the pit lane and got rid of its starting softs in favour of a set of mediums. He was the only one to do so as Verstappen continued on into the lead, with Russell's Mercedes some 4.5s behind. Leclerc had a big gap to drop into before Ricciardo's McLaren when the race went green again, rejoining third after a quick 2.2s Ferrari stop.

It was difficult to decide whether the "tight" situation that the Ferrari team leader had referred to was getting out still ahead of Ricciardo, or managing 40 laps on a set of Pirelli mediums. The latter promised to be a tall order. Behind him, Sainz continued his inexorable progress by relegating Ricciardo and taking fourth, now just 2s behind his freshly reshod team-mate.

Red Bull, of course, was fully cognisant of the situation Ferrari's early-stop gamble had created, engineer 'GP' Lambiase getting on the blower to tell Verstappen, "That's a long stint required for Leclerc on this medium tyre, and I think his front left was in slightly worse shape than yours, so back into your rhythm." Verstappen now led with a 5s margin over Russell and Leclerc 17.5s off the lead, with a pit stop taking approximately 24.5s.

With 14 laps down, Gasly made a bold bid to separate Ricciardo from fifth place down the inside into Turn One, but ran wide and had to give the place back.

Save for the flat-spotted Pérez, Gasly and Lance Stroll became the first of the medium-tyre starters to pit, after 18 laps, McLaren being forced to respond with Ricciardo next time around to successfully defend the undercut. De Vries, meanwhile, was continuing to impress on his F1 debut, storming along in eighth place, right with Norris and Alonso as McLaren and Alpine continued their scrap over fourth place in the constructors' championship. The Dutchman had started on the softs and was in for a set of mediums after 19 laps.

A few laps later, Alonso radioed Alpine: "We have a problem with the deployment, or everything is normal?"

"Everything looks okay from our side," they told him.

"Wow!" was his response as he felt a lack of power.

Russell, after 23 laps on his starting set of softs, now stopped for some mediums.

Two laps later, after a long opening stint on his softs, Verstappen was in for a set of mediums, some 13 laps after Leclerc's VSC-assisted stop, rejoining 10s behind the leading Ferrari.

The second Ferrari came in after an impressive 30-lap opening stint from the back on mediums, Sainz locking up quite spectacularly before taking on a set of softs for the remaining 22 laps. He rejoined just behind Pérez's hard-compound-shod Red Bull.

Alonso, in his 349th GP, equalled Kimi Räikkönen's total to become the most experienced F1 driver ever, but it was not a race to remember. A ten-race sequence of finishing in the points came to an end when he was told to pit with a power unit issue.

Above: Nyck de Vries made a dream debut, taking ninth place for Williams, ahead of much more experienced opposition.
Photo: XPB Images

Top left: No smoke without fire. Sergio Pérez had to contend with some debris becoming lodged in his brake duct. It soon ignited, but was swiftly extinguished on the Monza straights.

Above left: Starting fifth on the grid helped Pierre Gasly into the points; the AlphaTauri driver finished eighth.

Left: By the fourth lap, Max Verstappen's Red Bull easily slipped inside George Russell's Mercedes.
Photos: Red Bull Content Pool/Getty Images

Above: With all the penalties taken, Lando Norris lined up third on the grid. He ran a long first stint, pushing his Pirelli mediums to the limit.
Photo: McLaren F1 Team

Top right: Just off the podium, Carlos Sainz takes the opportunity to capture the atmosphere on his mobile.
Photo: Scuderia Ferrari

Above right: Third place for George Russell kept him well ahead of team-mate Lewis Hamilton in the championship standings.
Photo: Mercedes-AMG Petronas F1 Team

Right: Slow train coming. Verstappen leads the lapped cars of Bottas and Tsunoda across the line at the finish.
Photo: XPB Images

With Verstappen halving Leclerc's lead in eight laps after his stop and 20 laps still remaining, Ferrari made the call to pit Charles again while he still had a pit window to third-placed Russell, who was lapping competitively. A brand-new set of softs was fitted to the Ferrari.

Hamilton came in from seventh place a lap later, also going for softs and rejoining behind a Ricciardo/Gasly/deVries/Zhou train.

Norris stopped even later than Hamilton, after a 35-lap opening stint, which should have worked for him and promoted him to sixth, but a problem at the rear resulted in a slow 5s stop. He emerged just as Ricciardo, Gasly and Hamilton arrived down the main straight and was beaten into the first chicane by his team-mate. Then Gasly went around his outside into T2 and he lost a further place to Hamilton on exit, Lewis also managing to displace Gasly before the Roggia chicane.

Next time around, Hamilton was inside Ricciardo into Turn One and up to sixth place, while Norris, on his fresh softs, made short work of Gasly.

It was a bad afternoon for Aston Martin. With Vettel already out of the race thanks to a power unit issue, Stroll now received the instruction to cool the brakes, then pit and retire the car.

With Hamilton lapping quickly and just 10s behind the hard-tyred Pérez with 12 laps to go, Red Bull elected to pit the Mexican for a set of softs. In the process, he lost track position to Hamilton and Norris.

Further back, de Vries was still running tenth for Williams, looking set to score on his debut, but he had Zhou's Alfa breathing down his neck. He got a good break when Leclerc arrived to lap the pair of them, and in the process, Zhou lost DRS.

With six laps remaining, we had a yellow flag in sector two when Ricciardo came to a halt between the two Lesmos and radioed in that he'd lost the engine.

When the full safety car notification was posted, Verstappen and Leclerc had gone through to start lap 48, but Russell and Sainz were far enough back to pit. Norris stopped as well.

Verstappen had a 23s margin over Leclerc, and when he asked if he could make a free stop, he was told that he could. Ferrari was in discussion with Leclerc, telling him that he wouldn't gain a position by staying out, so to box as well. Both took on softs – Verstappen's new, but Leclerc's, used.

De Vries, meanwhile, had reported a long brake pedal, so the safety car intervention was good news for the man who now occupied ninth after Ricciardo's demise.

On the penultimate lap, Ferrari told Leclerc, "We will finish the race behind the safety car."

"Come on, it's clear. Come on!" complained the Monégasque.

Around the circuit, the boos rang out, and you could not help but think back to Abu Dhabi at the end of 2021. On that occasion, the rule book had not been followed. After the outrage that had followed, the removal of Michael Masi from his race director role and the worldwide spotlight that had shone on Formula 1, there was never any chance that the conclusion of the Italian GP was ever going to go any other way than by the book. It was an unsatisfactory conclusion, just as Abu Dhabi had been for very different reasons.

Anticlimactic though it was, Verstappen stood on the Monza podium for the first time in his career, having taken a fifth successive GP victory and the 30th of his career. Leclerc, Russell, Sainz, Hamilton, Pérez, Norris, Gasly, a delighted de Vries – the Driver of the Day – and Zhou were the points scorers. It just didn't seem a very appropriate way for the Monza/Ferrari anniversary celebrations to conclude.

Verstappen's second successive world championship was pretty much a foregone conclusion, as now he was a mammoth 116 points clear of Leclerc in the table. It meant that, mathematically, it could all be tied up at the following race, in Singapore.

Tony Dodgins

VIEWPOINT
FINISHING SCHOOL

YOU could say that the aftershock of Abu Dhabi, 2021 continued to reverberate during the closing laps at Monza. As at Zandvoort the week before, the presence of a stranded car triggered disagreement, this time over the method chosen by officials to deal with it. Or, put another way, that was the view of the eternally optimistic *tifosi*, keen to witness a Ferrari victory in such a disappointing season for Maranello and Italy.

When Daniel Ricciardo's McLaren rolled to a halt, it not only summed up the Australian's increasingly dire situation, but also triggered hope that the subsequent safety car would allow a grandstand finish in the Temple of Speed. It didn't work out that way.

The safety car had been called because a truck was needed to remove the McLaren, which was stuck in gear. Adding to the confusion, the safety car had been scrambled just as George Russell was exiting the pits, the Mercedes having stopped for tyres one lap after the leaders, who now were at the back of the pack.

Normally, those ahead of the leader would have been waved through by the safety car, but, given the potentially hazardous presence of the rescue truck, it was important to keep the field bunched to allow recovery to continue as safely as possible. Meanwhile, the final laps were counting down, and there simply was not enough time to re-establish the race order for the final shootout viewers and spectators wanted.

Later, there would be suggestions that a red flag would have provided all the answers – much as it would have done in Abu Dhabi. Conscious of the uproar that continued to reverberate around social media, however, the Monza officials executed this one exactly by the book. Disappointing as it was, this was the result – with the proviso that Max Verstappen's pace all weekend had suggested that a victory for Charles Leclerc was as unlikely as this race director making decisions driven solely by the wish to lay on a dramatic finish.

Maurice Hamilton

16

Official Timepiece

FORMULA 1 PIRELLI GRAN PREMIO D'ITALIA 2022

MONZA 9-11 SEPTEMBER

RACE DISTANCE: 53 laps, 190.587 miles/306.720km

RACE WEATHER: Dry/sunny (track 41-44°C, air 29-31°C)

AUTODROMO NAZIONALE DI MONZA

Circuit: 3.600 miles/5.793km, 53 laps

RACE – OFFICIAL CLASSIFICATION

Pos.	Driver	Nat.	No.	Entrant	Car/Engine	Laps	Time/Retirement	Speed (mph/km/h)	Gap to winner	Fastest race lap
1	**Max Verstappen**	NL	1	Oracle Red Bull Racing	Red Bull RB18-RBPTH001 V6	53	1h 20m 27.511s	142.126/228.729		1m 24.745s 38
2	**Charles Leclerc**	MC	16	Scuderia Ferrari	Ferrari F1-75-066/7 V6	53	1h 20m 29.957s	142.054/228.613	2.446s	1m 24.336s 38
3	**George Russell**	GB	63	Mercedes-AMG Petronas F1 Team	Mercedes-AMG F1 W13-M13 E Perf. V6	53	1h 20m 30.916s	142.025/228.567	3.405s	1m 25.288s 40
4	**Carlos Sainz**	E	55	Scuderia Ferrari	Ferrari F1-75-066/7 V6	53	1h 20m 32.572s	141.976/228.489	5.061s	1m 24.446s 41
5	**Lewis Hamilton**	GB	44	Mercedes-AMG Petronas F1 Team	Mercedes-AMG F1 W13-M13 E Perf. V6	53	1h 20m 32.891s	141.967/228.474	5.380s	1m 24.434s 43
6	**Sergio Pérez**	MEX	11	Oracle Red Bull Racing	Red Bull RB18-RBPTH001 V6	53	1h 20m 33.602s	141.946/228.440	6.091s	1m 24.030s 46
7	**Lando Norris**	GB	4	McLaren F1 Team	McLaren MCL36-Mercedes F1 M13 E Perf. V6	53	1h 20m 33.718s	141.943/228.435	6.207s	1m 24.718s 43
8	**Pierre Gasly**	F	10	Scuderia AlphaTauri	AlphaTauri AT03-RBPTH001 V6	53	1h 20m 33.907s	141.937/228.426	6.396s	1m 26.718s 30
9	**Nyck de Vries**	NL	45	Williams Racing	Williams FW44-Mercedes F1 M13 E Perf. V6	53	1h 20m 34.633s	141.916/228.392	7.122s	1m 26.624s 41
10	**Zhou Guanyu**	CHN	24	Alfa Romeo F1 Team ORLEN	Alfa Romeo C42-Ferrari 066/7 V6	53	1h 20m 35.421s	141.893/228.354	7.910s	1m 26.361s 41
11	Esteban Ocon	F	31	BWT Alpine F1 Team	Alpine A522-Renault E-Tech RE22 V6	53	1h 20m 35.834s	141.881/228.335	8.323s	1m 26.593s 37
12	Mick Schumacher	D	47	Haas F1 Team	Haas VF-22-Ferrari 066/7 V6	53	1h 20m 36.060s	141.874/228.324	8.549s	1m 25.298s 43
13	Valtteri Bottas	FIN	77	Alfa Romeo F1 Team ORLEN	Alfa Romeo C42-Ferrari 066/7 V6	52			1 lap	1m 25.706s 45
14	Yuki Tsunoda	J	22	Scuderia AlphaTauri	AlphaTauri AT03-RBPTH001 V6	52			1 lap	1m 26.857s 43
15	Nicholas Latifi	CDN	6	Williams Racing	Williams FW44-Mercedes F1 M13 E Perf. V6	52			1 lap	1m 26.798s 17
16	Kevin Magnussen	DK	20	Haas F1 Team	Haas VF-22-Ferrari 066/7 V6	52	*		1 lap	1m 26.798s 37
	Daniel Ricciardo	AUS	3	McLaren F1 Team	McLaren MCL36-Mercedes F1 M13 E Perf. V6	45	*oil leak*			1m 26.603s 39
	Lance Stroll	CDN	18	Aston Martin Aramco Cognizant F1 Team	Aston Martin AMR22-Mercedes F1 M13 E Perf. V6	39	*engine*			1m 27.467s 34
	Fernando Alonso	E	14	BWT Alpine F1 Team	Alpine A522-Renault E-Tech RE22 V6	31	*water pump*			1m 27.203s 7
	Sebastian Vettel	D	5	Aston Martin Aramco Cognizant F1 Team	Aston Martin AMR22-Mercedes F1 M13 E Perf. V6	10	*power unit*			1m 27.501s 4
EW	Alexander Albon	T	23	Williams Racing	Williams FW44-Mercedes F1 M13 E Perf. V6		*unwell with appendicitis*			

The race ended behind the safety car.

* Magnussen: 5s time penalty for leaving the track and gaining an advantage (served at pit stop).

DHL Fastest race lap (scores 1 point): Sergio Pérez on lap 46, 1m 24.030s, 154.214mph/248.182km/h.

Lap record: Rubens Barrichello (Ferrari F2004 V10), 1m 21.046s, 159.892mph/257.320km/h (2004)

19 · HAMILTON · Mercedes
Used additional power unit elements; required to start from the back of the grid

17 · SCHUMACHER · Haas
Used additional power unit element and restricted-number components; 15-place grid penalty

15 · BOTTAS · Alfa Romeo
Used additional power unit elements; 15-place grid penalty

13 · PÉREZ · Red Bull
Used additional power unit element; 10-place grid penalty

11 · VETTEL · Aston Martin

20 · TSUNODA · AlphaTauri
Used additional power unit elements; required to start from the back of the grid; accumulation of 5 reprimands and failing to slow for yellow flags; 13-place grid penalty;

18 · SAINZ · Ferrari
Used additional power unit elements; required to start from back of the grid; Used restricted-number components; 10-place grid penalty

16 · MAGNUSSEN · Haas
Used additional power unit elements; 15-place grid penalty

14 · OCON · Alpine
Used additional power unit element; 5-place grid penalty

12 · STROLL · Aston Martin

Grid order	1	2	3	4	5	6	7	8	9	10	11	12	13	14	15	16	17	18	19	20	21
16 LECLERC	16	16	16	16	16	16	16	16	16	16	16	1	1	1	1	1	1	1	1	1	1
63 RUSSELL	63	63	63	63	1	1	1	1	1	1	1	16	63	63	63	63	63	63	63	63	63
4 NORRIS	3	1	1	1	63	63	63	63	63	63	63	63	16	16	16	16	16	16	16	16	16
3 RICCIARDO	1	3	3	3	3	3	3	3	3	3	3	3	55	55	55	55	55	55	55	55	55
10 GASLY	10	10	10	10	10	10	10	10	10	10	10	55	3	3	3	3	3	3	4	4	4
14 ALONSO	4	4	4	4	4	4	4	4	4	4	55	10	10	10	10	10	10	4	14	14	14
1 VERSTAPPEN	14	14	14	14	14	14	14	14	14	55	4	4	14	14	14	14	14	14	3	44	44
45 DE VRIES	45	45	45	45	45	45	45	45	55	14	14	14	4	4	4	4	4	45	44	47	47
24 ZHOU	24	24	24	24	24	24	24	55	45	45	45	45	45	45	45	45	45	10	45	77	77
6 LATIFI	5	18	18	18	18	55	55	24	24	24	24	24	24	24	24	24	24	44	31	11	11
5 VETTEL	18	5	5	5	55	18	18	18	18	18	18	18	18	18	18	18	44	24	47	20	20
18 STROLL	20	31	31	31	5	5	5	5	5	31	31	31	31	31	31	44	18	31	22	3	3
11 PEREZ	31	20	20	55	31	11	31	31	31	5	44	44	44	44	44	31	31	22	77	10	10
31 OCON	6	55	55	11	11	31	20	22	22	22	22	22	22	22	22	22	22	18	20	45	45
77 BOTTAS	11	6	11	20	20	20	22	20	44	44	20	20	6	6	20	47	47	47	11	24	24
20 MAGNUSSEN	55	11	6	6	6	6	6	44	20	20	6	6	20	20	47	20	20	77	10	31	31
47 SCHUMACHER	47	22	22	22	22	22	44	6	6	6	47	47	47	47	77	77	77	20	24	18	22
55 SAINZ	22	44	44	44	44	44	11	47	47	47	77	77	77	77	6	11	11	11	18	22	18
44 HAMILTON	44	47	47	47	47	47	47	77	77	77	11	11	11	11	11	6	6	6	6	6	6
22 TSUNODA	77	77	77	77	77	77	77	11	11	11											

Grid order	22	23	24	25	26	27	28	29	30	31	32	33	34	35	36	37	38	39	40	41
16 LECLERC	1	1	1	1	16	16	16	16	16	16	16	16	1	1	1	1	1	1	1	1
63 RUSSELL	63	16	16	16	1	1	1	1	1	1	1	1	16	16	16	16	16	16	16	16
4 NORRIS	16	63	55	55	55	55	55	55	63	63	63	63	63	63	63	63	63	63	63	63
3 RICCIARDO	55	55	63	63	63	63	63	63	55	4	4	4	4	4	55	55	55	55	55	55
10 GASLY	4	4	4	4	4	4	4	4	4	44	44	55	55	55	11	11	11	11	11	11
14 ALONSO	14	14	14	14	14	44	44	44	44	11	11	11	11	11	3	44	44	44	44	44
1 VERSTAPPEN	44	44	44	44	44	14	14	14	14	55	55	44	77	3	44	4	4	4	4	4
45 DE VRIES	47	47	11	11	11	11	11	11	11	14	47	77	3	10	10	3	3	3	3	3
24 ZHOU	11	11	47	47	47	47	47	47	47	47	77	47	10	44	4	10	10	10	10	10
6 LATIFI	77	77	77	77	77	77	77	77	77	77	3	3	45	45	45	45	45	45	45	45
5 VETTEL	20	20	3	3	3	3	3	3	3	3	10	10	24	77	24	24	24	24	24	24
18 STROLL	3	3	10	10	10	10	10	10	10	10	45	45	44	24	31	31	31	31	31	31
11 PEREZ	10	10	45	45	45	45	45	45	45	45	24	24	31	31	22	22	22	22	22	22
31 OCON	45	45	20	24	24	24	24	24	24	24	31	31	22	22	6	6	6	6	6	47
77 BOTTAS	24	24	24	31	31	31	31	31	31	31	22	22	6	6	47	47	47	47	47	6
20 MAGNUSSEN	31	31	31	22	22	22	22	22	22	22	6	6	18	47	18	77	77	77	77	77
47 SCHUMACHER	22	22	22	6	6	6	6	6	6	6	18	18	47	18	77	18	18	18	20	20
55 SAINZ	18	18	6	18	18	18	18	18	18	18	20	20	20	20	20	20	20	20		
44 HAMILTON	6	6	18	20	20	20	20	20	20	20										
22 TSUNODA																				

VSC VSC (laps 12, 13)

VSC Virtual safety car deployed on laps shown

TIME SHEETS

PRACTICE 1 (FRIDAY)

Weather: Dry/cloudy

Temperatures: track 33-41°C, air 27-29°C

Pos.	Driver	Laps	Time
1	Charles Leclerc	25	1m 22.410s
2	Carlos Sainz	23	1m 22.487s
3	George Russell	27	1m 22.689s
4	Lewis Hamilton	24	1m 22.831s
5	Max Verstappen	27	1m 22.840s
6	Esteban Ocon	28	1m 23.075s
7	Fernando Alonso	26	1m 23.099s
8	Yuki Tsunoda	26	1m 23.260s
9	Valtteri Bottas	27	1m 23.394s
10	Daniel Ricciardo	26	1m 23.511s
11	Alexander Albon	24	1m 23.529s
12	Zhou Guanyu	28	1m 23.570s
13	Pierre Gasly	27	1m 23.640s
14	Sergio Pérez	21	1m 23.661s
15	Lance Stroll	28	1m 23.688s
16	Lando Norris	27	1m 23.856s
17	Kevin Magnussen	24	1m 24.006s
18	Antonio Giovinazzi	25	1m 24.317s
19	Nyck de Vries	22	1m 24.731s
20	Nicholas Latifi	24	1m 24.941s

PRACTICE 2 (FRIDAY)

Weather: Dry/sunny

Temperatures: track 33-36°C, air 28-30°C

Pos.	Driver	Laps	Time
1	Carlos Sainz	24	1m 21.664s
2	Max Verstappen	27	1m 21.807s
3	Charles Leclerc	23	1m 21.857s
4	Lando Norris	29	1m 22.338s
5	George Russell	24	1m 22.386s
6	Sergio Pérez	26	1m 22.394s
7	Lewis Hamilton	25	1m 22.503s
8	Esteban Ocon	29	1m 22.728s
9	Fernando Alonso	28	1m 22.752s
10	Alexander Albon	24	1m 22.835s
11	Daniel Ricciardo	26	1m 22.911s
12	Zhou Guanyu	30	1m 22.938s
13	Valtteri Bottas	26	1m 22.993s
14	Pierre Gasly	25	1m 23.135s
15	Yuki Tsunoda	31	1m 23.217s
16	Kevin Magnussen	25	1m 23.557s
17	Sebastian Vettel	26	1m 23.731s
18	Lance Stroll	27	1m 23.785s
19	Nicholas Latifi	23	1m 23.982s
20	Mick Schumacher	9	1m 24.586s

PRACTICE 3 (SATURDAY)

Weather: Dry/sunny

Temperatures: track 38-43°C, air 26-29°C

Pos.	Driver	Laps	Time
1	Max Verstappen	19	1m 21.252s
2	Charles Leclerc	15	1m 21.599s
3	Sergio Pérez	26	1m 21.848s
4	Carlos Sainz	17	1m 21.897s
5	Fernando Alonso	17	1m 22.306s
6	Lando Norris	19	1m 22.319s
7	George Russell	24	1m 22.357s
8	Yuki Tsunoda	27	1m 22.430s
9	Esteban Ocon	17	1m 22.506s
10	Lewis Hamilton	22	1m 22.567s
11	Zhou Guanyu	14	1m 22.657s
12	Pierre Gasly	21	1m 22.755s
13	Nicholas Latifi	19	1m 22.776s
14	Nyck de Vries	21	1m 22.869s
15	Daniel Ricciardo	19	1m 22.871s
16	Valtteri Bottas	26	1m 22.950s
17	Sebastian Vettel	20	1m 23.104s
18	Kevin Magnussen	17	1m 23.203s
19	Mick Schumacher	8	1m 23.392s
20	Lance Stroll	16	1m 23.739s

QUALIFYING (SATURDAY))

Weather: Dry/sunny Temperatures: track 36-41°C, air 28-31°C

Pos.	Driver	First	Second	Third	Qualifying Tyre
1	Charles Leclerc	1m 21.280s	1m 21.208s	1m 20.161s	Soft (n)
2	Max Verstappen	1m 20.922s	1m 21.265s	1m 20.306s	Soft (n)
3	Carlos Sainz	1m 21.348s	1m 20.878s	1m 20.429s	Soft (n)
4	Sergio Pérez	1m 21.495s	1m 21.358s	1m 21.206s	Soft (n)
5	Lewis Hamilton	1m 22.048s	1m 21.708s	1m 21.524s	Soft (n)
6	George Russell	1m 21.785s	1m 21.747s	1m 21.542s	Soft (n)
7	Lando Norris	1m 22.130s	1m 21.831s	1m 21.584s	Soft (n)
8	Daniel Ricciardo	1m 22.139s	1m 21.855s	1m 21.925s	Soft (n)
9	Pierre Gasly	1m 22.010s	1m 22.062s	1m 22.648s	Soft (u)
10	Fernando Alonso	1m 22.089s	1m 21.861s	no time	
11	Esteban Ocon	1m 22.166s	1m 22.130s		
12	Valtteri Bottas	1m 22.254s	1m 22.235s		
13	Nyck de Vries	1m 22.567s	1m 22.471s		
14	Zhou Guanyu	1m 22.003s	1m 22.577s		
15	Yuki Tsunoda	1m 22.020s	no time		
16	Nicholas Latifi	1m 22.587s			
17	Sebastian Vettel	1m 22.636s			
18	Lance Stroll	1m 22.748s			
19	Kevin Magnussen	1m 22.908s			
20	Mick Schumacher	1m 23.005s			

QUALIFYING: head to head

Hamilton	9	7	Russell
Verstappen	13	3	Pérez
Ricciardo	2	14	Norris
Leclerc	12	4	Sainz
Gasly	10	6	Tsunoda
Hülkenberg	1	1	Stroll
Vettel	9	5	Stroll
Alonso	10	6	Ocon
Bottas	11	5	Zhou
Albon	13	2	Latifi
de Vries	1	0	Latifi
Magnussen	12	4	Schumacher

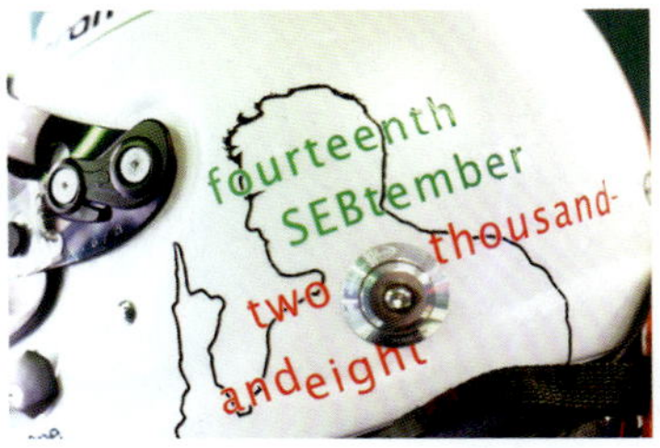

FOR THE RECORD

1st GRAND PRIX & FIRST POINT: Nyck de Vries.

10,000th POINT: Ferrari drivers.

350th GRAND PRIX START: Fernando Alonso

20th PODIUM: Charles Leclerc.

DID YOU KNOW?

Max Verstappen becomes the 9th driver to win 5 consecutive championship GPs

Other than Nyck de Vries, car number 45 has only appeared in championship grands prix once before: Andre Lotterer (Caterham) at the 2014 Belgian GP.

POINTS

DRIVERS

1	Max Verstappen	335
2	Charles Leclerc	219
3	Sergio Pérez	210
4	George Russell	203
5	Carlos Sainz	187
6	Lewis Hamilton	168
7	Lando Norris	88
8	Esteban Ocon	66
9	Fernando Alonso	59
10	Valtteri Bottas	46
11	Pierre Gasly	22
12	Kevin Magnussen	22
13	Sebastian Vettel	20
14	Daniel Ricciardo	19
15	Mick Schumacher	12
16	Yuki Tsunoda	11
17	Zhou Guanyu	6
18	Lance Stroll	5
19	Alexander Albon	4
20	Nyck de Vries	2

CONSTRUCTORS

1	Red Bull	545
2	Ferrari	406
3	Mercedes	371
4	Alpine	125
5	McLaren	107
6	Alfa Romeo	52
7	Haas	34
8	AlphaTauri	33
9	Aston Martin	25
10	Williams	6

9 · ZHOU · Alfa Romeo

7 · VERSTAPPEN · Red Bull
Used additional power unit element;
5-place grid penalty

5 · GASLY · AlphaTauri

3 · NORRIS · McLaren

1 · LECLERC · Ferrari

10 · LATIFI · Williams

8 · DE VRIES · Williams

6 · ALONSO · Alpine

4 · RICCIARDO · McLaren

2 · RUSSELL · Mercedes

42	43	44	45	46	47	48	49	50	51	52	53	
1	1	1	1	1	1	1	1	1	1	1	1	1
16	16	16	16	16	16	16	16	16	16	16	16	2
63	63	63	63	63	63	63	63	63	63	63	63	3
55	55	55	55	55	55	55	55	55	55	55	55	4
11	44	44	44	44	44	44	44	44	44	44	44	5
44	4	4	4	4	4	11	11	11	11	11	11	6
4	11	11	11	11	11	4	4	4	4	4	4	7
3	3	3	3	10	10	10	10	10	10	10	10	8
10	10	10	10	45	45	45	45	45	45	45	45	9
45	45	45	45	24	24	24	24	24	24	24	24	10
24	24	24	24	31	31	31	31	31	31	31	31	
31	31	31	31	47	47	47	47	47	47	47	47	
22	22	22	47	22	77	77	77	77	77	77		
47	47	47	22	77	22	22	22	22	22	22		
77	77	77	77	6	6	6	6	6	6	6		
6	6	6	6	20	20	20	20	20	20	20		
20	20	20	20									

11 = Pit stop 6 = *One lap or more behind*

SC Safety car deployed on laps shown

						SC	SC	SC	SC	SC	SC	

RACE TYRE STRATEGIES

PIRELLI

	Driver	Race Stint 1	Race Stint 2	Race Stint 3	Race Stint 4
1	Verstappen	Soft (n): 1-25	Medium (n): 26-48	Soft (n): 49-53	
2	Leclerc	Soft (n): 1-12	Medium (n): 13-33	Soft (n): 34-48	Soft (u): 49-53
3	Russell	Soft (n): 1-23	Hard (n): 24-47	Soft (u): 48-53	
4	Sainz	Medium (n): 1-30	Soft (n): 31-47	Soft (n): 48-53	
5	Hamilton	Medium (n): 1-33	Soft (n): 34-53		
6	Pérez	Medium (n): 1-7	Hard (n): 8-42	Soft (n): 43-53	
7	Norris	Medium (n): 1-35	Soft (n): 36-47	Soft (u): 48-53	
8	Gasly	Medium (n): 1-18	Hard (u): 19-53		
9	de Vries	Soft (n): 1-19	Medium (n): 20-53		
10	Zhou	Medium (n): 1-18	Hard (n): 19-53		
11	Ocon	Soft (n): 1-19	Hard (n): 20-53		
12	Schumacher	Medium (n): 1-33	Soft (n): 34-53		
13	Bottas	Medium (n): 1-35	Soft (n): 36-52		
14	Tsunoda	Medium (n): 1-19	Hard (n): 20-47	Soft (u): 48-52	
15	Latifi	Medium (n): 1-15	Hard (n): 16-47	Soft (u): 48-52	
16	Magnussen	Medium (n): 1-24	Hard (n): 25-46	Soft (n): 47-52	
	Ricciardo	Medium (n): 1-19	Hard (n): 20-45 (dnf)		
	Stroll	Medium (u): 1-18	Hard (u): 19-39 (dnf)		
	Alonso	Medium (n): 1-31 (dnf)			
	Vettel	Medium (u): 1-10 (dnf)			

The tyre regulations stipulate that at least two of three dry tyre specifications must be used during a dry race. Selected compounds for Monza: Red = Soft (C4); Yellow = Medium (C3); White = Hard (C2). (n) new (u) used

Red Bull Content Pool/Getty Images

Main photo: Sergio Pérez overcame the mixed conditions to post his finest victory to date.

Inset: How was it for you? Leclerc and Pérez discuss their races.
Photos: Red Bull Content Pool/Getty Images

FIA FORMULA 1 WORLD CHAMPIONSHIP · ROUND 17

SINGAPORE GRAND PRIX

MARINA BAY CIRCUIT

MARINA BAY QUALIFYING

THE Marina Bay race is the most challenging of the year: the longest in terms of time, hot, humid and bumpy. "The vibrations make it hard to keep the eyeline," Carlos Sainz explained, "and to get the last two- or three-tenths of performance is really draining. If you survive Singapore, then you are fit for anything else in F1."

Throw in a wet, but drying track, with intermediate/slick tyre crossover during the qualifying hour, and you had all the ingredients for an epic session, which is what we witnessed.

For the first time in 2022, Lewis Hamilton had topped a practice session in FP1, but both Max Verstappen and Charles Leclerc had experienced set-up issues, so he didn't consider that it had been entirely representative. It's a track where the driver can make a difference, but Hamilton thought that a top-five grid slot was a more realistic target than pole.

For team-mate George Russell, there was disappointment. In FP1, he had struggled with a phenomenon known as 'torque following', whereby the car pushes on mid-corner. It didn't appear for FP2 and FP3, but reared its head again in qualifying, limiting George to 11th on the grid, only the third time in 17 races that he had missed out on the top-ten shootout. The car had seemed particularly gripless through Turn Eight.

If Russell was disappointed, Max Verstappen was fit to be tied when he could qualify no better than eighth. In fact, he'd been on what was clearly a pole-position lap when Red Bull suddenly told him to 'box'.

Everyone had fuelled for the entire Q3 session, knowing that the track would evolve throughout as it dried, and, as Christian Horner explained, in such circumstances, it's always difficult to know precisely how much fuel will be left for the last lap because it depends on so many different factors. The concern was that if Verstappen had finished his lap, he would have had insufficient juice to provide the requisite 1-litre fuel sample, risking having his times deleted and starting from the pits. Eighth was not an ideal place to start in Singapore, where overtaking is tough, but it was much the lesser of two evils.

Verstappen, who had never taken victory in Singapore, was deeply unimpressed: "We should have seen it way earlier..."

It meant that Leclerc, who had bounced back from his bitty Friday to top Saturday morning's wet FP3 session, took his ninth 2022 pole position in a spellbinding Q3. The Ferrari stopped the clock in 1m 49.412s. Sergio Pérez lapped the second Red Bull just 0.02s slower to start on the front row for the first time since Azerbaijan, while Hamilton managed 1m 49.446s to make it just five-hundredths covering the top three.

"I'm very happy after such a limited Friday," Leclerc explained. "It was on the limit with the damp surface, losing the rear, but I did a very clean lap and it was enough."

Pérez was frustrated to miss a second pole of the year by those two-hundredths, and Hamilton grimaced at how close he'd come: "I was pushing so hard and it was so, so close. I knew we'd be closer than we were at Monza, but I didn't know it would be that close."

A couple more tenths would have given Sainz pole, too, and he reckoned he knew where they were: "I probably should have waited a couple of more minutes because the track was getting quicker all the time. A podium is the target."

Fernando Alonso was a superb fifth, just over half a second from pole. Alpine had brought an upgraded floor, and both drivers reckoned it was working well, as had all of the team's 2022 upgrades. Unfortunately for team-mate Esteban Ocon, a brake problem caused his car to pull strongly to the right and feel badly disconnected. He was desperately disappointed to go out in Q1, along with Williams pair Alex Albon and Nicholas Latifi, Daniel Ricciardo and Valtteri Bottas. It was brave of Albon to come to F1's most physical circuit just ten days after suffering a respiratory failure following an allergic reaction to anaesthetic for an appendix operation, and a spell in intensive care!

Lando Norris is always dynamite in changeable conditions, and in stark contrast to his struggling team-mate, he put his McLaren sixth on the grid. "Slicks and wet patches around here don't add up to a nice feeling in the cockpit," he admitted candidly.

Seventh for Pierre Gasly's AlphaTauri was the Frenchman's best starting slot since Azerbaijan, while team-mate Yuki Tsunoda also qualified in the top ten. The pair actually had topped Q3 early on, when they had gone out on the intermediate tyre, but as the track dried, the soft-compound Pirelli became the tyre of choice.

Damp conditions are usually right up Lance Stroll's street, and the Canadian put his Aston Martin 12th on the grid, 0.17s and two places better off than team-mate Sebastian Vettel. The German had taken his 53rd and last GP win around Marina Bay for Ferrari in 2019.

Zhou Guanyu, newly confirmed for a second season with Alfa Romeo, did another strong job to haul himself into Q2 when team-mate Bottas could not.

After an absorbing session, there were seven different chassis in the top ten grid positions: Ferrari, Red Bull, Mercedes, Alpine, McLaren, AlphaTauri and Haas. Max Verstappen had been making a habit of winning races from outside the top ten, but the question was, could he win from eighth around the tight, hot, challenging confines of Singapore?

WITH heavy rain falling at Marina Bay, it appeared initially as though there might not be a Singapore Grand Prix at all, but after a 65-minute delay, we were treated to a grid start, with the whole field on Pirelli's intermediate rubber.

As the lights blinked out, Charles Leclerc and Sergio Pérez, both starting in second gear, recorded almost identical reaction times, but in the second phase of the start, the Ferrari encountered a damper patch of tarmac and suffered from wheelspin. Sergio took full advantage to snatch the lead on the inside line. Behind, Lewis Hamilton had a look around the outside of Carlos Sainz, but the Spaniard ran him wide. Meanwhile, Lando Norris made a good start to slot into fifth, ahead of Pierre Gasly's AlphaTauri as Fernando Alonso dropped back a couple of places to seventh. Circuit specialist and five-time race winner Sebastian Vettel ran eighth for Aston Martin – up five places! – ahead of Yuki Tsunoda and Lance Stroll.

What of the world champion? As if starting eighth was not bad enough, Max Verstappen's Red Bull went into anti-stall off the grid and lost another three places. Kevin Magnussen was not at all accommodating by elbowing him down another slot, with Daniel Ricciardo also going by before the Dutchman sorted himself out and quickly retook the place.

"Magnussen has an endplate loose," Max radioed in. He wasn't about to be behind him for any length of time, though, and he passed the Haas and Stroll's Aston Martin on lap two to put himself back in the top ten, making a mockery of assertions that it is impossible to pass around Marina Bay. Tsunoda, unsurprisingly, did not try too hard to hinder his progress, allowing Max to set off after Vettel.

Meanwhile, Hamilton was on the radio, unhappy. "I told you about these tyres," he complained. "In future, you need to listen to me. No grip…" He had wanted to start on scrubbed rather than new intermediates.

On lap seven, we had a yellow flag in sector one after Zhou and Nicholas Latifi had made contact at Turn Five.

"I just got squeezed into the wall, guys. I don't know what he was doing," Zhou told Alfa Romeo.

"I didn't see him, I have a puncture," Latifi informed Williams, his left rear cocked askew. He would receive a five-place grid drop for the forthcoming Japanese GP from the race stewards and be miffed not to be summoned to present a defence. "He was in my blind spot and should have known I wouldn't see him," he added.

In the meantime, Magnussen had received the black and orange flag and had pitted to change the front wing that had been damaged in the opening-lap contact with Verstappen.

At the front, Pérez and Leclerc seemed to be in a different race from the rest, opening a 10s margin to the second Ferrari over the first eight laps. That was a surprise, given Sainz's career-long aplomb on a slippery surface. The margin was wiped out, however, when the safety car was deployed to allow retrieval of Zhou's Alfa, while Latifi retired with damaged left rear suspension.

The intervention lasted for only a couple of laps, and as it came to an end, Pérez backed up everyone through the tight final sector to allow the safety car time to get into the pits. He overdid it, however, dropping back further than the ten car lengths within which he was supposed to remain behind Bernd Maylander.

Hamilton was quickly on the radio to point out the transgression. "Lights haven't gone out yet and he's pulled a big gap," he snitched. As the race got under way again, the order was Pérez, Leclerc, Sainz, Hamilton, Norris, Alonso, Gasly, Vettel, Verstappen, Tsunoda, Stroll, Ricciardo, Mick

Above: With the track still wet, and the field on Pirelli intermediates, the leading quartet of Pérez, Leclerc, Sainz and Hamilton breaks clear.
Photo: Atsuo Sakurai

Left: Lewis Hamilton put in a great effort to place his Mercedes third on the grid.
Photo: Mercedes-AMG Petronas F1 Team

Above: The Ferraris of Leclerc and Sainz cross the Anderson Bridge.
Photo: Scuderia Ferrari

Top right: A welcome fifth place in a troubled season for Daniel Ricciardo.
Photo: McLaren F1 Team

Above right: Sebastian Vettel brought his Aston Martin home eighth.
Photo: Aston Matin Aramco Cognizant F1 Team

Right: Max Verstappen elbows aside Kevin Magnussen's Haas as he begins his climb through the field.
Photo: Red Bull Content Pool/Getty Images

Schumacher, Esteban Ocon, Valtteri Bottas, George Russell and Magnussen.

Verstappen continued to make ground by dispatching Vettel at the restart, no easy task around Singapore, to move up into the top eight. The next target was Gasly who, like Tsunoda earlier in the race, didn't make his AlphaTauri too wide. Next on his radar was Alonso's Alpine, which would prove a lot more obstructive.

With the track refusing to dry out to any significant degree as the race approached 20 laps, there was still only one real line – but not for Verstappen – and the game was all about trying to look after the starting set of intermediates so that the opening stint could be extended as long as possible. That was confirmed when Norris's race engineer, Will Joseph, told his man, "The goal is to make these inters last longer than anyone else's." Race leader Pérez, meanwhile, was informing the Red Bull pit-wall crew that the right front was starting to wear.

"The tyres are becoming more slick, especially in the dry areas, and it's becoming more and more slippery in the wet areas," Norris confirmed.

With 21 laps on the board, Verstappen was up to sixth place when Alonso's Alpine lost an engine and coasted to a halt, prompting a VSC period. Russell, with nothing much to lose, took advantage of the 10s pit stop saving, electing to roll the dice and change to slicks. He headed back out on the yellow-walled medium-compound Pirelli.

Verstappen's race engineer, Gianpiero Lambiase, keeping his man appraised, passed on the information. "Okay," said Verstappen. "Brave at the moment…"

"No grip," Russell confirmed.

The next little drama involved Alex Albon, who had been complaining about a brake issue, before understeering off and bringing out a yellow. He managed to reverse his Williams back out of the tyre wall and continue, without his front wing, but with a left front puncture. We had another VSC while the wing was recovered. With Russell still losing substantial time on his slicks, that was a good indication that track conditions were still not dry enough to make it worth taking advantage of a shortened pit stop.

With 27 laps down, Pérez had managed to gain some breathing space over Leclerc, the Ferrari dropping 4s behind as its intermediates continued to wear. Sainz, experiencing a similar situation, was now 15s behind his team-mate, with Hamilton's Mercedes harrying him.

"I'm just losing so much time behind this guy. He's really slow," was Hamilton's assessment. Norris's McLaren, meanwhile, was a further 10s behind Lewis and had Verstappen all over it.

For the moment, though, it was still status quo as far as track conditions ruling out an early stop for Hamilton to take on slicks. Then Ocon in the second Alpine also ground to a halt with a power unit issue at Turn 13.

"The tyres will come in eventually, yes," radioed Lewis's team-mate, Russell, sounding frustrated. He was now six laps into his medium-tyre stint, but still 5s off the pace. Another VSC for the stricken Alpine didn't help, and he began to lose the tyre temperature he had built.

On lap 33, Hamilton made a very rare mistake when he ran too deep on to the slippery stuff behind Sainz at Turn Seven and the Mercedes ploughed into the barrier. He kept the engine running and extricated himself just as Norris and

Verstappen arrived on the scene, Lando going by. Lewis managing to keep the Red Bull behind him, however, as he rejoined with a damaged left front wing.

Meanwhile, Russell set his first purple sector, tipping everyone the wink that the track was just about ready for a swap to slicks.

Now it was Hamilton's turn to be snitched upon. "His front wing is completely loose. It's dangerous, it's going to fly off," Verstappen informed Red Bull.

Handily for Hamilton, his mistake had come just at the slick-tyre crossover point, Leclerc heading into the pits for a set of mediums on lap 35, with 26 still to go. It was not the greatest of Ferrari stops, at just over 5s, Charles having gone a bit long on the slippery surface. Hamilton's stop, for a new wing as well as tyres, occupied just under 14s, dropping him a place to Vettel.

Race leader Pérez responded on the next lap, while Verstappen gave the instruction to do the opposite of Norris on stop timing. When the McLaren carried on around, car No.1 was in.

Just as the pit stops began, Tsunoda, who had already switched to slicks, understeered straight on at Turn Ten and buried his AlphaTauri in the tyres, creating a second safety car period and cheap stops for those still to make them.

When the safety car period ended and everyone was on slicks, there were 35 minutes left on the clock before the end of the two-hour maximum. The order was Pérez, Leclerc, Sainz, Norris, Verstappen, Ricciardo, Stroll, Vettel, Hamilton, Gasly, Schumacher, Bottas, Magnussen and Russell, with six cars out of the race.

"Can you just check the right rear brake temperature because I can see a tear-off hanging in there?" Verstappen asked Red Bull.

"We're okay for the moment, Max," Lambiase told him.

On the restart lap, the Dutchman immediately attacked Norris, but locked up as he tried to go past on the inside of Turn Seven, sliding down the escape road, his left front wreathed in smoke. He spun the car around and resumed, but had dropped to eighth, behind Vettel's Aston and just ahead of old sparring partner Hamilton.

Above: Lance Stroll comes out on medium slicks on lap 36, after his single pit stop. The Canadian recorded his best result of the season in sixth.
Photo: Aston Martin Aramco Cognizant F1 Team

Above right: A good day for McLaren. Lando Norris took fourth place ahead of team-mate Ricciardo, putting the team ahead of Alpine in the constructors' battle.
Photo: McLaren F1 Team

Right: "A super job." Pérez earned the plaudits of his team boss, Christian Horner, after victory in Singapore.
Photo: Red Bull Content Pool/Getty Images

"I completely bottomed out," Verstappen explained, referring to tyres that were not fully up to temperature and hence pressure, lowering the ride height in turn. He pitted again to get rid of his flat-spotted mediums in favour of a set of softs.

Next in trouble was Russell, the Mercedes crawling around with a right front puncture after contact with Schumacher at Turn One.

At the front, Pérez was under heavy pressure from Leclerc. Just as they had done on the intermediates, the pair left Sainz gasping on slicks, the Spaniard dropping 10s adrift in as many minutes. Clearly, both were giving their all, first Pérez and then Leclerc flirting with the walls and barriers. Twice, Pérez locked his left front going into Turn 14, but got away with it.

Then it was Leclerc's turn, going a little too deep into Turn 17, the time loss taking him out of DRS range and giving Pérez some respite. The Mexican made the most of it, opening a 2s advantage for the first time since the slicks had gone on.

With ten minutes left on the clock, Ferrari told Leclerc, "We need to stay within 5s from Pérez. He may have a penalty at the end of the race, safety car infringement."

Pérez's engineer, Hugh Bird, meanwhile, told his man, "There may be an investigation for a safety car infringement after the race, so let's disappear."

Further behind, Verstappen was now back on Hamilton's rear wing for eighth place, with Lewis himself trapped behind Vettel's Aston Martin, the trio boasting 12 world titles between them!

With just over a minute left on the clock, Hamilton had a look down Vettel's inside at Turn Eight, but got on the slippery stuff and ran wide, letting a grateful Verstappen by. Then Max made it seventh with a DRS pass of Vettel on the last lap.

Time ran out after 58 of the scheduled 61 laps, Pérez taking the chequer some 7.3s to the good, Leclerc having backed off as Sergio achieved his 5s margin. With two safety car transgressions being looked into, though, might he have needed 10s?

Behind Sainz, Norris was a fine fourth, while both Ricciardo and Stroll achieved their best finishes of the season so far with fifth and sixth respectively. Verstappen, Vettel, Hamilton and Gasly completed the scorers.

Pérez's fourth GP victory had been the greatest of his career to date.

"Without a doubt, it was," said Christian Horner. "The way he looked after the intermediates, the safety car restarts, the crossover on to slicks and his pace at the end. Charles threw everything at him, and he was world class. It even surpasses Monaco. Under massive pressure. A super job."

Verstappen had shown searing pace on the rare occasions he found himself in free air, but Pérez and Leclerc had traded fastest laps with him, even in the closing laps when Max was on softs and Sergio on mediums.

There followed a tense hour or two when Pérez was summoned to the stewards to explain why he'd dropped more than ten car lengths behind Bernd Maylander's safety car. Twice. He was looking at a potential 5s penalty for each offence…

In mitigation, Pérez explained that in those conditions, he did not want to restart with cold tyres and brakes, and that while there were places where the safety car was much slower than the race cars, that didn't apply to the final sector, which hadn't dried.

While the stewards weren't fully satisfied with the explanation, they cut Pérez some slack. He received a reprimand for the first offence and a 5s penalty plus two penalty points for the second. Thus his winning margin ended up at 2.5s. His closing-lap efforts, right on the limit, had been decisive.

"In the car, I didn't feel the tiredness, but when I got out, I certainly did!" said the exhausted-looking Mexican. If ever a driver deserved a slice of good fortune, it was Pérez in Singapore.

Tony Dodgins

VIEWPOINT
PEERLESS PÉREZ

THE relentlessly taxing 23 turns of the Marina Bay circuit are difficult enough when it's hot and humid. Throw in a track that has dried in parts and remains resolutely wet in others, and you have the most demanding race of the year. That much was evident by the state of Sergio Pérez and Charles Leclerc as they cooled down to the point of near collapse after two hours of intense concentration. It had been a superb drive by Pérez; his best so far.

It was also timely, given the manner in which Sergio's performances since his win in Monaco had been shaded – considerably on occasions – by Max Verstappen in the other RB18. If you want to talk figures, he had been 0.68s slower on average than the Dutchman in qualifying; not completely out of court on the one hand (given Max's step on to another level of confidence in both himself and his car); but on the other, this – and the dearth of points expected by Red Bull – had been a performance deficiency serious enough to have Pierre Gasly and Alex Albon demoted in the past.

With Pérez's sense of responsibility heightened by Verstappen being back on the fourth row and effectively out of the equation, the pressure came not from the gimlet eye of Dr Helmut Marko, but from the perpetual presence of Leclerc.

From the moment Pérez assumed the lead at the first corner, the Ferrari was a threat while 'Checo' tried not to take too much out of his inters early on. He also had to deal with two safety cars and three VSCs, which presented Leclerc with attacking opportunities every time. On each occasion, he remained cool.

The best – or the worst, depending on your point of view – came in the final phase when exhaustion was countered by adrenalin as Pérez stayed on the dry line and avoided the small, but crucial errors that could have put him on to the wet and into the wall in an instant.

"It was super-tricky," he said. It was also quite brilliant.

Maurice Hamilton

17

ROLEX

Official Timepiece

FORMULA 1 SINGAPORE AIRLINES SINGAPORE GRAND PRIX 2022

SINGAPORE 30 SEPTEMBER-2 OCTOBER

RACE DISTANCE: 59 laps, 185.529 miles/298.580km

RACE WEATHER: Wet-drying track, cloudy (track 29°C, air 26°C)

MARINA BAY STREET CIRCUIT, SINGAPORE

Circuit: 3.146 miles/5.063km, 61 laps

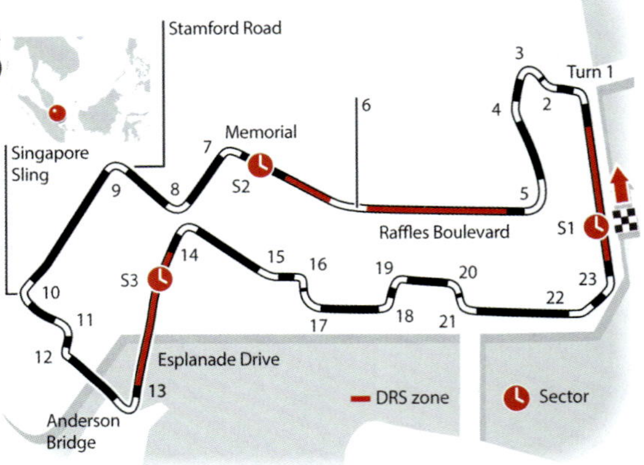

RACE – OFFICIAL CLASSIFICATION

Pos.	Driver	Nat.	No.	Entrant	Car/Engine	Laps	Time/Retirement	Speed (mph/km/h)	Gap to winner	Fastest race lap	
1	**Sergio Pérez**	MEX	11	Oracle Red Bull Racing	Red Bull RB18-RBPTH001 V6	59	2h 02m 20.238s *	90.992/146.437		1m 48.165s	57
2	**Charles Leclerc**	MC	16	Scuderia Ferrari	Ferrari F1-75-066/7 V6	59	2h 02m 22.833s	90.960/146.386	2.595s	1m 48.753s	54
3	**Carlos Sainz**	E	55	Scuderia Ferrari	Ferrari F1-75-066/7 V6	59	2h 02m 30.543s	90.864/146.232	10.305s	1m 48.414s	59
4	**Lando Norris**	GB	4	McLaren F1 Team	McLaren MCL36-Mercedes F1 M13 E Perf. V6	59	2h 02m 41.371s	90.731/146.017	21.133s	1m 49.212s	56
5	**Daniel Ricciardo**	AUS	3	McLaren F1 Team	McLaren MCL36-Mercedes F1 M13 E Perf. V6	59	2h 03m 13.520s	90.336/145.382	53.282s	1m 51.006s	57
6	**Lance Stroll**	CDN	18	Aston Martin Aramco Cognizant F1 Team	Aston Martin AMR22-Mercedes F1 M13 E Perf. V6	59	2h 03m 16.568s	90.299/145.322	56.330s	1m 50.283s	58
7	**Max Verstappen**	NL	1	Oracle Red Bull Racing	Red Bull RB18-RBPTH001 V6	59	2h 03m 19.063s	90.268/145.273	58.825s	1m 49.142s	52
8	**Sebastian Vettel**	D	5	Aston Martin Aramco Cognizant F1 Team	Aston Martin AMR22-Mercedes F1 M13 E Perf. V6	59	2h 03m 20.270s	90.254/145.249	1m 00.032s	1m 50.669s	58
9	**Lewis Hamilton**	GB	44	Mercedes-AMG Petronas F1 Team	Mercedes-AMG F1 W13-M13 E Perf. V6	59	2h 03m 21.753s	90.236/145.220	1m 01.515s	1m 50.622s	58
10	**Pierre Gasly**	F	10	Scuderia AlphaTauri	AlphaTauri AT03-RBPTH001 V6	59	2h 03m 29.814s	90.137/145.062	1m 09.576s	1m 50.569s	56
11	Valtteri Bottas	FIN	77	Alfa Romeo F1 Team ORLEN	Alfa Romeo C42-Ferrari 066/7 V6	59	2h 03m 49.082s	89.904/144.686	1m 28.844s	1m 51.864s	52
12	Kevin Magnussen	DK	20	Haas F1 Team	Haas VF-22-Ferrari 066/7 V6	59	2h 03m 52.848s	89.858/144.613	1m 32.610s	1m 52.067s	59
13	Mick Schumacher	D	47	Haas F1 Team	Haas VF-22-Ferrari 066/7 V6	58			1 lap	1m 50.290s	58
14	George Russell	GB	63	Mercedes-AMG Petronas F1 Team	Mercedes-AMG F1 W13-M13 E Perf. V6	57	*withdrawn*		2 laps	1m 46.458s	54
	Yuki Tsunoda	J	22	Scuderia AlphaTauri	AlphaTauri AT03-RBPTH001 V6	34	*accident*			1m 58.716s	32
	Esteban Ocon	F	31	BWT Alpine F1 Team	Alpine A522-Renault E-Tech RE22 V6	26	*power unit*			2m 01.105s	24
	Alexander Albon	T	23	Williams Racing	Williams FW44-Mercedes F1 M13 E Perf. V6	25	*accident damage*			2m 02.121s	24
	Fernando Alonso	E	14	BWT Alpine F1 Team	Alpine A522-Renault E-Tech RE22 V6	20	*power unit*			2m 00.463s	19
	Nicholas Latifi	CDN	6	Williams Racing	Williams FW44-Mercedes F1 M13 E Perf. V6	7	*accident damage*			2m 05.585s	5
	Zhou Guanyu	CHN	24	Alfa Romeo F1 Team ORLEN	Alfa Romeo C42-Ferrari 066/7 V6	6	*accident*			2m 05.556s	5

The start of the race was delayed by 65 minutes, due to heavy rain, and was ended on reaching the two-hour limit, at 59 of the scheduled 61 laps.

* Pérez: 5s time penalty for falling more than 10 car lengths behind the safety car..

DHL Fastest race lap: George Russell on lap 54, 1m 46.458s, 106.386mph/171.211km/h.

Lap record: Kevin Magnussen (Haas VF-18-Ferrari V6), 1m 41.905s, 111.139mph/178.860km/h (2018).

20 · RUSSELL · Mercedes
Car modified in parc fermé; required to start from the pit lane; used additional power unit elements

18 · ALBON · Williams

16 · RICCIARDO · McLaren

14 · ZHOU · Alfa Romeo

12 · SCHUMACHER · Haas

19 · LATIFI · Williams

17 · OCON · Alpine

15 · BOTTAS · Alfa Romeo

13 · VETTEL · Aston Martin

11 · STROLL · Aston Martin

Grid order	1	2	3	4	5	6	7	8	9	10	11	12	13	14	15	16	17	18	19	20	21	22	23	24	25	26	27	28	29	30	31	32	33	34	35	36	37	38	39	40	41	42	43	44	45	46	47	48	49
16 LECLERC	11	11	11	11	11	11	11	11	11	11	11	11	11	11	11	11	11	11	11	11	11	11	11	11	11	11	11	11	11	11	11	11	11	11	11	11	11	11	11	11	11	11	11	11	11	11	11	11	11
11 PEREZ	16	16	16	16	16	16	16	16	16	16	16	16	16	16	16	16	16	16	16	16	16	16	16	16	16	16	16	16	16	16	16	16	16	16	55	16	16	16	16	16	16	16	16	16	16	16	16	16	16
44 HAMILTON	55	55	55	55	55	55	55	55	55	55	55	55	55	55	55	55	55	55	55	55	55	55	55	55	55	55	55	55	55	55	55	55	55	55	16	4	55	55	55	55	55	55	55	55	55	55	55	55	55
55 SAINZ	44	44	44	44	44	44	44	44	44	44	44	44	44	44	44	44	44	44	44	44	44	44	44	44	44	44	44	44	44	44	44	44	4	4	4	55	4	4	4	4	4	4	4	4	4	4	4	4	4
14 ALONSO	4	4	4	4	4	4	4	4	4	4	4	4	4	4	4	4	4	4	4	4	4	4	4	4	4	4	4	4	4	4	4	4	44	1	1	3	1	1	1	3	3	3	3	3	3	3	3	3	3
4 NORRIS	14	14	14	14	14	14	14	14	14	14	14	14	14	14	14	14	14	14	14	14	1	1	1	1	1	1	1	1	1	1	1	1	1	44	3	1	3	3	3	18	18	18	18	18	18	18	18	18	18
10 GASLY	10	10	10	10	10	10	10	10	10	10	1	1	1	1	1	1	1	1	1	1	10	10	10	10	10	10	10	10	10	10	10	10	5	18	18	18	18	18	18	5	5	5	5	5	5	5	5	5	5
1 VERSTAPPEN	5	5	5	5	5	5	5	5	5	5	10	10	10	10	10	10	10	10	10	10	5	5	5	5	5	5	5	5	5	5	5	5	18	5	5	5	5	5	5	44	44	44	44	44	44	44	44	44	44
20 MAGNUSSEN	22	22	1	1	1	1	1	1	1	1	5	5	5	5	5	5	5	5	5	5	18	18	18	18	18	18	18	18	18	18	18	18	10	3	44	44	44	44	44	10	10	10	10	10	10	10	10	10	10
22 TSUNODA	18	1	22	22	22	22	22	22	22	22	22	22	22	22	22	22	22	22	22	22	3	3	3	3	3	3	3	3	3	3	3	3	3	47	10	10	10	10	10	47	77	77	77	77	77	77	77	77	77
18 STROLL	20	18	18	18	18	18	18	18	18	18	18	18	18	18	18	18	18	18	18	18	47	47	47	47	47	47	47	47	47	47	47	47	47	10	47	47	47	47	47	63	20	20	20	20	20	20	1	1	1
47 SCHUMACHER	1	20	20	20	20	20	3	3	3	3	3	3	3	3	3	3	3	3	3	3	22	22	22	22	22	22	22	22	22	22	22	22	22	22	77	77	77	77	77	77	1	1	1	1	1	1	20	20	20
5 VETTEL	3	3	3	3	3	3	47	47	47	47	47	47	47	47	47	47	47	47	47	47	31	31	31	31	31	31	77	77	77	77	77	77	77	77	20	20	20	20	20	1	47	*47*	*47*	*47*	*47*	*63*	*63*	*63*	*63*
24 ZHOU	47	47	47	47	47	47	31	31	31	31	31	31	31	31	31	31	31	31	31	31	77	77	77	77	77	77	20	20	20	20	20	20	20	20	63	63	63	63	63	20	63	*63*	*63*	*63*	*63*	*47*	*47*	*47*	*47*
77 BOTTAS	31	31	31	31	31	31	77	77	77	77	77	77	77	77	77	77	77	77	77	77	63	20	20	20	20	20	63	63	*63*	*63*	*63*	*63*	*63*	*63*															
3 RICCIARDO	77	77	77	77	77	77	20	63	63	63	63	63	63	63	63	63	63	63	63	63	23	23	23	23	63	63																							
31 OCON	6	6	6	63	63	63	63	23	23	23	23	23	23	23	23	23	23	23	23	23	20	63	63	63	23																								
23 ALBON	24	63	63	6	6	6	23	20	20	20	20	20	20	20	20	20	20	20	20	20																													
6 LATIFI	63	24	24	24	24	24	6l																																										
63 RUSSELL	23	23	23	23	23	23																																											
								SC	SC	SC												VSC	VSC			VSC	VSC	VSC	VSC	VSC						SC	SC	SC	SC										

TIME SHEETS

PRACTICE 1 (FRIDAY)

Weather: Dry/sunny

Temperatures: track 35-37°C, air 29°C

Pos.	Driver	Laps	Time
1	Lewis Hamilton	20	1m 43.033s
2	Max Verstappen	20	1m 43.117s
3	Charles Leclerc	17	1m 43.435s
4	Sergio Pérez	15	1m 43.839s
5	George Russell	21	1m 44.066s
6	Carlos Sainz	24	1m 44.138s
7	Esteban Ocon	24	1m 44.736s
8	Lance Stroll	12	1m 45.221s
9	Pierre Gasly	24	1m 45.258s
10	Fernando Alonso	11	1m 45.336s
11	Sebastian Vettel	22	1m 45.354s
12	Daniel Ricciardo	21	1m 45.724s
13	Valtteri Bottas	24	1m 45.725s
14	Kevin Magnussen	22	1m 46.028s
15	Yuki Tsunoda	26	1m 46.081s
16	Alexander Albon	20	1m 46.119s
17	Zhou Guanyu	25	1m 46.408s
18	Mick Schumacher	23	1m 46.601s
19	Lando Norris	22	1m 46.680s
20	Nicholas Latifi	18	1m 47.092s

PRACTICE 2 (FRIDAY)

Weather: Dry/dark

Temperatures: track 33°C, air 29°C

Pos.	Driver	Laps	Time
1	Carlos Sainz	23	1m 42.587s
2	Charles Leclerc	14	1m 42.795s
3	George Russell	26	1m 42.911s
4	Max Verstappen	8	1m 42.926s
5	Lewis Hamilton	22	1m 43.182s
6	Esteban Ocon	23	1m 43.412s
7	Valtteri Bottas	26	1m 43.431s
8	Fernando Alonso	23	1m 43.520s
9	Sergio Pérez	13	1m 43.906s
10	Lance Stroll	21	1m 43.982s
11	Lando Norris	16	1m 44.013s
12	Sebastian Vettel	24	1m 44.249s
13	Kevin Magnussen	22	1m 44.422s
14	Pierre Gasly	22	1m 44.469s
15	Zhou Guanyu	25	1m 44.524s
16	Alexander Albon	25	1m 45.144s
17	Yuki Tsunoda	11	1m 45.211s
18	Daniel Ricciardo	18	1m 45.447s
19	Mick Schumacher	23	1m 45.623s
20	Nicholas Latifi	25	1m 46.553s

PRACTICE 3 (SATURDAY)

Weather: Wet/overcast

Temperatures: track 28-29°C, air 26-27°C

Pos.	Driver	Laps	Time
1	Charles Leclerc	11	1m 57.782s
2	Max Verstappen	12	1m 58.308s
3	Carlos Sainz	12	1m 58.848s
4	Fernando Alonso	9	1m 59.429s
5	Sergio Pérez	11	1m 59.526s
6	Lance Stroll	11	2m 00.373s
7	Esteban Ocon	9	2m 00.911s
8	Sebastian Vettel	11	2m 01.007s
9	George Russell	10	2m 01.010s
10	Daniel Ricciardo	13	2m 01.036s
11	Kevin Magnussen	13	2m 01.089s
12	Lewis Hamilton	8	2m 01.220s
13	Pierre Gasly	15	2m 01.245s
14	Mick Schumacher	13	2m 01.502s
15	Yuki Tsunoda	14	2m 01.679s
16	Lando Norris	13	2m 01.791s
17	Alexander Albon	13	2m 01.907s
18	Valtteri Bottas	11	2m 02.066s
19	Zhou Guanyu	11	2m 02.599s
20	Nicholas Latifi	10	2m 03.510s

QUALIFYING (SATURDAY))

Weather: : Wet-drying/dark and mostly cloudy Temperatures: track 27-28°C, air 26-27°C

Pos.	Driver	First	Second	Third	Qualifying Tyre
1	Charles Leclerc	1m 54.129s	1m 52.343s	1m 49.412s	Soft (n)
2	Sergio Pérez	1m 54.404s	1m 52.818s	1m 49.434s	Soft (n)
3	Lewis Hamilton	1m 53.161s	1m 52.691s	1m 49.466s	Soft (n)
4	Carlos Sainz	1m 54.559s	1m 53.219s	1m 49.583s	Soft (n)
5	Fernando Alonso	1m 55.360s	1m 53.127s	1m 49.966s	Soft (n)
6	Lando Norris	1m 55.914s	1m 53.942s	1m 50.584s	Soft (n)
7	Pierre Gasly	1m 55.606s	1m 53.546s	1m 51.211s	Soft (u)
8	Max Verstappen	1m 53.057s	1m 52.723s	1m 51.395s	Soft (n)
9	Kevin Magnussen	1m 55.103s	1m 54.006s	1m 51.573s	Soft (n)
10	Yuki Tsunoda	1m 55.314s	1m 53.848s	1m 51.983s	Soft (n)
11	George Russell	1m 54.633s	1m 54.012s		
12	Lance Stroll	1m 55.629s	1m 54.211s		
13	Mick Schumacher	1m 55.736s	1m 54.370s		
14	Sebastian Vettel	1m 55.602s	1m 54.380s		
15	Zhou Guanyu	1m 55.375s	1m 55.518s		
16	Valtteri Bottas	1m 56.083s			
17	Daniel Ricciardo	1m 56.226s			
18	Esteban Ocon	1m 56.337s			
19	Alexander Albon	1m 56.985s			
20	Nicholas Latifi	1m 57.532s			

QUALIFYING: head to head

Hamilton	10	7	Russell
Verstappen	13	4	Pérez
Ricciardo	2	15	Norris
Leclerc	13	4	Sainz
Gasly	11	6	Tsunoda
Hülkenberg	1	1	Stroll
Vettel	9	6	Stroll
Alonso	11	6	Ocon
Bottas	11	6	Zhou
Albon	14	2	Latifi
de Vries	1	0	Latifi
Magnussen	13	4	Schumacher

Haas F1 Team

FOR THE RECORD

1st RACE OF LEADING EVERY LAP: Sergio Pérez

DID YOU KNOW?

Pérez became the first winner to receive an end-of-race time penalty and not lose his victory.

POINTS

DRIVERS

1	Max Verstappen	341
2	Charles Leclerc	237
3	Sergio Pérez	235
4	George Russell	203
5	Carlos Sainz	202
6	Lewis Hamilton	170
7	Lando Norris	100
8	Esteban Ocon	66
9	Fernando Alonso	59
10	Valtteri Bottas	46
11	Daniel Ricciardo	29
12	Sebastian Vettel	24
13	Pierre Gasly	23
14	Kevin Magnussen	22
15	Lance Stroll	13
16	Mick Schumacher	12
17	Yuki Tsunoda	11
18	Zhou Guanyu	6
19	Alexander Albon	4
20	Nyck de Vries	2

CONSTRUCTORS

1	Red Bull	576
2	Ferrari	439
3	Mercedes	373
4	McLaren	129
5	Alpine	125
6	Alfa Romeo	52
7	Aston Martin	37
8	Haas	34
9	AlphaTauri	34
10	Williams	6

10 · TSUNODA · AlphaTauri

8 · VERSTAPPEN · Red Bul

6 · NORRIS · McLaren

4 · SAINZ · Ferrari

2 · PÉREZ · Red Bull

9 · MAGNUSSEN · Haas

7 · GASLY · AlphaTauri

5 · ALONSO · Alpine

3 · HAMILTON · Mercedes

1 · LECLERC · Ferrari

50	51	52	53	54	55	56	57	58	59	
11	11	11	11	11	11	11	11	11	11	1
16	16	16	16	16	16	16	16	16	16	2
55	55	55	55	55	55	55	55	55	55	3
4	4	4	4	4	4	4	4	4	4	4
3	3	3	3	3	3	3	3	3	3	5
18	18	18	18	18	18	18	18	18	18	6
5	5	5	5	5	5	5	5	5	1	7
44	44	44	44	44	44	44	1	1	5	8
10	1	1	1	1	1	1	44	44	44	9
1	10	10	10	10	10	10	10	10	10	10
77	77	77	77	77	77	77	77	77	77	
20	20	20	20	20	20	20	20	20	20	
63	47	47	47	47	47	47	47	47		
47	63	63	63	63	63	63	63			

20 = Pit stop 63 = One lap or more behind

SC Safety car deployed on laps shown

VSC Virtual safety car deployed on laps shown

RACE TYRE STRATEGIES

PIRELLI

	Driver	Race Stint 1	Race Stint 2	Race Stint 3	Race Stint 4	Race Stint 5
1	Pérez	Inter (n): 1-35	Medium (n): 36-59			
2	Leclerc	Inter (n): 1-34	Medium (n): 35-59			
3	Sainz	Inter (n): 1-35	Medium (n): 36-59			
4	Norris	Inter (n): 1-36	Medium (n): 37-59			
5	Ricciardo	Inter (n): 1-36	Soft (n): 37-59			
6	Stroll	Inter (n): 1-35	Medium (n): 36-59			
7	Verstappen	Inter (n): 1-35	Medium (n): 36-40	Soft (n): 41-59		
8	Vettel	Inter (n): 1-34	Medium (n): 35-59			
9	Hamilton	Inter (n): 1-34	Medium (n): 35-59			
10	Gasly	Inter (u): 1-33	Medium (n): 34-59			
11	Bottas	Inter (n): 1-33	Soft (n): 34-59			
12	Magnussen	Inter (n): 1-7	Inter (u): 8-33	Medium (n): 34-59		
13	Schumacher	Inter (n): 1-34	Medium (n): 35-41	Soft (n): 42-58		
14	Russell	Inter (n): 1-21	Medium (n): 22-35	Medium (n): 36-41	Soft (n): 42-51	Soft (n): 52-57 (dnf)
	Tsunoda	Inter (u): 1-33	Medium (n): 34 (dnf)			
	Ocon	Inter (n): 1-26 (dnf)				
	Albon	Inter (n): 1-25 (dnf)				
	Alonso	Inter (n): 1-20 (dnf)				
	Latifi	Inter (n): 1-7 (dnf)				
	Zhou	Inter (n): 1-6 (dnf)				

The tyre regulations stipulate that at least two of three dry tyre specifications must be used during a dry race.

Selected compounds for Singapore: Red = Soft (C5); Yellow = Medium (C4); White = Hard (C3). (n) new (u) used

MAX
WORLD
CHAMPION
WORLD CHAMPION 2022
Red Bull
TAG HEUER

FIA FORMULA 1 WORLD CHAMPIONSHIP · ROUND 18

JAPANESE GRAND PRIX

SUZUKA CIRCUIT

SUZUKA QUALIFYING

AS the F1 circus returned to the circuit that most drivers rate the best on the calendar, Max Verstappen had a second world championship almost within his grasp. To clinch it, he needed to outscore Charles Leclerc by eight points, and Red Bull team-mate Sergio Pérez by six. A win with fastest lap would suffice.

The opening day at Suzuka was a washout, with Fernando Alonso's Alpine topping the first session and George Russell's Mercedes, the second. With teams and drivers on varying programmes because of the inconsistent conditions, it all amounted to not a lot. But Mick Schumacher, under pressure for his seat at Haas, did himself a power of no good when he lost his car on an out-lap at the end of FP1, cracking the chassis and missing FP2.

Saturday morning's practice hour was the only opportunity for teams and drivers to dial into the dry conditions that had greeted them for the final session of free practice and qualifying, although Friday's wet-weather intermediate running was potentially valuable, as mixed conditions were predicted for qualifying.

It was the expected Verstappen-versus-Leclerc battle once more, with Carlos Sainz also joining in with the second Ferrari, and it could barely have been tighter. When the chequer came down on Q3, Verstappen had taken his first Suzuka pole position with a lap in 1m 29.304s. That was good enough to pip Leclerc by a hundredth of a second and Sainz by six-hundredths, Max's first Q3 run better than his second.

"I lost a part, a bit of a brake duct on my final lap, so that's why I couldn't improve," Verstappen explained, "but the first lap was good enough – just."

The race stewards looked into an incident when Max, trying to warm his tyres at the end of his prep lap, almost lost the Red Bull and impeded Lando Norris's McLaren, which was attempting to go by at the same time. After an explanation, he got away with it.

Both Ferrari drivers were frustrated to miss out on pole by such a small margin. "It's a very tricky lap around here because whenever you are very quick in the first sector, then you lose out in the last sector," Leclerc explained. "I tried to find that balance on the last run, but lost the tyres a little bit in the last sector."

"Mine was a very clean lap all the way until the last corner," Sainz added. "Then I picked up quite a bit of wheelspin. It's a shame to be half a tenth again from pole. It's been so many qualifyings now with Max and Charles that we're all within half a tenth. And that last half-tenth tends to fall more to the other side. Hopefully, towards the end of the season, this half a tenth falls a bit more to my side and I can get a pole!" He would be as good as his word.

Sergio Pérez was three-and-a-half tenths off in the second Red Bull, but still comfortably on the second row, with 'best of the rest' honours claimed by Esteban Ocon, who put his Alpine fifth on the grid. He was a tenth clear of Lewis Hamilton, who split the two Alpines by pipping Fernando Alonso to a third-row slot by just 0.06s.

George Russell flirted with missing out on Q3, but found a lap when it mattered, ending up eighth quickest, just 0.12s adrift of his team-mate.

Sebastian Vettel continued Aston Martin's late-season upturn in form and maintained his 100 per cent record of reaching Q3 at Suzuka, with Lando Norris the lone McLaren driver to reach the top-ten shootout.

Team-mate Daniel Ricciardo missed out on Q3 by just 0.003s, and Valtteri Bottas was only five-hundredths away in the first of the Alfa Romeos. Yuki Tsunoda can boast plenty of Suzuka experience, and he used it to good effect by putting the first of the AlphaTauris 13th on the grid, ahead of Zhou Guanyu and Mick Schumacher in the Haas, who made up for his Friday indiscretion by outqualifying team-mate Kevin Magnussen for the fifth time in 2022.

Those to fall at the first hurdle were Alex Albon – who nevertheless impressed in the Williams with a lap that missed Q2 by just 0.055s – Pierre Gasly, Magnussen, Lance Stroll and Nicholas Latifi.

Gasly was fit to be tied. With his move to Alpine confirmed and Dutchman Nyck de Vries rewarded for his excellent Monza Williams showing by an AlphaTauri deal to replace the Frenchman, Gasly had been looking forward to Suzuka. But he was not impressed with either the team's decision to put him out too early for his final Q1 run, in traffic, or the performance of his brakes, as he locked up into the hairpin with a front left that was not quite up to working temperature.

"Why didn't we wait? Why?" he ranted over team radio. "This is what you get with this s*. What a joke!"**

On Sunday afternoon, he would be upset all over again, about matters altogether more serious...

Right: False start. The race finally begins with the field all on intermediate tyres. Leclerc is about to lose his early lead to Verstappen, but the race would be halted after just two laps.
Photo: Red Bull Content Pool/Getty Images

Below: Samurai Seb continued his love affair with all things Japanese.
Photo: Aston Martin Aramco Cognizant F1 Team

Bottom: The spear-like shape of Leclerc's Ferrari is well illustrated by this overhead pit-lane shot.
Photo: Scuderia Ferrari

Opening spread: Max Verstappen and his Red Bull crew share their second world championship triumph.
Photo: Red Bull Content Pool/Getty Images

A DARK, dank Suzuka meant a two-hour delay to the start before Max Verstappen and Charles Leclerc could prepare to share the front row for the eighth time in 2022. Pierre Gasly's qualifying woes meant that, with rain set for the race, he took the decision to change the AlphaTauri's rear wing and start from the pit lane.

Differing grip levels between the right- and left-hand sides of the grid experienced on the wet Friday led to much talk of a rolling start behind the safety car, but when the race finally did get under way, it was with the whole field on intermediates for a grid start – just as the rain began to intensify.

As the lights blinked out, Charles Leclerc made a slightly better getaway from P2 on the inside than pole-man Verstappen. In the wet, though, there was grip on the outside line, and Max kept his boot in to run all the way around the outside of the Ferrari through Turns One and Two, snatching the lead.

Further back, there was drama for Sebastian Vettel, who had made a great getaway in the Aston Martin, but then suffered wheelspin with his left rear wheel on the grass as he ran alongside Fernando Alonso's Alpine. Unsighted amid the spray, they made light contact and Vettel spun on the run to Turn One. If his getaway had been great, team-mate Lance Stroll's had been even better, the Canadian having gone from 18th to 11th as, fully committed, he blasted down the inside, millimetres from the pit wall. Brave stuff in severely compromised visibility!

Carlos Sainz aquaplaned at Turn 12 and lost his Ferrari, exiting stage left into the tyre barrier and simultaneously releasing an advertising banner on to the track, which was collected by Pierre Gasly's AlphaTauri. "What the hell is that?" the Frenchman yelled. "I can't see anything. I've got a f***ing board stuck in the way!"

Further around the opening lap, Zhou Guanyu spun his Alfa Romeo, and Alex Albon parked his Williams with a misfiring engine. On lap two, race control threw the red flag.

Meanwhile, Gasly had been into the pits to have the offending hoarding removed, and a new front wing and set of full wets fitted. Told that the leaders were at Turn 13 and driving at racing speed to catch the pack, he was dismayed to find a recovery vehicle on the track for Sainz's Ferrari.

"God, what is this tractor on the track?" Gasly radioed amid the murk. "This is unacceptable! Can't believe this..."

His thoughts were echoed by Leclerc, who asked, "Guys, what the f**k is this crane?" Charles, of course, had lost his godfather and mentor, Jules Bianchi, to injuries sustained at Suzuka in 2014, when the Marussia driver had collided with a tractor that had been sent out to recover Adrian Sutil's crashed Sauber.

It was painful to see Bianchi's father, Philippe, posting on social media, "No respect for the life of the driver, no respect for Jules' memory. Incredible."

The fact that Gasly was given a 20s penalty and two penalty points for speeding under red-flag conditions was a red herring. The problem arose well before that, the red light only appearing on Gasly's dash as he turned in to the high-speed section of track where Sainz had gone off.

As the cars filed into the pit lane and the drivers climbed out, there was widespread anger that a potential Bianchi situation had been allowed to reoccur, prompting a post-race FIA investigation. The governing body determined that in future, no recovery vehicles would be deployed unless all cars

Above: Just ten minutes into the race, proceedings were brought to a halt for over two hours.
Photo: XPB Images

Above right: For the Japanese Grand Prix, Red Bull reintroduced the Honda wording on their car.
Photo: Red Bull Content Pool/Getty Images

Right: During the lengthy break, Mick Schumacher chats with Fernando Alonso and Esteban Ocon in the Alpine garage.
Photo: XPB Images

were aligned behind the safety car. As they had been focused on the safe recovery of the Ferrari, Gasly's AlphaTauri, in the pit lane, had not been immediately detected.

"In hindsight, as the weather conditions were changing, it would have been prudent to have delayed the deployment of recovery vehicles," the FIA concluded. It also intended to put in place safety car/VSC monitoring to be used by race control and its Geneva-based ROC (Remote Operations Centre) – introduced in the aftermath of Abu Dhabi, 2021 – which would ensure that all cars, not just those behind the safety car, were properly monitored.

In addition, the rotation of the race director role between German former DTM/F2 race director Neils Wittich and Portugal's ex-WEC race director, Eduardo Freitas, instituted after the removal of Michael Masi, would no longer continue. Freitas had been directing in Suzuka, but Wittich would now take over the role on his own.

When it was decided that the race could be restarted, it was behind the safety car, with the whole field on full wets, and with just 40 minutes ahead of them before the three-hour maximum race time window would be reached. The drivers reported that conditions were okay, and as the safety car pulled off and the race went green, Verstappen was leading the field from Leclerc, Sergio Pérez, Esteban Ocon, Lewis Hamilton, Alonso, George Russell, Daniel Ricciardo, Yuki Tsunoda, Mick Schumacher, Stroll, Kevin Magnussen, Lando Norris, Valtteri Bottas, Nicholas Latifi and Vettel (both in at the end of the lap to go on to intermediates), Zhou and Gasly.

Norris and Bottas were in for inters next time around as Latifi set a sector best, with the first four – Verstappen, Leclerc, Pérez and Ocon – plus Hamilton and Russell following suit next time, while Alonso elected to stay out for another lap.

The inter was now definitely the tyre of choice. Witness Vettel, the early adopter, setting the race's fastest lap thus far and finding himself in tenth place as the pit stops started to shake out. One unhappy man was Russell, who had lost time stacked behind Hamilton and surrendered positions not only to Vettel, but also to Latifi, Norris and Tsunoda.

"That is the worst decision we have made," was Russell's terse assessment over the radio.

Those still on wets – Alonso, Ricciardo and Schumacher – now led as Haas explained the thinking to its driver: "Mick, lots of drivers have gone on to the other tyre, but we are hoping for a safety car."

As Alonso and Ricciardo pitted, Verstappen retook the lead from Schumacher, who would lose out on his gamble and rejoin 10s off the back of the field when he finally admitted defeat and pitted for inters.

The irked Russell was no respecter of the home fans as he made up for lost ground, pulling off a fine outside pass of Tsunoda at Turn Six, the end of the sweeping first-sector 'S' Curves. "That was a nice move," he radioed in, complimenting himself.

With 20 minutes remaining on the clock, Verstappen, who had come under early pressure from Leclerc as the Ferrari heated its tyres more rapidly, now had a comfortable 10s advantage over the Monégasque, with Pérez 5s further behind in the second Red Bull.

Ocon was 7s adrift of the Mexican, doing a sterling job with the lead Alpine and fending off Hamilton. The Mercedes was quicker, but it did not have sufficient straight-line speed to trouble the Frenchman, with DRS disabled in the conditions. Vettel was just 5s in arrears, with Alonso in close attendance. Latifi's early stop had put the Canadian in a solid seventh place, on course for his first points of 2022, although Norris, Russell, Tsunoda and Stroll were closing in.

Leclerc's intermediates were struggling soonest, and he was on the radio asking how many places he would lose if he pitted. The answer was five, which would have dropped him behind Alonso, so he stuck with it, despite Pérez starting to reduce the deficit to second place. Alonso, meanwhile, despite the relatively late first stop, did elect to pit for a second set of inters.

Russell was now on terms with old mate Norris and promoted himself to eighth down the inside into the chicane, without personal commentary this time! It didn't take him long to catch Latifi, on whom he repeated his excellent earlier pass of Tsunoda to go seventh.

With six minutes remaining, Verstappen was 20s clear of the struggling Leclerc, who had Pérez on his rear wing and looking to go by. Alonso, meanwhile, was making progress back through the field on his new tyres, and had passed Norris and Latifi to go eighth, although Russell was a further 11s up the road.

As the clock ticked down and Verstappen passed the chequer to take a consummate victory, his 12th of the year, Leclerc was still defending manfully, seeking out damp patches to cool his complaining intermediates. With Pérez pushing for all he was worth, Charles outbraked himself into the final chicane, ran off the road, rejoined and got his elbows out to force Pérez to lift off as they shot across the line. Ocon held off Hamilton right to the death for fourth, Vettel finished top six and Alonso demoted Russell to get back to seventh – where he had been before he pitted. Latifi took his hard earned first 2022 points and Norris completed the scorers.

To win the championship if Leclerc was second, Verstappen also needed fastest lap and had asked the team about a late-race stop, as he had a pit window, but he was told not to bother. Red Bull, like the rest of the paddock, believed that this was going to be a half-points race.

As Max conducted his post-race interview with Johnny Herbert, news came of a 5s time penalty for Leclerc, for leaving the track and gaining an advantage. That was enough to promote Pérez to second, which meant that Max was a two-time champion. But nobody realised.

The entire paddock 'got it wrong'. For the first time in F1 history, full points were awarded for a race that had not completed 75 per cent of its distance.

The wording of the rule in question was not new and said: 'If a race is suspended and cannot be resumed… half points will be awarded if the leader has completed more than two laps but less than 75% of the original race distance, and full points will be awarded if the leader has completed 75% or more of the original race distance.'

The important bit is 'cannot be resumed'. The Japanese GP was resumed, so none of it applied.

It could be argued that it's all perfectly clear, and that nobody – teams, broadcasters, media – read the rule book properly, while the FIA got it completely right. In fact, after the aggravation following Abu Dhabi 2021, it was imperative that everything was done by the book.

But there were problems with that. First, after the Spa debacle in 2021, when half-points had been awarded after three laps behind a safety car with no actual racing, a new regulation was introduced, intended to avoid a repeat and

Above: Sebastian Vettel took sixth place for Aston Martin, ahead of Fernando Alonso in the Alpine.
Photo: Aston Martin Aramco Cognizant F1 Team

Top right: Points at last for Nicholas Latifi, who brought his Williams home in ninth place.
Photo: Williams Racing

Above right: Fourth was a season's best result for Alpine's Esteban Ocon.
Photo: Alpine F1 Team

Right: Red Bull celebrates a 1-2 finish for Max Verstappen and Sergio Pérez.
Photo: Red Bull Content Pool/Getty Images

award points commensurate with race distance.

The more complex rule said that for any points to be allocated, a minimum of two laps must be completed by the leader without safety car or VSC intervention. If at least two laps, but less than 25 per cent of the scheduled distance, were completed, points would be 6-4-3-2-1 to just the first five finishers. If between 25 and 50 per cent was completed, the points allocation would change to 13-10-8-6-5-4-3-2-1 for the first nine. If at least 50 per cent distance, but less than 75 per cent, it would become 19-14-12-9-8-6-5-3-2-1 to the top ten, with anything over 75 per cent distance bringing full points.

The intent made sense, but only if the 'cannot be resumed' part was removed, which it wasn't. Otherwise, taking things to extremes, there could have been a situation at Suzuka where the rain delay lasted long enough that only three laps were possible before the race timed out, yet full points would still have been awarded. Clearly not the intention and a nonsense.

Thus, as soon as it became evident that the rain delay had got to the point where a full race was impossible within the three-hour time frame, teams, commentators and media all started taking note of the anticipated number of laps and the key milestones – laps 14, 27 and 40.

Muddying the picture were sporadic on-screen FOM graphics throughout the race showing full points. It was assumed by most that this was an error. Even when Leclerc was penalised, Red Bull did not think that Verstappen was champion (*see* Viewpoint).

Christian Horner: "I think it's a mistake after the issues in Spa last year, that the regulations obviously haven't been mopped up. We were under the strong impression that only with 75 per cent of the race would full points be scored. We felt we were going to be one point short."

McLaren's team principal, Andreas Seidl, added, "How the points were awarded today wasn't what we all had in mind [at a meeting about points revisions]. That wasn't the intention from the FIA or the team side, but in the end, it seems like we all overlooked this and therefore we are all responsible. We must try to do, together, a better job next time."

Complicating matters further, the race timing out after 28 laps of the scheduled 53 could also have been interpreted as it having been suspended once again, rather than completed, bringing the reduced-points scenario into play – the interpretation of most of the paddock.

For historical perspective, only six races in F1 history have resulted in half-points being awarded: Spain and Austria, 1975, when Vittorio Brambilla had been so excited at seeing the chequered flag that he had crashed on the slowdown lap; the famous 1984 Monaco where Alain Prost, frantically pointing at the rainy sky as Ayrton Senna reeled him in, succeeded in getting the race stopped, which cost him a world title by scoring four-and-a-half points for the win instead of six for finishing second to Senna (He lost the championship to McLaren team-mate Lauda by half a point.); then there was the shortened 14-lap 1991 Australian GP, Malayasia, 2009 and Spa in 2021.

Of all those races that have been red-flagged and restarted, but not gone the full scheduled distance, none has run less than the requisite 75 per cent for full points. The closest to it was Monza in 1978, after the first-lap pile-up that ultimately claimed the life of Ronnie Peterson. Under the threat of darkness, it ran 40 of the scheduled 52 laps (76.9 per cent).

The others were Detroit, 1982 (96.8 per cent); Britain, 1984 (93.8 per cent); Mexico, 1987 (92.6 per cent); San Marino, 1989 (95 per cent); France, 1992 (95.8 per cent); Japan, 1994 (94 per cent); France, 1998 (98.6 per cent); Spa, 2001 (81.8 per cent); and Monaco, 2022 (82 per cent).

In that regard, the 52.8 per cent-distance Suzuka race was unique in F1 history. Another box ticked by Max Verstappen. Not that F1's newest two-time champion cared!

Tony Dodgins

VIEWPOINT
GOING BY THE BOOK

As a new champion's crowning moment goes, this one was feeble and confused. No flood of emotion across the airwaves as the victor took the flag to release several months of relentless pressure. No tears or gushing messages of thanks delivered in a tremulous voice. Nothing, except the almost perfunctory of exchanges that come with win number 12 and a victory that hasn't quite managed to clinch the title. "Only one point in it. Never mind, we'll finish the job next time out at CoTA."

Championship arithmetic elsewhere on the Suzuka pit wall had come to the same conclusion, thanks to the three-hour limit (including the early red-flag period) coming into force. With less than 75 per cent of the scheduled race distance having been completed, half-points would be awarded. This had been the accepted procedure in the past, and there seemed no reason to believe it would be any different on this rain-soaked day.

But wait! Officials are saying full points will be applied. The top three finishers have no idea what's going on. The sense of anti-climax is actually accelerated in the lull as team managers urgently thumb through the relevant section of the sporting regulations (rewritten following the debacle at Spa in 2021, when half points were handed out after three miserable laps behind the safety car).

At Suzuka, they found elaborate tables showing columns of points to be awarded at various stages when a race fails to reach full distance. But this, as everyone quickly discovered, only applied when a red flag brought the race to an early conclusion. If the race was resumed and the chequered shown – as happened here – full points would be the reward.

This was not the intention of the revision since, taken to the letter, it meant that full points could be awarded even if the race lasted a mere three laps – but finished under a chequered flag. A correction was urgently needed.

In the meantime, Max Verstappen was 2022 world champion – and a most worthy one, regardless of when or how the points were added up.

Maurice Hamilton

18

FORMULA 1 HONDA JAPANESE GRAND PRIX 2022

ROLEX

Official Timepiece

SUZUKA INTERNATIONAL RACING COURSE, SUZUKA-CITY

Circuit: 3.608 miles/5.807km, 53 laps

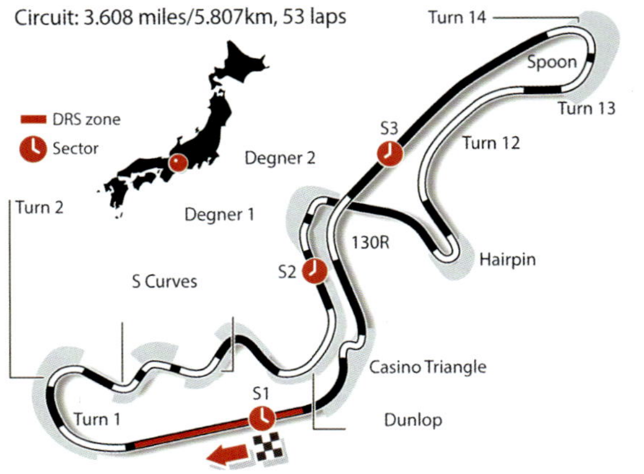

SUZUKA 7-9 OCTOBER

RACE DISTANCE: 28 laps, 100.846 miles/162.296km

RACE WEATHER: Wet/cloudy (track 18-21°C, air 16-18°C)

RACE – OFFICIAL CLASSIFICATION

Pos.	Driver	Nat.	No.	Entrant	Car/Engine	Laps	Time/Retirement	Speed (mph/km/h)	Gap to winner	Fastest race lap	
1	**Max Verstappen**	NL	1	Oracle Red Bull Racing	Red Bull RB18-RBPTH001 V6	28	3h 01m 44.004s	33.294/53.582		1m 44.911s	10
2	**Sergio Pérez**	MEX	11	Oracle Red Bull Racing	Red Bull RB18-RBPTH001 V6	28	3h 02m 11.070s	33.212/53.449	27.066s	1m 46.120s	11
3	**Charles Leclerc**	MC	16	Scuderia Ferrari	Ferrari F1-75-066/7 V6	28	3h 02m 15.767s *	33.198/53.427	31.763s	1m 44.489s	10
4	**Esteban Ocon**	F	31	BWT Alpine F1 Team	Alpine A522-Renault E-Tech RE22 V6	28	3h 02m 23.689s	33.174/53.388	39.685s	1m 46.559s	11
5	**Lewis Hamilton**	GB	44	Mercedes-AMG Petronas F1 Team	Mercedes-AMG F1 W13-M13 E Perf. V6	28	3h 02m 24.330s	33.172/53.385	40.326s	1m 45.530s	11
6	**Sebastian Vettel**	D	5	Aston Martin Aramco Cognizant F1 Team	Aston Martin AMR22-Mercedes F1 M13 E Perf. V6	28	3h 02m 30.362s	33.153/53.355	46.358s	1m 46.964s	13
7	**Fernando Alonso**	E	14	BWT Alpine F1 Team	Alpine A522-Renault E-Tech RE22 V6	28	3h 02m 30.373s	33.153/53.355	46.369s	1m 44.412s	25
8	**George Russell**	GB	63	Mercedes-AMG Petronas F1 Team	Mercedes-AMG F1 W13-M13 E Perf. V6	28	3h 02m 31.665s	33.150/53.349	47.661s	1m 47.004s	21
9	**Nicholas Latifi**	CDN	6	Williams Racing	Williams FW44-Mercedes F1 M13 E Perf. V6	28	3h 02m 54.147s	33.082/53.240	1m 10.143s	1m 48.371s	12
10	**Lando Norris**	GB	4	McLaren F1 Team	McLaren MCL36-Mercedes F1 M13 E Perf. V6	28	3h 02m 54.786s	33.080/53.237	1m 10.782s	1m 48.175s	8
11	Daniel Ricciardo	AUS	3	McLaren F1 Team	McLaren MCL36-Mercedes F1 M13 E Perf. V6	28	3h 02m 56.881s	33.073/53.226	1m 12.877s	1m 47.843s	11
12	Lance Stroll	CDN	18	Aston Martin Aramco Cognizant F1 Team	Aston Martin AMR22-Mercedes F1 M13 E Perf. V6	28	3h 02m 57.908s	33.070/53.221	1m 13.904s	1m 45.205s	21
13	Yuki Tsunoda	J	22	Scuderia AlphaTauri	AlphaTauri AT03-RBPTH001 V6	28	3h 02m 59.603s	33.065/53.213	1m 15.599s	1m 45.893s	22
14	Kevin Magnussen	DK	20	Haas F1 Team	Haas VF-22-Ferrari 066/7 V6	28	3h 03m 10.020s	33.034/53.163	1m 26.016s	1m 48.072s	10
15	Valtteri Bottas	FIN	77	Alfa Romeo F1 Team ORLEN	Alfa Romeo C42-Ferrari 066/7 V6	28	3h 03m 10.500s	33.032/53.160	1m 26.496s	1m 47.820s	11
16	Zhou Guanyu	CHN	24	Alfa Romeo F1 Team ORLEN	Alfa Romeo C42-Ferrari 066/7 V6	28	3h 03m 11.047s	33.031/53.158	1m 27.043s	1m 44.411s	20
17	Mick Schumacher	D	47	Haas F1 Team	Haas VF-22-Ferrari 066/7 V6	28	3h 03m 16.527s	33.014/53.131	1m 32.523s	1m 46.545s	13
18	Pierre Gasly	F	10	Scuderia AlphaTauri	AlphaTauri AT03-RBPTH001 V6	28	3h 03m 32.095s *	32.967/53.056	1m 48.091s	1m 45.387s	22
	Carlos Sainz	E	55	Scuderia Ferrari	Ferrari F1-75-066/7 V6	0	*accident*			no time	
	Alexander Albon	T	23	Williams Racing	Williams FW44-Mercedes F1 M13 E Perf. V6	0	*accident damage*			no time	

The race was red-flagged on the second lap due to heavy rain. After around 2 hours and 10 minutes the race resumed from a rolling start.
The race had been scheduled for 53 laps, but was ended at 28 laps on reaching the three-hour limit. Full points were awarded.

* Gasly: Drive-through converted to 20s time penalty for speeding under red flag conditions (originally finished 17th).

* Leclerc: 5s time penalty for leaving the track and gaining an advantage (originally finished 2nd).

DHL Fastest race lap: Zhou Guanyu on lap 20, 1m 44.411s, 124.411mph/200.220km/h.

Lap record: Lewis Hamilton (Mercedes F1 W10 V6), 1m 30.983s, 142.773mph/229.770km/h (2019).

19 · LATIFI · Williams
5-place grid penalty for causing a collision at the Singapore GP

17 · MAGNUSSEN · Haas

15 · SCHUMACHER · Haas

13 · TSUNODA · AlphaTauri

11 · RICCIARDO · McLaren

20 · GASLY · AlphaTauri
Car modified in parc fermé; required to start from the pit lane.

18 · STROLL · Aston Martin

16 · ALBON · Williams

14 · ZHOU · Alfa Romeo

12 · BOTTAS · Alfa Romeo

Grid order	1	2	3	4	5	6	7	8	9	10	11	12	13	14	15	16	17	18	19	20	21	22	23	24	25	26	27	28	
1 VERSTAPPEN	1	1	1	1	1	1	1	14	1	1	1	1	1	1	1	1	1	1	1	1	1	1	1	1	1	1	1	1	1
16 LECLERC	16	16	16	16	16	16	16	47	16	16	16	16	16	16	16	16	16	16	16	16	16	16	16	16	16	16	16	16	2
55 SAINZ	11	11	11	11	11	11	11	3	47	11	11	11	11	11	11	11	11	11	11	11	11	11	11	11	11	11	11	11	3
11 PEREZ	31	31	31	31	31	31	31	1	11	31	31	31	31	31	31	31	31	31	31	31	31	31	31	31	31	31	31	31	4
31 OCON	44	44	44	44	44	44	14	16	31	44	44	44	44	44	44	44	44	44	44	44	44	44	44	44	44	44	44	44	5
44 HAMILTON	14	14	14	14	14	14	44	24	44	47	5	5	5	5	5	5	5	5	5	5	5	5	5	5	5	5	5	5	6
14 ALONSO	63	63	63	63	63	63	63	11	24	5	14	14	14	14	14	14	14	14	14	14	14	14	63	63	63	63	63	14	7
63 RUSSELL	3	3	3	3	3	3	3	31	5	14	6	6	6	6	6	6	6	6	6	63	63	63	6	14	14	14	14	63	8
5 VETTEL	22	22	22	22	22	22	47	44	14	6	4	4	4	4	63	63	63	63	63	6	6	6	14	6	6	6	6	6	9
4 NORRIS	47	47	47	47	47	47	22	5	6	4	22	22	22	22	4	4	4	4	4	4	4	4	4	4	4	4	4	4	10
3 RICCIARDO	18	18	18	18	18	20	20	6	4	22	63	63	63	63	22	22	22	22	22	22	3	3	3	3	3	3	3	3	
77 BOTTAS	20	20	20	20	20	18	24	4	22	63	18	18	18	18	18	18	18	18	18	3	20	20	20	18	18	18	18	18	
22 TSUNODA	4	4	4	4	4	4	18	22	63	18	47	3	3	3	3	3	3	3	3	20	77	77	18	20	22	22	22	22	
24 ZHOU	77	77	77	77	77	24	10	63	18	3	3	20	20	20	20	20	20	20	20	77	47	18	77	77	20	20	20	20	
47 SCHUMACHER	6	6	6	6	24	10	5	18	3	20	20	77	77	77	77	77	77	77	77	47	18	47	22	22	77	77	77	77	
23 ALBON	5	5	5	5	10	77	6	77	20	77	77	10	10	10	10	10	10	10	10	18	22	22	47	24	24	24	24	24	
20 MAGNUSSEN	24	24	24	24	6	5	4	20	77	10	10	24	24	24	24	24	24	24	47	24	24	24	24	10	10	10	10	10	
18 STROLL	10	10	10	10	5	6	77	10	10	24	24	47	47	47	47	47	47	47	24	10	10	10	10	47	47	47	47	47	
6 LATIFI																													
	SC	SC	SC	SC	SC																								

Race red-flagged on lap 2

SC Safety car deployed on laps shown

10 = Pit stop

Alfa Romeo ORLEN

TIME SHEETS

PRACTICE 1 (FRIDAY)

Weather: Wet/cloudy

Temperatures: track 19-22°C, air 15-17°C

Pos.	Driver	Laps	Time
1	Fernando Alonso	7	1m 42.248s
2	Carlos Sainz	15	1m 42.563s
3	Charles Leclerc	16	1m 42.634s
4	Esteban Ocon	5	1m 43.022s
5	Kevin Magnussen	15	1m 43.258s
6	Max Verstappen	4	1m 43.362s
7	Mick Schumacher	13	1m 43.761s
8	Lando Norris	7	1m 43.889s
9	Valtteri Bottas	13	1m 43.969s
10	Sergio Pérez	4	1m 44.234s
11	Zhou Guanyu	15	1m 44.429s
12	Daniel Ricciardo	8	1m 44.486s
13	Lewis Hamilton	6	1m 44.558s
14	Lance Stroll	10	1m 44.570s
15	Alexander Albon	9	1m 44.791s
16	Pierre Gasly	12	1m 44.878s
17	Nicholas Latifi	11	1m 45.424s
18	George Russell	4	1m 46.103s
19	Yuki Tsunoda	16	1m 46.192s
20	Sebastian Vettel	8	1m 48.090s

PRACTICE 2 (FRIDAY)

Weather: Wet/cloudy

Temperatures: track 18-19°C, air 16-17°C

Pos.	Driver	Laps	Time
1	George Russell	23	1m 41.935s
2	Lewis Hamilton	22	1m 42.170s
3	Max Verstappen	24	1m 42.786s
4	Sergio Pérez	26	1m 42.834s
5	Kevin Magnussen	17	1m 43.187s
6	Carlos Sainz	23	1m 43.204s
7	Fernando Alonso	14	1m 43.533s
8	Valtteri Bottas	20	1m 43.733s
9	Esteban Ocon	13	1m 43.884s
10	Zhou Guanyu	17	1m 44.525s
11	Charles Leclerc	10	1m 44.709s
12	Nicholas Latifi	16	1m 44.962s
13	Alexander Albon	15	1m 45.039s
14	Yuki Tsunoda	27	1m 45.257s
15	Sebastian Vettel	24	1m 45.261s
16	Lando Norris	11	1m 45.885s
17	Daniel Ricciardo	9	1m 46.030s
18	Lance Stroll	21	1m 46.776s
19	Pierre Gasly	13	1m 47.109s
-	Mick Schumacher	-	-

PRACTICE 3 (SATURDAY)

Weather: Dry/cloudy

Temperatures: track 28-30°C, air 21-22°C

Pos.	Driver	Laps	Time
1	Max Verstappen	22	1m 30.671s
2	Carlos Sainz	27	1m 30.965s
3	Charles Leclerc	27	1m 30.980s
4	Fernando Alonso	20	1m 31.320s
5	Sergio Pérez	25	1m 31.514s
6	George Russell	28	1m 31.530s
7	Lewis Hamilton	25	1m 31.589s
8	Lando Norris	27	1m 31.747s
9	Esteban Ocon	22	1m 31.750s
10	Lance Stroll	25	1m 31.838s
11	Daniel Ricciardo	28	1m 31.860s
12	Alexander Albon	26	1m 31.946s
13	Valtteri Bottas	24	1m 31.971s
14	Sebastian Vettel	25	1m 32.222s
15	Kevin Magnussen	23	1m 32.290s
16	Mick Schumacher	24	1m 32.366s
17	Yuki Tsunoda	26	1m 32.377s
18	Zhou Guanyu	24	1m 32.385s
19	Nicholas Latifi	26	1m 32.868s
20	Pierre Gasly	24	1m 32.881s

QUALIFYING (SATURDAY))

Weather: Dry/mostly cloudy Temperatures: track 26°C, air 19°C

Pos.	Driver	First	Second	Third	Qualifying Tyre
1	Max Verstappen	1m 30.224s	1m 30.346s	1m 29.304s	Soft (n)
2	Charles Leclerc	1m 30.402s	1m 30.486s	1m 29.314s	Soft (n)
3	Carlos Sainz	1m 30.336s	1m 30.444s	1m 29.361s	Soft (n)
4	Sergio Pérez	1m 30.622s	1m 29.925s	1m 29.709s	Soft (n)
5	Esteban Ocon	1m 30.696s	1m 30.357s	1m 30.165s	Soft (u)
6	Lewis Hamilton	1m 30.906s	1m 30.443s	1m 30.261s	Soft (u)
7	Fernando Alonso	1m 30.603s	1m 30.343s	1m 30.322s	Soft (n)
8	George Russell	1m 30.865s	1m 30.465s	1m 30.389s	Soft (n)
9	Sebastian Vettel	1m 31.256s	1m 30.656s	1m 30.554s	Soft (u)
10	Lando Norris	1m 30.881s	1m 30.473s	1m 31.003s	Soft (n)
11	Daniel Ricciardo	1m 30.880s	1m 30.659s		
12	Valtteri Bottas	1m 31.226s	1m 30.709s		
13	Yuki Tsunoda	1m 31.130s	1m 30.808s		
14	Zhou Guanyu	1m 30.894s	1m 30.953s		
15	Mick Schumacher	1m 31.152s	1m 31.439s		
16	Alexander Albon	1m 31.311s			
17	Pierre Gasly	1m 31.322s			
18	Kevin Magnussen	1m 31.352s			
19	Lance Stroll	1m 31.419s			
20	Nicholas Latifi	1m 31.511s			

QUALIFYING: head to head

Hamilton	11	7	Russell
Verstappen	14	4	Pérez
Ricciardo	2	16	Norris
Leclerc	14	4	Sainz
Gasly	11	7	Tsunoda
Hülkenberg	1	1	Stroll
Vettel	10	6	Stroll
Alonso	11	7	Ocon
Bottas	12	6	Zhou
Albon	15	2	Latifi
de Vries	1	0	Latifi
Magnussen	13	5	Schumacher

Alfa Romeo ORLEN

FOR THE RECORD

2nd DRIVERS' WORLD TITLE: Max Verstappen

1st FASTEST LAP: Zhou Guanyu

DID YOU KNOW?

Zhou's fastest lap was the first by an Alfa Romeo-named car since Andrea De Cesaris at the 1983 Belgian GP.

POINTS

DRIVERS

1	Max Verstappen	366
2	Sergio Pérez	253
3	Charles Leclerc	252
4	George Russell	207
5	Carlos Sainz	202
6	Lewis Hamilton	180
7	Lando Norris	101
8	Esteban Ocon	78
9	Fernando Alonso	65
10	Valtteri Bottas	46
11	Sebastian Vettel	32
12	Daniel Ricciardo	29
13	Pierre Gasly	23
14	Kevin Magnussen	22
15	Lance Stroll	13
16	Mick Schumacher	12
17	Yuki Tsunoda	11
18	Zhou Guanyu	6
19	Alexander Albon	4
20	Nicholas Latifi	2
21	Nyck de Vries	2

CONSTRUCTORS

1	Red Bull	619
2	Ferrari	454
3	Mercedes	387
4	Alpine	143
5	McLaren	130
6	Alfa Romeo	52
7	Aston Martin	45
8	Haas	34
9	AlphaTauri	34
10	Williams	8

9 · VETTEL · Aston Martin

7 · ALONSO · Alpine

5 · OCON · Alpine

3 · SAINZ · Ferrari

1 · VERSTAPPEN · Red Bull

10 · NORRIS · McLaren

8 · RUSSELL · Mercedes

6 · HAMILTON · Mercedes

4 · PÉREZ · Red Bull

2 · LECLERC · Ferrari

RACE TYRE STRATEGIES

PIRELLI

	Driver	Race Stint 1	Race Stint 2	Race Stint 3	Race Stint 4
1	Verstappen	Inter (n): 1-2	Wet (n): 3-7	Inter (n): 8-28	
2	Pérez	Inter (n): 1-2	Wet (n): 3-7	Inter (n): 8-28	
3	Leclerc	Inter (n): 1-2	Wet (n): 3-7	Inter (n): 8-28	
4	Ocon	Inter (n): 1-2	Wet (n): 3-7	Inter (n): 8-28	
5	Hamilton	Inter (n): 1-2	Wet (n): 3-7	Inter (n): 8-28	
6	Vettel	Inter (u): 1-2	Wet (n): 3-5	Inter (n): 6-28	
7	Alonso	Inter (n): 1-2	Wet (n): 3-8	Inter (n): 9-22	Inter (n): 23-28
8	Russell	Inter (n): 1-2	Wet (n): 3-7	Inter (u): 8-28	
9	Latifi	Inter (n): 1-2	Wet (n): 3-5	Inter (n): 6-28	
10	Norris	Inter (n): 1-2	Wet (n): 3-6	Inter (n): 7-28	
11	Ricciardo	Inter (n): 1-2	Wet (n): 3-8	Inter (n): 9-28	
12	Stroll	Inter (n): 1-2	Wet (n): 3-7	Inter (n): 8-28	
13	Tsunoda	Inter (n): 1-2	Wet (n): 3-7	Inter (n): 8-20	Inter (n): 21-28
14	Magnussen	Inter (n): 1-2	Wet (n): 3-7	Inter (n): 8-28	
15	Bottas	Inter (n): 1-2	Wet (n): 3-6	Inter (n): 7-28	
16	Zhou	Inter (n): 1-2	Wet (n): 3-9	Inter (n): 10-28	
17	Gasly	Inter (n): 1	Wet (n): 2-7	Inter (n): 8-19	Inter (n): 20-28
18	Schumacher	Inter (n): 1-2	Wet (n): 3-11	Inter (n): 12-28	
	Albon	Inter (n): 0 (dnf)			
	Sainz	Inter (n): 0 (dnf)			

The tyre regulations stipulate that at least two of three dry tyre specifications must be used during a dry race. Selected compounds for Suzuka: Red = Soft (C3); Yellow = Medium (C2); White = Hard (C1). (n) new (u) used

Red Bull Content Pool/Getty Images

FIA FORMULA 1 WORLD CHAMPIONSHIP · ROUND 19

UNITED STATES GRAND PRIX

CIRCUIT OF THE AMERICAS

Red Bull drivers past and present line up with Christian Horner, Adrian Newey and Dr Helmut Marko to lead the applause in appreciation of the late Dietrich Mateschitz.
Photo: Red Bull Content Pool/Getty Images

CIRCUIT OF THE AMERICAS QUALIFYING

WITH the second F1 practice session in Austin devoted entirely to testing the 2023-generation Pirelli tyres, the first session offered the only real pointers to qualifying.

Carlos Sainz's Ferrari headed the times from Max Verstappen's Red Bull and Lewis Hamilton's Mercedes. Charles Leclerc was absent from the session, to make way for Ferrari Academy driver Robert Shwartzman, one of five 'junior' drivers taking part in FP1, with 2021 IndyCar champion Alex Palou in Daniel Ricciardo's McLaren, Theo Pourchaire in Valtteri Bottas's Alfa Romeo, and prospective full-time 2023 Williams recruit Logan Sergeant in the car normally piloted by Nicholas Latifi. There was also a brief appearance by Antonio Giovinazzi, who put Kevin Magnussen's Haas into the barriers and wasn't seen again.

Palou was the standout among the rookies. The headline times didn't reflect how good a job he had done because he didn't manage a run on the softs, but he was straight into it, attacking, and only a couple of tenths shy of Lando Norris on the medium compound.

The compressed programme meant that the long runs comprised no more than three or four laps in most cases. Verstappen didn't make a long run at all, that duty falling to Sergio Pérez, who averaged a couple of tenths slower than Sainz on the soft-compound tyres.

When Anthony Davidson had driven the 2021 Mercedes at CoTA in June for a sponsor day, he remarked that resurfacing could help the team with a new smoothness from Turn Two to the exit of T9/10, and also in the final sector, from Turn 12 to the exit of Turn 15. On the other hand, there are two lengthy straights, and the W13 was draggy, to the extent that even in the wet, Hamilton had been unable to pass Esteban Ocon at Suzuka. But, according to Jenson Button, who was Hamilton's McLaren team-mate for three years, CoTA is his strongest circuit, more so even than Silverstone. So, could Austin provide the opportunity for him to maintain that unbroken sequence of winning in every year he had competed in F1 since 2007?

The evidence of qualifying suggested that while Mercedes was closer, it wasn't close enough. After the first Q3 runs, it was a familiar story, with Leclerc heading Verstappen. On the final run, however, it was Sainz who delivered for Ferrari, stopping the clock in 1m 34.356s to his team-mate's 1m 34.421s.

"I knew it was coming, guys, I knew it!" grinned a delighted Sainz. "It was a lot of fun, but a bit gusty, with every corner a bit of an adventure. Pole has been a long time coming for me, but I'd say that Red Bull are still probably pre-race favourites."

Although Leclerc pipped Verstappen by two-hundredths, it would not be an all-red front row, as Charles suffered a ten-place engine penalty, his third grid drop of the 2022 season.

"With the wind, the car changes every lap," Leclerc confirmed, "but Carlos did a better job."

Thus Verstappen would be promoted to the front row and was happy enough: "In the low-speed stuff, I was running out of tyres, but the car will be quick tomorrow."

The two-time champion had another reason to want to win the race: the news that Red Bull founder Dietrich Mateschitz had died, aged 78, which was released on qualifying day. "It's hard news for everyone," Max said, "but I want to pay tribute to him and acknowledge what he has done for so many, and for me and my life."

Sergio Pérez was fourth quickest, a couple of tenths shy of Verstappen, but three-tenths clear of Hamilton's fifth-placed Mercedes. The seven-time champion appeared to have found a better balance than his team-mate, although in the final analysis, Russell was just 0.04s adrift.

The big three teams had a considerable advantage over the rest, headed by Lance Stroll, who produced comfortably his best qualifying performance of the season to put the first Aston Martin seventh on the grid, albeit more than half a second from Russell. Norris was a tenth behind with the first of the McLarens, while team-mate Daniel Ricciardo had fallen at the first hurdle, in Q1, almost six-tenths behind his team-mate at a circuit he loves, and could do no better than 17th.

The other surprise Q1 elimination was Ocon, who went out along with the two Haas drivers (Kevin Magnussen 16th and Mick Schumacher 19th after a quick spin) and Nicholas Latifi.

Completing the top ten qualifiers were Alpine's Fernando Alonso and Alfa Romeo's Valtteri Bottas, the Finn attempting to turn around a topsy-turvy year in which he had scored 42 points in the first nine races, and none since...

Alex Albon failed to make into the top-ten shootout by only two-hundredths, while Sebastian Vettel was another driver to miss out by less than a tenth. Zhou Guanyu was within striking distance, too, until he was penalised by having a lap deleted for exceeding track limits. Pierre Gasly and Yuki Tsunoda qualified their AlphaTauris 13th and 15th respectively.

That, though, was not quite how the grid would look. As well as a ten-place penalty for Leclerc (12th), Pérez (9th) and Alonso (14th) also took five-place hits for excessive power unit components, as did Zhou (18th). Tsunoda (19th) attracted a similar penalty for an additional gearbox, while a sixth engine, fourth energy store and seventh exhaust, with work conducted outside of *parc fermé* regulations, condemned Ocon to start from the pit lane.

WITH less than 250m from pole position to the apex of CoTA's wide, uphill Turn One, a 'busy' first corner is always standard fare in Austin. Max Verstappen got better traction off the line between the front-row men, the Red Bull comfortably down the inside of pole-man Carlos Sainz's Ferrari as they turned in.

Realising that he'd lost the corner, Sainz jinked right to try for a better exit, but was tagged in the middle of the road and spun around by George Russell, who had braked late and momentarily locked up as he went into T1 wheel to wheel with Lewis Hamilton's sister Mercedes.

Amid the confusion, Lance Stroll had his Aston Martin up to third as they disappeared through the sweeping Esses, while team-mate Sebastian Vettel, who had started tenth after grid penalties had been applied, had the second Aston up to fifth! Behind him, Valtteri Bottas only just avoided contact when he found Sergio Pérez on his inside, the Mexican making up opening-lap positions following his five-place grid drop to ninth.

As they streamed across the line at the end of lap one, Verstappen led from Hamilton, then Stroll, Russell, Vettel, Lando Norris, Pérez, Pierre Gasly, Alex Albon, Charles Leclerc (up from 12th), Bottas, Fernando Alonso, Daniel Ricciardo, Yuki Tsunoda, Nicholas Latifi, Mick Schumacher, Zhou Guanyu, Kevin Magnussen and Esteban Ocon. Sainz trailed forlornly into the pits, where his damaged Ferrari was pushed away. It was a bitter blow after his overdue pole position. Russell, meanwhile, was awarded a 5s penalty for the contact.

Second time around, and Norris had no answer to the straight-line speed of Pérez's Red Bull into Turn 12 as the Mexican moved himself into the top six. Leclerc, meanwhile, improved to ninth when he demoted Albon's Williams.

At the front, Verstappen was able to open a 2s gap to Hamilton before DRS was enabled, while Russell dropped almost 5s further back in as many laps, before going by Stroll's Aston into Turn 12. But rather than the Mercedes twins, Max's main concern seemed to be the weather. "The wind is making it very tricky," he said of gusts approaching 30mph. Proving the point, Latifi was blown off the road in the Esses, the Williams spinning just at the point where downforce was most needed.

On the strategy front, everyone in the top ten had gone to the grid on Pirelli's medium-compound tyre, while Alonso, running 11th from his penalised 14th starting slot, was on the hard compound. Team-mate Ocon, who had started from the pit lane, and the two Haas drivers had also opted for the same route.

Pérez had the second Red Bull into the top four by lap seven, when he bumped Stroll down to fifth, the Red Bull missing a right front wing endplate that did not appear to be hampering its progress too severely.

With a dozen laps on the board, Verstappen's lead over Hamilton was out to 4.5s, with Russell a further 6.5s further back and Pérez just outside DRS range of the second Mercedes. Stroll was another 4.5s adrift, a couple of seconds ahead of Aston Martin team-mate Vettel, who had been caught by Leclerc's seventh-placed Ferrari.

Then there was an 8s gap to Norris's McLaren, which had a 3s advantage over the hard-tyred Alonso, with Alpine team-mate Ocon completing the top ten. The Haas drivers ran 11th and 12th, Schumacher ahead of Magnussen, who had yet to stop, while Gasly and Bottas were some 6s further back, the Frenchman just managing to cover off the Finn at their first stops.

"Lewis, it's hammer time," was not a message we'd heard too many times from race engineer Pete Bonnington in 2022, but that was the instruction to the seven-time champion. Hamilton was indeed the first of the leaders to pit, going on to the hard-compound Pirelli after a 2.9s stop.

"What do you want me to do?" Verstappen asked the Red Bull team.

"You're free to push," engineer 'GP' Lambiase told him.

Verstappen and Russell were into the pits next time around, Max covering off Hamilton with a 2.6s Red Bull stop and rejoining just in front of Stroll.

Pérez relinquished his brief lead after 15 laps, with Stroll stopping a lap later. That left Verstappen back in front with a

Above: Carlos Sainz spins out on the opening lap while the pack takes avoiding action.
Photo: Lukas Gorys

Top left: Ed Sheeran poses for a photo with Christian and Geri Horner.
Photo: Red Bull Content Pool/Getty Images

Above far left: Théo Pourchaire handled the Alfa in FP1.
Photo: Alfa Romeo ORLEN

Above left: IndyCar champion Alex Palou impressed with his handling of Ricciardo's McLaren in FP1.
Photo: McLaren F1 Team

Centre far left: Logan Sargeant, hoping to graduate to Formula 1 with Williams in 2023.
Photo: Williams Racing

Centre left: Robert Schwartzman, a member of Ferrari's Driver Academy, was given an FP1 run in Charles Leclerc's car.
Photo: Scuderia Ferrari

Left: Ride 'em Cowboy! Daniel Ricciardo suitably dressed Texan style in the pit lane.
Photo: Lukas Gorys

Above: In front of the massive Austin crowd, George Russell and Sergio Pérez battle over fourth place.
Photo: Red Bull Content Pool/Getty Images

Top right: Lando Norris started sixth and finished sixth.
Photo: McLaren F1 Team

Above right: A welcome point for Yuki Tsunoda after a bad run of races for the Japanese driver.
Photo: Red Bull Content Pool/Getty Images

Right: Second place for Lewis Hamilton, still looking for that elusive first win of the season.
Photo: Mercedes-AMG Petronas F1 Team

3.3s margin to the yet-to-pit Leclerc and then, 2.5s further back, Hamilton.

"These tyres don't feel great," Hamilton told Mercedes. Verstappen, when asked his opinion about the hard, was non-committal.

Then Leclerc received a useful break when Bottas, also hit by a gust of wind, lost the rear end of his Alfa and ended up beached in the gravel between Turns 19 and 20, prompting a full safety car. In came Leclerc for a set of hard Pirellis, the Ferrari returning only just behind Pérez's third-placed Red Bull and ahead of Russell's Mercedes. Vettel also benefited from a cheap stop to jump team-mate Stroll, as did the Alpines of Alonso and Ocon, who jettisoned starting hards and went on to a set of the yellow-walled mediums.

The restart came 22 laps into the race's 56 and was handled well by Verstappen. The order behind him now: Hamilton, Pérez, Leclerc, Russell, Vettel, Stroll, Gasly, Alonso, Norris, Tsunoda, Ocon, the Haas pair, Zhou, Ricciardo and the two Williams drivers.

Those on the reverse-strategy medium Pirellis generated tyre temperature more rapidly and got better exits from Turn One. Alonso slingshotted his way past Gasly to go eighth, while Tsunoda did likewise to Norris's McLaren for tenth.

Next on Alonso's radar was Stroll. The Alpine had always been pretty slippery and, out of Turn 11, Fernando was quickly into a tow from the Aston. Just as he flicked left to pass, Stroll went the same way to defend and, in a trice, Alonso was airborne. Fortunately, not quite enough air got under the car to send it into a somersault and the Alpine thumped back down diffuser-first, smiting the barrier on the left a substantial blow. Stroll, meanwhile, exited stage right, clouting the barrier before shedding bodywork and coming to a halt in the middle of the circuit, thankfully uninjured. Out came the safety car again.

It had been a relatively late jink to the left by Stroll and a scary contact. Such incidents are not nice, and while F1 has done a great job of improving safety, it's never possible to legislate for a flying car. A bit of a rant might have been expected from Alonso, but when it came, his calm response – "a very late move" – was more in keeping with receiving a minor tap at somewhere like Monaco's hairpin. Then it dawned. Obviously, Fernando had quickly assimilated whose father would be writing his pay cheques in 2023... Undeterred, he pitted for a punctured left rear and rejoined in 16th.

We were racing again on lap 25, the first five all on the hard-compound tyres and remaining in the order Verstappen, Hamilton, Pérez, Leclerc and Russell. George was forced to go defensive at Turn 12, however, as the medium-shod Vettel had a quick look down his inside. Behind Sebastian, Gasly was running seventh, but soon received notification of a 5s penalty for falling more than ten car lengths behind while under safety car conditions.

Verstappen was soon on the radio asking, "What happened to my drivability? It's ****."

"Strat 2," Lambiase told him by way of reply.

Leclerc was now hassling Pérez, going around the outside of the Red Bull to take third at Turn 12, only to run wide and be obliged to hand back the position. Next time around, with DRS, Leclerc went for the inside with a super-late dive, and pulled it off.

With 25 laps to go, Verstappen, not looking quite so convincing on the hard-compound Pirelli, had a 2s lead over Hamilton, with Leclerc's Ferrari just over 3.5s behind the Mercedes. Pérez was still in touch, with Russell just outside DRS range. Then came Vettel, with the two AlphaTauris and Norris's McLaren scrapping over seventh.

With the second stops approaching, Hamilton started to push. He closed Verstappen's lead to just over a second before diving into the pits for a second set of hard-compound tyres after a 2.7s stop.

Verstappen responded immediately with a fastest first sector of the race as he tried to cover off Lewis again, Leclerc also pitting on the same lap. But while the Ferrari was stationary for just 2.8s, Red Bull had a gun problem on the left front and Verstappen remained immobile for over 11s! Not only did he lose track position to Hamilton, but also he pitted out behind Leclerc. To claim a record-equalling 13th win in a single season, he needed to pass both on track.

"Beautiful, beautiful," Max radioed, sarcastically.

Two laps later, Pérez pitted after another short-lived lead, while Hamilton set the race's fastest lap. Russell had attempted to undercut the second Red Bull by stopping a couple of laps earlier, and they were neck and neck into Turn One as Sergio rejoined, the Red Bull on the inside. Russell switched back to pass him on exit, but Pérez bravely kept his boot in and ran back around the outside of the Merc through the sweepers to hold on. Brave stuff!

Verstappen, knowing that he would have to close down Hamilton, was keen to dispense with Leclerc as quickly as possible. On lap 39, he got down the inside into Turn One, but the Ferrari made a better exit and retook the position. Tucked right under the Ferrari rear wing out of Turn 11 and with the benefit of DRS, however, there was no resisting the Red Bull any more, and Verstappen was through.

Vettel, with a stop to make, now led the race by a couple of seconds from Hamilton, but Lewis was past the Aston with 15 laps to go. With Verstappen 4s back, it appeared as though he had a realistic shot at maintaining that unique win-every-season record.

Further back, Kevin Magnussen was 'best of the rest', seventh, on course to become the only driver to pull off a one-stopper (hards and then a 38-lap medium stint!), but he was under investigation for failing to observe yellow flags. Meanwhile, things had gone from bad to worse for Gasly, who received a 10s penalty for incorrectly serving his earlier 5s penalty.

Vettel made his second pit stop on lap 42 and, heartbreakingly, was stationary for 16.8s due to a recalcitrant right front and a jack problem. When he rejoined, it was down in 13th position.

Norris was now on a charge on his second set of hards,

Left: Mediums go on, but a problematic pit stop for Max Verstappen allowed Charles Leclerc's Ferrari to jump him.
Photo: Red Bull Content Pool/Getty Images

Right: The leaders continue their race as, behind, Fernando Alonso's Alpine clouts the barrier after a collision with Lance Stroll's Aston Martin.
Photo: XPB Images

Below: True legend. Mario Andretti, 82 years young.
Photo: Peter J. Fox

Bottom: Backstage before the celebrations begin, Helmut Marko chats with the winner, while Charles Leclerc contemplates Ferrari losing ground to Mercedes in the constructors' race.
Photo: Red Bull Content Pool/Getty Images

making a late move to pass Tsunoda into Turn One, before relegating Zhou, Albon and Magnussen as he closed in on the irrepressible Alonso, who had his Alpine back up to sixth (*see* Viewpoint)! In the immortal words of Martin Brundle, commentating on Sky TV, "What is Alonso doing in the top six when, not long since, he was appearing on the radar at Austin International Airport?"

With six laps to go, Verstappen was within DRS range of the leading Mercedes for the first time. Leclerc, after running with the Dutchman for a number of laps, was falling away as the Ferrari began to degrade its mediums.

Into Turn 12 on lap 50, Verstappen went for the inside, and Hamilton, moving late, had no real chance to fend him off. Lewis made a bid to retake the lead out of the corner, but Verstappen covered him off. He fought hard through the twisty section, but, on the hard-compound tyres, didn't quite have the grip.

In one last bid, Hamilton was on the radio, pointing out, "He's gone off again!" – a reference to Verstappen exceeding track limits while attempting to keep the Mercedes out of DRS range.

"You need to make sure you're safe on track limits now, please, Max," Lambiase radioed his driver.

Vettel, far from being deflated by his lengthy final stop, was frantically making up lost ground, pulling off a great outside pass of Albon to go ninth. There were four laps left, and Magnussen was 4s up the road on his old mediums.

Verstappen now received a black-and-white flag for track limits, 'GP' telling him a little more urgently, "You've used up all your strikes now, Max, so we need to be safe on track limits." Another transgression would bring a 5s penalty.

Hamilton was still only 1.2s behind the lead Red Bull, but he, too, received a black-and-white warning flag with just two laps remaining. With Leclerc's Ferrari 4.5s behind, he needed to be careful.

Leclerc had managed to keep a 2s margin to Pérez, while Russell, with a pit window behind him to Alonso, stopped for a third time with two to go to bolt on a set of softs and successfully chase the extra fastest-lap point.

Norris, meanwhile, struck a blow for McLaren in the fight for fourth place in the constructors' championship with a last-lap, Turn One pass of Alonso's Alpine on hard tyres that were a dozen laps fresher than the Spaniard's.

As the chequered flag came down on Verstappen's 33rd GP win and that record-equalling 13th in a single season, it meant that Red Bull were constructors' champions for the first time since 2013, a fitting tribute to team founder Dietrich Mateschitz.

"Congrats, guys. I was a bit upset after that stop, but I just kept pushing, and you guys really deserve it," said Verstappen, perhaps a tad sheepishly after his earlier moment of frustration.

"So close, but so far," was Hamilton's reaction.

Leclerc, meanwhile, was relatively happy with a fifth consecutive podium, having started 12th, but not thrilled that the underlying pace hadn't been quite there when Verstappen's pit stop delay had provided an opportunity.

With the championships wrapped up against a backdrop of developing 2021 budget cap controversy, Verstappen could not be distracted. There were three to go, and he wanted to win them all.

Tony Dodgins

VIEWPOINT
ALONSO'S UPS AND DOWNS

FERNANDO ALONSO had had eventful races in his time, but few could come close to this one. Starting 14th, he was immediately on a typical charge, working his way into the points and staying there after the first scheduled stop on lap 18. The impetus continued as he quickly caught Lance Stroll and was set to make a DRS move for seventh on the back straight. As he rushed up to the back of the Aston Martin and flicked left, Stroll made the same move. Wheel-on-wheel contact sent the front of the Alpine into the air, Alonso doing a wheelie as he headed at a shallow angle towards the wall.

He might have narrowly missed what could have been catastrophic contact with the end of the barrier at an access point, but he seemed a certain retirement as the front wheels slammed on to the ground and the Alpine brushed against the wall. As Stroll prepared to evacuate his damaged car and a VSC came into play, Alonso headed for the pits, a lengthy stop for a new nose and fresh tyres dropping him to 17th and last. Surely he could go no further with a car that must have suffered serious structural damage.

Proving that the A522 was as resilient as its driver, however, Alonso carried on as if nothing had happened, taking just 11 laps to reach the top ten once more. By the end of the race, he was a remarkable seventh, earning valuable points for Alpine in their battle with McLaren for fourth in the championship.

Along the way, however, Alonso's right-hand mirror had vibrated loose before being whipped up and over the car. Fernando probably didn't notice, since he hadn't had much need of it. But Haas, having suffered at least three enforced pit stops to remove damaged parts, objected to the Alpine being allowed to run free. A subsequent 30-second penalty dropped Alonso to 15th. A counter claim by Alpine a week later over the timing of the Haas protest resulted in the place being reinstated. It was a messy end, but somehow appropriate after such a wild ride.

Maurice Hamilton

19

FORMULA 1 ARAMCO UNITED STATES GRAND PRIX 2022

ROLEX

Official Timepiece

AUSTIN 21-23 OCTOBER

RACE DISTANCE: 56 laps, 191.634 miles/308.405km

RACE WEATHER: Dry/sunny (track 34-39°C, air 29-33°C)

CIRCUIT OF THE AMERICAS
AUSTIN, TEXAS
Circuit: 3.426 miles/5.513km, 56 laps

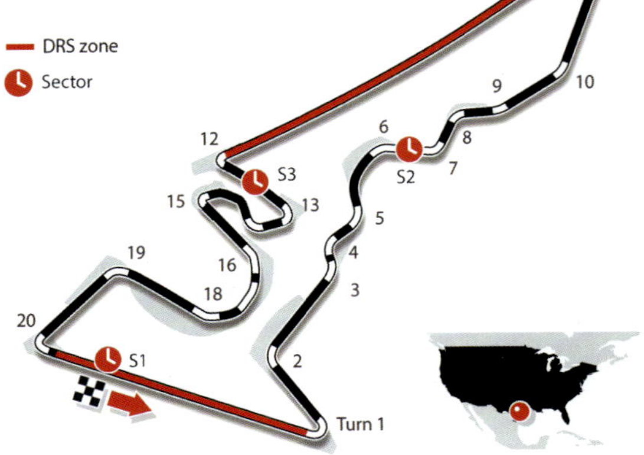

RACE – OFFICIAL CLASSIFICATION

Pos.	Driver	Nat.	No.	Entrant	Car/Engine	Laps	Time/Retirement	Speed (mph/km/h)	Gap to winner	Fastest race lap	
1	**Max Verstappen**	NL	1	Oracle Red Bull Racing	Red Bull RB18-RBPTH001 V6	56	1h 42m 11.687s	112.510/181.068		1m 39.541s	37
2	**Lewis Hamilton**	GB	44	Mercedes-AMG Petronas F1 Team	Mercedes-AMG F1 W13-M13 E Perf. V6	56	1h 42m 16.710s	112.418/180.920	5.023s	1m 39.830s	45
3	**Charles Leclerc**	MC	16	Scuderia Ferrari	Ferrari F1-75-066/7 V6	56	1h 42m 19.188s	112.373/180.847	7.501s	1m 39.731s	37
4	**Sergio Pérez**	MEX	11	Oracle Red Bull Racing	Red Bull RB18-RBPTH001 V6	56	1h 42m 19.980s	112.359/180.824	8.293s	1m 39.563s	44
5	**George Russell**	GB	63	Mercedes-AMG Petronas F1 Team	Mercedes-AMG F1 W13-M13 E Perf. V6	56	1h 42m 56.502s *	111.695/179.755	44.815s	1m 38.788s	56
6	**Lando Norris**	GB	4	McLaren F1 Team	McLaren MCL36-Mercedes F1 M13 E Perf. V6	56	1h 43m 05.472s	111.532/179.494	53.785s	1m 41.322s	49
7	**Fernando Alonso**	E	14	BWT Alpine F1 Team	Alpine A522-Renault E-Tech RE22 V6	56	1h 43m 06.765s *	111.509/179.456	55.078s	1m 41.804s	51
8	**Sebastian Vettel**	D	5	Aston Martin Aramco Cognizant F1 Team	Aston Martin AMR22-Mercedes F1 M13 E Perf. V6	56	1h 43m 17.041s	111.324/179.159	1m 05.354s	1m 41.538s	39
9	**Kevin Magnussen**	DK	20	Haas F1 Team	Haas VF-22-Ferrari 066/7 V6	56	1h 43m 17.521s	111.316/179.145	1m 05.834s	1m 42.546s	35
10	**Yuki Tsunoda**	J	22	Scuderia AlphaTauri	AlphaTauri AT03-RBPTH001 V6	56	1h 43m 22.606s	111.224/178.998	1m 10.919s	1m 42.206s	36
11	Esteban Ocon	F	31	BWT Alpine F1 Team	Alpine A522-Renault E-Tech RE22 V6	56	1h 43m 24.562s	111.189/178.942	1m 12.875s	1m 41.243s	49
12	Zhou Guanyu	CHN	24	Alfa Romeo F1 Team ORLEN	Alfa Romeo C42-Ferrari 066/7 V6	56	1h 43m 27.851s	111.130/178.847	1m 16.164s	1m 42.394s	39
13	Alexander Albon	T	23	Williams Racing	Williams FW44-Mercedes F1 M13 E Perf. V6	56	1h 43m 31.744s *	111.061/178.735	1m 20.057s	1m 42.471s	46
14	Pierre Gasly	F	10	Scuderia AlphaTauri	AlphaTauri AT03-RBPTH001 V6	56	1h 43m 33.450s *	111.030/178.686	1m 21.763s	1m 41.674s	55
15	Mick Schumacher	D	47	Haas F1 Team	Haas VF-22-Ferrari 066/7 V6	56	1h 43m 36.177s *	110.981/178.607	1m 24.490s	1m 42.320s	55
16	Daniel Ricciardo	AUS	3	McLaren F1 Team	McLaren MCL36-Mercedes F1 M13 E Perf. V6	56	1h 43m 42.174s	110.874/178.435	1m 30.487s	1m 42.420s	55
17	Nicholas Latifi	CDN	6	Williams Racing	Williams FW44-Mercedes F1 M13 E Perf. V6	56	1h 43m 55.275s *	110.641/178.060	1m 43.588s	1m 43.485s	54
	Lance Stroll	CDN	18	Aston Martin Aramco Cognizant F1 Team	Aston Martin AMR22-Mercedes F1 M13 E Perf. V6	21	*accident*			1m 43.080s	3
	Valtteri Bottas	FIN	77	Alfa Romeo F1 Team ORLEN	Alfa Romeo C42-Ferrari 066/7 V6	16	*accident*			1m 43.391s	4
	Carlos Sainz	E	55	Scuderia Ferrari	Ferrari F1-75-066/7 V6	1	*accident*			no time	

* Alonso: Originally 10s stop/go converted to 30s time penalty for car being in an unsafe condition, but the penalty was overturned on appeal.

* Albon: 5s time penalty for leaving the track and gaining an advantage. * Russell: 5s time penalty for causing a collision with Sainz (served at pit stop).

* Gasly: 5s time penalty for falling more than 10 car lengths behind the safety car (served at pit stop). * Gasly: 10s time penalty for failing to properly serve a penalty (originally finished 11th).

* Latifi: 5s time penalty for causing a collision with Schumacher. * Schumacher: 5s time penalty for leaving the track without a justifiable reason four times.

DHL Fastest race lap (scores 1 point): George Russell on lap 56, 1m 38.788s, 124.835mph/200.902km/h.

Lap record: Charles Leclerc (Ferrari SF90 V6), 1m 36.169s, 128.235mph/206.374km/h (2019).

19 · TSUNODA · AlphaTauri
Used additional restricted-number components; 5-place grid penalty

17 · LATIFI · Williams

15 · RICCIARDO · McLaren

13 · MAGNUSSEN · Haas

11 · GASLY · AlphaTauri

20 · OCON · Alpine
Car modified in parc fermé; required to start from the pit lane; used additional power unit elements

18 · ZHOU · Alfa Romeo

16 · SCHUMACHER · Haas

14 · ALONSO · Alpine
Used additional power unit element; 5-place grid penalty

12 · LECLERC · Ferrari
Used additional power unit elements; 10-place grid penalty

Grid order	1	2	3	4	5	6	7	8	9	10	11	12	13	14	15	16	17	18	19	20	21	22
55 SAINZ	1	1	1	1	1	1	1	1	1	1	1	1	1	11	1	1	1	16	1	1	1	1
1 VERSTAPPEN	44	44	44	44	44	44	44	44	44	44	44	44	63	1	16	16	16	1	44	44	44	44
44 HAMILTON	18	18	18	18	63	63	63	63	63	63	63	63	11	16	18	44	44	44	11	11	11	11
63 RUSSELL	63	63	63	63	18	11	11	11	11	11	11	11	18	18	5	5	5	5	16	16	16	16
18 STROLL	5	5	5	11	11	18	18	18	18	18	18	18	16	5	44	11	11	11	63	63	63	63
4 NORRIS	4	11	11	5	5	5	5	5	5	5	5	16	5	44	11	63	63	63	5	5	5	5
77 BOTTAS	11	4	4	10	16	16	16	16	16	16	16	5	44	4	14	14	14	14	18	18	18	10
23 ALBON	10	10	10	4	4	4	10	10	10	10	10	4	4	14	63	18	18	18	10	10	10	22
11 PÉREZ	23	16	16	16	10	10	4	4	4	4	4	14	14	63	47	31	31	31	14	14	14	4
5 VETTEL	16	23	23	77	77	77	77	77	77	77	14	31	47	47	31	47	47	47	4	4	4	47
10 GASLY	77	77	77	23	14	14	14	14	14	14	31	47	31	31	20	20	10	10	22	22	22	31
16 LECLERC	14	14	14	14	23	23	23	23	23	22	47	20	20	20	10	10	20	20	31	31	31	20
20 MAGNUSSEN	3	3	3	3	22	22	22	22	22	3	20	10	10	10	77	77	4	4	47	47	47	24
14 ALONSO	22	22	22	22	3	24	24	24	24	31	77	77	77	77	4	4	22	22	24	24	24	14
3 RICCIARDO	47	6	6	6	24	3	3	3	3	47	23	23	23	23	23	22	23	23	20	20	20	3
47 SCHUMACHER	6	24	24	24	47	47	47	47	47	20	22	22	22	22	22	23	24	24	3	3	3	23
6 LATIFI	24	47	47	47	31	31	31	31	31	23	24	24	24	24	24	24	3	3	23	23	23	6
24 ZHOU	20	20	31	31	20	20	20	20	20	24	3	3	3	3	3	3	6	6	6	6	6	
22 TSUNODA	55	31	20	20	6	6	6	6	6	6	6	6	6	6	6	6						
31 OCON	31																					
																		SC	SC	SC	SC	SC

Grid order	23	24	25	26	27	28	29	30	31	32	33	34	35	36	37	38	39	40	41	42	43	44
55 SAINZ	1	1	1	1	1	1	1	1	1	1	1	1	1	11	11	11	5	5	44	44	44	44
1 VERSTAPPEN	44	44	44	44	44	44	44	44	44	44	44	44	16	63	5	5	44	44	5	1	1	1
44 HAMILTON	11	11	11	11	11	11	11	16	16	16	16	16	11	5	44	44	1	1	1	16	16	16
63 RUSSELL	16	16	16	16	16	16	16	11	11	11	11	11	63	44	16	16	16	16	16	11	11	11
18 STROLL	63	63	63	63	63	63	63	63	63	63	63	63	5	16	1	1	11	11	11	63	63	63
4 NORRIS	5	5	5	5	5	5	5	5	5	5	5	5	44	1	63	63	63	63	63	20	20	20
77 BOTTAS	10	10	10	10	10	10	10	10	10	10	22	4	20	20	20	20	20	20	20	14	14	14
23 ALBON	22	22	22	22	22	22	22	22	22	22	4	20	31	31	31	31	31	14	14	31	31	31
11 PÉREZ	24	4	4	4	4	4	4	4	4	4	47	31	14	14	14	14	14	31	31	23	23	4
5 VETTEL	4	47	47	47	47	47	47	47	47	47	20	14	23	23	23	23	23	23	23	24	4	23
10 GASLY	47	31	31	20	20	20	20	20	20	20	31	23	3	24	24	24	24	24	24	4	24	24
16 LECLERC	31	20	20	31	31	31	31	31	31	31	14	3	24	22	22	22	22	22	22	22	22	22
20 MAGNUSSEN	20	3	3	3	3	3	3	23	23	23	23	24	6	6	4	4	4	4	4	5	5	5
14 ALONSO	3	23	23	23	23	23	23	3	14	14	3	6	22	4	6	47	47	10	10	10	10	10
3 RICCIARDO	23	6	6	6	6	14	14	14	3	3	24	22	4	47	47	10	10	47	47	47	47	47
47 SCHUMACHER	6	14	14	14	14	6	6	6	6	6	6	47	47	10	10	6	6	6	6	6	6	6
6 LATIFI	14	24	24	24	24	24	24	24	24	24	10	10	10	3	3	3	3	3	3	3	3	3
24 ZHOU																						
22 TSUNODA																						
31 OCON																						
	SC	SC	SC																			

TIME SHEETS

PRACTICE 1 (FRIDAY)

Weather: Dry/sunny

Temperatures: track 39-40°C, air 29-31°C

Pos.	Driver	Laps	Time
1	Carlos Sainz	19	1m 36.857s
2	Max Verstappen	15	1m 37.081s
3	Lewis Hamilton	20	1m 37.332s
4	Lance Stroll	23	1m 37.460s
5	Sergio Pérez	19	1m 37.515s
6	Fernando Alonso	25	1m 37.713s
7	George Russell	23	1m 37.802s
8	Pierre Gasly	24	1m 37.810s
9	Lando Norris	23	1m 37.856s
10	Sebastian Vettel	25	1m 38.041s
11	Esteban Ocon	24	1m 38.102s
12	Zhou Guanyu	21	1m 38.276s
13	Alexander Albon	21	1m 38.422s
14	Yuki Tsunoda	23	1m 38.898s
15	Mick Schumacher	20	1m 38.922s
16	Robert Shwartzman	21	1m 38.951s
17	Alex Palou	21	1m 39.911s
18	Théo Pourchaire	19	1m 40.175s
19	Logan Sargeant	23	1m 40.325s
20	Antonio Giovinazzi	4	1m 43.063s

PRACTICE 2 (FRIDAY)

Weather: Dry/dusk

Temperatures: track 30-37°C, air 28-31°C

Pos.	Driver	Laps	Time
1	Charles Leclerc	37	1m 36.810s
2	Valtteri Bottas	37	1m 37.525s
3	Daniel Ricciardo	40	1m 37.627s
4	Carlos Sainz	26	1m 38.232s
5	Mick Schumacher	26	1m 39.507s
6	Lando Norris	26	1m 39.547s
7	Max Verstappen	26	1m 39.575s
8	Lewis Hamilton	26	1m 39.698s
9	Pierre Gasly	26	1m 39.840s
10	Sergio Pérez	26	1m 39.852s
11	Kevin Magnussen	24	1m 40.084s
12	Yuki Tsunoda	26	1m 40.178s
13	George Russell	26	1m 40.562s
14	Zhou Guanyu	26	1m 40.664s
15	Lance Stroll	26	1m 40.806s
16	Esteban Ocon	26	1m 41.310s
17	Fernando Alonso	26	1m 41.334s
18	Alexander Albon	26	1m 41.853s
19	Sebastian Vettel	26	1m 41.857s
20	Nicholas Latifi	26	1m 42.317s

PRACTICE 3 (SATURDAY)

Weather: Dry/sunny

Temperatures: track 39-40°C, air 30-31°C

Pos.	Driver	Laps	Time
1	Max Verstappen	22	1m 35.825s
2	Charles Leclerc	18	1m 36.145s
3	Carlos Sainz	24	1m 36.271s
4	Sergio Pérez	20	1m 36.397s
5	Lewis Hamilton	17	1m 36.401s
6	Fernando Alonso	14	1m 36.928s
7	George Russell	21	1m 37.064s
8	Sebastian Vettel	19	1m 37.151s
9	Lance Stroll	20	1m 37.215s
10	Pierre Gasly	18	1m 37.290s
11	Valtteri Bottas	23	1m 37.310s
12	Lando Norris	19	1m 37.449s
13	Esteban Ocon	18	1m 37.468s
14	Kevin Magnussen	21	1m 37.519s
15	Daniel Ricciardo	16	1m 37.622s
16	Yuki Tsunoda	19	1m 37.888s
17	Alexander Albon	18	1m 37.904s
18	Nicholas Latifi	18	1m 38.028s
19	Mick Schumacher	12	1m 38.132s
20	Zhou Guanyu	3	1m 39.735s

QUALIFYING (SATURDAY))

Weather: Dry/dusk Temperatures: track 31-38°C, air 30-32°C

Pos.	Driver	First	Second	Third	Qualifying Tyre
1	Carlos Sainz	1m 35.297s	1m 35.590s	1m 34.356s	Soft (n)
2	Charles Leclerc	1m 35.795s	1m 35.246s	1m 34.421s	Soft (n)
3	Max Verstappen	1m 35.864s	1m 35.294s	1m 34.448s	Soft (n)
4	Sergio Pérez	1m 36.163s	1m 35.864s	1m 34.645s	Soft (n)
5	Lewis Hamilton	1m 36.148s	1m 35.732s	1m 34.947s	Soft (n)
6	George Russell	1m 36.195s	1m 35.692s	1m 34.988s	Soft (n)
7	Lance Stroll	1m 36.860s	1m 36.032s	1m 35.598s	Soft (n)
8	Lando Norris	1m 36.465s	1m 36.341s	1m 35.690s	Soft (n)
9	Fernando Alonso	1m 36.446s	1m 35.988s	1m 35.876s	Soft (n)
10	Valtteri Bottas	1m 36.746s	1m 36.321s	1m 36.319s	Soft (n)
11	Alexander Albon	1m 36.932s	1m 36.368s		
12	Sebastian Vettel	1m 36.695s	1m 36.398s		
13	Pierre Gasly	1m 36.577s	1m 36.740s		
14	Zhou Guanyu	1m 36.656s	1m 36.970s		
15	Yuki Tsunoda	1m 36.808s	1m 37.147s		
16	Kevin Magnussen	1m 36.949s			
17	Daniel Ricciardo	1m 37.046s			
18	Esteban Ocon	1m 37.068s			
19	Mick Schumacher	1m 37.111s			
20	Nicholas Latifi	1m 37.244s			

QUALIFYING: head to head

Hamilton	12	7	Russell
Verstappen	15	4	Pérez
Ricciardo	2	17	Norris
Leclerc	14	5	Sainz
Gasly	12	7	Tsunoda
Hülkenberg	1	1	Stroll
Vettel	10	7	Stroll
Alonso	12	7	Ocon
Bottas	13	6	Zhou
Albon	16	2	Latifi
de Vries	1	0	Latifi
Magnussen	14	5	Schumacher

Red Bull Content Pool/Getty Images

FOR THE RECORD

5th CONSTRUCTORS' WORLD TITLE: Red Bull

40th FRONT ROW: Max Verstappen

10th GRAND PRIX: Austin Circuit of the Americas

DID YOU KNOW?

Verstappen equals the record of 13 wins in a season set by Michael Schumacher (2004) and equalled by Sebastian Vettel (2013).

POINTS

DRIVERS

1	Max Verstappen	391
2	Charles Leclerc	267
3	Sergio Pérez	265
4	George Russell	218
5	Carlos Sainz	202
6	Lewis Hamilton	198
7	Lando Norris	109
8	Esteban Ocon	78
9	Fernando Alonso	71
10	Valtteri Bottas	46
11	Sebastian Vettel	36
12	Daniel Ricciardo	29
13	Kevin Magnussen	24
14	Pierre Gasly	23
15	Lance Stroll	13
16	Mick Schumacher	12
17	Yuki Tsunoda	12
18	Zhou Guanyu	6
19	Alexander Albon	4
20	Nicholas Latifi	2
21	Nyck de Vries	2

CONSTRUCTORS

1	Red Bull	656
2	Ferrari	469
3	Mercedes	416
4	Alpine	149
5	McLaren	138
6	Alfa Romeo	52
7	Aston Martin	49
8	Haas	36
9	AlphaTauri	35
10	Williams	8

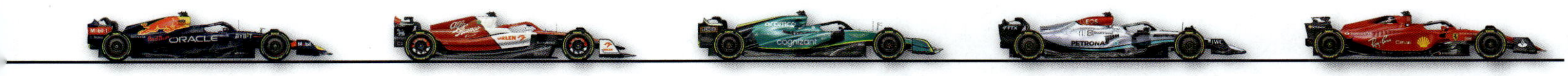

9 · PÉREZ · Red Bull
Used additional power unit element;
5-place grid penalty

7 · BOTTAS · Alfa Romeo

5 · STROLL · Aston Martin

3 · HAMILTON · Mercedes

1 · SAINZ · Ferrari

10 · VETTEL · Aston Martin

8 · ALBON · Williams

6 · NORRIS · McLaren

4 · RUSSELL · Mercedes

2 · VERSTAPPEN · Red Bull

45	46	47	48	49	50	51	52	53	54	55	56	
44	44	44	44	44	1	1	1	1	1	1	1	1
1	1	1	1	1	44	44	44	44	44	44	44	2
16	16	16	16	16	16	16	16	16	16	16	16	3
11	11	11	11	11	11	11	11	11	11	11	11	4
63	63	63	63	63	63	63	63	63	63	63	63	5
20	20	20	14	14	14	14	14	14	14	4	4	6
14	14	14	20	4	4	4	4	4	4	14	14	7
4	4	4	4	20	20	20	20	20	20	20	5	8
31	23	23	23	23	23	5	5	5	5	5	20	9
23	24	24	24	5	5	23	23	23	22	22	22	10
24	22	22	5	24	24	22	22	22	23	10	10	
22	5	5	22	22	22	24	24	10	10	23	31	
5	10	10	10	10	10	10	10	24	24	31	23	
10	47	47	47	47	47	47	31	31	31	24	24	
47	6	31	31	31	31	31	47	47	47	47	47	
6	31	6	6	6	6	3	3	3	3	3	3	
3	3	3	3	3	3	6	6	6	6	6	6	

55 = Pit stop

SC Safety car deployed on laps shown

RACE TYRE STRATEGIES

PIRELLI

	Driver	Race Stint 1	Race Stint 2	Race Stint 3	Race Stint 4
1	Verstappen	Medium (n): 1-13	Hard (n): 14-35	Medium (n): 36-56	
2	Hamilton	Medium (n): 1-12	Hard (n): 13-34	Hard (n): 35-56	
3	Leclerc	Medium (n): 1-18	Hard (n): 19-35	Medium (n): 36-56	
4	Pérez	Medium (n): 1-14	Hard (n): 15-38	Medium (n): 39-56	
5	Russell	Medium (n): 1-13	Hard (n): 14-36	Hard (n): 37-54	Soft (u): 55-56
6	Norris	Medium (n): 1-14	Hard (n): 15-34	Hard (n): 35-56	
7	Alonso	Hard (n): 1-18	Medium (n): 19-22	Hard (n): 23-56	
8	Vettel	Medium (u): 1-18	Medium (u): 19-41	Hard (u): 42-56	
9	Magnussen	Hard (n): 1-18	Medium (n): 19-56		
10	Tsunoda	Medium (n): 1-10	Medium (n): 11-33	Hard (n): 34-56	
11	Ocon	Hard (n): 1-18	Hard (n): 19-45	Medium (n): 46-56	
12	Albon	Medium (n): 1-9	Medium (n): 10-18	Hard (n): 19-56	
13	Zhou	Medium (n): 1-9	Hard (n): 10-23	Hard (n): 24-56	
14	Gasly	Medium (n): 1-11	Hard (n): 12-32	Hard (u): 33-56	
15	Schumacher	Hard (n): 1-18	Medium (n): 19-33	Hard (n): 34-56	
16	Ricciardo	Medium (n): 1-10	Hard (n): 11-35	Medium (n): 36-56	
17	Latifi	Medium (n): 1-5	Medium (n): 6-18	Hard (n): 19-56	
	Stroll	Medium (u): 1-15	Medium (u): 16-21 (dnf)		
	Bottas	Medium (n): 1-10	Hard (n): 11-16 (dnf)		
	Sainz	Medium (n): 1 (dnf)			

The tyre regulations stipulate that at least two of three dry tyre specifications must be used during a dry race. Selected compounds for Austin: Red = Soft (C4); Yellow = Medium (C3; White = Hard (C2). (n) new (u) used

Mercedes AMG Petronas F1 Team

Pure theatre for the fans as the battle between Red Bull and Mercedes commences under the Mexican sun.
Photo: Red Bull Content Pool/Getty Images

FIA FORMULA 1 WORLD CHAMPIONSHIP · ROUND 20

MEXICO CITY GRAND PRIX

MEXICO CITY CIRCUIT

MEXICO CITY QUALIFYING

MERCEDES arrived in Mexico City from an Austin race that Lewis Hamilton had led, even though ultimately Max Verstappen and Red Bull could not be resisted. Mexico's 2,200m altitude and thin air gave the team hope that they might be real contenders for the win.

The track has low grip, but is smooth, and even though the cars run Monaco-type maximum wings, they have less downforce than at Monza running skinny wings! The DRS and slipstreaming are less effective due to the low air density, but the real positive for Mercedes was that its naturally draggy car would be less heavily penalised than usual.

And so it proved in free practice, when Mercedes had its most convincing session of 2022, topping Saturday's FP3 and serving notice that Verstappen might have a pole-position rival. Ferrari, by contrast, seemed to be in more trouble than at any other circuit, Charles Leclerc in particular complaining of huge understeer.

When the chips were down, though, Verstappen – chasing a new 14-wins-in-a-single-season record – had the answer. And by no narrow margin, the two-time champion being the only man to break 1m 18s, his 1m 17.775s lap leaving him with a three-tenths advantage.

"We made a few adjustments after FP3, and it was a good qualifying," Verstappen said. "It's a long run down to Turn One, and pole might not be the best starting position, but we have a quick car."

The man closest to him was George Russell, who had outqualified team-mate Hamilton for the first time since the summer break, by a hundredth. Russell, though, was anything but happy. "Sorry, sorry, guys," he said over the radio. "The car has been feeling so good. After the first three corners of my last Q3 run, it felt great and I thought it was going to be one of those laps, but then in Turn Four, I lost a couple of tenths. I got it back and then I lost it again in Turn 12. It was just a chaotic lap from me. I believe we had the fastest car this weekend, but having Lewis up there as well, hopefully we can go aggressive on strategy because I don't think we can pass the Red Bull on the track."

Hamilton was a bit nonplussed at the sudden gap to Verstappen: "I had some engine problems in Q3 and felt like I left quite a bit of time on the table, but not three-tenths. I don't know where that came from. Some of it was engine, but... I just hope we can race these guys tomorrow."

Local hero Sergio Pérez had given a demo run in his home town of Guadalajara in the lead-up to the race, when 140,000 spectators had turned up! The Autodromo Hermanos Rodriguez had never been his best circuit, however, and fourth on the grid, 0.04s adrift of Hamilton, was the best he could do.

Carlos Sainz, in the quicker of the two Ferraris, was nearly six-tenths behind the Red Bull pace. "We're fighting it a bit too much over the kerbs," he admitted. "When I put all my sectors together, there is the potential for a 1m 18s flat, but it's so hard to put a lap together."

And indication of the strife Ferrari was suffering came when Valtteri Bottas managed to split the Maranello cars on the grid with his Alfa Romeo. Sixth was his best starting position since Miami, back in May.

"The upgrade felt good at the last race, and it's an uplifting performance for the team," he said. "The car felt easy, good over the kerbs and gave me confidence right from the start of FP1. We just carried that on."

The Ferrari predicament was a bit of a conundrum, given that at other high-downforce circuits, such as Barcelona and Monaco, they had been really strong.

Leclerc, who was losing time on the straight relative to Sainz, said, "We have to look into it because there are some engine problems and the drivability is not there. The car is not responding to what I'm doing with the throttle." He could only qualify seventh, comfortably his worst non-penalised starting slot of the year.

Lando Norris did his usual excellent job to put the McLaren eighth on the grid, a couple of tenths faster than team-mate Daniel Ricciardo, who would start 11th.

After his heroics in Austin en route to seventh, Fernando Alonso was more than galled to receive a 30s penalty from the US stewards for driving a car in an unsafe condition (minus a wing mirror), which relegated him to 15th, out of the points, despite the protest from Haas being outside the permitted 30-minute time frame. Alpine appealed and, in Mexico, the stewards reversed the decision, reinstating him. The team's battle for fourth in the constructors' championship was as keen as ever in Mexico, with Alonso and team-mate Esteban Ocon lining up ninth and tenth.

Behind Ricciardo, Zhou Guanyu did a solid job to put the second Alfa 12th on the grid, ahead of the AlphaTauri pair, with Yuki Tsunoda outqualifying Pierre Gasly for the ninth time in 2022.

Kevin Magnussen had received a five-place grid penalty for taking a sixth Ferrari power unit, so team-mate Mick Schumacher was less than impressed to be bounced out of Q2 by his team-mate, who would be starting at the back.

Aston Martin's impressive performance level from Austin did not translate, with Sebastian Vettel and Lance Stroll qualifying 17th and 18th. The Canadian also took a three-place grid drop following his incident with Alonso in Austin, ahead only of the Williams twins, Alex Albon (who, having been tenth in FP3, was disappointed) and Nicholas Latifi.

WITH an 800m-plus run down to the first turn, Max Verstappen knew only too well just how vulnerable he was to a slipstream, but when the lights went out, he got the power down well and wasted no time in moving right to force any potential attackers to go the long way around. George Russell tucked in behind the Red Bull, with Lewis Hamilton, in turn, towing his team-mate. Sergio Pérez, meanwhile, shaped up to go around the outside of the second Mercedes as they piled into Turn One.

Verstappen successfully fended off the Mercedes challenge as the two Mercs ran side by side into Turn Two. When Russell lost a bit of time on the kerb, Hamilton blasted around his outside, nipping his team-mate over the kerb on the exit of Turn Three. That gave Pérez a run on Russell into Turn Four, George dropping from second to fourth. Behind him, the two Ferraris were running side by side through Turns 5/6, with Carlos Sainz only just managing to repel the advances of team-mate Charles Leclerc.

Fernando Alonso was next up with the first of the Alpines, ahead of Valtteri Bottas, Esteban Ocon, Lando Norris, Yuki Tsunoda, Zhou Guanyu, Daniel Ricciardo, Sebastian Vettel, Lance Stroll (up five places), Pierre Gasly, the two Haas drivers and finally the Williams pair.

Once the first-corner sort-out had run its course, strategy would play a key part. With Mexico a tight call between a one- and two-stopper, it was widely believed that a medium/hard run was the most feasible one-stopper, even though the hard was not thought to be the greatest race tyre, many drivers believing that Pirelli should have gone a step softer with the compounds. Hamilton, therefore, was a little surprised when the tyre blankets came off to reveal both Red Bulls and both Ferraris on softs. Further down the field, Tsunoda, Vettel, Schumacher and Latifi had chosen the same route.

During the early laps, the soft-tyred Verstappen did not drop the medium-shod Hamilton as much as might have been expected, and you started to wonder whether Max was conserving his tyres in the hope of pulling off a one-stopper. Had it been a cast-iron two-stopper, he might have been expected to push more.

Behind Hamilton, Pérez stayed in touch, with Russell dropping about 2.5s behind the second Red Bull over the first ten laps. There was stalemate pretty much through the whole field until Ricciardo managed to force the second McLaren ahead of Zhou, using the approximate 12mph advantage generated by DRS down the main straight.

Gasly was also hassling Stroll for 15th place, but an attempt to get down the inside of the Aston Martin in Turn Four led to a lock-up and both cars running off the road. The Frenchman took the position, but soon was hit with a 5s time penalty for his trouble.

Approaching one-third-distance in the 71-lap race, Verstappen was telling Red Bull, “My left front does not want to turn.” The graining was clear to see.

The Red Bull crew were soon out in the pit lane, but it was Pérez, not Verstappen, who appeared, from some 2.5s behind Hamilton’s second-placed Mercedes. Mediums, rather than hard-compound Pirellis, went back on, but the stop was not one of the team’s best, Sergio stationary for 5s after a problem with the left rear.

Having started on the mediums, it was unlikely that Mercedes would respond to the Pérez stop. Sure enough, Hamilton was straight on the radio to Pete Bonnington: “My tyres are okay.”

Bonnington told his driver, “Let’s just see what we can do on these tyres, Lewis. Target, plus six.”

As soon as Verstappen had a pit window to Carlos Sainz’s fourth-placed Ferrari – also on softs – he was in for a much better 2.5s stop, with mediums going on to the lead Red Bull, requiring a 45-lap stint to the end.

Pérez, as in qualifying, was having intermittent problems with his DRS, but it worked well enough on the front straight to allow him to go by Charles Leclerc’s Ferrari with ease, to take back fifth place. Soon after, the Monégasque was into the pits to change his 29-lap-old softs for mediums.

Above: Max Verstappen takes advantage of the kerfuffle between the Mercedes pair, which leaves George Russell off-track at the start.
Photo: Red Bull Content Pool/Getty Images

Top left: There was much concern that the paddock was overcrowded, fans leaving drivers such as Lewis Hamilton to run the gauntlet.
Photo: Peter J. Fox

Above left: Pierre Gasly obliges a youngster with a selfie, but he needed to take refuge in the AlphaTauri motor home to avoid the throng.

Left: Father and son 1: Sergio Pérez gives Sergio Jr a hug post-race.
Photos: Red Bull Content Pool/Getty Images

Below left: Father and son 2: Five-time 500cc motorcycle world champion Mick Doohan with Jack, the Alpine reserve driver.
Photo: Alpine F1 Team

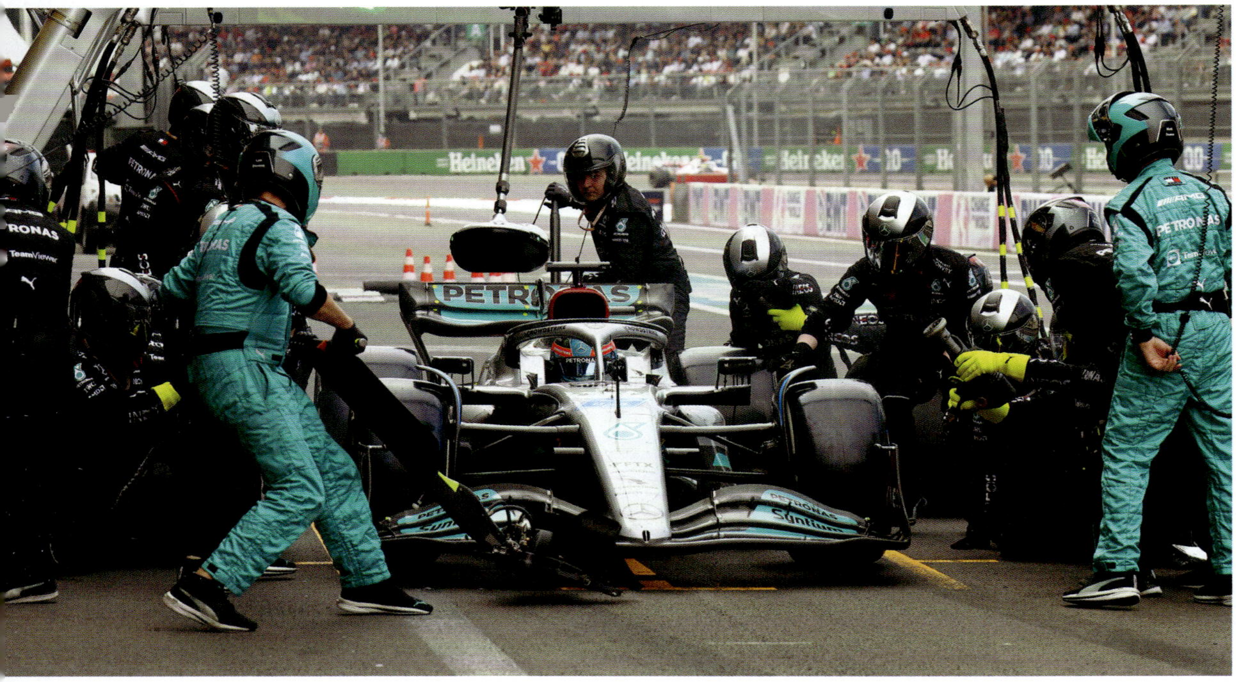

With Red Bull's medium-tyre pace really strong, Mercedes reacted and pitted Hamilton after 30 laps, bolting on hard-compound rubber in a 3.3s stop. Lewis rejoined still some 3s ahead of Pérez, who now was back up to fourth place as Sainz made his stop to go on to mediums one lap after Leclerc, The Spaniard retained track position over his team-mate, despite a slight problem with the front right.

Russell, meanwhile, was on to Mercedes, telling them, "Tyres are good, let's extend." He seemed keen to prolong his opening medium stint sufficiently to run the soft-compound Pirellis to the end. Norris, meanwhile, running eighth in the first McLaren, some 5.5s ahead of team-mate Ricciardo, was into the pits for the hard compound. At Alpine, Esteban Ocon was in, too, also for the hard compound, with Fernando Alonso being told that the data from the hard, after Hamilton's stop, suggested that it was okay. "Yes," he responded, "I think we are okay on any tyre. The car feels good today."

When Mercedes brought in Russell on lap 35, he also took the hard compound, which, perhaps, was a little conservative. It was another three laps before Vettel, who had started on the softs, pitted for mediums, having run the red-walled tyre for 38 heavily-fuelled laps!

Hamilton, meanwhile, was not thrilled with the hard compound. "This tyre is not as good as the medium," he told the team.

"Copy, Lewis," replied Bonnington. "We did see some drop-off at the end of life, so some may struggle to get to the end on that." Another medium, of course, was not an option after he had started on it, unless Mercedes committed to the two-stop route.

Team-mate Russell agreed. "I'm not happy with this tyre. I'm sliding around a lot," he reported.

Given the longevity of Vettel's opening soft-tyre stint, it was a surprise that Alonso went for a set of hards when he pitted after a 40-lap, medium-tyre opening stint, with just 31 laps remaining. At McLaren, meanwhile, Ricciardo went as far as lap 45, then took a set of softs and was soon flying. By lap 51, he'd caught Yuki Tsunoda's 11th-placed AlphaTauri and tried what appeared to be an unfeasible move down the inside of Turn Six from way back. It was never on, and Tsunoda's right rear rode up over the McLaren's left front.

"What the **** was he doing?" Tsunoda wanted to know, with some justification. The Japanese driver toured back to the pits and posted a retirement with damaged right-rear suspension. Soon after, Ricciardo received notification of a 10s penalty.

On lap 53, with 18 to go, Hamilton was 10.5s behind Verstappen, with the medium-tyred Pérez just 1.6s behind, and again was questioning the Mercedes strategy. "Are we on the wrong tyre, mate?" he asked. "No, Lewis, we think we're on the right tyre. You'll get to the end on this, no sweat."

Meanwhile, three others to opt for the medium/soft route were Pierre Gasly, Alex Albon and Zhou Guanyu, who ran 40-, 38- and 45-lap opening stints respectively and now were all lapping competitively. Albon was 12th and Gasly 13th after relegating Vettel's now medium-shod Aston Martin, which was under pressure from the Alfa Romeo.

Ricciardo, meanwhile, was a great advertisement for the effectiveness of the soft-compound Pirelli at this stage of the race, no doubt helped by ambient temperature that was almost 10 degrees lower than on Friday. Ten laps into his stint, it had lost none of its edge, allowing him to demote team-mate Norris to move into the points and then relegate Bottas's Alfa to take ninth.

With ten laps to go, it had dawned on Hamilton that hopes of the Red Bull medium tyres dropping off were forlorn. "That medium looks quick, mate," he told Bonnington. "They're gonna go to the end."

Alonso, having been 'best of the rest' behind the Red Bulls, Mercs and Ferraris all afternoon, was now under pressure from both team-mate Ocon and the flying Ricciardo. Coming

Above: More reliability woes forced Fernando Alonso out of the race.
Photo: XPB Images

Top Left: Valtteri Bottas qualified the Alfa in sixth place and stayed the course to pick up the final championship point on offer.
Photo: Alfa Romeo ORLEN

Above left: Mid-race pit stop for George Russell, about to take on hard Pirellis after a long opening stint on mediums.
Photo: Mercedes-AMG Petronas F1 Team

Right: Despite earning a ten-second penalty for his collision with Tsunoda, Daniel Ricciardo drove brilliantly to seventh place.
Photo: McLaren F1 Team

#MexicoGP
Emirates
BWT
Castrol
BWT

Above: Lewis Hamilton and Mercedes took the gamble of starting on medium Pirellis, which ultimately failed to pay off in their attempt to overcome Max Verstappen's Red Bull.
Photo: Mercedes-AMG Petronas F1 Team

Top right: A record-breaking win number 14 for Max.

Above right: The calming presence of Gianpiero Lambiase was a big factor in helping Verstappen to his dominance in 2022.

Right: Golden days for F1, which has never been so popular.
Photos: Red Bull Content Pool/Getty Images

down the main straight on lap 62, he lost places to both of them to drop to ninth. Despite having seven-lap-fresher hard-compound tyres, the Spaniard had been reeled in by Ocon at almost a second a lap and obviously had a power unit issue.

"Engine…" he said, disconsolately, as he pulled off into Turn One with six to go, prompting a VSC. In the battle with McLaren for fourth place in the constructors' championship, it was a blow for Alpine, with Ricciardo running so well and Norris also overtaking Bottas to move up to ninth.

"What a season," the frustrated Alonso radioed in, way more disappointed than you might have expected a 41-year-old two-time world champion to be over a lost seventh place. Then, when Ricciardo went flying by Ocon, it was he who would end the afternoon 'best of the rest' as he managed to put 10s between himself and the Alpine by race-end, thereby overcoming his Tsunoda penalty.

The hoped-for medium drop-off just didn't happen for Mercedes, and with three laps to go, Verstappen was 4s further in front of Hamilton than when the Englishman had emerged from the pits on his hard tyres. Further back, Gasly took his AlphaTauri past Albon's Williams and moved to within a couple of seconds of tenth-placed Bottas. Meanwhile, Russell, with a pit window behind him to Sainz's Ferrari after Maranello's least competitive showing of the season, made an 11th-hour stop in an attempt to claim the extra point for fastest lap on a set of softs, which he accomplished easily.

As well as the ride and balance issues the Ferrari drivers had experienced since first thing on Friday, it seemed as though their power train was not as potent in the thin air of Mexico City. The suggestion was that perhaps the turbocharger was less efficient than those of Honda and Mercedes, forcing Ferrari to open up the cooling and dial back the power. Both drivers were left hoping that the sub-par display was a one-off.

But the records just carried on falling to the imperious Verstappen. As he crossed the line, it was a record 14th victory in a single season. He also broke the record 413 points scored by Lewis Hamilton in 2019. That had been over a 21-race season; this was round 20 of 2022, a year when the Dutchman had started with a couple of mechanical failures and then had to cope with the challenge of a very quick Ferrari, and Charles Leclerc. Hugely impressive.

"You do not cease to amaze me, I have to say," was the comment from 'GP' Lambiase as Max drove his slow-down lap after a 34th F1 victory. The thing that had so impressed was his ability to drive quickly enough and yet sensitively enough to make a soft/medium strategy work – something that had been considered a long shot. Certainly by Mercedes.

"When I saw them on softs at the start, I thought, 'Oh, shoot,'" Hamilton admitted. "I think we should have started on them as well, because while the medium tyre was okay, the hard was an offset. But still, great to be able to split the Red Bulls."

In front of his home faithful, Pérez had to be content with third and a 25th F1 podium, some 3s behind Hamilton. "We had a bit of a bad pit stop, and that prevented us from being able to undercut Lewis," he explained. "And after that, it was hard to follow and overtaking was difficult." It was enough, however, to move him into second place in the championship, five points clear of Leclerc with two rounds remaining as Red Bull chased its first ever 1-2 championship finish.

Behind Russell and the two Ferraris, the last unlapped runners, Ricciardo won 'driver of the day' for his seventh place, ahead of Ocon, team-mate Norris and Bottas, who managed to keep Gasly at bay for the last point. The fact that the Australian had been able to finish 15s in front of team-mate Norris, having been 5s behind when he took on his softs, did make you wonder what Mercedes might have achieved if they'd gone the same route with Russell. The gap between Alpine and McLaren in their battle for fourth in the constructors' championship was now down to seven points.

Verstappen had beaten the 13 wins by Michael Schumacher in 2004 and Sebastian Vettel in 2013. If he could win the last two races, he would finish the season with the best ever winning percentage, too. That was the new target.

Tony Dodgins

VIEWPOINT
CHAMPION RECORD BREAKER

MEXICO marked Max Verstappen's 14th win in 2022, allowing him to overtake Michael Schumacher and Sebastian Vettel on 13 each in a single season. It is significant that Vettel should be mentioned, since the German was the last driver to work hand in hand with Red Bull's technical dominance as he claimed four titles on the trot. Verstappen now had two and, on the evidence of 2022, there seemed no reason why he should not eclipse Vettel by every performance metric.

The season was markedly different to the raw meat of the previous year, when Verstappen and Lewis Hamilton had taken an often bitter contest to the final lap. In 2022, circumstances were such that Verstappen could use the confidence inspired by his first title (regardless of how it had been achieved) to mature into a truly world-class driver, capable of winning on any type of track, in a variety of conditions, and from anywhere on the grid.

By honing the RB18 to his absolute liking and building further on the reassuring influence of Gianpiero Lambiase (who had been promoted to Red Bull's head of race engineering in 2022), Verstappen brought a calmness and deadly precision to his work in the cockpit.

Right from the moment of his early battles with Charles Leclerc, it was clear that Verstappen's drive and determination were more powerful than ever – particularly in reaction to Red Bull's initial problems with the RB18. But the most telling aspect was that any public outbursts of frustration were brief and quickly superseded by a coolness that was also evident in his driving. Underpinning all of this was a vivid hunger that lasted through the season and was evidenced by his anger over the lengthy pit stop at CoTA. Typically, he put that behind him immediately and went on to win – almost as a matter of course.

In Mexico, Verstappen also topped Hamilton's single-season record points total. He played that down by saying that he wasn't interested in stats. His preference was finishing a weekend knowing that he'd done his absolute best. That became a consistently impressive theme in 2022.

Maurice Hamilton

20

FORMULA 1 GRAN PREMIO DE LA CIUDAD DE MÉXICO 2022

ROLEX

Official Timepiece

MEXICO CITY 28-30 OCTOBER

RACE DISTANCE: 71 laps, 189.738 miles/305.354km

RACE WEATHER: Dry/sunny (track 35-45°C, air 25-30°C)

AUTÓDROMO HERMANOS RODRÍGUEZ, MEXICO CITY

Circuit: 2.674 miles/4.304 Km 71 laps

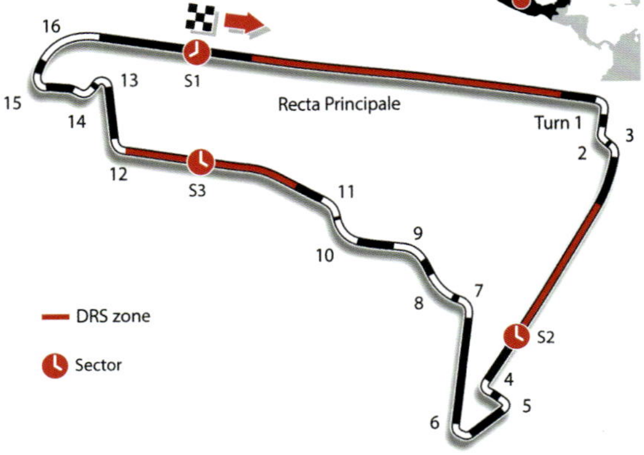

RACE – OFFICIAL CLASSIFICATION

Pos.	Driver	Nat.	No.	Entrant	Car/Engine	Laps	Time/Retirement	Speed (mph/km/h)	Gap to winner	Fastest race lap
1	**Max Verstappen**	NL	1	Oracle Red Bull Racing	Red Bull RB18-RBPTH001 V6	71	1h 38m 36.729s	115.445/185.790		1m 22.046s 36
2	**Lewis Hamilton**	GB	44	Mercedes-AMG Petronas F1 Team	Mercedes-AMG F1 W13-M13 E Perf. V6	71	1h 38m 51.915s	115.149/185.315	15.186s	1m 22.062s 32
3	**Sergio Pérez**	MEX	11	Oracle Red Bull Racing	Red Bull RB18-RBPTH001 V6	71	1h 38m 54.826s	115.093/185.224	18.097s	1m 21.775s 30
4	**George Russell**	GB	63	Mercedes-AMG Petronas F1 Team	Mercedes-AMG F1 W13-M13 E Perf. V6	71	1h 39m 26.160s	114.488/184.251	49.431s	1m 20.153s 71
5	**Carlos Sainz**	E	55	Scuderia Ferrari	Ferrari F1-75-066/7 V6	71	1h 39m 34.852s	114.322/183.983	58.123s	1m 22.199s 32
6	**Charles Leclerc**	MC	16	Scuderia Ferrari	Ferrari F1-75-066/7 V6	71	1h 39m 45.503s	114.119/183.656	1m 08.774s	1m 22.603s 48
7	**Daniel Ricciardo**	AUS	3	McLaren F1 Team	McLaren MCL36-Mercedes F1 M13 E Perf. V6	70	*		1 lap	1m 22.022s 48
8	**Esteban Ocon**	F	31	BWT Alpine F1 Team	Alpine A522-Renault E-Tech RE22 V6	70			1 lap	1m 23.279s 48
9	**Lando Norris**	GB	4	McLaren F1 Team	McLaren MCL36-Mercedes F1 M13 E Perf. V6	70			1 lap	1m 23.402s 48
10	**Valtteri Bottas**	FIN	77	Alfa Romeo F1 Team ORLEN	Alfa Romeo C42-Ferrari 066/7 V6	70			1 lap	1m 23.363s 43
11	Pierre Gasly	F	10	Scuderia AlphaTauri	AlphaTauri AT03-RBPTH001 V6	70	*		1 lap	1m 22.277s 42
12	Alexander Albon	T	23	Williams Racing	Williams FW44-Mercedes F1 M13 E Perf. V6	70			1 lap	1m 22.914s 48
13	Zhou Guanyu	CHN	24	Alfa Romeo F1 Team ORLEN	Alfa Romeo C42-Ferrari 066/7 V6	70			1 lap	1m 22.260s 47
14	Sebastian Vettel	D	5	Aston Martin Aramco Cognizant F1 Team	Aston Martin AMR22-Mercedes F1 M13 E Perf. V6	70			1 lap	1m 23.086s 45
15	Lance Stroll	CDN	18	Aston Martin Aramco Cognizant F1 Team	Aston Martin AMR22-Mercedes F1 M13 E Perf. V6	70			1 lap	1m 22.463s 42
16	Mick Schumacher	D	47	Haas F1 Team	Haas VF-22-Ferrari 066/7 V6	70			1 lap	1m 23.641s 30
17	Kevin Magnussen	DK	20	Haas F1 Team	Haas VF-22-Ferrari 066/7 V6	70			1 lap	1m 23.300s 49
18	Nicholas Latifi	CDN	6	Williams Racing	Williams FW44-Mercedes F1 M13 E Perf. V6	69			2 laps	1m 23.709s 56
19	Fernando Alonso	E	14	BWT Alpine F1 Team	Alpine A522-Renault E-Tech RE22 V6	63	*power unit*		8 laps	1m 22.866s 48
	Yuki Tsunoda	J	22	Scuderia AlphaTauri	AlphaTauri AT03-RBPTH001 V6	50	*accident damage*			1m 23.403s 48

Gasly: 5s time penalty for leaving the track and gaining an advantage (served at pit stop). * Ricciardo: 10s time penalty for causing a collision with Tsunoda.

DHL Fastest race lap (scores 1 point): George Russell on lap 71, 1m 20.153s, 120.117mph/193.310km/h.

Lap record: Nigel Mansell (Williams FW14-Renault V10), 1m 16.788s, 128.790mph/207.267km (1991, 2.747-mile/4.421km circuit).

Lap record (current configuration): Valtteri Bottas (Mercedes F1 W12 V6), 1m 17.774s, 123.792mph/199.223km/h (2021).

19 · MAGNUSSEN · Haas
Used additional power unit element; 5-place grid penalty

17 · ALBON · Williams

15 · SCHUMACHER · Haas

13 · TSUNODA · AlphaTauri

11 · RICCIARDO · McLaren

20 · STROLL · Aston Martin
3-place grid penalty for causing a collision with Alonso at the United States GP

18 · LATIFI · Williams

16 · VETTEL · Aston Martin

14 · GASLY · AlphaTauri

12 · ZHOU · Alfa Romeo

Grid order	1	2	3	4	5	6	7	8	9	10	11	12	13	14	15	16	17	18	19	20	21	22	23	24	25	26	27	28	29	30	31	32	33	34	35	36	37	38	39	40	41	42	43	44	45	46	47	48	49	50	51	52	53	54	55
1 VERSTAPPEN	1	1	1	1	1	1	1	1	1	1	1	1	1	1	1	1	1	1	1	1	1	1	1	1	44	44	44	44	44	63	63	63	63	63	1	1	1	1	1	1	1	1	1	1	1	1	1	1	1	1	1	1	1	1	1
63 RUSSELL	44	44	44	44	44	44	44	44	44	44	44	44	44	44	44	44	44	44	44	44	44	44	44	44	1	63	63	63	63	1	1	1	1	1	44	44	44	44	44	44	44	44	44	44	44	44	44	44	44	44	44	44	44	44	44
44 HAMILTON	11	11	11	11	11	11	11	11	11	11	11	11	11	11	11	11	11	11	11	11	11	11	63	63	63	1	1	1	1	44	44	44	44	44	11	11	11	11	11	11	11	11	11	11	11	11	11	11	11	11	11	11	11	11	11
11 PEREZ	63	63	63	63	63	63	63	63	63	63	63	63	63	63	63	63	63	63	63	63	63	63	11	55	55	55	55	55	11	11	11	11	11	11	63	63	63	63	63	63	63	63	63	63	63	63	63	63	63	63	63	63	63	63	63
55 SAINZ	55	55	55	55	55	55	55	55	55	55	55	55	55	55	55	55	55	55	55	55	55	55	55	16	16	16	11	11	55	14	14	14	14	14	14	14	14	14	14	55	55	55	55	55	55	55	55	55	55	55	55	55	55	55	55
77 BOTTAS	16	16	16	16	16	16	16	16	16	16	16	16	16	16	16	16	16	16	16	16	16	16	16	11	11	11	16	16	14	77	77	77	77	77	77	77	77	55	55	16	16	16	16	16	16	16	16	16	16	16	16	16	16	16	16
16 LECLERC	14	14	14	14	14	14	14	14	14	14	14	14	14	14	14	14	14	14	14	14	14	14	14	14	14	14	14	14	77	31	31	31	55	55	55	55	55	77	16	14	3	3	3	14	14	14	14	14	14	14	14	14	14	14	14
4 NORRIS	77	77	77	77	77	77	77	77	77	77	77	77	77	77	77	77	77	77	77	77	77	77	77	77	77	77	77	77	31	4	55	55	31	16	16	16	16	16	77	3	14	14	14	3	31	31	31	31	31	31	31	31	31	31	31
14 ALONSO	31	31	31	31	31	31	31	31	31	31	31	31	31	31	31	31	31	31	31	31	31	31	31	31	31	31	31	31	4	55	16	16	16	3	3	3	3	3	3	24	24	24	24	24	77	77	77	77	77	77	77	77	77	77	77
31 OCON	4	4	4	4	4	4	4	4	4	4	4	4	4	4	4	4	4	4	4	4	4	4	4	4	4	4	4	4	3	3	4	3	3	24	24	24	24	24	24	77	31	31	31	31	4	4	4	4	4	4	4	4	4	4	3
3 RICCIARDO	22	22	22	22	22	22	22	22	22	22	22	22	22	22	22	22	22	22	22	22	22	22	22	22	22	22	22	22	16	16	3	24	24	5	5	5	5	31	31	31	77	77	77	77	24	22	22	22	22	3	3	3	3	3	4
24 ZHOU	24	24	24	24	24	24	24	24	3	3	3	3	3	3	3	3	3	3	3	3	3	3	3	3	3	3	3	3	22	24	24	5	5	10	10	10	10	10	10	4	4	4	4	4	22	3	3	3	3	5	23	23	23	23	23
22 TSUNODA	3	3	3	3	3	3	3	3	24	24	24	24	24	24	24	24	24	24	24	24	24	24	24	24	24	24	24	24	24	5	5	10	10	31	31	31	31	5	4	22	22	22	22	22	3	5	5	5	5	23	5	5	10	10	10
10 GASLY	5	5	5	5	5	5	5	5	5	5	5	5	5	5	5	5	5	5	5	5	5	5	5	5	5	5	5	5	5	10	10	23	23	23	23	23	23	4	22	10	5	5	5	5	5	23	23	23	23	10	10	10	5	5	5
47 SCHUMACHER	18	18	18	18	18	18	18	18	18	18	18	18	10	10	10	10	10	10	10	10	10	10	10	10	10	10	10	10	10	23	23	4	4	4	4	4	4	22	18	5	23	23	23	23	23	10	10	10	10	24	24	24	24	24	24
5 VETTEL	10	10	10	10	10	10	10	10	10	10	10	10	18	18	18	18	23	23	23	23	23	23	23	23	23	23	23	23	23	22	22	22	22	22	22	22	22	23	5	18	10	10	10	10	10	24	24	24	24	22	18	18	18	18	18
23 ALBON	47	47	47	47	47	47	47	47	23	23	23	23	23	23	23	23	18	47	47	47	47	47	47	20	20	20	20	20	20	20	20	20	18	18	18	18	18	18	23	23	47	47	47	47	47	47	47	47	47	47	47	47	47	47	47
6 LATIFI	20	20	20	20	23	23	23	23	47	47	47	47	47	47	47	47	47	6	6	6	6	6	20	47	18	18	18	18	18	18	18	18	20	20	20	20	20	20	47	47	18	18	18	18	18	18	18	18	18	18	20	20	20	20	20
20 MAGNUSSEN	23	23	23	23	20	20	6	6	6	6	6	6	6	6	6	6	6	20	20	20	20	20	6	18	47	47	47	47	47	47	47	47	47	47	47	47	47	47	20	20	20	20	20	20	20	20	20	20	20	20	6	6	6	6	6
18 STROLL	6	6	6	6	6	6	20	20	20	20	20	20	20	20	20	20	20	18	18	18	18	18	18	6	6	6	6	6	6	6	6	6	6	6	6	6	6	6	6	6	6	6	6	6	6	6	6	6	6	6					

11 = Pit stop

TIME SHEETS

PRACTICE 1 (FRIDAY)

Weather: Dry/sunny

Temperatures: track 46-49°C, air 27-30°C

Pos.	Driver	Laps	Time
1	Carlos Sainz	25	1m 20.707s
2	Charles Leclerc	20	1m 20.753s
3	Sergio Pérez	22	1m 20.827s
4	Max Verstappen	22	1m 20.827s
5	Lewis Hamilton	17	1m 20.849s
6	Fernando Alonso	26	1m 20.899s
7	Valtteri Bottas	23	1m 21.083s
8	Lando Norris	21	1m 21.120s
9	Pierre Gasly	25	1m 21.310s
10	Sebastian Vettel	24	1m 21.525s
11	Daniel Ricciardo	16	1m 21.762s
12	Zhou Guanyu	20	1m 21.820s
13	Lance Stroll	24	1m 21.865s
14	Mick Schumacher	22	1m 21.952s
15	Nicholas Latifi	20	1m 22.912s
16	Liam Lawson	19	1m 23.861s
17	Logan Sargeant	22	1m 24.246s
18	Nyck de Vries	20	1m 24.582s
19	Jack Doohan	13	1m 24.615s
20	Pietro Fittipaldi	9	1m 26.766s

PRACTICE 2 (FRIDAY)

Weather: Dry/overcast

Temperatures: track 34-41°C, air 26-29°C

Pos.	Driver	Laps	Time
1	George Russell	32	1m 19.970s
2	Yuki Tsunoda	30	1m 20.798s
3	Esteban Ocon	31	1m 21.177s
4	Lewis Hamilton	32	1m 21.509s
5	Sergio Pérez	34	1m 21.579s
6	Max Verstappen	34	1m 21.588s
7	Charles Leclerc	13	1m 21.618s
8	Carlos Sainz	34	1m 21.693s
9	Valtteri Bottas	36	1m 21.993s
10	Pierre Gasly	36	1m 22.104s
11	Fernando Alonso	31	1m 22.337s
12	Sebastian Vettel	32	1m 22.371s
13	Alexander Albon	24	1m 22.447s
14	Lando Norris	31	1m 22.738s
15	Daniel Ricciardo	27	1m 22.763s
16	Lance Stroll	23	1m 22.840s
17	Mick Schumacher	31	1m 22.879s
18	Kevin Magnussen	21	1m 23.316s
19	Nicholas Latifi	34	1m 23.320s
20	Zhou Guanyu	34	1m 23.369s

PRACTICE 3 (SATURDAY)

Weather: Dry/sunny

Temperatures: track 37-43°C, air 23-26°C

Pos.	Driver	Laps	Time
1	George Russell	22	1m 18.399s
2	Lewis Hamilton	23	1m 18.543s
3	Max Verstappen	18	1m 18.876s
4	Charles Leclerc	23	1m 19.123s
5	Sergio Pérez	24	1m 19.241s
6	Carlos Sainz	20	1m 19.301s
7	Lando Norris	22	1m 19.317s
8	Valtteri Bottas	28	1m 19.390s
9	Yuki Tsunoda	24	1m 19.882s
10	Alexander Albon	18	1m 19.917s
11	Esteban Ocon	19	1m 19.960s
12	Zhou Guanyu	25	1m 20.019s
13	Fernando Alonso	16	1m 20.037s
14	Daniel Ricciardo	22	1m 20.139s
15	Pierre Gasly	24	1m 20.330s
16	Lance Stroll	20	1m 20.477s
17	Mick Schumacher	24	1m 20.598s
18	Nicholas Latifi	21	1m 20.848s
19	Sebastian Vettel	22	1m 20.986s
20	Kevin Magnussen	25	1m 21.271s

QUALIFYING (SATURDAY)

Weather: Dry/sunny Temperatures: track 44-48°C, air 27-30°C

Pos.	Driver	First	Second	Third	Qualifying Tyre
1	Max Verstappen	1m 19.222s	1m 18.566s	1m 17.775s	Soft (n)
2	George Russell	1m 19.583s	1m 18.565s	1m 18.079s	Soft (n)
3	Lewis Hamilton	1m 19.169s	1m 18.552s	1m 18.084s	Soft (n)
4	Sergio Pérez	1m 19.706s	1m 18.615s	1m 18.128s	Soft (n)
5	Carlos Sainz	1m 19.566s	1m 18.560s	1m 18.351s	Soft (n)
6	Valtteri Bottas	1m 19.523s	1m 18.762s	1m 18.401s	Soft (n)
7	Charles Leclerc	1m 19.505s	1m 19.109s	1m 18.555s	Soft (n)
8	Lando Norris	1m 19.857s	1m 19.119s	1m 18.721s	Soft (n)
9	Fernando Alonso	1m 20.006s	1m 19.272s	1m 18.939s	Soft (n)
10	Esteban Ocon	1m 19.945s	1m 19.081s	1m 19.010s	Soft (n)
11	Daniel Ricciardo	1m 20.279s	1m 19.325s		
12	Zhou Guanyu	1m 20.283s	1m 19.476s		
13	Yuki Tsunoda	1m 19.907s	1m 19.589s		
14	Pierre Gasly	1m 20.256s	1m 19.672s		
15	Kevin Magnussen	1m 20.293s	1m 19.833s		
16	Mick Schumacher	1m 20.419s			
17	Sebastian Vettel	1m 20.419s			
18	Lance Stroll	1m 20.520s			
19	Alexander Albon	1m 20.859s			
20	Nicholas Latifi	1m 21.167s			

QUALIFYING: head to head

Hamilton	12	8	Russell
Verstappen	16	4	Pérez
Ricciardo	2	18	Norris
Leclerc	14	6	Sainz
Gasly	12	8	Tsunoda
Hülkenberg	1	1	Stroll
Vettel	11	7	Stroll
Alonso	13	7	Ocon
Bottas	14	6	Zhou
Albon	17	2	Latifi
de Vries	1	0	Latifi
Magnussen	15	5	Schumacher

Red Bull Content Pool/Getty Images

FOR THE RECORD

100th GRAND PRIX START: Charles Leclerc

190th PODIUM: Lewis Hamilton

DID YOU KNOW?

Verstappen, now with 14 wins in a season, has created a new record.

POINTS

DRIVERS

1	Max Verstappen	416
2	Sergio Pérez	280
3	Charles Leclerc	275
4	George Russell	231
5	Lewis Hamilton	216
6	Carlos Sainz	212
7	Lando Norris	111
8	Esteban Ocon	82
9	Fernando Alonso	71
10	Valtteri Bottas	47
11	Sebastian Vettel	36
12	Daniel Ricciardo	35
13	Kevin Magnussen	24
14	Pierre Gasly	23
15	Lance Stroll	13
16	Mick Schumacher	12
17	Yuki Tsunoda	12
18	Zhou Guanyu	6
19	Alexander Albon	4
20	Nicholas Latifi	2
21	Nyck de Vries	2

CONSTRUCTORS

1	Red Bull	696
2	Ferrari	487
3	Mercedes	447
4	Alpine	153
5	McLaren	146
6	Alfa Romeo	53
7	Aston Martin	49
8	Haas	36
9	AlphaTauri	35
10	Williams	8

9 · ALONSO · Alpine

7 · LECLERC · Ferrari

5 · SAINZ · Ferrari

3 · HAMILTON · Mercedes

1 · VERSTAPPEN · Red Bull

10 · OCON · Alpine

8 · NORRIS · McLaren

6 · BOTTAS · Alfa Romeo

4 · PÉREZ · Red Bull

2 · RUSSELL · Mercedes

56	57	58	59	60	61	62	63	64	65	66	67	68	69	70	71	
1	1	1	1	1	1	1	1	1	1	1	1	1	1	1	1	1
44	44	44	44	44	44	44	44	44	44	44	44	44	44	44	44	2
11	11	11	11	11	11	11	11	11	11	11	11	11	11	11	11	3
63	63	63	63	63	63	63	63	63	63	63	63	63	63	63	63	4
55	55	55	55	55	55	55	55	55	55	55	55	55	55	55	55	5
16	16	16	16	16	16	16	16	16	16	16	16	16	16	16	16	6
14	14	14	14	31	3	3	3	3	3	3	3	3	3	3		7
31	31	31	31	3	31	31	31	31	31	31	31	31	31	31		8
77	3	3	3	14	14	14	14	4	4	4	4	4	4	4		9
3	77	77	77	77	77	77	77	77	77	77	77	77	77	77		10
4	4	4	4	4	4	4	4	23	23	23	23	10	10	10		
23	23	23	23	23	23	23	23	10	10	10	10	23	23	23		
10	10	10	10	10	10	10	10	24	24	24	24	24	24	24		
5	24	24	24	24	24	24	24	5	5	5	5	5	5	5		
24	5	5	5	5	15	5	5	18	18	18	18	18	18	18		
18	18	18	18	18	18	18	18	47	47	47	47	47	47	47		
47	47	47	47	47	47	47	47	20	20	20	20	20	20	20		
20	20	20	20	20	20	20	20	6	6	6	6	6	6			
6	6	6	6	6	6	6	6									
									VSC	VSC						

6 = One lap or more behind

VSC Virtual safety car deployed on laps shown

RACE TYRE STRATEGIES

PIRELLI

	Driver	Race Stint 1	Race Stint 2	Race Stint 3
1	Verstappen	Soft (u): 1-25	Medium (n): 26-71	
2	Hamilton	Medium (n): 1-29	Hard (n): 30-71	
3	Pérez	Soft (u): 1-23	Medium (n): 24-71	
4	Russell	Medium (n): 1-34	Hard (n): 35-69	Soft (u): 70-71
5	Sainz	Soft (u): 1-29	Medium (n): 30-71	
6	Leclerc	Soft (u): 1-28	Medium (n): 29-71	
7	Ricciardo	Medium (n): 1-44	Soft (n): 45-70	
8	Ocon	Medium (n): 1-33	Hard (n): 34-70	
9	Norris	Medium (n): 1-31	Hard (n): 32-70	
10	Bottas	Medium (n): 1-39	Hard (u): 40-70	
11	Gasly	Medium (n): 1-40	Soft (n): 41-70	
12	Albon	Medium (n): 1-38	Soft (n): 39-70	
13	Zhou	Medium (n): 1-45	Soft (n): 46-70	
14	Vettel	Soft (n): 1-38	Medium (u): 39-70	
15	Stroll	Medium (u): 1-17	Soft (u): 18-40	Soft (n): 41-70
16	Schumacher	Soft (n): 1-24	Medium (n): 25-70	
17	Magnussen	Medium (n): 1-38	Soft (u): 39-70	
18	Latifi	Soft (n): 1-23	Hard (n): 24-52	Soft (n): 53-69
19	Alonso	Medium (n): 1-40	Hard (n): 41-63 (dnf)	
	Tsunoda	Soft (n): 1-29	Medium (n): 30-50 (dnf)	

The tyre regulations stipulate that at least two of three dry tyre specifications must be used during a dry race.

Selected compounds for Mexico: Red = Soft (C4); Yellow = Medium (C3); White = Hard (C2). (n) new (u) used

Scuderia Ferrari

FIA FORMULA 1 WORLD CHAMPIONSHIP · ROUND 21

SÃO PAULO GRAND PRIX

INTERLAGOS CIRCUIT

TeamViewer
AMG
UBS
PETRONAS
PETRONAS
INEOS
TeamViewer

INTERLAGOS QUALIFYING/SPRINT QUALIFYING

INTERLAGOS might be a bit ragged around the edges, but it pretty much guarantees passion and good racing. As such, it's a no-brainer as a sprint-race venue. And with mixed conditions for the Friday qualifying session, all the right ingredients were there.

A damp, but drying circuit greeted drivers for Q1, with everyone venturing out initially on intermediate Pirellis. Mid-way through, Pierre Gasly switched to soft-compound slicks and went a second quicker, prompting everyone to follow suit. Lando Norris ended up with quickest time, 1m 13.106s, as the racing line slowly dried, ahead of a trio with 13 world championships between them: Lewis Hamilton, Fernando Alonso and Sebastian Vettel. The fact that Nicholas Latifi had been fastest, with 1m 45s on the clock, but then was eliminated, along with Zhou Guanyu, Valtteri Bottas, Yuki Tsunoda and Mick Schumacher, indicated just how quickly the track was evolving.

Into Q2, the racing line continued to grip up, and suddenly it was the usual suspects at the top of the time sheet. Max Verstappen was quickest on 1m 10.881s, from Carlos Sainz and Charles Leclerc, the trio separated by just 0.07s. George Russell was the quicker Mercedes, fourth fastest on 1m 11.318s. Alex Albon did a super job for Williams, missing out on the Q3 shootout by just five-hundredths, with Gasly, Vettel, Daniel Ricciardo and Lance Stroll the other Q2 eliminees.

As Q3 began, light rain was just starting to fall once more as the field ventured out. This time, everyone was on slicks except Leclerc, Ferrari having opted to split strategies, sending Sainz out on softs with Charles on intermediates.

"Am I the only one on inters?" asked a distinctly unimpressed Leclerc. Ferrari's strategy was highly questionable, and it was immediately obvious that by the time Leclerc came back in for slicks, he wouldn't get a lap in as the rain intensified. And, even then, the team put him on new softs when he wanted scrubbed ones...

Step forward Kevin Magnussen and Haas. They might have been at the right end of the pit lane, but the team did a fine job to get the Dane to the head of the queue. First out, he truly delivered. Both he and the car had demonstrated that they shone in the wet – he qualified fourth at Imola and fifth in Canada. Committed and aggressive, he was fastest on that all-important first lap, stopping the clock in 1m 11.674s. Verstappen, lamenting a lock-up at Turn Eight, could only manage 1m 11.877s. When George Russell, third quickest at the time, went off at Turn Four and beached his Mercedes in the gravel, bringing out the red flag as the rain became heavier, it meant that Haas had its first pole position at the 143rd time of asking – the longest such wait for any constructor.

"Where am I?" Magnussen asked on the radio.

"You're P1, mate."

"You're kidding me?" But they weren't, and there was general delirium in the Haas pit as the little team achieved the first F1 pole position for an American constructor since Tom Pryce had put his Shadow on the Silverstone pole in 1975. And it was the first pole for a Scandinavian since Ronnie Peterson for Lotus in Austria '78.

Behind Russell, Norris was an excellent fourth, ahead of Sainz (who would suffer a five-place main-race grid drop for a sixth internal-combustion engine), the Alpines of Esteban Ocon and Alonso, Hamilton, Sergio Pérez and the fuming Leclerc, with no time.

With six 'Sprint' Saturdays planned for 2023, Verstappen had been explaining that he was not a particular fan of them. He thought that with just a handful of points available, the risk versus reward balance was out of kilter, so drivers didn't really race. There are no pit stops or strategy involved. The big points come on Sunday, and a driver doesn't want to be starting at the back. So, thought was being given to separating out the two races on Sprint weekends – with Friday qualifying dictating the grid for both, and the Saturday sprint being a stand-alone event with more points on offer.

But nobody had told the Alpine drivers that they weren't expected to race in the sprint... The team was separated from McLaren by just seven points in the battle for fourth place in the constructors' championship, and no doubt team principal Otmar Szafnauer would not have appreciated what he saw on the opening lap, when Alonso attempted to go around the outside of team-mate Ocon at Turn Four.

Esteban, who was challenging Norris at the time, was not keen on giving Fernando racing room and ran him wide on exit, the Spaniard almost losing the car as the rear end fish-tailed on the kerb. He made contact with his team-mate's right rear floor as he sorted himself out. Then, quicker out of the Juncao final corner, he misjudged the tow and clipped the

Left: A moment of quiet satisfaction for Guenther Steiner.
Photo: Haas F1 Team

Centre left: A stunned Magnussen took pole position for the sprint race. The Dane is joined by Felipe Massa for Pirelli's tyre signing.
Photo: Peter J. Fox

Below left: George Russell soon took command of the sprint qualifying race to ensure his front-row start for the grand prix itself.
Photo: Mercedes-AMG Petronas F1 Team

Bottom left: Magnussen briefly held the lead in the sprint race, before the Haas was gobbled up by the pursuing Verstappen, Russell and Sainz.
Photo: Red Bull Content Pool/Getty Images

Far left: In a frantic Q3 session, Magnussen, on soft slicks, heads the queue of cars waiting for the green light. Behind, Leclerc had arrived on Pirelli intermediates.
Photo: XPB Images

Opening spread: A carnival atmosphere among the fans on track as Russell captures the moment with team-mate Hamilton.
Photo: Peter J. Fox

back of Ocon's car, damaging his own front wing in the process, necessitating a stop for a new one. Alonso drove aggressively back up to 16th, but the race stewards held him wholly responsible for the collision and awarded a five-second time penalty, which dropped him to 19th in the final classification, one slot behind Ocon.

"Today, both drivers have let the team down," Szafnauer stated. With a car not potentially as quick as the slippery Alpine around Interlagos, McLaren had Norris seventh and Ricciardo 11th for the main race...

At the sharp end, pretty much everyone had started on the red-walled soft-compound Pirelli for the 24-lap dash, based on data from FP2 on Saturday morning, but Verstappen had opted for the medium, Red Bull wanting to save two sets of softs for the main race.

The performance on the medium was not quite strong enough, and after initially rebuffing Russell, the Dutchman had to give best on the run to Turn Four, with George closing out the laps to see the chequer first for the first time in his F1 career.

"To be quicker than Max was unexpected," said Andrew Shovlin at Mercedes, "but much of that was down to the medium tyre."

Verstappen was not so sure: "At first, it felt okay, but I think that even on the soft, I would have been slow. We just had too much degradation today."

As Max fell to fourth, Sainz managed to resist the challenge of Lewis Hamilton to cross the line second, but his grid penalty would mean seventh for the main race and an all-Mercedes front row, with Verstappen and team-mate Sergio Pérez on row two.

Leclerc improved to sixth, which would become fifth to share row three with Norris.

And what of pole-man Magnussen? He launched the Haas off the line beautifully and had his moment of glory leading the first couple of laps, but he raced with a strong slice of pragmatism. Once DRS was enabled, he wasted no time in racing cars he knew he couldn't live with, letting them go and concentrating on losing as little race time as possible as the Mercs, Red Bulls, Ferraris and Norris went by.

The target was a point, and that's exactly what Magnussen got, moving his team two points ahead of AlphaTauri in the battle for eighth in the constructors' championship. Just behind was Vettel, who survived a scare when team-mate Stroll put him on the grass on the flat-out run out of Turn Three, for which Lance received a 10s time penalty. Gasly completed the top ten and, already on ten penalty points, was relieved to receive just a warning for driving too slowly on the formation lap.

Above: Leader Russell makes his first stop to take on mediums.
Photo: Mercedes-AMG Petronas F1 Team

Top right: Magnussen's race ended on the opening lap, after he was hit by Daniel Ricciardo's McLaren.
Photo: Haas F1 Team

Above right: Zhou and Ocon side by side through the Esses.
Photo: Alfa Romeo ORLEN

Right: Crunch! Max Verstappen came off second best after his collision with Lewis Hamilton left the Red Bull with a damaged front wing.
Photo: Peter J. Fox

As the grid formed up, Mercedes had its first front-row lock-out of the season, with George Russell starting from 'pole' position for the second time in 2022, while team-mate Lewis Hamilton had only his second front-row start.

Russell made a perfect getaway and Hamilton tucked in behind him through the Senna Esses, both Mercs having started on soft Pirellis, in keeping with the Max Verstappen/Sergio Pérez Red Bulls in hot pursuit, ahead of Lando Norris, also on softs and celebrating his 23rd birthday, but not feeling 100 per cent. Right behind him were the two medium-tyred Ferraris, Charles Leclerc ahead of Carlos Sainz.

Further around the lap, we had a yellow flag after Daniel Ricciardo made a bad misjudgement and clobbered the back of Saturday pole-man Kevin Magnussen's Haas into Turn Eight, taking both out.

Out came the safety car while the debris was cleared. We had green-flag conditions after five slow laps, and Russell coped admirably with the restart, going late and quickly opening a margin to his team-mate. Hamilton, though, had Verstappen right on his tail.

Max ran the Red Bull around the outside of the Mercedes into Turn One, attempting to take the inside for T2. Hamilton wasn't keen on ceding racing room, however, and they made contact at the apex of the right-hander, both briefly off on the left, losing multiple places.

"He left me no space, I have front wing damage," Verstappen radioed. The Red Bull was straight into the pits.

"That was no racing incident, mate," Hamilton opined.

There was more drama further around the lap when Norris got squirrelly through Turn Four, allowing Leclerc's Ferrari alongside. They ran side by side through T5, the Ferrari slightly ahead as they went into the uphill T6, which is where Norris went wide over the inside kerb and made contact with the Ferrari's right rear. Leclerc was flicked into a spin and then relatively gently nose-first into the tyres, from which the Monégasque was able to extricate himself and carry on. McLaren told Norris that all seemed okay on the telemetry, but he felt that the steering was awry.

The picture now was looking much rosier for Russell, with three of his quickest potential challengers all badly compromised. By lap eight of the 71, he had a 1.5s advantage over Pérez's Red Bull, from Norris, Sainz, Sebastian Vettel's Aston in a strong fifth, then Pierre Gasly, Mick Schumacher, Hamilton, Lance Stroll, Valtteri Bottas, Esteban Ocon, Fernando Alonso, Zhou Guanyu, Nicholas Latifi, Yuki Tsunoda and Alex Albon. Verstappen and Leclerc, both back out with new front wings, were some 25s behind the pack.

By lap 13, Mercedes was on the radio to Russell, telling him that it was important to run long to open a gap, while Hamilton, fighting back, had relegated Schumacher and Gasly, and was attacking Vettel. The German was now right on the back of the struggling Norris's McLaren, Lando having been forced to cede third place to Sainz's Ferrari.

It seemed that the race stewards agreed with Hamilton's assessment of his spat with Verstappen, as news came through of a 5s time penalty for the Red Bull driver for causing a collision. That was debatable, whereas the same penalty for Norris's contact with Leclerc was much more of a slam-dunk.

"You've been given a 5s time penalty for the collision at Turn One," 'GP' Lambiase told Verstappen.

"Where did they expect me to go?" Max wanted to know. "He just closed the door on me. But it doesn't matter..." I'll just get on with it was the inference.

By lap 14, Hamilton, who had been made an honorary citizen of Brazil and was very popular there, had slipstreamed past Vettel into Turn One and was all over Norris, easily demoting the McLaren on the main straight next time around. Vettel soon did likewise as Norris slipped to sixth.

Alpine's big boss, Laurent Rossi, had been as unimpressed as Otmar Szafnauer with the shenanigans between his two drivers in the sprint race and must have been watching with a degree of trepidation as McLaren rival Norris circulated in a strong points-scoring position while the Alpines ran nose to tail again, Ocon tenth and Alonso eleventh...

Esteban had started on the soft-compound Pirellis,

whereas Alonso was on the mediums, so it was a bit of a surprise when the Spaniard was first to pit, for another set of the yellow-walled tyres, after just 14 laps.

Sainz was in from third place three laps later, swapping his starting mediums for a set of softs. He rejoined 12th with his right rear brake duct still smoking, a visor tear-off having been removed during the 4.1s stop.

Team-mate Leclerc had made it as far as 15th, with the fastest race lap after his opening-lap dramas, and was in for another set of mediums after 21 laps, which dropped him back down to 17th.

At one-third-distance, Pérez pitted the second-placed Red Bull to get rid of his starting softs and take on a set of mediums, the Mexican covering off Sainz, and resuming right behind Norris and Bottas, both of whom had yet to pit.

Russell was in from the lead a lap later, rejoining just in front of Vettel's yet-to-stop Aston Martin, with team-mate Hamilton now briefly leading the race before making his own soft-to-medium stop five laps later. Norris and Bottas pitted at the same time as Russell, with Lando delayed by taking the 5s penalty for his incident with Leclerc.

Verstappen, too, had to serve his penalty, the world champion further delayed by a sticking right rear tyre.

It was lap 30 before Hamilton appeared in the pit lane to go on to the medium-compound tyre, comfortably the longest opening stint of anyone who had started on the soft, and six laps further than team-mate Russell, which suggested that Mercedes might have been splitting strategy for the 71-lap race, with Lewis going for a one-stopper.

One of those certainly stopping twice was Sainz, the Ferrari back for a second set of mediums after a 19-lap stint on softs, his race seemingly damaged by that earlier need to pit sooner than planned on his opening medium stint to

Right: A long time coming. George Russell had to wait nearly four seasons for his maiden grand prix victory.
Photo: Mercedes-AMG Petronas F1 Team

Top right: Valtteri Bottas took ninth place for Alfa Romeo, ahead of the Aston Martins in their tightly-poised constructors' battle.
Photo: Alfa Romeo ORLEN

Above right: The Alpines of Alonso and Ocon were in the top ten.
Photo: XPB Images

Centre right: Ferrari old boys Barrichello and Massa were reunited at Interlagos.
Photo: Scuderia Ferrari

Right: No problems for Verstappen and his crew.
Photo: Red Bull Content Pool/Getty Images

have the tear-off removed. He rejoined still fifth, just after half-distance.

At the front, Russell now had an 8.8s advantage over Pérez, with Hamilton right on the Red Bull's tail on six-lap-fresher tyres. Then there was a 15s gap to Sainz, who had a 13s margin over Bottas's Alfa.

"I think our race is with Checo now," radioed Sainz.

"Yes," the team agreed, "we are looking to come back on Checo at the end of the race."

Although Pérez was able to defend his second place from Hamilton into Descido de Lago (Turn Four), there was no stopping the Mercedes with DRS down the main straight, and as they started lap 45, we had a Mercedes 1-2, with Lewis's pace bringing back memories of 2021!

With 23 laps remaining, Sainz had taken 6s out of Pérez's advantage, and Red Bull decided it was time to pit Sergio for a second time. By this stage, Leclerc had worked himself into the points after relieving Gasly's AlphaTauri of tenth place down the main straight.

On lap 49, just 20 laps into his medium stint, having run so long on his starting softs, Hamilton seemed nonplussed to be called in for a second time.

"My tyres are good, my tyres are good!" he proclaimed over the radio. The move was to cover off Pérez's stop, although for the time being, Hamilton fell behind Sainz's Ferrari as he came back out on a set of used softs.

A lap later, Mercedes pitted Russell from the lead, but he maintained it after taking on used softs to the end. He pitted out just in front of Sainz, who would need to stop for a third time.

On lap 52, Norris pulled over at exactly the same spot where his team-mate had taken out Magnussen on the opening lap. "I've lost power," he told the team. Soon enough came notice of a Virtual Safety Car, which would save anyone making a stop around 11s versus full race conditions.

Alonso and Gasly took full advantage and dived into the pits, while Sainz was back for his third stop, too, a set of used softs being bolted on for the remaining 16 laps. It was not the work of a moment to recover Norris, however, and suddenly things turned very interesting – a full safety car!

When the safety car came in, Russell, who'd led convincingly all afternoon and had been within touching distance of his first victory, had Hamilton right behind him, trying to maintain his record of winning a GP in every season he had competed.

"Are we taking the 1-2?" Russell asked the Mercedes pit-wall crew.

"You're free to race," was the response he didn't want to hear. Neither Mercedes driver had new softs available and both were on used ones, but Russell's were three laps newer than Hamilton's.

Behind them, Pérez was on new mediums, Sainz on used softs, then came Bottas's Alfa and Leclerc's Ferrari on used softs, Vettel on new mediums and Ocon's Alpine. Behind the Frenchman, on a brand-new set of softs, was Alonso. And, completing the top ten, Verstappen on relatively new softs. This was going to be interesting!

"Shoot, guys," radioed Hamilton. "We've got people with brand-new tyres behind us!"

When it was time to race again, with 11 laps remaining, Russell went as late as he could, not wanting to offer any semblance of a tow to Hamilton. He judged the restart beautifully to get through Turn One with his nose still well in front. Pérez fended off Sainz to stay third, while Leclerc got his Ferrari down the inside of Bottas to take fifth.

"Esteban, do not hold up Fernando," was a sufficiently clear message from Alpine, and Ocon took heed. Alonso was quickly up to seventh as he went through, with Vettel falling back, struggling on his mediums. Then the Spaniard was all over Bottas, getting a run on the Alfa out of Turn Five and sweeping around the outside at Turn Six.

With nine to go, DRS was re-enabled, and it was vital that Russell kept Hamilton far enough back not to be able to benefit from it.

After some characteristically robust defence from Pérez, Sainz eventually battled his way back past into third, and Verstappen was soon on the move, too, up to seventh as he demoted Ocon and Bottas with the one move down the inside of Turn One.

Pérez could do nothing to stop Leclerc from displacing him

into Turn One and, on the next lap, Alonso swept past on the run to Turn Four, the Alpine losing precious little time to the Ferraris.

Verstappen was next to reel in Pérez, who was told to allow Max through to see if he could hunt down Alonso, but on the understanding that if he could not, the place would be returned.

Russell had driven beautifully to keep Hamilton at bay and was a more-than-deserved recipient of the chequered flag, which was waved by 1972/74 world champion Emerson Fittipaldi.

Behind, Leclerc was asking the Ferrari team to swap him around with Sainz to help his championship battle with Pérez for runner-up spot. "Please think about the championship. Every point," he requested.

"We believe it's too risky," was the response, with Alonso just behind Leclerc and only just out of DRS range.

Then came a radio instruction to Verstappen: "Max, if we don't pass Fernando, on the exit of T12, can we let Checo through please?"

Red Bull wanted to assist Pérez in his bid to beat Leclerc to runner-up spot in the drivers' championship, and also to achieve their first ever team 1-2 finish, but Max wasn't playing. They flashed across the line in the order Russell, Hamilton, Sainz, Leclerc, Alonso, Verstappen, Pérez, Ocon, Bottas and Stroll.

When Verstappen's engineer, Lambiase, asked him what had happened, he received short shrift in an apparent reference to Monaco qualifying, when the Dutchman had thought that Pérez had spun deliberately on his second Q3 run to ensure that the track was blocked and he could not beat his time (see Viewpoint).

"It shows who he really is," was Pérez's scathing response.

The minor spat, interesting though it was, could and should not have detracted from a fabulous weekend and emotional first win for the classy Russell, who had not put a foot wrong.

"That's only the beginning!" he told his team over the radio. And, somehow, you believed him.

Tony Dodgins

VIEWPOINT I'M IN CHARGE

WHILE Mercedes celebrated taking a major, if belated, step forward, Red Bull staggered backwards. Before getting into a serious post-race technical debrief about degradation on their front tyres, the 2022 world champions had to deal with a domestic issue that had gone viral.

Due to Max Verstappen's early clash with his nemesis, Lewis Hamilton, Sergio Pérez had been the leading Red Bull runner, always in contention for a podium until his mediums eventually gave up during the final ten laps. As he fell back, he allowed his team-mate through to have a go at Fernando Alonso in fifth place. When Verstappen failed to make any impact on the Alpine, he was asked to let Pérez return to sixth and claim the extra two points that were potentially vital in his fight with Charles Leclerc for second in the championship. Verstappen refused, leaving Leclerc and Pérez tied on 290 points with one race to go.

There was a polite, but puzzled inflection in Gianpiero Lambiase's voice when, during the slow-down lap, Verstappen's race engineer asked, "What happened, Max?" There was no mystery about the response.

"I told you already last time, guys," Verstappen fired back, "don't ask that to me. Okay? Are we clear about that? I gave my reasons and I stand by it."

In subsequent interviews, neither Verstappen nor Christian Horner would enlarge on the "reasons". The matter had been discussed internally, and that was the end of it. Not so on social media. Verstappen and Horner were still trending 12 hours later.

The world champion's defenders made repeated mentions of Dutch media reports in connection with Pérez's spin during qualifying in Monaco. Sergio was alleged to have admitted to the team that it had been a deliberate move to induce the red flag and scupper Max's final chance of improving on fourth. Pérez had started third, won the race – and, coincidentally, an extension to his contract.

In the light of, "Are we clear about that?", Sergio could be forgiven for wondering just who was running the team he had agreed to remain with for another two years.

Maurice Hamilton

21

FORMULA 1 HEINEKEN GRANDE PRÊMIO DE SÃO PAULO 2022

Official Timepiece

SÃO PAULO 11-13 NOVEMBER

RACE DISTANCE: 71 laps, 190.064 miles/305.879km

RACE WEATHER: Dry/sunny (track 34-35°C, air 22-26°C)

AUTODROMO JOSÉ CARLOS PACE, INTERLAGOS, BRAZIL

Circuit: 2.677 miles/4.309km, 71 laps

RACE – OFFICIAL CLASSIFICATION

Pos.	Driver	Nat.	No.	Entrant	Car/Engine	Laps	Time/Retirement	Speed (mph/km/h)	Gap to winner	Fastest race lap	
1	**George Russell**	GB	63	Mercedes-AMG Petronas F1 Team	Mercedes-AMG F1 W13-M13 E Perf. V6	71	1h 38m 34.044s	115.696/186.194		1m 13.785s	61
2	**Lewis Hamilton**	GB	44	Mercedes-AMG Petronas F1 Team	Mercedes-AMG F1 W13-M13 E Perf. V6	71	1h 38m 35.573s	115.666/186.146	1.529s	1m 13.942s	63
3	**Carlos Sainz**	E	55	Scuderia Ferrari	Ferrari F1-75-066/7 V6	71	1h 38m 38.095s	115.617/186.067	4.051s	1m 13.953s	65
4	**Charles Leclerc**	MC	16	Scuderia Ferrari	Ferrari F1-75-066/7 V6	71	1h 38m 42.485s	115.531/185.929	8.441s	1m 14.253s	63
5	**Fernando Alonso**	E	14	BWT Alpine F1 Team	Alpine A522-Renault E-Tech RE22 V6	71	1h 38m 43.605s	115.509/185.894	9.561s	1m 14.164s	62
6	**Max Verstappen**	NL	1	Oracle Red Bull Racing	Red Bull RB18-RBPTH001 V6	71	1h 38m 44.100s *	115.499/185.878	10.056s	1m 14.195s	64
7	**Sergio Pérez**	MEX	11	Oracle Red Bull Racing	Red Bull RB18-RBPTH001 V6	71	1h 38m 48.124s	115.421/185.752	14.080s	1m 14.283s	62
8	**Esteban Ocon**	F	31	BWT Alpine F1 Team	Alpine A522-Renault E-Tech RE22 V6	71	1h 38m 52.734s	115.331/185.608	18.690s	1m 15.093s	65
9	**Valtteri Bottas**	FIN	77	Alfa Romeo F1 Team ORLEN	Alfa Romeo C42-Ferrari 066/7 V6	71	1h 38m 56.596s	115.256/185.487	22.552s	1m 15.511s	62
10	**Lance Stroll**	CDN	18	Aston Martin Aramco Cognizant F1 Team	Aston Martin AMR22-Mercedes F1 M13 E Perf. V6	71	1h 38m 57.596s	115.237/185.456	23.552s	1m 14.831s	50
11	Sebastian Vettel	D	5	Aston Martin Aramco Cognizant F1 Team	Aston Martin AMR22-Mercedes F1 M13 E Perf. V6	71	1h 39m 00.227s	115.186/185.374	26.183s	1m 15.549s	64
12	Zhou Guanyu	CHN	24	Alfa Romeo F1 Team ORLEN	Alfa Romeo C42-Ferrari 066/7 V6	71	1h 39m 03.369s	115.125/185.276	29.325s	1m 15.802s	64
13	Mick Schumacher	D	47	Haas F1 Team	Haas VF-22-Ferrari 066/7 V6	71	1h 39m 03.943s	115.114/185.258	29.899s	1m 15.251s	63
14	Pierre Gasly	F	10	Scuderia AlphaTauri	AlphaTauri AT03-RBPTH001 V6	71	1h 39m 05.911s *	115.075/185.196	31.867s	1m 15.327s	64
15	Alexander Albon	T	23	Williams Racing	Williams FW44-Mercedes F1 M13 E Perf. V6	71	1h 39m 10.060s	114.995/185.067	36.016s	1m 15.613s	49
16	Nicholas Latifi	CDN	6	Williams Racing	Williams FW44-Mercedes F1 M13 E Perf. V6	71	1h 39m 11.082s	114.975/185.035	37.038s	1m 15.327s	59
17	Yuki Tsunoda	J	22	Scuderia AlphaTauri	AlphaTauri AT03-RBPTH001 V6	70			1 lap	1m 15.508s	63
	Lando Norris	GB	4	McLaren F1 Team	McLaren MCL36-Mercedes F1 M13 E Perf. V6	50	*electrics* *			1m 15.855s	48
	Kevin Magnussen	DK	20	Haas F1 Team	Haas VF-22-Ferrari 066/7 V6	0	*accident*			no time	
	Daniel Ricciardo	AUS	3	McLaren F1 Team	McLaren MCL36-Mercedes F1 M13 E Perf. V6	0	*accident*			no time	

* Gasly: 5s time penalty for pit lane speeding (originally finished 12th). * Norris: 5s time penalty for causing a collision with Leclerc (served at pit stop).

* Verstappen: 5s time penalty for causing a collision with Hamilton (served at pit stop).

DHL Fastest race lap (scores 1 point): George Russell on lap 61, 1m 13.785s, 130.636mph/210.237km/h.

Lap record: Valtteri Bottas (Mercedes F1 W09 V6), 1m 10.540s, 136.645mph/219.909km/h (2018).

20 · TSUNODA · AlphaTauri
Car modified in parc fermé; required to start from the pit lane.

18 · LATIFI · Williams

16 · OCON · Alpine

14 · BOTTAS · Alfa Romeo

12 · SCHUMACHER · Haas

19 · ALBON · Williams

17 · ALONSO · Alpine

15 · STROLL · Aston Martin

13 · ZHOU · Alfa Romeo

11 · RICCIARDO · McLaren

Grid order	1	2	3	4	5	6	7	8	9	10	11	12	13	14	15	16	17	18	19	20	21	22	23	24	25	26	27	28	29	30	31	32	33	34	35	36	37	38	39	40	41	42	43	44	45	46	47	48	49	50	51	52	53	54	55
63 RUSSELL	63	63	63	63	63	63	63	63	63	63	63	63	63	63	63	63	63	63	63	63	63	63	63	63	44	44	44	44	44	63	63	63	63	63	63	63	63	63	63	63	63	63	63	63	63	63	63	63	63	63	63	63	63	63	63
44 HAMILTON	44	44	44	44	44	44	11	11	11	11	11	11	11	11	11	11	11	11	11	11	11	11	11	44	63	63	63	63	63	11	11	11	11	11	11	11	11	11	11	11	11	11	11	11	44	44	44	44	55	55	55	55	55	44	44
1 VERSTAPPEN	1	1	1	1	1	1	4	4	55	55	55	55	55	55	55	55	44	44	44	44	44	44	44	5	5	11	11	11	11	55	55	55	55	55	55	44	44	44	44	44	44	44	44	44	11	11	11	55	44	44	44	44	44	11	11
11 PEREZ	11	11	11	11	11	11	55	55	4	4	4	4	4	4	44	44	55	5	5	5	5	5	5	11	11	55	55	55	55	44	44	44	44	44	44	55	55	55	55	55	55	55	55	55	55	55	55	11	11	11	11	11	11	55	55
16 LECLERC	4	4	4	4	4	4	5	5	5	5	5	5	5	44	4	4	5	4	4	4	4	4	4	55	55	5	18	18	14	14	14	14	14	14	77	77	77	77	77	77	77	77	77	77	77	31	31	14	14	14	14	14	77	77	77
4 NORRIS	16	16	16	16	16	16	10	10	44	44	44	44	44	5	5	5	4	10	77	77	77	77	77	4	18	18	14	14	77	77	77	77	77	77	5	5	5	5	5	5	5	5	5	5	31	1	1	1	77	77	77	77	16	16	16
55 SAINZ	55	55	55	55	55	55	47	47	10	10	10	10	10	10	10	10	10	77	31	31	31	31	31	77	14	14	10	77	18	5	5	5	5	5	14	31	31	31	31	31	31	31	31	31	5	14	14	77	5	5	16	16	5	5	5
20 MAGNUSSEN	5	5	5	5	5	5	44	44	47	47	47	47	47	47	47	47	77	31	10	47	55	55	55	31	10	10	77	10	5	31	31	31	31	31	31	4	4	4	4	4	4	4	16	4	1	18	77	5	16	16	5	5	31	31	31
5 VETTEL	10	10	10	10	10	10	18	18	18	18	18	77	77	77	77	77	47	47	47	55	47	47	47	18	24	77	5	5	10	10	10	10	10	10	4	16	16	16	16	16	16	16	4	1	14	77	18	16	31	31	31	31	14	14	14
10 GASLY	47	47	47	47	47	47	77	77	77	77	77	18	31	31	31	31	31	18	18	18	18	18	18	47	77	24	31	31	31	4	4	4	4	4	10	24	47	47	47	47	1	1	1	16	4	47	5	18	10	10	1	1	1	1	1
3 RICCIARDO	77	77	77	77	77	77	31	31	31	31	31	31	18	18	18	18	18	55	55	23	23	23	23	23	23	31	24	24	24	24	24	24	24	24	24	47	1	1	1	1	47	47	47	14	47	5	16	31	1	1	10	10	24	24	24
47 SCHUMACHER	18	18	18	18	18	18	14	14	14	14	14	14	14	24	24	24	23	23	23	1	1	1	14	14	31	4	4	4	4	47	47	47	47	47	16	1	24	18	18	18	14	14	14	47	18	10	10	10	4	4	24	24	47	47	47
24 ZHOU	24	24	24	24	24	24	24	24	24	24	24	24	24	14	23	23	22	22	22	22	14	14	10	10	4	47	47	47	47	16	16	16	16	16	47	18	18	14	14	14	18	18	18	18	10	16	*24*	4	24	24	47	47	18	18	18
77 BOTTAS	31	31	31	31	31	31	6	6	6	6	6	22	23	23	22	22	6	6	1	14	10	10	1	24	47	22	22	22	16	22	22	22	18	18	18	22	14	22	22	10	10	10	10	10	16	23	*4*	*24*	47	47	18	18	10	10	10
18 STROLL	14	14	14	14	14	14	22	22	22	22	22	23	22	22	6	6	1	1	6	10	24	24	24	22	22	16	16	16	22	18	18	18	1	1	1	14	22	23	23	23	23	23	23	23	23	*24*	*23*	*47*	18	18	*22*	*22*	*22*	*22*	*23*
31 OCON	6	6	6	6	6	6	23	23	23	23	23	6	6	6	1	1	14	14	14	16	16	22	22	16	16	23	23	23	23	1	1	1	22	22	22	23	23	10	10	22	24	24	24	24	24	*4*	*47*	*22*	22	22	*23*	*23*	*23*	*23*	*22*
14 ALONSO	23	23	23	22	22	22	1	1	1	1	1	1	1	1	14	14	16	16	16	6	22	16	16	1	1	1	1	1	1	23	23	23	23	23	23	10	10	24	24	24	*22*	*22*	*22*	*22*	*22*	*22*	*22*	*23*	*23*	*23*	6	6	6	6	6
6 LATIFI	22	22	22	23	23	23	16	16	16	16	16	16	16	16	16	16	24	24	24	24	6	6	6	6	6	6	6	6	6	6	6	6	*6*	*6*	*6*	*6*	*6*	*6*	*6*	*6*	*6*	*6*	*6*	*6*	*6*	*6*	*6*	*6*	*6*	*6*					
23 ALBON																																																							
22 TSUNODA																																																							
	SC	SC	SC	SC	SC	SC																																															VSC	VSC	SC

SC Safety car deployed on laps shown VSC Virtual safety car deployed on laps shown

TIME SHEETS

PRACTICE 1 (FRIDAY)

Weather: Dry/cloudy

Temperatures: track 41-48°C, air 24-27°C

Pos.	Driver	Laps	Time
1	Sergio Pérez	29	1m 11.853s
2	Charles Leclerc	31	1m 11.857s
3	Max Verstappen	28	1m 11.861s
4	Carlos Sainz	30	1m 12.039s
5	Lewis Hamilton	25	1m 12.040s
6	George Russell	24	1m 12.055s
7	Sebastian Vettel	30	1m 12.157s
8	Mick Schumacher	27	1m 12.314s
9	Valtteri Bottas	31	1m 12.466s
10	Pierre Gasly	32	1m 12.467s
11	Fernando Alonso	25	1m 12.554s
12	Alexander Albon	29	1m 12.633s
13	Esteban Ocon	30	1m 12.705s
14	Lance Stroll	26	1m 12.759s
15	Lando Norris	28	1m 12.955s
16	Kevin Magnussen	25	1m 12.997s
17	Nicholas Latifi	32	1m 13.019s
18	Zhou Guanyu	30	1m 13.115s
19	Yuki Tsunoda	32	1m 13.347s
20	Daniel Ricciardo	28	1m 13.359s

PRACTICE 2 (SATURDAY)

Weather: Dry/cloudy

Temperatures: track 43-50°C, air 27-30°C

Pos.	Driver	Laps	Time
1	Esteban Ocon	28	1m 14.604s
2	Sergio Pérez	36	1m 14.788s
3	George Russell	31	1m 14.916s
4	Fernando Alonso	29	1m 15.049s
5	Max Verstappen	30	1m 15.098s
6	Lewis Hamilton	33	1m 15.137s
7	Pierre Gasly	32	1m 15.636s
8	Mick Schumacher	40	1m 15.684s
9	Kevin Magnussen	38	1m 15.815s
10	Lando Norris	25	1m 15.851s
11	Carlos Sainz	38	1m 15.856s
12	Yuki Tsunoda	32	1m 15.865s
13	Charles Leclerc	37	1m 15.868s
14	Daniel Ricciardo	28	1m 15.994s
15	Valtteri Bottas	34	1m 16.047s
16	Nicholas Latifi	34	1m 16.181s
17	Lance Stroll	43	1m 16.263s
18	Sebastian Vettel	44	1m 16.400s
19	Zhou Guanyu	37	1m 16.468s
20	Logan Sargeant	28	1m 16.480s

QUALIFYING (FRIDAY)

Weather: Rainy/overcast Temperatures: track 23-25°C, air 19-20°C

Pos.	Driver	First	Second	Third	Qualifying Tyre
1	Kevin Magnussen	1m 13.954s	1m 11.410s	1m 11.674s	Soft (n)
2	Max Verstappen	1m 13.625s	1m 10.881s	1m 11.877s	Soft (n)
3	George Russell	1m 14.427s	1m 11.318s	1m 12.059s	Soft (n)
4	Lando Norris	1m 13.106s	1m 11.377s	1m 12.263s	Soft (n)
5	Carlos Sainz	1m 14.680s	1m 10.890s	1m 12.357s	Soft (n)
6	Esteban Ocon	1m 14.663s	1m 11.587s	1m 12.425s	Soft (n)
7	Fernando Alonso	1m 13.542s	1m 11.394s	1m 12.504s	Soft (n)
8	Lewis Hamilton	1m 13.403s	1m 11.539s	1m 12.611s	Soft (n)
9	Sergio Pérez	1m 13.613s	1m 11.456s	1m 15.601s	Soft (n)
10	Charles Leclerc	1m 14.486s	1m 10.950s	no time	
11	Alexander Albon	1m 14.324s	1m 11.631s		
12	Pierre Gasly	1m 14.371s	1m 11.675s		
13	Sebastian Vettel	1m 13.597s	1m 11.678s		
14	Daniel Ricciardo	1m 14.931s	1m 12.140s		
15	Lance Stroll	1m 14.398s	1m 12.210s		
16	Nicholas Latifi	1m 15.095s			
17	Zhou Guanyu	1m 15.197s			
18	Valtteri Bottas	1m 15.486s			
19	Yuki Tsunoda	1m 16.264s			
20	Mick Schumacher	1m 16.361s			

POINTS

DRIVERS

	Driver	Points
1	Max Verstappen	429
2	Charles Leclerc	290
3	Sergio Pérez	290
4	George Russell	265
5	Lewis Hamilton	240
6	Carlos Sainz	234
7	Lando Norris	113
8	Esteban Ocon	86
9	Fernando Alonso	81
10	Valtteri Bottas	49
11	Sebastian Vettel	36
12	Daniel Ricciardo	35
13	Kevin Magnussen	25
14	Pierre Gasly	23
15	Lance Stroll	14
16	Mick Schumacher	12
17	Yuki Tsunoda	12
18	Zhou Guanyu	6
19	Alexander Albon	4
20	Nicholas Latifi	2
21	Nyck de Vries	2

CONSTRUCTORS

	Constructor	Points
1	Red Bull	719
2	Ferrari	524
3	Mercedes	505
4	Alpine	167
5	McLaren	148
6	Alfa Romeo	55
7	Aston Martin	50
8	Haas	37
9	AlphaTauri	35
10	Williams	8

QUALIFYING: head to head

Hamilton	12	9	Russell
Verstappen	17	4	Pérez
Ricciardo	2	19	Norris
Leclerc	14	7	Sainz
Gasly	13	8	Tsunoda
Hülkenberg	1	1	Stroll
Vettel	12	7	Stroll
Alonso	13	8	Ocon
Bottas	14	7	Zhou
Albon	18	2	Latifi
de Vries	1	0	Latifi
Magnussen	16	5	Schumacher

SPRINT QUALIFYING RACE (SATURDAY)

RACE DISTANCE: 24 laps, 64.223 miles/103.356km Dry/sunny (track 31-34°C, air 22-23°C)

Pos.	Driver	Tyre	Laps	Time/Retirement	Speed (mph/km/h)	Gap to Leader	Fastest race lap	
1	**George Russell**		24	30m 11.307s	127.643/205.421		1m 14.233s	4
2	**Carlos Sainz**		24	30m 15.302s	127.362/204.969	3.995s	1m 14.522s	2
3	**Lewis Hamilton**		24	30m 15.799s	127.327/204.913	4.492s	1m 14.317s	3
4	**Max Verstappen**		24	30m 21.801s	126.908/204.238	10.494s	1m 14.507s	5
5	**Sergio Pérez**		24	30m 23.162s	126.813/204.085	11.855s	1m 14.699s	5
6	**Charles Leclerc**		24	30m 24.440s	126.724/203.942	13.133s	1m 15.236s	4
7	**Lando Norris**		24	30m 36.931s	125.862/202.556	25.624s	1m 15.380s	4
8	**Kevin Magnussen**		24	30m 40.075s	125.647/202.210	28.768s	1m 15.110s	2
9	Sebastian Vettel		24	30m 41.525s	125.548/202.050	30.218s	1m 15.451s	4
10	Pierre Gasly		24	30m 45.477s	125.280/201.618	34.170s	1m 15.290s	3
11	Daniel Ricciardo		24	30m 50.702s	124.925/201.048	39.395s	1m 15.385s	5
12	Mick Schumacher		24	30m 52.466s	124.807/200.857	41.159s	1m 15.771s	5
13	Zhou Guanyu		24	30m 53.070s	124.766/200.791	41.763s	1m 15.765s	7
14	Valtteri Bottas		24	30m 53.645s	124.727200.729	42.338s	1m 15.980s	8
15	Yuki Tsunoda		24	31m 01.613s	124.193/199.870	50.306s	1m 16.413s	4
16	Lance Stroll		24	31m 02.007s *	124.167/199.828	50.700s	1m 15.425s	4
17	Esteban Ocon		24	31m 03.063s	124.097/199.714	51.756s	1m 16.097s	5
18	Fernando Alonso		24	31m 05.292s *	123.949/199.476	53.985s	1m 14.764s	5
19	Nicholas Latifi		24	31m 28.157s	122.447/197.060	1m 16.850s	1m 16.525s	4
	Alexander Albon		12	debris damage			1m 15.998s	4

* Alonso: 5-second time penalty for causing a collision with Ocon (originally finished 16th).

* Stroll: 10-second time penalty for dangerous manoeuvre on Vettel (originally finished 12th).

Fastest race lap: George Russell on lap 4, 1m 14.233s, 129.847mph/208.969km/h.

10 · GASLY · AlphaTauri

8 · MAGNUSSEN · Haas

6 · NORRIS · McLaren

4 · PÉREZ · Red Bull

2 · HAMILTON · Mercedes

9 · VETTEL · Aston Martin

7 · SAINZ · Ferrari
Used additional power unit element;
5-place grid penalty

5 · LECLERC · Ferrari

3 · VERSTAPPEN · Red Bull

1 · RUSSELL · Mercedes

56	57	58	59	60	61	62	63	64	65	66	67	68	69	70	71	
63	63	63	63	63	63	63	63	63	63	63	63	63	63	63	63	1
44	44	44	44	44	44	44	44	44	44	44	44	44	44	44	44	2
11	11	11	11	11	11	11	55	55	55	55	55	55	55	55	55	3
55	55	55	55	55	55	55	11	16	16	16	16	16	16	16	16	4
77	77	77	77	16	16	16	16	11	14	14	14	14	14	14	14	5
16	16	16	16	77	14	14	14	14	11	11	1	1	1	1	1	6
5	5	5	5	14	77	77	1	1	1	1	11	11	11	11	11	7
31	31	31	31	31	31	31	31	31	31	31	31	31	31	31	31	8
14	14	14	14	1	1	1	77	77	77	77	77	77	77	77	77	9
1	1	1	1	5	5	5	5	5	18	18	18	18	18	18	18	10
24	24	24	24	24	24	24	18	18	5	5	5	5	5	5	5	
47	47	47	47	18	18	18	24	24	24	24	24	10	10	10	10	
18	18	18	18	47	47	47	47	47	47	10	10	24	24	24	24	
10	10	10	10	10	10	10	10	10	10	47	47	47	47	47	47	
23	23	23	23	23	23	23	23	23	23	23	23	23	23	23	23	
22	6	6	6	6	6	6	6	6	6	6	6	6	6	6	6	
6	22	22	22	22	22	22	22	22	22	22	22	22	22	22		
SC	SC	SC	SC													

11 = Pit stop

6 = One lap or more behind

RACE TYRE STRATEGIES

PIRELLI

	Driver	Race Stint 1	Race Stint 2	Race Stint 3	Race Stint 4
1	Russell	Soft (n): 1-24	Medium (n): 25-49	Soft (u): 50-71	
2	Hamilton	Soft (n): 1-29	Medium (n): 30-48	Soft (u): 49-71	
3	Sainz	Medium (n): 1-17	Soft (n): 18-36	Medium (n): 37-53	Soft (u): 54-71
4	Leclerc	Medium (n): 1-7	Soft (n): 8-44	Soft (u): 45-71	
5	Alonso	Medium (n): 1-14	Medium (n): 15-35	Medium (n): 36-52	Soft (n): 53-71
6	Verstappen	Soft (n): 1-7	Medium (n): 8-23	Soft (u): 24-48	Soft (n): 49-71
7	Pérez	Soft (n): 1-23	Medium (n): 24-47	Medium (n): 48-71	
8	Ocon	Soft (n): 1-24	Medium (n): 25-47	Soft (u): 48-71	
9	Bottas	Soft (u): 1-24	Medium (n): 25-45	Soft (n): 46-71	
10	Stroll	Medium (u): 1-29	Medium (n): 30-48	Soft (u): 49-71	
11	Vettel	Soft (n): 1-25	Medium (u): 26-45	Medium (u): 46-71	
12	Zhou	Soft (u): 1-16	Medium (n): 17-37	Soft (n): 38-71	
13	Schumacher	Medium (n): 1-24	Soft (u): 25-46	Soft (u): 47-71	
14	Gasly	Soft (n): 1-19	Medium (n): 20-35	Soft (u): 36-52	Medium (n): 53-71
15	Albon	Hard (n): 1-4	Medium (n): 5-25	Medium (n): 26-47	Medium (n): 48-71
16	Latifi	Medium (n): 1-20	Hard (n): 21-32	Medium (n): 33-52	Soft (n): 53-71
17	Tsunoda	Medium (n): 1-20	Soft (n): 21-40	Soft (u): 41-54	Medium (n): 55-70
	Norris	Soft (n): 1-24	Medium (n): 25-45	Soft (u): 46-50 (dnf)	
	Magnussen	Medium (n): 1 (dnf)			
	Ricciardo	Soft (n): 1 (dnf)			

The tyre regulations stipulate that at least two of three dry tyre specifications must be used during a dry race. Selected compounds for Interlagos: Red = Soft (C4); Yellow = Medium (C3); White = Hard (C2). (n) new (u) used

FOR THE RECORD

1st WIN: George Russell

100th FASTEST LAP: Mercedes

1st POLE POSITION: Kevin Magnussen & Haas (awarded as fastest Q3 qualifier)

Haas F1 Team

DID YOU KNOW?

Russell became the 20th British driver to win a F1 championship race.

The last occasion of British drivers finishing 1-2 was the 2010 Canadian GP (Hamilton and Button).

The last occasion of a US-owned team on pole was Shadow at the 1975 British GP.

FIA FORMULA 1 WORLD CHAMPIONSHIP · ROUND 22

ABU DHABI GRAND PRIX

YAS MARINA CIRCUIT

aramco
cognizant
SentinelOne
PERONI
BOMBARDIER
FINAL LAP
BOSS
Porto Seguro

YAS MARINA QUALIFYING

THE slight intra-team Red Bull implosion had caused a distracting few days for Milton Keynes, but come the season finale in Abu Dhabi, it had been patched up and the goal was clear – a 1-2 in the drivers' championship for the first time in the team's illustrious history.

Charles Leclerc and Sergio Pérez arrived at Yas Marina with 290 points each, but with Charles ahead by dint of his three victories to Sergio's two. It was, of course, Sebastian Vettel's 299th and final F1 start. Lewis Hamilton had organised a night out for Seb and, as a mark of just how highly he is regarded among his peers, it was a full house – all 20 of them. To add a bit of spice, it had emerged that Leclerc had a bonus clause in his contract for finishing championship runner-up.

The track layout, with its straights and slow corners, was expected to play to the myriad strengths of Red Bull's RB18, and so it proved. Max Verstappen took a 20th career pole and his seventh of 2022, even having time to give Pérez a tow while doing so! It helped the team to a front-row lock-out, as Pérez beat Leclerc to second place by four-hundredths.

"I didn't make the final step in Q3 that I had been expecting," Pérez explained after qualifying a couple of tenths behind his team-mate, "but Max did a good job for me and we worked together as a team really well." A week, as they say, is a long time in motor racing...

Leclerc was a bit disappointed with himself: "I locked up in Turn 6/7," he admitted, "but I think it's going to be close with Checo."

Carlos Sainz, after being the quicker Ferrari driver on the first Q3 run, ultimately found himself 0.15s behind his team-mate as Maranello claimed the second row, but he was not as optimistic as Leclerc about the team's prospects on Sunday afternoon. "Red Bull has a faster car," he said. "If the gap is three-tenths in qualifying [Verstappen's approximate margin over Leclerc], then it's normally five-tenths in the race, but at least we beat Mercedes, which is good. I would love to finish the season with a podium."

On the evidence of Friday practice, it looked as though Mercedes might have the legs of Ferrari around Yas Marina. The three-pointed star had closed to within 19 points of the Italians for second place in the constructors' championship after Brazil, but the qualifying performance was not as strong as many had expected. Lewis Hamilton and Interlagos winner George Russell shared row three, split by just a hundredth.

The silver cars were seven-tenths off, almost half a second of that in sector two alone – the sector containing the straights. After doing much experimentation with low-versus-higher downforce set-ups on Friday, the Mercs were loaded up with rear wing. With Pirelli tyres from the softest part of the range, and the race on the cusp between a one- and two-stopper, had they taken that approach in an attempt to look after the tyres and stop just the once?

But there was more to it than that after the morale-boosting 1-2 in Brazil. "The bouncing is back, which is costing us time, and I also had brake issues," Hamilton reported.

"I've heard it's World Toilet Day [a UN observance day to encourage tackling of the global sanitation crisis, apparently]," Toto Wolff smiled, "and that was definitely a session for the toilet..."

McLaren had the same 19-point deficit to Alpine as did Mercedes to Ferrari, this time over the championship's fourth place. Overhauling that margin was a big ask, but Lando Norris started the quest well by putting the first papaya-orange car seventh on the grid.

"I thought I might actually get one of the Mercs," he said, "but I was a couple of tenths from George. In the actual corner, the car wasn't so bad, but I was struggling to attack much. I couldn't come off the brakes, couldn't really push it, kind of the opposite from what you want in qualifying."

Just 0.07s behind was the first of the Alpine rivals, this time Esteban Ocon, as Fernando Alonso had missed out on Q3 by 0.03s to Daniel Ricciardo in the second McLaren, who qualified tenth in his 44th and last start for McLaren as news emerged that in 2023, the Australian would return to Red Bull as third driver.

But perhaps the standout performance of qualifying came from the departing Vettel (Yas Marina winner in 2009, '10 and '13), who put his Aston Martin into the top ten, equalling his best qualifying performance of the season. It included having to run the gauntlet in Q1 as he kept his boot in on the racing line as four or five other cars tooled around doing tyre-preparation laps, barely moving. His ire was directed particularly at the team with which he had won four world championships!

"It was all a bit emotional leading up to qualifying," he admitted, "but there was a job to do, beating the Alfas, and the car came alive. I would have liked another set of tyres in Q3, but all good!"

Yuki Tsunoda, Mick Schumacher (confirmed as axed by Haas in favour of Niko Hülkenberg for 2023), Lance Stroll and Zhou Guanyu went out in Q2, with Kevin Magnussen, Pierre Gasly, Valtteri Bottas, Alexander Albon and Nicholas Latifi the Q1 eliminees.

WITH the big prizes already claimed, Abu Dhabi was all about who would finish second. In the drivers' championship, would it be Charles Leclerc or Sergio Pérez? And could Mercedes, after its 1-2 finish in Brazil, overcome Ferrari's 19-point advantage in the bid to finish runner-up in the constructors' championship? Further back, Alpine came into the race with the self-same advantage over McLaren for fourth place. And Aston Martin and Alfa Romeo were battling for sixth.

With Red Bull taking a front-row lock-out for the first time since Mexico 2018, it was Advantage Pérez in the drivers' tussle, but despite clear-the-air talks after their Brazil spat, could Checo rely on any kind of help from Max Verstappen?

As the lights went out on the 2022 season, both Red Bulls got away well, Pérez slightly better than Verstappen, but Max came across and claimed his line for Turn One. Sergio tucked in behind and Leclerc slotted into third with the first Ferrari. Lewis Hamilton ran fourth ahead of Carlos Sainz, while George Russell found himself boxed in and lost a position to his old mate, Lando Norris.

Down into Turn Six, Sainz picked up a tow and went down the inside of Hamilton's Mercedes, Lewis being forced over the rumble strip on the outside of the tight left-right, but managing to rejoin still in front.

Sainz was not slow to offer his opinion: "He overtook me off the track, he needs to give the position back. He did exactly the same last year with Verstappen."

Meanwhile, the timing screens revealed an investigation into forcing another driver off the track. Sainz, quite rightly, was found not guilty of that, and then the stewards decided to have a look at the real issue – Hamilton going off-track and gaining an advantage. Peter Bonnington was on the radio to his driver on lap four, telling him, "Okay, Lewis, we've been told to give the position back to Sainz."

Officially, the FIA message was that there would be no further action on the second count. By lap five, however, the situation was reversed and now Hamilton got a strong DRS tow on Sainz. He didn't quite make it by into T6, but got a much better exit from Turn Seven and had the Mercedes decisively back ahead by the left-hander at Turn Nine.

In terms of strategy, Abu Dhabi was on the cusp between a one- and two-stop race, and all the front-runners had started on the medium-compound Pirelli. The only variation throughout the entire field was Kevin Magnussen and Valtteri Bottas starting on the hards, while Pierre Gasly had rolled the dice and opted for a set of softs.

Three laps later, and the Hamilton/Sainz battle had taken another twist, with Carlos doing to Lewis exactly what he'd had done to him to retake fourth place on lap eight of the 56. All the while, Russell was closing in on the pair of them, having broken a couple of seconds clear of a gaggle comprising Norris and the Alpines of Esteban Ocon and Fernando Alonso, the blue cars sandwiching Sebastian Vettel's Aston Martin.

Remember the feisty battle between old foes Vettel and Alonso in Suzuka? Well, this all seemed a bit different. There

Above: With Max Verstappen off in the lead, the battle for second place is on. Sergio Pérez keeps his Red Bull in front of Charles Leclerc's Ferrari, while Carlos Sainz and Lewis Hamilton dispute fourth.
Photo: Pirelli

Left: Farewell F1. A wistful-looking Nicholas Latifi surveys the scene on his last appearance for Williams.
Photo: Williams Racing

Opening spread, main photo: Burning rubber. Sebastian Vettel donuts the Aston after his final F1 lap.
Photo: Aston Martin Aramco Cognizant F1 Team

Opening spread, inset, left: Verstappen and Pérez celebrate their 1-3 finish for Red Bull.
Photo: Red Bull Content Pool/Getty Images

Opening spread, inset, right: Vettel takes the applause from the crowd at the end of his last F1 race.
Photo: Aston Martin Aramco Cognizant F1 Team

Above: Men at work. A total of 20 McLaren mechanics complete a pit stop for Lando Norris.
Photo: McLaren F1 Team

Top right: After two seasons with Haas, Mick Schumacher was left looking for another opportunity in F1.
Photo: Haas F1 Team

Above right: Daniel Ricciardo also found himself without a full-time ride after being released from McLaren. He joins Red Bull in a test and reserve role for 2023.
Photo: McLaren F1 Team

Right: Esteban Ocon finished the season strongly with Alpine, helping the team to fourth in the consructors' championship.
Photo: Alpine F1 Team

was a lot of good feeling towards Seb from his peers in what was his 299th and final GP start (see Viewpoint).

His rivals had been delighted when Vettel had equalled his best qualifying performance of the season to start ninth. "We all tried to have an eye on him when we saw him in the mirror in qually, when he was on a fast lap or whatever, because we wanted a smooth weekend for him," Alonso said. "Even in the race, I took care of him at the start and on the first lap. I was hoping we'd both see the chequered flag."

On lap nine, the two Mercs swapped position in the now-standard manner, a better exit out of the chicane at T7 and a relatively easy DRS pass around the outside through T8 on the run to T9.

"I'm losing power, man. What's going on," Hamilton wanted to know.

Alonso, despite his empathy with Vettel, wanted to make some forward progress – he came into the race five points behind team-mate Ocon in the championship, largely down to no fewer than six reliability retirements. If he wasn't going to monster Vettel, he wanted to go by the Aston and Ocon another way: "At his phase, let's think about Plan B," he told the Alpine pit-wall crew. "We are so slow."

"Yep, we're looking into it," they responded.

Alonso was probably looking for an early stop to undercut both Vettel and Ocon, but Alpine stuck with giving pit-stop priority to the driver ahead and brought in Ocon for a set of Pirelli hards. As well as that, you couldn't be surprised at the team prioritising the driver who was staying rather than the one who was leaving!

Russell, meanwhile, was on to Mercedes: "The fronts are gone. Consider Plan B." Which, presumably, meant going to a two-stopper.

Evidently, Pérez was thinking the same way. So well suited was the Red Bull to the Abu Dhabi layout, with its long straights and slow corners through the last sector, that many had expected Verstappen to simply disappear. That's not what happened, though, Max seldom more than 2–3s ahead of Checo as he took care of his starting set of mediums. In fact, Pérez's tyres were in worse shape, the front right graining considerably, which had allowed Leclerc to come back at him. The Monégasque was just back within undercut range when Red Bull reacted by pitting Pérez on lap 16.

Russell and Norris were also in, the Mercedes stationary for more than 5s. There was a problem at the back of the car, and when George was finally released, it was into the patch of Norris's McLaren, for which he would earn a 5s time penalty.

Pérez did himself no favours in his race with Leclerc by outbraking himself at Turn Seven on his out-lap. Vettel's Aston towed past him on the run to T9, and the Mexican lost some time behind the green car before he went by again.

With 18 laps on the board, Verstappen led by almost 8s from Leclerc, then Hamilton, who had fallen 11.5s behind the Ferrari, which was disappointing race pace after the highs of Interlagos. Sainz, in the second Ferrari, pitted, while Leclerc stayed out to maximise a tyre offset to the earlier-stopping Pérez.

Hamilton felt that he might have had floor damage from clattering the car over the Turn Seven kerbs on the opening lap, the team having a cursory look as he made a lap-19 stop to go on to the hard-compound Pirellis.

Verstappen was in a lap later and on his way again after a 3s stop, pitting out still just ahead of team-mate Pérez, despite the much later stop. Alpine pitted Alonso at this point, but Aston Martin left Vettel out.

Leclerc gave up his brief lead to pit after 21 laps for hards and, like Verstappen and Pérez, pitted out just in front of Sainz's Ferrari, despite the longer first stint.

Aston Martin finally brought in Vettel on lap 26, which dropped him down the field on his one-stopper. Alonso,

meanwhile, was back in the pit lane two laps later. That could only be unscheduled, and it was, Fernando's Alpine career ending with another water leak and his seventh retirement of the season.

Now it was becoming interesting in the Pérez/Leclerc battle as the first three closed up together. Sainz, always on top of a race tactically, had spotted that Verstappen's leading pace was not quick enough to be a two-stopper. Pérez, meanwhile, had pitted earlier and was going a bit quicker, while Leclerc, with hards that were six laps fresher than the Mexican's, was closing in to the point where he was an undercut threat once more.

You would have imagined that, on a planned two-stop, Pérez would have had the pace and tyres simply to go past the one-stopping Verstappen, but that didn't seem to be happening. And, perhaps unsurprisingly after the events of Brazil, there were no radio messages to Max asking that he get out of the way!

The other possibility, of course, was that the two-stopper might actually have turned out to be the better strategy – that was unknown at this stage – and if Red Bull had moved Max out of the way, and then Pérez had beaten him, imagine the ructions!

On lap 33, with 25 remaining, Ferrari told Leclerc, "Box opposite Pérez." Which meant do the opposite to the Red Bull – "If Pérez pits, keep going, and if he doesn't, come in."

Red Bull responded to the call – which Ferrari claimed later had been a dummy designed to push Pérez into the two-stopper – and pitted Pérez for hards. Leclerc kept going. Sergio, after a 2.4s stop, rejoined around 20s behind the Ferrari with 24 laps remaining.

Ferrari was on the phone to Leclerc: "Question: can you keep this pace with Plan C?"

"Yes, I think," replied Charles. He was committing to the one-stopper.

Latifi and Schumacher had a brief tangle at the Turn Five hairpin on lap 39, and for a brief moment, you wondered

Above: Fireworks light up the pit straight as Max Verstappen takes his Red Bull to victory number 15 after a remarkable season.
Photo: Peter Nygaard/GP Photo

Top right: A hug from girlfriend Kelly and the winner's trophy for Max.
Photo: Red Bull Content Pool/Getty Images

Above right: A winner and a loser. Charles Leclerc took three wins in a season that had promised so much, but ended with him a distant second to Verstappen in the championship.
Photo: Scuderia Ferrari

Right: Mutual respect. Seb joins the drivers for their end-of-year photo, bringing a round of applause from his competitors.
Photo: Aston Martin Aramco Cognizant F1 Team

about Latifi and late-race safety cars in Abu Dhabi all over again! But the fault had been Schumacher's, and both got going again after just a brief yellow.

Sainz and Russell were in for second stops on lap 40, George being delayed by his 5s penalty for the unsafe release at his first stop. Hamilton, who had been hassling Russell just before he stopped, was on the radio, telling the team, "Don't leave me on a one-stop, mate." But they did.

With 15 laps remaining, Pérez wanted to know, "At this pace, are we going to catch Leclerc?"

"Yeah, we're catching him, we're catching him," replied race engineer Hugh Bird. "This pace is good."

Further back, Zhou Guanyou was defending manfully from the one-stopping Vettel, both on hard Pirellis, while the two-stopping Stroll closed in on mediums as the teams fought out sixth in the constructors'.

Ferrari, meanwhile, was having second thoughts about the one-stopper for Leclerc.

"I don't think I'll come back if we box," Charles told them.

"We believe we'll get overtaken at the end of the race," the team told him. Putting him in the awkward position of needing to speed up without destroying his rubber.

With 13 laps remaining, Pérez had caught Hamilton's third-placed Mercedes, and Red Bull wanted him past as quickly as possible. Sergio obliged down the inside into T6, but suffered a bit of a lock-up and was repassed on the way out, Hamilton getting DRS.

Next time around, Pérez tried a different approach, staying behind through T6, picking up DRS and overtaking Hamilton into T9. The battle had cost him time, and the gap to Leclerc was now 10s with 12 laps to go. Charles now set his quickest lap of the race, proving that he still had tyre life and was doing a great job of managing the hards.

Vettel's final race was turning into a frustrating one, as he dropped out of the points when passed by team-mate Stroll. "How did we get the strategy so wrong?" Sebastian wanted to know.

"We need to increase tyre saving at Turn Three," Leclerc was told.

"Yes, leave me alone, please," he requested.

As the laps ticked by, Pérez was 3.6s behind the Ferrari with three to go. "You're going to be on him the last lap. You got him," Pérez was informed. Which was starting to look a tad optimistic.

Sainz, by this stage, was all over fourth-placed Hamilton, who was destined not to make it to the end in his last race with the W13, a Mercedes that Lewis was keen to be rid of.

"I've lost shifts, they aren't working properly," he told the team shortly before the Ferrari steamed by. The Mercedes toured into the pits to record the team's first mechanical failure of 2022. So near to a clean sheet...

With two laps remaining, Pérez was within 2.2s of Leclerc, but could have done without encountering the scrapping Albon and Gasly. He was just going to fall short.

The season-ending fireworks in Abu Dhabi started their spectacular display as Verstappen shot across the line to take a new record 15th win in a single season, with Leclerc just edging Pérez for second place in the race and the championship.

"That was sublime, Max, a perfect way to sum up your season," Lambiase told Verstappen.

Sainz took fourth, 14s adrift of Pérez and 10s clear of a lonely Russell. Norris held on to sixth ahead of Ocon, then Stroll, with Daniel Ricciardo just getting to the line ahead of the departing Vettel, who scored a point in his last race.

It all meant that Aston Martin and Alfa Romeo were tied on 55 points in the constructors' championship, with Alfa taking it on count-back. Valtteri Bottas's fifth place at Imola turned out to be worth an estimated $10m!

Tony Dodgins

VIEWPOINT
THE LAST SUPPER

On the night before practice began, all 20 regular F1 drivers dined together at Hakkasan Abu Dhabi in the Emirates Palace. Such unusual unity had very little to do with the restaurant's Michelin-star status, but said everything about the principal guest, Sebastian Vettel. Since this was his final race and championship pressure had been removed, it was a rare opportunity for the drivers to relax together and pay tribute to a universally respected colleague.

This sense of warm approval within such a competitive cabal had been evident at the drivers' press conference that afternoon. With Vettel on the panel, Lewis Hamilton had been asked for his views on the career of the four-time world champion. "What do I think of Seb?" mused Lewis. "He was a bit of a nuisance back then!"

It was widely assumed that Hamilton had been making light reference to their controversial collision when Vettel had used his Ferrari as a battering ram during the 2017 Baku GP. Sebastian did not dodge the issue when he responded. "I'm actually quite sorry," he said. "It's your answer ... but I think Baku wasn't a great moment because what I did wasn't right." "Our friendship got better!" Lewis chimed in, summing up the reasoned and responsible attitude that characterised Seb's career, particularly during the latter part of his 17 seasons in F1.

Come Sunday, Vettel initially followed one of his best qualifying performances of 2022 with a hard-charging race until a strategy call by Aston Martin failed to work and sent him sliding down the order. He spent his final racing laps in a tense fight with Daniel Ricciardo, the McLaren driver managing to defend ninth place.

Sebastian might have scored a point, but you could tell from his slightly terse comment about the team tactic that a racer is always a racer, even after 299 starts, 53 wins, a distinguished career – and a heart-warming dinner with his mates.

Maurice Hamilton

22

FORMULA 1 ETIHAD AIRWAYS ABU DHABI GRAND PRIX 2022

ROLEX

Official Timepiece

YAS MARINA 18-20 NOVEMBER

RACE DISTANCE: 58 laps, 190.253 miles/306.183km

RACE WEATHER: Dry/dusk-dark (track 31-34°C, air 30°C)

YAS MARINA CIRCUIT, YAS ISLAND

Circuit: 3.281miles/5.281km, 58 laps

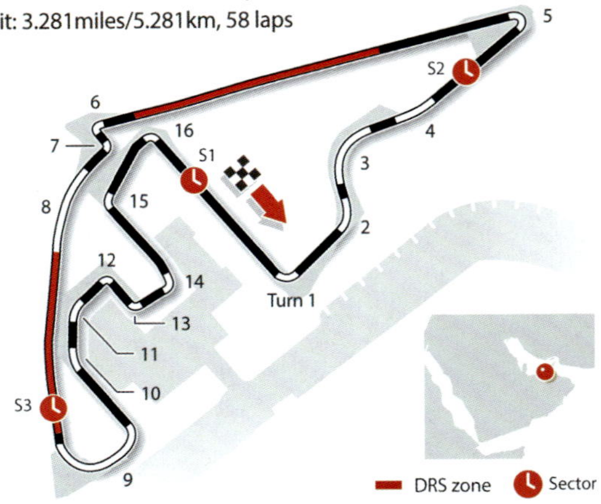

RACE – OFFICIAL CLASSIFICATION

Pos.	Driver	Nat.	No.	Entrant	Car/Engine	Laps	Time/Retirement	Speed (mph/km/h)	Gap to winner	Fastest race lap
1	**Max Verstappen**	NL	1	Oracle Red Bull Racing	Red Bull RB18-RBPTH001 V6	58	1h 27m 45.914s	130.065/209.319		1m 29.392s 54
2	**Charles Leclerc**	MC	16	Scuderia Ferrari	Ferrari F1-75-066/7 V6	58	1h 27m 54.685s	129.849/208.971	8.771s	1m 29.719s 48
3	**Sergio Pérez**	MEX	11	Oracle Red Bull Racing	Red Bull RB18-RBPTH001 V6	58	1h 27m 56.007s	129.816/208.919	10.093s	1m 28.972s 52
4	**Carlos Sainz**	E	55	Scuderia Ferrari	Ferrari F1-75-066/7 V6	58	1h 28m 10.806s	129.453/208.334	24.892s	1m 28.879s 50
5	**George Russell**	GB	63	Mercedes-AMG Petronas F1 Team	Mercedes-AMG F1 W13-M13 E Perf. V6	58	1h 28m 21.802s *	129.184/207.902	35.888s	1m 28.836s 48
6	**Lando Norris**	GB	4	McLaren F1 Team	McLaren MCL36-Mercedes F1 M13 E Perf. V6	58	1h 28m 42.148s	128.690/207.107	56.234s	1m 28.391s 44
7	**Esteban Ocon**	F	31	BWT Alpine F1 Team	Alpine A522-Renault E-Tech RE22 V6	58	1h 28m 43.154s	128.666/207.068	57.240s	1m 29.333s 45
8	**Lance Stroll**	CDN	18	Aston Martin Aramco Cognizant F1 Team	Aston Martin AMR22-Mercedes F1 M13 E Perf. V6	58	1h 29m 02.845s	128.192/206.305	1m 16.931s	1m 29.620s 42
9	**Daniel Ricciardo**	AUS	3	McLaren F1 Team	McLaren MCL36-Mercedes F1 M13 E Perf. V6	58	1h 29m 09.182s	128.040/206.061	1m 23.268s	1m 30.785s 45
10	**Sebastian Vettel**	D	5	Aston Martin Aramco Cognizant F1 Team	Aston Martin AMR22-Mercedes F1 M13 E Perf. V6	58	1h 29m 09.812s	128.025/206.036	1m 23.898s	1m 30.312s 35
11	Yuki Tsunoda	J	22	Scuderia AlphaTauri	AlphaTauri AT03-RBPTH001 V6	58	1h 29m 15.285s	127.894/205.826	1m 29.371s	1m 29.489s 40
12	Zhou Guanyu	CHN	24	Alfa Romeo F1 Team ORLEN	Alfa Romeo C42-Ferrari 066/7 V6	57			1 lap	1m 29.600s 53
13	Alexander Albon	T	23	Williams Racing	Williams FW44-Mercedes F1 M13 E Perf. V6	57			1 lap	1m 29.939s 40
14	Pierre Gasly	F	10	Scuderia AlphaTauri	AlphaTauri AT03-RBPTH001 V6	57			1 lap	1m 31.081s 16
15	Valtteri Bottas	FIN	77	Alfa Romeo F1 Team ORLEN	Alfa Romeo C42-Ferrari 066/7 V6	57			1 lap	1m 30.352s 47
16	Mick Schumacher	D	47	Haas F1 Team	Haas VF-22-Ferrari 066/7 V6	57	*		1 lap	1m 29.833s 39
17	Kevin Magnussen	DK	20	Haas F1 Team	Haas VF-22-Ferrari 066/7 V6	57			1 lap	1m 31.158s 40
18	Lewis Hamilton	GB	44	Mercedes-AMG Petronas F1 Team	Mercedes-AMG F1 W13-M13 E Perf. V6	55	*hydraulics*		3 laps	1m 29.788s 42
19	Nicholas Latifi	CDN	6	Williams Racing	Williams FW44-Mercedes F1 M13 E Perf. V6	55	*electrics*		3 laps	1m 30.309s 45
	Fernando Alonso	E	14	BWT Alpine F1 Team	Alpine A522-Renault E-Tech RE22 V6	27	*water leak*			1m 30.579s 24

* Russell: 5s time penalty for unsafe release from a pit stop (served at pit stop). * Schumacher: 5s time penalty for causing a collision with Latifi.

DHL Fastest race lap (scores 1 point): Lando Norris on lap 44, 1m 28.391s, 133.648mph/215.085km/h.

Lap record: Max Verstappen (Red Bull RB16B-Honda V6), 1m 26.103s, 137.199mph/220.800km/h (2021).

20 · LATIFI · Williams

18 · BOTTAS · Alfa Romeo

16 · MAGNUSSEN · Haas

14 · STROLL · Aston Martin

12 · SCHUMACHER · Haas

19 · ALBON · Williams

17 · GASLY · AlphaTauri

15 · ZHOU · Alfa Romeo

13 · RICCIARDO · McLaren
3-place grid penalty for causing a collision with Magnussen at the São Paulo GP

11 · TSUNODA · AlphaTauri

Grid order		1	2	3	4	5	6	7	8	9	10	11	12	13	14	15	16	17	18	19	20	21	22	23
1	VERSTAPPEN	1	1	1	1	1	1	1	1	1	1	1	1	1	1	1	1	1	1	1	1	16	1	1
11	PEREZ	11	11	11	11	11	11	11	11	11	11	11	11	11	11	16	16	16	16	16	16	1	11	11
16	LECLERC	16	16	16	16	16	16	16	16	16	16	16	16	16	16	11	55	55	44	11	11	11	16	16
55	SAINZ	44	44	44	55	44	44	44	55	55	55	55	55	55	55	55	44	44	11	5	55	55	55	55
44	HAMILTON	55	55	55	44	55	55	55	44	63	63	63	63	63	63	63	5	11	5	55	5	63	63	63
63	RUSSELL	4	4	4	4	63	63	63	63	44	44	44	44	44	44	44	11	5	14	63	63	5	5	44
4	NORRIS	63	63	63	63	4	4	4	4	4	4	4	4	4	4	4	14	14	55	14	44	44	44	5
31	OCON	31	31	31	31	31	31	31	31	31	31	31	31	31	5	5	3	3	63	3	4	4	4	4
5	VETTEL	5	5	5	5	5	5	5	5	5	5	5	5	5	14	14	63	63	3	44	31	31	31	31
14	ALONSO	14	14	14	14	14	14	14	14	14	14	14	14	14	31	3	20	20	4	4	77	18	18	18
22	TSUNODA	22	22	22	22	22	22	22	22	22	22	22	22	22	22	24	77	4	20	31	18	77	77	22
47	SCHUMACHER	18	18	18	18	18	18	18	18	18	18	18	18	3	3	20	4	77	77	20	20	22	22	14
3	RICCIARDO	47	3	3	3	3	3	3	3	3	3	3	3	18	24	77	31	31	31	77	22	20	14	77
18	STROLL	3	47	47	24	24	24	24	24	24	24	24	24	24	47	31	18	18	18	18	14	14	20	23
24	ZHOU	24	24	24	47	23	23	23	23	23	23	23	47	47	20	18	22	22	22	22	23	23	23	20
20	MAGNUSSEN	20	23	23	23	47	47	47	47	47	47	47	23	10	77	22	23	23	23	23	24	24	24	24
10	GASLY	23	20	10	10	10	10	10	10	10	10	10	10	20	10	6	24	24	24	24	47	47	47	3
77	BOTTAS	10	10	20	20	20	20	20	20	20	20	20	20	77	6	23	47	47	47	47	3	3	3	47
23	ALBON	6	6	6	6	6	6	6	6	77	77	77	77	6	18	47	10	10	10	10	10	10	10	10
6	LATIFI	77	77	77	77	77	77	77	77	6	6	6	6	23	23	10	6	6	6	6	6	6	6	6

Grid order		24	25	26	27	28	29	30	31	32	33	34	35	36	37	38	39	40	41	42	43	44	45	46
1	VERSTAPPEN	1	1	1	1	1	1	1	1	1	1	1	1	1	1	1	1	1	1	1	1	1	1	1
11	PEREZ	11	11	11	11	11	11	11	11	11	16	16	16	16	16	16	16	16	16	16	16	16	16	16
16	LECLERC	16	16	16	16	16	16	16	16	16	11	55	55	55	55	55	55	44	44	44	44	44	44	11
55	SAINZ	55	55	55	55	55	55	55	55	55	55	63	63	63	63	63	44	11	11	11	11	11	11	44
44	HAMILTON	63	63	63	63	63	63	63	63	63	63	44	44	44	44	44	63	55	55	55	55	55	55	55
63	RUSSELL	44	44	44	44	44	44	44	44	44	44	11	11	11	11	11	11	4	4	4	63	63	63	63
4	NORRIS	4	4	4	4	4	4	4	4	4	4	4	4	4	4	4	4	31	63	63	4	4	4	4
31	OCON	5	31	31	31	31	31	31	31	31	31	31	31	31	31	31	31	63	31	3	31	31	31	31
5	VETTEL	31	5	18	18	18	18	18	18	18	18	18	18	18	18	18	18	18	3	31	3	3	3	3
14	ALONSO	18	18	14	14	22	22	22	22	22	22	22	22	22	22	22	3	3	24	24	5	5	5	5
22	TSUNODA	14	14	22	22	23	23	23	23	23	23	23	3	3	3	3	24	24	5	5	24	18	18	18
47	SCHUMACHER	22	22	23	23	24	24	3	3	3	3	3	23	24	24	24	5	5	18	18	18	22	22	22
3	RICCIARDO	77	23	24	24	3	3	24	24	24	24	24	24	5	5	5	10	10	10	10	22	24	10	23
18	STROLL	23	77	77	3	47	47	47	47	47	47	5	5	10	10	10	22	22	22	22	10	10	23	10
24	ZHOU	24	24	3	77	77	77	5	5	5	5	47	10	23	23	23	23	23	23	23	23	23	47	47
20	MAGNUSSEN	20	3	47	47	5	5	10	10	10	10	10	6	6	6	77	47	47	47	47	47	47	24	24
10	GASLY	3	47	10	10	10	10	77	6	6	6	6	47	47	47	47	77	77	77	77	77	77	77	77
77	BOTTAS	47	20	20	5	20	6	6	77	77	77	77	77	77	77	20	20	20	20	20	20	20	20	20
23	ALBON	10	10	5	20	6	20	20	20	20	20	20	20	20	20	6	6	6	6	6	6	6	6	6
6	LATIFI	6	6	6	6																			

TIME SHEETS

PRACTICE 1 (FRIDAY)

Weather: Dry/sunny

Temperatures: track 44-48°C, air 35-37°C

Pos.	Driver	Laps	Time
1	Lewis Hamilton	21	1m 26.633s
2	George Russell	30	1m 26.853s
3	Charles Leclerc	22	1m 26.888s
4	Sergio Pérez	23	1m 26.967s
5	Liam Lawson	22	1m 27.201s
6	Sebastian Vettel	20	1m 27.268s
7	Robert Shwartzman	24	1m 27.429s
8	Daniel Ricciardo	21	1m 27.619s
9	Valtteri Bottas	23	1m 27.655s
10	Alexander Albon	26	1m 27.840s
11	Pierre Gasly	28	1m 27.845s
12	Esteban Ocon	27	1m 27.891s
13	Yuki Tsunoda	28	1m 27.991s
14	Robert Kubica	22	1m 28.064s
15	Logan Sargeant	23	1m 28.098s
16	Kevin Magnussen	20	1m 28.142s
17	Pietro Fittipaldi	26	1m 28.204s
18	Patricio O'Ward	22	1m 28.350s
19	Jack Doohan	25	1m 28.484s
20	Felipe Drugovich	23	1m 28.672s

PRACTICE 2 (SATURDAY)

Weather: Dry/dusk

Temperatures: track 36-39°C, air 30-32°C

Pos.	Driver	Laps	Time
1	Max Verstappen	25	1m 25.146s
2	George Russell	27	1m 25.487s
3	Charles Leclerc	30	1m 25.599s
4	Lewis Hamilton	22	1m 25.761s
5	Sergio Pérez	26	1m 25.852s
6	Carlos Sainz	31	1m 25.932s
7	Esteban Ocon	28	1m 26.038s
8	Fernando Alonso	29	1m 26.043s
9	Daniel Ricciardo	14	1m 26.124s
10	Valtteri Bottas	29	1m 26.300s
11	Lando Norris	28	1m 26.377s
12	Sebastian Vettel	28	1m 26.395s
13	Zhou Guanyu	30	1m 26.479s
14	Lance Stroll	27	1m 26.547s
15	Yuki Tsunoda	30	1m 26.680s
16	Alexander Albon	29	1m 26.750s
17	Mick Schumacher	26	1m 26.839s
18	Kevin Magnussen	25	1m 26.915s
19	Pierre Gasly	29	1m 27.036s
20	Nicholas Latifi	30	1m 27.262s

PRACTICE 3 (SATURDAY)

Weather: Dry/sunny

Temperatures: track 40-42°C, air 31-34°C

Pos.	Driver	Laps	Time
1	Sergio Pérez	15	1m 24.982s
2	Max Verstappen	15	1m 25.134s
3	Lewis Hamilton	20	1m 25.222s
4	George Russell	15	1m 25.395s
5	Lando Norris	16	1m 25.518s
6	Charles Leclerc	24	1m 25.571s
7	Carlos Sainz	23	1m 25.605s
8	Daniel Ricciardo	18	1m 25.950s
9	Sebastian Vettel	13	1m 26.012s
10	Alexander Albon	16	1m 26.051s
11	Esteban Ocon	17	1m 26.073s
12	Fernando Alonso	18	1m 26.076s
13	Yuki Tsunoda	19	1m 26.170s
14	Valtteri Bottas	17	1m 26.189s
15	Pierre Gasly	12	1m 26.239s
16	Lance Stroll	20	1m 26.298s
17	Kevin Magnussen	21	1m 26.356s
18	Mick Schumacher	19	1m 26.473s
19	Zhou Guanyu	17	1m 26.482s
20	Nicholas Latifi	14	1m 26.646s

QUALIFYING (FRIDAY)

Weather: Dry/dark Temperatures: track 32-33°C, air 28-29°C

Pos.	Driver	First	Second	Third	Qualifying Tyre
1	Max Verstappen	1m 24.754s	1m 24.622s	1m 23.824s	Soft (n)
2	Sergio Pérez	1m 24.820s	1m 24.419s	1m 24.052s	Soft (n)
3	Charles Leclerc	1m 25.211s	1m 24.517s	1m 24.092s	Soft (n)
4	Carlos Sainz	1m 25.090s	1m 24.521s	1m 24.242s	Soft (n)
5	Lewis Hamilton	1m 25.594s	1m 24.774s	1m 24.508s	Soft (n)
6	George Russell	1m 25.545s	1m 24.940s	1m 24.511s	Soft (n)
7	Lando Norris	1m 25.387s	1m 24.903s	1m 24.769s	Soft (n)
8	Esteban Ocon	1m 25.735s	1m 25.007s	1m 24.830s	Soft (n)
9	Sebastian Vettel	1m 25.523s	1m 24.974s	1m 24.961s	Soft (n)
10	Daniel Ricciardo	1m 25.766s	1m 25.068s	1m 25.045s	Soft (n)
11	Fernando Alonso	1m 25.782s	1m 25.096s		
12	Yuki Tsunoda	1m 25.630s	1m 25.219s		
13	Mick Schumacher	1m 25.711s	1m 25.225s		
14	Lance Stroll	1m 25.741s	1m 25.359s		
15	Zhou Guanyu	1m 25.594s	1m 25.408s		
16	Kevin Magnussen	1m 25.834s			
17	Pierre Gasly	1m 25.859s			
18	Valtteri Bottas	1m 25.892s			
19	Alexander Albon	1m 26.028s			
20	Nicholas Latifi	1m 26.054s			

QUALIFYING: head to head

Hamilton	13	9	Russell
Verstappen	18	4	Pérez
Ricciardo	2	20	Norris
Leclerc	15	7	Sainz
Gasly	13	9	Tsunoda
Hülkenberg	1	1	Stroll
Vettel	13	7	Stroll
Alonso	13	9	Ocon
Bottas	14	8	Zhou
Albon	19	2	Latifi
de Vries	1	0	Latifi
Magnussen	16	6	Schumacher

Scuderia Ferrari

FOR THE RECORD

200th GRAND PRIX START: Valtteri Bottas

20th POLE POSITION: Max Verstappen

POINTS

DRIVERS

1	Max Verstappen	454
2	Charles Leclerc	308
3	Sergio Pérez	305
4	George Russell	275
5	Carlos Sainz	246
6	Lewis Hamilton	240
7	Lando Norris	122
8	Esteban Ocon	92
9	Fernando Alonso	81
10	Valtteri Bottas	49
11	Daniel Ricciardo	37
12	Sebastian Vettel	37
13	Kevin Magnussen	25
14	Pierre Gasly	23
15	Lance Stroll	18
16	Mick Schumacher	12
17	Yuki Tsunoda	12
18	Zhou Guanyu	6
19	Alexander Albon	4
20	Nicholas Latifi	2
21	Nyck de Vries	2

CONSTRUCTORS

1	Red Bull	759
2	Ferrari	554
3	Mercedes	515
4	Alpine	173
5	McLaren	159
6	Alfa Romeo	55
7	Aston Martin	55
8	Haas	37
9	AlphaTauri	35
10	Williams	8

10 · ALONSO · Alpine 8 · OCON · Alpine 6 · RUSSELL · Mercedes 4 · SAINZ · Ferrari 2 · PÉREZ · Red Bull

9 · VETTEL · Aston Martin 7 · NORRIS · McLaren 5 · HAMILTON · Mercedes 3 · LECLERC · Ferrari 1 · VERSTAPPEN · Red Bull

47	48	49	50	51	52	53	54	55	56	57	58	
1	1	1	1	1	1	1	1	1	1	1	1	1
16	16	16	16	16	16	16	16	16	16	16	16	2
11	11	11	11	11	11	11	11	11	11	11	11	3
44	44	44	44	44	44	44	44	55	55	55	55	4
55	55	55	55	55	55	55	55	63	63	63	63	5
63	63	63	63	63	63	63	63	4	4	4	4	6
4	4	4	4	4	4	4	4	31	31	31	31	7
31	31	31	31	31	31	31	31	44	18	18	18	8
3	3	3	18	18	18	18	18	18	3	3	3	9
5	18	18	3	3	3	3	3	3	5	5	5	10
18	5	5	5	5	5	5	5	5	22	22	22	
22	22	22	22	22	22	22	22	22	23	24		
23	23	23	23	23	23	23	23	23	24	23		
10	10	10	10	10	10	10	10	10	10	10		
47	24	24	24	24	24	24	24	24	77	77		
24	47	47	47	47	47	77	77	77	47	47		
77	77	77	77	77	77	47	47	47	20	20		
20	20	20	20	20	20	20	20	20				
6	6	6	6	6	6	6	6	6				

23 = Pit stop *6 = One lap or more behind*

RACE TYRE STRATEGIES

PIRELLI

	Driver	Race Stint 1	Race Stint 2	Race Stint 3
1	Verstappen	Medium (n): 1-20	Hard (n): 21-58	
2	Leclerc	Medium (n): 1-21	Hard (n): 22-58	
3	Pérez	Medium (n): 1-15	Hard (n): 16-33	Hard (n): 34-58
4	Sainz	Medium (n): 1-17	Hard (n): 18-39	Hard (n): 40-58
5	Russell	Medium (n): 1-15	Hard (n): 16-39	Medium (n): 40-58
6	Norris	Medium (n): 1-15	Hard (n): 16-42	Medium (n): 43-58
7	Ocon	Medium (n): 1-14	Hard (n): 15-41	Hard (n): 42-58
8	Stroll	Medium (n): 1-13	Hard (n): 14-40	Medium (u): 41-58
9	Ricciardo	Medium (n): 1-19	Hard (n): 20-58	
10	Vettel	Medium (n): 1-25	Hard (u): 26-58	
11	Tsunoda	Medium (n): 1-14	Hard (n): 15-38	Soft (n): 39-58
12	Zhou	Medium (n): 1-15	Hard (n): 16-44	Soft (n): 45-57
13	Albon	Medium (n): 1-12	Hard (n): 13-35	Medium (n): 36-57
14	Gasly	Soft (n): 1-14	Hard (n): 15-57	
15	Bottas	Hard (n): 1-30	Medium (n): 31-57	
16	Schumacher	Medium (n): 1-14	Hard (n): 15-34	Medium (u): 35-57
17	Magnussen	Hard (n): 1-28	Medium (n): 29-57	
18	Hamilton	Medium (n): 1-18	Hard (n): 19-55 (dnf)	
19	Latifi	Medium (n): 1-15	Hard (n): 16-38	Medium (n): 39-55 (dnf)
	Alonso	Medium (n): 1-19	Hard (n): 20-27 (dnf)	

The tyre regulations stipulate that at least two of three dry tyre specifications must be used during a dry race. Selected compounds for Abu Dhabi: Red = Soft (C5); Yellow = Medium (C4); White = Hard (C3). (n) new (u) used

Alfa Romeo ORLEN

STATISTICS: Compiled by DAVID HAYHOE

DRIVERS' POINTS TABLE: 2022

Place	Driver	Nationality	Date of birth	Car	Bahrain	Saudi Arabia	Australia	Emilia Romagna	Miami	Spain	Monaco	Azerbaijan	Canada	Britain	Austria	France	Hungary	Belgium	Netherlands	Italy	Singapore	Japan	United States	Mexico City	São Paulo	Abu Dhabi	Points
1	**Max VERSTAPPEN**	NL	30/9/97	Red Bull	19*	1	R	1pf	1f	1	3	1	1p	7	2pf	1	1	1f	1pf	1	7	1p	1	1p	6	1p	**454**
2	**Charles LECLERC**	MC	16/10/97	Ferrari	1pf	2f	1pf	6	2p	Rp	4p	Rp	5	4	1	Rp	6	6	3	2p	2p	3	3	6	4	2	**308**
3	**Sergio PÊREZ**	MEX	26/1/90	Red Bull	18*	4p	2	2	4	2f	1	2f	R	2	R	4	5	2	5	6f	1	2	4	3	7	3	**305**
4	**George RUSSELL**	GB	15/2/98	Mercedes	4	5	3	4	5	3	5	3	4	R	4	3	3p	4	2	3	14*f	8	5f	4f	1pf	5	**275**
5	**Carlos SAINZ**	E	1/9/94	Ferrari	2	3	R	R	3	4	2	R	2f	1p	R	5f	4	3p	8	4	3	R	Rp	5	3	4	**246**
6	**Lewis HAMILTON**	GB	7/1/85	Mercedes	3	10	4	13	6	5	8	4	3	3f	3	2	2f	R	4	5	9	5	2	2	2	18*	**240**
7	**Lando NORRIS**	GB	13/11/99	McLaren-Mercedes	15	7	5	3	R	8	6f	9	15	6	7	7	7	12	7	7	4	10	6	9	R	6f	**122**
8	**Esteban OCON**	F	17/9/96	Alpine-Renault	7	6	7	14	8	7	12	10	6	R	5	8	9	7	9	11	R	4	11	8	8	7	**92**
9	**Fernando ALONSO**	E	29/7/81	Alpine-Renault	9	R	17	R	11	9	7	7	9	5	10	6	8	5	6	R	R	7	7	19*	5	R	**81**
10	**Valtteri BOTTAS**	FIN	28/8/89	Alfa Romeo-Ferrari	6	R	8	5	7	6	9	11	7	R	11	14	20*	R	R	13	11	15	R	10	9	15	**49**
11	**Daniel RICCIARDO**	AUS	1/7/89	McLaren-Mercedes	14	R	6	18	13	12	13	8	11	13	9	9	15	15	17	R	5	11	16	7	R	9	**37**
12	**Sebastian VETTEL**	D	3/7/87	Aston Martin-Mercedes	-	-	R	8	17*	11	10	6	12	9	17	11	10	8	14	R	8	6	8	14	11	10	**37**
13	**Kevin MAGNUSSEN**	DK	5/10/92	Haas-Ferrari	5	9	14	9	16*	17	R	R	17	10	8	R	16	16	15	16	12	14	9	17	Rp+	17	**25**
14	**Pierre GASLY**	F	7/2/96	AlphaTauri-Red Bull	R	8	9	12	R	13	11	5	14	R	15	12	12	9	11	8	10	18	14	11	14	14	**23**
15	**Lance STROLL**	CDN	29/10/98	Aston Martin-Mercedes	12	13	12	10	10	15	14	16*	10	11	13	10	11	11	10	R	6	12	R	15	10	8	**18**
16	**Mick SCHUMACHER**	D	22/3/99	Haas-Ferrari	11	NS	13	17	15	14	R	14	R	8	6	15	14	17	13	12	13	17	15	16	13	16	**12**
17	**Yuki TSUNODA**	J	11/5/00	AlphaTauri-Red Bull	8	NS	15	7	12	10	17	13	R	14	16	R	19	13	R	14	R	13	10	R	17	11	**12**
18	**ZHOU Guanyu**	CHN	30/5/99	Alfa Romeo-Ferrari	10	11	11	15	R	R	16	R	8	R	14	16*	13	14	16	10	R	16f	12	13	12	12	**6**
19	**Alexander ALBON**	T	23/3/96	Williams-Mercedes	13	14*	10	11	9	18	R	12	13	R	12	13	17	10	12	EW	R	R	13	12	15	13	**4**
20	**Nicholas LATIFI**	CDN	29/6/95	Williams-Mercedes	16	R	16	16	14	16	15	15	16	12	R	R	18	18	18	15	R	9	17	18	16	19*	**2**
21	**Nyck de VRIES**	NL	6/2/95	Williams-Mercedes	-	-	-	-	-	-	-	-	-	-	-	-	-	-	-	9	-	-	-	-	-	-	**2**
	Nico HÜLKENBERG	D	19/8/87	Aston Martin-Mercedes	17	12	-	-	-	-	-	-	-	-	-	-	-	-	-	-	-	-	-	-	-	-	**-**

TESTERS

Driver	Nationality	Date of birth	Car	Bahrain	Saudi Arabia	Australia	Emilia Romagna	Miami	Spain	Monaco	Azerbaijan	Canada	Britain	Austria	France	Hungary	Belgium	Netherlands	Italy	Singapore	Japan	United States	Mexico City	São Paulo	Abu Dhabi
Nyck de VRIES	NL	6/2/95	Williams-Mercedes	-	-	-	-	-	AP	-	-	-	-	-	-	-	-	-	-	-	-	-	-	-	-
			Mercedes	-	-	-	-	-	-	-	-	-	-	-	AP	-	-	-	-	-	-	-	AP	-	-
			Aston Martin-Mercedes	-	-	-	-	-	-	-	-	-	-	-	-	-	-	-	AP	-	-	-	-	-	-
Jack DOOHAN	AUS	20/1/03	Alpine-Renault	-	-	-	-	-	-	-	-	-	-	-	-	-	-	-	-	-	-	-	AP	-	AP
Felipe DRUGOVICH	BR	23/5/00	Aston Martin-Mercedes	-	-	-	-	-	-	-	-	-	-	-	-	-	-	-	-	-	-	-	-	-	AP
Pietro FITTIPALDI	BR	25/6/96	Haas-Ferrari	-	-	-	-	-	-	-	-	-	-	-	-	-	-	-	-	-	-	-	AP	-	AP
Antonio GIOVINAZZI	I	14/12/93	Haas-Ferrari	-	-	-	-	-	-	-	-	-	-	-	-	-	-	-	AP	-	-	AP	-	-	-
Robert KUBICA	PL	7/12/84	Alfa Romeo-Ferrari	-	-	-	-	-	AP	-	-	-	-	-	AP	AP	-	-	-	-	-	-	-	-	AP
Liam LAWSON	NZ	11/2/02	AlphaTauri-Red Bull	-	-	-	-	-	-	-	-	-	-	-	-	-	AP	-	-	-	-	-	AP	-	-
			Red Bull	-	-	-	-	-	-	-	-	-	-	-	-	-	-	-	-	-	-	-	-	-	AP
Patricio O'WARD	MEX	6/5/99	McLaren-Mercedes	-	-	-	-	-	-	-	-	-	-	-	-	-	-	-	-	-	-	-	-	-	AP
Alex PALOU	E	1/4/97	McLaren-Mercedes	-	-	-	-	-	-	-	-	-	-	-	-	-	-	-	-	-	-	AP	-	-	-
Théo POURCHAIRE	F	20/8/03	Alfa Romeo-Ferrari	-	-	-	-	-	-	-	-	-	-	-	-	-	-	-	-	-	-	AP	-	-	-
Logan SARGEANT	USA	31/12/00	Williams-Mercedes	-	-	-	-	-	-	-	-	-	-	-	-	-	-	-	-	-	-	AP	AP	AP	AP
Robert SHWARTZMAN	IL	16/9/99	Ferrari	-	-	-	-	-	-	-	-	-	-	-	-	-	-	-	-	-	-	AP	-	-	AP
Jüri VIPS	EST	10/8/00	Red Bull	-	-	-	-	-	AP	-	-	-	-	-	-	-	-	-	-	-	-	-	-	-	-

KEY: AP – Also practised EW – Entry withdrawn NS – Non-starter R – Retired * – Placed, but retired f – fastest lap p – pole position p+ – official pole position (sprint race)

POINTS AND PERCENTAGES

GRID POSITIONS: 2022

Pos	Driver	Starts	Best	Worst	Average
1	Max Verstappen	22	1	14	3.4
2	Charles Leclerc	22	1	19	3.9
3	Carlos Sainz	22	1	19	4.7
4	Sergio Pérez	22	1	13	4.8
5	George Russell	22	1	20	6.4
6	Lewis Hamilton	22	2	19	6.5
7	Nyck de Vries	1	8	8	8.0
8	Lando Norris	22	3	17	8.0
9	Fernando Alonso	22	2	20	9.4
10	Valtteri Bottas	22	5	20	11.4
11	Daniel Ricciardo	22	4	18	11.4
12	Esteban Ocon	22	5	20	11.6
13	Pierre Gasly	22	5	20	12.2
14	Kevin Magnussen	22	5	20	12.9
15	Sebastian Vettel	20	9	19	13.3
16	Mick Schumacher	21	6	20	13.8
17	Yuki Tsunoda	21	8	20	13.8
18	Zhou Guanyu	22	9	20	14.3
19	Lance Stroll	22	5	20	14.6
20	Alexander Albon	21	6	20	15.6
21	Nico Hülkenberg	2	17	17	17.0
22	Nicholas Latifi	22	10	20	17.5

RETIREMENTS: 2022

Number of cars to have retired

Grand Prix	Starters	At 1/4-distance	At 1/2-distance	At 3/4-distance	At full distance	Percentage of finishers
Bahrain	20	-	-	-	3	85.0
Saudi Arabia	18	-	1	4	5	72.2
Australia	20	1	2	3	3	85.0
Emilia Romagna	20	2	2	2	2	90.0
Miami	20	1	1	2	5	75.0
Spain	20	-	2	2	2	90.0
Monaco	20	-	2	3	3	85.0
Azerbaijan	20	1	3	4	5	75.0
Canada	20	1	2	3	3	85.0
Britain	20	3	5	6	6	70.0
Austria	20	-	1	2	3	85.0
France	20	-	2	3	5	75.0
Hungary	20	-	-	-	1	95.0
Belgium	20	2	2	2	2	90.0
Netherlands	20	-	-	2	2	90.0
Italy	20	1	1	3	4	80.0
Singapore	20	2	5	6	7	65.0
Japan	20	2	2	2	2	90.0
United States	20	1	3	3	3	85.0
Mexico City	20	-	-	1	2	90.0
Sao Paulo	20	2	2	3	3	85.0
Abu Dhabi	20	-	1	1	3	85.0

LAP LEADERS: 2022

Grand Prix	Verstappen	Leclerc	Pérez	Russell	Sainz	Hamilton	Vettel	Alonso	Total
Bahrain	-	55	-	-	2	-	-	-	57
Saudi Arabia	6	30	14	-	-	-	-	-	50
Australia	-	58	-	-	-	-	-	-	58
Emilia Romagna	63	-	-	-	-	-	-	-	63
Miami	48	8	-	-	1	-	-	-	57
Spain	25	26	11	4	-	-	-	-	66
Monaco	-	17	44	-	3	-	-	-	64
Azerbaijan	36	1	14	-	-	-	-	-	51
Canada	53	-	-	-	17	-	-	-	70
Britain	4	13	-	-	27	8	-	-	52
Austria	18	51	-	-	2	-	-	-	71
France	35	17	-	-	-	1	-	-	53
Hungary	20	14	-	24	8	4	-	-	70
Belgium	31	-	1	-	12	-	-	-	44
Netherlands	58	-	-	-	-	14	-	-	72
Italy	34	19	-	-	-	-	-	-	53
Singapore	-	-	59	-	-	-	-	-	59
Japan	27	-	-	-	-	-	-	1	28
United States	40	1	4	-	-	9	2	-	56
Mexico City	61	-	-	5	-	5	-	-	71
Sao Paulo		-	-	66	-	5	-	-	71
Abu Dhabi	57	1	-	-	-	-	-	-	58
Total	**616**	**311**	**147**	**99**	**72**	**46**	**2**	**1**	**1,294**
(Per cent)	**47.6**	**24.0**	**11.4**	**7.7**	**5.6**	**3.6**	**0.2**	**0.1**	**100.0**

CAREER PERFORMANCES: 2022

Driver	Nationality	Races	Championships	Wins	2nd places	3rd places	4th places	5th places	6th places	7th places	8th places	9th places	10th places	Pole positions	Fastest laps	Points
Alexander Albon	T	**59**	-	-	-	2	3	6	6	1	3	2	5	-	-	**201**
Fernando Alonso	E	**356**	2	32	37	29	27	26	21	24	17	12	13	22	23	**2061**
Valtteri Bottas	FIN	**200**	-	10	29	28	13	24	9	5	12	7	4	20	19	**1787**
Nyck de Vries	NL	**1**	-	-	-	-	-	-	-	-	-	1	-	-	-	**2**
Pierre Gasly	F	**108**	-	1	1	1	4	5	10	8	7	8	5	-	3	**332**
Lewis Hamilton	GB	**310**	7	103	53	35	25	23	7	10	5	7	3	103	61	**4405.5**
Nico Hülkenberg	D	**181**	-	-	-	-	3	9	20	19	19	10	17	1	2	**521**
Nicholas Latifi	CDN	**61**	-	-	-	-	-	-	-	1	-	2	-	-	-	**9**
Charles Leclerc	MC	**102**	-	5	9	10	15	9	9	7	4	2	5	18	7	**868**
Kevin Magnussen	DK	**141**	-	-	1	-	-	4	3	6	8	10	9	1	2	**183**
Lando Norris	GB	**82**	-	-	1	5	5	8	7	12	9	6	8	1	5	**428**
Esteban Ocon	F	**111**	-	1	1	-	2	5	12	10	13	15	9	-	-	**364**
Sergio Pérez	MEX	**235**	-	4	10	12	13	15	16	26	18	18	19	1	9	**1201**
Daniel Ricciardo	AUS	**232**	-	8	6	18	24	16	16	13	8	12	10	3	16	**1311**
George Russell	GB	**82**	-	1	2	6	6	5	-	-	2	2	1	1	5	**294**
Carlos Sainz	E	**162**	-	1	5	9	6	12	17	13	19	10	9	3	3	**782.5**
Mick Schumacher	D	**43**	-	-	-	-	-	-	1	-	1	-	-	-	-	**12**
Lance Stroll	CDN	**122**	-	-	-	3	3	-	4	3	8	10	11	1	-	**194**
Yuki Tsunoda	J	**42**	-	-	-	-	1	-	1	2	1	2	4	-	-	**44**
Max Verstappen	NL	**163**	2	35	26	16	14	12	6	4	6	5	3	20	21	**2011.5**
Sebastian Vettel	D	**299**	4	53	36	33	34	21	13	6	11	4	9	57	38	**3098**
Zhou Guanyu	CHN	**22**	-	-	-	-	-	-	-	-	1	-	2	-	1	**6**

Note: Drivers retiring on the formation lap are not counted as having started. At the 2001 Belgian GP, which was subjected to a restart, Alonso is counted as starting, having started the initial race.

From 2022, for events with Sprint races, Pole position is counted as the pole for the Sprint.

ALL–TIME RECORDS: 2022

STARTS

Fernando Alonso	356
Kimi Räikkönen	350
Rubens Barrichello	323
Lewis Hamilton	310
Michael Schumacher	307
Jenson Button	306
Sebastian Vettel	299
Felipe Massa	269
Riccardo Patrese	256
Jarno Trulli	252
David Coulthard	246
Sergio Pérez	235

WINS

Lewis Hamilton	103
Michael Schumacher	91
Sebastian Vettel	53
Alain Prost	51
Ayrton Senna	41
Max Verstappen	35
Fernando Alonso	32
Nigel Mansell	31
Jackie Stewart	27
Jim Clark	25
Niki Lauda	25
Juan Manuel Fangio	24

POLE POSITIONS

Lewis Hamilton	103
Michael Schumacher	68
Ayrton Senna	65
Sebastian Vettel	57
Jim Clark	33
Alain Prost	33
Nigel Mansell	32
Nico Rosberg	30
Juan Manuel Fangio	29
Mika Häkkinen	26
Niki Lauda	24
Nelson Piquet	24

YOUNGEST STARTERS

Max Verstappen	17y 166d
Lance Stroll	18y 148d
Lando Norris	19y 124d
Jaime Alguersuari	19y 125d
Mike Thackwell	19y 182d
Ricardo Rodríguez	19y 208d
Fernando Alonso	19y 218d
Esteban Tuero	19y 320d
Chris Amon	19y 324d
Daniil Kvyat	19y 324d
Esteban Ocon	19y 346d
Sebastian Vettel	19y 349d

YOUNGEST WINNERS

Max Verstappen	18y 228d
Sebastian Vettel	21y 73d
Charles Leclerc	21y 320d
Fernando Alonso	22y 26d
Bruce McLaren	22y 104d
Lewis Hamilton	22y 154d
Kimi Räikkönen	23y 157d
Robert Kubica	23y 184d
Jacky Ickx	23y 188d
Michael Schumacher	23y 240d
Emerson Fittipaldi	23y 296d
Mike Hawthorn	24y 86d

YOUNGEST ON POLE

Sebastian Vettel	21y 73d
Charles Leclerc	21y 166d
Fernando Alonso	21y 237d
Max Verstappen	21y 308d
Lando Norris	21y 317d
Lance Stroll	22y 17d
Rubens Barrichello	22y 97d
Lewis Hamilton	22y 154d
Andrea De Cesaris	22y 308d
Nico Hülkenberg	23y 80d
Robert Kubica	23y 121d
Jacky Ickx	23y 216d

PODIUMS

Lewis Hamilton	191
Michael Schumacher	155
Sebastian Vettel	122
Alain Prost	106
Kimi Räikkönen	103
Fernando Alonso	98
Ayrton Senna	80
Max Verstappen	77
Rubens Barrichello	68
Valtteri Bottas	67
David Coulthard	62
Nelson Piquet	60

FASTEST LAPS

Michael Schumacher	77
Lewis Hamilton	61
Kimi Räikkönen	46
Alain Prost	41
Sebastian Vettel	38
Nigel Mansell	30
Jim Clark	28
Mika Häkkinen	25
Niki Lauda	24
Fernando Alonso	23
Juan Manuel Fangio	23
Nelson Piquet	23

YOUNGEST CHAMPIONS

Sebastian Vettel	23y 134d
Lewis Hamilton	23y 300d
Fernando Alonso	24y 58d
Max Verstappen	24y 73d
Emerson Fittipaldi	25y 273d
Michael Schumacher	25y 314d
Niki Lauda	26y 197d
Jacques Villeneuve	26y 200d
Jim Clark	27y 188d
Kimi Räikkönen	28y 4d
Jochen Rindt	28y 169d
Ayrton Senna	28y 223d

MULTIPLE WORLD CHAMPIONS

Lewis Hamilton	7	Jackie Stewart	3
Michael Schumacher	7	Fernando Alonso	2
Juan Manuel Fangio	5	Alberto Ascari	2
Alain Prost	4	Jim Clark	2
Sebastian Vettel	4	Emerson Fittipaldi	2
Jack Brabham	3	Mika Häkkinen	2
Niki Lauda	3	Graham Hill	2
Nelson Piquet	3	Max Verstappen	2
Ayrton Senna	3		

F2 REVIEW by CRAIG LLEWELLYN

SUPER DRUG

Above: Felipe Drugovich returned to MP Motorsport and ran a convincing campaign, winning five races. The Brazilian's consistency paid dividends, with 14 other top-six finishes to put him over 100 points clear at the top of the championship.

Top right: Richard Verschoor was a late arrival at Trident, but he lost no time in securing a win in the season-opener in Bahrain.
Photos: XPB Images

Above right: The highly rated Théo Pourchaire remained with ART Grand Prix and was the closest challenger to Drugovitch.
Photo: Formula 2

Centre right: Jack Doohan, under the Alpine Academy's wing, made a slow start to the season with Virtuosi Racing, but steadily improved as the season progressed.
Photo: Alpine

Right: Big things were expected of F3 graduate Dennis Hauger, and the Norwegian delivered with a win for Prema at Monaco.
Photo: Red Bull Content Pool/Getty Images

FELIPE DRUGOVICH'S decision to return to the MP Motorsport fold for the 2022 FIA F2 Championship was personal. After a year away at UNI-Virtuosi, moving back to Sander Dorsman's operation just felt right, comfortable, the best place from which to launch a title bid in his third year at this level. And he was right.

As if to lay down a marker for the rest of the field, the 21-year-old finished inside the top ten in four out of the five pre-season test sessions and ended the final day at the very top of the time sheets. From that point, he went on a tear through the first half of the season, racking up more wins before round six than anyone else would manage throughout the season, allowing for a more reasoned view of the run-in to the title. And it was a title double at that, as MP Motorsport became only the second outfit in the short history of FIA F2 to take home both the drivers' and teams' titles in the same season, improving from a best of sixth in the standings as Drugovich converted ninth overall in 2021 into a stepping stone to F1.

The Brazilian wasn't the highest placed returnee to the series for 2022. That 'honour' went to 2021 rookie sensation Théo Pourchaire, who wound up fifth in the table and landed an F1 test role with Alfa Romeo, while Jüri Vips, Jehan Daruvala and Liam Lawson all came back for another crack at the title, having finished above Drugovich in the standings. Pourchaire remained with ART Grand Prix for a second season, while Vips did likewise at Hitech Grand Prix, but both Lawson and Daruvala were on the move, to Carlin and Prema Racing respectively, as they sought the edge that might lead to ultimate success.

With reigning champion Oscar Piastri ineligible to return, having slipped into a reserve role with Alpine F1, and team-mate Robert Shwartzman having decided to focus on his testing duties with Ferrari in the top flight, teams' champion Prema was forced to field an all-new line-up, promoting reigning FIA F3 champion Dennis Hauger alongside Red Bull stablemate Daruvala.

Runners-up in 2021, Carlin also needed to start afresh, landing Kiwi Lawson to partner American Logan Sargeant, who had made his F2 debut at the 2021 finale after impressing in a last-minute F3 seat during the season. Virtuosi Racing, too, had to bring in two new faces, as Drugovich's 2021 team-mate, Zhou Guanyu, had graduated to F1 with Alfa Romeo. In their stead came second-year F2 racer Marino Sato and FIA F3 runner-up Jack Doohan, who had scored points on his series debut with MP Motorsport at the 2021 finale. Hitech tabbed former Ferrari protégé Marcus Armstrong to replace compatriot Lawson, while ART added Mercedes Junior Team driver – and 2021 FIA F3 front-runner – Frederik Vesti to fill the seat previously occupied by Indycar graduate Christian Lundgaard.

With Drugovich returning, MP Motorsport also retained Clément Novolak, who had made his series debut with the team after claiming third overall in the 2021 F3 standings, while DAMS replaced Armstrong with Red Bull Junior Ayumu Iwasa, who also stepped up from F3 to partner Israel's Roy Nissany. Campos kept F3 graduate Olli Caldwell on its roster alongside Ralph Boschung; Trident signed both the under-rated Richard Verschoor and Australian hopeful Calan Williams; while Charouz Racing System took the most left-field turn of all by inking F1 Esports competitor – and erstwhile Euroformula Open front-runner – Cem Bölükbasi alongside Enzo Fittipaldi.

The only new team in the series, Van Amersfoort Racing, took over the entry previously held by HWA Racelab (as it did in FIA F3) and signed one of the German team's on again/off again drivers, Jake Hughes, for continuity alongside Belgian Amaury Cordeel.

F2's chassis and engine package remained unchanged for a fifth straight campaign, with the venerable Dallara F2-2018 and Mecachrome V6 turbo already confirmed to remain in use until the end of 2023. Pirelli also continued as official tyre supplier as the series moved into a third year of using 18in rims.

Meanwhile, the calendar underwent a major shake-up, almost doubling the number of events, at 14, but reverting to the more familiar double-header format to consist of 28 individual races, split evenly between sprint and feature. Running largely alongside the FIA F3 series, the original schedule also featured a return to Sochi, which was canned as soon as the Russian invasion of Ukraine became reality. Eventually, that round was replaced by one at Paul Ricard, shoehorned between the Austrian and Hungarian events, to keep the European portion of the schedule at 11 rounds, sandwiched between flyaways in Bahrain, Saudi Arabia and Abu Dhabi. Imola returned for the first time since the old GP2 Series days, while Zandvoort made its belated debut after falling victim to Covid-19 in 2020 and then being scheduled as an F3-only event in 2021. Likewise, Barcelona, Austria, Hungary and Belgium all returned after a year off the rotation, with five back-to-back combinations featuring across the year.

Testing gave a hint of what was to come during the season as Drugovich set the fastest time of the final day of three in Bahrain. The Brazilian's pace wasn't the fastest of the test, however, and he was prevented from improving in the sixth and final session when it was cancelled due to a sandstorm and low visibility. A day earlier, Lawson had posted what would become the benchmark lap of the test, the first driver to duck under the 1m 42s barrier to finish atop the day-two times, as the majority of teams opted to use the afternoon session to run qualifying simulations.

Drugovich remained at the top of the times in the first official practice session of the season, but it was Doohan, who had failed to crack the top ten in practice, who claimed a first F2 pole to add to the points he had scored in two end-of-season outings with MP Motorsport in 2021. The Australian made the most of a tactic too few seem to employ, capitalising on an almost empty Sakhir circuit to post a 1m 40.542s lap – extending Virtuosi's record of claiming pole at the opening round to four straight years – while the majority of the field were otherwise occupied in the pit lane. Meanwhile, Drugovich only made the top ten by the margin of 0.008s, but at least would have the benefit of starting at the front of the grid in Saturday's sprint race once the top ten had been reversed.

The Brazilian would line up alongside former MP Motorsport man Verschoor on the grid for the shorter of the weekend's two races, but it was the Dutchman who would leave with the spoils. It was a case of 'last in, first out of the gate' for Verschoor, who had secured his deal with Trident later than anyone else on the grid, but then found himself in the ideal position to claim top spot in the opening race. Vaulting past the slow-starting Drugovich and then making a perfect safety car restart, Verschoor remained in front throughout to claim Trident's first win at the level since GP2, although Daruvala tried his best to cut into the Dutchman's advantage after a mid-race VSC.

There would be no win for Sunday's pole-sitter either, as Doohan along with front-row partner Pourchaire both fell victim to a lightning start by Vips. Ahead by the first corner, the Estonian immediately looked favourite to take all 25 points, only to be undone by a slow mandatory pit stop when victory had appeared to be his for the taking. Doohan's chances of recovering to top spot were also undone in the pits, the Aussie clashing with Pourchaire in the race to rejoin and breaking his front wing. Pourchaire, who had been forced to retire from the sprint, escaped without damage and would go on to claim victory – and the points lead – from Lawson, with Vips recovering to a fine third.

While the accompanying F3 series got a break to reflect – and test – before its second round, the F2 circus immediately decamped from one emirate to another, setting up shop on the Jeddah corniche in Saudi Arabia. Again, it was Drugovich to the fore in free practice, and this time he also clinched the fastest time in qualifying. With red flags interrupting proceedings again, Drugovich literally saved his best

Above: Drugovich leads the field on his way to winning the feature race at Monaco, his fourth victory from the first ten races.

Top right: Marcus Armstrong celebrates his win at the Red Bull Ring.

Above right: Much was expected of Frederik Vesti, but the Danish driver could only manage a couple of wins for ART Grand Prix.

Right: Williams junior driver Logan Sargeant was paired with Liam Lawson at Carlin. They were pretty evenly matched throughout the season, with the American taking wins at Silverstone and the Red Bull Ring.

Photos: XPB Images

for last to dislodge Verschoor and Doohan, and claim his first pole position in almost two years.

With Doohan banished to the back of the field, Hauger and Hughes would line up on the front row for Saturday's sprint race, and the reigning FIA F3 champion showed his potential by twice getting the jump on the pack. The next time the race was suspended, however, proved to be Hauger's undoing, since he was hit with a stop-go penalty amid confusion as to whether the pit lane was open under the safety car. Then Williams, Hughes and Lawson took turns to lead, and the last only needed to survive a single lap at the third and final restart to take his first win of the year, completing a trio of 2022 podium visits in neat 3-2-1 fashion. Vips, from third on the grid, also got the better of Hughes in the latter stages, but worse was to come for the Briton, as his car failed post-race scrutineering and was disqualified, allowing Drugovich (from tenth at the start) to inherit the final podium place ahead of Williams and Verschoor.

The Brazilian made no mistake as the lights went out to start the feature race on the following day, leading from the front and eventually winning by 2.3s. Behind him, Verschoor started and finished second, unable to get the jump either at the initial start or by making the pit-stop overcut work to his advantage.

Remarkably, the final step of the podium went to Daruvala, who had played the alternate strategy of starting on the medium Pirellis best of all, rising from 13th to finish ahead of Hughes, who employed similar tactics in rising from ninth to fourth. From the back of the grid, Doohan headed Vips in the final two scoring positions, but both Pourchaire and Lawson, having run third, left empty-handed after retiring, giving Drugovich a useful points advantage heading back to Europe.

Almost exactly halfway between Jeddah and round three at Imola, the teams returned to the track for only their second test since the turn of the year, running for three days at the Circuit de Catalunya-Barcelona, where Drugovich topped the times during sun-blessed qualifying simulations on the third and final morning.

The sun failed to follow the paddock east to Imola in time for the start of round three, and persistent rainfall at the Autodromo Enzo e Dino Ferrari resulted in both Friday sessions being pushed deep into the evening. With the rain returning in earnest shortly before qualifying, it was surprising that only one red flag was required as Vips claimed his first F2 pole by just over a tenth from Iwasa.

Conditions had improved slightly by the time the sprint-race grid lined up on Saturday afternoon, and it was Armstrong who made the better getaway from the front row as pole-man Sargeant bogged down. While the American dropped to fifth, his Australian rival – despite losing communication with his pit crew – then aced both a safety car restart and VSC equivalent to retain his advantage over Daruvala on the run to the flag. Behind the Prema driver, Hauger rose to a maiden F2 podium, ahead of a best ever fourth for Nissany, while Drugovich took fifth ahead of Sargeant, Pouchaire and Lawson.

Sunday morning's feature race was also run on the slick Pirellis, with the usual division of strategies up and down the grid. Again, the pole-sitter made a poor start, as Vips was passed by both Nissany (from sixth) and Boschung, who had lined up two spots ahead of the Israeli. Nissany was unable to stretch his legs immediately, however, as the safety car was required to clear up after a clash between Hauger and Doohan – who had hoped to bounce back from his Jeddah woes – and again to cover the removal of Vips's car almost as soon as the race had gone green once more.

Tyre changes from soft to medium under the second safety car helped shape the result of the race, Pourchaire emerging with a net lead once Nissany, who had also stopped early, crashed out. With Lawson also bailing with three laps remaining, Drugovich became the last man to pit as the race ended under another safety car, but only managed tenth as Pourchaire claimed his second feature win of the year, and the championship lead. Meanwhile, Fittipaldi (from 15th on the grid) and Boschung, on the same strategy, had been propelled into podium positions.

Drugovich having topped the times in testing at the Circuit de Catalunya not six weeks previously, it came as little surprise to see him at the head of the practice session times on the Friday of race weekend, but the MP Motorsport driver was unable to put it all together in qualifying for the Barcelona race, coming in only tenth fastest in a session that was only decided when Vips fell 0.023s short of Doohan on a last-ditch lap. Behind the Estonian (who had made his F1 practice debut with Red Bull Racing earlier in the day), Vesti, Daruvala and Sargeant rounded out the top five, with Pourchaire seventh.

Although his best lap had been more than half a second slower than Doohan's pole mark, and a subsequent three-place penalty for impeding Pourchaire meant that he would start from fourth in Saturday evening's sprint event, Drugovich was not going to be denied a second win of the campaign. Leading by the first turn, the Brazilian was unfazed by an early safety car and then proceeded to reel off the laps until he saw the chequered flag some two seconds ahead of Iwasa, with Sargeant having moved up to claim his maiden F2 podium.

Pourchaire was a distant fifth, behind Daruvala, allowing Drugovich to reclaim the points lead, and the Brazilian further extended his new-found advantage by completing a round-four double on Sunday. Despite starting from the outside of row five, Drugovich made a risky strategy work, taking his soft-shod opening stint further than anyone imagined possible before making a late stop for fresh rubber and hunting down leader Doohan for the win. While he appeared to have left nothing to chance in pursuit of his first victory at this level, Doohan simply had no answer to his rival, having pitted five laps earlier, and had to settle for second, ahead of Vesti, Sargeant and Novalak, while Pourchaire managed only eighth.

There was little time for either Drugovich or Pourchaire to reflect on their changing championship circumstances – the Brazilian now leading by 26 from his closest rival – as the second back-to-back of the season took the field immediately to Monaco. After a ballot determined that the traditional qualifying groups would be split into odd- and even-numbered cars, the first of the two sessions boiled down to a shootout between Drugovich and Lawson, which initially appeared to have gone the Australian's way after his rival had hit the wall in his effort to keep up. Subsequently, however, the stewards determined that both Lawson and second-placed Iwasa had failed to slow for yellow flags covering the incident and, in penalising the pair, inadvertently promoted the hapless Drugovich to pole, as the second group failed to produce similarly rapid times. As a result, the championship's top two would line up on the front row for its blue riband event after Pourchaire had set the Group B pace prior to a session-ending red flag brought about by Hughes, who would go on to claim reverse-grid pole for the sprint.

As it happened, the Briton was unable to cash in on his good fortune, stalling at the start and handing the advantage to Hauger. The Norwegian wasn't about to waste the opportunity and, having overcome an early safety car interruption, proceeded to pull fully six seconds clear of the chasing pack, which was headed throughout by Prema team-mate Daruvala, with Armstrong completing the podium. Pourchaire took the points for sixth to close back in on Drugovich, who failed to score after sustaining a first-lap puncture.

There was no such misjudgement on Sunday, however, as the championship leader took his advantage to new heights with a fourth race win, and third in four races. Withstanding the pressure of starting alongside his main rival – and winner of the corresponding race in 2021 – Drugovich converted pole into a lead that he would not lose, even if it meant en-

Above: Sauber Academy driver Théo Pourchaire claimed three wins in a season when he took on a reserve F1 role with the Alfa Romeo team.
Photo: Alfa Romeo ORLEN

Top right: Jehan Daruvala's only win of the season came in the feature race at Monza.
Photo: Red Bull Content Pool/Getty Images

Top far right: Series veteran Ralph Boschung bounced in and out at Campos Racing.

Above right: No wins, but Enzo Fittipaldi made six trips to the podium, including this one in Hungary.

Above far right: Estonian Jüri Vips lost his Red Bull patronage in controversial circumstances, but he came good with a win at Monza for Hitech.

Centre right: Marcus Armstrong took three wins, but only one further podium during a frustrating year for the New Zealander.
Photos: XPB Images

Right: Young Japanese hotshot Ayumu Iwaza showed tremendous speed throughout the season and was rewarded with a win in the finale at Yas Marina.
Photo: Red Bull Content Pool/Getty Images

tering a game of rubber roulette with Pourchaire that resulted in the pair pushing their tyres to the limit in the latter stages.

Finishing behind the top two in Monaco appeared to energise Vips, as the Estonian topped both a truncated free practice session and qualifying two weeks later in Baku. Lawson had to settle for second this time around, while Hauger – also on the up after Monaco – claimed third. For the second event in a row, Hughes found himself on reverse-grid pole for the sprint race, but although he didn't stall this time, Daruvala took the lead into the first corner. The Indian would lead until the inevitable safety car, but a lock-up allowed Vesti to take advantage. The race finished under yellow flags after a multi-car crash at Turn One, with Drugovich claiming fifth and Pourchaire seventh.

Once the field had gathered itself after the chaos, it was ready to do it all again on Sunday, starting with an opening-lap accident that required the immediate intervention of the safety car. Another appearance was required amid multiple incidents after the pit-stop window opened, and the race finished under Bernd Mayländer's control after Vips crashed out of the lead at the narrowest part of the circuit while under pressure from Hauger, handing victory to the Norwegian. Sargeant and Drugovich duly completed the podium, which, with Pourchaire sustaining damage and missing the points, allowed the Brazilian to strengthen his championship advantage further.

Sargeant quietly rounding into form set up the American perfectly for the series' return to Silverstone, where he'd secured back-to-back pole positions during the F3 double-header in 2020. The Carlin driver set the pace from the off, topping practice before laying down a qualifying pace few could match, even though the field was closely packed in his wake. Daruvala's tenth place put the Prema driver on sprint-race pole, but on a damp-but-drying track, tyre management became the biggest factor in determining the result, and it was Doohan who came through to win, even as Iwasa was closing in. Fittipaldi hung on from Pourchaire to join the rookies in their celebration.

After moving up from tenth to seventh on Saturday, Sargeant was ready to create another bit of history in the feature and, having already become the first American pole-sitter, duly dominated from pole to become the first to claim victory in FIA F2. Unfortunately, his success was largely overshadowed by a frightening accident that only added to the merit of the originally unloved halo device. On this occasion, Nissany was both instigator and victim as an unsafe return to the track at Vale tagged Hauger into a moment of his own, the Prema machine being launched over a kerb and striking Nissany's at head height. Fortunately, neither driver was seriously injured, but the incident went viral in the four-lap period it took the safety car to release the pack once more.

Sargeant, meanwhile, remained unfazed, pacing the field on the restart and opening enough of a gap that his pit stop could pass off untroubled. Although Pourchaire got back within DRS distance of the American towards the end, Sargeant had him covered, crossing the line 1.6s clear of his rival. Lawson claimed the final step in a Carlin 1-3, having snatched third on the opening lap, while Drugovich limited his losses to Pourchaire by passing Vesti for fourth on the final tour.

As the season passed its halfway point, Drugovich sat on a 42-point lead over Pourchaire, 148–106, with Sargeant's Silverstone success having lifted him above Daruvala and into third, although still around a feature win adrift of second overall. There was little time for the drivers to work out the implications of the standings, however, as round eight was just days away. Hughes and VAR went fastest in a red-flag-interrupted Austrian practice session, but it was Vesti who claimed pole later in the day, edging Vips – recently dropped by Red Bull over the use of a slur during a video game session – by 0.035s, with Sargeant continuing his surge in third.

Armstrong would start the sprint race from the very front and, without the need for a safety car, proceeded to lead from lights to flag to claim his second win of the campaign, just over a second clear of Pourchaire. The Frenchman clawed back a couple more points in the title fight, despite Drugovich nipping at Doohan's podium place during the closing stages.

Saturday's sunshine was replaced by trickier conditions ahead of Sunday's feature race, leaving the grid divided over tyre choice. Almost all those at the front, no doubt mindful of not throwing away their hard-fought qualifying advantage,

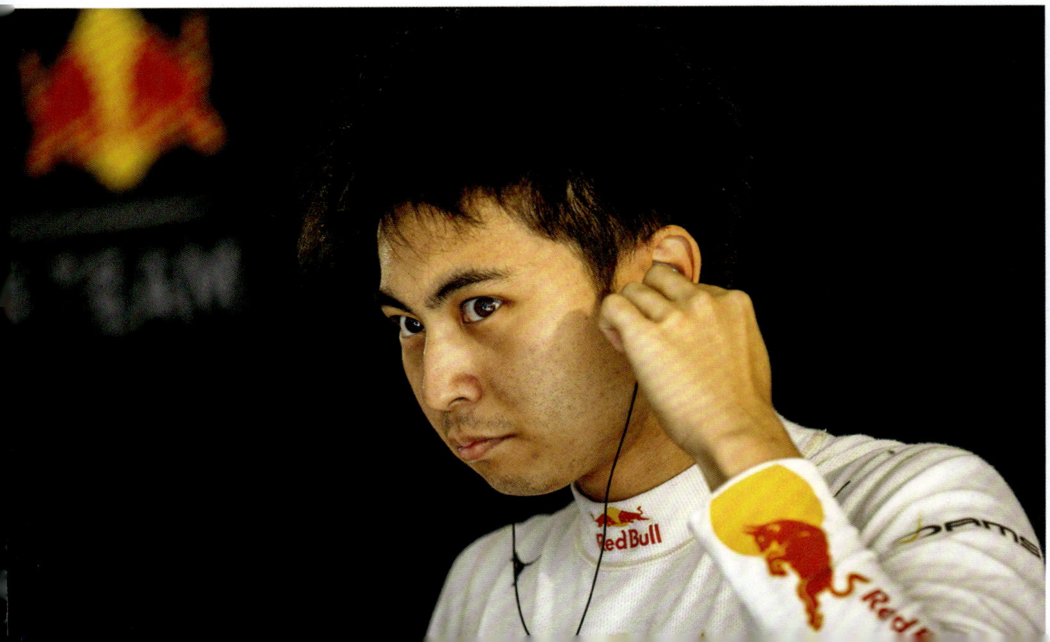

opted for the safer course of action, but taking a chance proved the correct bet, with Verschoor fairly galloping through the front-runners to win – on the road – by nearly 14s.

The Dutchman was joined on the podium by Daruvala and Sargeant, the latter the best of those to have started on wets, but there was still drama to come at the front of the field, as Verschoor and Daruvala were removed from first and second – for failing to provide a fuel sample and drying their grid slot respectively – promoting Sargeant to his second consecutive feature-race win. The American, who gained significant ground in the standings, was joined at the top of the revised result by Fittipaldi and Roberto Mehri, the Spaniard fumbling a fairy-tale win for both team and driver as, having started 21st, he fell foul of track limits shortly after taking second from Daruvala…

Drugovich's non-score in Austria was only his second such result in 2022, while a penalised sixth in qualifying at Paul Ricard two weeks later didn't ease his mood, especially as Sargeant was beginning to loom in the championship battle. Grabbing pole in France only set up the American for another decent haul of points, and the Carlin team's potential was further underlined by Lawson taking the sister entry to victory in the sprint race. Initially, Pourchaire thought he had held off Drugovich for third, until the stewards intervened and punished the Frenchman with a driving-standards penalty for a forceful pass on Armstrong.

Pourchaire was able to make some amends for his sprint error the following morning when, starting from fifth, he charged through to claim runner-up honours in the feature, although his gains were limited by Drugovich securing fourth. Between the two title contenders, Vesti held on to his starting position, despite increasing pressure from Drugovich in the latter stages. There was no one to rival race-winner Iwasa, however, who, having capitalised on a poor getaway by pole-sitter Sargeant, fairly bolted away from the field to beat Pouchaire by over eight seconds.

France to Hungary is not a route usually followed by motorsport's premier travelling circus, but regardless of the detour, Iwasa remained the man to catch, only ceding top spot in practice by 0.001s to Doohan before blasting the field with a scintillating lap in qualifying. While the DAMS team

Above: Liam Lawson led the Carlin challenge, taking four wins in a successful season that put him third in the final standings.

Top right: The Red Bull junior driver moves to Japan in 2023 to further his promising career.
Photos: Red Bull Content Pool/Getty Images

Above right: Jack Doohan was hoping his affiliation with Alpine would lead to a full-time F1 ride in the future.
Photo: XPB Images

Centre right: Sheer delight for Drugovich after securing the F2 title at Monza. The newly-crowned champion secured a full-time test and reserve driver role at Aston Martin for the 2023 season.
Photo: Lukas Gorys

Right: In Japanese Super Formula, the title was retained by Mugen team driver Tomoki Nojiri.
Photo: Japan Super Formula

celebrated, former driver Armstrong had to settle for second in his Hitech entry, with Drugovich and Pourchaire again hard to separate as they filled row two from Sargeant and Vips.

Doohan started the sprint race on pole and, apart from the run to Turn One, led from start to finish after Fittipaldi locked up into the corner, also allowing Vips to gain a spot. Further back, Sargeant and Hauger were forced into retirement after a three-way moment that also included the championship leader, who somehow escaped terminal damage and piled up points in fourth.

Pourchaire, frustrated at missing out on Saturday, poured it all into Sunday's feature, going forward from his second-row spot while his title rival went in the opposite direction. Again, tyre choice was divided after overnight rain, but Pourchaire would remain first to the finish, despite light precipitation, with Fittipaldi pipping pole-man Iwasa for second, having nursed his original soft rubber as far as it would go. With Drugovich sinking to an eventual ninth, the points difference between the contenders closed to just 21 heading into the four-week summer break.

The return to action would come under similarly grey skies at Spa-Francorchamps, where Drugovich took the bonus points for pole, while Pourchaire languished in eighth with a lot resting on his sprint-race result. Unfortunately for the Frenchman, not only did reverse-grid pole-sitter Boschung get away well, but also the absence of the other front-row starter, Daruvala, allowed Lawson to capitalise from fifth, diving through to take second into La Source before sailing into the lead at the top of the hill. With Doohan moving to third, the rest of the field became bottled up behind Verschoor, prompting the MP Motorsport crew to react radically when Sargeant spun out, pitting Drugovich for fresh soft rubber in a move that the Brazilian used to carve his way to fourth, two spots ahead of Pourchaire.

Things wouldn't get any better for the ART driver either, as a gearbox-induced retirement from the feature race left him at the mercy of whatever result Drugovich could achieve from pole. The only reprieve for Pourchaire was the Brazilian's inability to resist a charging Doohan, as the Virtuosi team made the undercut work in his favour, with Lawson overcoming a slow tyre change to complete the podium from Verschoor and Sargeant.

Spa marked the start of three rounds in as many weeks for the F2 field, which pitched up at Zandvoort on the opening weekend of September, only to see Doohan lead practice and Drugovich claim another two points for pole. Sargeant, Verschoor and Iwasa completed the top five, but there was no sign of Pourchaire, who had crashed out of the session before the second runs and would have to come from 16th if he was to stop Drugovich from putting one hand on the title.

A single point from the sprint was not enough for the Brazilian to start celebrating, but with Pourchaire trailing home 20th after a second-lap brush with the gravel, it was enough to extend his advantage. At the front, Armstrong got a better jump than pole-man Novalak, and the top two remained unchanged to the end, coming home ahead of Hauger as all found passing hard on the twisty confines of the Dutch track.

Pourchaire and the ART team knew they had to try every trick in the book to find a way of slowing Drugovich's march to the title, opting for an alternate strategy for the feature race – only to have their tactic thwarted by a series of accidents that started with Sargeant crashing out on lap one, bringing out the red flags. While Drugovich and Doohan had headed the field into the pit-stop window, the reappearance of the safety car afterwards scuppered not only Pourchaire, but also the ambitions of Lawson, Armstrong and Vesti, as the individual circuit rules prevented stops from being taken under such circumstances. Subsequently, Doohan was forced out in a series of later incidents, and the race headed towards a timed finish that resulted in Drugovich being joined by Verschoor and Iwasa on a podium that was enjoyed by the massed ranks of Dutch fans.

If Drugovich were to clinch the crown at Monza, he would have to do it from the disadvantage of a five-place penalty, picked up for setting his best qualifying lap under yellow flags covering the crashed car of Iwasa at Parabolica. The Brazilian had posted the fourth-best time of the session to sit behind pace-setter Doohan and fellow antipodeans Lawson and Armstrong, but having started from 12th rather than seventh in the sprint, he found himself in the thick of the mêlée and

failed to complete the opening lap after a clash with Cordeel. Sensing an opportunity, Pourchaire pushed to make up places, but only made it as far as 11th before running out of road. Unable to score points, his title ambitions were over, allowing the spectating Drugovich to become Brazil's first second-tier champion since Bruno Junqueira in 2000.

"When you start racing, you always have a dream of being in F1, but then, going through [the ranks], you realise how difficult it is to be an F2 champion, and that becomes a dream as well," Drugovich reflected. "Since a kid, I was already dreaming about this moment, so it's such an unreal feeling to be here, but for sure, this is not how I expected [to win] it. I had no idea what I was going to do without F2 this year, but I think, for sure, this title will open up a lot of opportunities for me, an, hopefully one day I can be in F1."

The championship drama overshadowed Vips's first race win of the year, as he had remained out of reach of Vesti and Daruvala, with Sargeant fourth, the American now with his sights set on a possible F1 seat with Williams. Monza also proved to be good for Daruvala, as he finally found the top step in a feature race dominated by drama from the start. The Indian was involved in the incident that ended Doohan and Sargeant's weekend, but escaped serious damage to remain out front. Pourchaire, too, exited early, caught up in an incident with Boschung and DAMS stand-in Luca Ghiotto, but Vesti escaped the carnage to bring home another second-place finish, this time ahead of Fittipaldi (from 15th on the grid) after Iwasa was removed from third over a technical non-compliance.

Although the individual title had been decided, the F2 paddock could not pack up and go home after Monza, with the now-traditional season finale scheduled for Abu Dhabi more than two months down the road. The wait gave Iwasa time to mull over his disqualification, and he came out fighting at Yas Marina, pacing practice and then claiming his second pole of the season. Remarkably, he was joined on the front row by DAMS team-mate Nissany, while Pourchaire and Drugovich again found themselves together on row two.

The entire weekend proved to be good for those in Red Bull colours, with Lawson waiting out a red-flagged opening to the sprint before seeing off pole-sitter Verschoor by almost eight seconds. Meanwhile, Drugovich moved up from the outside of row four to complete the podium, ahead of row-two starters Hauger and Cordeel, while Sargeant took another step towards his F1 superlicence in sixth.

Although he still had to wait for official confirmation that he was to replace Nicholas Latifi in the top flight, the American earned the necessary paperwork with fifth in the feature, but was a sideshow as Drugovich took his search for a sixth and final victory right to the wire, hounding pole-sitter Iwasa all the way. Lawson came through to claim both the final podium position and third in the final standings by a point from Sargeant, but there would be no happy send-off for Pourchaire, whose mid-race meeting with the local wildlife did not end well for either.

Drugovich might not have bowed out on the top step, but his second place was enough to cement MP Motorsport as teams' champion, eight points clear of Carlin, whose brace of top-five finishes was enough to leapfrog ART, with reigning champions Prema only fourth.

As in 2021, some 29 drivers made at least one appearance in FIA F2 in 2022, some predominantly in stand-in roles, and often with multiple teams, as in the case of David Beckmann. Three drivers – Cordeel, Caldwell and Nissany – fell foul of the FIA's penalty points rule and had to sit out a round, while others failed to see out an entire season. In all, 23 of the 29 scored points, with 12 different race winners and four others making at least one podium appearance. Fittipaldi, eighth overall, was the highest-placed driver not to see the chequered flag first.

JAPANESE SUPER FORMULA

JAPAN'S F2 equivalent, running under the Super Formula banner for a tenth season, also marked the 50th year of premier open-wheel racing in the country. The title was retained by Tomoki Nojiri, who became the first driver to defend a title successfully since Tsugio Matsude in 2007 and 2008. This time around, however, Nojiri's Mugen team also claimed the teams' title for the first time after running a two-car assault featuring Ukyo Sasahara alongside the champion.

With points from all eight rounds counting in the 2022 season, the two Mugen drivers took a brace of wins apiece, with Nojiri triumphing in round two at Fuji and then closing the season out – with the titles already won – with a second victory in the Suzuka finale. His win ensured a clean sweep of the finale after Sasahara had added his own success to victory in round six at Fuji.

Sasahara's other results were not enough for him to keep pace with his team-mate over the course of the season, with French interloper Sacha Fenestraz (Kondo Racing) claiming second overall, just two points clear of series veteran Ryo Hirakawa, despite the Carenex Team Impul driver winning two races to his one. Former F2 pilot Nobuharu Matsushita (B-Max Racing), Naoki Yamamoto (TCS Nakajima Racing) and Hirakawa's Carenex team-mate, Yuhi Sekiguchi, claimed the remaining race wins, but none finished ahead of the more consistent Ritomo Miyata (Kuo Vantelin Team TOM'S) and Tadasuke Makino (DoCoMo Team Dandelion Racing) in the final standings.

The 2021 season's runner-up, Nirei Fukuzumi (ThreeBond Drago Corse), languished down in 19th overall after a nightmare campaign that resulted in four DNFs and a disqualification, leaving him tied on just three points with the other *gaijin* in the series, Giuliano Alesi (Kuo Vantelin Team TOM'S).

F3 REVIEW by CRAIG LLEWELLYN

TO VICTOR, THE SPOILS

Above: ART Grand Prix's Victor Martins emerged as the Formula 3 champion, having shown admirable consistency in a season that produced no fewer than 11 different winners.

Top right: Argentine Franco Colapinto celebrates on the podium after his sprint-race win at Monza.

Above right: Martins shows his joy after being confirmed as champion, following a chaotic race at Monza.
Photos: XPB Images

Centre right: After three early-season podiums, Red Bull's Jak Crawford scored a sprint-race win in Spielberg.
Photo: Red Bull Content Pool/Getty Images

Right: Spaniard David Vidales scored his only win on home soil, at the Circuit de Catalunya.
Photo: XPB Images

A SEVEN-WAY battle for the title heading into the final round of the 2022 FIA Formula 3 Championship was more than even the most invested individual could have imagined when the series kicked off in March, but it provided the perfect culmination for one of the more closely-contested campaigns in recent memory.

With the expected new chassis having been put on hold due to post-Covid cost-saving measures, nine of the ten teams found themselves on familiar ground when it came to technical matters. The tenth, former F3 giant Van Amersfoort Racing, would start slightly on the back foot, having purchased the assets of the HWA Racelab outfit at the end of the previous season, but it possessed the experience to quickly get to grips with the venerable Dallara F3-2019.

While the car remained the same, the 2022 calendar displayed some expected changes from the previous year. Perhaps in tacit admission that splitting the F2 and F3 schedules for a season hadn't worked, the two series were back in the same paddock for 2022, with the junior partner reverting to double-header rounds (from 2021's timetable-filling triples) at nine venues on the F1 circuit.

Reverting to the familiar sprint and feature-race format, the F3 season opened on new ground in Bahrain and Imola, while Silverstone and Monza returned in place of Paul Ricard and Sochi. Changes were also made to the sprint-race scoring system, which now rewarded the top ten finishers in single-point increments, while the previously high-powered bonuses for pole and fastest laps were cut in half, from four and two points respectively.

With two members of its triumphant 2021 line-up – Jack Doohan and Clément Novolak – having graduated to F2, and the third, David Schumacher, having moved to the DTM, Trident would field an all-new trio of drivers for 2022, bringing Red Bull Junior Jonny Edgar over from Carlin, and teaming him with Formula Regional European graduate Zane Maloney and F3 veteran Roman Stanek, now entering his third season at this level.

Previous champion Prema countered with two changes of its own, as both 2021 champion Dennis Hauger and team-mate Ollie Caldwell had stepped up to F2. While Arthur Leclerc remained on board for a second campaign, Prema brought in Red Bull protégé Jak Crawford and promoted Ferrari Academy member Oliver Bearman, who had cruised to the 2021 ADAC and Italian F4 titles with the team.

Perennial title challenger ART Grand Prix also had to field two new faces to partner Juan Manuel Correa, who continued his return from serious injuries sustained in F2 at Spa in 2020. The seats vacated by Frederik Vesti – who had finished fourth overall in 2021 – and Alexander Smolyar would be filled by reigning Formula Regional European champion Grégoire Saucy, already a member of the ART programme, and Victor Martins, who effectively swapped places with Smolyar in moving over from MP Motorsport.

Martins was the highest remaining driver from the 2021 season, having edged Smolyar by one spot in the table, with Leclerc and Caio Collet (MP Motorsport) the only other top-ten points finishers to return. Carlin, Hitech Grand Prix, Campos Racing and Jenzer Motorsport all required fresh line-ups, signing, among others, Red Bull Junior Isack Hadjar, 2020 British F3 champion Kaylen Frederick, reigning UAE F4 title holder Enzo Trulli and new GB3 champ Zak O'Sullivan.

Meanwhile, Van Amersfoort reunited with former Euroformula Open charge Rafael Villagómez, who had raced in FIA F3 with HWA in 2021, and signed up series newcomers Franco Colapinto (Formula Regional European) and Reece Ushijima (GB3) for their first campaign.

An all-British front row to the opening race, generated by the familiar reversal of the top 12 times from qualifying, resulted in new boys O'Sullivan and Bearman battling early on, but while the former faded, Bearman raced on to claim what

he thought was a debut victory – until the stewards intervened with a track-limits penalty, which promoted Hadjar to his own first-time success and Smolyar to the podium.

Meanwhile, Martins ended race one on the sidelines, having come together with team-mate Saucy at Turn One while battling over eighth place. With Saucy and Kush Maini both having picked up penalties between qualifying and the feature race, however, the Alpine protégé found himself elevated to the inside of row two for Sunday's longer event. Having passed front-row starter Stanek at an early safety car restart, Martins then sat on pole-sitter Colapinto's tail for 14 laps before eventually taking control. Leclerc completed another strong recovery drive in second from 13th on the grid, and there was further disappointment for Colapinto as a maiden F3 podium became fifth thanks to his own track-limits penalty, allowing Saucy to join team-mate Martins in the top three.

Colapinto's form, which continued through to in-season tests at Valencia and Barcelona, was rewarded just a couple of weeks later when he came out on top of a frantic sprint race at Imola. VAR's rookie started from pole courtesy of the partially reversed grid, but in the midst of three safety car interruptions, both lost and regained the top spot in a battle with Collet, eventually securing the win a lap from home. Subsequently, Collet collided with a feisty Hadjar and posted a DNF, while Martins and Crawford completed the podium, split by just 0.06s as they took the chequered flag.

Starting from the outside of row six on Sunday, Colapinto was unlikely to repeat the success of the day before, but in damp conditions, the VAR driver was one of those on the move in the early stages, joining the similarly wet-shod Collet in carving through the field. From ninth on the grid, Collet vaulted into a four-second lead within the space of a lap, only for the first of several safety car appearances to negate his advantage. As the leaders took the opportunity to pit for slicks, front-row starters Maloney and Stanek returned to the head of the field – only to be overhauled once again by the charging Collet.

When Maloney spun out at the head of the next safety car pack, Bearman briefly seized the upper hand, but eventually ceded the lead to Stanek as the remaining podium positions became the focus of a five-car battle. Crawford quickly overhauled Bearman for second, but Saucy's attempt to do likewise ended with the pair colliding at the final corner of the race, which dropped Bearman to fourth behind Hadjar, while Leclerc – again needing a stellar recovery drive, this time from 21st – completed the top five.

Despite not featuring in the podium fight as he recovered from 29th to 11th, Martins continued to lead the drivers' standings into the short break before round three in Barcelona, and the championship positions were mirrored when the action resumed at the Circuit de Catalunya, with Martins ending practice fastest from Leclerc, Stanek and Crawford. Come qualifying, however, and it was Stanek to the fore, adding a maiden pole to his Imola victory, while Martins held firm in P2.

While the reversed grid allowed home favourite David Vidales to beat Crawford and take sprint-race victory for Campos Racing, the main story centred on another Martins retirement and Leclerc, whose fourth-place finish behind Collet was enough for him to assume top spot in the points.

Martins wasn't going to go quietly, however, and a great start to the feature allowed the Alpine Junior to slipstream past Stanek at Turn One and, after two safety car restarts, pull a couple of seconds clear to claim his second feature-race win of the season. Stanek spent the morning looking mostly in his mirrors before ultimately resisting the attentions of Hadjar, who had to settle for third. Meanwhile, Leclerc blew his chance of retaining top spot in the standings, as a poor getaway dropped him into the pack before a series of erratic decisions eventually resulted in a penalised 16th, while Stanek took up the points pursuit of Martins.

With rounds more evenly spread than in recent seasons, it was only a matter of weeks before the paddock reconvened at Silverstone, where opening practice produced an enticing mix of points leaders and those with 'home advantage'. The theme continued into qualifying, where O'Sullivan surprised the pack by emerging fastest to claim not only his first pole at this level, but also a first for a Carlin team synonymous with success. Leclerc gave his chances a boost with a front-row spot, but the top ten was also peppered with former British championship runners in Maloney, Frederick and Maini.

Martins' 11th on the grid might not have looked ideal for another big points haul on Sunday, but the Frenchman made the most of a front-row spot in the sprint to jump pole-man Ushijima off the line and assume a lead that was only erased by the appearance of a safety car, which allowed Hadjar to surge around the outside of the ART driver on the penultimate lap. That left Martins to fend off Ushijima, who claimed his maiden F3 podium.

The safety car also intervened on Sunday, but could not stop Leclerc from taking his only win of an otherwise up-and-down season. The Monégasque needed two attempts to pass O'Sullivan, but was able to control the race from the front, leaving the pole-sitter to fend off compatriot Bearman by just 0.051s at the flag. Martins salvaged seventh place from row six, and with Stanek forced to retire after contact with Saucy, it was Leclerc back up to second in the points, now ahead of Hadjar, who added fifth in the feature to his win on Saturday.

For the first time all season, the teams faced a quick turnaround, with the British and Austrian grands prix running back to back. It proved to be no hindrance to Hadjar, however, who, once everyone had attempted to find a tow conducive to a good lap time, gave Red Bull a pole position on home soil. He was joined on the front row by countryman Martins, with Bearman – another to carry his Silverstone form to Austria – heading Leclerc and Frederick in the top five.

Collet's 12th place in qualifying enabled him to hold the initial lead in the sprint race, but Correa was quick to seize the advantage on the opening lap. Any hopes of a dream victory were dashed five tours later, however, when the ART coasted to a halt, handing the lead back to Collet, while Crawford moved past Colapinto for second. With Leclerc, Bearman and Maloney causing a second safety car period, the American was given an unexpected shot at the lead, and he wasted little time in taking it to claim his first F3 win, coming home ahead of Collet and Colapinto.

Seventh on Saturday left Martins with the knowledge that he had to get something from Sunday morning's feature, but although he started from the front row, there would be no third win for the Alpine protégé. Instead, it was pole-man and compatriot Hadjar who stole the show, producing a virtuoso wet-weather performance to overcome a safety car and ensure that he was never headed en route to a first feature.race win, and a second for Red Bull drivers across the weekend. Behind him, Martins retained a slim points advantage – now by one point over Hadjar

Above: Trident's Zane Maloney produced a strong run of results towards the end of the year, including three wins. The Barbadian finished five points shy of Martins in the title race.
Photo: XPB Images

Top right: Williams-backed youngster Zak O'Sullivan visited the podium at Silverstone and Zandvoort.
Photo: Williams Racing

Above right: Red Bull Junior driver Isack Hadjar's season tailed off after three wins, which had made him appear a serious championship contender mid-season.
Photo: Red Bull Content Pool/Getty images

Centre right: A win at Silverstone for Arthur Leclerc, who enjoyed Ferrari Academy backing as he followed in the footsteps of brother Charles.

Right: In wet conditions, Alexander Smolyar took the honours for MP Motorsport in Hungary's feature race.
Photos: XPB Images

– as Bearman held off Prema team-mate Leclerc to complete the podium.

Bearman's second third place in a row was a portent of things to come, although it was Smolyar, racing under a neutral flag, who claimed pole in a red-flagged Hungarian qualifying session blighted, again, by track-limits violations that left Maloney, Bearman, Leclerc and Saucy to round out the top five.

Having missed an opportunity to open his FIA F3 victory account in Austria, Collet was in no mood to let another slip through his fingers, arguing over second with Hadjar for the first part of a largely wet race that had started behind the safety car, before capitalising on a Colapinto error to take the lead as those behind ran into trouble. Maini charged through to eventually claim third, and a maiden F3 podium, from Hadjar, with Bearman gaining most from a collision between Prema team-mates Leclerc and Crawford to finish fifth, ahead of Martins, Saucy and series debutant Oliver Goethe.

The feature race also started on a damp track, allowing pole-sitter Smolyar to pull away once he had survived two- and three-wide passing attempts at the opening corners. With the track drying beneath him, the MP Motorsport driver's only concern appeared to be whether he needed to consider slicks, but such was his lead that he never made the change. Those who did – and did so at the right time – were reaping the rewards in Smolyar's mirrors, however, with O'Sullivan rising from 17th to fourth in a matter of laps – including passing Maini, Leclerc and Crawford on the final tour – and Correa doing likewise to take sixth. Around them, Maloney and Bearman fought over second right to the line, with the Bajan holding on by 0.025s to net his best result of the season.

Quiet through the Austrian and Hungarian weekends, Ushijima opened a few eyes with a stunning practice lap that put him over a second clear of the pack as times tumbled at Spa-Francorchamps, but the Japanese-American couldn't better 16th in qualifying as the rain returned with a vengeance between sessions. Instead, it was Collet who made the best of the conditions, timing his final lap perfectly to claim pole and the bonus points that accompanied it. Maloney, whose own late effort temporarily took top spot, had to settle for second, ahead of Charouz Racing System's Francesco Pizzi, whose only notable performance to that point had been squeaking tenth out of the Imola sprint race. The topsy-turvy nature of the session was highlighted further by Leclerc heading the championship leaders – in 20th! Hadjar and Martins would share row 12, while Crawford was consigned to the very back after spinning out of the session.

The sprint race started with Hungaroring stars O'Sullivan and Correa on the front row, but contact at Les Combes led to both dropping down the order, briefly promoting Carlin's Brad Benevides into the lead until Bearman – who had started fifth – swept by down the Kemmel Straight. The race was neutralised at that point for barrier repairs after a heavy collision between Goethe and Maloney, who had been battling over sixth at the time, but a good rolling restart allowed Bearman to retain his lead ahead of Stanek and Smolyar, in second and third respectively. Edgar should have finished in the top three, but a five-second penalty for spinning Colapinto on lap one came back to haunt him, as he was relegated to fourth, just ahead of a charging Leclerc.

Hadjar's ninth-place finish was enough to promote him ahead of Martins overall, the ART man finishing a lowly 21st after being penalised for an alleged jump start – and worse was to come, as contact from Maini in the feature left him unable to do anything about his championship situation. The Frenchman got off lightly, however, as the leading quartet's qualifying struggles ensured that Leclerc (11th), Hadjar (14th) and Crawford (17th) also went home scoreless.

This was the race, therefore, that marked a changing

of the guard in the title fight, with Bearman climbing from eighth on the grid to grab a second podium of the weekend at the expense of Goethe on the final lap. The Briton was not alone in making a play for big points, however, as Maloney – his car having been rebuilt overnight – overcame having to hand back the lead after passing Collet while off the road at Les Combes to return to the front and take a first win for the nation of Barbados at the head of a Trident 1-2. Goethe was fourth in the final cameo appearance.

With the drivers who led the championship when it arrived at Spa all failing to add significant points – Leclerc and Hadjar managed six and two respectively from the sprint – Bearman's consistency, which had quietly allowed him to score six podiums among ten points finishes from the 14 outings to date, promoted him over Martins to second spot and just a single score from pulling level with Hadjar. Only five points separated the top four, however, with Martins, Leclerc and even Stanek holding on to title ambitions as the series moved into the second part of another back-to-back.

At Zandvoort's return in 2021, Martins had claimed his first win at this level, but it was form-man Maloney who ultimately annexed pole position ahead of the ART driver this time around, with Crawford, Stanek, Colapinto and Hadjar next up. Meanwhile, Bearman had it all to do from P14 in both races, while Leclerc would need to fight back through the field again, having also been caught out by a late red flag.

An all-ART front row for the sprint race didn't last long, although pole-man Correa did what he could to resist the fast-starting Collet for a lap or so. Without a safety car interruption, the Brazilian was able to ease away to a four-second victory, while Correa claimed his maiden F3 podium ahead of O'Sullivan. Crucially, Martins made it into the points, rising from 11th to seventh by the flag, while his major rivals all failed to add to their totals.

Maloney wasn't included in that group as the series hit the Netherlands, but by the time it was packing up and thinking of the Monza finale, the Bajan was most definitely in the frame. Despite losing top spot in the feature to Martins early on, he drove patiently before reclaiming the lead and, having survived the inevitable safety car breaks, held on to land his second successive win in the high-points race, moving into the top five overall. Martins held off Colapinto to the line for 18 points and a return to the top of the championship table, while Stanek, Hadjar and Crawford kept themselves in the hunt with fourth, fifth and sixth respectively.

With the principal results having been shared throughout the season, seven drivers retained a mathematical chance of lifting the title as the F3 paddock set up just a week later at the Autodromo Nazionale – and nothing could be decided in the sprint, ensuring the battle would go to the wire on the final Sunday of the season.

Bearman, having had his tenth-place finish at Zandvoort commuted to 25th by a post-race penalty, was the first to show at Monza, claiming top spot in another wet-dry practice session by 0.048s from Hadjar, but it was Smolyar who claimed pole, coming out on top of a qualifying session that had been cut in two by a lengthy red flag after Hadjar had crashed heavily at the Parabolica. With a tow essential to a notable time, Maloney kept up his good run by slotting into second, ahead of Stanek, while Martins, Leclerc and Bearman ensured that the title fight remained hot by taking fourth through sixth, with Crawford eighth.

The close nature of qualifying left Colapinto to pick up the reverse-grid pole, and the Argentine wasn't about to waste an opportunity to bolster VAR's solid debut season. Leading from start to finish, his main concern was the safety car, but behind him, the title contenders were in the thick of it. While Bearman raced forward to finish a very close second – following a scintillating double pass on Edgar and Collet to take the position – and Maloney strengthened his claim in fourth, Martins and Leclerc made contact on the opening lap, necessitating fight-backs to score points, while Hadjar's nightmare continued with the need for a new front wing. Crawford, despite being sixth on the road, dropped out of contention.

Despite coming home 27th, Hadjar remained Martins' closest rival with one race remaining, but Bearman's second place closed the gap to the top spot to just 13 points, with Maloney and Stanek five further back. Leclerc remained an outside bet, but he needed Lady Luck to ride aboard his Prema entry.

As expected, with the contenders all bunched towards the front of the grid, no quarter was given in the feature race, even between team-mates. Out front, Martins, Smolyar and Malonely all took turns to lead, while further back, Prema partners Leclerc and Bearman were going wheel to wheel until the Monégasque tangled with Stanek, dropping both down the order and opening the door for another Bearman charge. The Briton was on it immediately, catching and passing Martins for second while eyeing up a move on Maloney for the lead.

Then Maini and Benavides crashed out at the second Lesmo, and the season ended five laps early, under cover of a red flag.

With no restart, the only drama remained with possible post-race penalties, but despite picking up a five-second slap for exceeding track limits, which dropped him off the podium, Martins remained untouchable in the points, eventually clinching the championship 139–134 over Maloney, who duly ended the year with three straight feature-race wins. Bearman was only a couple more points adrift in third overall, ahead of the hapless Hadjar and Stanek, who had been ninth and sixth on the road respectively when racing was suspended.

"I knew I had the car, the consistency and the team behind me, and the potential to do it," Martins reflected, having dedicated his title to the late Anthoine Hubert, with whom he had shared time at Renault's academy. "I was trying to manage things a bit too much early in the season, and losing points because of it, so for the last two rounds, I said 'Give it everything, just push and not think about the championship,'

Above: Spa feature-race winner Zak Maloney is flanked on the podium by Trident's serious-looking Roman Stanek and Prema's Oliver Bearman.
Photo: XPB Images

Top right: Dino Beganovic took the Formula Regional European F3 title for Prema.
Photo: Ferrari Media

Above right (left & centre): Arthur Leclerc started his season in fine fettle by claiming the F3 Asian title, just pipping prodigious young talent Pepi Marti.
Photo: F3 Asian Championship

Above far right: Art Grand Prix's Gabriele Mini battled for honours with Beganovic in the European series.
Photo: Art Grand Prix

Centre right: Luke Browning emerged as top dog in the renamed British GP3 series.
Photo: Britsh GP3

Right: Japan's Miki Koyama made history by becoming the first female driver to win an FIA-sanctioned Formula Regional title.
Photo: Japan Regional F3

Far right: Rookie Noah Sands (Gilmour Racing) was on target to take the Australian F3 title with races to spare.
Photo: Australian F3

and that's how it's ended. To go right to the end reflected a season full of ups and downs."

The seven final-round contenders shared 12 of the 18 possible victories between them, with Maloney matching Hadjar's season-leading three, although the Bajan's all came in feature races. Bearman's consistency, with one win among eight podium finishes, earned him third overall, while Stanek, Leclerc and Crawford all managed a win apiece. Stanek and Crawford enjoyed four and five total podium appearances respectively, but Leclerc's ability to hang in the title race came from seven top-five finishes, often from lower grid positions, to add to his three podiums.

With Smolyar victorious in Hungary's feature, the season's other wins, all in sprint races courtesy of the reversed grid, went to Colapinto (2), Collet (2) and Vidales, while a further five drivers – O'Sullivan, Correa, Maini, Saucy and Ushijima – made at least one podium appearance each. Goethe deserves mention, too, for narrowly missing out in Belgium on only his second appearance.

Although the teams' title fight also went all the way to the last race of the season, Prema's ability to thrust all three of its drivers into the scrap for individual honours eventually paid dividends, as the Italian operation regained the trophy from Trident by 54 points. ART Grand Prix remained third in the standings, albeit 93 points adrift of second, with MP Motorsport and Hitech Grand Prix completing the top five.

In all, 40 drivers took part in at least one round – a figure boosted by Charouz's running no fewer than seven different names, six in the No.15 car alone – while 27 managed at least a point across the nine double-headers.

With the F2 season extending through to the F1 finale in Abu Dhabi, there was little in the way of graduation news for the F3 pack. However, Bearman's stellar debut season had already earned him a slot in Prema's senior team, and It is inconceivable that Martins won't find a ride in the higher series, while Maloney was handed the keys to Trident's F2 car for the season finale (as was Correa at VAR). Crawford and Hadjar are both likely to step up with Red Bull for 2023, when a revised ten-round F3 campaign will visit both Melbourne and Monaco for the first time.

ROUND-UP

PRIOR to returning to the FIA F3 Championship, Arthur Leclerc (Mumbai Falcons) took a first career title by seeing off the threat of Spaniard Pepe Marti in the winter's Formula Regional Asia series. Although 16-year-old Marti took the Monégasque to the final round in Abu Dhabi before accepting defeat, and duly claimed the Rookie Cup, he was a relative non-factor in the FIA F3 series, finishing 26th overall courtesy of two points picked up at the Monza finale. Isack Hadjar (Hitech GP) finished third overall, ahead of team-mate Gabriele Mini and Dino Beganovic (Mumbai Falcons), while Khaled Al Qubaisi (Abu Dhabi Racing by Prema) claimed the Master Cup crown.

Mini and Beganovic would lock horns again throughout the summer as they chased the Formula Regional European title. Tied on points in the final Asian standings, it was Sweden's Beganovic (Prema Racing) who came off best closer to home, eventually taking the championship by 40 points courtesy of no fewer than 12 podium finishes. Mini (ART Grand Prix) reached the top three on nine occasions, but only secured second overall by a single point from Beganovic's team-mate, Paul Aron, who racked up a season-leading six race wins, with Hadrien David (R-ace GP) and Kas Haverkort (VAR) rounding out the top five. Unlike the main championship, the Rookie Cup went all the way to the wire, with Leonardo Fornaroli (Trident) holding on in the face of a late charge from VAR's Joshua Dufek.

The other Formula Regional series, in Japan and the Americas, both ran later into the year than their European counterpart, with Miki Koyama (Super License) creating history in the former by becoming the first female driver to win an FIA-sanctioned Formula Regional title. Koyama had to wait until race five of the season, at the second triple-header in Okayama, to claim her first win, but then took five on the bounce before adding two more for good measure in the penultimate round at Fuji. At the time of writing, the series had a December double-header at Suzuka still to run. The enigmatic 'Hirobon' likewise wrapped up the Masters class with eight wins in the 15 races run to date.

Raoul Hyman (TJ Speed Motorsports) made his own unique mark on the American series, the South African having returned from a two-year hiatus to claim the crown with races to spare and earning himself a Honda-backed Super Formula seat in Japan for 2023. Hyman's margin of victory was 81 points over American Dylan Tavella (Crosslink Kiwi Motorsport), with TJ Speed team-mate Jason Alder third.

As his brief foray into the FIA F3 series hinted, Oliver Goethe could be a name to reckon with in 2023, the Dane wrapping up the Euroformula Open title at the season finale in Barcelona. Running with series stalwart Team Motopark, Goethe took 11 wins from 27 races, with seven further podium appearances. Closest rival Vladislav Lomko and third-placed Aussie Christian Mansell (both CryptoTower Racing) were regular podium finishers, but they trailed the champion by 57 points in the final reckoning.

The final true international F3 series, the women-only W Series, once again went the way of Jamie Chadwick (Jenner Racing), the Briton having taken a hat trick of titles across a Covid-interrupted four-year span. More dominant than ever before, Williams F1-affiliated Chadwick piled up five straight wins to open a season that took the field to Miami and Singapore, as well as more traditional European venues before Alice Powell (Click2Drive Bristol Street Motors Racing) and Beitske Visser (Sirin Racing) found their way to the top step. Chadwick was 50 points clear of the Dutch driver when series organisers cancelled the final two flyaway rounds in Austin and Mexico City on financial grounds, following the loss of a potential sponsor.

The British F3 series, now in its first full year under the GB3 banner, included an 'away day' at Spa-Francorchamps among its eight triple-header rounds, while drivers had to get to grips with an updated chassis and engine package. The title fight went to the wire as Luke Browning (Hitech GP) and Sweden's Joel Granfors (Fortec Motorsport) duked it out, but the Briton's five wins and seven second places from 24 outings proved insurmountable.

Tom Lebbon (Elite Motorsport) edged fellow countryman Callum Voisin (Carlin) for third overall, but both were well adrift of the champion, despite multiple trips to the top step of the podium. Brazil's Roberto Faria (Fortec) was fifth, despite being unable to find his winning form from 2021, but there were champagne moments for Matthew Rees (JHR Developments), Americans Max Esterson (Douglas Motorsports) and Bryce Aron (Hitech), Canada's Nick Gilkes (Hillspeed), Douglas Motorsport's Australian duo of Tommy Smith and Marcos Flack, Denmark's Mikkel Grundvig (Fortec), and Britons Cian Shields (Hitech) and Brandon Lee Oxley (Chris Dittman Racing).

Japan's Super Formula Lights went the way of Kazuto Kotaka (TOM'S), who edged Kakunoshin Ohta (Toda Racing) by just six points in the final reckoning, despite taking eight race wins to his rival's four. Nobuhiro Imada (B-Max Racing Team) retained the Masters Cup by a relatively more comfortable 17 points from 'Dragon'.

The Australian F3 Championship was run in earnest for the first time since 2019, after two Covid-blighted campaigns bit the dust. As AUTOCOURSE went to press, the Gold Star class was being led comfortably by rookie Noah Sands (Gilmour Racing) with one triple-header round remaining. Likewise, the National class was all but sealed by Roman Krumins (R-Tek Motorsport Services), who enjoyed a 130-point lead over his nearest rival.

Finally, the Drexel Automotive Formel Cup – previously the Austrian Formula 3 Cup – was claimed for a seventh successive season by Sandro Zeller (Jo Zeller Racing), who was well ahead of Canada's David Richert (Franz Woss Racing) and Tomas Chabr (Chabr Motorsport) of the Czech Republic after the Mugello finale. Benjamin Berta (Team Hoffmann Racing) of Hungary won the Formel 3 Open class.

The Macau Grand Prix was again the preserve of the Chinese F4 series rather than an international F3 event.

FORMULA E REVIEW by SAM SMITH

SIMPLY THE BEST

Above: Stoffel Vandoorne brought all his years of experience to bear, his calm and methodical approach bringing rich rewards.
Photo: Mercedes-AMG

Top right: The season got under way in Saudi Arabia, where defending champion Nyck de Vries fired the opening salvo with a race-one win.

Above right: ROKiT Venturi's Edoardo Mortara and Lucas di Grassi celebrate their 1-3 finish in Riyadh.
Photos: Formula E

Right: Porsche was untouchable in Mexico City, where Pascal Wehrlein and André Lotterer gave the Stuttgart team its maiden Formula E win.
Photo: Porsche

IN years to come, it might be tempting to view Stoffel Vandoorne's 2022 ABB FIA Formula E Championship success as a kind of electric version of Keke Rosberg's 1982 F1 title win. The constituent parts of it are not dissimilar. A single victory in a 16-round season and an emphasis on consistency abounded for both. But perhaps the single most significant trait is that each fully deserved their silverware because, pound for pound, over the course, they were clearly the best performers.

Vandoorne was in his fourth Formula E season and his third with Mercedes. He'd long since banished the misery of his career nadir at McLaren over the course of 2016–18 and instantly became engaged with a brand-new all-electric world in conjunction with some sports car outings and occasional F1 support work with Mercedes.

Having turned 30 in March, Vandoorne had matured noticeably into a polished professional. He had been popular in the Mercedes EQ set-up from the beginning, and he had an air of title favourite from the very start of the season.

Yet the fact was that over his then three-season stint, he had mustered just two victories, in Berlin in 2020 and Rome a few months later. He'd also watched team-mate Nyck de Vries converting a crazy 2021 campaign to his advantage, although Vandoorne was universally accepted as at least his equal in capability, if not in good fortune.

During the 2021/22 off-season, the Belgian had toyed with IndyCar and been given a test with Arrow McLaren. At that stage, he also knew that the Mercedes Formula E advantage would be ending at the end of the 2022 season. That was because the three-pointed star had taken the decision to pour all of its resources into F1 and seemingly disregard its automotive strategy to go all-electric by 2030 (where market conditions allowed).

It should have set a volatile scene for Vandoorne, but none of that was on show. In fact, quite the opposite, as Mercedes embraced the more stable qualifying format that rewarded the quickest drivers, rather than the most fortunate through circumstance.

This related to a necessary change to the previous 'tombola-style' system, which had pooled drivers into groups by dint of their championship points position from the previous round. Instead, a new World Cup-style knock-out programme was drawn up, whereby the four quickest drivers from two 12-car sessions would form quarter-final, semi-final and a final to decide the order of the top eight

The new arrangement played nicely into Vandoorne's hands, and immediately he began to thrive in the high-pressure sessions, honing a mostly effective qualifying strategy to ensure a strong average grid start. At the very first round in Riyadh, however, he was beaten again by team-mate de Vries, who took victory after Vandoorne messed up his attack-mode boost deployment by missing the crucial in-track transponder loop.

While this could have knocked others off their stride, Vandoorne didn't panic and executed his own calculated drive to ensure only a second ever Merc 1-2.

With Mercedes-powered cars also locking out the top four positions, as ROKiT Venturi's duo of Edoardo Mortara and Lucas di Grassi followed, the omens for a Mercedes cakewalk looked foreboding for the opposition.

Twenty-four hours later at the same track, it was Mortara who reigned supreme, the Swiss/Italian now having to be described as an ex-firebrand after maturing noticeably since his series debut in 2017. He overtook a sluggish de Vries to nail his third EPrix victory, leading home Envison's Robin Frijns and team-mate di Grassi.

Curiously, Mercedes EQ faltered, with Vandoorne fading to seventh and de Vries to a dispirited tenth. After the dominance of the day before, this was hearty encouragement for the likes of Riyadh underachievers Jean-Éric Vergne (DS

Techeetah) and Mitch Evans (Jaguar TCS), who were little more than bit-part players in the Saudi desert. This was significant, because as the season panned out, both of these drivers forged a serious title challenge to Vandoorne. In addition, Mortara made it a 'gang of four' from relatively early on.

Crucially, though, the paltry points score of Evans and Vergne in that first weekend in Riyadh set the tone. Vandoorne simply hit his straps sooner, and although at the third race in Mexico, he non-scored after being punted off in the Foro Sol stadium by an over-eager di Grassi, this proved to be the Belgian's only non-score of the season.

Mexico City was all about Porsche and its breakthrough win. Pascal Wehrlein and team-mate André Lotterer completely dominated at the Circuit Hermanos Rodriguez, leaving the opposition gasping more readily amid the thin air of the imposing Autodromo.

For Wehrlein in particular, there was a redemption of sorts after he had had a debut victory in 2019 cruelly snatched away on the finishing line by a more energy-rich Lucas di Grassi, then with Audi. This time, the former Manor and Sauber F1 driver made sure with a sublime performance, and Lotterer followed him home for a long overdue big result for the Stuttgart marque, which had entered Formula E two years before. Although it had ticked off milestones with a debut pole at Riyadh in 2019 and then a podium soon after, it had massively underachieved since, finishing seventh and eighth in its first two seasons in the all-electric category.

Mexico changed all that, and for a fleeting moment, it seemed that Porsche could mount a title challenge. That was a complete false dawn, however, and despite being close to the ultimate pace, a litany of errors and subdued races dulled the Mexican joy.

But on that day in February, Wehrlein totally dominated the encounter from the front, with Lotterer riding shotgun. The dominance was such that the team elected to stretch the race an extra lap, and in doing so, compromised several rivals who in part had gambled on Porsche backing off

Above: Mitch Evans ruled in Rome, the New Zealander taking both race wins for Jaguar.

Top right: Evans and his team pose for a celebratory photo after their double.
Photos: Formula E

Above right: Stoffel Vandoorne took the honours in Monaco, but only after misfortune struck Pascal Wehrlein.
Photo: Mercedes-AMG

Centre right: Wehrlein's season never really recovered after his disappointment in Monte Carlo.
Photo: Porsche

Centre far right: Envision Racing's Robin Frijns and Nick Cassidy were also kept busy in sports and GT racing throughout the season.

Right: Jean-Éric Vergne leads André Lotterer and Jake Dennis at the start of race two in Rome. Two second places for the Frenchman, at this race and in Jakarta, were his best results of the season.
Photos: Formula E

in the final lap so as not to risk an extra circulation of the 45-minutes-plus-one-lap timed race.

One of the victims was Mitch Evans, who faded badly with critical energy levels on the final tour. That meant one of the pre-season title favourites had but a single point from the first three rounds and was seriously on the back foot, as Mortara led with 43 to his name.

As ever with Formula E, its weak point was the calendar. While new races in Jakarta and Seoul were introduced for 2022, the planned Vancouver EPrix became a car-crash that played out in real time. As the paddock gathered in Rome in April, word came that all was not well for the race that was intended to be part of a north American double-header in just ten weeks' time.

A shambolic breakdown of communications between the local promoters and city officials resulted in the necessary permits not being obtained in time, and initially the race was postponed, then cancelled. That meant that the Berlin race in May would become a double-header, but with ongoing Covid-19 disruption still rendering a planned race at Sanya in March impossible, there was a mammoth nine-week gap between Mexico in February and Rome just before Easter.

For Jaguar and Mitch Evans, this was a godsend. In that break, the Kiwi was finally able to visit family and friends back home in New Zealand, the first time he had been able to do so since the end of 2019! It proved to be a major tonic and played a large part in rejuvenating Evans, who arrived in Rome in an ultra-focused frame of mind.

Yet it seemed that his 2022 hoodoo would continue when he qualified a disappointing ninth after failing to get to grips again with the new brutally competitive qualifying format.

The race was a different matter, however, and conclusively so, as Evans eased to the front, picking off both Mercs, both DS Techeetahs, Andretti's Jake Dennis and the Audi-powered Envision driver, Robin Frijns.

Evans held such an advantage on the undulating Rome track – a kind of homage to the fearsome Monjuich Park street circuit in Barcelona – that he took the chequered flag over five seconds ahead of Frijns.

Aiming for a cut-and-paste performance a day later, Evans delivered again. This time, his qualifying was much better, and from fourth on the grid, he soon made short work of Vergne, Dennis and Lotterer to romp home for a rare Formula E double-bubble victory.

This win came with some crucial help from Jaguar teammate Sam Bird, who held off Vergne in the later stages to give Evans the buffer he needed to resist late-race pressure.

The mammoth 50-point haul meant that Evans leapt from the lower reaches of the 22-driver order to fourth. just nine points off new leader Vergne, who offered only a measured appraisal of his Roman adventures, which netted him a fourth and a second, the former having prompted memorable radio fury

"It was a bit of a mess at times," said the double Formula E champion. "We have to do better in the coming races and convert our promise into wins. It's all very well scoring points every race, but we need to get some big ones soon."

While Vergne was always there or thereabouts, that wish would never be realised, and despite being in strong positions such as in Rome, the black and gold of his side of the garage never took to the top step.

That disappointment, though, was nothing compared to Alfa Romeo F1 refugee Antonio Giovinazzi, who endured a kind of slow torture in his season with Dragon Penske Racing. He never looked particularly engaged with the backmarker team, and it ended with no points and with the Italian giving up in Seoul when he bruised his thumb in the first encounter. That allowed debutant Sacha Fenestraz to show more grit in one race than Giovinazzi had done in the entire season.

A second venture on the full Monaco track, this time with-

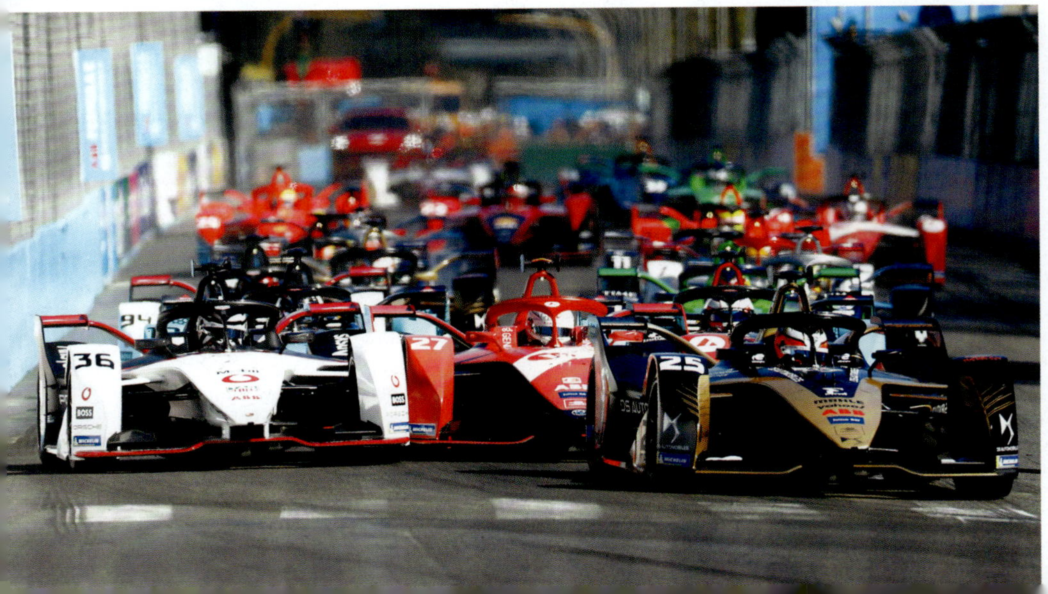

out the unnecessary tweaks to the harbour-front Nouvelle Chicane of 2021, brought another memorable EPrix to the principality in late April.

As well as Vandoorne's present, his future was a hive of speculation at this time. Knowing that his place in the Mercedes family would be limited at best, following its withdrawal from Formula E, he jumped early and signed a deal with DS to become Vergne's team-mate just prior to Monaco.

While not formalised publicly until later in the year, it ensured stability in his Formula E career after the uncertainty of the previous nine months in a championship that was feeling the full whirls and eddies of manufacturer hokey-cokey, which is so common in international motor sport.

With his long-term future assured, Vandoorne seemed to hit another gear as far as his title quest went. In Monaco, he was sublime, applying a deft race strategy that outfoxed rivals Evans and Vergne, and seizing the points lead again.

It should have been all so different, though, because by rights, Porsche should have been celebrating its second victory in as many rounds. Pascal Wehrlein had just been pipped to pole by Evans' Jaguar, but after the first of the attack-mode deployments, and just after he had taken and seemingly built an unassailable lead, his Porsche 99X Electric simply shut off on the descent from Mirabeau to the hairpin. It was a complex fault, which was traced to his car's inverter. That brought no relief, however, as his day was done and he was forced to trudge forlornly back to the paddock.

That left Vandoorne to maximise his fortune, and subsequently he was able to deploy his second attack-mode boost without losing the lead and then defend reasonably comfortably from a flying Evans.

Monaco was also notable for an intra-team flare-up between Venturi team-mates Mortara and di Grassi. They had been dicing for position in the lower reaches of the top ten when the Brazilian had glanced the left rear of Mortara's car, causing a puncture. The fact that Mortara had scythed his way through the field after a troublesome qualifying and that this was Venturi's home race tipped the normally unflappable Swiss/Italian over the edge.

"I had a close encounter with the butcher of Formula E," was Mortara's amusing, but deadpan comment later.

It meant that he lost some impetus in the title race, and Venturi boss and former EPrix winner Jérôme d'Ambrosio was forced to scold his drivers in private after what turned out to be the only spat between the two all season. The set-to had come as a surprise to many, as both drivers were in the higher echelons of the most combative in the series. Post-Monaco, whatever d'Ambrosio had done behind the scenes seemed to work.

Mortara's disappointment only lasted a couple of weeks, because at Berlin Tempelhof, he left everyone else floundering in the departure lounge.

Mercedes-powered cars had a clear advantage on energy management and vehicle dynamics upon the quirky bitumen-heavy asphalt at the location of the iconic Berlin airlift. From the very start of proceedings, Mortara banished the ghost of the previous season by waltzing to a pole and win in the first of the double-headers. Noticeably more efficient at piloting his car through the hairpins of the specially created airport circuit, he was in a different class entirely.

While Vandoorne and Vergne joined him on the podium, and Evans executed a damage-limiting drive to fifth, the 'gang of four' narrative that would run like a seam through the championship began to take shape.

The following day, Mortara took another pole, and the script seemed merely to duplicate that of the day before. Yet this time, the Venturi had a more durable challenger in the shape of reigning champion Nyck de Vries.

After his opening win in Riyadh, the Dutch ace had netted just 14 points, but also the ire of some of his rivals for excessively brawny defending. This was especially the case in Rome, where his name rang like a cursed bell throughout the mixed-zone interview area after both races.

Above: Edoardo Mortara takes control of proceedings ahead of Jean-Éric Vergne in Marrakesh.

Top right: Mitch Evans celebrates his triumph in Jakarta.
Photos: Formula E

Above centre right: Berlin brought more success for Mercedes, with a 1-3 finish for de Vries and Vandoorne in race two.
Photo: Mercedes-AMG

Above right: Mortara reaches out to the crowd after his race-one win at Tempelhof.

Right: Another new venue for Formula E, but Evans and Mortara continued to trade blows in Jakarta.
Photos: Formula E

On the Sunday of the Berlin double-header, however, flashes of the old de Vries converged to make a bright start, devoid of the erratic battle tactics. This was largely because he was much more comfortable with the brake splits that had stymmied his Saturday, and he was able to match Mortara for pace in the most crucial phases of the second encounter.

Such was de Vries' disappointing start to the season, though, that his Berlin success only took him to the outer edges of the Vandoorne/Mortara/Vergne/Evans group at the head of the table.

Robin Frijns was clinging gamely to those four, but his position in the team was fading after he elected to join the returning ABT team for 2023. This clearly unsettled both parties, and the normally phlegmatically benign Dutchman became an unhappy soul for the remainder of the season.

Vandoorne had driven perhaps the best effort of his season in the second Berlin race. He'd been there or thereabouts in qualifying, but was knocked out at the quarter-final stage by Vergne's DS E-Tense FE21, which was nimbler, especially in the first sector.

Still, eighth on the grid was decent. What wasn't decent was his start: he was shuffled back to 12th, remaining there until he was able to read the race and get a rhythm going. This he did expertly, picking off his prey brilliantly – Sam Bird, de Vries, Sérgio Sette Câmara, Jake Dennis, di Grassi, Evans and António Félix da Costa all fell to the silver scythe.

His move on da Costa at Turn One was especially sweet, and he also resisted becoming too involved with a fired-up Vergne, who was limbering up for some do-or-die heroics in the closing stages.

Vandoorne settled for third, but given his position in the first quarter of the race, it was an expertly achieved result, one that his engineer, Stephen Lane, professed to be "the best drive I've ever seen in Formula E."

The big news away from the track in Berlin was that effectively McLaren would be taking over the outgoing title-winning Mercedes EQ entry. Formula E founder and chairman Alejandro Agag had brokered a deal between Zak Brown and the remnants of the Merc team, and secured backing from one of its commercial partners, NEOM.

The transaction effectively ensured that the majority of the Mercedes team would move from the Brackley base that also housed the F1 squad to a new facility in Bicester by the end of 2022. But that is where the continuity ended, as both its race seats would change hands. Vandoorne's deal with DS was already done, while de Vries was exploring a variety of options, ranging from the Venturi team, which would become Maserati, to the Toyota Gazoo Racing FIA World Endurance Championship squad.

That was only the start of the options for the reigning champion, however, and while he did sign a planned deal with Maserati, all that became obsolete in September when he wowed the F1 world with his remarkable cameo for Williams. That set in motion a deal with AlphaTauri for 2023 and probably beyond.

Mercedes EQ team principal Ian James, who would be in charge of the new NEOM McLaren operation, acted swiftly and signed former Audi driver René Rast. At the time of writing, it seemed highly likely that the German would be joined by former F3 and F2 front-runner Jake Hughes, who had acted as a full-time reserve and development driver for Mercedes EQ throughout 2022.

Against many predictions, Formula E's first visit to Jakarta was a resounding success. The build-up to the event in early June had been troublesome, with a location change from central downtown to a beach resort north of the city. Come race day, however, a healthy crowd awaited the grid, and with terrestrial TV coverage in the city, all eyes were on the country's first international single-seater motor race since A1 GP had visited Sentul some 15 years before.

Held in almost unbearable humidity, the race was perhaps the best of the season, developing into a scrap between three of the four title contenders.

Surprisingly, Vandoorne was not in the cut and thrust of the battle as Evans, Vergne and Mortara duelled it out on the Jakartan streets.

Ultimately, the race came down to a magical move made by Evans on a surprised Vergne. He described it as "risky, but at the same time, it felt I had it nailed from the moment the opportunity came to me."

That was only one facet of his third win of the season, however. With the all-weather Michelins screaming in the mid-afternoon in Jakarta's furnace, he had a whole different challenge to contend with thereafter.

"The balance was incredible until the last five laps, where I started to really struggle with my rear tyres," said a drained Evans after the race. "This was challenging, as I needed to defend from Jean-Éric Vergne and Edoardo Mortara. Overall, the team delivered another amazing race for me."

With his title rivals second (Vergne), third (Mortara) and fifth (Vandoorne), the points situation was ultra-close, the quartet being covered by 12 points and Vandoorne heading Vergne by a mere five.

The looming massive seven-week break in the calendar, due to the Vancouver debacle, actually became four when Formula E's go-to super-sub race in Marrakesh, Morocco, was plugged in at short notice for the first weekend of July. It would be the start a seven-race odyssey that also took in New York, London and Seoul. Although the schedule was intense, ultimately it would shape where the title would land.

On the dusty streets of Marrakesh, Mortara channelled his Berlin form and took control from the first time he entered the track. Again, highly impressive on slow-speed sections, he produced a dominant win once again. Yet he had to fight for it due to the return of form that was being enjoyed by 2019–20 champion António Félix da Costa.

The DS Techeetah driver had been a bit-part player during the first half of the season, perhaps having become unsettled at the Sino-French operation after the financial taps had been turned off by the sports marketing business side of the squad's ownership.

This played a major part in pushing da Costa Porsche's way, a deal being forged between the two early in 2022, although it was not confirmed until just after the season's end.

Da Costa seemed to wake up just in time to assist team-mate Vergne's title credentials, but trying to orchestrate two cars in Formula E is far from a simple task. DS Techeetah had tied themselves in knots before, particularly at the Berlin finale weekend in 2021. They contrived to do so again on occasion in 2022, particularly in London. But in Marrakesh, pole-sitter da Costa was simply unable to match the flying Mortara. Despite losing some time being positioned with team-mate Vergne, second seemed to be the best that he could achieve.

Vandoorne's Marrakesh was a roller coaster. Trouble with the infamous brake-splitting issues, due to the spec material, niggled at most competitors at some stage in 2022. In Morocco, it was Vandoorne's turn, as he qualified a lowly 20th, having been dogged by brake locking. While in the previous season, that would have spelled disaster, in 2022's more meritorious racing, especially on a passing-friendly track like Marrakesh, the Belgian could make some hay.

So it proved, as he drove a stellar race to limit the damage of his title rivals finishing first, third (Evans) and fourth (Vergne) grabbing four crucial points for eighth.

The first of the three crucial double-headers took place amid the industrial landscape of Red Hook near Brooklyn, New York, a popular venue for the Formula E travelling circus due to its ferry-ride proximity to Manhattan. The disappointing news on arrival, though, was that the 2022 event would very likely be the last, due to land reclamation for the burgeoning cruise industry.

It posed another problem for Formula E, and at the time of writing, no 'Plan B' has been announced, meaning that the

Above: It's not quicker by train! Formula E throws up some quirky venues, none more so than London's ExCeL Arena.

Top right: New York car crash. Vandoorne's Mercedes is lifted out of the tangled mess after a number of cars slithered off the wet track, causing the race to be red-flagged.

Above right: Despite crashing in the abandoned race, Nick Cassidy was declared the winner.

Above far right: In race two in NYC, António Félix da Costa triumphed. It was the first win in over a year for the DS Techeetah driver.

Right: Lucas di Grassi scored his only victory of the season in the second race in London.

Photos: Formula E

first Gen 3 season, in 2023, looks set not to feature any US race, a situation that has been received with huge discontent by the stakeholders.

But if Formula E wanted to 'start spreading the news' in the Big Apple, it went about it in the most spectacular fashion on the first day of action.

Envision Racing's Nick Cassidy had effectively announced himself at the 2021 New York City EPrix with a superb pole position in an otherwise quiet debut season. A year on, and he did it again, scorching his Audi around the Red Hook track to maintain his 'King of New York' status.

He had appeared to be in total control of the race from a resurgent Lucas di Grassi and Vandoorne when a localised rain shower swept over the circuit with approximately 15 minutes of the race remaining. Such was the ferocity of the shower that it turned the track into what Cassidy described as "a wall of water", and he sailed haplessly into the Turn Six barriers.

While the impact was not especially vicious, what immediately transpired was initially sickening, as di Grassi and Vandoorne aquaplaned straight into the stricken Kiwi. Thankfully, he emerged unhurt, as did the other two. Heroically, a stranded da Costa, who had stopped with an issue on his DS a few laps earlier, rushed to the scene to help with the extrication of his rivals. It stood as one of the most uplifting scenes of the season.

While Cassidy, di Grassi and Vandoorne were clearly out of contention, Mitch Evans had come through the carnage in the top six after qualifying a lowly 14th, and with Mortara also having spun down the order and suffered damage, Jaguar were praying for a restart.

It never came. In a baffling twist, the FIA decided that, despite the race having started earlier than usual, it could not be concluded.

The decision was contentious, and it was rebutted by Jaguar. What it meant was that Cassidy, with a shattered car, won his first EPrix, while Vandoorne picked up 15 points to get to within five points of Mortara in the standings. For both drivers, however, there was little time for celebration as spare chassis were prepared for all-night rebuilds by their respective teams.

The following day, there would be drama for Cassidy. Remarkably, he took pole again in his rebuilt Envision Audi, but during his post-session live TV interview, he was informed by the presenters that he would be starting from the back of the grid. It was possibly the most uncomfortable moment of the season, and one that made something of a mockery of the championship in the full glare of the TV cameras.

It underlined a cruel sanction that could only be applied after the grid had been set, a grid that provisionally the Kiwi headed – in a new car that Envision had built around a spare chassis late the previous night. But mere minutes after the session, notification came that the replacement of the rechargeable energy storage system (RESS) pack and radiator damaged in Saturday's accident had triggered the penalty.

Although Envision Racing lodged an appeal, the facts were that this was the fifth RESS radiator used during the season for the No.37 Audi, and that was subject to the penalty under the regulations.

As a result, Cassidy was confined to the role of bit-part player in a race he had been convinced he could have won. One Kiwi's misfortune, however, triggered good luck for the other, Evans playing a central part in a thrilling Sunday race.

Ultimately, it was won by António Félix da Costa, who finally broke a 14-month victory famine for the DS Techeetah team by converting his second pole in three races to lead home Vandoorne and Evans.

The Jaguar driver had fought tooth and nail for his podium,

engaging in a tumultuous battle with de Vries. The Dutch driver defended stoutly on one occasion, forcing Evans off line on the bumpy back straight, which triggered the mother and father of all lurid moments under braking. In a supreme piece of car control, he caught the slide with armfuls of opposite lock and then booted the power around the following corner to send the raucous Big Apple wild.

After Evans cleared a briefly resurgent Alexander Sims' Mahindra, he was able to savour perhaps the hardest-won podium place of his entire career.

With Mortara and Vergne enduring self-confessed "nightmare" weekends in New York, where the former had registered a paltry five points and the latter none at all after a tetchy two days, the four title protagonists looked like being whittled down to just Vandoorne and Evans as they continued to accrue consistent points finishes.

London hosted perhaps the biggest and best EPrix of the season at the monolithic ExCeL Arena in the UK capital's East End. Although being the second visit for Formula E, it was the first to be attended by a full quota of fans, and it didn't disappoint.

Previous Formula E races had largely been confined to genuine city-centre circuits, like Paris, Santiago and Montreal. This time, however, the promoters turned on the stye with a flashy pre-race show and an engaging festival feel in the vast exhibition halls.

The unique nature of racing inside and outside the halls had been a novelty in 2021. A year later, with a modified circuit to do away with the ludicrously tight double-backed hairpins, which had been replaced by a quick double chicane, there was a sense that finally Formula E had found a home in London.

The track action lived up to the peripheral activity by re-crowning the acknowledged master of the all-action ExCeL track – Jake Dennis. The Avalanche Andretti driver had been the surprise star of 2021, winning two races, one at the inaugural London event. A year on, and he'd lost none of his potency, as he crushed the opposition comprehensively in the first event, almost casting the title race into the shadows as he did so.

Dennis had started the 2022 season brightly by being one of the best qualifiers and snaffling a podium in Riyadh. But from Rome onwards, his campaign fell away, possibly a legacy of the recalibrated team that was now devoid of its former total BMW support.

Although Dennis still enjoyed BMW power, the team was very much an independent one, with many new staffers settling in during the early season. This contributed to a dearth of points for Dennis, resulting in any notion of an unlikely tilt at the title being over by mid-season. He didn't let that get him down, however, and although his negotiations over a contract extension with Andretti for 2023 were long and complex, eventually he decided to stick rather than twist.

It paid off, because in the final two events of the season, he was one of the biggest points scorers, helping Andretti to vault their future powertrain and tech supplier, Porsche, in the standings.

In London, Dennis eyed a double after he took his second consecutive pole, but di Grassi had something to say about that as the two made the race their own. Ultimately, di Grassi triumphed after a slight miscalculation by Dennis on his final attack mode opened the way for him to take his first victory for Venturi.

While there was elation on one side of the Venturi pit box, there was dejection on the other. Mortara had self-sabotaged his first race with an erratic start and then a collision at the first corner, before not really turning up for the second. Mathematically, he all but cancelled himself out of the title hunt, as did Vergne, who was caught up in several incidents and registered his second consecutive double-header dud.

That left Vandoorne and Evans to fight for the prize in Seoul, but each of them had heart-stopping moments in London. Crucially, though, while Vandoorne was able to play

Above: Oliver Rowland leads the Envision Racing pair Nick Cassidy and Robin Frijns through a ridiculously tight chicane on Seoul's temporary Olympic stadium track.

Top right: Late-season joy for Jake Dennis as he takes the race-one win at London's ExCeL track.
Photos: Formula E

Above right: For Mercedes team principal Ian James, the championship was the culmination of years of dedicated hard work.
Photo: Mercedes-AMG

Above far right: A glimpse into the future. A mock-up of the third-generation Formula E car due to be raced in 2023.
Photo: Formula E

Right: A champion again at last. A hint of tears in the eyes of Stoffel Vandoorne, 2022's King of Formula E.
Photo: Mercedes-AMG

the percentage game to a point, Evans' second London encounter ended in a rare Jaguar retirement. An issue with an inverter component had stopped him while he was eyeing up Vandoorne for a crack at fourth place.

It was a bitter, yet familiar feeling for Evans, who had lost any chance of the title 12 months previously when an inverter issue had left him stranded on the starting grid, to be struck by Mortara.

The drama left Vandoorne heading to the first ever races in Seoul with a healthy 36-point cushion and the momentum firmly on his side. It could have been an even greater lead had team-mate de Vries heeded a team instruction to relinquish his third place in the closing stages at ExCeL. He wouldn't play ball, however, denying Vandoorne an extra three points, protesting on the radio, "Why? Give me one reason. He's got the points. I'm prepared to drive for Stoffel, but with three rounds to go and 25 points lead, I see no reason to give up a podium."

That left a tetchy atmosphere in the Mercedes EQ garage afterwards, but to be fair to Vandoorne, he didn't make a fuss over the matter, choosing instead to put full focus on getting the championship done.

So, it all came to the 1988 Seoul Olympic stadium at Jamsil in the Korean capital in mid-August. After nine months, the epic contest would be resolved once and for all.

Evans made a decent fist of extending the agony for Vandoorne with a well-crafted victory in the first encounter, after audaciously taking the lead from di Grassi on the first lap in treacherously damp conditions. He even controlled a restart after an early red flag, caused by no fewer than eight Formula E cars in the barriers after encountering soaked asphalt. But with Vandoorne relatively cruising to fifth, the gap was only reduced to 11 points. However, it did put extra pressure on Vandoorne and the Mercedes EQ team, with 29 points to play for on the final day of the season.

The nerves were palpable in the all-important qualifying, but the pressure switched to Evans after his drier set-up soon proved less than ideal on the highly technical and narrow Seoul track. When the Jaguar TCS driver glanced a wall, the title was effectively decided. He was forced to start 13th, while Vandoorne was comfortably ensconced in fourth.

The Belgian was always in control of the final round from the perspective of what he had to do to ward off any late challenge from Evans. In fact, he cruised to the silverware, even able to take another podium by following Jake Dennis home third on the road, but being safe in the knowledge that the Andretti driver had been docked five seconds for an earlier incident that had sent da Costa's DS spinning off the road.

Mortara offered some well-deserved redemption by equalling Evans' haul of four race wins with a final flourish for Venturi, which bowed out of Formula E at season's end as it metamorphosed into Maserati for 2023 and beyond.

Mercedes EQ also bade farewell, and in the best possible way by defending its titles brilliantly in its swan-song season. Savouring the adulation afterwards, team principal Ian James gave a fascinating perspective on the achievement, saying that the team had "set an internal target, it wasn't even communicated internally, it was almost just at board level. It was securing a first championship by season ten [2024], so to have done it in such a short space of time was pretty admirable."

That seemed remarkable in the context of what it had actually achieved, and the thought that Mercedes wouldn't stand atop the pile until its fifth season seemed incongruous. But they had become double champions, and all within three seasons. Seoul had the air of the end of an epoch, and with good reason.

The third-generation of Formula E car will herald the 2023 season, beginning in January, and while the cars are set to be faster, lighter and more technically interesting than ever, initially there will be a backdrop of turmoil and issues. Problems and accidents plagued the manufacturer's tests between June and December, 2022, and the long-awaited fast-charging pit stops will have to wait as a result.

That was only the start, however. By November, one of the project leaders and driving forces of Formula E had vacated

his position at the FIA. Frederic Bertrand was one of the most senior of the FIA's old guard, from a sporting perspective, and his move to replace Mahindra team principal Dilbagh Gill was seen with more than a bit of concern by Mahindra's rivals.

Practically, the Gen 3 car also had myriad problems to get over, and despite the hyperbole from the promoters, it is likely that it will not hit the ground running in 2023. A kind of hand-to-mouth situation with spares, the delayed introduction of fast-charging pit stops and some nervousness over RESS reliability could make it a season for Formula E to just get through, making the most of what it has.

Also new for 2023 will be a fixed total duration of the attack mode, which can be used in one of a predefined combination of periods of activation for teams and drivers. This will be introduced ahead of the fast-charging pit stops. The divisive Fanboost initiative of getting fans to vote for their favourite driver for an extra surge of power will be discontinued. With some drivers rumoured to be spending upwards of 2,500 euros per race weekend on collating 'bot votes', Fanboost will not be missed.

From an existential point of view, Formula E was also braced for some major decisions in the final weeks of 2022. The problems with the Gen 3 project management had left several manufacturers dissatisfied, Porsche being particularly vocal on the matter. With manufacturers having to work to double homologations, they are set until the end of the 2024 season, but as was seen with Audi, BMW and Mercedes in 2020 and 2021, manufacturers wait for no one.

Looking further ahead, rumours of clandestine meetings between Formula E chairman Alejandro Agag and F1 supremo Stefano Domenicali gathered momentum in the first two quarters of 2022, but then seemed to peter out. Word was that at one stage, some form of future amalgamation might occur. That now seems unlikely due to F1's accelerated global popularity and Formula E's constant struggle to gain a larger and more engaged audience.

Overall, Formula E had a reasonably strong year in 2022, compared to its *annus horibilis* of 2021, when the energy debacle of Valencia and the races at a shabby Puebla showed this vibrant and immensely competitive championship in its worst light. If the issues with Gen 3 can be overcome, there is little doubt that other manufacturers could be attracted to the championship.

Equally, if its first season of a fresh epoch reveals any of the old Formula E problems, such as the inconsistent calendar, and not getting the basics of the cars and technology right, then it will start to operate on thin ice as far as a genuinely credible world championship is concerned.

ROLEX
ROLEX
ROLEX
MICHELIN
24h LE
ROLEX
ROLEX
ROLEX
DENSO
DENSO
MICHELIN
AISIN
RAYS
MICHELIN
Mobil 1
8
HYPER CAR
HAYASHI
MICHELIN

SPORTS & GT REVIEW by GARY WATKINS

TOYOTA'S TREASURE

Above: The start of the 2022 WEC season at Sebring, with the winning Alpine edging ahead of the Glickenhaus-Pipo of Pla, Dumas and Briscoe.
Photo: WEC

Above right: The Alpine driver trio of André Negrão, Matthieu Vaxivière and Nicolas Lapierre, outright winners in two races – Sebring and Monza (pictured here).

Top right: Dipping their toes in the water? Team Penske's LMP2 entry, with drivers Dane Cameron, Felipe Nasr and Emmanuel Collard, finished eighth in class at Sebring and later fourth in class at Spa-Francorchamps. After Le Mans, however, Penske withdrew from the series to concentrate on its LMDh programme for 2023.

Right: The race having been stopped three times, Toyota reasserted its authority at a rain-soaked Spa, where the No.7 GR010, driven by Mike Conway, Kamui Kobayashi and José María López was victorious.

Opening spread: Toyota triumphed at Le Mans once more. Winners Sébastien Buemi, Brendon Hartley and Ryo Hirakawa pose for the photographers.
Photos: WEC

TOYOTA picked up all the shiny baubles on offer in the World Endurance Championship in 2022. For yet another season, the Japanese marque maintained its stranglehold on the drivers' and manufacturers' titles, and made it five wins on the trot at the Le Mans 24 Hours. Yet it would be wrong to say that Toyota had everything all its own way in the second season for its Le Mans Hypercar. In 2021, it had taken a clean sweep of the six WEC races. This time, it won only four and went into the final weekend of the season equal on points with its only full-season competitor. Alpine, represented by the French Signature team with its downspecced Oreca LMP1 design, made a fight of it.

Sébastien Buemi, Brendon Hartley and Ryo Hirakawa, in his first season with the the team, claimed the title in Bahrain aboard their Toyota GR010 Hybrid, and admittedly with some ease courtesy of a solid second place behind their team-mates in the sister car. The Alpine-Gibson A480, which had formerly raced in the WEC as the Rebellion R-13, wasn't in the game over the eight hours of the championship finale in November. Yet there were races over the course of the season where the roles were reversed, and the French car driven by Nicolas Lapierre, Matthieu Vaxivière and André Negrão had the advantage over the Japanese LMH contender.

A see-sawing Balance of Performance sometimes put Alpine at the forefront of the pack and sometimes left it nowhere. What the rule makers, the FIA and WEC promoter the Automobile Club de l'Ouest, were trying to achieve wasn't exactly clear: they never explained their intentions or just how competitive they thought an old car 'grandfathered' in from the P1 category should be against the new breed of LMH machinery.

Their ideas certainly didn't conform to the generally held notion that such grandfathered machinery should be there to pick up the pieces if the new cars hit problems. At the Sebring 1000 Miles season-opener in March, back on the schedule after a two-year COVID-enforced hiatus, the Alpine had a clear advantage over both the Toyota and Glickenhaus-Pipo 007 LMH, the only other entry in the slender four-car Hypercar class.

The lighter Alpine, with more downforce to boot, was always going to be better suited to the bumpy surface of the Florida airfield circuit, or so argued Toyota. It claimed that the BoP didn't take into account the unique circuit characteristics after the Alpine took a clear victory. The car had been on pole position by more than a second, and the eventual 37-second victory said more about the interrupted nature of the race – it was red-flagged three times and ended early as a result of the threat of lightning strikes in the area – than the Alpine's pace advantage. It had been more than a minute up the road on the Toyotas when the first of those reds came in the third hour.

Next time out at Spa in May, however, a revised BoP left the Alpine with little chance in another rain-affected race also with three red flags. The A480 was off the pace again in practice at Le Mans in June, received a performance break for Thursday's Hyperpole qualifying and suddenly went from being a couple of seconds back on the Toyotas to only a few tenths, and was promptly pegged back again ahead of the race. Lapierre and his team-mates finished 18 laps down in 23rd position overall, after suffering a series of technical glitches and time lost in the pits following an off-track excursion. Yet the truth was they weren't in the game before they started running into problems.

At Monza, and with a further revision to the BoP in its favour, the Alpine won again, though this time in a close fight with Toyota. Suddenly, Lapierre, Vaxivière and Negrão found themselves with a ten-point lead in the championship. Thereafter, however, they never challenged the Toyotas, thanks to a BoP hit ahead of Fuji that was only partially reversed before Bahrain, and finished a distant third both times.

A championship challenge that would have been considered unlikely ahead of the season was helped by Toyota's failure to get one of its revised cars – now running narrower front and wider rear wheels and tyres, rather than the equal

sizes of 2021 – to the finish in the opening two races. Kamui Kobayashi, newly installed as team principal of the WEC squad over the winter, Mike Conway and José María López made a faltering start to their championship defence – and bid for a hat trick of WEC titles. López had a coming together with a GTE Am-class car, tagged the barriers and then had the front splitter collapse on him as he negotiated the quick Bishop Bend. The dramatic-looking accident ended with the No.7 car on its roof and a no-score for its drivers in a race with extra points on offer over a regular six-hour WEC round.

Things were pretty much levelled up in the battle between the two Toyotas at Spa. The No.8 GR010 went out of the race with a hybrid system failure early in the second hour, after Buemi had led the opening exchanges. The Toyota crews headed for Le Mans separated by only a couple of points, No.7 ahead of No.8, though down in third and fourth places in the championship, behind the Alpine trio and Glickenhaus drivers Oliver and Romain Dumas.

The destination of the title in favour of Buemi and co was effectively decided at the double-points Le Mans round, a race that skewed the championship battle more than in the days when the WEC was made up of eight races. The No.8 Toyota triumphed in a close battle, at least for the first 15-and-a-bit hours. There wasn't much between the two Japanese cars over the first two-thirds of the race. Then an electrical glitch forced López to bring the car to a complete stop just after Arnage to undertake a systems reboot. He had to do it twice more when he arrived back in the pits. The gap between the GR010s stood at the better part of three minutes after the next scheduled stop for No.8. There was no way back for the previous year's winners, who ended up two minutes down on completion of the 24 hours.

The No.7 car finished behind No.8 at both Monza and Fuji, the result of a clash with the Alpine while Kobayashi was at the wheel in Italy, and then a set-up that didn't prove as effective in the hotter conditions of race-day in Japan. That meant the only way for the reigning champs to retain their

Above: Five go racing. The start at Le Mans, with the Hypercars of Toyota, Glickenhaus and Alpine setting the pace. The LMP2 brigade follows at a respectful distance.

Top right: JOTA ended the season as LMP2 Endurance Trophy winner, with a class win at Le Mans and top-six finishes in five of the six rounds.

Above right: The sinister-looking Peugeot 9X8 made an underwhelming debut at Monza, but all the manufacturer's efforts are being thrown behind the 2023 campaign.

Right: The winning Toyota speeds through the night at Le Mans.
Photos: WEC

title in Bahrain was for their team-mates not to finish. They did win the race to level the score at two victories apiece, but that wasn't enough to overhaul the Alpine trio in the championship table. Kobayashi, Conway and López ended up 11 points behind, in third place.

Glickenhaus drivers Dumas and Pla took fourth in the points, though a long way back after contesting only four of the six races. Their No.708 entry was on the podium for the first two, at Sebring (shared with Ryan Briscoe) and at Spa (with Pipo Derani). Then they were fourth at Le Mans, behind the sister No.709 car in which Briscoe was joined by Richard Westbrook and Franck Mailleux, but they took points for third because the team's additional car was ineligible to score as a one-off entry.

There were plenty of highs for the plucky *garagistes* running out of Italy. Pole positions were taken by Pla and Dumas respectively at Spa and Monza, which sandwiched the most meaningful result, third place at Le Mans, which had nothing to do with a Toyota failing to make the finish. Yet Glickenhaus might have ended up with a world championship victory to its name. Pla, Dumas and Derani had had the pace to pull it off, only for a turbo-related engine problem to intervene. Then the team decided not to take part in the Asian leg of the series.

Glickenhaus had committed to a full-season entry and duly received a second entry for Le Mans, which claimed its historic result, despite an early problem with delaminating tyres. It trailed the regular entry until 11pm, when Pla looped No.708, which was within a couple of minutes of the Toyotas, at Tertre Rouge and damaged a toe-link against the barriers, necessitating a nine-minute stop for repairs.

The run of podiums from Glickenhaus looked even more impressive when Peugeot pitched up at Monza to end a ten-season hiatus from the sportscar big-time with its avant-garde 9X8 LMH. The French manufacturer, a force in endurance racing in 1990–93 with the 905 3.5-litre Group C car and again in 2007–11 with two iterations of its 908 LMP1 turbodiesel, could do no better than three fourth positions over the second half of the championship.

Peugeot chose not to take up its full-season entries until after Le Mans. Although described as a delay in some quarters, that ignored the timeline of the Peugeot LMH programme. It had been announced in November, 2019, with the intent that what became the 9X8 would be ready for the start of the 2022/23 campaign – the WEC was in the midst of its first season run to the winter-series calendar when the decision was made. That would have meant a start date at the end of the summer, so arguably Peugeot was a tad ahead of schedule with a July debut at Monza.

To be able to compete in 2022, Peugeot had to enter the full series, but it always reserved judgement on when it would join the fray. Rules that limit technical upgrades during the life of an LMH design caused it to opt against rushing into homologation and, to a greater degree, freezing the specification of a car that ran without a rear wing, courtesy of the LMH rules that allow significant freedoms while laying down modest aero targets.

The disappointment for Peugeot was that it failed to get a car to finish a race cleanly and registered two retirements. The 9X8 increasingly came into play, however, helped at Bahrain by a BoP change in its favour and another that penalised Toyota. There was a front-row starting slot in the Middle East, secured by Paul di Resta, and then a fastest race lap from Jean-Éric Vergne in the same No.93 car, but the 9X8 looked slightly less of a competitive proposition over the course of a double stint on a set of tyres than over a single lap. Come the end of the season, Peugeot admitted that there was work to be done over the winter before its first full campaign – and a return to Le Mans – in 2023.

The British Jota team took its first WEC title in the LMP2 division after being a class front-runner for years and winning the class at Le Mans on two previous occasions. A third triumph at the French enduro formed the foundation of the championship victory for António Félix da Costa, Will Ste-

vens and Roberto González on a weekend when their closest championship rivals failed to score big or at all.

Jota's lead crew, which had been joined by Stevens after the retirement of Anthony Davidson at the end of 2021, dominated at the French enduro, leading all but 11 of the 369 laps they completed. Da Costa took the lead during the first round of pit stops, and a series of 'slow zones', where the cars run under virtual safety car conditions for a prescribed section of the track, fell in favour of the No.38 Jota Oreca-Gibson 07, allowing it to stretch its lead. The car was briefly a full lap ahead, though the winning margin over the Oreca fielded for Robert Kubica, Louis Delétraz and Lorenzo Colombo by Le Mans debutant Prema was 2m 20s.

The title-winning Jota crew had already finished third at Spa and were on the podium again with two seconds and a third in each of the final three races. With the big score at the double-points Le Mans round, that made them pretty much unbeatable over the course of a season in which no one could match their consistency.

The Belgian WRT had dominated the class in its maiden campaign in the WEC in 2021, and won four of the six races with an expanded operation in 2022, an additional car run under the Realteam by WRT banner. The lead entry shared by Robin Frijns, Sean Gelael and René Rast (who was replaced by Dries Vanthoor at Fuji) took three of those victories, but retirement at Le Mans, after Frijns crashed negotiating Indianapolis, and a finish out of the points at Monza, following a water leak, meant that there could never be a repeat of the championship won by Frijns, Ferdinand Habsburg and Charles Milesi in '21. Back-to-back victories in the final two races hauled the car to second in the final points, however.

The Realteam by WRT entry shared by Habsburg, Norman Nato and Rui Andrade was also a winner, at Monza. A further two podiums were enough to give them fourth in the points.

United Autosports, winner of the P2 title in 2019/20, was

Above: World Endurance GTE drivers' champions for Ferrari were Alessandro Pier Guidi and James Calado.
Photo: Ferrari Racing

Above right: Porsche's Kévin Estre and Michael Christensen finished just three points shy in the GTE Pro battle.
Photo: Porsche

Top: The WRT LMP2, driven throughout by Robin Frijns and Sean Galeal, augmented by René Rast and Dries Vanthoor, won three of the six rounds.

Top right: The winning LMP2 trio of Will Stevens, António Félix da Costa and Roberto González.

Top far right: Porsche's Gianmaria Bruni and Richard Leitz took GTE Pro glory with their win at Le Mans.
Photos: WEC

Above far right: The Audi Sport Team Phoenix R8 LMS, driven by Robin Frijns, Kelvin van der Linde, Dries Vanthoor and Frédéric Vervisch, won the Nürburgring 24-hour race.
Photo: Audi Motorsport Communications

Right: Raffaele Marciello, Daniel Juncadella and Jules Gounon, winners of the Spa 24-hour race for Mercedes.
Photo: Mercedes

the other class winner over the course of the season. The British team pretty much dominated the series-opener at Sebring. Either of its two Orecas might have won, but Oliver Jarvis, 16-year-old Josh Pierson and Paul di Resta (who was standing in for Alex Lynn) prevailed. Pierson became the youngest ever driver to start Le Mans in June. Though there were no more wins or even podiums for this crew, the young American and Jarvis were second in the points and nominally in the title hunt going into the season finale at Bahrain. However, even a strong runner-up finish with Lynn wasn't enough to stop them from slipping to third in the points, behind Frijns and Gelael.

The pro/am LMP2 sub-class for line-ups, including a bronze-rated driver, was won by Nicklas Nielsen, Alessio Rovera and François Perrodo in an AF Corse-run Oreca. They won three times to beat the Algarve Pro line-up of René Binder, James Allen and Steven Thomas into second place.

The final season of the GTE Pro class was a strange one. Ferrari appeared to be nowhere at the start of the season, after a BoP reset following the introduction of a new biofuel from WEC supplier TotalEnergies. The two AF Corse-run factory Ferrari 488 Evos were off the pace at Sebring and again at Spa until rain arrived. The course of the race – and ultimately Ferrari's season – changed on the wet track. Pier Guidi, who drove the first four-and-a-half hours of the race, took the car through the field and into the lead on wet-weather Michelins. Then it was Calado's job over the final laps to hang on to the lead on slicks. He proved equal to the task, holding off Michael Christensen in the best of the Porsches over a thrilling final ten minutes.

Pier Guidi and Calado followed this victory with second place at Le Mans (with Daniel Serra). The Ferrari wasn't a truly competitive proposition after a race-week BoP change robbed it of engine power (though it got some of it back ahead of the race), but problems for others allowed the lead Ferrari crew to pick up a big score in the double-points round. First, the best of the Manthey-run Porsche 911 RSRs, shared by Christensen, Kévin Estre and Laurens Vanthoor, lost three laps after Christensen locked up at Mulsanne Corner and then suffered a dramatic front-right blowout that ripped apart the front end.

The Porsche had been battling with the Chevrolet Corvette C8.R shared by class pole-winner Nick Tandy, Tommy Milner and Alexander Sims at the time of the delay, just before the two-thirds mark of the race. That left the remaining Corvette Racing entry – the other car was already out with suspension problems – in a clear lead. A first class win for the team at Le Mans since 2015 appeared to be on the cards when Sims was unceremoniously sideswiped into the barriers by François Perrodo in the AF Corse-run LMP2 Oreca. Victory went to the second Porsche of Gianmaria Bruni, Richard Lietz and Frédéric Makowiecki by 42s, though the Ferrari would have run it closer but for a late puncture.

The two Porsches headed the championship table after Le Mans, Bruni and Lietz three points ahead of Estre and Christensen, but the pendulum swung in Fersarri's favour over the remainder of the season. A BoP tweak that gave the Italian car a little more power changed the balance at the front of the field, and the 911 wasn't a competitive proposition thereafter. Pier Guidi and Calado headed to the season's curtain closer in the Middle East with a handy 11-point lead after another win at Fuji. But their championship victory ended up being almost as dramatic as 12 months before when Pier Guidi controversially tapped Christensen into a spin in the closing stages of the Bahrain finale.

This time, the loss of fourth gear threatened to derail their hopes when they had appeared to be cruising to the title. Pier Guidi drove much of the last 90 minutes using fifth gear only and managed to nurse the car home in fifth, which was just enough to secure the title. Estre and Christensen ended

up second in the championship, but only after Porsche had swapped the positions of its two cars on the final lap. A last-gasp problem for Pier Guidi could still have given the Frenchman and the Dane the title if they had been third.

The second Ferrari pairing of Antonio Fuoco and Miguel Molina took their first WEC victory in Bahrain and ended up third in the points, ahead of Bruni and then Lietz (who had missed the Monza round with Covid). Tandy and Milner brought up the rear of the GTE Pro pack for Corvette Racing, which contested a full WEC schedule for the first time with a solo C8.R, though if you added the 50 points they had lost when they were pushed off at Le Mans, they would have been champions. The highpoint of their season was a last-gasp victory at Monza, where Fuoco had come in from the lead for a splash-and-dash pit stop. The Corvette didn't need to stop, much to the disbelief of everyone in the Ferrari camp.

The TF Sport Aston Martin squad claimed the GTE Am title with Ben Keating and factory driver Marco Sørensen. Key to their success was victory at Le Mans together with Henrique Chaves, who had replaced Florian Latorre in the line-up for round two. A second victory aboard their Aston Martin Vantage GTE at Fuji made the title more or less a foregone conclusion.

The championship challenge from the works-run NorthWest AMR Aston trio of Nicki Thiim, David Pittard and Paul Dalla Lana faded after they finished runner-up at Le Mans, but they still ended up second in the points. The all-female Iron Dames Ferrari became increasingly competitive over the second half of the year, taking a podium in each of the final three races with Sarah Bovy, Rahel Frey and Michelle Gatting. Apart from TF, the only other double winners were Harry Tincknell, Sebastien Priaulx and Christian Ried in the best of the Dempsey-Proton Porsches.

On the other side of the sportscar divide in Europe, Mercedes took the big prize at the Spa 24 Hours, the centrepiece round of the GT World Challenge Europe for GT3 machinery. Raffaele Marciello, Jules Gounon and Daniel Juncadella won the race with the French Auto Sport Promotion team, which took its maiden win in the Belgian classic after near misses in both 2017 and '18.

Gounon and then Marciello had the edge on pace over the second-place GetSpeed Mercedes-AMG GT3 shared by Maximilian Götz, Luca Stolz and Steijn Schothorst when push came to shove in the closing stages of the double-points encounter. The two German cars were on different refuelling strategies over the final hours, but Marciello was able to pass Stolz for the lead at the end of the penultimate hour to secure the victory.

The win at Spa, coupled with the points garnered for running third at six and then 12 hours, anchored victory for Marciello, Gounon and Juncadella in the GTWCE Endurance Cup. They were only fifth in the Barcelona season-finale, but that was just enough for them to seal the title from the Iron Lynx Ferrari 488 GT3 Evo driven by Fuoco, Serra and Davide Rigon, who'd won the Paul Richard 1000Km six-hour event in June.

The Sprint Cup segment of the GTWCE went to Dries Vanthoor and Charles Weerts, and the WRT Audi team for a third year in succession. They won half the races aboard their Audi R8 GT3 evo II and only finished off the podium on one occasion. Second were double race winners Marciello and Timur Boguslavskiy for the ASP Merc squad. That meant Marciello also took the overall title, which combined the points from the Endurance and Sprint legs of the GTWCE, to go with his 2018 crown.

Sportscar racing stood on the verge of a bright new era as 2022 drew to a close. The manufacturers of the new LMDh hybrid prototypes set to join the WEC in 2023 – Porsche and Cadillac – as well as Ferrari with its 499P LMH were all well advanced with their testing regimes. Toyota finally faced an unlikely threat for championship honours in 2022, but it was nothing compared with what lay ahead.

TOURING CAR REVIEW by MATT SALISBURY

DRAMA KINGS

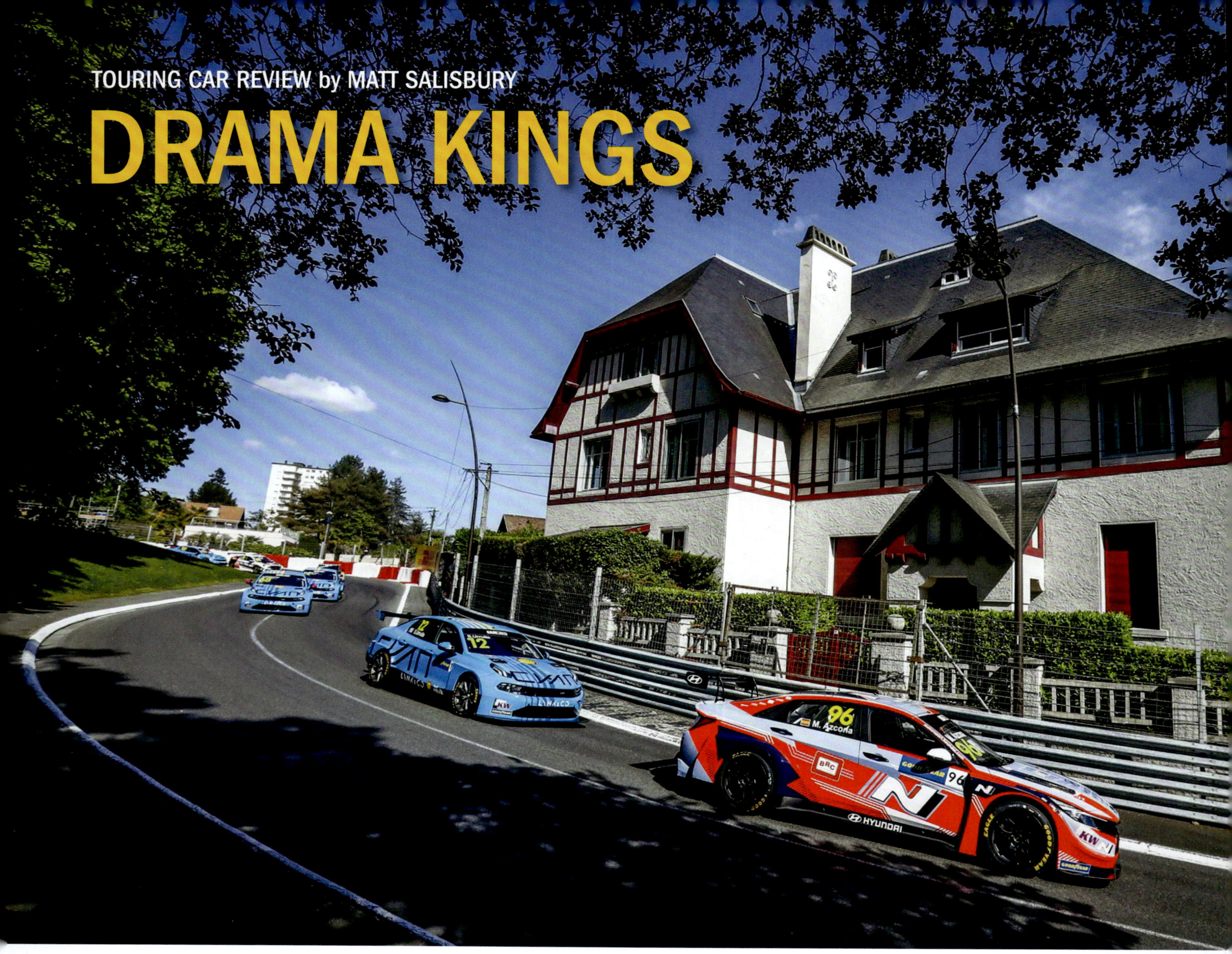

Above: Resplendent under sunny skies, Pau hosted the series-opener. Mikel Azcona leads a trio of Lynk & Co pursuers, headed by Santiago Urrutia.

Top right: All-Inkl.com team-mates Néstor Girolami and Esteban Guerreri celebrate their 1-2 finish at Pau.

Above centre right: Mehdi Bennani flies to pole position at the Nürburgring – for the race that never was...

Above right: Reigning champion Yann Erlacher's bid for a third successive title was scuppered when his team withdrew suddenly mid-season.

Right: Anneau du Rhin played host to a major international meeting for the first time. Nathanaël Berthon, in the Comtoyou Racing DHL Audi, leads Girolami, Azcona and Guerreri through the chicane.

Photos: Courtesy WTCR

ONCE again, the touring car world was the place to be if you were looking for drama during the course of the 2022 season – and not all of it took place on the racetrack...

New champions emerged in both the World Touring Car Cup and the British Touring Car Championship after battles that raged throughout the year, although only one of those them would go into 2023 in a position to defend the title. New champions were also crowned in the newly renamed eTouring Car World Cup and in the German-based DTM series, although it was a familiar name who emerged on top of the Supercars Championship in record-breaking fashion.

WORLD TOURING CAR CUP

Anyone who had hoped that 2022 would be a season of recovery for the World Touring Car Cup, after two campaigns ravaged by the impact of the pandemic, would have been sorely disappointed, as various issues over the course of the year hammered the final nails into WTCR's coffin...

Organisers had been optimistic about a return to normality in terms of the calendar, which initially included a return to Asia for events in Korea, China and on the famous streets of Macau, but news of the entry list was thin on the ground as the new year arrived.

It would be mid-January before Honda became the first manufacturer to confirm an unchanged driver line-up, and eventually a 17-car entry was revealed by the series that – while low on numbers – had plenty of talent.

Alongside the Honda quartet, Cyan Racing Lynk & Co retained the four drivers it had run in 2021 while adding a fifth car for Chinese racer Ma Qing Hua. Comtoyou Audi was also largely unchanged, the only difference being a return to the series for Mehdi Bennani, who took the place of the departed Frédéric Vervisch.

Team Engstler's switch from Hyundai to Honda resulted in the Korean marque being represented by just two cars as Mikel Azcona joined forces with Norbert Michelisz at BRC Racing. Azcona's former outfit, Zengo Motorsport, fielded only two cars, Dániel Nagy returning to partner Rob Huff in the two Cupras.

Before the season had even started, the calendar had been revised, with Russia's invasion of Ukraine leading to the cancellation of the planned opening round in the Czech Republic and also the event that had been due to take place in Sochi. Instead, rounds were added at Vallelunga and Anneau du Rhin.

Consequently, the campaign kicked off in early May on the streets of Pau, where Néstor Girolami topped the times in a truncated qualifying session that featured a lengthy stoppage after Thed Björk buried his Lynk & Co entry in the barriers. Girolami converted his pole into victory in the opening race of the campaign, ahead of Münnich Motorsport team-mate Esteban Guerrieri, before Azcona took advantage of an early clash between team-mate Michelisz and the Honda of Attila Tassi to grab honours in race two, ahead of Santiago Urrutia's Lynk & Co.

The French results gave Girolami a seven-point lead over Guerrieri and Azcona heading to the Nürburgring for round two, but it would be a weekend that grabbed headlines for all the wrong reasons.

A number of drivers – including Yvan Muller, Gilles Mag-

nus and defending champion Yann Ehrlacher – reported tyre issues during the two practice sessions, resulting in an additional 15-minute test being added to the schedule prior to qualifying. Bennani grabbed pole in his Audi, but it was clear that there were still concerns over the tyres, with Lynk & Co restricting its running, and further issues affecting the likes of Girolami and Huff; the latter crashed out after suffering from a vibration.

After overnight discussions between Goodyear, the teams, the FIA and promoters Discovery Sports Events, both races on the Nordschleife were cancelled on safety grounds less than an hour before the first was due to begin, with plenty of questions needing to be answered as the series moved to Hungary for round three.

Azcona grabbed pole in a dramatic qualifying session, controlling the race from the front to win ahead of Ehrlacher and Nathanaël Berthon, who swapped places on the penultimate lap. Warm conditions had led to drivers being forced to manage their tyres, and it was a similar story in race two, where Urrutia nursed a vibration to keep Huff's Cupra at bay for his first victory of the year.

A technical directive relating to damper settings ahead of round four in Spain led to frustration among the Audi drivers, but didn't stop Magnus from heading Berthon for a 1-2 in qualifying at Motorland Aragon. The Belgian driver won the opening race from Huff, who added another podium to his tally. Then Azcona took victory on home soil in race two for a third success of the season as the series headed straight for Vila Real.

Between the two meetings came news that all the Asian races were to be cancelled for logistical reasons. More issues would emerge in Portugal, where arguments over Balance of Performance and the use of Compensation Weight bubbled to the surface.

Urrutia converted pole into victory in race one, but that win was tinged with controversy after a team-orders call from Cyan Racing resulted in Ehrlacher being forced to let the Uruguayan through. That enabled him to close the gap to Azcona at the top to six points, while the defending champion found himself 12 points off the Spaniard in third. Then Huff took the honours in race two – which ended behind the

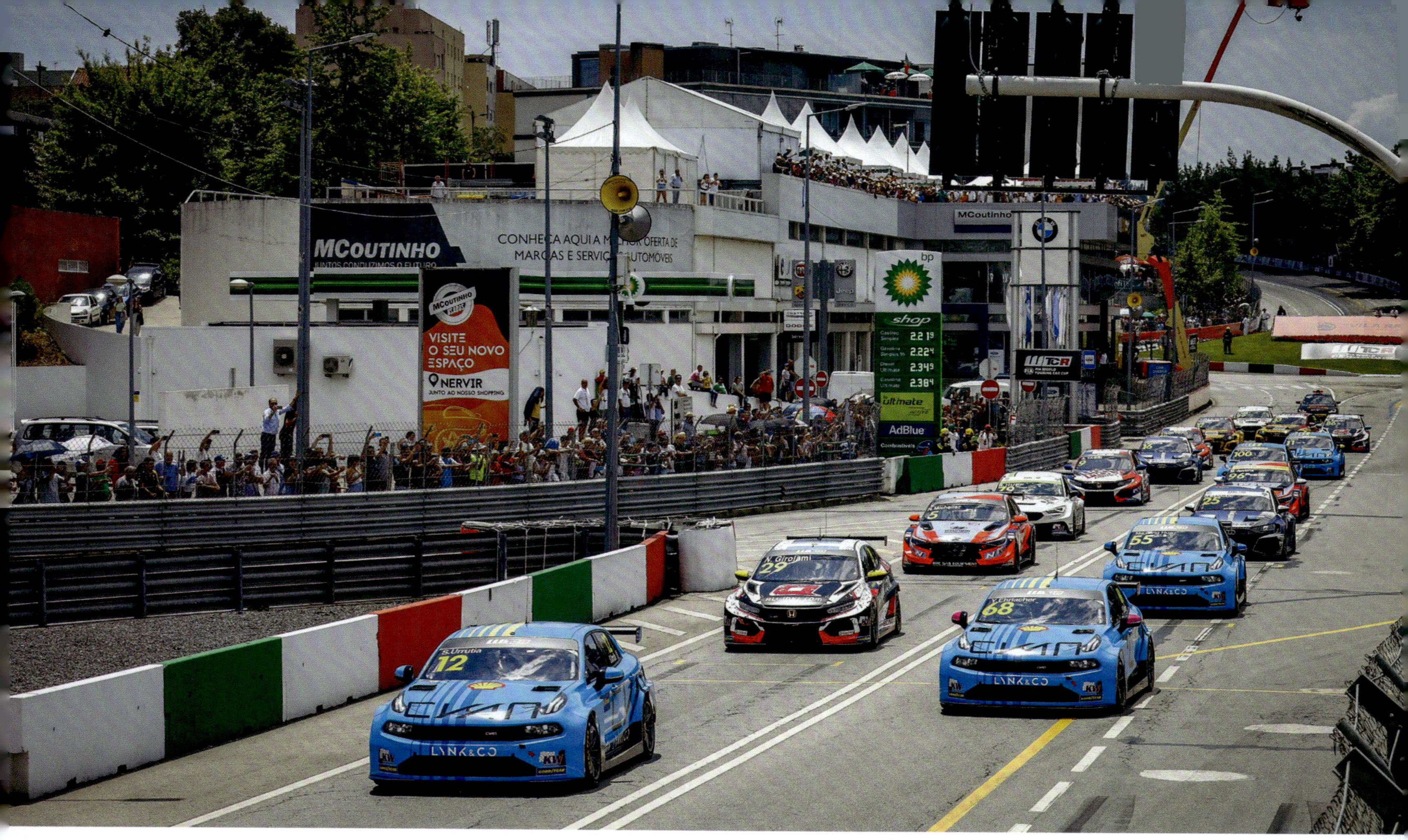

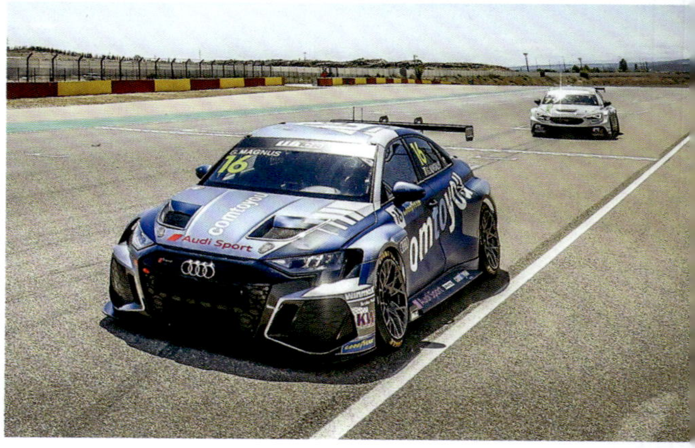

Above: Santiago Urrutia heads Lynk & Co team-mate Yann Erlacher at the start of the race in Vila Real. Somewhat controversially, the Uruguayan took the win on team orders.

Top right: Overblown? Mikel Azcona kisses the huge trophy after clinching the title in Saudi Arabia.

Above right: Nathanaël Berthon leads under the lights in Saudi Arabia.

Centre row, from left: Zengo Motorsport's Rob Huff picked up the pieces to win race two in Portugal; Gilles Magnus crosses the line to win in Aragon; Urrutia sprays the bubbly after his second place at Pau; Frenchman Nathaniël Berthon was eventually placed third in the final rankings.

Photos: Courtesy WTCR

safety car after an off for team-mate Nagy – with a podium for Azcona enabling him to retain his points lead.

The tyre issue that had blighted the German weekend reared its head again in Italy, with a high-speed off for Muller in opening practice calling into question whether Lynk & Co would race on safety grounds. The team took part in qualifying, where Girolami put his Honda on pole, but then all five cars retired to the pits ahead of race one, having elected not to compete.

That opening race proved to be chaotic, with multiple drivers forced to make unscheduled stops as a result of tyre concerns as Girolami beat Azcona to the win. There were further problems in race two, where Magnus led Berthon home for a Comtoyou 1-2.

Cyan Racing's decision not to race resulted in Azcona extending his lead at the top to 36 points over Girolami. Worse was to come ahead of the Alsace meeting when the Lynk & Co entries withdrew from the series with immediate effect over the ongoing concerns about tyre safety and Balance of Performance.

That left just a dozen cars on the grid as Anneau du Rhin played host to a major international meeting for the first time, with Berthon and Huff sharing the wins, and Azcona scoring a double podium to hold on to his points lead.

The final two meetings would be scheduled for Bahrain and Saudi Arabia, but before they took place came the bombshell announcement that the series would be halted at the end of the year. A combination of the various issues encountered over the previous two seasons and an inability to make a hoped-for switch to fossil-free fuels ultimately became the final straw.

Back on track, Azcona moved closer to the title when he led Michelisz home to a Hyundai 1-2 in the opening race in Sakhir, while Michelisz won race two to take a first victory of the campaign. Although Azcona missed out on a podium on the road, points for third, thanks to Nicky Catsburg being a guest entrant, meant that the Spaniard had one hand on the championship trophy when the field assembled in Jeddah for the final WTCR event.

When Azcona made it into Q3 in the final qualifying session and Girolami dropped out in Q2, the Hyundai man successfully clinched the crown before racing even began. Audi pair Berthon and Magnus emerged victorious in two action-packed races, but the fact that the finale ended behind the safety car meant WTCR bowed out with something of a whimper.

Where touring car racing at a global level goes next remains to be seen, with the FIA set to re-evaluate its World Touring Car category for combustion-engined cars. However, TCR creators WSC have announced the launch of a new TCR World Tour, incorporating events in various national and regional TCR series around the world.

Above: The ETCR Cupras of Adrien Tambay and Tom Blomqvist lead the Alfas of Maxime Martin and Luca Filippi off the line at Pau.

Left: Tambay was crowned champion after only six rounds had been held in a truncated season.

Photos: Courtesy ETCR

Running alongside a new TCR Ranking system, the World Tour will help select a field of 60 drivers, who then will take part in a four-day TCR World Ranking Final to determine who comes out on top at the end of the year.

eTOURING CAR WORLD CUP

After a single season under the Pure ETCR name, the series for electric touring cars evolved into the FIA ETCR - eTouring Car World Cup for 2022, with two manufacturer entries from Hyundai and Cupra once again joined by the Alfa Romeo Giulia developed by the Romeo Ferraris team.

Despite the new name, the series continued to run a unique format under which the field was split into two pools for a series of 'battles' that would help to set the field for the main Super Finals. With points scored across each race over a weekend, the highest scorer from the two pools would then be declared the overall winner.

A planned seven-round calendar kicked off on the streets of Pau in May, where defending champion Mattias Ekström held off the challenge of Hyundai's Mikel Azcona to win the Pool Furious final and with it, the opening round ahead of Cupra team-mate – and Pool Fast winner – Adrien Tambay.

After round two in Istanbul was rescheduled at the last minute for organisational reasons, the series headed for Hungary. There, it was Tambay who emerged victorious as he took Pool Furious honours, outscoring Ekström to grab the points lead.

They were split by just two points heading to Jarama a week later, where the Cupra squad made it three wins from three. Again, Tambay and Ekström shared the pool victories, and a maximum score for the Swede allowed him to reclaim the top spot.

At the halfway stage of the season, Ekström led Tambay by just six points in the standings, with Hyundai's Mikel Azcona nearly 70 points further back in third – only a handful clear of Alfa Romeo man Maxime Martin.

On home soil at Zolder, Martin ended the run of Cupra wins for Romeo Ferraris, securing a comfortable victory in the Pool Furious final to top the points with a maximum score ahead of Tambay. Meanwhile, Ekström lost ground in the standings when he was hit with a penalty after clashing with Azcona in his semi-final.

At the penultimate meeting of the year, at Vallelunga, the ETCR field was affected by tyre issues, with Tambay, Jordi Gené and Luca Filippi all suffering problems in their quarter-finals. Then, in a chaotic Pool Fast Super Final, Bruno Spengler suffered a high-speed off at Turn Two – which resulted in the Romeo Ferraris cars being withdrawn from the remainder of the action – while Norbert Michelisz and Filippi were both affected by tyre troubles.

Then Ekström grabbed the Pool Furious win when Nicky Castburg picked up a puncture while leading on the final lap, although Pool Fast winner Azcona took the round victory.

With the planned event in Korea having been canned because of logistical concerns, the delayed Istanbul meeting should have rounded out the campaign, but it was cancelled in August and replaced by an event at the Sachsenring.

Arriving in Germany, Tambay held a lead of 14 points over Ekström, and while Azcona and Martin were still in mathematical contention, realistically it was a two-way battle between the Cupras for the crown.

Tambay extended his lead when he outscored Ekström in qualifying, and moved further clear after the quarter- and semi-finals with a pair of wins. When Ekström could only take third in the Pool Fast Super Final, Tambay was confirmed as the champion. He duly celebrated with victory in the Pool Furious Super Final, taking second for the round behind Tom Blomqvist on fastest laps after both drivers grabbed a maximum score.

With Tambay, Ekström and Blomqvist rounding out the top three in the points, it was little surprise that Cupra also grabbed the manufacturers' crown, well ahead of Hyundai.

Above: Six wins and a further six podiums helped Tom Ingram clinch the BTCC crown in his Bristol Street Motors-backed Hyundai i30.

Top right: Defending champion Ash Sutton switched from his successful Infiniti to a Ford Focus for 2022. He was just 12 points shy in his bid for a third consecutive title.

Above right: Jake Hill took third overall in the series with his Rokit-backed BMW 330e M Sport.

Above far right: BTCC champion Tom Ingram surveys his hard-earned silverware.

Right: Colin Turkington leads BMW team-mate Daniel Lloyd and the rest of the pack at Croft.

Photos: BTCC/Jakob Ebrey

BRITISH TOURING CAR CHAMPIONSHIP

The British Touring Car Championship entered a new era in 2022 with the introduction of hybrid technology, but one thing that didn't change was the frenetic on-track action as the fight for the title went to the wire.

The new hybrid system was brought in to replace success ballast, offering drivers an extra boost of power each lap that could be used to both attack and defend over the course of qualifying and a race. Just how much hybrid power was available would come down to championship positions and race results, with the top ten penalised with a reduced amount to level the playing field.

With plans to expand the grid having come to nothing, a 29-car field was assembled, with several intriguing changes to the entry – not least defending champion Ash Sutton swapping the Infiniti that had carried him to back-to-back titles for a Motorbase Performance-run Ford Focus.

Sutton was joined by series returnee Dan Cammish in two cars backed by US automotive brand NAPA, with 2021 Motorbase racer Jake Hill – once again supported by ex-F1 racer Mark Blundell – having switched to West Surrey Racing after Tom Oliphant had left the series to move to Australia. Other notable changes included Daniel Lloyd and Tom Chilton moving to the EXCELR8 team, while the elder statesman of the grid, Jason Plato, joined forces with BTC Racing for what he insisted would be his final year. Meanwhile, race winners Senna Proctor, Chris Smiley and Jack Goff had all bowed out of the series.

After a hectic pre-season as teams and drivers tried to get their heads around the new hybrid systems, the racing action kicked off in late April at Donington Park. Immediately, Hill demonstrated impressive pace in his BMW to grab pole position in a dramatic session punctuated by Cammish's Focus going up in flames after a fuel fire.

When Hill became embroiled in a wheel-to-wheel dice with team-mate Colin Turkington in the early laps of race one, Tom Ingram was able to nip ahead of the pair to grab the first hybrid victory in his Hyundai. Turkington had to settle for second, while Hill battled back from being run wide to grab third.

Then Hill was excluded from the results for failing the ride-height check, promoting the Honda of Gordon Shedden on to the podium, before the Scot fought his way to victory ahead of Ingram and impressive rookie George Gamble in race two, with Turkington plummeting down the order when he failed to get away at the start. By contrast, Hill stormed from the back into the top ten before being drawn on the reverse-grid pole – and he promptly led race three from start to finish for a comfortable victory.

Turkington made it two straight poles for WSR when he headed a 1-2-3 in qualifying at Brands Hatch, ahead of Hill and Stephen Jelley, with the similar BMW of Adam Morgan in fourth spot. Come race one, however, it was the Honda of Josh Cook that emerged victorious as he mastered tricky track conditions after morning rain to become the fourth winner in four races, ahead of Ingram and Cammish, who picked up his first podium of the year.

Then Cook doubled up in race two after a race-long battle with Hill and Cammish, with Hill pushing the BTC Racing man throughout before spinning down to eighth late on. Race three went the way of Turkington, ahead of Hill, with Bobby Thompson grabbing a first career podium in his Team HARD Cupra.

Having moved up to second in the standings with his double win, Cook hit the top spot at Thruxton as he continued his love affair with the fastest circuit on the calendar in record-breaking fashion. Having scored pole position on Saturday, he saw off the challenge of Hill's BMW in the opening two races as he became the most successful driver in series history at the circuit with his eighth and ninth wins. Adam Morgan rounded out the weekend with victory in race three, having celebrated his 300th start earlier in the day.

Despite hitting the front in the points – and retaining the championship lead at Oulton Park – straight-line speed is-

CARLYLE TOOLS
NAPA
KwikFit
CATACLEAN

uniserve
ROKiT
ROKiT
ABK BEER
ABK BEER
KwikFit

MARON
S2M

BMW FIRST
50
Allianz Assistance
KwikFit
ONE PLM
ONE PLM
CATACLEAN
EXCELR8
123
LASER

Above: Series veteran Gordon Shedden could still hold his own against younger opposition. The Scot claimed two victories in his Halfords Racing Honda Civic.

Right: BTCC chief executive Alan Gow has overseen the growth of the series, which attracts both in-person and TV audiences in large numbers.

Centre right: Jason Plato signs for the fans. The twice BTCC champion announced his retirement from the series, in which he had clocked up over 650 races and 97 wins.

Photos: BTCC/Jakob Ebrey

Left: Rory Butcher almost bounces his Toyota off the track in his efforts to stave off the advances of Gordon Shedden at Knockhill.

Below left: Ash Sutton might have surrendered his crown, but with the help of Dan Cammish, NAPA Racing UK took the teams' championship ahead of Team BMW.

Below: Josh Cook claimed top independent honours, and sixth overall in the series, in his Rich Energy Honda.

Bottom: A great weekend at Croft for Daniel Lloyd, who took two wins for BMW at the North Yorkshire track.

Photos: BTCC/Jakob Ebrey

sues with the new M-Sport TOCA engine would begin to hamper Cook's title challenge. As a result, at the fourth meeting of the year, Ingram returned to the top of the podium. At a circuit where he had struggled for results previously, the Hyundai man grabbed a pair of victories, beating Sutton in races two and three, the latter enjoying a solid run of form that resulted in him grabbing five podium finishes in a row.

Race three – eventually won by Stephen Jelley – proved to be a chaotic affair, with early contact between Lloyd and the Toyota of Ricky Collard resulting in Lloyd's car being turned around in front of the field, where it was collected by Turkington's BMW and the Vauxhall of Michael Crees. All three drivers were lucky to escape injury, although EXCELR8 was left with a race against time to fix Lloyd's car for the following weekend at Croft. Turkington's car wouldn't race again all season. Instead, he reverted to his title-winning chassis from 2019.

Not only was Lloyd's car fixed for the trip to North Yorkshire, but also he rewarded his team for their efforts with a stunning weekend on track, snatching a pair of wins on home soil, the highlight a battling drive in race one to keep Turkington at bay. Shedden took his second win of the year in race three, while Ingram would head into the summer break on top as he took advantage of another tough weekend for Cook to secure the championship lead.

When the action resumed in late July at Knockhill, it did so with two of the most memorable races of the season as Hill and Sutton went wheel to wheel for victory. Race one went the way of Hill after he had overhauled Sutton's Focus mid-way through, but Sutton turned the tables in race two when he took advantage of a small error by his rival to grab his first victory of the campaign. Hill rounded out a strong weekend with another second-place finish in race three, this time behind Gamble, who took full advantage of the reverse-grid draw to claim a maiden victory.

The results north of the border had resulted in Turkington becoming the third championship leader in as many rounds, leaving him as the man to beat going to Snetterton, where he would hit the landmark of 500 races in the series. In sweltering weather conditions, the Northern Irishman grabbed pole position in qualifying and produced two fine drives to win the opening pair of races – the second after a stunning battle with Hill on lap one, during which they ran side by side for more than half a lap.

Then Sutton recovered from dropping behind Dan Rowbottom at the start to win race three and strengthen his championship challenge, although Turkington's high-scoring weekend meant that he extended his advantage at the front to 15 points over Ingram, who would battle hard to take three podium finishes.

With both Turkington and Ingram having struggled in qualifying at Thruxton, it was Cammish who grabbed pole, converting it into a comfortable race-one win ahead of Shedden, after a chaotic opening lap in which Hill, Sutton and Cook had made early contact, allowing the pole-sitter to build an early lead that he retained to the finish.

Cammish appeared set to double up in race two before he let Sutton through to grab the win and extra championship points. Meanwhile, Cook – who had spun down the order after contact with Sutton in race one – made it back on to the top step as he won again at his home circuit in race three.

Salvaging a podium in race three meant that Turkington held on to his lead, but contact in race one at Silverstone, followed by hybrid issues in race two, came at the worst possible time. He went from leading in the points to the role of title outsider in one afternoon.

After Rory Butcher's Toyota won the opening race of the weekend, title contenders Hill and Ingram won races two and three. It was Sutton, however, who picked up a 12th podium of the campaign and topped the standings as the field headed to Brands Hatch for the big finale.

Just seven points covered Sutton, Hill and Ingram going into the weekend, with Turkington also retaining an outside chance of the title. Come qualifying, though, it was Ingram who blasted his way to pole by more than four-tenths of a second, converting it to victory in race one to move into the championship lead.

Then he held off the challenge of Hill to extend his advantage with a third successive victory in race two. Finally, fifth spot in the finale – won by team-mate Lloyd – resulted in the EXCELR8 racer being crowned overall champion for the first time.

"I've been thinking about this moment for literally my entire life," he said. "The BTCC is what I always wanted to do. It's what I always wanted to win. I've had a few years of coming into the finale with a chance and it not quite working out, so I honestly can't put into words what this means and what an incredible feeling it is.

"I fell in love with the BTCC when I was just five years old, and when you've devoted your whole life to something, as my family and I have done… I simply don't have the words. This isn't going to sink in for quite some time."

Sutton ended the year as runner-up, with his NAPA Racing UK team winning the teams' title, while third for Hill helped BMW to take the manufacturers' crown for the seventh successive season. Cook and his BTC Racing squad grabbed both of the independents' titles, with the Jack Sears Trophy going the way of Thompson.

As AUTOCOURSE closed for press, changes to the hybrid system and a return of the option tyre had both been confirmed for 2023, along with a revised calendar that included a return for the Donington Park GP layout. As ever, rumours abound about potential driver news and new cars, although little had been officially confirmed.

Above: Sheldon van der Linde's red Schubert Motorsport BMW heads the pack at the Lautsitzring. The South African won both races at the track in May and added another win at the Nürburgring on his way to the title.

Top right: Former DTM champion Marco Wittmann could only score a single victory in the BMW M4 GT3.
Photos: BMW Motorsport

Top far right: Mercedes' Lucas Auer was the closest challenger to van der Linde in the championship.

Above right: Mercedes pair Luca Stolz and Maro Engel celebrate their success at the Red Bull Ring.
Photos: Mercedes-AMG

Above far right: Thomas Preining campaigned a Porsche on behalf of Team Bernhard, taking a win in Austria.
Photo: Red Bull Content Pool

Right: The 2022 DTM season was run under a variety of weather. Rain hit the start of race two at Spielberg in September, leaving the field to explore the limits of adhesion.
Photo: Mercedes-AMG

DEUTSCHE TOURENWAGEN MASTERS

The 2022 season marked the second year for the new-look version of the DTM, with the series attempting to recover from the controversy surrounding the way in which the 2021 title had been decided.

Such had been the reaction to the way in which Mercedes had asked Lucas Auer and Philip Ellis to slow and let Maximilian Götz through, to ensure that he was able to lift the title, that the organisers took decisive action for 2022 by introducing a complete ban on team orders. Teams were warned that any attempt to impose them during the season could result in exclusion from the championship, which would prove to be one of the biggest and most competitive since the DTM had been revived more than 20 years earlier.

A field of nearly 30 cars was assembled ahead of round one, with a number of new teams joining the party, including Lamborghini outfit Grasser Racing, Timo Bernhard's eponymous Porsche squad and long-time BMW runner Schubert Motorsport, which was one of three teams fielding the new BMW M4 GT3.

Returning three-time champion René Rast was a major addition to the driver line-up, having been drafted in by the Abt team to replace the retiring Mike Rockenfeller, while the likes of Philip Eng, Maro Engel, Mirko Bortolotti and Nicki Thiim were among those appearing in the GT3 version of the DTM for the first time

Götz was also back to defend his title, although he would move from Team HRT to fellow Mercedes outfit Winward.

Although initial plans had been for the series to expand to nine rounds, the calendar would again feature 16 races spread across eight events, although there were a number of changes compared to 2021.

Monza, Zolder and Assen had been dropped from the schedule, with Spa returning after a year away, and Portimão and Imola each hosting a DTM round for the first time.

The season got under way in Portugal, where Bortolotti grabbed the first pole position of the campaign for Grasser, ahead of the Mercedes of fellow newcomer Mikaël Grenier, running alongside Engel in an expanded GruppeM line-up.

Bortolotti led the early stages of the race before a loss of power on a mid-race restart cost him valuable time. That allowed Auer through to claim the win for Team Winward as Mercedes clinched the first victory of the year.

Race two resulted in a relatively straightforward win for the Audi of Nico Müller, the Swiss racer having beaten Bortolotti to pole position and then leading the majority of the race to score victory ahead of Felipe Fraga's Ferrari. Third for Bortolotti, however – a repeat of his race-one result – meant that he picked up the early championship lead.

Auer followed up his Portimao victory by grabbing pole for the opening race at the Lausitzring, although it was a close-run affair, the top three on the grid being covered by less than seven-hundredths of a second. Having qualified on the front row, Sheldon van der Linde got the jump on Auer at the start and ultimately grabbed a comfortable first win for the new BMW, ahead of Luca Stolz, who headed four Mercedes drivers behind.

Van der Linde grabbed pole in a red-flagged second qualifying session and held off the late challenge of Maro Engel in race two to grab a double win, with Rast scoring his first podium finish of the campaign in third. With Bortolotti only able to claim a best finish of sixth from the two races, and Auer having struggled for pace in race two, van der Linde moved into the points lead ahead of the visit to Imola for round three.

Rast became the fifth different driver to score pole when he topped the times in qualifying for race one, ahead of Müller. The former champion kept his cool in baking hot conditions to lead his fellow Audi driver home for a 1-2 finish. The star, however, was Bortolotti, who fought back from a ten-place grid penalty, handed out for a tyre issue in practice, to storm through the pack from 16th spot to third, having elected to run long on his first stint and then benefit from fresher tyres towards the end.

Then rookie Ricardo Feller grabbed a maiden win from

AUTOHERO
11
SCHAEFFLER
MAHLE
Motorsport

DTM
AUTOHERO
KNAUS

DEKRA
DEKRA
DTM
AUTOHERO
BILSTEIN
DTM
AUTOHERO
IWC
BWT
BEST WATER TECHNOLOGY

AUTOHERO
24
KÜS
PAUL
MAHLE
PAUL
HYLO
ixo

SCHAEFFLER
BWT
PAUL

Above: The thunder of machines at the start of the Hockenheim race. The Mercedes of Lucas Auer (22) and Luca Stolz (4) head the pack.
Photo: Mercedes-AMG

Top right: René Rast returned to the series with Audi, and the experienced racer took third in the final standings.
Photo: Audi Communications Motorsport

Top far right: Sheldon van der Linde, 2022 DTM champion with BMW.
Photo: BMW Motorsport

Above right: Brazilian Felipe Fraga raced a Red Bull-backed Ferrari 448, taking a win for his sponsor at its home track.

Above far right: The mix of cars on the grid was enlivened by the vivid green Lamborghini of Mirko Bortolotti.

Right: Down under, it was business as usual for Shane van Gisbergen, who trounced the opposition to take his third V8 Supercar title.
Photos: Red Bull Content Pool

pole in race two, despite having lost the lead early on, with Dev Gore benefiting from a fine call from Team Rosberg to bounce back from a lap-one puncture to take an unexpected second place finish.

Van der Linde maintained the points lead, despite being hampered by the additional ballast on his BMW. However, he was one of a number of drivers to suffer a weekend to forget on what would prove to be a chaotic return to the Norisring, scene of the controversial 2021 finale, for round four.

Kelvin van der Linde became the latest pole-sitter in race-one qualifying, but he failed to finish the race after contact from Bortolotti, with points leader Sheldon van der Linde and Müller eliminated in a multi-car shunt shortly after the start, while Auer was tipped into a spin by debutant Ayhancan Guven. With less than half the field making it to the finish, Thomas Preining emerged through the carnage to grab a first Porsche win of the year.

Race two proved to be a more straightforward affair, Felipe Fraga winning from pole in his Red Bull-backed Ferrari, with Bortolotti following him home in second to move back ahead of Sheldon van der Linde, who failed to score again.

The South African fought back at the Nürburgring, however, where poor weather conditions led to the grid for race one being set by championship positions. That left Bortolotti to start from pole, and he was running second to Fraga late on when an opportunistic move at the final corner caused both to spin, handing victory to van der Linde ahead of his brother.

Then the pair lined up on the front row for race two, but it was Stolz who took advantage of a well-timed pit stop during an early caution period to win. Eighth for Sheldon van der Linde extended his advantage over Borotolotti, who again failed to score after a contact-induced puncture.

Dennis Olsen added his name to the 2022 winners list after surviving a late rain shower in the opening race at Spa, ahead of defending champion Götz. Meanwhile, van der Linde saw his lead in the standings cut by both Bortolotti – who came through impressively from well down the grid to take eighth – and Rast, who moved level on points with the Italian after taking fourth.

Then Nick Cassidy took his first win of the year in race two, ahead of van der Linde, the pair enjoying a huge battle at the front that ultimately went the way of the Kiwi. However, second was good enough for van der Linde to extend his lead, Rast having dropped out of third with a puncture, while Bortolotti could only manage tenth. As a result, Auer jumped the pair to move up to second in the standings.

At the Red Bull Ring, Cassidy made it two wins in a row with victory in the opening race, before Preining vaulted into championship contention by picking up a second win of the campaign in race two, which was held in tricky wet-to-dry conditions. Things tightened up in the points, as van der Linde failed to score in either race, with Rast and Bortolotti both claiming podiums in race one and Auer fighting hard to score a pair of top-six finishes to close the gap at the top.

Just 16 points covered the top five in the standings as the field arrived at Hockenheim, and it was Auer who grabbed pole for race one. Bortolotti was third, Preining and Rast in seventh and eighth, but van der Linde back in 16th after being hit with a ten-place grid penalty.

The race was red-flagged after multiple incidents during the early laps, the most serious of which ruled four drivers out of the finale, including title hopeful Preining. Auer emerged victorious in the restarted race, ahead of a charging van der Linde, to bring the gap between the pair down to two points. Rast took fifth and Bortolotti seventh to remain in contention.

Rast grabbed pole for race two in a session halted early by an incident for Fraga, which occurred before a number of drivers had been able to set their quickest time. That left van der Linde back in sixth, with Auer in 11th and outsider Bortolotti all the way down in 18th.

Although Marco Wittmann won the race ahead of Rast, third for van der Linde was enough for him to be crowned champion. Meanwhile, hampered by the success ballast he was carrying after race one, Auer could only take seventh, which left him to end the year as runner-up.

"I have to admit that the pressure of going into the weekend as championship leader was massive," van der Linde

admitted afterwards. "It feels fantastic now that this weight is off my shoulders. Ever since I was a child, I have dreamed of driving in the DTM. I am unbelievably proud and delighted now that I have won it. Growing up in South Africa, making the leap to the DTM seemed a very long way away.

"Now it has all worked out. I can barely believe it!"

SUPERCARS CHAMPIONSHIP

With the start of the new Gen3 era delayed until 2023, fans of the Supercars Championship were treated to one more year of the famous rivalry between Ford and Holden. The season would be dominated by one man, a record-breaking display from Shane van Gisbergen allowing him to grab a third championship title, with his title defence kicking off with victory in the opening race of the year in Sydney.

Although Chaz Mostert won race two, it was followed by a hat trick for van Gisbergen at Symmons Plains and two further victories at Albert Park during the Australian Grand Prix support event as the Triple Eight driver stamped his early authority on proceedings. It would take until the 11th race of the year before Ford grabbed a win, thanks to Will Davison in Perth, and it would be the sixth meeting of the campaign at Hidden Valley before a race weekend passed without a van Gisbergen win.

That started an astonishing run for the Kiwi, however, who won five races in a row across the meetings at Townsville and The Bend, then took double wins at Sandown and Pukekohe as the latter played host to the series for the final time before closing its doors.

Although van Gisbergen battled to victory in the biggest race of the year at Bathurst, alongside Garth Tander, after holding off Mostert, it wasn't quite enough to wrap up the championship title. He didn't have to wait long, however, grabbing his third title with a double win at Surfers Paradise.

Having broken Scott McLaughlin's record for most wins in a season, van Gisbergen ensured that Holden would bow out of the series on a high, Gen3 leading to the introduction of the Chevrolet Camaro for 2023 to go wheel to wheel with the latest incarnation of the Ford Mustang.

UNITED STATES RACING REVIEW by GORDON KIRBY

WINNERS & LOSERS

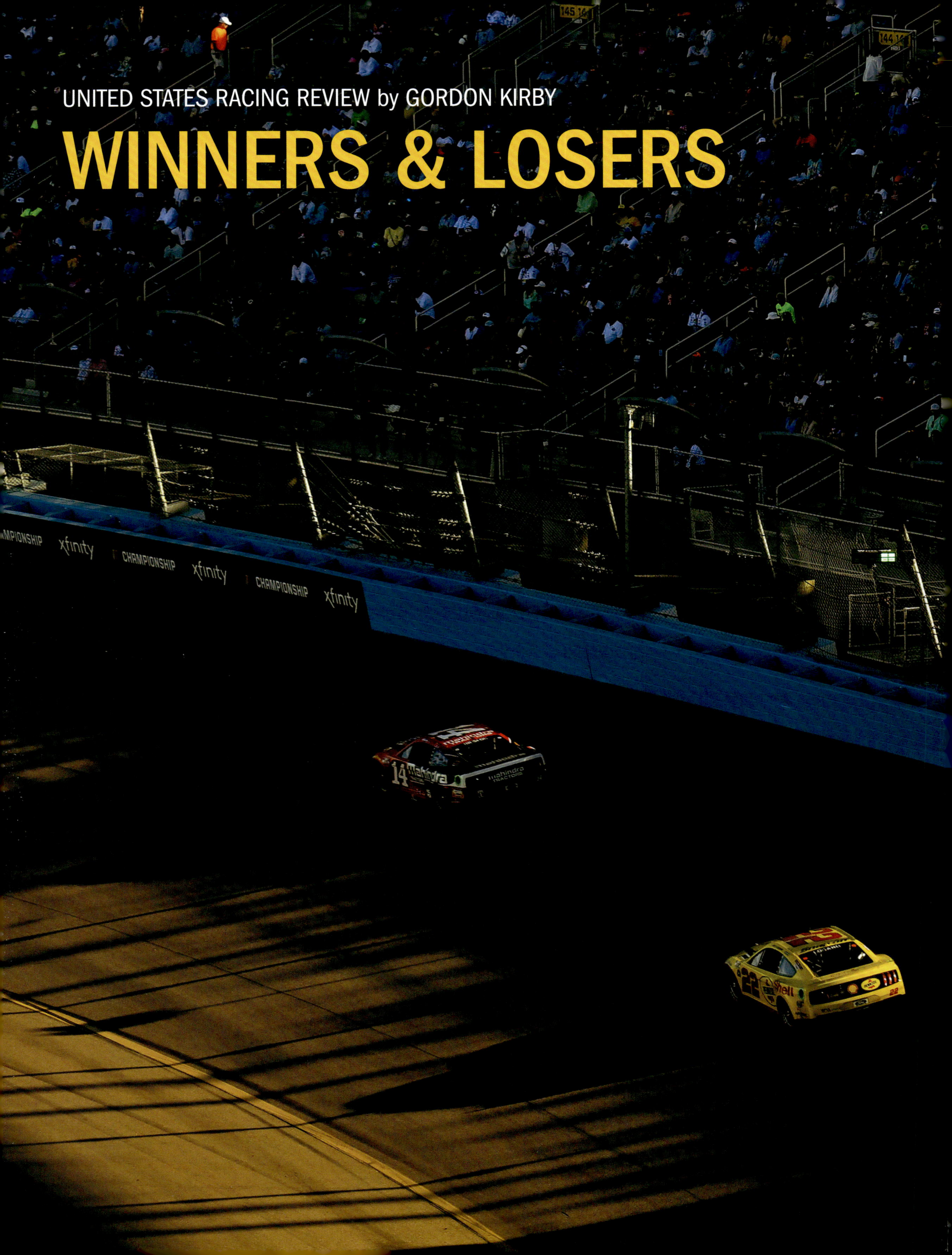

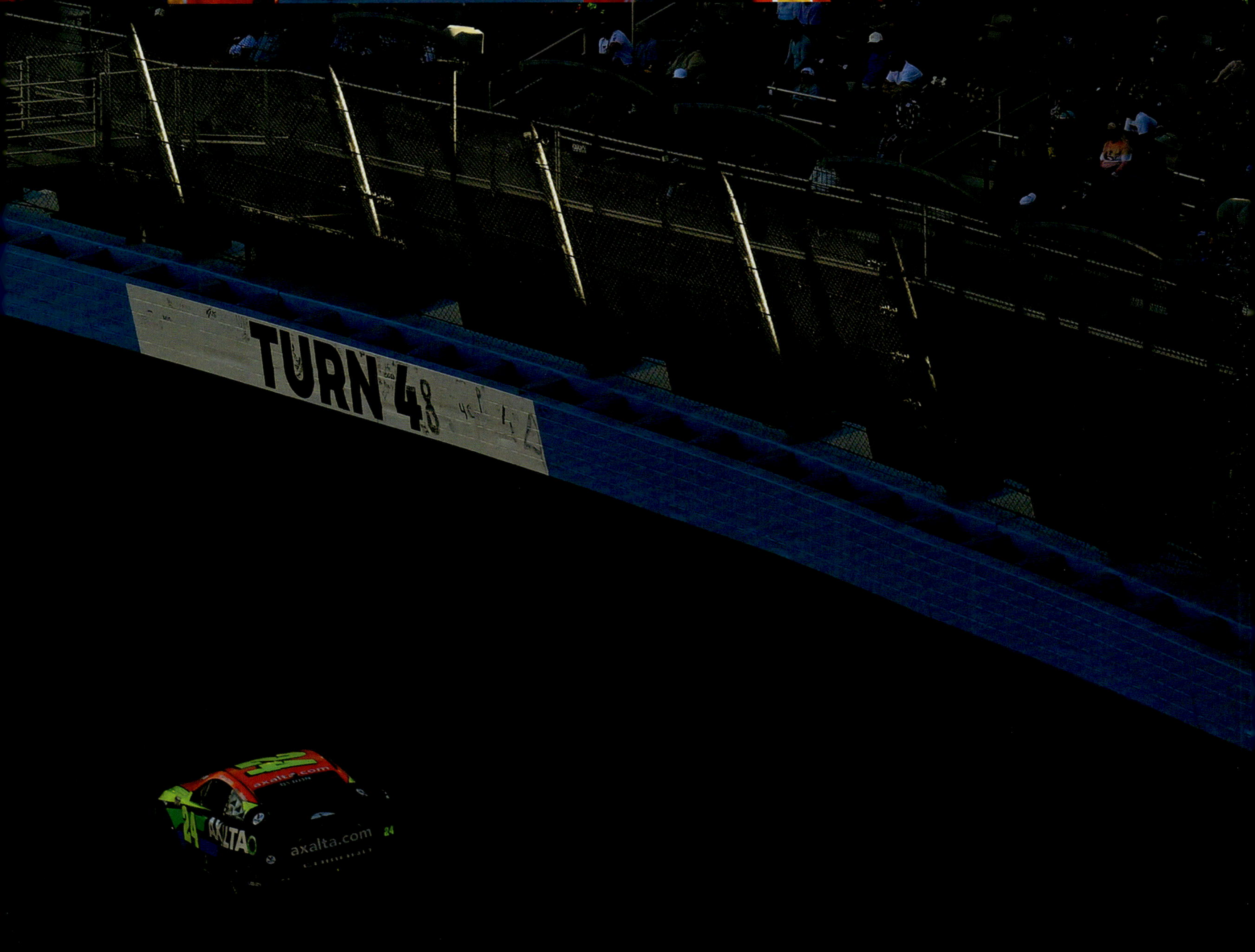

Main photo: Joey Logano's yellow Ford is sandwiched between the cars of Briscoe (14) and Byron (24) in the season finale at Phoenix.
Photo: Nigel Kinrade/NKP/LAT Images

Inset: Logano's son is wide-eyed at the size of the winner's trophy.
Photo: Matthew T. Thacker/Motorsport Images

PENNZOIL
Mazak
SIEMENS
TEAM PENSKE

xfinity
DISCOUNT TIRE
tires.com
GOODYEAR
CINDRIC

KYLE BUSCH
CAMRY

BLANEY
PENNZOIL
Ford

JOEY LOGANO dominated NASCAR's 2022 season finale on the one-mile Phoenix oval to win his second Cup Series championship. Having qualified on pole, he led most of the 312-lap race, adding a second NASCAR Cup championship to his first title from 2018. He and team-mate Ryan Blaney finished 1-2, driving a pair of Team Penske's three Fords, the team winning both NASCAR and IndyCar championships for the first time in its 56-year history.

NASCAR's 'play-off' format takes place over the final ten races of the 36-race Cup season and is designed to ensure that the championship goes down to the year's last race. The top 16 drivers in points qualify for the play-offs and are whittled down to 12 after three races, then eight after three more. The following round of three races determines the final four contenders for the season finale at Phoenix; if any of the top eight win one of those races, they qualify for the final four.

Logano turned the trick at Las Vegas in the middle of October, while Christopher Bell put himself into the final four by winning at Martinsville, Virginia, at the end of the month. In all, Logano won four races and also took the non-championship, pre-season Busch Clash in February.

"We did it!" Logano exclaimed. "We're champions again. Oh, my God, I'm so excited! Thank you to everybody on my team. You guys are amazing. You gave me a good race-car and a good pit stop there at the end, which got us up in front. Boy! It was just intense there at the end. We worked so hard the last couple weeks trying to put ourselves in position. I knew we just wanted to have a solid run and do this today. I can't thank Ford, Shell-Pennzoil and all our partners at Team Penske enough for supporting me over the last ten years and getting us a championship today."

Logano's Penske team-mates, Blaney and Austin Cindric, often ran well. Blaney led many races, but was unable to score a victory, although he did win one of two non-championship All-Star races in Texas in May. Cindric ran his first full Cup season and scored a victory in the season-opening Daytona 500, but he was unable to win another race.

Second in the championship was Ross Chastain, who drove for Trackhouse Racing, which had been founded two years before by Justin Marks and rap star Pitbull. Trackhouse had bought the assets of Chip Ganassi's NASCAR team towards the end of the 2021 season and ran its second season in NASCAR in 2022, fielding two Chevrolets for

Above: The rookie takes the 'big one'. Austin Cindric just beats Bubba Wallace across the line to win the Daytona 500.

Top left: A disbelieving Joey Logano with Roger Penske and Tim Cindric after his championship win at Phoenix.
Photos: Michael R. Levitt/Images

Above left: Austin Cindric celebrates his maiden Daytona 500 victory.
Photo: Rusty Jarrett/NKP/LAT Images

Left: Penske's Ryan Blaney failed to secure a win in 2022.

Far left: Kyle Busch left Joe Gibbs's team after 15 seasons.
Photos: John K. Harrelson/NKP/LAT Images

1
KESELOWSKI
Ford
6
RFK
LOGANO
Ford
24
11

SIMPSON
NASCAR
SERIES
CHAMPION
NAPA
HOOTERS
LLumar
SIMPSON
NAPA

sparco
NASCAR
CUP SERIES
GOODYEAR
JOCKEY
AdventHealth
MOOSE
FRATERNITY
Kubota
sparco

Daniel Suarez and Chastain. Suarez had shown promise for a few years and scored his first win at the Sonoma, California road course in June. Chastain came on strong from the start of the season, claiming his first win on the CoTA road course in March and a second at Talladega in May.

Chastain is a very aggressive driver and he got into some arguments after a few run-ins, most notably with Denny Hamlin. He and his Trackhouse Chevrolet earned their place among the final four in spectacular style at Martinsville at the end of October. Needing to pass four cars on the final lap of the little half-mile oval, he attacked the last turn in unique style, slamming his car along the wall all the way through Turns Three and Four at what looked like inhuman speed and rocketing past five cars as they took the chequered flag. It was a display of Dale Earnhardt-style fender-bashing stock car racing at its best. He went on to run a strong race in the Phoenix season-closer, finishing third behind the leading pair of Penske Fords.

Third in the championship went to Christopher Bell, a new star who drives one of Joe Gibbs Racing's four factory Toyotas. He won three races and is a fast, tidy racer with a rosy future. In 2022, he emerged as Gibbs's most successful driver, as team-mates Hamlin, Kyle Busch and Martin Truex Jr endured disappointing years. Hamlin was very competitive in many races and won twice. He had appeared likely to make the final-four championship shootout, but was knocked out at the last second when Chastain passed him at the chequered flag at Martinsville.

Two-time champion (2015 and 2019) Busch also had a poor year. He was a midfielder in many races, and before the end of the season, after protracted contract negotiations with Joe Gibbs had gone nowhere, he announced a move from Gibbs's team after 15 years to Richard Childress's Chevrolet team for 2023. Over the years, Busch had won 60 Cup races and a total of 162 races, including in the second-division Xfinity and third-division Truck Series.

Truex was another veteran who struggled in 2022 in Gibbs's fourth Toyota. The 2017 champion was uncompetitive in many races and failed to win one.

Above: Aggressive or what? Ross Chastain runs his Chevrolet along the wall in an audacious move at the finish in Martinsville.
Photo: Lesley Ann Miller/LAT Images)

Left: Tough and ucompromising , Chastain was old-style NASCAR.
Photo: Matthew T. Thacker/NKP/LAT Images

Far left: Chase Elliott was unimpressed by the introduction of the next-generation stock cars, due to race in 2023.

Right: A new star for Joe Gibbs Raceing emerged in the form of Christopher Bell. The fresh-faced 27-year-old appears to have a very bright future.
Photos: Nigel Kinrade/NKP/LAT Images

The remaining final-four qualifier was 2020 Cup champion Chase Elliott, the son of the great Bill Elliott, NASCAR's most popular driver. Driving one of Hendrick Motorsports' four Chevrolets, he won five races in 2022, more than any other driver. He lost his chance of a second title, however, when he tangled with Bell on a restart in the Phoenix season finale. He spun and clipped the wall, damaging his car and falling to the tail of the field.

Hendrick's four Chevrolets usually ran at or near the front, and each of Elliott's team-mates – Kyle Larson, William Byron and Alex Bowman – won races, although none of them was able to put together a championship challenge. Defending champion Larson had dominated in 2021, winning ten races, but he was less strong in '22. He won three races, but was eliminated from the championship battle early in the play-off process. Byron and Bowman won a race apiece, the former finishing sixth in points behind Elliott and Hamlin. Larson was seventh.

Chase Briscoe was another driver to win once in 2022. He drove for Tony Stewart's team and often ran near the front. Stewart-Haas fielded four Fords for Briscoe, Kevin Harvick, Aric Almirola and Cole Custer. Harvick had been racing Cup cars for more than 20 years, winning the championship in 2014, but he was conspicuously uncompetitive in many races. Harvick scored a couple of mid-season wins, but failed to make the play-offs.

The other leading Ford team was Roush-Fenway-Keselowski Racing, which ran a pair of cars for 2012 Cup champion Brad Keselowski, a part-owner of RFK, and Chris Buescher. Keselowski was unable to win in 2022, while Buescher won once, at Bristol in September.

Tyler Reddick won the second-division Xfinity championship in 2018 and '19, and had raced in the Cup series for Richard Childress's team for three years. He scored his first Cup win on the Elkhart Lake road course in July and went on to win two more races. He would move to 23XI Racing for 2023, where he would be teamed with Bubba Wallace, the only black driver in NASCAR. Wallace won at Kansas in September and showed good form in many races for Denny Hamlin and Michael Jordan's 23XI team. He was suspended for one race near the end of the year after an altercation with Larson following a collision between the two at Las Vegas.

Five drivers won two races apiece, and ten drivers scored single wins, so a record-equalling 19 drivers won Cup races in 2022. NASCAR might not be what it once was, but it remains by far America's most visible form of racing, as well as being the most competitive and unpredictable racing series on earth, with substantial fields and plenty of young stars taking the places of established names.

Kyle Busch's older brother, Kurt, announced in mid-October that he would not compete full-time in the NASCAR Cup Series in 2023. In July, he suffered a concussion during a qualifying crash at Pocono and did not race again in 2022. He had started racing in NASCAR's top series in 2000, winning the championship in 2004 with Team Penske, and in total, he had won 34 Cup races over 23 seasons.

"I'm not 100 per cent in my ability to go out and race at the top level in the NASCAR Cup series," Busch admitted. "Lately, I haven't felt my best. The doctors have come to the conclusion that it is best for me to 'shut it down' for this season. As I continue to focus on my health and work towards being cleared, I will be stepping away from full-time NASCAR Cup series competition in 2023. My long-term health is priority number one, and I don't feel committing to compete for a championship next year is in my best interest or the best interest of the team. If I'm cleared, maybe you'll see me at select races."

However, Busch would continue to work with 23XI Racing and the team's drivers, Wallace and Reddick. The latter had been released from Richard Childress Racing to drive Busch's car at 23XI Racing in 2023. He was slated to join the organisation proper in 2024. Busch would also continue as a brand ambassador for sponsor Monster Energy.

Above: Christopher Bell, in the Joe Gibbs Racing Toyota Camry, and Chase Briscoe, in the Stewart-Haas Ford, head the field at Bristol.
Photo: Matthew T. Thacker/NKP/LAT Images

Top right: Kyle Larson, in the Hendrick Motorsports Chevrolet Camaro, won on the road course at Watkins Glen.

Above right: Younger talents emerged strongly in 2023, in the form of Chase Briscoe *(left)* and William Byron.
Photos: LAT Images

Right: Denny Hamlin is very much one of the 'old guard'. He just missed out on the play-offs, but placed fifth in the series
Photo: Matthew T. Thacker/NKP/LAT Images

Unhappy drivers

Hendrick driver Alex Bowman also suffered a concussion in a mid-season accident. As a result, he was compelled to sit out five races before returning for the season finale. Meanwhile, NASCAR's latest NextGen spec car (the third in a series of increasingly tightly-regulated spec cars since 2008) drew a lot of criticism for the poor reliability of many components and for not being as safe as previous cars. Denny Hamlin and Kevin Harvick were among those who criticised the new car, and towards the end of the year, NASCAR's most popular driver, Chase Elliott, spoke out about the matter.

"I don't feel like we should have ever been in this position to need to go forward [with the car]," Elliott said. "In my opinion, we should have gone forward with a new opportunity at a new car. You have all these years of experience and knowledge, and time of racing and crashing these cars, and teams working on them and building them. And it just blows me away that we can have something new in 2022 that offers all this technology and all this time and experience of so many super-talented people in this sport, and we allow it to go backward, especially with safety.

"I think it's just super-surprising to me that we allowed that to happen. But we did, and now it's just about how do we go forward from here, making sure we make the right choices to improve what we have, and keep things like what happened to Kurt and Alex from happening. I'm confident that we will, but it's crucial that we do, because having guys out in the play-offs, or any time for that matter, shouldn't be happening. I think it's taking away from our product on Sunday, which should be the focus.

"There's no excuse for going backward. We have too many smart people, too much technology and too much experience with these cars. We should not be in the position that we are in. When you come out with a new product, you should take steps forward, not stay the same or go backward."

Unhappy team owners

Meanwhile, NASCAR's team owners became serious in 2022 about pushing for a new financial agreement. In June, a committee of team representatives made a request to NASCAR for a better economic model that would allow for greater longevity and sustainability for the team owners. "We've gotten to this point where the teams realise we can't keep going on," said Curtis Polk, an investor in Michael Jordan and Denny Hamlin's 23XI Racing. "The sustainability of the teams in this sport is not very long-term unless we have a fundamental change in the model."

Polk was new to NASCAR, but not the sports business. He has a stake in the Charlotte Hornets NBA team and is a long-time financial advisor to Michael Jordan. "It's become fundamentally clear to me that there is a total misalignment of interest, and as a result, the economic model is really broken for the teams," he said.

He is one of 16 NASCAR Cup series team owners who between them hold 36 NASCAR charters. The group's steering committee includes Polk, four-time NASCAR champion Jeff Gordon (now vice-chairman of Hendrick Motorsports), Steve Newman (president of Roush-Fenway-Keselowski Racing) and Dave Alpern (president of Joe Gibbs Racing).

The committee submitted a seven-point proposal to

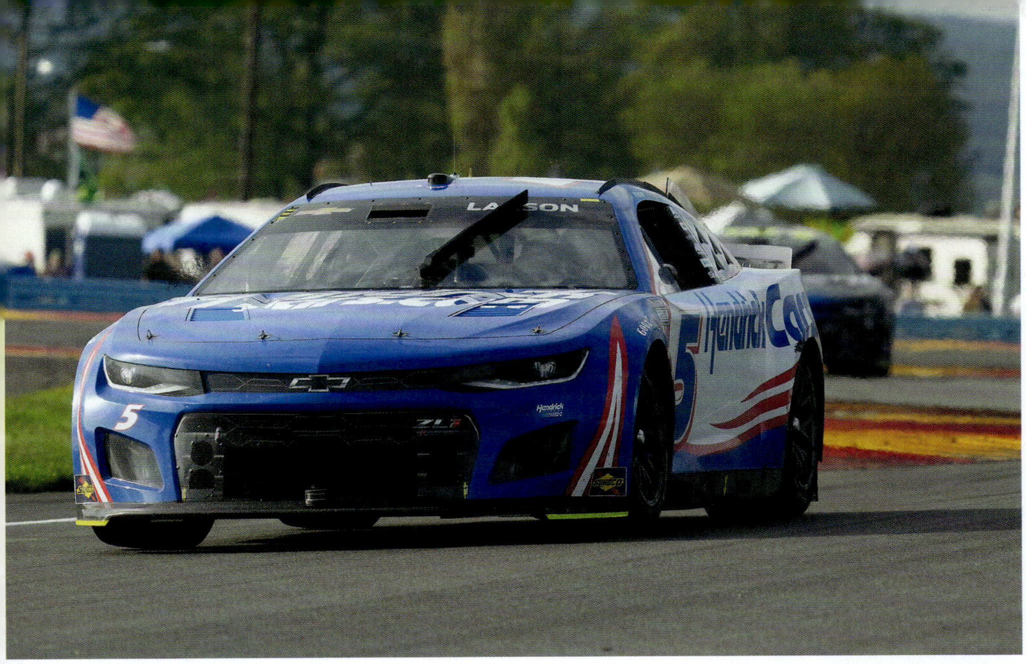

NASCAR in June, but received no response until October. Polk said the committee was very disappointed with NASCAR's reply. "We received a proposal with a minimal increase in revenue, and the emphasis was on cutting costs dramatically," he said.

NASCAR has enjoyed a pair of eight-year TV contracts with Fox and NBC that expire at the end of 2024. It's widely believed that the series will be compelled to accept much smaller cheques from the TV networks, because ratings have sagged substantially in recent decades.

The teams are targeting 2025 for a new financial deal and other changes. The committee acknowledged that it's going to take time and effort for everyone to reach an equitable agreement. Polk said that the committee had determined that 93 per cent of the value of NASCAR is possessed by the France family and the racetracks, and that the team owners share in only seven per cent of NASCAR's total value.

"Most of the teams have a very difficult time breaking even," he continued. "All well-managed teams should be able to compete for a Cup championship and make a reasonable profit. I think the sport is a sleeping giant, but we all have to get the interest aligned because we need to grow it together. We need to grow more revenue, and we need to create great sharing and an arrangement where every dollar that is created benefits the drivers, benefits the teams, benefits the tracks, benefits NASCAR. That's not how it's set up right now."

RFK's Newman added, "We have expressed a willingness to entertain cost caps and other measurements as long as it's part of an overall structure that is a fair model, and provides the stability and longevity for the teams."

NASCAR responded with the following statement:

"NASCAR acknowledges the challenges currently facing race teams. A key focus moving forward is an extension to the Charter agreement, one that will further increase revenue and help lower team expenses. Collectively, the goal is a strong, healthy sport, and we will accomplish that together."

In November, NASCAR president Steve Phelps elaborated: "There are two areas to do it – increasing revenue, which we have every intention of doing with our race teams, and controlling expenses," he said. "The teams have asked us to control expenses. Where those come from, I don't know. That will be up to the race teams to determine the best way to figure out how they would control those expenses.

"I'm not suggesting that we have a specific discussion around what that would be or the mechanisms that we put in place. The teams have thrown out the idea of having caps, floors and ceilings, and luxury taxes. There are all kinds of different things and levers we could pull, but those conversations will be between ourselves and our race teams. We'll continue to have a dialogue with our race teams.

"The charters go through the end of 2024. We will have meaningful dialogue with our teams next year, I'm sure. We'll figure out what is going to be a fair opportunity for all stakeholders. Moving forward in 2025, what that looks like, I don't know, but it will absolutely have to be around both revenue increases as well as some type of expense restriction in some way."

A healthy ladder system

One of the NASCAR's greatest strengths is its ladder system, which includes two long-running championships: the second-division Xfinity Series and third-division Camping World Truck Series. At most NASCAR race weekends, the Xfinity and Truck series run as support races on Saturday and Friday nights. They attract a useful fan following, and the Xfinity's TV ratings are consistently better than both IndyCar and F1 in the USA. The Xfinity series is ranked second only to the Cup Series in domestic auto racing TV ratings. The 2022 Xfinity championship was won by Ty Gibbs, the 20-year-old grandson of Joe Gibbs, while the Truck title went to Zane Smith, a 23-year-old Californian.

Above: Life begins at forty for Will Power, who took his second IndyCar title with a mature and measured approach to his season.

Top right: Scott McLaughlin opened his season's account with a victory at St Petersburg.

Top far right: Six hundred up for Roger Penske. Texas marked a victory milestone for 'The Captain'.

Above right: Joy for Pato O'Ward after his victory in Alabama.

Above far right: So close to a first win. Romain Grosjean took his DHL Andretti car to second in Long Beach.

Right: Colton Herta heads the field off Aquarium Way at the start of the Grand Prix of Long Beach.

Photos: IndyCar/Penske Entertainment Corp.

Power's second IndyCar championship

The NTT IndyCar Series developed into a fierce battle between the Penske and Ganassi teams, with Team Penske ultimately finishing 1-2-4 in championship points, and Chip Ganassi Racing coming home third, fifth and sixth. Penske's trio of Chevrolet-powered Dallaras won ten races, while Ganassi's four Honda-powered Dallaras won four, including the Indianapolis 500.

In the end, the championship was taken by Australian Will Power, who won two races and added seven more podium finishes on the way to his second title in 12 years with Penske. He had earned his first championship in 2014. Power enjoyed probably his most consistently competitive season in 2022. He also broke Mario Andretti's record of 67 pole positions by taking five poles in 2022 and qualifying fastest for the season finale to establish himself as the leading pole-winner in IndyCar history.

"It's so surreal," Power said after wrapping up the championship with a third-place finish in the Laguna Seca season-closer. "In the off-season, my wife said to me, 'I believe you're going to beat Mario's record and you're going to win the championship.' It actually gave me confidence that I could do it. That's how much confidence I have in her gut feel. I just couldn't believe that they came true.

"I just knew I had to get the most out of those stints today and not lose any more positions. I had to drive the thing today. It was on the edge, very loose. What a relief to get that done. I can't thank Verizon enough. They've been with me for close to 12 years now, and without them, I would never have had this career, and obviously, Roger Penske, the whole team and Chevrolet."

Team-mate Josef Newgarden finished second in the championship, 16 points behind Power. He was the winningest IndyCar driver of the year, scoring five wins and leading 527 laps, substantially more than any other driver, having bounced back from a big crash on the Iowa oval in July caused by a broken driveshaft. He was sidelined for a few days, but was back in action the following weekend on the Indy road course, where he qualified and finished fifth.

Kiwi Scott McLaughlin completed Penske's line-up and won three races in his second IndyCar season, after dominating the Australian Supercar championship for many years. He won the 2022 season-opener and led the championship for a few months before slipping back to finish fourth in points behind Scott Dixon.

Six-time champion Dixon led Ganassi's team, scoring two wins, but often struggling for speed in qualifying. He suffered a heart-breaker at Indianapolis, where he had started from pole and dominated the race, leading most of the way until he locked his brakes while coming into the pits for his final stop. As a result, he broke the pit-lane speed limit marginally and was given a stop/go penalty, ultimately finishing 21st.

Dixon, 42, has been racing Indy cars for 22 years and remains one of IndyCar's strongest racers. He also completed every lap of every race in 2022. "As a group effort, everybody did a hell of a job this season," he said. "We finished every lap this year, which is definitely a huge milestone in itself. That's kudos to the team, but also to our partners, too, with Honda and HPD, and the effort that goes into making it all possible. We'll keep after it, and we know exactly what we need to do in the off-season."

Team-mate Alex Palou was able to win only one race in 2022, after sweeping to the 2021 IndyCar championship in his first season with Ganassi's team. His year was disrupted by a mid-season squabble between Ganassi and McLaren team boss Zak Brown over the Spaniard's 2023 contract. The teams made contradictory announcements on the same day that Palou had signed for them for the coming season, and for a few months, the matter fell into the hands of lawyers. Eventually, the matter was resolved in Ganassi's favour, and Palou showed his true abilities with a dominant drive to win the season-closer by more than half a minute. He finished fifth in points.

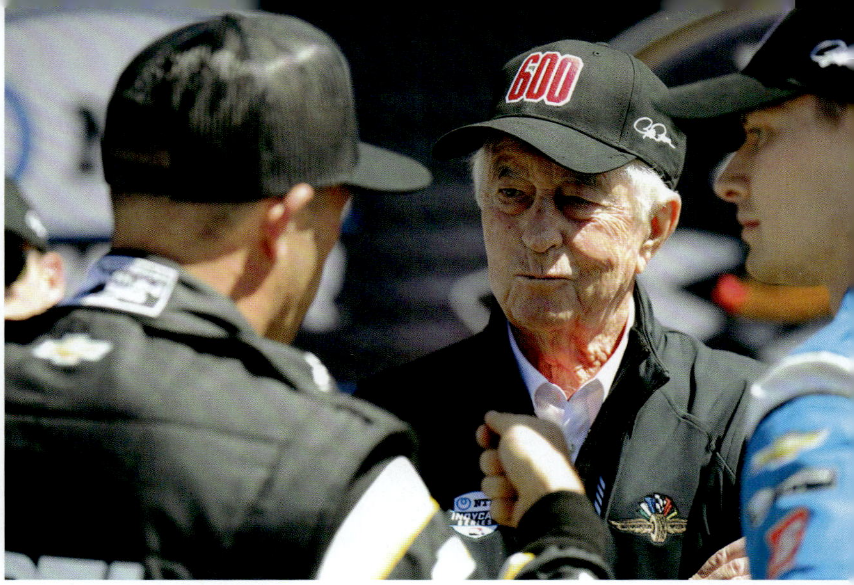

ACURA
DHL

Aquarium Way
ACURA

Above: Marcus Ericsson holds his nerve ahead of Pato O'Ward as the '500' enters its decisive phase.

Clockwise, from top right: Indy 500 veterans had contrasting fortunes on Memorial Day: Tony Kanaan rolled back the years to finish a brilliant third; Juan Pablo Montoya, seeking a third victory, was a respectable 11th; Ed Carpenter was still left seeking an elusive win across the 'Yard of Bricks'; Scott Dixon could have won but for a speed-lane infraction.

Right: "I drank the milk!" Marcus Ericsson went from F1 reject to Indy 500 winner on a gloriously sunny day in May.

Photos: IndyCar/Penske Entertainment Corp.

Ericsson wins the Indy 500

Swede Marcus Ericsson drove Ganassi's third car with personal sponsorship from Huski chocolate. He was very competitive in most races and led the championship for a few months, after scoring an excellent victory in the 105th Indianapolis 500 following a fierce battle with Pato O'Ward and Ganassi team-mate Tony Kanaan, which followed a red-flag for an accident.

"I think we did a really good last pit sequence," Ericsson said. "The car was fast. We came out third and caught Felix [Rosenqvist] and Pato, and passed them, pulled a gap. I was hoping that was the race-winning move. We had that three-second gap and had it covered. The only thing that could stop us was a caution and, of course, that caution came.

"It's not supposed to be easy to win the 500. Those ten minutes sitting there in the pit lane during that red flag was some of the hardest ten minutes of my life probably, thinking what to do, thinking that I'm leading the biggest race in the world, and I'm that close to win it.

"I knew Pato was going to have a run on me, because we've seen all month it's really hard to defend when you're up front. I was actually sitting during dinner here at the Speedway on the infield last night, talking with Dario [Franchitti] about this type of scenario: if I'm leading when it's towards the end of the race, the last couple laps, what to do, how to break the tow of the car behind, how to place the car? We had that very conversation last night. That was in my mind when I was sitting there during that red flag.

"I just tried to go out and execute that plan I had made in my head. Pato had a really good run on me. I wanted to put him on the outside because I knew it was going to be hard to go around my outside. I was not going to lift. There was no way I was going to lift. I just kept my foot down and that was the race-winning move."

Ericsson also talked about his transition from Formula 1 to Indy cars. "It's been tough. I did five years in Formula 1, almost a hundred grands prix, running for small teams towards the back most of it. You don't get a lot of credit running in the back in Formula 1. People think you are not very good.

"I came over here, and people probably didn't think much of that. I had to work my way here as well, learning American racing. I moved here, put my whole life into trying to become an IndyCar and mainly Indianapolis 500 champion. It's been tough, it's been not easy, but I've been working extremely hard. It feels good to show that hard work pays off. Winning the Indy 500 is not bad for a pay driver! It's good.

"When I came to IndyCar and American racing, one of the big reasons was the ovals, because I always thought the ovals were something that would suit me. I always enjoyed the tracks in Europe that had a lot of high-speed content.

"When I was going towards the end of my Formula 1 career, my goal was to get to IndyCar. I came here, had a very open mind about ovals, wanted to learn everything I could about it, and enjoyed it from the first moment. I learned very quickly that on the ovals, experience is very important, and the small details in the way you drive, the way you set up the car, the way you have to adjust your car in a race, those were things that I didn't really understand at the beginning. So it took me some time to understand that and learn, but I think we showed today that I did those things well."

Seven-time NASCAR champion Jimmie Johnson ran his second IndyCar season in Ganassi's fourth car. He struggled for speed in many races and had a few embarrassing incidents, but he enjoyed his IndyCar adventure before announcing his retirement from full-time racing at the end of 2022. He has become a part owner of the Petty GMS NASCAR team and may run in a few races in 2023.

Pato O'Ward came home seventh in IndyCar points, after an up-and-down season with McLaren. O'Ward won on the Barber road course and Iowa oval, and was very quick at Indianapolis. But in some races, he was mired in the midfield. If he wants to achieve his goal of racing in F1, he must show more consistency and do better in 2023. Team-mate Felix Rosenqvist's season was much like O'Ward's, running hot and cold. He led some races and finished on the podium twice, finishing eighth in points.

mission

PNC
NTT
INDYCAR SERIES
sparco
S. DIXON
PNC BANK

E. CARPENTER
BITNILE
Speedway

American
Dairy
Association
Indiana
WINNERS
DRINK
MILK
HUSKI
CHOCOLATE

PALOU
INDY 500
GAINBRIDGE
Sports
PNC BANK
PNC BANK GANASSI RACING

Take your seat. 'The greatest spectacle in racing' gets under way at the Indianapolis Motor Speedway.
Photo: IndyCar/Penske Entertainment Corp.

Above: Will Power took his only win of the season in Detroit, but the Penske stalwart broke Mario Andretti's record of 67 pole positions on his way to the championship.

Clockwise, from top right: Winners all: Scott McLaughlin took three wins for Penske, including Portland; Alex Palou put aside his contractual issues with Ganassi to win the final race of the 'season at Laguna Seca; Josef Newgarden won the most races throughout the season, but fell just short in the championship chase; Colton Herta emerged with only a single victory, at the IMS road course meeting in May.

Right: Alexander Rossi's season was largely forgettable, but it was rescued somewhat by his last win for Andretti Autosport in the Gallagher Grand Prix at Indianapolis in July.

Far right: You can never discount Scott Dixon. Even though the Ganassi driver struggled for ultimate pace, the six-time champion still managed to notch up two wins, in Toronto (*pictured*) and Nashville.

Photos: IndyCar/Penske Entertainment Corp.

FREIGHTLINER
PPG
HITACHI

GAINBRIDGE
GROUP 1001

TEAM
PENSKE

PNC
Firestone

Above: Harum-scarum at Nashville as Jack Harvey nearly rear-ends the car of Alex Palou. The venue was terrific, but the track was found wanting in many respects.

Right: Rahal-Lannigan-Letterman's Christian Lundgaard was Rookie of the Year. Second place on the Indianapolis road course was the highlight of his season.

Below right: Equally meritorious was David Malukas's driving. He also scored a brilliant second place, in a thrilling finish just behind Josef Newgarden at Gateway.

Centre right: Linus Lundqvist took the Indy Lights championship with six wins from 14 races.

Far right: Andretti's Sting Ray Robb (*top*) was runner-up, having overcome the challenge of Matthew Brabham (*bottom*).

Photos: IndyCar/Penske Entertainment Corp.

Michael Andretti's team ran four cars in all races, plus an occasional fifth entry, but 2022 was a very disappointing year for Andretti Autosport. Alexander Rossi won once on the Indianapolis road course, but usually ran in the midfield; he finished ninth in points. In mid-season, he announced that he would be moving to McLaren for 2023, hoping to reignite his career. He would be replaced by 2021 Indy Lights champion Kyle Kirkwood. Colton Herta had a similarly up-and-down year, winning just once on the Indy road course (two races were run ot the track during the year) and finishing a disappointing tenth in points. Like O'Ward, he must do better if he wants to break into F1.

Romain Grosjean ran his second IndyCar season with Andretti's team and was its strongest card in many races. He finished second at Long Beach, having challenged Newgarden for the win, but had a disappointing year otherwise, finishing 13th in points. Canadian rookie Devlin DeFrancesco drove Andretti's fourth car and ran well in some races, but had few results, finishing 23rd in points.

Dane Christian Lundgaard beat David Malukas to IndyCar's rookie-of-the-year honors. Driving for Rahal-Letterman-Lanigan Racing's three-car team, the 21-year-old was often the fastest of RLL's three drivers. He finished second on the Indy road course in August and wrapped up the rookie award with a strong drive to fifth in the season finale. Malukas also enjoyed an impressive rookie season, often running in the top ten and taking a brilliant second place at Gateway, hounding the winner Newgarden to the chequered flag.

Lundgaard's team leader, Graham Rahal, had a disappointing season, finishing 11th in points and often struggling well outside the top ten. Aged, 33, he has been racing Indy cars for 15 years and appears to be approaching the end of his IndyCar career.

Swede Linus Lundqvist prevailed in the Indy Lights championship. He won five of 14 races and took six poles to beat American Sting Ray Robb and Australian Matthew Brabham (Jack's grandson) to the title. Englishman Louis Foster won the Indy Pro championship, with Michael d'Orlando taking the US F2000 title.

The same old problems

IndyCar continued its struggle to attract crowds, TV ratings and any major media coverage. Some races drew good crowds, but many were very weak, and TV ratings remain tepid at best. Most IndyCar practice and qualifying sessions are broadcast on NBC's Peacock streaming service.

A few of the races were also on Peacock in 2022, drawing audiences of barely 100,000. IndyCar has endured a steady, sad decline over the last 20 years and appears to have no plan to reverse this unfortunate trend.

The fact is that IndyCar is America's smallest, least relevant professional sport, with champions like Will Power, Josef Newgarden and Scott Dixon largely unknown to the general public. And in the last two years, Formula 1 has pulled better TV ratings in America than IndyCar, as well as attracting regular coverage in the New York Times, where IndyCar simply doesn't exist.

As I've noted before, the Indy cars were no fewer than 13 seconds per lap slower than F1 cars on their only appearance at the Circuit of The Americas in 2019. Nor did anyone show up to watch that particular race in great numbers. The bottom line is that IndyCar lost its spectacular, high-performance car 20 years ago amid the CART/IRL war, and now there is neither the money nor the motivation to recreate the formula with multiple car builders and much more powerful engines. Until that happens, IndyCar will continue to languish as a minor sporting attraction in the US.

I also have to add that in my 50 years covering the US racing scene for AUTOCOURSE, I have never encountered such a poorly conceived or absurdly "Mickey Mouse" excuse for a racetrack as IndyCar's street circuit located in downtown Nashville, first run in 2021. The circuit is way too narrow, ridiculously tight, and by its very nature, it breeds incidents, accidents and yellow flags. The 2022 race in Nashville was littered with full-course yellows and interruptions, trailing well on beyond its TV time slot. In all, it was an absolute embarrassment of the first order and should not be repeated.

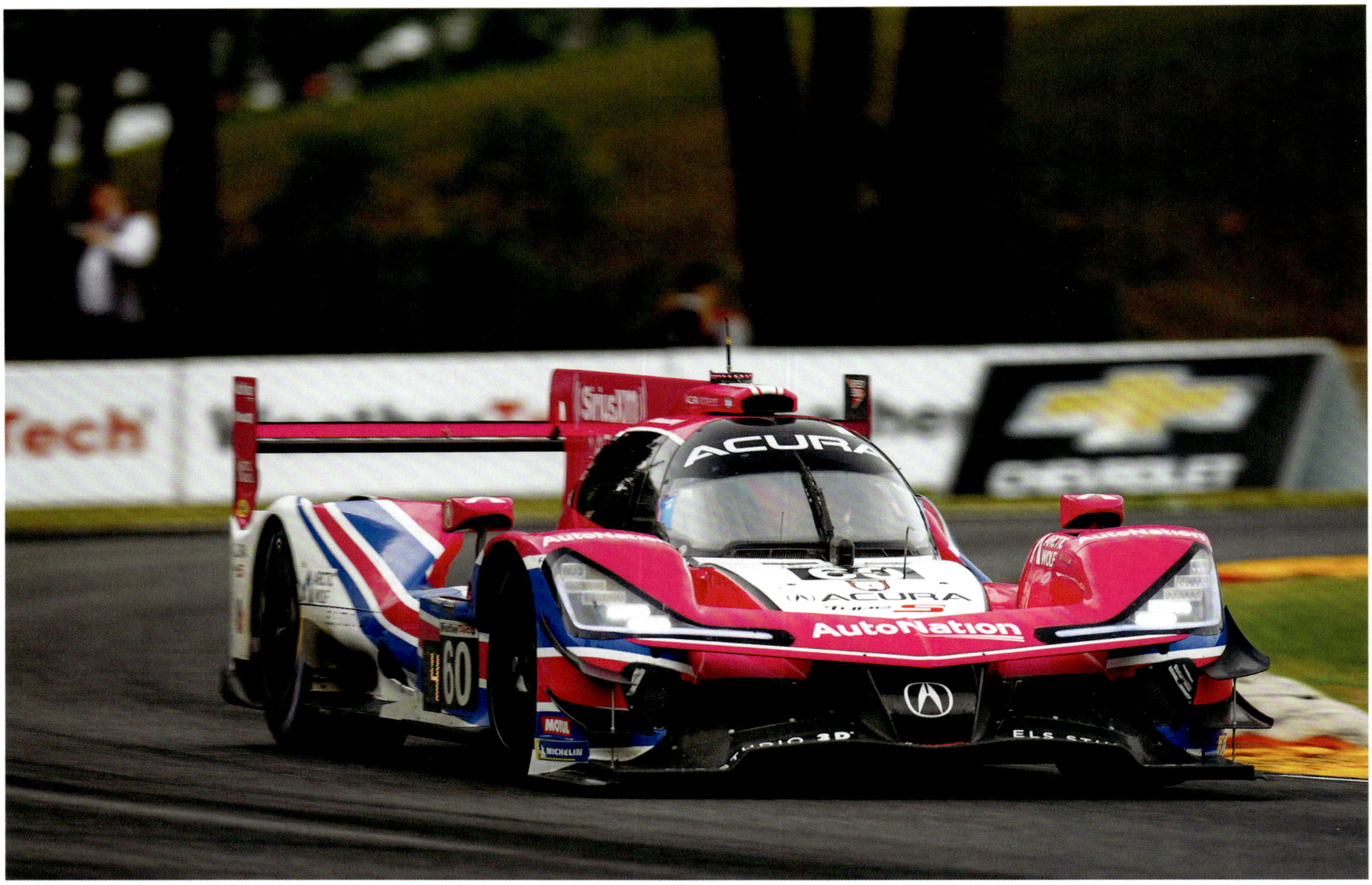

Above: Consistency was the key for the Meyer Shank Racing team as its Acura DPi, driven by Oliver Jarvis and Tom Blomqvist, took the 2022 WeatherTech IMSA championship honours.
Photo: Jake Galstad LAT Images)

Jarvis and Blomqvist take IMSA title

IMSA offers a healthy alternative to IndyCar. The WeatherTech Sports Car Championship enjoys the benefits of an active, customer-orientated series sponsor that energetically promotes IMSA. There is also an impressive array of 18 manufacturers, who compete in one of five WeatherTech series categories or any one of IMSA's six additional supporting championships. The manufacturers are required to participate in a multi-faceted commercial mid-way, which is a central part of all IMSA races. IMSA also benefits from a solid, proven schedule of a dozen races run at North America's most historic road courses. All these elements contribute to a very healthy fan base and good crowds at every race weekend.

The 2022 WeatherTech Championship was sewn up in the closing laps of the ten-hour Petit Le Mans at Road Atlanta, with the title going to Meyer Shank Racing's Acura DPi driven by Oliver Jarvis and Tom Blomqvist, with Helio Castroneves joining them for the long-distance races. Blomqvist stood out as he qualified on the pole for the season finale and won the ten-hour race with some aggressive driving. He joined Jarvis, Castroneves and Simon Pagenaud to win the season-opening Daytona 24 Hours as well as Petit Le Mans, while with Jarvis, he added five second-place finishes and three more top-fives.

Runner-up in points was Wayne Taylor Racing's Acura DPi, driven by Ricky Taylor and Filipe Albuquerque, who were joined by Will Stevens and Alexander Rossi at Daytona, and Brendan Hartley at Petit Le Mans. Taylor and Albuquerque were the men to beat in most races, claiming four wins, a second and a pair of fourth places. The championship was lost in the final 15 minutes of the season-closer, however, when Albuquerque crashed while attempting to lap a slower GTD car.

Also winning races in 2022 were Chip Ganassi's pair of Cadillac DPis. Sébastien Bourdais and Renger van der Zande won three races and added three more top-fives, while Alex Lynn and Earl Bamber won the Sebring 12 Hours and finished in the top six in another half-a-dozen races. Cadillac's DPi cars were built by Dallara, but they were beaten to IMSA's primary manufacturers' championship by the pair of Acura DPis run by Meyer Shank and Wayne Taylor's team.

Tower Motorsport's Oreca, driven by John Farano, Louis Delétraz and Rui Pinto de Andrade, finished fifth overall at Road Atlanta, with Farano winning IMSA's LMP2 championship. The LMP3 title was taken by Jon Bennett's CORE Autosport Ligier JS P320, driven by Bennett and Colin Braun, George Kurtz joining them for the endurance races.

The GTD Pro championship went to Matt Campbell and Mathieu Jaminet's Pfaff Motorsport's Porsche 911 GT3R, with Felipe Nasr on board for the long-distance grinds. The GTD championship was won by Roman de Angelis's Heart of Racing Aston Martin, which he shared with Maxime Martin and Ian James.

The 2022 season was the last for IMSA's premier DPi category. It will be replaced in 2023 by the new LMDh (Le Mans Daytona hybrid) GTP class. The LMDh rules stipulate a car weight of 1,030kg with 500kW peak combined power from engine and hybrid systems. LMDh also requires a single bodywork package, a single tyre supplier (Michelin) and a complex global BoP system to balance out LMDh and LMH cars. The LMDh gearbox hybrid system is supplied by Xtrac, with an integrated motor generator unit supplied by Bosch and batteries from Williams Advanced Engineering. LMDh approved chassis suppliers are Dallara, Ligier, Multimatic and Oreca. Factory-backed teams will be run by Acura, Cadillac, Audi, BMW and Porsche.

APPRECIATIONS · by Gordon Kirby

Kevin Kalkhoven

1944–2022

KEVIN KALKHOVEN was an Australian venture capitalist, and Champ Car team owner and series boss based in Alamo, California. He served as CEO and chairman of JDS Uniphase, a manufacturer of industrial lasers, and supplier of components and modules for fibre-optic telecommunications networks.

Kalkhoven oversaw JDS's transformation from a privately-owned entity to a publicly-traded company on the NASDAQ stock exchange. During his tenure, the company's annual sales increased from US$23 million in 1991 to US$394 million in 2000, while its market cap grew from US$35 million to US$100 billion. Kalkhoven was named in the May 2000 edition of *Worth* magazine as one of America's Top 50 CEOs.

He became a CART Indy car team owner in 2002, in partnership with Craig Pollock. The following year, he became a co-owner with Gerry Forsythe and Paul Gentilozzi of the Champ Car organisation. With Forsythe, he also bought the Long Beach and Toronto Champ Car races. In 2004, he and Forsythe bought Cosworth and the PI electronics group. Kalkhoven served as chairman of the merged companies and led the transition of Cosworth from a motor racing-centric company to a profitable automotive technology company providing LIDAR sensor technology and hybrid powertrains.

In 2008, Kalkhoven hatched an agreement with Tony George to merge Champ Car with the Indy Racing League, ending a 12-year civil war between the two groups. He also partnered with Jimmy Vasser during this time to establish KV Racing, which won the 2013 Indy 500 with Tony Kanaan.

Roger Rager

1948–2022

ROGER RAGER was a veteran sprint car driver who hailed from Minnesota. He was the only driver to have won a feature race at the famed Knoxville speedway in every one of the five decades from the 1960s to the 2000s.

In 1973, Rager was captain of a sprint car team that competed in South Africa. He won Knoxville's season championship in 1975 and raced into his fifties at the turn of the century. In 1980, he qualified his own Chevrolet stock-block-powered Wildcat an impressive tenth fastest for the Indy 500, but crashed in the race.

In 1987, Rager moved his family to Pequot Lakes in Florida and purchased Loon Lake Campland. He built the property into a seasonal RV park named Rager's Acres.

Rager is survived by a brother, two sisters, two daughters, a son and eight grandchildren.

Vince Granatelli

1942–2022

VINCE GRANATELLI was the son of STP impresario Andy Granatelli, who won the 1969 Indy 500 with Mario Andretti. Vince worked as a chief mechanic on Andy's team and later bought an existing Indy car team from Dan Cotter, owner of True Value hardware stores.

The younger Granatelli operated his Indy car team for four years, from 1987 to 1991, and won two races with Roberto Guerrero driving, and two races with Arie Luyendyk. He sold his team in 1992 to Bob Tezak. Granatelli died on 22nd January, aged 80, as a result of complications from pneumonia and Covid-19.

Eldon Rasmussen

1936–2022

A WELL-KNOWN fabricator and car builder, ELDON RASMUSSEN was a Canadian who spent his working years and driving career in Indianapolis. He built his own Indy car, the Rascar, which he qualified on the last row at the Indy 500 in 1975, '77 and '79. He raced Indy cars from 1971 to 1979, making 23 starts. His best finish was seventh at the Ontario Motor Speedway in 1975.

Rasmussen was best known for being involved in Tom Sneva's giant accident during the 1975 Indy 500. While attempting to lap Rasmussen in Turn Two, Sneva hit his left front wheel and was launched into the wall. His car burned briefly before tumbling to a stop in several pieces, but Sneva survived unhurt. The spectacular accident was often replayed on television over the following years, giving the softly-spoken Rasmussen the kind of notoriety he did not deserve.

Danny Ongais

1942–2022

DANNY ONGAIS enjoyed one of the most wide-ranging careers of any modern racing driver. Known as 'On-the-gas', he won races in Indy cars, IMSA sports cars, NHRA top fuel dragsters and on motorcycles. Born and raised in Hawaii, Ongais began his career on two wheels, winning the Hawaiian motorcycle championship in 1960, before moving to California and making his name in drag racing.

He won the AHRA's AA Gas Dragster championship in 1963 and '64, and took the NHRA's AA Dragster title the following year. In 1969, he won two major NHRA Funny Car races, driving a Ford Mustang for Mickey Thompson. Over the next decade, Ongais raced Formula 5000, IMSA GT cars and Indy cars sponsored by wealthy Californian Ted Field, under the Interscope Racing banner.

His career reached its height in 1977 and '78. He took eight poles and won five Indy car races in 1978, driving Interscope Parnelli-Cosworths. He also started six F1 grands prix in 1977 and '78, driving an Ensign and Shadow for Field. Ongais and Field also won the Daytona 24 Hours with Hurley Haywood in 1979, aboard an Interscope Porsche 935.

His career was sidetracked in 1981 when he crashed badly, suffering a concussion and critical injuries to his legs and lower extremities. Ongais made a comeback in 1983, however, and raced Indy cars irregularly until 1987. He started the Indy 500 for the last time in 1996, aged 54, finishing seventh. Ongais died from congestive heart failure in February, aged 79.

Bruton Smith

1927–2022

WITHOUT doubt, the second most powerful and important man in NASCAR's history was BRUTON SMITH, who was Bill France Sr's biggest rival during American stock car racing's formative years. In the late 1940s and early 1950s, Smith ran the rival National Stock Car Racing Association (NSCRA) and promoted races across the South. In 1959, he built the Charlotte Motor Speedway, followed quickly by the Atlanta Motor Speedway, and these tracks joined Daytona as the USA's first high-banked super-speedways built specifically for NASCAR.

Later, Smith founded and ran Speedway Motorsports, which operates eight NASCAR tracks and a dozen Cup races. SMI owns Charlotte, Atlanta, Bristol, Sonoma, Kentucky, Las Vegas, New Hampshire and Texas Motor Speedways. Near the end of the 20th century, Smith took SMI public, but 15 years later, he privatised the company. He also established Sonic Automotive, a group of 100 American automobile dealerships.

Smith was ranked in the top 200 of the Forbes 400 list of America's wealthiest businessmen, with an estimated net worth of $1.5 billion. Smith was divorced with four children. His oldest son, Marcus, runs SMI today. He died of natural causes on 22nd June.

Bobby East

1984–2022

BOBBY EAST achieved considerable success in midgets and sprint cars, winning USAC's national midget championship in 2004 when he was just 19. He was the youngest driver ever to win the title, and he won 15 races that year in midgets, sprint cars and championship dirt cars.

Over the following four years, East moved to NASCAR, competing in the second-division Nationwide series and the third-division truck series. He won the last race he started, a Nationwide event, at Memphis in 2008.

East died on 13th July while filling his car with gasoline at a gas station in Westminster, California. He had been accosted by a knife-wielding vagrant who was running from an arrest warrant for a parole violation. The two men exchanged words, during which East was stabbed fatally in his chest. He was rushed to hospital, but died from his injuries shortly thereafter. Later, his attacker was found hiding in a nearby apartment and was killed in a shootout with the police.

Ted Prappas

1955–2022

TED PRAPPAS raced Indy cars in 1991 and '92, making 26 starts, including the 1992 Indy 500. His best finish was sixth at Long Beach in 1991. He had three other top-ten results.

Prappas started his racing career in Formula Super Vee in 1983, going on to win the 1986 West Coast Formula Atlantic championship and finishing second in the 1990 Indy Lights championship.

He died in April after a battle with colon cancer.

Lee Brayton

1933–2022

LEE BRAYTON raced Indy cars from 1972 to 1975, making 16 starts. His best finishes were a trio of tenth places. After his racing career, he founded his own engineering company, which built engines and ran Indy cars for his son, Scott, who was killed during practice for the 1996 Indy 500.

Later, in 2001 and 2002, Brayton campaigned cars in the Indy Racing League, but failed to make the Indy 500 field.

He died at the end of April, at a nursing home in his hometown, Coldwater, Michigan

MAJOR RESULTS

OTHER CHAMPIONSHIP RACING SERIES WORLDWIDE

Compiled by DAVID HAYHOE and JOÃO PAULO CUNHA – www.forix.com

ABB FIA Formula E World Championship

Officially designated as the 2021-22 season, but all races were held in 2022

DIRIYAH E-PRIX, Diriyah (Riyadh) Street Circuit, Saudi Arabia, 28/29 January. Round 1. 41 and 35 laps of the 1.550-mile/2.495km circuit.

Race 1 (63.930 miles/102.885km).

1 Nyck de Vries, NL (Mercedes EQ Silver Arrow 02), 52m 14.642s, 73.003mph/117.488km/h; **2** Stoffel Vandoorne, B (Mercedes EQ Silver Arrow 02), +0.636s; **3** Jake Dennis, GB (BMW iFE.21), +8.802s; **4** Sam Bird, GB (Jaguar I-TYPE 5), +14.925s; **5** Lucas di Grassi, BR (Mercedes EQ Silver Arrow 02), +15.152s; **6** Edoardo Mortara, CH (Mercedes EQ Silver Arrow 02), +16.015s; **7** Nick Cassidy, NZ (Audi e-tron FE07), +17.265s; **8** Jean-Éric Vergne, F (DS E-Tense FE21), +25.076s; **9** Oliver Askew, USA (BMW iFE.21), +25.699s; **10** Mitch Evans, NZ (Jaguar I-TYPE 5), +27.320s; **11** Pascal Wehrlein, D (Porsche 99X Electric), +28.781s; **12** Maximilian Günther, D (Nissan IM03), +30.536s; **13** André Lotterer, D (Porsche 99X Electric), +31.521s; **14** Alexander Sims, GB (Mahindra M7Electro), +34.572s; **15** Sérgio Sette Câmara, BR (Penske EV-5), +36.781s; **16** Robin Frijns, NL (Audi e-tron FE07), +39.953s; **17** Sébastien Buemi, CH (Nissan IM03), +41.334s; **18** Dan Ticktum, GB (NIO 333 001), +49.222s; **19** Oliver Turvey, GB (NIO 333 001), +50.965s; **20** Antonio Giovinazzi, I (Penske EV-5), +1m 16.527s; Oliver Rowland, GB (Mahindra M7Electro), -34 laps (DNF-accident); António Félix da Costa, P (DS E-Tense FE21), -41 (DNF-accident damage).

Fastest race lap: Cassidy, 1m 09.207s, 80.644mph/129.784km/h.

Pole position: Vandoorne, 1m 08.626s, 81.327mph/130.883km/h.

Race 2 (54.628 miles/87.915km).

1 Edoardo Mortara, CH (Mercedes EQ Silver Arrow 02), 47m 02.131s, 69.222mph/111.402km/h; **2** Robin Frijns, NL (Audi e-tron FE07), +0.451s; **3** Lucas di Grassi, BR (Mercedes EQ Silver Arrow 02), +0.912s; **4** André Lotterer, D (Porsche 99X Electric), +1.125s; **5** Jake Dennis, GB (BMW iFE.21), +1.646s; **6** Jean-Éric Vergne, F (DS E-Tense FE21), +3.166s; **7** Stoffel Vandoorne, B (Mercedes EQ Silver Arrow 02), +3.568s; **8** Oliver Rowland, GB (Mahindra M7Electro), +4.235s; **9** Pascal Wehrlein, D (Porsche 99X Electric), +4.962s; **10** Nyck de Vries, NL (Mercedes EQ Silver Arrow 02), +5.294s; **11** Oliver Askew, USA (BMW iFE.21), +6.732s; **12** António Félix da Costa, P (DS E-Tense FE21), +8.693s; **13** Sébastien Buemi, CH (Nissan IM03), +9.015s; **14** Maximilian Günther, D (Nissan IM03), +9.464s; **15** Sam Bird, GB (Jaguar I-TYPE 5), +11.690s; **16** Nick Cassidy, NZ (Audi e-tron FE07), +13.973s; **17** Sérgio Sette Câmara, BR (Penske EV-5), +14.521s; **18** Oliver Turvey, GB (NIO 333 001), +15.005s; **19** Dan Ticktum, GB (NIO 333 001), +16.744s; **20** Antonio Giovinazzi, I (Penske EV-5), +17.681s; **21** Mitch Evans, NZ (Jaguar I-TYPE 5), +29.872s *; Alexander Sims, GB (Mahindra M7Electro), -6 laps (DNF-accident).

* 24s penalty for failing to activate the second activation of the Attack Mode.

Fastest race lap: Bird, 1m 08.723s, 81.212mph/130.698km/h.

Pole position: de Vries, 1m 07.154s, 83.109mph/133.752km/h.

Championship points: Drivers: 1 Mortara, 33; **2** de Vries, 29; **3** Vandoorne, 28; **4** di Grassi, 25; **4** Dennis, 25; **6** Frijns, 18.

Teams: 1 ROKiT Venturi Racing, 58; **2** Mercedes-EQ Formula E Team, 57; **3** Avalanche Andretti Formula E, 27.

MEXICO CITY E-PRIX, Autódromo Hermanos Rodríguez, Mexico City, D.F., Mexico, 12 February. Round 2. 40 laps of the 1.619-mile/2.606km circuit, 64.772 miles/104.240km.

1 Pascal Wehrlein, D (Porsche 99X Electric), 47m 20.404s, 82.093mph/132.116km/h; **2** André Lotterer, D (Porsche 99X Electric), +0.302s; **3** Jean-Éric Vergne, F (DS E-Tense FE21), +9.051s; **4** António Félix da Costa, P (DS E-Tense FE21), +9.975s; **5** Edoardo Mortara, CH (Mercedes EQ Silver Arrow 02), +18.356s; **6** Nyck de Vries, NL (Mercedes EQ Silver Arrow 02), +19.020s; **7** Robin Frijns, NL (Audi e-tron FE07), +20.232s; **8** Sébastien Buemi, CH (Nissan IM03), +23.394s; **9** Maximilian Günther, D (Nissan IM03), +26.497s; **10** Jake Dennis, GB (BMW iFE.21), +26.829s; **11** Stoffel Vandoorne, B (Mercedes EQ Silver Arrow 02), +27.086s; **12** Lucas di Grassi, BR (Mercedes EQ Silver Arrow 02), +27.525s *; **13** Nick Cassidy, NZ (Audi e-tron FE07), +28.794s; **14** Oliver Turvey, GB (NIO 333 001), +32.978s; **15** Sam Bird, GB (Jaguar I-TYPE 5), +35.677s; **16** Oliver Rowland, GB (Mahindra M7Electro), +36.047s; **17** Oliver Askew, USA (BMW iFE.21), +36.395s; **18** Dan Ticktum, GB (NIO 333 001), +44.607s; **19** Mitch Evans, NZ (Jaguar I-TYPE 5), +1m 02.458s; **20** Sérgio Sette Câmara, BR (Penske EV-5), +1m 21.406s; Antonio Giovinazzi, I (Penske EV-5), -19 laps (DNF-mechanical); Alexander Sims, GB (Mahindra M7Electro), -39 (DNF-accident).

* 5s penalty for causing a collision.

Fastest race lap: di Grassi, 1m 09.487s, 83.892mph/135.012km/h.

Pole position: Wehrlein, 1m 07.100s, 86.877mph/139.815km/h.

Championship points: Drivers: 1 Mortara, 43; **2** de Vries, 38; **3** Wehrlein, 30; **4** Lotterer, 30; **5** Vandoorne, 28; **6** Vergne, 27.

Teams: 1 ROKiT Venturi Racing, 68; **2** Mercedes-EQ Formula E Team, 66; **3** TAG Heuer Porsche Formula E Team, 60.

ROME E-PRIX, Circuit Cittadino dell'EUR, Rome, Italy, 9/10 April. Round 3. 2 x 27 laps of the 2.100-mile/3.380km circuit.

Race 1 (56.706 miles/91.260km).

1 Mitch Evans, NZ (Jaguar I-TYPE 5), 51m 59.632s, 65.438mph/105.312km/h; **2** Robin Frijns, NL (Audi e-tron FE07), +5.703s; **3** Stoffel Vandoorne, B (Mercedes EQ Silver Arrow 02), +6.966s; **4** Jean-Éric Vergne, F (DS E-Tense FE21), +7.553s; **5** Sam Bird, GB (Jaguar I-TYPE 5), +7.877s; **6** António Félix da Costa, P (DS E-Tense FE21), +8.971s; **7** Edoardo Mortara, CH (Mercedes EQ Silver Arrow 02), +13.356s *; **8** Pascal Wehrlein, D (Porsche 99X Electric), +14.216s; **9** Nick Cassidy, NZ (Audi e-tron FE07), +14.543s; **10** André Lotterer, D (Porsche 99X Electric), +19.339s; **11** Lucas di Grassi, BR (Mercedes EQ Silver Arrow 02), +19.731s; **12** Alexander Sims, GB (Mahindra M7Electro), +24.758s; **13** Jake Dennis, GB (BMW iFE.21), +25.029s *; **14** Oliver Askew, USA (BMW iFE.21), +28.039s; **15** Sérgio Sette Câmara, BR (Penske EV-5), +28.645s **; **16** Sébastien Buemi, CH (Nissan IM03), +28.865s; **17** Oliver Turvey, GB (NIO 333 001), +58.372s; **18** Dan Ticktum, GB (NIO 333 001), +1m 19.306s **; **19** Antonio Giovinazzi, I (Penske EV-5), +1m 37.231s ***; Nyck de Vries, NL (Mercedes EQ Silver Arrow 02), -2 laps (DNF-accident damage); Oliver Rowland, GB (Mahindra M7Electro), -10 (DNF-accident damage); Maximilian Günther, D (Nissan IM03), -27 (DNF-accident).

* 5s penalty for causing a collision.

** 5s penalty due to Safety Car procedure.

*** 5s penalty due to Safety Car procedure & 30s penalty for exceeding the FCY speed and gaining an advantage.

Fastest race lap: di Grassi, 1m 41.653s, 74.378mph/119.701km/h.

Pole position: Vandoorne, 1m 39.151s, 76.255mph/122.721km/h.

Race 2 (56.706 miles/91.260km).

1 Mitch Evans, NZ (Jaguar I-TYPE 5), 52m 55.224s, 64.292mph/103.468km/h; **2** Jean-Éric Vergne, F (DS E-Tense FE21), +0.584s; **3** Robin Frijns, NL (Audi e-tron FE07), +1.606s; **4** André Lotterer, D (Porsche 99X Electric), +2.093s; **5** Stoffel Vandoorne, B (Mercedes EQ Silver Arrow 02), +2.756s; **6** Pascal Wehrlein, D (Porsche 99X Electric), +4.655s; **7** Oliver Turvey, GB (NIO 333 001), +7.097s; **8** Lucas di Grassi, BR (Mercedes EQ Silver Arrow 02), +8.680s *; **9** Sébastien Buemi, CH (Nissan IM03), +8.796s; **10** Dan Ticktum, GB (NIO 333 001), +11.130s; **11** Maximilian Günther, D (Nissan IM03), +11.221s; **12** Sérgio Sette Câmara, BR (Penske EV-5), +12.309s; **13** António Félix da Costa, P (DS E-Tense FE21), +13.134s *; **14** Nyck de Vries, NL (Mercedes EQ Silver Arrow 02), +14.207s **; **15** Oliver Askew, USA (BMW iFE.21), +20.429s ***; Sam Bird, GB (Jaguar I-TYPE 5), -1 lap (DNF-accident damage); Nick Cassidy, NZ (Audi e-tron FE07), -2 (DNF-accident damage); Jake Dennis, GB (BMW iFE.21), -6 (DNF-accident damage); Alexander Sims, GB (Mahindra M7Electro), -11 (DNF-accident); Oliver Rowland, GB (Mahindra M7Electro), -13 (DNF-accident damage); Edoardo Mortara, CH (Mercedes EQ Silver Arrow 02), -20 (DNF-accident); Antonio Giovinazzi, I (Penske EV-5), -20 (DNF-mechanical).

* 5s penalty for causing a collision.

** 10s penalty for causing a collision.

*** 5s penalty for overtaking during Safety Car period & 5s penalty for causing a collision.

Fastest race lap: Frijns, 1m 41.256s, 74.670 mph/120.170km/h.

Pole position: Vergne, 1m 38.268s, 76.941mph/123.824km/h.

Championship points: Drivers: 1 Vergne, 60; **2** Frijns, 58; **3** Vandoorne, 56; **4** Evans, 51; **5** Mortara, 49; **6** Lotterer, 43.

Teams: 1 Mercedes-EQ Formula E Team, 94; **2** TAG Heuer Porsche Formula E Team, 85; **3** DS TECHEETAH, 80.

MONACO E-PRIX, Circuit de Monaco, Monaco, 30 April. Round 4. 30 laps of the 2.074-mile/3.337km circuit, 62.205 miles/100.110km.

1 Stoffel Vandoorne, B (Mercedes EQ Silver Arrow 02), 51m 12.473s, 72.885mph/117.298km/h; **2** Mitch Evans, NZ (Jaguar I-TYPE 5), +1.285s; **3** Jean-Éric Vergne, F (DS E-Tense FE21), +3.293s; **4** Robin Frijns, NL (Audi e-tron FE07), +3.467s; **5** António Félix da Costa, P (DS E-Tense FE21), +3.952s; **6** Lucas di Grassi, BR (Mercedes EQ Silver Arrow 02), +8.133s; **7** Nick Cassidy, NZ (Audi e-tron FE07), +15.273s; **8** Sébastien Buemi, CH (Nissan IM03), +17.773s; **9** Jake Dennis, GB (BMW iFE.21), +17.820s; **10** Nyck de Vries, NL (Mercedes EQ Silver Arrow 02), +18.283s; **11** Alexander Sims, GB (Mahindra M7Electro), +19.350s; **12** Dan Ticktum, GB (NIO 333 001), +19.756s; **13** Sérgio Sette Câmara, BR (Penske EV-5), +22.894s; **14** Oliver Turvey, GB (NIO 333 001), +23.198s; **15** Oliver Askew, USA (BMW iFE.21), +23.432s; **16** Antonio Giovinazzi, I (Penske EV-5), +27.987s *; **17** Maximilian Günther, D (Nissan IM03), +39.668s; Edoardo Mortara, CH (Mercedes EQ Silver Arrow 02), -7 laps (DNF-puncture); André Lotterer, D (Porsche 99X Electric), -12 (DNF-accident); Oliver Rowland, GB (Mahindra M7Electro), -12 (DNF-accident damage); Pascal Wehrlein, D (Porsche 99X Electric), -15 (DNF-lost power); Sam Bird, GB (Jaguar I-TYPE 5), -23 (DNF-steering track rod).

* 5s penalty for overtaking outside the track and gaining an advantage.

Fastest race lap: Frijns, 1m 32.707s, 80.518mph/129.582km/h.

Pole position: Evans, 1m 29.839s, 83.089mph/133.719km/h.

Championship points: Drivers: 1 Vandoorne, 81; **2** Vergne, 75; **3** Evans, 72; **4** Frijns, 71; **5** Mortara, 49; **6** Lotterer, 43.

Teams: 1 Mercedes-EQ Formula E Team, 120; **2** DS TECHEETAH, 105; **3** Jaguar TCS Racing, 94.

SHELL RECHARGE BERLIN E-PRIX, Tempelhof Airport Street Circuit, Berlin, Germany, 14/15 May. Round 5. 2 x 40 laps of the 1.463-mile/2.355km circuit.

Race 1 (58.533 miles/94.200km).

1 Edoardo Mortara, CH (Mercedes EQ Silver Arrow 02), 46m 16.175s, 75.902mph/122.153km/h; **2** Jean-Éric Vergne, F (DS E-Tense FE21), +1.782s; **3** Stoffel Vandoorne, B (Mercedes EQ Silver Arrow 02), +1.987s; **4** André Lotterer, D (Porsche 99X Electric), +2.579s; **5** Mitch Evans, NZ (Jaguar I-TYPE 5), +3.189s; **6** Pascal Wehrlein, D (Porsche 99X Electric), +5.405s; **7** Sam Bird, GB (Jaguar I-TYPE 5), +5.683s; **8** António Félix da Costa, P (DS E-Tense FE21), +6.400s; **9** Alexander Sims, GB (Mahindra M7Electro), +6.569s; **10** Nyck de Vries, NL (Mercedes EQ Silver Arrow 02), +6.602s; **11** Oliver Rowland, GB (Mahindra M7Electro), +8.141s; **12** Robin Frijns, NL (Audi e-tron FE07), +9.879s; **13** Jake Dennis, GB (BMW iFE.21), +13.314s; **14** Sébastien Buemi, CH (Nissan IM03), +15.275s; **15** Oliver Askew, USA (BMW iFE.21), +22.071s; **16** Oliver Turvey, GB (NIO 333 001), +22.662s; **17** Sérgio Sette Câmara, BR (Penske EV-5), +24.120s; **18** Maximilian Günther, D (Nissan IM03), +28.716s; **19** Dan Ticktum, GB (NIO 333 001), +30.393s; **20** Antonio Giovinazzi, I (Penske EV-5), +52.025s; Lucas di Grassi, BR (Mercedes EQ Silver Arrow 02), -2 laps (DNF-puncture); Nick Cassidy, NZ (Audi e-tron FE07), -9 (DNF-suspension).

Fastest race lap: di Grassi, 1m 07.880s, 77.607mph/124.896km/h.

Pole position: Mortara, 1m 06.093s, 79.705mph/128.273km/h.

Race 2 (58.533 miles/94.200km).

1 Nyck de Vries, NL (Mercedes EQ Silver Arrow 02), 46m 12.268s, 76.009mph/122.325km/h; **2** Edoardo Mortara, CH (Mercedes EQ Silver Arrow 02), +2.454s; **3** Stoffel Vandoorne, B (Mercedes EQ Silver Arrow 02), +6.936s; **4** Lucas di Grassi, BR (Mercedes EQ Silver Arrow 02), +8.165s; **5** Robin Frijns, NL (Audi e-tron FE07), +13.829s; **6** António Félix da Costa, P (DS E-Tense FE21), +14.387s; **7** Oliver Rowland, GB (Mahindra M7Electro), +15.518s; **8** André Lotterer, D (Porsche 99X Electric), +15.845s; **9** Jean-Éric Vergne, F (DS E-Tense FE21), +18.831s; **10** Mitch Evans, NZ (Jaguar I-TYPE 5), +21.722s; **11** Sam Bird, GB (Jaguar I-TYPE 5), +22.875s; **12** Pascal Wehrlein, D (Porsche 99X Electric), +25.412s; **13** Jake Dennis, GB (BMW iFE.21), +27.012s; **14** Sébastien Buemi, CH (Nissan IM03), +29.559s; **15** Oliver Askew, USA (BMW iFE.21), +33.359s; **16** Maximilian Günther, D (Nissan IM03), +35.775s; **17** Oliver Turvey, GB (NIO 333 001), +40.044s; **18** Alexander Sims, GB (Mahindra M7Electro), +41.542s; **19** Sérgio Sette Câmara, BR (Penske EV-5), +41.860s; **20** Dan Ticktum, GB (NIO 333 001), +51.648s; **21** Nick Cassidy, NZ (Audi e-tron FE07), +55.192s; **22** Antonio Giovinazzi, I (Penske EV-5), +1m 01.933s.

Fastest race lap: Cassidy, 1m 07.849s, 77.642mph/124.953km/h.

Pole position: Mortara, 1m 05.972s, 79.851mph/128.509km/h.

Championship points: Drivers: 1 Vandoorne, 111; **2** Mortara, 99; **3** Vergne, 95; **4** Evans, 83; **5** Frijns, 81; **6** de Vries, 65.

Teams: 1 Mercedes-EQ Formula E Team, 176; **2** ROKiT Venturi Racing, 148; **3** DS TECHEETAH, 137.

JAKARTA E-PRIX, Jakarta International e-Prix Circuit, Indonesia, 4 June. Round 6. 40 laps of the 1.473-mile/2.370km circuit, 58.906 miles/94.800km.

1 Mitch Evans, NZ (Jaguar I-TYPE 5), 48m 28.424s, 72.912mph/117.341km/h; **2** Jean-Éric Vergne, F (DS E-Tense FE21), +0.733s; **3** Edoardo Mortara, CH (Mercedes EQ Silver Arrow 02), +0.967s; **4** António Félix da Costa, P (DS E-Tense FE21), +3.350s; **5** Stoffel Vandoorne, B (Mercedes EQ Silver Arrow 02), +4.038s; **6** Jake Dennis, GB (BMW iFE.21), +4.635s; **7** Lucas di Grassi, BR (Mercedes EQ Silver Arrow 02), +5.253s; **8** Pascal Wehrlein, D (Porsche 99X Electric), +8.191s; **9** André Lotterer, D (Porsche 99X Electric), +11.089s; **10** Sam Bird, GB (Jaguar I-TYPE 5), +13.348s; **11** Sébastien Buemi, CH (Nissan IM03), +14.766s; **12** Oliver Turvey, GB (NIO 333 001), +20.922s; **13** Oliver Askew, USA (BMW iFE.21), +23.020s; **14** Maximilian Günther, D (Nissan IM03), +25.184s; **15** Alexander Sims, GB (Mahindra M7Electro), +29.520s; **16** Nick Cassidy, NZ (Audi e-tron FE07), +29.873s; **17** Robin Frijns, NL (Audi e-tron FE07), +30.854s; **18** Dan Ticktum, GB (NIO 333 001), +31.827s; **19** Sérgio Sette Câmara, BR (Penske EV-5), +38.218s; Antonio Giovinazzi, I (Penske EV-5), -5 laps (DNF-withdrew); Nyck de Vries, NL (Mercedes EQ Silver Arrow 02), -11 (DNF-accident); Oliver Rowland, GB

(Mahindra M7Electro), -39 (DNF-wheel).
Fastest race lap: Evans, 1m 09.786s, 75.968mph/122.259km/h.
Pole position: Vergne, 1m 08.523s, 77.368mph/124.512km/h.
Championship points: Drivers: 1 Vandoorne, 121; **2** Vergne, 116; **3** Mortara, 114; **4** Evans, 109; **5** Frijns, 81; **6** de Vries, 65.
Teams: 1 Mercedes-EQ Formula E Team, 186; **2** DS TECHEETAH, 170; **3** ROKiT Venturi Racing, 169.

MARRAKESH E-PRIX, Circuit International Automobile Moulay El Hassan, Agdal, Marrakesh, Morocco, 2 July. Round 7. 34 laps of the 1.846-mile/2.971km circuit, 62.704 miles/100.913km.
1 Edoardo Mortara, CH (Mercedes EQ Silver Arrow 02), 46m 45.410s, 80.544mph/129.623km/h; **2** António Félix da Costa, P (DS E-Tense FE21), +2.297s; **3** Mitch Evans, NZ (Jaguar I-TYPE 5), +6.270s; **4** Jean-Éric Vergne, F (DS E-Tense FE21), +6.965s; **5** Lucas di Grassi, BR (Mercedes EQ Silver Arrow 02), +7.787s; **6** Nyck de Vries, NL (Mercedes EQ Silver Arrow 02), +8.394s; **7** Jake Dennis, GB (BMW iFE.21), +12.084s; **8** Stoffel Vandoorne, B (Mercedes EQ Silver Arrow 02), +14.541s; **9** Sam Bird, GB (Jaguar I-TYPE 5), +15.048s; **10** Oliver Rowland, GB (Mahindra M7Electro), +15.270s; **11** Oliver Askew, USA (BMW iFE.21), +16.336s; **12** Pascal Wehrlein, D (Porsche 99X Electric), +30.043s; **13** Nick Cassidy, NZ (Audi e-tron FE07), +31.970s; **14** Alexander Sims, GB (Mahindra M7Electro), +32.332s; **15** André Lotterer, D (Porsche 99X Electric), +32.364s; **16** Sébastien Buemi, CH (Nissan IM03), +33.707s; **17** Oliver Turvey, GB (NIO 333 001), +35.018s; **18** Robin Frijns, NL (Audi e-tron FE07), +35.686s; **19** Antonio Giovinazzi, I (Penske EV-5), +40.887s; **20** Sérgio Sette Câmara, BR (Penske EV-5), +42.764s; Maximilian Günther, D (Nissan IM03), -2 laps (DNF-accident damage); Dan Ticktum, GB (NIO 333 001), -6 (DNF-out of energy).
Fastest race lap: di Grassi, 1m 20.909s, 82.140mph/132.192km/h.
Pole position: da Costa, 1m 17.070s, 86.232mph/138.777km/h.
Championship points: Drivers: 1 Mortara, 139; **2** Vergne, 128; **3** Vandoorne, 125; **4** Evans, 124; **5** Frijns, 81; **6** da Costa, 75.
Teams: 1 ROKiT Venturi Racing, 205; **2** DS TECHEETAH, 203; **3** Mercedes-EQ Formula E Team, 198.

NEW YORK CITY E-PRIX, Brooklyn Street Circuit, New York, USA, 16/17 July. Round 8. 29 and 39 laps of the 1.442-mile/2.320km circuit.
Race 1 (41.806 miles/67.280km).
1 Nick Cassidy, NZ (Audi e-tron FE07), 35m 04.095s, 71.527mph/115.112km/h; **2** Lucas di Grassi, BR (Mercedes EQ Silver Arrow 02), +1.123s; **3** Robin Frijns, NL (Audi e-tron FE07), +1.671s; **4** Stoffel Vandoorne, B (Mercedes EQ Silver Arrow 02), +3.693s; **5** Sébastien Buemi, CH (Nissan IM03), +5.570s; **6** Pascal Wehrlein, D (Porsche 99X Electric), +5.783s; **7** Sam Bird, GB (Jaguar I-TYPE 5), +7.207s; **8** Nyck de Vries, NL (Mercedes EQ Silver Arrow 02), +7.503s; **9** Edoardo Mortara, CH (Mercedes EQ Silver Arrow 02), +9.734s *; **10** Jake Dennis, GB (BMW iFE.21), +11.595s *; **11** Mitch Evans, NZ (Jaguar I-TYPE 5), +13.605s *; **12** Maximilian Günther, D (Nissan IM03), +13.763s; **13** Oliver Rowland, GB (Mahindra M7Electro), +14.924s; **14** Alexander Sims, GB (Mahindra M7Electro), +16.648s; **15** Oliver Turvey, GB (NIO 333 001), +19.707s; **16** André Lotterer, D (Porsche 99X Electric), +24.384s **; **17** Dan Ticktum, GB (NIO 333 001), +25.312s; **18** Jean-Éric Vergne, F (DS E-Tense FE21), +53.018s; **19** Oliver Askew, USA (BMW iFE.21), +1m 22.282s ***; António Félix da Costa, P (DS E-Tense FE21), -1 lap (DNF-puncture); Antonio Giovinazzi, I (Penske EV-5), -29 (DNF-suspension).
* 5s penalty for overspeeding under FCY.
** 10s penalty for causing a collision.
*** Drive-through penalty converted into a 21s penalty for not activating the second activation of the Attack Mode.
Did not start: Sérgio Sette Câmara, BR (Penske EV-5) - accident damage.
Fastest race lap: Mortara, 1m 10.843s, 73.256mph/117.894km/h.
Pole position: Cassidy, 1m 08.980s, 75.234mph/121.078km/h.

Race 2 (56.222 miles/90.480km).
1 António Félix da Costa, P (DS E-Tense FE21), 46m 55.511s, 71.886mph/115.690km/h; **2** Stoffel Vandoorne, B (Mercedes EQ Silver Arrow 02), +0.929s; **3** Mitch Evans, NZ (Jaguar I-TYPE 5), +3.524s; **4** Alexander Sims, GB (Mahindra M7Electro), +3.631s; **5** Sam Bird, GB (Jaguar I-TYPE 5), +4.412s; **6** Robin Frijns, NL (Audi e-tron FE07), +4.979s; **7** Nyck de Vries, NL (Mercedes EQ Silver Arrow 02), +6.233s; **8** Jake Dennis, GB (BMW iFE.21), +6.316s; **9** André Lotterer, D (Porsche 99X Electric), +6.590s; **10** Edoardo Mortara, CH (Mercedes EQ Silver Arrow 02), +13.449s; **11** Pascal Wehrlein, D (Porsche 99X Electric), +18.469s; **12** Dan Ticktum, GB (NIO 333 001), +23.002s; **13** Sébastien Buemi, CH (Nissan IM03), +30.216s; **14** Oliver Rowland, GB (Mahindra M7Electro), +32.676s; **15** Nick Cassidy, NZ (Audi e-tron FE07), +39.699s; **16** Oliver Turvey, GB (NIO 333 001), +43.255s *; **17** Sérgio Sette Câmara, BR (Penske EV-5), +1m 08.193s; Jean-Éric Vergne, F (DS E-Tense FE21), -3 laps (DNF-accident damage); Lucas di Grassi, BR (Mercedes EQ Silver Arrow 02), -3 (DNF-accident damage); Oliver Askew, USA (BMW iFE.21), -3 (DNF-accident damage); Antonio Giovinazzi, I (Penske EV-5), -12 (DNF-mechanical).
Disqualified: Maximilian Günther, D (Nissan IM03), +45.934s, energy used over regulatory limit - finished 17th.
Fastest race lap: Mortara, 1m 10.378s, 73.740mph/118.673km/h.
Pole position: da Costa, 1m 08.751s, 75.485mph/121.481km/h.
Championship points: Drivers: 1 Vandoorne, 155; **2** Mortara, 144; **3** Evans, 139; **4** Vergne, 128; **5** Frijns, 104; **6** da Costa, 100.
Teams: 1 Mercedes-EQ Formula E Team, 238; **2** ROKiT Venturi Racing, 228; **3** DS TECHEETAH, 228.

SABIC LONDON E-PRIX, ExCel, London, Great Britain, 30/31 July. Round 9. 37 and 38 laps of the 1.330-mile/2.141km circuit.
Race 1 (49.223 miles/79.217km).
1 Jake Dennis, GB (BMW iFE.21), 46m 56.557s, 62.914mph/101.251km/h; **2** Stoffel Vandoorne, B (Mercedes EQ Silver Arrow 02), +2.223s; **3** Nick Cassidy, NZ (Audi e-tron FE07), +12.663s; **4** Oliver Askew, USA (BMW iFE.21), +14.904s; **5** Mitch Evans, NZ (Jaguar I-TYPE 5), +17.128s; **6** Nyck de Vries, NL (Mercedes EQ Silver Arrow 02), +17.367s *; **7** António Félix da Costa, P (DS E-Tense FE21), +17.733s; **8** Maximilian Günther, D (Nissan IM03), +22.067s; **9** Lucas di Grassi, BR (Mercedes EQ Silver Arrow 02), +32.139s **; **10** Pascal Wehrlein, D (Porsche 99X Electric), +34.347s; **11** Sébastien Buemi, CH (Nissan IM03), +35.307s **; **12** André Lotterer, D (Porsche 99X Electric), +35.508s; **13** Alexander Sims, GB (Mahindra M7Electro), +40.345s; **14** Jean-Éric Vergne, F (DS E-Tense FE21), +41.057s **; **15** Oliver Turvey, GB (NIO 333 001), +41.293s; **16** Robin Frijns, NL (Audi e-tron FE07), +44.023s ***; **17** Dan Ticktum, GB (NIO 333 001), +51.947s; **18** Edoardo Mortara, CH (Mercedes EQ Silver Arrow 02), +1m 18.796s; Sérgio Sette Câmara, BR (Penske EV-5), +1m 06.394s (DNF-out of energy); Antonio Giovinazzi, I (Penske EV-5), -11 laps (DNF-powertrain) **; Oliver Rowland, GB (Mahindra M7Electro), -20 (DNF-accident); Sam Bird, GB (Jaguar I-TYPE 5), -37 (DNF-accident damage).
* 5s penalty for defending his position on the straight with more than one move.
** 5s penalty for causing a collision.
*** 5s penalty for moving under braking.
Fastest race lap: Dennis, 1m 14.429s, 64.346mph/103.556km/h.
Pole position: Dennis, 1m 13.161s, 65.462mph/105.351km/h.

Race 2 (50.554 miles/81.358km).
1 Lucas di Grassi, BR (Mercedes EQ Silver Arrow 02), 49m 28.805s, 61.301mph/98.655km/h; **2** Jake Dennis, GB (BMW iFE.21), +3.191s; **3** Nyck de Vries, NL (Mercedes EQ Silver Arrow 02), +4.508s; **4** Stoffel Vandoorne, B (Mercedes EQ Silver Arrow 02), +10.358s; **5** António Félix da Costa, P (DS E-Tense FE21), +13.946s; **6** Sébastien Buemi, CH (Nissan IM03), +20.399s; **7** Robin Frijns, NL (Audi e-tron FE07), +20.850s; **8** Sam Bird, GB (Jaguar I-TYPE 5), +21.748s *; **9** Sérgio Sette Câmara, BR (Penske EV-5), +28.913s; **10** Pascal Wehrlein, D (Porsche 99X Electric), +29.685s; **11** Alexander Sims, GB (Mahindra M7Electro), +30.611s; **12** André Lotterer, D (Porsche 99X Electric), +31.644s; **13** Edoardo Mortara, CH (Mercedes EQ Silver Arrow 02), +35.147s **; **14** Oliver Turvey, GB (NIO 333 001), +37.285s; **15** Maximilian Günther, D (Nissan IM03), +1m 19.833s ***; Mitch Evans, NZ (Jaguar I-TYPE 5), -3 laps (DNF-electrics); Nick Cassidy, NZ (Audi e-tron FE07), -8 (DNF-suspension); Oliver Askew, USA (BMW iFE.21), -17 (DNF-mechanical) **; Antonio Giovinazzi, I (Penske EV-5), -19 (DNF-withdew) ****; Jean-Éric Vergne, F (DS E-Tense FE21), -35 (DNF-accident damage); Dan Ticktum, GB (NIO 333 001), -37 (DNF-accident); Oliver Rowland, GB (Mahindra M7Electro), -37 (DNF-accident).
* 5s penalty.
** 5s penalty for forcing Günther off track.
*** 10s penalty for mechanic working on the car while the car is in ready to move status.
**** 5s penalty for causing a collision.
Fastest race lap: Cassidy, 1m 14.349s, 64.416mph/103.667km/h.
Pole position: Dennis, 1m 12.535s, 66.027mph/106.260km/h.
Championship points: Drivers: 1 Vandoorne, 185; **2** Evans, 149; **3** Mortara, 144; **4** Vergne, 128; **5** da Costa, 116; **6** di Grassi, 111.
Teams: 1 Mercedes-EQ Formula E Team, 291; **2** ROKiT Venturi Racing, 255; **3** DS TECHEETAH, 244.

HANA BANK SEOUL E-PRIX, Seoul Street Circuit, South Korea, 13/14 August. Round 10. 30 and 34 laps of the 1.629-mile/2.621km circuit.
Race 1 (49.090 miles/79.002km).
1 Mitch Evans, NZ (Jaguar I-TYPE 5), 1h 29m 55.478s, 32.601mph/52.466km/h; **2** Oliver Rowland, GB (Mahindra M7Electro), +0.820s; **3** Lucas di Grassi, BR (Mercedes EQ Silver Arrow 02), +1.393s; **4** Jake Dennis, GB (BMW iFE.21), +1.902s; **5** Stoffel Vandoorne, B (Mercedes EQ Silver Arrow 02), +2.470s; **6** Jean-Éric Vergne, F (DS E-Tense FE21), +3.957s; **7** Pascal Wehrlein, D (Porsche 99X Electric), +4.149s; **8** Robin Frijns, NL (Audi e-tron FE07), +4.508s; **9** António Félix da Costa, P (DS E-Tense FE21), +4.970s; **10** Nick Cassidy, NZ (Audi e-tron FE07), +5.325s; **11** Maximilian Günther, D (Nissan IM03), +5.610s; **12** Sérgio Sette Câmara, BR (Penske EV-5), +6.121s; **13** Norman Nato, F (Jaguar I-TYPE 5), +57.545s *; Alexander Sims, GB (Mahindra M7Electro), -4 laps (DNF-accident) **; Antonio Giovinazzi, I (Penske EV-5), -6 (DNF-withdrew); Edoardo Mortara, CH (Mercedes EQ Silver Arrow 02), -10 (DNF-puncture) ***; Sébastien Buemi, CH (Nissan IM03), -30 (DNF-accident); Dan Ticktum, GB (NIO 333 001), -30 (DNF-accident); Nyck de Vries, NL (Mercedes EQ Silver Arrow 02), -30 (DNF-accident); Oliver Turvey, GB (NIO 333 001), -30 (DNF-accident); André Lotterer, D (Porsche 99X Electric), -30 (DNF-accident); Oliver Askew, USA (BMW iFE.21), -30 (DNF-accident).
* 5s penalty for failing to keep **10** car lengths behind Safety Car.
** 5s penalty for causing a collision.
*** 5s penalty for changing of direction more than once.
Fastest race lap: Dennis, 1m 25.497s, 68.575mph/110.361km/h.
Pole position: Rowland, 1m 35.406s, 61.453mph/98.899km/h.

Race 2 (55.604 miles/89.486km).
1 Edoardo Mortara, CH (Mercedes EQ Silver Arrow 02), 53m 31.680s, 62.070mph/99.892km/h; **2** Stoffel Vandoorne, B (Mercedes EQ Silver Arrow 02), +3.756s; **3** Jake Dennis, GB (BMW iFE.21), +6.649s *; **4** Robin Frijns, NL (Audi e-tron FE07), +7.021s; **5** Oliver Askew, USA (BMW iFE.21), +7.850s; **6** Jean-Éric Vergne, F (DS E-Tense FE21), +9.471s; **7** Mitch Evans, NZ (Jaguar I-TYPE 5), +10.243s; **8** Nick Cassidy, NZ (Audi e-tron FE07), +14.208s; **9** Sébastien Buemi, CH (Nissan IM03), +16.629s; **10** António Félix da Costa, P (DS E-Tense FE21), +22.226s; **11** Lucas di Grassi, BR (Mercedes EQ Silver Arrow 02), +24.546s; **12** Alexander Sims, GB (Mahindra M7Electro), +26.513s; **13** Sérgio Sette Câmara, BR (Penske EV-5), +27.813s **; **14** Norman Nato, F (Jaguar I-TYPE 5), +31.526s; **15** Oliver Turvey, GB (NIO 333 001), +31.565s *; **16** Sacha Fenestraz, F (Penske EV-5), +36.270s; Maximilian Günther, D (Nissan IM03), -22 laps (DNF-accident damage); Nyck de Vries, NL (Mercedes EQ Silver Arrow 02), -27 (DNF-accident damage) *; Pascal Wehrlein, D (Porsche 99X Electric), -28 (DNF-accident); Dan Ticktum, GB (NIO 333 001), -32 (DNF-accident damage); André Lotterer, D (Porsche 99X Electric), -34 (DNF-accident damage) ***; Oliver Rowland, GB (Mahindra M7Electro), -34 (DNF-accident damage).
* 5s penalty for causing a collision.
** 5s penalty for changing of direction more than once.
*** Drive-through penalty converted to 18s penalty for failure to respect the start procedure regulations.
Fastest race lap: Cassidy, 1m 22.401s, 71.152mph/114.508km/h.
Pole position: da Costa, 1m 21.078s, 72.313mph/116.376km/h.

Final championship points
Drivers
1 Stoffel Vandoorne, B, 213; **2** Mitch Evans, NZ, 180; **3** Edoardo Mortara, CH, 169; **4** Jean-Éric Vergne, F, 144; **5** Lucas di Grassi, BR, 126; **6** Jake Dennis, GB, 126; **7** Robin Frijns, NL, 126; **8** António Félix da Costa, P, 122; **9** Nyck de Vries, NL, 106; **10** Pascal Wehrlein, D, 71; **11** Nick Cassidy, NZ, 68; **12** André Lotterer, D, 63; **13** Sam Bird, GB, 51; **14** Oliver Rowland, GB, 32; **15** Sébastien Buemi, CH, 30; **16** Oliver Askew, USA, 24; **17** Alexander Sims, GB, 14; **18** Oliver Turvey, GB, 6; **19** Maximilian Günther, D, 6; **20** Sérgio Sette Câmara, BR, 2; **21** Dan Ticktum, GB, 1.

Teams
1 Mercedes-EQ Formula E Team, 319; **2** ROKiT Venturi Racing, 295; **3** DS TECHEETAH, 266; **4** Jaguar TCS Racing, 231; **5** Envision Racing, 194; **6** Avalanche Andretti Formula E, 150; **7** TAG Heuer Porsche Formula E Team, 134; **8** Mahindra Racing, 46; **9** Nissan e.Dams, 36; **10** NIO 333 FE Team, 7; **11** DRAGON / PENSKE AUTOSPORT, 2.

Race cancelled: Vancouver, 2 July (unable to meet tight deadlines, following the Covid-19 pandemic).

FIA Formula 2 Championship

All cars are Dallara F2 2018-Mecachrome F2.

FIA FORMULA 2 CHAMPIONSHIP, Bahrain International Circuit, Sakhir, Bahrain, 19/20 March. Round 1. 23 and 31 laps of the 3.363-mile/5.412km circuit.
Race 1 (77.193 miles/124.230km).
1 Richard Verschoor, NL, 43m 34.983s, 106.478mph/171.360km/h; **2** Jehan Daruvala, IND, +1.853s; **3** Liam Lawson, NZ, +4.975s; **4** Ralph Boschung, CH, +6.981s; **5** Felipe Drugovich, BR, +8.801s; **6** Logan Sargeant, USA, +9.263s; **7** Jüri Vips, EST, +13.350s; **8** Ayumu Iwasa, J, +15.749s; **9** Dennis Hauger, N, +17.665s; **10** Jack Doohan, AUS, +21.472s; **11** Enzo Fittipaldi, BR, +22.902s; **12** Roy Nissany, IL, +26.574s; **13** Frederik Vesti, DK, +27.490s; **14** Cem Bölükbasi, TR, +31.921s; **15** Calan Williams, AUS, +49.959s; **16** Marino Sato, J, +50.640s *; **17** Amaury Cordeel, B, +52.671s; **18** Clément Novalak, GB, +1m 18.205s **; **19** Olli Caldwell, GB, -1 lap; Jake Hughes, GB, -9 (DNF) **; Théo Pourchaire, F, -17 (DNF); Marcus Armstrong, NZ, -21 (DNF).
* 5s penalty for exceeding track limits.
** 10s penalty for causing a collision.
Fastest race lap: Cordeel, 1m 43.848s, 116.577mph/187.612km/h.
Pole position: Drugovich.

Race 2 (104.096 miles/167.526km).
1 Théo Pourchaire, F, 1h 01m 54.454s, 101.034mph/162.600km/h; **2** Liam Lawson, NZ, +0.925s; **3** Jüri Vips, EST, +1.714s; **4** Ralph Boschung, CH, +3.863s; **5** Marcus Armstrong, NZ, +4.606s; **6** Felipe Drugovich, BR, +5.722s; **7** Logan Sargeant, USA, +6.539s; **8** Roy Nissany, IL, +7.256s; **9** Jake Hughes, GB, +8.008s; **10** Jack Doohan, AUS, +8.854s; **11** Marino Sato, J, +11.353s; **12** Jehan Daruvala, IND, +14.361s *; **13** Enzo Fittipaldi, BR, +15.074s **; **14** Cem Bölükbasi, TR, +15.965s; **15** Amaury Cordeel, B, +22.704s ***; **16** Ayumu Iwasa, J, +31.170s; **17** Olli Caldwell, GB, -1 lap ****; **18** Calan Williams, AUS, -4; **19** Dennis Hauger, N, -4; Richard Verschoor, NL, -5 (DNF); Clément Novalak, GB, -19 (DNF); Frederik Vesti, DK, -30 (DNF).
* 5s penalty for exceeding track limits.
** 5s penalty for causing a collision.
*** 15s penalty for speeding in the pit lane.
**** 5s penalty because the team failed to wait the correct period of time before carrying out the pit stop.
Fastest race lap: Vips, 1m 46.845s, 113.307mph/182.350km/h.
Pole position: Doohan, 1m 40.542s, 120.410mph/193.781km/h.
Championship points: Drivers: 1 Pourchaire, 25; **2** Lawson, 24; **3** Vips, 18; **4** Boschung, 17; **5** Drugovich, 12; **6** Verschoor, 10.
Teams: 1 Carlin, 33; **2** Hitech Grand Prix, 28; **3** ART Grand Prix, 25.

FIA FORMULA 2 CHAMPIONSHIP, Jeddah Corniche Circuit, Jeddah, Saudi Arabia, 26/27 March. Round 2. 20 and 27 laps of the 3.836-mile/6.174km circuit.
Race 1 (76.572 miles/123.230km).
1 Liam Lawson, NZ, 47m 55.487s, 96.057mph/154.589km/h; **2** Jüri Vips, EST, +3.166s; **3** Felipe Drugovich, BR, +4.846s; **4** Calan Williams, AUS, +6.277s; **5** Richard Verschoor, NL, +12.121s; **6** Ayumu Iwasa, J, +13.520s; **7** Jehan Daruvala, IND, +15.237s; **8** Marino Sato, J, +16.040s; **9** Roy Nissany, IL, +17.390s; **10** Enzo Fittipaldi, BR, +17.441s; **11** Clément Novalak, GB, +18.739s; **12** Frederik Vesti, DK, +20.298s; **13** Théo Pourchaire, F, +20.569s; **14** Olli Caldwell, GB, +25.495s; **15** Ralph Bos-

chung, CH, +34.454s *; **16** Dennis Hauger, N, +51.495s; Marcus Armstrong, NZ, -3 laps (DNF); Logan Sargeant, USA, -15 (DNF-accident); Jack Doohan, AUS, -15 (DNF-accident); Amaury Cordeel, B, -19 (DNF-accident).
Disqualified: Jake Hughes, GB, +3.224s, technical infringement, plank thickness - finished 3rd.
Withdrawn: Cem Bölükbasi, TR.
* Drive through converted to 20s penalty for out of position on the grid.
Fastest race lap: Vips, 1m 43.284s, 133.717mph/215.196km/h.
Pole position: Hauger.

Race 2 (103.426 miles/166.448km).
1 Felipe Drugovich, BR, 47m 41.485s, 130.312mph/209.717km/h; **2** Richard Verschoor, NL, +2.379s; **3** Jehan Daruvala, IND, +15.358s; **4** Jake Hughes, GB, +19.117s; **5** Marcus Armstrong, NZ, +20.595s; **6** Dennis Hauger, N, +21.071s; **7** Ayumu Iwasa, J, +27.108s; **8** Roy Nissany, IL, +28.428s; **9** Jack Doohan, AUS, +28.861s; **10** Jüri Vips, EST, +32.173s; **11** Enzo Fittipaldi, BR, +32.647s; **12** Logan Sargeant, USA, +37.612s; **13** Calan Williams, AUS, +38.282s; **14** Clément Novalak, GB, +42.370s; **15** Ralph Boschung, CH, +47.601s; **16** Olli Caldwell, GB, +48.706s; **17** Marino Sato, J, +50.384s; **18** Frederik Vesti, DK, -1 lap (DNF-spun off); Liam Lawson, NZ, -18 (DNF-wheel); Théo Pourchaire, F, -22 (DNF).
Withdrawn: Amaury Cordeel, B.
Fastest race lap: Doohan, 1m 43.098s, 133.958mph/215.585km/h.
Pole position: Drugovich, 1m 40.422s, 137.528mph/221.329km/h.
Championship points: Drivers: 1 Drugovich, 45; **2** Lawson, 34; **3** Verschoor, 32; **4** Vips, 28; **5** Pourchaire, 25; **6** Daruvala, 25.
Teams: 1 Hitech Grand Prix, 48; **2** MP Motorsport, 45; **3** Carlin, 43.

FIA FORMULA 2 CHAMPIONSHIP, Autodromo Enzo e Dino Ferrari, Imola, Italy, 23/24 April. Round 3. 25 and 35 laps of the 3.050-mile/4.909km circuit.
Race 1 (76.122 miles/122.507km).
1 Marcus Armstrong, NZ, 40m 50.545s, 112.025mph/180.287km/h; **2** Jehan Daruvala, IND, +1.431s; **3** Dennis Hauger, N, +2.243s; **4** Roy Nissany, IL, +2.803s; **5** Felipe Drugovich, BR, +7.045s; **6** Logan Sargeant, USA, +9.821s; **7** Théo Pourchaire, F, +12.372s; **8** Liam Lawson, NZ, +12.826s; **9** Ayumu Iwasa, J, +13.436s; **10** Frederik Vesti, DK, +17.714s; **11** Jack Doohan, AUS, +20.179s; **12** Enzo Fittipaldi, BR, +21.059s; **13** Richard Verschoor, NL, +21.493s; **14** Calan Williams, AUS, +22.942s; **15** Jüri Vips, EST, +23.275s; **16** Marino Sato, J, +24.216s; **17** Olli Caldwell, GB, +24.637s; **18** Jake Hughes, GB, +25.856s; **19** Clément Novalak, GB, +26.299s; Ralph Boschung, CH, -16 laps (DNF); David Beckmann, D, -25 (DNF).
Did not start: Amaury Cordeel, B.
Fastest race lap: Vips, 1m 28.841s, 123.604mph/198.921km/h.
Pole position: Sargeant.

Race 2 (106.625 miles/171.597km).
1 Théo Pourchaire, F, 1h 01m 56.611s, 103.409mph/166.422km/h; **2** Enzo Fittipaldi, BR, +0.388s; **3** Ralph Boschung, CH, +0.729s; **4** Clément Novalak, GB, +1.497s; **5** Ayumu Iwasa, J, +1.806s; **6** Frederik Vesti, DK, +2.122s; **7** Logan Sargeant, USA, +2.592s; **8** David Beckmann, D, +3.229s; **9** Jehan Daruvala, IND, +4.191s; **10** Felipe Drugovich, BR, +4.396s; **11** Marino Sato, J, +4.893s; **12** Jake Hughes, GB, +5.044s; **13** Olli Caldwell, GB, +6.745s; **14** Richard Verschoor, NL, +7.271s; **15** Calan Williams, AUS, +7.763s; **16** Marcus Armstrong, NZ, +11.287s *; **17** Amaury Cordeel, B, +1m 26.403s **; Liam Lawson, NZ, -5 laps (DNF); Roy Nissany, IL, -15 (DNF); Jüri Vips, EST, -30 (DNF); Jack Doohan, AUS, -34 (DNF); Dennis Hauger, N, -35 (DNF).
* 5s penalty for unsafe release.
** 15s penalty for exceeding track limits, 10s stop and go penalty converted to 30s penalty for speeding in the pit lane, 5s penalty for speeding in the pit lane.
Fastest race lap: Daruvala, 1m 28.353s, 124.286mph/200.020km/h.
Pole position: Vips, 1m 40.221s, 109.569mph/176.334km/h.
Championship points: Drivers: 1 Pourchaire, 52; **2** Drugovich, 50; **3** Daruvala, 36; **4** Lawson, 35; **5** Verschoor, 32; **6** Boschung, 32.
Teams: 1 MP Motorsport, 62; **2** ART Grand Prix, 60; **3** Hitech Grand Prix, 60.

FIA FORMULA 2 CHAMPIONSHIP, Circuit de Catalunya, Montmeló, Barcelona, Spain, 21/22 May. Round 4. 26 and 37 laps of the 2.905-mile/4.675km circuit.
Race 1 (75.449 miles/121.424km).
1 Felipe Drugovich, BR, 44m 12.635s, 102.500mph/164.958km/h; **2** Ayumu Iwasa, J, +2.109s; **3** Logan Sargeant, USA, +4.165s; **4** Jehan Daruvala, IND, +8.493s; **5** Théo Pourchaire, F, +9.251s; **6** Jack Doohan, AUS, +10.481s; **7** Frederik Vesti, DK, +16.430s; **8** Enzo Fittipaldi, BR, +17.256s; **9** Liam Lawson, NZ, +17.705s; **10** Marcus Armstrong, NZ, +18.524s; **11** Richard Verschoor, NL, +25.321s; **12** Dennis Hauger, N, +25.997s; **13** Olli Caldwell, GB, +26.476s; **14** Clément Novalak, GB, +29.315s; **15** Roy Nissany, IL, +31.490s; **16** Calan Williams, AUS, +33.781s; **17** Marino Sato, J, +37.436s; **18** Cem Bölükbasi, TR, +53.281s; **19** Amaury Cordeel, B, +1m 05.926s; **20** Jake Hughes, GB, -2 laps; Jüri Vips, EST, -21 (DNF).
Withdrawn: Ralph Boschung, CH.
Fastest race lap: Drugovich, 1m 35.211s, 109.836mph/176.765km/h.
Pole position: Williams.

Race 2 (107.403 miles/172.849km).
1 Felipe Drugovich, BR, 1h 02m 14.874s, 103.599mph/166.727km/h; **2** Jack Doohan, AUS, +5.630s; **3** Frederik Vesti, DK, +23.169s; **4** Logan Sargeant, USA, +24.720s; **5** Clément Novalak, GB, +25.060s; **6** Enzo Fittipaldi, BR, +31.430s; **7** Marcus Armstrong, NZ, +32.199s; **8** Théo Pourchaire, F, +35.607s; **9** Liam Lawson, NZ, +37.174s; **10** Roy Nissany, IL, +37.275s; **11** Calan Williams, AUS, +38.754s; **12** Ayumu Iwasa, J, +54.848s; **13** Dennis Hauger, N, +55.049s; **14** Olli Caldwell, GB, +56.548s; **15** Amaury Cordeel, B, +59.627s; **16** Jake Hughes, GB, +1m 03.353s; **17** Jüri Vips, EST, +1m 14.803s; **18** Richard Verschoor, NL, +1m 20.062s; **19** Marino Sato, J, +1m 30.518s; **20** Cem Bölükbasi, TR, +1m 33.835s; Jehan Daruvala, IND, -35 laps (DNF).
Fastest race lap: Doohan, 1m 34.231s, 110.979mph/178.603km/h.
Pole position: Doohan, 1m 28.612s, 118.016mph/189.929km/h.
Championship points: Drivers: 1 Drugovich, 86; **2** Pourchaire, 60; **3** Daruvala, 41; **4** Lawson, 37; **5** Armstrong, 36; **6** Sargeant, 36.
Teams: 1 MP Motorsport, 108; **2** ART Grand Prix, 85; **3** Carlin, 73.

FIA FORMULA 2 CHAMPIONSHIP, Monte-Carlo Street Circuit, Monaco, 28/29 May. Round 5. 30 and 42 laps of the 2.074-mile/3.337km circuit.
Race 1 (62.205 miles/100.110km).
1 Dennis Hauger, N, 44m 28.491s, 83.919mph/135.056km/h; **2** Jehan Daruvala, IND, +6.711s; **3** Marcus Armstrong, NZ, +7.267s; **4** Enzo Fittipaldi, BR, +13.164s; **5** Jüri Vips, EST, +14.566s; **6** Théo Pourchaire, F, +15.829s; **7** Jack Doohan, AUS, +17.365s; **8** Liam Lawson, NZ, +21.670s; **9** Roy Nissany, IL, +22.838s; **10** Logan Sargeant, USA, +23.031s; **11** Frederik Vesti, DK, +26.356s; **12** Cem Bölükbasi, TR, +31.338s; **13** Richard Verschoor, NL, +32.414s; **14** Calan Williams, AUS, +44.226s; **15** Marino Sato, J, +44.652s; **16** Olli Caldwell, GB, +45.245s; **17** Amaury Cordeel, B, +47.270s; **18** Jake Hughes, GB, +55.403s; **19** Ayumu Iwasa, J, +55.751s *; Felipe Drugovich, BR, -19 laps (DNF); Clément Novalak, GB, -22 (DNF).
Withdrawn: Ralph Boschung, CH.
* 10s penalty for causing a collision.
Fastest race lap: Doohan, 1m 22.832s, 90.118mph/145.030km/h.
Pole position: Hughes.

Race 2 (87.088 miles/140.154km).
1 Felipe Drugovich, BR, 1h 02m 35.675s, 83.477mph/134.344km/h; **2** Théo Pourchaire, F, +0.827s; **3** Jüri Vips, EST, +8.042s; **4** Jack Doohan, AUS, +12.954s; **5** Enzo Fittipaldi, BR, +13.534s; **6** Marcus Armstrong, NZ, +14.746s; **7** Dennis Hauger, N, +15.301s; **8** Jehan Daruvala, IND, +15.721s; **9** Logan Sargeant, USA, +16.164s; **10** Marino Sato, J, +24.165s; **11** Cem Bölükbasi, TR, +27.670s; **12** Richard Verschoor, NL, +27.755s; **13** Jake Hughes, GB, +30.513s; **14** Frederik Vesti, DK, +31.625s; **15** Olli Caldwell, GB, +32.609s; **16** Calan Williams, AUS, -1 lap; **17** Ayumu Iwasa, J, -1 *; Liam Lawson, NZ, -6 (DNF); Clément Novalak, GB, -20 (DNF); Amaury Cordeel, B, -25 (DNF); Roy Nissany, IL, -29 (DNF).
* 5s penalty for causing a collision.
Fastest race lap: Verschoor, 1m 22.862s, 90.085mph/144.978km/h.
Pole position: Drugovich, 1m 21.348s, 91.762mph/147.676km/h.
Championship points: Drivers: 1 Drugovich, 113; **2** Pourchaire, 81; **3** Daruvala, 53; **4** Armstrong, 50; **5** Vips, 49; **6** Doohan, 45.
Teams: 1 MP Motorsport, 135; **2** ART Grand Prix, 106; **3** Hitech Grand Prix, 99.

FIA FORMULA 2 CHAMPIONSHIP, Baku City Circuit, Azerbaijan, 11/12 June. Round 6. 21 and 26 laps of the 3.730-mile/6.003km circuit.
Race 1 (78.267 miles/125.959km).
1 Frederik Vesti, DK, 48m 36.014s, 96.704mph/155.631km/h; **2** Jehan Daruvala, IND, +0.380s; **3** Liam Lawson, NZ, +1.102s; **4** Marcus Armstrong, NZ, +1.517s; **5** Felipe Drugovich, BR, +1.764s; **6** Logan Sargeant, USA, +2.178s; **7** Théo Pourchaire, F, +2.668s; **8** Ayumu Iwasa, J, +3.246s; **9** Jake Hughes, GB, +5.496s; **10** Roy Nissany, IL, +7.381s; **11** Jack Doohan, AUS, +7.573s; **12** Jüri Vips, EST, +8.027s; **13** Amaury Cordeel, B, +8.997s; **14** Clément Novalak, GB, +9.290s; **15** Ralph Boschung, CH, -1 lap (DNF-accident); **16** Calan Williams, AUS, -1 (DNF-accident); **17** Marino Sato, J, -1 (DNF-accident); **18** Cem Bölükbasi, TR, -1 (DNF-accident); **19** Olli Caldwell, GB, -1; **20** Richard Verschoor, NL, -3 (DNF-accident); Enzo Fittipaldi, BR, -5 (DNF-accident); Dennis Hauger, N, -8 (DNF-accident).
Fastest race lap: Hauger, 1m 57.308s, 114.470mph/184.222km/h.
Pole position: Hughes.

Race 2 (96.918 miles/155.974km).
1 Dennis Hauger, N, 1h 03m 29.334s, 91.652mph/147.500km/h; **2** Logan Sargeant, USA, +0.492s; **3** Felipe Drugovich, BR, +0.946s; **4** Jehan Daruvala, IND, +1.664s; **5** Richard Verschoor, NL, +2.776s; **6** Enzo Fittipaldi, BR, +2.970s; **7** Frederik Vesti, DK, +3.149s; **8** Marino Sato, J, +4.791s; **9** Ralph Boschung, CH, +4.911s; **10** Jake Hughes, GB, +5.263s; **11** Théo Pourchaire, F, +5.307s; **12** Marcus Armstrong, NZ, +6.015s; **13** Jack Doohan, AUS, +6.902s *; **14** Ayumu Iwasa, J, +7.279s; **15** Liam Lawson, NZ, +11.575s; **16** Calan Williams, AUS, +12.198s; Jüri Vips, EST, -4 laps (DNF); Roy Nissany, IL, -15 (DNF); Cem Bölükbasi, TR, -15 (DNF); Clément Novalak, GB, -18 (DNF); Amaury Cordeel, B, -26 (DNF); Olli Caldwell, GB, -26 (DNF).
* 5s penalty for causing a collision.
Fastest race lap: Vips, 1m 56.429s, 115.334mph/185.613km/h.
Pole position: Vips, 1m 53.762s, 118.038mph/189.965km/h.
Championship points: Drivers: 1 Drugovich, 132; **2** Pourchaire, 83; **3** Daruvala, 73; **4** Sargeant, 59; **5** Hauger, 55; **6** Armstrong, 55.
Teams: 1 MP Motorsport, 154; **2** Prema Racing, 128; **3** ART Grand Prix, 124.

FIA FORMULA 2 CHAMPIONSHIP, Silverstone Arena Grand Prix Circuit, Towcester, Northamptonshire, Great Britain, 2/3 July. Round 7. 20 and 29 laps of the 3.660-mile/5.891km circuit.
Race 1 (73.127 miles/117.686km).
1 Jack Doohan, AUS, 40m 42.488s, 107.903mph/173.653km/h; **2** Ayumu Iwasa, J, +0.932s; **3** Enzo Fittipaldi, BR, +16.722s; **4** Théo Pourchaire, F, +17.888s; **5** Felipe Drugovich, BR, +21.717s; **6** Frederik Vesti, DK, +26.830s; **7** Logan Sargeant, USA, +28.284s; **8** Jehan Daruvala, IND, +36.291s; **9** Marcus Armstrong, NZ, +38.699s; **10** Richard Verschoor, NL, +43.770s; **11** Jake Hughes, GB, +44.611s; **12** Jüri Vips, EST, +48.113s *; **13** Clément Novalak, GB, +49.448s; **14** Roy Nissany, IL, +54.509s; **15** Dennis Hauger, N, +55.235s; **16** David Beckmann, D, +58.703s; **17** Calan Williams, AUS, +1m 06.077s; **18** Olli Caldwell, GB, +1m 06.411s; **19** Cem Bölükbasi, TR, +1m 21.711s; **20** Liam Lawson, NZ, +1m 35.025s; Marino Sato, J, -9 laps (DNF).
Withdrawn: Ralph Boschung, CH.
* 5s penalty for abusing track limits.
Fastest race lap: Iwasa, 1m 58.954s, 110.780mph/178.284km/h.
Pole position: Daruvala.

Race 2 (106.071 miles/170.705km).
1 Logan Sargeant, USA, 53m 50.586s, 118.292mph/190.372km/h; **2** Théo Pourchaire, F, +1.681s; **3** Liam Lawson, NZ, +8.994s; **4** Felipe Drugovich, BR, +11.312s; **5** Frederik Vesti, DK, +11.961s; **6** Jüri Vips, EST, +12.276s; **7** Jehan Daruvala, IND, +13.899s; **8** Marcus Armstrong, NZ, +17.320s; **9** Jack Doohan, AUS, +21.033s; **10** Jake Hughes, GB, +28.297s; **11** Enzo Fittipaldi, BR, +29.117s; **12** Ayumu Iwasa, J, +30.586s; **13** Clément Novalak, GB, +34.161s; **14** Richard Verschoor, NL, +35.004s; **15** Marino Sato, J, +35.426s; **16** Calan Williams, AUS, +36.391s; **17** Olli Caldwell, GB, +51.166s; **18** Cem Bölükbasi, TR, +1m 01.078s; **19** David Beckmann, D, +1m 03.207s; Roy Nissany, IL, -29 laps (DNF-accident); Dennis Hauger, N, -29 (DNF-accident).
Fastest race lap: Beckmann, 1m 40.842s, 130.677mph/210.305km/h.
Pole position: Sargeant, 1m 38.432s, 133.877mph/215.454km/h.
Championship points: Drivers: 1 Drugovich, 148; **2** Pourchaire, 106; **3** Sargeant, 88; **4** Daruvala, 80; **5** Lawson, 59; **6** Armstrong, 59.
Teams: 1 MP Motorsport, 170; **2** ART Grand Prix, 160; **3** Carlin, 147.

FIA FORMULA 2 CHAMPIONSHIP, Red Bull Ring, Spielberg, Austria, 9/10 July. Round 8. 28 and 40 laps of the 2.683-mile/4.318km circuit.
Race 1 (75.048 miles/120.778km).
1 Marcus Armstrong, NZ, 36m 38.856s, 122.996mph/197.943km/h; **2** Théo Pourchaire, F, +1.098s; **3** Jack Doohan, AUS, +2.169s; **4** Felipe Drugovich, BR, +5.053s; **5** Jüri Vips, EST, +11.972s; **6** Richard Verschoor, NL, +14.832s; **7** Logan Sargeant, USA, +15.291s; **8** Enzo Fittipaldi, BR, +17.538s; **9** Dennis Hauger, N, +19.337s; **10** Ayumu Iwasa, J, +20.891s *; **11** Jehan Daruvala, IND, +21.644s; **12** Frederik Vesti, DK, +22.036s **; **13** Roy Nissany, IL, +31.700s; **14** Calan Williams, AUS, +34.565s; **15** Clément Novalak, GB, +38.673s; **16** Jake Hughes, GB, +40.245s; **17** Olli Caldwell, GB, +53.559s **; **18** Amaury Cordeel, B, +1m 10.121s ***; **19** Roberto Merhi, E, -2 laps (DNF) **; Cem Bölükbasi, TR, -5 (DNF); Liam Lawson, NZ, -17 (DNF); Marino Sato, J, -26 (DNF).
* 5s penalty for forcing another driver off the track.
** 5s penalty for exceeding track limits.
*** 5s penalty for exceeding track limits & 10s stop and go penalty converted to a 30s penalty for overtaking in a double waved yellow flag zone after the chequered flag.
Fastest race lap: Drugovich, 1m 17.328s, 124.910mph/201.024km/h.
Pole position: Armstrong.

Race 2 (107.245 miles/172.594km).
1 Logan Sargeant, USA, 55m 44.500s, 115.521mph/185.913km/h; **2** Enzo Fittipaldi, BR, +0.514s; **3** Roberto Merhi, E, +1.618s *; **4** Dennis Hauger, N, +5.999s; **5** Jake Hughes, GB, +10.137s; **6** Olli Caldwell, GB, +12.152s; **7** Ayumu Iwasa, J, +13.145s *; **8** Jüri Vips, EST, +13.872s; **9** Roy Nissany, IL, +14.442s; **10** Liam Lawson, NZ, +15.964s **; **11** Felipe Drugovich, BR, +19.006s; **12** Jehan Daruvala, IND, +19.635s ***; **13** Théo Pourchaire, F, +19.842s; **14** Frederik Vesti, DK, +26.760s ****; **15** Calan Williams, AUS, +28.949s *; **16** Marino Sato, J, +32.056s; **17** Clément Novalak, GB, +58.606s; **18** Amaury Cordeel, B, -1 lap; **19** Jack Doohan, AUS, -1; Cem Bölükbasi, TR, -37 (DNF); Marcus Armstrong, NZ, -40 (DNF).
* 5s penalty for exceeding track limits.
** 15s penalty for exceeding track limits.
*** Drive through penalty converted to a 20s penalty, attempted to alter the grip of the track surface at their grid position document.
**** 5s penalty for leaving the track and gaining an advantage & 15s penalty for exceeding track limits.
Disqualified: Richard Verschoor, NL (finished 1st in 55m 30.399s, but failed to provide sufficient fuel sample).
Fastest race lap: Doohan, 1m 16.536s, 126.203mph/203.104km/h.
Pole position: Vesti, 1m 14.123s, 130.311mph/209.716km/h.
Championship points: Drivers: 1 Drugovich, 154; **2** Sargeant, 115; **3** Pourchaire, 114; **4** Daruvala, 80; **5** Fittipaldi, 75; **6** Armstrong, 69.
Teams: 1 MP Motorsport, 176; **2** Carlin, 175; **3** ART Grand Prix, 170.

FIA FORMULA 2 CHAMPIONSHIP, Circuit ASA Paul Ricard, Le Beausset, France, 23/24 July. Round 9. 21 and 30 laps of the 3.630-mile/5.842km circuit.
Race 1 (76.271 miles/122.746km).
1 Liam Lawson, NZ, 41m 22.995s, 110.525mph/177.872km/h; **2** Jehan Daruvala, IND, +3.206s; **3** Felipe Drugovich, BR, +4.835s; **4** Jack Doohan, AUS, +5.709s; **5** Frederik Vesti, DK, +7.948s; **6** Ayumu Iwasa, J, +8.260s; **7** Théo Pourchaire, F, +9.552s *; **8** Logan Sargeant, USA, +9.654s; **9** Marino Sato, J, +10.586s; **10** David Beckmann, D, +10.979s; **11** Jüri Vips, EST, +12.087s *; **12** Dennis Hauger, N, +12.477s; **13** Calan Williams, AUS, +12.530s; **14** Marcus Armstrong, NZ, +14.433s **; **15** Cem Bölükbasi, TR, +15.861s; **16** Roy Nissany, IL, +16.536s; **17** Clément Novalak, F, +16.643s; **18** Olli Caldwell, GB, +17.338s; Roberto Merhi, E, -4 laps (DNF); Richard Verschoor, NL, -5 (NC); Enzo Fittipaldi, BR, -13 (DNF); Amaury Cordeel, B, -13 (DNF).
* 5s penalty for forcing another driver off the track.
** 5s penalty for causing a collision.
Fastest race lap: Lawson, 1m 47.984s, 121.019mph/194.762km/h.
Pole position: Daruvala.

Race 2 (108.941 miles/175.324km).
1 Ayumu Iwasa, J, 57m 54.568s, 112.833mph/181.587km/h; **2** Théo Pourchaire, F, +8.649s;

3 Frederik Vesti, DK, +9.887s; **4** Felipe Drugovich, BR, +10.253s; **5** Jack Doohan, AUS, +16.050s; **6** Liam Lawson, NZ, +19.680s; **7** Jehan Daruvala, IND, +27.558s; **8** Clément Novalak, F, +32.852s; **9** Roy Nissany, IL, +36.514s *; **10** Enzo Fittipaldi, BR, +37.686s; **11** Calan Williams, AUS, +40.214s; **12** Jüri Vips, EST, +45.584s; **13** Olli Caldwell, GB, +46.476s; **14** David Beckmann, D, +48.501s; **15** Amaury Cordeel, B, +49.092s; **16** Dennis Hauger, N, +1m 25.136s; **17** Richard Verschoor, NL, -2 laps (DNF); Cem Bölükbasi, TR, -6 (DNF); Logan Sargeant, USA, -19 (DNF); Roberto Merhi, E, -21 (DNF); Marcus Armstrong, NZ, -30 (DNF); Marino Sato, J, -30 (DNF).
* 5s penalty for leaving the track and gaining an advantage.
Fastest race lap: Drugovich, 1m 46.901s, 122.245mph/196.735km/h.
Pole position: Sargeant, 1m 43.871s, 125.811mph/202.474km/h.
Championship points: Drivers: 1 Drugovich, 173; **2** Pourchaire, 134; **3** Sargeant, 118; **4** Daruvala, 94; **5** Lawson, 79; **6** Doohan, 78.
Teams: 1 ART Grand Prix, 209; **2** MP Motorsport, 199; **3** Carlin, 197.

FIA FORMULA 2 CHAMPIONSHIP, Hungaroring, Mogyoród, Budapest, Hungary, 30/31 July. Round 10. 28 and 37 laps of the 2.722-mile/4.381km circuit.
Race 1 (76.198 miles/122.628km).
1 Jack Doohan, AUS, 45m 42.642s, 100.049mph/161.013km/h; **2** Jüri Vips, EST, +5.275s; **3** Enzo Fittipaldi, BR, +6.325s; **4** Felipe Drugovich, BR, +7.792s; **5** Frederik Vesti, DK, +9.266s; **6** Liam Lawson, NZ, +13.550s; **7** Marcus Armstrong, NZ, +20.185s; **8** Ayumu Iwasa, J, +20.723s; **9** Théo Pourchaire, F, +21.715s; **10** Olli Caldwell, GB, +29.794s; **11** Calan Williams, AUS, +31.056s; **12** David Beckmann, D, +31.839s; **13** Amaury Cordeel, B, +32.290s; **14** Roberto Merhi, E, +48.884s; **15** Marino Sato, J, +51.818s; **16** Cem Bölükbasi, TR, +1m 07.163s; **17** Jehan Daruvala, IND, +1m 17.268s; **18** Richard Verschoor, NL, +1m 27.022s *; **19** Roy Nissany, IL, -1 lap; **20** Clément Novalak, F, -1; Logan Sargeant, USA, -27 (DNF); Dennis Hauger, N, -28 (DNF).
* 10s penalty for leaving the track without justifiable reason & Drive through penalty converted to 20s penalty for not serving a time penalty correctly.
Fastest race lap: Verschoor, 1m 30.414s, 108.390mph/174.437km/h.
Pole position: Doohan.

Race 2 (100.698 miles/162.057km).
1 Théo Pourchaire, F, 58m 56.681s, 102.525mph/164.998km/h; **2** Enzo Fittipaldi, BR, +3.641s; **3** Ayumu Iwasa, J, +5.927s; **4** Frederik Vesti, DK, +6.760s; **5** Jüri Vips, EST, +9.624s; **6** Marcus Armstrong, NZ, +13.542s; **7** Liam Lawson, NZ, +14.755s; **8** Richard Verschoor, NL, +20.156s; **9** Felipe Drugovich, BR, +28.627s; **10** Logan Sargeant, USA, +29.230s; **11** Jehan Daruvala, IND, +42.499s; **12** Clément Novalak, F, +42.805s; **13** Cem Bölükbasi, TR, +45.736s; **14** David Beckmann, D, +47.459s; **15** Marino Sato, J, +47.669s; **16** Calan Williams, AUS, +51.200s; **17** Amaury Cordeel, B, +56.084s; **18** Roy Nissany, IL, +58.388s *; **19** Dennis Hauger, N, +1m 17.981s; **20** Olli Caldwell, GB, -1 lap (DNF) **; **21** Roberto Merhi, E, -3 (DNF); Jack Doohan, AUS, -35 (DNF).
* 10s penalty for causing a collision.
** 5s penalty for exceeding track limits.
Fastest race lap: Hauger, 1m 31.204s, 107.451mph/172.926km/h.
Pole position: Iwasa, 1m 27.930s, 111.452mph/179.365km/h.
Championship points: Drivers: 1 Drugovich, 180; **2** Pourchaire, 159; **3** Sargeant, 119; **4** Fittipaldi, 100; **5** Daruvala, 94; **6** Vesti, 91.
Teams: 1 ART Grand Prix, 250; **2** Carlin, 207; **3** MP Motorsport, 206.

FIA FORMULA 2 CHAMPIONSHIP, Circuit de Spa-Francorchamps, Stavelot, Belgium, 27/28 August. Round 11. 18 and 25 laps of the 4.352-mile/7.004km circuit.
Race 1 (78.260 miles/125.948km).
1 Liam Lawson, NZ, 40m 22.343s, 116.421mph/187.361km/h; **2** Jack Doohan, AUS, +3.868s; **3** Ralph Boschung, CH, +5.718s; **4** Felipe Drugovich, BR, +6.360s; **5** Richard Verschoor, NL, +8.407s; **6** Théo Pourchaire, F, +8.686s; **7** Marcus Armstrong, NZ, +9.422s; **8** David Beckmann, D, +10.065s; **9** Ayumu Iwasa, J, +10.833s; **10** Dennis Hauger, N, +11.134s; **11** Roy Nissany, IL, +11.615s; **12** Marino Sato, J, +14.089s; **13** Enzo Fittipaldi, BR, +15.801s; **14** Jüri Vips, EST, +16.393s; **15** Frederik Vesti, DK, +16.767s; **16** Calan Williams, AUS, +17.669s; **17** Clément Novalak, F, +18.553s; **18** Amaury Cordeel, B, +18.594s; **19** Tatiana Calderón, CO, +19.044s; **20** Lirim Zendeli, D, +23.207s *; Logan Sargeant, USA, -8 laps (DNF).
* 5s penalty for exceeding track limits.
Did not start: Jehan Daruvala, IND.
Fastest race lap: Lawson, 2m 01.740s, 128.696mph/207.116km/h.
Pole position: Boschung.

Race 2 (108.725 miles/174.976km).
1 Jack Doohan, AUS, 52m 16.133s, 124.894mph/200.997km/h; **2** Felipe Drugovich, BR, +1.942s; **3** Liam Lawson, NZ, +8.714s; **4** Richard Verschoor, NL, +12.479s; **5** Logan Sargeant, USA, +21.266s; **6** David Beckmann, D, +22.365s; **7** Ayumu Iwasa, J, +22.498s; **8** Jüri Vips, EST, +23.899s; **9** Clément Novalak, F, +24.746s; **10** Enzo Fittipaldi, BR, +25.481s *; **11** Frederik Vesti, DK, +31.001s; **12** Dennis Hauger, N, +37.471s **; **13** Marcus Armstrong, NZ, +39.756s ***; **14** Ralph Boschung, CH, +40.683s; **15** Marino Sato, J, +43.718s; **16** Calan Williams, AUS, +45.683s; **17** Amaury Cordeel, B, +52.243s; **18** Tatiana Calderón, CO, +57.384s; **19** Roy Nissany, IL, +1m 02.827s; **20** Jehan Daruvala, IND, +1m 46.358s; **21** Lirim Zendeli, D, -3 laps; Théo Pourchaire, F, -22 (DNF).
* 5s penalty for leaving the track and gaining an advantage.
** 5s penalty for forcing another driver off the track & 5s penalty for exceeding track limits.
*** 5s penalty for forcing another driver off the track.
Fastest race lap: Daruvala, 2m 00.677s, 129.830mph/208.941km/h.
Pole position: Drugovich, 1m 58.232s, 132.514mph/213.262km/h.
Championship points: Drivers: 1 Drugovich, 205; **2** Pourchaire, 162; **3** Sargeant, 129; **4** Doohan, 121; **5** Lawson, 114; **6** Fittipaldi, 101.
Teams: 1 ART Grand Prix, 253; **2** Carlin, 243; **3** MP Motorsport, 233.

FIA FORMULA 2 CHAMPIONSHIP, Circuit Park Zandvoort, Netherlands, 3/4 September. Round 12. 29 and 38 laps of the 2.646-mile/4.259km circuit.
Race 1 (76.708 miles/123.450km).
1 Marcus Armstrong, NZ, 43m 42.549s, 105.349mph/169.543km/h; **2** Clément Novalak, F, +0.880s; **3** Dennis Hauger, N, +1.990s; **4** Liam Lawson, NZ, +2.517s; **5** Jüri Vips, EST, +3.026s; **6** Ayumu Iwasa, J, +3.318s; **7** Richard Verschoor, NL, +4.268s; **8** Logan Sargeant, USA, +4.650s; **9** Jack Doohan, AUS, +4.840s; **10** Felipe Drugovich, BR, +5.458s; **11** Frederik Vesti, DK, +6.287s; **12** Amaury Cordeel, B, +6.719s; **13** Enzo Fittipaldi, BR, +7.416s; **14** David Beckmann, D, +8.103s; **15** Roy Nissany, IL, +8.940s; **16** Jehan Daruvala, IND, +9.719s; **17** Ralph Boschung, CH, +9.818s; **18** Calan Williams, AUS, +10.445s; **19** Marino Sato, J, +11.288s; **20** Théo Pourchaire, F, +11.470s; Tatiana Calderón, CO, -4 laps (DNF); Olli Caldwell, GB, -18 (DNF).
Fastest race lap: Drugovich, 1m 25.808s, 111.028mph/178.682km/h.
Pole position: Novalak.

Race 2 (100.526 miles/161.781km).
1 Felipe Drugovich, BR, 1h 25m 22.484s, 70.674mph/113.739km/h; **2** Richard Verschoor, NL, +2.405s; **3** Ayumu Iwasa, J, +3.645s; **4** Dennis Hauger, N, +6.947s; **5** Enzo Fittipaldi, BR, +7.987s; **6** Amaury Cordeel, B, +10.872s; **7** Jüri Vips, EST, +12.400s; **8** Olli Caldwell, GB, +14.609s; **9** Théo Pourchaire, F, +15.562s; **10** Jehan Daruvala, IND, +17.281s; **11** Calan Williams, AUS, +18.499s; **12** Liam Lawson, NZ, +20.264s; **13** David Beckmann, D, +23.196s *; **14** Marcus Armstrong, NZ, +25.601s; **15** Frederik Vesti, DK, +29.385s; **16** Roy Nissany, IL, +37.144s *; **17** Ralph Boschung, CH, +50.639s; Tatiana Calderón, CO, -17 laps (DNF); Clément Novalak, F, -17 (DNF); Jack Doohan, AUS, -18 (DNF); Marino Sato, J, -22 (DNF); Logan Sargeant, USA, -38 (DNF).
* 10s penalty for driving in a dangerous manner during the safety car period.
Fastest race lap: Vesti, 1m 23.078s, 114.676mph/184.554km/h.
Pole position: Drugovich, 1m 20.713s, 118.036mph/189.961km/h.
Championship points: Drivers: 1 Drugovich, 233; **2** Pourchaire, 164; **3** Sargeant, 130; **4** Doohan, 121; **5** Lawson, 119; **6** Iwasa, 114.
Teams: 1 MP Motorsport, 269; **2** ART Grand Prix, 255; **3** Carlin, 249.

FIA FORMULA 2 CHAMPIONSHIP, Autodromo Nazionale di Monza, Milan, Italy, 10/11 September. Round 13. 21 and 30 laps of the 3.600-mile/5.793km circuit.
Race 1 (75.400 miles/121.344km).
1 Jüri Vips, EST, 35m 29.646s, 127.778mph/205.639km/h; **2** Frederik Vesti, DK, +1.035s; **3** Jehan Daruvala, IND, +7.684s; **4** Logan Sargeant, USA, +9.022s; **5** Liam Lawson, NZ, +13.129s; **6** Jack Doohan, AUS, +13.306s; **7** David Beckmann, D, +14.391s; **8** Richard Verschoor, NL, +14.462s *; **9** Dennis Hauger, N, +14.723s; **10** Marcus Armstrong, NZ, +17.621s *; **11** Marino Sato, J, +19.195s; **12** Enzo Fittipaldi, BR, +22.604s; **13** Luca Ghiotto, I, +24.186s; **14** Calan Williams, AUS, +24.687s; **15** Amaury Cordeel, B, +25.907s; **16** Ayumu Iwasa, J, +28.155s *; **17** Théo Pourchaire, F, +30.385s **; Ralph Boschung, CH, -14 laps (DNF); Clément Novalak, F, -14 (DNF); Felipe Drugovich, BR, -20 (DNF); Olli Caldwell, GB, -21 (DNF); Tatiana Calderón, CO, -21 (DNF).
* 5s penalty for leaving the track and gaining an advantage.
** 5s penalty for causing a collision.
Fastest race lap: Hauger, 1m 33.739s, 138.240mph/222.477km/h.
Pole position: Vesti.

Race 2 (107.796 miles/173.481km).
1 Jehan Daruvala, IND, 1h 06m 39.193s, 97.207mph/156.439km/h; **2** Frederik Vesti, DK, +1.970s; **3** Enzo Fittipaldi, BR, +6.491s; **4** Dennis Hauger, N, +7.249s; **5** David Beckmann, D, +7.801s; **6** Felipe Drugovich, BR, +10.502s; **7** Amaury Cordeel, B, +12.738s; **8** Clément Novalak, F, +27.950s; **9** Richard Verschoor, NL, +35.184s; **10** Jüri Vips, EST, +45.692s; **11** Marino Sato, J, +47.522s; **12** Marcus Armstrong, NZ, +54.718s *; **13** Liam Lawson, NZ, +1m 31.534s; Calan Williams, AUS, -24 laps (DNF); Jack Doohan, AUS, -29 (DNF); Logan Sargeant, USA, -30 (DNF); Théo Pourchaire, F, -30 (DNF); Luca Ghiotto, I, -30 (DNF); Ralph Boschung, CH, -30 (DNF); Olli Caldwell, GB, -30 (DNF).
* 10s penalty for failing to follow Race Director's instructions.
Disqualified: Ayumu Iwasa, J, +5.738s, technical non-conformity - finished 3rd.
Did not start: Tatiana Calderón, CO.
Fastest race lap: Verschoor, 1m 33.155s, 139.107mph/223.872km/h.
Pole position: Doohan, 1m 31.641s, 141.405mph/227.570km/h.
Championship points: Drivers: 1 Drugovich, 241; **2** Pourchaire, 164; **3** Sargeant, 135; **4** Doohan, 126; **5** Daruvala, 126; **6** Fittipaldi, 126.
Teams: 1 MP Motorsport, 281; **2** ART Grand Prix, 281; **3** Carlin, 258.

FIA FORMULA 2 CHAMPIONSHIP, Yas Marina Circuit, Abu Dhabi, United Arab Emirates, 19/20 November. Round 14. 23 and 33 laps of the 3.281-mile/5.281km circuit.
Race 1 (75.402 miles/121.348km).
1 Liam Lawson, NZ, 1h 11m 53.868s, 62.983mph/101.362km/h; **2** Richard Verschoor, NL, +7.943s; **3** Felipe Drugovich, BR, +8.803s; **4** Dennis Hauger, N, +14.937s; **5** Amaury Cordeel, B, +15.449s; **6** Logan Sargeant, USA, +15.938s; **7** Jack Doohan, AUS, +16.501s; **8** Roy Nissany, IL, +17.313s; **9** Théo Pourchaire, F, +17.579s; **10** Marcus Armstrong, NZ, +17.968s; **11** Frederik Vesti, DK, +19.213s; **12** Jüri Vips, EST, +22.031s; **13** Ayumu Iwasa, J, +24.162s; **14** Clément Novalak, F, +27.095s; **15** Zane Maloney, BB, +33.860s; **16** Olli Caldwell, GB, +34.034s; **17** Ralph Boschung, CH, +36.430s; **18** Juan Manuel Correa, USA, +38.164s; **19** Marino Sato, J, +58.710s; **20** Tatiana Calderón, CO, +1m 14.890s; Jehan Daruvala, IND, -23 laps (DNF-accident); Enzo Fittipaldi, BR, -23 (DNF-accident).
Fastest race lap: Lawson, 1m 39.292s, 118.974mph/191.471km/h.
Pole position: Verschoor.

Race 2 (108.217 miles/174.158km).
1 Ayumu Iwasa, J, 57m 02.908s, 113.890mph/183.288km/h; **2** Felipe Drugovich, BR, +0.830s; **3** Liam Lawson, NZ, +1.348s; **4** Dennis Hauger, N, +13.440s; **5** Logan Sargeant, USA, +14.064s; **6** Amaury Cordeel, B, +15.719s; **7** Richard Verschoor, NL, +18.162s; **8** Jüri Vips, EST, +20.279s; **9** Marcus Armstrong, NZ, +20.684s; **10** Roy Nissany, IL, +22.181s *; **11** Frederik Vesti, DK, +22.732s; **12** Clément Novalak, F, +23.489s; **13** Jehan Daruvala, IND, +24.298s; **14** Enzo Fittipaldi, BR, +27.616s; **15** Marino Sato, J, +28.246s; **16** Zane Maloney, BB, +31.754s; **17** Juan Manuel Correa, USA, +37.446s; **18** Tatiana Calderón, CO, +45.116s; **19** Théo Pourchaire, F, -2 laps (DNF); **20** Olli Caldwell, GB, -4 (DNF); Jack Doohan, AUS, -8 (DNF); Ralph Boschung, CH, -33 (DNF).
* 5s penalty for failing to respect track limits.
Fastest race lap: Novalak, 1m 39.146s, 119.150mph/191.753km/h.
Pole position: Iwasa, 1m 36.290s, 122.684mph/197.441km/h.

Final championship points
Drivers
1 Felipe Drugovich, BR, 265; **2** Théo Pourchaire, F, 164; **3** Liam Lawson, NZ, 149; **4** Logan Sargeant, USA, 148; **5** Ayumu Iwasa, J, 141; **6** Jack Doohan, AUS, 128; **7** Jehan Daruvala, IND, 126; **8** Enzo Fittipaldi, BR, 126; **9** Frederik Vesti, DK, 117; **10** Dennis Hauger, N, 115; **11** Jüri Vips, EST, 114; **12** Richard Verschoor, NL, 103; **13** Marcus Armstrong, NZ, 93; **14** Clément Novalak, F, 40; **15** Ralph Boschung, CH, 40; **16** Jake Hughes, GB, 26; **17** Amaury Cordeel, B, 26; **18** David Beckmann, D, 25; **19** Roy Nissany, IL, 20; **20** Roberto Merhi, E, 15; **21** Olli Caldwell, GB, 12; **22** Marino Sato, J, 6; **23** Calan Williams, AUS, 5.

Teams
1 MP Motorsport, 305; **2** Carlin, 297; **3** ART Grand Prix, 281; **4** Prema Racing, 241; **5** Hitech Grand Prix, 207; **6** DAMS, 161; **7** Virtuosi Racing, 134; **8** Charouz Racing System, 130; **9** Trident, 108; **10** Van Amersfoort Racing, 73; **11** Campos Racing, 67.

Japanese Championship Super Formula

All cars are Dallara SF19.

JAPANESE CHAMPIONSHIP SUPER FORMULA, Fuji International Speedway, Sunto-gun, Shizuoka Prefecture, Japan, 9/10 April. Round 1. 2 x 41 laps of the 2.835-mile/4.563km circuit.
Race 1 (116.059 miles/186.779km).
1 Ryo Hirakawa, J (-Toyota), 58m 25.743s, 119.372mph/192.110km/h; **2** Tomoki Nojiri, J (-Honda), +5.623s; **3** Sacha Fenestraz, F (-Toyota), +6.717s; **4** Yuhi Sekiguchi, J (-Toyota), +19.396s; **5** Ritomo Miyata, J (-Toyota), +22.288s; **6** Tadasuke Makino, J (-Honda), +32.351s; **7** Toshiki Oyu, J (-Honda), +33.991s; **8** Sho Tsuboi, J (-Toyota), +35.293s; **9** Ren Sato, J (-Honda), +35.575s; **10** Atsushi Miyake, J (-Honda), +43.676s.
Fastest race lap: Hirakawa, 1m 22.941s, 123.065mph/198.054km/h.
Pole position: Ukyo Sasahara, J (-Honda), 1m 21.404s, 125.389mph/201.794km/h.

Race 2 (116.059 miles/186.779km).
1 Tomoki Nojiri, J (-Honda), 1h 01m 10.882s, 114.001mph/183.468km/h; **2** Ryo Hirakawa, J (-Toyota), +1.659s; **3** Ritomo Miyata, J (-Toyota), +2.494s; **4** Kenta Yamashita, J (-Toyota), +15.042s; **5** Atsushi Miyake, J (-Honda), +15.839s; **6** Yuhi Sekiguchi, J (-Toyota), +18.206s; **7** Hiroki Ohtsu, J (-Honda), +31.087s; **8** Giuliano Alesi, F (-Toyota), +35.048s; **9** Kamui Kobayashi, J (-Toyota), +35.940s; **10** Ukyo Sasahara, J (-Honda), +36.338s.
Fastest race lap: Sekiguchi, 1m 23.665s, 122.000mph/196.340km/h.
Pole position: Nojiri, 1m 21.522s, 125.207mph/201.501km/h.

JAPANESE CHAMPIONSHIP SUPER FORMULA, Suzuka International Racing Course, Suzuka-shi, Mie Prefecture, Japan, 24 April. Round 2. 31 laps of the 3.608-mile/5.807km circuit, 111.857 miles/180.017km.
1 Nobuharu Matsushita, J (-Honda), 1h 01m 18.681s, 109.465mph/176.167km/h; **2** Tomoki Nojiri, J (-Honda), +5.053s; **3** Tadasuke Makino, J (-Honda), +8.113s; **4** Sacha Fenestraz, F (-Toyota), +18.419s; **5** Kamui Kobayashi, J (-Toyota), +21.894s; **6** Yuji Kunimoto, J (-Toyota), +44.604s; **7** Ryo Hirakawa, J (-Toyota), +46.381s; **8** Hiroki Ohtsu, J (-Honda), +47.809s; **9** Naoki Yamamoto, J (-Honda), +51.564s; **10** Ren Sato, J (-Honda), +52.487s.
Fastest race lap: Nojiri, 1m 55.285s, 112.676mph/181.335km/h.
Pole position: Nojiri, 1m 36.352s, 134.817mph/216.967km/h.

JAPANESE CHAMPIONSHIP SUPER FORMULA, Autopolis International Racing Course, Kamit-sue-mura, Hita-gun, Oita Prefecture, Japan, 22 May. Round 3. 42 laps of the 2.904-mile/4.674km circuit, 121.980 miles/196.308km.
1 Ryo Hirakawa, J (-Toyota), 1h 11m 58.025s, 101.697mph/163.665km/h; **2** Sacha Fenestraz, F (-Toyota), +2.310s; **3** Atsushi Miyake, J (-Honda), +12.508s; **4** Tomoki Nojiri, J (-Honda), +21.821s; **5** Ritomo Miyata, J (-Toyota), +22.391s; **6** Tadasuke Makino, J (-Honda), +32.569s; **7** Ukyo Sasahara, J (-Honda), +33.571s; **8** Sena Sakaguchi, J (-Toyota), +34.647s; **9** Hiroki Ohtsu, J (-Honda), +35.577s; **10** Nobuharu Matsushita, J (-Honda), +36.410s.
Fastest race lap: Miyake, 1m 28.747s, 117.812mph/189.600km/h.

Pole position: Nojiri, 1m 24.529s, 123.691mph/199.061km/h.

JAPANESE CHAMPIONSHIP SUPER FORMULA, Sportsland-SUGO International Course, Shibata-gun, Miyagi Prefecture, Japan, 19 June. Round 4. 49 laps of the 2.229-mile/3.587km circuit, 109.199 miles/175.738km.

1 Sacha Fenestraz, F (-Toyota), 1h 10m 32.529s, 92.880mph/149.475km/h; **2** Toshiki Oyu, J (-Honda), +5.304s; **3** Tomoki Nojiri, J (-Honda), +7.021s; **4** Tadasuke Makino, J (-Honda), +7.146s; **5** Hiroki Ohtsu, J (-Honda), +10.887s; **6** Ritomo Miyata, J (-Toyota), +11.654s; **7** Ryo Hirakawa, J (-Toyota), +14.965s; **8** Nirei Fukuzumi, J (-Honda), +18.071s; **9** Yuji Kunimoto, J (-Toyota), +19.162s; **10** Ukyo Sasahara, J (-Honda), +19.474s.

Fastest race lap: Yuhi Sekiguchi, J (-Toyota), 1m 07.125s, 119.520mph/192.349km/h.

Pole position: Nojiri, 1m 04.349s, 124.676mph/200.646km/h.

JAPANESE CHAMPIONSHIP SUPER FORMULA, Fuji International Speedway, Sunto-gun, Shizuoka Prefecture, Japan, 17 July. Round 5. 40 laps of the 2.835-mile/4.563km circuit, 113.224 miles/182.216km.

1 Ukyo Sasahara, J (-Honda), 1h 10m 52.708s, 96.004mph/154.504km/h; **2** Sho Tsuboi, J (-Toyota), +2.098s; **3** Tomoki Nojiri, J (-Honda), +7.549s; **4** Ritomo Miyata, J (-Toyota), +8.854s; **5** Tadasuke Makino, J (-Honda), +13.454s; **6** Ren Sato, J (-Honda), +14.116s; **7** Kenta Yamashita, J (-Toyota), +15.660s; **8** Yuji Kunimoto, J (-Toyota), +18.438s; **9** Naoki Yamamoto, J (-Honda), +19.258s; **10** Toshiki Oyu, J (-Honda), +21.269s.

Fastest race lap: Oyu, 1m 23.886s, 121.679mph/195.823km/h.

Pole position: Yuhi Sekiguchi, J (-Toyota), 1m 35.951s, 106.379mph/171.200km/h.

JAPANESE CHAMPIONSHIP SUPER FORMULA, Twin Ring Motegi, Motegi-machi, Haga-gun, Tochigi Prefecture, Japan, 20/21 August. Round 6. 2 x 37 laps of the 2.983-mile/4.801km circuit.

Race 7 (110.379 miles/177.637km).

1 Naoki Yamamoto, J (-Honda), 1h 14m 32.841s, 88.839mph/142.972km/h; **2** Sacha Fenestraz, F (-Toyota), +5.337s; **3** Tomoki Nojiri, J (-Honda), +7.210s; **4** Tadasuke Makino, J (-Honda), +12.628s; **5** Sho Tsuboi, J (-Toyota), +13.575s; **6** Kenta Yamashita, J (-Toyota), +16.112s; **7** Ukyo Sasahara, J (-Honda), +17.622s; **8** Ritomo Miyata, J (-Toyota), +19.323s; **9** Yuhi Sekiguchi, J (-Toyota), +29.138s; **10** Hiroki Ohtsu, J (-Honda), +29.911s.

Fastest race lap: Yamamoto, 1m 49.399s, 98.168mph/157.987km/h.

Pole position: Yamamoto, 1m 30.423s, 118.770mph/191.142km/h.

Race 8 (110.379 miles/177.637km).

1 Yuhi Sekiguchi, J (-Toyota), 59m 31.699s, 111.253mph/179.045km/h; **2** Ryo Hirakawa, J (-Toyota), +0.943s; **3** Tadasuke Makino, J (-Honda), +2.450s; **4** Tomoki Nojiri, J (-Honda), +4.713s; **5** Toshiki Oyu, J (-Honda), +5.985s; **6** Sacha Fenestraz, F (-Toyota), +7.222s; **7** Ren Sato, J (-Honda), +8.096s; **8** Ukyo Sasahara, J (-Honda), +14.316s; **9** Sena Sakaguchi, J (-Toyota), +25.715s; **10** Sho Tsuboi, J (-Toyota), +26.211s.

Fastest race lap: Kazuya Oshima, J (-Toyota), 1m 33.930s, 114.335mph/184.005km/h.

Pole position: Oyu, 1m 30.313s, 118.915mph/191.374km/h.

JAPANESE CHAMPIONSHIP SUPER FORMULA, Suzuka International Racing Course, Suzuka-shi, Mie Prefecture, Japan, 29/30 October. Round 7. 2 x 31 laps of the 3.608-mile/5.807km circuit.

Race 9 (111.857 miles/180.017km).

1 Ukyo Sasahara, J (-Honda), 53m 00.126s, 126.626mph/203.785km/h; **2** Tomoki Nojiri, J (-Honda), +12.589s; **3** Ren Sato, J (-Honda), +14.212s; **4** Toshiki Oyu, J (-Honda), +19.638s; **5** Ritomo Miyata, J (-Toyota), +19.995s; **6** Yuhi Sekiguchi, J (-Toyota), +21.206s; **7** Tadasuke Makino, J (-Honda), +23.151s; **8** Sho Tsuboi, J (-Toyota), +25.941s; **9** Ryo Hirakawa, J (-Toyota), +26.423s; **10** Sena Sakaguchi, J (-Toyota), +27.631s.

Fastest race lap: Atsushi Miyake, J (-Honda), 1m 40.056s, 129.826mph/208.935km/h.

Pole position: Nojiri, 1m 36.020s, 135.283mph/217.717km/h.

Race 10 (111.857 miles/180.017km).

1 Tomoki Nojiri, J (-Honda), 1h 01m 20.630s, 109.407mph/176.073km/h; **2** Hiroki Ohtsu, J (-Honda), +6.857s; **3** Ritomo Miyata, J (-Toyota), +8.000s; **4** Sacha Fenestraz, F (-Toyota), +10.549s; **5** Ryo Hirakawa, J (-Toyota), +13.862s; **6** Naoki Yamamoto, J (-Honda), +14.803s; **7** Toshiki Oyu, J (-Honda), +18.707s; **8** Atsushi Miyake, J (-Honda), +31.953s; **9** Tadasuke Makino, J (-Honda), +32.799s; **10** Kamui Kobayashi, J (-Toyota), +33.017s.

Fastest race lap: Ren Sato, J (-Honda), 1m 39.362s, 130.733mph/210.394km/h.

Pole position: Nojiri, 1m 36.003s, 135.307mph/217.756km/h.

Final championship points

Drivers

1 Tomoki Nojiri, J, 154; **2** Sacha Fenestraz, F, 89; **3** Ryo Hirakawa, J, 87; **4** Ritomo Miyata, J, 64; **5** Tadasuke Makino, J, 61; **6** Ukyo Sasahara, J, 57; **7** Yuhi Sekiguchi, J, 43; **8** Toshiki Oyu, J, 43; **9** Hiroki Ohtsu, J, 33; **10** Naoki Yamamoto, J, 32; **11** Sho Tsuboi, J, 30; **12** Ren Sato, J, 25; **13** Nobuharu Matsushita, J, 21; **14** Atsushi Miyake, J, 21; **15** Kenta Yamashita, J, 19; **16** Yuji Kunimoto, J, 10; **17** Kamui Kobayashi, J, 9; **18** Sena Sakaguchi, J, 6; **19** Nirei Fukuzumi, J, 3; **20** Giuliano Alesi, F, 3.

Teams

1 Team Mugen, 187; **2** carenex Team Impul, 126; **3** Kondo Racing, 99; **4** DoCoMo Team Dandelion Racing, 91; **5** TCS Nakajima Racing, 67; **6** Kuo Vantelin Team TOM'S, 59; **7** Team Goh, 44; **8** P.mu/cerumo-INGING, 34; **9** B-MAX Racing Team, 21; **10** KCMG, 19; **11** ThreeBond Drago Corse, 3.

FIA Formula 3 Championship

All cars are Dallara F3 2019-Mecachrome V634.

FIA FORMULA 3 CHAMPIONSHIP, Bahrain International Circuit, Sakhir, Bahrain, 19/20 March. Round 1. 20 and 23 laps of the 3.363-mile/5.412km circuit.

Race 1 (67.104 miles/107.994km).

1 Isack Hadjar, F, 37m 30.285s, 107.595mph/173.158km/h; **2** Ollie Bearman, GB, +1.589s *; **3** Alexander Smolyar, RUS, +3.593s; **4** Zane Maloney, BB, +5.649s; **5** Arthur Leclerc, MC, +5.664s; **6** Zak O'Sullivan, GB, +8.850s; **7** Caio Collet, BR, +9.140s; **8** Kaylen Frederick, USA, +11.479s; **9** Juan Manuel Correa, USA, +12.153s; **10** David Vidales, E, +19.134s; **11** William Alatalo, FIN, +21.251s; **12** Reece Ushijima, USA, +21.871s; **13** Jonny Edgar, GB, +28.399s; **14** Ido Cohen, IL, +29.919s; **15** Kush Maini, IND, +30.741s; **16** Nazim Azman, MAL, +34.890s; **17** Rafael Villagómez, MEX, +34.911s; **18** Ayrton Simmons, GB, +44.886s; **19** Francesco Pizzi, I, +45.648s; **20** Enzo Trulli, I, +51.577s *; **21** Brad Benavides, GCA, +53.412s; **22** László Tóth, H, +53.720s *; **23** Hunter Yeany, USA, +59.278s **; **24** Roman Stanek, CZ, +1m 07.166s; **25** Franco Colapinto, RA, +1m 16.651s; **26** Niko Kari, FIN, +1m 39.371s; **27** Jak Crawford, USA, +1m 40.417s; **28** Pepe Martí, E, -1 lap; Grégoire Saucy, CH, -14 (DNF); Victor Martins, F, -15 (DNF).

* 5s penalty for exceeding track limits.

** 15s penalty for exceeding track limits.

Fastest race lap: Maloney, 1m 51.231s, 108.839mph/175.159km/h.

Pole position: O'Sullivan.

Race 2 (77.193 miles/124.230km).

1 Victor Martins, F, 46m 47.389s, 99.180mph/159.616km/h; **2** Arthur Leclerc, MC, +1.543s; **3** Grégoire Saucy, CH, +6.812s; **4** Juan Manuel Correa, USA, +9.084s; **5** Franco Colapinto, RA, +11.193s *; **6** Ollie Bearman, GB, +14.582s; **7** Jak Crawford, USA, +18.765s; **8** David Vidales, E, +23.004s; **9** William Alatalo, FIN, +23.665s; **10** Kaylen Frederick, USA, +23.843s; **11** Jonny Edgar, GB, +26.906s; **12** Rafael Villagómez, MEX, +28.274s; **13** Pepe Martí, E, +30.194s *; **14** Niko Kari, FIN, +35.044s; **15** Ido Cohen, IL, +35.068s; **16** Kush Maini, IND, +35.111s; **17** Reece Ushijima, USA, +35.790s; **18** Zak O'Sullivan, GB, +36.274s; **19** Ayrton Simmons, GB, +36.792s; **20** Brad Benavides, GCA, +38.167s; **21** Hunter Yeany, USA, +38.297s **; **22** Roman Stanek, CZ, +38.303s; **23** Alexander Smolyar, RUS, +38.795s ***; **24** László Tóth, H, +49.781s; **26** Enzo Trulli, I, +1m 51.611s ****; Nazim Azman, MAL, -19 laps (DNF); Caio Collet, BR, -22 (DNF); Zane Maloney, BB, -23 (DNF); Francesco Pizzi, I, -23 (DNF).

* 5s penalty for exceeding track limits.

** 5s penalty for causing a collision.

*** 20s penalty for causing a collision twice

**** 10s penalty for causing a collision.

Fastest race lap: Stanek, 1m 51.634s, 108.446mph/174.527km/h.

Pole position: Colapinto, 1m 46.249s, 113.942mph/183.373km/h.

Championship points: Drivers: 1 Martins, 25; **2** Leclerc, 24; **3** Bearman, 17; **4** Saucy, 15; **5** Correa, 14; **6** Colapinto, 12.

Teams: 1 ART Grand Prix, 54; **2** Prema Racing, 47; **3** Hitech Grand Prix, 14.

FIA FORMULA 3 CHAMPIONSHIP, Autodromo Enzo e Dino Ferrari, Imola, Italy, 23/24 April. Round 2. 20 and 24 laps of the 3.050-mile/4.909km circuit.

Race 1 (60.871 miles/97.962km).

1 Franco Colapinto, RA, 36m 38.273s, 99.904mph/160.780km/h; **2** Victor Martins, F, +2.640s; **3** Jak Crawford, USA, +2.700s; **4** Roman Stanek, CZ, +3.634s; **5** Isack Hadjar, F, +4.088s; **6** Zane Maloney, BB, +4.651s; **7** Oliver Rasmussen, DK, +5.156s; **8** Alexander Smolyar, RUS, +5.844s; **9** Rafael Villagómez, MEX, +6.420s; **10** Francesco Pizzi, I, +6.614s; **11** David Vidales, E, +6.990s; **12** Ollie Bearman, GB, +7.185s; **13** Arthur Leclerc, MC, +7.663s; **14** Brad Benavides, GCA, +9.341s; **15** William Alatalo, FIN, +10.261s; **16** Kaylen Frederick, USA, +10.500s *; **17** Hunter Yeany, USA, +10.901s; **18** David Schumacher, D, +11.372s; **19** László Tóth, H, +13.988s; **20** Kush Maini, IND, +15.008s; **21** Nazim Azman, MAL, +16.253s; **22** Enzo Trulli, I, +20.913s **; **23** Ido Cohen, IL, +21.137s ***; **24** Caio Collet, BR, -1 lap; Grégoire Saucy, CH, -3 (DNF); Federico Malvestiti, I, -8 (DNF); Reece Ushijima, USA, -8 (DNF); Zak O'Sullivan, GB, -13 (DNF); Pepe Martí, E, -13 (DNF).

* 5s penalty for causing a collision.

** 5s penalty for overtaking under yellow flag conditions.

*** 5s penalty for exceeding track limits.

Fastest race lap: Bearman, 1m 33.573s, 117.353mph/188.862km/h.

Pole position: Colapinto.

Race 2 (73.072 miles/117.598km).

1 Roman Stanek, CZ, 45m 37.829s, 96.259mph/154.914km/h; **2** Jak Crawford, USA, +0.654s; **3** Isack Hadjar, F, +4.247s; **4** Arthur Leclerc, MC, +6.515s; **5** Kush Maini, IND, +12.566s; **6** Zak O'Sullivan, GB, +13.285s; **7** Kaylen Frederick, USA, +14.289s; **8** David Vidales, E, +14.945s; **9** Victor Martins, F, +15.893s; **10** William Alatalo, FIN, +16.613s; **11** Caio Collet, BR, +18.587s; **12** David Schumacher, D, +18.848s; **13** Ido Cohen, IL, +20.446s *; **14** Alexander Smolyar, RUS, +21.050s; **15** Pepe Martí, E, +21.969s; **16** Hunter Yeany, USA, +22.963s; **17** Ollie Bearman, GB, +24.728s **; **18** Reece Ushijima, USA, +27.704s; **19** Nazim Azman, MAL, +28.761s; **20** Rafael Villagómez, MEX, +30.406s; **21** Federico Malvestiti, I, +32.374s; **22** Franco Colapinto, RA, +1m 12.566s; **23** Grégoire Saucy, CH, -1 lap; **24** Enzo Trulli, I, -1; **25** László Tóth, H, -3 ***; Zane Maloney, BB, -15 (DNF); Brad Benavides, GCA, -18 (DNF) ****; Oliver Rasmussen, DK, -19 (DNF); Francesco Pizzi, I, -23 (DNF).

* 5s penalty for failing to respect track limits.

** 20s penalty for causing a collision.

*** 30s penalty for violation of minimum delta time under Safety Car.

**** 10s penalty for causing a collision.

Fastest race lap: Stanek, 1m 33.129s, 117.913mph/189.762km/h.

Pole position: Maloney, 1m 41.180s, 108.530mph/174.662km/h.

Championship points: Drivers: 1 Martins, 36; **2** Leclerc, 36; **3** Stanek, 33; **4** Crawford, 32; **5** Hadjar, 31; **6** Colapinto, 22.

Teams: 1 Prema Racing, 85; **2** ART Grand Prix, 65; **3** Trident, 52.

FIA FORMULA 3 CHAMPIONSHIP, Circuit de Catalunya, Montmeló, Barcelona, Spain, 21/22 May. Round 3. 20 and 24 laps of the 2.905-mile/4.675km circuit.

Race 1 (58.020 miles/93.374km).

1 David Vidales, E, 32m 38.784s, 106.775mph/171.838km/h; **2** Jak Crawford, USA, +1.268s; **3** Caio Collet, BR, +6.482s; **4** Arthur Leclerc, MC, +9.081s; **5** Juan Manuel Correa, USA, +10.326s; **6** Alexander Smolyar, RUS, +11.239s; **7** Kaylen Frederick, USA, +11.839s; **8** Roman Stanek, CZ, +12.370s; **9** Reece Ushijima, USA, +15.274s; **10** Isack Hadjar, F, +16.057s; **11** Grégoire Saucy, CH, +16.908s; **12** Ollie Bearman, GB, +17.427s; **13** Pepe Martí, E, +18.137s; **14** Rafael Villagómez, MEX, +19.983s; **15** William Alatalo, FIN, +23.465s; **16** Oliver Rasmussen, DK, +24.284s; **17** Kush Maini, IND, +24.858s; **18** Zak O'Sullivan, GB, +25.438s; **19** Federico Malvestiti, I, +29.713s; **20** Lirim Zendeli, D, +32.164s; **21** Zane Maloney, BB, +35.784s; **22** Enzo Trulli, I, +36.292s; **23** Ido Cohen, IL, +39.535s; **24** Francesco Pizzi, I, +39.941s; **25** Brad Benavides, GCA, +41.105s; **26** László Tóth, H, +42.196s; **27** Hunter Yeany, USA, +1m 08.603s; Nazim Azman, MAL, -4 laps (DNF); Franco Colapinto, RA, -10 (DNF); Victor Martins, F, -13 (DNF).

Fastest race lap: Crawford, 1m 36.788s, 108.047mph/173.885km/h.

Pole position: Vidales.

Race 2 (69.640 miles/112.074km).

1 Victor Martins, F, 43m 43.673s, 95.660mph/153.950km/h; **2** Roman Stanek, CZ, +2.368s; **3** Isack Hadjar, F, +3.026s; **4** Alexander Smolyar, RUS, +3.624s; **5** Ollie Bearman, GB, +4.348s; **6** Jak Crawford, USA, +5.420s; **7** Caio Collet, BR, +6.633s; **8** Franco Colapinto, RA, +6.899s; **9** Kaylen Frederick, USA, +8.431s; **10** Juan Manuel Correa, USA, +12.094s; **11** Grégoire Saucy, CH, +14.186s; **12** William Alatalo, FIN, +15.236s; **13** Zane Maloney, BB, +17.510s; **14** Oliver Rasmussen, DK, +18.747s; **15** Lirim Zendeli, D, +21.287s; **16** Arthur Leclerc, MC, +23.398s *; **17** Francesco Pizzi, I, +26.651s; **18** Nazim Azman, MAL, +27.867s; **19** Reece Ushijima, USA, +28.281s; **20** Pepe Martí, E, +28.482s; **21** Federico Malvestiti, I, +29.713s; **22** Ido Cohen, IL, +31.079s **; **23** László Tóth, H, +31.123s; **24** Enzo Trulli, I, +34.906s ***; **25** Kush Maini, IND, +54.804s ****; **26** Hunter Yeany, USA, +1m 25.486s ***; **27** Zak O'Sullivan, GB, -2 laps (DNF); David Vidales, E, -9 (DNF); Brad Benavides, GCA, -14 (DNF); Rafael Villagómez, MEX, -22 (DNF).

* 5s penalty for causing a collision & 5s penalty for erratic driving.

** 5s penalty for erratic driving.

*** 5s penalty for causing a collision.

**** 10s penalty for causing a collision.

Fastest race lap: Martins, 1m 37.030s, 107.777mph/173.451km/h.

Pole position: Stanek, 1m 33.516s, 111.827mph/179.969km/h.

Championship points: Drivers: 1 Martins, 62; **2** Stanek, 56; **3** Crawford, 50; **4** Hadjar, 47; **5** Leclerc, 43; **6** Smolyar, 28.

Teams: 1 Prema Racing, 120; **2** ART Grand Prix, 98; **3** Trident, 75.

FIA FORMULA 3 CHAMPIONSHIP, Silverstone Arena Grand Prix Circuit, Towcester, Northamptonshire, Great Britain, 2/3 July. Round 4. 17 and 22 laps of the 3.660-mile/5.891km circuit.

Race 1 (62.145 miles/100.013km).

1 Isack Hadjar, F, 32m 24.707s, 115.194mph/185.387km/h; **2** Victor Martins, F, +0.757s; **3** Reece Ushijima, USA, +1.359s; **4** Kush Maini, IND, +2.916s; **5** Kaylen Frederick, USA, +5.827s; **6** Roman Stanek, CZ, +6.549s; **7** Zane Maloney, BB, +7.296s; **8** Arthur Leclerc, MC, +7.693s; **9** Ollie Bearman, GB, +7.988s; **10** Jak Crawford, USA, +8.552s; **11** Caio Collet, BR, +9.252s; **12** David Vidales, E, +10.966s; **13** Franco Colapinto, RA, +11.235s; **14** Zak O'Sullivan, GB, +12.320s; **15** Jonny Edgar, GB, +12.909s; **16** Hunter Yeany, USA, +13.364s; **17** Ido Cohen, IL, +14.009s; **18** Grégoire Saucy, CH, +14.367s; **19** William Alatalo, FIN, +14.999s; **20** Pepe Martí, E, +15.247s; **21** Juan Manuel Correa, USA, +16.901s; **22** Nazim Azman, MAL, +17.739s; **23** Filip-Ioan Ugran, RO, +18.932s; **24** Francesco Pizzi, I, +21.127s; **25** Federico Malvestiti, I, +21.369s; **26** Rafael Villagómez, MEX, +23.276s; **27** Enzo Trulli, I, +23.319s; Brad Benavides, GCA, -5 laps (DNF); László Tóth, H, -7 (DNF); Zdenek Chovanec, YV, -9 (DNF).

Fastest race lap: Hadjar, 1m 46.643s, 123.569mph/198.865km/h.

Pole position: Ushijima.

Race 2 (80.448 miles/129.468km).

1 Arthur Leclerc, MC, 45m 23.209s, 106.458mph/171.328km/h; **2** Zak O'Sullivan, GB, +0.913s; **3** Ollie Bearman, GB, +0.964s; **4** Caio Collet, BR, +1.273s; **5** Isack Hadjar, F, +1.658s; **6** Jak Crawford, USA, +2.349s; **7** Victor Martins, F, +4.012s; **8** Jonny Edgar, GB, +4.658s; **9** David Vidales, E, +5.847s; **10** Reece Ushijima, USA, +6.616s; **11** Zane Maloney, BB, +8.011s; **12** Kaylen Frederick, USA, +9.878s; **13** Federico Malvestiti, I, +14.364s; **14** Francesco Pizzi, I, +15.097s; **15** Ido Cohen, IL, +15.591s; **16** William Alatalo, FIN, +16.562s; **17** Enzo Trulli, I, +17.102s; **18** Filip-Ioan Ugran, RO, +17.957s; **19** Hunter Yeany, USA, +20.445s; **20** Brad Benavides, GCA, +22.522s; **21** László Tóth, H, +24.304s; **22** Kush Maini, IND, +25.179s; **23** Pepe Martí, E, +29.432s; **24** Zdenek Chovanec, YV, +30.100s; **25** Grégoire Saucy, CH, +37.328s; Nazim Azman, MAL, -13 laps (DNF); Rafael Villagómez, MEX, -13 (DNF); Roman Stanek, CZ, -13 (DNF); Juan Manuel Correa, USA, -21 (DNF); Franco Colapinto, RA, -22 (DNF).

Fastest race lap: Crawford, 1m 46.713s, 123.488mph/198.734km/h.

Pole position: O'Sullivan, 1m 44.597s, 125.986mph/202.755km/h.

Championship points: Drivers: 1 Martins, 77; **2** Leclerc, 71; **3** Hadjar, 68; **4** Stanek, 61; **5** Crawford, 60; **6** Bearman, 44.
Teams: 1 Prema Racing, 175; **2** ART Grand Prix, 113; **3** Hitech Grand Prix, 90.

FIA FORMULA 3 CHAMPIONSHIP, Red Bull Ring, Spielberg, Austria, 9/10 July. Round 5. 21 and 25 laps of the 2.683-mile/4.318km circuit.
Race 1 (56.266 miles/90.552km).
1 Jak Crawford, USA, 32m 50.011s, 102.962mph/165.702km/h; **2** Caio Collet, BR, +0.626s; **3** Franco Colapinto, RA, +1.020s; **4** Arthur Leclerc, MC, +1.265s; **5** Roman Stanek, CZ, +2.351s; **6** Kaylen Frederick, USA, +6.178s; **7** Jonny Edgar, GB, +7.207s; **8** Victor Martins, F, +7.582s; **9** Alexander Smolyar, RUS, +8.111s; **10** Isack Hadjar, F, +8.568s; **11** Grégoire Saucy, CH, +8.959s; **12** Zak O'Sullivan, GB, +9.362s; **13** Pepe Martí, E, +9.752s; **14** Ido Cohen, IL, +10.311s; **15** Francesco Pizzi, I, +10.585s; **16** Ollie Bearman, GB, +10.606s; **17** Reece Ushijima, USA, +11.280s; **18** David Vidales, E, +11.637s; **19** Kush Maini, IND, +12.495s; **20** Brad Benavides, GCA, +16.133s; **21** Federico Malvestiti, I, +17.119s; **22** Hunter Yeany, USA, +19.716s; **23** László Tóth, H, +19.964s; **24** Nazim Azman, MAL, +21.141s; **25** Enzo Trulli, I, +50.504s; **26** Zdenek Chovanec, YV, +54.445s; Zane Maloney, BB, -12 laps (DNF); William Alatalo, FIN, -14 (DNF); Juan Manuel Correa, USA, -16 (DNF); Rafael Villagómez, MEX, -21 (DNF).
Fastest race lap: Leclerc, 1m 21.200s, 118.954mph/191.438km/h.
Pole position: Collet.

Race 2 (66.999 miles/107.824km).
1 Isack Hadjar, F, 40m 34.535s, 99.187mph/159.626km/h; **2** Victor Martins, F, +3.251s; **3** Ollie Bearman, GB, +4.881s; **4** Arthur Leclerc, MC, +5.383s; **5** Zane Maloney, BB, +6.457s; **6** Franco Colapinto, RA, +9.113s; **7** Alexander Smolyar, RUS, +9.882s; **8** William Alatalo, FIN, +10.852s; **9** Ido Cohen, IL, +12.286s; **10** Juan Manuel Correa, USA, +12.706s; **11** Roman Stanek, CZ, +13.067s; **12** David Vidales, E, +13.901s; **13** Reece Ushijima, USA, +14.095s; **14** Grégoire Saucy, CH, +14.738s; **15** Rafael Villagómez, MEX, +15.442s; **16** Nazim Azman, MAL, +15.722s; **17** Zak O'Sullivan, GB, +16.765s; **18** Enzo Trulli, I, +19.446s; **19** László Tóth, H, +21.368s; **20** Brad Benavides, GCA, +24.273s; **21** Jonny Edgar, GB, +50.679s; **22** Jak Crawford, USA, +1m 00.379s; **23** Kaylen Frederick, USA, +1m 13.566s; **24** Francesco Pizzi, I, -1 lap; **25** Kush Maini, IND, -2; **26** Federico Malvestiti, I, -2; **27** Caio Collet, BR, -3; Zdenek Chovanec, YV, -7 (DNF); Pepe Martí, E, -8 (DNF).
Withdrawn: Hunter Yeany, USA.
Fastest race lap: Hadjar, 1m 32.041s, 104.943mph/168.889km/h.
Pole position: Hadjar, 1m 19.759s, 121.103mph/194.897km/h.
Championship points: Drivers: 1 Martins, 98; **2** Hadjar, 97; **3** Leclerc, 91; **4** Crawford, 70; **5** Stanek, 67; **6** Bearman, 59.
Teams: 1 Prema Racing, 220; **2** ART Grand Prix, 135; **3** Hitech Grand Prix, 124.

FIA FORMULA 3 CHAMPIONSHIP, Hungaroring, Mogyoród, Budapest, Hungary, 30/31 July. Round 6. 18 and 24 laps of the 2.722-mile/4.381km circuit.
Race 1 (48.975 miles/78.818km).
1 Caio Collet, BR, 37m 34.616s, 78.239mph/125.913km/h; **2** Franco Colapinto, RA, +8.789s; **3** Kush Maini, IND, +9.694s; **4** Isack Hadjar, F, +12.004s; **5** Ollie Bearman, GB, +13.915s; **6** Victor Martins, F, +14.607s; **7** Grégoire Saucy, CH, +15.561s; **8** Oliver Goethe, DK, +19.682s; **9** Roman Stanek, CZ, +20.082s; **10** Zane Maloney, BB, +21.180s; **11** Reece Ushijima, USA, +22.208s; **12** Juan Manuel Correa, USA, +22.877s; **13** Jonny Edgar, GB, +24.797s; **14** Pepe Martí, E, +27.122s; **15** Alexander Smolyar, RUS, +29.104s; **16** William Alatalo, FIN, +29.590s; **17** Rafael Villagómez, MEX, +31.696s; **18** Zak O'Sullivan, GB, +31.956s; **19** Kaylen Frederick, USA, +37.123s; **20** Jak Crawford, USA, +38.362s; **21** Francesco Pizzi, I, +38.718s; **22** Christian Mansell, AUS, +39.394s; **23** Nazim Azman, MAL, +40.281s; **24** Enzo Trulli, I, +43.663s; **25** Federico Malvestiti, I, +48.834s; **26** László Tóth, H, +49.526s; **27** Arthur Leclerc, MC, +52.437s; Ido Cohen, IL, -12 laps (DNF); Brad Benavides, GCA, -14 (DNF); David Vidales, E, -18 (DNF).
Fastest race lap: Collet, 1m 50.440s, 88.736mph/142.806km/h.
Pole position: Goethe.

Race 2 (65.309 miles/105.104km).
1 Alexander Smolyar, RUS, 45m 02.423s, 87.032mph/140.065km/h; **2** Zane Maloney, BB, +5.560s; **3** Ollie Bearman, GB, +5.585s; **4** Zak O'Sullivan, GB, +7.316s; **5** Jak Crawford, USA, +8.705s; **6** Juan Manuel Correa, USA, +10.059s; **7** Kush Maini, IND, +10.578s; **8** Arthur Leclerc, MC, +10.983s; **9** Caio Collet, BR, +19.452s; **10** Victor Martins, F, +19.614s; **11** Grégoire Saucy, CH, +22.570s; **12** Roman Stanek, CZ, +23.027s; **13** David Vidales, E, +32.473s; **14** Reece Ushijima, USA, +35.487s; **15** Franco Colapinto, RA, +38.020s; **16** William Alatalo, FIN, +39.532s; **17** Ido Cohen, IL, +40.124s; **18** Isack Hadjar, F, +40.642s; **19** Enzo Trulli, I, +40.978s; **20** Kaylen Frederick, USA, +41.152s; **21** Rafael Villagómez, MEX, +41.691s; **22** Brad Benavides, GCA, +47.360s; **23** Christian Mansell, AUS, +57.609s; **24** Jonny Edgar, GB, +1m 09.334s; **25** Federico Malvestiti, I, +1m 10.674s; **26** Nazim Azman, MAL, +1m 14.488s; **27** Francesco Pizzi, I, +1m 16.800s; **28** Oliver Goethe, DK, +1m 27.064s; **29** Pepe Martí, E, -1 lap; László Tóth, H, -22 (DNF).
Fastest race lap: O'Sullivan, 1m 38.070s, 99.928mph/160.819km/h.
Pole position: Smolyar, 1m 32.740s, 105.671mph/170.062km/h.
Championship points: Drivers: 1 Hadjar, 104; **2** Martins, 104; **3** Leclerc, 95; **4** Crawford, 80; **5** Bearman, 80; **6** Stanek, 69.
Teams: 1 Prema Racing, 255; **2** ART Grand Prix, 153; **3** MP Motorsport, 146.

FIA FORMULA 3 CHAMPIONSHIP, Circuit de Spa-Francorchamps, Stavelot, Belgium, 27/28 August. Round 7. 15 and 18 laps of the 4.352-mile/7.004km circuit.
Race 1 (65.204 miles/104.936km).
1 Ollie Bearman, GB, 1h 07m 07.734s, 58.347mph/93.901km/h; **2** Roman Stanek, CZ, +4.762s; **3** Alexander Smolyar, RUS, +5.689s; **4** Jonny Edgar, GB, +6.339s; **5** Arthur Leclerc, MC, +7.586s; **6** William Alatalo, FIN, +10.609s; **7** David Vidales, E, +12.294s; **8** Brad Benavides, GCA, +12.326s; **9** Isack Hadjar, F, +12.538s; **10** Caio Collet, BR, +13.231s; **11** Jak Crawford, USA, +14.118s; **12** Grégoire Saucy, CH, +14.276s; **13** Kush Maini, IND, +14.670s; **14** Reece Ushijima, USA, +16.969s; **15** Franco Colapinto, RA, +17.887s; **16** Nazim Azman, MAL, +19.147s; **17** Juan Manuel Correa, USA, +20.061s; **18** Federico Malvestiti, I, +20.876s; **19** Francesco Pizzi, I, +21.857s; **20** Zak O'Sullivan, GB, +26.173s; **21** Victor Martins, F, +27.345s; **22** László Tóth, H, +28.710s; **23** Rafael Villagómez, MEX, +32.465s; **24** Ido Cohen, IL, -2 laps; Pepe Martí, E, -4 (DNF); Oliver Goethe, DK, -10 (DNF); Zane Maloney, BB, -10 (DNF); Christian Mansell, AUS, -14 (DNF); Kaylen Frederick, USA, -14 (DNF).
Disqualified: Enzo Trulli, I, +18.668s, the team conducted non-authorised work during the race - finished 16th.
Fastest race lap: Edgar, 2m 07.266s, 123.108mph/198.123km/h.
Pole position: O'Sullivan.

Race 2 (78.260 miles/125.948km).
1 Zane Maloney, BB, 45m 33.153s, 103.182mph/166.055km/h; **2** Roman Stanek, CZ, +1.046s; **3** Ollie Bearman, GB, +5.684s; **4** Oliver Goethe, DK, +6.737s; **5** Jonny Edgar, GB, +7.433s; **6** Caio Collet, BR, +9.297s; **7** William Alatalo, FIN, +10.879s; **8** David Vidales, E, +10.831s; **9** Alexander Smolyar, RUS, +11.665s; **10** Reece Ushijima, USA, +13.360s; **11** Arthur Leclerc, MC, +13.608s; **12** Franco Colapinto, RA, +14.855s; **13** Zak O'Sullivan, GB, +15.784s; **14** Isack Hadjar, F, +16.423s; **15** Juan Manuel Correa, USA, +16.909s; **16** Kaylen Frederick, USA, +17.952s; **17** Jak Crawford, USA, +18.311s; **18** Brad Benavides, GCA, +20.101s; **19** Rafael Villagómez, MEX, +20.610s; **20** Nazim Azman, MAL, +20.940s; **21** Francesco Pizzi, I, +21.568s; **22** Pepe Martí, E, +23.753s; **23** Christian Mansell, AUS, +24.691s; **24** Enzo Trulli, I, +24.908s; **25** László Tóth, H, +25.404s; **26** Federico Malvestiti, I, +1m 13.968s; Grégoire Saucy, CH, -12 laps (DNF); Ido Cohen, IL, -17 (DNF); Victor Martins, F, -17 (DNF); Kush Maini, IND, -18 (DNF).
Fastest race lap: Maloney, 2m 07.838s, 122.557mph/197.237km/h.
Pole position: Collet, 2m 11.289s, 119.335mph/192.052km/h.
Championship points: Drivers: 1 Hadjar, 106; **2** Bearman, 105; **3** Martins, 104; **4** Leclerc, 101; **5** Stanek, 96; **6** Crawford, 80.
Teams: 1 Prema Racing, 286; **2** Trident, 200; **3** MP Motorsport, 167.

FIA FORMULA 3 CHAMPIONSHIP, Circuit Park Zandvoort, Netherlands, 3/4 September. Round 8. 21 and 26 laps of the 2.646-mile/4.259km circuit.
Race 1 (55.537 miles/89.378km).
1 Caio Collet, BR, 30m 55.183s, 107.842mph/173.556km/h; **2** Juan Manuel Correa, USA, +4.057s; **3** Zak O'Sullivan, GB, +4.935s; **4** Jonny Edgar, GB, +5.888s; **5** Grégoire Saucy, CH, +6.628s; **6** Isack Hadjar, F, +7.593s; **7** Victor Martins, F, +8.184s; **8** Sebastian Montoya, CO, +9.903s; **9** Jak Crawford, USA, +10.599s; **10** Roman Stanek, CZ, +11.028s; **11** Ollie Bearman, GB, +12.399s; **12** Arthur Leclerc, MC, +15.688s; **13** Franco Colapinto, RA, +17.290s; **14** Alexander Smolyar, RUS, +17.941s; **15** Kaylen Frederick, USA, +19.994s; **16** Francesco Pizzi, I, +20.638s; **17** Zane Maloney, BB, +21.116s; **18** Kush Maini, IND, +23.870s; **19** Pepe Martí, E, +23.930s; **20** David Schumacher, D, +24.193s; **21** David Vidales, E, +24.583s; **22** Reece Ushijima, USA, +27.177s; **23** Enzo Trulli, I, +30.780s; **24** Federico Malvestiti, I, +31.218s; **25** Nazim Azman, MAL, +34.656s; **26** Brad Benavides, GCA, +44.181s; **27** László Tóth, H, +1m 03.611s; **28** Rafael Villagómez, MEX, +1m 15.548s *; **29** Ido Cohen, IL, -1 lap; **30** William Alatalo, FIN, -1.
* 10s penalty for causing a collision.
Fastest race lap: Collet, 1m 27.259s, 109.181mph/175.711km/h.
Pole position: Correa.

Race 2 (68.769 miles/110.673km).
1 Zane Maloney, BB, 44m 04.515s, 93.666mph/150.742km/h; **2** Victor Martins, F, +1.091s; **3** Franco Colapinto, RA, +1.417s; **4** Roman Stanek, CZ, +2.188s; **5** Isack Hadjar, F, +2.750s; **6** Jak Crawford, USA, +2.978s; **7** Caio Collet, BR, +4.378s; **8** Sebastian Montoya, CO, +5.275s; **9** Jonny Edgar, GB, +5.568s; **10** Alexander Smolyar, RUS, +9.368s; **11** Kush Maini, IND, +10.822s; **12** Arthur Leclerc, MC, +11.222s; **13** Kaylen Frederick, USA, +12.218s; **14** Pepe Martí, E, +12.930s; **15** David Schumacher, D, +13.624s; **16** Ido Cohen, IL, +14.797s; **17** Enzo Trulli, I, +15.456s; **18** Francesco Pizzi, I, +15.607s; **19** Reece Ushijima, USA, +16.075s; **20** Federico Malvestiti, I, +16.456s; **21** Nazim Azman, MAL, +17.013s; **22** László Tóth, H, +17.529s; **23** Zak O'Sullivan, GB, +20.128s *; **24** Juan Manuel Correa, USA, +24.299s *; **25** Ollie Bearman, GB, +28.495s **; Grégoire Saucy, CH, -4 laps (DNF); Rafael Villagómez, MEX, -5 (DNF); David Vidales, E, -10 (DNF); Brad Benavides, GCA, -23 (DNF); William Alatalo, FIN, -23 (DNF).
* 10s penalty for causing a collision.
** Drive through converted to a 20s penalty for failing to maintain the proper gap behind Safety Car.
Fastest race lap: Maloney, 1m 27.100s, 109.381mph/176.032km/h.
Pole position: Maloney, 1m 24.386s, 112.899mph/181.693km/h.
Championship points: Drivers: 1 Martins, 126; **2** Hadjar, 121; **3** Stanek, 109; **4** Bearman, 105; **5** Maloney, 102; **6** Leclerc, 101.
Teams: 1 Prema Racing, 296; **2** Trident, 250; **3** ART Grand Prix, 190.

FIA FORMULA 3 CHAMPIONSHIP, Autodromo Nazionale di Monza, Milan, Italy, 10/11 September. Round 9. 18 and 15 laps of the 3.600-mile/5.793km circuit.
Race 1 (64.601 miles/103.965km).
1 Franco Colapinto, RA, 34m 09.813s, 113.789mph/183.126km/h; **2** Ollie Bearman, GB, +0.433s; **3** Caio Collet, BR, +2.109s; **4** Zane Maloney, BB, +3.404s; **5** Jonny Edgar, GB, +4.122s; **6** Grégoire Saucy, CH, +4.279s; **7** Jak Crawford, USA, +4.615s; **8** Arthur Leclerc, MC, +6.062s; **9** Pepe Martí, E, +6.547s; **10** Victor Martins, F, +6.879s; **11** Kush Maini, IND, +7.756s; **12** Roman Stanek, CZ, +7.984s; **13** Juan Manuel Correa, USA, +8.158s; **14** William Alatalo, FIN, +9.252s; **15** Ido Cohen, IL, +12.317s; **16** Federico Malvestiti, I, +12.999s; **17** Francesco Pizzi, I, +13.469s; **18** Brad Benavides, GCA, +13.750s *; **19** Reece Ushijima, USA, +15.953s; **20** Enzo Trulli, I, +17.477s; **21** Nazim Azman, MAL, +18.711s; **22** László Tóth, H, +22.363s; **23** Alessandro Famularo, YV, +30.913s; **24** Hunter Yeany, USA, +50.937s; **25** Alexander Smolyar, RUS, +1m 09.800s; **26** Rafael Villagómez, MEX, +1m 10.264s; **27** Isack Hadjar, F, +1m 10.410s; Kaylen Frederick, USA, -7 laps (DNF); Zak O'Sullivan, GB, -15 (DNF).
* 5s penalty for leaving the track and gaining an advantage.
Did not start: David Vidales, E.
Fastest race lap: Smolyar, 1m 39.160s, 130.683mph/210.314km/h.
Pole position: Colapinto.

Race 2 (53.802 miles/86.586km).
1 Zane Maloney, BB, 28m 00.288s, 115.677mph/186.165km/h; **2** Ollie Bearman, GB, +0.587s; **3** Jak Crawford, USA, +5.024s; **4** Victor Martins, F, +6.061s *; **5** Arthur Leclerc, MC, +6.086s; **6** Roman Stanek, CZ, +6.420s; **7** William Alatalo, FIN, +9.628s *; **8** Jonny Edgar, GB, +12.080s; **9** Isack Hadjar, F, +13.555s; **10** Reece Ushijima, USA, +14.228s; **11** Zak O'Sullivan, GB, +14.696s; **12** Ido Cohen, IL, +15.613s; **13** Kush Maini, IND, +15.958s; **14** Brad Benavides, GCA, +16.820s; **15** Franco Colapinto, RA, +18.031s *; **16** Francesco Pizzi, I, +21.196s; **17** Hunter Yeany, USA, +21.298s **; **18** Federico Malvestiti, I, +21.807s; **19** László Tóth, H, +23.790s; **20** Caio Collet, BR, +24.324s ***; **21** Nazim Azman, MAL, +29.215s; **22** Enzo Trulli, I, +30.145s; **23** Alessandro Famularo, YV, +43.109s; **24** Juan Manuel Correa, USA, +1m 01.827s; **25** Kaylen Frederick, USA, +1m 02.568s; **26** Pepe Martí, E, +1m 33.017s; **27** Alexander Smolyar, RUS, -1 lap; **28** Grégoire Saucy, CH, -2; David Vidales, E, -15 (DNF); Rafael Villagómez, MEX, -15 (DNF).
* 5s penalty for exceeding track limits.
** 5s penalty for forcing another driver off the track.
*** 15s penalty for exceeding track limits.
Fastest race lap: Edgar, 1m 38.887s, 131.044mph/210.895km/h.
Pole position: Smolyar, 1m 37.559s, 132.828mph/213.766km/h.

Final championship points
Drivers
1 Victor Martins, F, 139; **2** Zane Maloney, BB, 134; **3** Ollie Bearman, GB, 132; **4** Isack Hadjar, F, 123; **5** Roman Stanek, CZ, 117; **6** Arthur Leclerc, MC, 114; **7** Jak Crawford, USA, 109; **8** Caio Collet, BR, 88; **9** Franco Colapinto, RA, 76; **10** Alexander Smolyar, RUS, 76; **11** Zak O'Sullivan, GB, 54; **12** Jonny Edgar, GB, 46; **13** Juan Manuel Correa, USA, 39; **14** Kush Maini, IND, 31; **15** Grégoire Saucy, CH, 30; **16** David Vidales, E, 29; **17** Kaylen Frederick, USA, 27; **18** William Alatalo, FIN, 24; **19** Oliver Goethe, DK, 15; **20** Reece Ushijima, USA, 13; **21** Sebastian Montoya, CO, 7; **22** Oliver Rasmussen, DK, 4; **23** Brad Benavides, GCA, 3; **24** Ido Cohen, IL, 2; **25** Rafael Villagómez, MEX, 2; **26** Pepe Martí, E, 2; **27** Francesco Pizzi, I, 1.

Teams
1 Prema Racing, 355; **2** Trident, 301; **3** ART Grand Prix, 208; **4** MP Motorsport, 195; **5** Hitech Grand Prix, 150; **6** Van Amersfoort Racing, 91; **7** Carlin, 57; **8** Campos Racing, 53; **9** Jenzer Motorsport, 26; **10** Charouz Racing System, 1.

GB3 Championship

All cars are Tatuus MSV-022-Cosworth.

GB3 CHAMPIONSHIP, Oulton Park Circuit, Tarporley, Cheshire, Great Britain, 16/18 April. 3 x 14 laps of the 2.692-mile/4.332km circuit.
Round 1 (37.688 miles/60.653km).
1 Luke Browning, GB, 21m 05.607s, 107.202mph/172.526km/h; **2** Roberto Faria, BR, +10.258s; **3** Matthew Rees, GB, +10.719s; **4** McKenzy Cresswell, GB, +13.414s; **5** John Bennett, GB, +20.988s; **6** Joel Granfors, S, +23.243s; **7** Zak Taylor, GB, +23.627s; **8** Branden Lee Oxley, GB, +24.905s; **9** Marcos Flack, AUS, +29.538s; **10** David Morales, USA, +30.831s.
Fastest race lap: Browning, 1m 29.766s, 107.960mph/173.745km/h.
Pole position: Browning, 1m 28.929s, 108.976mph/175.381km/h.

Round 2 (37.688 miles/60.653km).
1 Luke Browning, GB, 20m 59.933s, 107.685mph/173.303km/h; **2** Roberto Faria, BR, +8.924s; **3** Joel Granfors, S, +10.305s; **4** Matthew Rees, GB, +10.736s; **5** John Bennett, GB, +14.583s; **6** Tom Lebbon, GB, +14.992s; **7** McKenzy Cresswell, GB, +16.195s; **8** Francisco Javier Sagrera, E, +16.698s; **9** Callum Voisin, CH, +20.013s; **10** James Hedley, GB, +30.230s.
Fastest race lap: Browning, 1m 29.205s, 108.639mph/174.838km/h.
Pole position: Browning, 1m 29.091s, 108.778mph/175.062km/h.

Round 3 (37.688 miles/60.653km).
1 Mikkel Grundtvig, DK, 21m 19.131s, 106.069mph/170.702km/h; **2** Tom Smith, AUS, +5.841s; **3** David Morales, USA, +6.208s; **4** Nick Gilkes, CDN, +7.743s; **5** Branden Lee Oxley, GB, +8.490s; **6** Zak Taylor, GB, +11.796s; **7** Cian Shields, GB, +12.974s; **8** Maxwell Esterson, USA, +14.221s; **9** Francisco Javier Sagrera, E, +14.429s; **10** John Bennett, GB, +16.817s.
Fastest race lap: Morales, 1m 30.419s, 107.181mph/172.491km/h.
Pole position: Grundtvig.

GB3 CHAMPIONSHIP, Silverstone Arena Grand Prix Circuit, Towcester, Northampton-

shire, Great Britain, 7/8 May. 3 x 10 laps of the 3.660-mile/5.891km circuit.
Round 4 (36.604 miles/58.908km).
1 Joel Granfors, S, 19m 02.131s, 115.375mph/185.679km/h; **2** Luke Browning, GB, +0.721s; **3** Tom Lebbon, GB, +5.738s; **4** Maxwell Esterson, USA, +8.800s; **5** James Hedley, GB, +9.320s; **6** John Bennett, GB, +11.069s; **7** Roberto Faria, BR, +11.829s; **8** Branden Lee Oxley, GB, +14.732s; **9** McKenzy Cresswell, GB, +14.982s; **10** Callum Voisin, CH, +17.229s.
Fastest race lap: Browning, 1m 53.441s, 116.161mph/186.943km/h.
Pole position: Granfors, 1m 53.086s, 116.525mph/187.530km/h.

Round 5 (36.604 miles/58.908km).
1 Tom Lebbon, GB, 18m 56.436s, 115.954mph/186.610km/h; **2** Joel Granfors, S, +1.013s; **3** Luke Browning, GB, +2.882s; **4** Maxwell Esterson, USA, +8.409s; **5** Callum Voisin, CH, +10.311s; **6** Roberto Faria, BR, +13.607s; **7** James Hedley, GB, +16.130s; **8** Matthew Rees, GB, +16.523s; **9** John Bennett, GB, +17.980s; **10** Alex Connor, GB, +18.612s.
Fastest race lap: Browning, 1m 52.783s, 116.838mph/188.033km/h.
Pole position: Granfors, 1m 53.121s, 116.489mph/187.472km/h.

Round 6 (36.604 miles/58.908km).
1 Cian Shields, GB, 19m 13.449s, 114.243mph/183.857km/h; **2** Nick Gilkes, CDN, +0.434s; **3** Bryce Aron, USA, +3.248s; **4** David Morales, USA, +5.575s; **5** Francisco Javier Sagrera, E, +7.342s; **6** McKenzy Cresswell, GB, +7.485s; **7** Alex Connor, GB, +8.212s; **8** Callum Voisin, CH, +13.739s *; **9** Joel Granfors, S, +14.300s; **10** Maxwell Esterson, USA, +14.560s.
* 5s penalty for gaining an unfair advantage.
Fastest race lap: Voisin, 1m 54.290s, 115.298mph/185.554km/h.
Pole position: Morales.

GB3 CHAMPIONSHIP, Donington Park National Circuit, Castle Donington, Great Britain, 28/29 May. 3 x 12 laps of the 2.487-mile/4.003km circuit.
Round 7 (29.848 miles/48.035km).
1 Callum Voisin, CH, 16m 51.913s, 106.186mph/170.890km/h; **2** Roberto Faria, BR, +2.262s; **3** Maxwell Esterson, USA, +2.964s; **4** Alex Connor, GB, +5.217s; **5** Tom Lebbon, GB, +8.569s; **6** James Hedley, GB, +9.520s; **7** McKenzy Cresswell, GB, +13.650s; **8** Matthew Rees, GB, +14.086s; **9** Zak Taylor, GB, +21.303s; **10** Branden Lee Oxley, GB, +24.934s.
Fastest race lap: Esterson, 1m 23.543s, 107.181mph/172.492km/h.
Pole position: Joel Granfors, S, 1m 22.745s, 108.215mph/174.155km/h.

Round 8 (29.848 miles/48.035km).
1 Maxwell Esterson, USA, 16m 47.380s, 106.664mph/171.659km/h; **2** Luke Browning, GB, +0.762s; **3** Joel Granfors, S, +3.357s; **4** James Hedley, GB, +5.540s; **5** Roberto Faria, BR, +5.983s; **6** Matthew Rees, GB, +6.506s; **7** Callum Voisin, CH, +8.369s; **8** Tom Lebbon, GB, +10.143s; **9** Alex Connor, GB, +10.712s; **10** Francisco Javier Sagrera, E, +13.147s.
Fastest race lap: Esterson, 1m 23.123s, 107.723mph/173.363km/h.
Pole position: Esterson, 1m 22.893s, 108.022mph/173.844km/h.

Round 9 (29.848 miles/48.035km).
1 Bryce Aron, USA, 16m 59.361s, 105.410mph/169.641km/h; **2** Branden Lee Oxley, GB, +2.359s; **3** Mikkel Grundtvig, DK, +7.022s; **4** John Bennett, GB, +7.627s; **5** Tom Smith, AUS, +16.195s*; **6** Callum Voisin, CH, +16.913s; **7** Matthew Rees, GB, +17.391s; **8** Alex Connor, GB, +17.584s; **9** Luke Browning, GB, +18.134s; **10** Joel Granfors, S, +18.781s.
* 10s penalty for false start
Disqualified: Zak Taylor, GB, manouevres liable to hinder other drivers - finished 5th.
Fastest race lap: Roberto Faria, BR, 1m 23.810s, 106.840mph/171.942km/h.
Pole position: Aron.

GB3 CHAMPIONSHIP, Snetterton Circuit, Thetford, Norfolk, Great Britain, 25/26 June. 12, 12 and 10 laps of the 2.969-mile/4.778km circuit.
Round 10 (35.627 miles/57.336km).
1 Callum Voisin, CH, 20m 42.159s, 103.252mph/166.169km/h; **2** Luke Browning, GB, +0.526s; **3** Joel Granfors, S, +0.942s; **4** Roberto Faria, BR, +2.265s; **5** Tom Lebbon, GB, +8.333s; **6** John Bennett, GB, +8.504s; **7** Francisco Javier Sagrera, E, +9.070s; **8** Alex Connor, GB, +10.222s; **9** McKenzy Cresswell, GB, +11.669s; **10** Maxwell Esterson, USA, +11.864s.
Fastest race lap: Faria, 1m 42.363s, 104.413mph/168.036km/h.
Pole position: Voisin, 1m 41.442s, 105.361mph/169.562km/h.

Round 11 (35.627 miles/57.336km).
1 Luke Browning, GB, 20m 36.960s, 103.686mph/166.867km/h; **2** Joel Granfors, S, +0.235s; **3** Francisco Javier Sagrera, E, +1.463s; **4** Matthew Rees, GB, +1.946s; **5** Tom Lebbon, GB, +6.864s; **6** Alex Connor, GB, +7.607s; **7** Roberto Faria, BR, +7.844s; **8** Nico Christodoulou, CDN, +8.226s; **9** Branden Lee Oxley, GB, +10.467s; **10** Maxwell Esterson, USA, +10.790s.
Fastest race lap: Sagrera, 1m 41.885s, 104.902mph/168.824km/h.
Pole position: Browning, 1m 41.639s, 105.156mph/169.233km/h.

Round 12 (29.689 miles/47.780km).
1 Mikkel Grundtvig, DK, 20m 58.789s, 84.907mph/136.645km/h; **2** Marcos Flack, AUS, +0.253s; **3** James Hedley, GB, +0.786s; **4** Tom Smith, AUS, +1.753s; **5** McKenzy Cresswell, GB, +1.997s; **6** Zak Taylor, GB, +4.335s; **7** Maxwell Esterson, USA, +5.883s; **8** David Morales, USA, +6.046s; **9** Francisco Javier Sagrera, E, +6.416s; **10** Nico Christodoulou, CDN, +7.042s.
Disqualified: Bryce Aron, USA, caused a collision - finished 6th.
Fastest race lap: Roberto Faria, BR, 1m 43.301s, 103.465mph/166.510km/h.
Pole position: Grundtvig.

GB3 CHAMPIONSHIP, Circuit de Spa-Francorchamps, Stavelot, Belgium, 23/24 July. 8, 9 and 1 laps of the 4.352-mile/7.004km circuit.
Round 13 (34.816 miles/56.031km).
1 Luke Browning, GB, 21m 01.224s, 99.377mph/159.932km/h; **2** Joel Granfors, S, +6.095s; **3** Branden Lee Oxley, GB, +9.347s; **4** Maxwell Esterson, USA, +9.584s; **5** Francisco Javier Sagrera, E, +10.822s; **6** Tom Lebbon, GB, +9.986s *; **7** Cian Shields, GB, +11.846s **; **8** Callum Voisin, CH, +12.751s; **9** Bryce Aron, USA, +12.891s; **10** Marcos Flack, AUS, +13.793s.
* 1-position penalty.
** 5s penalty for exceeding track limits.
Fastest race lap: Browning, 2m 16.329s, 114.921mph/184.949km/h.
Pole position: Browning, 2m 15.627s, 115.516mph/185.906km/h.

Round 14 (39.168 miles/63.035km).
1 Luke Browning, GB, 20m 33.326s, 114.328mph/183.994km/h; **2** Maxwell Esterson, USA, +10.105s; **3** McKenzy Cresswell, GB, +11.441s; **4** Joel Granfors, S, +11.531s *; **5** John Bennett, GB, +15.604s; **6** Marcos Flack, AUS, +15.973s **; **7** Matthew Rees, GB, +16.930s; **8** Francisco Javier Sagrera, E, +17.506s; **9** Cian Shields, GB, +17.856s; **10** Callum Voisin, CH, +18.676s.
* 10s penalty for crowding another competitor.
** 1s penalty for causing a collision.
Fastest race lap: Browning, 2m 16.176s, 115.051mph/185.156km/h.
Pole position: Browning, 2m 15.925s, 115.263mph/185.498km/h.

Round 15 (4.352 miles/7.004km).
1 Tom Smith, AUS, 2m 22.596s, 109.871mph/176.820km/h; **2** Callum Voisin, CH, +0.235s; **3** Zak Taylor, GB, +0.694s; **4** Roberto Faria, BR, +1.071s; **5** Nick Gilkes, CDN, +1.631s; **6** Alex Connor, GB, +2.071s; **7** Mikkel Grundtvig, DK, +2.811s; **8** Francisco Javier Sagrera, E, +3.167s; **9** Marcos Flack, AUS, +3.364s; **10** Nico Christodoulou, CDN, +3.981s.
Pole position: Taylor.

GB3 CHAMPIONSHIP, Silverstone Arena Grand Prix Circuit, Towcester, Northamptonshire, Great Britain, 30/31 July. 3 x 10 laps of the 3.660-mile/5.891km circuit.
Round 16 (36.604 miles/58.908km).
1 Joel Granfors, S, 19m 05.651s, 115.021mph/185.109km/h; **2** Callum Voisin, CH, +1.116s; **3** Roberto Faria, BR, +6.752s; **4** Francisco Javier Sagrera, E, +7.307s; **5** John Bennett, GB, +7.982s; **6** Tom Lebbon, GB, +8.323s; **7** Nico Christodoulou, CDN, +8.646s; **8** Matthew Rees, GB, +9.082s; **9** Maxwell Esterson, USA, +9.875s; **10** Luke Browning, GB, +10.223s.
Fastest race lap: Voisin, 1m 53.635s, 115.962mph/186.624km/h.
Pole position: Voisin, 1m 53.229s, 116.378mph/187.293km/h.

Round 17 (36.604 miles/58.908km).
1 Tom Lebbon, GB, 21m 51.380s, 100.485mph/161.715km/h; **2** Callum Voisin, CH, +0.448s; **3** Joel Granfors, S, +0.571s; **4** Francisco Javier Sagrera, E, +1.306s; **5** Roberto Faria, BR, +1.747s; **6** Matthew Rees, GB, +2.229s; **7** Nico Christodoulou, CDN, +3.743s; **8** John Bennett, GB, +3.881s; **9** Alex Connor, GB, +5.778s; **10** Maxwell Esterson, USA, +6.543s.
Fastest race lap: Voisin, 1m 54.077s, 115.513mph/185.901km/h.
Pole position: Voisin, 1m 53.280s, 116.326mph/187.208km/h.

Round 18 (36.604 miles/58.908km).
1 Marcos Flack, AUS, 19m 27.513s, 112.867mph/181.642km/h; **2** Roberto Faria, BR, +6.176s; **3** Joel Granfors, S, +8.132s; **4** Callum Voisin, CH, +9.232s; **5** Luke Browning, GB, +9.761s; **6** Matthew Rees, GB, +10.548s; **7** Tom Smith, AUS, +15.053s; **8** Mikkel Grundtvig, DK, +16.522s; **9** David Morales, USA, +19.150s; **10** Zak Taylor, GB, +19.642s.
Fastest race lap: Nico Christodoulou, CDN, 1m 55.024s, 114.562mph/184.370km/h.
Pole position: Ori.

GB3 CHAMPIONSHIP, Brands Hatch GP Circuit, West Kingsdown, Dartford, Kent, Great Britain, 10/11 September. 14, 14 and 10 laps of the 2.433-mile/3.916km circuit.
Round 19 (34.065 miles/54.822km).
1 Matthew Rees, GB, 18m 45.228s, 108.985mph/175.394km/h; **2** Luke Browning, GB, +0.723s; **3** Joel Granfors, S, +7.846s; **4** John Bennett, GB, +11.560s; **5** Nico Christodoulou, CDN, +11.863s; **6** Tom Lebbon, GB, +15.360s; **7** Alex Connor, GB, +15.784s; **8** Bryce Aron, USA, +16.364s; **9** Callum Voisin, CH, +16.904s; **10** Maxwell Esterson, USA, +20.101s.
Fastest race lap: Browning, 1m 19.425s, 110.286mph/177.489km/h.
Pole position: Rees, 1m 18.749s, 111.233mph/179.012km/h.

Round 20 (34.065 miles/54.822km).
1 Tom Lebbon, GB, 18m 44.047s, 109.099mph/175.579km/h; **2** Luke Browning, GB, +0.718s; **3** Matthew Rees, GB, +1.252s; **4** Joel Granfors, S, +6.955s; **5** Alex Connor, GB, +7.628s; **6** John Bennett, GB, +8.076s; **7** Bryce Aron, USA, +8.721s; **8** Francisco Javier Sagrera, E, +9.296s; **9** Roberto Faria, BR, +12.362s; **10** Nico Christodoulou, CDN, +14.000s.
Fastest race lap: Rees, 1m 19.231s, 110.556mph/177.923km/h.
Pole position: Lebbon, 1m 18.813s, 111.143mph/178.867km/h.

Round 21 (24.332 miles/39.159km).
1 Branden Lee Oxley, GB, 13m 29.579s, 108.198mph/174.128km/h; **2** Cian Shields, GB, +0.923s; **3** Roberto Faria, BR, +2.023s; **4** Zak Taylor, GB, +4.486s; **5** Francisco Javier Sagrera, E, +4.857s; **6** Nick Gilkes, CDN, +5.875s; **7** McKenzy Cresswell, GB, +6.160s; **8** Alex Connor, GB, +8.660s; **9** Luke Browning, GB, +9.911s; **10** Bryce Aron, USA, +13.668s.
Fastest race lap: Browning, 1m 19.602s, 110.041mph/177.094km/h.
Pole position: Flack.

GB3 CHAMPIONSHIP, Donington Park National Circuit, Castle Donington, Great Britain, 15/16 October. 14, 13 and 13 laps of the 2.487-mile/4.003km circuit.
Round 22 (34.822 miles/56.041km).
1 Callum Voisin, CH, 20m 45.927s, 100.615mph/161.925km/h; **2** Luke Browning, GB, +2.036s; **3** John Bennett, GB, +3.922s; **4** Tom Lebbon, GB, +5.532s *; **5** Joel Granfors, S, +5.646s; **6** Bryce Aron, USA, +7.058s; **7** Francisco Javier Sagrera, E, +7.577s; **8** Zak Taylor, GB, +14.444s; **9** Nico Christodoulou, CDN, +15.123s; **10** Alex Connor, GB, +16.912s.
* 5s penalty for exceeding track limits.
Fastest race lap: Lebbon, 1m 23.620s, 107.082mph/172.333km/h.
Pole position: Voisin, 1m 23.629s, 107.071mph/172.314km/h.

Round 23 (32.335 miles/52.038km).
1 Tom Lebbon, GB, 20m 07.788s, 96.379mph/155.107km/h; **2** Luke Browning, GB, +1.952s; **3** Bryce Aron, USA, +2.684s; **4** McKenzy Cresswell, GB, +5.655s; **5** Cian Shields, GB, +5.756s; **6** Matthew Rees, GB, +8.180s; **7** Nico Christodoulou, CDN, +9.215s; **8** Max Esterson, USA, +12.988s *; **9** Callum Voisin, CH, +13.379s; **10** Zak Taylor, GB, +20.233s.
* 5s penalty for exceeding track limits.
Fastest race lap: Rees, 1m 27.540s, 102.287mph/164.616km/h.
Pole position: Voisin, 1m 23.802s, 106.850mph/171.959km/h.

Round 24 (32.335 miles/52.038km).
1 Nick Gilkes, CDN, 20m 17.698s, 95.594mph/153.844km/h; **2** Cian Shields, GB, +0.903s; **3** Alex Connor, GB, +1.198s; **4** Nico Christodoulou, CDN, +1.507s; **5** Joel Granfors, S, +1.671s; **6** Ayato Iwasaki, J, +3.235s; **7** Luke Browning, GB, +3.952s; **8** McKenzy Cresswell, GB, +4.699s; **9** Matthew Rees, GB, +5.264s; **10** David Morales, USA, +5.680s.
Fastest race lap: Christodoulou, 1m 24.046s, 106.540mph/171.459km/h.
Pole position: Gilkes.

Final championship points
Drivers
1 Luke Browning, GB, 507; **2** Joel Granfors, S, 460.5; **3** Tom Lebbon, GB, 363.5; **4** Callum Voisin, CH, 359; **5** Roberto Faria, BR, 316.5; **6** Matthew Rees, GB, 310.5; **7** Max Esterson, USA, 292.5; **8** John Bennett, GB, 262.5; **9** Francisco Javier Sagrera, E, 257.5; **10** Alex Connor, GB, 252.5; **11** McKenzy Cresswell, GB, 221; **12** Bryce Aron, USA, 215; **13** Cian Shields, GB, 186.5; **14** Nick Gilkes, CDN, 165.5; **15** Branden Lee Oxley, GB, 163; **16** Nico Christodoulou, CDN, 163; **17** James Hedley, GB, 156; **18** Zak Taylor, GB, 154.5; **19** Marcos Flack, AUS, 136.5; **20** Tom Smith, AUS, 136.5; **21** Mikkel Grundtvig, DK, 135.5; **22** David Morales, USA, 130; **23** Ayato Iwasaki, J, 24; **24** Ayrton Ori, USA, 3.

Teams
1 Hitech Grand Prix, 805.5; **2** Carlin, 794.5; **3** Elite Motorsport, 697; **4** Fortec Motorsports, 648; **5** Douglas Motorsport, 514; **6** Arden Motorsport, 493.5; **7** Chris Dittmann Racing, 423; **8** JHR Developments, 340.5; **9** Hillspeed, 165.5.

Super Formula Lights Championship

All cars are Dallara F320.

SUPER FORMULA LIGHTS, Fuji International Speedway, Sunto-gun, Shizuoka Prefecture, Japan, 9/10 April. 21, 15 and 15 laps of the 2.835-mile/4.563km circuit.
Round 1 (59.353 miles/95.519km).
1 Seita Nonaka, J (-Toyota), 33m 24.795s, 106.915mph/172.063km/h; **2** Iori Kimura, J (-Spiess), +0.624s; **3** Hibiki Taira, J (-Toyota), +2.623s; **4** Kazuto Kotaka, J (-Toyota), +3.626s; **5** Togo Suganami, J (-Spiess), +8.439s; **6** Reiji Hiraki, J (-Tomei), +15.358s; **7** Yuga Furutani, J (-Toyota), +15.665s; **8** Yuya Hiraki, J (-Tomei), +23.623s; **9** Masayuki Ueda, J (-Spiess), +1m 25.141s; Dragon, J (-Spiess), -11 laps (DNF).
Fastest race lap: Kotaka, 1m 34.717s, 107.765mph/173.430km/h.
Pole position: Kohta Kawaai, J (-Spiess), 1m 33.248s, 109.462mph/176.162km/h.

Round 2 (42.341 miles/68.141km).
1 Kazuto Kotaka, J (-Toyota), 23m 39.179s, 107.879mph/173.615km/h; **2** Kakunoshin Ohta, J (-Spiess), +0.631s; **3** Hibiki Taira, J (-Toyota), +5.646s; **4** Kohta Kawaai, J (-Spiess), +6.726s; **5** Seita Nonaka, J (-Toyota), +7.942s; **6** Iori Kimura, J (-Spiess), +10.279s; **7** Yuga Furutani, J (-Toyota), +11.850s; **8** Reiji Hiraki, J (-Tomei), +15.081s; **9** Togo Suganami, J (-Spiess), +15.439s; **10** Yuya Hiraki, J (-Tomei), +19.685s.
Fastest race lap: Ohta, 1m 34.146s, 108.418mph/174.482km/h.
Pole position: Kotaka, 1m 33.365s, 109.325mph/175.942km/h.

Round 3 (42.341 miles/68.141km).
1 Hibiki Taira, J (-Toyota), 23m 39.775s, 107.834mph/173.542km/h; **2** Iori Kimura, J (-Spiess), +2.964s; **3** Seita Nonaka, J (-Toyota), +3.768s; **4** Kakunoshin Ohta, J (-Spiess), +10.325s; **5** Togo Suganami, J (-Spiess), +10.768s *; **6** Kohta Kawaai, J (-Spiess), +18.518s; **7** Kazuto Kotaka, J (-Toyota), +19.690s; **8** Reiji Hiraki, J (-Tomei), +20.867s; **9** Yuga Furutani, J (-Toyota), +21.811s; **10** Yuya Hiraki, J (-Tomei), +25.287s.
* 5s penalty.
Fastest race lap: Taira, 1m 34.196s, 108.361mph/174.390km/h.
Pole position: Nonaka.

SUPER FORMULA LIGHTS, Suzuka International Racing Course, Suzuka-shi, Mie Prefecture, Japan, 23/24 April. 12, 12 and 17 laps of the 3.608-mile/5.807km circuit.
Round 4 (43.300 miles/69.684km).
1 Kazuto Kotaka, J (-Toyota), 22m 45.426s, 114.161mph/183.725km/h; **2** Kakunoshin Ohta, J (-Spiess), +0.570s; **3** Seita Nonaka, J (-Toyota), +1.137s; **4** Yuga Furutani, J (-Toyota), +5.004s; **5** Iori Kimura, J (-Spiess), +5.346s; **6** Togo Suganami, J (-Spiess), +8.711s; **7** Hibiki Taira, J (-Toyota), +13.406s; **8** Seiya Motojima, J (-Spiess), +17.388s; **9** Reiji Hiraki, J (-Tomei), +30.647s; **10** Yuya Hiraki, J (-Tomei), +30.852s.

Fastest race lap: Ohta, 1m 53.223s, 114.728mph/184.637km/h.
Pole position: Kotaka, 1m 51.450s, 116.554mph/187.575km/h.

Round 5 (43.300 miles/69.684km).
1 Kakunoshin Ohta, J (-Spiess), 28m 55.931s, 89.795mph/144.512km/h; **2** Kazuto Kotaka, J (-Toyota), +1.129s; **3** Yuga Furutani, J (-Toyota), +3.407s; **4** Hibiki Taira, J (-Toyota), +4.187s; **5** Iori Kimura, J (-Spiess), +6.174s; **6** Togo Suganami, J (-Spiess), +8.765s; **7** Reiji Hiraki, J (-Tomei), +15.878s; **8** Nobuhiro Imada, J (-Spiess), +22.200s; **9** Yuya Hiraki, J (-Tomei), +22.946s; **10** Dragon, J (-Spiess), +25.338s.
Fastest race lap: Ohta, 2m 09.996s, 99.925mph/160.814km/h.
Pole position: Ohta, 1m 52.045s, 115.935mph/186.579km/h.

Round 6 (61.341 miles/98.719km).
1 Kazuto Kotaka, J (-Toyota), 37m 50.811s, 97.246mph/156.503km/h; **2** Kakunoshin Ohta, J (-Spiess), +1.228s; **3** Yuga Furutani, J (-Toyota), +2.049s; **4** Togo Suganami, J (-Spiess), +4.274s; **5** Hibiki Taira, J (-Toyota), +5.850s; **6** Seita Nonaka, J (-Toyota), +6.820s; **7** Iori Kimura, J (-Spiess), +12.147s; **8** Seiya Motojima, J (-Spiess), +20.468s; **9** Reiji Hiraki, J (-Tomei), +25.567s; **10** Yuya Hiraki, J (-Tomei), +37.376s.
Fastest race lap: Kimura, 2m 12.161s, 98.288mph/158.180km/h.
Pole position: Kotaka.

SUPER FORMULA LIGHTS, Autopolis International Racing Course, Kamit-sue-mura, Hitagun, Oita Prefecture, Japan, 21/22 May. 13, 14 and 21 laps of the 2.904-mile/4.674km circuit.
Round 7 (37.756 miles/60.762km).
1 Iori Kimura, J (-Spiess), 21m 23.978s, 105.859mph/170.364km/h; **2** Kakunoshin Ohta, J (-Spiess), +6.059s; **3** Seita Nonaka, J (-Toyota), +7.238s; **4** Hibiki Taira, J (-Toyota), +11.723s; **5** Togo Suganami, J (-Spiess), +12.793s; **6** Kazuto Kotaka, J (-Toyota), +16.192s; **7** Reiji Hiraki, J (-Tomei), +22.919s; **8** Yuga Furutani, J (-Toyota), +23.321s; **9** Kohta Kawaai, J (-Spiess), +24.156s; **10** Yuya Hiraki, J (-Tomei), +35.337s.
Fastest race lap: Kimura, 1m 38.359s, 106.299mph/171.071km/h.
Pole position: Ohta, 1m 36.608s, 108.225mph/174.172km/h.

Round 8 (40.660 miles/65.436km).
1 Kakunoshin Ohta, J (-Spiess), 26m 58.774s, 90.424mph/145.523km/h; **2** Yuga Furutani, J (-Toyota), +4.875s; **3** Seita Nonaka, J (-Toyota), +8.962s; **4** Reiji Hiraki, J (-Tomei), +20.876s; **5** Yuya Hiraki, J (-Tomei), +29.521s; **6** Kazuto Kotaka, J (-Toyota), +30.083s; **7** Dragon, J (-Spiess), +35.536s; **8** Iori Kimura, J (-Spiess), +1m 02.037s *; **9** Nobuhiro Imada, J (-Spiess), +1m 17.638s **; **10** Togo Suganami, J (-Spiess), -1 lap.
* 60s penalty.
** 35s penalty.
Fastest race lap: Ohta, 1m 38.918s, 105.698mph/170.105km/h.
Pole position: Ohta, 1m 36.932s, 107.864mph/173.590km/h.

Round 9 (60.990 miles/98.154km).
1 Iori Kimura, J (-Spiess), 34m 47.773s, 105.167mph/169.249km/h; **2** Kakunoshin Ohta, J (-Spiess), +16.571s; **3** Seita Nonaka, J (-Toyota), +17.414s; **4** Togo Suganami, J (-Spiess), +18.275s; **5** Hibiki Taira, J (-Toyota), +19.994s; **6** Kazuto Kotaka, J (-Toyota), +20.707s; **7** Yuga Furutani, J (-Toyota), +32.451s; **8** Reiji Hiraki, J (-Tomei), +32.916s; **9** Kohta Kawaai, J (-Spiess), +34.017s; **10** Yuya Hiraki, J (-Tomei), +46.087s.
Fastest race lap: Kimura, 1m 38.736s, 105.893mph/170.418km/h.
Pole position: Kimura.

SUPER FORMULA LIGHTS, Sportsland-SUGO International Course, Shibata-gun, Miyagi Prefecture, Japan, 18/19 June. 25, 19 and 19 laps of the 2.229-mile/3.587km circuit.
Round 10 (55.714 miles/89.662km).
1 Kazuto Kotaka, J (-Toyota), 1h 18m 16.722s, 42.704mph/68.726km/h; **2** Hibiki Taira, J (-Toyota), +1.012s; **3** Reiji Hiraki, J (-Tomei), +9.822s; **4** Seita Nonaka, J (-Toyota), +9.958s; **5** Yuga Furutani, J (-Toyota), +15.652s; **6** Nobuhiro Imada, J (-Spiess), +24.683s; **7** Dragon, J (-Spiess), +24.973s; **8** Yuya Hiraki, J (-Tomei), +25.594s; **9** Kohta Kawaai, J (-Spiess), -13 laps; Kakunoshin Ohta, J (-Spiess), -20 (DNF).
Fastest race lap: Kotaka, 1m 14.832s, 107.210mph/172.538km/h.
Pole position: Ohta, 1m 13.399s, 109.304mph/175.907km/h.

Round 11 (42.342 miles/68.144km).
1 Kazuto Kotaka, J (-Toyota), 23m 51.460s, 106.488mph/171.375km/h; **2** Yuga Furutani, J (-Toyota), +5.125s; **3** Kakunoshin Ohta, J (-Spiess), +6.941s; **4** Hibiki Taira, J (-Toyota), +10.665s; **5** Iori Kimura, J (-Spiess), +11.020s; **6** Seita Nonaka, J (-Toyota), +15.207s; **7** Togo Suganami, J (-Spiess), +16.814s; **8** Kohta Kawaai, J (-Spiess), +17.551s; **9** Nobuhiro Imada, J (-Spiess), +1m 02.978s; **10** Yuya Hiraki, J (-Tomei), +1m 03.677s.
Fastest race lap: Ohta, 1m 14.529s, 107.646mph/173.240km/h.
Pole position: Kotaka, 1m 13.590s, 109.020mph/175.450km/h.

Round 12 (42.342 miles/68.144km).
1 Kazuto Kotaka, J (-Toyota), 27m 41.688s, 91.734mph/147.631km/h; **2** Hibiki Taira, J (-Toyota), +2.347s; **3** Seita Nonaka, J (-Toyota), +3.377s; **4** Yuga Furutani, J (-Toyota), +6.962s; **5** Kakunoshin Ohta, J (-Spiess), +8.070s; **6** Iori Kimura, J (-Spiess), +10.713s; **7** Reiji Hiraki, J (-Tomei), +18.569s; **8** Togo Suganami, J (-Spiess), +20.115s; **9** Nobuhiro Imada, J (-Spiess), +30.899s; **10** Dragon, J (-Spiess), +31.262s.
Fastest race lap: Nonaka, 1m 15.426s, 106.366mph/171.180km/h.
Pole position: Kotaka.

SUPER FORMULA LIGHTS, Twin Ring Motegi, Motegi-machi, Haga-gun, Tochigi Prefecture, Japan, 20/21 August. 20, 14 and 14 laps of the 2.983-mile/4.801km circuit.
Round 13 (59.664 miles/96.020km).
1 Kazuto Kotaka, J (-Toyota), 41m 32.357s, 86.180mph/138.693km/h; **2** Kakunoshin Ohta, J (-Spiess), +39.515s; **3** Iori Kimura, J (-Spiess), +44.489s; **4** Yuga Furutani, J (-Toyota), +53.210s *; **5** Kohta Kawaai, J (-Spiess), +54.833s; **6** Dragon, J (-Spiess), +1m 42.215s; **7** Togo Suganami, J (-Spiess), +1m 44.441s; **8** Nobuhiro Imada, J (-Spiess), +2m 03.017s; **9** Seita Nonaka, J (-Toyota), +2m 04.112s; **10** Hibiki Taira, J (-Toyota), -1 lap.
* 10s penalty.
Fastest race lap: Kotaka, 2m 03.588s, 86.898mph/139.849km/h.
Pole position: Kimura, 1m 44.439s, 102.831mph/165.490km/h.

Round 14 (41.765 miles/67.214km).
1 Hibiki Taira, J (-Toyota), 24m 53.099s, 100.699mph/162.059km/h; **2** Seita Nonaka, J (-Toyota), +2.177s; **3** Togo Suganami, J (-Spiess), +6.734s; **4** Kazuto Kotaka, J (-Toyota), +7.742s; **5** Yuga Furutani, J (-Toyota), +10.138s; **6** Kohta Kawaai, J (-Spiess), +15.544s; **7** Nobuhiro Imada, J (-Spiess), +43.101s; **8** Dragon, J (-Spiess), +55.369s; **9** Kakunoshin Ohta, J (-Spiess), +1m 18.637s; Iori Kimura, J (-Spiess), -14 laps (DNF).
Fastest race lap: Ohta, 1m 45.601s, 101.699mph/163.669km/h.
Pole position: Ohta, 1m 44.817s, 102.460mph/164.893km/h.

Round 15 (41.765 miles/67.214km).
1 Iori Kimura, J (-Spiess), 24m 55.239s, 100.555mph/161.827km/h; **2** Kazuto Kotaka, J (-Toyota), +1.959s; **3** Yuga Furutani, J (-Toyota), +8.351s; **4** Kakunoshin Ohta, J (-Spiess), +8.645s; **5** Kohta Kawaai, J (-Spiess), +14.358s; **6** Togo Suganami, J (-Spiess), +15.131s; **7** Hibiki Taira, J (-Toyota), +15.846s; **8** Seita Nonaka, J (-Toyota), +16.425s; **9** Nobuhiro Imada, J (-Spiess), -1 lap; Dragon, J (-Spiess), -5 (DNF).
Fastest race lap: Kimura, 1m 46.148s, 101.175mph/162.825km/h.
Pole position: Kotaka.

SUPER FORMULA LIGHTS, Okayama International Circuit (TI Circuit Aida), Aida Gun, Okayama Prefecture, Japan, 24/25 September. 25, 18 and 18 laps of the 2.301-mile/3.703km circuit.
Round 16 (57.523 miles/92.575km).
1 Kakunoshin Ohta, J (-Spiess), 35m 04.459s, 98.403mph/158.364km/h; **2** Iori Kimura, J (-Spiess), +1.036s; **3** Kazuto Kotaka, J (-Toyota), +5.916s; **4** Seita Nonaka, J (-Toyota), +7.551s; **5** Togo Suganami, J (-Spiess), +11.980s; **6** Hibiki Taira, J (-Toyota), +15.215s; **7** Yuga Furutani, J (-Toyota), +17.412s; **8** Seiya Motojima, J (-Spiess), +25.572s; **9** Roberto Merhi, E (-Spiess), +26.208s; **10** Nobuhiro Imada, J (-Spiess), +52.255s.
Fastest race lap: Ohta, 1m 23.588s, 99.098mph/159.482km/h.
Pole position: Ohta, 1m 21.137s, 102.091mph/164.300km/h.

Round 17 (41.417 miles/66.654km).
1 Kazuto Kotaka, J (-Toyota), 28m 28.249s, 87.283mph/140.468km/h; **2** Iori Kimura, J (-Spiess), +0.961s; **3** Kakunoshin Ohta, J (-Spiess), +7.352s; **4** Togo Suganami, J (-Spiess), +8.990s; **5** Yuga Furutani, J (-Toyota), +11.761s; **6** Hibiki Taira, J (-Toyota), +13.410s; **7** Seita Nonaka, J (-Toyota), +19.747s; **8** Seiya Motojima, J (-Spiess), +20.300s; Roberto Merhi, E (-Spiess), -6 laps (DNF); Dragon, J (-Spiess), -18 (DNF).
Fastest race lap: Kimura, 1m 22.281s, 100.672mph/162.016km/h.
Pole position: Kimura, 1m 21.229s, 101.976mph/164.114km/h.

Round 18 (41.417 miles/66.654km).
1 Kakunoshin Ohta, J (-Spiess), 25m 14.493s, 98.449mph/158.439km/h; **2** Iori Kimura, J (-Spiess), +1.099s; **3** Seita Nonaka, J (-Toyota), +2.659s; **4** Kazuto Kotaka, J (-Toyota), +5.000s; **5** Hibiki Taira, J (-Toyota), +11.492s; **6** Yuga Furutani, J (-Toyota), +12.631s; **7** Seiya Motojima, J (-Spiess), +18.188s; **8** Togo Suganami, J (-Spiess), +19.115s; **9** Roberto Merhi, E (-Spiess), +19.613s; **10** Dragon, J (-Spiess), +33.339s.
Fastest race lap: Kimura, 1m 23.492s, 99.212mph/159.666km/h.
Pole position: Ohta.

Final championship points
Drivers
1 Kazuto Kotaka, J, 114; **2** Kakunoshin Ohta, J, 108; **3** Iori Kimura, J, 85; **4** Seita Nonaka, J, 63; **5** Hibiki Taira, J, 62; **6** Yuga Furutani, J, 45; **7** Togo Suganami, J, 25; **8** Kohta Kawaai, J, 10; **9** Reiji Hiraki, J, 9; **10** Yuya Hiraki, J, 2; **11** Dragon, J, 1; **12** Nobuhiro Imada, J, 1.

Drivers (Masters)
1 Nobuhiro Imada, J, 143; **2** Dragon, J, 126; **3** Masayuki Ueda, J, 35.

Teams
1 TOM'S, 131; **2** Toda Racing, 98; **3** B-MAX Racing Team, 84; **4** HELM Motorsports, 9; **5** Rn-Sports, 9.

FIA World Endurance Championship

1000 MILES OF SEBRING, Sebring International Raceway, Florida, USA, 18 March. Round 1. 194 laps of the 3.740-mile/6.019km circuit, 725.566 miles/1167.686km.
1 André Negrão/Nicolas Lapierre/Matthieu Vaxivière, BR/F/F (Alpine A480-Gibson), 7h 15m 37.293s, 99.935mph/160.830km/h; **2** Sébastien Buemi/Brendon Hartley/Ryo Hirakawa, CH/NZ/J (Toyota GR010 HYBRID), +37.466s; **3** Olivier Pla/Romain Dumas/Ryan Briscoe, F/F/AUS (Glickenhaus 007 LMH-Pipo), -1 lap; **4** Paul Di Resta/Oliver Jarvis/Josh Pierson, GB/GB/USA (ORECA 07-Gibson), -2; **5** Sean Gelael/Robin Frijns/René Rast, RI/NL/D (ORECA 07-Gibson), -2; **6** Rui Andrade/Ferdinand Habsburg/Norman Nato, P/A/F (ORECA 07-Gibson), -2; **7** Robert Kubica/Louis Delétraz/Lorenzo Colombo, PL/CH/I (ORECA 07-Gibson), -2; **8** Oliver Rasmussen/Ed Jones/Jonathan Aberdein, DK/GB/ZA (ORECA 07-Gibson), -2; **9** Roberto González/António Félix da Costa/Will Stevens, MEX/P/GB (ORECA 07-Gibson), -2; **10** Phil Hanson/Filipe Albuquerque/Will Owen, GB/P/USA (ORECA 07-Gibson), -2.
Fastest race lap: Vaxivière, 1m 49.033s, 123.486mph/198.732km/h.
Pole position: Negrão/Lapierre/Vaxivière, 1m 47.407s, 125.356mph/201.741km/h.

TOTAL ENERGIES 6 HOURS OF SPA-FRANCORCHAMPS, Circuit de Spa-Francorchamps, Stavelot, Belgium, 7 May. Round 2. 103 laps of the 4.352-mile/7.004km circuit, 448.258 miles/721.402km.
1 Mike Conway/Kamui Kobayashi/José María López, GB/J/RA (Toyota GR010 HYBRID), 6h 00m 31.052s, 74.602mph/120.061km/h; **2** André Negrão/Nicolas Lapierre/Matthieu Vaxivière, BR/F/F (Alpine A480-Gibson), +27.473s; **3** Sean Gelael/Robin Frijns/René Rast, RI/NL/D (ORECA 07-Gibson), +1m 06.185s; **4** Rui Andrade/Ferdinand Habsburg/Norman Nato, P/A/F (ORECA 07-Gibson), +1m 40.676s; **5** Roberto González/António Félix da Costa/Will Stevens, MEX/P/GB (ORECA 07-Gibson), +1m 48.571s; **6** Dane Cameron/Emmanuel Collard/Felipe Nasr, USA/F/BR (ORECA 07-Gibson), +1m 57.610s; **7** Phil Hanson/Filipe Albuquerque/Will Owen, GB/P/USA (ORECA 07-Gibson), +1m 57.901s; **8** Alex Lynn/Oliver Jarvis/Josh Pierson, GB/GB/USA (ORECA 07-Gibson), -1 lap; **9** Olivier Pla/Romain Dumas/Pipo Derani, F/F/BR (Glickenhaus 007 LMH-Pipo), -1; **10** Robert Kubica/Louis Delétraz/Lorenzo Colombo, PL/CH/I (ORECA 07-Gibson), -1.
Fastest race lap: Sébastien Buemi, CH (Toyota GR010 HYBRID), 2m 05.298s, 125.040mph/201.232km/h.
Pole position: Pla/Dumas/Derani, 2m 02.771s, 127.613mph/205.374km/h.

24 HEURES DU MANS, Circuit International Du Mans, Les Raineries, Le Mans, France, 12 June. Round 3. 380 laps of the 8.467-mile/13.626km circuit, 3217.385 miles/5177.880km.
1 Sébastien Buemi/Brendon Hartley/Ryo Hirakawa, CH/NZ/J (Toyota GR010 HYBRID), 24h 02m 07.996s, 133.859mph/215.426km/h; **2** Mike Conway/Kamui Kobayashi/José María López, GB/J/RA (Toyota GR010 HYBRID), +2m 01.222s; **3** Ryan Briscoe/Richard Westbrook/Franck Mailleux, AUS/GB/F (Glickenhaus 007 LMH-Pipo), -5 laps; **4** Olivier Pla/Romain Dumas/Pipo Derani, F/F/BR (Glickenhaus 007 LMH-Pipo), -10; **5** Roberto González/António Félix da Costa/Will Stevens, MEX/P/GB (ORECA 07-Gibson), -11; **6** Robert Kubica/Louis Delétraz/Lorenzo Colombo, PL/CH/I (ORECA 07-Gibson), -11; **7** Oliver Rasmussen/Ed Jones/Jonathan Aberdein, DK/GB/ZA (ORECA 07-Gibson), -12; **8** Nyck de Vries/Mathias Beche/Tijmen van der Helm, NL/CH/NL (ORECA 07-Gibson), -12; **9** Dane Cameron/Emmanuel Collard/Felipe Nasr, USA/F/BR (ORECA 07-Gibson), -12; **10** Alex Lynn/Oliver Jarvis/Josh Pierson, GB/GB/USA (ORECA 07-Gibson), -12; **11** Yifei Ye/Ricky Taylor/Niklas Krütten, CHN/USA/D (ORECA 07-Gibson), -13; **12** Paul Lafargue/Paul-Loup Chatin/Patrick Pilet, F/F/F (ORECA 07-Gibson), -14; **13** Lilou Wadoux/Sébastien Ogier/Charles Milesi, F/F/F (ORECA 07-Gibson), -14; **14** Phil Hanson/Filipe Albuquerque/Will Owen, GB/P/USA (ORECA 07-Gibson), -14; **15** Rolf Ineichen/Mirko Bortolotti/Dries Vanthoor, CH/I/B (ORECA 07-Gibson), -14; **16** Julien Canal/Nicolas Jamin/Job van Uitert, F/F/NL (ORECA 07-Gibson), -14; **17** Jakub Smiechowski/Alex Brundle/Esteban Gutiérrez, PL/GB/MEX (ORECA 07-Gibson), -15; **18** David Heinemeier Hansson/Fabio Scherer/Pietro Fittipaldi, DK/CH/BR (ORECA 07-Gibson), -16; **19** Steven Thomas/James Allen/Rene Binder, USA/AUS/A (ORECA 07-Gibson), -17; **20** Rodrigo Sales/Matthew Bell/Ben Hanley, USA/GB/GB (ORECA 07-Gibson), -18; **21** Rui Andrade/Ferdinand Habsburg/Norman Nato, P/A/F (ORECA 07-Gibson), -18; **22** Laurents Hörr/Jean Glorieux/Alexandre Cougnaud, D/B/F (ORECA 07-Gibson), -18; **23** André Negrão/Nicolas Lapierre/Matthieu Vaxivière, BR/F/F (Alpine A480-Gibson), -18; **24** François Perrodo/Nicklas Nielsen/Alessio Rovera, F/DK/I (ORECA 07-Gibson), -19; **25** Sophia Flörsch/John Falb/Jack Aitken, D/USA/GB (ORECA 07-Gibson), -19; **26** Miro Konopka/Bent Viscaal/Tristan Vautier, SK/NL/F (ORECA 07-Gibson), -20; **27** Nico Müller/Ryan Cullen/Sébastien Bourdais, CH/IRL/F (ORECA 07-Gibson), -23; **28** Gianmaria Bruni/Richard Lietz/Frédéric Makowiecki, I/A/F (Porsche 911 RSR-19), -30; **29** Alessandro Pier Guidi/James Calado/Daniel Serra, I/GB/BR (Ferrari 488 GTE Evo), -30; **30** Miguel Molina/Antonio Fuoco/Davide Rigon, E/I/I (Ferrari 488 GTE Evo), -31; **31** Michael Christensen/Kévin Estre/Laurens Vanthoor, DK/F/B (Porsche 911 RSR-19), -32; **32** Felipe Fraga/Sam Bird/Shane van Gisbergen, BR/GB/NZ (Ferrari 488 GTE Evo), -33; **33** Eric Trouillet/Sebastien Page/David Droux, F/CH/CH (ORECA 07-Gibson), -36; **34** Ben Keating/Henrique Chaves Jr./Marco Sørensen, USA/P/DK (Aston Martin Vantage AMR), -37; **35** Cooper MacNeil/Julien Andlauer/Thomas Merrill, USA/F/USA (Porsche 911 RSR-19), -37; **36** Paul Dalla Lana/Nicki Thiim/David Pittard, CDN/DK/GB (Aston Martin Vantage AMR), -38; **37** Mike Wainwright/Ben Barker/Riccardo Pera, GB/GB/I (Porsche 911 RSR-19), -40; **38** Fred Poordad/Maxwell Root/Jan Heylen, USA/USA/B (Porsche 911 RSR-19), -40; **39** Thomas Flohr/Francesco Castellacci/Nick Cassidy, CH/I/NZ (Ferrari 488 GTE Evo), -40; **40** Rahel Frey/Michelle Gatting/Sarah Bovy, CH/DK/B (Ferrari 488 GTE Evo), -41; **41** Simon Mann/Christoph Ulrich/Toni Vilander, USA/CH/FIN (Ferrari 488 GTE Evo), -41; **42** Louis Prette Jr./Conrad Grunewald/Vincent Abril, MC/USA/F (Ferrari 488 GTE Evo), -41; **43** Duncan Cameron/Matt Griffin/David Perel, GB/IRL/ZA (Ferrari 488 GTE Evo), -41; **44** Andrew Haryanto/Alessio Picariello/Martin Rump, RI/B/EST (Porsche 911 RSR-19), -42; **45** Takeshi Kimura/Mikkel Jensen/Frederik Schandorff, J/DK/DK (Ferrari 488 GTE Evo), -44; **46** Matteo Cressoni/Giancarlo Fisichella/Richard Heistand, I/I/USA (Ferrari 488 GTE Evo), -44; **47** Christian Ried/Seb Priaulx/Harry Tincknell, D/GB/GB (Porsche 911 RSR-19), -44; **48** Jean-Baptiste Lahaye/Matthieu Lahaye/François Heriau, F/F/F (ORECA 07-Gibson), -45; **49** Christophe Crespo/Michael Jensen/Steven Palette, F/DK/F (Ligier JS P217-Gibson), -47; **50** Renger van der Zande/

Mark Kvamme/Jason Hart, NL/USA/USA (Ferrari 488 GTE Evo), -49; **51** Michael Fassbender/Matt Campbell/Zacharie Robichon, D/AUS/CDN (Porsche 911 RSR-19), -51; **52** Richard Bradley/Memo Rojas/Reshad De Gerus, GB/MEX/F (ORECA 07-Gibson), -54; **53** Pierre Ehret/Christian Hook/Nicolás Varrone, D/D/RA (Ferrari 488 GTE Evo), -56; Claudio Schiavoni/Alessandro Balzan/Raffaele Giammaria, I/I/I (Ferrari 488 GTE Evo), -91 (NC); Sean Gelael/Robin Frijns/René Rast, RI/NL/D (ORECA 07-Gibson), -95 (DNF-accident); Nick Tandy/Tommy Milner/Alexander Sims, GB/USA/GB (Chevrolet Corvette C8.R), -120 (DNF-accident); Brendan Iribe/Ollie Millroy/Ben Barnicoat, USA/GB/GB (Porsche 911 RSR-19), -139 (DNF-accident); Antonio García/Jordan Taylor/Nicky Catsburg, E/USA/NL (Chevrolet Corvette C8.R), -166 (DNF-suspension); Alexander West/Côme Ledogar/Marvin Klein, S/F/F (Ferrari 488 GTE Evo), -190 (DNF-axle); Franck Dezoteux/Pierre Ragues/Gabriel Aubry, F/F/F (Ferrari 488 GTE Evo), -253 (DNF-cooling); Satoshi Hoshino/Tomonobu Fujii/Charlie Fagg, J/J/GB (Aston Martin Vantage AMR), -268 (DNF-accident damage); Matteo Cairoli/Mikkel Overgaard Pedersen/Niki Leutwiler, I/DK/CH (Porsche 911 RSR-19), -303 (DNF-vibrations).
Fastest race lap: López, 3m 27.749s, 146.718mph/236.120km/h.
Pole position: Buemi/Hartley/Hirakawa, 3m 24.408s, 149.116mph/239.979km/h.

6 HOURS OF MONZA, Autodromo Nazionale di Monza, Milan, Italy, 10 July. Round 4. 194 laps of the 3.600-mile/5.793km circuit, 698.323 miles/1123.842km.
1 André Negrão/Nicolas Lapierre/Matthieu Vaxivière, BR/F/F (Alpine A480-Gibson), 6h 00m 47.738s, 116.130mph/186.893km/h; **2** Sébastien Buemi/Brendon Hartley/Ryo Hirakawa, CH/NZ/J (Toyota GR010 HYBRID), +2.762s; **3** Mike Conway/Kamui Kobayashi/José María López, GB/J/RA (Toyota GR010 HYBRID), -2 laps; **4** Rui Andrade/Ferdinand Habsburg/Norman Nato, P/A/F (ORECA 07-Gibson), -6; **5** Roberto González/António Félix da Costa/Will Stevens, MEX/P/GB (ORECA 07-Gibson), -6; **6** Nico Müller/Ryan Cullen/Sébastien Bourdais, CH/IRL/F (ORECA 07-Gibson), -6; **7** Jakub Smiechowski/Alex Brundle/Esteban Gutiérrez, PL/GB/MEX (ORECA 07-Gibson), -6; **8** Alex Lynn/Oliver Jarvis/Josh Pierson, GB/GB/USA (ORECA 07-Gibson), -6; **9** Robert Kubica/Louis Delétraz/Lorenzo Colombo, PL/CH/I (ORECA 07-Gibson), -6; **10** Steven Thomas/James Allen/Rene Binder, USA/AUS/A (ORECA 07-Gibson), -7.
Fastest race lap: Romain Dumas, F (Glickenhaus 007 LMH-Pipo), 1m 36.589s, 134.161mph/215.912km/h.
Pole position: Olivier Pla/Romain Dumas/Pipo Derani, F/F/BR (Glickenhaus 007 LMH-Pipo), 1m 35.416s, 135.811mph/218.567km/h.

6 HOURS OF FUJI, Fuji International Speedway, Sunto-gun, Shizuoka Prefecture, Japan, 11 September. Round 5. 232 laps of the 2.835-mile/4.563km circuit, 657.793 miles/1058.616km.
1 Sébastien Buemi/Brendon Hartley/Ryo Hirakawa, CH/NZ/J (Toyota GR010 HYBRID), 6h 01m 23.341s, 109.210mph/175.757km/h; **2** Mike Conway/Kamui Kobayashi/José María López, GB/J/RA (Toyota GR010 HYBRID), +1m 08.382s; **3** André Negrão/Nicolas Lapierre/Matthieu Vaxivière, BR/F/F (Alpine A480-Gibson), -2 laps; **4** Paul Di Resta/Mikkel Jensen/Jean-Éric Vergne, GB/DK/F (Peugeot 9X8), -7; **5** Sean Gelael/Robin Frijns/Dries Vanthoor, RI/NL/B (ORECA 07-Gibson), -7; **6** Roberto González/António Félix da Costa/Will Stevens, MEX/P/GB (ORECA 07-Gibson), -8; **7** Oliver Rasmussen/Ed Jones/Jonathan Aberdein, DK/GB/ZA (ORECA 07-Gibson), -8; **8** Rui Andrade/Ferdinand Habsburg/Norman Nato, P/A/F (ORECA 07-Gibson), -8; **9** Alex Lynn/Oliver Jarvis/Josh Pierson, GB/GB/USA (ORECA 07-Gibson), -8; **10** Robert Kubica/Louis Delétraz/Lorenzo Colombo, PL/CH/I (ORECA 07-Gibson), -8.
Fastest race lap: Kobayashi, 1m 30.735s, 112.493mph/181.041km/h.
Pole position: Conway/Kobayashi/López, 1m 29.234s, 114.386mph/184.086km/h.

BAPCO 8 HOURS OF BAHRAIN, Bahrain International Circuit, Sakhir, Bahrain, 12 November. Round 6. 245 laps of the 3.363-mile/5.412km circuit, 823.901 miles/1325.940km.
1 Mike Conway/Kamui Kobayashi/José María López, GB/J/RA (Toyota GR010 HYBRID), 8h 00m 40.920s, 102.841mph/165.507km/h; **2** Sébastien Buemi/Brendon Hartley/Ryo Hirakawa, CH/NZ/J (Toyota GR010 HYBRID), +45.471s; **3** André Negrão/Nicolas Lapierre/Matthieu Vaxivière, BR/F/F (Alpine A480-Gibson), -2 laps; **4** Loïc Duval/Gustavo Menezes/Nico Müller, F/USA/CH (Peugeot 9X8), -6; **5** Sean Gelael/Robin Frijns/René Rast, RI/NL/D (ORECA 07-Gibson), -8; **6** Alex Lynn/Oliver Jarvis/Josh Pierson, GB/GB/USA (ORECA 07-Gibson), -8; **7** Roberto González/António Félix da Costa/Will Stevens, MEX/P/GB (ORECA 07-Gibson), -9; **8** Robert Kubica/Louis Delétraz/Lorenzo Colombo, PL/CH/I (ORECA 07-Gibson), -9; **9** Rui Andrade/Ferdinand Habsburg/Norman Nato, P/A/F (ORECA 07-Gibson), -9; **10** Phil Hanson/Filipe Albuquerque/Will Owen, GB/P/USA (ORECA 07-Gibson), -9.
Fastest race lap: Jean-Éric Vergne, F (Peugeot 9X8), 1m 49.709s, 110.349mph/177.589km/h.
Pole position: Buemi/Hartley/Hirakawa, 1m 46.800s, 113.354mph/182.426km/h.

Final championship points
Drivers (LMP2)
1 António Félix da Costa, P, 137; **1** Roberto González, MEX, 137; **1** Will Stevens, GB, 137; **2** Robin Frijns, NL, 116; **2** Sean Gelael, RI, 116; **3** Josh Pierson, USA, 113; **3** Oliver Jarvis, GB, 113; **4** Ferdinand Habsburg, A, 96; **4** Norman Nato, F, 96; **4** Rui Andrade, P, 96; **5** Lorenzo Colombo, I, 94; **5** Louis Delétraz, CH, 94; **5** Robert Kubica, PL, 94; **6** René Rast, D, 91; **7** Alex Lynn, GB, 75; **8** Ed Jones, GB, 70; **8** Jonathan Aberdein, ZA, 70; **8** Oliver Rasmussen, DK, 70; **9** Filipe Albuquerque, P, 50; **9** Phil Hanson, GB, 50; **9** Will Owen, USA, 50; **10** Dane Cameron, USA, 42; **10** Emmanuel Collard, F, 42; **10** Felipe Nasr, BR, 42.

Drivers (LMP2 Pro/Am)
1 Alessio Rovera, I, 177; **1** François Perrodo, F, 177; **1** Nicklas Nielsen, DK, 177; **2** James Allen, AUS, 154; **2** Rene Binder, A, 154; **2** Steven Thomas, USA, 154; **3** François Heriau, F, 129; **3** Jean-Baptiste Lahaye, F, 129; **3** Matthieu Lahaye, F, 129.

Drivers (Hypercar)
1 Brendon Hartley, NZ, 149; **1** Ryo Hirakawa, J, 149; **1** Sébastien Buemi, CH, 149; **2** André Negrão, BR, 144; **2** Matthieu Vaxivière, F, 144; **2** Nicolas Lapierre, F, 144; **3** José María López, RA, 133; **3** Kamui Kobayashi, J, 133; **3** Mike Conway, GB, 133.

Drivers (LMGTE)
1 Alessandro Pier Guidi, I, 135; **1** James Calado, GB, 135; **2** Kévin Estre, F, 132; **2** Michael Christensen, DK, 132; **3** Antonio Fuoco, I, 131; **3** Miguel Molina, E, 131;.

Drivers (LMGTE Am)
1 Ben Keating, USA, 141; **1** Marco Sørensen, DK, 141; **2** David Pittard, GB, 118; **2** Nicki Thiim, DK, 118; **2** Paul Dalla Lana, CDN, 118; **3** Henrique Chaves Jr., P, 113.

Manufacturers (Hypercar)
1 Toyota, 186; **2** Alpine, 144; **3** Glickenhaus/Pipo, 70.

Manufacturers (LMGTE)
1 Ferrari, 269; **2** Porsche, 257; **3** Chevrolet, 102.

Teams (LMP2)
1 JOTA (car 38), 137; **2** WRT (31), 116; **3** United Autosports USA (23), 113.

Teams (LMP2 Pro/Am)
1 AF Corse (car 83), 177; **2** Algarve Pro Racing (45), 154; **3** Ultimate (35), 129.

Teams (LMGTE Am)
1 TF Sport (car 33), 141; **2** Northwest AMR (98), 118; **3** Iron Dames (85), 93.

European Le Mans Series

4 HOURS OF LE CASTELLET, Circuit ASA Paul Ricard, Le Beausset, France, 17 April. Round 1. 120 laps of the 3.586-mile/5.771km circuit, 430.312 miles/692.520km.
1 Lorenzo Colombo/Louis Delétraz/Ferdinand Habsburg, I/CH/A (ORECA 07-Gibson), 4h 00m 43.565s, 107.253mph/172.607km/h; **2** Sophia Flörsch/Bent Viscaal, D/NL (ORECA 07-Gibson), +10.936s; **3** Julien Canal/Nicolas Jamin/Job van Uitert, F/F/NL (ORECA 07-Gibson), +13.484s; **4** Paul Lafargue/Paul-Loup Chatin/Patrick Pilet, F/F/F (ORECA 07-Gibson), +30.027s; **5** Nicolas Lapierre/Niklas Krütten/Yifei Ye, F/D/CHN (ORECA 07-Gibson), +30.537s; **6** Salih Yoluc/Charlie Eastwood/Jack Aitken, TR/GB/GB (ORECA 07-Gibson), +33.737s; **7** Phil Hanson/Tom Gamble/Duncan Tappy, GB/GB/GB (ORECA 07-Gibson), +1m 01.958s; **8** François Perrodo/Nicklas Nielsen/Alessio Rovera, F/DK/I (ORECA 07-Gibson), +1m 12.820s; **9** Matthias Kaiser/Thomas Laurent/Ugo De Wilde, FL/F/B (ORECA 07-Gibson), -1 lap; **10** Philippe Cimadomo/Mathias Beche/Tijmen van der Helm, F/CH/NL (ORECA 07-Gibson), -1.
Fastest race lap: Delétraz, 1m 44.370s, 123.688mph/199.057km/h.
Pole position: Cimadomo/Beche/Helm, 1m 43.038s, 125.287mph/201.630km/h.

4 HOURS OF IMOLA, Autodromo Enzo e Dino Ferrari, Imola, Italy, 15 May. Round 2. 127 laps of the 3.050-mile/4.909km circuit, 387.390 miles/623.443km.
1 Lorenzo Colombo/Louis Delétraz/Ferdinand Habsburg, I/CH/A (ORECA 07-Gibson), 4h 00m 39.273s, 96.583mph/155.436km/h; **2** Phil Hanson/Tom Gamble/Duncan Tappy, GB/GB/GB (ORECA 07-Gibson), +4.659s; **3** Nicolas Lapierre/Niklas Krütten/Yifei Ye, F/D/CHN (ORECA 07-Gibson), +29.182s; **4** Julien Canal/Nicolas Jamin/Job van Uitert, F/F/NL (ORECA 07-Gibson), +29.981s; **5** Paul Lafargue/Paul-Loup Chatin/Patrick Pilet, F/F/F (ORECA 07-Gibson), +1m 04.130s; **6** Memo Rojas/Reshad De Gerus/Richard Bradley, MEX/F/GB (ORECA 07-Gibson), +1m 28.794s; **7** Salih Yoluc/Charlie Eastwood/Jack Aitken, TR/GB/GB (ORECA 07-Gibson), +1m 29.192s; **8** Sophia Flörsch/Bent Viscaal, D/NL (ORECA 07-Gibson), -1 lap; **9** David Heinemeier Hansson/Fabio Scherer/Pietro Fittipaldi, DK/CH/BR (ORECA 07-Gibson), -1; **10** Philippe Cimadomo/Mathias Beche/Tijmen van der Helm, F/CH/NL (ORECA 07-Gibson), -2.
Fastest race lap: Colombo, 1m 33.702s, 117.191mph/188.602km/h.
Pole position: François Perrodo/Nicklas Nielsen/Alessio Rovera, F/DK/I (ORECA 07-Gibson), 1m 32.269s, 119.012mph/191.531km/h.

4 HOURS OF MONZA, Autodromo Nazionale di Monza, Milan, Italy, 3 July. Round 3. 121 laps of the 3.600-mile/5.793km circuit, 435.552 miles/700.953km.
1 Paul Lafargue/Paul-Loup Chatin/Patrick Pilet, F/F/F (ORECA 07-Gibson), 4h 00m 54.476s, 108.477mph/174.577km/h; **2** Julien Canal/Job van Uitert/Nicolas Jamin, F/NL/F (ORECA 07-Gibson), +13.209s; **3** Matthias Kaiser/Thomas Laurent/Ugo De Wilde, FL/F/B (ORECA 07-Gibson), +28.177s; **4** Phil Hanson/Tom Gamble/Duncan Tappy, GB/GB/GB (ORECA 07-Gibson), +29.066s; **5** Lorenzo Colombo/Louis Delétraz/Ferdinand Habsburg, I/CH/A (ORECA 07-Gibson), +29.496s *; **6** Rodrigo Sales/Matthew Bell/Ben Hanley, USA/GB/GB (ORECA 07-Gibson), +29.702s; **7** Salih Yoluc/Charlie Eastwood/Jack Aitken, TR/GB/GB (ORECA 07-Gibson), +29.768s; **8** Nicolas Lapierre/Niklas Krütten/Yifei Ye, F/D/CHN (ORECA 07-Gibson), +31.790s; **9** John Falb/James Allen/Alex Peroni, USA/AUS/AUS (ORECA 07-Gibson), +33.875s; **10** Sophia Flörsch/Bent Viscaal, D/NL (ORECA 07-Gibson), +44.459s.
* 10s penalty.
Fastest race lap: Habsburg, 1m 39.531s, 130.196mph/209.530km/h.
Pole position: Philippe Cimadomo/Mathias Beche/Tijmen van der Helm, F/CH/NL (ORECA 07-Gibson), 1m 38.032s, 132.187mph/212.734km/h.

4 HOURS OF BARCELONA, Circuit de Catalunya, Montmeló, Barcelona, Spain, 28 August. Round 4. 132 laps of the 2.905-mile/4.675km circuit, 383.448 miles/617.100km.
1 Lorenzo Colombo/Ferdinand Habsburg/Louis Delétraz, I/A/CH (ORECA 07-Gibson), 4h 00m 43.527s, 95.573mph/153.810km/h; **2** Julien Canal/Nicolas Jamin/Job van Uitert, F/F/NL (ORECA 07-Gibson), +22.926s; **3** Nicolas Lapierre/Niklas Krütten/Yifei Ye, F/D/CHN (ORECA 07-Gibson), +1m 17.973s; **4** Phil Hanson/Tom Gamble/Duncan Tappy, GB/GB/GB (ORECA 07-Gibson), -1 lap; **5** François Perrodo/Nicklas Nielsen/Alessio Rovera, F/DK/I (ORECA 07-Gibson), -1; **6** Memo Rojas/Anders Fjordbach/Richard Bradley, MEX/DK/GB (ORECA 07-Gibson), -1; **7** Rodrigo Sales/Matthew Bell/Ben Hanley, USA/GB/GB (ORECA 07-Gibson), -1; **8** John Falb/James Allen/Alex Peroni, USA/AUS/AUS (ORECA 07-Gibson), -1; **9** Matthias Kaiser/Thomas Laurent/Ugo De Wilde, FL/F/B (ORECA 07-Gibson), -1; **10** Salih Yoluc/Charlie Eastwood/Jack Aitken, TR/GB/GB (ORECA 07-Gibson), -2.
Fastest race lap: Patrick Pilet, F (ORECA 07-Gibson), 1m 37.536s, 107.218mph/172.551km/h.
Pole position: Canal/Jamin/Uitert, 1m 34.802s, 110.310mph/177.527km/h.

4 HOURS OF SPA-FRANCORCHAMPS, Circuit de Spa-Francorchamps, Stavelot, Belgium, 25 September. Round 5. 97 laps of the 4.352-mile/7.004km circuit, 422.146 miles/679.378km.
1 Tom Gamble/Duncan Tappy/Phil Hanson, GB/GB/GB (ORECA 07-Gibson), 4h 00m 31.833s, 105.303mph/169.469km/h; **2** David Heinemeier Hansson/Pietro Fittipaldi/Fabio Scherer, DK/BR/CH (ORECA 07-Gibson), +23.508s *; **3** Juan Manuel Correa/Louis Delétraz/Ferdinand Habsburg, USA/CH/A (ORECA 07-Gibson), +24.661s; **4** Nicolas Jamin/Job van Uitert/Julien Canal, F/NL/F (ORECA 07-Gibson), +35.904s; **5** Niklas Krütten/Yifei Ye/Nicolas Lapierre, D/CHN/F (ORECA 07-Gibson), +48.995s; **6** Salih Yoluc/Charlie Eastwood/Will Stevens, TR/GB/GB (ORECA 07-Gibson), +1m 04.217s; **7** François Perrodo/Nicklas Nielsen/Alessio Rovera, F/DK/I (ORECA 07-Gibson), +1m 04.259s; **8** Bent Viscaal/Filip-Ioan Ugran, NL/RO (ORECA 07-Gibson), +1m 35.290s; **9** Memo Rojas/Richard Bradley/Mathieu de Barbuat, MEX/GB/F (ORECA 07-Gibson), +1m 47.745s; **10** John Falb/Alex Peroni/James Allen, USA/AUS/AUS (ORECA 07-Gibson), +2m 17.167s **.
* 5-second penalty for overtaking before the start line at the start.
** Drive-through penalty converted into 30-second penalty due to track limits.
Fastest race lap: Paul-Loup Chatin, F (ORECA 07-Gibson), 2m 05.893s, 124.449mph/200.281km/h.
Pole position: Krütten/Ye/Lapierre, 2m 03.544s, 126.815mph/204.089km/h.

4 HOURS OF PORTIMÃO, Autódromo Internacional do Algarve, Portimão, Portugal, 16 October. Round 6. 126 laps of the 2.891-mile/4.653km circuit, 364.296 miles/586.278km.
1 Juan Manuel Correa/Louis Delétraz/Ferdinand Habsburg, USA/CH/A (ORECA 07-Gibson), 4h 00m 17.688s, 90.962mph/146.389km/h; **2** Nicolas Jamin/Job van Uitert/Julien Canal, F/NL/F (ORECA 07-Gibson), +49.262s; **3** Yifei Ye/Niklas Krütten/Nicolas Lapierre, CHN/D/F (ORECA 07-Gibson), +51.296s; **4** David Heinemeier Hansson/Fabio Scherer/Pietro Fittipaldi, DK/CH/BR (ORECA 07-Gibson), -1 lap; **5** Bent Viscaal/Filip-Ioan Ugran, NL/RO (ORECA 07-Gibson), -1; **6** Jack Aitken/Charlie Eastwood/Salih Yoluc, GB/GB/TR (ORECA 07-Gibson), -1; **7** Paul Lafargue/Paul-Loup Chatin/Patrick Pilet, F/F/F (ORECA 07-Gibson), -2; **8** François Perrodo/Alessio Rovera/Nicklas Nielsen, F/I/DK (ORECA 07-Gibson), -2; **9** Memo Rojas/Richard Bradley/Rui Andrade, MEX/GB/P (ORECA 07-Gibson), -2; **10** Rodrigo Sales/Matthew Bell/Ben Hanley, USA/GB/GB (ORECA 07-Gibson), -4.
Fastest race lap: Correa, 1m 33.547s, 111.264mph/179.062km/h.
Pole position: Aitken/Eastwood/Yoluc, 1m 32.375s, 112.676mph/181.334km/h.

Final championship points
Drivers (LMP2)
1 Ferdinand Habsburg, A, 125; **1** Louis Delétraz, CH, 125; **2** Julien Canal, F, 94; **2** Job van Uitert, NL, 94; **2** Nicolas Jamin, F, 94; **3** Lorenzo Colombo, I, 85; **4** Duncan Tappy, GB, 73; **4** Phil Hanson, GB, 73; **4** Tom Gamble, GB, 73; **5** Nicolas Lapierre, F, 70; **5** Niklas Krütten, D, 70; **5** Yifei Ye, CHN, 70; **6** Patrick Pilet, F, 53; **6** Paul-Loup Chatin, F, 53; **6** Paul Lafargue, F, 53; **7** Juan Manuel Correa, USA, 40; **8** Charlie Eastwood, GB, 38; **8** Salih Yoluc, TR, 38; **9** Bent Viscaal, NL, 37; **10** Pietro Fittipaldi, BR, 32; **10** David Heinemeier Hansson, DK, 32; **10** Fabio Scherer, CH, 32.

Drivers (LMP3)
1 Maurice Smith, USA, 86; **1** Malthe Jakobsen, DK, 86; 1 Michael Benham, GB, 86; **2** Nico Pino, RCH, 79; **2** CR Crews, USA, 79; **2** Guilherme Oliveira, P, 79; **3** Alexander Bukhantsov, RUS, 60; **3** Sebastián Álvarez, MEX, 60; **4** Nick Adcock, GB, 59; **4** Michael Jensen, DK, 59; **4** Alex Kapadia, GB, 59; **5** Tom Van Rompuy, B, 56; **6** Andrew Bentley, GB, 53; **6** Kay van Berlo, NL, 53; **7** Nicolas Maulini, CH, 53; **7** Jean-Ludovic Foubert, F, 53; **7** Antoine Doquin, F, 53; **8** Finn Gehrsitz, D, 48; **8** Bailey Voisin, GB, 48; **8** Josh Caygill, GB, 48; **9** Terrence Woodward, GB, 46; **9** Ross Kaiser, GB, 46; **10** Mark Richards, GB, 46.

Drivers (LMP2 Pro-Am)
1 Charlie Eastwood, GB, 131; **1** Salih Yoluc, TR, 131; **2** Jack Aitken, GB, 106; **3** Alessio Rovera, I, 101; **3** François Perrodo, F, 101; **3** Nicklas Nielsen, DK, 101; **4** Ben Hanley, GB, 97; **4** Matthew Bell, GB, 97; **4** Rodrigo Sales, USA, 97; **5** Mathias Beche, CH, 76; **5** Philippe Cimadomo, F, 76; **5** Tijmen van der Helm, NL, 76; **6** Alex Peroni, AUS, 59; **6** James Allen, AUS, 59; **6** John Falb, USA, 59; **7** Gabriel Aubry, F, 34; **7** Rob Hodes, USA, 34; **8** David Droux, CH, 26; **8** Eric Trouillet, F, 26; **8** Sebastien Page, CH, 26; **9** Will Stevens, GB, 25; **10** Jazeman Jaafar, MAL, 18; **11** Ian Geoffrey Rodriguez, GCA, 8.

Drivers (LMGTE)
1 Lorenzo Ferrari, I, 82; **1** Christian Ried, D, 82; 1 Gianmaria Bruni, I, 82; **2** Frederik Schandorff, DK, 78; **2** Mikkel Jensen, DK, 78; **3** Sarah Bovy, B, 70; **3** Michelle Gatting, DK, 70; **4** Davide Rigon, I, 63; **4** Matteo Cressoni, I, 63; **4** Claudio Schiavoni, I, 63; **5** Ahmad Al Harthy, OM, 59; **5** Marco Sørensen, DK, 59; **5** Sam De Haan, GB,

59; **6** Takeshi Kimura, J, 52; **7** Martin Rump, EST, 49; **7** Alessio Picariello, B, 49; **7** Andrew Haryanto, RI, 49; **8** Giacomo Petrobelli, I, 48; **8** Sean Hudspeth, SGP, 48; **9** Doriane Pin, F, 44; **10** Nicolás Varrone, RA, 39.

Teams (LMP2)
1 Prema Racing (car 9), 125; **2** Panis Racing (65), 94; **3** United Autosports (22), 73; **4** COOL Racing (37), 70; **5** Idec Sport (28), 53; **6** Racing Team Turkey (34), 38.

Teams (LMP3)
1 COOL Racing (car 17), 86; **2** Inter Europol Competition (13), 79; **3** DKR Engineering (4), 60; **4** RLR MSport (5), 59; **5** United Autosports (3), 53; **6** COOL Racing (27), 53.

Teams (LMP2 Pro-Am)
1 Racing Team Turkey (car 34), 131; **2** AF Corse (88), 101; **3** Nielsen Racing (24), 97; **4** TDS Racing x Vaillante (31), 76; **5** Algarve Pro Racing (47), 59; **6** Team Virage (51), 34; **7** Graff Racing (40), 26.

Teams (LMGTE)
1 Proton Competition (car 77), 82; **2** Kessel Racing (57), 78; **3** Iron Lynx (83), 70; **4** Iron Lynx (60), 63; **5** Oman Racing with TF Sport (69), 59; **6** Absolute Racing (18), 49.

IMSA WeatherTech Sportscar Championship

MOTUL POLE AWARD 100, Daytona International Speedway, Daytona Beach, Florida, USA, 23 January. 61 laps of the 3.560-mile/5.729km circuit, 217.160 miles/ 349.485km.
1 Ricky Taylor/Filipe Albuquerque, USA/P (Acura ARX-05), 1h 40m 45.641s, 129.312mph/ 208.108km/h; **2** Tristan Vautier/Richard Westbrook, F/GB (Cadillac DPi-V.R), +7.900s; **3** Jimmie Johnson/Kamui Kobayashi, USA/J (Cadillac DPi-V.R), +9.569s; **4** Oliver Jarvis/Tom Blomqvist, GB/GB (Acura ARX-05), +15.643s; **5** Renger van der Zande/Sébastien Bourdais, NL/F (Cadillac DPi-V.R), +22.680s; **6** Earl Bamber/ Alex Lynn, NZ/GB (Cadillac DPi-V.R), +25.550s; **7** Pipo Derani/Tristan Nunez, BR/USA (Cadillac DPi-V.R), +56.737s; **8** Ben Keating/Mikkel Jensen, USA/DK (ORECA 07-Gibson), -1 lap; **9** Steven Thomas/Jonathan Bomarito, USA/USA (ORECA 07-Gibson), -1; **10** François Heriau/ René Rast, F/D (ORECA 07-Gibson), -1.
Fastest race lap: Bamber, 1m 34.628s, 135.436mph/217.962km/h.
Pole position: Vautier/Westbrook, 1m 34.034s, 136.291mph/219.339km/h.

IMSA WEATHERTECH SPORTSCAR CHAMPIONSHIP, Daytona International Speedway, Daytona Beach, Florida, USA, 30 January. 761 laps of the 3.560-mile/5.729km circuit, 2709.160 miles/4359.970km.
1 Oliver Jarvis/Tom Blomqvist/Hélio Castroneves/ Simon Pagenaud, GB/GB/BR/F (Acura ARX-05), 24h 00m 23.026s, 112.852mph/181.617km/h; **2** Ricky Taylor/Filipe Albuquerque/Alexander Rossi/Will Stevens, USA/P/USA/GB (Acura ARX-05), +3.028s; **3** Tristan Vautier/Richard Westbrook/ Loïc Duval/Ben Keating, F/GB/F/USA (Cadillac DPi-V.R), +4.420s; **4** Pipo Derani/Tristan Nunez/ Mike Conway, BR/USA/GB (Cadillac DPi-V.R), +5.615s; **5** Eric Lux/Devlin Defrancesco/Patricio O'Ward/Colton Herta, USA/CDN/MEX/USA (ORECA 07-Gibson), -10 laps; **6** Frits van Eerd/Giedo van der Garde/Dylan Murry/Rinus Van Kalmthout, NL/NL/USA/NL (ORECA 07-Gibson), -10; **7** John Farano/Louis Delétraz/Rui Andrade/Ferdinand Habsburg, CDN/CH/P/A (ORECA 07-Gibson), -10; **8** Ben Keating/Mikkel Jensen/Scott Huffaker/Nicolas Lapierre, USA/DK/USA/F (ORECA 07-Gibson), -10; **9** François Heriau/Oliver Rasmussen/Ed Jones/René Rast, F/DK/GB/D (ORECA 07-Gibson), -17; **10** Jim McGuire/Guy Smith/ Phil Hanson/Will Owen, USA/GB/GB/USA (ORECA 07-Gibson), -21.
Fastest race lap: Alex Palou, E (Cadillac DPi-V.R), 1m 33.724s, 136.742mph/220.065km/h.
Pole position: Taylor/Albuquerque/Rossi/Stevens.

70TH ANNUAL MOBIL 1 TWELVE HOURS OF SEBRING PRESENTED BY ADVANCE AUTO PARTS, Sebring International Raceway, Florida, USA, 19 March. 351 laps of the 3.740-mile/6.019km circuit, 1312.740 miles/ 2112.650km.
1 Earl Bamber/Alex Lynn/Neel Jani, NZ/GB/ CH (Cadillac DPi-V.R), 12h 01m 46.148s, 109.127mph/175.623km/h; **2** Tristan Vautier/ Richard Westbrook/Loïc Duval, F/GB/F (Cadillac DPi-V.R), +6.471s; **3** Pipo Derani/Tristan Nunez/ Mike Conway, BR/USA/GB (Cadillac DPi-V.R), +14.616s; **4** Ricky Taylor/Filipe Albuquerque/Will Stevens, USA/P/GB (Acura ARX-05), +26.958s; **5** Oliver Jarvis/Tom Blomqvist/Stoffel Vandoorne, GB/GB/B (Acura ARX-05), +27.621s; **6** Mike Rockenfeller/Kamui Kobayashi/José María López, D/J/RA (Cadillac DPi-V.R), -5 laps; **7** Ben Keating/Mikkel Jensen/Scott Huffaker, USA/DK/USA (ORECA 07-Gibson), -6; **8** Frits van Eerd/Giedo van der Garde/Dylan Murry, NL/NL/USA (ORECA 07-Gibson), -7; **9** Dwight Merriman/Kyle Tilley/ Ryan Dalziel, USA/GB/GB (ORECA 07-Gibson), -7; **10** Steven Thomas/Josh Pierson/Jonathan Bomarito, USA/USA/USA (ORECA 07-Gibson), -8.
Fastest race lap: Conway, 1m 47.018s, 125.811mph/202.473km/h.
Pole position: Renger van der Zande/Sébastien Bourdais/Ryan Hunter-Reay, NL/F/USA (Cadillac DPi-V.R), 1m 45.166s, 128.026mph/ 206.038km/h.

ACURA GRAND PRIX OF LONG BEACH, Long Beach Street Circuit, California, USA, 9 April. 73 laps of the 1.968-mile/3.167km circuit, 143.664 miles/231.205km.
1 Renger van der Zande/Sébastien Bourdais, NL/F (Cadillac DPi-V.R), 1h 40m 48.134s, 85.512mph/137.619km/h; **2** Earl Bamber/ Alex Lynn, NZ/GB (Cadillac DPi-V.R), +3.761s; **3** Tristan Vautier/Richard Westbrook, F/GB (Cadillac DPi-V.R), +9.048s; **4** Oliver Jarvis/Tom Blomqvist, GB/GB (Acura ARX-05), +10.014s; **5** Pipo Derani/Tristan Nunez, BR/USA (Cadillac DPi-V.R), +10.535s; **6** Ricky Taylor/Filipe Albuquerque, USA/P (Acura ARX-05), +11.979s; **7** Ross Gunn/Alex Riberas, GB/E (Aston Martin Vantage AMR GT3), -4 laps; **8** Jack Hawksworth/ Ben Barnicoat, GB/GB (Lexus RC F GT3), -4; **9** Bryan Sellers/Madison Snow, USA/USA (BMW M4 GT3), -4; **10** Antonio García/Jordan Taylor, E/ USA (Chevrolet Corvette C8.R GTD), -4.
Fastest race lap: Bourdais, 1m 10.317s, 100.755mph/162.150km/h.
Pole position: van der Zande/Bourdais, 1m 09.472s, 101.981mph/164.122km/h.

HYUNDAI MONTEREY SPORTS CAR CHAMPIONSHIP PRESENTED BY MOTUL, Mazda Raceway Laguna Seca, Monterey, California, USA, 1 May. 117 laps of the 2.238-mile/3.602km circuit, 261.846 miles/421.400km.
1 Ricky Taylor/Filipe Albuquerque, USA/P (Acura ARX-05), 2h 41m 05.230s, 97.530mph/ 156.959km/h; **2** Oliver Jarvis/Tom Blomqvist, GB/GB (Acura ARX-05), +1.080s; **3** Pipo Derani/Tristan Nunez, BR/USA (Cadillac DPi-V.R), +26.744s; **4** Tristan Vautier/Richard Westbrook, F/GB (Cadillac DPi-V.R), +33.375s; **5** Earl Bamber/Alex Lynn, NZ/GB (Cadillac DPi-V.R), -1 lap; **6** John Farano/Louis Delétraz, CDN/CH (ORECA 07-Gibson), -3; **7** Dwight Merriman/Ryan Dalziel, USA/GB (ORECA 07-Gibson), -3; **8** Henrik Hedman/Juan Pablo Montoya, S/CO (ORECA 07-Gibson), -4; **9** Josh Pierson/Patrick Kelly, USA/USA (ORECA 07-Gibson), -4; **10** Steven Thomas/ Jonathan Bomarito, USA/USA (ORECA 07-Gibson), -4.
Fastest race lap: Blomqvist, 1m 15.546s, 106.648mph/171.633km/h.
Pole position: Taylor/Albuquerque, 1m 13.924s, 108.988mph/175.399km/h.

LEXUS GRAND PRIX AT MID-OHIO, Mid-Ohio Sports Car Course, Lexington, Ohio, USA, 15 May. 121 laps of the 2.258-mile/3.634km circuit, 273.218 miles/439.702km.
1 Ricky Taylor/Filipe Albuquerque, USA/P (Acura ARX-05), 2h 40m 20.108s, 102.243mph/ 164.544km/h; **2** Oliver Jarvis/Tom Blomqvist, GB/GB (Acura ARX-05), +2.098s; **3** Pipo Derani/Tristan Nunez, BR/USA (Cadillac DPi-V.R), +16.910s; **4** Earl Bamber/Alex Lynn, NZ/GB (Cadillac DPi-V.R), +36.916s; **5** Renger van der Zande/Sébastien Bourdais, NL/F (Cadillac DPi-V.R), +37.104s; **6** Tristan Vautier/Richard Westbrook, F/GB (Cadillac DPi-V.R), +1m 02.301s; **7** Henrik Hedman/Juan Pablo Montoya, S/CO (ORECA 07-Gibson), -3 laps; **8** Steven Thomas/ Jonathan Bomarito, USA/USA (ORECA 07-Gibson), -3; **9** Dennis Andersen/Anders Fjordbach, DK/DK (ORECA 07-Gibson), -3; **10** John Farano/ Will Stevens, CDN/GB (ORECA 07-Gibson), -4.
Fastest race lap: Blomqvist, 1m 12.264s, 112.488mph/181.031km/h.
Pole position: van der Zande/Bourdais, 1m 10.439s, 115.402mph/185.721km/h.

CHEVROLET SPORTS CAR CLASSIC, The Raceway at Belle Isle, Detroit, Michigan, USA, 4 June. 73 laps of the 2.350-mile/3.782km circuit, 171.550 miles/276.083km.
1 Renger van der Zande/Sébastien Bourdais, NL/F (Cadillac DPi-V.R), 1h 40m 45.972s, 102.147mph/164.390km/h; **2** Oliver Jarvis/Tom Blomqvist, GB/GB (Acura ARX-05), +0.398s; **3** Earl Bamber/Alex Lynn, NZ/GB (Cadillac DPi-V.R), +0.783s; **4** Ricky Taylor/Filipe Albuquerque, USA/P (Acura ARX-05), +15.942s; **5** Tristan Vautier/Richard Westbrook, F/GB (Cadillac DPi-V.R), +44.888s; **6** Olivier Pla/Pipo Derani, F/BR (Cadillac DPi-V.R), +1.663s *; **7** Ben Barnicoat/ Kyle Kirkwood, GB/USA (Lexus RC F GT3), -6 laps; **8** Roman De Angelis/Ross Gunn, CDN/GB (Aston Martin Vantage AMR GT3), -6; **9** Bryan Sellers/Madison Snow, USA/USA (BMW M4 GT3), -6; **10** Frankie Montecalvo/Aaron Telitz, USA/USA (Lexus RC F GT3), -6.
* Moved to the back of its class for failing to meet the minimum weight requirement.
Fastest race lap: Derani, 1m 18.877s, 107.256mph/172.611km/h.
Pole position: van der Zande/Bourdais, 1m 18.818s, 107.336mph/172.740km/h.

SAHLEN'S SIX HOURS OF THE GLEN, Watkins Glen International, New York, USA, 26 June. 162 laps of the 3.400-mile/5.472km circuit, 550.800 miles/886.427km.
1 Ricky Taylor/Filipe Albuquerque, USA/P (Acura ARX-05), 6h 10m 17.401s, 89.249mph/ 143.632km/h; **2** Oliver Jarvis/Tom Blomqvist, GB/GB (Acura ARX-05), +0.861s; **3** Renger van der Zande/Sébastien Bourdais, NL/F (Cadillac DPi-V.R), +2.267s; **4** Earl Bamber/Alex Lynn, NZ/GB (Cadillac DPi-V.R), +4.176s; **5** Olivier Pla/Pipo Derani/Mike Conway, F/BR/GB (Cadillac DPi-V.R), +4.211s; **6** Mike Rockenfeller/Kamui Kobayashi/Jimmie Johnson, D/J/USA (Cadillac DPi-V.R), -1 lap; **7** Tristan Vautier/Richard Westbrook/Loïc Duval, F/GB/F (Cadillac DPi-V.R), -2; **8** Ben Keating/Mikkel Jensen/Scott Huffaker, USA/ DK/USA (ORECA 07-Gibson), -2; **9** John Farano/ Louis Delétraz/Rui Andrade, CDN/CH/P (ORECA 07-Gibson), -2; **10** Frits van Eerd/Giedo van der Garde/Dylan Murry, NL/NL/USA (ORECA 07-Gibson), -2.
Fastest race lap: Albuquerque, 1m 30.790s, 134.817mph/216.966km/h.
Pole position: Jarvis/Blomqvist, 1m 29.580s, 136.638mph/219.897km/h.

CHEVROLET GRAND PRIX, Mosport International Raceway, Bowmanville, Ontario, Canada, 3 July. 123 laps of the 2.459-mile/3.957km circuit, 302.457 miles/ 486.757km.
1 Renger van der Zande/Sébastien Bourdais, NL/F (Cadillac DPi-V.R), 2h 40m 31.158s, 113.054mph/181.943km/h; **2** Oliver Jarvis/Tom Blomqvist, GB/GB (Acura ARX-05), +3.509s; **3** Olivier Pla/Pipo Derani, F/BR (Cadillac DPi-V.R), +4.272s; **4** Earl Bamber/Alex Lynn, NZ/ GB (Cadillac DPi-V.R), +4.704s; **5** Tristan Vautier/Richard Westbrook, F/GB (Cadillac DPi-V.R), +5.785s; **6** Ricky Taylor/Filipe Albuquerque, USA/P (Acura ARX-05), +15.025s; **7** Jon Bennett/Colin Braun, USA/USA (Ligier JS P320-Nissan), -8 laps; **8** Jarett Andretti/Gabby Chaves, USA/CO (Ligier JS P320-Nissan), -8; **9** Ari Balogh/Garett Grist, USA/CDN (Ligier JS P320-Nissan), -8; **10** Orey Fidani/Kyle Marcelli, CDN/CDN (Duqueine M30-D08-Nissan), -9.
Fastest race lap: Blomqvist, 1m 05.987s, 134.154mph/215.899km/h.
Pole position: Jarvis/Blomqvist, 1m 04.394s, 137.472mph/221.240km/h.

NORTHEAST GRAND PRIX, Lime Rock Park, Lakeville, Connecticut, USA, 16 July. 174 laps of the 1.474-mile/2.372km circuit, 256.476 miles/412.758km.
1 Matt Campbell/Mathieu Jaminet, AUS/F (Porsche 911 GT3 R), 2h 40m 43.134s, 95.748mph/154.092km/h; **2** Ross Gunn/ Alex Riberas, GB/E (Aston Martin Vantage AMR GT3), +1.883s; **3** Jack Hawksworth/Ben Barnicoat, GB/GB (Lexus RC F GT3), +4.078s; **4** Bryan Sellers/Madison Snow, USA/USA (BMW M4 GT3), +8.842s; **5** Roman De Angelis/Maxime Martin, CDN/B (Aston Martin Vantage AMR GT3), +9.473s; **6** Robert Megennis/Jeff Westphal, USA/USA (Lamborghini Huracán GT3 Evo), +9.532s; **7** Mike Skeen/Stevan McAleer, USA/ GB (Mercedes AMG GT3 Evo), +9.641s; **8** Russell Ward/Philip Ellis, USA/GB (Mercedes AMG GT3 Evo), +17.960s; **9** Ryan Hardwick/Jan Heylen, USA/B (Porsche 911 GT3 R), +22.317s; **10** Cooper MacNeil/Jules Gounon, USA/F (Mercedes AMG GT3 Evo), +33.800s.
Fastest race lap: Gounon, 51.733s, 102.573mph/165.075km/h.
Pole position: Campbell/Jaminet, 51.079s, 103.886mph/167.189km/h.

IMSA SPORTS CAR WEEKEND, Road America, Elkhart Lake, Wisconsin, USA, 7 August. 64 laps of the 4.048-mile/6.515km circuit, 259.072 miles/416.936km.
1 Ricky Taylor/Filipe Albuquerque, USA/P (Acura ARX-05), 2h 40m 44.167s, 96.707mph/ 155.635km/h; **2** Earl Bamber/Alex Lynn, NZ/GB (Cadillac DPi-V.R), +1.463s; **3** Renger van der Zande/Sébastien Bourdais, NL/F (Cadillac DPi-V.R), +1.981s; **4** Oliver Jarvis/Tom Blomqvist, GB/GB (Acura ARX-05), +3.819s; **5** Tristan Vautier/Richard Westbrook, F/GB (Cadillac DPi-V.R), +7.003s; **6** Olivier Pla/Pipo Derani, F/BR (Cadillac DPi-V.R), +7.189s; **7** Dwight Merriman/Ryan Dalziel, USA/GB (ORECA 07-Gibson), +19.642s; **8** John Farano/Louis Delétraz, CDN/CH (ORECA 07-Gibson), +20.358s; **9** Dennis Andersen/ Fabio Scherer, DK/CH (ORECA 07-Gibson), +21.147s; **10** Steven Thomas/Tristan Nunez, USA/USA (ORECA 07-Gibson), +21.944s.
Fastest race lap: Lynn, 1m 51.636s, 130.539mph/210.081km/h.
Pole position: Taylor/Albuquerque, 1m 48.915s, 133.800mph/215.330km/h.

MICHELIN GT CHALLENGE AT VIR, Virginia International Raceway, Alton, Virginia, USA, 28 August. 86 laps of the 3.270-mile/5.263km circuit, 281.220 miles/452.580km.
1 Matt Campbell/Mathieu Jaminet, AUS/F (Porsche 911 GT3 R), 2h 40m 37.906s, 105.043mph/ 169.050km/h; **2** Antonio García/Jordan Taylor, E/ USA (Chevrolet Corvette C8.R GTD), +0.823s; **3** Russell Ward/Philip Ellis, USA/GB (Mercedes AMG GT3 Evo), +4.463s; **4** Roman De Angelis/ Maxime Martin, CDN/B (Aston Martin Vantage AMR GT3), +10.799s; **5** Bryan Sellers/Madison Snow, USA/USA (BMW M4 GT3), +12.960s; **6** Frankie Montecalvo/Aaron Telitz, USA/USA (Lexus RC F GT3), +14.475s; **7** Ryan Hardwick/Jan Heylen, USA/B (Porsche 911 GT3 R), +15.136s; **8** Cooper MacNeil/Jules Gounon, USA/F (Mercedes AMG GT3 Evo), +15.454s; **9** Jack Hawksworth/Ben Barnicoat, GB/GB (Lexus RC F GT3), +18.029s; **10** Robby Foley/Bill Auberlen, USA/ USA (BMW M4 GT3), +25.791s.
Fastest race lap: Taylor, 1m 45.455s, 111.631mph/179.652km/h.
Pole position: Ross Gunn/Alex Riberas, GB/E (Aston Martin Vantage AMR GT3), 1m 43.953s, 113.243mph/182.248km/h.

MOTUL PETIT LE MANS, Road Atlanta Motorsports Center, Braselton, Georgia, USA, 1 October. 423 laps of the 2.540-mile/4.088km circuit, 1074.420 miles/1729.111km.
1 Oliver Jarvis/Tom Blomqvist/Hélio Castroneves, GB/GB/BR (Acura ARX-05), 10h 00m 14.591s, 107.398mph/172.841km/h; **2** Olivier Pla/Pipo Derani/Mike Conway, F/BR/GB (Cadillac DPi-V.R), +4.369s; **3** Mike Rockenfeller/Kamui Kobayashi/Jimmie Johnson, D/J/USA (Cadillac DPi-V.R), -1 lap; **4** Renger van der Zande/Sébastien Bourdais/Scott Dixon, NL/F/NZ (Cadillac DPi-V.R), -4; **5** John Farano/Louis Delétraz/Rui Andrade, CDN/CH/P (ORECA 07-Gibson), -5; **6** Henrik Hedman/Juan Pablo Montoya/Sebastian Montoya, S/CO/CO (ORECA 07-Gibson), -5; **7** Steven Thomas/Josh Pierson/Tristan Nunez, USA/USA/ USA (ORECA 07-Gibson), -5; **8** Earl Bamber/ Alex Lynn/Ryan Hunter-Reay, NZ/GB/USA (Cadillac DPi-V.R), -5; **9** Ricky Taylor/Filipe Albuquerque/Brendon Hartley, USA/P/NZ (Acura ARX-05), -9; **10** Dennis Andersen/Anders Fjordbach/Fabio Scherer, DK/DK/CH (ORECA 07-Gibson), -9.
Fastest race lap: Bamber, 1m 09.664s, 131.259mph/211.240km/h.
Pole position: Jarvis/Blomqvist/Castroneves, 1m 08.555s, 133.382mph/214.657km/h.

Final championship points.
Drivers (Daytona Prototype international)
1 Oliver Jarvis, GB, 3432; **1** Tom Blomqvist, GB, 3432; **2** Filipe Albuquerque, P, 3346; **2** Ricky Taylor, USA, 3346; **3** Renger van der Zande, NL, 3220; **3** Sébastien Bourdais, F, 3220; **4** Alex Lynn, GB, 3191; **4** Earl Bamber, NZ, 3191; **5** Pipo Derani, BR, 3083; **6** Richard Westbrook, GB, 2979; **6** Tristan Vautier, F, 2979; **7** Tristan Nunez, USA, 1575; **8** Olivier Pla, F, 1508; **9** Mike Conway, GB, 1266; **10** Loïc Duval, F, 1209.

Drivers (Le Mans Prototype 2)
1 John Farano, CDN, 2018; **2** Dwight Merriman, USA, 1892; **2** Ryan Dalziel, GB, 1892; **3** Steven Thomas, USA, 1882.

Drivers (Le Mans Prototype 3)
1 Colin Braun, USA, 2002; **1** Jon Bennett, USA, 2002; **2** Gar Robinson, USA, 1948; **3** Ari Balogh, USA, 1942; **3** Garett Grist, CDN, 1942.

Drivers (GT Daytona Pro)
1 Mathieu Jaminet, F, 3497; **1** Matt Campbell, AUS, 3497; **2** Ben Barnicoat, GB, 3277; **3** Antonio García, E, 3194; **3** Jordan Taylor, USA, 3194.

Drivers (GT Daytona)
1 Roman De Angelis, CDN, 2898; **2** Jan Heylen, B, 2875; **2** Ryan Hardwick, USA, 2875; **3** Stevan McAleer, GB, 2860.

Manufacturers (Daytona Prototype international)
1 Acura, 3718; **2** Cadillac, 3652.

Manufacturers (GT Daytona Pro)
1 Porsche, 3497; **2** Lexus, 3307; **3** Chevrolet, 3204.

Manufacturers (GT Daytona)
1 BMW, 3307; **2** Mercedes, 3235; **3** Aston Martin, 3193.

Teams (Daytona Prototype international)
1 Meyer Shank Racing with Curb-Agajanian (car 60), 3432; **2** Konica Minolta Acura (10), 3346; **3** Cadillac Racing (01), 3220.

Teams (Le Mans Prototype 2)
1 Tower Motorsport (car 8), 2018; **2** PR1/Mathiasen Motorsports (52), 1939; **3** Era Motorsport (18), 1892.

Teams (Le Mans Prototype 3)
1 CORE Autosport (car 54), 2002; **2** Riley Motorsports (74), 1948; **3** Jr III Racing (30), 1942.

Teams (GT Daytona Pro)
1 Pfaff Motorsports (car 9), 3497; **2** Vasser Sullivan (14), 3277; **3** Corvette Racing (3), 3194.

Teams (GT Daytona)
1 Heart of Racing Team (car 27), 2898; **2** Wright Motorsports (16), 2875; **3** Gilbert Korthoff Motorsports (32), 2860.

Autobacs Super GT Series (Japan)

OKAYAMA GT 300KM RACE, Okayama International Circuit (TI Circuit Aida), Aida Gun, Okayama Prefecture, Japan, 17 April. Round 1. 82 laps of the 2.301-mile/3.703km circuit, 188.677 miles/303.646km.
1 Kazuya Oshima/Kenta Yamashita, J/J (Toyota GR Supra), 1h 58m 54.464s, 95.205mph/153.217km/h; **2** Naoki Yamamoto/Tadasuke Makino, J/J (Honda NSX-GT), +1.798s; **3** Tsugio Matsuda/Ronnie Quintarelli, J/I (Nissan Fairlady Z), +3.478s; **4** Yuji Tachikawa/Hiroaki Ishiura, J/J (Toyota GR Supra), +9.761s; **5** Katsumasa Chiyo/Mitsunori Takaboshi, J/J (Nissan Fairlady Z), +11.701s; **6** Sho Tsuboi/Giuliano Alesi, J/F (Toyota GR Supra), +13.534s; **7** Kazuki Hiramine/Bertrand Baguette, J/B (Nissan Fairlady Z), +20.789s; **8** Yuhi Sekiguchi/Yuichi Nakayama, J/J (Toyota GR Supra), +20.943s; **9** Koudai Tsukakoshi/Nobuharu Matsushita, J/J (Honda NSX-GT), +24.697s; **10** Tomoki Nojiri/Nirei Fukuzumi, J/J (Honda NSX-GT), +25.339s.
Fastest race lap: Oshima, 1m 20.632s, 102.730mph/165.328km/h.
Pole position: Oshima/Yamashita, 1m 17.251s, 107.226mph/172.564km/h.

FUJI GT 450KM RACE, Fuji International Speedway, Sunto-gun, Shizuoka Prefecture, Japan, 4 May. Round 2. 62 laps of the 2.835-mile/4.563km circuit, 175.790 miles/282.906km.
1 Tomoki Nojiri/Nirei Fukuzumi, J/J (Honda NSX-GT), 3h 45m 40.807s, 46.735mph/75.214km/h; **2** Sho Tsuboi/Giuliano Alesi, J/F (Toyota GR Supra), +2.570s; **3** Kazuki Hiramine/Bertrand Baguette, J/B (Nissan Fairlady Z), +3.151s; **4** Tsugio Matsuda/Ronnie Quintarelli, J/I (Nissan Fairlady Z), +3.614s; **5** Naoki Yamamoto/Tadasuke Makino, J/J (Honda NSX-GT), +4.326s; **6** Yuji Kunimoto/Sena Sakaguchi, J/J (Toyota GR Supra), +4.522s; **7** Kazuya Oshima/Kenta Yamashita, J/J (Toyota GR Supra), +4.781s; **8** Daiki Sasaki/Kohei Hirate, J/J (Nissan Fairlady Z), +4.913s; **9** Koudai Tsukakoshi/Nobuharu Matsushita, J/J (Honda NSX-GT), +5.534s; **10** Ukyo Sasahara/Toshiki Oyu, J/J (Honda NSX-GT), +5.701s.
Fastest race lap: Tsuboi, 1m 28.803s, 114.941mph/184.980km/h.
Pole position: Kunimoto/Sakaguchi, 1m 26.137s, 118.498mph/190.705km/h.

SUZUKA GT 300KM RACE, Suzuka International Racing Course, Suzuka-shi, Mie Prefecture, Japan, 29 May. Round 3. 52 laps of the 3.608-mile/5.807km circuit, 187.632 miles/301.964km.
1 Katsumasa Chiyo/Mitsunori Takaboshi, J/J (Nissan Fairlady Z), 1h 55m 50.895s, 97.178mph/156.392km/h; **2** Koudai Tsukakoshi/Nobuharu Matsushita, J/J (Honda NSX-GT), +4.549s; **3** Sacha Fenestraz/Ritomo Miyata, F/J (Toyota GR Supra), +4.832s; **4** Yuhi Sekiguchi/Yuichi Nakayama, J/J (Toyota GR Supra), +4.880s; **5** Yuji Kunimoto/Sena Sakaguchi, J/J (Toyota GR Supra), +8.357s; **6** Daiki Sasaki/Kohei Hirate, J/J (Nissan Fairlady Z), +10.429s; **7** Tomoki Nojiri/Nirei Fukuzumi, J/J (Honda NSX-GT), +10.472s; **8** Kazuya Oshima/Kenta Yamashita, J/J (Toyota GR Supra), +13.278s; **9** Naoki Yamamoto/Tadasuke Makino, J/J (Honda NSX-GT), +14.304s; **10** Sho Tsuboi/Giuliano Alesi, J/F (Toyota GR Supra), +15.362s.
Fastest race lap: Chiyo, 1m 48.055s, 120.215mph/193.468km/h.
Pole position: Kunimoto/Sakaguchi, 1m 44.112s, 124.768mph/200.795km/h.

FUJI GT 450KM RACE, Fuji International Speedway, Sunto-gun, Shizuoka Prefecture, Japan, 7 August. Round 4. 99 laps of the 2.835-mile/4.563km circuit, 280.696 miles/451.737km.
1 Sacha Fenestraz/Ritomo Miyata, F/J (Toyota GR Supra), 2h 34m 24.270s, 109.075mph/175.540km/h; **2** Kazuki Hiramine/Bertrand Baguette, J/B (Nissan Fairlady Z), +7.542s; **3** Daiki Sasaki/Kohei Hirate, J/J (Nissan Fairlady Z), +12.863s; **4** Sho Tsuboi/Giuliano Alesi, J/F (Toyota GR Supra), +15.822s; **5** Tomoki Nojiri/Nirei Fukuzumi, J/J (Honda NSX-GT), +41.978s; **6** Yuhi Sekiguchi/Yuichi Nakayama, J/J (Toyota GR Supra), +45.334s; **7** Kazuya Oshima/Kenta Yamashita, J/J (Toyota GR Supra), +47.184s; **8** Naoki Yamamoto/Tadasuke Makino, J/J (Honda NSX-GT), +1m 08.814s; **9** Yuji Kunimoto/Sena Sakaguchi, J/J (Toyota GR Supra), +1m 24.628s; **10** Koudai Tsukakoshi/Nobuharu Matsushita, J/J (Honda NSX-GT), -1 lap.
Fastest race lap: Fenestraz/Miyata, 1m 29.948s, 113.478mph/182.625km/h.
Pole position: Kunimoto/Sakaguchi, 1m 26.178s, 118.442mph/190.614km/h.

SUZUKA GT 450KM RACE, Suzuka International Racing Course, Suzuka-shi, Mie Prefecture, Japan, 28 August. Round 5. 77 laps of the 3.608-mile/5.807km circuit, 277.839 miles/447.139km.
1 Kazuki Hiramine/Bertrand Baguette, J/B (Nissan Fairlady Z), 2h 35m 39.339s, 107.097mph/172.356km/h; **2** Koudai Tsukakoshi/Nobuharu Matsushita, J/J (Honda NSX-GT), +6.630s; **3** Yuhi Sekiguchi/Yuichi Nakayama, J/J (Toyota GR Supra), +7.747s; **4** Katsumasa Chiyo/Mitsunori Takaboshi, J/J (Nissan Fairlady Z), +8.257s; **5** Tsugio Matsuda/Ronnie Quintarelli, J/I (Nissan Fairlady Z), +13.747s; **6** Ukyo Sasahara/Toshiki Oyu, J/J (Honda NSX-GT), +33.508s; **7** Yuji Kunimoto/Sena Sakaguchi, J/J (Toyota GR Supra), +48.668s; **8** Sacha Fenestraz/Ritomo Miyata, F/J (Toyota GR Supra), +49.750s; **9** Sho Tsuboi/Giuliano Alesi, J/F (Toyota GR Supra), +1m 27.350s; **10** Daiki Sasaki/Kohei Hirate, J/J (Nissan Fairlady Z), +1m 30.122s.
Fastest race lap: Quintarelli, 1m 48.910s, 119.271mph/191.949km/h.
Pole position: Matsuda/Quintarelli, 1m 45.169s, 123.514mph/198.777km/h.

SUGO GT 300KM RACE, Sportsland-SUGO International Course, Shibata-gun, Miyagi Prefecture, Japan, 18 September. Round 6. 84 laps of the 2.228-mile/3.586km circuit, 187.172 miles/301.224km.
1 Katsumasa Chiyo/Mitsunori Takaboshi, J/J (Nissan Fairlady Z), 1h 58m 41.824s, 94.613mph/152.265km/h; **2** Tsugio Matsuda/Ronnie Quintarelli, J/I (Nissan Fairlady Z), +9.114s; **3** Ukyo Sasahara/Toshiki Oyu, J/J (Honda NSX-GT), +46.720s; **4** Yuji Tachikawa/Hiroaki Ishiura, J/J (Toyota GR Supra), +1m 05.148s; **5** Kazuki Hiramine/Bertrand Baguette, J/B (Nissan Fairlady Z), -1 lap; **6** Yuhi Sekiguchi/Yuichi Nakayama, J/J (Toyota GR Supra), -1; **7** Takuya Izawa/Hiroki Ohtsu, J/J (Honda NSX-GT), -1; **8** Naoki Yamamoto/Tadasuke Makino, J/J (Honda NSX-GT), -1; **9** Sacha Fenestraz/Ritomo Miyata, F/J (Toyota GR Supra), -1; **10** Sho Tsuboi/Giuliano Alesi, J/F (Toyota GR Supra), -1 *.
* 80s penalty.
Fastest race lap: Tachikawa, 1m 13.194s, 109.594mph/176.375km/h.
Pole position: Yuji Kunimoto/Sena Sakaguchi, J/J (Toyota GR Supra), 1m 09.627s, 115.208mph/185.410km/h.

AUTOPOLIS GT 300KM RACE, Autopolis International Racing Course, Kamit-sue-mura, Hita-gun, Oita Prefecture, Japan, 2 October. Round 7. 65 laps of the 2.904-mile/4.674km circuit, 188.779 miles/303.810km.
1 Koudai Tsukakoshi/Nobuharu Matsushita, J/J (Honda NSX-GT), 1h 54m 02.414s, 99.322mph/159.843km/h; **2** Naoki Yamamoto/Tadasuke Makino, J/J (Honda NSX-GT), +13.162s; **3** Daiki Sasaki/Kohei Hirate, J/J (Nissan Fairlady Z), +13.453s; **4** Kazuya Oshima/Kenta Yamashita, J/J (Toyota GR Supra), +19.045s; **5** Yuji Kunimoto/Sena Sakaguchi, J/J (Toyota GR Supra), +19.621s; **6** Kazuki Hiramine/Bertrand Baguette, J/B (Nissan Fairlady Z), +20.348s; **7** Katsumasa Chiyo/Mitsunori Takaboshi, J/J (Nissan Fairlady Z), +31.560s; **8** Sho Tsuboi/Giuliano Alesi, J/F (Toyota GR Supra), +38.330s; **9** Sacha Fenestraz/Ritomo Miyata, F/J (Toyota GR Supra), +39.762s; **10** Yuhi Sekiguchi/Yuichi Nakayama, J/J (Toyota GR Supra), +40.849s.
Fastest race lap: Sasaki, 1m 35.854s, 109.076mph/175.541km/h.
Pole position: Sasaki/Hirate, 1m 31.679s, 114.044mph/183.536km/h.

MOTEGI GT 300KM RACE, Twin Ring Motegi, Motegi-machi, Haga-gun, Tochigi Prefecture, Japan, 6 November. Round 8. 63 laps of the 2.983-mile/4.801km circuit, 187.957 miles/302.487km.
1 Naoki Yamamoto/Tadasuke Makino, J/J (Honda NSX-GT), 2h 04m 58.929s, 90.232mph/145.214km/h; **2** Kazuki Hiramine/Bertrand Baguette, J/B (Nissan Fairlady Z), +1.212s; **3** Kazuya Oshima/Kenta Yamashita, J/J (Toyota GR Supra), +1.888s; **4** Katsumasa Chiyo/Mitsunori Takaboshi, J/J (Nissan Fairlady Z), +2.795s; **5** Koudai Tsukakoshi/Nobuharu Matsushita, J/J (Honda NSX-GT), +16.005s; **6** Sacha Fenestraz/Ritomo Miyata, F/J (Toyota GR Supra), +26.476s; **7** Yuji Kunimoto/Sena Sakaguchi, J/J (Toyota GR Supra), +33.939s; **8** Tomoki Nojiri/Nirei Fukuzumi, J/J (Honda NSX-GT), +40.295s; **9** Sho Tsuboi/Giuliano Alesi, J/F (Toyota GR Supra), +45.265s; **10** Yuji Tachikawa/Hiroaki Ishiura, J/J (Toyota GR Supra), +50.036s.
Fastest race lap: Makino, 1m 38.350s, 109.205mph/175.749km/h.
Pole position: Yamamoto/Makino, 1m 35.194s, 112.826mph/181.576km/h.

Final championship points
Drivers (GT500)
1 Kazuki Hiramine, J, 70.5; 1 Bertrand Baguette, B, 70.5; **2** Katsumasa Chiyo, J, 66; **2** Mitsunori Takaboshi, J, 66; **3** Naoki Yamamoto, J, 62; **3** Tadasuke Makino, J, 62; **4** Koudai Tsukakoshi, J, 60; **4** Nobuharu Matsushita, J, 60; **5** Kazuya Oshima, J, 49; **5** Kenta Yamashita, J, 49; **6** Sacha Fenestraz, F, 43; **6** Ritomo Miyata, J, 43; **7** Ronnie Quintarelli, I, 37; **7** Tsugio Matsuda, J, 37; **8** Yuichi Nakayama, J, 33; **8** Yuhi Sekiguchi, J, 33; **9** Daiki Sasaki, J, 30.5; **9** Kohei Hirate, J, 30.5; **10** Giuliano Alesi, F, 29.5; **10** Sho Tsuboi, J, 29.5.

Drivers (GT300)
1 João Paulo de Oliveira, BR, 52; **1** Kiyoto Fujinami, J, 52; **2** Takuto Iguchi, J, 49.5; **2** Hideki Yamauchi, J, 49.5; **3** Riki Okusa, J, 49.

Teams (GT500)
1 Team Impul (car 12), 89; **2** NDDP Racing (3), 86.5; **3** Team Kunimitsu (100), 81.5.

Teams (GT300)
1 Kondo Racing (car 56), 74.5; **2** Gainer (10), 68.5; **3** R&D Sport (61), 68.

Other Sports Car races

ADAC-ZüRICH-24H-RENNEN, Nürburgring, Nürburg/Eifel, Germany, 28 May. 159 laps of the 15.769-mile/25.378km circuit, 2507.296 miles/4035.102km.
1 Kelvin van der Linde/Dries Vanthoor/Frédéric Vervisch/Robin Frijns, ZA/B/B/NL (Audi R8 LMS Evo2), 24h 06m 41.822s, 103.987mph/167.351km/h; **2** Adam Christodoulou/Maximilian Götz/Fabian Schiller, GB/D/D (Mercedes AMG GT3), +55.276s; **3** Maro Engel/Jules Gounon/Daniel Juncadella, D/F/E (Mercedes AMG GT3), +4m 05.519s; **4** Christopher Haase/Nico Müller/Patric Niederhauser/René Rast, D/CH/CH/D (Audi R8 LMS Evo2), +5m 12.864s; **5** Kuba Giermaziak/Kim-Luis Schramm/Michele Beretta/Markus Winkelhock, PL/D/I/D (Audi R8 LMS Evo2), +7m 25.468s; **6** Patrick Kolb/Mattia Drudi/Christopher Mies/Patric Niederhauser, D/I/D/CH (Audi R8 LMS Evo2), +7m 33.159s; **7** Raffaele Marciello/Philip Ellis/Luca Stolz, I/GB/D (Mercedes AMG GT3), -1 lap; **8** Hubert Haupt/Gabriele Piana/Nico Bastian, D/I/D (Mercedes AMG GT3), -1; **9** Jaxon Evans/Sven Müller/Patrick Pilet/Marco Seefried, NZ/D/F/D (Porsche 911 GT3 R), -2; **10** Axcil Jefferies/Jordan Pepper/Michele Di Martino, ZW/ZA/D (Lamborghini Huracán GT3 Evo), -3.
Fastest race lap: Marciello/Ellis/Stolz, 8m 11.639s, 115.469mph/185.829km/h.
Pole position: Björn Grossmann/Simon Trummer/Jonathan Hirschi/Luca Ludwig, D/CH/CH/D (Ferrari 488 GT3 Evo), 8m 09.469s, 115.981mph/186.653km/h.

SPA 24 HOURS, Circuit de Spa-Francorchamps, Stavelot, Belgium, 30 July. 536 laps of the 4.352-mile/7.004km circuit, 2332.717 miles/3754.144km.
1 Raffaele Marciello/Daniel Juncadella/Jules Gounon, I/E/F (Mercedes AMG GT3), 536 laps; **2** Maximilian Götz/Steijn Schothorst/Luca Stolz, D/NL/D (Mercedes AMG GT3), 536; **3** Davide Rigon/Daniel Serra/Antonio Fuoco, I/BR/I (Ferrari 488 GT3), 536; **4** Maro Engel/Mikaël Grenier/Maximilian Buhk, D/CDN/D (Mercedes AMG GT3), 536; **5** Neil Verhagen/Max Hesse/Daniel Harper, USA/D/GB (BMW M4 GT3), 536; **6** Augusto Farfus/Nick Yelloly/Nicky Catsburg, BR/GB/NL (BMW M4 GT3), 536; **7** Nick Tandy/Laurens Vanthoor/Dennis Olsen, GB/B/N (Porsche 911 GT3 R), 536; **8** Rob Bell/Ollie Wilkinson/Marvin Kirchhöfer, GB/GB/D (McLaren 720S GT3), 536; **9** Miguel Molina/Nicklas Nielsen/James Calado, E/DK/GB (Ferrari 488 GT3), -1; **10** Maxime Martin/Marco Sørensen/Nicki Thiim, B/DK/DK (Aston Martin Vantage AMR GT3), -2.
Fastest race lap: Stefano Costantini/Louis Machiels/Andrea Bertolini/Alessio Rovera, I/B/I/I (Ferrari 488 GT3), 2m 17.480s, 113.962mph/183.404km/h.
Pole position: Marciello/Juncadella/Gounon, 2m 16.375s, 114.885mph/184.890km/h.

Repco Supercars Championship

Cars are: Holden Commodore ZB; Ford Mustang

BEAUREPAIRES SYDNEY SUPER600, Sydney Motorsport Park, Eastern Creek, New South Wales, Australia, 5/6 March. Round 1. 2 x 77 laps of the 2.442-mile/3.930km circuit.
Race 1 (188.033 miles/302.610km).
1 Shane van Gisbergen, NZ (Holden), 2h 03m 01.4868s, 91.705mph/147.584km/h; **2** Anton De Pasquale, AUS (Ford), +19.5575s; **3** Chaz Mostert, AUS (Holden), +31.0525s; **4** Will Davison, AUS (Ford), +37.5003s; **5** Brodie Kostecki, AUS (Holden), +38.8060s; **6** Nick Percat, AUS (Holden), +39.3928s; **7** William Brown, AUS (Holden), +41.1128s; **8** Tim Slade, AUS (Ford), +50.7901s; **9** Broc Feeney, AUS (Holden), +52.4770s; **10** James Courtney, AUS (Ford), +54.5231s.
Fastest race lap: Andre Heimgartner, NZ (Holden), 1m 31.6249s, 95.947mph/154.412km/h.
Pole position: Pasquale, 1m 29.3599s, 98.379mph/158.326km/h.

Race 2 (188.033 miles/302.610km).
1 Chaz Mostert, AUS (Holden), 2h 15m 28.2868s, 83.279mph/134.025km/h; **2** Brodie Kostecki, AUS (Holden), +2.7663s; **3** Anton De Pasquale, AUS (Ford), +4.4336s; **4** Cameron Waters, AUS (Ford), +4.9738s; **5** Andre Heimgartner, NZ (Holden), +6.8468s; **6** Shane van Gisbergen, NZ (Holden), +7.8728s; **7** Will Davison, AUS (Ford), +9.3467s; **8** William Brown, AUS (Holden), +9.8057s; **9** David Reynolds, AUS (Ford), +10.7733s; **10** Tim Slade, AUS (Ford), +11.5799s.
Fastest race lap: Broc Feeney, AUS (Holden), 1m 32.0958s, 95.456mph/153.622km/h.
Pole position: Kostecki, 1m 39.5216s, 88.334mph/142.160km/h.

TASMANIA SUPERSPRINT, Symmons Plains Raceway, Launceston, Tasmania, Australia, 26/27 March. Round 2. 3 x 44 laps of the 1.491-mile/2.400km circuit.
Race 3 (65.617 miles/105.600km).
1 Shane van Gisbergen, NZ (Holden), 38m 54.6722s, 101.179mph/162.832km/h; **2** Will Davison, AUS (Ford), +2.8302s; **3** Cameron Waters, AUS (Ford), +6.2856s; **4** Brodie Kostecki, AUS (Holden), +8.8610s; **5** Broc Feeney, AUS (Holden), +11.6976s; **6** Anton De Pasquale, AUS (Ford), +13.7417s; **7** Scott Pye, AUS (Holden), +16.0783s; **8** Andre Heimgartner, NZ (Holden), +16.1006s; **9** Lee Holdsworth, AUS (Ford), +19.0540s; **10** Todd Hazelwood, AUS (Holden), +19.3518s.
Fastest race lap: David Reynolds, AUS (Ford), 51.6935s, 103.855mph/167.139km/h.
Pole position: Waters, 50.5363s, 106.233mph/170.966km/h.

Race 4 (65.617 miles/105.600km).
1 Shane van Gisbergen, NZ (Holden), 58m 56.1767s, 66.801mph/107.505km/h; **2** Broc Feeney, AUS (Holden), +2.4175s; **3** David Reynolds, AUS (Ford), +3.7173s; **4** Chaz Mostert, AUS (Holden), +4.2382s; **5** Anton De Pasquale, AUS (Ford), +9.0123s; **6** Mark Winterbottom, AUS (Holden), +11.5154s; **7** Scott Pye, AUS (Holden), +14.5569s; **8** James Courtney, AUS (Ford), +17.4306s; **9** Lee Holdsworth, AUS (Ford), +17.6979s; **10** Todd Hazelwood, AUS (Holden), +19.3207s.
Fastest race lap: van Gisbergen, 51.6528s, 103.937mph/167.270km/h.
Pole position: van Gisbergen, 50.4840s, 106.343mph/171.143km/h.

Race 5 (65.617 miles/105.600km).
1 Shane van Gisbergen, NZ (Holden), 39m 08.3251s, 100.591mph/161.885km/h; **2** Will Davison, AUS (Ford), +1.1882s; **3** Anton De Pasquale, AUS (Ford), +2.7833s; **4** David Reynolds, AUS (Ford), +3.1970s; **5** Todd Hazelwood, AUS (Holden), +5.9936s; **6** Cameron Waters, AUS (Ford), +7.5416s; **7** Mark Winterbottom, AUS (Holden), +9.6794s; **8** Broc Feeney, AUS (Holden), +10.3647s; **9** James Courtney, AUS (Ford), +11.6524s; **10** Nick Percat, AUS (Holden), +15.4170s.

Fastest race lap: van Gisbergen, 52.0117s, 103.219mph/166.116km/h.
Pole position: Davison, 50.5515s, 106.201mph/170.914km/h.

MELBOURNE 400, Albert Park Circuit, Melbourne, Victoria, Australia, 8/10 April. Round 3. 20, 19, 20 and 20 laps of the 3.280-mile/5.278km circuit.
Race 6 (65.592 miles/105.560km).
1 Chaz Mostert, AUS (Holden), 37m 15.6301s, 105.621mph/169.981km/h; **2** David Reynolds, AUS (Ford), +7.6838s; **3** Shane van Gisbergen, NZ (Holden), +9.4731s; **4** Tim Slade, AUS (Ford), +11.1534s; **5** Nick Percat, AUS (Holden), +13.0285s; **6** Macauley Jones, AUS (Holden), +17.9486s; **7** Mark Winterbottom, AUS (Holden), +18.2434s; **8** Broc Feeney, AUS (Holden), +24.7155s; **9** Garry Jacobson, AUS (Holden), +29.4764s; **10** Bryce Fullwood, AUS (Holden), +31.5081s.
Fastest race lap: William Brown, AUS (Holden), 1m 46.8130s, 110.534mph/177.888km/h.
Pole position: Reynolds, 1m 45.6781s, 111.721mph/179.798km/h.

Race 7 (62.312 miles/100.282km).
1 Shane van Gisbergen, NZ (Holden), 41m 54.8962s, 89.198mph/143.550km/h; **2** David Reynolds, AUS (Ford), +2.0375s; **3** Lee Holdsworth, AUS (Ford), +7.0899s; **4** Scott Pye, AUS (Holden), +9.9748s; **5** Todd Hazelwood, AUS (Holden), +12.9927s; **6** Garry Jacobson, AUS (Holden), +13.4971s; **7** Brodie Kostecki, AUS (Holden), +14.4582s; **8** Tim Slade, AUS (Ford), +14.6946s; **9** James Courtney, AUS (Ford), +15.2008s; **10** Bryce Fullwood, AUS (Holden), +16.8638s.
Fastest race lap: van Gisbergen, 1m 46.6866s, 110.665mph/178.099km/h.
Pole position: Will Davison, AUS (Ford), 1m 44.9418s, 112.505mph/181.060km/h.

Race 8 (65.592 miles/105.560km).
1 Shane van Gisbergen, NZ (Holden), 36m 51.5320s, 106.772mph/171.833km/h; **2** Will Davison, AUS (Ford), +5.6474s; **3** David Reynolds, AUS (Ford), +6.5366s; **4** Anton De Pasquale, AUS (Ford), +10.6672s; **5** Chaz Mostert, AUS (Holden), +13.2716s; **6** Broc Feeney, AUS (Holden), +13.5495s; **7** Tim Slade, AUS (Ford), +15.8526s; **8** Cameron Waters, AUS (Ford), +21.2471s; **9** James Courtney, AUS (Ford), +23.1066s; **10** Garry Jacobson, AUS (Holden), +24.3597s.
Fastest race lap: Scott Pye, AUS (Holden), 1m 46.0060s, 111.376mph/179.242km/h.
Pole position: Pasquale, 1m 45.8031s, 111.589mph/179.586km/h.

Race 9 (65.592 miles/105.560km).
1 Chaz Mostert, AUS (Holden), 39m 09.2815s, 100.512mph/161.758km/h; **2** Will Davison, AUS (Ford), +5.2168s; **3** Anton De Pasquale, AUS (Ford), +6.8791s; **4** Tim Slade, AUS (Ford), +8.1296s; **5** Brodie Kostecki, AUS (Holden), +8.7869s; **6** Nick Percat, AUS (Holden), +9.6997s; **7** Cameron Waters, AUS (Ford), +12.6092s *; **8** William Brown, AUS (Holden), +12.6759s; **9** Mark Winterbottom, AUS (Holden), +13.9282s; **10** Lee Holdsworth, AUS (Ford), +15.6673s.
* 5s penalty.
Fastest race lap: Todd Hazelwood, AUS (Holden), 1m 46.3008s, 111.067mph/178.745km/h.
Pole position: Davison, 1m 45.3792s, 112.038mph/180.308km/h.

BUNNINGS TRADE PERTH SUPERNIGHT, Barbagallo Raceway Wanneroo, Perth, Western Australia, Australia, 30 April/1 May. Round 4. 3 x 46 laps of the 1.504-mile/2.420km circuit.
Race 10 (69.171 miles/111.320km).
1 Shane van Gisbergen, NZ (Holden), 42m 58.7302s, 96.565mph/155.406km/h; **2** Anton De Pasquale, AUS (Ford), +2.3077s; **3** Cameron Waters, AUS (Ford), +7.3180s; **4** David Reynolds, AUS (Ford), +12.3540s; **5** Broc Feeney, AUS (Holden), +14.0598s; **6** Will Davison, AUS (Ford), +15.9682s; **7** James Courtney, AUS (Ford), +21.7293s; **8** Brodie Kostecki, AUS (Holden), +22.5669s; **9** Todd Hazelwood, AUS (Holden), +22.8757s; **10** Andre Heimgartner, NZ (Holden), +26.3838s.
Fastest race lap: van Gisbergen, 54.7858s, 98.810mph/159.019km/h.
Pole position: Pasquale, 53.5982s, 100.999mph/162.542km/h.

Race 11 (69.171 miles/111.320km).
1 Will Davison, AUS (Ford), 1h 41m 34.0509s, 40.862mph/65.761km/h; **2** Anton De Pasquale, AUS (Ford), +2.0984s; **3** Andre Heimgartner, NZ (Holden), +2.5291s; **4** Cameron Waters, AUS (Ford), +3.5909s *; **5** Shane van Gisbergen, NZ (Holden), +4.2602s; **6** Brodie Kostecki, AUS (Holden), +5.7866s; **7** James Courtney, AUS (Ford), +6.7384s; **8** Broc Feeney, AUS (Holden), +6.9346s; **9** Jake Kostecki, AUS (Ford), +7.3494s; **10** Todd Hazelwood, AUS (Holden), +7.6989s.
* 5s penalty.
Fastest race lap: Heimgartner, 55.3024s, 97.886mph/157.533km/h.
Pole position: Davison, 53.6293s, 100.940mph/162.448km/h.

Race 12 (69.171 miles/111.320km).
1 Shane van Gisbergen, NZ (Holden), 46m 06.4143s, 90.013mph/144.863km/h; **2** James Courtney, AUS (Ford), +1.9130s; **3** Will Davison, AUS (Ford), +2.2131s; **4** Anton De Pasquale, AUS (Ford), +2.4760s; **5** William Brown, AUS (Holden), +4.2573s; **6** David Reynolds, AUS (Ford), +5.2374s; **7** Cameron Waters, AUS (Ford), +5.5096s; **8** Todd Hazelwood, AUS (Holden), +5.9719s; **9** Andre Heimgartner, NZ (Holden), +6.4009s; **10** Tim Slade, AUS (Ford), +6.8339s.
Fastest race lap: van Gisbergen, 54.8584s, 98.679mph/158.808km/h.
Pole position: van Gisbergen, 53.4632s, 101.254mph/162.953km/h.

PIZZA HUT WINTON SUPERSPRINT, Winton Motor Raceway, Benalla, Victoria, Australia, 21/22 May. Round 5. 3 x 36 laps of the 1.864-mile/3.000km circuit.
Race 13 (67.108 miles/108.000km).
1 Cameron Waters, AUS (Ford), 49m 10.3624s, 81.884mph/131.780km/h; **2** Shane van Gisbergen, NZ (Holden), +0.4000s; **3** David Reynolds, AUS (Ford), +3.0329s; **4** Chaz Mostert, AUS (Holden), +11.3465s; **5** Lee Holdsworth, AUS (Ford), +15.9295s; **6** Scott Pye, AUS (Holden), +18.0761s; **7** Brodie Kostecki, AUS (Holden), +20.7115s; **8** Anton De Pasquale, AUS (Ford), +22.7910s; **9** Andre Heimgartner, NZ (Holden), +22.9426s; **10** Broc Feeney, AUS (Holden), +25.5335s.
Fastest race lap: Reynolds, 1m 19.9093s, 83.980mph/135.153km/h.
Pole position: van Gisbergen, 1m 18.2644s, 85.745mph/137.993km/h.

Race 14 (67.108 miles/108.000km).
1 Shane van Gisbergen, NZ (Holden), 49m 18.2907s, 81.665mph/131.427km/h; **2** Cameron Waters, AUS (Ford), +5.2987s; **3** David Reynolds, AUS (Ford), +8.5425s; **4** Lee Holdsworth, AUS (Ford), +15.0572s; **5** Chaz Mostert, AUS (Holden), +19.9167s; **6** William Brown, AUS (Holden), +21.8308s; **7** Andre Heimgartner, NZ (Holden), +21.9690s; **8** James Courtney, AUS (Ford), +24.8262s; **9** Mark Winterbottom, AUS (Holden), +24.9473s; **10** Anton De Pasquale, AUS (Ford), +26.8026s.
Fastest race lap: Courtney, 1m 20.0046s, 83.880mph/134.992km/h.
Pole position: Waters, 1m 18.5503s, 85.433mph/137.491km/h.

Race 15 (67.108 miles/108.000km).
1 Cameron Waters, AUS (Ford), 49m 11.5491s, 81.851mph/131.727km/h; **2** Shane van Gisbergen, NZ (Holden), +0.4422s; **3** Andre Heimgartner, NZ (Holden), +10.7326s; **4** David Reynolds, AUS (Ford), +15.2561s; **5** William Brown, AUS (Holden), +25.5654s; **6** Lee Holdsworth, AUS (Ford), +27.7565s; **7** Broc Feeney, AUS (Holden), +28.7059s; **8** Anton De Pasquale, AUS (Ford), +29.0243s; **9** Mark Winterbottom, AUS (Holden), +34.1904s; **10** Will Davison, AUS (Ford), +35.4370s.
Fastest race lap: van Gisbergen, 1m 20.1318s, 83.747mph/134.777km/h.
Pole position: Waters, 1m 18.3425s, 85.659mph/137.856km/h.

MERLIN DARWIN TRIPLE CROWN, Hidden Valley Raceway, Darwin, Northern Territory, Australia, 18/19 June. Round 6. 38, 37 and 38 laps of the 1.783-mile/2.870km circuit.
Race 16 (67.767 miles/109.060km).
1 Anton De Pasquale, AUS (Ford), 43m 47.1156s, 92.862mph/149.447km/h; **2** Will Davison, AUS (Ford), +1.1831s; **3** Shane van Gisbergen, NZ (Holden), +1.4784s; **4** Andre Heimgartner, NZ (Holden), +6.6768s; **5** Mark Winterbottom, AUS (Holden), +14.4053s; **6** Scott Pye, AUS (Holden), +18.3171s; **7** Cameron Waters, AUS (Ford), +19.3786s; **8** Broc Feeney, AUS (Holden), +23.9295s; **9** James Courtney, AUS (Ford), +24.4053s; **10** Brodie Kostecki, AUS (Holden), +24.9411s.
Disqualified: Chaz Mostert, AUS, finished 3rd.
Fastest race lap: van Gisbergen, 1m 07.2234s, 95.502mph/153.696km/h.
Pole position: Davison, 1m 04.9542s, 98.838mph/159.065km/h.

Race 17 (65.983 miles/106.190km).
1 Cameron Waters, AUS (Ford), 56m 57.8420s, 69.500mph/111.849km/h; **2** Will Davison, AUS (Ford), +0.6170s; **3** Shane van Gisbergen, NZ (Holden), +1.8496s; **4** Anton De Pasquale, AUS (Ford), +2.7476s; **5** David Reynolds, AUS (Ford), +3.6527s; **6** Jack Le Brocq, AUS (Holden), +10.5375s; **7** Mark Winterbottom, AUS (Holden), +11.0661s; **8** Chaz Mostert, AUS (Holden), +12.2348s; **9** Andre Heimgartner, NZ (Holden), +12.6211s; **10** Nick Percat, AUS (Holden), +17.3743s.
Fastest race lap: Reynolds, 1m 07.3003s, 95.393mph/153.520km/h.
Pole position: Waters, 1m 05.2552s, 98.383mph/158.332km/h.

Race 18 (67.767 miles/109.060km).
1 Chaz Mostert, AUS (Holden), 47m 06.0030s, 86.326mph/138.929km/h; **2** Anton De Pasquale, AUS (Ford), +0.9580s; **3** Cameron Waters, AUS (Ford), +1.1035s; **4** Will Davison, AUS (Ford), +1.4933s; **5** Andre Heimgartner, NZ (Holden), +3.3056s; **6** Broc Feeney, AUS (Holden), +3.3158s; **7** William Brown, AUS (Holden), +8.8692s; **8** Jake Kostecki, AUS (Ford), +9.0464s; **9** Mark Winterbottom, AUS (Holden), +9.2514s; **10** Nick Percat, AUS (Holden), +9.3879s.
Fastest race lap: Davison, 1m 07.0532s, 95.744mph/154.086km/h.
Pole position: Davison, 1m 04.8114s, 99.056mph/159.416km/h.

NTI TOWNSVILLE 500, Townsville Street Circuit, Queensland, Australia, 9/10 July. Round 7. 2 x 88 laps of the 1.777-mile/2.860km circuit.
Race 19 (156.387 miles/251.680km).
1 Shane van Gisbergen, NZ (Holden), 1h 52m 39.1086s, 83.293mph/134.048km/h; **2** Will Davison, AUS (Ford), +5.1967s; **3** Cameron Waters, AUS (Ford), +20.4891s; **4** Andre Heimgartner, NZ (Holden), +21.0855s; **5** Scott Pye, AUS (Holden), +29.9100s; **6** Anton De Pasquale, AUS (Ford), +31.7876s; **7** Broc Feeney, AUS (Holden), +47.6101s; **8** Tim Slade, AUS (Ford), +49.0992s; **9** Chaz Mostert, AUS (Holden), +53.3283s; **10** Jack Le Brocq, AUS (Holden), +56.1749s.
Fastest race lap: Lee Holdsworth, AUS (Ford), 1m 13.7195s, 86.783mph/139.664km/h.
Pole position: van Gisbergen, 1m 13.3674s, 87.200mph/140.334km/h.

Race 20 (156.387 miles/251.680km).
1 Shane van Gisbergen, NZ (Holden), 1h 54m 58.0390s, 81.616mph/131.348km/h; **2** Anton De Pasquale, AUS (Ford), +4.4989s *; **3** Cameron Waters, AUS (Ford), +6.1402s; **4** James Courtney, AUS (Ford), +12.7414s; **5** Chaz Mostert, AUS (Holden), +14.0978s; **6** Broc Feeney, AUS (Holden), +18.1361s; **7** Will Davison, AUS (Ford), +30.0153s; **8** Tim Slade, AUS (Ford), +40.7548s; **9** Andre Heimgartner, NZ (Holden), +43.4468s; **10** Mark Winterbottom, AUS (Holden), +44.3432s.
* 5s penalty.
Fastest race lap: Davison, 1m 13.7668s, 86.727mph/139.574km/h.
Pole position: Waters, 1m 13.8604s, 86.617mph/139.398km/h.

OTR SUPERSPRINT, The Bend Motorsport Park, Tailem Bend, South Australia, 30/31 July. Round 8. 24, 18 and 24 laps of the 3.073-mile/4.945km circuit.
Race 21 (73.744 miles/118.680km).
1 Shane van Gisbergen, NZ (Holden), 45m 08.7762s, 98.007mph/157.727km/h; **2** Will Davison, AUS (Ford), +2.2227s; **3** Chaz Mostert, AUS (Holden), +4.0888s; **4** Cameron Waters, AUS (Ford), +10.4553s; **5** Zak Best, AUS (Ford), +10.8632s; **6** Brodie Kostecki, AUS (Holden), +11.4282s; **7** Broc Feeney, AUS (Holden), +11.7643s; **8** David Reynolds, AUS (Ford), +13.2936s; **9** Anton De Pasquale, AUS (Ford), +13.7233s; **10** Andre Heimgartner, NZ (Holden), +14.4812s.
Fastest race lap: van Gisbergen, 1m 50.1133s, 100.456mph/161.669km/h.
Pole position: Best, 1m 47.8168s, 102.596mph/165.113km/h.

Race 22 (55.308 miles/89.010km).
1 Shane van Gisbergen, NZ (Holden), 34m 00.4156s, 97.582mph/157.044km/h; **2** Chaz Mostert, AUS (Holden), +2.5737s; **3** James Courtney, AUS (Ford), +3.4936s; **4** Cameron Waters, AUS (Ford), +4.3036s; **5** Anton De Pasquale, AUS (Ford), +7.8496s; **6** Broc Feeney, AUS (Holden), +8.3776s; **7** William Brown, AUS (Holden), +12.2901s; **8** David Reynolds, AUS (Ford), +12.4195s; **9** Mark Winterbottom, AUS (Holden), +20.0378s; **10** Bryce Fullwood, AUS (Holden), +20.7462s.
Fastest race lap: van Gisbergen, 1m 50.1787s, 100.397mph/161.573km/h.
Pole position: Waters, 1m 48.3481s, 102.093mph/164.303km/h.

Race 23 (73.744 miles/118.680km).
1 Shane van Gisbergen, NZ (Holden), 56m 35.1526s, 78.193mph/125.840km/h; **2** Cameron Waters, AUS (Ford), +8.7109s; **3** Brodie Kostecki, AUS (Holden), +17.2306s; **4** Will Davison, AUS (Ford), +25.5051s; **5** Broc Feeney, AUS (Holden), +31.8322s; **6** William Brown, AUS (Holden), +32.6306s; **7** Anton De Pasquale, AUS (Ford), +32.8623s; **8** Chaz Mostert, AUS (Holden), +33.3410s; **9** Nick Percat, AUS (Holden), +34.8295s; **10** Lee Holdsworth, AUS (Ford), +38.4134s.
Fastest race lap: van Gisbergen, 2m 06.7465s, 87.273mph/140.453km/h.
Pole position: Waters, 1m 48.3372s, 102.103mph/164.320km/h.

PENRITE OIL SANDOWN SUPERSPRINT, Sandown International Motor Raceway, Melbourne, Victoria, Australia, 20/21 August. Round 9. 3 x 36 laps of the 1.926-mile/3.100km circuit.
Race 24 (69.345 miles/111.600km).
1 Will Davison, AUS (Ford), 41m 58.7286s, 99.114mph/159.509km/h; **2** Shane van Gisbergen, NZ (Holden), +8.4920s; **3** Anton De Pasquale, AUS (Ford), +9.0175s; **4** William Brown, AUS (Holden), +15.3172s; **5** Cameron Waters, AUS (Ford), +15.5330s; **6** James Courtney, AUS (Ford), +15.7716s; **7** Scott Pye, AUS (Holden), +16.2331s; **8** Mark Winterbottom, AUS (Holden), +16.6513s; **9** Tom Randle, AUS (Ford), +17.6355s; **10** Chaz Mostert, AUS (Holden), +18.2569s.
Fastest race lap: Broc Feeney, AUS (Holden), 1m 08.4474s, 101.311mph/163.044km/h.
Pole position: Davison, 1m 07.6500s, 102.505mph/164.966km/h.

Race 25 (69.345 miles/111.600km).
1 Shane van Gisbergen, NZ (Holden), 42m 03.8337s, 98.913mph/159.186km/h; **2** Chaz Mostert, AUS (Holden), +7.5168s; **3** William Brown, AUS (Holden), +11.9971s; **4** David Reynolds, AUS (Ford), +13.9855s; **5** Scott Pye, AUS (Holden), +16.1845s; **6** Andre Heimgartner, NZ (Holden), +16.1860s; **7** Cameron Waters, AUS (Ford), +27.5696s; **8** Anton De Pasquale, AUS (Ford), +28.5089s; **9** James Golding, AUS (Holden), +31.3972s; **10** Broc Feeney, AUS (Holden), +33.5710s.
Fastest race lap: van Gisbergen, 1m 08.6630s, 100.993mph/162.532km/h.
Pole position: van Gisbergen, 1m 07.4467s, 102.814mph/165.463km/h.

Race 26 (69.345 miles/111.600km).
1 Shane van Gisbergen, NZ (Holden), 42m 06.0656s, 98.826mph/159.045km/h; **2** Will Davison, AUS (Ford), +0.4611s; **3** Broc Feeney, AUS (Holden), +11.8048s; **4** Chaz Mostert, AUS (Holden), +15.2635s; **5** Mark Winterbottom, AUS (Holden), +15.4090s; **6** Tim Slade, AUS (Ford), +16.9619s; **7** Scott Pye, AUS (Holden), +18.5781s; **8** Tom Randle, AUS (Ford), +22.3954s; **9** David Reynolds, AUS (Ford), +24.0920s; **10** Cameron Waters, AUS (Ford), +25.7157s.
Fastest race lap: Davison, 1m 08.6132s, 101.066mph/162.650km/h.
Pole position: Davison, 1m 07.2078s, 103.180mph/166.052km/h.

ITM AUCKLAND SUPERSPRINT, Pukekohe Park Raceway, Auckland, New Zealand, 10/11 September. Round 10. 41, 36 and 41 laps of the 1.808-mile/2.910km circuit.
Race 27 (74.136 miles/119.310km).
1 Will Davison, AUS (Ford), 48m 16.5957s, 92.138mph/148.283km/h; **2** Andre Heimgartner, NZ (Holden), +0.8650s; **3** Cameron Waters, AUS (Ford), +1.7629s; **4** Chaz Mostert, AUS (Holden), +2.5772s; **5** Shane van Gisbergen, NZ (Holden), +2.8857s; **6** Anton De Pasquale, AUS (Ford), +4.7146s; **7** Broc Feeney, AUS (Holden), +5.2480s; **8** Nick Percat, AUS (Holden), +5.8731s; **9** David Reynolds, AUS (Ford), +6.8853s; **10** Scott Pye, AUS (Holden), +7.9966s.
Fastest race lap: van Gisbergen, 1m 02.9504s, 103.406mph/166.416km/h.
Pole position: Waters, 1m 01.9984s, 104.994mph/168.972km/h.

Race 28 (65.095 miles/104.760km).
1 Shane van Gisbergen, NZ (Holden), 1h 01m 06.3736s, 63.916mph/102.863km/h; **2** Chaz Mostert, AUS (Holden), +2.3985s; **3** Cameron Waters, AUS (Ford), +4.4748s; **4** Will Davison, AUS (Ford), +6.9475s; **5** Scott Pye, AUS (Holden), +11.8097s; **6** Andre Heimgartner, NZ (Holden), +12.2090s; **7** David Reynolds, AUS (Ford), +19.7578s; **8** Broc Feeney, AUS (Holden), +22.0980s; **9** Jake Kostecki, AUS (Ford), +23.7598s; **10** James Golding, AUS (Holden), +24.1541s.
Fastest race lap: van Gisbergen, 1m 03.3351s,

102.778mph/165.405km/h.
Pole position: van Gisbergen, 1m 02.1092s, 104.807mph/168.670km/h.

Race 29 (74.136 miles/119.310km).
1 Shane van Gisbergen, NZ (Holden), 54m 40.0655s, 81.366mph/130.947km/h; **2** Cameron Waters, AUS (Ford), +1.1160s; **3** Andre Heimgartner, NZ (Holden), +1.6265s; **4** Broc Feeney, AUS (Holden), +3.2136s; **5** Anton De Pasquale, AUS (Ford), +5.6266s; **6** Chaz Mostert, AUS (Holden), +6.2275s; **7** Scott Pye, AUS (Holden), +7.4169s; **8** David Reynolds, AUS (Ford), +8.5180s; **9** Nick Percat, AUS (Holden), +12.6317s; **10** Tim Slade, AUS (Ford), +12.9635s.
Fastest race lap: van Gisbergen, 1m 03.0287s, 103.278mph/166.209km/h.
Pole position: Will Davison, AUS (Ford), 1m 01.9211s, 105.125mph/169.183km/h.

REPCO BATHURST 1000, Mount Panorama, Bathurst, New South Wales, Australia, 9 October. Round 11. 161 laps of the 3.861-mile/6.213km circuit.
Race 30 (621.553 miles/1000.293km).
1 Shane van Gisbergen/Garth Tander, NZ/AUS (Holden), 6h 41m 53.7221s, 92.793mph/149.336km/h; **2** Chaz Mostert/Fabian Coulthard, AUS/NZ (Holden), +1.0991s; **3** Cameron Waters/James Moffat, AUS/AUS (Ford), +5.9875s; **4** Brodie Kostecki/David Russell, AUS/AUS (Holden), +10.1572s; **5** Broc Feeney/Jamie Whincup, AUS/AUS (Holden), +15.0853s; **6** Lee Holdsworth/Matthew Payne, AUS/NZ (Ford), +15.7835s; **7** Anton De Pasquale/Tony D'Alberto, AUS/AUS (Ford), +18.8110s; **8** Craig Lowndes/Declan Fraser, AUS/AUS (Holden), +19.7505s; **9** Bryce Fullwood/Dean Fiore, AUS/AUS (Holden), +21.7230s; **10** William Brown/Jack Perkins, AUS/AUS (Holden), +22.6732s.
Fastest race lap: van Gisbergen/Tander, 2m 06.2663s, 110.069mph/177.139km/h.
Pole position: Waters/Moffat, 2m 23.6168s, 96.772mph/155.739km/h.

BOOST MOBILE GOLD COAST 500, Surfer's Paradise Street Circuit, Queensland, Australia, 29/30 October. Round 12. 2 x 85 laps of the 1.854-mile/2.984km circuit.
Race 31 (157.605 miles/253.640km).
1 Shane van Gisbergen, NZ (Holden), 1h 43m 27.5354s, 91.401mph/147.096km/h; **2** David Reynolds, AUS (Ford), +16.8514s; **3** Chaz Mostert, AUS (Holden), +17.7941s; **4** Will Davison, AUS (Ford), +18.1125s; **5** Cameron Waters, AUS (Ford), +32.5661s; **6** Anton De Pasquale, AUS (Ford), +34.4391s; **7** Brodie Kostecki, AUS (Holden), +34.9309s; **8** James Courtney, AUS (Ford), +42.6231s; **9** Mark Winterbottom, AUS (Holden), +58.9575s; **10** Nick Percat, AUS (Holden), +1m 06.1061s.
Fastest race lap: Reynolds, 1m 11.0219s, 93.985mph/151.254km/h.
Pole position: Reynolds, 1m 10.4319s, 94.772mph/152.521km/h.

Race 32 (157.605 miles/253.640km).
1 Shane van Gisbergen, NZ (Holden), 2h 19m 20.3212s, 67.865mph/109.218km/h; **2** Chaz Mostert, AUS (Holden), +2.1096s; **3** Will Davison, AUS (Ford), +3.5022s; **4** David Reynolds, AUS (Ford), +5.3727s; **5** Brodie Kostecki, AUS (Holden), +8.3008s; **6** Mark Winterbottom, AUS (Holden), +10.4124s; **7** Cameron Waters, AUS (Ford), +12.2384s; **8** Andre Heimgartner, NZ (Holden), +13.3424s; **9** Chris Pither, NZ (Holden), +14.1626s; **10** Tim Slade, AUS (Ford), +15.2888s.
Disqualified: Anton De Pasquale, AUS (Ford), failed to meet minimum tyre pressure requirement – finished 10th.
Fastest race lap: van Gisbergen, 1m 10.7908s, 94.292mph/151.748km/h.
Pole position: van Gisbergen, 1m 10.3133s, 94.932mph/152.779km/h.

Provisional championship points
1 Shane van Gisbergen, NZ, 3382; **2** Cameron Waters, AUS, 2722; **3** Chaz Mostert, AUS, 2547; **4** Will Davison, AUS, 2429; **5** Anton De Pasquale, AUS, 2407; **6** Broc Feeney, AUS, 2137; **7** David Reynolds, AUS, 2000; **8** Brodie Kostecki, AUS, 1932; **9** Mark Winterbottom, AUS, 1735; **10** Andre Heimgartner, NZ, 1682; **11** Tim Slade, AUS, 1678; **12** William Brown, AUS, 1573; **13** Lee Holdsworth, AUS, 1572; **14** James Courtney, AUS, 1565; **15** Scott Pye, AUS, 1449; **16** Nick Percat, AUS, 1436; **17** Bryce Fullwood, AUS, 1329; **18** Todd Hazelwood, AUS, 1303; **19** Jack Le Brocq, AUS, 1186; **20** Macauley Jones, AUS, 1174.

Teams
1 Red Bull Ampol Racing, 5519; **2** Shell V-Power Racing, 4836; **3** Monster Energy Racing & Opposite Lock Racing, 4287; **4** Mobil 1 Optus Racing & Mobil 1 NTI Racing, 3953; **5** Penrite Racing, 3572.

Results of the Adelaide races will be given in AUTOCOURSE 2023–2024.

Race cancelled: Newcastle, 20 November (due to the Covid-19 pandemic).

FIA World Touring Car Cup

FIA WORLD TOURING CAR CUP, Circuit de Pau Ville, Pau, France, 8 May. 23 and 21 laps of the 1.715-mile/2.760km circuit.
Round 1 (39.445 miles/63.480km).
1 Néstor Girolami, RA (Honda Civic Type-R TCR), 32m 03.148s, 73.837mph/118.830km/h; **2** Esteban Guerrieri, RA (Honda Civic Type-R TCR), +1.239s; **3** Yvan Muller, F (Lynk & Co 03 TCR), +2.314s; **4** Yann Ehrlacher, F (Lynk & Co 03 TCR), +2.991s; **5** Ma Qinghua, CHN (Lynk & Co 03 TCR), +6.001s; **6** Mikel Azcona, E (Hyundai Elantra N TCR), +6.285s; **7** Santiago Urrutia, U (Lynk & Co 03 TCR), +7.149s; **8** Gilles Magnus, B (Audi RS 3 LMS TCR), +10.280s; **9** Norbert Michelisz, H (Hyundai Elantra N TCR), +11.178s; **10** Mehdi Bennani, MA (Audi RS 3 LMS TCR), +11.634s.
Fastest race lap: Rob Huff, GB (Cupra León Competición TCR), 1m 22.293s, 75.023mph/120.739km/h.
Pole position: Girolami, 1m 19.783s, 77.384mph/124.537km/h.

Round 2 (36.015 miles/57.960km).
1 Mikel Azcona, E (Hyundai Elantra N TCR), 31m 55.170s, 67.697mph/108.949km/h; **2** Santiago Urrutia, U (Lynk & Co 03 TCR), +3.876s; **3** Ma Qinghua, CHN (Lynk & Co 03 TCR), +4.378s; **4** Nathanaël Berthon, F (Audi RS 3 LMS TCR), +6.563s; **5** Esteban Guerrieri, RA (Honda Civic Type-R TCR), +7.679s; **6** Yvan Muller, F (Lynk & Co 03 TCR), +8.406s; **7** Néstor Girolami, RA (Honda Civic Type-R TCR), +9.168s; **8** Rob Huff, GB (Cupra León Competición TCR), +9.455s; **9** Thed Björk, S (Lynk & Co 03 TCR), +10.147s; **10** Tiago Monteiro, P (Honda Civic Type-R TCR), +12.235s.
Fastest race lap: Azcona, 1m 21.331s, 75.911mph/122.167km/h.
Pole position: Michelisz.

FIA WORLD TOURING CAR CUP, Nürburgring, Nürburg/Eifel, Germany, 28 May. 2 x 3 laps of the 15.769-mile/25.378km circuit.

Both races were cancelled due to concerns over tyre safety.

Round 3 (47.307 miles/76.134km).
Pole position: Mehdi Bennani, MA (Audi RS 3 LMS TCR), 8m 50.527s, 107.004mph/172.207km/h.

Round 4 (47.307 miles/76.134km).

FIA WORLD TOURING CAR CUP, Hungaroring, Mogyoród, Budapest, Hungary, 12 June. 17 and 14 laps of the 2.722-mile/4.381km circuit.
Round 5 (46.278 miles/74.477km).
1 Mikel Azcona, E (Hyundai Elantra N TCR), 32m 38.095s, 85.082mph/136.927km/h; **2** Yann Ehrlacher, F (Lynk & Co 03 TCR), +1.895s; **3** Nathanaël Berthon, F (Audi RS 3 LMS TCR), +3.331s; **4** Gilles Magnus, B (Audi RS 3 LMS TCR), +4.829s; **5** Ma Qinghua, CHN (Lynk & Co 03 TCR), +5.259s; **6** Rob Huff, GB (Cupra León Competición TCR), +6.076s; **7** Néstor Girolami, RA (Honda Civic Type-R TCR), +11.483s; **8** Santiago Urrutia, U (Lynk & Co 03 TCR), +12.098s; **9** Esteban Guerrieri, RA (Honda Civic Type-R TCR), +15.109s; **10** Yvan Muller, F (Lynk & Co 03 TCR), +15.974s.
Fastest race lap: Azcona, 1m 53.163s, 86.600mph/139.370km/h.
Pole position: Azcona, 1m 52.020s, 87.484mph/140.792km/h.

Round 6 (38.111 miles/61.334km).
1 Santiago Urrutia, U (Lynk & Co 03 TCR), 28m 10.696s, 81.150mph/130.598km/h; **2** Rob Huff, GB (Cupra León Competición TCR), +0.380s; **3** Néstor Girolami, RA (Honda Civic Type-R TCR), +2.428s; **4** Norbert Michelisz, H (Hyundai Elantra N TCR), +3.173s; **5** Ma Qinghua, CHN (Lynk & Co 03 TCR), +5.880s; **6** Yann Ehrlacher, F (Lynk & Co 03 TCR), +6.518s; **7** Gilles Magnus, B (Audi RS 3 LMS TCR), +8.649s; **8** Mikel Azcona, E (Hyundai Elantra N TCR), +9.930s; **9** Yvan Muller, F (Lynk & Co 03 TCR), +10.250s; **10** Esteban Guerrieri, RA (Honda Civic Type-R TCR), +12.872s.
Fastest race lap: Huff, 1m 53.875s, 86.059mph/138.499km/h.
Pole position: Urrutia.

FIA WORLD TOURING CAR CUP, Ciudad del Motor de Aragón, Alcañiz, Aragon, Spain, 26 June. 16 and 12 laps of the 3.321-mile/5.345km circuit.
Round 7 (53.140 miles/85.520km).
1 Gilles Magnus, B (Audi RS 3 LMS TCR), 34m 09.551s, 93.338mph/150.214km/h; **2** Rob Huff, GB (Cupra León Competición TCR), +0.393s; **3** Mikel Azcona, E (Hyundai Elantra N TCR), +4.869s; **4** Nathanaël Berthon, F (Audi RS 3 LMS TCR), +9.351s *; **5** Yann Ehrlacher, F (Lynk & Co 03 TCR), +9.655s; **6** Norbert Michelisz, H (Hyundai Elantra N TCR), +10.548s *; **7** Yvan Muller, F (Lynk & Co 03 TCR), +16.558s; **8** Santiago Urrutia, U (Lynk & Co 03 TCR), +18.960s; **9** Thed Björk, S (Lynk & Co 03 TCR), +19.990s; **10** Mehdi Bennani, MA (Audi RS 3 LMS TCR), +20.571s.
* 5s penalty for causing a collision
Fastest race lap: Magnus, 2m 06.320s, 94.651mph/152.327km/h.
Pole position: Magnus, 2m 05.485s, 95.281mph/153.341km/h.

Round 8 (39.855 miles/64.140km).
1 Mikel Azcona, E (Hyundai Elantra N TCR), 27m 31.604s, 86.871mph/139.805km/h; **2** Rob Huff, GB (Cupra León Competición TCR), +0.802s; **3** Santiago Urrutia, U (Lynk & Co 03 TCR), +5.633s; **4** Dániel Nagy, H (Cupra León Competición TCR), +7.868s; **5** Yann Ehrlacher, F (Lynk & Co 03 TCR), +8.755s; **6** Ma Qinghua, CHN (Lynk & Co 03 TCR), +10.057s; **7** Yvan Muller, F (Lynk & Co 03 TCR), +12.525s; **8** Nathanaël Berthon, F (Audi RS 3 LMS TCR), +13.440s; **9** Mehdi Bennani, MA (Audi RS 3 LMS TCR), +13.810s; **10** Thed Björk, S (Lynk & Co 03 TCR), +17.014s.
Fastest race lap: Huff, 2m 07.880s, 93.497mph/150.469km/h.
Pole position: Ma.

FIA WORLD TOURING CAR CUP, Circuito Internacional de Vila Real, Portugal, 3 July. 16 and 15 laps of the 2.976-mile/4.790km circuit.
Round 9 (47.622 miles/76.640km).
1 Santiago Urrutia, U (Lynk & Co 03 TCR), 32m 55.515s, 86.781mph/139.661km/h; **2** Yann Ehrlacher, F (Lynk & Co 03 TCR), +0.264s; **3** Néstor Girolami, RA (Honda Civic Type-R TCR), +5.236s; **4** Norbert Michelisz, H (Hyundai Elantra N TCR), +5.911s; **5** Ma Qinghua, CHN (Lynk & Co 03 TCR), +6.651s; **6** Rob Huff, GB (Cupra León Competición TCR), +7.103s; **7** Mehdi Bennani, MA (Audi RS 3 LMS TCR), +14.495s; **8** Mikel Azcona, E (Hyundai Elantra N TCR), +14.693s; **9** Attila Tassi, H (Honda Civic Type-R TCR), +16.463s; **10** Nathanaël Berthon, F (Audi RS 3 LMS TCR), +22.489s.
Fastest race lap: Urrutia, 2m 01.999s, 87.827mph/141.345km/h.
Pole position: Urrutia, 1m 59.626s, 89.570mph/144.149km/h.

Round 10 (44.646 miles/71.850km).
1 Rob Huff, GB (Cupra León Competición TCR), 34m 41.616s, 77.211mph/124.259km/h; **2** Attila Tassi, H (Honda Civic Type-R TCR), +0.388s; **3** Mikel Azcona, E (Hyundai Elantra N TCR), +0.935s; **4** Yvan Muller, F (Lynk & Co 03 TCR), +1.474s; **5** Norbert Michelisz, H (Hyundai Elantra N TCR), +2.644s; **6** Mehdi Bennani, MA (Audi RS 3 LMS TCR), +3.435s; **7** Ma Qinghua, CHN (Lynk & Co 03 TCR), +3.916s; **8** Yann Ehrlacher, F (Lynk & Co 03 TCR), +5.125s; **9** Néstor Girolami, RA (Honda Civic Type-R TCR), +7.000s; **10** Santiago Urrutia, U (Lynk & Co 03 TCR), +7.305s.
Fastest race lap: Huff, 2m 01.525s, 88.170mph/141.896km/h.
Pole position: Muller.

FIA WORLD TOURING CAR CUP, Autodromo Vallelunga Piero Taruffi, Campagnano di Roma, Italy, 24 July. 22 and 21 laps of the 2.006-mile/3.228km circuit.
Round 11 (44.127 miles/71.016km).
1 Néstor Girolami, RA (Honda Civic Type-R TCR), 31m 21.344s, 84.438mph/135.890km/h; **2** Mikel Azcona, E (Hyundai Elantra N TCR), +0.248s; **3** Gilles Magnus, B (Audi RS 3 LMS TCR), +1.788s; **4** Norbert Michelisz, H (Hyundai Elantra N TCR), +2.099s; **5** Attila Tassi, H (Honda Civic Type-R TCR), +6.706s; **6** Tom Coronel, NL (Audi RS 3 LMS TCR), +12.152s; **7** Esteban Guerrieri, RA (Honda Civic Type-R TCR), +59.004s; **8** Rob Huff, GB (Cupra León Competición TCR), -1 lap; **9** Nathanaël Berthon, F (Audi RS 3 LMS TCR), -1; **10** Mehdi Bennani, MA (Audi RS 3 LMS TCR), -1.
Fastest race lap: Berthon, 1m 15.763s, 95.308mph/153.383km/h.
Pole position: Girolami, 1m 14.811s, 96.520mph/155.335km/h.

Round 12 (42.122 miles/67.788km).
1 Gilles Magnus, B (Audi RS 3 LMS TCR), 27m 10.386s, 93.007mph/149.680km/h; **2** Nathanaël Berthon, F (Audi RS 3 LMS TCR), +1.409s; **3** Mikel Azcona, E (Hyundai Elantra N TCR), +1.783s; **4** Norbert Michelisz, H (Hyundai Elantra N TCR), +11.857s; **5** Néstor Girolami, RA (Honda Civic Type-R TCR), +12.768s; **6** Rob Huff, GB (Cupra León Competición TCR), +13.366s; **7** Tom Coronel, NL (Audi RS 3 LMS TCR), +20.291s; **8** Attila Tassi, H (Honda Civic Type-R TCR), +55.093s; **9** Mehdi Bennani, MA (Audi RS 3 LMS TCR), +1m 04.012s; **10** Esteban Guerrieri, RA (Honda Civic Type-R TCR), +1m 12.993s.
Fastest race lap: Magnus, 1m 16.464s, 94.434mph/151.977km/h.
Pole position: Ehrlacher.

FIA WORLD TOURING CAR CUP, Anneau du Rhin, Biltzheim, Haut-Rhin, France, 7 August. 22 and 18 laps of the 2.249-mile/3.620km circuit.
Round 13 (49.486 miles/79.640km).
1 Nathanaël Berthon, F (Audi RS 3 LMS TCR), 32m 59.625s, 89.991mph/144.827km/h; **2** Néstor Girolami, RA (Honda Civic Type-R TCR), +0.299s; **3** Mikel Azcona, E (Hyundai Elantra N TCR), +1.047s; **4** Norbert Michelisz, H (Hyundai Elantra N TCR), +1.586s; **5** Rob Huff, GB (Cupra León Competición TCR), +2.408s; **6** Tom Coronel, NL (Audi RS 3 LMS TCR), +4.603s; **7** Gilles Magnus, B (Audi RS 3 LMS TCR), +5.660s *; **8** Dániel Nagy, H (Cupra León Competición TCR), +5.946s; **9** Tiago Monteiro, P (Honda Civic Type-R TCR), +6.505s; **10** Esteban Guerrieri, RA (Honda Civic Type-R TCR), +1m 04.602s.
* 5s penalty
Fastest race lap: Guerrieri, 1m 28.347s, 91.658mph/147.509km/h.
Pole position: Girolami, 1m 26.546s, 93.565mph/150.578km/h.

Round 14 (40.489 miles/65.160km).
1 Rob Huff, GB (Cupra León Competición TCR), 26m 53.763s, 90.322mph/145.359km/h; **2** Mehdi Bennani, MA (Audi RS 3 LMS TCR), +0.896s; **3** Mikel Azcona, E (Hyundai Elantra N TCR), +1.114s; **4** Norbert Michelisz, H (Hyundai Elantra N TCR), +3.990s; **5** Gilles Magnus, B (Audi RS 3 LMS TCR), +4.936s; **6** Tiago Monteiro, P (Honda Civic Type-R TCR), +7.591s; **7** Néstor Girolami, RA (Honda Civic Type-R TCR), +11.716s; **8** Nathanaël Berthon, F (Audi RS 3 LMS TCR), +12.289s; **9** Attila Tassi, H (Honda Civic Type-R TCR), +12.533s; **10** Esteban Guerrieri, RA (Honda Civic Type-R TCR), +13.817s.
Fastest race lap: Azcona, 1m 28.334s, 91.671mph/147.530km/h.
Pole position: Bennani.

FIA WORLD TOURING CAR CUP, Bahrain International Circuit, Sakhir, Bahrain, 11/12 November. 15 and 13 laps of the 3.363-mile/5.412km circuit.
Round 15 (50.443 miles/81.180km).
1 Mikel Azcona, E (Hyundai Elantra N TCR), 33m 34.107s, 90.161mph/145.100km/h; **2** Norbert Michelisz, H (Hyundai Elantra N TCR), +1.955s; **3** Nathanaël Berthon, F (Audi RS 3 LMS TCR), +3.443s; **4** Néstor Girolami, RA (Honda Civic Type-R TCR), +9.193s; **5** Nicky Catsburg, NL (Hyundai Elantra N TCR), +10.291s; **6** Tom Coronel, NL (Audi RS 3 LMS TCR), +11.336s *; **7** Mehdi Bennani, MA (Audi RS 3 LMS TCR), +12.247s; **8** Esteban Guerrieri, RA (Honda Civic Type-R TCR), +14.605s; **9** Attila Tassi, H (Honda Civic Type-R TCR), +19.527s; **10** Viktor Davidovski, MK (Audi RS 3 LMS TCR), +20.006s.
* 5s penalty for causing a collision.
Fastest race lap: Michelisz, 2m 11.155s, 92.305mph/148.550km/h.
Pole position: Azcona, 2m 11.061s, 92.371mph/148.657km/h.

Round 16 (43.717 miles/70.356km).
1 Norbert Michelisz, H (Hyundai Elantra N TCR), 29m 04.963s, 90.192mph/145.150km/h; **2** Esteban Guerrieri, RA (Honda Civic Type-R TCR), +1.046s; **3** Nicky Catsburg, NL (Hyundai Elantra N TCR), +3.677s; **4** Mikel Azcona, E (Hyundai Elantra N TCR), +7.811s; **5** Nathanaël Berthon, F (Audi RS 3 LMS TCR), +12.637s *; **6** Tom Coronel, NL (Audi RS 3 LMS TCR), +13.958s; **7** Franco Girolami, RA (Audi RS 3 LMS TCR), +15.776s; **8** Mehdi Bennani, MA (Audi RS 3 LMS TCR), +24.353s; **9** Néstor Girolami, RA (Honda Civic Type-R TCR), +24.739s; **10** Dániel Nagy, H (Cupra León Competición TCR), +24.975s.
* 5s penalty for gaining position out of track.
Fastest race lap: Michelisz, 2m 11.605s, 91.989mph/148.043km/h.
Pole position: Bennani.

FIA WORLD TOURING CAR CUP, Jeddah Corniche Circuit, Jeddah, Saudi Arabia, 27 November. 28 and 22 laps of the 2.144-mile/3.450km circuit.
Round 17 (60.024 miles/96.600km).
1 Nathanaël Berthon, F (Audi RS 3 LMS TCR),

37m 02.491s, 97.227mph/156.473km/h; **2** Norbert Michelisz, H (Hyundai Elantra N TCR), +1.869s; **3** Tom Coronel, NL (Audi RS 3 LMS TCR), +4.573s; **4** Franco Girolami, RA (Audi RS 3 LMS TCR), +5.758s; **5** Gilles Magnus, B (Audi RS 3 LMS TCR), +9.430s; **6** Mikel Azcona, E (Hyundai Elantra N TCR), +10.054s; **7** Nicky Catsburg, NL (Hyundai Elantra N TCR), +15.311s; **8** Viktor Davidovski, MK (Audi RS 3 LMS TCR), +15.616s; **9** Rob Huff, GB (Cupra León Competición TCR), +16.576s; **10** Néstor Girolami, RA (Honda Civic Type-R TCR), +28.840s.
Fastest race lap: Berthon, 1m 17.052s, 100.158mph/161.189km/h.
Pole position: Berthon, 1m 16.362s, 101.063mph/162.646km/h.

Round 18 (47.162 miles/75.900km).
1 Gilles Magnus, B (Audi RS 3 LMS TCR), 32m 55.427s, 85.947mph/138.319km/h; **2** Viktor Davidovski, MK (Audi RS 3 LMS TCR), +0.464s; **3** Mikel Azcona, E (Hyundai Elantra N TCR), +0.932s; **4** Norbert Michelisz, H (Hyundai Elantra N TCR), +1.314s; **5** Rob Huff, GB (Cupra León Competición TCR), +1.570s; **6** Tom Coronel, NL (Audi RS 3 LMS TCR), +1.788s; **7** Dániel Nagy, H (Cupra León Competición TCR), +2.217s; **8** Néstor Girolami, RA (Honda Civic Type-R TCR), +3.030s; **9** Tiago Monteiro, P (Honda Civic Type-R TCR), +3.621s; **10** Ahmed Bin-Khanen, SA (Audi RS 3 LMS TCR), +5.057s.
Fastest race lap: Magnus, 1m 16.986s, 100.244mph/161.328km/h.
Pole position: Tassi.

Final championship points.
Drivers
1 Mikel Azcona, E, 337; **2** Néstor Girolami, RA, 254; **3** Nathanaël Berthon, F, 240; **4** Norbert Michelisz, H, 222; **5** Gilles Magnus, B, 210; **6** Rob Huff, GB, 210; **7** Esteban Guerrieri, RA, 149; **8** Santiago Urrutia, U, 137; **9** Yann Ehrlacher, F, 133; **10** Tom Coronel, NL, 115; **11** Mehdi Bennani, MA, 112; **12** Ma Qinghua, CHN, 97; **13** Attila Tassi, H, 83; **14** Yvan Muller, F, 78; **15** Tiago Monteiro, P, 70; **16** Dániel Nagy, H, 62; **17** Thed Björk, S, 35; **18** Franco Girolami, RA, 16; **19** Bence Boldizs, H, 12.

Teams
1 BRC Hyundai N Squadra Corse, 559; **2** All-Inkl.com Münnich Motorsport, 403; **3** Comtoyou DHL Team Audi Sport, 355; **4** Comtoyou Team Audi Sport, 338; **5** Zengo Motorsport Services KFT, 284; **6** Cyan Performance Lynk & Co, 211; **7** Cyan Racing Lynk & Co, 211; **8** Liqui Moly Team Engstler, 153.

Races cancelled: Korea, 9 October; China, 6 November; Macau, 20 November (due to logistical challenges and Covid-19 restrictions).

German Touring Car Championship (DTM)

GERMAN TOURING CAR CHAMPIONSHIP (DTM), Autódromo Internacional do Algarve, Portimão, Portugal, 30 April/1 May. Round 1. 32 and 33 laps of the 2.891-mile/4.653km circuit.
Race 1 (92.520 miles/148.896km).
1 Lucas Auer, A (Mercedes AMG GT3 Evo), 57m 55.325s, 95.839mph/154.238km/h; **2** Luca Stolz, D (Mercedes AMG GT3 Evo), +0.851s; **3** Mirko Bortolotti, I (Lamborghini Huracán GT3 Evo), +1.811s; **4** Kelvin van der Linde, ZA (Audi R8 LMS Evo II), +3.053s; **5** Dennis Olsen, N (Porsche 911 GT3 R), +3.406s; **6** Ricardo Feller, CH (Audi R8 LMS Evo II), +4.405s; **7** Sheldon van der Linde, ZA (BMW M4 GT3), +4.768s; **8** Laurens Vanthoor, B (Porsche 911 GT3 R), +5.365s; **9** Philipp Eng, A (BMW M4 GT3), +7.399s; **10** Maro Engel, D (Mercedes AMG GT3 Evo), +7.468s *.
* 5s penalty for pit stop infringement.
Fastest race lap: Stolz, 1m 41.154s, 102.897mph/165.597km/h.
Pole position: Bortolotti, 1m 39.678s, 104.421mph/168.049km/h.

Race 2 (95.411 miles/153.549km).
1 Nico Müller, CH (Audi R8 LMS Evo II), 56m 59.568s, 100.445mph/161.651km/h; **2** Felipe Fraga, BR (Ferrari 488 GT3 Evo 2020), +3.415s; **3** Mirko Bortolotti, I (Lamborghini Huracán GT3 Evo), +8.447s; **4** Marco Wittmann, D (BMW M4 GT3), +10.283s; **5** Maximilian Götz, D (Mercedes AMG GT3 Evo), +12.734s; **6** Kelvin van der Linde, ZA (Audi R8 LMS Evo II), +13.553s; **7** Laurens Vanthoor, B (Porsche 911 GT3 R), +14.349s; **8** Sheldon van der Linde, ZA (BMW M4 GT3), +18.002s; **9** Ricardo Feller, CH (Audi R8 LMS Evo II), +19.754s; **10** Maro Engel, D (Mercedes AMG GT3 Evo), +21.579s.
Fastest race lap: Fraga, 1m 41.681s, 102.364mph/164.739km/h.
Pole position: Müller, 1m 39.794s, 104.300mph/167.854km/h.

LAUSITZRING TURN 1 POWERED BY AUTO-HERO, EuroSpeedway Lausitz, Klettwitz, Dresden, Germany, 21/22 May. Round 2. 2 x 36 laps of the 2.859-mile/4.601km circuit.
Race 1 (102.921 miles/165.636km).
1 Sheldon van der Linde, ZA (BMW M4 GT3), 56m 48.270s, 108.711mph/174.954km/h; **2** Luca Stolz, D (Mercedes AMG GT3 Evo), +3.590s; **3** Lucas Auer, A (Mercedes AMG GT3 Evo), +5.427s; **4** Arjun Maini, IND (Mercedes AMG GT3 Evo), +7.752s; **5** Maro Engel, D (Mercedes AMG GT3 Evo), +9.142s; **6** Mirko Bortolotti, I (Lamborghini Huracán GT3 Evo), +13.654s; **7** Laurens Vanthoor, B (Porsche 911 GT3 R), +17.577s; **8** René Rast, D (Audi R8 LMS Evo II), +19.056s; **9** Nick Cassidy, NZ (Ferrari 488 GT3 Evo 2020), +19.303s; **10** Maximilian Götz, D (Mercedes AMG GT3 Evo), +21.425s.
Fastest race lap: van der Linde, 1m 32.565s, 111.188mph/178.940km/h.
Pole position: Auer, 1m 30.654s, 113.532mph/182.712km/h.

Race 2 (102.921 miles/165.636km).
1 Sheldon van der Linde, ZA (BMW M4 GT3), 56m 42.296s, 108.902mph/175.261km/h; **2** Maro Engel, D (Mercedes AMG GT3 Evo), +0.347s; **3** René Rast, D (Audi R8 LMS Evo II), +1.817s; **4** Philipp Eng, A (BMW M4 GT3), +6.907s; **5** Nico Müller, CH (Audi R8 LMS Evo II), +7.338s; **6** Mirko Bortolotti, I (Lamborghini Huracán GT3 Evo), +7.682s; **7** Ricardo Feller, CH (Audi R8 LMS Evo II), +14.572s; **8** Lucas Auer, A (Mercedes AMG GT3 Evo), +14.872s; **9** Laurens Vanthoor, B (Porsche 911 GT3 R), +15.426s; **10** Marco Wittmann, D (BMW M4 GT3), +16.236s.
Fastest race lap: Engel, 1m 32.085s, 111.768mph/179.873km/h.
Pole position: van der Linde, 1m 30.998s, 113.103mph/182.022km/h.

GERMAN TOURING CAR CHAMPIONSHIP (DTM), Autodromo Enzo e Dino Ferrari, Imola, Italy, 18/19 June. Round 3. 2 x 33 laps of the 3.050-mile/4.909km circuit.
Race 1 (100.660 miles/161.997km).
1 René Rast, D (Audi R8 LMS Evo II), 57m 01.108s, 105.924mph/170.468km/h; **2** Nico Müller, CH (Audi R8 LMS Evo II), +3.809s; **3** Mirko Bortolotti, I (Lamborghini Huracán GT3 Evo), +7.936s; **4** Thomas Preining, A (Porsche 911 GT3 R), +9.323s; **5** Kelvin van der Linde, ZA (Audi R8 LMS Evo II), +10.605s; **6** Clemens Schmid, A (Lamborghini Huracán GT3 Evo), +13.289s; **7** Marco Wittmann, D (BMW M4 GT3), +17.853s; **8** Sheldon van der Linde, ZA (BMW M4 GT3), +32.103s; **9** Dennis Olsen, N (Porsche 911 GT3 R), +32.733s; **10** Maro Engel, D (Mercedes AMG GT3 Evo), +33.394s.
Fastest race lap: Bortolotti, 1m 40.957s, 108.770mph/175.049km/h.
Pole position: Rast, 1m 39.817s, 110.013mph/177.048km/h.

Race 2 (100.660 miles/161.997km).
1 Ricardo Feller, CH (Audi R8 LMS Evo II), 1h 01m 05.974s, 98.849mph/159.082km/h; **2** Dev Gore, USA (Audi R8 LMS Evo II), +1.873s; **3** Marco Wittmann, D (BMW M4 GT3), +3.188s; **4** Lucas Auer, A (Mercedes AMG GT3 Evo), +4.064s; **5** Sheldon van der Linde, ZA (BMW M4 GT3), +4.353s; **6** Philipp Eng, A (BMW M4 GT3), +4.651s; **7** Maro Engel, D (Mercedes AMG GT3 Evo), +5.286s; **8** Nico Müller, CH (Audi R8 LMS Evo II), +8.870s; **9** Maximilian Götz, D (Mercedes AMG GT3 Evo), +9.395s; **10** Mirko Bortolotti, I (Lamborghini Huracán GT3 Evo), +9.807s.
Fastest race lap: Nick Cassidy, NZ (Ferrari 488 GT3 Evo 2020), 1m 41.684s, 107.993mph/173.797km/h.
Pole position: Feller, 1m 39.814s, 110.016mph/177.053km/h.

DTM NORISRING POWERED BY BMW M, Norisring, Nürnberg (Nuremberg), Germany, 2/3 July. Round 4. 57 and 67 laps of the 1.343-mile/2.162km circuit.
Race 1 (76.574 miles/123.234km).
1 Thomas Preining, A (Porsche 911 GT3 R), 57m 57.354s, 79.275mph/127.580km/h; **2** Dennis Olsen, N (Porsche 911 GT3 R), +3.675s; **3** René Rast, D (Audi R8 LMS Evo II), +4.154s; **4** Laurens Vanthoor, B (Porsche 911 GT3 R), +7.030s; **5** Philipp Eng, A (BMW M4 GT3), +8.066s; **6** Maximilian Götz, D (Mercedes AMG GT3 Evo), +8.975s; **7** Luca Stolz, D (Mercedes AMG GT3 Evo), +9.859s; **8** Ricardo Feller, CH (Audi R8 LMS Evo II), +10.979s; **9** Mikaël Grenier, CDN (Mercedes AMG GT3 Evo), +12.013s; **10** Clemens Schmid, A (Lamborghini Huracán GT3 Evo), +13.119s.
Fastest race lap: Preining, 49.618s, 97.470mph/156.862km/h.
Pole position: Kelvin van der Linde, ZA (Audi R8 LMS Evo II), 49.236s, 98.226mph/158.079km/h.

Race 2 (90.008 miles/144.854km).
1 Felipe Fraga, BR (Ferrari 488 GT3 Evo 2020), 56m 17.533s, 95.937mph/154.395km/h; **2** Mirko Bortolotti, I (Lamborghini Huracán GT3 Evo), +2.709s; **3** René Rast, D (Audi R8 LMS Evo II), +5.747s; **4** Marco Wittmann, D (BMW M4 GT3), +9.505s; **5** Dennis Olsen, N (Porsche 911 GT3 R), +15.172s; **6** Maximilian Götz, D (Mercedes AMG GT3 Evo), +17.429s; **7** Ayhancan Guven, TR (Ferrari 488 GT3 Evo 2020), +18.011s; **8** Luca Stolz, D (Mercedes AMG GT3 Evo), +22.510s; **9** Thomas Preining, A (Porsche 911 GT3 R), +24.294s; **10** Maro Engel, D (Mercedes AMG GT3 Evo), +24.747s.
Fastest race lap: Bortolotti, 49.150s, 98.398mph/158.356km/h.
Pole position: Fraga, 48.717s, 99.272mph/159.764km/h.

GERMAN TOURING CAR CHAMPIONSHIP (DTM), Nürburgring, Nürburg/Eifel, Germany, 27/28 August. Round 5. 38 and 40 laps of the 2.255-mile/3.629km circuit.
Race 1 (85.688 miles/137.902km).
1 Sheldon van der Linde, ZA (BMW M4 GT3), 57m 04.374s, 90.083mph/144.975km/h; **2** Kelvin van der Linde, ZA (Audi R8 LMS Evo II), +1.928s; **3** Ricardo Feller, CH (Audi R8 LMS Evo II), +8.432s; **4** Maximilian Götz, D (Mercedes AMG GT3 Evo), +8.884s; **5** Lucas Auer, A (Mercedes AMG GT3 Evo), +11.151s; **6** Philipp Eng, A (BMW M4 GT3), +18.473s; **7** Nick Cassidy, NZ (Ferrari 488 GT3 Evo 2020), +19.120s; **8** Marco Wittmann, D (BMW M4 GT3), +19.553s; **9** René Rast, D (Audi R8 LMS Evo II), +20.968s; **10** Mikaël Grenier, CDN (Mercedes AMG GT3 Evo), +21.913s.
Fastest race lap: Mirko Bortolotti, I (Lamborghini Huracán GT3 Evo), 1m 26.820s, 93.502mph/150.477km/h.
Pole position: Bortolotti.

Race 2 (90.198 miles/145.160km).
1 Luca Stolz, D (Mercedes AMG GT3 Evo), 1h 00m 43.674s, 89.117mph/143.420km/h; **2** Dennis Olsen, N (Porsche 911 GT3 R), +4.507s; **3** Lucas Auer, A (Mercedes AMG GT3 Evo), +11.354s; **4** Kelvin van der Linde, ZA (Audi R8 LMS Evo II), +15.024s; **5** Maximilian Götz, D (Mercedes AMG GT3 Evo), +15.711s; **6** Nico Müller, CH (Audi R8 LMS Evo II), +16.457s; **7** Thomas Preining, A (Porsche 911 GT3 R), +19.523s; **8** Mikaël Grenier, CDN (Mercedes AMG GT3 Evo), +20.518s; **9** Sheldon van der Linde, ZA (BMW M4 GT3), +23.811s; **10** Marco Wittmann, D (BMW M4 GT3), +28.393s.
Fastest race lap: Stolz, 1m 26.927s, 93.387mph/150.292km/h.
Pole position: van der Linde, 1m 25.945s, 94.454mph/152.009km/h.

GERMAN TOURING CAR CHAMPIONSHIP (DTM), Circuit de Spa-Francorchamps, Stavelot, Belgium, 10/11 September. Round 6. 23 and 21 laps of the 4.352-mile/7.004km circuit.
Race 1 (100.098 miles/161.092km).
1 Dennis Olsen, N (Porsche 911 GT3 R), 54m 34.994s, 110.032mph/177.079km/h; **2** Maximilian Götz, D (Mercedes AMG GT3 Evo), +0.818s; **3** Thomas Preining, A (Porsche 911 GT3 R), +6.972s; **4** René Rast, D (Audi R8 LMS Evo II), +16.127s; **5** Kelvin van der Linde, ZA (Audi R8 LMS Evo II), +20.772s; **6** Nico Müller, CH (Audi R8 LMS Evo II), +21.102s; **7** Felipe Fraga, BR (Ferrari 488 GT3 Evo 2020), +22.504s; **8** Mirko Bortolotti, I (Lamborghini Huracán GT3 Evo), +27.636s; **9** Marco Wittmann, D (BMW M4 GT3), +29.319s; **10** Nick Cassidy, NZ (Ferrari 488 GT3 Evo 2020), +29.996s.
Fastest race lap: Götz, 2m 19.166s, 112.581mph/181.182km/h.
Pole position: Olsen, 2m 30.488s, 104.111mph/167.551km/h.

Race 2 (91.394 miles/147.084km).
1 Nick Cassidy, NZ (Ferrari 488 GT3 Evo 2020), 53m 20.316s, 102.808mph/165.453km/h; **2** Sheldon van der Linde, ZA (BMW M4 GT3), +0.680s; **3** Thomas Preining, A (Porsche 911 GT3 R), +1.673s; **4** Lucas Auer, A (Mercedes AMG GT3 Evo), +2.756s; **5** Luca Stolz, D (Mercedes AMG GT3 Evo), +3.013s; **6** Mikaël Grenier, CDN (Mercedes AMG GT3 Evo), +4.541s; **7** Philipp Eng, A (BMW M4 GT3), +5.863s; **8** Felipe Fraga, BR (Ferrari 488 GT3 Evo 2020), +6.565s; **9** Marco Wittmann, D (BMW M4 GT3), +6.837s; **10** Mirko Bortolotti, I (Lamborghini Huracán GT3 Evo), +7.096s.
Fastest race lap: Rolf Ineichen, CH (Lamborghini Huracán GT3 Evo), 2m 19.135s, 112.606mph/181.223km/h.
Pole position: René Rast, D (Audi R8 LMS Evo II), 2m 23.424s, 109.239mph/175.803km/h.

GERMAN TOURING CAR CHAMPIONSHIP (DTM), Red Bull Ring, Spielberg, Austria, 24/25 September. Round 7. 38 and 35 laps of the 2.683-mile/4.318km circuit.
Race 1 (101.957 miles/164.084km).
1 Nick Cassidy, NZ (Ferrari 488 GT3 Evo 2020), 57m 42.987s, 105.991mph/170.576km/h; **2** René Rast, D (Audi R8 LMS Evo II), +2.573s; **3** Mirko Bortolotti, I (Lamborghini Huracán GT3 Evo), +5.917s; **4** Lucas Auer, A (Mercedes AMG GT3 Evo), +6.465s; **5** Thomas Preining, A (Porsche 911 GT3 R), +7.167s; **6** Nico Müller, CH (Audi R8 LMS Evo II), +8.700s; **7** Maro Engel, D (Mercedes AMG GT3 Evo), +12.831s; **8** Kelvin van der Linde, ZA (Audi R8 LMS Evo II), +11.946s *; **9** Maximilian Götz, D (Mercedes AMG GT3 Evo), +15.626s; **10** Luca Stolz, D (Mercedes AMG GT3 Evo), +16.107s.
* Switch position with Engel.
Fastest race lap: Bortolotti, 1m 29.354s, 108.099mph/173.969km/h.
Pole position: Cassidy, 1m 27.800s, 110.012mph/177.048km/h.

Race 2 (93.908 miles/151.130km).
1 Thomas Preining, A (Porsche 911 GT3 R), 58m 02.943s, 97.064mph/156.209km/h; **2** Luca Stolz, D (Mercedes AMG GT3 Evo), +4.640s; **3** Maro Engel, D (Mercedes AMG GT3 Evo), +10.505s; **4** Arjun Maini, IND (Mercedes AMG GT3 Evo), +16.373s; **5** Philipp Eng, A (BMW M4 GT3), +16.481s; **6** Lucas Auer, A (Mercedes AMG GT3 Evo), +19.107s; **7** Maximilian Götz, D (Mercedes AMG GT3 Evo), +20.216s; **8** Nico Müller, CH (Audi R8 LMS Evo II), +21.003s; **9** Mirko Bortolotti, I (Lamborghini Huracán GT3 Evo), +23.051s; **10** Dennis Olsen, N (Porsche 911 GT3 R), +23.543s.
Fastest race lap: Auer, 1m 32.407s, 104.528mph/168.221km/h.
Pole position: Engel, 1m 40.776s, 95.847mph/154.251km/h.

GERMAN TOURING CAR CHAMPIONSHIP (DTM), Hockenheimring Grand Prix Circuit, Heidelberg, Germany, 8/9 October. Round 8. 30 and 34 laps of the 2.842-mile/4.574km circuit.
Race 1 (85.265 miles/137.220km).
1 Lucas Auer, A (Mercedes AMG GT3 Evo), 1h 34m 18.676s, 54.245mph/87.298km/h; **2** Sheldon van der Linde, ZA (BMW M4 GT3), +0.681s; **3** Marco Wittmann, D (BMW M4 GT3), +1.907s; **4** Dev Gore, USA (Audi R8 LMS Evo II), +3.099s; **5** René Rast, D (Audi R8 LMS Evo II), +5.053s; **6** Philipp Eng, A (BMW M4 GT3), +5.849s; **7** Mirko Bortolotti, I (Lamborghini Huracán GT3 Evo), +6.296s; **8** Nico Müller, CH (Audi R8 LMS Evo II), +9.324s; **9** Luca Stolz, D (Mercedes AMG GT3 Evo), +14.350s; **10** Maximilian Buhk, D (Mercedes AMG GT3 Evo), +19.652s.
Fastest race lap: van der Linde, 1m 38.369s, 104.014mph/167.394km/h.
Pole position: Auer, 1m 36.479s, 106.052mph/170.673km/h.

Race 2 (96.633 miles/155.516km).
1 Marco Wittmann, D (BMW M4 GT3), 57m 03.832s, 101.605mph/163.518km/h; **2** René Rast, D (Audi R8 LMS Evo II), +4.425s; **3** Sheldon van der Linde, ZA (BMW M4 GT3), +14.793s; **4** Marius Zug, D (Audi R8 LMS Evo II), +15.084s; **5** Kelvin van der Linde, ZA (Audi R8 LMS Evo II), +23.821s; **6** Nico Müller, CH (Audi R8 LMS Evo II), +41.011s; **7** Lucas Auer, A (Mercedes AMG GT3 Evo), +41.433s; **8** Leon Köhler, D (BMW M4 GT3), +41.557s; **9** Luca Stolz, D (Mercedes AMG GT3 Evo), +42.360s; **10** Alessio Deledda, I (Lamborghini Huracán GT3 Evo), +58.164s *.
* 15s penalty for abusing track limits.
Fastest race lap: Wittmann, 1m 38.640s, 103.728mph/166.934km/h.
Pole position: Rast, 1m 36.817s, 105.681mph/170.078km/h.

Final championship points
Drivers
1 Sheldon van der Linde, ZA, 164; **2** Lucas Auer, A, 153; **3** René Rast, D, 149; **4** Mirko Bortolotti, I, 121; **5** Thomas Preining, A, 116; **6** Luca Stolz, D, 108; **7** Nico Müller, CH, 105; **8** Marco Wittmann, D, 98; **9** Kelvin van der Linde, ZA, 90; **10** Dennis Olsen, N, 89; **11** Maximilian Götz, D, 74; **12** Maro Engel, D, 65; **13** Nick Cassidy, NZ, 64; **14** Philipp Eng, A, 64; **15** Ricardo Feller, CH, 63; **16** Felipe Fraga, BR, 60.

Manufacturers
1 Audi, 441; **2** Mercedes, 413; **3** BMW, 327;

4 Porsche, 234; **5** Lamborghini, 130; **6** Ferrari, 129.

Teams
1 Schubert Motorsport, 226; **2** Mercedes-AMG Team Winward, 152; **3** Team ABT Sportsline, 152.

British Touring Car Championship

BRITISH TOURING CAR CHAMPIONSHIP, Donington Park National Circuit, Castle Donington, Great Britain, 24 April. 19, 16 and 16 laps of the 1.979-mile/3.185km circuit.
Round 1 (37.563 miles/60.452km).
1 Tom Ingram, GB (Hyundai i30 Fastback N Performance), 24m 40.599s, 91.423mph/147.132km/h; **2** Colin Turkington, GB (BMW 330e M Sport), +0.659s; **3** Gordon Shedden, GB (Honda Civic Type-R), +4.122s; **4** Ash Sutton, GB (Ford Focus ST), +5.067s; **5** Adam Morgan, GB (BMW 330e M Sport), +5.466s; **6** George Gamble, GB (BMW 330e M Sport), +7.173s; **7** Stephen Jelley, GB (BMW 330e M Sport), +7.477s; **8** Josh Cook, GB (Honda Civic Type-R-TOCA), +13.266s; **9** Daniel Rowbottom, GB (Honda Civic Type-R), +14.668s; **10** Tom Chilton, GB (Hyundai i30 Fastback N Performance), +16.553s.
Disqualified: Jake Hill, GB, 3-position penalty for gaining an unfair advantage - finished 3rd
Fastest race lap: Ingram, 1m 09.440s, 102.597mph/165.115km/h.
Pole position: Jake Hill, GB (BMW 330e M Sport), 1m 08.418s, 104.130mph/167.581km/h.

Round 2 (31.626 miles/50.897km).
1 Gordon Shedden, GB (Honda Civic Type-R), 18m 42.545s, 101.545mph/163.421km/h; **2** Tom Ingram, GB (Hyundai i30 Fastback N Performance), +0.197s; **3** George Gamble, GB (BMW 330e M Sport), +2.250s; **4** Adam Morgan, GB (BMW 330e M Sport), +3.230s; **5** Josh Cook, GB (Honda Civic Type-R-TOCA), +5.712s; **6** Ash Sutton, GB (Ford Focus ST), +7.362s; **7** Bobby Thompson, GB (Cupra León-TOCA), +7.832s; **8** Daniel Lloyd, GB (Hyundai i30 Fastback N Performance), +7.988s; **9** Jake Hill, GB (BMW 330e M Sport), +10.230s; **10** Rory Butcher, GB (Toyota Corolla GR Sport-TOCA), +14.089s.
Fastest race lap: Shedden, 1m 09.214s, 102.932mph/165.654km/h.
Pole position: Ingram.

Round 3 (31.626 miles/50.897km).
1 Jake Hill, GB (BMW 330e M Sport), 18m 41.379s, 101.650mph/163.591km/h; **2** Ash Sutton, GB (Ford Focus ST), +2.148s; **3** Josh Cook, GB (Honda Civic Type-R-TOCA), +9.261s; **4** Daniel Lloyd, GB (Hyundai i30 Fastback N Performance), +9.878s; **5** Tom Ingram, GB (Hyundai i30 Fastback N Performance), +10.104s; **6** Adam Morgan, GB (BMW 330e M Sport), +10.466s; **7** Rory Butcher, GB (Toyota Corolla GR Sport-TOCA), +11.045s; **8** Colin Turkington, GB (BMW 330e M Sport), +11.247s; **9** Gordon Shedden, GB (Honda Civic Type-R), +12.314s; **10** Bobby Thompson, GB (Cupra León-TOCA), +14.651s.
Fastest race lap: Hill, 1m 09.211s, 102.937mph/165.661km/h.
Pole position: Hill.

BRITISH TOURING CAR CHAMPIONSHIP, Brands Hatch Indy Circuit, West Kingsdown, Dartford, Kent, Great Britain, 15 May. 24, 24 and 27 laps of the 1.208-mile/1.944km circuit.
Round 4 (28.990 miles/46.654km).
1 Josh Cook, GB (Honda Civic Type-R-TOCA), 21m 44.124s, 80.025mph/128.787km/h; **2** Tom Ingram, GB (Hyundai i30 Fastback N Performance), +0.802s; **3** Dan Cammish, GB (Ford Focus ST), +4.209s; **4** Jake Hill, GB (BMW 330e M Sport), +5.037s; **5** Colin Turkington, GB (BMW 330e M Sport), +7.691s; **6** Adam Morgan, GB (BMW 330e M Sport), +10.120s; **7** Rory Butcher, GB (Toyota Corolla GR Sport-TOCA), +10.848s; **8** Gordon Shedden, GB (Honda Civic Type-R), +11.670s; **9** Ash Sutton, GB (Ford Focus ST), +12.509s; **10** Dan Rowbottom, GB (Honda Civic Type-R), +14.385s.
Fastest race lap: Butcher, 49.515s, 87.820mph/141.333km/h.
Pole position: Turkington, 47.539s, 91.471mph/147.208km/h.

Round 5 (28.990 miles/46.654km).
1 Josh Cook, GB (Honda Civic Type-R-TOCA), 21m 48.632s, 79.749mph/128.344km/h; **2** Dan Cammish, GB (Ford Focus ST), +0.253s; **3** Rory Butcher, GB (Toyota Corolla GR Sport-TOCA), +0.932s; **4** Ash Sutton, GB (Ford Focus ST), +4.381s; **5** Tom Ingram, GB (Hyundai i30 Fastback N Performance), +7.185s; **6** Gordon Shedden, GB (Honda Civic Type-R), +10.086s; **7** Jake Hill, GB (BMW 330e M Sport), +10.384s; **8** Dan Lloyd, GB (Hyundai i30 Fastback N Performance), +10.889s; **9** George Gamble, GB (BMW 330e M Sport), +11.965s; **10** Colin Turkington, GB (BMW 330e M Sport), +12.666s.
Fastest race lap: Sutton, 52.657s, 82.580mph/132.900km/h.
Pole position: Cook.

Round 6 (32.613 miles/52.486km).
1 Colin Turkington, GB (BMW 330e M Sport), 26m 45.566s, 73.125mph/117.684km/h; **2** Jake Hill, GB (BMW 330e M Sport), +1.181s; **3** Bobby Thompson, GB (Cupra León-TOCA), +5.198s; **4** Tom Ingram, GB (Hyundai i30 Fastback N Performance), +5.808s; **5** Rory Butcher, GB (Toyota Corolla GR Sport-TOCA), +6.186s; **6** Ash Sutton, GB (Ford Focus ST), +6.488s; **7** George Gamble, GB (BMW 330e M Sport), +7.031s; **8** Josh Cook, GB (Honda Civic Type-R-TOCA), +8.256s; **9** Dan Lloyd, GB (Hyundai i30 Fastback N Performance), +9.062s; **10** Dan Cammish, GB (Ford Focus ST), +9.543s.
Fastest race lap: Turkington, 54.071s, 80.420mph/129.424km/h.
Pole position: Chilton.

BRITISH TOURING CAR CHAMPIONSHIP, Thruxton Circuit, Andover, Hampshire, Great Britain, 29 May. 16, 16 and 17 laps of the 2.356-mile/3.792km circuit.
Round 7 (37.696 miles/60.666km).
1 Josh Cook, GB (Honda Civic Type-R-TOCA), 20m 40.575s, 109.389mph/176.044km/h; **2** Jake Hill, GB (BMW 330e M Sport), +0.900s; **3** Ash Sutton, GB (Ford Focus ST), +8.957s; **4** Colin Turkington, GB (BMW 330e M Sport), +9.400s; **5** Dan Rowbottom, GB (Honda Civic Type-R), +9.816s; **6** Jason Plato, GB (Honda Civic Type-R-TOCA), +10.208s; **7** Adam Morgan, GB (BMW 330e M Sport), +14.615s; **8** Dan Lloyd, GB (Hyundai i30 Fastback N Performance), +15.032s; **9** Stephen Jelley, GB (BMW 330e M Sport), +15.625s; **10** Ash Hand, GB (Vauxhall Astra-TOCA), +18.254s.
Fastest race lap: Rowbottom, 1m 16.400s, 111.015mph/178.662km/h.
Pole position: Cook, 1m 15.310s, 112.622mph/181.248km/h.

Round 8 (37.696 miles/60.666km).
1 Josh Cook, GB (Honda Civic Type-R-TOCA), 20m 38.196s, 109.599mph/176.383km/h; **2** Jake Hill, GB (BMW 330e M Sport), +0.487s; **3** Ash Sutton, GB (Ford Focus ST), +3.067s; **4** Colin Turkington, GB (BMW 330e M Sport), +3.717s; **5** Dan Rowbottom, GB (Honda Civic Type-R), +7.806s; **6** Adam Morgan, GB (BMW 330e M Sport), +8.763s; **7** Jason Plato, GB (Honda Civic Type-R-TOCA), +10.488s; **8** Tom Ingram, GB (Hyundai i30 Fastback N Performance), +15.424s; **9** Dan Lloyd, GB (Hyundai i30 Fastback N Performance), +15.735s; **10** Ash Hand, GB (Vauxhall Astra-TOCA), +19.736s.
Fastest race lap: Cook, 1m 16.486s, 110.890mph/178.461km/h.
Pole position: Cook.

Round 9 (40.052 miles/64.457km).
1 Adam Morgan, GB (BMW 330e M Sport), 22m 49.005s, 105.322mph/169.500km/h; **2** Colin Turkington, GB (BMW 330e M Sport), +0.599s; **3** Ash Sutton, GB (Ford Focus ST), +1.003s; **4** Dan Rowbottom, GB (Honda Civic Type-R), +3.787s; **5** Josh Cook, GB (Honda Civic Type-R-TOCA), +4.535s; **6** Tom Ingram, GB (Hyundai i30 Fastback N Performance), +4.744s; **7** Dan Lloyd, GB (Hyundai i30 Fastback N Performance), +7.884s; **8** Michael Crees, GB (Vauxhall Astra-TOCA), +8.168s; **9** Ash Hand, GB (Vauxhall Astra-TOCA), +8.638s; **10** Rory Butcher, GB (Toyota Corolla GR Sport-TOCA), +15.793s.
Fastest race lap: Ingram, 1m 16.793s, 110.447mph/177.748km/h.
Pole position: Plato.

BRITISH TOURING CAR CHAMPIONSHIP, Oulton Park Circuit, Tarporley, Cheshire, Great Britain, 12 June. 18, 15 and 18 laps of the 2.226-mile/3.582km circuit.
Round 10 (40.068 miles/64.483km).
1 Tom Ingram, GB (Hyundai i30 Fastback N Performance), 28m 03.964s, 85.657mph/137.853km/h; **2** Ash Sutton, GB (Ford Focus ST), +3.370s; **3** Rory Butcher, GB (Toyota Corolla GR Sport-TOCA), +7.207s; **4** Colin Turkington, GB (BMW 330e M Sport), +7.307s; **5** Dan Cammish, GB (Ford Focus ST), +8.248s; **6** Gordon Shedden, GB (Honda Civic Type-R), +5.164s; **7** Dan Lloyd, GB (Hyundai i30 Fastback N Performance), +8.499s; **8** Josh Cook, GB (Honda Civic Type-R-TOCA), +8.767s; **9** Dan Rowbottom, GB (Honda Civic Type-R), +9.261s; **10** Ricky Collard, GB (Toyota Corolla GR Sport-TOCA), +9.836s.
Fastest race lap: Lloyd, 1m 26.279s, 92.880mph/149.475km/h.
Pole position: Ingram, 1m 25.468s, 93.761mph/150.894km/h.

Round 11 (33.390 miles/53.736km).
1 Tom Ingram, GB (Hyundai i30 Fastback N Performance), 21m 46.431s, 92.009mph/148.074km/h; **2** Ash Sutton, GB (Ford Focus ST), +0.979s; **3** Colin Turkington, GB (BMW 330e M Sport), +2.281s; **4** Rory Butcher, GB (Toyota Corolla GR Sport-TOCA), +9.482s; **5** Gordon Shedden, GB (Honda Civic Type-R), +10.037s; **6** Dan Cammish, GB (Ford Focus ST), +12.271s; **7** Jake Hill, GB (BMW 330e M Sport), +13.076s; **8** Dan Lloyd, GB (Hyundai i30 Fastback N Performance), +13.824s; **9** Josh Cook, GB (Honda Civic Type-R-TOCA), +14.913s; **10** Ricky Collard, GB (Toyota Corolla GR Sport-TOCA), +15.150s.
Fastest race lap: Sutton, 1m 26.132s, 93.038mph/149.731km/h.
Pole position: Ingram.

Round 12 (40.068 miles/64.483km).
1 Stephen Jelley, GB (BMW 330e M Sport), 28m 58.209s, 82.984mph/133.550km/h; **2** Aiden Moffat, GB (Infiniti Q50-TOCA), +1.541s; **3** Josh Cook, GB (Honda Civic Type-R-TOCA), +3.975s; **4** Gordon Shedden, GB (Honda Civic Type-R), +4.402s; **5** Rory Butcher, GB (Toyota Corolla GR Sport-TOCA), +5.196s; **6** Dan Cammish, GB (Ford Focus ST), +8.245s; **7** Ricky Collard, GB (Toyota Corolla GR Sport-TOCA), +8.261s *; **8** Adam Morgan, GB (BMW 330e M Sport), +8.453s; **9** Ash Hand, GB (Vauxhall Astra-TOCA), +11.503s; **10** Árón Taylor-Smith, IRL (Cupra León-TOCA), +16.670s.
* 5s penalty for false start.
Fastest race lap: Jake Hill, GB (BMW 330e M Sport), 1m 26.182s, 92.984mph/149.644km/h.
Pole position: Jelley.

BRITISH TOURING CAR CHAMPIONSHIP, Croft Racing Circuit, Croft-on-Tees, North Yorkshire, Great Britain, 26 June. 18, 18 and 15 laps of the 2.100-mile/3.380km circuit.
Round 13 (37.802 miles/60.836km).
1 Dan Lloyd, GB (Hyundai i30 Fastback N Performance), 28m 10.977s, 80.478mph/129.516km/h; **2** Colin Turkington, GB (BMW 330e M Sport), +0.377s; **3** Dan Rowbottom, GB (Honda Civic Type-R), +0.779s; **4** Tom Ingram, GB (Hyundai i30 Fastback N Performance), +1.167s; **5** Jake Hill, GB (BMW 330e M Sport), +2.209s; **6** Ash Sutton, GB (Ford Focus ST), +2.734s; **7** Rory Butcher, GB (Toyota Corolla GR Sport-TOCA), +3.447s; **8** Aiden Moffat, GB (Infiniti Q50-TOCA), +3.747s; **9** George Gamble, GB (BMW 330e M Sport), +4.345s; **10** Tom Chilton, GB (Hyundai i30 Fastback N Performance), +5.394s.
Fastest race lap: Ingram, 1m 22.327s, 91.833mph/147.791km/h.
Pole position: Turkington, 1m 21.468s, 92.801mph/149.349km/h.

Round 14 (37.802 miles/60.836km).
1 Dan Lloyd, GB (Hyundai i30 Fastback N Performance), 26m 55.725s, 84.226mph/135.549km/h; **2** Tom Ingram, GB (Hyundai i30 Fastback N Performance), +0.634s; **3** Colin Turkington, GB (BMW 330e M Sport), +1.156s; **4** Jake Hill, GB (BMW 330e M Sport), +2.490s; **5** Dan Rowbottom, GB (Honda Civic Type-R), +4.586s; **6** Ash Sutton, GB (Ford Focus ST), +5.516s; **7** Rory Butcher, GB (Toyota Corolla GR Sport-TOCA), +6.719s; **8** Aiden Moffat, GB (Infiniti Q50-TOCA), +9.905s; **9** Tom Chilton, GB (Hyundai i30 Fastback N Performance), +11.442s; **10** Stephen Jelley, GB (BMW 330e M Sport), +11.842s.
Fastest race lap: Ingram, 1m 21.863s, 92.353mph/148.629km/h.
Pole position: Lloyd.

Round 15 (31.502 miles/50.697km).
1 Gordon Shedden, GB (Honda Civic Type-R), 20m 52.233s, 90.562mph/145.746km/h; **2** Josh Cook, GB (Honda Civic Type-R-TOCA), +2.528s; **3** Rory Butcher, GB (Toyota Corolla GR Sport-TOCA), +3.251s; **4** Stephen Jelley, GB (BMW 330e M Sport), +3.837s; **5** Jake Hill, GB (BMW 330e M Sport), +4.093s; **6** Colin Turkington, GB (BMW 330e M Sport), +4.404s; **7** Tom Ingram, GB (Hyundai i30 Fastback N Performance), +10.404s; **8** Dan Cammish, GB (Ford Focus ST), +12.965s; **9** Tom Chilton, GB (Hyundai i30 Fastback N Performance), +13.472s; **10** Adam Morgan, GB (BMW 330e M Sport), +13.942s.
Fastest race lap: Shedden, 1m 22.165s, 92.014mph/148.082km/h.
Pole position: Shedden.

BRITISH TOURING CAR CHAMPIONSHIP, Knockhill Racing Circuit, Dunfermline, Fife, Scotland, Great Britain, 31 July. 24, 26 and 24 laps of the 1.267-mile/2.039km circuit.
Round 16 (30.406 miles/48.933km).
1 Jake Hill, GB (BMW 330e M Sport), 20m 52.156s, 87.417mph/140.684km/h; **2** Ash Sutton, GB (Ford Focus ST), +3.640s; **3** Colin Turkington, GB (BMW 330e M Sport), +3.784s; **4** Stephen Jelley, GB (BMW 330e M Sport), +5.979s; **5** George Gamble, GB (BMW 330e M Sport), +6.363s; **6** Tom Ingram, GB (Hyundai i30 Fastback N Performance), +6.933s; **7** Gordon Shedden, GB (Honda Civic Type-R), +13.008s; **8** Rory Butcher, GB (Toyota Corolla GR Sport-TOCA), +13.984s; **9** Dan Cammish, GB (Ford Focus ST), +14.242s; **10** Ricky Collard, GB (Toyota Corolla GR Sport-TOCA), +14.381s.
Fastest race lap: Hill, 51.316s, 88.877mph/143.034km/h.
Pole position: Hill, 50.726s, 89.911mph/144.698km/h.

Round 17 (32.939 miles/53.011km).
1 Ash Sutton, GB (Ford Focus ST), 23m 53.655s, 82.712mph/133.113km/h; **2** Jake Hill, GB (BMW 330e M Sport), +0.141s; **3** Colin Turkington, GB (BMW 330e M Sport), +0.758s; **4** Tom Ingram, GB (Hyundai i30 Fastback N Performance), +3.969s; **5** Gordon Shedden, GB (Honda Civic Type-R), +10.196s; **6** Rory Butcher, GB (Toyota Corolla GR Sport-TOCA), +11.269s; **7** George Gamble, GB (BMW 330e M Sport), +11.567s; **8** Stephen Jelley, GB (BMW 330e M Sport), +12.425s; **9** Dan Cammish, GB (Ford Focus ST), +14.629s; **10** Tom Chilton, GB (Hyundai i30 Fastback N Performance), +15.318s.
Fastest race lap: Turkington, 51.370s, 88.784mph/142.884km/h.
Pole position: Hill.

Round 18 (30.406 miles/48.933km).
1 George Gamble, GB (BMW 330e M Sport), 20m 52.392s, 87.400mph/140.658km/h; **2** Jake Hill, GB (BMW 330e M Sport), +4.332s; **3** Rory Butcher, GB (Toyota Corolla GR Sport-TOCA), +7.357s; **4** Colin Turkington, GB (BMW 330e M Sport), +7.883s; **5** Ash Sutton, GB (Ford Focus ST), +8.503s; **6** Gordon Shedden, GB (Honda Civic Type-R), +8.971s; **7** Stephen Jelley, GB (BMW 330e M Sport), +9.143s; **8** Josh Cook, GB (Honda Civic Type-R-TOCA), +13.901s; **9** Tom Chilton, GB (Hyundai i30 Fastback N Performance), +16.516s; **10** Aiden Moffat, GB (Infiniti Q50-TOCA), +18.437s.
Fastest race lap: Hill, 51.410s, 88.715mph/142.773km/h.
Pole position: Gamble.

BRITISH TOURING CAR CHAMPIONSHIP, Snetterton Circuit, Thetford, Norfolk, Great Britain, 14 August. 15, 14 and 12 laps of the 2.969-mile/4.778km circuit.
Round 19 (44.533 miles/71.670km).
1 Colin Turkington, GB (BMW 330e M Sport), 32m 10.063s, 83.064mph/133.680km/h; **2** Jake Hill, GB (BMW 330e M Sport), +1.098s; **3** Tom Ingram, GB (Hyundai i30 Fastback N Performance), +3.604s; **4** Adam Morgan, GB (BMW 330e M Sport), +4.171s; **5** Stephen Jelley, GB (BMW 330e M Sport), +5.133s; **6** Jason Plato, GB (Honda Civic Type-R-TOCA), +6.519s; **7** Dan Cammish, GB (Ford Focus ST), +6.975s; **8** Dan Rowbottom, GB (Honda Civic Type-R), +7.915s; **9** Ash Sutton, GB (Ford Focus ST), +7.945s; **10** Gordon Shedden, GB (Honda Civic Type-R), +8.037s.
Fastest race lap: Turkington, 1m 57.389s, 91.048mph/146.527km/h.
Pole position: Turkington, 1m 55.805s, 92.293mph/148.531km/h.

Round 20 (41.565 miles/66.892km).
1 Colin Turkington, GB (BMW 330e M Sport), 29m 02.147s, 85.889mph/138.226km/h; **2** Jake Hill, GB (BMW 330e M Sport), +1.287s; **3** Tom Ingram, GB (Hyundai i30 Fastback N Performance), +4.872s; **4** Adam Morgan, GB (BMW 330e M Sport), +5.919s; **5** Stephen Jelley, GB (BMW 330e M Sport), +6.310s; **6** Ricky Collard, GB (Toyota Corolla GR Sport-TOCA), +8.634s; **7** Jason Plato, GB (Honda Civic Type-R-TOCA), +9.838s; **8** Dan Rowbottom, GB (Honda Civic Type-R), +10.477s; **9** Ash Sutton, GB (Ford Focus ST), +10.717s; **10** Ash Hand, GB (Vauxhall Astra-TOCA), +14.191s.
Fastest race lap: Turkington, 1m 56.218s, 91.965mph/148.004km/h.
Pole position: Turkington.

Round 21 (35.627 miles/57.336km).
1 Ash Sutton, GB (Ford Focus ST), 23m 51.491s, 89.596mph/144.191km/h; **2** Jason Plato, GB (Honda Civic Type-R-TOCA), +4.556s; **3** Tom Ingram, GB (Hyundai i30 Fastback N Performance), +7.263s; **4** Ricky Collard, GB (Toyota Corolla GR Sport-TOCA), +7.475s *; **5** Jake Hill,

GB (BMW 330e M Sport), +8.677s; **6** Colin Turkington, GB (BMW 330e M Sport), +9.074s; **7** Rory Butcher, GB (Toyota Corolla GR Sport-TOCA), +12.094s; **8** Adam Morgan, GB (BMW 330e M Sport), +12.344s; **9** Ollie Jackson, GB (Ford Focus ST), +15.263s; **10** Dan Rowbottom, GB (Honda Civic Type-R), +15.551s.
* 1s penalty.
Fastest race lap: Sutton, 1m 57.772s, 90.751mph/146.051km/h.
Pole position: Sutton.

BRITISH TOURING CAR CHAMPIONSHIP, Thruxton Circuit, Andover, Hampshire, Great Britain, 28 August. 16, 14 and 14 laps of the 2.356-mile/3.792km circuit.
Round 22 (37.696 miles/60.666km).
1 Dan Cammish, GB (Ford Focus ST), 20m 42.490s, 109.220mph/175.773km/h; **2** Gordon Shedden, GB (Honda Civic Type-R), +1.050s; **3** Ash Sutton, GB (Ford Focus ST), +1.684s; **4** Jake Hill, GB (BMW 330e M Sport), +5.136s; **5** Ash Hand, GB (Vauxhall Astra-TOCA), +10.109s; **6** Rory Butcher, GB (Toyota Corolla GR Sport-TOCA), +13.243s; **7** Dan Rowbottom, GB (Honda Civic Type-R), +13.915s; **8** Michael Crees, GB (Vauxhall Astra-TOCA), +14.240s; **9** Tom Ingram, GB (Hyundai i30 Fastback N Performance), +16.047s; **10** Colin Turkington, GB (BMW 330e M Sport), +16.650s.
Fastest race lap: Shedden, 1m 16.609s, 110.712mph/178.175km/h.
Pole position: Cammish, 1m 15.303s, 112.632mph/181.265km/h.

Round 23 (32.984 miles/53.083km).
1 Ash Sutton, GB (Ford Focus ST), 18m 10.671s, 108.870mph/175.210km/h; **2** Dan Cammish, GB (Ford Focus ST), +1.283s; **3** Gordon Shedden, GB (Honda Civic Type-R), +2.215s; **4** Jake Hill, GB (BMW 330e M Sport), +2.894s; **5** Rory Butcher, GB (Toyota Corolla GR Sport-TOCA), +4.310s; **6** Tom Ingram, GB (Hyundai i30 Fastback N Performance), +7.501s; **7** Dan Rowbottom, GB (Honda Civic Type-R), +7.774s; **8** Josh Cook, GB (Honda Civic Type-R-TOCA), +10.067s; **9** Michael Crees, GB (Vauxhall Astra-TOCA), +10.398s; **10** Colin Turkington, GB (BMW 330e M Sport), +11.071s.
Fastest race lap: Sutton, 1m 16.693s, 110.591mph/177.979km/h.
Pole position: Cammish.

Round 24 (32.984 miles/53.083km).
1 Josh Cook, GB (Honda Civic Type-R-TOCA), 18m 07.311s, 109.207mph/175.752km/h; **2** Colin Turkington, GB (BMW 330e M Sport), +2.682s; **3** Stephen Jelley, GB (BMW 330e M Sport), +4.844s; **4** Rory Butcher, GB (Toyota Corolla GR Sport-TOCA), +6.043s; **5** Ash Sutton, GB (Ford Focus ST), +7.854s; **6** Dan Rowbottom, GB (Honda Civic Type-R), +8.179s; **7** Tom Ingram, GB (Hyundai i30 Fastback N Performance), +10.813s; **8** Michael Crees, GB (Vauxhall Astra-TOCA), +11.035s; **9** Gordon Shedden, GB (Honda Civic Type-R), +12.034s; **10** Dan Cammish, GB (Ford Focus ST), +12.766s.
Fastest race lap: Cook, 1m 16.529s, 110.828mph/178.361km/h.
Pole position: Jelley.

BRITISH TOURING CAR CHAMPIONSHIP, Silverstone National Circuit, Towcester, Northamptonshire, Great Britain, 25 September. 24, 25 and 24 laps of the 1.640-mile/2.640km circuit.
Round 25 (39.370 miles/63.359km).
1 Rory Butcher, GB (Toyota Corolla GR Sport-TOCA), 24m 26.524s, 96.643mph/155.533km/h; **2** Jake Hill, GB (BMW 330e M Sport), +0.299s; **3** Adam Morgan, GB (BMW 330e M Sport), +0.551s; **4** Gordon Shedden, GB (Honda Civic Type-R), +1.424s; **5** Tom Ingram, GB (Hyundai i30 Fastback N Performance), +1.714s; **6** Ash Sutton, GB (Ford Focus ST), +3.216s; **7** Dan Cammish, GB (Ford Focus ST), +3.404s; **8** Ricky Collard, GB (Toyota Corolla GR Sport-TOCA), +4.077s; **9** Stephen Jelley, GB (BMW 330e M Sport), +5.511s; **10** Tom Chilton, GB (Hyundai i30 Fastback N Performance), +6.077s.
Fastest race lap: Ingram, 57.783s, 102.200mph/164.475km/h.
Pole position: Butcher, 57.374s, 102.928mph/165.647km/h.

Round 26 (41.010 miles/65.999km).
1 Jake Hill, GB (BMW 330e M Sport), 27m 09.022s, 90.628mph/145.852km/h; **2** Rory Butcher, GB (Toyota Corolla GR Sport-TOCA), +2.092s; **3** Gordon Shedden, GB (Honda Civic Type-R), +2.452s; **4** Ash Sutton, GB (Ford Focus ST), +2.886s; **5** Tom Ingram, GB (Hyundai i30 Fastback N Performance), +3.078s; **6** Adam Morgan, GB (BMW 330e M Sport), +3.412s; **7** Dan Cammish, GB (Ford Focus ST), +4.189s; **8** Josh Cook, GB (Honda Civic Type-R-TOCA), +4.868s; **9** Bobby Thompson, GB (Cupra León-TOCA), +5.897s; **10** Árón Taylor-Smith, IRL (Cupra León-TOCA), +6.868s.
Fastest race lap: Ingram, 57.695s, 102.356mph/164.726km/h.
Pole position: Butcher.

Round 27 (39.370 miles/63.359km).
1 Tom Ingram, GB (Hyundai i30 Fastback N Performance), 26m 34.484s, 88.888mph/143.051km/h; **2** Ash Sutton, GB (Ford Focus ST), +1.539s; **3** Rory Butcher, GB (Toyota Corolla GR Sport-TOCA), +2.072s; **4** Jake Hill, GB (BMW 330e M Sport), +2.579s; **5** Dan Cammish, GB (Ford Focus ST), +4.724s; **6** Josh Cook, GB (Honda Civic Type-R-TOCA), +8.594s; **7** Tom Chilton, GB (Hyundai i30 Fastback N Performance), +8.924s; **8** Gordon Shedden, GB (Honda Civic Type-R), +9.680s; **9** Ollie Jackson, GB (Ford Focus ST), +13.997s; **10** Árón Taylor-Smith, IRL (Cupra León-TOCA), +14.458s.
Fastest race lap: Hill, 57.582s, 102.557mph/165.049km/h.
Pole position: Cook.

BRITISH TOURING CAR CHAMPIONSHIP, Brands Hatch GP Circuit, West Kingsdown, Dartford, Kent, Great Britain, 9 October. 18, 15 and 17 laps of the 2.433-mile/3.916km circuit.
Round 28 (43.798 miles/70.485km).
1 Tom Ingram, GB (Hyundai i30 Fastback N Performance), 32m 40.611s, 80.419mph/129.422km/h; **2** Rory Butcher, GB (Toyota Corolla GR Sport-TOCA), +0.581s; **3** Jake Hill, GB (BMW 330e M Sport), +8.644s; **4** Ash Sutton, GB (Ford Focus ST), +10.408s; **5** Colin Turkington, GB (BMW 330e M Sport), +10.524s; **6** Adam Morgan, GB (BMW 330e M Sport), +10.779s; **7** Bobby Thompson, GB (Cupra León-TOCA), +11.190s; **8** George Gamble, GB (BMW 330e M Sport), +11.504s; **9** Dan Cammish, GB (Ford Focus ST), +12.259s; **10** Stephen Jelley, GB (BMW 330e M Sport), +12.728s.
Fastest race lap: Ingram, 1m 31.293s, 95.949mph/154.415km/h.
Pole position: Ingram, 1m 29.529s, 97.840mph/157.458km/h.

Round 29 (36.498 miles/58.738km).
1 Tom Ingram, GB (Hyundai i30 Fastback N Performance), 23m 02.565s, 95.035mph/152.944km/h; **2** Jake Hill, GB (BMW 330e M Sport), +0.673s; **3** Colin Turkington, GB (BMW 330e M Sport), +0.981s; **4** Rory Butcher, GB (Toyota Corolla GR Sport-TOCA), +4.693s; **5** Ash Sutton, GB (Ford Focus ST), +6.758s; **6** Adam Morgan, GB (BMW 330e M Sport), +6.908s; **7** Josh Cook, GB (Honda Civic Type-R-TOCA), +9.854s; **8** Dan Cammish, GB (Ford Focus ST), +10.177s; **9** Bobby Thompson, GB (Cupra León-TOCA), +11.301s; **10** Dan Lloyd, GB (Hyundai i30 Fastback N Performance), +11.786s.
Fastest race lap: Ingram, 1m 30.875s, 96.390mph/155.126km/h.
Pole position: Ingram.

Round 30 (41.364 miles/66.570km).
1 Dan Lloyd, GB (Hyundai i30 Fastback N Performance), 27m 43.343s, 89.525mph/144.077km/h; **2** Josh Cook, GB (Honda Civic Type-R-TOCA), +0.724s; **3** Rory Butcher, GB (Toyota Corolla GR Sport-TOCA), +4.409s; **4** Ash Sutton, GB (Ford Focus ST), +8.555s; **5** Tom Ingram, GB (Hyundai i30 Fastback N Performance), +9.479s; **6** George Gamble, GB (BMW 330e M Sport), +9.831s; **7** Jake Hill, GB (BMW 330e M Sport), +10.327s; **8** Dan Cammish, GB (Ford Focus ST), +11.472s; **9** Stephen Jelley, GB (BMW 330e M Sport), +17.304s; **10** Aiden Moffat, GB (Infiniti Q50-TOCA), +21.511s.
Fastest race lap: Cook, 1m 30.568s, 96.717mph/155.651km/h.
Pole position: Lloyd.

Final championship points
Drivers
1 Tom Ingram, GB, 394; **2** Ash Sutton, GB, 382; **3** Jake Hill, GB, 381; **4** Colin Turkington, GB, 348; **5** Rory Butcher, GB, 318; **6** Josh Cook, GB, 296; **7** Gordon Shedden, GB, 248; **8** Dan Cammish, GB, 207; **9** Adam Morgan, GB, 193; **10** Dan Lloyd, GB, 192; **11** Stephen Jelley, GB, 181; **12** Dan Rowbottom, GB, 151; **13** George Gamble, GB, 123; **14** Bobby Thompson, GB, 99; **15** Tom Chilton, GB, 83; **16** Ricky Collard, GB, 81; **17** Jason Plato, GB, 77; **18** Aiden Moffat, GB, 69; **19** Ash Hand, GB, 55; **20** Michael Crees, GB, 50; **21** Árón Taylor-Smith, IRL, 38; **22** Ollie Jackson, GB, 33; **23** Dexter Patterson, GB, 5; **24** James Gornall, GB, 2; **25** Sam Osborne, GB, 1; **26** Jack Butel, GB, 1; **27** Jade Edwards, GB, 1.

Drivers (Independents)
1 Josh Cook, GB, 502; **2** Adam Morgan, GB, 400; **3** Bobby Thompson, GB, 354; **4** George Gamble, GB, 335; **5** Jason Plato, GB, 302; **6** Aiden Moffat, GB, 283; **7** Árón Taylor-Smith, IRL, 265; **8** Michael Crees, GB, 253; **9** Ash Hand, GB, 247; **10** Jade Edwards, GB, 182.

Drivers (Jack Sears Trophy)
1 Bobby Thompson, GB, 480; **2** George Gamble, GB, 445; **3** Ash Hand, GB, 365; **4** Sam Osborne, GB, 329; **5** Jade Edwards, GB, 300; **6** Dexter Patterson, GB, 280; **7** Jack Butel, GB, 242; **8** Nicolas Hamilton, GB, 192; **9** Rick Parfitt, GB, 178; **10** Will Powell, GB, 124; **11** James Gornall, GB, 28.

Manufacturers
1 BMW, 798; **2** Ford, 717; **3** Hyundai, 644; **4** Honda, 543; **5** Toyota, 483.

Teams
1 NAPA Racing UK, 582; **2** Team BMW, 525; **3** Bristol Street Motors with Excelr8 TradePriceCars.com, 497; **4** Halfords Racing with Cataclean, 388; **5** ROKiT MB Motorsport, 371; **6** Rich Energy BTC Racing, 366; **7** Car Gods with Ciceley Motorsport, 324; **8** Toyota Gazoo Racing UK, 302; **9** Autobrite Direct with JourneyHero, 110; **10** Laser Tools Racing, 74.

NTT IndyCar Series

All cars are Dallara DW12.

FIRESTONE GRAND PRIX OF ST. PETERSBURG PRESENTED BY RP FUNDING, St. Petersburg Street Circuit, Florida, USA, 27 February. Round 1. 100 laps of the 1.800-mile/2.897km circuit, 180.000 miles/289.682km.
1 Scott McLaughlin, NZ (-Chevrolet), 1h 51m 27.3466s, 96.899mph/155.944km/h; **2** Alex Palou, E (-Honda), +0.5095s; **3** Will Power, AUS (-Chevrolet), +2.4671s; **4** Colton Herta, USA (-Honda), +15.8442s; **5** Romain Grosjean, F (-Honda), +18.4525s; **6** Rinus Van Kalmthout, NL (-Chevrolet), +20.6514s; **7** Graham Rahal, USA (-Honda), +21.4181s; **8** Scott Dixon, NZ (-Honda), +22.0277s; **9** Marcus Ericsson, S (-Honda), +22.3674s; **10** Takuma Sato, J (-Honda), +23.2743s; **11** Christian Lundgaard, DK (-Honda), +24.4244s; **12** Patricio O'Ward, MEX (-Chevrolet), +26.2750s; **13** Jack Harvey, GB (-Honda), +31.6687s; **14** Hélio Castroneves, BR (-Honda), +33.5985s; **15** Simon Pagenaud, F (-Honda), +34.2147s; **16** Josef Newgarden, USA (-Chevrolet), +36.2603s; **17** Felix Rosenqvist, S (-Chevrolet), +39.0361s; **18** Kyle Kirkwood, USA (-Chevrolet), +58.1240s; **19** Callum Ilott, GB (-Chevrolet), +58.7223s; **20** Alexander Rossi, USA (-Honda), +59.1634s; **21** Conor Daly, USA (-Chevrolet), +1m 00.1358s; **22** Devlin Defrancesco, CDN (-Honda), +1m 02.8613s; **23** Jimmie Johnson, USA (-Honda), -1 lap; **24** Tatiana Calderón, CO (-Chevrolet), -3; **25** Dalton Kellett, CDN (-Chevrolet), -38 (DNF-mechanical); **26** David Malukas, USA (-Honda), -77 (DNF-accident).
Most laps led: McLaughlin, 49.
Fastest race lap: Daly, 1m 00.9868s, 106.253mph/170.997km/h.
Pole position: McLaughlin, 59.4821s, 108.940mph/175.322km/h.
Championship points: Drivers: 1 McLaughlin, 54; **2** Palou, 41; **3** Power, 36; **4** Herta, 32; **5** Grosjean, 30; **6** Kalmthout, 29.

XPEL 375, Texas Motor Speedway, Fort Worth, Texas, USA, 20 March. Round 2. 248 laps of the 1.440-mile/2.317km circuit, 357.120 miles/574.729km.
1 Josef Newgarden, USA (-Chevrolet), 2h 09m 29.7270s, 165.467mph/266.293km/h; **2** Scott McLaughlin, NZ (-Chevrolet), +0.0669s; **3** Marcus Ericsson, S (-Honda), +1.3537s; **4** Will Power, AUS (-Chevrolet), +15.2230s; **5** Scott Dixon, NZ (-Honda), +15.6736s; **6** Jimmie Johnson, USA (-Honda), +18.0939s; **7** Alex Palou, E (-Honda), +19.1937s; **8** Simon Pagenaud, F (-Honda), +22.4649s; **9** Santino Ferrucci, USA (-Honda), +24.4149s; **10** Rinus Van Kalmthout, NL (-Chevrolet), +25.4840s; **11** David Malukas, USA (-Honda), +26.0503s; **12** Colton Herta, USA (-Honda), -1 lap; **13** Ed Carpenter, USA (-Chevrolet), -1; **14** J.R. Hildebrand, USA (-Chevrolet), -1; **15** Patricio O'Ward, MEX (-Chevrolet), -1; **16** Callum Ilott, GB (-Chevrolet), -1; **17** Dalton Kellett, CDN (-Chevrolet), -2; **18** Conor Daly, USA (-Chevrolet), -3; **19** Christian Lundgaard, DK (-Honda), -15 (DNF-accident damage); **20** Takuma Sato, J (-Honda), -108 (DNF-accident damage); **21** Felix Rosenqvist, S (-Chevrolet), -110 (DNF-rear bodywork); **22** Graham Rahal, USA (-Honda), -120 (DNF-accident); **23** Hélio Castroneves, BR (-Honda), -120 (DNF-accident); **24** Devlin Defrancesco, CDN (-Honda), -120 (DNF-accident); **25** Kyle Kirkwood, USA (-Chevrolet), -135 (DNF-accident); **26** Romain Grosjean, F (-Honda), -145 (DNF-exhaust); **27** Alexander Rossi, USA (-Honda), -237 (DNF-electrics).
Withdrawn: Jack Harvey, GB (-Honda) (injured in practice).
Most laps led: McLaughlin, 186.
Fastest race lap: O'Ward, 23.4930s, 220.661mph/355.120km/h.
Pole position: Rosenqvist, 46.8906s, 221.110mph/355.843km/h (over 2 laps).
Championship points: Drivers: 1 McLaughlin, 97; **2** Power, 69; **3** Palou, 67; **4** Newgarden, 65; **5** Ericsson, 58; **6** Dixon, 55.

ACURA GRAND PRIX OF LONG BEACH, Long Beach Street Circuit, California, USA, 10 April. Round 3. 85 laps of the 1.968-mile/3.167km circuit, 167.280 miles/269.211km.
1 Josef Newgarden, USA (-Chevrolet), 1h 46m 48.0102s, 93.977mph/151.242km/h; **2** Romain Grosjean, F (-Honda), +1.2869s; **3** Alex Palou, E (-Honda), +1.7594s; **4** Will Power, AUS (-Chevrolet), +2.9654s; **5** Patricio O'Ward, MEX (-Chevrolet), +3.7122s; **6** Scott Dixon, NZ (-Honda), +5.0605s; **7** Graham Rahal, USA (-Honda), +5.3931s; **8** Alexander Rossi, USA (-Honda), +7.3084s; **9** Hélio Castroneves, BR (-Honda), +8.9521s; **10** Kyle Kirkwood, USA (-Chevrolet), +12.8631s; **11** Felix Rosenqvist, S (-Chevrolet), +14.2930s; **12** Conor Daly, USA (-Chevrolet), +15.2177s; **13** Rinus Van Kalmthout, NL (-Chevrolet), +16.2460s; **14** Scott McLaughlin, NZ (-Chevrolet), +17.9291s; **15** Jack Harvey, GB (-Honda), +18.7807s; **16** Tatiana Calderón, CO (-Chevrolet), -1 lap; **17** Takuma Sato, J (-Honda), -2 (DNF-accident); **18** Christian Lundgaard, DK (-Honda), -2; **19** Simon Pagenaud, F (-Honda), -4; **20** Jimmie Johnson, USA (-Honda), -12 (DNF-accident); **21** David Malukas, USA (-Honda), -13 (DNF-accident); **22** Marcus Ericsson, S (-Honda), -19 (DNF-accident); **23** Colton Herta, USA (-Honda), -30 (DNF-accident); **24** Callum Ilott, GB (-Chevrolet), -30 (DNF-accident); **25** Devlin Defrancesco, CDN (-Honda), -50 (DNF-accident); **26** Dalton Kellett, CDN (-Chevrolet), -80 (DNF-accident).
Most laps led: Newgarden, 32.
Fastest race lap: Palou, 1m 07.2359s, 105.372mph/169.580km/h.
Pole position: Herta, 1m 05.3095s, 108.480mph/174.582km/h.
Championship points: Drivers: 1 Newgarden, 118; **2** McLaughlin, 113; **3** Palou, 103; **4** Power, 102; **5** Dixon, 83; **6** Grosjean, 75.

HONDA INDY GRAND PRIX OF ALABAMA, Barber Motorsports Park, Birmingham, Alabama, USA, 1 May. Round 4. 90 laps of the 2.300-mile/3.701km circuit, 207.000 miles/333.134km.
1 Patricio O'Ward, MEX (-Chevrolet), 1h 48m 39.4368s, 114.304mph/183.955km/h; **2** Alex Palou, E (-Honda), +0.9800s; **3** Rinus Van Kalmthout, NL (-Chevrolet), +12.4819s; **4** Will Power, AUS (-Chevrolet), +15.2616s; **5** Scott Dixon, NZ (-Honda), +22.8297s; **6** Scott McLaughlin, NZ (-Chevrolet), +24.0649s; **7** Romain Grosjean, F (-Honda), +24.5161s; **8** Graham Rahal, USA (-Honda), +31.9173s; **9** Alexander Rossi, USA (-Honda), +33.2497s; **10** Colton Herta, USA (-Honda), +33.5102s; **11** Simon Pagenaud, F (-Honda), +33.7418s; **12** Marcus Ericsson, S (-Honda), +34.4738s; **13** Takuma Sato, J (-Honda), +34.9140s; **14** Josef Newgarden, USA (-Chevrolet), +35.6807s; **15** Christian Lundgaard, DK (-Honda), +37.0416s; **16** Felix Rosenqvist, S (-Chevrolet), +41.6145s; **17** Devlin Defrancesco, CDN (-Honda), +42.4511s; **18** Jack Harvey, GB (-Honda), +1m 02.3267s; **19** Conor Daly, USA (-Chevrolet), +1m 03.2947s; **20** David Malukas, USA (-Honda), +1m 03.7435s; **21** Hélio Castroneves, BR (-Honda), +1m 04.5322s; **22** Kyle Kirkwood, USA (-Chevrolet), -1 lap; **23** Dalton Kellett, CDN (-Chevrolet), -1; **24** Jimmie Johnson, USA (-Honda), -1; **25** Callum Ilott, GB (-Chevrolet), -2; **26** Tatiana Calderón, CO (-Chevrolet), -2.
Most laps led: Kalmthout, 57.
Fastest race lap: Palou, 1m 08.1541s, 121.489mph/195.518km/h.
Pole position: Kalmthout, 1m 06.2507s, 124.980mph/201.136km/h.
Championship points: Drivers: 1 Palou, 144; **2** McLaughlin, 141; **3** Newgarden, 135; **4** Power, 134; **5** O'Ward, 114; **6** Dixon, 113.

GMR GRAND PRIX, Indianapolis Motor Speedway, Speedway, Indiana, USA, 14 May. Round 5. 75 laps of the 2.439-mile/3.925km circuit, 182.925 miles/294.389km.
1 Colton Herta, USA (-Honda), 2h 01m 56.3273s, 90.008mph/144.854km/h; **2** Simon Pagenaud, F (-Honda), +3.0983s; **3** Will Power, AUS (-Chevrolet), +7.1538s; **4** Marcus Ericsson, S (-Honda), +7.8193s; **5** Conor Daly, USA (-Chevrolet), +9.6535s; **6** Felix Rosenqvist,

S (-Chevrolet), +11.0949s; **7** Takuma Sato, J (-Honda), +11.5104s; **8** Callum Ilott, GB (-Chevrolet), +11.5105s *; **9** Christian Lundgaard, DK (-Honda), +11.8047s; **10** Scott Dixon, NZ (-Honda), +13.9916s; **11** Alexander Rossi, USA (-Honda), +16.7300s; **12** David Malukas, USA (-Honda), +17.9817s; **13** Jack Harvey, GB (-Honda), +19.5748s; **14** Hélio Castroneves, BR (-Honda), +24.4881s; **15** Tatiana Calderón, CO (-Chevrolet), +31.9259s; **16** Graham Rahal, USA (-Honda), +41.8037s; **17** Romain Grosjean, F (-Honda), -1 lap; **18** Alex Palou, E (-Honda), -1; **19** Patricio O'Ward, MEX (-Chevrolet), -1; **20** Scott McLaughlin, NZ (-Chevrolet), -1; **21** Devlin Defrancesco, CDN (-Honda), -2; **22** Jimmie Johnson, USA (-Honda), -2; **23** Rinus Van Kalmthout, NL (-Chevrolet), -2; **24** Juan Pablo Montoya, CO (-Chevrolet), -3 (DNF-accident); **25** Josef Newgarden, USA (-Chevrolet), -15; **26** Kyle Kirkwood, USA (-Chevrolet), -22 (DNF-accident); **27** Dalton Kellett, CDN (-Chevrolet), -41 (DNF-accident).
Most laps led: Herta, 50.
* 1-position penalty for overtaking under yellow flag.
Fastest race lap: Herta, 1m 11.7415s, 122.389mph/196.967km/h.
Pole position: Power, 1m 09.7664s, 125.854mph/202.543km/h.
Championship points: Drivers: 1 Power, 170; **2** Palou, 156; **3** McLaughlin, 152; **4** Newgarden, 140; **5** Dixon, 133; **6** Herta, 132.

106TH INDIANAPOLIS 500 PRESENTED BY GAINBRIDGE, Indianapolis Motor Speedway, Speedway, Indiana, USA, 29 May. Round 6. 200 laps of the 2.500-mile/4.023km circuit, 500.000 miles/804.672km.
1 Marcus Ericsson, S (-Honda), 2h 51m 00.6432s, 175.428mph/282.323km/h; **2** Patricio O'Ward, MEX (-Chevrolet), +1.7929s; **3** Tony Kanaan, BR (-Honda), +3.5173s; **4** Felix Rosenqvist, S (-Chevrolet), +4.1267s; **5** Alexander Rossi, USA (-Honda), +4.9804s; **6** Conor Daly, USA (-Chevrolet), +5.0799s; **7** Hélio Castroneves, BR (-Honda), +6.5614s; **8** Simon Pagenaud, F (-Honda), +7.0937s; **9** Alex Palou, E (-Honda), +8.2446s; **10** Santino Ferrucci, USA (-Chevrolet), +9.8329s; **11** Juan Pablo Montoya, CO (-Chevrolet), +10.7647s; **12** J.R. Hildebrand, USA (-Chevrolet), +11.6554s; **13** Josef Newgarden, USA (-Chevrolet), +11.8276s; **14** Graham Rahal, USA (-Honda), +12.4253s; **15** Will Power, AUS (-Chevrolet), +13.3036s; **16** David Malukas, USA (-Honda), +13.6283s; **17** Kyle Kirkwood, USA (-Chevrolet), +14.5864s; **18** Christian Lundgaard, DK (-Honda), +16.3308s; **19** Ed Carpenter, USA (-Chevrolet), +16.5602s; **20** Devlin Defrancesco, CDN (-Honda), +16.8218s; **21** Scott Dixon, NZ (-Honda), +18.1238s; **22** Marco Andretti, USA (-Honda), +25.2002s; **23** Sage Karam, USA (-Chevrolet), -1 lap (DNF-accident); **24** Jack Harvey, GB (-Honda), -1; 25 Takuma Sato, J (-Honda), -1; **26** Stefan Wilson, GB (-Chevrolet), -2; **27** Dalton Kellett, CDN (-Chevrolet), -2; **28** Jimmie Johnson, USA (-Honda), -7 (DNF-accident); **29** Scott McLaughlin, NZ (-Chevrolet), -50 (DNF-accident); **30** Colton Herta, USA (-Honda), -71 (DNF-throttle); **31** Romain Grosjean, F (-Honda), -95 (DNF-accident); **32** Callum Ilott, GB (-Chevrolet), -132 (DNF-accident); **33** Rinus Van Kalmthout, NL (-Chevrolet), -162 (DNF-accident).
Most laps led: Dixon, 95.
Fastest race lap: Ericsson, 40.0263s, 224.852mph/361.864km/h.
Pole position: Dixon, 2m 33.8162s, 234.046mph/376.660km/h (over **4** laps).
Championship points: Drivers: 1 Ericsson, 226; **2** O'Ward, 213; **3** Palou, 212; **4** Power, 202; **5** Newgarden, 174; **6** Dixon, 166.

CHEVROLET DETROIT GRAND PRIX PRESENTED BY LEAR, The Raceway at Belle Isle, Detroit, Michigan, USA, 5 June. Round 7. 70 laps of the 2.350-mile/3.782km circuit, 164.500 miles/264.737km.
1 Will Power, AUS (-Chevrolet), 1h 32m 08.8183s, 107.111mph/172.379km/h; **2** Alexander Rossi, USA (-Honda), +1.0027s; **3** Scott Dixon, NZ (-Honda), +7.1239s; **4** Josef Newgarden, USA (-Chevrolet), +10.6716s; **5** Patricio O'Ward, MEX (-Chevrolet), +11.2348s; **6** Alex Palou, E (-Honda), +14.9056s; **7** Marcus Ericsson, S (-Honda), +40.8996s; **8** Colton Herta, USA (-Honda), +41.1286s; **9** Simon Pagenaud, F (-Honda), +41.2942s; **10** Felix Rosenqvist, S (-Chevrolet), +42.8774s; **11** David Malukas, USA (-Honda), +45.8916s; **12** Conor Daly, USA (-Chevrolet), +51.1769s; **13** Takuma Sato, J (-Honda), +52.2162s; **14** Christian Lundgaard, DK (-Honda), +1m 12.7763s; **15** Jack Harvey, GB (-Honda), +1m 28.2411s; **16** Rinus Van Kalmthout, NL (-Chevrolet), -1 lap; **17** Romain Grosjean, F (-Honda), -1; **18** Devlin Defrancesco, CDN (-Honda), -1; **19** Scott McLaughlin, NZ (-Chevrolet), -1; **20** Dalton Kellett, CDN (-Chevrolet), -1; **21** Santino Ferrucci, USA (-Chevrolet), -2; **22** Jimmie Johnson, USA (-Honda), -2; **23** Tatiana Calderón, CO (-Chevrolet), -2; **24** Kyle Kirkwood, USA (-Chevrolet), -21 (DNF-accident); **25** Hélio Castroneves, BR (-Honda), -49 (DNF-steering); **26** Graham Rahal, USA (-Honda), -68 (DNF-accident).
Most laps led: Power, 55.
Fastest race lap: Malukas, 1m 16.4034s, 110.728mph/178.200km/h.
Pole position: Newgarden, 1m 15.2153s, 112.477mph/181.014km/h.
Championship points: Drivers: 1 Power, 255; **2** Ericsson, 252; **3** O'Ward, 243; **4** Palou, 241; **5** Newgarden, 208; **6** Dixon, 202.

SONSIO GRAND PRIX PRESENTED BY AMR, Road America, Elkhart Lake, Wisconsin, USA, 12 June. Round 8. 55 laps of the 4.014-mile/6.460km circuit, 220.770 miles/355.295km.
1 Josef Newgarden, USA (-Chevrolet), 1h 53m 02.8097s, 117.174mph/188.574km/h; **2** Marcus Ericsson, S (-Honda), +3.3710s; **3** Alexander Rossi, USA (-Honda), +5.6348s; **4** Romain Grosjean, F (-Honda), +5.8490s; **5** Colton Herta, USA (-Honda), +8.7657s; **6** Felix Rosenqvist, S (-Chevrolet), +9.2835s; **7** Scott McLaughlin, NZ (-Chevrolet), +9.3064s; **8** Graham Rahal, USA (-Honda), +9.3728s; **9** Scott Dixon, NZ (-Honda), +9.7102s; **10** Christian Lundgaard, DK (-Honda), +10.0430s; **11** Callum Ilott, GB (-Chevrolet), +10.6025s; **12** Simon Pagenaud, F (-Honda), +11.7440s; **13** Jack Harvey, GB (-Honda), +13.4662s; **14** Conor Daly, USA (-Chevrolet), +14.7608s; **15** Takuma Sato, J (-Honda), +15.0849s; **16** David Malukas, USA (-Honda), +16.1401s; **17** Rinus Van Kalmthout, NL (-Chevrolet), +16.6505s; **18** Devlin Defrancesco, CDN (-Honda), +16.8028s; **19** Will Power, AUS (-Chevrolet), +17.2091s; **20** Kyle Kirkwood, USA (-Chevrolet), +18.6841s; **21** Simona de Silvestro, CH (-Chevrolet), +20.2548s; **22** Hélio Castroneves, BR (-Honda), +21.4368s; **23** Dalton Kellett, CDN (-Chevrolet), +23.3098s; **24** Jimmie Johnson, USA (-Honda), -1 lap; **25** Tatiana Calderón, CO (-Chevrolet), -1; **26** Patricio O'Ward, MEX (-Chevrolet), -9 (DNF-engine); **27** Alex Palou, E (-Honda), -19 (DNF-accident).
Most laps led: Newgarden, 26.
Fastest race lap: Newgarden, 1m 46.6212s, 135.530mph/218.115km/h.
Pole position: Rossi, 1m 44.8656s, 137.799mph/221.766km/h.
Championship points: Drivers: 1 Ericsson, 293; **2** Power, 266; **3** Newgarden, 261; **4** O'Ward, 248; **5** Palou, 246; **6** Dixon, 224.

HONDA INDY 200 AT MID-OHIO PRESENTED BY THE ALL-NEW 2023 CIVIC TYPE R, Mid-Ohio Sports Car Course, Lexington, Ohio, USA, 3 July. Round 9. 80 laps of the 2.258-mile/3.634km circuit, 180.640 miles/290.712km.
1 Scott McLaughlin, NZ (-Chevrolet), 1h 46m 43.3290s, 101.557mph/163.440km/h; **2** Alex Palou, E (-Honda), +0.5512s; **3** Will Power, AUS (-Chevrolet), +3.8415s; **4** Rinus Van Kalmthout, NL (-Chevrolet), +11.3742s; **5** Scott Dixon, NZ (-Honda), +12.3194s; **6** Marcus Ericsson, S (-Honda), +13.0700s; **7** Josef Newgarden, USA (-Chevrolet), +13.7717s; **8** Hélio Castroneves, BR (-Honda), +16.8590s; **9** David Malukas, USA (-Honda), +19.0958s; **10** Simon Pagenaud, F (-Honda), +26.1914s; **11** Christian Lundgaard, DK (-Honda), +27.0849s; **12** Graham Rahal, USA (-Honda), +28.9183s; **13** Conor Daly, USA (-Chevrolet), +29.4121s; **14** Takuma Sato, J (-Honda), +29.7488s; **15** Colton Herta, USA (-Honda), +35.6803s; **16** Jimmie Johnson, USA (-Honda), +36.6512s; **17** Devlin Defrancesco, CDN (-Honda), +39.6556s; **18** Simona de Silvestro, CH (-Chevrolet), +46.0278s; **19** Alexander Rossi, USA (-Honda), +46.9341s; **20** Jack Harvey, GB (-Honda), +1m 05.0242s; **21** Romain Grosjean, F (-Honda), -1 lap; **22** Dalton Kellett, CDN (-Chevrolet), -2; **23** Callum Ilott, GB (-Chevrolet), -23 (DNF-engine); **24** Patricio O'Ward, MEX (-Chevrolet), -28 (DNF-fuel feed); **25** Tatiana Calderón, CO (-Chevrolet), -29 (DNF-transmission); **26** Kyle Kirkwood, USA (-Chevrolet), -52 (DNF-accident); **27** Felix Rosenqvist, S (-Chevrolet), -72 (DNF-engine).
Most laps led: McLaughlin, 45.
Fastest race lap: Palou, 1m 08.3376s, 118.951mph/191.432km/h.
Pole position: O'Ward, 1m 06.7054s, 121.861mph/196.117km/h.
Championship points: Drivers: 1 Ericsson, 321; **2** Power, 301; **3** Newgarden, 287; **4** Palou, 286; **5** O'Ward, 256; **6** Dixon, 254.

HONDA INDY TORONTO, Toronto Street Circuit, Ontario, Canada, 17 July. Round 10. 85 laps of the 1.786-mile/2.874km circuit, 151.810 miles/244.315km.
1 Scott Dixon, NZ (-Honda), 1h 38m 45.3087s, 92.234mph/148.437km/h; **2** Colton Herta, USA (-Honda), +0.8106s; **3** Felix Rosenqvist, S (-Chevrolet), +1.3490s; **4** Graham Rahal, USA (-Honda), +4.4830s; **5** Marcus Ericsson, S (-Honda), +5.1260s; **6** Alex Palou, E (-Honda), +6.3629s; **7** Simon Pagenaud, F (-Honda), +8.7398s; **8** Christian Lundgaard, DK (-Honda), +9.3820s; **9** Scott McLaughlin, NZ (-Chevrolet), +10.2868s; **10** Josef Newgarden, USA (-Chevrolet), +10.6561s; **11** Patricio O'Ward, MEX (-Chevrolet), +12.4284s; **12** David Malukas, USA (-Honda), +13.3711s; **13** Rinus Van Kalmthout, NL (-Chevrolet), +18.2715s; **14** Callum Ilott, GB (-Chevrolet), +18.4471s; **15** Will Power, AUS (-Chevrolet), +19.0185s; **16** Romain Grosjean, F (-Honda), +19.7939s; **17** Hélio Castroneves, BR (-Honda), +20.3903s; **18** Devlin Defrancesco, CDN (-Honda), +21.2042s; **19** Jack Harvey, GB (-Honda), +21.9470s; **20** Conor Daly, USA (-Chevrolet), +24.2445s; **21** Jimmie Johnson, USA (-Honda), -12 laps (DNF-accident damage); **22** Kyle Kirkwood, USA (-Chevrolet), -27 (DNF-accident); **23** Alexander Rossi, USA (-Honda), -41 (DNF-accident); **24** Dalton Kellett, CDN (-Chevrolet), -55 (DNF-engine); **25** Takuma Sato, J (-Honda), -85 (DNF-accident damage).
Most laps led: Dixon, 40.
Fastest race lap: Malukas, 1m 00.8307s, 105.697mph/170.102km/h.
Pole position: Herta, 59.2698s, 108.480mph/174.582km/h.
Championship points: Drivers: 1 Ericsson, 351; **2** Power, 316; **3** Palou, 314; **4** Newgarden, 307; **5** Dixon, 307; **6** O'Ward, 276.

HY-VEEDEALS.COM 250 PRESENTED BY DOORDASH, Iowa Speedway, Newton, Iowa, USA, 23/24 July. Round 11. 250 and 300 laps of the 0.894-mile/1.439km circuit.
Race 1 (223.500 miles/359.688km).
1 Josef Newgarden, USA (-Chevrolet), 1h 39m 34.4218s, 134.674mph/216.737km/h; **2** Patricio O'Ward, MEX (-Chevrolet), +6.1784s; **3** Will Power, AUS (-Chevrolet), +20.2822s; **4** Rinus Van Kalmthout, NL (-Chevrolet), +20.3748s; **5** Scott Dixon, NZ (-Honda), +21.9744s; **6** Alex Palou, E (-Honda), -1 lap; **7** Romain Grosjean, F (-Honda), -1; **8** Marcus Ericsson, S (-Honda), -1; **9** Graham Rahal, USA (-Honda), -1; **10** Christian Lundgaard, DK (-Honda), -1; **11** Jimmie Johnson, USA (-Honda), -1; **12** Callum Ilott, GB (-Chevrolet), -1; **13** Alexander Rossi, USA (-Honda), -1; **14** David Malukas, USA (-Honda), -1; **15** Kyle Kirkwood, USA (-Chevrolet), -1; **16** Hélio Castroneves, BR (-Honda), -1; **17** Devlin Defrancesco, CDN (-Honda), -1; **18** Jack Harvey, GB (-Honda), -1; **19** Conor Daly, USA (-Chevrolet), -1; **20** Dalton Kellett, CDN (-Chevrolet), -3; **21** Takuma Sato, J (-Honda), -5; **22** Scott McLaughlin, NZ (-Chevrolet), -6; **23** Simon Pagenaud, F (-Honda), -6; **24** Colton Herta, USA (-Honda), -8; **25** Ed Carpenter, USA (-Chevrolet), -90 (DNF-accident); **26** Felix Rosenqvist, S (-Chevrolet), -141 (DNF-accident).
Most laps led: Newgarden, 208.
Fastest race lap: Power, 19.4571s, 165.410mph/266.202km/h.
Pole position: Power, 18.0607s, 178.199mph/286.784km/h.

Race 2 (268.200 miles/431.626km).
1 Patricio O'Ward, MEX (-Chevrolet), 1h 54m 23.2097s, 140.681mph/226.403km/h; **2** Will Power, AUS (-Chevrolet), +4.2476s; **3** Scott McLaughlin, NZ (-Chevrolet), +9.4464s; **4** Scott Dixon, NZ (-Honda), +11.1499s; **5** Jimmie Johnson, USA (-Honda), +12.3251s; **6** Marcus Ericsson, S (-Honda), +14.2340s; **7** Felix Rosenqvist, S (-Chevrolet), +17.6887s; **8** David Malukas, USA (-Honda), +18.3725s; **9** Romain Grosjean, F (-Honda), +19.5576s; **10** Takuma Sato, J (-Honda), +20.7325s; **11** Callum Ilott, GB (-Chevrolet), +21.4930s; **12** Colton Herta, USA (-Honda), -1 lap; **13** Alex Palou, E (-Honda), -1; **14** Graham Rahal, USA (-Honda), -1; **15** Devlin Defrancesco, CDN (-Honda), -2; **16** Conor Daly, USA (-Chevrolet), -2; **17** Ed Carpenter, USA (-Chevrolet), -3; **18** Alexander Rossi, USA (-Honda), -4; **19** Rinus Van Kalmthout, NL (-Chevrolet), -4; **20** Jack Harvey, GB (-Honda), -4; **21** Hélio Castroneves, BR (-Honda), -5; **22** Dalton Kellett, CDN (-Chevrolet), -6; **23** Simon Pagenaud, F (-Honda), -19; **24** Josef Newgarden, USA (-Chevrolet), -65 (DNF-accident); **25** Kyle Kirkwood, USA (-Chevrolet), -183 (DNF-accident); **26** Christian Lundgaard, DK (-Honda), -188 (DNF-mechanical).
Most laps led: Newgarden, 148.
Fastest race lap: Power, 19.2241s, 167.415mph/269.428km/h.
Pole position: Power, 18.0796s, 178.013mph/286.484km/h.
Championship points: Drivers: 1 Ericsson, 403; **2** Power, 395; **3** Newgarden, 369; **4** Dixon, 369; **5** O'Ward, 367; **6** Palou, 359.

GALLAGHER GRAND PRIX, Indianapolis Motor Speedway, Speedway, Indiana, USA, 30 July. Round 12. 85 laps of the 2.439-mile/3.925km circuit, 207.315 miles/333.641km.
1 Alexander Rossi, USA (-Honda), 1h 48m 39.1825s, 114.483mph/184.242km/h; **2** Christian Lundgaard, DK (-Honda), +3.5441s; **3** Will Power, AUS (-Chevrolet), +14.8481s; **4** Scott McLaughlin, NZ (-Chevrolet), +15.9694s; **5** Josef Newgarden, USA (-Chevrolet), +18.4253s; **6** Rinus Van Kalmthout, NL (-Chevrolet), +22.9626s; **7** Graham Rahal, USA (-Honda), +23.3542s; **8** Scott Dixon, NZ (-Honda), +23.6130s; **9** Felix Rosenqvist, S (-Chevrolet), +24.4659s; **10** Alex Palou, E (-Honda), +27.6401s; **11** Marcus Ericsson, S (-Honda), +35.0774s; **12** Patricio O'Ward, MEX (-Chevrolet), +43.0641s; **13** David Malukas, USA (-Honda), +50.1868s; **14** Callum Ilott, GB (-Chevrolet), +51.9201s; **15** Takuma Sato, J (-Honda), +57.1069s; **16** Romain Grosjean, F (-Honda), +59.0527s; **17** Conor Daly, USA (-Chevrolet), +1m 00.1316s; **18** Devlin Defrancesco, CDN (-Honda), +1m 01.7880s; **19** Hélio Castroneves, BR (-Honda), +1m 03.4684s; **20** Jack Harvey, GB (-Honda), +1m 04.5997s; **21** Dalton Kellett, CDN (-Chevrolet), -1 lap; **22** Jimmie Johnson, USA (-Honda), -1; **23** Kyle Kirkwood, USA (-Chevrolet), -1; **24** Colton Herta, USA (-Honda), -43 (DNF-drivetrain); **25** Simon Pagenaud, F (-Honda), -51 (DNF-out of fuel).
Most laps led: Rossi, 44.
Fastest race lap: Pagenaud, 1m 11.4537s, 122.882mph/197.760km/h.
Pole position: Rosenqvist, 1m 10.2265s, 125.030mph/201.216km/h.
Championship points: Drivers: 1 Power, 431; **2** Ericsson, 422; **3** Newgarden, 399; **4** Dixon, 393; **5** O'Ward, 385; **6** Palou, 379.

BIG MACHINE MUSIC CITY GRAND PRIX, Nashville Street Circuit, Tennessee, USA, 7 August. Round 13. 80 laps of the 2.100-mile/3.380km circuit, 168.000 miles/270.370km.
1 Scott Dixon, NZ (-Honda), 2h 06m 24.2439s, 79.744mph/128.336km/h; **2** Scott McLaughlin, NZ (-Chevrolet), +0.1067s; **3** Alex Palou, E (-Honda), +0.6100s; **4** Alexander Rossi, USA (-Honda), +0.9412s; **5** Colton Herta, USA (-Honda), +1.3942s; **6** Josef Newgarden, USA (-Chevrolet), +2.1828s; **7** Felix Rosenqvist, S (-Chevrolet), +2.8426s; **8** Christian Lundgaard, DK (-Honda), +3.2724s; **9** Simon Pagenaud, F (-Honda), +4.4000s; **10** Jack Harvey, GB (-Honda), +5.1560s; **11** Will Power, AUS (-Chevrolet), +6.7843s; **12** Rinus Van Kalmthout, NL (-Chevrolet), -1 lap; **13** Hélio Castroneves, BR (-Honda), -1; **14** Marcus Ericsson, S (-Honda), -4 (DNF-accident damage); **15** Callum Ilott, GB (-Chevrolet), -4; **16** Romain Grosjean, F (-Honda), -5 (DNF-accident); **17** Conor Daly, USA (-Chevrolet), -6; **18** Jimmie Johnson, USA (-Honda), -8 (DNF-accident); **19** Kyle Kirkwood, USA (-Chevrolet), -17 (DNF-accident); **20** David Malukas, USA (-Honda), -17 (DNF-accident); **21** Takuma Sato, J (-Honda), -48 (DNF-accident); **22** Devlin Defrancesco, CDN (-Honda), -48 (DNF-accident); **23** Graham Rahal, USA (-Honda), -51 (DNF-accident); **24** Patricio O'Ward, MEX (-Chevrolet), -55 (DNF-accident); **25** Dalton Kellett, CDN (-Chevrolet), -55 (DNF-accident); **26** Simona de Silvestro, CH (-Chevrolet), -55 (DNF-accident).
Most laps led: Palou, 31.
Fastest race lap: McLaughlin, 1m 15.7491s, 99.803mph/160.618km/h.
Pole position: McLaughlin, 1m 14.5555s, 101.401mph/163.189km/h.
Championship points: Drivers: 1 Power, 450; **2** Dixon, 444; **3** Ericsson, 438; **4** Newgarden, 428; **5** Palou, 417; **6** McLaughlin, 392.

BOMMARITO AUTOMOTIVE GROUP 500 PRESENTED BY AXALTA AND VALVOLINE, World Wide Technology Raceway, St Louis, Madison, Illinois, USA, 20 August. Round 14. 260 laps of the 1.250-mile/2.012km circuit, 325.000 miles/523.037km.
1 Josef Newgarden, USA (-Chevrolet), 2h 10m 40.1827s, 149.231mph/240.164km/h; **2** David Malukas, USA (-Honda), +0.4708s; **3** Scott McLaughlin, NZ (-Chevrolet), +1.5254s; **4** Patricio O'Ward, MEX (-Chevrolet), +5.2079s; **5** Takuma Sato, J (-Honda), +5.5365s; **6** Will Power, AUS (-Chevrolet), +11.8662s; **7** Marcus Ericsson, S (-Honda), +12.6189s; **8** Scott Dixon, NZ (-Honda), +15.8852s; **9** Alex Palou, E (-Honda), +21.8239s; **10** Graham Rahal, USA (-Honda), +26.1005s; **11** Colton Herta, USA (-Honda), -1 lap; **12** Devlin Defrancesco, CDN (-Honda), -1; **13** Romain Grosjean, F (-Honda), -1; **14** Jimmie Johnson, USA (-Honda), -1; **15** Hélio Castroneves, BR (-Honda), -1; **16** Felix Rosenqvist, S (-Chevrolet), -1; **17** Kyle Kirkwood, USA (-Chevrolet), -2; **18** Dalton Kellett, CDN (-Chevrolet), -2; **19** Christian Lundgaard, DK (-Honda), -2; **20** Simon Pagenaud, F (-Honda), -3; **21** Callum

Ilott, GB (-Chevrolet), -3; **22** Ed Carpenter, USA (-Chevrolet), -4; **23** Conor Daly, USA (-Chevrolet), -16 (DNF-electrics); **24** Jack Harvey, GB (-Honda), -21 (DNF-accident damage); **25** Alexander Rossi, USA (-Honda), -34 (DNF-fuel); **26** Rinus Van Kalmthout, NL (-Chevrolet), -207 (DNF-electrics).
Most laps led: Power, 128.
Fastest race lap: Newgarden, 25.5579s, 176.071mph/283.358km/h.
Pole position: Power, 49.2539s, 182.727mph/294.070km/h (over **2** laps).
Championship points: Drivers: 1 Power, 482; **2** Newgarden, 479; **3** Dixon, 468; **4** Ericsson, 465; **5** Palou, 439; **6** McLaughlin, 428.

GRAND PRIX OF PORTLAND, Portland International Raceway, Portland, Oregon, USA, 4 September. Round 15. 110 laps of the 1.964-mile/3.161km circuit, 216.040 miles/347.683km.
1 Scott McLaughlin, NZ (-Chevrolet), 1h 56m 15.6892s, 111.493mph/179.431km/h; **2** Will Power, AUS (-Chevrolet), +1.1792s; **3** Scott Dixon, NZ (-Honda), +1.6006s; **4** Patricio O'Ward, MEX (-Chevrolet), +13.8892s; **5** Graham Rahal, USA (-Honda), +14.8208s; **6** Colton Herta, USA (-Honda), +16.3039s; **7** Alexander Rossi, USA (-Honda), +17.0044s; **8** Josef Newgarden, USA (-Chevrolet), +17.6062s; **9** Callum Ilott, GB (-Chevrolet), +18.0978s; **10** Felix Rosenqvist, S (-Chevrolet), +18.6356s; **11** Marcus Ericsson, S (-Honda), +23.5169s; **12** Alex Palou, E (-Honda), +27.5282s; **13** Kyle Kirkwood, USA (-Chevrolet), +28.3322s; **14** David Malukas, USA (-Honda), +29.0288s; **15** Jack Harvey, GB (-Honda), +31.2329s; **16** Devlin Defrancesco, CDN (-Honda), +32.5754s; **17** Hélio Castroneves, BR (-Honda), +33.8121s; **18** Takuma Sato, J (-Honda), +34.0886s; **19** Romain Grosjean, F (-Honda), +34.7299s; **20** Rinus Van Kalmthout, NL (-Chevrolet), +35.4454s; **21** Christian Lundgaard, DK (-Honda), +44.5500s; **22** Dalton Kellett, CDN (-Chevrolet), -1 lap; **23** Simon Pagenaud, F (-Honda), -10; **24** Jimmie Johnson, USA (-Honda), -28 (DNF-accident); **25** Conor Daly, USA (-Chevrolet), -43 (DNF-clutch line/fire).
Most laps led: McLaughlin, 104.
Fastest race lap: Newgarden, 59.5874s, 118.656mph/190.958km/h.
Pole position: McLaughlin, 58.2349s, 121.412mph/195.393km/h.
Championship points: Drivers: 1 Power, 523; **2** Newgarden, 503; **3** Dixon, 503; **4** Ericsson, 484; **5** McLaughlin, 482; **6** Palou, 457.

FIRESTONE GRAND PRIX OF MONTEREY, Mazda Raceway Laguna Seca, Monterey, California, USA, 11 September. Round 16. 95 laps of the 2.238-mile/3.602km circuit, 212.610 miles/342.163km.
1 Alex Palou, E (-Honda), 2h 03m 31.0628s, 103.277mph/166.209km/h; **2** Josef Newgarden, USA (-Chevrolet), +30.3812s; **3** Will Power, AUS (-Chevrolet), +33.8528s; **4** Felix Rosenqvist, S (-Chevrolet), +35.5322s; **5** Christian Lundgaard, DK (-Honda), +50.8901s; **6** Scott McLaughlin, NZ (-Chevrolet), +56.1091s; **7** Romain Grosjean, F (-Honda), +57.9853s; **8** Patricio O'Ward, MEX (-Chevrolet), +59.9521s; **9** Marcus Ericsson, S (-Honda), +1m 02.6247s; **10** Alexander Rossi, USA (-Honda), +1m 05.3231s; **11** Colton Herta, USA (-Honda), +1m 07.6483s; **12** Scott Dixon, NZ (-Honda), +1m 07.9752s; **13** David Malukas, USA (-Honda), -1 lap; **14** Rinus Van Kalmthout, NL (-Chevrolet), -1; **15** Devlin Defrancesco, CDN (-Honda), -1; **16** Jimmie Johnson, USA (-Honda), -1; **17** Simon Pagenaud, F (-Honda), -1; **18** Graham Rahal, USA (-Honda), -1; **19** Hélio Castroneves, BR (-Honda), -1; **20** Jack Harvey, GB (-Honda), -1; **21** Kyle Kirkwood, USA (-Chevrolet), -1; **22** Simona de Silvestro, CH (-Chevrolet), -1; **23** Takuma Sato, J (-Honda), -1; **24** Conor Daly, USA (-Chevrolet), -2; **25** Dalton Kellett, CDN (-Chevrolet), -2; **26** Callum Ilott, GB (-Chevrolet), -58 (DNF-mechanical).
Most laps led: Palou, 67.
Fastest race lap: O'Ward, 1m 13.8486s, 109.099mph/175.578km/h.
Pole position: Power, 1m 11.6127s, 112.505mph/181.060km/h.

Final championship points
Drivers
1 Will Power, AUS, 560; **2** Josef Newgarden, USA, 544; **3** Scott Dixon, NZ, 521; **4** Scott McLaughlin, NZ, 510; **5** Alex Palou, E, 510; **6** Marcus Ericsson, S, 506; **7** Patricio O'Ward, MEX, 480; **8** Felix Rosenqvist, S, 393; **9** Alexander Rossi, USA, 381; **10** Colton Herta, USA, 381; **11** Graham Rahal, USA, 345; **12** Rinus Van Kalmthout, NL, 331; **13** Romain Grosjean, F, 328; **14** Christian Lundgaard, DK, 323; **15** Simon Pagenaud, F, 314; **16** David Malukas, USA, 305; **17** Conor Daly, USA, 267; **18** Hélio Castroneves, BR, 263; **19** Takuma Sato, J, 258; **20** Callum Ilott, GB, 219; **21** Jimmie Johnson, USA, 214; **22** Jack Harvey, GB, 209; **23** Devlin Defrancesco, CDN, 206; **24** Kyle Kirkwood, USA, 183; **25** Dalton Kellett, CDN, 133; **26** Tony Kanaan, BR, 78; **27** Ed Carpenter, USA, 75; **28** Santino Ferrucci, USA, 71; **29** Tatiana Calderón, CO, 58; **30** J.R. Hildebrand, USA, 53; **31** Juan Pablo Montoya, CO, 44; **32** Simona de Silvestro, CH, 34; **33** Marco Andretti, USA, 17; **34** Sage Karam, USA, 14; **35** Stefan Wilson, GB, 10.

Rookie of the Year
Christian Lundgaard, DK.

Manufacturers
1 Chevrolet, 1510; **2** Honda, 1299.

NASCAR Cup Series

MONSTER ENERGY NASCAR CUP SERIES, Daytona International Speedway, Daytona Beach, Florida, USA, 20 February. Round 1. 201 laps of the 2.500-mile/4.023km circuit, 502.500 miles/808.695km.
1 Austin Cindric, USA (Ford Mustang '22), 3h 31m 53s, 142.295mph/229.002km/h; **2** Darrell Wallace Jr., USA (Toyota Camry '22), +0.036s; **3** Chase Briscoe, USA (Ford Mustang '22), +0.091s; **4** Ryan Blaney, USA (Ford Mustang '22), +0.130s; **5** Aric Almirola, USA (Ford Mustang '22), +0.140s; **6** Kyle Busch, USA (Toyota Camry '22), +0.169s; **7** Michael McDowell, USA (Ford Mustang '22), +0.256s; **8** David Ragan, USA (Ford Mustang '22), +0.277s; **9** Brad Keselowski, USA (Ford Mustang '22), +0.290s; **10** Chase Elliott, USA (Chevrolet Camaro ZL1 '22), +0.391s.
Pole position: Kyle Larson, USA (Chevrolet Camaro ZL1 '22), 49.680s, 181.159mph/291.548km/h.
Drivers' championship points: 1 Cindric, 54; **2** Keselowski, 54; **3** Truex Jr., 49; **4** Wallace Jr., 47; **5** Briscoe, 41; **6** Blaney, 41.

25TH WISE POWER 400, Auto Club Speedway, Fontana, California, USA, 27 February. Round 2. 200 laps of the 2.000-mile/3.219km circuit, 400.000 miles/643.738km.
1 Kyle Larson, USA (Chevrolet Camaro ZL1 '22), 3h 30m 07s, 114.222mph/183.823km/h; **2** Austin Dillon, USA (Chevrolet Camaro ZL1 '22), +0.195s; **3** Erik Jones, USA (Chevrolet Camaro ZL1 '22), +0.445s; **4** Daniel Suárez, MEX (Chevrolet Camaro ZL1 '22), +1.768s; **5** Joey Logano, USA (Ford Mustang '22), +1.928s; **6** Aric Almirola, USA (Ford Mustang '22), +2.109s; **7** Kevin Harvick, USA (Ford Mustang '22), +2.155s; **8** Kurt Busch, USA (Toyota Camry '22), +2.239s; **9** Daniel Hemric, USA (Chevrolet Camaro ZL1 '22), +2.416s; **10** Ricky Stenhouse Jr., USA (Chevrolet Camaro ZL1 '22), +2.417s.
Pole position: Austin Cindric, USA (Ford Mustang '22), 41.226s, 174.647mph/281.067km/h.
Drivers' championship points: 1 Cindric, 85; **2** Logano, 77; **3** Truex Jr., 73; **4** Blaney, 70; **5** Briscoe, 69; **6** Jones, 68.

25TH ANNUAL PENNZOIL 400 PRESENTED BY JIFFY LUBE, Las Vegas Motor Speedway, Nevada, USA, 6 March. Round 3. 274 laps of the 1.500-mile/2.414km circuit, 411.000 miles/661.440km.
1 Alex Bowman, USA (Chevrolet Camaro ZL1 '22), 3h 29m 50s, 117.522mph/189.133km/h; **2** Kyle Larson, USA (Chevrolet Camaro ZL1 '22), +0.178s; **3** Ross Chastain, USA (Chevrolet Camaro ZL1 '22), +0.264s; **4** Kyle Busch, USA (Toyota Camry '22), +0.271s; **5** William Byron, USA (Chevrolet Camaro ZL1 '22), +0.419s; **6** Aric Almirola, USA (Ford Mustang '22), +0.829s; **7** Tyler Reddick, USA (Chevrolet Camaro ZL1 '22), +0.868s; **8** Martin Truex Jr., USA (Toyota Camry '22), +0.887s; **9** Chase Elliott, USA (Chevrolet Camaro ZL1 '22), +0.922s; **10** Christopher Bell, USA (Toyota Camry '22), +0.939s.
Pole position: Bell, 29.561s, 182.673mph/293.984km/h.
Drivers' championship points: 1 Larson, 113; **2** Truex Jr., 107; **3** Logano, 104; **4** Cindric, 103; **5** Busch (Kyle), 102; **6** Almirola, 97.

18TH ANNUAL RUOFF MORTGAGE 500, Phoenix Raceway, Arizona, USA, 13 March. Round 4. 312 laps of the 1.000-mile/1.609km circuit, 312.000 miles/502.115km.
1 Chase Briscoe, USA (Ford Mustang '22), 3h 06m 34s, 100.339mph/161.481km/h; **2** Ross Chastain, USA (Chevrolet Camaro ZL1 '22), +0.771s; **3** Tyler Reddick, USA (Chevrolet Camaro ZL1 '22), +0.787s; **4** Ryan Blaney, USA (Ford Mustang '22), +1.499s; **5** Kurt Busch, USA (Toyota Camry '22), +1.523s; **6** Kevin Harvick, USA (Ford Mustang '22), +1.903s; **7** Kyle Busch, USA (Toyota Camry '22), +2.149s; **8** Joey Logano, USA (Ford Mustang '22), +2.390s; **9** Daniel Suárez, MEX (Chevrolet Camaro ZL1 '22), +2.735s; **10** Chris Buescher, USA (Ford Mustang '22), +2.897s.
Pole position: Blaney, 27.127s, 132.709mph/213.575km/h.
Drivers' championship points: 1 Logano, 136; **2** Busch (Kyle), 132; **3** Elliott, 131; **4** Larson, 126; **5** Briscoe, 126; **6** Almirola, 122.

64TH ANNUAL FOLDS OF HONOR QUIKTRIP 500, Atlanta Motor Speedway, Hampton, Georgia, USA, 20 March. Round 5. 325 laps of the 1.540-mile/2.478km circuit, 500.500 miles/805.477km.
1 William Byron, USA (Chevrolet Camaro ZL1 '22), 3h 57m 14s, 126.584mph/203.718km/h; **2** Ross Chastain, USA (Chevrolet Camaro ZL1 '22), +0.145s; **3** Kurt Busch, USA (Toyota Camry '22), +0.243s; **4** Daniel Suárez, MEX (Chevrolet Camaro ZL1 '22), +0.255s; **5** Corey LaJoie, USA (Chevrolet Camaro ZL1 '22), +0.538s; **6** Chase Elliott, USA (Chevrolet Camaro ZL1 '22), +0.572s; **7** Chris Buescher, USA (Ford Mustang '22), +0.659s; **8** Martin Truex Jr., USA (Toyota Camry '22), +0.749s; **9** Joey Logano, USA (Ford Mustang '22), +0.763s; **10** Alex Bowman, USA (Chevrolet Camaro ZL1 '22), +0.799s.
Pole position: Chase Briscoe, USA (Ford Mustang '22).
Drivers' championship points: 1 Elliott, 171; **2** Logano, 164; **3** Briscoe, 156; **4** Byron, 150; **5** Busch (Kurt), 148; **6** Blaney, 148.

2ND ANNUAL ECHOPARK AUTOMOTIVE GRAND PRIX, Circuit of the Americas, Austin, Texas, USA, 27 March. Round 6. 69 laps of the 3.410-mile/5.488km circuit, 235.290 miles/378.663km.
1 Ross Chastain, USA (Chevrolet Camaro ZL1 '22), 3h 20m 57s, 70.253mph/113.062km/h; **2** Alex Bowman, USA (Chevrolet Camaro ZL1 '22), +1.331s; **3** Christopher Bell, USA (Toyota Camry '22), +1.871s; **4** Chase Elliott, USA (Chevrolet Camaro ZL1 '22), +2.661s; **5** Tyler Reddick, USA (Chevrolet Camaro ZL1 '22), +3.034s; **6** Ryan Blaney, USA (Ford Mustang '22), +3.458s; **7** Martin Truex Jr., USA (Toyota Camry '22), +3.874s; **8** Austin Cindric, USA (Ford Mustang '22), +3.997s; **9** Erik Jones, USA (Chevrolet Camaro ZL1 '22), +4.803s; **10** Austin Dillon, USA (Chevrolet Camaro ZL1 '22), +5.170s.
Pole position: Blaney, 2m 12.343s, 92.759mph/149.281km/h.
Drivers' championship points: 1 Elliott, 208; **2** Blaney, 195; **3** Logano, 185; **4** Bowman, 183; **5** Chastain, 180; **6** Byron, 175.

67TH ANNUAL TOYOTA OWNERS 400, Richmond Raceway, Virginia, USA, 3 April. Round 7. 400 laps of the 0.750-mile/1.207km circuit, 300.000 miles/482.803km.
1 Denny Hamlin, USA (Toyota Camry '22), 3h 04m 43s, 97.447mph/156.825km/h; **2** Kevin Harvick, USA (Ford Mustang '22), +0.552s; **3** William Byron, USA (Chevrolet Camaro ZL1 '22), +2.735s; **4** Martin Truex Jr., USA (Toyota Camry '22), +3.261s; **5** Kyle Larson, USA (Chevrolet Camaro ZL1 '22), +5.555s; **6** Christopher Bell, USA (Toyota Camry '22), +5.745s; **7** Ryan Blaney, USA (Ford Mustang '22), +11.184s; **8** Alex Bowman, USA (Chevrolet Camaro ZL1 '22), +11.790s; **9** Kyle Busch, USA (Toyota Camry '22), +12.668s; **10** Austin Dillon, USA (Chevrolet Camaro ZL1 '22), +14.113s.
Pole position: Blaney, 22.541s, 119.782mph/192.770km/h.
Drivers' championship points: 1 Blaney, 241; **2** Elliott, 241; **3** Truex Jr., 222; **4** Byron, 218; **5** Logano, 215; **6** Chastain, 214.

73RD ANNUAL BLUE-EMU MAXIMUM PAIN RELIEF 400, Martinsville Speedway, Ridgeway, Virginia, USA, 9 April. Round 8. 403 laps of the 0.526-mile/0.847km circuit, 211.978 miles/341.146km.
1 William Byron, USA (Chevrolet Camaro ZL1 '22), 2h 40m 30s, 79.244mph/127.531km/h; **2** Joey Logano, USA (Ford Mustang '22), +0.303s; **3** Austin Dillon, USA (Chevrolet Camaro ZL1 '22), +0.524s; **4** Ryan Blaney, USA (Ford Mustang '22), +0.732s; **5** Ross Chastain, USA (Chevrolet Camaro ZL1 '22), +1.427s; **6** Kurt Busch, USA (Toyota Camry '22), +1.520s; **7** Kyle Busch, USA (Toyota Camry '22), +1.639s; **8** Aric Almirola, USA (Ford Mustang '22), +1.773s; **9** Chase Briscoe, USA (Ford Mustang '22), +1.906s; **10** Chase Elliott, USA (Chevrolet Camaro ZL1 '22), +2.150s.
Pole position: Elliott, 19.694s, 96.151mph/154.740km/h.
Drivers' championship points: 1 Elliott, 288; **2** Blaney, 285; **3** Byron, 276; **4** Logano, 261; **5** Chastain, 246; **6** Bowman, 237.

62ND ANNUAL FOOD CITY DIRT RACE, Bristol Motor Speedway, Tennessee, USA, 17 April. Round 9. 250 laps of the 0.500-mile/0.805km circuit, 125.000 miles/201.168km.
1 Kyle Busch, USA (Toyota Camry '22), 3h 34m 27s, 34.973mph/56.284km/h; **2** Tyler Reddick, USA (Chevrolet Camaro ZL1 '22), +0.330s; **3** Joey Logano, USA (Ford Mustang '22), +4.004s; **4** Kyle Larson, USA (Chevrolet Camaro ZL1 '22), +4.186s; **5** Ryan Blaney, USA (Ford Mustang '22), +4.849s; **6** Alex Bowman, USA (Chevrolet Camaro ZL1 '22), +6.434s; **7** Christopher Bell, USA (Toyota Camry '22), +6.556s; **8** Chase Elliott, USA (Chevrolet Camaro ZL1 '22), +6.786s; **9** Michael McDowell, USA (Ford Mustang '22), +7.852s; **10** Ty Dillon, USA (Chevrolet Camaro ZL1 '22), +8.311s.
Pole position: Cole Custer, USA (Ford Mustang '22).
Drivers' championship points: 1 Elliott, 324; **2** Blaney, 321; **3** Logano, 303; **4** Byron, 295; **5** Bowman, 273; **6** Busch (Kyle), 273.

53RD ANNUAL GEICO 500, Talladega Superspeedway, Lincoln, Alabama, USA, 24 April. Round 10. 188 laps of the 2.660-mile/4.281km circuit, 500.080 miles/804.801km.
1 Ross Chastain, USA (Chevrolet Camaro ZL1 '22), 3h 21m 52s, 148.637mph/239.208km/h; **2** Austin Dillon, USA (Chevrolet Camaro ZL1 '22), +0.105s; **3** Kyle Busch, USA (Toyota Camry '22), +0.225s; **4** Kyle Larson, USA (Chevrolet Camaro ZL1 '22), +0.233s; **5** Martin Truex Jr., USA (Toyota Camry '22), +0.250s; **6** Erik Jones, USA (Chevrolet Camaro ZL1 '22), +0.311s; **7** Chase Elliott, USA (Chevrolet Camaro ZL1 '22), +0.357s; **8** Michael McDowell, USA (Ford Mustang '22), +0.445s; **9** Alex Bowman, USA (Chevrolet Camaro ZL1 '22), +0.458s; **10** Kevin Harvick, USA (Ford Mustang '22), +0.461s.
Pole position: Christopher Bell, USA (Toyota Camry '22), 52.927s, 180.928mph/291.176km/h.
Drivers' championship points: 1 Elliott, 368; **2** Blaney, 347; **3** Byron, 334; **4** Busch (Kyle), 312; **5** Bowman, 309; **6** Logano, 308.

53RD ANNUAL DURAMAX DRYDENE 400 PRESENTED BY RELADYNE, Dover Motor Speedway, Delaware, USA, 2 May. Round 11. 400 laps of the 1.000-mile/1.609km circuit, 400.000 miles/643.738km.
1 Chase Elliott, USA (Chevrolet Camaro ZL1 '22), 3h 49m 39s, 104.507mph/168.187km/h; **2** Ricky Stenhouse Jr., USA (Chevrolet Camaro ZL1 '22), +2.577s; **3** Ross Chastain, USA (Chevrolet Camaro ZL1 '22), +3.679s; **4** Christopher Bell, USA (Toyota Camry '22), +4.060s; **5** Alex Bowman, USA (Chevrolet Camaro ZL1 '22), +5.329s; **6** Kyle Larson, USA (Chevrolet Camaro ZL1 '22), +11.932s; **7** Kyle Busch, USA (Toyota Camry '22), +12.164s; **8** Chris Buescher, USA (Ford Mustang '22), +14.137s; **9** Kevin Harvick, USA (Ford Mustang '22), +14.549s; **10** Erik Jones, USA (Chevrolet Camaro ZL1 '22), +18.275s.
Pole position: Buescher, 22.479s, 160.149mph/257.736km/h.
Drivers' championship points: 1 Elliott, 418; **2** Blaney, 368; **3** Byron, 353; **4** Busch (Kyle), 353; **5** Bowman, 349; **6** Chastain, 338.

3RD ANNUAL GOODYEAR 400, Darlington Raceway, South Carolina, USA, 8 May. Round 12. 293 laps of the 1.366-mile/2.198km circuit, 400.238 miles/644.121km.
1 Joey Logano, USA (Ford Mustang '22), 3h 21m 32s, 119.158mph/191.766km/h; **2** Tyler Reddick, USA (Chevrolet Camaro ZL1 '22), +0.775s; **3** J.J. Haley, USA (Chevrolet Camaro ZL1 '22), +5.295s; **4** Kevin Harvick, USA (Ford Mustang '22), +5.633s; **5** Chase Elliott, USA (Chevrolet Camaro ZL1 '22), +5.882s; **6** Christopher Bell, USA (Toyota Camry '22), +6.129s; **7** Michael McDowell, USA (Ford Mustang '22), +7.394s; **8** Ricky Stenhouse Jr., USA (Chevrolet Camaro ZL1 '22), +8.132s; **9** Austin Dillon, USA (Chevrolet Camaro ZL1 '22), +8.728s; **10** Daniel Suárez, MEX (Chevrolet Camaro ZL1 '22), +10.389s.
Pole position: Logano, 28.805s, 170.720mph/274.748km/h.
Drivers' championship points: 1 Elliott, 453; **2** Byron, 388; **3** Blaney, 388; **4** Logano, 374; **5** Chastain, 364; **6** Busch (Kyle), 364.

3RD ANNUAL ADVENTHEALTH 400, Kansas Speedway, Kansas City, Kansas, USA, 15 May. Round 13. 267 laps of the 1.500-mile/2.414km circuit, 400.500 miles/644.542km.
1 Kurt Busch, USA (Toyota Camry '22), 3h 13m 03s, 124.476mph/200.324km/h; **2** Kyle Larson, USA (Chevrolet Camaro ZL1 '22), +1.413s; **3** Kyle Busch, USA (Toyota Camry '22), +1.991s; **4** Denny Hamlin, USA (Toyota Camry '22), +2.286s; **5** Christopher Bell, USA (Toyota Camry '22), +3.845s; **6** Martin Truex Jr., USA (Toyota Camry '22), +8.656s; **7** Ross Chastain,

USA (Chevrolet Camaro ZL1 '22), +13.539s; **8** Ricky Stenhouse Jr., USA (Chevrolet Camaro ZL1 '22), +15.158s; **9** Alex Bowman, USA (Chevrolet Camaro ZL1 '22), +15.958s; **10** Darrell Wallace Jr., USA (Toyota Camry '22), +16.498s.
Pole position: Bell, 30.071s, 179.575mph/288.998km/h.
Drivers' championship points: **1** Elliott, 475; **2** Blaney, 423; **3** Busch (Kyle), 417; **4** Byron, 415; **5** Chastain, 407; **6** Truex Jr., 400.

63RD ANNUAL COCA-COLA 600, Charlotte Motor Speedway, Concord, North Carolina, USA, 29 May. Round 14. 413 laps of the 1.500-mile/2.414km circuit, 619.500 miles/996.989km.
1 Denny Hamlin, USA (Toyota Camry '22), 5h 13m 08s, 118.703mph/191.035km/h; **2** Kyle Busch, USA (Toyota Camry '22), +0.119s; **3** Kevin Harvick, USA (Ford Mustang '22), +0.665s; **4** Chase Briscoe, USA (Ford Mustang '22), +0.785s; **5** Christopher Bell, USA (Toyota Camry '22), +1.217s; **6** Tyler Reddick, USA (Chevrolet Camaro ZL1 '22), +1.527s; **7** Ricky Stenhouse Jr., USA (Chevrolet Camaro ZL1 '22), +1.572s; **8** Michael McDowell, USA (Ford Mustang '22), +1.601s; **9** Kyle Larson, USA (Chevrolet Camaro ZL1 '22), +1.695s; **10** Alex Bowman, USA (Chevrolet Camaro ZL1 '22), +1.727s.
Pole position: Hamlin, 29.399s, 183.680mph/295.604km/h.
Drivers' championship points: **1** Elliott, 489; **2** Chastain, 455; **3** Busch (Kyle), 452; **4** Blaney, 436; **5** Truex Jr., 430; **6** Logano, 423.

INAUGURAL ENJOY ILLINOIS 300 PRESENTED BY TICKETSMARTER, World Wide Technology Raceway, St Louis, Madison, Illinois, USA, 5 June. Round 15. 245 laps of the 1.250-mile/2.012km circuit, 306.250 miles/492.862km.
1 Joey Logano, USA (Ford Mustang '22), 3h 07m 34s, 97.965mph/157.660km/h; **2** Kyle Busch, USA (Toyota Camry '22), +0.655s; **3** Kurt Busch, USA (Toyota Camry '22), +0.913s; **4** Ryan Blaney, USA (Ford Mustang '22), +0.937s; **5** Aric Almirola, USA (Ford Mustang '22), +1.475s; **6** Martin Truex Jr., USA (Toyota Camry '22), +1.857s; **7** Erik Jones, USA (Chevrolet Camaro ZL1 '22), +2.017s; **8** Ross Chastain, USA (Chevrolet Camaro ZL1 '22), +2.034s; **9** Christopher Bell, USA (Toyota Camry '22), +2.119s; **10** A.J. Allmendinger, USA (Chevrolet Camaro ZL1 '22), +2.176s.
Pole position: Chase Briscoe, USA (Ford Mustang '22), 32.544s, 138.274mph/222.531km/h.
Drivers' championship points: **1** Elliott, 507; **2** Busch (Kyle), 498; **3** Chastain, 490; **4** Blaney, 479; **5** Truex Jr., 470; **6** Logano, 467.

33RD ANNUAL TOYOTA/SAVE MART 350, Sonoma Raceway, California, USA, 12 June. Round 16. 110 laps of the 1.990-mile/3.203km circuit, 218.900 miles/352.285km.
1 Daniel Suárez, MEX (Chevrolet Camaro ZL1 '22), 2h 48m 22s, 78.008mph/125.542km/h; **2** Chris Buescher, USA (Ford Mustang '22), +3.849s; **3** Michael McDowell, USA (Ford Mustang '22), +5.682s; **4** Kevin Harvick, USA (Ford Mustang '22), +7.911s; **5** Austin Cindric, USA (Ford Mustang '22), +9.852s; **6** Ryan Blaney, USA (Ford Mustang '22), +12.975s; **7** Ross Chastain, USA (Chevrolet Camaro ZL1 '22), +13.966s; **8** Chase Elliott, USA (Chevrolet Camaro ZL1 '22), +16.141s; **9** William Byron, USA (Chevrolet Camaro ZL1 '22), +17.260s; **10** Brad Keselowski, USA (Ford Mustang '22), +17.734s.
Pole position: Kyle Larson, USA (Chevrolet Camaro ZL1 '22), 1m 17.776s, 92.111mph/148.238km/h.
Drivers' championship points: **1** Elliott, 536; **2** Chastain, 520; **3** Busch (Kyle), 513; **4** Blaney, 511; **5** Logano, 506; **6** Truex Jr., 481.

2ND ANNUAL ALLY 400, Nashville Superspeedway, Lebanon, Tennessee, USA, 26 June. Round 17. 300 laps of the 1.330-mile/2.140km circuit, 399.000 miles/642.128km.
1 Chase Elliott, USA (Chevrolet Camaro ZL1 '22), 3h 35m 15s, 111.220mph/178.990km/h; **2** Kurt Busch, USA (Toyota Camry '22), +0.551s; **3** Ryan Blaney, USA (Ford Mustang '22), +1.248s; **4** Kyle Larson, USA (Chevrolet Camaro ZL1 '22), +1.36s; **5** Ross Chastain, USA (Chevrolet Camaro ZL1 '22), +1.922s; **6** Denny Hamlin, USA (Toyota Camry '22), +2.156s; **7** Austin Cindric, USA (Ford Mustang '22), +2.485s; **8** Christopher Bell, USA (Toyota Camry '22), +2.728s; **9** Joey Logano, USA (Ford Mustang '22), +3.235s; **10** Kevin Harvick, USA (Ford Mustang '22), +3.338s.
Pole position: Hamlin, 29.848s, 160.413mph/258.159km/h.
Drivers' championship points: **1** Elliott, 586; **2** Chastain, 556; **3** Blaney, 555; **4** Busch (Kyle), 539; **5** Logano, 534; **6** Larson, 519.

2ND ANNUAL KWIK TRIP 250 PRESENTED BY JOCKEY MADE IN AMERICA, Road America, Elkhart Lake, Wisconsin, USA, 3 July. Round 18. 62 laps of the 4.048-mile/6.515km circuit, 250.976 miles/403.907km.
1 Tyler Reddick, USA (Chevrolet Camaro ZL1 '22), 2h 35m 51s, 96.622mph/155.498km/h; **2** Chase Elliott, USA (Chevrolet Camaro ZL1 '22), +3.304s; **3** Kyle Larson, USA (Chevrolet Camaro ZL1 '22), +21.138s; **4** Ross Chastain, USA (Chevrolet Camaro ZL1 '22), +25.641s; **5** Daniel Suárez, MEX (Chevrolet Camaro ZL1 '22), +32.080s; **6** Chris Buescher, USA (Ford Mustang '22), +32.482s; **7** Austin Cindric, USA (Ford Mustang '22), +32.782s; **8** Michael McDowell, USA (Ford Mustang '22), +42.348s; **9** A.J. Allmendinger, USA (Chevrolet Camaro ZL1 '22), +44.127s; **10** Kevin Harvick, USA (Ford Mustang '22), +45.463s.
Pole position: Elliott, 2m 14.427s, 108.407mph/174.464km/h.
Drivers' championship points: **1** Elliott, 624; **2** Blaney, 591; **3** Chastain, 589; **4** Larson, 553; **5** Logano, 551; **6** Busch (Kyle), 547.

53RD QUAKER STATE 400 PRESENTED BY WALMART, Atlanta Motor Speedway, Hampton, Georgia, USA, 10 July. Round 19. 260 laps of the 1.540-mile/2.478km circuit, 400.400 miles/644.381km.
1 Chase Elliott, USA (Chevrolet Camaro ZL1 '22), 3h 22m 18s, 118.754mph/191.117km/h; **2** Ross Chastain, USA (Chevrolet Camaro ZL1 '22), +0.081s; **3** Austin Cindric, USA (Ford Mustang '22), +0.541s; **4** Erik Jones, USA (Chevrolet Camaro ZL1 '22), +0.991s; **5** Ryan Blaney, USA (Ford Mustang '22), +1.165s; **6** Daniel Suárez, MEX (Chevrolet Camaro ZL1 '22), +1.515s; **7** J.J. Haley, USA (Chevrolet Camaro ZL1 '22), +2.283s; **8** Aric Almirola, USA (Ford Mustang '22), +2.531s; **9** Cole Custer, USA (Ford Mustang '22), +2.532s; **10** Harrison Burton, USA (Ford Mustang '22), +2.533s.
Pole position: Elliott.
Drivers' championship points: **1** Elliott, 684; **2** Blaney, 637; **3** Chastain, 634; **4** Larson, 579; **5** Busch (Kyle), 569; **6** Truex Jr., 566.

30TH ANNUAL AMBETTER 301, New Hampshire Motor Speedway, Loudon, New Hampshire, USA, 17 July. Round 20. 301 laps of the 1.058-mile/1.703km circuit, 318.458 miles/512.508km.
1 Christopher Bell, USA (Toyota Camry '22), 3h 14m 45s, 98.113mph/157.897km/h; **2** Chase Elliott, USA (Chevrolet Camaro ZL1 '22), +5.439s; **3** Darrell Wallace Jr., USA (Toyota Camry '22), +13.377s; **4** Martin Truex Jr., USA (Toyota Camry '22), +13.646s; **5** Kevin Harvick, USA (Ford Mustang '22), +15.398s; **6** Denny Hamlin, USA (Toyota Camry '22), +19.040s; **7** Brad Keselowski, USA (Ford Mustang '22), +22.482s; **8** Ross Chastain, USA (Chevrolet Camaro ZL1 '22), +23.307s; **9** Daniel Suárez, MEX (Chevrolet Camaro ZL1 '22), +23.982s; **10** Kurt Busch, USA (Toyota Camry '22), +24.638s.
Pole position: Truex Jr., 29.964s, 127.113mph/204.568km/h.
Drivers' championship points: **1** Elliott, 734; **2** Chastain, 667; **3** Blaney, 656; **4** Truex Jr., 619; **5** Larson, 616; **6** Busch (Kyle), 594.

49TH ANNUAL M&MS FAN APPRECIATION 400, Pocono Raceway, Long Pond, Pennsylvania, USA, 24 July. Round 21. 160 laps of the 2.500-mile/4.023km circuit, 400.000 miles/643.738km.
1 Chase Elliott, USA (Chevrolet Camaro ZL1 '22), 3h 16m 01s, 122.439mph/197.046km/h; **2** Tyler Reddick, USA (Chevrolet Camaro ZL1 '22), +3.118s; **3** Daniel Suárez, MEX (Chevrolet Camaro ZL1 '22), +3.900s; **4** Christopher Bell, USA (Toyota Camry '22), +5.772s; **5** Kyle Larson, USA (Chevrolet Camaro ZL1 '22), +7.417s; **6** Michael McDowell, USA (Ford Mustang '22), +9.734s; **7** Martin Truex Jr., USA (Toyota Camry '22), +10.29s; **8** Darrell Wallace Jr., USA (Toyota Camry '22), +11.17s; **9** Erik Jones, USA (Chevrolet Camaro ZL1 '22), +11.555s; **10** Austin Dillon, USA (Chevrolet Camaro ZL1 '22), +11.684s.
Pole position: Denny Hamlin, USA (Toyota Camry '22), 52.944s, 169.991mph/273.574km/h.
Drivers' championship points: **1** Elliott, 787; **2** Chastain, 682; **3** Blaney, 676; **4** Larson, 661; **5** Truex Jr., 654; **6** Bell, 605.

29TH ANNUAL VERIZON 200 AT THE BRICKYARD, Indianapolis Motor Speedway, Speedway, Indiana, USA, 31 July. Round 22. 86 laps of the 2.439-mile/3.925km circuit, 209.754 miles/337.566km.
1 Tyler Reddick, USA (Chevrolet Camaro ZL1 '22), 2h 40m 18s, 78.511mph/126.350km/h; **2** Austin Cindric, USA (Ford Mustang '22), +1.065s; **3** Harrison Burton, USA (Ford Mustang '22), +2.388s; **4** Todd Gilliland, USA (Ford Mustang '22), +3.337s; **5** Darrell Wallace Jr., USA (Toyota Camry '22), +4.422s; **6** Joey Logano, USA (Ford Mustang '22), +4.938s; **7** A.J. Allmendinger, USA (Chevrolet Camaro ZL1 '22), +5.069s; **8** Michael McDowell, USA (Ford Mustang '22), +5.681s; **9** Cole Custer, USA (Ford Mustang '22), +6.183s; **10** Chris Buescher, USA (Ford Mustang '22), +6.207s.
Pole position: Reddick, 1m 28.354s, 99.378mph/159.933km/h.
Drivers' championship points: **1** Elliott, 821; **2** Blaney, 696; **3** Chastain, 692; **4** Truex Jr., 671; **5** Larson, 667; **6** Bell, 640.

54TH ANNUAL FIREKEEPERS CASINO 400, Michigan International Speedway, Brooklyn, Michigan, USA, 7 August. Round 23. 200 laps of the 2.000-mile/3.219km circuit, 400.000 miles/643.738km.
1 Kevin Harvick, USA (Ford Mustang '22), 2h 54m 08s, 137.825mph/221.809km/h; **2** Darrell Wallace Jr., USA (Toyota Camry '22), +2.903s; **3** Denny Hamlin, USA (Toyota Camry '22), +3.910s; **4** Joey Logano, USA (Ford Mustang '22), +7.823s; **5** Ryan Blaney, USA (Ford Mustang '22), +8.152s; **6** Martin Truex Jr., USA (Toyota Camry '22), +8.236s; **7** Kyle Larson, USA (Chevrolet Camaro ZL1 '22), +9.951s; **8** Erik Jones, USA (Chevrolet Camaro ZL1 '22), +10.741s; **9** Alex Bowman, USA (Chevrolet Camaro ZL1 '22), +10.972s; **10** Ty Gibbs, USA (Toyota Camry '22), +11.229s.
Pole position: Wallace Jr., 37.755s, 190.703mph/306.907km/h.
Drivers' championship points: **1** Elliott, 847; **2** Blaney, 728; **3** Chastain, 710; **4** Truex Jr., 709; **5** Larson, 705; **6** Logano, 673.

65TH ANNUAL FEDERATED AUTO PARTS 400, Richmond International Raceway, Virginia, USA, 14 August. Round 24. 400 laps of the 0.750-mile/1.207km circuit, 300.000 miles/482.803km.
1 Kevin Harvick, USA (Ford Mustang '22), 3h 03m 27s, 98.119mph/157.908km/h; **2** Christopher Bell, USA (Toyota Camry '22), +0.441s; **3** Chris Buescher, USA (Ford Mustang '22), +2.492s; **4** Denny Hamlin, USA (Toyota Camry '22), +3.839s; **5** Chase Elliott, USA (Chevrolet Camaro ZL1 '22), +6.672s; **6** Joey Logano, USA (Ford Mustang '22), +12.152s; **7** Martin Truex Jr., USA (Toyota Camry '22), +13.205s; **8** Aric Almirola, USA (Ford Mustang '22), +13.848s; **9** Kyle Busch, USA (Toyota Camry '22), +15.978s; **10** Ryan Blaney, USA (Ford Mustang '22), +18.716s.
Pole position: Kyle Larson, USA (Chevrolet Camaro ZL1 '22), 23.042s, 117.177mph/188.579km/h.
Drivers' championship points: **1** Elliott, 882; **2** Blaney, 766; **3** Larson, 745; **4** Truex Jr., 740; **5** Chastain, 739; **6** Logano, 718.

36TH ANNUAL GO BOWLING AT THE GLEN, Watkins Glen International, New York, USA, 21 August. Round 25. 90 laps of the 2.450-mile/3.943km circuit, 220.500 miles/354.860km.
1 Kyle Larson, USA (Chevrolet Camaro ZL1 '22), 2h 17m 52s, 95.962mph/154.436km/h; **2** A.J. Allmendinger, USA (Chevrolet Camaro ZL1 '22), +0.882s; **3** Joey Logano, USA (Ford Mustang '22), +3.841s; **4** Chase Elliott, USA (Chevrolet Camaro ZL1 '22), +4.256s; **5** Daniel Suárez, MEX (Chevrolet Camaro ZL1 '22), +6.360s; **6** Michael McDowell, USA (Ford Mustang '22), +7.173s; **7** Tyler Reddick, USA (Chevrolet Camaro ZL1 '22), +7.579s; **8** Christopher Bell, USA (Toyota Camry '22), +8.823s; **9** Chris Buescher, USA (Ford Mustang '22), +8.975s; **10** Erik Jones, USA (Chevrolet Camaro ZL1 '22), +9.378s.
Pole position: Elliott, 1m 10.477s, 125.147mph/201.405km/h.
Drivers' championship points: **1** Elliott, 922; **2** Larson, 788; **3** Blaney, 779; **4** Logano, 767; **5** Chastain, 761; **6** Truex Jr., 754.

64TH ANNUAL COKE ZERO SUGAR 400, Daytona International Speedway, Daytona Beach, Florida, USA, 28 August. Round 26. 160 laps of the 2.500-mile/4.023km circuit, 400.000 miles/643.738km.
1 Austin Dillon, USA (Chevrolet Camaro ZL1 '22), 2h 52m 44s, 138.942mph/223.606km/h; **2** Tyler Reddick, USA (Chevrolet Camaro ZL1 '22), +0.128s; **3** Austin Cindric, USA (Ford Mustang '22), +0.140s; **4** Landon Cassill, USA (Chevrolet Camaro ZL1 '22), +0.262s; **5** Noah Gragson, USA (Chevrolet Camaro ZL1 '22), +0.284s; **6** Cody Ware, USA (Ford Mustang '22), +0.446s; **7** B.J. McLeod, USA (Ford Mustang '22), +0.555s; **8** Martin Truex Jr., USA (Toyota Camry '22), +0.575s; **9** David Ragan, USA (Ford Mustang '22), +0.579s; **10** Kyle Busch, USA (Toyota Camry '22), +41.745s.
Pole position: Larson.
Drivers' championship points: **1** Elliott, 2040; **2** Logano, 2025; **3** Chastain, 2020; **4** Larson, 2019; **5** Byron, 2014; **6** Hamlin, 2013.

73RD ANNUAL COOK OUT SOUTHERN 500, Darlington Raceway, South Carolina, USA, 4 September. Round 27. 367 laps of the 1.366-mile/2.198km circuit, 501.322 miles/806.800km.
1 Erik Jones, USA (Chevrolet Camaro ZL1 '22), 4h 09m 49s, 120.406mph/193.774km/h; **2** Denny Hamlin, USA (Toyota Camry '22), +0.252s; **3** Tyler Reddick, USA (Chevrolet Camaro ZL1 '22), +0.924s; **4** Joey Logano, USA (Ford Mustang '22), +2.361s; **5** Christopher Bell, USA (Toyota Camry '22), +2.751s; **6** Michael McDowell, USA (Ford Mustang '22), +3.965s; **7** Brad Keselowski, USA (Ford Mustang '22), +6.075s; **8** William Byron, USA (Chevrolet Camaro ZL1 '22), +6.878s; **9** Darrell Wallace Jr., USA (Toyota Camry '22), +7.741s; **10** Alex Bowman, USA (Chevrolet Camaro ZL1 '22), +8.360s.
Pole position: Logano, 29.181s, 168.521mph/271.208km/h.
Drivers' championship points: **1** Logano, 2065; **2** Byron, 2059; **3** Hamlin, 2057; **4** Bell, 2055; **5** Reddick, 2050; **6** Blaney, 2047.

22ND ANNUAL HOLLYWOOD CASINO 400 PRESENTED BY BARSTOOL SPORTSBOOK, Kansas Speedway, Kansas City, Kansas, USA, 11 September. Round 28. 267 laps of the 1.500-mile/2.414km circuit, 400.500 miles/644.542km.
1 Darrell Wallace Jr., USA (Toyota Camry '22), 3h 10m 03s, 126.440mph/203.486km/h; **2** Denny Hamlin, USA (Toyota Camry '22), +1.000s; **3** Christopher Bell, USA (Toyota Camry '22), +3.718s; **4** Alex Bowman, USA (Chevrolet Camaro ZL1 '22), +13.516s; **5** Martin Truex Jr., USA (Toyota Camry '22), +13.851s; **6** William Byron, USA (Chevrolet Camaro ZL1 '22), +17.240s; **7** Ross Chastain, USA (Chevrolet Camaro ZL1 '22), +17.984s; **8** Kyle Larson, USA (Chevrolet Camaro ZL1 '22), +20.143s; **9** Ryan Blaney, USA (Ford Mustang '22), +20.586s; **10** Daniel Suárez, MEX (Chevrolet Camaro ZL1 '22), +20.658s.
Pole position: Tyler Reddick, USA (Chevrolet Camaro ZL1 '22), 29.899s, 180.608mph/290.660km/h.
Drivers' championship points: **1** Bell, 2108; **2** Byron, 2098; **3** Hamlin, 2097; **4** Logano, 2090; **5** Blaney, 2086; **6** Bowman, 2080.

62ND ANNUAL BASS PRO SHOPS NIGHT RACE, Bristol Motor Speedway, Tennessee, USA, 17 September. Round 29. 500 laps of the 0.533-mile/0.858km circuit, 266.500 miles/428.890km.
1 Chris Buescher, USA (Ford Mustang '22), 3h 01m 07s, 88.286mph/142.082km/h; **2** Chase Elliott, USA (Chevrolet Camaro ZL1 '22), +0.458s; **3** William Byron, USA (Chevrolet Camaro ZL1 '22), +1.667s; **4** Christopher Bell, USA (Toyota Camry '22), +1.809s; **5** Kyle Larson, USA (Chevrolet Camaro ZL1 '22), +3.688s; **6** Ross Chastain, USA (Chevrolet Camaro ZL1 '22), +4.106s; **7** A.J. Allmendinger, USA (Chevrolet Camaro ZL1 '22), +5.994s; **8** Cole Custer, USA (Ford Mustang '22), +7.648s; **9** Denny Hamlin, USA (Toyota Camry '22), +7.884s; **10** Kevin Harvick, USA (Ford Mustang '22), +8.421s.
Pole position: Aric Almirola, USA (Ford Mustang '22), 14.946s, 128.382mph/206.611km/h.
Drivers' championship points: **1** Elliott, 3040; **2** Logano, 3025; **3** Chastain, 3020; **4** Larson, 3019; **5** Byron, 3015; **6** Hamlin, 3013.

18TH ANNUAL AUTOTRADER ECHOPARK AUTOMOTIVE 500, Texas Motor Speedway, Fort Worth, Texas, USA, 25 September. Round 30. 334 laps of the 1.500-mile/2.414km circuit, 501.000 miles/806.281km.
1 Tyler Reddick, USA (Chevrolet Camaro ZL1 '22), 4h 21m 53s, 114.784mph/184.727km/h; **2** Joey Logano, USA (Ford Mustang '22), +1.190s; **3** J.J. Haley, USA (Chevrolet Camaro ZL1 '22), +1.768s; **4** Ryan Blaney, USA (Ford Mustang '22), +2.365s; **5** Chase Briscoe, USA (Ford Mustang '22), +4.144s; **6** Erik Jones, USA (Chevrolet Camaro ZL1 '22), +4.326s; **7** William Byron, USA (Chevrolet Camaro ZL1 '22), +4.378s; **8** Brad Keselowski, USA (Ford Mustang '22), +5.037s; **9** Kyle Larson, USA (Chevrolet Camaro ZL1 '22), +5.504s; **10** Denny Hamlin, USA (Toyota Camry '22), +5.621s.
Pole position: Keselowski, 28.573s, 188.990mph/304.149km/h.
Drivers' championship points: **1** Logano, 3071; **2** Chastain, 3059; **3** Larson, 3057; **4** Blaney, 3056; **5** Hamlin, 3049; **6** Elliott, 3045.

54TH ANNUAL YELLAWOOD 500, Talladega Superspeedway, Lincoln, Alabama, USA, 2 October. Round 31. 188 laps of the 2.660-mile/4.281km circuit, 500.080 miles/ 804.801km.
1 Chase Elliott, USA (Chevrolet Camaro ZL1 '22), 3h 15m 23s, 153.569mph/247.145km/h; **2** Ryan Blaney, USA (Ford Mustang '22), +0.046s; **3** Michael McDowell, USA (Ford Mustang '22), +0.094s; **4** Ross Chastain, USA (Chevrolet Camaro ZL1 '22), +0.160s; **5** Denny Hamlin, USA (Toyota Camry '22), +0.183s; **6** Erik Jones, USA (Chevrolet Camaro ZL1 '22), +0.251s; **7** Todd Gilliland, USA (Ford Mustang '22), +0.284s; **8** Daniel Suárez, MEX (Chevrolet Camaro ZL1 '22), +0.296s; **9** Austin Cindric, USA (Ford Mustang '22), +0.312s; **10** Chase Briscoe, USA (Ford Mustang '22), +0.322s.
Pole position: Christopher Bell, USA (Toyota Camry '22), 53.026s, 180.591mph/290.632km/h.
Drivers' championship points: 1 Elliott, 3103; **2** Blaney, 3101; **3** Chastain, 3097; **4** Hamlin, 3090; **5** Logano, 3087; **6** Larson, 3087.

63RD ANNUAL BANK OF AMERICA ROVAL 400, Charlotte Motor Speedway, Concord, North Carolina, USA, 9 October. Round 32. 112 laps of the 2.320-mile/3.734km circuit, 259.840 miles/418.172km.
1 Christopher Bell, USA (Toyota Camry '22), 2h 59m 54s, 86.661mph/139.468km/h; **2** Kevin Harvick, USA (Ford Mustang '22), +1.790s; **3** Kyle Busch, USA (Toyota Camry '22), +1.976s; **4** A.J. Allmendinger, USA (Chevrolet Camaro ZL1 '22), +3.136s; **5** J.J. Haley, USA (Chevrolet Camaro ZL1 '22), +4.635s; **6** Chris Buescher, USA (Ford Mustang '22), +4.974s; **7** Darrell Wallace Jr., USA (Toyota Camry '22), +5.442s; **8** Tyler Reddick, USA (Chevrolet Camaro ZL1 '22), +6.839s; **9** Chase Briscoe, USA (Ford Mustang '22), +6.973s; **10** Austin Dillon, USA (Chevrolet Camaro ZL1 '22), +8.329s.
Pole position: Joey Logano, USA (Ford Mustang '22), 1m 20.755s, 103.424mph/166.445km/h.
Drivers' championship points: 1 Elliott, 4046; **2** Logano, 4026; **3** Chastain, 4021; **4** Bell, 4018; **5** Byron, 4015; **6** Blaney, 4015.

5TH ANNUAL SOUTH POINT 400, Las Vegas Motor Speedway, Nevada, USA, 16 October. Round 33. 267 laps of the 1.500-mile/2.414km circuit, 400.500 miles/ 644.542km.
1 Joey Logano, USA (Ford Mustang '22), 3h 04m 10s, 130.480mph/209.987km/h; **2** Ross Chastain, USA (Chevrolet Camaro ZL1 '22), +0.817s; **3** Kyle Busch, USA (Toyota Camry '22), +1.033s; **4** Chase Briscoe, USA (Ford Mustang '22), +2.062s; **5** Denny Hamlin, USA (Toyota Camry '22), +3.432s; **6** Tyler Reddick, USA (Chevrolet Camaro ZL1 '22), +3.775s; **7** Martin Truex Jr., USA (Toyota Camry '22), +4.547s; **8** Erik Jones, USA (Chevrolet Camaro ZL1 '22), +5.032s; **9** A.J. Allmendinger, USA (Chevrolet Camaro ZL1 '22), +5.101s; **10** Austin Dillon, USA (Chevrolet Camaro ZL1 '22), +5.723s.
Pole position: Reddick, 29.252s, 184.603mph/ 297.089km/h.
Drivers' championship points: 1 Logano, 4084; **2** Chastain, 4063; **3** Elliott, 4062; **4** Hamlin, 4051; **5** Byron, 4045; **6** Briscoe, 4042.

24TH ANNUAL DIXIE VODKA 400, Homestead-Miami Speedway, Florida, USA, 23 October. Round 34. 267 laps of the 1.500-mile/2.414km circuit, 400.500 miles/ 644.542km.
1 Kyle Larson, USA (Chevrolet Camaro ZL1 '22), 3h 05m 24s, 129.612mph/208.590km/h; **2** Ross Chastain, USA (Chevrolet Camaro ZL1 '22), +1.261s; **3** A.J. Allmendinger, USA (Chevrolet Camaro ZL1 '22), +1.362s; **4** Austin Dillon, USA (Chevrolet Camaro ZL1 '22), +2.671s; **5** Brad Keselowski, USA (Ford Mustang '22), +3.739s; **6** Martin Truex Jr., USA (Toyota Camry '22), +4.203s; **7** Denny Hamlin, USA (Toyota Camry '22), +4.429s; **8** Kevin Harvick, USA (Ford Mustang '22), +5.107s; **9** Kyle Busch, USA (Toyota Camry '22), +5.372s; **10** Daniel Suárez, MEX (Chevrolet Camaro ZL1 '22), +5.694s.
Pole position: William Byron, USA (Chevrolet Camaro ZL1 '22), 32.454s, 166.389mph/ 267.778km/h.
Drivers' championship points: 1 Logano, 4106; **2** Chastain, 4101; **3** Elliott, 4093; **4** Byron, 4087; **5** Hamlin, 4082; **6** Blaney, 4069.

74TH ANNUAL XFINITY 500, Martinsville Speedway, Ridgeway, Virginia, USA, 30 October. Round 35. 500 laps of the 0.526-mile/0.847km circuit, 263.000 miles/ 423.257km.
1 Christopher Bell, USA (Toyota Camry '22), 3h 24m 18s, 77.239mph/124.305km/h; **2** Kyle Larson, USA (Chevrolet Camaro ZL1 '22), +0.869s; **3** Ryan Blaney, USA (Ford Mustang '22), +2.228s; **4** Ross Chastain, USA (Chevrolet Camaro ZL1 '22), +2.919s; **5** Denny Hamlin, USA (Toyota Camry '22), +2.992s; **6** Joey Logano, USA (Ford Mustang '22), +3.341s; **7** William Byron, USA (Chevrolet Camaro ZL1 '22), +3.395s; **8** Darrell Wallace Jr., USA (Toyota Camry '22), +3.741s; **9** Chase Briscoe, USA (Ford Mustang '22), +4.862s; **10** Chase Elliott, USA (Chevrolet Camaro ZL1 '22), +5.283s.
Pole position: Larson, 19.709s, 96.078mph/ 154.622km/h.
Drivers' championship points: 1 Elliott, 5000; **2** Logano, 5000; **3** Bell, 5000; **4** Chastain, 5000; **5** Hamlin, 2350; **6** Byron, 2339.

35TH ANNUAL NASCAR CUP SERIES CHAMPIONSHIP RACE, Phoenix Raceway, Arizona, USA, 6 November. Round 36. 312 laps of the 1.000-mile/1.609km circuit, 312.000 miles/ 502.115km.
1 Joey Logano, USA (Ford Mustang '22), 2h 58m 42s, 104.757mph/168.589km/h; **2** Ryan Blaney, USA (Ford Mustang '22), +0.301s; **3** Ross Chastain, USA (Chevrolet Camaro ZL1 '22), +1.268s; **4** Chase Briscoe, USA (Ford Mustang '22), +3.206s; **5** Kevin Harvick, USA (Ford Mustang '22), +3.436s; **6** William Byron, USA (Chevrolet Camaro ZL1 '22), +4.494s; **7** Kyle Busch, USA (Toyota Camry '22), +5.133s; **8** Denny Hamlin, USA (Toyota Camry '22), +6.463s; **9** Kyle Larson, USA (Chevrolet Camaro ZL1 '22), +7.011s; **10** Christopher Bell, USA (Toyota Camry '22), +7.311s.
Pole position: Logano, 26.788s, 134.389mph/ 216.277km/h.

Final championship points
Drivers
1 Joey Logano, USA, 5040; **2** Ross Chastain, USA, 5034; **3** Christopher Bell, USA, 5027; **4** Chase Elliott, USA, 5009; **5** Denny Hamlin, USA, 2379; **6** William Byron, USA, 2378; **7** Kyle Larson, USA, 2354; **8** Ryan Blaney, USA, 2354; **9** Chase Briscoe, USA, 2292; **10** Daniel Suárez, MEX, 2272; **11** Austin Dillon, USA, 2228; **12** Austin Cindric, USA, 2226; **13** Kyle Busch, USA, 2224; **14** Tyler Reddick, USA, 2215; **15** Kevin Harvick, USA, 2126; **16** Alex Bowman, USA, 2107; **17** Martin Truex Jr., USA, 1037; **18** Erik Jones, USA, 831; **19** Darrell Wallace Jr., USA, 764; **20** Aric Almirola, USA, 760; **21** Chris Buescher, USA, 727; **22** J.J. Haley, USA, 699; **23** Michael McDowell, USA, 663; **24** Brad Keselowski, USA, 629; **25** Cole Custer, USA, 589; **26** Ricky Stenhouse Jr., USA, 580; **27** Harrison Burton, USA, 573; **28** Todd Gilliland, USA, 531; **29** Ty Dillon, USA, 518; **30** Kurt Busch, USA, 485.

Manufacturers
1 Chevrolet, 1324; **2** Ford, 1231; **3** Toyota, 1200.

Sunoco Rookie of the Year
Austin Cindric, USA.

Other NASCAR races

44TH ANNUAL BUSCH LIGHT CLASH AT THE COLISEUM, LA Memorial Coliseum, Los Angeles, California, USA, 6 February. 150 laps of the 0.250-mile/0.402km circuit, 37.500 miles/ 60.350km.
1 Joey Logano, USA (Ford Mustang '22), 57m 39s, 39.029mph/62.810km/h; **2** Kyle Busch, USA (Toyota Camry '22), +0.877s; **3** Austin Dillon, USA (Chevrolet Camaro ZL1 '22), 150 laps; **4** Erik Jones, USA (Chevrolet Camaro ZL1 '22), 150; **5** Kyle Larson, USA (Chevrolet Camaro ZL1 '22), 150; **6** William Byron, USA (Chevrolet Camaro ZL1 '22), 150; **7** Cole Custer, USA (Ford Mustang '22), 150; **8** Christopher Bell, USA (Toyota Camry '22), 150; **9** A.J. Allmendinger, USA (Chevrolet Camaro ZL1 '22), 150; **10** Kevin Harvick, USA (Ford Mustang '22), 150.
Fastest race lap: Logano, 13.336s, 67.487mph/ 108.609km/h.
Pole position: Busch.

BLUEGREEN VACATIONS DUEL 1 & DUEL 2, Daytona International Speedway, Daytona Beach, Florida, USA, 17 February. 2 x 60 laps of the 2.500-mile/4.023km circuit.
Duel 1 (150.000 miles/241.402km).
1 Brad Keselowski, USA (Ford Mustang '22), 48m 36s, 185.185mph/298.027km/h; **2** Austin Cindric, USA (Ford Mustang '22), +0.264s; **3** Ryan Blaney, USA (Ford Mustang '22), 60 laps; **4** Chase Briscoe, USA (Ford Mustang '22), 60; **5** Chase Elliott, USA (Chevrolet Camaro ZL1 '22), 60; **6** Erik Jones, USA (Chevrolet Camaro ZL1 '22), 60; **7** Kyle Larson, USA (Chevrolet Camaro ZL1 '22), 60; **8** Tyler Reddick, USA (Chevrolet Camaro ZL1 '22), 60; **9** Kurt Busch, USA (Toyota Camry '22), 60; **10** Ross Chastain, USA (Chevrolet Camaro ZL1 '22), 60.
Pole position: Larson.

Duel 2 (150.000 miles/241.402km).
1 Chris Buescher, USA (Ford Mustang '22), 48m 24s, 185.950mph/299.258km/h; **2** Michael McDowell, USA (Ford Mustang '22), 60 laps; **3** Harrison Burton, USA (Ford Mustang '22), 60; **4** Kyle Busch, USA (Toyota Camry '22), 60; **5** Christopher Bell, USA (Toyota Camry '22), 60; **6** Martin Truex Jr., USA (Toyota Camry '22), 60; **7** Darrell Wallace Jr., USA (Toyota Camry '22), 60; **8** Ricky Stenhouse Jr., USA (Chevrolet Camaro ZL1 '22), 60; **9** Joey Logano, USA (Ford Mustang '22), -1 (DNF-accident); **10** Kevin Harvick, USA (Ford Mustang '22), -1.
Pole position: Alex Bowman, USA (Chevrolet Camaro ZL1 '22).

NASCAR ALL-STAR OPEN, Texas Motor Speedway, Fort Worth, Texas, USA, 22 May. 50 laps of the 1.500-mile/2.414km circuit, 75.000 miles/120.701km.
1 Daniel Suárez, MEX (Chevrolet Camaro ZL1 '22), 54m 32s, 82.518mph/132.800km/h; **2** Austin Dillon, USA (Chevrolet Camaro ZL1 '22), +1.393s; **3** J.J. Haley, USA (Chevrolet Camaro ZL1 '22), 50 laps; **4** Corey LaJoie, USA (Chevrolet Camaro ZL1 '22), 50; **5** Erik Jones, USA (Chevrolet Camaro ZL1 '22), 50; **6** Ty Dillon, USA (Chevrolet Camaro ZL1 '22), 50; **7** Cole Custer, USA (Ford Mustang '22), 50; **8** Todd Gilliland, USA (Ford Mustang '22), 50; **9** Cody Ware, USA (Ford Mustang '22), 50; **10** Garrett Smithley, USA (Ford Mustang '22), 50.
Pole position: Tyler Reddick, USA (Chevrolet Camaro ZL1 '22), 28.880s, 186.981mph/ 300.916km/h.

NASCAR ALL-STAR RACE, Texas Motor Speedway, Fort Worth, Texas, USA, 22 May. 140 laps of the 1.500-mile/2.414km circuit, 210.000 miles/337.962km.
1 Ryan Blaney, USA (Ford Mustang '22), 2h 02m 47s, 102.620mph/165.151km/h; **2** Denny Hamlin, USA (Toyota Camry '22), +0.266s; **3** Austin Cindric, USA (Ford Mustang '22), 140 laps; **4** Joey Logano, USA (Ford Mustang '22), 140; **5** Daniel Suárez, MEX (Chevrolet Camaro ZL1 '22), 140; **6** Alex Bowman, USA (Chevrolet Camaro ZL1 '22), 140; **7** A.J. Allmendinger, USA (Chevrolet Camaro ZL1 '22), 140; **8** Chris Buescher, USA (Ford Mustang '22), 140; **9** Brad Keselowski, USA (Ford Mustang '22), 140; **10** Christopher Bell, USA (Toyota Camry '22), 140.
Pole position: Kyle Busch, USA (Toyota Camry '22), 28.554s, 189.115mph/304.352km/h.

Indy Lights Presented by Cooper Tires

All cars are Dallara IL15-AER IL-2.

INDY LIGHTS GP OF ST. PETERSBURG, St. Petersburg Street Circuit, Florida, USA, 27 February. Round 1. 45 laps of the 1.800-mile/2.897km circuit, 81.000 miles/ 130.357km.
1 Matthew Brabham, USA, 52m 27.3033s, 92.651mph/149.107km/h; **2** Benjamin Pedersen, DK, +2.4726s; **3** Linus Lundqvist, S, +3.7179s; **4** Sting Ray Robb, USA, +4.6470s; **5** Danial Frost, SGP, +9.6321s; **6** Manuel Sulaimán, MEX, +14.4322s; **7** Ernie Francis Jr., USA, +38.8998s; **8** Antonio Serravalle, CDN, +39.2926s; **9** Christian Bogle, USA, +40.4748s; **10** Jacob Abel, USA, +46.6426s.
Fastest race lap: Christian Rasmussen, DK, 1m 05.0427s, 99.627mph/160.334km/h.
Pole position: Hunter McElrea, AUS, 1m 05.2812s, 99.263mph/159.748km/h.

INDY LIGHTS GRAND PRIX OF ALABAMA, Barber Motorsports Park, Birmingham, Alabama, USA, 1 May. Round 2. 31 laps of the 2.300-mile/3.701km circuit, 71.300 miles/114.746km.
1 Linus Lundqvist, S, 45m 58.8139s, 93.040mph/149.733km/h; **2** Benjamin Pedersen, DK, +0.1782s; **3** Sting Ray Robb, USA, +7.7798s; **4** Danial Frost, SGP, +8.2787s; **5** Kyffin Simpson, BB, +24.9462s; **6** Jacob Abel, USA, +26.1443s; **7** Matthew Brabham, USA, +28.4906s; **8** Ernie Francis Jr., USA, +41.2256s; **9** Antonio Serravalle, CDN, +48.2387s; **10** Manuel Sulaimán, MEX, +1m 05.7804s.
Fastest race lap: Christian Rasmussen, DK, 1m 21.9787s, 101.002mph/162.547km/h.
Pole position: Lundqvist, 1m 12.5713s, 114.095mph/183.618km/h.

INDY LIGHTS GRAND PRIX OF INDIANAPOLIS, Indianapolis Motor Speedway, Speedway, Indiana, USA, 13/14 May. Round 3. 2 x 35 laps of the 2.439-mile/3.925km circuit.
Race 1 (85.365 miles/137.382km).
1 Danial Frost, SGP, 47m 28.6831s, 107.879mph/173.615km/h; **2** Hunter McElrea, AUS, +1.5449s; **3** Sting Ray Robb, USA, +3.3539s; **4** Christian Rasmussen, DK, +9.1499s; **5** Linus Lundqvist, S, +10.9835s; **6** Antonio Serravalle, CDN, +20.2883s; **7** Christian Bogle, USA, +21.1478s; **8** Jacob Abel, USA, +26.3739s; **9** Ernie Francis Jr., USA, +28.8987s; **10** Matthew Brabham, USA, +30.4664s.
Fastest race lap: Lundqvist, 1m 17.4895s, 113.311mph/182.356km/h.
Pole position: Lundqvist, 1m 16.3362s, 115.023mph/185.111km/h.

Race 2 (85.365 miles/137.382km).
1 Linus Lundqvist, S, 56m 23.7504s, 90.821mph/146.161km/h; **2** Christian Rasmussen, DK, +3.5993s; **3** Sting Ray Robb, USA, +7.6291s; **4** Benjamin Pedersen, DK, +12.8071s; **5** Jacob Abel, USA, +13.0001s; **6** Hunter McElrea, AUS, +14.4895s; **7** Danial Frost, SGP, +15.7282s; **8** Kyffin Simpson, BB, +15.8957s; **9** Matthew Brabham, USA, +16.0668s; **10** Ernie Francis Jr., USA, +27.6464s.
Fastest race lap: Brabham, 1m 17.8721s, 112.754mph/181.460km/h.
Pole position: Lundqvist, 1m 16.4266s, 114.887mph/184.892km/h.

INDY LIGHTS DETROIT GRAND PRIX, The Raceway at Belle Isle, Detroit, Michigan, USA, 4/5 June. Round 4. 25 and 30 laps of the 2.350-mile/3.782km circuit.
Race 1 (58.750 miles/94.549km).
1 Linus Lundqvist, S, 39m 47.9921s, 88.568mph/142.537km/h; **2** Benjamin Pedersen, DK, +3.7232s; **3** Matthew Brabham, USA, +4.7936s; **4** Christian Bogle, USA, +10.2362s; **5** Kyffin Simpson, BB, +10.8649s; **6** Antonio Serravalle, CDN, +11.4164s; **7** James Roe, IRL, +16.4810s; **8** Ryan Phinny, USA, +20.8913s; **9** Ernie Francis Jr., USA, -1 lap; **10** Danial Frost, SGP, -2 (DNF).
Fastest race lap: Lundqvist, 1m 22.3345s, 102.752mph/165.363km/h.
Pole position: Lundqvist, 1m 23.1190s, 101.782mph/163.802km/h.

Race 2 (70.500 miles/113.459km).
1 Linus Lundqvist, S, 44m 47.6446s, 94.432mph/151.974km/h; **2** Hunter McElrea, AUS, +3.7005s; **3** Sting Ray Robb, USA, +4.0130s; **4** Matthew Brabham, USA, +5.4745s; **5** Danial Frost, SGP, +11.4373s; **6** Benjamin Pedersen, DK, +12.1261s; **7** Kyffin Simpson, BB, +12.2142s; **8** Antonio Serravalle, CDN, +24.8361s; **9** James Roe, IRL, +25.7713s; **10** Ernie Francis Jr., USA, +1m 00.3121s.
Fastest race lap: Lundqvist, 1m 21.6294s, 103.639mph/166.791km/h.
Pole position: Lundqvist, 1m 22.6778s, 102.325mph/164.676km/h.

INDY LIGHTS GRAND PRIX AT ROAD AMERICA, Road America, Elkhart Lake, Wisconsin, USA, 12 June. Round 5. 20 laps of the 4.014-mile/6.460km circuit, 80.280 miles/ 129.198km.
1 Christian Rasmussen, DK, 45m 45.0401s, 105.284mph/169.438km/h; **2** Sting Ray Robb, USA, +2.3573s; **3** Hunter McElrea, AUS, +6.1310s; **4** Linus Lundqvist, S, +6.8120s; **5** Jacob Abel, USA, +10.7062s; **6** Matthew Brabham, USA, +12.6208s; **7** James Roe, IRL, +18.8083s; **8** Danial Frost, SGP, +19.6014s; **9** Kyffin Simpson, BB, +34.6822s; **10** Ernie Francis Jr., USA, -1 lap.
Fastest race lap: Robb, 1m 55.4791s, 125.134mph/201.384km/h.
Pole position: Robb, 1m 53.9743s, 126.786mph/204.043km/h.

INDY LIGHTS AT MID-OHIO, Mid-Ohio Sports Car Course, Lexington, Ohio, USA, 3 July. Round 6. 35 laps of the 2.258-mile/3.634km circuit, 79.030 miles/127.186km.
1 Hunter McElrea, AUS, 44m 36.1766s, 106.311mph/171.092km/h; **2** Matthew Brabham, USA, +2.6826s; **3** Linus Lundqvist, S, +7.1228s; **4** Christian Rasmussen, DK, +8.5555s; **5** Sting Ray Robb, USA, +14.0837s; **6** Benjamin Pedersen, DK, +14.7419s; **7** Christian Bogle, USA, +14.9304s; **8** Antonio Serravalle, CDN, +16.5518s; **9** Kyffin Simpson, BB, +16.8589s; **10** Ernie Francis Jr., USA, +24.5104s.
Fastest race lap: McElrea, 1m 12.5680s, 112.016mph/180.273km/h.
Pole position: McElrea, 1m 12.1926s, 112.599mph/181.210km/h.

INDY LIGHTS AT IOWA SPEEDWAY, Iowa Speedway, Newton, Iowa, USA, 23 July. Round 7. 75 laps of the 0.894-mile/1.439km circuit, 67.050 miles/107.907km.
1 Hunter McElrea, AUS, 29m 52.0797s, 134.693mph/216.767km/h; **2** Christian

Rasmussen, DK, +1.2171s; **3** Matthew Brabham, USA, +1.6030s; **4** Linus Lundqvist, S, +2.5742s; **5** Sting Ray Robb, USA, +4.0216s; **6** Jacob Abel, USA, +7.7754s; **7** Danial Frost, SGP, +8.5442s; **8** Ernie Francis Jr., USA, +14.1510s; **9** Benjamin Pedersen, DK, +16.1584s; **10** Christian Bogle, USA, +17.4177s.
Fastest race lap: Brabham, 20.3500s, 158.152mph/254.522km/h.
Pole position: McElrea, 40.3553s, 159.503mph/256.696km/h (over **2** laps).

INDY LIGHTS MUSIC CITY GRAND PRIX, Nashville Street Circuit, Tennessee, USA, 7 August. Round 8. 35 laps of the 2.100-mile/3.380km circuit, 73.500 miles/118.287km.
1 Linus Lundqvist, S, 48m 09.4677s, 91.574mph/147.374km/h; **2** Sting Ray Robb, USA, +7.2221s; **3** Hunter McElrea, AUS, +10.3944s; **4** Matthew Brabham, USA, +16.3765s; **5** Christian Rasmussen, DK, +25.6394s; **6** Benjamin Pedersen, DK, +41.4944s; **7** Christian Bogle, USA, +41.9224s; **8** Kyffin Simpson, BB, +42.5055s; **9** Jacob Abel, USA, +1m 12.8024s; **10** Danial Frost, SGP, -2 laps.
Fastest race lap: Robb, 1m 20.9801s, 93.356mph/150.242km/h.
Pole position: Lundqvist.

INDY LIGHTS AT WORLD WIDE TECHNOLOGY RACEWAY, World Wide Technology Raceway, St Louis, Madison, Illinois, USA, 20 August. Round 9. 75 laps of the 1.250-mile/2.012km circuit, 93.750 miles/150.876km.
1 Matthew Brabham, USA, 36m 01.6741s, 156.129mph/251.265km/h; **2** Linus Lundqvist, S, +0.6770s; **3** Benjamin Pedersen, DK, +11.6153s; **4** Danial Frost, SGP, +12.9299s; **5** Hunter McElrea, AUS, +21.0565s; **6** Sting Ray Robb, USA, +21.6109s; **7** Jacob Abel, USA, +28.8474s; **8** James Roe, IRL, -1 lap; **9** Ernie Francis Jr., USA, -1; **10** Kyffin Simpson, BB, -1.
Fastest race lap: Pedersen, 28.4820s, 157.995mph/254.268km/h.
Pole position: Lundqvist, 56.1590s, 80.130mph/128.956km/h.

INDY LIGHTS GRAND PRIX OF PORTLAND, Portland International Raceway, Portland, Oregon, USA, 4 September. Round 10. 35 laps of the 1.964-mile/3.161km circuit, 68.740 miles/110.626km.
1 Benjamin Pedersen, DK, 44m 18.7886s, 93.074mph/149.788km/h; **2** Matthew Brabham, USA, +0.9651s; **3** Linus Lundqvist, S, +6.4087s; **4** Jacob Abel, USA, +11.0037s; **5** Hunter McElrea, AUS, +11.3346s; **6** Sting Ray Robb, USA, +17.3661s; **7** Christian Rasmussen, DK, +19.4541s; **8** Ernie Francis Jr., USA, +21.1388s; **9** Kyffin Simpson, BB, +21.6544s; **10** Danial Frost, SGP, -30 laps (DNF-accident).
Fastest race lap: Brabham, 1m 03.8712s, 110.698mph/178.151km/h.
Pole position: Pedersen, 1m 03.6698s, 111.048mph/178.714km/h.

INDY LIGHTS GRAND PRIX OF MONTEREY, Mazda Raceway Laguna Seca, Monterey, California, USA, 10/11 September. Round 11. 2 x 35 laps of the 2.238-mile/3.602km circuit.
Race 1 (78.330 miles/126.060km).
1 Sting Ray Robb, USA, 46m 04.2826s, 102.011mph/164.171km/h; **2** Christian Rasmussen, DK, +11.0674s; **3** Hunter McElrea, AUS, +19.2306s; **4** Jacob Abel, USA, +20.1513s; **5** Benjamin Pedersen, DK, +24.5887s; **6** Linus Lundqvist, S, +27.6857s; **7** Danial Frost, SGP, +28.1225s; **8** Matthew Brabham, USA, +28.7642s; **9** Christian Bogle, USA, +45.2572s; **10** Nolan Siegel, USA, +55.7876s.
Fastest race lap: Robb, 1m 16.7720s, 104.945mph/168.892km/h.
Pole position: Robb, 1m 15.7209s, 106.401mph/171.236km/h.

Race 2 (78.330 miles/126.060km).
1 Christian Rasmussen, DK, 46m 16.3888s, 101.566mph/163.455km/h; **2** Sting Ray Robb, USA, +0.8893s; **3** Matthew Brabham, USA, +3.8933s; **4** Linus Lundqvist, S, +6.6970s; **5** Jacob Abel, USA, +12.5765s; **6** Benjamin Pedersen, DK, +22.3970s; **7** Danial Frost, SGP, +23.0611s; **8** Hunter McElrea, AUS, +28.4702s; **9** Nolan Siegel, USA, +41.0777s; **10** Christian Bogle, USA, +43.4502s.
Fastest race lap: Robb, 1m 18.3304s, 102.857mph/165.532km/h.
Pole position: Rasmussen, 1m 15.3618s, 106.908mph/172.052km/h.

Final championship points
Drivers
1 Linus Lundqvist, S, 575; **2** Sting Ray Robb, USA, 483; **3** Matthew Brabham, USA, 471; **4** Hunter McElrea, AUS, 460; **5** Benjamin Pedersen, DK, 443; **6** Christian Rasmussen, DK, 440; **7** Danial Frost, SGP, 382; **8** Jacob Abel, USA, 355; **9** Kyffin Simpson, BB, 312; **10** Ernie Francis Jr., USA, 299; **11** Christian Bogle, USA, 298; **12** James Roe, IRL, 219; **13** Antonio Serravalle, CDN, 204; **14** Ryan Phinny, USA, 77; **15** Flinn Lazier, USA, 54; **16** Manuel Sulaimán, MEX, 48; **17** Nolan Siegel, USA, 42.

Teams
1 Andretti Autosport, 454; **2** HMD Motorsports with Dale Coyne Racing, 406; **3** Global Racing Group with HMD Motorsports, 237; **4** Abel Motorsports, 163; **5** Force Indy, 119; **6** TJ Speed Motorsports, 92.

Indy Pro 2000 Presented by Cooper Tires

All cars are Tatuus IP22-Mazda.

ANDERSEN INTERIOR CONTRACTING GRAND PRIX OF ST. PETERSBURG, St. Petersburg Street Circuit, Florida, USA, 25/26 February. Round 1. 2 x 25 laps of the 1.800-mile/2.897km circuit.
Race 1 (45.000 miles/72.420km).
1 Josh Green, USA, 29m 37.0619s, 91.162mph/146.711km/h; **2** Enaam Ahmed, GB, +0.6150s; **3** Louis Foster, GB, +1.8226s; **4** Braden Eves, USA, +3.8042s; **5** Nolan Siegel, USA, +5.2548s; **6** Kiko Porto, BR, +8.5090s; **7** Reece Gold, USA, +10.3550s; **8** Jack William Miller, USA, +11.5268s; **9** Salvador de Alba, MEX, +16.5080s; **10** Matthew Round-Garrido, GB, +24.1315s.
Fastest race lap: Siegel, 1m 09.5905s, 93.116mph/149.856km/h.
Pole position: Green, 1m 09.6117s, 93.088mph/149.810km/h.

Race 2 (45.000 miles/72.420km).
1 Nolan Siegel, USA, 35m 57.7849s, 75.077mph/120.825km/h; **2** Louis Foster, GB, +0.7470s; **3** Braden Eves, USA, +1.6020s; **4** Kiko Porto, BR, +2.9505s; **5** Wyatt Brichacek, USA, +3.7309s; **6** Jack William Miller, USA, +4.3236s; **7** Yuven Sundaramoorthy, USA, +6.2772s; **8** Jordan Missig, USA, +6.8850s; **9** Matthew Round-Garrido, GB, +7.6391s; **10** Reece Gold, USA, +39.8745s.
Fastest race lap: Foster, 1m 09.4668s, 93.282mph/150.123km/h.
Pole position: Siegel, 1m 09.5905s, 93.116mph/149.856km/h.

ANDERSEN INTERIOR CONTRACTING GRAND PRIX OF ALABAMA, Barber Motorsports Park, Birmingham, Alabama, USA, 30 April/1 May. Round 2. 25 and 30 laps of the 2.300-mile/3.701km circuit.
Race 1 (57.500 miles/92.537km).
1 Reece Gold, USA, 33m 09.3892s, 104.052mph/167.456km/h; **2** Colin Kaminsky, USA, +4.8884s; **3** Enaam Ahmed, GB, +5.3197s; **4** Louis Foster, GB, +5.7561s; **5** Braden Eves, USA, +8.5971s; **6** Josh Green, USA, +9.6747s; **7** Nolan Siegel, USA, +10.0283s; **8** Kiko Porto, BR, +10.4142s; **9** Jordan Missig, USA, +20.0091s; **10** Jonathan Browne, IRL, +20.8589s.
Fastest race lap: Foster, 1m 18.6458s, 105.282mph/169.435km/h.
Pole position: Gold, 1m 17.3343s, 107.068mph/172.309km/h.

Race 2 (69.000 miles/111.045km).
1 Nolan Siegel, USA, 40m 03.5218s, 103.348mph/166.323km/h; **2** Braden Eves, USA, +0.7522s; **3** Louis Foster, GB, +1.1829s; **4** Enaam Ahmed, GB, +6.2271s; **5** Reece Gold, USA, +8.4850s; **6** Josh Green, USA, +10.1798s; **7** Kiko Porto, BR, +10.7470s; **8** Salvador de Alba, MEX, +11.1013s; **9** Jonathan Browne, IRL, +19.6183s; **10** Jack William Miller, USA, +20.6132s.
Fastest race lap: Foster, 1m 19.2563s, 104.471mph/168.130km/h.
Pole position: Siegel, 1m 17.8455s, 106.365mph/171.177km/h.

INDY PRO 2000 GRAND PRIX OF INDIANAPOLIS, Indianapolis Motor Speedway, Speedway, Indiana, USA, 13/14 May. Round 3. 3 x 25 laps of the 2.439-mile/3.925km circuit.
Race 1 (60.975 miles/98.130km).
1 Salvador de Alba, MEX, 39m 54.9582s, 91.655mph/147.504km/h; **2** Yuven Sundaramoorthy, USA, +0.0884s; **3** Colin Kaminsky, USA, +0.7072s; **4** Reece Gold, USA, +1.0353s; **5** Enaam Ahmed, GB, +2.9675s; **6** Kiko Porto, BR, +4.5070s; **7** Jordan Missig, USA, +5.5209s; **8** Lindsay Brewer, USA, +7.0552s; **9** Jonathan Browne, IRL, +26.1221s; **10** Wyatt Brichacek, USA, +27.8387s.
Fastest race lap: Brichacek, 1m 23.3035s, 105.403mph/169.629km/h.
Pole position: Browne, 1m 21.6771s, 107.501mph/173.007km/h.

Race 2 (60.975 miles/98.130km).
1 Reece Gold, USA, 38m 15.5740s, 95.623mph/153.891km/h; **2** Colin Kaminsky, USA, +1.4833s; **3** Nolan Siegel, USA, +2.7616s; **4** Kiko Porto, BR, +4.2867s; **5** Jack William Miller, USA, +8.0666s; **6** Salvador de Alba, MEX, +10.2206s; **7** Wyatt Brichacek, USA, +11.3871s; **8** Yuven Sundaramoorthy, USA, +12.9038s; **9** Braden Eves, USA, +15.1094s; **10** Jonathan Browne, IRL, +15.5567s.
Fastest race lap: Louis Foster, GB, 1m 22.4807s, 106.454mph/171.321km/h.
Pole position: Miller, 1m 21.7907s, 107.352mph/172.766km/h.

Race 3 (60.975 miles/98.130km).
1 Louis Foster, GB, 37m 26.3793s, 97.717mph/157.261km/h; **2** Braden Eves, USA, +2.5609s; **3** Jack William Miller, USA, +6.7533s; **4** Wyatt Brichacek, USA, +6.8192s; **5** Enaam Ahmed, GB, +7.2664s; **6** Nolan Siegel, USA, +7.6265s; **7** Josh Green, USA, +10.6693s; **8** Kiko Porto, BR, +11.3700s; **9** Jonathan Browne, IRL, +11.4995s; **10** Colin Kaminsky, USA, +11.8098s.
Fastest race lap: Brichacek, 1m 23.4866s, 105.171mph/169.257km/h.
Pole position: Miller, 1m 21.7907s, 107.352mph/172.766km/h.

COOPER TIRES FREEDOM 90, Lucas Oil Raceway, Indianapolis, USA, 27 May. Round 4. 90 laps of the 0.686-mile/1.104km circuit, 61.740 miles/99.361km.
1 Louis Foster, GB, 33m 20.2301s, 111.119mph/178.829km/h; **2** Reece Gold, USA, +1.4089s; **3** Josh Green, USA, +2.8177s; **4** Enaam Ahmed, GB, +8.8081s; **5** Nolan Siegel, USA, +9.3264s; **6** Jordan Missig, USA, +12.3952s; **7** Kiko Porto, BR, -1 lap; **8** Salvador de Alba, MEX, -1; **9** Jack William Miller, USA, -1; **10** Jonathan Browne, IRL, -1.
Fastest race lap: Foster, 20.8920s, 118.208mph/190.237km/h.
Pole position: Gold, 41.3426s, 119.470mph/192.268km/h (over 2 laps).

COOPER TIRES GRAND PRIX OF ROAD AMERICA POWERED BY ELITE ENGINES, Road America, Elkhart Lake, Wisconsin, USA, 11/12 June. Round 5. 2 x 15 laps of the 4.014-mile/6.460km circuit.
Race 1 (60.210 miles/96.899km).
1 Louis Foster, GB, 33m 58.2799s, 106.343mph/171.142km/h; **2** Josh Green, USA, +3.6090s; **3** Enaam Ahmed, GB, +8.0093s; **4** Salvador de Alba, MEX, +8.5468s; **5** Braden Eves, USA, +10.1126s; **6** Reece Gold, USA, +10.5438s; **7** Colin Kaminsky, USA, +12.1256s; **8** Jonathan Browne, IRL, +12.5979s; **9** Jordan Missig, USA, +13.3921s; **10** Yuven Sundaramoorthy, USA, +14.3819s.
Fastest race lap: Gold, 2m 05.6751s, 114.982mph/185.046km/h.
Pole position: Gold, 2m 04.3105s, 116.244mph/187.077km/h.

Race 2 (60.210 miles/96.899km).
1 Braden Eves, USA, 31m 33.7990s, 114.456mph/184.199km/h; **2** Jack William Miller, USA, +1.2538s; **3** Salvador de Alba, MEX, +14.4464s; **4** Enaam Ahmed, GB, +14.4465s; **5** Reece Gold, USA, +14.9743s; **6** Josh Green, USA, +16.1427s; **7** Nolan Siegel, USA, +16.4897s; **8** Yuven Sundaramoorthy, USA, +17.9505s; **9** Jonathan Browne, IRL, +18.5925s; **10** Colin Kaminsky, USA, +20.0931s.
Fastest race lap: Miller, 2m 04.8888s, 115.706mph/186.211km/h.
Pole position: Green, 2m 04.4308s, 116.132mph/186.896km/h.

COOPER TIRES GRAND PRIX OF MID-OHIO, Mid-Ohio Sports Car Course, Lexington, Ohio, USA, 2 July. Round 6. 30 and 25 laps of the 2.258-mile/3.634km circuit.
Race 1 (67.740 miles/109.017km).
1 Louis Foster, GB, 43m 05.8282s, 94.308mph/151.774km/h; **2** Salvador de Alba, MEX, +14.5615s; **3** Nolan Siegel, USA, +15.1053s; **4** Kiko Porto, BR, +15.7064s; **5** Josh Green, USA, +16.0460s; **6** Enaam Ahmed, GB, +16.5739s; **7** Reece Gold, USA, +16.8683s; **8** Braden Eves, USA, +17.8391s; **9** Wyatt Brichacek, USA, +20.3986s; **10** Jack William Miller, USA, +24.1290s.
Fastest race lap: Foster, 1m 18.9100s, 103.014mph/165.784km/h.
Pole position: Foster, 1m 18.2678s, 103.859mph/167.145km/h.
Race 2 (56.450 miles/90.847km).
1 Kiko Porto, BR, 33m 24.4424s, 101.385mph/163.163km/h; **2** Louis Foster, GB, +0.3423s; **3** Yuven Sundaramoorthy, USA, +4.6985s; **4** Enaam Ahmed, GB, +5.3610s; **5** Salvador de Alba, MEX, +5.8609s; **6** Reece Gold, USA, +6.9697s; **7** Nolan Siegel, USA, +8.8100s; **8** Braden Eves, USA, +11.5660s; **9** Josh Green, USA, +11.8732s; **10** Jordan Missig, USA, +15.9949s.
Fastest race lap: Alba, 1m 19.2694s, 102.547mph/165.033km/h.
Pole position: Foster, 1m 18.4328s, 103.640mph/166.793km/h.

L&W SUPPLY GRAND PRIX OF TORONTO, Toronto Street Circuit, Ontario, Canada, 16/17 July. Round 7. 2 x 25 laps of the 1.786-mile/2.874km circuit.
Race 1 (44.650 miles/71.857km).
1 Louis Foster, GB, 31m 02.2535s, 86.315mph/138.910km/h; **2** Enaam Ahmed, GB, +5.2348s; **3** Josh Green, USA, +5.9526s; **4** Reece Gold, USA, +6.9163s; **5** Nolan Siegel, USA, +7.2657s; **6** Yuven Sundaramoorthy, USA, +8.8901s; **7** Jordan Missig, USA, +13.7590s; **8** Jack William Miller, USA, +14.5445s; **9** Kiko Porto, BR, +17.6879s; **10** Jonathan Browne, IRL, +20.1073s.
Fastest race lap: Foster, 1m 08.8922s, 93.328mph/150.198km/h.
Pole position: Foster, 1m 09.4139s, 92.627mph/149.069km/h.

Race 2 (44.650 miles/71.857km).
1 Louis Foster, GB, 35m 43.4854s, 74.990mph/120.685km/h; **2** Jordan Missig, USA, +3.9205s; **3** Reece Gold, USA, +7.4653s; **4** Yuven Sundaramoorthy, USA, +8.0417s; **5** Jack William Miller, USA, +9.0458s; **6** Braden Eves, USA, +9.8684s; **7** Kiko Porto, BR, +11.7380s; **8** Enaam Ahmed, GB, +19.0516s; **9** Wyatt Brichacek, USA, +28.7903s; **10** Lindsay Brewer, USA, -1 lap.
Fastest race lap: Foster, 1m 08.6907s, 93.602mph/150.638km/h.
Pole position: Foster, 1m 08.6292s, 93.686mph/150.773km/h.

VP RACING FUELS OVAL CHALLENGE OF ST. LOUIS, World Wide Technology Raceway, St Louis, Madison, Illinois, USA, 20 August. Round 8. 55 laps of the 1.250-mile/2.012km circuit, 68.750 miles/110.642km.
1 Salvador de Alba, MEX, 29m 52.0692s, 138.109mph/222.264km/h; **2** Nolan Siegel, USA, +5.9398s; **3** Braden Eves, USA, +6.3174s; **4** Louis Foster, GB, +6.7537s; **5** Josh Green, USA, +9.9415s; **6** Reece Gold, USA, +17.1472s; **7** Enaam Ahmed, GB, +26.7828s; **8** Marcos Flack, AUS, +27.1056s; **9** Yuven Sundaramoorthy, USA, +28.9998s; **10** Bijoy Garg, USA, +31.8387s.
Fastest race lap: Alba, 32.1899s, 139.795mph/224.979km/h.
Pole position: Alba, 1m 04.9537s, 138.560mph/222.991km/h (over **2** laps).

COOPER TIRES INDY PRO 2000 GRAND PRIX OF PORTLAND, Portland International Raceway, Portland, Oregon, USA, 2/3 September. Round 9. 30, 22 and 30 laps of the 1.964-mile/3.161km circuit.
Race 1 (58.920 miles/94.823km).
1 Louis Foster, GB, 34m 54.4064s, 101.275mph/162.987km/h; **2** Reece Gold, USA, +2.1474s; **3** Enaam Ahmed, GB, +11.6947s; **4** Marcos Flack, AUS, +28.1933s; **5** Jonathan Browne, IRL, +29.1087s; **6** Jordan Missig, USA, +30.4428s; **7** Braden Eves, USA, +30.9413s; **8** Salvador de Alba, MEX, +32.8622s; **9** Josh Green, USA, +33.1841s; **10** Bijoy Garg, USA, +33.7361s.
Fastest race lap: Gold, 1m 09.3726s, 101.919mph/164.023km/h.
Pole position: Foster, 1m 08.2477s, 103.599mph/166.727km/h.

Race 2 (43.208 miles/69.537km).
1 Reece Gold, USA, 25m 42.1087s, 100.868mph/162.331km/h; **2** Louis Foster, GB, +3.5502s; **3** Kiko Porto, BR, +10.2385s; **4** Enaam Ahmed, GB, +11.0370s; **5** Jack William Miller, USA, +12.8453s; **6** Salvador de Alba, MEX, +20.7750s; **7** Jordan Missig, USA, +21.3239s; **8** Nolan Siegel, USA, +21.8212s; **9** Braden Eves, USA, +22.4040s; **10** Bijoy Garg, USA, +22.9929s.
Fastest race lap: Foster, 1m 09.3781s, 101.911mph/164.010km/h.
Pole position: Gold, 1m 08.4016s, 103.366mph/166.351km/h.

Race 3 (58.920 miles/94.823km).
1 Reece Gold, USA, 34m 48.4361s,

101.565mph/163.453km/h; **2** Kiko Porto, BR, +3.6582s; **3** Nolan Siegel, USA, +5.5860s; **4** Enaam Ahmed, GB, +6.2776s; **5** Jack William Miller, USA, +12.6487s; **6** Louis Foster, GB, +16.0585s; **7** Salvador de Alba, MEX, +16.7746s; **8** Josh Green, USA, +17.3287s; **9** Jordan Missig, USA, +20.4513s; **10** Yuven Sundaramoorthy, USA, +22.0479s.
Fastest race lap: Foster, 1m 08.9594s, 102.530mph/165.006km/h.
Pole position: Gold, 1m 08.4016s, 103.366mph/166.351km/h.

Final championship points
Drivers
1 Louis Foster, GB, 451; **2** Reece Gold, USA, 390; **3** Enaam Ahmed, GB, 338; **4** Nolan Siegel, USA, 333; **5** Braden Eves, USA, 304; **6** Josh Green, USA, 298; **7** Kiko Porto, BR, 290; **8** Salvador de Alba, MEX, 289; **9** Jack William Miller, USA, 251; **10** Yuven Sundaramoorthy, USA, 244; **11** Jordan Missig, USA, 199; **12** Jonathan Browne, IRL, 187; **13** Wyatt Brichacek, USA, 160; **14** Colin Kaminsky, USA, 144; **15** Lindsay Brewer, USA, 98; **16** Charles Finelli, USA, 59; **17** Marcos Flack, AUS, 51; **18** Bijoy Garg, USA, 47; **19** Matthew Round-Garrido, GB, 23; **20** Trey Burke, USA, 14.

Teams
1 Juncos Hollinger Racing, 419; **2** Jay Howard Driver Development, 324; **3** DEForce Racing, 314; **4** Exclusive Autosport, 307; **5** Pabst Racing, 185; **6** Turn 3 Motorsport, 172; **7** Miller Vinatieri Motorsports, 155; **8** FatBoy Racing!, 32.

Cooper Tires USF2000 Championship

All cars are Tatuus USF-22-Mazda.

COOPER TIRES GRAND PRIX OF ST. PETERSBURG, St. Petersburg Street Circuit, Florida, USA, 25/27 February. Round 1. 2 x 20 laps of the 1.800-mile/2.897km circuit.
Race 1 (36.000 miles/57.936km).
1 Jace Denmark, USA, 25m 18.5252s, 85.346mph/137.351km/h; **2** Billy Frazer, NZ, +0.8051s; **3** Bijoy Garg, USA, +1.3243s; **4** Michael D'Orlando, USA, +1.9173s; **5** Simon Sikes, USA, +3.4197s; **6** Spike Kohlbecker, USA, +11.0065s; **7** Trey Burke, USA, +11.0066s; **8** Jagger Jones, USA, +11.6497s; **9** Dylan Christie, USA, +14.9099s; **10** Christian Weir, USA, +15.7431s.
Fastest race lap: Myles Rowe, USA, 1m 13.1838s, 88.544mph/142.498km/h.
Pole position: Thomas Nepveu, CDN, 1m 12.7274s, 89.100mph/143.392km/h.

Race 2 (36.000 miles/57.936km).
1 Myles Rowe, USA, 36m 29.0001s, 59.205mph/95.281km/h; **2** Jace Denmark, USA, +1.0493s; **3** Jagger Jones, USA, +2.9011s; **4** Michael D'Orlando, USA, +3.9496s; **5** Thomas Nepveu, CDN, +7.2696s; **6** Billy Frazer, NZ, +7.6841s; **7** Jackson Lee, USA, +8.7914s; **8** Nicky Hays, USA, +9.7924s; **9** Simon Sikes, USA, +11.0887s; **10** Jorge Garcíarce, MEX, +11.4170s.
Fastest race lap: Rowe, 1m 12.8112s, 88.997mph/143.227km/h.
Pole position: Denmark, 1m 12.7399s, 89.085mph/143.368km/h.

COOPER TIRES GRAND PRIX OF ALABAMA, Barber Motorsports Park, Birmingham, Alabama, USA, 30 April/1 May. Round 2. 20 and 17 laps of the 2.300-mile/3.701km circuit.
Race 1 (46.000 miles/74.030km).
1 Myles Rowe, USA, 27m 48.1527s, 99.271mph/159.762km/h; **2** Billy Frazer, NZ, +1.7632s; **3** Michael D'Orlando, USA, +2.3057s; **4** Bijoy Garg, USA, +7.4099s; **5** Simon Sikes, USA, +7.9317s; **6** Thomas Nepveu, CDN, +9.1071s; **7** Christian Weir, USA, +9.9166s; **8** Nicky Hays, USA, +10.7225s; **9** Jagger Jones, USA, +11.3500s; **10** Spike Kohlbecker, USA, +12.5246s.
Fastest race lap: D'Orlando, 1m 22.8961s, 99.884mph/160.748km/h.
Pole position: Rowe, 1m 21.9164s, 101.079mph/162.670km/h.

Race 2 (39.100 miles/62.925km).
1 Jagger Jones, USA, 25m 24.8345s, 92.312mph/148.561km/h; **2** Michael D'Orlando, USA, +0.5455s; **3** Christian Weir, USA, +1.2888s; **4** Myles Rowe, USA, +1.8234s; **5** Simon Sikes, USA, +2.0295s; **6** Thomas Nepveu, CDN, +2.5243s; **7** Nicky Hays, USA, +4.9989s; **8** Dylan Christie, USA, +7.0421s; **9** Jackson Lee, USA, +7.4665s; **10** Bijoy Garg, USA, +7.8192s.
Fastest race lap: Billy Frazer, NZ, 1m 23.1475s, 99.582mph/160.262km/h.
Pole position: Weir, 1m 22.3788s, 100.511mph/161.757km/h.

USF2000 GRAND PRIX OF INDIANAPOLIS, Indianapolis Motor Speedway, Speedway, Indiana, USA, 13/14 May. Round 3. 3 x 15 laps of the 2.439-mile/3.925km circuit.
Race 1 (36.585 miles/58.878km).
1 Alex Quinn, GB, 28m 51.6842s, 76.057mph/122.401km/h; **2** Jagger Jones, USA, +2.4392s; **3** Billy Frazer, NZ, +3.1657s; **4** Christian Weir, USA, +3.6323s; **5** Thomas Nepveu, CDN, +3.7886s; **6** Spike Kohlbecker, USA, +4.3180s; **7** Jorge Garcíarce, MEX, +5.4113s; **8** Frankie Mossman, USA, +5.9011s; **9** Simon Sikes, USA, +6.5776s; **10** Trey Burke, USA, +6.6259s.
Fastest race lap: Quinn, 1m 26.4887s, 101.521mph/163.382km/h.
Pole position: Jones, 1m 25.4254s, 102.784mph/165.415km/h.

Race 2 (36.585 miles/58.878km).
1 Alex Quinn, GB, 25m 33.6215s, 85.879mph/138.209km/h; **2** Billy Frazer, NZ, +3.4115s; **3** Myles Rowe, USA, +3.7167s; **4** Jace Denmark, USA, +4.2312s; **5** Michael D'Orlando, USA, +6.9970s; **6** Spike Kohlbecker, USA, +7.7759s; **7** Bijoy Garg, USA, +8.5494s; **8** Nicky Hays, USA, +9.5757s; **9** Simon Sikes, USA, +10.1915s; **10** Chase Gardner, USA, +10.6149s.
Fastest race lap: Denmark, 1m 26.0748s, 102.009mph/164.167km/h.
Pole position: Jagger Jones, USA, 1m 25.4479s, 102.757mph/165.372km/h.

Race 3 (36.585 miles/58.878km).
1 Alex Quinn, GB, 21m 47.8372s, 100.705mph/162.069km/h; **2** Michael D'Orlando, USA, +2.2187s; **3** Jagger Jones, USA, +2.6928s; **4** Jace Denmark, USA, +8.3080s; **5** Thomas Nepveu, CDN, +8.7468s; **6** Myles Rowe, USA, +13.0387s; **7** Billy Frazer, NZ, +17.6304s; **8** Bijoy Garg, USA, +17.9316s; **9** Simon Sikes, USA, +18.9605s; **10** Spike Kohlbecker, USA, +19.2950s.
Fastest race lap: Quinn, 1m 26.7264s, 101.243mph/162.934km/h.
Pole position: Jones, 1m 25.4479s, 102.757mph/165.372km/h.

COOPER TIRES FREEDOM 75, Lucas Oil Raceway, Indianapolis, USA, 27 May. Round 4. 75 laps of the 0.686-mile/1.104km circuit, 51.450 miles/82.801km.
1 Michael D'Orlando, USA, 28m 30.4238s, 108.289mph/174.274km/h; **2** Bijoy Garg, USA, +0.2328s; **3** Myles Rowe, USA, +1.0138s; **4** Jace Denmark, USA, +6.1757s; **5** Jagger Jones, USA, +6.4224s; **6** Thomas Nepveu, CDN, +8.0341s; **7** Billy Frazer, NZ, +11.7888s; **8** Simon Sikes, USA, +11.8173s; **9** Spike Kohlbecker, USA, +12.7748s; **10** Dylan Christie, USA, +13.6525s.
Fastest race lap: Garg, 22.3544s, 110.475mph/177.792km/h.
Pole position: D'Orlando, 44.823s, 110.193mph/177.339km/h (over **2** laps).

COOPER TIRES GRAND PRIX OF ROAD AMERICA POWERED BY ELITE ENGINES, Road America, Elkhart Lake, Wisconsin, USA, 11 June. Round 5. 12 and 11 laps of the 4.014-mile/6.460km circuit.
Race 1 (48.168 miles/77.519km).
1 Jace Denmark, USA, 31m 49.9972s, 90.788mph/146.109km/h; **2** Myles Rowe, USA, +0.3126s; **3** Billy Frazer, NZ, +2.0737s; **4** Dylan Christie, USA, +2.4787s; **5** Thomas Nepveu, CDN, +3.6575s; **6** Bijoy Garg, USA, +3.9793s; **7** Christian Weir, USA, +4.0881s; **8** Jacob Douglas, NZ, +6.4009s; **9** Spike Kohlbecker, USA, +6.5711s; **10** Nicholas d'Orlando, USA, +7.4356s.
Fastest race lap: d'Orlando, 2m 11.9849s, 109.485mph/176.199km/h.
Pole position: Michael D'Orlando, USA, 2m 10.7439s, 110.524mph/177.872km/h.

Race 2 (44.154 miles/71.059km).
1 Michael D'Orlando, USA, 45m 03.7733s, 58.790mph/94.613km/h; **2** Myles Rowe, USA, +0.3907s; **3** Thomas Nepveu, CDN, +2.2057s; **4** Bijoy Garg, USA, +2.4154s; **5** Jace Denmark, USA, +3.4610s; **6** Dylan Christie, USA, +3.9618s; **7** Jagger Jones, USA, +4.3197s; **8** Nikita Johnson, USA, +4.9347s; **9** Nicky Hays, USA, +5.8121s; **10** Spike Kohlbecker, USA, +6.0942s.
Fastest race lap: Rowe, 2m 12.7089s, 108.888mph/175.238km/h.
Pole position: D'Orlando, 2m 11.1192s, 110.208mph/177.363km/h.

COOPER TIRES GRAND PRIX OF MID-OHIO, Mid-Ohio Sports Car Course, Lexington, Ohio, USA, 1/2 July. Round 6. 3 x 20 laps of the 2.258-mile/3.634km circuit.
Race 1 (45.160 miles/72.678km).
1 Myles Rowe, USA, 28m 41.1648s, 94.457mph/152.014km/h; **2** Jace Denmark, USA, +8.8492s; **3** Billy Frazer, NZ, +9.6396s; **4** Jagger Jones, USA, +10.8520s; **5** Jacob Douglas, NZ, +13.1643s; **6** Christian Weir, USA, +13.7940s; **7** Nicky Hays, USA, +14.1486s; **8** Dylan Christie, USA, +16.8203s; **9** Bijoy Garg, USA, +17.1978s; **10** Danny Dyszelski, USA, +18.4908s.
Fastest race lap: Michael D'Orlando, USA, 1m 22.8583s, 98.105mph/157.884km/h.
Pole position: Rowe, 1m 22.0932s, 99.019mph/159.356km/h.

Race 2 (45.160 miles/72.678km).
1 Myles Rowe, USA, 30m 58.6591s, 87.470mph/140.769km/h; **2** Michael D'Orlando, USA, +0.5031s; **3** Jace Denmark, USA, +0.7305s; **4** Nikita Johnson, USA, +1.5172s; **5** Nicky Hays, USA, +2.4869s; **6** Jagger Jones, USA, +3.4276s; **7** Jacob Douglas, NZ, +4.6838s; **8** Nicholas d'Orlando, USA, +5.7755s; **9** Spike Kohlbecker, USA, +6.3568s; **10** Jackson Lee, USA, +6.8511s.
Fastest race lap: Christian Weir, USA, 1m 22.5029s, 98.527mph/158.565km/h.
Pole position: D'Orlando, 1m 22.1603s, 98.938mph/159.226km/h.

Race 3 (45.160 miles/72.678km).
1 Michael D'Orlando, USA, 27m 56.4272s, 96.978mph/156.070km/h; **2** Jace Denmark, USA, +3.3923s; **3** Myles Rowe, USA, +5.7952s; **4** Lochie Hughes, AUS, +9.2965s; **5** Dylan Christie, USA, +12.8330s; **6** Thomas Nepveu, CDN, +13.5478s; **7** Jagger Jones, USA, +13.8649s; **8** Nikita Johnson, USA, +16.3401s; **9** Bijoy Garg, USA, +17.6376s; **10** Christian Weir, USA, +18.2416s.
Fastest race lap: D'Orlando, 1m 23.0211s, 97.912mph/157.575km/h.
Pole position: D'Orlando, 1m 22.1603s, 98.938mph/159.226km/h.

COOPER TIRES GRAND PRIX OF TORONTO, Toronto Street Circuit, Ontario, Canada, 16/17 July. Round 7. 2 x 20 laps of the 1.786-mile/2.874km circuit.
Race 1 (35.720 miles/57.486km).
1 Myles Rowe, USA, 24m 17.0226s, 88.257mph/142.035km/h; **2** Jace Denmark, USA, +5.8524s; **3** Jagger Jones, USA, +7.0781s; **4** Michael D'Orlando, USA, +8.4351s; **5** Jacob Douglas, NZ, +13.6064s; **6** Nicky Hays, USA, +14.1637s; **7** Spike Kohlbecker, USA, +18.8523s; **8** Christian Weir, USA, +20.8885s; **9** Nicholas d'Orlando, USA, +24.3994s; **10** Dylan Christie, USA, +25.5306s.
Fastest race lap: Rowe, 1m 12.0141s, 89.283mph/143.686km/h.
Pole position: Denmark, 1m 13.0629s, 88.001mph/141.624km/h.

Race 2 (35.720 miles/57.486km).
1 Jace Denmark, USA, 28m 06.6255s, 76.242mph/122.700km/h; **2** Thomas Nepveu, CDN, +1.7783s; **3** Dylan Christie, USA, +2.1194s; **4** Michael D'Orlando, USA, +2.4226s; **5** Myles Rowe, USA, +2.4227s; **6** Jagger Jones, USA, +5.4091s; **7** Jacob Douglas, NZ, +6.0737s; **8** Jorge Garcíarce, MEX, +7.1890s; **9** Christian Weir, USA, -1 lap; **10** Nicky Hays, USA, -1.
Fastest race lap: D'Orlando, 1m 12.0941s, 89.183mph/143.527km/h.
Pole position: Denmark, 1m 12.1898s, 89.065mph/143.337km/h.

COOPER TIRES USF2000 GRAND PRIX OF PORTLAND, Portland International Raceway, Portland, Oregon, USA, 2/3 September. Round 8. 25, 18 and 25 laps of the 1.964-mile/3.161km circuit.
Race 1 (49.100 miles/79.019km).
1 Jace Denmark, USA, 36m 44.9632s, 80.165mph/129.012km/h; **2** Nikita Johnson, USA, +2.2945s; **3** Thomas Nepveu, CDN, +3.1773s; **4** Mac Clark, CDN, +7.7876s; **5** Jacob Douglas, NZ, +9.2649s; **6** Danny Dyszelski, USA, +9.7984s; **7** Michael D'Orlando, USA, +10.1622s; **8** Nicky Hays, USA, +10.5551s; **9** Jorge Garcíarce, MEX, +11.1347s; **10** Myles Rowe, USA, +11.9432s.
Fastest race lap: Johnson, 1m 12.4810s, 97.548mph/156.989km/h.
Pole position: Denmark, 1m 11.8336s, 98.427mph/158.404km/h.

Race 2 (35.352 miles/56.894km).
1 Mac Clark, CDN, 24m 29.6622s, 86.596mph/139.363km/h; **2** Nicky Hays, USA, +0.8977s; **3** Billy Frazer, NZ, +2.6205s; **4** Michael D'Orlando, USA, +3.6175s; **5** Christian Weir, USA, +4.3620s; **6** Jacob Douglas, NZ, +4.5730s; **7** Dylan Christie, USA, +5.5052s; **8** Spike Kohlbecker, USA, +6.3628s; **9** Thomas Nepveu, CDN, +8.5805s; **10** Jorge Garcíarce, MEX, +8.8680s.
Fastest race lap: Myles Rowe, USA, 1m 12.7153s, 97.234mph/156.483km/h.
Pole position: Jace Denmark, USA, 1m 11.8365s, 98.424mph/158.397km/h.

Race 3 (49.100 miles/79.019km).
1 Michael D'Orlando, USA, 35m 00.8231s, 84.138mph/135.408km/h; **2** Nicky Hays, USA, +1.1008s; **3** Christian Weir, USA, +2.2125s; **4** Jagger Jones, USA, +2.4903s; **5** Myles Rowe, USA, +2.9216s; **6** Jorge Garcíarce, MEX, +6.4225s; **7** Spike Kohlbecker, USA, +7.8187s; **8** Danny Dyszelski, USA, +8.1990s; **9** Nicholas d'Orlando, USA, +8.9550s; **10** Joey Brienza, USA, +9.2022s.
Fastest race lap: Rowe, 1m 12.4152s, 97.637mph/157.131km/h.
Pole position: Jace Denmark, USA, 1m 11.8365s, 98.424mph/158.397km/h.

Final championship points
Drivers
1 Michael D'Orlando, USA, 387; **2** Myles Rowe, USA, 381; **3** Jace Denmark, USA, 363; **4** Jagger Jones, USA, 294; **5** Billy Frazer, NZ, 268; **6** Thomas Nepveu, CDN, 262; **7** Nicky Hays, USA, 235; **8** Christian Weir, USA, 229; **9** Bijoy Garg, USA, 203; **10** Spike Kohlbecker, USA, 200; **11** Dylan Christie, USA, 188; **12** Jacob Douglas, NZ, 179.

Teams
1 Pabst Racing, 463; **2** Cape Motorsports, 433; **3** DEForce Racing, 288; **4** Exclusive Autosport, 218.

Atlantic Championship

Final championship points
Drivers (016)
1 Keith Grant, USA, 253; **2** Flinn Lazier, USA, 212; **3** Rich Zober, USA, 153; **4** Dudley Fleck, USA, 122; **5** Chris Ash, USA, 111; **6** Larry Howard, USA, 110; **7** Tonis Kasemets, EST, 84; **8** Peter Ruggiero, USA, 65.

Drivers (Open)
1 Austin Hill, USA, 484; **2** Bob Corliss, USA, 187; **3** Kirk Kindsfater, USA, 184; **4** Bruce Hamilton, USA, 110; **5** Nathan Byrd, USA, 74; **5** Christian Lall Dass, TT, 74; **7** Robert Wright, USA, 39; **8** Hayden Bowlsbey, USA, 8.